THE MASS MEDIA SHAPE OUR WORLD

More on media ownership. Two new features help students understand media consolidation and the increasingly complex relationship between content and access:

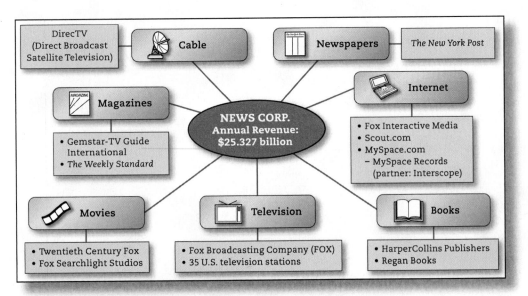

- ■ Media Ownership charts in Chapters 2–10 show the principal U.S. holdings of dominant media conglomerates.

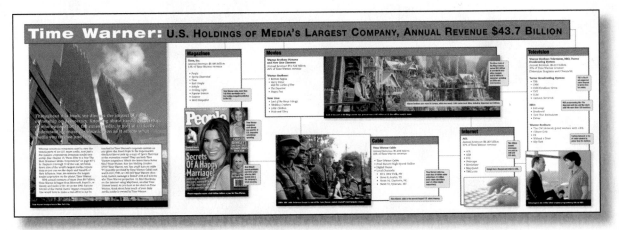

- ■ A new double-sided, fold-out chart appears at the front of the book. One side shows the holdings of the media colossus Time Warner; the reverse presents a timeline showing how media has been shaped by culture throughout time.

E-book and online resources. Please see the inside back cover or bedfordstmartins.com/communication for more information.

praise for media & culture

The feature boxes are excellent, and are indispensable to any classroom.
— Marvin Williams, *Kingsborough Community College*

The Critical Perspective has enlightened the perspective of all of us who study media, and Campbell has the power to infect students with his love of the subject.

— Roger Desmond, *University of Hartford*

I think the Campbell text is outstanding. It is a long-overdue media text that is grounded in pressing questions about American culture and its connection to the techniques and institutions of commercial communication. It is, indeed, an important book. At the undergraduate level, that's saying something.
— Steve M. Barkin, *University of Maryland*

This is one of the most up-to-date texts I've ever seen, and students certainly recognize this too.
— Karen Pitcher, University of Iowa

I found *Media & Culture* so intriguing I could hardly put it down.
— Dean A. Kruckeberg, *University of Northern Iowa*

I will switch to Campbell because it is a tour de force of coverage and interpretation, it is the best survey text in the field hands down, and it challenges students. Campbell's text is the most thorough and complete in the field. . . . No other text is even close.

—Russell Barclay,
Quinnipiac University

I am extremely impressed with *Media & Culture.*

—Laurie Fluker,
Texas State University

[Chapter outlines] provide a quick reference for discussion preparation. I can be more certain that students are getting the significant content issues if they can address these highlights.

—Peter Croisant,
Geneva College

This book is an outstanding contribution to the field. It allows students to build upon their own experiences with various media they use, to see the ways in which those media are active constructors of culture.

—*John Pantalone,*
University of Rhode Island

media & culture

media & culture

an introduction to mass communication

SIXTH EDITION

RICHARD CAMPBELL

Miami University

Christopher R. Martin

Miami University

Bettina Fabos

Miami University

BEDFORD/ST. MARTIN'S

Boston • New York

For Bedford/St. Martin's

Executive Editor for Communication: Erika Gutierrez
Executive Editor: Simon Glick
Developmental Editor: Noel Hohnstine
Production Editor: Ryan Sullivan
Senior Production Supervisor: Dennis J. Conroy
Executive Marketing Manager: Rachel Falk
Art Director: Lucy Krikorian
Text Design: Anne Carter
Copy Editor: Denise Quirk
Indexer: Kirsten Kite
Graphics: Burmar Technical Corporation
Photo Research: Joan Scafarello
Cover Design: Billy Boardman
Composition: Stratford/TexTech
Printing and Binding: R.R. Donnelley & Sons Company

President: Joan E. Feinberg
Editorial Director: Denise B. Wydra
Director of Development: Erica T. Appel
Director of Marketing: Karen Melton Soeltz
Director of Editing, Design, and Production: Marcia Cohen
Managing Editor: Shuli Traub

Library of Congress Control Number: 2006939563

Manufactured in the United States of America.

2 1 0 9 8 7
f e d c b a

For information, write: Bedford/St. Martin's, 75 Arlington Street,
Boston, MA 02116   (617-399-4000)

ISBN-10: 0-312-45586-0
ISBN-13: 978-0-312-45586-6

Acknowledgments

Acknowledgments and copyrights appear at the back of the book on pages C-1–C-4, which constitute an extension of the copyright page.

"WE ARE NOT ALONE."

For my family—Chris, Caitlin, and Dianna

"YOU MAY SAY I'M A DREAMER, BUT I'M NOT THE ONLY ONE."

For our daughters—Olivia and Sabine

about the authors

Richard Campbell, director of the journalism program at Miami University in Ohio, is the author of *60 Minutes and the News: A Mythology for Middle America* (1991) and coauthor of *Cracked Coverage: Television News, the Anti-Cocaine Crusade, and the Reagan Legacy* (1994). Campbell has written for numerous publications including *Columbia Journalism Review, Journal of Communication,* and *Media Studies Journal,* and he is on the editorial board of *Critical Studies in Mass Communication* and *Television Quarterly.* He holds a Ph.D. from Northwestern University and has also taught at the University of Wisconsin–Milwaukee, Mount Mary College, the University of Michigan, and Middle Tennessee State University.

Bettina Fabos, an award-winning video maker and former print reporter, is an assistant professor of journalism and interactive media studies at Miami University in Ohio. She is the author of *Wrong Turn on the Information Superhighway: Education and the Commercialized Internet* (2003). Her areas of expertise include critical media literacy, Internet commercialization, the role of the Internet in education, and media representations of popular culture. Her work has been published in *Library Trends, Review of Educational Research,* and *Harvard Educational Review.* Fabos has also taught at the University of Northern Iowa and has a Ph.D. from the University of Iowa.

Christopher R. Martin is an associate professor of journalism at Miami University in Ohio and author of *Framed! Labor and the Corporate Media* (2003). He has written articles and reviews on journalism, televised sports, the Internet, and labor for several publications including *Communication Research, Journal of Communication, Journal of Communication Inquiry, Labor Studies Journal,* and *Culture, Sport, and Society.* Martin holds a Ph.D. from the University of Michigan and has also taught at the University of Northern Iowa.

brief contents

preface

While revising this new edition of *Media and Culture*, I thought again about what an honor it is to work on a textbook that not only deals with subjects and ideas that I am passionate about but that also constantly evolves and provides new material to study. When I began writing the first edition in 1994, I was motivated by a general dissatisfaction with the introductory texts in our field. I wanted a book with a critical edge that also gave students a method for becoming better critics themselves. I also worked hard to place the facts about mass communication in a compelling narrative that would tell students the stories of mass media—how they came to be and how they affect our contemporary democracy. And finally, I tried to provide a larger cultural context—one that grows from understanding media from the viewpoint of a teacher and a scholar with some experience as a journalist.

The response to *Media and Culture* has been enthusiastic and overwhelming. From the first edition, the comments, suggestions, and diverse views of teachers using the book have reinforced the message of the text and have helped to shape it. Two of those teachers, Christopher Martin and Bettina Fabos, have been instrumental in bringing their own passion to the text from the very beginning. First as the supplement authors, then as contributors in the second and third editions, and finally as coauthors since the fourth edition, Chris and Bettina add creativity, energy, and expertise in journalism and multimedia technology to the project. We all believe that the critical and cultural perspective we present in *Media and Culture* helps students understand the media and their role in the larger ebb and flow of everyday life. And we hope the text enables students to become more knowledgeable as media consumers and to be more fully engaged as citizens with a critical stake in the shape of our culture and democracy.

We would also like to express our gratitude to all the teachers and students who have supported this book over the years and told us how the book has helped them become more aware of—and engaged with—mass media. We are particularly enthusiastic about the community of teachers that has developed around *Media and Culture*, helping us not only to stay current but also to take the project in important new directions—with fresh examples and practical experience from using the book in the classroom.

Media and Culture is both a personal and a global journey. As a textbook, it aims to provide students with maps for navigating our cultural terrain. It asks that we participate in the critical work of evaluating mass media and shaping their direction. In this journey, we have choices. We can watch the media as detached outsiders—as observers, we can praise them when they perform well and blame them for our social predicaments. Or we can become active participants—we can analyze the impact and investigate the consequences of the stories that media industries tell and sell. We can challenge our media to perform at high levels and steer them to serve and preserve democratic ideals. And as involved citizens, we can be aware of the consequences of the business of media, and we can give voice to the issues that matter most to us and that most affect our daily lives. That's where we hope this book makes a contribution.

A New Look at How the Media Shape Our World

For the sixth edition of *Media and Culture,* we wanted to emphasize macro-level media developments, such as the technological advances and legislative reforms that continue to influence the way media forms are created, distributed, shared, consumed, and owned. The new edition focuses on these changes and shows students how they shape the media industries and our shared political and cultural landscape.

- **An expanded focus on media convergence.** Chapter 1 introduces and defines the concept of convergence in which older media forms appear in newer platforms— for example, how we now read our newspapers, watch television and movies, and download music while online or on a cell phone. It then explores the cultural effects of this phenomenon and situates technological convergence in the context of cross-platform media.
- **A new look at the Internet.** Along with a focus on convergence, the heavily revised Chapter 2 offers a fresh look at the history of the medium from ARPAnet to Internet2. And now, Chapter 2 analyzes three of the biggest online players— Microsoft, Yahoo!, and Google—to help students understand the forces shaping the Internet today.
- **More on media ownership.** The sixth edition examines the consolidation of media outlets and explores how increasingly powerful media oligarchies may limit access to diverse topics and opinions. To help students understand the complex web of connections shaping content and access, Chapters 2–10 each include a new Media Ownership chart showing the principal U.S. operations of a major media conglomerate. In addition, a fold-out chart at the beginning of *Media and Culture* depicts the holdings of Time Warner, the world's largest media corporation, illustrating the staggering reach of this media colossus.
- **A deeper look at news media.** *Media and Culture* explores the new ground rules and the increased complexity of today's news culture. A new Extended Case Study, "The News Media and War," walks students through the five steps of the critical process to show them how to tackle complicated and broad media issues for a better understanding of the media's influence.
- **New section on fake news and satiric journalism.** Chapter 14 discusses the satiric turn in news reporting on shows like *The Colbert Report* and *The Daily Show* and explores why today's media consumers trust—and are attracted to—these "fake" sources.

Always the Most Current Text Available

Because the mass media are always changing, so does *Media and Culture.* From coverage of the Iraq war and the growth of the Internet in China, to the problem of copyright law in the digital era and the challenge of balancing First Amendment rights with issues of national security, the new edition gives students the information they need to analyze today's most pressing media trends.

- **Thirty percent new chapter openers** including an examination of the landmark 2006 midterm elections, the prime-time television battle between reality TV and scripted dramas, and the media storm surrounding *The Da Vinci Code.*
- **Thirty percent new or fully revised feature boxes.** The five types of feature boxes—Case Study, Tracking Technology, Examining Ethics, Global Village, and Media Literacy—now cover pressing new issues, such as the rise of blogs, the impact of digitally downloading music, product placement in video games, and controversies surrounding Wikipedia.

- **Updated tables and figures** track the latest economic, technological, and cultural changes across the media industries.
- **Fifty percent new images** and an award-winning design illustrate both contemporary media trends and historically significant events.
- **Updated and expanded coverage throughout** focuses on such topics as a la carte cable options; podcasting; the rise of MySpace.com, Facebook.com, and YouTube .com; and developments in digital publishing.

The *Media and Culture e-Book* Offers a New Learning Tool

The sixth edition of *Media and Culture* is also available as an online, interactive e-book. The e-book includes the complete text of the print book along with all of the figures and charts and most of the photographs. Even better, the innovative interface allows students to take notes, highlight text, search the book or the Internet, and link to the book's glossary. Instructors can add custom notes for their students and add their own material, including text and Web links. Please see the Supplements section in this preface for more information.

The Best and Broadest Introduction to the Mass Media

The sixth edition of *Media and Culture* retains the essential features that students and teachers alike have always praised. Since it was first published, each edition of *Media and Culture* has been recognized for its unique critical approach, its rich cultural perspective, and its comprehensive coverage of mass media industries.

- **A critical approach to media literacy.** *Media and Culture* introduces students to the five stages of the critical thinking and writing process: description, analysis, interpretation, evaluation, and engagement. The text uses these stages as a lens for examining the historical context and current processes that shape mass media as part of U.S. culture. This framework informs the writing throughout, including the Media Literacy and the Critical Process boxes that appear within each chapter and with end-of-chapter exercises.
- **A cultural perspective.** The text consistently focuses on the vital relationship between mass media and our shared culture—how cultural trends influence our mass media and how specific historical developments, technical innovations, and key decision makers in the history of the media have affected the ways our democracy and society have evolved.
- **Comprehensive coverage.** The text gives students the nuts and bolts content they need to understand each media industry's history, organizational structure, economic models, and market statistics.
- **Compelling storytelling.** Most mass media—whether news, prime-time television, magazines, film, paperback novels, digital games, or advertising—make use of storytelling to tap into our shared beliefs and values, and so does this book. Each chapter presents the events and issues surrounding media culture as intriguing and informative narratives rather than as a series of unconnected facts and feats. *Media and Culture* presents the history of mass media as compelling and complex stories that map the uneasy and parallel developments of consumer culture and democratic society.
- **The most accessible book available.** Learning tools in every chapter help students find and remember the information they need to know: chapter-opening outlines give students a roadmap to main points, annotated timelines offer powerful visual guides that highlight key events and refer to more coverage in the chapters, Media Literacy and the Critical Process boxes model the five-step process for students, and end-of-chapter exercises help students study and review.

The Organization and Themes of *Media and Culture*

The organization of *Media and Culture* takes into account the dramatic influences of digital forms of mass communication on the social world. Because intersecting forms of mass communication integrate aspects of print, electronic, and digital culture in our daily lives, we begin with the stories of convergence. Rather than starting chronologically with the book—society's oldest mass medium—the industry chapters open with the media students know best: the Internet, music, radio, television, cable, and film. Placing past and present communication developments within contemporary contexts, *Media and Culture* looks at older media against the backdrop of new forms that have reshaped printed culture.

- **A focus on media technology.** *Media and Culture* examines key technological developments that have changed the world, from the telegraph, our first binary communication system (with its electronic dots and dashes), to the Internet, our latest binary system (with its digital ones and zeros). The text studies our journey from the Industrial Age to the recent developments of the Information Age: e-mail, cell phones, digital games, MP3 players, radio, TV sets, VCRs and DVDs, newspapers, magazines, digital books, and communication satellites.

- **A concern for values and ethics.** To develop a critical perspective toward mass media, students must think about values and ethics as a routine and integrated part of the way they experience media in daily life. Media books often ghettoize the subject of ethics by treating it in a separate, isolated chapter near the end. *Media and Culture,* on the other hand, weaves into the media industry chapters compelling discussions about the values depicted in mass communication and the ethical implications faced by media practitioners.

- **An exploration of media economics and democracy.** To become better citizens and discerning consumers, students must attend to the complex relationship between democracy and capitalism, between the marketplace of ideas and the global consumer market. To that end, *Media and Culture* addresses the significance of the dramatic rise in multinational media systems. It invites students to explore the implications of the 1996 Telecommunications Act and the vast control that a handful of mammoth international companies exercise over the production and distribution of commercial mass media. Additionally, Chapter 13 looks critically at the global picture and encourages students to participate in the debates over ownership. Each chapter ends with a discussion of the effects of various mass media on the nature of democratic life.

Student Supplements

Book Companion Site at bedfordstmartins.com/mediaculture

Study aids on the book's Web site help students gauge their understanding of the text material through chapter summaries with accompanying study questions, visual activities that combine images and critical thinking analysis, and pre- and post-chapter quizzes to help students assess their strengths and weaknesses and focus their studying. In addition, streaming headlines from a variety of news sources keep students informed of recent developments in the mass media.

Media and Culture e-Book at bedfordstmartins.com/mediaculture

Print Book and e-Book ISBN-10: 0-312-47350-8; ISBN-13: 978-0-312-47350-1; Access Cards for e-Book Only ISBN-10: 0-312-47349-4; ISBN-13: 978-0-312-47349-5

This online e-book includes the complete text of the print book, along with all of the figures and charts and most of the photographs. Access cards with activation codes can be packaged at no extra cost with the print book or purchased separately.

Media Career Guide: Preparing for Jobs in the 21st Century, **Sixth Edition**
James Seguin, *Robert Morris College*; ISBN-10: 0-312-46914-4; ISBN-13: 978-0-312-46914-6
Practical and student-friendly, this revised guide includes a comprehensive directory of media jobs, practical tips, and career guidance for students considering a major in communication studies and mass media.

Instructor Supplements

About the Media: Video Clips DVD to Accompany *Media and Culture*
ISBN-10: 0-312-45173-3; ISBN-13: 978-0-312-45173-8
This unique instructor's resource includes more than fifty media clips, keyed to every chapter in *Media and Culture*. It provides historical and contemporary footage as well as excerpts from critical pieces about the media. The DVD is available upon adoption of *Media and Culture*; please contact your local sales representative.

Instructor Resources at bedfordstmartins.com/mediaculture
In addition to all student resources, the site offers instructors PowerPoint presentations for each chapter, the Instructor's Resource Manual, and student quiz tracking. And new Clicker Questions for every chapter help integrate the latest personal response systems (PRS) into the classroom and get instant feedback on students' understanding of course concepts as well as their opinions and perspectives.

Instructor's Resource Manual
Bettina Fabos, *Miami University*; Christopher R. Martin, *Miami University*; and Richard Campbell, *Miami University*; ISBN-10: 0-312-46348-0; ISBN-13: 978-0-312-46348-9
This updated manual improves on what has always been the best and most comprehensive instructor teaching tool available for the introduction to mass communication course. Every chapter in the new edition offers teaching tips and activities culled from dozens of instructors who use *Media and Culture* to teach thousands of students. In addition, this extensive resource provides a range of teaching approaches, tips for facilitating in-class discussions, writing assignments, outlines, lecture topics, lecture spin-offs, critical process exercises, classroom media resources, and an annotated list of more than 200 video resources.

Test Bank
Christopher R. Martin, *Miami University*, and Bettina Fabos, *Miami University*; Computerized Test Bank ISBN-10: 0-312-46347-2; ISBN-13: 978-0-312-46347-2; Print Test Bank ISBN-10: 0-312-46346-4; ISBN-13: 978-0-312-46346-5
A complete testing program is available both in print and as software formatted for Windows and Macintosh, with multiple-choice, true/false, fill-in-the-blank, and short and long essay questions.

Content for Course Management Systems
Instructors can access content for course management systems such as WebCT and Blackboard. Visit bedfordstmartins.com/cms for more information.

The Bedford/St. Martin's Video Resource Library
A wide selection of contemporary and historical media-related videos is organized around the issues explored in *Media and Culture*. Qualified instructors are eligible to select videos from the resource library upon adoption of the text.

Media Presentations CD-ROM
ISBN-10: 0-312-25045-2; ISBN-13: 978-0-312-25045-4
CD-ROM technology and PowerPoint software let you build classroom presentations around three case studies: "Popular Music and Freedom of Expression,"

"Newspapers: From Print to the Web," and "Photojournalism, Photography, and the Coverage of War." These case studies include visual and textual material that instructors can use as is for lectures or customize with additions from the Web or other sources.

Acknowledgments

We are very grateful to everyone at Bedford/St. Martin's who supported this project through its many stages. We wish that every textbook author could have the kind of experience we had with these people: Chuck Christensen, Joan Feinberg, Denise Wydra, Erika Gutierrez, Erica Appel, and Rachel Falk. We also collaborated with superb and supportive developmental editors: on the sixth edition, Noel Hohnstine, along with Simon Glick, who also worked on the first three editions of *Media and Culture*. We particularly appreciate the tireless work of Shuli Traub, managing editor, who oversaw the book's extremely tight schedule; Ryan Sullivan, project editor, who kept the book on schedule while making sure we got the details right; Dennis J. Conroy, senior production supervisor; and Anna Palchik, whose award-winning design keeps the book looking fresh from edition to edition. We are especially grateful to our Miami University research assistant, Susan Coffin, who functioned again as a one-person clipping service through the process.

We also want to thank the many fine and thoughtful reviewers who contributed ideas to the sixth edition of *Media and Culture*: Boyd Dallos, *Lake Superior College*; Roger George, *Bellevue Community College*; Osvaldo Hirschmann, *Houston Community College*; Ed Kanis, *Butler University*; Dean A. Kruckeberg, *University of Northern Iowa*; Larry Leslie, *University of South Florida*; Lori Liggett, *Bowling Green State University*; Steve Miller, *Rutgers University*; Robert Pondillo, *Middle Tennessee State University*; David Silver, *University of San Francisco*; Chris White, *Sam Houston State University*; and Marvin Williams, *Kingsborough Community College*.

For the fifth edition: Russell Barclay, *Quinnipiac University*; Kathy Battles, *University of Michigan*; Kenton Bird, *University of Idaho*; Ed Bonza, *Kennesaw State University*; Larry L. Burris, *Middle Tennessee State University*; Ceilidh Charleson-Jennings, *Collin County Community College*; Raymond Eugene Costain, *University of Central Florida*; Richard Craig, *San Jose State University*; Dave Deeley, *Truman State University*; Janine Gerzanics, *West Valley College*; Beth Haller, *Towson University*; Donna Hemmila, *Diablo Valley College*; Sharon Hollenback, *Syracuse University*; Marshall D. Katzman, *Bergen Community College*; Kimberly Lauffer, *Towson University*; Steve Miller, *Rutgers University*; Stu Minnis, *Virginia Wesleyan College*; Dave Perlmutter, *Louisiana State University–Baton Rouge*; Frank G. Perez, *University of Texas at El Paso*; Karen Pitcher, *University of Iowa*; Ronald C. Roat, *University of Southern Indiana*; Marshel Rossow, *Minnesota State University*; Roger Saathoff, *Texas Tech University*; Matthew Smith, *Wittenberg University*; and Marlane C. Steinwart, *Valparaiso University*.

For the fourth edition: Fay Y. Akindes, *University of Wisconsin–Parkside*; Robert Arnett, *Mississippi State University*; Charles Aust, *Kennesaw State University*; Russell Barclay, *Quinnipiac University*; Bryan Brown, *Southwest Missouri State University*; Peter W. Croisant, *Geneva College*; Mark Goodman, *Mississippi State University*; Donna Halper, *Emerson College*; Rebecca Self Hill, *University of Colorado*; John G. Hodgson, *Oklahoma State University*; Cynthia P. King, *American University*; Deborah L. Larson, *Southwest Missouri State University*; Charles Lewis, *Minnesota State University–Mankato*; Lila Lieberman, *Rutgers University*; Abbus Malek, *Howard University*; Anthony A. Olorunnisola, *Pennsylvania State University*; Norma Pecora, *Ohio University–Athens*; Elizabeth M. Perse, *University of Delaware*; Hoyt Purvis, *University of Arkansas*; Alison Rostankowski, *University of Wisconsin–Milwaukee*; Roger A. Soenksen, *James Madison University*; and Hazel Warlaumont, *California State University–Fullerton*.

For the third edition: Gerald J. Baldasty, *University of Washington*; Steve M. Barkin, *University of Maryland*; Ernest L. Bereman, *Truman State University*; Daniel Bernadi, *University of Arizona*; Kimberly L. Bissell, *Southern Illinois University*; Audrey Boxmann, *Merimack College*; Todd Chatman, *University of Illinois*; Ray Chavez, *University of Colorado*; Vic Costello, *Gardner–Webb University*; Paul D'Angelo, *Villanova University*; James Shanahan, *Cornell University*; and Scott A. Webber, *University of Colorado*.

For the second edition: Susan B. Barnes, *Fordham University*; Margaret Bates, *City College of New York*; Steven Alan Carr, *Indiana University/Purdue University, Fort Wayne*; William G. Covington Jr., *Bridgewater State College*; Roger Desmond, *University of Hartford*; Jules d'Hemecourt, *Louisiana State University*; Cheryl Evans, *Northwestern Oklahoma State University*; Douglas Gomery, *University of Maryland*; Colin Gromatzky, *New Mexico State University*; John L. Hochheimer, *Ithaca College*; Sheena Malhotra, *University of New Mexico*; Sharon R. Mazzarella, *Ithaca College*; David Marc McCoy, *Kent State University*; Beverly Merrick, *New Mexico State University*; John Pantalone, *University of Rhode Island*; John Durham Peters, *University of Iowa*; Lisa Pieraccini, *Oswego State College*; Susana Powell, *Borough of Manhattan Community College*; Felicia Jones Ross, *Ohio State University*; Enid Sefcovic, *Florida Atlantic University*; Keith Semmel, *Cumberland College*; Augusta Simon, *Embry–Riddle Aeronautical University*; Clifford E. Wexler, *Columbia–Greene Community College*.

For the first edition: Paul Ashdown, *University of Tennessee*; Terry Bales, *Rancho Santiago College*; Russell Barclay, *Quinnipiac University*; Thomas Beell, *Iowa State University*; Fred Blevens, *Southwest Texas State University*; Stuart Bullion, *University of Maine*; William G. Covington Jr., *Bridgewater State College*; Robert Daves, *Minneapolis Star Tribune*; Charles Davis, *Georgia Southern University*; Thomas Donahue, *Virginia Commonwealth University*; Ralph R. Donald, *University of Tennessee-Martin*; John P. Ferre, *University of Louisville*; Donald Fishman, *Boston College*; Elizabeth Atwood Gailey, *University of Tennessee*; Bob Gassaway, *University of New Mexico*; Anthony Giffard, *University of Washington*; Zhou He, *San Jose State University*; Barry Hollander, *University of Georgia*; Sharon Hollenbeck, *Syracuse University*; Anita Howard, *Austin Community College*; James Hoyt, *University of Wisconsin–Madison*; Joli Jensen, *University of Tulsa*; Frank Kaplan, *University of Colorado*; William Knowles, *University of Montana*; Michael Leslie, *University of Florida*; Janice Long, *University of Cincinnati*; Kathleen Maticheck, *Normandale Community College*; Maclyn McClary, *Humboldt State University*; Robert McGaughey, *Murray State University*; Joseph McKerns, *Ohio State University*; Debra Merskin, *University of Oregon*; David Morrissey, *Colorado State University*; Michael Murray, *University of Missouri at St. Louis*; Susan Dawson O'Brien, *Rose State College*; Patricia Bowie Orman, *University of Southern Colorado*; Jim Patton, *University of Arizona*; John Pauly, *St. Louis University*; Ted Pease, *Utah State University*; Janice Peck, *University of Colorado*; Tina Pieraccini, *University of New Mexico*; Peter Pringle, *University of Tennessee*; Sondra Rubenstein, *Hofstra University*; Jim St. Clair, *Indiana University Southeast*; Jim Seguin, *Robert Morris College*; Donald Shaw, *University of North Carolina*; Martin D. Sommernes, *Northern Arizona State University*; Linda Steiner, *Rutgers University*; Jill Diane Swensen, *Ithaca College*; Sharon Taylor, *Delaware State University*; Hazel Warlaumont, *California State University-Fullerton*; Richard Whitaker, *Buffalo State College*; and Lynn Zoch, *University of South Carolina*.

Special thanks from Richard Campbell: I would also like to acknowledge the number of fine teachers at both the *University of Wisconsin–Milwaukee* and *Northwestern University* who helped shape the way I think about many of the issues raised in this book, and I am especially grateful to my former students at the *University of Wisconsin–Milwaukee, Mount Mary College,* the *University of Michigan,* and *Middle Tennessee State University,* as well as my current students at *Miami University.* Some of my students have contributed directly to this text, and thousands have endured my courses over the years — and made them better. My all-time favorite former students, Chris

Martin and Bettina Fabos, are now Miami University colleagues and essential co-authors, as well as the creators of our book's Instructor's Resource Manual and the *About the Media* DVD, the new collection of short teaching clips related to each chapter. I am grateful for Chris and Bettina's fine writing, research savvy, good stories, and tireless work amid their own teaching schedules and writing careers (all while raising two spirited young daughters).

I remain most grateful, though, to the people I most love: my son, Chris; my daughter, Caitlin; and, most of all, my wife, Dianna, whose daily conversations, shared interests (especially her love of good music and crime stories), and ongoing support are resources I depend on to make this project go better with each edition.

Special thanks from Christopher Martin and Bettina Fabos: We would also like to thank Richard Campbell, with whom, as always, it has been a delight to work with on this project. We also appreciate the great energy, creativity, and talent that everyone at Bedford/St. Martin's brings to the book. From edition to edition, we also receive plenty of suggestions from *Media and Culture* users and reviewers and from our own journalism and media students. We would like to thank them for their input and for creating a community of sorts around the theme of critical perspectives on the media. Most of all, we'd like to thank our daughters, Olivia and Sabine, who bring us joy and laughter every day, and a sense of mission to better understand the world of media and culture in which they live.

contents

Sounds and Images

3 Sound Recording and Popular Music 72

Words and Pictures

 Newspapers and the Rise of Modern Journalism   **274**

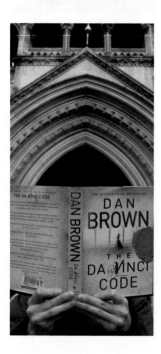

The Business of Mass Media

11 Advertising and Commercial Culture   386

Democratic Expression and the Mass Media

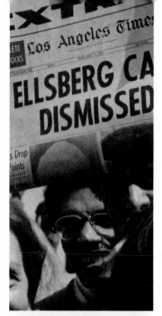

media & culture

mass communication

a critical approach

CHAPTER 1

In television, in newspapers, and online, the 2006 national midterm election featured great stories, including a lead narrative that highlighted disillusionment and anger over the Iraq war from both the American public and many conservative politicians (who traditionally stand for U.S. isolationism, fiscal responsibility, and lean government). This dissatisfaction resulted in the Democrats winning the majority position in both the House and Senate with promises of new legislation and investigations into the war, which by the end of 2006 had cost 3,000 American lives, 500,000-plus Iraqi lives, and more than $350 billion.

This dramatic political change rode in on a tide of political advertising that deluged radio and TV stations during the election. Most of these ads built up one candidate while tearing down another, turning genuine corruption—or sleazy innuendo— into thirty-second melodramas. The ads reached a peak in 2006 when many scandals surfaced before the election, from sordid instant messages sent by a disgraced congressman to young congressional pages to sexual

innuendo aimed at stirring up racial division and fear. For example, there was the narrow defeat of Tennessee Democrat Harold Ford, who was trying to become the first African American from the South to win a U.S. Senate seat since Civil War Reconstruction. A political moderate, Ford's loss was partially due to a widely televised thirty-second ad sponsored by the Republican Party that highlighted his brief attendance at a Playboy Mansion party—one that hosted political figures from across party lines. The ad ended with a scantily clad white woman whispering, "Harold, call me," conjuring up the kind of racial suspicion that had routinely prevented Southern black politicians from holding national office.

In a democracy, we often depend on political ads and the news media to provide information that helps us choose our elected leaders. We might expect that the media earning millions of dollars from political advertising would investigate carefully the main issues of the day. Did the news media's coverage help us better understand an election full of "mud-slinging" ads? Perhaps, but as critics rightly predicted,

little of the money earned by media outlets during the elections was invested in hiring more reporters and setting aside more time for analyzing major issues. Instead, through the lobbying efforts of the TV and cable industries, substantial amounts of that money would be "donated" back to politicians running for office. Why? These politicians vote on the laws that govern media ownership (how many media outlets one company can own), and they depend on TV exposure for their election. A Center for Public Integrity investigation of campaign contributions and lobbying expenditures revealed that the broadcasting, cable, and telecommunication industries spent $1.1 billion dollars between 1998 and 2004 "to affect election outcomes and influence legislation before Congress and the White House." Increasing this cycle of interdependence between politicians and the media, in the 2004 election alone, the presidential candidates, the major parties, and their supporters spent a record $1.5 billion on political ads on television.[1]

So, rather than increasing their news departments and critical political coverage with the money

earned from political ads, large media corporations today invest in acquiring new properties, such as additional TV stations, cable outlets, and small newspapers. It is no coincidence that since the 1996 Telecommunications Act, most rules restricting the number of media outlets that a single company can own have largely disappeared. And in many newsrooms and TV stations, investigative reporting units (which could do stories on the impact of media consolidation on politics) have also disappeared, making job reduction a means to maximize profits.

With citizens in need of complex narratives, documented information, and sharp analysis about the nation and the world—particularly since the terrorist attacks of 9/11—our major media instead sell astonishing amounts of time to political parties and fill twenty-four-hour cable news cycles with sensational crime stories. As media ownership laws are relaxed and as more money is exchanged between politicians and the news media, how will citizens be informed about the issues that matter most to them and that most affect our daily lives?

So what exactly are the roles and responsibilities of the media in the wake of the 2006 election, the aftermath of Hurricane Katrina, and the ongoing war in Iraq? In such times, how do we demand higher standards from our news media and popular culture? In this book, we take up such questions. In addition to international terrorism, foreign wars, and natural disasters, we can also examine the media's role.

At its worst, the media's appetite for telling and selling stories leads them not only to document tragedy but also to exploit or misrepresent it. Many social critics are uneasy with the way our culture—particularly TV and cable—seems to hurtle from one media event to another. News saturates the airwaves with twenty-four-hour coverage, accompanied by specially chosen theme music and catchy titles, such as the war in Iraq being packaged as "Operation Iraqi Freedom"—a Pentagon term. Rather than maintain a critical distance, most mainstream news media began using other government-inspired phrases as their own, such as "shock and awe" (the early bombing strikes on Baghdad) and "embedded" journalists (the nearly six hundred reporters the Pentagon permitted to accompany the troops to document the early stages of the war).

In this book, we examine media as a central force in shaping our culture and democracy. We investigate issues such as the media coverage of terrorism and war to see ways the mass media fail us as well as the ways they succeed. After all, they have an impact beyond reporting acts of terrorism or telling tragic stories. The media—in all their various forms, from mainstream newspapers to radio talk shows to Internet chat rooms—try to bring understanding to events that affect all of us. At their best, our media reflect and sustain the values and traditions of a vital democracy. Not only do the Harry Potter book series and TV shows like *CSI* or *American Idol* engage and entertain diverse audiences, but our newspapers and Internet Web sites also watch over society's institutions, making sense of important events and chronicling the ebb and flow of daily life.

> **❝** Embed, n. A war correspondent tagging along with a combat unit, who is said to be 'embedded' (a Pentagon term) or 'in bed with the Pentagon' (the journalism-school definition).**❞**
>
> –David Olive, *Toronto Star*, March 23, 2003

● In addition to the 600 radio, TV, and print reporters granted "embedded" status by the Pentagon, many journalists covered the war from known locations throughout the Middle East. This map illustrates the location of Cable News Network (CNN) reporters at the beginning of the war in Iraq.

The growth of media industries, commercial culture, and new converging technologies—fiber-optic cable, computers, digital television, satellites—offers a challenge to all of us. If we can learn to examine and critique the powerful dynamics of the media, we will be better able to monitor the rapid changes going on around us.

In this chapter, we will examine key concepts and introduce critical processes for investigating media industries and issues. In the chapters that follow, we will probe the history and structure of media's major institutions. In the process, we will develop an informed and critical view of the multiple impacts these institutions have had on community and global life. Our goal is to become *media literate*—more critical as consumers of mass media institutions and more engaged as citizens who accept part of the responsibility for the shape and direction of media culture.

Culture and the Evolution of Mass Communication

One way to understand the role and impact of the media in our lives is to understand the cultural context in which the media operate. Often, culture is narrowly associated with art, the unique forms of representational expression that give pleasure and raise awareness about what is true, good, and beautiful. Culture, however, can be viewed as a broader category that identifies the ways in which people live and represent themselves at particular historical times. This idea of culture encompasses fashion, sports, architecture, education, religion, and science, as well as mass media. Although we can study permanent cultural forms, such as novels or songs from various historical periods, culture is always changing. It includes a society's art, beliefs, customs, games, technologies, traditions, and institutions. It also encompasses a society's modes of **communication**: the process of creating symbol systems that convey information and meaning (for example, language systems, dot-dash Morse code, motion pictures, or one-zero binary computer codes).

Culture is made up of both the products that a society fashions and, perhaps more importantly, the processes that forge those products and reflect a culture's diverse values. Thus, **culture** may be defined as the symbols of expression that individuals, groups, and societies use to make sense of daily life and to articulate their values. According to this definition, when we listen to music, read a book, watch television, or scan the Internet, we are not asking, "Is this art?" but are instead trying to identify or connect with something or someone. In other words, we are assigning meaning to the song, book, TV program, or Internet site. Culture, therefore, is a process that delivers the values of a society through products or other meaning-making forms. For instance, the American ideal of "tough" or rugged individualism has been depicted for decades through a tradition of westerns and detective stories on television and in movies and books.

Culture links individuals to their society, providing shared and contested values, and the mass media help circulate those values. The **mass media** are the cultural industries—the channels of communication—that produce and distribute songs, novels, newspapers, movies, Internet services, and other cultural products to large numbers of people. The historical development of media and communication can be traced through several overlapping eras in which newer forms of technology and knowledge disrupted and modified older forms. These eras, which all still operate to greater or lesser degrees, are oral, written, print, electronic, and digital. The first two eras refer to the communication of tribal or feudal communities and agricultural economies. The last three phases feature the development of **mass communication**: the process of designing and delivering cultural messages and stories to large and diverse audiences through media channels as old as the book and as new as the Internet. Hastened by the growth of industry and modern technology, mass communication accompanied the gradual shift of rural populations to urban settings and the rise of a consumer culture.

Oral and Written Forms Begin the Dialogue

In most early societies, information and knowledge first circulated slowly through oral traditions passed on by poets, teachers, and tribal storytellers. As alphabets and the written word developed, however, a manuscript, or written, culture began to complement and then overshadow oral communication. Documented and transcribed by philosophers, monks, and stenographers, the manuscript culture served the ruling classes. Working people were generally illiterate, and the economic and educational gap between peasants and rulers was vast. These eras of oral and written communication developed slowly over many centuries. Although exact time frames are disputed, historians generally consider these eras as part of civilization's premodern period, spanning the epoch roughly from 1000 B.C. to the mid-fifteenth century.

Early tensions between oral and written communication played out among ancient Greek philosophers and writers. Socrates (470–399 B.C.), for instance, made his arguments through public conversations and debates. This dialogue style of communication became known as the Socratic method, and it is still used in university law schools and college classrooms. Many philosophers who supported the superiority of the oral tradition feared that the written word would threaten public discussion by offering fewer opportunities for the give-and-take of conversation. In fact, Socrates' most famous student, Plato (427–347 B.C.), sought to banish poets, whom he saw as purveyors of ideas less rigorous than those generated in oral, face-to-face, question-and-answer discussions. These debates foreshadowed similar discussions in the twentieth century regarding the dangers of television and the Internet. Does contemporary culture, such as TV talk shows and anonymous online chat rooms, cheapen public discussions and discourage face-to-face communication?

● Postmodern artist Barbara Kruger, famous for the epigram "I shop therefore I am," relays her concern that popular culture equals "checkbook" culture — under the control of giant media corporations and outside the control of citizens, who are defined only as consumers.

Printed Words Revolutionize Everyday Life

The invention of the printing press and movable metallic type in the fifteenth century provided the industrial seed that spawned modern mass communication. From the time of Johannes Gutenberg's invention, it took about four hundred years for the print era to evolve and to eclipse oral and manuscript traditions.

The printing press, among its many contributions, introduced a method for mass production. Presses and publications spread rapidly across Europe in the late 1400s and early 1500s. Many early books were large, elaborate, and expensive, taking months to illustrate and publish. They were usually purchased by wealthy aristocrats, royal families, church leaders, prominent merchants, and powerful politicians. Gradually, however, printers reduced the size and cost of books, making them available and affordable to more people.

With the print revolution, the book became the first mass-marketed product in history. The printing press combined three elements necessary for this innovation. First, duplication, or machine copying, replaced the tedious manuscript system in which scribes hand-copied a text several times to produce multiple copies. Second, duplication could be done rapidly, producing mass quantities of the same book. Third, the faster processing of multiple copies brought down the cost of each unit, making books more affordable to less affluent people. These three basic elements would provide the impetus for the Industrial Revolution, assembly-line production, modern capitalism, and the rise of consumer culture in the twentieth century.

The printing press also paved the way for major social and cultural changes by transmitting knowledge across national boundaries. Mass-produced printed materials spread information faster and farther than ever before, extending communication outside the realm of isolated tribal or community life. Printers and writers circulated views counter to traditional civic doctrine and to religious authority. Ultimately, the printing press and the wide distribution of knowledge jump-started large social movements, including the Protestant Reformation and the rise of modern nationalism, which prompted people to think of themselves not merely as members of families or tribes but as part of a country whose interests were broader than local or regional concerns.

With the revolution in industry came the rise of the middle class and an elite business class of owners and managers who gained the kind of clout once held only by the nobility or the clergy. Whereas oral and writing societies featured decentralized local governments, the print era marked the ascent of more centralized nation-states. As print media diminished the role of oral and manuscript communication, they also became key tools for commercial and political leaders to distribute information and maintain social order.

● Before the invention of the printing press, books were copied by hand in a labor-intensive process. This beautifully illuminated page is from an Italian Bible from the early 1300s.

As with the Internet today, however, it was difficult for a single business leader or political party in democratic societies to gain total control over books and technology (although the king did control printing press licenses in England until the early nineteenth century). Instead, the mass publication of pamphlets, magazines, and books helped spread the word and democratize knowledge. Literacy rates rose among the working and middle classes as publications of all sorts became affordable. Industrialization required a more educated workforce, but printed literature and textbooks also encouraged compulsory education, thus promoting literacy and extending learning beyond the world of wealthy upper-class citizens.

Just as the printing press fostered nationalism, it also nourished the competing ideal of individualism. With all sorts of ideas and treatises available, people came to rely less on their local community and their commercial, religious, and political leaders for guidance. By challenging tribal life, the printing press "fostered the modern idea of individuality," disrupting "the medieval sense of community and integration."[2] In urban and industrial environments, many individuals became cut off from the traditions of rural and small-town life, which had encouraged community cooperation in premodern times. By the mid-nineteenth century, the ideal of individualism affirmed the rise of commerce and increased resistance to government interference in the affairs of self-reliant entrepreneurs. The democratic impulse of individualism became a fundamental value in American society in the nineteenth and twentieth centuries.

Electronic and Digital Messages Deliver Immediacy

In Europe and America, the impact of industry's rise was enormous: Factories replaced farms as the main centers of work and production. During the 1880s, roughly 80 percent of Americans lived on farms and in small towns; by the 1920s and 1930s, most of this population had shifted to urban areas, where new industries and economic opportunities beckoned. The city had overtaken the country as the focus of national life.

In America, the gradual transformation from an industrial, print-based society to an informational era began with the development of the telegraph in the 1840s. Featuring dot-dash electronic signals (foreshadowing the ones and zeroes of our binary digital era), the telegraph made four key contributions to communication. First, it separated communication from transportation, making media messages instantaneous—unencumbered by stagecoaches, ships, or the pony express.[3] Second, the telegraph, in combination with the rise of mass-marketed newspapers, transformed "information into a commodity, a 'thing' that could be bought or sold irrespective of its uses or meaning."[4] By the time of the Civil War, news had become a valuable product, foreshadowing its contemporary role as a phenomenon that is both enormously profitable and ubiquitous. Third, the telegraph made it easier for military, business, and political leaders to coordinate commercial and military operations, especially after the installation of the transatlantic cable in the late 1860s. Finally, the telegraph foreshadowed future technological developments, such as wireless telegraphy, the fax machine, and the cellular phone. And in 2006, the Western Union telegraph offices sent their final message.

The rise of film at the turn of the twentieth century and the development of radio in the 1920s were early signposts, but the electronic phase of the Information Age really began in the 1950s and 1960s. The dramatic impact of television on daily life marked the arrival of a new visual and electronic era. With the coming of the latest communication gadgetry—ever smaller personal computers, cable television, DVDs, direct broadcast satellites, cellular phones, beepers, faxes, and e-mail—the Information Age passed into a digital phase. In **digital communication**, images, texts, and sounds are converted (encoded) into electronic signals (represented as varied combinations of binary numbers—ones and zeros), which are then reassembled (decoded) as a precise reproduction of, say, a TV picture, a magazine article, a song, or a telephone voice. On the Internet's various Web pages, image, text, and sound are all digitally reproduced and transmitted globally.

New electronic and digital technologies, particularly cable television and the Internet, have developed so quickly that traditional leaders in communication have lost some of their control over information. For example, starting with the 1992 presidential campaign, the network news began to lose its influence and audience to CNN's Larry King, Comedy Central, MTV, and radio talk shows, and by the 2004 election, Internet **bloggers'** personalized opinion sites had become a key element in news. Moreover, the technology of e-mail, which has assumed some of the functions of the postal service, is outpacing attempts to control it within national borders. A professor sitting at her desk in Oxford, Ohio, sends messages routinely to research scientists in Moscow, Russia. As recently as 1990, letters between citizens of the United States and former communist states might have been censored or taken months to reach their destinations.

Media Convergence: Citizen Choice or Corporate Control?

By 2006, the electronic and digital eras had fully ushered in the age of **media convergence**. And *convergence* today has come to mean two very different things. First, it means the technological merging of content in different mass media—for example,

> **" We are in great haste to construct a magnetic telegraph from Maine to Texas; but Maine and Texas, it may be, have nothing important to communicate. . . . We are eager to tunnel under the Atlantic and bring the old world some weeks nearer to the new; but perchance the first news that will leak through into the broad flapping American ear will be that Princess Adelaide has the whooping cough. "**
>
> —Henry David Thoreau, *Walden,* 1854

magazine articles and radio programs are also accessible on the Internet, and songs and TV programs are now available on iPods and cell phones. Such technical and media content convergence is not entirely new. For example, back in the late 1920s, the Radio Corporation of America (RCA) purchased the Victor Talking Machine Company and ushered in machines that could play both radio and recorded music. And in the 1950s, the radio and the recording industries again united during the emergence of television. This type of media convergence is also much broader than the simple merging of older and newer forms on the Internet. In fact, the various eras of communication are themselves reinvented in the Age of Convergence. Oral communication, for example, finds itself reconfigured, in part, as e-mail and in Internet instant messaging. And print communication is re-formed in the thousands of newspapers now available online. It is also important to keep in mind the wonderful irony of media convergence: That is, the first major digital retailer, Amazon.com, made its name by selling the world's oldest mass medium—the book—on the world's newest mass medium—the Internet.

Although this first meaning of convergence offers citizens the promise of wide choice and flexible control over how to use and access media, a second definition of media convergence—sometimes called **cross platform** by media marketers—describes a particular business model that is favored by corporate interests. Under this model, convergence is about consolidating various media holdings—such as cable connections, phone services, television transmissions, and Internet access—under one corporate umbrella. Here the goal is not necessarily to offer consumers more choice but to manage resources and maximize profits better. For example, a company that owns TV stations, radio outlets, and newspapers in multiple markets—as well as in the same cities—can deploy a reporter or producer to create three or four versions of the same story for various media outlets. So rather than each radio station, TV station, newspaper, and online news site all generating diverse and independent stories about an issue vital to a community or city, a media company can now use fewer employees to generate multiple versions of the same story. This means a company employing a convergence model needs fewer reporters, producers, and editors—not more. Therefore, the fewer stories generated from fewer perspectives under this business arrangement means that citizens have less choice in news coverage. This model offers more profits to those companies that downsize—or converge—their workforce while increasing their media holdings in many markets. (See Chapter 2 for more about convergence.)

● The rise of high-end cell phones—like T-Mobile's Sidekick (sometimes called a "hiptop")—has emerged as digital competition for laptops, allowing users to e-mail, take pictures, instant message, play games, edit documents, and browse the Web.

Mass Media and the Process of Communication

Although often labeled and discussed disparagingly as "the media," mass communication institutions are not a single entity. The mass media constitute a wide variety of industries and merchandise, from documentary news programs about famines in Africa to infomercials about vegetable slicers or psychic therapists. The word *media* is, after all, a Latin plural form for the singular noun *medium*. Television, newspapers, music, movies, magazines, books, billboards, direct mail, broadcast satellites, and the Internet are all part of the media; and they each remain quite capable of either producing worthy products or pandering to society's worst desires, prejudices, and stereotypes.

Considering the diversity of mass media, to paint them all with the same broad brush would be inaccurate and unfair. Yet that is often what we seem to do, which may in fact reflect the distrust many of us hold toward prominent social institutions, from local governments to daily newspapers. Of course, when one recent president has an extramarital affair with a young White House intern and another has appointees linked to unethical corporate misbehavior, our distrust of both our institutions and the media is understandable. (See "Examining Ethics: Covering the War" on page 24.) In this text, we will attempt to replace a sometimes misdirected and cynical perception of the media with an attitude of genuine criticism. To become media literate, we can begin by understanding competing models of mass communication.

A Linear Model of Mass Communication

To develop an interpretive or critical perspective toward the media, we need insight into how the mass communication process works. One of the older and more influential ideas about the way media work is depicted in a linear model of communication. In this model, mass communication is conceptualized as the process of producing and delivering messages to large audiences. According to the linear model, mass communication is a component system, made up of **senders** (the authors, producers, and organizations) who transmit **messages** (the programs, texts, images, sounds, and ads). Through a **mass media channel** (newspapers, books, magazines, radio, television, or the Internet), senders pitch their messages to large groups of **receivers** (readers, viewers, citizens, and consumers). In the process, **gatekeepers** (such as editors, producers, and other media managers) function as message filters. Media gatekeepers make decisions about what messages actually get produced for particular audiences. The process occasionally allows **feedback**, in which citizens and consumers return messages to senders or gatekeepers through letters to the editor, phone calls, e-mail, Web site postings, or as audience members of talk shows.

Although the linear model explains certain aspects of the communication process, media messages usually do not flow smoothly from a sender at point A to a receiver at point Z. Like fish in turbulent water, words and images are in flux, spilling into each other and crisscrossing in the flow of everyday life. Media messages and stories are encoded and sent in written and visual forms, but senders often have very little control over how their intended messages are decoded or whether the messages are ignored or misread by readers and viewers.

A Cultural Approach to Mass Communication

Moving beyond a simple sender-message-receiver model, we offer a cultural component to the study of the media. Working under this *cultural approach*, it is important to recognize that individuals and societies bring diverse meanings to messages, given varying factors such as gender, age, educational level, ethnicity, and occupation. For instance, when the rapper Ice-T's heavy-metal group Body Count produced the song "Cop Killer" in the early 1990s, police organizations and urban teens interpreted the lyrics in dramatically different ways. Some police groups wanted to ban the song, arguing that it would lead to violence, whereas fans of the band asserted that the song accurately portrayed the exercise of police authority in urban America.

It is sometimes easy to assume that producers of media messages are the active creators of communication and that audiences are passive receptacles. This may describe some situations, but as the "Cop Killer" example illustrates, audiences also shape media messages to fit their own values and viewpoints. This phenomenon is known as **selective exposure**: Audiences typically seek messages and produce meanings that correspond to their own cultural beliefs and values. Thus in the process of mass communication, audiences are actively interpreting, refashioning, or rejecting the cultural messages and stories that flow through various media channels.

> "" 2005 was something of a watershed. Looking back 10 years, the hype outweighed the reality of convergence. Like a lot of technology, the tech [part] was there but the business models and consumer habits hadn't gotten there. Now we are . . . into 2006, [and] the reality has caught up with the rhetoric of convergence. ""
>
> —Pete Winkler, Director, Global Marketing Entertainment and Media Practice, PricewaterhouseCoopers, 2006

The Stories Media Tell

At its most significant level, mass communication and its *stories* can alter a society's perception of events and attitudes. Throughout the twentieth century and during the recent wars in Afghanistan and Iraq, for instance, courageous journalists covered armed conflicts, telling stories that helped the public comprehend the magnitude and tragedy of such events. In the 1950s and 1960s, television news reports on the Civil Rights movement led to crucial legislation that transformed the way many white people viewed the problems and aspirations of African Americans. In the late 1990s, the President Clinton–Monica Lewinsky affair sparked heated debates over private codes of behavior and public abuses of authority. And in 2001–2002, the *Boston Globe*'s coverage of the Catholic Church's cover-up of sexual abuse by some of its priests demonstrated that a story that had been viewed as an occasional isolated regional occurrence was truly a major national problem and a nightmare for the Church. In 2005–2006, news stories about the Bush administration's secret domestic spying operation sparked debates about terrorism and privacy rights. In each of these instances and through all of these stories, the mass media played a key role in changing individual awareness, cultural attitudes, and even public policy.

To take a cultural approach to mass communication is to understand that our media institutions are basically in the narrative—or storytelling—business. As journalist-essayist Joan Didion reminded us at the beginning of *The White Album*: "We tell ourselves stories in order to live." Psychologist Jerome Bruner argues that we are storytelling creatures, that as children we acquire language to tell stories that we already have inside us. In his book *Making Stories,* he says, "Stories, finally, provide models of the world."

This text acknowledges the centrality—and limitations—of media stories in our daily lives and how they provide the models through which we understand the world. The common denominator, in fact, between our entertainment and information cultures is the narrative. It is the media's main cultural currency—from a Harry Potter tale to a Dixie Chicks ballad to a Fox News "exclusive" to a *New York Times* story. The point is that the popular narratives of our news and entertainment culture are complex and varied. Roger Rosenblatt, writing in *Time* magazine right around the time of the polarizing 2000 presidential election, made this observation about the importance of stories in our culture: "We are a narrative species. We exist by storytelling—by relating our situations—and the test of our evolution may lie in getting the story right."[5]

The Impact of Media in Everyday Life

The earliest debates about the impact of cultural narratives on daily life date from the ancient Greeks. Socrates, himself accused of corrupting youths, worried that children exposed to stories "without distinction" would "take into their souls teachings that are wholly opposite to those we wish them to be possessed of when they are grown up."[6] The playwright Euripides, on the other hand, believed that art should imitate life, that characters should be real, and that artistic works should reflect the actual world even when that reality was sordid.

In *The Republic,* Plato developed the classical view of art: It should aim to instruct and uplift. He worried that some staged performances glorified evil and that common folk watching might not be able to distinguish between art and reality. Aristotle, Plato's student, occupied a middle ground in these debates, arguing that art and stories should provide insight into the human condition but should entertain as well.

Since the time of the early Greeks, concerns about the impact of culture have continued. At the turn of the twentieth century, for example, newly arrived immigrants to the United States who spoke little English gravitated toward cultural events

> **" Stories matter, and matter deeply, because they are the best way to save our lives. "**
>
> –Frank McConnell,
> *Storytelling and Mythmaking,* 1979

● In the 1950s, television images of early Civil Rights struggles visually documented the inequalities faced by black citizens. In 1957, the governor of Arkansas refused to allow black students like Elizabeth Eckford to enter Little Rock's Central High School, even though racial segregation had been outlawed by the Supreme Court in 1954. In response, President Dwight Eisenhower sent in the army to integrate the school and control angry white mobs. Think about the ways in which TV images can make events (such as boxing, vaudeville, and the new medium of silent film) for which enjoyment did not depend solely on understanding the English language. Consequently, these popular events occasionally became a flash point for many groups, including the Daughters of the American Revolution, some local politicians, religious leaders, and police vice squads, who not only resented the commercial success of immigrant culture but also feared that these "low" cultural forms would undermine traditional American values.

In the United States in the 1950s, the emergence of television and rock and roll generated countless points of contention. For instance, the phenomenal popularity of Elvis Presley set the stage for many of today's debates over hip-hop lyrics and television's negative influence. In 1956 and 1957, Presley made three appearances on the *Ed Sullivan Show*. The public outcry against Presley's "lascivious" hip movements was so great that by the third show the camera operators were instructed to shoot the singer from the waist up. Thousands of protective parents refused to allow their children to watch Presley's performances. In some communities, objections to Presley were motivated by class bias and racism. Many white adults believed that this "poor white trash" singer from Mississippi was spreading rhythm and blues, a "dangerous" form of black popular culture.

Today, the stakes are higher. Given the reach and spread of print, electronic, and digital communication, culture and its myriad mutations play an even more controversial role in society (see Table 1.1 below). People used to share their common interests in radio or TV characters and major news stories in backyard, barroom, and coffee-shop conversations, but the proliferation of specialized publications and personalized channels has fragmented the media audience. Many citizens have also become critical of the lack of quality in so much contemporary culture and are concerned about the overwhelming amount of information now available. Even the computer, once heralded as the educational salvation of children, has created confusion. Today, when kids announce that they are "on the computer," parents may wonder whether they are writing a term paper, playing a video game, talking to cyberspace strangers, shopping for sneakers, or peeking at pornography.

● **Table 1.1 Hours per Person per Year Using Consumer Media**

Year	Total TV	Broadcast & Satellite Radio	Newspaper	Consumer Internet	Video Games	Total*
1999	1,427	939	205	65	58	3,280
2002	1,519	991	194	147	70	3,430
2004	1,546	986	188	176	77	3,480
2006	1,555	975	179	190	82	3,499
2009	1,562	984	165	203	96	3,555
Five-Year Change						
1999–2004	+119	+47	–17	+111	+19	+200
2004–2009	+16	–2	–23	+27	+19	+75

Source: Veronis Suhler Stevenson Communications Industry Forecast.

*Total hours includes time spent with recorded music, consumer magazines, consumer books, home video/DVD, box office, interactive TV and wireless content, and time spent media multitasking—using media simultaneously.

By 2006, the mass media had given the public much to be concerned about. Talk shows exploited personal problems for commercial gain, and so-called reality shows glamourized outlandish and often dangerous stunts. Television research once again documented the connection between aggression in children and violent entertainment programs. Children watched nearly forty thousand TV commercials each year. Debates also raged about curbing kids' exposure to pornography and adult subject matter on the Internet. Yet, although media depictions may worsen social problems, research has seldom demonstrated that the media directly cause our society's major afflictions. For instance, when a middle school student shoots a fellow student over a designer jacket, should society blame the ad that glamourized the clothing and the network that carried the ad? Or are parents, teachers, and religious leaders failing to instill strong moral values? Or are economic and social issues involving gun legislation, consumerism, and income disparity at work as well? Even if the clothing manufacturer bears responsibility as a corporate citizen, did the ad itself cause the tragedy, or is the ad symptomatic of larger problems?

With American mass media industries earning more than $200 billion annually, the economic stakes are high. Large portions of media resources now go toward studying audiences, capturing their attention through stories, and taking their consumer dollars. This process involves trying to influence everything from how people vote to how they shop. Like the air we breathe, the fallout from the mass media surrounds us. But to monitor the media's "air quality"—to become media literate—responsible citizens must attend more thoughtfully to diverse media stories that are too often taken for granted.

Surveying the Cultural Landscape

Some cultural phenomena gain wide popular appeal, and others do not. Some appeal to certain age groups or social classes; some, such as rock and roll, jazz, and classical music, are popular worldwide. Other cultural forms, such as Tejano, salsa, and Cajun music, are popular primarily in certain regions or communities. Some aspects of culture are considered elite in one place (opera in the United States) and popular in another (opera in Italy). Throughout history, however, most societies have arranged culture into hierarchical categories.

Culture as a Skyscraper

Throughout twentieth-century America, critics and audiences took for granted a hierarchy of culture that exists to this day and can be visualized, in some respects, as a modern skyscraper. The top floors of the building house **high culture**, such as ballet, the symphony, art museums, and classical literature. The bottom floors—and even the basement—house popular or **low culture**, including such icons as soap operas, rock music, radio shock jocks, and video games (see Figure 1.1 on page 16). High culture, identified with "good taste" and often supported by wealthy patrons and corporate donors (the kind of folks who might favor sky-boxes and penthouses), is associated with "fine art," which is available primarily in libraries, theaters, and museums. In contrast, low or popular culture is aligned with the questionable tastes of the "masses," who enjoy the commercial "junk" circulated by the mass media. Whether or not we agree with this cultural skyscraper model, the high-low hierarchy has become so entrenched that it often determines or limits the ways in which we view and discuss culture today.[7]

> **" Skyscrapers were citadels of the new power of finance capitalism. . . . Far above the thronging sidewalks, they elevated the men who controlled much of the capital that lubricated the workings of organized cultural enterprises — publishing companies, film studios, theatrical syndicates, symphony orchestras. Culture . . . was becoming increasingly organized during the twentieth century. And the model for that organization was the hierarchical, bureaucratic corporation."**
>
> —Jackson Lears, historian

Figure 1.1
Culture as a Skyscraper

Culture is diverse and difficult to categorize. Yet throughout the twentieth century we tended to think of culture not as a social process but as a set of products sorted into high, low, or middle positions on a cultural skyscraper. Look at this highly arbitrary arrangement and see if you agree or disagree. Write in some of your own examples.

Why do so many people view culture this way? Why do we categorize or classify culture in this way? Who controls this process? Is control of making cultural categories important—why or why not?

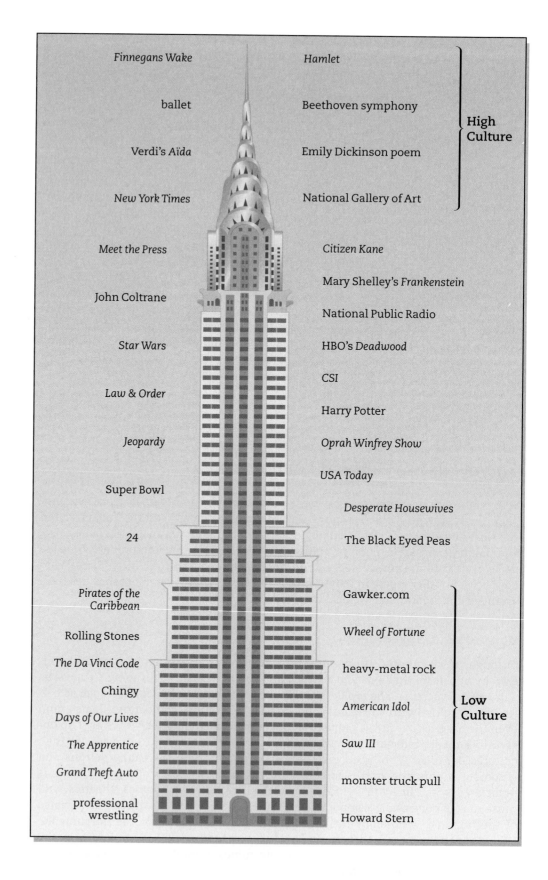

Finnegans Wake   Hamlet

ballet   Beethoven symphony

Verdi's Aïda   Emily Dickinson poem

New York Times   National Gallery of Art

High Culture

Meet the Press   Citizen Kane

Mary Shelley's Frankenstein

John Coltrane   National Public Radio

Star Wars   HBO's Deadwood

CSI

Law & Order   Harry Potter

Jeopardy   Oprah Winfrey Show

USA Today

Super Bowl   Desperate Housewives

24   The Black Eyed Peas

Pirates of the Caribbean   Gawker.com

Rolling Stones   Wheel of Fortune

The Da Vinci Code   heavy-metal rock

Chingy   American Idol

Low Culture

Days of Our Lives

The Apprentice   Saw III

Grand Theft Auto   monster truck pull

professional wrestling   Howard Stern

Some critics are concerned that popular culture in the form of contemporary movies, television, and rock music distracts students from serious literature and philosophy, thus ruining their imagination and undermining their ability to recognize great art.[8] Discounting a person's ability to value Bach and the Beatles or Shakespeare and *The Simpsons* concurrently, this critical view pits popular culture against the more traditional forms of high art and culture. The assumption is that because popular forms of culture are made for profit, they cannot be experienced as valuable artistic experiences in the way more elite art forms are.

Another concern is that popular culture exploits classic works of literature and art. The best example may be Mary Wollstonecraft Shelley's dark Gothic novel *Frankenstein,* written in 1818 and ultimately transformed into multiple popular forms. Today, the tale is best remembered by virtue of a 1931 film version starring Boris Karloff as the towering monster. In addition to the movies, television turned the tale into *The Munsters,* a mid-1960s situation comedy. Eventually, the monster was resurrected as sugar-coated Frankenberry cereal. In the recycled forms of the original story, Shelley's powerful themes about abusing science and judging people on the basis of appearances are often lost or trivialized.

Unlike an Italian opera or a Shakespearean tragedy, many elements of popular culture have a short life span. The average newspaper circulates for about twelve hours, then lands in a recycle bin or at the bottom of a cat litter tray; the average magazine circulates for about five to seven days; a new Top 40 song on the radio lasts about one month; and the typical TV series survives for less than ten weeks. Although endurance does not necessarily denote quality, in the view of many critics better forms of culture have more staying power. These critics argue that popular forms promote a culture that is unstable and fleeting, that they follow rather than lead public taste. In the television industry in the 1960s and 1970s, this was known as "least objectionable programming," or *LOP:* TV's network executives were often accused of pandering to mediocrity by airing bland, disposable programming that would not disturb or challenge a "normal" viewer.

A final concern is that popular culture not only undermines or exploits high culture but has inundated the cultural environment, driving out higher forms of culture and cheapening public life.[9] This concern is supported by data showing that TV sets are in use in the average American home for more than seven hours a day, exposing adults and children each year to thousands of hours of TV commercials and popular culture. According to critics, the prevalence of media products prevents the public from experiencing genuine art. Forty or more radio stations are available in most

● Mary Shelley, the author of *Frankenstein,* might not recognize our popular culture's mutations of her Gothic classic. First published in 1818, the novel has inspired numerous interpretations, everything from the scary—Boris Karloff in the classic 1931 movie—to the silly—the Munster family in the 1960s TV sitcom. Can you think of another example of a story that has developed and changed over time and through various media transformations?

● *Lost* (2004–)

The Sleeper Curve

In the 1973 science fiction comedy movie *Sleeper,* the film's director, Woody Allen, plays a character who reawakens 200 years after being cryogenically frozen (a routine ulcer operation had gone bad). The scientists who "unfreeze" Allen discuss how back in the 1970s people actually believed that "deep fat," "steaks," "cream pies," and "hot fudge" were thought to be unhealthy. But apparently in 2173, those food items will be good for us.

In Steven Johnson's 2005 book, *Everything Bad Is Good for You,* Johnson makes a controversial argument about TV and culture based on the movie. He calls his idea the "Sleeper Curve" and claims that "today's popular culture is actually making us smarter."[1] Johnson's ideas run counter to those of many critics who fret about popular culture and its potentially disastrous effects, particularly on young people. An influential argument in this strain of thinking appeared twenty years ago in Neil Postman's 1985 book, *Amusing Ourselves to Death.* Postman argued that we are moving from the "Age of Typology" to the "Age of Television," from the "Age of Exposition" to the "Age of Show Business."[2] Postman worried that an image-centered culture had overtaken words and a print-oriented culture, resulting in "all public discourse increasingly tak[ing] the form of entertainment." He pointed to the impact of adver-

tising and how "American businessmen discovered, long before the rest of us, that the quality and usefulness of their goods are subordinate to the artifice of their display."[3] For Postman, image making has become central to choosing our government leaders, including the way politicians are branded and packaged as commodity goods in political ads. Postman argued that the TV ad has become the "chief instrument" for presenting political ideas, with these results: "that short simple messages are preferable to long and complex ones; that drama is to be preferred over exposition; that being sold solutions is better than being confronted with questions about problems."[4]

Now that we are somewhere between the Age of Television and the Age of the Internet, Johnson's argument offers an opportunity to assess where our visual culture has taken us. According to Johnson, "For decades, we've worked under the assumption that mass culture follows a path declining steadily toward lowest-common-denominator standards, presumably because the 'masses' want dumb, simple pleasures and big media companies try to give the masses what they want. But, the exact opposite is happening: the culture is getting more cognitively demanding, not less."[5] While Johnson shares many of Postman's 1985 concerns, he disagrees with the point from *Amusing Ourselves to Death* that image-saturated media is only about "simple" messages and "trivial" culture. Instead, Johnson discusses the complexity of video and computer games and many of TV's dramatic prime-time series, especially when compared with this kind of TV programming from the 1970s and early 1980s.

As evidence, Johnson compares the plot complications of Fox's CIA/secret agent thriller *24* with *Dallas,* the prime-time soap opera that was America's most popular TV show in the early 1980s. "To make sense of an episode of *24,*" Johnson maintains, "you have to integrate far more information than you would have a few decades ago watching a comparable show. Beneath the violence and the ethnic stereotypes, another trend appears: to keep up with entertainment like *24,* you have to pay attention, make inferences, track shifting social relationships." Johnson argues that today's audience would be "bored" watching a show like *Dallas,* in part "because the show contains far less information in each scene, despite the fact that its soap-opera structure made it one of the most complicated narratives on television in its prime. With *Dallas,* the modern viewer doesn't have to think to make sense of what's going on, and not having to think is boring."

In addition to *24,* a number of contemporary programs offer complex narratives, including *Desperate Housewives, The West Wing, Alias, Lost, The Simpsons, E.R., Without a Trace,* and *CSI,* which air on the traditional broadcast networks; and *The Sopranos, Deadwood, Six Feet Under, Carnivale, Curb Your Enthusiasm,* and *Extras* on cable's HBO. Johnson says that in contrast to older popular programs like *Dallas* or *Dynasty,* contemporary TV storytelling layers "each scene with a thick network of affiliations. You have to focus to follow the plot, and in focusing you're exercising the parts of your brain that map social networks, that fill in missing information, that connect multiple narrative threads." Johnson argues that younger audiences today — brought up in the Age of the Internet and in an era of complicated interactive visual games — bring high expectations to other kinds of popular culture as well, including television. "The mind," Johnson writes, "likes to be challenged; there's real pleasure to be found in solving puzzles, detecting patterns or unpacking a complex narrative system."

In countering the cultural fears expressed by critics like Postman and by many parents trying to make sense of the intricate media world that their children encounter each day, Johnson sees a hopeful sign: "I believe that the Sleeper Curve is the single most important new force altering the mental development of young people today, and I believe it is largely a force for good: enhancing our cognitive faculties, not dumbing them down. And yet you almost never hear this story in popular accounts of today's media."

● *Dallas* (1978–1991)

Steven Johnson's theory is one of many about the impact of media on the way we live and learn. Do you buy Johnson's Sleeper Curve argument that certain TV programs — along with challenging interactive video and computer games — are intellectually demanding and are actually making us smarter? Why or why not? Are you more persuaded by Postman's 1985 account — that the world has been displaced by an image-centered culture and, consequently, that popular culture has been dumbed down by its oversimplified and visual triviality? As you consider Postman, think about the Internet: Is it word based or

> **"The Web has created a forum for annotation and commentary that allows more complicated shows to prosper, thanks to the fan sites where each episode of shows like *Lost* or *Alias* is dissected with an intensity usually reserved for Talmud scholars."**
>
> —Steven Johnson, 2005

image based? What kinds of opportunities for learning does it offer?

In thinking about both the 1985 and 2005 arguments by Postman and Johnson, consider as well generational differences. Do you enjoy TV shows and video games that your parents or grandparents don't understand? What types of stories and games do they enjoy? What did earlier generations value in storytelling and what is similar and dissimilar about storytelling today? Interview someone who is close to you but from an earlier generation about media and story preferences. Then discuss or write about both the common ground and the cultural differences that you discovered.

cities; cable systems with hundreds of channels are in place in more than 65 percent of all U.S. households; and MP3 players, Internet services, DVRs, and DVD players are increasing in popularity. Thus the chance of more refined culture transforming the media environment or even finding a substantial audience seems small.

There is also concern that the impact of popular culture, especially its visual forms (such as TV advertising and daytime talk shows), has undermined democratic reasoning. According to this view, popular media may inhibit social progress or reform by transforming audiences into cultural dupes, seduced by the promise of products. A few multinational conglomerates, which make large profits from media products, may be distracting citizens from examining economic disparity and implementing change. Seductive advertising images showcasing the buffed and airbrushed bodies of professional models frequently contradict the actual lives of many people, who cannot hope to achieve a particular "look" or may not have the financial means to obtain many of the cosmetic products offered on the market. In this environment, art and commerce have become blurred, restricting the audience's ability to make cultural distinctions. Sometimes called the "Big Mac" theory, this view suggests that people are so addicted to mass-produced media menus that they have lost not only the will to challenge social inequities but also their discriminating taste for finer fare.

Culture as a Map

To depict culture as an ongoing process—rather than as a vertically organized hierarchy of products—and to account for our diverse and individual tastes, it might help to imagine culture as a map rather than as a skyscraper. Maps represent large, unwieldy spaces that extend in all directions. Maps highlight main highways and familiar urban centers, but they also include scores of side roads and small towns, directing our focus to unexplored areas.

Whereas the hierarchical skyscraper model of culture too easily presents culture on a simple high-to-low scale, a map model depicts culture in a more complex way, spreading in more directions. On the one hand, cultural phenomena—such as the stories we read in books or watch at the movies—offer places to go that are conventional, recognizable, stable, and comforting. But on the other hand, our culture's storehouse of stories may tend toward the innovative, unfamiliar, unstable, and challenging. Most forms of culture, however, demonstrate both tendencies. For example, we may buy the CDs of a favorite artist or watch our favorite TV programs for both their innovation *and* their familiarity. We may listen to a song or watch a program to complement a mood, to distance ourselves from problems, or to reflect critically on the song's lyrics or the TV show's meanings.

The appeal of culture is often its familiar stories, pulling audiences toward the security of repetition and common landmarks on the cultural map. Consider, for instance, television's *Lassie* series. More than 500 episodes exist in syndication; many had a familiar and repetitive plot line: Timmy, who arguably possessed the poorest sense of direction and suffered more concussions than any TV character in history, gets lost or knocked unconscious. After finding Timmy and licking his face, Lassie goes for help and saves the day. Adult critics might mock this melodramatic formula, but many children find comfort in the predictability of the story. This quality is also illustrated when night after night children ask their parents to read Margaret Wise Brown's *Good Night, Moon* or Maurice Sendak's *Where the Wild Things Are*. Like children, adults also seek a kind of comfort, often returning to the same songs, the same plays, the same poems, and the same TV programs.

But we also like cultural adventure. We seek new stories and new places to go—those aspects of culture that may demonstrate originality and complexity. For instance, James Joyce's *Finnegans Wake* (1939) created language anew and challenged

> ❝ TV is a genre of reruns, a formulaic return to what we already know. Everything is familiar. Ads and old programs are constantly recycled. It's like mythology, like the Homeric epics, the oral tradition, in which the listener hears passages, formulae, and epithets repeated over and over again. There is a joy in repetition, as children know when they say, 'Mommy, tell me that story again.' ❞
>
> –Camille Paglia, *Harper's,* 1991

● *The Simpsons,* the longest-running prime-time cartoon in TV history, undermines the notion that cultural products fit into either "high" or "low" categories. Each episode about this cartoon family might contain references to serious playwrights and classical philosophers as well as to trendy rock bands and popular movies (the characters even appear at concerts). What do you think of this program's ability to blend both "high" and "low" forms of culture?

readers, as the novel's poetic first sentence illustrates: "riverrun, past Eve and Adam's, from swerve of shore to bend of bay, brings us by a commodius vicus of recirculation back to Howth Castle and Environs." A revolutionary work, crammed with historical names and topical references to events, myths, songs, jokes, and daily conversation, Joyce's novel remains a challenge to understand and decode. His work demonstrated that part of what culture provides is that impulse to explore new places. In our everyday lives we return to our favorite TV programs and recording artists, but we may also tire of old shows and favorite singers. So we strike out in new directions, searching for something different that may mirror our own growth.

We know that people have complex cultural tastes, needs, and interests based on different backgrounds and dispositions. It is not surprising, then, that our cultural forms and stories—from blues music and opera to comic books and classical literature—contain a variety of messages. Just as Shakespeare's plays were packed with both obscure and popular references, TV episodes of *The Simpsons* today include allusions to the Beatles, Kafka, the *Adventures of Ozzie & Harriet,* Tennessee Williams, talk shows, Aerosmith, *The X-Files,* and *Citizen Kane.* In other words, as part of an ongoing process, cultural products and their meanings are "all over the map." This suggests that in spite of many critics' tendencies to rank culture vertically, we should not think about our cultural environment merely as a product hierarchy but as a changing road map that spreads out in diverse directions.

Some critics of popular culture—often without presenting supportive evidence—assert that society was better off before the latest developments in mass media. They resist the idea of redrawing established cultural maps. The nostalgia for some imagined "better past" has often operated as a device for condemning new cultural phenomena. In the nineteenth century, in fact, a number of intellectuals and politicians worried that rising literacy rates among the working class might create havoc: How would the aristocracy and intellectuals maintain their authority and status if everyone could read? Throughout history, a call to return to familiar terrain, to "the good old days," has been a frequent response to new, "threatening" forms of popular culture, which over the years have included the waltz, silent movies, ragtime, jazz, comic books, rock and roll, soap operas, heavy metal, hip-hop, tabloid newspapers, "reality" television programs, and the Internet.

Shifting Values in Modern Culture

In contemporary life, cultural boundaries are being tested; the arbitrary lines between information and entertainment have become even more blurred. Consumers now read newspapers on their computer screens. Media corporations do business across vast geographic boundaries. We are witnessing *media convergence,* in which satellite dishes, TV screens, cable or computer modems, and cell phones easily access new and old forms of mass communication. For a fee, everything from magazines to movies is channeled into homes through computer modems, TV cables, or satellite transmissions. To place these shifts and this convergence in historical context, scholars have traced the meandering route of cultural values through the **modern** period (from the full-blown arrival of the Industrial Revolution in the nineteenth century) to one that is frequently labeled **postmodern**, or contemporary.

What it means to be "modern" is complicated. As we have seen, the process of modernization involved individuals and societies responding to changing economic circumstances. Captains of industry employed workforces and new technology, creating efficient manufacturing centers and inexpensive products aimed at making everyday life both better and more profitable. Printing presses and assembly lines made major contributions in this transformation, and modern advertising spread the word about new gadgets to American consumers.

Cultural responses to modernization often manifest themselves in the mass media. For example, Aldous Huxley, in *Brave New World* (1932), created a fictional world in which he cautioned readers that modern science and technology posed a threat to individual dignity. Charlie Chaplin's film *Modern Times* (1936), set in a futuristic manufacturing plant, also told the story of the dehumanizing impact of modernization and machinery. Writers and artists, in their criticisms of the modern world, often point to technology's ability to alienate people from one another, capitalism's tendency to foster greed, and government's inclination to create bureaucracies that oppress rather than help people.

Among the major values of the modern period, four typically manifest themselves in the cultural environment: celebrating the individual, believing in rational order, working efficiently, and rejecting tradition. These values of the modern period were originally embodied in the printing press and later in newspapers and magazines. The print media encouraged the vision of individual writers, publishers, and readers who circulated new ideas. Whereas the premodern period was guided by strong beliefs in a natural or divine order, becoming modern meant elevating individual self-expression to a central position. Along with democratic breakthroughs, however, individualism and the Industrial Revolution triggered modern forms of hierarchy, in which certain individuals and groups achieved higher standing in the social order. For example, those who managed commercial enterprises gained more control over the economic ladder, while an intellectual class of modern experts, who mastered specialized realms of knowledge, gained increasing power over the nation's social, political, and cultural agendas.

To be modern also meant to value the capacity of organized, scientific minds to solve problems efficiently. Progressive thinkers maintained that the printing press, the telegraph, and the railroad in combination with a scientific attitude would foster a new type of informed society. At the core of this society, the printed mass media, particularly newspapers, would educate the citizenry, helping to build and maintain an organized social framework.[10] Journalists strove for the modern ideal through a more fact-based and efficient approach to reporting. They discarded decorative writing and championed a lean look. Modern front-page news de-emphasized description, commentary, and historical context. The lead sentences that reported a presidential press conference began to look similar, whether they were on the front page in Tupelo, Mississippi, or Wahpeton, North Dakota. Just as modern architecture made many American skylines look alike, the front pages of newspapers began to resemble one another.

Finally, to be modern meant to throw off the rigid rules of the past, to break with tradition. Modern journalism became captivated by timely and immediate events. As a result, the more standardized forms of front-page journalism, on one hand, championed facts and current events while efficiently meeting deadlines. But on the other hand, modern newspapers often failed to take a historical perspective or to analyze sufficiently the ideas underlying these events.

Shifting Values in Postmodern Culture

For many people, the changes occurring in contemporary, or postmodern, society are identified only by a confusing array of examples: music videos, remote controls, Nike ads, shopping malls, fax machines, e-mail, video games, *South Park, USA Today,* cell phones, *TRL,* hip-hop, and reality TV. Some critics argue that postmodern culture represents a way of seeing—a condition (or malady) of the human spirit. Chiefly a response to the modern world, controversial postmodern values are playing increasingly pivotal roles in our daily lives. Four values, in particular, are identified here as markers of the so-called postmodern period: opposing hierarchy, diversifying and recycling culture, questioning scientific reasoning, and embracing paradox (see Table 1.2 below).

● Table 1.2 Trends across Historical Periods

	Premodern (pre-1800s)	Modern Industrial Revolution (post-1800s–1950s)	Postmodern (1950s–present)
Work hierarchies	peasants/ merchants/ rulers	factory workers/ managers/ national CEOs	temp workers/ managers/ global CEOs
Major work sites	field/farm	factory/office	office/home/"Virtual" or mobile office
Communication reach	local	national	global
Communication transmission	oral/manuscript	print/electronic	electronic/digital
Communication channels	storytellers/elders/ town criers	books/newspapers/ magazines/radio	television/cable/ Internet/multimedia
Communication at home	quill pen	typewriter/office computer	personal computer/ laptop/cell phone
Key social values	belief in natural or divine order	individualism/ rationalism/ efficiency/ anti-tradition	anti-hierarchy/ skepticism (about science)/diversity/ multiculturalism/irony & paradox
Journalism	oral & print-based/ partisan/decorative/ controlled by political parties	print-based/ objective/efficient/ timely/controlled by publishing families	TV-Internet based/ opinionated/ conversational/ controlled by giant media corporations

EXAMINING ETHICS

Covering the War

Early in 2006—with the war in Iraq about to begin its fourth year—President Bush criticized the national news media for not showing enough "good news" about the U.S. efforts to bring democracy to Iraq. Bush's remarks raised ethical questions about the complex relationship between the government and news media during times of war: How much freedom should the news media have to cover the war? What topics should they report on? How much control should the military have over the media's reports on the war? Are there topics that should not be covered?

These kinds of questions have also spurred ethical quagmires for local TV stations that cover the war and its effects on communities where soldiers have been called to war and then injured or killed. Sometimes, many station managers—out of fear of alienating viewers—encourage their news division not to seem critical of the war, wanting the station to appear "patriotic." In one extreme 2004 case, the nation's largest TV station owner—Sinclair Broadcast Group—would not air the ABC news program *Nightline* because it devoted an episode to reading the names of all U.S. soldiers killed in the war up to that time. Here is an excerpt from a *New York Times* account of that event:

> Sinclair Broadcast Group, one of the largest owners of local television stations, will pre-empt tonight's edition of the ABC News program "Nightline," saying the program's plan to have Ted Koppel read aloud the names of every member of the armed forces killed in action in Iraq was motivated by an antiwar agenda and threatened to undermine American efforts there.
>
> The decision means viewers in eight cities, including St. Louis and Columbus, Ohio, will not see "Nightline."
>
> ABC News disputed that the program carried a political message, calling it in a statement "an expression of respect which simply seeks to honor those who have laid down their lives for their country."
>
> But Mark Hyman, the vice president of corporate relations for Sinclair, who is also a conservative commentator on the company's newscasts, said tonight's edition of "Nightline" is biased journalism. "Mr. Koppel's reading of the fallen will have no proportionality,"

he said in a telephone interview, pointing out that the program will ignore other aspects of the war effort.

The company's reaction to "Nightline" is consistent with criticism from some conservatives, who are charging ABC with trying to influence opinion against the war.

Mr. Koppel and the producers of "Nightline" said earlier this week that they had no political motivation behind the decision to devote an entire show, expanded to 40 minutes, to reading the names and displaying the photos of those killed. They said they only intended to honor the dead and document what Mr. Koppel called "the human cost" of the war.[1]

Given such a case, how might a local TV news director—under pressure from the station's manager or owner—formulate guidelines to help negotiate such treacherous ethical territory? While most TV news divisions have ethical codes to guide journalists' behavior in certain situations, should ordinary citizens help shape ethical discussions and decisions? Below is a general plan for dealing with an array of ethical dilemmas that face media practitioners and for finding ways in which we might insert ourselves into this decision-making process.

Arriving at ethical decisions is a particular kind of criticism involving several steps. These include (1) laying out the case; (2) pinpointing the key issues; (3) identifying the parties involved, their intent, and their competing values; (4) studying ethical models and theories; (5) presenting strategies and options; and (6) formulating a decision or policy.[2] As a test case, let's look at how local TV news directors might establish ethical guidelines for war-related events. Following the six steps above, our goal is to make some ethical decisions and to lay the groundwork for policies that address TV images or photographs used for war coverage (for example, protesters, supporters, or memorial/funeral images). (See Chapter 14, page 494, for details on confronting ethical problems.)

Examining Ethics Activity

As a class or in smaller groups, design policies that address at least one of the issues raised above. Start by researching the topic; find as much information as possible. For example, you can research guidelines that local stations already use by contacting local news directors and TV journalists. Do they have guidelines? If so, are they adequate? Are there images they will not show? How are protesters and supporters of the war treated? Finally, if time allows, send the policies to various TV news directors and/or stations managers; ask for their evaluations and whether they would consider implementing them.

● Films often reflect the key social values of an era—as represented by the modern and postmodern movies pictured. Charlie Chaplin's *Modern Times* (1936) satirized modern industry and the dehumanizing impact of a futuristic factory on its overwhelmed workers. Similarly, Ridley Scott's *Blade Runner* (1982), set in futurist Los Angeles in 2019, questions the impact on humanity when technology overwhelms the natural world. As author William Romanowski said of *Blade Runner* in *Pop Culture Wars,* "It managed to quite vividly capture some postmodern themes that were not recognized at the time. . . . We are constantly trying to balance the promise of technology with the threats of technology."

One of the main values of contemporary culture is an opposition to hierarchy. Many artists are challenging the sometimes arbitrary line between high and low culture, and others are blurring the distinctions between fact and fiction or art and commerce. For example, a new television vocabulary now includes *infotainment* (*Entertainment Tonight, Access Hollywood*) and *infomercials* (fading celebrities selling anti-wrinkle cream). On cable, MTV's Tom Green produced a dark comedic documentary on his personal battle with testicular cancer, and Comedy Central's fake news program, *The Daily Show with Jon Stewart,* often does a better job covering real news than the regular networks. In magazines, arresting clothing or cigarette ads combine stark social commentaries with low-key sales pitches. At the movies, *Pulp Fiction* (1994), *Fargo* (1996), *Moulin Rouge* (2001), and *The Hitchhiker's Guide to the Galaxy* (2005) fused the comic and the tragic in film tributes to postmodern style. And in music, Madonna (who in 2004 took the Hebrew name Esther) championed oppressed groups at the same time that her songs made her a wealthy global icon for consumer culture.

Another contemporary value (or vice) of the so-called postmodern period emphasizes diversity and fragmentation, including the wild juxtaposition of old and new cultural styles. In a suburban shopping mall, for instance, Waldenbooks and Gap clothes border a Vietnamese, Italian, and Mexican food court, while a Muzak version of the Beatles' "Revolution" plays in the background and CDs are for sale at Starbucks. Part of this stylistic diversity involves borrowing and then transforming earlier ideas from the modern period. In music, hip-hop deejays and performers sample old R&B, soul, and rock classics to reinvent songs. Borrowing in hip-hop is often so pronounced that the original artists and record companies have frequently filed for copyright infringement. Critics of postmodern style contend that such borrowing devalues originality, emphasizing surface over depth and recycled ideas over new ones. Throughout the twentieth century, for example, films were adapted from books and short stories. Now, films often derive from popular TV series: *The Brady Bunch, The Mask of Zorro, Mission Impossible, Charlie's Angels,* and *The Dukes of Hazzard,* to name just a few. And in 2006, director Robert Altman (*M*A*S*H, Nashville, Gosford Park*) even made a movie, *Prairie Home Companion,* based on Garrison Keillor's long-running public radio program.

Another tendency of postmodern culture is to raise doubts about scientific reasoning. Rather than seeing science purely as enlightened thinking, postmodernists view it as laying the groundwork for modern bureaucratic problems. They reject rational thought as "the answer" to every social problem, lauding instead the premodern values of small communities and mystical experiences. Internet users, for example, are seen as reclaiming in digital form lost conversational skills and letter-writing habits. Even the current popularity of radio and TV talk shows, according to this view, is partly an attempt to recover lost aspects of oral traditions. Given the feelings of powerlessness and alienation that mark the contemporary age, one attraction of the talk-show format has been the way it encourages ordinary people to participate in discussions with celebrities, experts, and each other.

Although some forms of contemporary culture raise questions about rational science, other postmodern cultural forms warmly embrace technology. Blockbuster films such as *Jurassic Park, The Matrix,* and the Harry Potter movies do both, presenting stories that challenge modern science but depend on technological wizardry for their execution. During the modern period, art and literature criticized the dangers of machines. Postmodern style, however, often embraces new technologies.

Many forms of contemporary culture generally accept technology. There is, however, a fundamental paradox in this uneasy postmodern alliance. As modern writers and artists have pointed out, new technologies often eliminate jobs and physically isolate us from one another. Conversely, new technologies can draw people together to discuss politics on radio talk shows, electronic town-hall meetings, or Internet newsgroups. Our lives today are full of such incongruities.

> **"** A cynic is a man who, when he smells flowers, looks around for a coffin.**"**
>
> —H. L. Mencken

Critiquing Media and Culture

Just as communication is not always reducible to the linear sender-message-receiver model, many forms of media and culture are not easily represented by the high-low metaphor. We should, perhaps, strip culture of such adjectives as *high, low, popular,* and *mass.* These modifiers may artificially force media forms and products into predetermined categories. Rather than focusing on these worn-out labels, we might instead look at a wide range of issues generated by culture, from the role of storytelling in the mass media to the global influences of media industries on the consumer marketplace. We should also be moving toward media literacy and a critical perspective that takes into account the intricacies of the cultural landscape.

A fair critique of any cultural form, regardless of its social or artistic reputation, requires a working knowledge of the particular book, program, or music under scrutiny. For example, to understand W. E. B. DuBois's essays, critics immerse themselves in his work and in the historical context in which he wrote. Similarly, if we want to develop a meaningful critique of *The Simpsons* or *CSI,* it is essential to understand the contemporary context in which these programs are produced.

To begin this process of critical assessment, we must imagine culture as more complicated and richer than the high-low model allows. We must also assume a critical stance that enables us to get outside our own preferences. We may like or dislike Tim McGraw's pop country, Usher's urban R&B, or Chuck D's political rap, but if we want to criticize these musical styles intelligently, we should understand what the various types of music have to say and why their messages have appeal for particular audiences. The same approach applies to other cultural forms. If we critique a newspaper article, we must account for the language that is chosen and what it means; if we analyze a film or TV program, we need to slow down the images in order to understand how they try to make sense.

It is easy to form a cynical view of the stream of TV advertising, talk shows, rock stars, and news tabloids that floods the cultural landscape. But cynicism is no substitute for criticism. To become literate about media involves striking a balance between taking a critical position (developing knowledgeable interpretations and judgments) and becoming tolerant of diverse forms of expression (appreciating the distinctive variety of cultural products and processes). A cynical view usually involves some form of intolerance and either too little or too much information. For example, after enduring the glut of news coverage devoted to the 2004 presidential election, we might easily have become cynical about our political system. However, *information* in the form of news facts and *knowledge* about a complex social process such as a national election are not the same thing. The **critical process** stresses the subtle distinctions between amassing information and becoming knowledgeable or attaining **media literacy**.

Developing a media-literate critical perspective involves mastering five overlapping stages that build on each other:

- *Description*: paying close attention, taking notes, and researching the subject under study
- *Analysis*: discovering and focusing on significant patterns that emerge from the description stage
- *Interpretation*: asking and answering the "What does that mean?" and "So what?" questions about one's findings
- *Evaluation*: arriving at a judgment about whether something is good, bad, or mediocre, which in-

volves subordinating one's personal taste to the critical assessment resulting from the first three stages
- *Engagement*: taking some action that connects our critical perspective with our role as citizens to question our media institutions, adding our own voice to the process of shaping the cultural environment

Let's look at each of these stages in greater detail.

Description

If we decide to focus on how well the news media serve democracy, we might critique the fairness of several programs or individual stories from *60 Minutes* or the *New York Times*. We start by describing the programs or articles, accounting for their reporting strategies, and noting what persons are featured as interview subjects. We might further identify central characters, conflicts, topics, and themes. From the notes taken at this stage, we can begin comparing what we have found to other stories on similar topics. We can also document what we think is missing from these news narratives—the questions, viewpoints, and persons that were not included—and other ways to tell the story.

Analysis

In the second stage of the critical process, we isolate patterns that call for closer attention. At this point, we decide how to focus the critique. Because *60 Min-*

Benefits of a Critical Perspective

Developing an informed critical perspective and becoming media literate allow us to participate in a debate about media culture as a force for both democracy and consumerism (see "Case Study: The Sleeper Curve" on pages 18–19). On the one hand, the media can be a catalyst for democratic tendencies. Consider the role of television in documenting racism and injustice in the 1960s; the use of video technology to reveal oppressive conditions in China and Eastern Europe or to document crimes by urban police departments; the appearance of hip-hop as black-produced commerce drawing attention to social injustice; the public hearings on the 9/11 tragedy carried on cable TV; and congressional hearings on the utes has produced thousands of hours of programs, our critique might spotlight just a few key patterns. For example, many of the program's reports are organized like detective stories, reporters are almost always visually represented at a medium distance, and interview subjects are generally shot in tight close-ups. In studying the *New York Times*, on the other hand, we might limit our analysis to countries that get covered more regularly than others, recurring topics chosen for front-page treatment, or the number of quotes from male and female experts.

Interpretation

In the interpretive stage, we try to determine the *meanings* of the patterns we have analyzed. The most difficult stage in criticism, interpretation demands an answer to the "So what?" question. For instance, the greater visual space granted to *60 Minutes* reporters—compared with the close-up shots used for interview subjects—might mean that the reporters appear to be in control. They are given more visual space in which to operate, whereas interview subjects have little room to maneuver within the visual frame. As a result, the subjects often look guilty and the reporters look heroic—or, at least, in charge. Likewise, if we look again at the *New York Times*, its attention to particular countries could mean that the paper tends to cover nations in which the United States has more vital political or economic interests, even though the *Times* might claim to be neutral and even-handed in its reporting of news from around the world.

Evaluation

The fourth stage of the critical process focuses on making an informed judgment. Building on description, analysis, and interpretation, we are better able to evaluate the fairness of a group of *60 Minutes* or *New York Times* reports. At this stage, we can grasp the strengths and weaknesses of the news media under study and make critical judgments measured against our own frames of reference—what we like and dislike as well as what seems good or bad about the stories and coverage we analyzed.

This fourth stage differentiates the reviewer (or *previewer*) from the critic. Most newspaper reviews, for example, are limited by daily time or space constraints. Although these reviews may give us important information about particular programs, they often begin and end with personal judgments—"This is a quality show" or "That was a piece of trash"—which should be the *final* stage in any substantial critical process. Regrettably, many reviews do not reflect such a process; they do not move much beyond the writer's own frame of reference.

Engagement

To be fully media literate, we must actively work to create a media world that best serves democracy—the fifth stage of the critical process. In our *60 Minutes* and *New York Times* examples, engagement might involve something as simple as writing a formal or e-mail letter to these media outlets to offer a critical take on the news narratives we are studying. But engagement can also mean participating in Web discussions, contacting various media producers or governmental bodies like the Federal Communications Commission (FCC) with critiques and ideas, organizing or participating in public media literacy forums, or learning to construct different types of media narratives ourselves—either in print, audio, video, or online—to participate directly in the creation of mainstream or alternative media. The key to this stage is to challenge our civic imaginations, to refuse to sit back and cynically complain about media without taking some action that lends our own voices and critiques to the process.

government's slow response to Hurricane Katrina victims in 2005. The media have also helped to renew interest in diverse cultures around the world (see "The Global Village: Bedouins, Camels, Transistors, and Coke" on page 30).

On the other hand, competing against these democratic tendencies is a powerful commercial culture that reinforces a world economic order controlled by fewer and fewer multinational corporations. For instance, when Poland threw off the shackles of the Soviet Union in the late 1980s, one of the first things its new leadership did was buy and dub the American soap operas *Santa Barbara* and *Dynasty*. For some Poles, these shows were a relief from sober Soviet political propaganda, but other Poles worried that they might inherit another kind of indoctrination—one

THE GLOBAL VILLAGE

Bedouins, Camels, Transistors, and Coke

Upon receiving the Philadelphia Liberty Medal in 1994, President Václav Havel of the Czech Republic described postmodernism as the fundamental condition of global culture, "when it seems that something is on the way out and something else is painfully being born." He described this "new world order" as a "multicultural era" or state in which consistent value systems break into mixed and blended cultures:

> For me, a symbol of that state is a Bedouin mounted on a camel and clad in traditional robes under which he is wearing jeans, with a transistor radio in his hands and an ad for Coca-Cola on the camel's back. . . . New meaning is gradually born from the . . . intersection of many different elements.[1]

Many critics, including Havel, think that there is a crucial tie between global politics and postmodern culture. They contend that the people who overthrew governments in the former Yugoslavia and the Soviet Union were the same people who valued American popular culture—especially movies, rock music, and television—for its free expression and democratic possibilities.

As modern communist states were undermined by the growth and influence of transnational corporations, citizens in these nations capitalized on the developing global market, using portable video and audio technology to smuggle out tapes of atrocities perpetrated by totalitarian regimes. Thus it was difficult for political leaders to hide repressive acts from the rest of the world. In *Newsweek*, CBS news anchor Dan Rather wrote about the role of television in the 1989 student uprising in China:

> Television brought Beijing's battle for democracy to Main Street. It made students who live on the other side of the planet just as human, just as vulnerable as the boy on the next block. The miracle of television is that the triumph and tragedy of Tiananmen Square would not have been any more vivid had it been Times Square.[2]

At the same time, we need to examine the impact on other nations of the influx of popular culture—the second-biggest American export (after military and airplane equipment). Has access to an American consumer lifestyle fundamentally altered Havel's Bedouin on the camel? What happens when CNN or MTV is transported to remote African villages that share a single community TV set? What happens when Westernized popular culture encroaches on the rituals of Islamic countries where the spread of American music, movies, and television is viewed as a danger to tradition? These questions still need answers. A global village, which through technology shares culture and communication, can also alter traditional rituals forever.

To try to grasp this phenomenon, we might imagine how we would feel if the culture from a country far away gradually eroded our own established habits. This, in fact, is happening all over the world as American culture becomes the world's global currency. Although newer forms of communication such as instant messaging have in some ways increased citizen participation in global life, in what ways have they muted the values of older cultures? Our current postmodern period is double-coded: It is an agent both for the renewed possibilities of democracy and for the worldwide spread of consumerism and American popular culture.

starring American consumer culture and dominated by large international media companies.

This example illustrates that contemporary culture cannot easily be characterized as one thing or another. Binary terms such as *liberal* and *conservative* or *high* and *low* have less meaning in an environment where so many boundaries have been blurred, so many media forms have converged, and so many diverse cultures coexist. Modern distinctions between print and electronic culture have begun to break down largely because of the increasing number of individuals who have come of age in *both* a print *and* an electronic culture.[11] Either/or models of culture, such as the high-low perspective, are making room for more inclusive models, similar to the map metaphor for culture discussed earlier.

What are the social implications of the new, blended, and merging cultural phenomena? How do we deal with the fact that public debate and news about everyday life now seem as likely to come from Oprah, Jon Stewart, or popular music as from the *New York Times, Nightline,* or *Newsweek?*[12] Clearly, such changes challenge us to reassess and rebuild the standards by which we judge our culture. The search for answers lies in recognizing the links between cultural expression and daily life. The search also involves monitoring how well the mass media serve democratic practices and involve a rich variety of people, not just as educated consumers but also as engaged citizens.

A healthy democracy requires the active participation of interested citizens. Part of this involvement means watching over the role and impact of the mass media, a job that belongs to each citizen, not just to paid media critics and watchdog organizations. In this textbook, we will begin the job by examining the historical contexts and current processes that shape media products. By probing various media industries, we can then develop a framework for tracking the ways in which they perform. By becoming more critical consumers and engaged citizens, we will be in a better position to influence the relationships among mass media, democratic participation, and the cultural landscape that we inhabit.

www.

For review questions and activities for Chapter 1, go to the interactive *Media and Culture* Online Study Guide at *bedfordstmartins.com/mediaculture*

REVIEW QUESTIONS

Culture and the Evolution of Mass Communication

1. Define *culture, mass communication,* and *mass media,* and explain their interrelationships.

2. What are the key technological breakthroughs that accompanied the transition to the print and electronic eras? Why were these changes significant?

Mass Media and the Process of Communication

3. Explain the linear model of mass communication and its limitations.

4. In looking at the history of popular culture, explain why newer forms of media seem to threaten status quo values.

Surveying the Cultural Landscape

5. Describe the skyscraper model of culture. What are its strengths and limitations?

6. Describe the map model of culture. What are its strengths and limitations?

7. What are the chief differences between modern and postmodern values?

Critiquing Media and Culture

8. What are the five steps in the critical process? Which of these is the most difficult and why?

9. What is the difference between cynicism and criticism?

10. Why is the critical process important?

QUESTIONING THE MEDIA

1. Using music or television as an example, identify a performer or program you once liked but began to dislike as you grew older and your tastes changed. Why do you think this happened? Do you think your early interests in popular music or television have had an impact on shaping your identity? Explain.

2. From your own experience, cite examples in which you think the media have been treated unfairly. Draw on comments from parents, teachers, religious leaders, friends, news media, etc. Discuss whether these criticisms have been justified.

3. Pick an example of a popular media product that you think is harmful to children. How would you make your concerns known? Should the product be re-moved from circulation? Why or why not? If you think the product should be banned, how would you do it?

4. Make a critical case either defending or condemning Comedy Central's *South Park,* a TV talk show, professional wrestling, a hip-hop group, a soap opera, or TV news coverage of the U.S. occupation of Iraq. Use the five-step critical process to develop your position.

5. Although in some ways postmodern forms of communication, such as e-mail, MTV, and CNN, have helped citizens participate in global life, in what ways might these forms harm more traditional or native cultures?

SEARCHING THE INTERNET

http://www.mediahistory.umn.edu

Hosted by the University of Minnesota, the Media History Project was founded to discover and understand trends in various media practices. You'll find information about media research and theory, historical time lines, key terms and concepts, and links to related sites.

http://www.aml.ca

Canada's Association for Media Literacy offers a site de-signed to teach students and citizens about the signifi-cance of media education. Broadly international in flavor, this site tracks the worldwide media literacy movement, offering notes and summaries from a variety of confer-ences and panels.

http://www.mediaed.org

The Media Education Foundation site features a guide to critical video resources, study guides, current articles, a free catalogue, and job/internship information.

http://www.media-awareness.ca

The Media Awareness Network is another cutting-edge Canadian site, offering an array of critical strategies for teaching children and students how to deal with media. Featuring news about media developments and issues, the site also has specific ideas for teachers, students, parents, and community leaders.

http://www.acmecoalition.org

ACME—the Action Coalition for Media Education—offers this site that links citizens in working groups around is-sues such as media curriculum ideas for schools; support for independent and alternative media initiatives; sup-port for media reform and legislative campaigns; and training in media education for students, parents, and community groups.

Media Literacy
and the Critical Process

In Brief

Develop a model or metaphor for categorizing culture other than the skyscraper model offered on page 16. How would your model help us better understand the ways in which culture works? Discuss your model.

In Depth

In small groups, or as a class, write the headings *Quality* and *Trash* on the board or on a sheet of paper. As a group, agree on several television shows that serve as examples of trashy programs and quality programs. In another column, if necessary, place any programs that are in dispute—those that may divide group opinion. (Films, books, magazines, and advertisements can be used here as well.) Your column headings should look like this:

Quality   *Trash*   *In Dispute*

1. For each set of programs, gather information and evidence. On a separate piece of paper, *describe* the programs by listing their narrative features: basic plots, central conflicts or tensions, typical subject matter, major themes, main characters, and how tensions are resolved.

2. Now return to your listing of programs. Under each category, name and *analyze* the attributes that led your group to classify the programs as you did. Identify as many characteristics as you can, and then summarize which virtues are essential to a quality show, which vices make a show trashy, and which elements make a particular show hard to classify.

3. Examine the patterns among the characteristics you have chosen, and *interpret* what this means. Why did you pick the characteristics you did for each category? Why did you associate particular features with quality or with trash? What made your disputed programs a problem for different members of your group? Why do some viewers (or readers) gravitate toward trashy shows (or books)? What might the programs mean to those audiences? For the programs you could not easily categorize, what led to their disputed standing?

4. *Evaluate* the programs on your lists. Assess whether these shows are good or bad. Should restrictions be placed on some programs even if this means testing the First Amendment protections of the press and free speech?

    Discuss the differences that were evident in your group between individual tastes and the critical standards used to make judgments. Are more categories needed to evaluate programs adequately? If so, what categories should be added?

    What standards did your group use to judge merit? Is there such a thing as a "good" trashy program? Give an example. Why is it important to make critical judgments of this kind?

5. Pick a program from the "trash" category and organize a group to write a letter or make a call to the producers of that program. Report your findings and offer your critical suggestions to them, *engaging* them in a discussion of the program and its contributions to consumer culture and to democracy.

KEY TERMS

communication, 6
culture, 6
mass media, 6
mass communication, 6
digital communication, 9
bloggers, 9
media convergence, 9

cross platform, 10
senders, 11
messages, 11
mass media channel, 11
receivers, 11
gatekeepers, 11
feedback, 11

selective exposure, 11
high culture, 15
low culture, 15
modern, 22
postmodern, 22
critical process, 28
media literacy, 28

media and
culture

an extended case study

VIDEO GAMES AND STORYTELLING

Step 1: Description

Step 2: Analysis

Step 3: Interpretation

Step 4: Evaluation

Step 5: Engagement

A powerful story that circulates frequently in mainstream media is the "demon" or "death" narrative—that is, some new development in popular culture that threatens children and portends the downfall of civilization. As Chapters 1, 3, 5, and 10 explain, this has been true (since at least the time of the early Greek philosophers) of developments in dance, music, television, and even poetry and books. Among the latest villains are digital video and computer games.

Author Stephen Poole reported in *Trigger Happy* that after the ap-

pearance of *Grand Theft Auto* in Great Britain in 1997, the British Police Federation described the game—"in which the player steals cars, runs over lines of Hare Krishna and shoots cops"— as "sick, deluded and beneath contempt."[1] In Alabama in 2005, lawyers for a twenty-year-old man claimed that playing *Grand Theft Auto* was a factor in his killing of three small-town police officers. (The jury didn't buy the argument and convicted the man of capital murder.)

On another level of this debate, some stories are told that under-

Attendees try new video games at the E3 Electronic Entertainment Expo in May 2006.

mine the game industry's research and tell how digital games hurt the educational and cultural development of children and teens. In this critique, educators and politicians often cite research on the decline in reading for pleasure. Other adults complain about the "addiction" of these games and about the hours young people spend in front of image-infested screens.

Finally, another group of stories circulates that supports the game industry. They make claims for the positive cultural impact of digital games, citing the familiar studies about improved levels of eye-hand coordination that come with game mastery. There are also games for educational or military purposes. Fans of the *SimCity* computer game praise the knowledge of basic government, tax systems, and population control required to skillfully simulate the construction of a fictional city. In his book *Everything Bad Is Good for You*, Steven Johnson reports that these games stimulate interactivity and problem solving among their participants, drawing players into complex situations that require difficult choices in order to reach workable solutions.

Perhaps the most powerful story here—and the major allure of digital games—is the opportunities digital games provide for players to tell their own complicated stories. Although critics argue that *The Sims* offers "some of the voyeuristic kicks of a reality TV show" and over-celebrates "the brutal rules of free-market capitalism,"[2] young people interviewed about the pleasure (and frustration) of playing digital games discuss the intricate and detailed stories that game players command.

a s developed in Chapter 1, a media-literate perspective involves mastering five overlapping critical stages that build on each other: (1) *description*, (2) *analysis*, (3) *interpretation*, (4) *evaluation*, and (5) *engagement*. See the Media Literacy box on pages 28–29 for an explanation of each stage.

The case before us here is the dynamic relationships (and collisions) among the digital game industry, the popular tastes/interests of young people, adult responsibilities for supervising youth culture, and the ideals of free expression. Digital games are a massive media-related industry that earned $7 billion in 2005, nearly rivaling the domestic movie business. (In fact, a 2005 study found that summer movie attendance for men under age twenty-five decreased by 24 percent from summer 2003 and attributed part of the decline to game playing.)[3] For this extended case study illustrating the value of the critical process, we put forward several important questions: First, who are the major players in the lucrative digital game business, and how do they figure out what attracts and holds players? Second, how are video and computer games like and unlike older mass media forms (such as the book or television), and what are the ramifications of these games for the larger culture? Third, what kinds of stories do digital games tell, to whom do these stories appeal, and how central is storytelling to their allure? Fourth, what are our responsibilities as students of the media—and as citizens with a stake in the quality of the cultural environment—in the creation, consumption, and circulation of digital games?

Step 1: Description

Using video and computer games as the subject under study, let's examine aspects of the up- and downsides of games through the lens of the critical process. The idea here is to offer a template for taking stock of the influence of such games and making critical assessments of the relationships among technology, business, culture, and storytelling. First, for the **description** phase, we might study and take notes on a variety of crucial topics, such as the ways in which digital games are similar to and different from other mass media technologies. We might also look at the companies that manufacture games, scholars who research games, and stories that games tell.

Next, focus on what gets said: What stories do video and computer games tell? For this, interview students, relatives, friends, or strangers who are avid game players and ask them to describe the storytelling that unfolds in digital games. Try to talk to both male and female players whose ages vary. Limit your focus here to two or three selected games. Remember that most of us make sense of the world through stories—from the song lyrics we enjoy, to the novels we read, to the news reports we view, to the movies and TV shows we watch. And the cultural industries that produce video and computer games understand that the best way to succeed is to pay attention to storytelling. Ask the subjects you interview why they play the games and what kinds of stories the games offer. In this descriptive phase of the critical process, identify central characters, conflicts, topics, and themes that emerge in the games under study. From the notes you take at this stage, document particular kinds of stories and characters that dominate in the games—and note what kind of stories and characters are *not* featured. Here you might look at ways in which games draw on our familiarity with older media storytelling forms, such as serialized children's books or TV programs. Compare as well the stories and characters found in the games to character portrayals in network or cable television and in feature Holly-

wood films. For example, look at the influence of digital games like *Tomb Raider* on the movie business or the impact of the latest *Madden NFL* on pro football and how that sport is presented to fans (who also might play the video game).

Finally, consider some of the larger cultural discussions surrounding these types of games. For example, state legislators have gotten involved by passing laws that restrict video and computer game sales. In October 2005—following the lead of Illinois and Michigan—California's Governor Arnold Schwarzenegger signed legislation that outlaws "the sale to teenagers of electronic games featuring reckless mayhem and explicit sexuality." Specifically, the bill targets teens under eighteen and bans games that "depict serious injury to human beings in a manner that is especially heinous, atrocious or cruel."[4] As a counterpoint, the video and computer game industry's main trade group, the Entertainment Software Association (ESA), reported research in 2005 that video and computer "gamers" devoted 23.4 hours per week (in 2004) "to exercise, playing sports, volunteering in the community, religious activities, creative endeavors, cultural activities, and reading," compared with just 6.8 hours per week playing games.[5]

● According to the Entertainment Software Association, the four best-selling video game genres in 2005 were: Action (30.1 percent), Sports (17.3 percent), Racing (11.1 percent), and Children and Family Entertainment (9.3 percent). What could be the compelling narratives behind games in each of these genres? (For example, pictured from left: *Grand Theft Auto, Halo 2,* and *The Sims.*)

Step 2: Analysis

Second, in the **analysis** phase we are looking for patterns or themes that emerge from the selected games under study. In this second stage of the critical process, we isolate those patterns that call for closer attention. For example, what types of games tended to be the most popular among the people you interviewed, and why? In what ways do games in different genres differ; for example, how are strategy games different from storytelling games? How is the storytelling in games like the kinds of stories found on network television or in Hollywood movies? How are the stories different? Do the stories that unfold in the selected digital games feature lone heroic individuals as the main characters, or do they require team or group solutions to various problems posed in the games? Look too at gender and age patterns among players. What kinds of stories do male game players prefer compared with female players? In the interviews conducted, what kind of stories do younger players (say, adolescents and teens) like compared with older players in their twenties or thirties? For this analysis, focus on two or three of the above questions. Or, based on what was uncovered in the description phase of the study, suggest other patterns or themes that emerged that are worthy of study and focus.

Step 3: Interpretation

Third, in the **interpretation** stage we try to determine the meanings of the patterns or themes we have analyzed. For example, what does it mean that certain kinds of stories tend to dominate video and computer games? And what does it mean that male and female players often seem to prefer different kinds of stories in their games of choice? Possible interpretations might derive from particular narratives that celebrate heroic individuals or that offer complex depictions of social interaction. If we find patterns of storytelling that celebrate the adventurous hero versus game stories that require teamwork, what does this mean? And if game storytelling differs from network television and Hollywood films, what does that mean? After all, courageous heroes saving towns from villains and cities from corruption dominate our main fictional forms—particularly our prime-time television and mainstream movies. What does it mean that these patterns are not always replicated in digital games?

The central value that emerges in so much of our popular storytelling is the ideal of individualism: the notion that one person can stand in for all of us and make a difference in our lives. Of course, one of the limits of narrative is that our lives don't usually play out like fictional stories. In fact, most progress—whether it is small cultural change at work or big political shifts that affect our legal or military system—is the result of collective action. Rather than the initiative of one heroic person (which does occasionally happen) as played out in television, movies, video games, and other mainstream narratives, communities and societies usually move forward because a group of people—a number of individuals—work together to make such movement possible. In this analysis, did certain kinds of video and computer games come to light that resisted the mainstream cultural myths of the powerful hero character? If so, what might that suggest?

There are, of course, other possible interpretations and other patterns that can be investigated as part of this particular phase of the critical process. For example, do digital games that involve complicated strategy and calculation fit into conventional ideas of narrative? What might this mean? In more conventional storytelling games, do narrative and character types surface in games that celebrate something other than heroic individualism or the benefits of team play? Were there values other than individualism and teamwork at the core of the narratives featured in some of the games under study? Are there alternative versions of video and computer games that are sharply different from most of the games that circulate in our popular culture? If so, what does the presence and production of such alternative games suggest and mean?

Step 4: Evaluation

Fourth, the **evaluation** stage of the critical process focuses on making informed judgments. Building on description, analysis, and interpretation, we become better able to evaluate the place of games in society and their impact on our culture. At this stage, we try to make judgments on whether games—or at least those under study here—are good or bad and what their positive and negative impact might be. Here we make critical judgments: what we like and dislike about the stories that we tell through video and computer games. For our current case study, evaluate the ways in which games celebrate individual character or the virtues of team play. Are these features positive or negative aspects of these games? Assess the violent or sexual content of some games against the problem-solving skills and narrative imagination needed to play these games. Evaluate the different ways men, women, and children seem to be portrayed in the games under study. Evaluate differences and similarities between strategy games and storytelling games. Should we distinguish among different categories of video and computer games? What would those categories look like?

Step 5: Engagement

Fifth, the **engagement** stage invites us to take some action that connects our critical interpretations and evaluations with our responsibility as citizens to question the cultural industries that manufacture digital games and the voices in culture that seek to regulate them. In this stage, we add our own voices to the process of shaping the cultural environment. For example, after researching a number of these games you might call or e-mail game manufacturers about your findings. Or together with other students, you may want to write a letter about your findings and submit it to a newspaper, magazine, radio station, or Web site. Or your class may want to convene a forum on the state of video and computer gaming that raises questions about the cultural contributions and drawbacks of these games. Such a forum might probe the range of storytelling and strategies that exist in digital games or explore the various ways gender, age, authority, politics, economics, or some other issue is portrayed in games. Finally, your class might produce a strategy—or media narrative—that would draw news media attention, allowing the class to marshal a collective voice that might offer a competing point of view to the knee-jerk demon and death narratives that tend to dominate mainstream media stories about video and computer games.

● Hollywood has traditionally used books and theatrical productions as the basis for movie projects. With the rising popularity of digital games, Hollywood has discovered a new source for narrative material. For example, the movies *Lara Croft: Tomb Raider* (2001) and *Lara Croft: Cradle of Life* (2003) were based on the successful *Tomb Raider* game series. A common challenge in turning a game into a movie is hiring actors who physically resemble the idealized digital heroes. These heroes are often represented as a culture's "ideal" man or woman: extremely fit, muscular, and unrealistically proportioned. How do you think gender roles play into digital representations of these characters? How are these roles transformed or adapted for another medium, such as movies?

> ❝ Most video games differ from traditional games like chess or *Monopoly* in the way they withhold information about the underlying rules of the system. ❞
>
> –Steven Johnson, *Everything Bad Is Good for You*, 2005

the internet and new technologies

media at the crossroads

Visionaries of the Internet have long heralded the new online world as one without traditional geographic, political, or legal limits.

Media theorist Marshall McLuhan wrote in 1972 that "the wired planet has no boundaries and no monopolies of knowledge."[1] William Gibson, the novelist who coined the word *cyberspace* in the 1980s to represent the virtual reality environment of computing networks, similarly argued "the Internet is transnational. Cyberspace has no borders."[2] And in 2000, Microsoft leader Bill Gates said, "The Internet is a constantly changing global network that knows no borders."[3]

But as the Internet has matured and global communications have grown more widespread in the 2000s, the real, political borders of nations are making themselves known. This trend became most evident in 2006 with the operation of the Internet in China. Over 111 million Chinese are online, only a fraction of the country's 1.3 billion population, but with enough Internet users to be second only to the United States. But in rapidly modernizing China, where for decades the Communist

Party has tightly controlled mass communication, the openness of the Internet has led to a clash of cultures. As *Washington Post* reporter Philip Pan writes, "The party appears at once determined not to be left behind by the global information revolution and fearful of being swept away by it."[4]

As more and more Chinese citizens take to the Internet, an estimated thirty thousand government censors monitor their use of Web pages, blogs, chat rooms, and e-mails. This surveillance constitutes what some now call the "Great Firewall of China." Internet police give warning calls to people posting material critical of the government, force Internet service providers to axe unfavorable blogs, and block thousands of international sites. Many Chinese Internet service providers and Webmasters learn to self-censor to avoid attracting attention. For those who persist in practicing "subversive" free speech, there can be severe penalties: Paris-based Reporters without Borders (www.rsf.org) reports that more than eighty-one cyberdissidents and journalists are in Chinese prisons for writing articles and blogs that criticized the government.

Into this regulated environment enter U.S. Internet corporations eager to establish a foothold in the massive Chinese market. Yahoo!, Google, and Microsoft are three of the leading U.S. Internet companies, and they have long promoted the liberating possibilities of the Internet — Google's famous corporate motto even states, "Do no evil."

Yet in much-criticized decisions, all three companies are censoring information to appease Chinese authorities. In 2006, Google created a new search engine for the China market, Google.cn, that filters out offending sites, including many relating to Tibetan independence, the Tiananmen Square massacre, the Falun Gong religion, and even BBC News. Moreover, the Google.cn site stripped away e-mail and blog features because they might be used for political protest. According to the Open Net Initiative, Microsoft did much the same, prohibiting the creation of blogs with politically unacceptable titles (such as "freedom of speech," "democracy," and "human rights"), and deleting Chinese MSN Space blogs that criticized the government.[5]

Yahoo! censored Web sites on its Chinese-language search portal, too, and also made a controversial decision: assisting Chinese Internet police in linking computer addresses to the owners of Yahoo! e-mail accounts. Yahoo's complicity led to the jailing of at least three cyberdissidents. One of them, journalist Shi Tao, is now serving a ten-year sentence.

China isn't the only country to impose borders on the Internet. As the Open Net Initiative reports, the governments of Bahrain, Burma, Iran, Saudi Arabia, Singapore, Tunisia, and the United Arab Emirates are also conducting Internet filtering.

While governments may impose virtual borders on the Internet, attempts of any country to block free speech on the medium may ultimately be futile. As major U.S. Internet firms yield to the government's repressive rules, hundreds of thousands of Chinese citizens are bravely evading them, using free services like Hushmail, Freegate, and Ultrasurf (the latter two produced by Chinese immigrants in the United States) to break through China's Great Firewall.

he **Internet**—the vast network of telephone and cable lines and satellite systems designed to link and carry computer information worldwide—has often been described as an *information highway*. Imagine the traditional media—books, newspapers, television, and radio—as an older interstate highway system now intersected by a sprawling, poorly planned major freeway system (the Internet), much of which is still under construction and is fed by thousands of new capillary roads, some paved, some dirt, some extending into remote locations around the globe. In addition, many side roads along the highway are virtually unregulated, while others are as highly policed, such as China.

Unlike interstate highways built by federal and state governments, however, the information highway has been taken over and expanded by private enterprise, although it was initially established and subsidized by the government. What difference will this make? If we look to the history of another medium, we know that when private commercial managers took over radio broadcasting in the 1920s and 1930s, they helped build the United States into the world's foremost producer of communication technology and content. At the same time, though, they dramatically thwarted the growth of nonprofit and educational broadcasting.

The full impact of the Internet and the expanding information highway, like that of all emerging mass media, will evolve over time. Cable TV, for example, which operated in only 13 percent of American households in 1975, took nearly twenty years to reach 60 percent of U.S. homes. As a mass medium, the Internet has had a much more rapid ascent: More than 60 percent of U.S. adults were connected to the Internet by 2003, just ten years after the introduction of the first Web browsers. By 2006, about 75 percent of American adults used the Internet.

Unlike cable and earlier mass media, the Internet is also unique in that there is no limit on how large its databases of content can grow. And while the Internet is a major medium for the global economy, the slowing of the dot-com business world in 2000 and the September 11 attacks a year later have led to a new caution about the Internet. On October 26, 2001, the United States enacted a new antiterrorism law—called the USA PATRIOT Act—that granted sweeping new powers to law-enforcement agencies for intercepting computer communications, including e-mail messages and Web browsing. Other nations followed the United States' lead on increasing Internet surveillance. Congress renewed the law in 2006, making most of its provisions permanent, thus reshaping the debate over security measures versus civil liberties on the Internet and in the entire world for years to come.

In later chapters we will explore the impact of traditional media such as books, radio, and television—and how they evolved to their current state. But first we will analyze the ongoing Internet revolution, as we both witness and participate in the emergence of this dynamic medium. As governments, corporations, and public and private interests vie to shape the Internet's evolution, answers to many questions remain ambiguous. Who will have access to the Internet, and who will be left behind? Who or what will manage the Internet, and what are the implications for the future and for democracy? The task for critical media consumers is to sort through competing predictions about the Internet and new technology, analyzing and determining how the "new and improved" Information Age can best serve the majority of citizens and communities.

> **❝** We had a choice to enter the country and follow the law. Or we had a choice to not enter the country. **❞**
>
> –Eric E. Schmidt, Google CEO, on why the company chose to comply with China's censorship, 2006

Origins of the Internet

Although many branches of the Internet still resemble dirt roads on the information highway, the rapid technological advances that accompany the new routes pose a major challenge to cable TV and to the more traditional media. From its humble origins as an attack-proof military communications network in the 1960s, the Internet had become increasingly interactive by the 1990s, allowing immediate two-way communication (like telephones) and one-to-many communication (like radio and television) between senders and receivers of media messages. With its ability to transport both personal conversation and mass communication, the Internet has begun to break down conventional distinctions among various media and between private and public modes of communication.

The Evolution of a New Mass Medium

The term *Industrial Age* usually refers to the period spanning the development of the steam engine in the 1760s to mass assembly-line production in the 1900s, an era that transformed manufacturing and consumer culture. By a similar measuring stick, the *Information Age* has barely begun. It has passed through an early phase marked by broadcasting to a phase that features the convergence of computers, cell phones, e-mail, cable television, satellite transmission, and the Internet.

Most mass media evolve through various stages, which are initiated not only by the diligence of great inventors, such as Thomas Edison, but also by social, cultural, political, and economic circumstances. For instance, both telegraph and radio developed as newly industrialized nations sought to expand military and economic control over colonies and to transmit information more rapidly. The phonograph, too, emerged because of the social and economic conditions of a growing middle class with more money and leisure time. Today, the Internet is a contemporary response to new concerns: transporting messages more rapidly for an increasingly mobile and interconnected global population.

Typically, media innovations emerge in three stages. First is the *novelty* or *development stage* in which inventors and technicians try to solve a particular problem, such as making pictures move, transmitting voices through the air without wires, or sending mail electronically. Second is the *entrepreneurial stage* in which inventors and investors determine a practical and marketable use for the new device. For example,

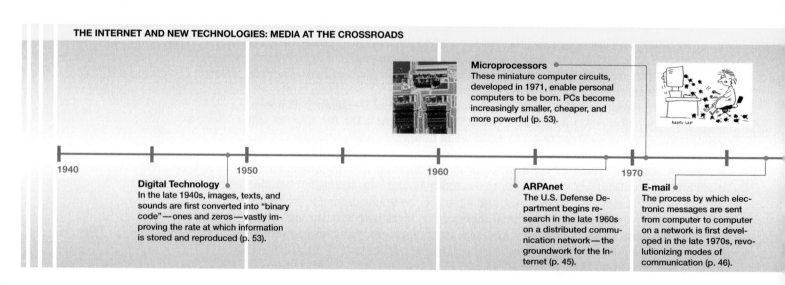

THE INTERNET AND NEW TECHNOLOGIES: MEDIA AT THE CROSSROADS

Microprocessors
These miniature computer circuits, developed in 1971, enable personal computers to be born. PCs become increasingly smaller, cheaper, and more powerful (p. 53).

1940   1950   1960   1970

Digital Technology
In the late 1940s, images, texts, and sounds are first converted into "binary code"—ones and zeros—vastly improving the rate at which information is stored and reproduced (p. 53).

ARPAnet
The U.S. Defense Department begins research in the late 1960s on a distributed communication network—the groundwork for the Internet (p. 45).

E-mail
The process by which electronic messages are sent from computer to computer on a network is first developed in the late 1970s, revolutionizing modes of communication (p. 46).

early radio or wireless technology relayed messages to and from places where telegraph wires and cables could not go, such as military ships at sea. Part of the Internet also had its roots in the ideas of military leaders who wanted a communication system that could survive nuclear wars or natural disasters.

The third phase in a new medium's development involves a breakthrough to the *mass medium stage*. At this point, businesses figure out how to market the new device as an appealing consumer product. Although the government and the navy played a central role in radio's early years, it was commercial entrepreneurs who eventually took radio into its broadcasting phase, where it began reaching millions of people. In the same way, Pentagon and government researchers developed the prototype for the Internet, but commercial interests took it over, extending its reach nationally and globally. With the release of the World Wide Web in 1991, and the introduction of user-friendly graphic browsers like Mosaic in 1993 and Netscape in 1994, the Internet entered its mass medium stage.

By the late 1980s and 1990s, online computer services and the Internet had begun featuring all sorts of mass communication—and advertising—services and marketing them through computers, modems, and phone lines. Following this innovation, the Internet grew rapidly, becoming "the most wide-ranging interactive mass medium in history."[6] By 2006, a projected 1.08 billion people worldwide (roughly 205 million of them in the United States) had access to the Internet regularly. Global Internet access is expected to rise to 1.8 billion by 2008.[7]

> **❝** The medium, or process, of our time—electric technology—is reshaping and restructuring patterns of social interdependence and every aspect of our personal life. **❞**
>
> –Marshall McLuhan, 1967

The Birth of the Internet

The Internet originated as a military-government project with national security as one of its goals. Begun in the late 1960s by the Defense Department's Advanced Research Projects Agency (ARPA), the original Internet—called **ARPAnet** and nicknamed the Net—enabled military and academic researchers to communicate on a distributed network system (see Figure 2.1 on page 47). The network design of what would become the Internet differed from the centralized style of telephone communication at the time, whereby calls were routed through a central switcher. A distributed network system offered two advantages to the researchers and military units developing the Net. First, because multiple paths linked one computer site to another, communications "traffic" would be less likely to get clogged at a single point.

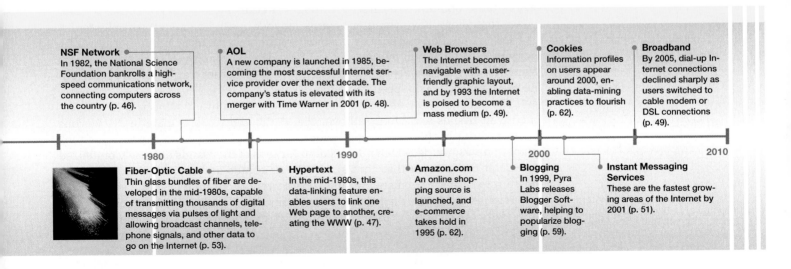

NSF Network
In 1982, the National Science Foundation bankrolls a high-speed communications network, connecting computers across the country (p. 46).

AOL
A new company is launched in 1985, becoming the most successful Internet service provider over the next decade. The company's status is elevated with its merger with Time Warner in 2001 (p. 48).

Web Browsers
The Internet becomes navigable with a user-friendly graphic layout, and by 1993 the Internet is poised to become a mass medium (p. 49).

Cookies
Information profiles on users appear around 2000, enabling data-mining practices to flourish (p. 62).

Broadband
By 2005, dial-up Internet connections declined sharply as users switched to cable modem or DSL connections (p. 49).

1980   1990   2000   2010

Fiber-Optic Cable
Thin glass bundles of fiber are developed in the mid-1980s, capable of transmitting thousands of digital messages via pulses of light and allowing broadcast channels, telephone signals, and other data to go on the Internet (p. 53).

Hypertext
In the mid-1980s, this data-linking feature enables users to link one Web page to another, creating the WWW (p. 47).

Amazon.com
An online shopping source is launched, and e-commerce takes hold in 1995 (p. 62).

Blogging
In 1999, Pyra Labs releases Blogger Software, helping to popularize blogging (p. 59).

Instant Messaging Services
These are the fastest growing areas of the Internet by 2001 (p. 51).

This helped convince computer researchers in the 1960s to sign on to the project—they could share research and data on the new network without their computers becoming overrun by the traffic of others' messages. Second, because the network was like an interconnected web, it offered a communication system that was more impervious to technical screwups, natural disasters, or military attacks.

In developing one of the Net prototypes for the military, the Rand Corporation, a Cold War think tank, conceptualized a communications network that had no central authority. Ironically, one of the most hierarchically structured and centrally organized institutions in our culture, the national defense industry, created the Internet, possibly the least hierarchical and most decentralized social network ever conceived. Each computer hub in the Internet has similar status and power, so nobody can own the system outright and nobody has the power to kick others off the network. There isn't even a master power switch, so authority figures cannot shut off the Internet during an emergency.

During its developmental stage, the military computer network permitted different people in separate locations to communicate with one another. One of the most common ways of communicating over the network—**e-mail** (electronic mail)—was invented in 1971 by computer engineer Ray Tomlinson, who developed software to send electronic mail messages to any computer on ARPAnet. He decided to use the @ symbol to signify the location of the computer user, thus establishing the "login name@host computer" convention for e-mail addresses. At this stage, the Internet was primarily used by universities and government research labs, and later by corporations—especially companies involved in computer software and other high-tech products—to transmit and receive e-mail and to post information on computer *bulletin boards,* sites that listed information about particular topics such as health issues, computer programs, or employment services.

By 1982, the Net had hit its entrepreneurial stage: The National Science Foundation invested in a high-speed communications network designed to link computer centers around the country. This innovation led to a dramatic increase in Internet use. Then, after the dissolution of the Soviet Union in the late 1980s, the ARPAnet military venture officially ended. By that time, however, a growing network of researchers, computer programmers, commercial interests, and amateur hackers had tapped into the Net, creating tens of thousands of decentralized intersections. As the military had predicted, the absence of a central authority meant that the Net could not be knocked out.

Just as most radio pioneers did not foresee the potential of radio, many pioneers of the Net did not predict how rapidly its mass appeal would spread beyond national and military interests. The Internet system comprises worldwide computer networks that communicate directly through Internet Protocol (IP), a computer language that allows any computer on any network to send data electronically to any other computer on an equal basis.[8] These networks link computers known as **servers**, which are run by individuals, universities, corporations, and government agencies. The servers operate as entry points for Internet traffic and are interconnected by special high-speed data lines.

The Net enables users to find information on virtually any subject, to chat and e-mail with friends and family all over the world, and to participate in discussions about favorite hobbies and social issues. In the beginning, such connections took place in **newsgroups**, which now account for tens of thousands of loosely organized computer conferences that consist of bulletin boards and individual messages, or postings, which are circulated to subscribers twenty-four hours a day.

Prior to the 1990s, the Internet's look consisted mostly of computer command lines, with the green or orange text of the era's monochromatic computer monitors. Most of the Internet's traffic was for e-mail, file transfers, and remote access of com-

> ❝ The dream behind the Web is of a common information space in which we communicate by sharing information. Its universality is essential: the fact that a hypertext link can point to anything, be it personal, local, or global, be it draft or highly polished. ❞
>
> –Tim Berners-Lee, inventor of the World Wide Web, 2000

Figure 2.1 Distributed Networks

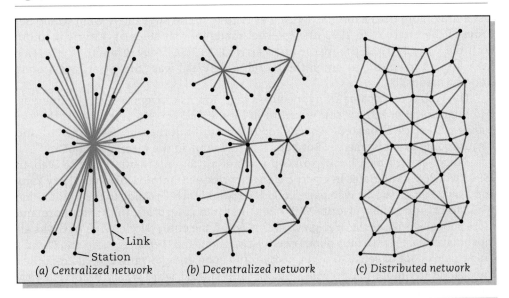

Link
Station
(a) Centralized network   (b) Decentralized network   (c) Distributed network

Source: Katie Hafner and Matthew Lyon, *Where Wizards Stay Up Late* (New York: Simon & Schuster, 1996).

Paul Baran, a computer scientist at the Rand Corporation in the Cold War era, worked on developing a national communication system that could survive a nuclear attack. Centralized networks (a) are vulnerable because all the paths lead to a single nerve center. Decentralized networks (b) are less vulnerable because they contain several main nerve centers. In a distributed network (c), which resembles a net, there are no nerve centers; if any connection is severed, information can be immediately rerouted and delivered to its destination. But is there a downside to distributed networks when it comes to the circulation of network viruses?

puter databases. The **World Wide Web** changed all of that. Developed in the late 1980s by software engineer Tim Berners-Lee at the CERN particle physics lab in Switzerland in order to help scientists better collaborate, the Web was initially a text data-linking system that allowed computer-accessed information to associate with, or link to, other information no matter where it was on the Internet. Known as *hypertext*, this data-linking feature of the Web was a breakthrough for those attempting to use the Internet.

Hypertext is a nonlinear way of organizing information, enabling a user to click on a highlighted word, phrase, picture, or icon and skip directly to other files related to that subject in other computer systems. **HTML (HyperText Markup Language)**, the written code that creates Web pages and links, is a language that all computers can read, so computers with varying operating systems, such as Windows and Macintosh, can communicate easily. XHTML, a form of HTML, first released in 2000, brings graphically rich Web pages to small-device platforms such as cell phones, palmtop computers, and cars.

The release of Web **browsers**—the software packages that help users navigate the Web—brought the Web to mass audiences. In 1993, computer programmers at the National Center for Supercomputing Applications (NCSA) at the University of Illinois in Urbana-Champaign released Mosaic, the first window-based browser to load text and graphics together in a magazine-like layout, with attractive fonts and easy-to-use back, forward, home, and bookmark buttons at the top. Together, the World Wide Web and Mosaic gave the Internet basic multimedia capability, enabling users to transmit pictures, sound, and video.

With HTML and Mosaic in place, the Internet experienced extraordinarily rapid growth. The number of servers (which can host multiple Web sites) on the Web jumped from just 130 in 1993 to more than 80 million in 2006.[9]

> **❝** One woman who entered the classroom with her walker got so inspired by the [Internet] class that she left without it. We have people leaving their canes behind all the time. **❞**
>
> —Leonard Krauss, 74,
> **president of the Computer Club, Rossmoor retirement community (California), 2004**

● One of the latest attempts to make the Internet accessible as an on-the-go service is a line of tablet computers that merge the functions of a laptop and a media player. These light, handheld devices run all the same software as a conventional PC and come equipped with wireless capability and Bluetooth technology. These converged devices are an attempt to move into the market where converged cell phones, iPods, and the BlackBerry are the portable devices of choice.

The Internet Grows Up

Just a little more than a decade ago, it was hard to figure out exactly what would become of the Internet. In 1993, the Internet made its first steps as a mass medium with the Web. By 1994, the masses had arrived. As *USA Today* wrote that year, this "new way to travel the Internet, the World Wide Web," was "the latest rage among Net aficionados."[10]

The Web soon became everyone else's rage, too, as universities and businesses, and later home users, got connected to it. By the end of 1994, a writer for the *San Francisco Chronicle* lamented, "There's too much stuff out there to keep track of, and it's just going to get worse. . . . But help is to be found, in the form of Yahoo!"[11]

Yahoo! started as a hobby to keep track of all the information on the Web. In 1994, two Ph.D. candidates in electrical engineering at Stanford University, Jerry Yang and David Filo, created a Web page, called "Jerry and David's Guide to the World Wide Web," to organize their favorite Web sites, first into categories, then into more and more subcategories as the Web grew. At this point, the entire World Wide Web was almost manageable, with only about twenty-two thousand Web sites. Jerry and David's Guide made a lot of sense to other people, and soon enough Yang and Filo renamed their guide the more memorable "Yahoo!" and started what would become a very profitable corporation.

Like Yahoo!, the Web's most popular sites have helped us make sense of the overwhelming information available, organizing it for certain functions such as searching for other Web sites, shopping, finding people, reading the news, booking airline tickets, and sending and receiving e-mail—or in the case of Yahoo!, all of these things.

As with other mass media forms, the Internet has become increasingly commercial, leading to battles between corporations over attracting the most users. By the end of the 1990s, four companies—Yahoo!, Microsoft, AOL, and Google—emerged as the leading forces on the Internet. Yahoo!'s method has been to make itself an all-purpose entry point—or **portal**—to the Internet. Computer software behemoth Microsoft's approach began by integrating its Windows software with its new Internet Explorer Web browser in 1995, drawing users to its MSN.com site and other Microsoft applications. AOL, founded in 1985, attempted to dominate the Internet as the top **Internet service provider** (ISP), connecting millions of home users to its proprietary Web system through dial-up access. Google, launched in 1998 by two other Ph.D. students at Stanford, Larry Page and Sergey Brin, made its play to seize the Internet with a more elegant, robust **search engine**, which helps users find sites on the Web.

The Structure of the Internet Today

Although government and nonprofit Web sites and newsgroups make up part of the Internet, most of the Internet is now structured around businesses' attempts to reach the millions of people around the world who regularly use the Internet.

Internet Service Providers

One of the first ways businesses got involved with the Internet was by offering connections to it. Although many individuals access the Internet through their university or business accounts, home users often purchase a commercial online service or Internet service provider (ISP). The largest is AOL, which began in 1985 and merged with the world's largest media company, Time Warner, in 2001. By 2006, AOL had about 20 million U.S. subscribers—still more than any other ISP, but down from more than 33 million in 2002, as AOL's dial-up service customers migrated to ISPs with faster **broadband** connections. In fact, the next leading ISP is Comcast, the nation's top cable company, with more than 8 million broadband customers.

Other major online services include the giant regional telephone company SBC Communications, which has more than 6.5 million broadband customers on its digital subscriber lines (DSL); Earthlink, which has 5.3 million DSL, cable, satellite, and dial-up customers; Time Warner's Roadrunner, with 4.8 million cable broadband clients, and Verizon, with 4.5 million DSL customers. Alongside the national online services, hundreds of local services, many of them operated by regional telephone companies, compete to offer consumers access to the Internet.

Web Browsers

In the early 1990s, as the Web became the most popular part of the Internet, many thought that the key to commercial success on the Net would be through the Web browser, since it is the most common interface with the Internet. For at least a short time in the 1990s, the browser business caused one of the first battles for control of the Internet, in this case between Netscape and Internet Explorer. Within a year of developing Mosaic, Marc Andreessen and several of his graduate school colleagues from NCSA relocated to Silicon Valley in California and teamed with venture capital firms to start Netscape, a company built on a browser inspired by the government-funded Mosaic. By 1995, they led a wave of young Internet entrepreneurs who became overnight millionaires as Wall Street invested billions of speculative dollars in the new dot-com economy. But, in that same year, Microsoft released its own Web browser, Internet Explorer, which also was based on Mosaic. Within a few years, Internet Explorer—strategically bundled with Microsoft operating system software—overtook Netscape as the most popular Web browser. AOL later purchased Netscape in 1998, and today Netscape survives only as a minor brand of AOL and its parent company, Time Warner.

Internet Explorer continues to dominate the Web browser business, and although it clearly forced out Netscape, other browsers offer alternatives. Apple Computer

> **"In less than three years, the Internet's World Wide Web has spawned some 10 million electronic documents at a quarter million Web sites. By contrast, the Library of Congress has taken 195 years to collect 14 million books."**
>
> –Tim Miller,
> New Media Resources, 1995

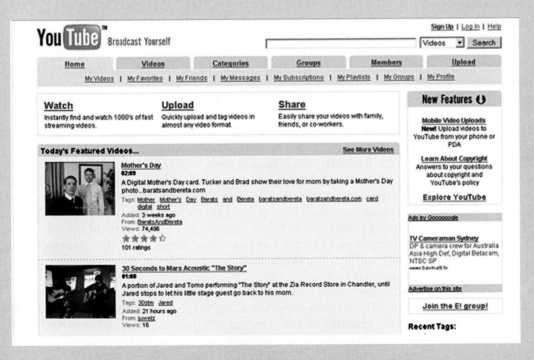

● As one of the most popular Web sites, YouTube.com was drawing twenty-five million hits a day in 2006, only one year after the site launched. The site allows users to post homemade video clips to share with anyone who wants to watch. As a venue for user-made content, YouTube began to partner with other media companies to offer contests for homemade videos, such as the 2006 deal with Matador Records to feature a Make a Video contest for the band Pretty Girls Make Graves, and to provide film previews for major studios.

"I can't explain it—it's just a funny feeling that I'm being Googled."

offers Safari to Mac users, and Opera, Firefox, and Konqueror exist as alternatives to Microsoft's Internet Explorer.

Directories and Search Engines

Browsers display the Web on your computer screen, but how do you find the appropriate pages to visit? **Directories**, one of the original methods to find your way around the Web, rely on people to review and catalogue Web sites, creating categories with hierarchical topic structures that can be browsed. Directories such as Yahoo!, LookSmart, and Ask.com (formerly AskJeeves.com) maintain staffs of paid editors to review and catalogue the sites, whereas open directory projects at Netscape and Lycos depend on volunteers from around the world to maintain certain topic areas.

> **"** Call it the Google Effect. Expectations of search engines have skyrocketed. Whether it involves complex specialist knowledge or the completely trivial, there is a general belief that everything should be available instantly, at the click of a mouse. **"**
>
> —Richard Waters,
> technology writer, 2004

Search engines offer a different route to finding content by allowing users to enter key words or queries to locate related Web pages. Search engines work in two different ways. First, some return search information from their directory catalogues. Yahoo! used to do this exclusively, and was initially known early on as a search service bringing results that were highly relevant, but relatively low in number. The second kind of search engine, based on a precise algorithm (mathematical formula), sends out computer "spiders" that search through the search engine's massive proprietary indexes—billions of pages—that are constantly increasing in size. These search engines deliver millions of results, but relatively few of the results are completely relevant.

Alta Vista and Inktomi, both released in 1995, were the first algorithmic search engines, and both had formulas that awarded relevance based on the number of times a search term appeared on a Web page. Contrary to popular belief, there are few of these powerful search services, because it's difficult to create an algorithm. Thus, while there are many portals that claim to be search engines, most of them rely on one of the other companies to do the computer-intensive work of their searches. For example, Alta Vista and Inktomi syndicated their services to larger portals, such as AOL and Yahoo!, respectively.

But soon, searches began to be corrupted by Web sites that tried to trick search engines in order to get their Web sites ranked higher on the results list. One common way was to embed a popular search term in the page, often typed over and over again in the tiniest font possible, and in the same color as the site's background. Although users didn't see the word, the search engines did, and their formula ranked the page higher even if the actual page had little to do with the search term.

The release of Google in 1998 introduced a new algorithm that mathematically ranked a page's "popularity" based on how many other pages link to it. Users immediately recognized Google's algorithm as an improvement. Leading portal Yahoo! dropped Inktomi in favor of Google, and many other portals chose to syndicate Google's search engine as well. Google became the favorite branded search portal almost overnight and made its early money through syndication.

The search engine business became more complicated—and more lucrative—with the onset of commercial search engine providers. These companies, beginning with Goto in 1998, commercialize search results by brokering three-way deals between a particular key word, an algorithmic search list, and an advertiser. Paid links appear as "sponsored links" at the top, bottom, and side of search engine lists, and even, depending on the portal, within the "objective" result list itself. Every time a user clicks on any sponsored link, whether it's clearly distinguished as sponsored or not, money changes hands.

Key-word advertising quickly became regarded as a critical marketing strategy for every business venture, large and small. And all search engines, seeing enormous potential revenue as advertising venues, jumped on the bandwagon. Goto (now Overture) invested in two leading algorithmic search engines (Alta Vista and the European favorite, AlltheWeb) to feature its own paid listings service. Overture was ultimately purchased by the much larger Yahoo!, which in turn purchased Inktomi to further gain its independence from Google. With these deals, Yahoo! quickly secured an Internet advertising empire. Meanwhile, Google responded by creating its own index of sponsored links alongside each search results list, and like Yahoo! morphed into an advertising firm. By 2006, Google's and Yahoo!'s respective market shares accounted for more than 70 percent of Web searches in the United States.

For online shopping, having paid placement in searches could be a good thing. But search engines doubling as ad brokers may undermine the utility of search engines as locators of Web content. As search engines increasingly ensure that the best-financed Web sites get the most visitors, nonprofit Web sites that can't afford priority placement become increasingly marginalized. Although this practice generates funds for commercial search engines, it does not bode well for search engines as education and research tools (see "Media Literacy and the Critical Process: Search Engines and Their Commercial Bias" on page 57). While there are increasingly sophisticated nonprofit directories across which a user can search using a single search term—such as the Open Directory Project (dmoz.org)—there are currently no algorithmic search engines that operate in the nonprofit sphere.

E-mail and Instant Messaging Services

The Pew Internet & American Life Project has noted that "sending and reading e-mail is by far the single most popular use of the Internet," and is practiced by more than nine out of ten Internet users. Moreover, e-mail is often the first activity for online users, and draws new users to the Internet.[12] Major Web portals such as Yahoo!, AOL, and Microsoft (Hotmail) have offered free Web-based e-mail accounts to draw users to their sites; each has more than thirty million users. Google introduced a similar free e-mail service in 2004 called Gmail. All of the e-mail services also include advertisements in their users' e-mail messages, one of the costs of the "free" e-mail accounts.

One of the Internet's fastest-growing features since the late 1990s is a cousin of e-mail—**instant messaging**, or IM, which enables users to send and receive real-time computer messages. Users assemble personalized buddy lists of friends, and depending on who is also online, they can chat with their buddies in real time. Mes-

> **"** Twenty-four percent of IM users say they have IM-ed a person who was in the same location as they were—such as their home, an office, or a classroom. **"**
>
> –Pew Internet & American Life Project, 2004

sages tend to be short and conversational, with one small window assigned to each buddy and with users often negotiating many conversations at a time. Although instant messaging can organize immediate Web conversations among coworkers or family members, its most popular use is as an extended social scene among teenagers, who log on after school and chat for hours with their friends. Major IM services include AOL Instant Messenger (AIM), Microsoft's MSN Messenger Service, Yahoo!'s Messenger, and Skype (an Internet telephone service owned by eBay). In 2006, Google joined the growing IM market by launching Gmail Chat, while MySpace added its MySpaceIM service. Instant messaging is one of the Internet's "stickiest" portal services, with users tending to remain on the same advertising-strewn screen for hours. IM windows also operate as full-service portals, providing buttons linking users to their e-mail, news briefs, and Web search engines. In addition, IM users fill out detailed profiles when signing up for the service, providing advertisers with multiple ways to target them as they chat with their friends.

The Internet's Next Step

While corporations continue to change the face of the Internet, behind the scenes the next generation of the Internet's core structure is already under way. A consortium of more than two hundred research universities, the federal government, and technology companies are developing **Internet2 (I2)**, a more advanced, second generation of the Internet. I2 was first deployed on an experimental basis in 1999 and is still being developed for advanced applications run on the cross-country, high-bandwidth Abilene Network. An even faster network, with ten times the fiber-optic capacity, is scheduled to replace the Abilene Network in late 2007. In addition to an updated Internet Protocol system that will add trillions more IP addresses to an already burgeoning Internet, I2 supports two-way interactive digital video—enabling virtual laboratories, remote control of telescopes, and increased use of online meetings. Like the first Internet, I2's technology will eventually be deployed to the global Internet for widespread use.

Digital Technology and Converging Media

What generally distinguishes the Internet from older media is not only the revolutionary ways in which data are stored and retrieved but also the convergence of media forms. Three innovations make the Internet a particularly distinct mass medium, offering unprecedented opportunities to communicate. First, it is interactive, enabling receivers to respond almost immediately to senders' messages. The second way in which the Internet is innovative is that it has become a hub for converging media—connecting consumers to other media and personalizing this experience by calling up mass media on demand. Third, the Internet allows individuals to create and distribute their own messages, in what has been called **participatory media**, allowing people to become producers rather than just consumers of media content. (Because the Internet is decentralized and unhierarchical, there are no gatekeepers to prevent individuals from creating and displaying their own messages.)

Technological Breakthroughs

Three key technological developments allow today's online media convergence. The first innovation involved **digital communication**, which was central to the development of the first computers in the 1940s. In digital technology an image, text, or sound is converted into electronic signals represented as a series of binary numbers—ones and zeros—which are then reassembled as a precise reproduction of an image, text, or sound. Digital signals operate as pieces, or bits (from BInary digiTS), of information representing two values, such as yes/no, on/off, or 0/1. For example, a typical compact disc track uses a binary code system in which zeros are microscopic pits in the surface of the disc and ones are represented on the unpitted surface. Used in various combinations, these digital codes can duplicate, store, and play back any kind of media content.

The second technological breakthrough occurred in 1971 with the introduction of **microprocessors**, miniature circuits that can process and store electronic signals. This innovation facilitated the integration of thousands of transistors and related circuitry into thin strands of silicon along which binary codes traveled. With this innovation, manufacturers were able to introduce the first personal computers (PCs), relatively inexpensive machines that consumers could purchase for home use. PCs were smaller, cheaper, and increasingly more powerful and were no longer just a tool for the office. According to Moore's Law (coined in 1965 by Gordon Moore, a former chairman of Intel, which is a leading builder of microprocessors), computer chip power doubles about every eighteen months. Because of microtechnology, a single PC that now fits on an individual's lap is more than 400,000 times more powerful than the bulky computer systems that occupied entire floors of office buildings during the 1960s.[13]

In the mid-1980s, the third technological development, **fiber-optic cable**, featured thin glass bundles of fiber capable of transmitting thousands of messages that had been digitally converted into shooting pulses of light. Fiber-optic technology has allowed information to be transported via lasers. With their ability to carry broadcast channels, telephone signals, and all sorts of digital codes, thin fiber-optic cables began replacing the older, bulkier copper wire used by phone and cable companies. Nicholas Negroponte, the founding director of MIT's Media Lab, points out that "a fiber the size of a human hair can deliver every issue ever made of the *Wall Street Journal* in less than one second."[14] With the increased speeds of the new media technology, few limits exist with regard to the amount of information that digital technology can transport.

Media Convergence Online

The technological breakthroughs of digital communication, microprocessors, high-speed fiber-optic cables, and wireless systems positioned the Internet as the hub of **media convergence**. Multimedia content—mixing audio, video, and data—can be delivered in a number of forms, including through telephone, cable, and satellite

66 **It's a different life on IM than in person. We have long conversations that we won't mention in school.** 99
–Matt, age 11, quoted in the *Boston Globe*, 2005

66 **Often, IM is where gossip starts.** 99
–Mark, Matt's 17-year-old brother, quoted in the *Boston Globe*, 2005

● Continuing the trend of media convergence on portable devices, cell phones are now capable of receiving digital television. Instead of downloading an episode of a show at home before leaving the house, the new phones will allow users to watch any show, at any time, at any place they receive a cell phone signal. While early devices look like traditional flip-top cell phones, this new technology is expected to have an impact on mobile phones' look, design, and function.

broadband; cell phone services; and wireless WiFi connections. And there are an ever-increasing array of devices on which to play multimedia content: portable digital players such as iPods, personal digital assistants, mobile phones, laptop and desktop computers, Internet-ready game consoles (for example, Playstation, Xbox, and GameCube), handheld game players, in-dash automobile systems, portable DVD players, digital video recorders, and digital television sets and radios.

Media convergence represents dramatic cultural and economic changes. Some of the best-known forms of convergence emerged democratically (although not always legally). In the late 1990s, music enthusiasts around the world began sharing music files over the Internet, much to the dismay of the music industry, which still wanted to sell its product on CDs. But, as usually happens, corporate media adjusted to keep up with culture. In a few years, Apple Computer capitalized on the cultural shift by creating a new online music source, the iTunes music store (selling legal music downloads) and the iPod, the now-ubiquitous digital player. This new multibillion-dollar music market expanded to include downloading music through cell phones, too.

A similar story is being replayed in the television and movie industries, after TV and movie fans started to swap these larger multimedia files online and watch them on computers and other devices. As the *New York Times* technology columnist David Pogue argued, the "networks and cable companies are only fueling the illegal download racket by letting most already-broadcast shows rot in their warehouses."[15] But in 2005, Apple's iTunes began selling episodes from TV programs (playable on video iPods, of course). ABC later streamed free "encore" episodes on its own Web site, and Disney movie studios were the first to sell downloadable films in fall 2006.

Thus, the cultural shifts of media convergence have shaken up old cultural industries and created new markets and practices. The centrality of the Internet to media convergence helps to explain why companies like Google and Yahoo! are worth billions in the stock market: investors believe these corporations will be essential to the future of the media. Other traditional media corporations continue to invest in converging media to help ensure they will hold a stake in the future of the industry as well.

Some critics note that media convergence has not created much in the way of new content. Instead, they argue, convergence brings us the same song or the same movie, just with new routes to obtain it and hear or see it. Critics also note that the economics of media convergence affects media workers, too. In news organizations, for example, journalists who once worked for one medium are now often stretched to create content for a converged newsroom that feeds print, television, radio, and Internet outlets. For the audience though, the product is not necessarily better—it can be the same story across all four outlets.

But the culture of media convergence centered on the Internet has also created some unique content that isn't easily controlled or replicated by commercial interests. Bloggers, videomakers, independent musical artists, and others continue to circulate original, free content—content that without media convergence would not likely have an audience.

Ownership Issues on the Internet

The contemporary era is distinguished not only by the revolutionary ways in which data are transmitted but also by the increasing convergence of owners and players in mass media industries. Large media firms, such as Disney, Time Warner, and Microsoft, are buying up or investing in smaller companies and spreading their economic interests among books, magazines, music, movies, radio, television, cable, and Internet channels.

As with the automobile or film industries of an earlier era, many players and companies are jockeying for position (see Table 2.1 below). With the passage of the sweeping overhaul of the nation's communication regulations in the **Telecommunications Act of 1996**, most regional and long-distance phone companies now participate in both cable and Internet-access businesses. The phone companies, like cable TV firms, have the added advantage of controlling the wires into most American homes and businesses. As cable and phone companies gradually convert older wiring into high-speed fiber-optic lines, they are wrestling for control of Internet circuitry and intensifying the battle over mass communication delivery systems.

Given the paucity of regulations governing the Internet industry, and the industry's rapid growth, it is not surprising to see a recent spate of mergers, joint ventures, consolidations, and power grabs. Although all of these mergers were an attempt to find a dominant position in the Information Age, some companies have loomed larger than others. Microsoft, for example, built a near-monopoly dominance of its Windows operating systems and Web browser software throughout the 1990s. The U.S. Department of Justice brought an antitrust lawsuit against Microsoft in 1997, arguing that it used its computer operating system dominance to sabotage its competitors. But Microsoft prevailed in 2001, when the Department of Justice dropped its

> **"** One of the more remarkable features of the computer network on which much of the world has come to rely is that nobody owns it. That does not mean, however, that no one controls it. **"**
>
> —Amy Harmon,
> *New York Times*, 1998

● **Table 2.1 Top 10 Internet Parent Companies in the United States, 2006**

Parent	Unique Audience (in millions)	Time per Person (hh:mm:ss)*
1. Microsoft	112,388	2:04:09
2. Yahoo!	102,826	3:10:12
3. Time Warner	100,015	4:50:21
4. Google	90,490	0:54:31
5. eBay	59,120	1:49:13
6. InterActiveCorp	55,906	0:25:58
7. News Corp. Online	52,767	1:23:37
8. Amazon	45,693	0:23:59
9. Walt Disney Internet Group	41,249	0:34:05
10. New York Times Company	38,559	0:15:37

*Average time a person spent per month at one or more of the company's sites or applications.

Note: Parent companies can own a number of unique Web sites. For example, InterActiveCorp's operations include Ask.com, Bloglines.com, Excite.com, iWon.com, and Myway.

Source: "Nielsen//Netratings Top 10 Web Sites by Parent Company," March 14, 2006, http://www.nielsen-netratings.com/pr/pr_060314.pdf.

As the largest software company in the world, Microsoft has been both applauded and jeered for its role in computing and digital media. With more than 63,000 worldwide employees and about $40 billion in annual revenue, Microsoft dominates the computer software business, but has spread its interests to the Internet, computer games, and television.

Today, Microsoft is among just a few major corporations positioned at the center of media convergence, particularly as digital media content is created, played, and distributed on personal computers and related digital devices. But does Microsoft's enormous size and financial reserves make it more or less likely to be an important innovator in the future?

Figure 2.2 Media Ownership: Principal Operations for Microsoft Corporation

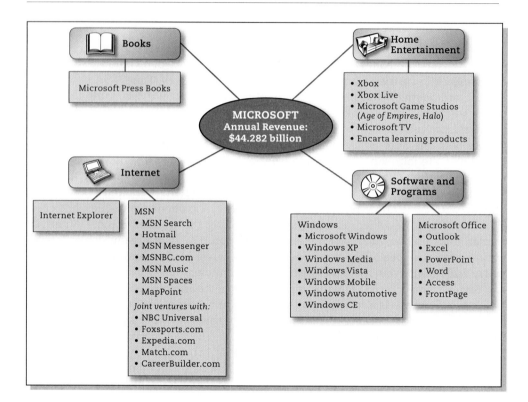

efforts to break Microsoft into two independent companies. Today Microsoft's Internet dominance is considerable: The company continues to operate the most popular Web browser (Microsoft Explorer); one of the leading free Web e-mail services (Hotmail); a top Internet service provider (MSN); a popular instant messaging service (MSN Messenger); and a new search engine, which is poised to compete with Google (see Figure 2.2).

Another heavyweight is AOL. Although the company has struggled in the last few years, its Internet presence is still ubiquitous. The company remains the leading ISP worldwide, dwarfing competitors. With this dominance comes dominance in other areas: AOL Mail, AOL Instant Messenger, AOL's shopping directory, AOL@School. As part of the largest media conglomerate, Time Warner, AOL routinely steers its users to Time Warner subsidiaries, such as its book and magazine publishing empires and its film and television businesses.

Yahoo! has surged past other Internet start-ups since its beginnings in 1994. Yahoo! has branched out into e-mail, instant messaging, Internet telephone service, audio and video streaming, shopping partnerships, and Web site tools. Its latest strategy has been to become the dominant corporation in the search industry. After acquiring key search indexes Overture and Inktomi in 2003, Yahoo! began to compete directly with Google and aggressively market to users by including sponsored links with search result lists. According to Nielsen//NetRatings, the Yahoo.com Web site regularly ranks among the top Internet sites in terms of its audience reach.

Finally, Google has quickly risen to the ranks of the Internet's top properties. The company was established in 1998, offered public stock in 2004, and by 2006 had a market value of more than $100 billion. Starting with the strength of its immensely popular search engine, Google has become more of an all-purpose portal like Yahoo!,

Media Literacy
and the Critical Process

Search Engines and Their Commercial Bias

How valuable are search engines for doing research? Are they the best resources for academic information?

Description: We're going to do a search for the topic "obesity," which has been prevalent in the news lately, and a topic we know is highly controversial. Here's what we find in the first thirty results from Google: numerous sites for obesity research organizations (e.g., American Obesity Association, Obesity Research, and Obesity-online.com), many of which are government funded. Here's what we find in the top-rated results from Yahoo!: numerous sponsored sites (e.g., eDiets: Your diet, Your way) and the same obesity research organizations.

Analysis: A closer look at these results reveals a subtle but interesting pattern: All the sites listed in the top ten results (of both search engine result lists) offer loads of advice to help an *individual* lose weight (e.g., change eating habits, exercise, undergo surgery, take drugs). These sites all frame obesity as either a disease, a genetic disorder, or the result of personal inactivity. In other words, they put the blame squarely on the individual. But where is all the other research that links high obesity rates to social factors (e.g., constant streams of advertising for junk food, government subsidies of the giant corn syrup food sweetener industry, deceptive labeling practices—see Chapter 11)? These society-level views are not apparent in our Web searches.

Interpretation: What does it mean that our searches are so biased? Consider this series of connections:

Obesity research organizations manufacture drugs and promote surgery treatments to "cure" obese individuals. They are backed by Big Business, which is interested in selling more junk food (not taking social responsibility), and then promoting drugs to treat the problem. A wealthy site can pay for placement, either directly (via Yahoo!) or indirectly (by promoting itself through various marketing channels and ensuring its popularity—Google ranks pages by popularity). As a result, search results today are skewed toward Big Business. Money speaks.

Evaluation: Commercial search engines have evolved to be much like the commercial mass media: They tend to reflect the corporate perspective that finances them. This does not bode well for the researcher, who is interested in many angles of a single issue. Controversy is at the heart of every important research question.

Engagement: What to do? Start by including the word *controversy* next to the search term, as in *obesity and controversy.* Or, learn about where alternative information sources exist on the Web. A search for *obesity* on the independent media publications AlterNet, MediaChannel, Common Dreams, and Salon, for example, will offer countless other perspectives to the obesity epidemic. The Resource Discovery Network, http://www.rdn.ac.uk, a powerful subject gateway from Britain; Wikipedia, a collaboratively built encyclopedia; ibiblio; and the National Science Digital Library are other valuable resources that weed out much of the commercial incursions and offer valuable and diverse perspectives.

as it has branched out to provide financial data (Google Finance), shopping (Froogle), mapping (Google Local), and e-mail (Gmail) services, all designed to draw users and advertisers. But, Google's most significant recent development is its desktop software, which is in direct competition with Microsoft's main software business.

The desire of corporations to tap into the Internet economy is clear. The increasing dominance of commercial interests on the Internet is affecting the way in which the information highway—once a nonprofit, government-subsidized medium known for freely accessible information—is evolving. Indeed, the phenomenon of a fifteen-year-old Internet start-up like AOL in 2000 acquiring Time Warner, the world's largest media conglomerate, certainly speaks to the power of the Internet in the twenty-first century. But as the Internet economic bubble burst in 2001, it became clear that not all ambitious corporate strategies to cash in on the information high-way would be successful.

Alternative Voices

Independent hackers and programmers continue to invent new ways to use and to communicate on the Internet, and while some of these products have retained their corporate-free environments, others have been taken over by commercial interests. Despite the commercial traffic and interests, the pioneering spirit of the Internet's early days endures; the Internet continues to be a participatory medium where any-one can be involved.

Open-Source Software

Microsoft has become the predominant corporation of the digital age, but indepen-dent software creators persist in developing alternate options. One of the best exam-ples of this is the development of **open-source software**. In the early days of computer code writing, amateur hackers collec-tively developed software on an open-source ethic, freely sharing the program source code and ideas to upgrade and improve pro-grams. Beginning in the 1970s, Microsoft put an end to much of this activity by making software development a business in which programs were developed privately and users were re-quired to pay for them—and all the necessary upgrades.

● Linus Torvalds, the Finnish software developer, holds a license plate bear-ing the name of his inven-tion, the Linux computer operating system. Since Torvalds's first version of Linux in 1991, hundreds of other developers around the world have contributed improvements to this open-source software rival of Mi-crosoft's Windows.

Programmers are still developing noncommercial, open-source software. As Microsoft fought an antitrust lawsuit by the U.S. Justice Department between 1999 and 2001, some experts ar-gued that Linux (pronounced linn-ucks), a free, open-source soft-ware operating system, might be a significant challenger to Windows.[16] Linux was established in 1991 by Linus Torvalds, a twenty-one-year-old student at the University of Helsinki. Since then, professional computer programmers and hobbyists around the world have e-mailed improvements back and forth, creating a sophisticated software system that even Microsoft has ac-knowledged is a credible alternative to expensive commercial programs. Linux can operate across disparate platforms and companies such as IBM, Dell, and Sun Microsystems, as well as other corporations and governmental organizations, have embraced Linux. Still, the greatest impact of Linux is not on the PC desktops of everyday computer users, but instead on the op-eration of behind-the-scenes computer servers.

Wiki Web Sites

Another open-source movement involves *wiki* (which means "quick" in Hawaiian) technology. Wiki Web sites enable anyone to edit and contribute to them. The most notable example is Wikipedia, www.wikipedia.org, an online encyclopedia that is constantly updated and revised by interested volunteers. All previous page versions of the Wikipedia are stored, allowing users to see how each individual topic devel-ops. The largest version of Wikipedia, in English, has more than one million articles. Wikipedias are also being developed in about two hundred different languages.

Although Wikipedia has become one of the most popular resources on the Web, there have been some criticisms of its open editing model. In 2005, John Seigenthaler Sr., a former editor of the *Nashville Tennessean* newspaper, discovered that the biogra-phical article about him on Wikipedia falsely claimed he may have had a role in the assassinations of John F. Kennedy and Robert F. Kennedy. Investigators later identified the man who had posted the false biography content as a joke. The false copy was corrected, and Wikipedia now carries an entry covering the entire Seigenthaler biography controversy.[17] But Seigenthaler and many in the mainstream media continue to criticize Wikipedia's open architecture as an invitation to inaccuracies and disinformation. Ironically, a follow-up study by *Nature* magazine that reviewed science entries found Wikipedia's articles were sometimes poorly written, but only slightly less accurate than the traditionally edited *Encyclopaedia Britannica*.[18]

Blogs

The biggest phenomenon in user-created content on the Internet has been Web logs, more commonly known as **blogs**. Blogs are sites that contain articles in chronological, journal-like form, often with reader comments and links to other articles on the Web. Ideally, blogs are updated frequently, often with daily posts that keep readers coming back to them. A 2005 study by the Pew Internet & American Life Project found that more than eight million U.S. adults have created a blog, and 27 percent of Internet users report that they read blogs.[19] (See "Case Study: A Blog's Life" on page 67.) Blogs have become personal and corporate multimedia sites, sometimes with photos, graphics, and downloadable audio podcasts that can be played on computers and portable digital devices such as iPods. More recently, *vlogs* have emerged, bringing video to blog pages.

Social Networking Web Sites

The do-it-yourself content of the Internet doesn't end with blogs. A whole host of social networking sites like MySpace, Facebook, Friendster, LiveJournal, Hi5, and Xanga have sprung up on the Web. MySpace and Facebook, in particular, have been two of the fastest growing sites on the Internet. Both sites allow users to create personal profiles with photos and lists of favorite things, to connect in posted messages with old friends and to meet new friends.

● The most popular Web site for social networking, MySpace.com exploded onto the Internet scene in 2003 and is now often cited as being the fifth most-viewed English-language Web site. The News Corporation–owned site has attracted major advertising dollars and claims to post more than 8 percent of all Internet advertisements, which ranks the site with AOL, Google, and Yahoo!.

MySpace, founded in 2003, is the leading social networking site. By 2006, My-Space boasted more than 106 million profiles, making it one of the leading Web sites in user traffic. In addition to personal profiles, MySpace is known for its music listings, where more than three million unsigned, independent, and mainstream artists such as the Yeah, Yeah, Yeahs; Weezer; and the Black Eyed Peas set up profiles to promote their music, launch new albums, and allow users to buy songs. Its popularity with teens made it a major site for online advertising, and it attracted the attention of media conglomerate News Corporation. In 2005, News Corporation bought Intermix Media, the parent company of MySpace, for $580 million to strengthen the company's new Fox Interactive Media unit. Shortly after, the company announced the formation of MySpace Records, a new label that releases compilation recordings with partner Interscope Records. Hoping to tap into the United Kingdom music scene, News Corporation launched a UK version of MySpace in 2006.

Similar to MySpace, Facebook is an online directory that creates online social networks through schools. Started at Harvard in 2004 as an online substitute to the printed facebooks the school created for incoming freshmen, Facebook was instantly a hit, and has since expanded to more than ten million users at nearly every college in the United States (and at colleges in other countries). In 2006, the site expanded to include high school students and business-based networks.

Although both sites enable users to limit access to only their friends and block others, there is concern by schools, law-enforcement officials, and parents that the photos and personal information in the profiles are an invitation to predators. In response to these concerns, News Corporation hired a safety consultant in 2006 to improve the site's security and announced an advertising campaign to educate users and parents about Internet safety. Public disclosures on social networking sites have also led to assorted real-world consequences: an applicant was denied admission to Reed College in Oregon for criticizing the school on his LiveJournal site, two Louisiana State swimmers were kicked off the team after disparaging their coaches on Facebook, and a sixteen-year-old in Colorado was arrested after police saw him holding guns in MySpace photos. They later found the same guns in his house.[20]

Linux, wikis, blogs, and social networking sites illustrate that although the information highway has become a mass medium, it is evolving in such an open way that individuals can still make an impact and have an online presence.

Free Expression, Security, and Access

In recent years, three issues about the Internet have commanded the most attention: the suitability of online material, the security of personal and private information, and the accessibility of the Internet. With each of these issues there have been heated debates, with many questions but no easy answers: Should the Internet be a completely open forum, or should certain types of communications be limited or prohibited? Should personal or sensitive government information be private, or should the Internet be an enormous public record? Should all people have equal access to the Internet, or should it be available only to those who can afford it?

The Battle over Inappropriate Material

The question of what constitutes appropriate content has been part of the story of most mass media, from debates over lurid pulp fiction in the nineteenth century to opposition to sexually explicit themes and images during film's early years. The de-

MARTIN /•uH'

● The open architecture of the Internet is both its strength and one of its failings, in that it allows all kinds of electronic viruses to circulate freely. Viruses are small programs that can attach themselves to programs, causing them to break down. They are often replicated by automatically mailing themselves to everyone in the victim's e-mail address book. In 2006, viruses with names like MyJob, Lovgate, and Netsky infected millions of Windows-based computers worldwide. The most common were variants of Netsky, which showed up in e-mail in-boxes with subject lines such as "re: here is the document" and "Auction successful!" and carried a malicious .pif file attached.

mand for X-rated movies also helped drive the VCR–video store boom of the 1980s, and today eliminating some forms of sexual content from television remains a top priority for many politicians and public interest groups. It is not surprising that public objection to indecent and obscene Internet material has led to various legislative efforts to tame the Web, including the Communications Decency Act in 1996 and the Child Online Protection Act in 1998. Both efforts were judged unconstitutional.

Congress tried again in 2000 with the Children's Internet Protection Act, which required schools and libraries that received federal funding for Internet access to use software to filter out visual content that is deemed obscene, pornographic, or harmful to minors. In 2003 the U.S. Supreme Court upheld the law, as long as libraries disable the filtering software at the request of adult users.

Still, pornography continues to flourish on the Internet on commercial pornography sites and even on individuals' blogs and social networking pages. On file-sharing sites such as KaZaA, more people swap pornography than audio files. Yet, the difficulty is that filtering technology simply doesn't work well. As the American Library Association notes, there is "no filtering technology that will block out all illegal content, but allow access to constitutionally protected materials."[21]

Although the "back alleys of sex" of the Internet have caused considerable public concern, Internet sites that carry potentially dangerous information (e.g., bomb-building instructions, hate speech) have also incited calls for Internet censorship, particularly after the 1999 high school shootings in Littleton, Colorado, and the terrorism of September 11, 2001.

The Challenge to Keep Personal Information Private

As personal computers increasingly become gateways into our private lives, government and commercial surveillance, online fraud, and unethical data-gathering methods have made the Internet treacherous at times. Government agencies around the world have obtained communication logs, Web browser histories, and private online records of individual users who thought their online activities were private. In the United States, for example, the USA PATRIOT Act, which became law about a month after the September 11 attacks and was renewed in 2006, grants sweeping powers to law-enforcement agencies to intercept computer communications, including e-mail messages and Web browsing.

Besides surveillance, the Internet is also increasingly a conduit for online robbery and identity theft—illegally obtaining personal credit and identity information. Computer hackers have infiltrated Internet databases from banks and hospitals to the Pentagon, stolen credit card numbers from online retailers, and shut down entire companies for days. Identity theft victimizes hundreds of thousands of people a year, and clearing one's name can take countless hours and hundreds of dollars. More than $12 billion worldwide is lost to online fraud artists every year.

Another problem is **spam** and spurious "news"—the Internet equivalent of unwanted junk mail and backroom gossip. Unlike traditional media, which routinely employ editors as information gatekeepers, information distributed on the Internet is typically not checked by anyone. Most media outlets screen material for accuracy, fairness, appropriateness, and decency, but such screening is more difficult on the Internet.

Thus, the Internet is rife with scams. One particularly costly Internet scam is what fraud investigators call **phishing**—a new twist on identity theft. The scam begins with phony e-mail messages that pretend to be from an official site—such as eBay or AOL—and request that customers send their credit card numbers and other personal information to update their account. Phishing is just one type of spam that increasingly clogs up users' e-mail inboxes. By 2006, one Internet security company reported that only 15.5 percent of all e-mail messages were legitimate. The rest were spam, phishing scams, and viruses.[22] (See "Tracking Technology: Keylogging" on opposite page.)

Other privacy problems concern undisclosed data-collection practices. Despite justifiable concerns about transmitting personal information online, people are increasingly warming to the idea of **e-commerce**, selling and purchasing products and services on the Internet, especially as more companies offer products online and assure customers of online security with more rigorous data-encryption standards. With the growth in e-commerce, however, comes the growth of online marketing strategies and attempts to collect information on Web users for commercial purposes. One common method of gathering information on users is through **cookies**, information profiles about a user that are usually automatically accepted by the Web browser and stored on the user's own computer hard drive. Cookies work as "spies," sending back information to track the user's subsequent visits within that Web site. In a relatively benign situation, cookies can tell a Web site that the user is cleared for access to an authorized site, such as a library database that is open only to university faculty and students. More intrusive are Web sites that use cookies to record the user's Internet account, the last several Web pages visited, and other information stored in that person's Web browser directory. In these cases, the Web sites create a marketing profile of users and can target them for certain advertisements. Cookies are automatically accepted by most browsers, although preference commands can be set to reject cookies or provide warnings when a Web site is trying to set such a system. Nevertheless, many Web sites require the user to accept cookies in order to gain access to the site. Even more intrusive is **spyware**, which is often secretly bundled with free downloaded software, such as the peer-to-peer file-sharing programs eDonkey, BitTorrent, Limewire, KaZaA, and Morpheus, and permits a third party to retrieve personal information on computer users and send pop-up ads to users' computer screens.

In 1998, the U.S. Federal Trade Commission (FTC) developed fair information practice principles for online privacy to address the issues of notice, choice, access, and security. These principles require Web sites to (1) disclose their data-collection

TRACKING TECHNOLOGY

Keylogging

By Tom Zeller Jr.

Most people who use e-mail now know enough to be on guard against "phishing" messages that pretend to be from a bank or business but are actually attempts to steal passwords and other personal information. But there is evidence that among global cybercriminals, phishing may already be passé.

In some countries, like Brazil, it has been eclipsed by an even more virulent form of electronic con—the use of keylogging programs that silently copy the keystrokes of computer users and send that information to the crooks. These programs are often hidden inside other software and then infect the machine, putting them in the category of malicious programs known as Trojan horses, or just Trojans.

The twist here is that the keylogging programs exploit security flaws and monitor the path that carries data from the keyboard to other parts of the computer. This is a more invasive approach than phishing, which relies on deception rather than infection, tricking people into giving their information to a fake Web site.

The monitoring programs are often hidden inside ordinary software downloads, e-mail attachments or files shared over peer-to-peer networks. They can even be embedded in Web pages, taking advantage of browser features that allow programs to run automatically.

"It's the wave of the future," said Peter Cassidy, the secretary general of the Anti-Phishing Working Group, a consortium of industry and law enforcement partners that fights online fraud and identity theft. "All this stuff is becoming more and more automated and more and more opaque."

Mr. Cassidy's group found that the number of Web sites known to be hiding this kind of malicious code nearly doubled between November and December [2005], rising to more than 1,900. The antivirus company Symantec has reported that half of the malicious software it tracks is designed not to damage computers but to gather personal data. Over the course of 2005, iDefense, a unit of Verisign that provides information on computer security to government and industry clients, counted over 6,000 different keylogger variants—a 65 percent increase over 2004.

About one-third of all malicious code tracked by the company now contains some keylogging component, according to Ken Dunham, the company's rapid-response director.

And the SANS Institute, a group that trains and certifies computer security professionals, estimated that at a single moment last fall, as many as 9.9 million machines in the United States were infected with keyloggers of one kind or another, putting as much as $24 billion in bank account assets—and probably much more—literally at the fingertips of fraudsters. John Bambenek, the SANS researcher who made the estimate, suggested that the infection rate was probably much higher.

"I get concerned that we're scaring people off the Internet," said Alex Eckelberry, the president of Sun-Belt Software, a maker of antispyware software based in Clearwater, Fla. Mr. Eckelberry believes that the infection rate is probably far lower than most estimates indicate, in part because the trend is hard to measure and so many computers are already protected.

In fact, keylogging's simplicity may be why it is suddenly so popular among thieves. "Phishing takes a lot of time and effort," said David Thomas, the chief of the computer intrusion division at the Federal Bureau of Investigation. "This type of software is a much more efficient way to get what they're after."

The programming, too, is often trivial. "These can be developed by a 12-year-old hacker," said Eugene Kaspersky, a cofounder of Kaspersky Labs, an international computer security and antivirus company based in Moscow.

"I'm afraid that if the number of criminals grows with this same speed, the antivirus companies will not be able to create adequate protection," said Mr. Kaspersky, who added that the time has come for increased investment in law enforcement and far better cross-border cooperation among investigators, who are overwhelmed by the global nature of cybercrime. "There are more criminals on the Internet street than policemen," he said.

Source: Excerpted from Tom Zeller Jr., "Cyberthieves Silently Copy as You Type," *New York Times,* February 27, 2006, A1.

practices, (2) give consumers options for choosing whether and how personal data may be collected, (3) permit individuals access to their records to ensure data accuracy, and (4) secure personal data from unauthorized use. Unfortunately, the FTC has no power to enforce fair information practices on the Internet, and most Web sites' own self-enforcement has been dismal. When they post privacy policies about not selling consumer data, for example, most Web sites will not mention that they rent the information instead, or that they don't abide by their own policy at all.[23]

One of the most important elements in the online data-collection debate is whether Web sites should be required to use **opt-in** or **opt-out** policies. Opt-in data policies, favored by consumer and privacy advocates, require that the Web site gain explicit permission from online consumers before the site can collect their personal data. Opt-out data policies, favored by data-mining corporations, involve the automatic collection of personal data unless the consumer goes to the trouble of filling out a specific form to "opt out" of the practice. According to the FTC, most Web sites follow opt-out policies, and the opt-out consent is often buried at the end of long pages in prechecked click boxes that the consumer has to take the time to uncheck.[24]

> " These two syllables — 'opt in' — strike terror in the hearts of Google, Microsoft, AOL, and everyone else in the interactive marketing field. "
>
> –Jeff Chester, Center for Digital Democracy, 2006

The Economics of Access and the Digital Divide

A key economic issue of our times is whether the cost of getting on the Internet will undermine equal access. Mimicking the economic disparity between rich and poor that grew more pronounced during the 1980s and 1990s, the term **digital divide** refers to the growing contrast between "information haves," or Internet users who can afford to acquire multiple media services, and "information have-nots," or people who may not be able to afford a computer or the monthly bills for Internet service connections, much less the many options now available.

Although about 75 percent of U.S. households are connected to the Internet, there are big gaps in access, particularly in terms of age and education. For example, a recent study found that only 26 percent of Americans age sixty-five and older go online, compared with 67 percent of those aged fifty to sixty-four, 80 percent of those aged thirty to forty-nine, and 84 percent of those aged eighteen to twenty-nine. Education has an even more pronounced effect: only 29 percent of those who did not graduate from high school have access, compared with 61 percent of high school graduates and 89 percent of college graduates.

Another digital divide has developed in the United States as Americans have switched over from slow dial-up connections to high-speed broadband service. By 2006, 68 percent of all Internet users in the United States had broadband connections, but those in lower income households were much less likely to have high-speed service. The Pew Internet & American Life Project concluded that American adults split into three tiers — "the truly offline (22% of American adults); those with relatively more modest connections, such as dial-up users, intermittent users, and non-users who live with an internet user (40%); and the highly-wired broadband elite (33%)."[25]

One way of improving access is by making Internet connection available in public libraries. The Bill and Melinda Gates Foundation has been the leading advocate of funding networked computers in libraries since 1997. Now, more than 95 percent of public libraries in the United States offer Internet access. About 10 percent of all Internet users gain access to the Internet through public libraries, which rank fifth as an access point, behind home, work, school, and someone else's home. Libraries have helped to close the digital divide for low-income citizens and remote rural residents.[26]

Another alternative for Internet access is **Wi-Fi**, a standard for short-distance wireless networking, enabling users of notebook computers and other devices to connect to the Internet in cafés, hotels, airports, and parks. What began as a home wireless technology is now heralded as a citizen's utility. Entire cities are developing Wi-Fi mesh systems—often by attaching Wi-Fi cells to streetlight posts—and enabling citizens with Wi-Fi devices to make free or low-cost seamless Internet connections throughout a municipal area. Throughout the world, and in U.S. cities such as Chaska, Minnesota; Dayton, Ohio; St. Cloud, Florida; Philadelphia, San Francisco, and Washington, D.C., municipal Wi-Fi systems have been either planned or built.

In those locations, Wi-Fi is viewed as an inexpensive and essential utility for the community's citizens, bridging the digital divide and giving them easy and mobile access to high-speed broadband Internet service. However, some media corporations see municipal Wi-Fi as a threat because Wi-Fi challenges the almost complete control that the cable industry (via cable modems) and telephone companies (through DSL) have over access to broadband Internet service.

In one of the largest planned municipal Wi-Fi services, Philadelphia is building a 135-square-mile hotspot to blanket the city in low-cost wireless Internet service. Verizon, the state's largest telephone company, balked, arguing that existing commercial broadband providers, such as itself, should control the Wi-Fi business. After heavy lobbying from Verizon, the state of Pennsylvania ultimately passed a law prohibiting Pennsylvania cities from starting their own Wi-Fi networks without giving existing phone or cable broadband providers the first rights to the opportunity. But Philadelphia was exempted from the new state law and will build a system and charge city residents $10–$20 for monthly Wi-Fi access.

Globally, though, the have-nots face an even greater obstacle in connecting to the Internet. Although the Web claims to be worldwide, countries like the United States, Norway, Sweden, Finland, Japan, South Korea, Israel, Australia, the United Kingdom, and Germany account for most of its international flavor. In nations such as Jordan,

> 66 [The Internet] is a way for . . . the struggle in our country, and the many other countries where there are a lot of human rights abuses, to be brought out into the open. 99
>
> —Janai Robert Orina, Kenyan human rights worker, 1998

● Nicolas Negroponte, founder of the Media Lab at MIT, began a project to provide $100 laptops to children in developing countries. These laptops, the first supply of which was funded by Negroponte, need to survive in rural environments where challenges include adverse weather conditions (dust and high heat), reliable power, Internet access, and maintenance.

Saudi Arabia, Syria, and Myanmar (Burma), the governments permit limited or no access to the Web. In countries like Argentina, Colombia, Brazil, and Mexico, an inadequate telecommunications infrastructure means that consumers must endure painfully long waits to get online. In other countries, phone lines and computers are almost nonexistent. For example, in Sierra Leone, a nation of about six million in West Africa with poor public utilities and intermittent electrical service, only about twenty thousand people—about 0.3 percent of the population—are Internet users.[27]

Even as the Internet matures and becomes more accessible, wealthy users are still able to buy higher levels of privacy, specialty access, and capability than other users. Whereas traditional media made the same information available to everyone who owned a radio or a TV set, the Internet creates economic tiers and classes of service. Policy groups, media critics, and concerned citizens continue to debate the implications of media access for democratic societies, which have traditionally valued the equal opportunity to acquire knowledge.

"In Africa, there are only three computers for every 1,000 people."

–Computers for Africa, 2005

CASE STUDY

Wonkette!

HOT: ABRAMOFF CRAIGSLIST EAVESDROPPING IRAQ NSA SUPREME COURT   tip your editors: tips@wonkette

Friday
05 12 06

Must Be a Small Table

Just so we're clear.

☞ **Impeachment:** Off the table.
☞ **Nuking Iran:** On the table.

Democrats Won't Try to Impeach President [WP]
Iran Leader Says Attack On His Country Unlikely [WP]

READ MORE: GEORGE W. BUSH, IMPEACHMENT, IRAN, NANCY PELOSI,
NUCLEAR APOCALYPSE, TABLES, WAR

(comment on this post) ♡ ✉ 🔖

Wonk'd: Everything Old is New Again

This week DC was packed with has-beens and also-rans, still probably
looking better than everyone else. **Chuck Norris** enjoyed a steak, but
wasn't on a stake-out. **Bo Derek** has traded in the couture for the sale
down the street. **Madeleine Albright** has a book to hawk (but she's a
dove), **Ari Fleischer** thinks his Blackberry has too many buttons, and
Grover Norquist wants everyone to know how his name is spelled. Plus

A Blog's Life

As the blogging phenomenon has grown into more than
8 million sites representing the perspectives of more than 8
million individuals, we are struck with the question of where
blogs fit into the culture of the mass media landscape. The
vast majority of blogs do not have many readers, and typically read like a diary — a diary that bloggers sometimes
forget millions of people can access. For example, while one
posting complains "Today was a boring day. I'm awfully sick
& I hate Tina," other blogs rant: "Today's pet peeve: People
who won't wash their hands in the office bathroom. Yes, I
know who you are."

But blogs also tackle more compelling issues and have
emerged as widely read reports on technology, politics, and
journalism. One of the earliest blogs — call it a *proto-blog,*
since it lacks a reader comment tool — was Matt Drudge's
The Drudge Report, a Web site created in 1995 to write
about entertainment business news, and later about politics
from a conservative stance. Drudge forced some stories
into the public eye, such as his January 17, 1998, posting
that *Newsweek* magazine editors had killed a story about a
relationship between a White House intern and President
Clinton. But at the same time, *The Drudge Report* is also
known for its lack of journalistic standards and inaccurate
stories — a common paradox on blogs.[1]

Blogs were popularized by the Blogger software developed by Pyra Labs in 1999. Users sign up for free accounts
and easily create their own blogs in a Web browser environment in just a few minutes. When Google noticed the blogging phenomenon, it bought Blogger in 2003 and raised the
profile of blogging. In just a few years, several top bloggers,
attracting many loyal readers, emerged in the blogosphere
(the blogging community), such as Andrew Sullivan.com,
Daily Kos, Engadget, Eschaton, Instapundit, Joshua Micah
Marshall's Talking Points Memo, Romenesko, and Won-
kette.

Recently, political blogs have flourished as they responded to events such as the U.S. invasions of Afghanistan
and Iraq. Like *The Drudge Report,* newer blogs have also
succeeded in pushing stories into the mainstream news
media, resulting in serious outcomes such as the fall of
Trent Lott as Senate Majority Leader, the exit of Dan Rather
as the anchor of CBS Evening News, and the recall of Kryp-
tonite U-shaped bicycle locks (which, Engadget revealed,
could be opened with a Bic pen).

Despite earlier controversy about the validity of their
content, blogs gained credibility as news outlets in 2004,
when some bloggers were invited to cover the major political party conventions. Picking up on the trend, political candidates also used blogs to promote their candidacies, and
news personalities like CNN's Anderson Cooper and NBC's
Brian Williams also began blogging. As journalism, blogs
can be unreliable because they do not go through an editorial verification process. But an advantage of blogs is maximum transparency, connecting journalists directly with
readers.

Some of the most compelling blogs offer insights beyond
typical news reports, like the posts from ordinary people in
the South Pacific offering firsthand accounts of life after the
horrific tsunami disaster in December 2004, or the reports
from a young woman in Iraq whose blog, *Baghdad Burning,*
is so riveting it has been published as a book.

While personal blogs have had noted inaccuracies, some
blogs have been revealed as outright frauds masking as
commentary. In 2006 it was reported that blogs had acted
as shills for Wal-Mart, representing Wal-Mart public relations messages as original blog writing.[2] While advertising
already appears on some blogs, the issue of having sponsored content on blogs — and whether that sponsorship is
clearly disclosed to readers — raises ethical questions.
Should we judge blogs by journalistic standards, advertising
standards, or just as ordinary speech?

In many ways, the blogosphere is much like the public
sphere we live in. There are self-indulgent gossips and
ranters, there are commentators of every political stripe,
there are people who get paid to tell someone else's story,
and — finally — there are people who have a good, honest
story of their own to share.

ⓑ Blogger

Already have an account? Sign in:
Username: Password: ?
SIGN IN   ☐ Remember me ?

Search blogs from across the web with Google Blog Search.

Explore blogs

BLOGS   Rollin' Waters   BLOGS OF NOTE   RANDOM BLOGS
UPDATED AT   ๑าฬัๅอ-ววไลๅ   ◄ ◄ **Mighty Optical Illusions**   **NEXT BLOG >>**
12:42 PM   SEARCH BLOGS

What's a **blog**?   [TAKE A QUICK TOUR]   Create a **blog** in 3
easy steps:

① Create an account
② Name your blog
③ Choose a template

Publish   **Get**   **Post**   **Go**
thoughts   feedback   photos   mobile

A **blog** is your easy-to-use web site, where you can quickly post
thoughts, interact with people, and more. All for **FREE**.

[CREATE YOUR BLOG NOW →]

RECENT NEWS   QUICK CASH

★ **Citizens, the Internet, and Democracy**

Throughout the twentieth century, Americans closely examined emerging mass media for their potential contributions to democracy and culture. As radio became more affordable in the 1920s and 1930s, we hailed the medium for its ability to reach and entertain even the poorest Americans caught in the Great Depression. When television developed in the 1950s and 1960s, it also held promise as a medium that could reach everyone, even those who were illiterate or cut off from printed information. Despite the criticisms of the Internet's accessibility and continuing national and international digital divides, many have praised the Internet for its democratic possibilities and for its accessibility. Some advocates even tout it as the most decentralized social network ever conceived.

> **" If television took the grass roots out of politics, the Internet will put it back in. "**
>
> —Joe Trippi, campaign manager for Democratic presidential candidate Howard Dean, 2003

The biggest threat to the Internet's democratic potential may well be its increasing commercialization. Similar to what happened with the radio and television media, the growth of commercial "channels" on the Internet has far outpaced the emergence of viable nonprofit channels, as fewer and fewer corporations have gained more and more control. The passage of the 1996 Telecommunications Act cleared the way for cable TV systems, computer firms, and telephone companies to merge their interests in advancing communication technology. Although there was a great deal of buzz about lucrative Internet start-ups in the 1990s, it has been large corporations such as Microsoft, Time Warner, Yahoo!, and Google that have weathered the low points of the dot-com economy and maintained a controlling hand in the new information systems.

About three-quarters of households in the United States are now linked to the Internet—up from 50 percent in 2000—thus greatly increasing its democratic possibilities, but also tempting commercial interests to gain even greater control over it and intensifying problems for agencies that are trying to regulate it. If the past is any predictor, it seems realistic to expect that the Internet's potential for widespread democratic use could be partially preempted by narrower commercial interests. As media economist Douglas Gomery warns, "Technology alone does not a communication revolution make. Economics trumps technology every time."[28]

On the more positive side of the ledger, the new technologies may be so uniquely accessible that they offer at least the potential for enriching democratic processes. Books, newspapers, magazines, radio, film, and television widened and expanded the reach of media, but they did not generate equivalent avenues for response and debate. Defenders of the digital age argue that newer media forms—from the MP3 music of emerging musicians to online streaming of independent short films to an array of blogs—allow greater participation. Individuals can create their own Web sites or blogs and seek the social networking sites of others, joining and encouraging conversations about such things as movies, politics, or why they hate *American Idol*. In response to these new media forms, older media are using Internet technology to increase their access to and feedback from varied audiences, soliciting e-mail from users and fostering discussions in sponsored chat rooms and blogs.

Despite the potential of new media forms, skeptics raise doubts about the participatory nature of discussions on the Internet. For instance, critics warn that Internet users may be searching out only those people whose beliefs and values are similar to their own. Although it is important to be able to communicate across vast distances with people who have similar viewpoints, these kinds of discussions may not serve to extend the diversity and tolerance that are central to democratic ideals.

To take a critical position on the debates, we must analyze and judge the Internet's possibilities and limitations. Such a position should be grounded in the knowledge that the media are converging nationally and globally, changing the nature of mass communication. One of these changes is **mass customization**, whereby product companies and content providers can customize a Web page or media form for an individual consumer. For example, Internet portals such as Yahoo! allow users to personalize their front-page services by choosing their own channels of information—their favorite newspapers or sports teams, local movie listings and weather broadcasts, and many other categories—within the Yahoo! interface. Users of My Yahoo! and similar services have the benefits of a personal home page without going through the steps of creating a home page of their own. They are, however, subject to the banner ads of Yahoo!, which are also customized for the user on the basis of his or her shopping and surfing habits. Such mass customization services blur the boundary between one-to-one communication, which we generally associate with an office conversation or a telephone call, and mass communication, which we associate with daily newspapers or TV programs.

It is also no longer very useful to discuss print media and electronic or digital media as if they were completely segregated forms. We live in a world in which a ten-year-old can simultaneously watch an old TV rerun on cable and read the latest Harry Potter book; in which a twenty-year-old can make sense of a nineteenth-century poem while wearing a portable MP3 player blasting out recently downloaded music. Moreover, it is now possible to access old TV reruns, horror thrillers, classic literary texts, and alternative music—all through a home computer and Internet connection. Today, developments in word processing, e-mail, audio books, cable-access channels, DVDs, children's pictorial literature, magazine advertising, and Internet social networking sites are integrating aspects of both print and electronic culture at the crossroads of everyday life.

> 66 The Internet will soon be so pervasive that not having access to the technology or not knowing how to use it will be the equivalent of not knowing how to read or write. 99
>
> —Michael Fleisher, chief executive of Gartner Group, a technology consulting firm, 2000

www.

For review questions and activities for Chapter 2, go to the interactive *Media and Culture* Online Study Guide at *bedfordstmartins.com/ mediaculture*

REVIEW QUESTIONS

Origins of the Internet

1. What are the three stages in the development of a mass medium?

2. How did the Internet originate? What does its development have in common with earlier mass media?

3. How does the World Wide Web work? Why is it significant in the development of the Internet?

4. What are the four main features of the structure of the Internet? How do they help users access and navigate the Internet?

Digital Technology and Converging Media

5. How does media convergence distinguish a different phase in mass media history?

6. What three key technological developments have made possible today's intersection of mass media along the information highway?

Ownership Issues on the Internet

7. What are the key issues involving ownership of the Internet? How do these issues differ from earlier ownership issues in other mass media?

8. Who are the major players vying for control of the Internet?

9. What are the major alternative voices on the Internet?

Free Expression, Security, and Access

10. What are the central concerns about the Internet regarding freedom of expression, security, and access?

11. What is the digital divide, and what does it have to do with the information highway?

Citizens, the Internet, and Democracy

12. What are the key problems involving the expansion of the information highway? How can the information highway make democracy work better?

QUESTIONING THE MEDIA

1. What was your first encounter with the Internet like? How did it compare with your first encounters with other mass media?

2. What features of the information highway are you most excited about? Why? What features are most troubling? Why?

3. What are the advantages of an electronic-digital highway that links televisions, computers, phones, audio equipment, homes, schools, and offices?

4. Do you think virtual communities are genuine communities? Why or why not?

5. As we move from a print-oriented Industrial Age to a digitally based Information Age, how do you think individuals, communities, and nations will be affected?

SEARCHING THE INTERNET

http://www.cdt.org

The Center for Democracy and Technology, a nonprofit group, works to promote "democratic values and constitutional liberties in the digital age" by tracking industry and legislative actions that affect such issues as privacy, bandwidth, domain names, and free expression.

http://www.eff.org

The Electronic Frontier Foundation was formed to protect civil liberties on the Internet and "to help civilize the electronic frontier; to make it truly useful and beneficial not just to a technical elite, but to everyone."

http://www.internet2.edu

Detailing the latest developments of Internet2, this site offers information on the private consortium of more than two hundred universities and corporations that are building and testing the Internet's multimedia-friendly second generation.

http://dmoz.org

The Open Directory Project is the largest human-edited directory of the Web, maintained by a global network of more than seventy thousand volunteers.

http://www.pewinternet.org

The Pew Internet & American Life Project is a nonprofit organization that funds research exploring the impact of the Internet on children, families, communities, the workplace, schools, health care, and civic/political life.

http://www.isoc.org/internet/

The Internet Society is an international organization concerned with the future of the Internet. Its site contains excellent links to several Internet histories.

In Brief

This "think-pair-share" exercise focuses on the Internet and its content.

Think: On your own, spend two to three minutes writing down what kind of content—if any—you think should not be on the World Wide Web. Be sure to consider pornography, hate speech, and potentially violent information, such as how to make bombs.

Pair: Turn to your neighbor and compare notes. Are you concerned about certain kinds of Internet content matter that children might see? Did either of you list excessive commercialism as a problem? What are the most valuable things about the Internet?

Share: As a class, consider the content of the Internet. Should anything on the Internet be censored? What is the value of the Internet to our society? The Internet is fairly new—does it seem to be developing in a positive direction? If you could rethink the direction and uses of the Internet, what would they be?

In Depth

Description. Interview a sample of people about their online privacy. In what kinds of ways has their privacy been violated through their Internet use? Do they regularly have to divulge personal information to gain access to certain Web sites? Do they enter contests, play games, download files, or register on sites that require them to enter their e-mail address or disclose specific interests? What types of Web sites try to gather the most personal information from them? Have they noticed any Internet advertising targeting their personal tastes? Do they contend with increasing amounts of spam e-mail? What is their biggest complaint about being online? Does it have anything to do with privacy?

Analysis. What sort of patterns emerge from your interviews? Are there common ways that online privacy seems to be consistently violated? Are there certain strategies for maintaining privacy on the Internet? Do these work pretty well? Do the interviewees generally seem to be concerned, or unconcerned, about their online privacy? Do your questions make them consider their online privacy for the first time?

Interpretation. What do these patterns mean? Are current marketing practices merely inconvenient, or is there something more insidious going on? Do Internet privacy incursions undercut the usefulness of the medium?

Evaluation. Are data mining, spam, and other invasions of privacy tolerable "costs" for the benefits of the Internet? What should be the standards of privacy for the Internet? How should they be enforced?

Engagement. Learn about and take action against privacy infringements. Visit the Center for Democracy and Technology, http://cdt.org/privacy, and GetNetWise, http://www.privacy.getnetwise.org, to learn how to prevent and delete unwanted cookies, spyware, spam, and online fraud, and how to report violations to the FTC. Share your knowledge with your peers.

KEY TERMS

Internet, 43
ARPAnet, 45
e-mail, 46
servers, 46
newsgroups, 46
World Wide Web, 47
HTML (HyperText Markup Language), 47
browsers, 47
portal, 48
Internet service provider, 48

search engine, 48
broadband, 49
directories, 50
instant messaging, 51
Internet2, 52
participatory media, 53
digital communication, 53
microprocessors, 53
fiber-optic cable, 53
media convergence, 53
Telecommunications Act of 1996, 55

open-source software, 58
blogs, 59
spam, 62
phishing, 62
e-commerce, 62
cookies, 62
spyware, 62
opt-in or opt-out policies, 64
digital divide, 64
Wi-Fi, 65
mass customization, 69

sound recording

and popular music

Apple revolutionized the early personal computer market in the 1970s with the introduction of the Apple II, the first mass-produced personal computer. The company transformed the PC again in the 1980s with the Macintosh, teaching the world how to point and click with a mouse.

In the 1990s, with company co-founder Steve Jobs back as CEO (after he successfully launched Pixar Animation Studios), Apple returned to the vanguard of personal computing with the debut of the iMac, Internet-ready computers with eye-catching colorful translucent plastic cases that challenged the hegemony of beige in computer design.

Then in 2003, Apple brought its characteristic ease-of-use and contemporary design to the online music industry. Millions of music fans worldwide had been downloading songs, mostly illegally, since the late 1990s. But no one in the music industry had figured out how to successfully design a business that sold legitimate downloads of songs.

Jobs was able to convince the five top music-industry corpora-

tions that Apple, with only about 2 percent of the personal computer market and its proprietary operating system, could be a safe, self-contained testing ground for an online music distribution business.

By early 2006, Apple had clearly revolutionized another industry: Apple's iTunes online music store had sold more than 1 billion songs at ninety-nine cents each, captured 75 percent of the legal download market in the United States (70 percent in Europe), and held a U.S. catalogue of more than 1.5 million songs from the four major labels and a thousand-plus independent labels. In its arrangement with the labels, Apple gets between twenty-five and thirty cents per legal download, with the labels getting the rest.

After the initial success of their music store, Apple upgraded iTunes to enable Windows-based computers to download songs. Apple has since launched iTunes music stores in more than eighteen other countries, reaching 70 percent of the global music market.

The chief accessory to the iTunes music store is Apple's iPod, a portable digital music player that plays songs downloaded from iTunes. By the first half of 2006, Apple had sold 50 million iPods—including 14 million iPods in the last three months of 2005 alone. The TV ads for iPods have themselves become part of music culture. The dark silhouetted figures dancing with an iPod against a full screen of vivid color feature popular artists including Eminem, Rinôçérôse, Gorillaz, and the Black Eyed Peas.

The digital download market in the United States accounted for 6 percent of the music industry's sales in 2006, up from 2 percent in 2004–05. Apple's latest innovations established the legitimate side of music downloading, integrated it into people's lifestyles, and ignited competition for an industry that's forecast to be worth $4.4 billion by 2008—about a third of all U.S. music sales. Still, illegal downloads far outpaced legal downloads in 2006.

The ubiquity of the iPod has given rise to new forms of prerecorded audio programs called *podcasts* that are posted on the Web and can be played on a computer or an iPod (or a similar digital music player). Apple continues to release variants of the iPod, such as the iPod Shuffle, which holds only 240 songs but dropped the iPod price below $80. The iPod Nano, which replaced the iPod Mini, features a color screen to display album art and stores photos as well as music. The latest generation of the original iPod also has a color screen and can play music videos, television shows, movies, and video games downloaded from iTunes as Apple attempts to make its popular portable music player also a popular tool for video.

he medium of sound recording has had an immense impact on our culture. The music that helps to shape our identities and comfort us during the transition from childhood to adulthood resonates throughout our lives. It stirs debate among parents and teenagers, teachers and students, politicians and performers.

Throughout its history, popular music has been banned by parents, business outlets, radio stations, school officials, and even governments seeking to protect young people from the raw language and corrupting excesses of the music world. At a time when various forms of rock music have become an ever-present annoyance to many, it is easy to forget that in the late 1700s authorities in Europe, thinking that it was immoral for young people to dance close together, outlawed the waltz as "savagery." A hundred years later, the Argentinean upper class tried to suppress the tango, the urban roots of which could be traced to the bars and bordellos of Buenos Aires. The first Latin music and dance to gain international popularity, the tango migrated to Paris in the early twentieth century and was condemned by the clergy for its impact on French youth. During the 1920s, some adults criticized the Charleston, a dance that featured cheek-to-cheek contact by partners. Rock and roll in the 1950s and hip-hop in the 1980s and 1990s added their chapters to the age-old battle between generations.

To place the impact of popular music in context, we will begin by investigating the origins of recording's technological "hardware." We will review Thomas Edison's early phonograph, Emile Berliner's invention of the flat disk record, and the development of audiotape and compact discs. We will study radio's early threat to sound recording and the subsequent alliance between the two media when television arrived in the 1950s.

In this chapter we will also examine the content and culture of the music industry. The predominant role of rock music is a key point of reference. Many important forms of music have become popular—including classical, tango, jazz, salsa, country, blues, gospel, hip-hop, and folk—but no other musical expression has had such an extraordinary impact on other mass media forms. With the introduction of music videos in the early 1980s, rock music dramatically changed the cable and TV landscapes. More significant, rock simultaneously linked and transformed the fundamental structure of two mass media industries: sound recording and radio. Beginning in the 1950s, rock created an enormous and enduring consumer youth market for sound recordings, and it provided much-needed content for radio at a time when television had "borrowed" most of radio's longtime programming. Rock has influenced a diverse array of international cultures, operating as a kind of common ground for fans worldwide. In this chapter, we will look at rock and other contemporary forms of popular music as we survey the growth of sound recording as a mass medium. Finally, we will examine economic and democratic issues facing the recording industry.

> **"If people knew what this stuff was about, we'd probably all get arrested."**
>
> **–Bob Dylan, 1966, talking about rock and roll**

● An Edison Standard Phonograph, circa 1900, for playing wax cylinders.

Technology and the Development of Sound Recording

New mass media have often been defined in terms of the communication technology that preceded them. For example, movies were initially called motion pictures, a term that derived from photography; radio was referred to as wireless telegraphy; and television was often called *picture radio*. Sound recording instruments were initially labeled "talking machines" and later called phonographs, when Thomas Edison made a recording device in 1877 that played back voices. Edison's invention was the result of tinkering with existing innovations, the tele*phone* and the tele*graph*. The origin of *tele-* is the Greek word for "far off"; *phono-* and *-graph* come from the Greek words for "sound" and "writing." This early blending of technology foreshadowed our contemporary era, in which media as diverse as newspapers and movies are converging on the Internet. Before the Internet, however, the first major media convergence involved the relationship between the sound recording and radio industries.

From Wax Cylinders to Flat Disks: Sound Recording Becomes a Mass Medium

In the 1850s, the French printer Leon Scott de Martinville conducted the first experiments with sound recording. Using a hog's hair bristle as a needle, he tied one end to a thin membrane stretched over the narrow part of a funnel. When the inventor spoke into the funnel, the membrane vibrated and the free end of the bristle made grooves on a revolving cylinder coated with a thick liquid called *lamp black*. Different sounds made different trails in the lamp black. However, de Martinville could not figure out how to play back the sound. That is what Thomas Edison did in 1877. He recorded his own voice by using a needle to press his voice's sound waves onto tinfoil wrapped around a metal cylinder about the size of a cardboard toilet-paper roll. After recording his voice, Edison played it back by repositioning the needle to retrace the grooves in the foil, a material he later replaced with wax.

As we discussed in Chapter 2, most new media pass through three developmental stages. The first is the novelty stage, in which inventors experiment to solve a particular problem, such as how to play back recorded music. In the second, or entrepreneurial, stage, inventors and investors work out a practical and marketable use for the new device. Edison, for example, initially thought of his phonograph as a kind of answering machine; he envisioned a "telephone repeater" that would "provide invaluable records, instead of being the recipient of momentary and fleeting communication."[1]

In the third stage, entrepreneurs figure out how to market the new device as a consumer product. For sound recording, a key breakthrough at this stage came from Emile Berliner, a German engineer who had immigrated to America. In the late 1880s, he began using a flat spinning five-inch disk to trace voices. Through a photo-engraving process, he recorded the sounds onto disks made of metal and shellac.

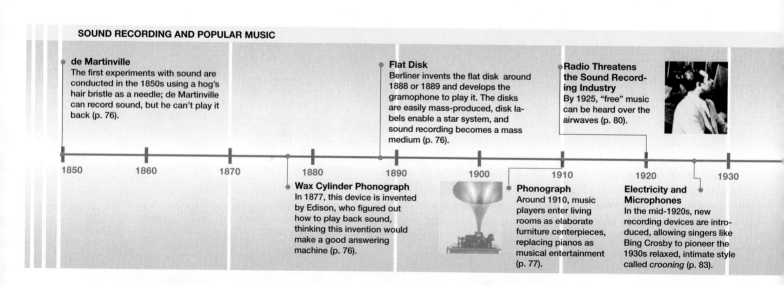

SOUND RECORDING AND POPULAR MUSIC

de Martinville
The first experiments with sound are conducted in the 1850s using a hog's hair bristle as a needle; de Martinville can record sound, but he can't play it back (p. 76).

Flat Disk
Berliner invents the flat disk around 1888 or 1889 and develops the gramophone to play it. The disks are easily mass-produced, disk labels enable a star system, and sound recording becomes a mass medium (p. 76).

Radio Threatens the Sound Recording Industry
By 1925, "free" music can be heard over the airwaves (p. 80).

1850   1860   1870   1880   1890   1900   1910   1920   1930

Wax Cylinder Phonograph
In 1877, this device is invented by Edison, who figured out how to play back sound, thinking this invention would make a good answering machine (p. 76).

Phonograph
Around 1910, music players enter living rooms as elaborate furniture centerpieces, replacing pianos as musical entertainment (p. 77).

Electricity and Microphones
In the mid-1920s, new recording devices are introduced, allowing singers like Bing Crosby to pioneer the 1930s relaxed, intimate style called *crooning* (p. 83).

These disks became the first records. Using Edison's ideas, Berliner developed a machine for playing his disks on the first turntable, which he called a *gramophone*.

Berliner also developed a technique that enabled him to stamp and mass-produce his round records. Previously, using Edison's cylinder, performers had to play or sing into the speaker for each separate recording. Berliner's technique featured a master recording from which copies could be easily duplicated in mass quantities. In addition, the industry realized that disks needed to have places for labels, so that the music could be differentiated by title, performer, and songwriter. This led to the development of a "star system," because fans could identify and choose their favorite sounds and artists.

Another breakthrough occurred in the early twentieth century when the Victor Talking Machine Company placed the hardware, or "guts," of the record player inside a piece of furniture. These early record players, known as Victrolas, were mechanical and had to be primed with a crank handle. Electric record players, first available in 1925, gradually replaced Victrolas in the late 1920s as more homes were wired for electricity.

In the 1940s, because shellac was needed for World War II munitions production, the record industry turned to a polyvinyl plastic record. The vinyl recordings turned out to be more durable than shellac records, which broke easily. In 1948, CBS Records introduced the 33 1/3-revolutions-per-minute (rpm) *long-playing record* (LP), with about twenty minutes of music on each side. This was an improvement over the three to four minutes of music contained on the existing 78-rpm records. The next year, RCA developed a competing 45-rpm record, featuring a quarter-size hole (best suited for jukebox use). The two new standards were technically incompatible, meaning they could not be played on each other's machines. A five-year marketing battle ensued, similar to the VHS vs. Beta war over consumer video standards in the 1980s, or the Macintosh vs. Windows battle over computer-operating-system standards in the 1980s and 1990s. In 1953, CBS and RCA compromised. The 33 1/3 record became the standard for long-playing albums and collections of music, and 45s became the format for two-sided singles. Record players were designed to accommodate 45s, 33 1/3 LPs, and, for a while, 78s. The 78-rpm record, however, eventually became obsolete, doomed to antique collections along with Edison's wax cylinders.

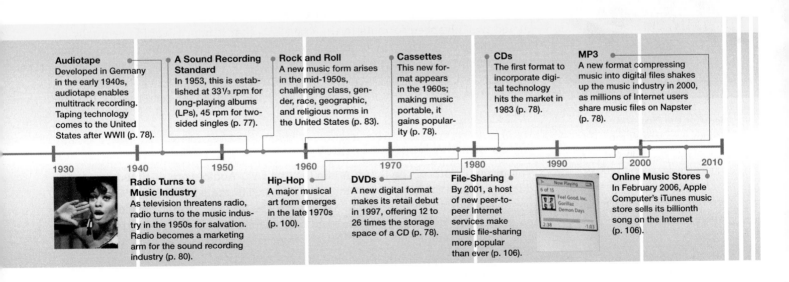

Audiotape
Developed in Germany in the early 1940s, audiotape enables multitrack recording. Taping technology comes to the United States after WWII (p. 78).

A Sound Recording Standard
In 1953, this is established at 33⅓ rpm for long-playing albums (LPs), 45 rpm for two-sided singles (p. 77).

Rock and Roll
A new music form arises in the mid-1950s, challenging class, gender, race, geographic, and religious norms in the United States (p. 83).

Cassettes
This new format appears in the 1960s; making music portable, it gains popularity (p. 78).

CDs
The first format to incorporate digital technology hits the market in 1983 (p. 78).

MP3
A new format compressing music into digital files shakes up the music industry in 2000, as millions of Internet users share music files on Napster (p. 78).

1930   1940   1950   1960   1970   1980   1990   2000   2010

Radio Turns to Music Industry
As television threatens radio, radio turns to the music industry in the 1950s for salvation. Radio becomes a marketing arm for the sound recording industry (p. 80).

Hip-Hop
A major musical art form emerges in the late 1970s (p. 100).

DVDs
A new digital format makes its retail debut in 1997, offering 12 to 26 times the storage space of a CD (p. 78).

File-Sharing
By 2001, a host of new peer-to-peer Internet services make music file-sharing more popular than ever (p. 106).

Online Music Stores
In February 2006, Apple Computer's iTunes music store sells its billionth song on the Internet (p. 106).

From Audiotape to CDs and DVDs: Analog Goes Digital

Berliner's flat disk would be the key recording advancement until the advent of **audiotape** in the 1940s, when German engineers developed the technology for making plastic magnetic tape (which U.S. soldiers then confiscated at the end of the war). Audiotape's lightweight magnetized strands of plastic finally made possible sound editing and multiple-track mixing, in which instrumentals or vocals could be recorded at one location and later mixed onto a master recording in another studio.

The first machines developed to play magnetized audiotape were bulky reel-to-reel devices. But by the mid-1960s, engineers had placed reel-to-reel audiotapes inside small plastic cassettes. Audiotape also permitted "home dubbing": Consumers could copy their favorite records onto tape or record songs from the radio. This practice denied sales to the recording industry; during the period from the mid to late 1970s, record sales dropped by 20 percent. Meanwhile, blank audiotape sales doubled. Some thought audiotape would mean the demise of record albums because of its superior sound and editing capability, but commercial sales of albums did not plummet until the compact disc came along in the 1980s.

In 1958, engineers developed stereophonic sound, or **stereo**, which eventually made monophonic (one-track) records obsolete. Stereo permitted the recording of two separate channels, or tracks, of sound. Recording-studio engineers, using audiotape, could now record many instrumental or vocal tracks, which they "mixed down" to the two stereo tracks. Playing the channels back through two loudspeakers creates a more natural sound distribution that fills a room.

The biggest recording advancement came in the 1970s, when electrical engineer Thomas Stockham developed **digital recording**, in which music is played back by laser beam rather than by needle or magnetic tape. Digital recorders translate sound waves into computer-like on/off impulses and store the impulses on disks in binary code. When these are played back, the laser decodes, or "reads," the stored impulses; a microprocessor translates these numerical codes into sound and sends them through the loudspeakers. This technique began replacing Edison's **analog recording** technique, which merely captured the fluctuations of the original sound waves and stored those signals on records or cassettes as a continuous stream of magnetization—analogous to the actual sound. Incorporating purer, more precise digital techniques (which do not add noise during recording and editing sessions), **compact discs**, or **CDs**, hit the market in 1983.

By 1987, CD sales had doubled LP record album sales (see Figure 3.1). Although audiocassette sales outnumbered CD sales by two to one as recently as 1988, by 2000 CDs outsold cassettes by more than ten to one and more than three hundred to one in 2005. In an effort to create new consumer product lines, the music industry promoted two advanced formats in the late 1990s that it hoped would eventually replace standard compact discs. Sony's Super Audio CD and the DVD-Audio format both offered greater storage capacity than a regular CD; additional capabilities included better fidelity, multichannel music, and in the case of the **DVD**, graphics, music lyrics, music videos, and artist interviews, as well as the potential for interactivity.

MP3s and the Napster Legacy

The introductions of the Super Audio CD and DVD-Audio were ill-timed for the industry, because the biggest development in music formats in the late 1990s was one popularized by music enthusiasts—the **MP3**. The MP3 file format, developed in 1992 as part of a video compression standard, enables music to be compressed into smaller, more manageable files. With the increasing popularity of the Internet in the

● After the iPod and iTunes popularized the portability of MP3s, cell phones were soon to follow with multifunction phones that could store and play these music files.

Figure 3.1
Annual Record, Tape, CD, DVD, and Digital Sales

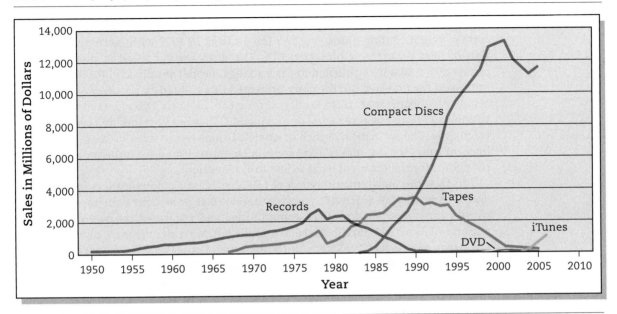

Source: Recording Industry Association of America, 2005 Year-end Statistics.

mid-1990s, computer users began adapting the MP3 format to swap music online, because a song encoded in the MP3 format could be uploaded or downloaded on the Internet in a fraction of the time it took to send or receive noncompressed music.

By the end of 1999, the year the Internet's now infamous Napster free file-sharing service brought the MP3 format to popular attention, music files were widely available on the Internet—some for sale, some of them legally available for free downloading, and many traded in violation of copyright rules—and music fans typically downloaded MP3 files and "burned" the songs to CDs, even when industry-manufactured CDs and DVDs had higher quality. Some music fans skipped CDs altogether, keeping their music on computer hard drives and essentially using their computer as a stereo system. The music industry fought the proliferation of the MP3 format with an array of lawsuits, but the format's popularity continued to increase, as other Internet file-sharing systems such as KaZaA, Morpheus, Limewire, and Grokster have succeeded Napster (see "Tracking Technology: The Rise of MP3s and Digital Downloading" on page 81).

In 2001 the U.S. Supreme Court ruled in favor of the music industry and against Napster, declaring free music file-swapping illegal and in violation of music copyrights held by recording labels and artists. Napster (which has since relaunched as a legal service) had required users to log into a centralized system. But new software since that ruling provides decentralized—or peer-to-peer (P2P)—systems that also enable free music file-sharing. By conservative estimates, even with the success of Apple's iTunes, ninety out of one hundred music downloads on the Internet are still free and probably in violation of copyright law. And in 2005, P2P service Grokster was fined $50 million by U.S. federal courts and, in upholding the lower court rulings, the Supreme Court reaffirmed that big entertainment companies could pursue legal action against any P2P service that encouraged its users to illegally download music, videotapes, and music on the Internet.

> **❝** Our best guess, is that for every legal song download there are 75 illegal downloads.**❞**
>
> —Gene Munster, music industry analyst, 2006

Despite the legal complexities, new styles of MP3 players spread the format to home-stereo component systems, cars, portable devices, and even cell phones, making computer audio files an increasingly viable music format, and leading the music industry to begrudgingly realize that it needed to somehow adapt its business to the format. The recording industry again fought back in 2002 with increasing distribution of releases on copy-protected CDs. The discs are supposed to prevent digital copies of the CDs being burned to CD for illegal resale, or uploaded for illegal distribution on the Internet. But the copy-protected CDs created controversy because they also prevent consumers from legally copying CDs for their own personal use (similar to copying LPs to cassette tapes) or making MP3 files out of tracks for their own digital players. The successful launch of Apple's iTunes music store in 2003, with downloads of songs for just ninety-nine cents each, transformed the industry and became the model for the future of legal online music distribution.

In fact, the independent action of millions of music downloaders is also influencing radio airplay. Since 2002, Internet service BigChampagne.com has tracked the world's most popular download communities and published the week's ten most popular file-shared songs (both legal and illegal). Most significantly, BigChampagne has begun selling its "Top Swaps" information and other download data to the radio industry, which has, in turn, adjusted radio playlists to incorporate what is popular on the Internet. Ironically, the download-influenced radio playlists spur legitimate music sales, and recording companies have begun to use BigChampagne's data to hone their marketing campaigns.

Records and Radio: First Hate, Then Love, Then Component Marriages

By 1915, the phonograph had become a popular form of entertainment. The recording industry sold thirty million records that year, and by the end of the decade sales more than tripled each year. By 1924, though, record sales were only half of what they had been the previous year. Radio had arrived as a competing mass medium.

To the alarm of the sound recording industry, radio stations had begun broadcasting recorded music, but without any compensation to the music industry. The American Society of Composers, Authors, and Publishers (ASCAP), founded in 1914 to collect copyright fees for publishers and writers, charged that radio was contributing to plummeting sales of records and sheet music. So, by 1925, music rights fees were established, charging stations between $250 and $2,500 a week, and causing many stations to leave the air. But other stations started their own live, in-house orchestras, disseminating "free" music to listeners and giving radio an edge over the recording industry.

Throughout the late 1920s and the onset of the Depression, record and phonograph sales continued to fall. The industry got a boost when Prohibition ended in 1933 and record-playing jukeboxes became the standard musical entertainment in neighborhood taverns. The music industry's biggest boost came in the 1950s. Television had arrived, pilfering radio's variety shows, crime dramas, and comedy programs, as well as its advertising revenue. Radio turned to the record industry for a cheap source of content. This time, when songs were played on the air, record sales rose. Once the threatened medium in the 1930s, the music industry saved radio in the 1950s. The marriage of the two media would eventually enable both to prosper economically at record levels.

Just as radio would later seek improved sound quality (through FM and stereo) to retain an edge over television, the recording industry survived during radio's golden age by continually improving sound reproduction. With RCA's acquisition of the Victrola company in 1929 came the development of radio-phonograph players. Then, in the 1930s, RCA began experimenting with *high-fidelity systems,* which improved

The Rise of MP3s and Digital Downloading

By John Dougan

When 16-year-old Alex Ostrovsky received a call from a representative of the iTunes Music Store informing him that his selection of Coldplay's "Speed of Sound" was the digital music store's one billionth download, he thought it was a joke—it wasn't. In a brief interview with *Rolling Stone,* the elated Ostrovsky articulated a pro-downloading sentiment common among his peers, "CDs are kind of a hassle." While it took iTunes a little more than two years to reach this milestone (the last 500 million tracks were downloaded in just seven months, a pace that shows no sign of slowing), the significance of the event reaffirmed what many music industry observers predicted would happen in the late '90s during the Napster file trading controversy. Namely that the music industry's distribution model, predicated upon consumers going to record stores or big box retailers (e.g., Best Buy, Wal-Mart) for their purchases, would be seriously challenged by online retail sites, as well as legal (and illegal) digital music sources. Frustrated by escalating CD prices and convinced that most releases contained only a few good songs and too much filler, digital music sites offer consumers an a la carte menu where they can cherry-pick their favorite tracks and build a music library that is easily stored on a hard drive and transfer it to an MP3 player. In its short history, iTunes Music Store has gone from intriguing concept to one of the world's ten largest music retailers— meteoric growth indicating that many younger consumers have quite happily adapted to downloading and prefer it to purchasing CDs.

Digital downloading has also made a significant impact on locating and accessing non-mainstream music and recordings by unsigned bands. If iTunes resembles a traditional retailer with a deep catalogue, then a competitor such as eMusic (which primarily focuses on artists on independent labels) is the online equivalent of a specialty record store, designed for connoisseurs, who are uninterested in mass mar-

keted pop "product." The success of MySpace (106 million member profiles and counting), though not a music site *per se,* has become an important, if controversial, gathering place for an active virtual community of fans with dozens of genres and subgenres represented. By capitalizing on the Internet's ability to, "marginalize the traditional bodies of mediation between those who make music and those who listen to it,"[1] MySpace (and other online sources such as podcasts and music-oriented blogs) makes searching for new music and performers much easier, changing not only how consumers are exposed to music, but how record label A&R (Artist & Repertoire) departments scout talent. Unsigned performers now come with a built-in community of fans, and A&R reps, who no longer travel as much to locate talent, are searching for acts who have done their own marketing and development and can deliver an audience.

Almost none of the technological shifts created by digital downloading bode well for traditional retail locations. Over the next decade record stores (already battered and bruised by virtual retailers such as Amazon) will face a battle for survival in a marketplace populated by a generation of consumers who regard compact discs as "a hassle." Now that digital downloading has altered the music industry's long-established methods of production and distribution, it is only reasonable to assume that a similar seismic shift will occur in retailing. For the music industry, a future where entire music collections will be portable, loaded on MP3 players, and always accessible means accepting and embracing the inevitability (and increased speed) of technological change, while remaining mindful of how it affects consumer attitudes, expectations, and, most importantly, buying habits.

John Dougan is an Associate Professor in the Department of the Recording Industry at Middle Tennessee State University.

phonographic sound dramatically. In the 1950s, these "hi-fi" systems were intro-duced to the consumer market. Designed to produce the best fidelity (that is, faith-fulness to the music or voice without noise or distortion), the systems came in two varieties: console and component.

A variation on the Victrola, *console systems* combined several elements—radio tuner, turntable, speakers, and amplifier—all hardwired inside a piece of furniture. Hi-fis looked like dining-room sideboards and, based on the market research of the day, were marketed primarily to women. By the 1950s, when this consumer market was saturated, manufacturers "unpacked" the furniture and introduced *component systems*, which enabled consumers to mix and match different models and parts. These systems also permitted easier replacement of various elements. Once again, based on research that tapped into existing gender stereotypes, component systems featured lots of dials, chrome, and control panels—new marketing ploys aimed at men. Today, companies have created another market by melding the console and component concepts into *entertainment systems*. These systems allow users to stack various components, including a CD and a tape player, a television, a radio, and a DVD player, within a large piece of furniture.

U.S. Popular Music and the Formation of Rock

In general, **pop music** appeals either to a wide cross section of the public or to siz-able subdivisions within the larger public based on age, region, or ethnic background (for example, teenagers, southerners, Mexican Americans). U.S. popular music today encompasses styles as diverse as blues, country, Tejano, salsa, jazz, rock, reggae, punk, hip-hop, and electronica. The word *pop* has also been used to distin-guish popular music from classical music, which is written primarily for ballet, opera, ensemble, or symphony. As various subcultures have intersected, U.S. popular music has devel-oped organically, constantly creating new forms and reinvigo-rating older musical styles.

> **❝ Music should never be harmless. ❞**
>
> –Robbie Robertson,
> The Band

The Rise of Pop Music

Although we sometimes assume that popular music depended on the phonograph and the radio for success, it actually existed prior to the development of these media. In the late nineteenth century, the sale of sheet music for piano and other in-struments spread rapidly in an area of Manhattan along Broadway known as Tin Pan Alley. During the popular ragtime era in the early 1900s, *tin pan* was a derisive term used to describe the way that quickly produced tunes supposedly sounded like cheap pans clanging together. The tradition of song publishing that began in Tin Pan Alley in the late 1800s continued through the 1950s, with such rock-and-roll writing teams as Jerry Lieber–Mike Stoller and Carole King–Gerry Goffin. Major influences during the earlier period included the marches of John Philip Sousa, the ragtime piano pieces of Scott Joplin, and the show tunes and vocal ballads of Irving Berlin, Hoagy Carmichael, George Gershwin, and Cole Porter.

At the turn of the twentieth century, with the newfound ability of song publish-ers to mass-produce sheet music for a growing middle class captivated by a piano craze, popular songs moved from novelty stage to business enterprise. With the emergence of the phonograph, song publishers also discovered that recorded tunes boosted interest in and sales of sheet music. Although the popularity of sheet music would decline rapidly with the development of the radio in the 1920s, songwriting along Tin Pan Alley played a key role in transforming popular music into a mass medium.

As sheet music grew in popularity, **jazz** developed in New Orleans. An improvisational and mostly instrumental musical form, jazz absorbed and integrated a diverse body of musical styles, including African rhythms, blues, and gospel. Jazz influenced many bandleaders throughout the 1930s and 1940s. Groups led by Louis Armstrong, Count Basie, Tommy Dorsey, Duke Ellington, Benny Goodman, and Glenn Miller were among the most popular of the jazz, or "swing," bands, whose music also dominated radio and recording in their day.

The first vocal stars of popular music in the twentieth century were products of the vaudeville circuit (which radio, movies, and the Depression would bring to an end in the 1930s). In 1929, Rudy Vallee wrapped himself in a raccoon coat and sang popular songs into a megaphone. In the 1930s, the bluesy harmonies of a New Orleans vocal trio, the Boswell Sisters, influenced the Andrews Sisters, whose boogie-woogie style helped them sell more than sixty million records in the late 1930s and 1940s. Also in the 1930s, Bing Crosby pioneered a relaxed, intimate style called *crooning*; he popularized Irving Berlin's "White Christmas," one of the most *covered* songs in recording history. (A song recorded or performed by another artist is known as **cover music**.) In one of the first mutually beneficial alliances between sound recording and radio, many early pop vocalists had network or regional radio programs, which vastly increased their exposure. Ironically, their record sales, promoted on radio, boosted sound recording at a time when the record industry was threatened by the growing popularity of radio.

Frank Sinatra arrived in the 1940s. His romantic ballads foreshadowed the teen love songs of rock and roll's early years. Nicknamed "The Voice" early in his career, Sinatra, like Crosby, parlayed his music and radio exposure into movie stardom. (Both singers made more than fifty films apiece.) Helped by radio, Vallee, the Andrews Sisters, Crosby, and Sinatra were among the first vocalists to become popular with a large national teen audience. Their record sales helped stabilize the industry, and in the early 1940s, Sinatra's concerts alone caused the kind of audience riots that would later characterize rock-and-roll performances.

● Louis Armstrong (1901–1971) transformed jazz with astonishing improvised trumpet solos and scat singing.

> ❝ Frank Sinatra was categorized in 1943 as 'the glorification of ignorance and musical illiteracy.' ❞
>
> –Dick Clark,
> *The First 25 Years
> of Rock & Roll*

Rock and Roll Is Here to Stay

The cultural storm called **rock and roll** hit in the 1950s. (Like the early meaning of *jazz*, *rock and roll* was a blues slang term that sometimes meant "sex.") It combined the vocal and instrumental traditions of popular music with the rhythm-and-blues sounds of Memphis and the country beat of Nashville. Early rock and roll was therefore considered the first "integrationist music," merging the black sounds of rhythm and blues, gospel, and Robert Johnson's screeching blues guitar with the white influences of country, folk, and pop vocals.[2] Only a few musical forms have ever sprung from such a diverse set of influences, and no new style of music has ever had such a widespread impact on so many different cultures. From an economic perspective, no single musical form prior to rock and roll had ever simultaneously transformed the structure of two mass media industries: sound recording and radio.

Blues and R&B: The Foundation of Rock and Roll

Many social, cultural, economic, and political factors contributed to the growth of rock and roll around the 1940s and 1950s. The migration of southern blacks to northern cities in search of better jobs during the first half of the twentieth century had

● Duke Ellington (1899–1974), writer of more than fifteen hundred compositions, from pop songs (including the catchy "It Don't Mean a Thing [If It Ain't Got That Swing]") to symphonies and ballets. Most of his work, though, was composed for his sixteen-member dance band, which over fifty years featured many of the greatest talents of jazz.

helped spread different popular music styles. In particular, **blues** music came to the North, influenced by African American spirituals, ballads, and work songs from the rural South, and exemplified in the music of Robert Johnson, Son House, and Charley Patton. Starting in the late 1930s, the electric guitar—a major contribution to rock music—made it easier for musicians "to cut through the noise in ghetto taverns" and gave southern blues its urban style, popularized in the work of Muddy Waters, Howlin' Wolf, B.B. King, and Buddy Guy.

During this time, **rhythm and blues**, or **R&B**, developed in various cities. Featuring "huge rhythm units smashing away behind screaming blues singers," R&B merged urban blues and big-band sounds.[3] As with hip-hop today, young listeners were fascinated by the explicit (and forbidden) sexual lyrics in songs like "Annie Had a Baby," "Sexy Ways," and "Wild Wild Young Men." Although it was banned on some stations, by 1953 R&B aired on 25 percent of all radio stations for at least a few hours each week. In those days, black and white musical forms were segregated: Trade magazines tracked R&B record sales on "race" charts, which were kept separate from white record sales tracked on "pop" charts.

Youth Culture Cements Rock's Place

Another reason for the growth of rock and roll can be found in the repressive and uneasy atmosphere of the 1950s. With the constant concern over the atomic bomb, the Cold War, and communist witch-hunts, young people were seeking forms of escape from the menacing world created by adults. Teens have traditionally sought out music that has a beat—music they can dance to. In Europe in the late 1700s they popularized the waltz, and in America during the 1890s they took up a dance called the cakewalk. The trend continued during the 1920s with the Charleston, in the 1930s and 1940s with the jazz swing bands and the jitterbug, in the 1970s with disco, and in the 1980s and 1990s with hip-hop. Each of these twentieth-century musical forms began as dance and party music before its growing popularity eventually energized both record sales and radio formats.

Rock and Race

Perhaps most significant to the growth of rock and roll, the border that had separated white and black cultures began to break down. Radio, which saw its network programs converting to television, was seeking inexpensive forms of content. Radio deejays, particularly Alan Freed in Cleveland (and later on WINS in New York), began exposing more white people to black music. Some white teens cruising the radio dial had already discovered black-oriented stations, however, and had adopted the different rhythms as dance music. This process got another boost during the Korean War in the early 1950s when President Truman signed an executive order integrating the armed forces. Young men drafted into the service were thrown together with others from very different ethnic and economic backgrounds. The biggest legal change, though, came with the *Brown v. Board of Education* decision in 1954. With this ruling the Supreme Court ruled unconstitutional "separate but equal" laws, which had kept white and black schools, hotels, restaurants, rest rooms, and drinking fountains segregated for decades. Thus mainstream America began to wrestle seriously with the legacy of slavery and the unequal treatment of African American citizens. A cultural reflection of the times, rock and roll would burst from the midst of these social and political tensions.

● Among the most influential and innovative American guitarists, Robert Johnson (1911–1938) played the Mississippi delta blues and was a major influence on early rock and rollers, especially the Rolling Stones and Eric Clapton. His intense slide-guitar and finger-style playing also inspired generations of blues artists, including Muddy Waters, Howlin' Wolf, Bonnie Raitt, and Stevie Ray Vaughan. To get a sense of his style, visit The Robert Johnson Notebooks, http://xroads.virginia .edu/~MUSIC/rjhome.html.

Rock Muddies the Waters

In the 1950s, legal integration accompanied a cultural shift, and the industry's race and pop charts blurred. White deejay Alan Freed had been playing black music for his young audiences since the early 1950s, and such white performers as Johnnie Ray and Bill Haley had crossed over to the race charts to score R&B hits. Black artists like Chuck Berry were performing country songs, and for a time Ray Charles even played in an otherwise all-white country band. Revitalizing record sales and changing the sound of radio, rock and roll exploded old distinctions and tested traditional boundaries in five critical ways.

High and Low Culture

In 1956, Chuck Berry's song "Roll Over Beethoven" introduced rock and roll to high culture: "You know my temperature's risin' / the jukebox is blowin' a fuse . . . Roll over Beethoven / and tell Tchaikovsky the news." Although such early rock-and-roll lyrics seem tame by today's standards, at the time these lyrics were written, rock and rollers were challenging music decorum and the rules governing how musicians should behave (or misbehave): Berry's "duck walk" across the stage; Elvis Presley's pegged pants and gyrating hips, influenced by blues performers he admired; and Bo Diddley's use of the guitar as a phallic symbol, another old blues tradition. An affront to well-behaved audiences of classical music, such acts and antics would be imitated endlessly throughout rock's history. In fact, rock and roll's live exhibitions and the legends about them became key ingredients in promoting record sales.

Masculine and Feminine

Rock and roll was also the first popular music that overtly confused issues of sexuality. Al-

● A major influence on early rock and roll, Chuck Berry, born in 1926, scored major hits between 1955 and 1958, writing "Maybellene," "Roll Over Beethoven," "School Day," "Sweet Little Sixteen," and "Johnny B. Goode." At the time, he was criticized by some black artists for sounding white and by conservative critics for his popularity among white teenagers. Today, young guitar players routinely imitate his style.

❝Listening to my idol Nat [King] Cole prompted me to sing sentimental songs with distinct diction. The songs of Muddy Waters impelled me to deliver the down-home blues in the language they came from, Negro dialect. When I played hillbilly songs, I stressed my diction so that it was harder and whiter. All in all it was my intention to hold both the black and white clientele.**❞**

–Chuck Berry,
The Autobiography, 1987

though early rock largely attracted males as performers, the most fascinating feature of Elvis Presley, according to the Rolling Stones' Mick Jagger, was his androgynous appearance.[4] During this early period, though, the most sexually outrageous rock-and-roll performer was Little Richard (Penniman), who influenced a generation of extravagant rock stars.

Wearing a pompadour hairdo and assaulting his Steinway piano, Little Richard was considered rock's first drag queen, blurring the boundary between masculinity and femininity (although his act had been influenced by a flamboyant 6½-foot-tall gay piano player named Esquerita who hosted drag-queen shows in New Orleans in the 1940s).[5] Little Richard has said that given the reality of American racism, he feared the consequences of becoming a sex symbol for white girls: "I decided that my image should be crazy and way out so that adults would think I was harmless. I'd appear in one show dressed as the Queen of England and in the next as the pope."[6] By the end of the 1950s, although white parents may not have been overly concerned about their daughters falling for Little Richard, most adults did not view rock and roll as harmless.

Black and White

Rock and roll also blurred geographic borders between country and city, and between black urban rhythms from Memphis and white country & western music from Nashville. Early white rockers such as Buddy Holly and Carl Perkins combined country or hillbilly music, southern gospel, and Mississippi delta blues to create a sound called **rockabilly**. Raised on bluegrass music and radio's Grand Old Opry, Perkins (a sharecropper's son from Tennessee) mixed these influences with music he heard from black cotton-field workers and blues singers like Muddy Waters and John Lee Hooker, both of whom used electric guitars in their performances. In 1956, Perkins recorded "Blue Suede Shoes"; a Presley cover version made the song famous.

Conversely, rhythm and blues spilled into rock and roll. The urban R&B influences on early rock came from Fats Domino ("Blueberry Hill"), Willie Mae "Big Mama" Thornton ("Hound Dog"), and Big Joe Turner ("Shake, Rattle, and Roll"). Many of these songs, first popular on R&B labels, crossed over to the pop charts during the mid to late 1950s (although many were performed by more widely known white artists). Chuck Berry, who originally played country music to supplement his day jobs as a beautician and carpenter, tore down these boundaries. His first hit was "Maybellene," modeled on an old country song called "Ida Red." To earn royalties, since the country version was too old for copyright, Chess Records asked Berry to make some changes, and he renamed the song after a popular cosmetic product. Chess gave the record to Alan Freed, who attached his name to the credits in exchange for radio play. "Maybellene" became a No. 1 R&B hit in July 1955 and crossed over to the pop charts the next month, where it climbed to No. 5.

● Richard Wayne Penniman (Little Richard) was inducted into the Rock and Roll Hall of Fame in 1986. Little Richard played a key role in getting black music played on white radio stations and sold in mainstream record stores. His flamboyant, gender-tweaking style has been a major influence on many performers—notably Elton John and David Bowie in the 1970s, Culture Club and Prince in the 1980s, and Marilyn Manson and OutKast in the 1990s and 2000s.

● Although his unofficial title, "King of Rock and Roll," has been challenged by Little Richard and Chuck Berry, Elvis Presley remains the most popular solo artist of all time. From 1956 to 1962, he recorded seventeen No. 1 hits, from "Heartbreak Hotel" to "Good Luck Charm." According to Little Richard, Presley's main legacy was that he opened doors for many young performers and made black music popular in mainstream America.

Although rock lyrics in the 1950s may not have been especially provocative or overtly political, soaring record sales and the crossover appeal of the music itself represented an enormous threat to long-standing racial and class boundaries. In 1956, the secretary of the North Alabama White Citizens Council bluntly spelled out the racism and white fear concerning the new prominence of African American culture: "Rock and roll is a means of pulling the white man down to the level of the Negro. It is part of a plot to undermine the morals of the youth of our nation."[7]

North and South

Not only did rock and roll muddy the urban and rural terrain, but in doing so it combined northern and southern influences as well. In fact, with so much blues, R&B, and rock and roll rising from the South, this region regained some of the cultural standing that it had lost after the Civil War. With many northern middle-class teens influenced by southern "lower-class" music, rock and roll challenged stereotypes regarding class as well as race. Like the many white male teens today who are fascinated by hip-hop (buying the majority of hip-hop CDs on the commercial market), Carl Perkins, Elvis Presley, and Buddy Holly—all from the rural South—were fascinated with and influenced by the black urban styles they had heard on the radio or seen in nightclubs.

But the key to record sales and the spread of rock and roll, according to famed record producer Sam Phillips of Sun Records, was to find a white man who sounded black. Phillips found that man in Elvis Presley. Commenting on Presley's cultural importance, one critic wrote: "White rockabillies like Elvis took poor white southern mannerisms of speech and behavior deeper into mainstream culture than they had ever been taken, at the same time he was being reviled for seducing white youth with black music."[8]

❝ [Elvis Presley's] kind of music is deplorable, a rancid smelling aphrodisiac. ❞

–Frank Sinatra, 1956

The Sacred and the Secular

Just as the new music confronted racial, sexual, regional, and class taboos, for many mainstream adults it also constituted an offense against God. In fact, many early rock figures had close ties to religion. As a boy, Elvis Presley had dreamed of joining the Blackwoods, one of country-gospel's most influential groups. As a teen, Jerry Lee Lewis was thrown out of a Bible institute in Texas. Also influenced by church gospel music, Ray Charles changed the lyrics of an old gospel tune: "I've got a Savior / way over Jordan / he's saved my soul, oh yeah!" became "I got a woman / way over town / she's good to me." A top R&B hit in 1955, "I Got a Woman" became one of Charles's signature songs. The recording drew criticism from many African American church leaders and members, who worried about the impact of such worldly music on black youths.

Many people in the 1950s thought that rock and roll violated the boundary between the sacred and the secular. In the late 1950s, public outrage was so great that even Little Richard and Jerry Lee Lewis, both sons of southern preachers, became convinced that they were playing the "devil's music." By 1959, Little Richard had left rock and roll to become a minister. Lewis, too, feared that rock was no way to salvation. He had to be coerced into recording "Great Balls of Fire," a song by Otis Blackwell that turned an apocalyptic biblical phrase into a highly charged sexual teen love song. The tune, banned by many radio stations, nevertheless climbed to No. 2 on the pop charts late in 1957.

> **❝** There have been many accolades uttered about his talent and performances through the years, all of which I agree with wholeheartedly.**❞**
>
> –Frank Sinatra, 1977

Battles in Rock and Roll

With the blurring of racial lines, performers and producers played a tricky game as they tried to get R&B music accepted in the 1950s. Two prominent white disc jockeys used different methods. Alan Freed, credited with popularizing the term *rock and roll*, played original R&B songs from the race charts and the black versions of early rock and roll. In contrast, Philadelphia deejay Dick Clark believed that making black music acceptable to white audiences required cover versions by white artists.

Some music historians point to Jackie Brenston's "Rocket 88" and other R&B songs from the early 1950s as examples of the first rock and roll. But Bill Haley and the Comets, a former country group, scored the first No. 1 rock-and-roll hit on the Billboard pop chart in May 1955 with "Rock Around the Clock." The record had been an R&B hit in 1954, but it gained popularity and notoriety in the 1955 teen rebellion movie *Blackboard Jungle*. For many parents, the song became a symbol of juvenile delinquency and raised concerns about negative influences in the changing recording industry.

Cover Music Undermines Black Artists

Since the integration of popular music in the 1960s, black and white artists have recorded and performed each other's original tunes. For example, Otis Redding, an established R&B songwriter, covered the Rolling Stones' "Satisfaction" in 1966. Both the Rolling Stones and Eric Clapton covered Robert Johnson's 1930s blues songs, and Clapton had a No. 1 hit in 1974 with Bob Marley's reggae tune "I Shot the Sheriff." In 2005, humorist Jonathan Coulton recorded a soft-rock version of Sir Mix-a-Lot's 1992 hit "Baby Got Back."

Although today we take such rerecordings for granted, in the 1950s cover music was racially coded. Almost all popular covers were attempts by white producers and

● Pat Boone, the squeaky-clean recording artist who topped the charts with many songs that covered black artists' recordings.

● Ray Charles (1930–2004) merged the sounds of rhythm & blues, gospel, country, jazz, and pop.

artists to capitalize on popular songs from the R&B charts and transform them into hits on the pop charts. Occasionally, white producers would list white performers like Elvis Presley, who never wrote songs himself, as co-writers for the tunes they covered. More often, dishonest producers would buy the rights to potential hits from naive songwriters, who seldom saw a penny in royalties or received credit as the writers.

During this period, black R&B artists, working for small record labels, saw many of their popular songs covered by white artists working for major labels. These cover records, boosted by better marketing and ties to white deejays, usually outsold the original black versions. Covers also slowed sales of the original releases and hampered smaller labels. For instance, the 1954 R&B song "Sh-Boom," by the Chords on Atlantic's Cat label, was immediately covered by a white group, the Crew Cuts, for the major Mercury label. Record sales declined for the Chords, although jukebox and R&B radio play remained strong for their original version. As rock critic Ed Ward suggested: "With 'Sh-Boom,' the pop establishment had found itself a potent weapon to use against R&B records—whiten them up and use the corporate might of a major label to get them to places a hapless [small label] caught with a hit on its hands could never reach."[9]

By 1955, R&B hits regularly crossed over to the pop charts, but inevitably the cover music versions were more successful. Pat Boone's cover of Fats Domino's "Ain't That a Shame" went to No. 1 and stayed on the Top 40's pop chart for twenty weeks, whereas Domino's original made it only to No. 10. During this time, Pat Boone ranked as the king of cover music, with thirty-eight Top 40 songs between 1955 and 1962. His records were second in sales only to Presley's. Slowly, however, the cover situation changed. After watching Boone outsell his song "Tutti-Frutti" in 1956, Little Richard wrote "Long Tall Sally," which included lyrics written and delivered in such a way that he believed Boone would not be able to adequately replicate them. "Long Tall Sally" went to No. 6 for Little Richard and charted for twelve weeks; Boone's version got to No. 8 and stayed there for nine weeks.

Overt racism lingered in the music business well into the 1960s. When the Marvelettes scored a No. 1 hit with "Please Mr. Postman" in 1961, their Tamla/Motown label had to substitute a cartoon album cover because many record-store owners feared customers would not buy a recording that pictured four black women. A turning point, however, came in 1962, the last year that Pat Boone, then age twenty-eight, ever had a Top 40 rock-and-roll hit. That year Ray Charles covered "I Can't Stop Loving You," a 1958 country song by the Grand Old Opry's Don Gibson. This marked the first time that a black artist, covering a white artist's song, had notched a No. 1 pop hit. With Charles's cover, the rock-and-roll merger between gospel and R&B, on one hand, and white country and pop, on the other, was complete. In fact, the relative acceptance of black crossover music provided a more favorable cultural context for the political activism that spurred important Civil Rights legislation in the mid-1960s.

Payola Creates the Hits

Besides the overt racism evident in the business of rock and roll, in the 1950s, the recording and radio industries generated the **payola** scandals. In the music industry, payola is the practice of record promoters paying deejays or radio programmers to play particular songs. (The term originated as slang, combining the bribery term *pay-off* with the generic ending of *Victrola*.) As recorded rock and roll became central to commercial radio in the 1950s, independent promoters hired by record labels used payola to pressure deejays to play songs by the artists whom they represented. In the 1950s, as today, fewer than 10 percent of new releases became hits or sold more than the fifty thousand copies needed for a major label to make money on them. With the industry releasing a hundred new singles per week by the end of the 1950s, the demand for airplay—essential to establishing hit-record sales—was enormous. Although payola was considered unethical and a form of bribery, no laws prohibited its practice.

Following closely on the heels of television's quiz-show scandals, congressional hearings on radio payola began in December 1959. After a November announcement of the upcoming hearings, stations across the country fired deejays, and many others resigned. The hearings were partly a response to generally fraudulent business practices and partly an opportunity to blame deejays and radio for rock and roll's negative impact on teens.

In 1959, shortly before the hearings, a Chicago deejay decided to clear the air. He broadcast secretly taped discussions in which a representative of a small independent record label acknowledged that it had paid $22,000 to ensure that a record would get airplay. The deejay, Phil Lind of WAIT, got calls threatening his life and had to have police protection. At the hearings in 1960, Alan Freed admitted to participating in payola, although he said he did not believe there was anything illegal about such deals. His career soon ended. Dick Clark, then an influential twenty-nine-year-old deejay and the host of TV's *American Bandstand,* would not admit to practicing payola. But the hearings committee chastised Clark and alleged that some of his complicated business deals were ethically questionable. Congress eventually added a law concerning payola to the Federal Communications Act, prescribing a $10,000 fine and/or a year in jail for each violation. But given both the interdependence between radio and recording and the high stakes involved in creating a hit, the practice of payola persists. In 2005, for example, Sony BMG and Warner Music paid millions to settle payola cases brought by New York State. (See Chapter 4.)

Taming Rock and Roll's Rebels

By late 1959, many key figures in rock and roll had been tamed, partly by mounting social pressure against the music so often accused of undermining the morals of U.S. youths. Jerry Lee Lewis was exiled from the industry, labeled southern "white trash" for marrying his thirteen-year-old third cousin; Elvis Presley was drafted into the army; Chuck Berry was run out of Mississippi and eventually jailed for gun possession and transporting a minor (with a prostitution record) across state lines; and Little Richard left rock and roll to sing gospel music. Then, in February 1959, in a plane crash in Iowa, Buddy Holly ("Peggy Sue"), Richie Valens ("La Bamba"), and the Big Bopper ("Chantilly Lace") all died—a tragedy mourned in Don McLean's 1971 hit "American Pie" as "the day the music died."

Although rock and roll did not die in the late 1950s, the U.S. recording industry decided that it needed a makeover. To protect the enormous profits the new music had been generating, record companies began to discipline some of rock's rebellious impulses. In the early 1960s, the industry tried to clone Pat Boone by featuring a new generation of clean-cut white singers, including Frankie Avalon, who made beach-movie musicals, and Ricky Nelson, from TV's popular series *Adventures of Ozzie & Harriet.* Rock and roll's explosive violations of class and racial

> **"** The idea of payola being back, that's like saying that the gravity is especially strong this year or something.**"**
>
> —Cliff Doerksen, music historian, 2004

> **"** This is not a pretty picture; what we see is that payola is pervasive. . . . It is omnipresent. It is driving the industry and it is wrong.**"**
>
> —Eliot Spitzer, New York's attorney general on his investigation into payola in 2005

boundaries were transformed into simpler generation gap problems. By the early 1960s, the music had developed a milder reputation for merely fostering disagreements among parents and teens.

A Changing Industry: Reformations in Popular Music

As the 1960s began, rock and roll may have been tamer and "safer," as reflected in the surf and road music of the Beach Boys and Jan & Dean, but it was beginning to branch out in several directions. For instance, the success of producer Phil Spector's so-called all-girl groups, such as the Crystals ("He's a Rebel") and the Ronettes ("Be My Baby"), and other groups, such as the Shangri-Las ("Leader of the Pack"), challenged the male-dominated world of early rock. In addition, rock music and other popular styles went through cultural reformations that significantly changed the industry. We will consider them in this section, including the internationalization of sound recording during the "British invasion," the development of soul and Motown, the political impact of folk-rock, the rejection of music's mainstream by punk, grunge, and other alternative rock performers, and the reassertion of black urban style in hip-hop.

The British Are Coming!

Rock recordings today remain among America's largest economic exports, bringing in billions of dollars a year from abroad. In cultural terms, the global trade of rock and roll is even more evident in exchanges of rhythms, beats, vocal styles, and musical instruments to and from the United States, Latin America, Europe, Africa, and Asia. The origin of rock's global impact can be traced to England in the late 1950s, when the young Rolling Stones listened to the urban blues of Robert Johnson and Muddy Waters, and the young Beatles tried to imitate Chuck Berry and Little Richard.

Until 1964, rock-and-roll recordings had traveled on a one-way ticket to Europe. Even though American artists regularly reached the top of the charts overseas, no British performers had yet appeared on any Top 10 pop lists in the States. This changed almost overnight. In 1964, the Beatles invaded with their mop haircuts and pop reinterpretations of American blues and rock and roll. By the end of the year, more than thirty British hits had landed on American Top 10 lists.

Ed Sullivan, who booked the Beatles several times on his TV variety show in 1964, helped promote their early success. Sullivan, though, reacted differently to the Rolling Stones, who had initially been rejected by British television because lead singer Mick Jagger sounded "too black." Before the Stones performed on Sullivan's program in 1964, he made them change a lyric from "let's spend the night together" to "let's spend some time together"; then he issued an apology to viewers following the Stones' performance. The Stones were not invited back. Performing black-influenced music and struggling for acceptance, the band was cast as the "bad boys" of rock in contrast to the "good" Beatles. Despite Sullivan's lack of support, the Stones would go on to inspire harder versions of rock music in the 1970s — what one conservative critic called "a relentless percussive assault on the human ear."[10]

With the British invasion, rock and roll unofficially became *rock*, sending popular music and the industry in two directions. On the one hand, the Stones, influenced by both blues and 1950s rock and roll, emphasized hard rhythms and vocals in their performances. Their music would influence a generation of hard-rock and heavy-metal performers, two of the many subgenres of rock that developed in the 1970s. The Beatles, on the other hand, influenced by Frank Sinatra as well as by rock and

roll, more often stressed melody. Their music inspired rock's softer digressions. With the Beatles arriving shortly after the assassination of John F. Kennedy, America welcomed their more melodic and innocent recordings.

In the end, the British invasion verified what Chuck Berry and Little Richard had already demonstrated—that rock-and-roll performers could write and produce popular songs as well as Tin Pan Alley had. The success of British groups helped change an industry arrangement in which most pop music was produced by songwriting teams hired by major labels and matched with selected performers. Even more important, however, the British invasion showed the recording industry how older American musical forms, especially blues and R&B, could be repackaged as rock and exported around the world.

● The Beatles led the British invasion of America's pop charts in 1964 and made several appearances on the *Ed Sullivan Show*. They championed innovations that are still found in music today, such as thematic albums, multi-track recording, and looping (a forerunner to sampling).

Motor City Music: Detroit Gives America Soul

Ironically, the British invasion, which drew much of its inspiration from black influences, siphoned off many white listeners from a new generation of black performers. Gradually, however, throughout the 1960s, black singers like James Brown, Sam Cooke, Aretha Franklin, Ben E. King, and Wilson Pickett found large and diverse audiences. Transforming the rhythms and melodies of older R&B, pop vocals, and early

● Following on the heels of the Beatles came the Rolling Stones, whose name was inspired by a Muddy Waters song. The blatant sexuality of strutting lead vocalist Mick Jagger helped ensure the "bad boy" reputation of the group, which charted its first No. 1 hit in the summer of 1965 with "(I Can't Get No) Satisfaction." The band was still together and touring 40 years later in 2006.

rock and roll into what became labeled as **soul**, they countered the British invaders with powerful vocal performances. It is hard to define soul music, which mixes gospel, blues, and urban and southern black styles with slower, more emotional and melancholic lyrics. Soul contrasted sharply with the emphasis on loud, fast instrumentals that had become so important to rock music.[11]

The main independent label that nourished soul and black popular music was Motown, started by former Detroit autoworker and songwriter Berry Gordy with a $700 investment in 1960. "Motown" is a nickname for Detroit—the Motor City—the capital of auto production in the United States. Beginning with Smokey Robinson and the Miracles, whose "Shop Around" hit No. 2 late in 1960, Motown groups rivaled the pop success of British bands throughout the decade. Robinson, who later became a vice president of Motown, also wrote "My Girl" for the Temptations and "My Guy" for Mary Wells—both No. 1 hits in the mid-1960s. In the 1960s and 1970s, Motown produced the Four Tops, Martha and the Vandellas, and the Jackson 5. But the label's most successful group was the Supremes, featuring Diana Ross. Between 1964 and 1969, this group scored twelve No. 1 singles. These Motown groups had a more stylized, softer sound than the grittier southern soul (or funk) of Brown and Pickett. Mo-

❝ Hard rock was rock's blues base electrified and upped in volume . . . heavy metal wanted to be the rock music equivalent of a horror movie—loud, exaggerated, rude, out for thrills only. ❞

—Ken Tucker,
Rock of Ages, 1986

town producers realized at the outset that by cultivating romance and dance over rebellion and politics, black music could attract a young, white audience.

Popular Music Reflects the Times

Popular music has always been part of its time. So, in the social upheavals that the Civil Rights movement, the women's movement, the environmental movement, and the Vietnam War all brought to the 1960s and early 1970s, music did not remain politically quiet. Even Motown acts sounded edgy, with hits like Edwin Starr's "War" (1970) and Marvin Gaye's "What's Goin' On" (1971). But the music genre that most clearly responded to the political happenings was folk music, which had long been the sound of social activism. In the 1960s, folk blended with rock and roll to create a new sound for the era. Later, rock became entwined with the drug counterculture, but by the 1970s it was increasingly part of mainstream consumer culture.

● One of the most successful groups in rock-and-roll history, the Supremes started out as the Primettes in Detroit in 1959. They signed with Motown's Tamla label in 1960 and changed their name in 1961. Between 1964 and 1969 they recorded twelve No. 1 hits, including "Where Did Our Love Go," "Baby Love," "Come See about Me," "Stop! In the Name of Love," " I Hear a Symphony," "You Can't Hurry Love," and "Someday We'll Be Together." Lead singer Diana Ross (*center*) left the group in 1969 for a solo career. The group was inducted into the Rock and Roll Hall of Fame in 1988.

Folk Inspires Protest

In its broadest sense, **folk music** in any culture refers to songs performed by untrained musicians and passed down mainly through oral traditions. Folk encompasses old-time music from the banjo and fiddle tunes of Appalachia to the accordion-led zydeco of Louisiana and the folk-blues of the legendary Leadbelly (Huddie Ledbetter). Given its rough edges and amateur quality, folk is considered a more democratic and participatory musical form. Folk, in fact, inspired many writers and performers of popular music to become more socially aware.

During the 1930s, folk became defined by a white musician named Woody Guthrie ("This Land Is Your Land"). Like many blues singers, Guthrie also brought folk music from the country to the city. He wrote his own songs, promoted social reforms, and played acoustic guitar. Groups such as the Weavers, featuring labor activist and songwriter Pete Seeger, carried on Guthrie's legacy. In 1950, before rock and roll, the Weavers' cover of Leadbelly's "Good Night, Irene" stayed at the top of the pop charts for thirteen weeks. Although the group was regularly blacklisted for political activism, the Weavers' comeback concert at Carnegie Hall in 1955 reenergized folk and inspired a new generation of singer-songwriters, including Joan Baez, Bob Dylan, Simon & Garfunkel, James Taylor, Carly Simon, and Joni Mitchell.

Significantly influenced by the blues, Bob Dylan identified folk as "finger pointin'" music that addressed current social circumstances, such as the growing Civil Rights movement and the Vietnam War. For many folk followers who had grown up on less overtly political rock and roll, acoustic folk music represented both a maturing process and a return to traditional, de-amplified values.

Folk Gets Electrified

When the Byrds electrified folk recordings in the 1960s, they invented **folk-rock**, a sound that went on to influence a long list of performers, from the Grateful Dead to R.E.M. Partly a response to the British invasion, amplified folk-rock earned the Byrds a No. 1 hit in 1965 with a cover of Dylan's folk song "Mr. Tambourine Man." The Byrds had grabbed the attention of Dylan, who had also been influenced by a British group, the Animals, and their 1964 hit "The House of the Rising Sun."

Dylan's career as a folk artist had begun with his performances in New York's Greenwich Village in 1961. His notoriety as a songwriter was spurred by his measured nonchalance and his unique nasal voice. Then, at a key moment in popular music's history, Dylan walked onstage at the 1965 Newport Folk Festival fronting a full, electric rock band. He was booed and cursed by traditional "folkies," who saw amplified music as a sellout to the commercial recording industry. For many critics, however, Dylan's move to rock was aimed at reaching a broader and younger constituency. For Dylan, who would later experiment with country and gospel music before returning to the blues, it was a matter of changing with the times and finding sounds that matched his interests. By 1965, Dylan had his first major hit, "Like a Rolling Stone," a six-minute blues-rock tune boosted by new "progressive rock" radio stations that played longer cuts.

Rock Turns Psychedelic

Alcohol and drugs have long been associated with the private lives of blues, jazz, country, and rock musicians. These links, however, became much more public in the late 1960s and early 1970s, when authorities busted members of the Rolling Stones and the Beatles. With the increasing role of drugs in youth culture and the availability of LSD (not made illegal until the mid-1960s), more and more rock musicians experimented with and sang about drugs in what were frequently labeled rock's psychedelic years. A number of performers believed, as did various writers and artists from other eras, that artistic expression could be enhanced by mind-altering drugs. The music of this period fed on liberal drug laws and a large college-student population, the targeted consumers for much of this music. In the past, musicians had not publicized their drug and alcohol habits. The 1960s drug explorations, however, coincided with the free-speech movement, in which taking drugs was seen by some artists as a form of personal expression and a public challenge to traditional values.

The rock-drug connection was also a cultural response to the perceived failure of traditional institutions to deal with social problems such as racism and political issues such as America's involvement in the Vietnam War. Students and musicians used drugs not only to experiment or get high, or out of boredom or addiction, but to

● Born Robert Allen Zimmerman in Minnesota, Bob Dylan took his stage name from Welsh poet Dylan Thomas. He led a folk music movement in the early 1960s with engaging, socially provocative lyrics. He also was an astute media critic, as is evident in the seminal documentary, *Don't Look Back* (1967).

drop out of conventional society. Some dropped all the way out. During this time, incidents involving drugs or alcohol claimed the lives of several artists, including Janis Joplin, Jimi Hendrix, and the Doors' Jim Morrison.

At the time, the recording industry generally did little to confront the problem of drug dependency and alcoholism among musicians. As long as artists produced hits, record companies either ignored the problem or, in a few cases, made sure that musicians were supplied with drugs to sustain their routines and energy levels. With the rise in cocaine and heroin addiction among musicians in the 1980s and 1990s, the industry faced a new set of challenges. Critics and scholars alike linked the 80 percent rise in drug use among twelve- to seventeen-year-olds between 1992 and 1997 to increased drug use among their rock-group role models.[12] In this case, though, the National Academy of Recording Arts and Sciences, which sponsors the Grammy Awards, brought together hundreds of industry managers and agents to discuss drug issues. Many critics contend, however, that until record companies are willing to terminate contracts and drop their support of artists unwilling to take responsibility for their addictions, problems and tragedies will persist.

Rock Becomes Mainstream

Following the historic Woodstock concert in August 1969, which drew more than 400,000 fans to a New York farm, the deaths of Joplin and Hendrix in 1970, and the announcement late in 1970 that the Beatles had officially disbanded, rock music reached a crossroads. Considered a major part of the rebel counterculture in the 1960s (despite its profits), rock music in the 1970s was increasingly viewed as the centerpiece of mainstream consumer culture. With major music acts earning huge profits, rock soon became another product line for manufacturers and retailers to promote, package, and sell.

Nevertheless, some rock musicians continued the traditions of early rock. In the 1970s, stars like Bruce Springsteen emerged to carry on rock's integrationist legacy, combining the influences of Chuck Berry and Elvis Presley with the folk-rock poetry of Bob Dylan. Britain's Elton John drew upon the outrageous stage performances of Little Richard and the melodic influences of the Beatles. Generally, though, in the 1970s business concerns steered rock and its stars toward a new form of segregation, one that divided popular music along lines of class and race. Both the recording industry and album-oriented rock formats on radio began to aggressively market and program harder rock music and to aim it primarily toward middle-class white male teens.

Another sign that rock and roll had become synonymous with mainstream culture was the continued blurring of the distinction between the sacred and the secular. By the 1970s, rock and roll's earliest foes—religious institutions—had begun to embrace forms of rock as a means of retaining and attracting young churchgoers. In some Catholic churches, rock infiltrated via special church services that featured folk guitar versions of hymns. In many Protestant churches, where gospel music was already a familiar style, contemporary Christian gospel and Christian rock emerged, melding Bible-based lyrics with music that mimicked R&B, Top 40 pop, and even heavy metal. By the mid-1990s, Christian rock boasted a number of acts that featured newly minted contracts with major labels, and by 2000, it was one of the

● Janis Joplin, performing in 1968 at the Newport Folk Festival with her band, Big Brother and the Holding Company. Her brief but brilliant career as a blues-rock singer ended with a heroin overdose in 1970. Her only top single, "Me and Bobby McGee," was released posthumously in 1971.

● Patti Smith, often referred to as "punk rock's poet laureate," fused poetry and rock with the release of 1975's *Horses,* considered the first art-punk album. Smith, who was born in Chicago in 1946 and raised in New Jersey, was known for her androgynous appearance and, despite never achieving commercial success, is considered one of the genre's most influential musicians. (Smith's only Top 40 hit, 1978's "Because the Night," was co-written with Bruce Springsteen.)

fastest-growing segments of the music industry. Bands like Jars of Clay, Evanescence, and MercyMe even crossed over into mainstream radio and MTV.

Alternative Sounds of Punk and Grunge

In the United States and Britain in the mid-1970s, **punk rock** challenged the orthodoxy and commercialism of the record business. Punk has generally been characterized by loud, unpolished distortions, a jackhammer beat, primal vocal screams, crude aggression, and defiant or comic lyrics. By this time, the glory days of rock's competitive independent labels had ended, and rock music was controlled by six major companies: CBS, Warner, Polygram, RCA, Capitol-EMI, and MCA. According to critic Ken Tucker, this situation gave rise to "faceless rock—crisply recorded, eminently catchy," featuring anonymous hits by bands with "no established individual personalities outside their own large but essentially discrete audiences" of young white males.[13]

In avoiding rock's consumer popularity, punk attempted to recover the early amateurish and offensive energies of rock and roll. Essentially, any teenager with a few weeks of guitar practice could learn the sound, making music that was both more democratic and more discordant than rock. In the early 1970s, pre-punk groups like the Velvet Underground set the stage for the Ramones and the Dead Kennedys. In England, the music of the Sex Pistols ("Anarchy in the U.K."), one of the most controversial groups in rock history, was eventually banned for offending British decorum.

Punk, of course, was not a commercial success in the United States in the 1970s, lack of widespread popularity being one of punk's goals. Nevertheless, punk made contributions, especially by "defining the big business of the rock industry and then condemning it." Punk also offered women the opportunity "to participate fully in the rock world for the first time in the history of the music."[14] In the United States, for instance, poet and rocker Patti Smith helped pioneer punk in the mid-1970s, and in Britain, Siouxsie & the Banshees assaulted commercial rock's fixation on all-male groups.

Taking the spirit of punk and infusing it with attention to melody, **grunge** represented a significant development in rock in the 1990s. Grunge's commercial breakthrough can be traced to the "Smells Like Teen Spirit" cut on the album *Nevermind* by

Nirvana, led by songwriter and vocalist Kurt Cobain. In 1992, *Nevermind* was the top-selling album in America, its popular success ironically built on satirizing some of the rock music of the 1970s and 1980s. One critic described a Cobain song as "stunning, concise bursts of melody and rage that occasionally spilled over into haunting, folk-styled acoustic ballad."[15] Suffering from stomach problems, drug addiction, and severe depression, Cobain committed suicide in 1994.

Influenced by punk, grunge groups adopted an alienated performing style that was in direct contrast to the slick theatrics of 1970s and 1980s rock. Taking a cue from low-key folk singers and 1960s rock bands like the Grateful Dead, grunge spoke the low-maintenance language of the garage: torn jeans, T-shirts, long underwear, worn sneakers, and old flannel shirts. But with the music's success, grunge's antistyle became commercially viable as hundreds of new garage bands emulated it. Nirvana's influences paved the way for a variety of punk and alternative groups in the 1990s, including Nine Inch Nails, Smashing Pumpkins, Soundgarden, Stone Temple Pilots, Pearl Jam, and Green Day.

In some critical circles, both punk and grunge are considered subcategories or fringe movements of **alternative rock**. This vague label describes many types of experimental rock music that offered a departure from the theatrics and staged extravaganzas of 1970s glam rock, which showcased such performers as David Bowie and Kiss. Appealing chiefly to college students, alternative rock has traditionally opposed the sounds of Top 40 and commercial FM radio. In the 1980s and 1990s, U2 and R.E.M. emerged as successful groups often associated with alternative rock. A key dilemma for successful alternative performers, however, is that their popularity results in commercial success, ironically a situation that their music often criticizes. Caught in this very predicament, Pearl Jam in 1993 tried to play down its commercial success by refusing to release any music-video singles from its No. 1 album, Vs., which sold more than five million copies. Pearl Jam also chose to perform in smaller arenas and on college campuses rather than in the gigantic, impersonal sports stadiums preferred by established rock bands.

In more recent times, critics argue that alternative rock has fragmented. While rock music has more variety than ever, it is also not producing mega groups like Nirvana, Pearl Jam, and Green Day. One reason is that the venues that used to produce top alt-rock acts are fragmented and dispersed. With both legal and illegal downloading running rampant today, music fans often go their own ways, discovering independent or unsigned bands on regional Web sites. Commercialized rock radio—such as the

● Nirvana's lead singer, Kurt Cobain, during his brief career in the early 1990s. The release of Nirvana's *Nevermind* in September 1991 bumped Michael Jackson's *Dangerous* from the top of the charts and signaled a new direction in popular music. Other grunge bands soon followed Nirvana onto the charts, including Pearl Jam, Alice in Chains, Stone Temple Pilots, and Soundgarden.

● After producing hit songs for artists such as Alicia Keys and Jay-Z, Kanye West released his first album in 2004. Known as much for his persona as his music, West was described by *Rolling Stone* magazine in 2006 as ". . . one of the most popular and polarizing artists in music today . . . he is as known for his out-spokenness as he is for his hitmaking ability. His temper tantrum at the 2004 American Music Awards after Gretchen Wilson beat him out for Best New Artist, his no-holds-barred takedown of George Bush after the Hurricane Katrina disaster—not since Tupac Shakur has a rapper been so compelling, so ridiculously brash, so irresistibly entertaining."

❝ We're like reporters. We give them [our listeners] the truth. People where we come from hear so many lies the truth stands out like a sore thumb.❞

–Eazy-E, N.W.A., 1989

mega radio chain Clear Channel—often only plays the reliable names from rock's recent past, forcing music fans interested in new music to roam the Internet. *Billboard Radio Monitor*'s Bram Teitelman argued in 2005 that "even though there's a lot of high-quality rock music out there, there's no Nirvana or Seattle scene that's getting people excited about it. . . . There's no 50 Cent in rock radio."[16] *Denver Post* music critic Ricardo Baca, though, reminded rock fans in 2005 about the nature of rock and its varied alternatives: "entangled and cross-referenced, varied and genre-bending, mining mass appeal and musical subcultures alike."[17]

Hip-Hop Redraws Musical Lines

With the growing segregation of radio formats and the dominance of mainstream rock by white male performers, the place of black artists in the rock world diminished. By the late 1980s, no major popular black successor to Chuck Berry or Jimi Hendrix had emerged in rock. These trends, combined with the rise of "safe" dance disco by white bands (the Bee Gees), black artists (Donna Summer), and integrated groups (the Village People), created a space for the culture that produced hip-hop music.

In some ways a black counterpart to the spirit of white punk, **hip-hop music** also stood in direct opposition to the polished, professional, and less political world of soul. Hip-hop's combination of social politics, male swagger, and comic lyrics carried forward long-standing traditions in blues, R&B, soul, and rock and roll. Like punk, hip-hop was driven by a democratic, nonprofessional spirit—accessible to anyone who could talk (or "rap") to a funky beat in street dialect. But rap is just one part of the hip-hop sound, which can also include cutting (or "sampling") records on a turntable. Hip-hop deejays emerged in Jamaica and New York, scratching and re-cueing old reggae, disco, soul, and rock albums. As dance music, hip-hop developed MCs (masters of ceremony) who used humor, boasts, and "trash talking" to entertain and keep the peace at parties.

When the Sugarhill Gang released "Rapper's Delight" in 1979, the music industry viewed it as a novelty song, even though the music was rooted in a long tradition of party deejays playing soul and funk music through powerful sound systems. Then, in 1982, Grandmaster Flash and the Furious Five released "The Message" and infused rap with a political take on ghetto life. Rap also continued the black musical tradition of elevating the spoken word over conventional instruments, which were displaced by turntables. Although hip-hop was at first considered party music, its early political voices, including Public Enemy and Ice-T, addressed Civil Rights issues and the worsening economic conditions facing urban America.

Hip-hop exploded as a popular genre in 1986 with the commercial successes of groups like Run-DMC, the Fat Boys, and LL Cool J. That year, Run-DMC's album *Raising Hell* became a major crossover hit, the first No. 1 hip-hop album on the popular charts (thanks in part to a collaboration with Aerosmith on a rap version of the group's 1976 hit "Walk This Way"). Like punk and early rock and roll, hip-hop was cheap to produce, requiring only a few mikes, speakers, amps, turntables, and vinyl record albums. With CDs displacing LPs as the main recording format in the 1980s, partially obsolete hardware was "reemployed" for use by hip-hop artists, many of whom had trained in vocational colleges for industrial jobs that evaporated in the 1970s and 1980s.

Because most major labels and many black radio stations rejected the rawness of hip-hop, the music spawned hundreds of new independent labels. Although initially dominated by male performers, hip-hop was open to women, and some—Salt-N-Pepa and Queen Latifah (Dana Owens) among them—quickly became major players. Soon white groups like the Beastie Boys, Limp Bizkit, and Kid Rock were combining hip-hop and punk-rock in commercially successful music, along with the first virtual cartoon band, Gorillaz. Today, hip-hop is a commercial success with best-selling artists including Eminem (a.k.a. Marshall Mathers), whose 2004 *Encore* album sold nearly five million copies by early 2006, and 50 Cent (a.k.a. Curtis Jackson), whose album *The Massacre* was the top-selling CD in 2005. That year 50 Cent became the first artist since the Beatles in 1964 to have four songs in one year in the Top 10 on *Billboard's* popular music charts.

Hip-hop, like punk, defies mainstream culture. Some rap has drawn criticism from both the white and black communities for lyrics that degrade women or applaud violence. Rappers respond that punk has often been more explicit and offensive but that punk's lyrics are less discernible under the guitar distortion. The conversational style of rap, however, makes it a forum in which performers can debate such issues as gender, class, and drugs. A few hip-hop artists have also fought extended battles over copyright infringement, since their music continues to sample rock, soul, funk, and disco records.

Although hip-hop encompasses many different styles, including various Latin offshoots, its most controversial subgenre is probably **gangster rap**. This style developed in Los Angeles in 1987, partly in response to drug-related news stories that represented, at least for many African American communities, a one-sided portrait of life in urban America. This offshoot of rap drew major national attention in 1996 with the shooting death of Tupac Shakur, a performer, actor, and ex-con who lived the violent life he sang about on albums like *Thug Life*. But although Shakur was criticized for his criminal lifestyle, he was revered by many fans for telling hard truths about urban problems and street life. In 1997, Notorious B.I.G. (Christopher Wallace, a.k.a. Biggie Smalls), whose followers were prominent suspects in Shakur's death, was shot to death in Hollywood. He was considered Shakur's main rival.[18]

In the wake of Shakur's and B.I.G.'s still unsolved murders, the business and sound of hip-hop changed with the rise of Sean "P. Diddy" Combs. He led Bad Boy Entertainment (former home of Notorious B.I.G.) away from gangster rap to a more danceable hip-hop that combined singing and rapping with musical elements of rock and soul. In the late 1990s, Bad Boy was New York's hottest label. But Combs's increasingly commercialized, sample-heavy style angered many in the hard-line hip-hop community, who blamed him for diluting a purist urban art form. Then the emergence of 50 Cent as the top-selling rapper in the early 2000s marked the return of the hard-core gangster genre. In a well-publicized event, 50 Cent survived being shot nine times in 2000 as he sat in a car outside his grandmother's house in Queens, New York. Similarly, Kimberly (Lil' Kim) Jones marked a prominent woman rap artist's central involvement in the gangster scene; in 2005 she was sentenced to a year in federal prison and fined $50,000 for perjury (she had lied to a grand jury investigating a 2001 gunfight among rival rappers in front of a Manhattan radio station in which one person was injured).

Throughout hip-hop's history, artists have occasionally characterized themselves as street reporters who tell alternative stories of city life. Chuck D of Public Enemy has maintained that most hip-hop music offers interpretations of urban experience and the war on drugs that are very different from network-news portrayals. Despite the conflicts generated around hip-hop, it remains a major development in popular music. Like early rock and roll, hip-hop's crossover appeal, particularly to white male adolescents, seems rooted in a cultural style that questions class and racial boundaries and challenges status quo values.

> **"** The creative and commercial emergence of women has been rivaled only by the growth of hip-hop as the most vital development in pop music in the '90s. **"**
>
> –Robert Hilburn,
> *New York Times*, 1999

The Business of Sound Recording

For many artists in the recording industry, the relationship between music's business and artistic elements is an uneasy one. The lyrics of hip-hop or alternative rock, for example, often question the commercial values of popular music. Both hip-hop and rock are built on the assumption that musical integrity requires a separation between business and art. But, in fact, the line between commercial success and artistic expression grows hazier each day. When the questioning of commercialism resonates with enough fans, popular artists often stand to make a lot of money. In order to understand this situation, we will examine the business of sound recording.

The Internet and file-swapping software have revolutionized the music industry—for better or worse, depending on one's perspective. Some see it as a legitimate new medium to sample, sell, and distribute music. Others view it as the scourge of the music industry. After several years of steady growth, global revenues for the industry experienced significant losses beginning in 2000 as file-sharing began to undercut CD sales. By 2005, global music sales were valued at under $34 billion (down from a peak of $38.5 billion in 1999), with the leading U.S. market accounting for about one-third of global sales, followed by Japan, the United Kingdom, France, Germany, and Canada. Despite the losses, the U.S. and global music business still constitutes a powerful **oligopoly**: a business situation in which a few firms control most of an industry's production and distribution resources. This global reach gives these firms enormous influence over what types of music gain worldwide distribution and popular acceptance.

Four Major Labels Control Most of the World's Popular Music

From the 1970s to the late 1990s, six companies controlled popular music. Then, in 1998, Universal acquired Polygram, leaving five corporations that produced about 85 percent of all American recordings and controlled 80 percent of the global market. The largest music corporation is Universal, which controls nearly one-third of the recorded music market. Between 1995 and 2002, Universal was owned by the Canadian company Seagram, which was shifting its core business from distilled beverages to entertainment media with the 1995 purchase of MCA, better known as Universal Studios. In 2000, however, Seagram itself was swallowed up in a takeover by Vivendi, a French utility company. After Vivendi Universal lost billions of dollars due to mismanagement, in 2003 it sold Universal's film and television companies to General Electric, but it retained Universal Music Group.

Time Warner, which had also suffered billions in corporate losses, reduced its debt by selling Warner Music in 2003 to a group of investors led by Edgar Bronfman Jr., the Seagram family heir who had built Universal into a media giant and then lost billions of his family's wealth in the decline of Vivendi Universal. In addition to Universal and Warner, the other global players are Sony, the Japanese company that bought CBS Records in the 1980s; BMG, owned by Bertelsmann in Germany, which bought RCA Records in the 1980s; and EMI, owned by Britain's EMI Group (see Figure 3.2). Each "major" owns and operates several labels, most of them formerly independent companies. The music industry as a whole—the majors and the independents—produced more than 60,000 albums in 2005—an increase of 35 percent over the 44,000-plus titles issued in 2004.[19]

In late 2003, BMG and Sony agreed to combine their music units into a single company, a move that reduced the number of majors to four (see Figure 3.3 on page 104). The joint corporation gained regulatory approval in the United States and Europe in 2004, creating a fifty-fifty partnership that rivaled Universal in size. But in July 2006, the European Union ended the merger and broke the companies apart.

The Indies Spot the Trends

The rise of rock and roll in the 1950s and early 1960s showcased a rich diversity of independent labels, all vying for a share of the new music. These labels included Sun, Stax, Chess, Motown, and Atlantic. Today, most of these independents have folded or have been absorbed by majors. However, in contrast to the four global players, some five thousand large and small production houses—sometimes called **indies**—record less commercially viable music, or music they hope will become commercially viable. Often struggling enterprises, indies require only a handful of people to operate them. They identify forgotten older artists and record new innovative performers. To keep costs down, indies usually depend on wholesale distributors to promote and sell their music. Producing about 18 percent of America's music, indies often enter into deals with majors to gain the widest distribution for their artists. They may also entrust their own recordings or contracts to independent distributors, who ship new recordings to various retail outlets and radio stations. The Internet has also become a low-cost distribution and promotion outlet for independent labels, which often use Web sites for recording and merchandise sales, fan discussion groups, regular e-mail updates of tour schedules, new releases, and MP3 downloads of new songs.

In the music business, the majors frequently rely on indies to discover and initiate distinctive musical trends that first appear on a local level. For instance, although hip-hop was rejected by many radio stations and major labels, indies such as Sugarhill, Tommy Boy, and Uptown emerged in the 1980s to produce this music for regional markets. In the early 1990s, punk faced similar problems and relied on labels such as Kill Rock Stars, Dischord, and Aargh! Records. In the early 2000s, bands of the so-called indie-rock movement, such as Interpol and Arcade Fire, found their home on indie labels Matador and Merge. Indies play a major role as the music industry's risk-takers, since major labels are reluctant to invest in lost or commercially unproven artists.

Once indies become successful, the financial inducement to sell out to a major label is enormous. Seattle indie Sub Pop (Nirvana's initial recording label), faced with the commercial success of alternative rock, sold 49 percent of its stock to Time Warner for $20 million in 1994. Throughout the 1990s, Polygram, Sony, and EMI aggressively pursued the punk label Epitaph, which rejected takeover offers as high as $50 million and remains independent. All four majors remain busy looking for and swallowing up independent labels that have successfully developed artists with national or global appeal.

Making, Distributing, and Profiting from a Recording

Like most mass media, the music business is divided into several areas, including artist development, technical facilities, sales and distribution, advertising and promotion, and administrative operations. Recording companies, whether major or minor, are generally driven by **A&R (artist & repertoire) agents**: the talent scouts of the music business who discover, develop, and sometimes manage artists. A&R executives listen to demonstration tapes, or

Figure 3.2
U.S. Market Share of the Major Labels in the Recording Industry, First Quarter 2006

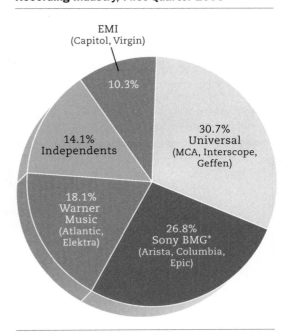

EMI (Capitol, Virgin)
10.3%

14.1% Independents

18.1% Warner Music (Atlantic, Elektra)

30.7% Universal (MCA, Interscope, Geffen)

26.8% Sony BMG* (Arista, Columbia, Epic)

Source: Nielsen SoundScan. Billboard.com, April 22, 2006.

*European Union dissolved the Sony BMG music merger in 2006.

> **"** The one good thing I can say about file-sharing is it affords us a chance to get our music heard without the label incurring crazy marketing expenses. **"**
>
> –Gerard Cosley, co-president of the indie record label Matador, 2003

Figure 3.3
Media Ownership: Principal Operations for Sony Corporation of America

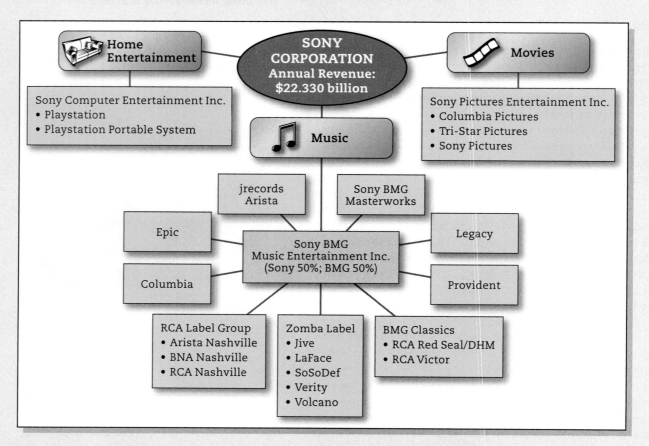

Sony uses a media convergence—or cross platform—business model to integrate its media hardware holdings—TVs, DVDs, CD players, radios, Playstation, and other electronics (where it makes most of its money)—with its media "software": the content it produces to run on its equipment, such as movies, TV programs, digital games, and music. The "software" or content piece of Sony's corporate empire is depicted above, listing its music label partnership with another media giant—BMG (Bertelsmann).

Discuss or examine the implications of how this kind of cross platform model allows Sony to make and market movies that can be turned into digital games (and digital games that can become movies), and TV programs that carry—as background ambience—and promote Sony's music labels and artists

demos, from new artists; and they decide whom to hire and which songs to record. Before Chuck Berry, Little Richard, and rock's British invasion, few commercially successful performers wrote their own music, so A&R agents had to match them with songs and writers—a practice still prevalent in country music.

The technical group at a recording label oversees the entire production process. A typical recording session is a complex process that involves musicians and audio technicians and is directed by a session engineer and a producer. A chief engineer oversees the technical aspects of the recording session, everything from choosing recording equipment to arranging microphone placement. In charge of the overall recording process, the producer handles most nontechnical elements of the session, including reserving studio space and hiring musicians. During recording, the producer takes command and in most cases decides whether certain vocal or instrumental parts work well or need to be rerecorded.

● Matador Records, a large indie label, began in 1989 in New York City. Primarily known for its indie rock focus, the label has expanded into the United Kingdom and is currently home to musical acts such as Belle and Sebastian, Interpol (*pictured*), Pretty Girls Make Graves, and Yo La Tengo.

Most popular albums are now produced part by part. Using separate microphones, the vocalists, guitarists, drummers, and other musical sections are digitally recorded onto audio tracks. To produce one song, as many as two or three dozen tracks might be recorded, often at different times and in different studios. Controlling the overall sound quality, the chief engineer mixes the parts onto a two-track stereo master tape. Mixing engineers specialize in other postproduction editing; they mix the multiple tracks after the recording sessions. Mastering engineers prepare the song for transfer to a final version on audiotape and CD. Remix engineers work with tapes that are already mastered, removing flaws or adding new instrumental or vocal parts. Because digital keyboard synthesizers are able to reproduce most instrumental sounds, engineers can now duplicate many instrumental parts without recalling studio musicians.

Throughout the recording and postproduction process, the marketing department plans strategies for packaging, promoting, and selling a recording. In addition to arranging advertising in various media, this department might design point-of-purchase displays that use signs, posters, and other gimmicks to encourage in-store impulse buying, which accounts for nearly 15 percent of all CD sales.

❝ Teenagers listen to five and a half hours of music daily but only listen to their parents five minutes a day. ❞
—CNN survey, 2000

Selling the Music

Distributing and selling CDs and tapes is a tricky part of the business. For years, the traditional sales outlet was direct retail record stores, which offer variety but now account for only about 33 percent of all record sales—down from a 70 percent share of record sales in 1990. The record store business is led by large but struggling chains such as Sam Goody and Tower Records, each of which operates hundreds of stores nationally, mostly in high-rent shopping malls, in urban centers, and near college campuses. Direct retailers specialize in music, carefully monitoring new releases by major labels and independents. Like chain bookstores, direct music retailers keep a large inventory. Their staffs can also track down and order obscure recordings that the store may not have on hand. In addition, used-CD stores and inventories have developed as a by-product of the durability of digital recordings. Book chains such as Barnes & Noble and Borders are also direct retailers of recordings as part of their "superstore" books and media product mix.

Overwhelming direct retail record stores are general retail outlets, like Wal-Mart, Target, and Best Buy, which have also captured about 54 percent of CD and tape sales. Because music is not the main focus of these stores, general retail outlets contract with *rack jobbers* to stock their stores’ music racks or shelves with the latest CDs, audiocassettes, and music videos. Rack jobbers either lease shelf space from the stores or sell recordings directly to them. By managing inventories and orders, rack jobbers perform record-keeping tasks that many retailers prefer to avoid. To earn the highest profits, rack jobbers generally stock the most popular music, screen controversial titles for some of their clients, and ignore obscure musical forms.

Another 4 percent of recording sales each year come from *music clubs* such as BMG and Columbia. Like book clubs, music clubs use direct mail and inserts in Sunday newspapers to offer prospective members ten CDs for the price of one as an incentive to join. In exchange, consumers agree to buy at least three or four CDs at the regular price (about $15 to $17, plus shipping charges). Like major book clubs, music clubs sort through many possible new releases, identifying the commercial hits or “hot” groups. Through clubs, consumers are generally offered music by only the most popular and profitable performers.

Internet Distribution Outlets

In 1997, the recording industry began to track Internet sales of music for the first time. Although Net-based sales accounted for only 0.3 percent of music purchases that year, sales had climbed to more than 6 percent of the U.S. market in 2005. Internet music purchases are made on independent music sites such as InSound, or through such retailers as Amazon.com. Music sites typically allow computer users to download and listen to short segments of songs for free as they browse among possible purchases.

By the late 1990s, though, getting music from the Internet had taken on another meaning. Music fans engaged in digital music file-sharing, popularized by the easy-to-use Napster Web site service. Napster and other file-sharing services had put millions of songs on the Internet that could be downloaded directly to computer hard drives for free. The enormous popularity of online digital swapping services called attention to the fact that the industry had failed to adapt quickly to the Internet as a new for-profit distribution outlet. Initial attempts to sell music on the Web by the music industry were assailed for their high prices and inflexibility, as they confined listening to the computer only, via streaming or downloads that couldn’t be burned to CDs. In 2003, though, Apple Computer opened the first successful major online music store, iTunes, selling songs for just ninety-nine cents each. By 2006 digital music sales soared with consumers legally downloading more than 1 billion tracks.

MTV’s Influence Goes International . . . and Digital

When the MTV cable network was launched in 1981, it had immediate impact on the music business, especially bringing rock acts—24/7—to mainstream TV audiences via the three-minute music video. Many newer artists who could not get songs played on radio turned to MTV and found another route to rock music fans. But by the 1990s, the cable channel was turning more and more to producing TV programs like *Real World* and *Laguna Beach,* and so MTV networks (owned by Viacom) expanded in new directions. By 2006, MTV networks had created a hundred channels that specialized in particular genres—MTV Jams (hip-hop), MTV Hits (top hits), MTV Espanol, and mtvU (college progressive rock)—and across international borders—MTV Latin America (launched in 1993), MTV China (1995), MTV Southeast Asia (1995), MTV India (1996), MTV Australia (1997) MTV Korea (2001), MTV Canada (2001), and MTV Base (Africa, 2005). By 2005, MTV had forty-two channels in other countries.

Although still dominant in the television music video business, MTV also entered the Internet and cell phone music video service. In response to competitors like Fuse, who began offering a "rotating free catalogue" of "music videos on demand and other music-related content" to customers via cable companies like Comcast,[20] MTV and its sister channel VH1 started their own online on-demand broadband services, MTV Overdrive and VSpot, respectively. In 2005, MTV expanded to phone-delivered music videos by launching MTV Flux—"the world's first mobile phone-based music video series"[21]—to compete with a deal between Warner Music and Verizon Wireless that provided cell phone and multimedia subscribers access to Warner's music video collection at $3.99 per download. By that time, MTV ran ninety Web sites as part of its growing services in "PC broadband mobile phones, personal digital assistants and other emerging technology."[22] So as a music delivery system, music videos continue to offer competition to radio. And with access to the Internet and mobile phones, new artists and regional bands continue to make their own videos, circulating them on the Web and developing their own following outside the mainstream music business.

> **❝ When MTV started, it was primarily an outlet for rock. But just think of all the genres that have evolved over the years. As our audience's needs change, we've been evolving and reinventing MTV.❞**
>
> —Christina Norman, MTV president, 2005

Dividing the Profits

The upheaval in the music industry in recent years has shaken up the once predictable (and high) cost of CDs. With general retail outlets now the primary sellers of CDs, the music industry's suggested retail price of $15 to $17 is often not the actual sale price, as stores like Wal-Mart and Best Buy lure customers by selling CDs near wholesale rates ranging from $9.49 to $12.00. Moreover, Universal Music Group, the leading recording company, announced in 2004 that it would compete with online digital music stores by discounting their wholesale price so retailers could sell Universal recordings (such as those by Eminem) at a suggested retail price of $13.98. None of the other major music companies followed Universal in cutting prices.

The pricing of new CDs now varies widely depending on the music label and the retailer. But for the sake of example, we will look at the various costs and profits

Figure 3.4
Where Money Goes on a $16.98 CD

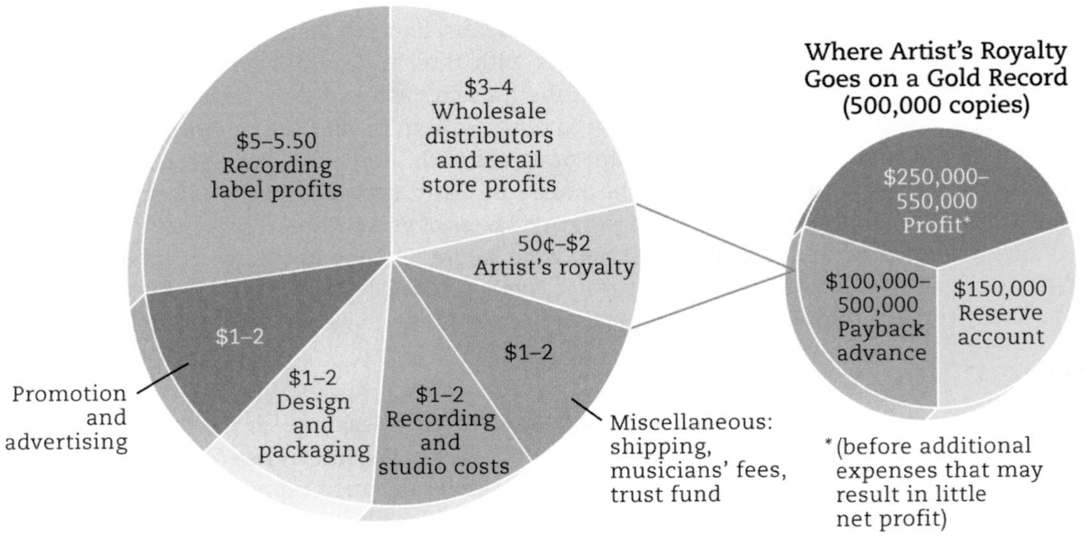

$3–4 Wholesale distributors and retail store profits

$5–5.50 Recording label profits

50¢–$2 Artist's royalty

$1–2

$1–2

Promotion and advertising

$1–2 Design and packaging

$1–2 Recording and studio costs

Miscellaneous: shipping, musicians' fees, trust fund

Where Artist's Royalty Goes on a Gold Record (500,000 copies)

$250,000–550,000 Profit*

$100,000–500,000 Payback advance

$150,000 Reserve account

*(before additional expenses that may result in little net profit)

Media Literacy
and the Critical Process

Music Preferences across Generations

We make judgments about music all the time. Older generations don't like some of the music younger people prefer, and young people often dismiss some of the music of their parents' and grandparents' generations. Even among our peers, we have different tastes in music and often reject certain kinds of music that have become too popular or that don't conform to our own preferences. The following exercise aims to understand musical tastes beyond our own individual choices.

Description. Arrange to interview four to eight friends or relatives of different ages about their musical tastes and influences. Devise questions about what music they listen to and have listened to *at different stages of their lives.* While interviewing your subjects, have them trace the changes in their musical interests and tastes. What music do they buy? What's the first album (or single) they purchased? What's the latest album they have purchased? Find out if they have stories to tell about any strong or vivid memories related to particular songs or artists. Always include yourself in this project. Also, collect demographic and consumer information: what is their age, gender, occupation, and educational background? Where did they grow up and where do they live now?

Analysis. Chart and organize your results. Do you recognize any patterns emerging from these data, recollections, and stories? What kinds of music did they listen to when they were younger? What kinds of music do they listen to now? What formed/influenced their music interests? If their musical interests changed, what happened? (If they stopped listening to music, note that and find out why.) Do they have any associations between music and their everyday lives? Are these music associations and lifetime interactions with songs and artists important to them? As they got older, did they reject music they once liked—or did they come to like music that they once rejected or never listened to?

Interpretation. Based on what you have discovered and the patterns you have charted, determine what the patterns mean about your interview subjects. Does age, gender, geographic location, or education matter in musical tastes? Over time, are the changes in music tastes and buying habits significant? Why or why not? What kind of music is most important to your subjects? Finally, and most importantly, why do you think their music preferences developed as they did? Remember to include yourself in the interpretation as you try to make sense of the stories and answers.

Evaluation. Determine how your interview subjects came to like particular kinds of music. What constitutes "good" and "bad" music for them? Did their ideas about good and bad music change over time? How? Are they open- or closed-minded about music? How do they form judgments about music? What criteria did your interview subjects offer for making judgments about music? Do you think their criteria are a valid way to judge music? Again, include your own tastes and criteria in this evaluation.

Engagement. To expand on your findings and see how they match up with industry practices, contact music professionals. Track down record label representatives from both a small indie label and a larger mainstream label and ask them who they are trying to target with their music and how they find out about the musical tastes of their consumers. Share your findings with them and discuss whether it violates or agrees with their practices. Speculate about the music industry and whether it is serving the needs and tastes of you and your interview subjects. If not, what might be done to change or modify the current system? Finally, write an assessment or general overview about your findings.

from a typical CD that retails at $16.98. The wholesale price for that CD is about $10.70, leaving the remainder as retail profit. The more heavily discounted the CD, the less retail profit there is. The wholesale price represents the actual cost of producing and promoting the recording, plus the recording label's profits. The

record company reaps the highest profit (close to $5.50 on a typical CD) but, along with the artist, bears the bulk of the expenses: manufacturing costs, packaging and CD design, advertising and promotion, and artists' royalties (see Figure 3.4 on page 107 for proportional breakdown of costs). The physical product of the CD itself costs less than a quarter to manufacture.

New artists usually negotiate a royalty rate of between 8 and 12 percent on the retail price of a cassette or CD. A more established performer might negotiate a 15 percent rate, and popular artists might get more than 15 percent. An artist who has negotiated a typical 11 percent royalty rate would earn about $1.80 for a CD whose suggested list retail price is $16.98. So, a CD that "goes gold"—that is, sells 500,000 units—would net the artist around $900,000. But out of this amount, the artist repays the record company the money it has advanced him or her—from $100,000 to $500,000—for recording and music video costs, travel expenses, and promotional efforts. Another $150,000 might have to be set aside in a reserve account to cover any unsold recordings returned by record stores. After the artist pays band members, managers, and attorneys with the remaining money, it's quite possible that the artist will have almost nothing—even after a certified gold CD.

Independent producers or labels sign songwriters, singers, or groups and then advance them money to cover expenses, hoping for a hit song or album. More than 95 percent of all musicians who receive advances, however, do not recoup them through recording sales. Indeed, large numbers of artists fall gravely in debt or declare bankruptcy when their cut of record sales fails to cover their costs. Toni Braxton and TLC, for example, sold eighteen million CDs between them in the late 1990s but had to declare bankruptcy because of disadvantageous recording contracts: TLC received less than 2 percent of the gross, and Braxton received only $0.35 per album, far lower than the typical royalty rate.

In addition to sales royalties received by artists from their recording companies, two other kinds of royalty payments exist: mechanical and performance royalties. Songwriters protect their work by obtaining an exclusive copyright on each song, ensuring that it will not be copied or performed without permission. To protect their copyrights, songwriters assign their creations to a publisher, who represents the songs by trying to sell them in printed form or by having them recorded by a major label or indie. Songwriters and publishers receive a *mechanical royalty* when they allow a song to be recorded. They are paid at a rate of about $0.08 per song, or about $0.85 for each CD or audiotape sold.

The owner of a song's copyright, which is not always the songwriter, also receives a *performance royalty* whenever the music is used on radio or television. Because songwriters are seldom wealthy enough to underwrite the original costs of producing a CD or tape, they often sell their copyrights to music publishers. On behalf of songwriters and publishers, performance royalties are collected by three national licensing associations: ASCAP, Society of European Stage Authors and Composers (SESAC), and Broadcast Music, Inc. (BMI). These groups keep track of recording rights, collect copyright fees, and license music for use in TV commercials or films. Radio stations annually pay licensing fees of between 1.5 and 2 percent of their gross annual revenues, and they generally play only licensed music. Even

● The Black Eyed Peas are one of the most successful groups in hip-hop history, with their breakthrough 2003 album, *Elephunk*, selling 7.5 million copies worldwide. Although their 2005 album, *Monkey Business*, had sold nearly 7 million copies by early 2006, they were sometimes criticized for their commercial endorsements, which included licensing their music to Best Buy, the NBA, cell phones, and even a digital game where they were turned into characters for "The Urbz: Sims in the City."

restaurants and dentist offices paid an average of $2,000 and $182 respectively in 2005 to play licensed background music.

Pirates, Counterfeits, and Bootlegs

Not surprisingly, the music industry is less than thrilled when music lovers obtain or share music without paying for it. One of the biggest challenges facing sound recording today is online **piracy**, that is, the illegal uploading, downloading, or streaming of copyrighted material. Industry groups have blamed unauthorized downloads via file-sharing software like KaZaA and Morpheus for a 20 percent drop in CD sales since 2001. In 2003, the Recording Industry Association of America began to criminalize peer-to-peer (P2P) file-sharing by suing thousands of song swappers—a move that has deterred some digital thefts and steered music lovers to legitimate commercial services such as iTunes. Meanwhile, other studies suggest the music industry is exaggerating the online piracy problem. Some economists argue that file-sharing has actually created music fans and helped CD sales; other analysts cite another compelling reason for the decline in CD sales: the end of the "CD upgrade cycle," as people have finished upgrading their favorite albums and cassettes to the CD format.

Unauthorized recordings have been a part of the music industry for much of the twentieth century. Besides online file-sharing, piracy involves any kind of unofficial recording that skirts official copyright permissions—the illegal reissue, for example, of out-of-print material into "greatest hits" albums. Another form of illicit copying is **counterfeiting**, the unauthorized copying of CDs, cassettes, and their packaging. In the late 1980s, the collapse of the communist governments throughout Eastern Europe and the growth of wide-open economies worldwide led to a flourishing illegal market in the music industry. In the absence of international policing of copyright laws, manufacturing plants were set up, especially throughout China and other parts of Asia, to duplicate recordings and photocopy jacket materials. These illegal firms sell recordings at cut-rate prices, with no profits going to the original recording companies or the artists. Although China passed a law that criminalized piracy and counterfeiting in 2004, enforcing the law has been difficult as China develops as a market-driven economy—especially since counterfeit products drive much of that new economy.

Finally, **bootlegging** occurs from unauthorized or stolen tape recordings—sometimes called "gray tracks"—of live concerts, informal studio sessions, or live radio or TV appearances. Individuals duplicate these recordings and then sell them for profit without paying fees to the artists. The recent popularity of digital technologies has made illegal copies both better in quality and easier to make. By some estimates, twenty-five million unique bootleg recordings are available digitally on various file-sharing networks.[23] An estimated one in three CDs sold worldwide is an unauthorized recording.[24]

Alternative Voices

Even as major labels continue to see profits decline, independent labels have recently enjoyed major successes. For example, the Washington, D.C., punk band Fugazi has become nationally prominent while shunning offers from the majors and running its own label. Likewise, the Omaha-based band Bright Eyes has stuck with its tiny label, Saddle Creek, despite the promise of lucrative major label contracts. "No one in any of our bands wants to sacrifice a whole lot of control over what we're doing for a whole bunch of money when we've already sort of achieved a really huge dream of ours, like, growing up, which was just to play music for a living," lead singer Conor Oberst says. "You don't really need a million dollars, you know, if you're doing everything you want."[25]

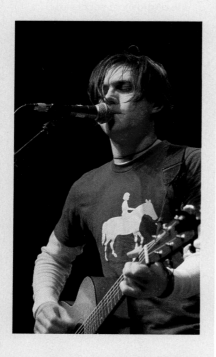

● Despite his success and substantial impact on the current rock scene, Conor Oberst remains dedicated to independent music. Currently involved in a boycott of Clear Channel Communications, he is also a champion of independent music labels and has helped to found two of his own, Saddle Creek and Team-Love.

The Internet and Indie Labels

Labels such as Rounder Records (They Might Be Giants, who did the quirky theme song to Fox TV's *Malcolm in the Middle*) and Matador Records (Interpol, Pretty Girls Make Graves) court much smaller niche audiences than major labels. They have benefited from file-swapping networks and people actively seeking alternative music. Consequently, bands that in previous years would have signed to a major label (losing creative control) have demonstrated another path to success in the music industry. Unlike the case for a band with a major label needing to sell 500,000 copies in order to recoup expenses and make a profit, an indie band using word-of-mouth, music blog sites, and online message boards "can turn a profit after selling roughly 25,000 copies of an album."[26] The Internet lets fans share new music and discover obscure artists, who in turn post their music (and inexpensive homemade videos) online, bypassing the traditional and expensive promotion-marketing structure of the major labels. Indie labels also use the Internet to run fan clubs, notify fans of new music (plus sell albums and merchandise), and post tour dates to boost attendance at shows. While the indie share of the music sales market declined from roughly 18 to 20 percent in the 1990s to around 15 percent by 2004, 2005 marked the first upward spike in five years—back up to 18 percent. Meanwhile, the four major music corporations saw their sales fall 8 percent.[27]

The Internet and Self-Promotion

Alternative artists and unsigned bands now build online communities around their personal Web sites—listing shows, news, tours, photos, downloadable songs, and locations where fans can buy albums—a key self-promotional tool. But the biggest new players in the online music scene are social networking sites like MySpace.com— "the prime convergence point for bands and fans."[28] MySpace (and sites like Friendster, Pure Volume, and TagWorld) have created spaces for unsigned and signed bands to promote their music (and themselves with blog features). By 2006, more than 3 million bands and individual artists were using MySpace "to upload songs and videos, announce shows, promote albums and interact with fans."[29] As Tom Anderson, who cofounded MySpace in 2003 at age twenty-six, noted, "Bands join because it is free, they don't have to know how to run a website, and most importantly— there are 43 million people on MySpace."[30] In 2005, Rupert Murdoch and News Corporation bought MySpace for $580 million. Already a major player in television, movies, newspapers, and book publishing, News Corporation bought MySpace to expand its new Internet division, called Fox Interactive.

> " Exploiting online message boards, music blogs, and social networks, independent music companies are making big advances at the expense of the four global music conglomerates, whose established business model of blockbuster hits through radio airplay now looks increasingly outdated. "
>
> –Jeff Leeds,
> *New York Times*, 2005

Recordings, Free Expression, and Democracy

From sound recording's earliest stages as a mass medium, when the music industry began stamping out flat records with labels—which identified artists and turned them into stars—to the breakthrough of MP3s and Internet-based music services, fans have been sharing music and pushing culture in unpredictable directions. Sound recordings allowed for the formation of rock and roll, a genre drawing from such a diverse range of musical styles that its impact on culture is unprecedented: Low culture challenged high-brow propriety; black culture spilled into white; southern culture infused the North; masculine and feminine stereotypes broke down; and artists reconfigured sacred songs into sexually charged (and deeply threatening) lyrics and rhythms. Attempts to tame the music were met by new affronts, including those from Britain, Detroit, and the political and psychedelic fringe. The gradual mainstreaming of rock led to the establishment of other culture-shaking genres, including punk and grunge, hip-hop, and electronica.

CASE STUDY

In the Jungle, the Unjust Jungle, a Small Victory

By Sharon LaFraniere

As Solomon Linda first recorded it in 1939, it was a tender melody, almost childish in its simplicity—three chords, a couple of words and some baritones chanting in the background.

But the saga of the song now known worldwide as "The Lion Sleeps Tonight" is anything but a lullaby. It is fraught with racism and exploitation and, in the end, 40-plus years after his death, brings a measure of justice. Were he still alive, Solomon Linda might turn it into one heck of a ballad.

Born in 1909 in the Zulu heartland of South Africa, Mr. Linda never learned to read or write, but in song he was supremely eloquent. After moving to Johannesburg in his mid-20's, he quickly conquered the weekend music scene at the township beer halls and squalid hostels that housed much of the city's black labor force.

He sang soprano over a four-part harmony, a vocal style that was soon widely imitated. By 1939, a talent scout had ushered Mr. Linda's group, the Original Evening Birds, into a recording studio where they produced a startling hit called "Mbube," Zulu for "The Lion." Elizabeth Nsele, Mr. Linda's youngest surviving daughter, said it had been inspired by her father's childhood as a herder protecting cattle in the untamed hinterlands.

From there, it took flight worldwide. In the early 50's, Pete Seeger recorded it with his group, the Weavers. His version differed from the original mainly in his misinterpretation of the word "mbube" (pronounced "EEM-boo-beh"). Mr. Seeger sang it as "wimoweh," and turned it into a folk music staple.

There followed a jazz version, a nightclub version, another folk version by the Kingston Trio, a pop version and finally, in 1961, a reworking of the song by an American songwriter, George Weiss. Mr. Weiss took the last 20 improvised seconds of Mr. Linda's recording and transformed it into the melody. He added lyrics beginning "In the jungle, the mighty jungle." A teen group called the Tokens sang it with a doo-wop beat—and it topped charts worldwide.

Some 150 artists eventually recorded the song. It was translated into languages from Dutch to Japanese. It had a role in more than 13 movies. By all rights, Mr. Linda should have been a rich man.

Instead, he lived in Soweto with barely a stick of furniture, sleeping on a dirt floor carpeted with cow dung. Mr. Linda received 10 shillings—about 87 cents today—when he signed over the copyright of "Mbube" in 1952 to Gallo Studios, the company that produced his record. When Mr. Linda died in 1962, at 53, with the modern equivalent of $22 in his bank account, his widow had no money for a gravestone.

How much he should have collected is in dispute. Over the years, he and his family have received royalties for "Wimoweh" from the Richmond Organization, the publishing house that holds the rights to that song, though not as much as they should have, Mr. Seeger said. But where Mr. Linda's family really lost out, his lawyers claim, was in "The Lion Sleeps Tonight," a megahit. From 1991 to 2000, the years when "The Lion King" began enthralling audiences in movie theaters and on Broadway, Mr. Linda's survivors received a total of perhaps $17,000 in royalties, according to Hanro Friedrich, the family's lawyer.

The Lindas filed suit in 2004, demanding $1.5 million in damages, but their case was no slam-dunk. Not only had Mr. Linda signed away his copyright to Gallo in 1952, Mr. Dean said, but his wife, who was also illiterate, signed them away again in 1982, followed by his daughters several years later. In their lawsuit, the Lindas invoked an obscure 1911 law under which the song's copyright reverted to Mr. Linda's estate 25 years after his death. On a separate front, they criticized the Walt Disney Company, whose 1994 hit movie "The Lion King" featured a meerkat and warthog singing "The Lion Sleeps Tonight." Disney argued that it had paid Abilene Music for permission to use the song, without knowing its origins.

In February 2006, Abilene agreed to pay Mr. Linda's family royalties from 1987 onward, ending the suit. No amount has been disclosed, but the family's lawyers say their clients should be quite comfortable.

Source: Excerpted from Sharon Lafraniere, "In the Jungle, the Unjust Jungle, a Small Victory," *New York Times*, March 22, 2006, p. A1.

The battle over popular music's controversial lyrics and visual styles speaks to the heart of democratic expression. Indeed, popular recordings have a history of confronting stereotypes and questioning conventions. Nevertheless, popular recordings—like other art forms—also have a history of reproducing old stereotypes: limiting women's access as performers, fostering racist or homophobic attitudes, and celebrating violence and misogyny.

Popular musical forms that test cultural boundaries face a dilemma: how to uphold a legacy of free expression while resisting co-optation by giant companies bent on consolidating independents and maximizing profits. For example, since the 1950s forms of rock music have been teetering at the edge of what's acceptable—becoming commercial, pulling back, reemerging as rebellious, and then repeating the pattern. The congressional payola hearings of 1959 and the Senate hearings of the mid-1980s triggered by Tipper Gore's Parents Music Resource Center (which led to music advisory labels) are a few of the many attempts to rein in popular music, whereas the infamous antics of heavy metal's Ozzy Osbourne, the blunt rap lyrics of Public Enemy, and the independent path of Conor Oberst are among those actions that pushed popular music's boundaries.

Still, this dynamic between popular music's clever innovations and capitalism's voracious appetite is crucial to sound recording's constant innovation and mass appeal. The major labels need resourceful independents to develop new talent. So, ironically, successful commerce requires periodic infusions of the diverse sounds that come from ethnic communities, backyard garages, dance parties, and neighborhood clubs. At the same time, nearly all musicians need the major labels if they want wide distribution or national popularity. Such an interdependent pattern is common in contemporary media economics.

No matter how it is produced and distributed, popular music endures because it speaks to both individual and universal themes, from a teenager's first romantic adventure to a nation's outrage over social injustice. Music often reflects the personal or political anxieties of a society. It also breaks down artificial or hurtful barriers better than many government programs do. Despite its tribulations, music at its best continues to champion a democratic spirit. Writer and free-speech advocate Nat Hentoff addressed this issue in the 1970s when he wrote: "Popular music always speaks, among other things, of dreams—which change with the times."[31] The recording industry continues to capitalize on and spread those dreams globally, but in each generation musicians and their fans keep imagining new ones.

www.

For review questions and activities for Chapter 3, go to the interactive *Media and Culture* Online Study Guide at *bedfordstmartins.com/ mediaculture*

REVIEW QUESTIONS

Technology and the Development of Sound Recording

1. The technological configuration of a particular medium sometimes elevates it to mass market status. Why did Emile Berliner's flat disk replace Edison's wax cylinder, and why did this reconfiguration of records matter in the history of the mass media? Can you think of other mass media examples in which the size and shape of the technology have made a difference?

2. How did sound recording survive the advent of radio?

U.S. Popular Music and the Formation of Rock

3. How did rock and roll significantly influence two mass media industries?

4. Although many rock-and-roll lyrics from the 1950s are tame by today's standards, this new musical development represented a threat to many parents and adults at that time. Why?

5. What moral and cultural boundaries were blurred by rock and roll in the 1950s?

6. Why did cover music figure so prominently in the development of rock and roll and the record industry in the 1950s?

A Changing Industry: Reformations in Popular Music

7. Explain the British invasion. What was its impact on the recording industry?

8. How did soul music manage to survive the British invasion in the 1960s?

9. What were the major influences of folk music on the recording industry?

10. Why did hip-hop and punk rock emerge as significant musical forms in the late 1970s and 1980s? What do their developments have in common, and how are they different?

The Business of Sound Recording

11. What companies control the bulk of worldwide music production and distribution?

12. Why are independent labels so important to the music industry?

13. What accounts for the cost of a typical CD recording? Where do the profits go?

14. What are the three types of unauthorized recordings that plague the recording business?

Recordings, Free Expression, and Democracy

15. Why is it ironic that so many forms of alternative music become commercially successful?

QUESTIONING THE MEDIA

1. Who was your first favorite group or singer? How old were you at the time? What was important to you about this music?

2. If you ran a noncommercial campus radio station, what kind of music would you play and why?

3. Think about the role of the 1960s drug culture in rock's history. How are drugs and alcohol treated in contemporary and alternative forms of rock and hip-hop today?

4. Is it healthy for or detrimental to the music business that so much of the recording industry is controlled by four large international companies? Explain.

5. Do you think the Internet as a technology helps or hurts musical artists? Why do so many contemporary musical performers differ in their opinions about the Internet?

6. Do you think the global popularity of rock music is mainly a positive or a negative cultural influence? What are the pros and cons of rock's influence?

SEARCHING THE INTERNET

http://www.riaa.com

Web site of the Recording Industry Association of America, a trade group that promotes U.S. recording companies; loaded with updated statistics and industry legislation.

http://www.allmusic.com

With more than a half-million album recordings listed in its database, plus more than 200,000 album reviews, the All Music Guide is an excellent resource for researching recorded music of all genres.

http://www.billboard.com

The online site for *Billboard* magazine, which charts music recordings according to weekly sales.

http://www.bigchampagne.com

The Web site lists the ten most popular downloads each week for music, videos, movies, TV, games, and soft-

ware, and has become a significant player in market research.

http://www.podcast.net

A leading directory of podcast content, with links to submit your own podcasts.

http://www.rockhall.com

The site includes a virtual tour of Cleveland's Rock and Roll Hall of Fame museum, audio files and biographies of inductees, and an interactive timeline.

http://www.npr.org/programs/specials/vote/list100.html

The National Public Radio 100—NPR's list of the one hundred most important American musical works of the twentieth century, including jazz, rock and roll, country, R&B, musical theater, film score, and classical genres.

Media Literacy
and the Critical Process

In Brief

Survey the class to discover how many individuals download copyrighted digital audio files from the Internet.

1. Even though the unauthorized downloading of copyrighted music is inherently unethical, why are so many people doing it?

2. Considering how the profits on a typical CD sale are divided, who is getting hurt by online piracy?

3. If most music becomes distributed on the Internet, how much would you pay per month for a service allowing unlimited downloads of music?

In Depth

In small groups, take on the investigation of a small independent recording company (of which there are tens of thousands throughout the United States and the world). Visit their Web site, and/or e-mail them or telephone them. In your investigation, try to proceed through the five steps of the critical process:

Description. What kind of music does this label specialize in? Is the label limited to only one genre? What are some of the groups the label produces? Where and how does the label identify its musical artists? How does the label describe itself? How does the label distribute its recordings to consumers?

Analysis. Look at the variety of groups the label produces. Is there a kind of fan the label is trying to target? How does this label go about promoting its artists and getting a recording to the consumer?

Does the label face any obstacles in popularizing its artists? Is the label fiercely independent, or is its goal to eventually sell to a major label? Is the label struggling, or is it financially viable?

Interpretation. From what you've gathered so far from your research, what are the major problems facing independent labels in the recording industry? Do you see independent labels overcoming these problems? How?

Evaluation. What is the value of small independent recording companies to the entire recording industry? What would be different about the recording industry as a whole if small independent labels didn't exist?

Add other questions and information as you go along. Meet with the members of your group to discuss your findings. Your group might want to prepare a chart or provide information on your label that can be shared with the rest of the class.

Engagement. Now that you know about indies, give some a try. Sample independent label artists on Web sites such as http://wiki.etree.org (all music is free and legal to download and trade). Better yet, buy some music and request that local radio stations play quality local independent artists so that other people can hear them. (This will be more effective if several people make requests over a sustained period of time.) You might also talk with retailers about carrying local independent music CDs, if they don't already do so.

(*Note:* This assignment can be adapted to other media industries covered in this text.)

KEY TERMS

audiotape, 78
stereo, 78
digital recording, 78
analog recording, 78
compact discs (or CDs), 78
DVD, 78
MP3, 78
pop music, 82
jazz, 83
cover music, 83

rock and roll, 83
blues, 84
rhythm and blues (or R&B), 84
rockabilly, 87
payola, 90
soul, 94
folk music, 95
folk-rock, 96
punk rock, 98
grunge, 98

alternative rock, 99
hip-hop music, 100
gangster rap, 101
oligopoly, 102
indies, 103
A&R (artist & repertoire) agents, 103
piracy, 110
counterfeiting, 110
bootlegging, 110

popular radio

and the origins of broadcasting

In 1995, the San Antonio–based Clear Channel Communications owned just 42 radio stations nationwide, prohibited by Federal Communications Commission (FCC) rules from owning more than 48 broadcast stations (24 AM and 24 FM) and, with some exceptions, from owning more than one station per market.

By 2006, however, the radio giant owned more than 1,100 stations, including outlets in Anchorage (6), Atlanta (7), Chicago (6), Cincinnati (8), Denver (8), Detroit (7), Houston (7), Los Angeles (11), Louisville (8), Memphis (8), Phoenix (8), Salt Lake City (7), San Diego (9), Tulsa (6), and Washington, D.C. (8).

How did this happen? The 1996 Telecommunications Act wiped away most radio and TV ownership rules, some of which had existed for more than fifty years. The advocates for deregulation, including then President Bill Clinton, argued that with so many channels of information, such as the Internet and satellite TV and radio, there was no longer any need to ensure diversity of ownership in broadcast radio.

> **"** If anyone said we were in the radio business, it wouldn't be someone from our company. We're not in the business of providing news and information. We're not in the business of providing well-researched music. We're simply in the business of selling our customers products. **"**
>
> – Clear Channel CEO,
> Lowry Mays

4

Today, owners applaud the relaxed rules that allow them to consolidate their radio station operations, while critics complain that this downsizing has led radio's giant companies to rely more on automation and on predictable national music formats, with less attention to local interests.

In some cases the consolidation of the stations has even had deadly consequences. Take the case of Minot, North Dakota (population 37,000), where in 2002, Clear Channel owned all 6 of the town's commercial radio stations. Sometime after 1 A.M. on January 18, 2002, a train derailed near Minot, spilling 210,000 gallons of liquid anhydrous ammonia farm fertilizer, which immediately vaporized into the frigid air and spread over the city in a toxic white cloud.

Anhydrous ammonia delivers caustic burns when it comes in contact with body tissue. A blast to the face can swell the throat shut, suffocating the victim, or touch the eyes and cause blindness.

That night, one man died when he walked outside and was overcome by the ammonia gas in his front yard. More than one thousand people received medical aid, and thirty-two were hospitalized, some in intensive care units. In the weeks afterward, hundreds of residents returned to hospitals for more testing to assess the long-term damage to their lungs.

Normally, in an emergency situation, citizens would tune in to their radios for information and to get safety instructions. But when local police tried to reach the city's commercial radio stations early that morning, no one answered. All of the stations were on automation, playing music through the night with no live deejays. The 6 stations started emergency broadcasts only after safety officials were able to reach station employees at home.

The owner of those 6 commercial stations (Minot also had a public radio station and a Christian radio station), Clear Channel is the largest owner of radio stations in the United States. At the time, Clear Channel claimed one

employee was on duty overseeing the automated operations, but he didn't answer the phone.

The train disaster in Minot has since become the prime example of the dangers of lost localism in radio. Since 1996, large radio corporations like Clear Channel have grown to dominate radio airwaves in markets across the country, typically dropping news programs, laying off deejays, and piping in content from centralized studios.

As North Dakota Senator Byron Dorgan later commented, "They tried to sound an emergency alarm and couldn't get anyone at the radio station to pick up and—Why? Because they're running homogenized music through a board from, you know, a thousand miles away. In my judgment, local control of . . . broadcast properties . . . is something that's very important to the community, and we've gotten far away from that."[1]

ven with the arrival of TV in the 1950s and the recent "corporatization" of broadcasting, the historical and contemporary roles played by radio have been immense. From the early days of network radio, which gave us "a national identity" and "a chance to share in a common experience,"[2] to the more customized, demographically segmented medium today, radio's influence continues to reverberate throughout the airwaves. Though television displaced radio as our most common media experience, radio specialized and survived. The daily music and persistent talk that resonate from radios all over the world continue to play a key role in contemporary culture.

> **❝** The common bond [with the local community] is you're hearing people talking from your town, things important to your life. You can't get that from satellite radio. **❞**
>
> —Mark Remington, market manager, Clear Channel of Colorado, 2005

The story of radio from its invention in the late nineteenth century to its survival in the age of television is one of the most remarkable in media history. In this chapter, we will examine the cultural, political, and economic factors surrounding radio's development and perseverance. We will explore the origins of broadcasting, from the early theories about mysterious radio waves to the critical formation of RCA as a national radio monopoly. We will then probe the evolution of commercial radio, including the rise of NBC as the first network, the development of CBS, and the establishment of the first federal radio acts. Reviewing the fascinating ways in which radio reinvented itself in the 1950s, we will examine television's impact on radio programming and its advertising base, focusing on the invention of FM radio, radio's convergence with sound recording, and the influence of various formats. Finally, we will survey the economic health, increasing conglomeration, and cultural impact of commercial and noncommercial radio today, including the emergence of noncommercial low-power FM service.

Early Technology and the Development of Broadcasting

The wired and electronic transmissions of media messages have always required three ingredients: power (electricity); symbols (Morse code, music, or language); and a transmission reception system (such as radio and TV stations and sets). Because of these requirements, radio did not emerge as a full-blown mass medium until the 1920s, though it had been evolving for a number of years.

Inventions Leading to the Modern Age of Mass Media

The **telegraph**—the precursor of radio technology—was invented in the 1840s. American artist-inventor Samuel Morse developed the first practical system, sending electrical impulses from a transmitter through a cable to a reception point. Using a symbol system that became known as **Morse code**—a series of dots and dashes that stood for letters in the alphabet—telegraph operators transmitted news and messages simply by interrupting the electrical current along a wire cable. By 1844, Morse had set up the first telegraph line between Washington, D.C., and Baltimore, Maryland. By 1861, lines ran coast to coast. By 1866, the first transatlantic cable ran between Newfoundland and Ireland along the ocean floor. Although it transmitted only about six words per minute, this cable was the forerunner of today's global communication technologies, including the Internet, faxes, and satellite transmissions.

Along with this revolution came a recognition of the telegraph's limitations. For instance, the telegraph dispatched complicated language codes, but it was unable to

Figure 4.1
The Electromagnetic Spectrum

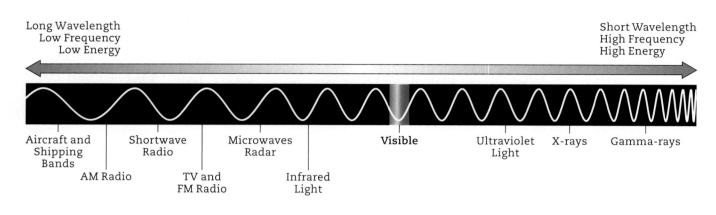

Long Wavelength
Low Frequency
Low Energy

Short Wavelength
High Frequency
High Energy

Aircraft and Shipping Bands

Shortwave Radio

Microwaves Radar

Visible

Ultraviolet Light

X-rays

Gamma-rays

AM Radio

TV and FM Radio

Infrared Light

Source: NASA, http://imagine.gsfc.nasa.gov/docs/science/know_l1/emspectrum.html.

transmit the human voice. Armies benefited from telegraphed information, but ships still had no contact with the rest of the world. As a result, navies could not find out that wars had ceased on land and often continued fighting for months. Commercial shipping interests also lacked an efficient way to coordinate and relay information from land and between ships. What was needed was a telegraph without the wires.

The key development in wireless transmissions came from James Maxwell, a Scottish physicist who in the mid-1860s elaborated on some earlier ideas about electricity and magnetism. Maxwell theorized that there existed **electromagnetic waves**: invisible electronic impulses similar to visible light. Maxwell's equations showed that electricity, magnetism, light, and heat are part of the same electromagnetic spectrum and radiate in space at the speed of light, about 186,000 miles per second (see Figure 4.1). Maxwell further theorized that a portion of these phenomena, later known as **radio waves**, could be harnessed so that signals could be sent from a transmission point and obtained at a reception point. As one historian commented on the significance of Maxwell's ideas: "Every appliance we have today, from

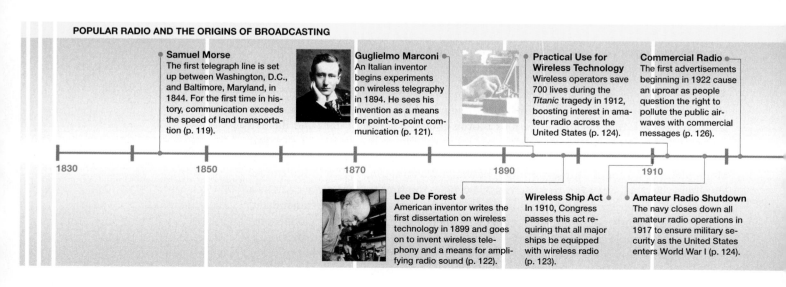

POPULAR RADIO AND THE ORIGINS OF BROADCASTING

Samuel Morse
The first telegraph line is set up between Washington, D.C., and Baltimore, Maryland, in 1844. For the first time in history, communication exceeds the speed of land transportation (p. 119).

Guglielmo Marconi
An Italian inventor begins experiments on wireless telegraphy in 1894. He sees his invention as a means for point-to-point communication (p. 121).

Practical Use for Wireless Technology
Wireless operators save 700 lives during the *Titanic* tragedy in 1912, boosting interest in amateur radio across the United States (p. 124).

Commercial Radio
The first advertisements beginning in 1922 cause an uproar as people question the right to pollute the public airwaves with commercial messages (p. 126).

1830   1850   1870   1890   1910

Lee De Forest
American inventor writes the first dissertation on wireless technology in 1899 and goes on to invent wireless telephony and a means for amplifying radio sound (p. 122).

Wireless Ship Act
In 1910, Congress passes this act requiring that all major ships be equipped with wireless radio (p. 123).

Amateur Radio Shutdown
The navy closes down all amateur radio operations in 1917 to ensure military security as the United States enters World War I (p. 124).

an electric generator to the microwave oven in the kitchen—and, of course, the radio—operates according to his fundamental equations. As Newton revolutionized mechanical science in the seventeenth century, so Maxwell revolutionized electrical science in the nineteenth."[3]

It was German physicist Heinrich Hertz, however, who in the 1880s proved Maxwell's theories. Hertz created a crude device that permitted an electrical spark to leap across a small gap between two steel balls. As the electricity jumped the gap, it emitted electromagnetic waves and marked the first recorded transmission and reception of a radio wave. Hertz's experiments profoundly influenced two inventor-entrepreneurs, Guglielmo Marconi and Lee De Forest, who in the late 1800s began marketing wireless communication systems for businesses.

Marconi Invents Wireless Telegraphy

In 1894, Guglielmo Marconi, a twenty-year-old, self-educated Italian engineer, read Hertz's work and set about trying to make wireless technology practical. Marconi understood that developing a way to send high-speed messages over great distances would transform communication, the military, and commercial shipping. Although revolutionary, the telephone and the telegraph were limited by their wires.

Marconi improved on Hertz in a number of important ways. First, he attached the spark-gap transmitter to a Morse telegraph key, which could send out dot-dash signals. The electrical impulses traveled into a Morse inker, the machine that telegraph operators used to record the dots and dashes onto narrow strips of paper. Second, Marconi discovered that grounding—connecting the transmitter and receiver to the earth—greatly increased the distance over which he could send signals.

The Italian government, not understanding what Marconi had accomplished, refused to patent his invention. Thus in 1896 he left for England, where he finally received a patent on **wireless telegraphy**, a form of voiceless point-to-point communication. In London, in 1897, he formed the Marconi Wireless Telegraph Company, later known as British Marconi, and began installing wireless technology on British naval and private commercial ships. In 1899, he opened a branch in the United States, establishing a company nicknamed American Marconi. That same year, he sent the first wireless Morse code signal across the English Channel to France, and in 1901 he relayed the first wireless signal across the Atlantic Ocean.

> **❝** The telegraph and the telephone were instruments for private communication between two individuals. The radio was democratic; it directed its message to the masses and allowed one person to communicate with many.
>
> The new medium of radio was to the printing press what the telephone had been to the letter: it allowed immediacy. It enabled listeners to experience an event as it happened. **❞**
>
> –Tom Lewis,
> *Empire of the Air,* 1991

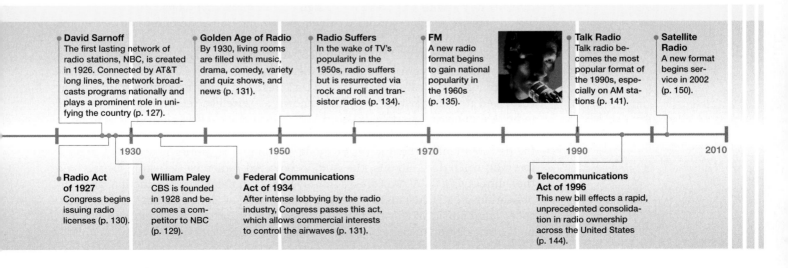

David Sarnoff
The first lasting network of radio stations, NBC, is created in 1926. Connected by AT&T long lines, the network broadcasts programs nationally and plays a prominent role in unifying the country (p. 127).

Golden Age of Radio
By 1930, living rooms are filled with music, drama, comedy, variety and quiz shows, and news (p. 131).

Radio Suffers
In the wake of TV's popularity in the 1950s, radio suffers but is resurrected via rock and roll and transistor radios (p. 134).

FM
A new radio format begins to gain national popularity in the 1960s (p. 135).

Talk Radio
Talk radio becomes the most popular format of the 1990s, especially on AM stations (p. 141).

Satellite Radio
A new format begins service in 2002 (p. 150).

1930   1950   1970   1990   2010

Radio Act of 1927
Congress begins issuing radio licenses (p. 130).

William Paley
CBS is founded in 1928 and becomes a competitor to NBC (p. 129).

Federal Communications Act of 1934
After intense lobbying by the radio industry, Congress passes this act, which allows commercial interests to control the airwaves (p. 131).

Telecommunications Act of 1996
This new bill effects a rapid, unprecedented consolidation in radio ownership across the United States (p. 144).

● Italian wireless pioneer Guglielmo Marconi (1897–1937) was a major figure in developing radio. In 1901 he transmitted the first radio signal across the Atlantic Ocean—from England to Newfoundland. Marconi shared the 1909 Nobel Prize for Physics for his contributions to wireless telegraphy, soon required on all seagoing ships and credited with saving more than seven hundred lives when the *Titanic* sank in 1912.

Although Marconi was a successful innovator and entrepreneur, his vision was limited. He saw wireless telegraphy only as point-to-point communication, much like the telegraph and the telephone, and not as a one-to-many mass medium. He also confined his applications to military and commercial ships. In limiting his patents to Morse-code transmission, Marconi left others to explore the wireless transmission of voice and music.

De Forest Invents Wireless Telephony

> **❝ I discovered an Invisible Empire of the Air, intangible, yet solid as granite. ❞**
>
> –Lee De Forest, inventor

In 1899, inventor Lee De Forest (who subsequently liked to call himself "the father of radio") wrote the first Ph.D. dissertation on wireless technology. Understanding the extent and influence of Marconi's innovations, De Forest decided that he could ensure his future livelihood and place in history by going beyond Marconi. In 1901, De Forest challenged the Italian inventor, who had contracted with the Associated Press to cover New York's International Yacht Races. De Forest signed up to report the races for a rival news service. The two rivals' transmitters jammed each other's signals so badly, however, that officials ended up relaying information on the races the premodern way—with flags and hand signals. The event symbolized a problem that would persist throughout radio's early development: noise and interference from too much competition for a finite supply of radio waves.

In 1902, De Forest set up the Wireless Telephone Company to compete head-on with American Marconi, by then the leader in the field of wireless communication. A major difference between Marconi and De Forest was the latter's interest in wireless voice and music transmissions, later known as **wireless telephony** and, then, as radio. Although occasionally accused of stealing others' ideas, De Forest went on to patent more than three hundred inventions. De Forest's biggest breakthrough was the development of the Audion, or triode, vacuum tube. Until the arrival of transistors and solid-state circuits, the Audion powered radios by detecting signals and then amplifying them. De Forest's improvements in detection, conduction, and amplification greatly increased listeners' ability to hear dots and dashes and, later, speech and music on a receiver set. His modifications were essential to the development of voice transmission, long-distance radio, and television. In fact, many historians consider De Forest's improvements to the vacuum tube the beginning of modern electronics.

The credit for the first voice broadcast belongs to Canadian engineer Reginald Fessenden, formerly a chief chemist for Thomas Edison. Fessenden went to work for the U.S. Navy and eventually for General Electric (GE), where he played a central role in improving wireless signals. Both the navy and GE, however, were interested in the potential for voice transmissions that did not require Morse code. On Christmas Eve in 1906, after GE had built Fessenden a powerful transmitter, he gave his first public demonstration, sending a voice through the airwaves from his station at Brant Rock, Massachusetts. A radio historian describes what happened:

> That night, ship operators and amateurs around Brant Rock heard the results: "someone speaking! . . . a woman's voice rose in song. . . . Next someone was heard reading a poem." Fessenden himself played "O Holy Night" on his violin. Though the fidelity was not all that it might be, listeners were captivated by the voices and notes they heard. No more would sounds be restricted to mere dots and dashes of the Morse code.[4]

Ship operators, who had not seen the publicity announcing Fessenden's broadcast, were astonished to hear voices rather than the familiar Morse code. (Some operators actually thought they were having a supernatural encounter.) The wireless medium was quickly moving from its use as a point-to-point communication tool (wireless operator to wireless operator) toward a one-to-many communication tool. As a medium for mass communication, radio broadcasts offered the possibility of sending voice and music to thousands of people. **Broadcasting**, once an agricultural term that referred to the process of casting seeds over a large area, would come to mean the transmission of radio waves (and, later, TV signals) to a broad public audience. Prior to radio broadcasting, wireless was considered a form of **narrowcasting**, or person-to-person communication, like the telegraph and telephone.

In 1907, De Forest followed Fessenden's first broadcast by sending radio voices and music—actually, a performance by Metropolitan Opera tenor Enrico Caruso—to his friends in New York. The next year, De Forest and his wife, Nora, played records into a microphone from atop the Eiffel Tower in Paris. The signals were picked up four hundred miles away. Radio had passed from an inventor's toy to a business venture and was now poised to explode as a mass medium.

Regulating a New Medium

The two most important international issues affecting radio in the 1900s were ship radio requirements and signal interference. Congress passed the Wireless Ship Act in 1910, which required that all major U.S. seagoing ships carrying more than fifty passengers and traveling more than two hundred miles off the coast be equipped with wireless equipment with a one-hundred-mile range. The importance of this act was underscored by the *Titanic* disaster two years later. A brand-new British luxury steamer, the *Titanic* sank in 1912. Although fifteen hundred people died in the tragedy, wireless reports played a critical role in pinpointing the *Titanic*'s location, enabling rescue ships to save seven hundred lives.

● Inventor Lee De Forest (1873–1961) continued working in his Los Angeles workshop well into the 1950s. His lengthy radio career was marked by incredible innovations, missed opportunities, and poor business practices. In the end, De Forest was upset that radio content had stooped, in his opinion, to such low standards. With a passion for opera, he had hoped radio would be a tool for elite culture. If De Forest were alive today, what might be his reaction to the state of modern radio?

St. Louis Post-Dispatch — HOME EDITION

1302 LIVES LOST WHEN "TITANIC" SANK; 868 SAVED

Carpathia Steaming to New York With Survivors; None on Other Ships

2-THIRDS WOMEN IN PARTIAL LIST OF THOSE RESCUED

7 ST. LOUISANS ARE REPORTED SAFE ON BOARD CARPATHIA

● Despite the headline in the *St. Louis Post-Dispatch*, actually 1,523 people died and only 705 were rescued when the *Titanic* hit an iceberg on April 14, 1912 (the ship technically sank at 2:20 A.M. on April 15). The crew of the *Titanic* used the Marconi Wireless equipment on board to send distress signals to other ships. Of the eight ships nearby, the *Carpathia* was the first to respond with lifeboats.

In the wake of the *Titanic* tragedy, Congress also passed the **Radio Act of 1912**, which addressed the problem of amateur radio operators increasingly cramming the airwaves. A short policy guide, this first Radio Act required all wireless stations to obtain radio licenses from the Commerce Department. Because radio waves crossed state and national borders, legislators determined that broadcasting constituted a "natural resource"—a kind of interstate commerce. With this act, America also formally adopted the SOS Morse-code distress signal that other countries had been using for several years. The Radio Act of 1912 governed radio's development and regulated the new medium until 1927.

The Deals That Made Radio an American Medium

By 1915, more than twenty American companies sold point-to-point communication systems, primarily for use in ship-to-shore communication. Having established a reputation for efficiency and honesty, American Marconi, the U.S. subsidiary of British Marconi, was the biggest and best of these companies. But in 1914, with World War I beginning in Europe and with America warily watching the conflict, the U.S. Navy questioned the wisdom of allowing a foreign-controlled company to wield so much power. American corporations in competition with Marconi, especially General Electric and AT&T, capitalized on the navy's xenophobia and succeeded in undercutting Marconi's influence.

Wireless telegraphy played an increasingly large role in military operations as the navy sought tight controls on information. When the United States entered the war in 1917, the navy closed down all amateur radio operations and took control of key radio transmitters to ensure military security. As the war was nearing its end in 1919, British Marconi placed an order with GE for twenty-four potent new alternators, which were strong enough to power a transoceanic system of radio stations that could connect the world. But the U.S. Navy, influenced by Franklin Roosevelt, at that time the navy's assistant secretary, grew concerned and moved to ensure that such powerful new radio technology would not fall under foreign control. Roosevelt was guided by President Woodrow Wilson's goal of developing the United States as an international power, a position greatly enhanced by American military successes during the war. Wilson and the navy saw an opportunity to slow Britain's influence over communication and to promote a U.S. plan for the control of the emerging wireless operations. Thus corporate heads and government leaders conspired to make sure radio communication would serve American interests.

Some members of Congress and the corporate community opposed federal legislation that would grant the government or the navy a radio monopoly. Consequently, General Electric developed a compromise plan that would create a private sector monopoly. First, GE broke off negotiations to sell key radio technologies to European-owned companies like British Marconi, thereby limiting those companies' global reach. Second, GE took the lead in founding a new company, **Radio Corporation of America (RCA)**, which soon acquired the holdings of American Marconi and radio patents of other U.S. companies. By the end of 1919, RCA had pooled the necessary technology and patents to monopolize the wireless industry and expand American communication technology throughout the world.[5]

Under RCA's patents pool arrangement, wireless patents from the navy, AT&T, GE, the former American Marconi, and other companies were combined to ensure U.S. control over the manufacture of transmitters and receivers. Initially AT&T man-

ufactured most transmitters, while GE (and later Westinghouse) made radio receivers. RCA administered the pool, collecting and distributing patent royalties to pool members. To protect individual profits from existing patents, the government did not permit RCA to manufacture equipment or to operate radio stations under its own name for several years. Instead, RCA's initial function was to ensure that radio parts were standardized by manufacturers and to control frequency interference by amateur radio operators, which became an increasing problem after the war.

At this time, the control of patents, amateur radio operators, and foreign radio competitors was among RCA's major concerns. A government restriction mandated that no more than 20 percent of RCA—and eventually any U.S. broadcasting facility—could be owned by foreigners. This restriction, later raised to 25 percent, became law in 1934 and applied to all U.S. broadcasting stocks and facilities. Because of this rule, in 1985 Rupert Murdoch, the head of Australia's giant News Corporation, became a U.S. citizen so that he could buy a number of TV stations as well as form the Fox television network.

RCA's most significant impact was that it gave the United States almost total control over the emerging mass medium of broadcasting, which had not been anticipated by most wireless companies. At the time, the United States was the only country that placed broadcasting under the care of commercial, rather than military or government, interests. By pooling more than two thousand patents and sharing research developments, RCA ensured the global dominance of the United States in mass communication, a position it maintained in electronic hardware into the 1960s and maintains in program content today.

The Evolution of Commercial Radio

When Westinghouse engineer Frank Conrad set up a crude radio studio above his Pittsburgh garage in 1916, placing a microphone in front of a phonograph to broadcast music and news to his friends (whom Conrad supplied with receivers) two evenings a week on experimental station 8XK, he unofficially became one of the medium's first disc jockeys. In 1920, a Westinghouse executive who had become intrigued by Conrad's curious hobby realized the potential of radio as a mass medium, and a new opportunity to sell radio receivers to the general public. Westinghouse then established station KDKA, which is generally regarded as the first commercial broadcast station. KDKA is most noted for airing national returns from the Cox-Harding presidential election on November 2, 1920, an event most historians consider the first professional broadcast. Other amateur broadcasters could also lay claim to being first. One of the earliest stations, operated by Charles "Doc" Herrold in San Jose, California, began in 1909 and later became KCBS. Additional experimental stations—in places like New York; Detroit; Medford, Massachusetts; and Pierre, South Dakota—broadcast voice and music prior to the establishment of KDKA. But KDKA's success, with the financial backing of Westinghouse, signaled the transformation of the age of point-to-point wireless into the age of broadcast radio.

In 1921, the U.S. Commerce Department officially licensed five radio stations for operation; by early 1923, more than six hundred commercial and noncommercial stations were operating. Some stations were owned by AT&T, GE, and Westinghouse, but many were run by amateurs or were independently owned by universities or businesses. Later, the government permitted RCA to acquire its own stations. By the end of 1923, as many as 550,000 radio receivers, most manufactured by GE and Westinghouse, had been sold for about $55 each. Just as the "guts" of the phonograph had been put inside a piece of furniture to create a consumer product, the vacuum tubes, electrical posts, and bulky batteries that made up the radio receiver were placed inside stylish furniture and marketed to households. By 1925, 5.5 million radio sets were in use across America, and radio was a mass medium.

The RCA Partnership Unravels

In 1922, in a major power grab, AT&T, which already had a government-sanctioned monopoly in the telephone business, decided to break its RCA agreements in an attempt to monopolize radio as well. Identifying the new medium as the "wireless telephone," AT&T argued that broadcasting was merely an extension of its control over the telephone. Ultimately, the corporate giant complained that RCA had gained too much monopoly power. In violation of its early agreements with RCA, AT&T began making and selling its own radio receivers.

In the same year, AT&T started WEAF (now WNBC) in New York, the first radio station to regularly sell commercial time to advertisers. AT&T claimed that under the RCA agreements, it had the exclusive right to sell ads, which AT&T called *toll broadcasting*. Most people in radio at the time recoiled at the idea of using the medium for crass advertising, viewing it instead as a public information service. In fact, stations that had earlier tried to sell ads received "cease and desist" letters from the Department of Commerce. But by August 1922, AT&T had nonetheless sold its first ad to a New York real estate developer for $50. The idea of promoting the new medium as a public service, along the lines of today's noncommercial National Public Radio (NPR), ended when executives realized that radio ads offered another opportunity for profits. Advertising would in fact ensure profits long after radio-set sales had saturated the consumer market.

> **❝ I believe the quickest way to kill broadcasting would be to use it for direct advertising. ❞**
>
> —Herbert Hoover,
> Secretary of Commerce,
> 1924

The initial strategy behind AT&T's toll broadcasting idea, however, was its effort to conquer radio. By its agreements with RCA, AT&T retained the rights to interconnect the signals between two or more radio stations via telephone wires. In 1923, when AT&T aired a program simultaneously on its flagship WEAF station and on WNAC in Boston, the phone company created the first **network**: a cost-saving operation that links, through special phone lines (and, later, satellite relays), a group of broadcast stations that share programming produced at a central location. By the end of 1924, AT&T had interconnected twenty-two stations in order to air a talk by President Calvin Coolidge. Some of these stations were owned by AT&T, but most simply consented to become AT&T "affiliates," agreeing to air the phone company's programs. These network stations informally became known as the *telephone group* and later as the Broadcasting Corporation of America (BCA).

● Westinghouse engineer Frank Conrad, broadcasting from his garage. His hobby evolved into Pittsburgh's KDKA, one of the first radio stations. Although this early station is widely celebrated in history books as the first broadcasting outlet, one can't underestimate the influence Westinghouse had in promoting this "historical first." Westinghouse clearly saw the celebration of Conrad's garage as a way to market the company and its radio equipment. The resulting legacy of Conrad's garage has thus overshadowed other individuals who also experimented with radio broadcasting.

In response, GE, Westinghouse, and RCA interconnected a smaller set of competing stations, known as the *radio group*. Initially, their network linked WGY in Schenectady, New York (then GE's national headquarters), and WJZ in Manhattan. The radio group had to use inferior Western Union telegraph lines when AT&T denied them access to telephone wires. By this time, AT&T had sold its stock in RCA and refused to lease its lines to competing radio networks. The telephone monopoly was now enmeshed in a battle to defeat RCA for control of radio. This, among other problems, eventually led to a government investigation and an arbitration settlement in 1925. In the agreement, the Justice Department, irritated by AT&T's power grab, redefined patent agreements. AT&T received a monopoly on providing the wires, known as *long lines*, to interconnect stations nationwide. In exchange, AT&T sold its BCA network to RCA for $1 million and agreed not to reenter broadcasting for eight years (a banishment that actually extended into the mid-1990s).

Sarnoff and NBC: Building the "Blue" and "Red" Networks

After Lee De Forest, David Sarnoff was among the first to envision the wireless as a modern mass medium. From the time he served as Marconi's fifteen-year-old personal messenger, Sarnoff rose rapidly at American Marconi. He became a wireless operator, helping to relay information about the *Titanic* survivors in 1912. Promoted to a series of management positions, Sarnoff was closely involved in RCA's creation in 1919, when most radio executives saw wireless merely as point-to-point communication. But with Sarnoff as RCA's first commercial manager, radio's potential as a mass medium was quickly realized. In 1921, at age thirty, Sarnoff became RCA's general manager.

After RCA bought AT&T's telephone group network, Sarnoff created a new subsidiary in September 1926 called the National Broadcasting Company (NBC). Its ownership was shared by RCA (50 percent), General Electric (30 percent), and Westinghouse (20 percent). This loose network of stations would be hooked together by AT&T long lines. Shortly thereafter, the original telephone group became known as the NBC-Red network, and the radio group became the NBC-Blue network.

Although NBC owned a number of stations by the late 1920s, many independent stations also began affiliating with the NBC networks to receive programming. An

"I have in mind a plan of development which would make radio a 'household utility' in the same sense as the piano or phonograph. The idea is to bring music into the house by wireless."

—David Sarnoff, age 24, 1915 memo

● A young David Sarnoff, who had taught himself Morse code and learned as much as possible in Marconi's experimental shop in New York, was given a job as wireless operator for the station on Nantucket Island. He went on to create NBC and network radio. Sarnoff's calculated ambition in the radio industry can easily be compared to Bill Gates's drive to control the computer software and Internet industries.

affiliate station, though independently owned, signs a contract to be part of a network and receives money to carry the network's programs. In exchange, the network reserves time slots, which it sells to national advertisers. By 1933, NBC-Red had twenty-eight affiliates; NBC-Blue had twenty-four.

Recall that the rationale behind a network is an economic one: A network enables stations to control program costs and avoid unnecessary duplication. As early as 1923, AT&T had realized that it would be cheaper to produce programs at one station and broadcast them simultaneously over a network of owned or affiliated stations than for each station to generate its own programs. Such a network centralized costs and programming by bringing the best musical, dramatic, and comedic talent to one place, where programs could be produced and then distributed all over the country.

In fact, network radio may have helped modernize America by de-emphasizing the local and the regional in favor of national programs broadcast to nearly everyone. For example, when Charles Lindbergh returned from the first solo transatlantic flight in 1927, an estimated twenty-five to thirty million people listened to his welcome-home party on the six million radio sets then in use. At the time, it was the largest shared audience experience in the history of any mass medium.

David Sarnoff's leadership at RCA was capped by two other negotiations that solidified his stature as the driving force behind radio's development as a modern medium. In 1929, Sarnoff cut a deal with General Motors for the manufacture of car radios, which had been invented a year earlier by William Lear (later the designer of the Learjet), who sold the radios under the name Motorola. Sarnoff also merged RCA with the Victor Talking Machine Company. Afterward, until the mid-1960s, the company was known as RCA Victor, adopting as its corporate symbol the famous terrier sitting alertly next to a Victrola radio-phonograph. The merger gave RCA control over Victor's records and recording equipment, making the radio company a major player in the sound recording industry. In 1930, David Sarnoff became president of RCA. He ran the company for the next forty years.

Government Scrutiny Ends RCA's Monopoly

As early as 1923, the Federal Trade Commission had charged RCA with violations of antitrust laws but allowed the monopoly to continue. By the late 1920s, the government, concerned about NBC's growing control over radio content, intensified its scrutiny. Then, in 1930, when RCA bought out the GE and Westinghouse interests in the two NBC networks, federal marshals charged RCA/NBC with a number of violations, including exercising too much control over manufacturing and programming. Although the government had originally sanctioned a closely supervised monopoly for wireless communication, RCA products, its networks, and the growth of the new mass medium dramatically changed the radio industry by the late 1920s. After the collapse of the stock market in 1929, the public became increasingly distrustful of big business. In 1932, the government revoked RCA's monopoly status.

RCA acted quickly. To eliminate its monopolizing partnerships, Sarnoff's company bought out GE's and Westinghouse's remaining shares in RCA's manufacturing business. Now RCA would compete directly against GE, Westinghouse, and other radio manufacturers, encouraging more competition in the radio manufacturing industry. Ironically, in the mid-1980s, General Electric bought back RCA, a shell of its former self and no longer competitive with foreign electronics firms. GE was chiefly interested in RCA's brand-name status and its still-lucrative subsidiary, NBC.

Paley and CBS: Challenging NBC

Even with RCA's head start and its favored status, the company's two NBC networks faced competitors in the late 1920s. The competitors all found it tough going. One group, United Independent Broadcasters (UIB), even lined up twelve prospective affiliates and offered them $500 a week for access to ten hours of station time in exchange for quality programs. UIB was cash-poor, however, and AT&T would not rent the new company line services to link the affiliates. Enter the Columbia Phonograph Company, which was looking for a way to preempt RCA's merger with the Victor Company, then Columbia's major competitor. With backing from the record company, UIB and the new Columbia Phonograph Broadcasting System launched a wobbly sixteen-affiliate network in 1927, nicknamed CPBS. But after losing $100,000 in the first month, the record company pulled out. Later, CPBS dropped the word *phonograph* from the title, creating the Columbia Broadcasting System (CBS).

In 1928, William Paley, the twenty-seven-year-old son of Sam Paley, owner of a Philadelphia cigar company, bought a controlling interest in CBS to sponsor the cigar manufacturer's La Palina brand. One of Paley's first moves was to hire the public relations pioneer Edward Bernays, Sigmund Freud's nephew, to polish the new network's image. Paley and Bernays modified a concept called **option time**, in which CBS paid affiliate stations $50 per hour for an option on any portion of their time. The network provided programs to them and sold ad space or sponsorships to various product companies. In theory, CBS could now control up to twenty-four hours a day of its affiliates' radio time. Some affiliates received thousands of dollars per

● William S. Paley (*top*) ran CBS for more than fifty years. He first took control of the struggling radio network in 1928 and saw CBS through its transition into TV and helped earn CBS the label "Tiffany Network" for his early support of quality programming and network news. But he was also criticized for undermining his news division to sidestep controversy or to increase profits. In the 2005 film *Good Night, and Good Luck* (*bottom*, with director George Clooney) Paley, played by Frank Langella, is portrayed as unsupportive of CBS newsman Edward R. Murrow, who took on Wisconsin Senator and communist witch hunter Joseph McCarthy in the 1950s CBS program *See It Now*, which Paley eventually canceled.

week merely to serve as conduits for CBS programs and ads. Because NBC was still charging some of its affiliates as much as $96 a week to carry network programs, the CBS offer was extremely appealing.

By 1933, Paley's efforts had netted CBS more than ninety affiliates, many of them defecting from NBC. Paley also concentrated on developing news programs and entertainment shows, particularly soap operas and comedy-variety series. In the process, CBS successfully raided NBC, not just for affiliates but for top talent as well. Throughout the 1930s and 1940s, Paley lured a number of radio stars from NBC, including Jack Benny, Frank Sinatra, George Burns and Gracie Allen, and Groucho Marx. During World War II, Edward R. Murrow's powerful firsthand news reports from bomb-riddled London established CBS as the premier radio news network, a reputation it carried forward to television. In 1949, near the end of big-time network radio, CBS finally surpassed NBC as the highest-rated network. Although William Paley had intended to run CBS only for six months to help get it off the ground, he ultimately ran it for more than fifty years.

A Cooperative Network: The Mutual Broadcasting System

While the major networks were building their dynasties during the 1930s, many stations were content to produce their own regional and local programs. In 1934, four powerful independent stations — WGN in Chicago, WOR in Newark, WLW in Cincinnati, and WXYZ in Detroit — formed the Mutual Broadcasting System as a venue for promoting the radio program *The Lone Ranger*. Sharing programs and functioning as a cooperative venture, not as a regular network, three stations operated 50,000-watt "clear channels" that reached most of North America. Among the first AM stations established in the United States, clear channels claimed the most powerful AM signals. Other stations operating on the same channels were required to reduce their signal power at night, allowing clear channel stations to broadcast with minimal interference across hundreds of miles, giving them huge potential audiences.

Mutual offered a small central news service and a few entertainment programs. It mostly served smaller stations, often in remote areas that were ignored by NBC and CBS. In 1968, Mutual became the first network to offer a news service, the Mutual Black Network, that raised issues of interest to black listeners. Westwood One, the nation's largest radio network, acquired Mutual in 1985, operating it as a separate program service through the 1990s, although Mutual was just a brand name (like RCA). Westwood One also acquired NBC's network radio operations in 1987 and stopped using the Mutual and NBC name in favor of CNN Radio in 1999. By 2006, CBS Radio was managing Westwood One's radio networks.

Bringing Order to Chaos with the Radio Act of 1927

In the 1920s, as radio moved from narrowcasting to broadcasting, the battle for more frequency space and less channel interference intensified. Manufacturers, engineers, station operators, network executives, and the listening public demanded action. Many wanted more sweeping regulation than the simple licensing function granted under the Radio Act of 1912, which gave the Commerce Department little power to deny a license or to unclog the airwaves.

Beginning in 1924, Commerce Secretary Herbert Hoover ordered radio stations to share time and to set aside certain frequencies for entertainment and news and others for farm and weather reports. To challenge Hoover, a station in Chicago jammed the airwaves, intentionally moving its signal onto an unauthorized frequency. In 1926, the courts decided that based

> **"** Overnight, it seemed, everyone had gone into broadcasting: newspapers, banks, public utilities, department stores, universities and colleges, cities and towns, pharmacies, creameries, and hospitals.**"**
>
> —Tom Lewis, radio historian

on the existing Radio Act, Hoover had the power only to grant licenses, not to restrict stations from operating. Within the year, two hundred new stations clogged the airwaves, creating a chaotic period in which nearly all radios had poor reception. By early 1927, sales of radio sets had declined sharply.

To restore order to the airwaves, Congress passed the **Radio Act of 1927**, the precursor to the **Federal Communications Act of 1934**. The 1927 act stated that licensees did not *own* their channels but could license them as long as they operated to serve the "public interest, convenience, or necessity." To oversee licenses and negotiate channel problems, the 1927 act created the **Federal Radio Commission (FRC)**, whose members were appointed by the president. Although the FRC was intended as a temporary committee, it grew into a powerful regulatory agency. In 1934, with passage of the Federal Communications Act, the FRC became the **Federal Communications Commission (FCC)**. Its jurisdiction covered not only radio but also the telephone and the telegraph (and later television, cable, and the Internet).

In 1941, an activist FCC went after the networks. Declaring that NBC and CBS could no longer force affiliates to carry programs they did not want, the government outlawed the practice of option time that Paley had used to build CBS into a major network. The FCC also demanded that RCA sell one of its two NBC networks. RCA and NBC claimed that the rulings would bankrupt them. The Supreme Court sided with the FCC, however, and RCA eventually sold NBC-Blue to a group of businessmen for $8 million in the mid-1940s. It became the American Broadcasting Company (ABC). These government crackdowns brought long-overdue reform to the radio industry. But they had not come soon enough to prevent considerable damage to noncommercial radio.

> 66 It is my personal opinion that American listeners would not stand for the payment of a receiving-set tax. It is my judgment that it would be most unpopular in this country. It is not the American way of accomplishing things. 99
>
> –Anning S. Prall, chairman of the FCC, 1936

The Golden Age of Radio

Many ingredients in television today were initially formulated for radio. The term *veejay*, or *video jockey*, used on cable's MTV and VH1, derives from *deejay*, or *disc jockey*, a term first used in 1941 to describe someone who played recorded music on radio programs. In addition, the first weather forecasts and farm reports on radio began in the 1920s. Regularly scheduled radio news analysis started in 1927, with H. V. Kaltenborn, a reporter for the *Brooklyn Eagle*, providing commentary on AT&T's WEAF. The first regular *network* news analysis began on CBS in 1930, featuring Lowell Thomas, who would remain on radio for forty-four years. Thomas's first report began, "Adolf Hitler, the German fascist chief, is snorting fire. There are now two Mussolinis in the world, which seems to offer a rousing time."[6]

Radio in this golden age was not the portable medium it would later become, however. Prior to transistors and solid-state integrated circuits, most radio sets required large glass tubes housed in heavy wooden pieces of furniture. Like television today, the radio commanded a central position in most American living rooms in the 1930s and 1940s. At the time, only a handful of stations operated in most large radio markets, and popular stations were affiliated with either CBS or one of the two NBC networks. Many large stations employed their own in-house orchestras and aired live music daily. Listeners had favorite evening programs, usually fifteen minutes long, which they would tune in each night. Families gathered around the radio to hear such shows as *Amos 'n' Andy*, *The Shadow*, *The Lone Ranger*, *The Green Hornet*, and *Fibber McGee and Molly*, or one of President Franklin Roosevelt's fireside chats.

Among the most popular early forms on radio, the *variety show* was the forerunner to such popular TV shows as the *Ed Sullivan Show*. The variety show, developed

● This giant bank of radio network microphones makes us wonder today how President Franklin D. Roosevelt managed to project such an intimate and re-assuring tone in his famous fireside chats. Conceived originally to promote FDR's New Deal policies amid the Great Depression, these chats were delivered be-tween 1933 and 1944 and touched on national topics. Roosevelt was the first president to effectively use broadcasting to communi-cate with citizens; he also gave nearly a thousand press conferences during his twelve-plus years as president, revealing a strong commitment to use media and news to speak early and often with the American people.

> ❝ There are three things which I shall never forget about America — the Rocky Mountains, Niagara Falls, and *Amos 'n' Andy.* ❞
>
> —George Bernard Shaw,
> Irish playwright

from stage acts and vaudeville, began with the *Eveready Hour* in 1923 on WEAF. Con-sidered experimental, the program presented classical music, minstrel shows, com-edy sketches, and dramatic readings. Stars from vaudeville, musical comedy, and New York theater and opera would occasionally make guest appearances.

By the 1930s, studio-audience *quiz shows—Professor Quiz* and the *Old Time Spelling Bee*—had emerged. Other quiz formats, used on *Information Please* and *Quiz Kids,* featured guest panelists. The quiz formats were later copied by television, par-ticularly in the 1950s. *Truth or Consequences,* based on a nineteenth-century parlor game, began in 1940 and featured guests performing goofy stunts. It ran for seven-teen years on radio and another twenty-seven on television, influencing TV stunt shows like CBS's *Beat the Clock* in the 1950s and NBC's *Fear Factor* in the early 2000s.

Dramatic programs, mostly radio plays that were broad-cast live from theaters, developed as early as 1922. Historians mark the appearance of *Clara, Lu, and Em* on WGN in 1931 as the first *soap opera.* One year later, Colgate-Palmolive bought the program, put it on NBC, and began selling the soap prod-ucts that gave this dramatic genre its distinctive nickname. Early "soaps" were fifteen minutes in length and ran five or six days a week. It wasn't until mid-1960s television that soaps were extended to thirty minutes, and by the late 1970s some had expanded to sixty minutes. Still a fixture on CBS, *Guiding Light* actually began on radio in 1937 and moved to television in 1952 (the only radio soap to suc-cessfully make the transition). By 1940, sixty different soap operas occupied nearly eighty hours of network radio time each week.

The *situation comedy,* a major staple of TV programming today, also began on radio in the mid-1920s. By the early 1930s, the most popular comedy was *Amos 'n'*

Andy, which started on Chicago radio in 1925 before moving to NBC-Blue in 1929. By today's standards, *Amos 'n' Andy* can be described as a nineteenth-century minstrel show that often stereotyped black characters as shiftless and stupid. Created as a blackface stage act by two white comedians, Charles Correll and Freeman Gosden, the program was criticized as racist. But NBC and the program's producers claimed that *Amos 'n' Andy* was as popular among black audiences as among white listeners.

A pioneering program in many ways, *Amos 'n' Andy* launched the idea of the *serial show*: a program that featured continuing story lines from one day to the next. The format was soon copied by soap operas and other radio dramas. *Amos 'n' Andy* aired six nights a week from 7:00 to 7:15 P.M. During the show's first year on the network, radio-set sales rose nearly 25 percent nationally. To keep people coming to restaurants and movie theaters, owners broadcast *Amos 'n' Andy* in lobbies, rest rooms, and entryways. Early radio research estimated that the program aired in more than half of all radio homes in the nation during the 1930–31 season, making it the most popular radio series in history. From 1951 to 1953, it made a brief transition to television (Correll and Gosden sold the rights to CBS for $1 million), becoming the first TV series to have an entirely black cast.

While *Amos 'n' Andy* was the most popular series, the most famous single broadcast featured an adaptation of H. G. Wells's *War of the Worlds* on the radio series *Mercury Theater of the Air*. Orson Welles produced, hosted, and acted in this popular series, which adapted science fiction, mystery, and historical adventure dramas for radio. On Halloween eve in 1938, the twenty-three-year-old Welles aired the 1898 Martian invasion novel in the style of a radio news program. For people who missed the opening disclaimer, the program sounded like a real news report, with eyewitness accounts of pitched battles between Martian invaders and the U.S. Army.

The program created a panic that lasted several hours. In New Jersey, some people walked through the streets with wet towels around their heads for protection from deadly Martian heat rays. In New York, young men reported to their National Guard headquarters to prepare for battle. Across the nation, calls jammed police

● On Halloween eve in 1938, Orson Welles's radio dramatization of *War of the Worlds* (*inset*) created a panic up and down the East Coast, especially in Grover's Mill, New Jersey — the setting for the fictional Martian invasion that many listeners assumed was real. Above, a seventy-six-year-old Grover's Mill resident guards a warehouse against alien invaders.

● Aviator Amelia Earhart was one of a number of people to speak via radio with explorer Richard Byrd and his expedition team as they explored the Antarctic in 1929. These conversations were broadcast to the American public every two weeks. The Byrd expedition (1928–30) brought the novelty of advanced radio systems to a captivated home audience.

switchboards. Afterward, Orson Welles, once the radio voice of *The Shadow*, used the notoriety of this broadcast to launch a film career. Meanwhile, the FCC called for stricter warnings both before and during programs that imitated the style of radio news.

Most programs in those days had a single sponsor that created and produced each show. The networks distributed these programs live around the country, charging the sponsors advertising fees. Many shows—the *Palmolive Hour*, *General Motors Family Party*, the *Lucky Strike Orchestra*, and the *Eveready Hour* among them—were named after the sole sponsor's product.

Radio Reinvents Itself

The history of American mass media reveals that older media forms do not disappear when confronted by newer forms. Instead, mass media adapt. Although radio threatened sound recording in the 1920s and television threatened radio in the 1950s, both older forms adjusted to the economic and social challenges posed by the arrival of a newer medium. Remarkably, the arrival of television in the 1950s marked the only time in media history in which a new medium virtually stole every national programming and advertising strategy from the older medium. Television snatched radio's advertisers, its program genres, its major celebrities, and its large evening audiences. In the process, the TV set physically displaced the radio as the living room centerpiece across America.

New Technologies Bring Portability and Clarity to Radio

The story of radio's evolution and survival provides a fascinating look at the impact of one medium on another. This history is especially important today, as newspapers and magazines appear online and as publishers produce books on tape and e-books for new generations of "readers." In contemporary culture, we have grown accustomed to such media convergence as the norm. To understand this blurring of the boundaries between media forms, it is useful to look at the 1950s and the ways in which radio responded to the advent of television.

The Transistor: A Revolution of Small Proportions

A key development in radio's adaptation occurred with the invention of the transistor by Bell Laboratories in 1947. **Transistors**, like De Forest's vacuum tubes, were small electrical devices that could receive and amplify radio signals. They used less power and heat than vacuum tubes, and they were more durable and less expensive. Best of all, they were tiny. Transistors, which also revolutionized hearing aids, represented the first step in replacing bulky and delicate tubes, leading eventually to today's silicon-chip integrated circuits. Texas Instruments marketed the first transistor radios in 1953, at about $40 apiece. Using even smaller transistors, Sony introduced the pocket radio in 1957. But it wasn't until the 1960s that transistor radios became cheaper than conventional tube and battery radios. For a while, the term *transistor* became a synonym for a small, portable radio.

The development of transistors let radio go where television could not—to the beach, to the office, into bedrooms and bathrooms, and into nearly all new cars. (Before the transistor, car radios were a luxury item.) By the 1960s, most radio listening took place outside the home. For economic reasons, radio turned to the recording industry for content to replace the shows it had lost to television.

Edwin Armstrong's FM Revolution

By the time the broadcast industry launched commercial television in the 1950s, many people, including David Sarnoff of RCA, were predicting radio's demise. To fund television's development and protect his radio holdings, Sarnoff had even delayed a dramatic breakthrough in broadcast sound, what he himself called a "revolution"—FM radio.

Edwin Armstrong, who first discovered and developed FM radio in the 1920s and early 1930s, is often considered the most prolific and influential inventor in radio history. He alone understood the impact of De Forest's vacuum tube, and he used it to invent an amplifying system that enabled radio receivers to pick up distant signals. Armstrong's innovations rendered obsolete the enormous alternators used for generating power in early radio transmitters. In 1922, he sold a "super" version of his circuit to RCA for $200,000 and sixty thousand shares of RCA stock, making him a millionaire as well as RCA's largest private stockholder.

Armstrong also worked on the major problem of radio reception—electrical interference. Between 1930 and 1933, the inventor filed five patents on **FM**, or frequency modulation. Offering static-free radio reception, FM supplied greater fidelity and clarity than AM, making FM ideal for music. **AM**, or amplitude modulation, stressed the volume, or height, of radio waves; FM accentuated the pitch, or distance, between radio waves (see Figure 4.2 on page 136). Although David Sarnoff, by then the

● *Radio Broadcast* magazine (cover, December 1926) was a trade magazine that disseminated information among industry insiders. Today mass media have similar trade magazines, such as *Broadcasting & Cable*.

Figure 4.2
AM and FM Waves

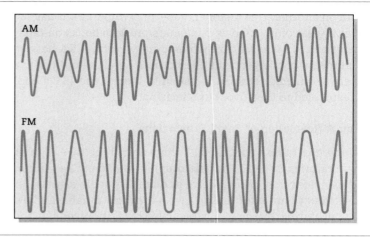

Source: Adapted from David Cheshire, *The Video Manual*, 1982.

chairman of RCA, thought that television would replace radio, he helped Armstrong set up the first experimental FM station atop the Empire State Building in New York City. Eventually, though, the RCA chief thwarted FM's development (which he was able to do because RCA had an option on Armstrong's new patents). In 1935, Sarnoff threw RCA's considerable weight behind the development of television. With the FCC allocating and reassigning scarce frequency spaces, RCA wanted to ensure that channels went to television before they went to FM. But most of all, Sarnoff wanted to protect RCA's existing AM empire. Given the high costs of converting to FM and the revenue needed for TV experiments, Sarnoff decided to close down Armstrong's station.

Armstrong forged ahead without RCA. He founded a new FM station and advised other engineers, who started more than twenty experimental stations between 1935 and the early 1940s. In 1941, the FCC approved limited space allocations for commercial FM licenses. During the next few years, FM grew in fits and starts. Between 1946 and early 1949, the number of commercial FM stations expanded from 48 to 700. But then the FCC moved FM's frequency space to a new band on the electromagnetic spectrum, rendering some 400,000 prewar FM receiver sets useless. FM's future became uncertain, and by 1954 the number of FM stations had fallen to 560.

> **"** Armstrong was a lone experimenter, Sarnoff a company man. **"**
>
> –Erik Barnouw,
> media historian

On January 31, 1954, Edwin Armstrong, weary from years of legal skirmishes over patents, wrote a note apologizing to his wife, removed the air conditioner from his thirteenth-story New York apartment, and jumped to his death. A month later, David Sarnoff announced record profits of $850 million for RCA, with TV sales accounting for 54 percent of the company's earnings. In the early 1960s, the FCC opened up more spectrum space for the superior sound of FM, infusing new life into radio. Although AM stations had greater reach, they could not match the crisp fidelity of FM, which would gradually make FM the preferred broadcast medium for music. In the early 1970s, about 70 percent of listeners tuned almost exclusively to AM radio. By the 1980s, however, FM had surpassed AM in profitability. By the 2000s, more than 75 percent of all listeners reportedly preferred FM, and about sixty-two hundred commercial and twenty-four hundred educational FM stations were in operation. The expansion of FM represented one of the chief ways by which radio survived television and Sarnoff's gloomy predictions.

Changes in Programming

Live and recorded music had long been radio's single biggest staple, accounting for 48 percent of all programming in 1938. Although network affiliates in large markets carried many drama, comedy, and variety series, smaller independent stations had always relied heavily on music. As noted earlier, in the 1920s many stations even hired their own house bands and studio musicians. In the 1930s and 1940s, lean economic times forced more stations to play recorded music, either older music in the public domain (not under copyright) or music that was marginally popular and was not closely monitored by ASCAP. (See Chapter 3.)

Although live music on radio was generally considered superior to recorded music, early disc jockeys made a significant contribution to the latter. They demonstrated that music alone could drive radio. In fact, when television snatched radio's program ideas and national sponsors, radio's dependence on recorded music became a necessity and helped the medium survive in the 1950s.

The Rise of Format and Top 40 Radio

As early as 1949, station owner Todd Storz in Omaha, Nebraska, experimented with formula-driven radio, or **format radio**. Under this system, management rather than deejays controlled programming each hour. When Storz and his program manager noticed that bar patrons and waitresses repeatedly played certain favorite songs from the forty records available in a jukebox, they began researching record sales to identify the most popular tunes. From observing jukebox culture, Storz hit on the idea of **rotation**: playing the top songs many times during the day. By the mid-1950s, the management-control idea had combined with the rock-and-roll explosion. The *Top 40 format* was born. Although the term *Top 40* derived from the number of records stored in a jukebox, this format came to refer to the forty most popular hits in a given week as measured by record sales.

As format radio grew, program managers combined rapid deejay chatter with the best-selling songs of the day and occasional *oldies*—popular songs from a few months earlier. By the early 1960s, to avoid "dead air," managers asked deejays to talk over the beginning and the end of a song so that listeners would feel less compelled to switch stations. Ads, news, weather forecasts, and station identifications were all designed to fit a consistent station environment. Listeners, tuning in at any moment, would recognize the station by its distinctive sound.

In format radio, management carefully coordinates, or programs, each hour, dictating what the deejay will do at various intervals throughout each hour of the day (see Figure 4.3 on page 138). Management creates a program log—once called a *hot clock* in radio jargon—that deejays must follow. By the mid-1960s, one study had determined that in a typical hour on Top 40, listeners could expect to hear about twenty ads; numerous weather, time, and contest announcements; multiple recitations of the station's call letters; about three minutes of news; and approximately twelve songs.

Radio managers further sectioned off programming into *day parts*, which typically consisted of time blocks covering 6 to 10 A.M., 10 A.M. to 3 P.M., 3 to 7 P.M., and 7 P.M. to 12 midnight. Each day part, or block, was programmed through ratings research according to who was listening. For instance, a Top 40 station would feature its top deejays in the morning and afternoon periods when audiences, many riding in cars, were largest. From 10 A.M. to 3 P.M., research determined that women at home and secretaries at work usually controlled the dial, so program managers, capitalizing on the gender stereotypes of the day, played more romantic ballads and less hard rock. Teenagers tended to be heavy evening listeners, so program managers often discarded news breaks at this time, since research showed that teens turned the dial when news came on.

Figure 4.3
Radio Program Log for an Adult Contemporary (AC) Station

```
CART/CD           TITLE                                    ARTIST              YEAR  IN/TOT/END
================================================================================================
00:00   7433      Legal I.D. - Jingle 1
-----------------------------------------------------------------------------------------------
10552             Don't Stop Believin'                     Journey             81    :17/4:04/F J10
-----------------------------------------------------------------------------------------------
04:16   38        *Live* Intro of *SOFT ROCK FAVORITE*
-----------------------------------------------------------------------------------------------
10003             (Everything I Do) I Do It F              Bryan Adams         91    :5/4:02/S 9202
-----------------------------------------------------------------------------------------------
08:18   1099      Family Flyaway Sweeper
-----------------------------------------------------------------------------------------------
10944             Breakaway                                Kelly Clarkson      05    :01/3:54/s
-----------------------------------------------------------------------------------------------
12:32   103       ***Warm 98 Traffic***
-----------------------------------------------------------------------------------------------
14:02   60        Traffic Merge :10 [09-17]
-----------------------------------------------------------------------------------------------
18:02   7402      Weather Intro
-----------------------------------------------------------------------------------------------
18:30   7404      Weather Close
-----------------------------------------------------------------------------------------------
10497             While You See A Chance                   Steve Winwood       81    :55/3:52/F 147
-----------------------------------------------------------------------------------------------
22:28   8006      SRF - Work Along With
-----------------------------------------------------------------------------------------------
10166             If I Can't Have You                      Yvonne Elliman      04    :16/2:53/F P1
-----------------------------------------------------------------------------------------------
25:33   38        *Live* Intro of *SOFT ROCK FAVORITE*
-----------------------------------------------------------------------------------------------
10101             I Can See Clearly                        Jimmy Cliff         94    :09/2:59/F 952
-----------------------------------------------------------------------------------------------
28:32   100       ***Warm 98-Second Update***
-----------------------------------------------------------------------------------------------
10:47   61        Traffic Merge :27 [25-33]
-----------------------------------------------------------------------------------------------
10363             Wind Beneath My Wings                    Bette Midler        89    :16/4:14/S 167
-----------------------------------------------------------------------------------------------
39:01   2         *Live* Intro of the latest Soft Rock Favorite from ...
-----------------------------------------------------------------------------------------------
```

Source: WWRM-FM, CIncinnati, OH, 2005.

Critics of format radio argued that only the top songs received play and that lesser-known songs deserving air time received meager attention. Although a few popular star deejays continued to play a role in programming, many others quit when managers introduced formats. Owners approached programming as if it were a science, but deejays considered it an art form. Program managers argued that deejays had different tastes than the average listener and therefore could not be fully trusted to know popular audience tastes. The owners' position, which generated more revenue, triumphed.

Payola Then and Now

According to management, format radio had another big advantage over deejays who simply played their favorite music: It helped curb **payola**, the practice by which record promoters paid deejays to play particular records. As we noted in Chapter 3, payola was rampant during the 1950s, as record companies sought to guarantee record sales. When management took control of programming, however, individual deejays had less impact on what records would be played and became less susceptible to bribery. In response, record promoters showered their favors on a few influential, high-profile deejays, whose backing could make or break a record nationally, or on key program managers in charge of Top 40 formats in large urban markets.

Despite congressional hearings and new rules designed to eliminate the problem, payola persisted. In the 1970s, for example, payola scandals involved exchang-

> **"** Please be sure all callers are male, preferably under 25 (or sounding like it!), and that the bulk of the calls are made between 6 P.M. and midnight. **"**
>
> –E-mail from an Arista Records employee to the coordinator of a phone team paid to call radio stations and request a specific song be played, 2005

ing airplay for drugs as well as cash. Although a 1984 congressional hearing determined that there was "no credible evidence" of payola practices in the recording industry, NBC News broke a story in 1986 about independent promoters who had alleged ties to the Mafia. A subsequent investigation led major recording companies to break most of their ties with independent promoters. Prominent record labels had been paying such promoters up to $80 million per year to help records become hits.

In recent years, the U.S. Department of Justice and the FCC have been lax in enforcing payola laws. But in 2004, a high-profile payola case emerged in Denver against radio conglomerate Clear Channel. In the suit, a Denver concert promoter alleged that Clear Channel coerced bands with a novel form of payola: requesting that musical acts book concerts with Clear Channel's concert promotions subsidiary in exchange for airplay. The suit later ended in a confidential settlement. Then in 2005, two major labels—Sony-BMG and Warner Music—paid $10 million and $5 million respectively to settle payola cases brought by New York Attorney General Eliot Spitzer. He had discovered label executives bribing radio station programmers to play songs by particular artists and bands. And in 2006, demonstrating that payola worked in two directions, New York went after radio chain Entercom Communications, the nation's fifth largest radio station operator, "for soliciting money and gifts from record companies in exchange for playing songs." Evidence in the case revealed a 2003 e-mail from a Buffalo, New York, pop music station owned by Entercom to an executive at Columbia Records: "Do you need help on Jessica [Simpson] this week? 1250? If you don't need help, I certainly don't need to play it." Another case involved a Rochester, New York, country station asking executives at Universal Music to provide a $2,500 laptop in exchange for playing certain songs.[7]

In 1998, a "legal" alternative to payola emerged that has been hotly debated in the radio and recording industries. The promotional strategy, called **pay-for-play**, typically involves up-front payments from record companies to radio stations to play a song a specific number of times.[8] Stations that use pay-for-play sidestep FCC regulations by broadcasting disclosures that state that the song has been sponsored or paid for by the record company. In effect, the time to play the song is being purchased, not unlike the paid programming of television infomercials. If the station's listeners ultimately like the pay-for-play song, the song can become part of the station's regular, unsponsored lineup. Another form of pay-for-play involves a weekly, infomercial-like music program sponsored by a music label or department store that airs in several markets of a national radio chain. Although some see pay-for-play as a direct, honest way to introduce new music on radio stations, others object to having commercial interests blatantly tamper with playlists and the weekly *Billboard* music charts.

The Sounds of Radio Today

Contemporary radio sounds very different from its predecessors. In contrast to the few stations per market in the 1930s, most large markets today include more than forty receivable signals that vie for listener loyalty. With the exception of national network–sponsored news segments and nationally syndicated programs, most programming is locally produced and heavily dependent on the music industry for content. Although a few radio personalities, such as Howard Stern, Rush Limbaugh, Don Imus, Tom Joyner, Dr. Laura Schlessinger, and Jim Rome, are nationally prominent, local deejays and their music are the stars at most radio stations.

However, unlike listeners in the 1930s, who tuned in their favorite shows at set times, listeners today do not say, "Gee, my favorite song is coming on at 8 P.M., so I'd better be home to listen." Instead, radio has become a secondary, or background, medium that follows the rhythms of daily life. In the 1930s, radio often dictated those rhythms, particularly with its popular evening programs. Today, radio programmers worry about channel cruising—when listeners search the dial until they find a song they like.

Today, stations are more specialized. Listeners in the 1940s were loyal to favorite programs, but now we are loyal to favorite stations, music formats, and even radio personalities. We generally listen to only four or five stations that target us, usually based on our age, gender, or race. In the 1930s, peak listening time occurred during evening hours—dubbed *prime time* in the TV era—when people were home from work and school. Now, the heaviest radio listening occurs during **drive time**, between 6 and 9 A.M. and 4 and 7 P.M., when people are commuting to and from work or school. Today, more than thirteen thousand radio stations operate in the United States, customizing their sounds to reach mobile niche audiences. With radio as a truly portable medium, Americans are still tuning in, but the youth audience has been declining—15 percent between 1999 and 2006 among 12–24 year olds, who have embraced iPods and the Internet.

● Tom Joyner has the nation's No. 1 urban radio show, targeting African Americans between the ages of twenty-five and fifty-four with a mix of comedy, soap opera sketches, social activism, and old-school R&B music. The syndicated program can be heard in more than a hundred broadcast markets, including Chicago, Dallas, Detroit, Miami, Washington, D.C., and Los Angeles.

The Economics of Broadcast Radio

About 8 percent of all U.S. spending on media advertising goes to radio stations. Like newspapers, radio generates its largest profits by selling local and regional ads. Thirty-second radio spot ads range from $1,500 or more in large markets to just a few dollars in the smallest markets. Today, gross advertising receipts for radio are close to $20 billion (more than three-quarters of the revenues from local ad sales, with the remainder in national spot and network sales), up from about $12.4 billion in 1996. The industry is economically healthy, with approximately 13,500 stations (almost 4,800 AM stations, about 6,200 FM commercial stations, and about 2,500 FM educational stations). Unlike television, where nearly 40 percent of a station's expenses goes to buy syndicated programs, local radio stations get much of their content free from the recording industry. Therefore, only about 20 percent of a typical radio station's budget goes to cover programming costs.

When radio stations want to purchase programming, they often turn to national network radio, which generates more than $1 billion in ad sales annually by offering dozens of specialized services. For example, Westwood One, the nation's largest radio network service, managed and owned by CBS Radio (formerly Viacom's Infinity Broadcasting), syndicates more than 150 programs, including regular news features (e.g., *CBS Radio News*, *CNN Radio News*), entertainment programs (e.g., *Country Countdown USA, Saturday Night All Request*

80s), talk shows to fill entire day parts (e.g., the *G. Gordon Liddy Show, Loveline,* and the *Tom Leykis Show*), and complete twenty-four-hour formats (e.g., adult rock and roll, bright adult contemporary, hot country, mainstream country, and CNN Headline News). More than sixty companies offer national program and format services, typically providing local stations with programming in exchange for time slots for national ads. The most successful radio network programs are the shows broadcast by affiliates in the Top 20 markets, which offer advertisers half of the country's radio audience. As mergers and buyouts continue, creating huge national radio groups in the wake of the 1996 Telecommunications Act, national network radio is expected to produce a larger portion of radio revenues.

Commercial Radio and Format Specialization

Although Top 40 managers pioneered format radio, stations today use a variety of formats based on managed program logs and day parts, as explained earlier. All told, more than forty different radio formats, plus variations, serve diverse groups of listeners. To please advertisers, who want to know exactly who's listening, formats are usually targeted at audiences according to their age and income, gender, or race/ethnicity. Radio's specialization enables advertisers to reach smaller target audiences at costs that are much lower than those for television. This process has become extremely competitive, however, because forty or fifty stations may be available in a large radio market. In the last decade, according to the Center for Radio Information, more than one thousand stations a year (roughly 10 percent of all stations) switched formats in an effort to find the formula that would generate more advertising money. Some stations, particularly those in large cities, have also been renting blocks of time to various local ethnic and civic groups; this enables the groups to dictate their own formats and sell ads.

● The most popular radio format among people ages twelve and older is news/talk, which includes call-in shows where listeners ask questions of the host. Broadcasting from New York City, Dr. Joy Browne is a psychologist whose daily syndicated show attracts nine million listeners, and she has won awards for Best Female Talk Show Host and Female Talk Show Host of the Year.

The nation's fastest-growing format throughout much of the 1990s was the **news/talk format** (see "Case Study—Host: The Origins of Talk Radio" on page 143). In 1987, only 170 radio stations operated formats dominated by either news programs or talk shows, which tend to appeal to adults over age thirty-five (except for sports talk programs, which draw both younger and older, mostly male, sports fans). By 2005, buoyed by the notoriety and popularity of personalities like Dr. Laura Schlessinger and Rush Limbaugh, more than 1,200 stations used some combination of news and talk. With many of the most powerful AM stations in the country programming the format, and with a large portion of listeners being over age thirty-five, news/talk reigns as the most popular format in the nation. A news/talk format, though more expensive to produce than a music format, appeals to advertisers looking to target working- and middle-class adult consumers. Nevertheless, most radio stations continue to be driven by a variety of less expensive music formats. (See Figure 4.4 on page 142.)

Just behind news/talk in popularity is the **adult contemporary (AC)** format. Known first as middle-of-the-road, or MOR, AC is among radio's oldest and most popular format, reaching almost 15 percent of all listeners, most of them older than forty. In the early 1970s, *Broadcasting* magazine described AC's eclectic mix of news, talk, oldies, and soft rock music as "not too soft, not too loud, not too fast, not too slow, not too hard, not too lush, not too old, not too new."

Figure 4.4
Most Popular Radio Formats in the United States

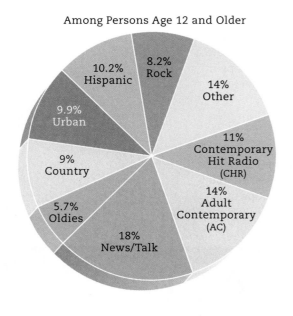

Among Persons Age 12 and Older

- 8.2% Rock
- 14% Other
- 11% Contemporary Hit Radio (CHR)
- 14% Adult Contemporary (AC)
- 18% News/Talk
- 5.7% Oldies
- 9% Country
- 9.9% Urban
- 10.2% Hispanic

Source: Arbitron, http://www.arbitron.com, Fall 2005.

Although Top 40 radio—also called **contemporary hit radio (CHR)**—is in decline, it still appeals to many teens and young adults, and advertisers continue to buy time from Top 40 stations. Since the mid-1980s, however, these stations have lost ground steadily as younger generations have followed music on MTV and now online rather than on radio. In addition, Top 40 music has become so diverse, encompassing everything from gangster rap to children's songs, that "no commercial radio station could ever play it all and hold on to an audience."[9]

The **country** format does not reach as many total listeners as news/talk, AC, or CHR radio, but country claims by far the most stations—more than two thousand, about twice as many stations as those that have the news/talk format. Many of these stations are in tiny markets where country has traditionally reigned as the default format for communities with only one radio station. Country music has old roots in radio, starting in 1925 with the influential Grand Ole Opry program on WSM in Nashville. Although Top 40 drove country music out of many radio markets in the 1950s, the growth of FM in the 1960s brought it back as station managers looked for market niches not served by rock music. As diverse as rock, country music today includes such subdivisions as old-time, progressive country, country-rock, western swing, and country-gospel.

Many formats target by age or gender, but some also appeal to particular ethnic or racial groups. For example, formats featuring jazz, gospel, rhythm and blues, hip-hop, and dance music have targeted various audience segments of African American listeners over the years. In 1947, WDIA in Memphis was the first station to program exclusively for black listeners. Now called **urban**, this format targets a wide variety of African American listeners, primarily in large cities. Urban, which typically plays popular dance, rap, R&B, and hip-hop music (featuring performers like Siagon and Kanye West), also subdivides by age, featuring an Urban AC category with performers like Faith Evans, India.Arie, and Mary J. Blige.

Spanish-language radio, one of radio's fastest-growing formats, targets large Cuban populations in Miami, Puerto Rican and Dominican listeners in New York, and Mexican American audiences in Chicago, California, and Texas (where KCOR, the first all-Spanish-language station, originated in San Antonio in 1947). Besides talk shows and news segments in Spanish, Hispanic formats feature a variety of Spanish, Caribbean, and Latin American musical styles, including calypso, flamenco, mariachi, merengue, reggae, samba, salsa, and Tejano.

Resisting the Top 40

Accompanying the expansion of the FM spectrum in the mid-1960s, *progressive rock* emerged as an alternative to conventional formats. Many of the noncommercial stations broadcast from college campuses, where student deejays and managers, unencumbered by ads and format radio, rejected the commercialism associated with Top 40 tunes. Instead, they began playing lesser-known alternative music and longer album cuts. Until that time, most rock on radio had been consigned almost exclusively to Top 40 AM formats, with song length averaging about three minutes.

The expansion of FM created room for experimenting, particularly with classical music, jazz, blues, and non–Top 40 rock songs. Experimental FM stations, both commercial and noncommercial, served as a venue for Bob Dylan's 1965 song "Desolation Row," which ran eleven minutes. In 1967, the Doors' "Light My Fire," a No. 1 hit,

Case Study

Host: The Origins of Talk Radio

By David Foster Wallace

The origins of contemporary political talk radio can be traced to three phenomena of the 1980s. The first of these involved AM music stations' getting absolutely murdered by FM, which could broadcast music in stereo and allowed for much better fidelity on high and low notes. The human voice, on the other hand, is mid-range and doesn't require high fidelity. The eighties' proliferation of talk formats on the AM band also provided new careers for some music deejays—e.g., Don Imus, Morton Downey Jr.—whose chatty personas didn't fit well with FM's all-about-the-music ethos.

The second big factor was the repeal, late in Ronald Reagan's second term, of what was known as the Fairness Doctrine. This was a 1949 FCC rule designed to minimize any possible restrictions on free speech caused by limited access to broadcasting outlets. The idea was that, as one of the conditions for receiving an FCC broadcast license, a station had to "devote reasonable attention to the coverage of controversial issues of public importance," and consequently had to provide "reasonable, although not necessarily equal" opportunities for opposing sides to express their views. Because of the Fairness Doctrine, talk stations had to hire and program symmetrically: if you had a three-hour program whose host's politics were on one side of the ideological spectrum, you had to have another long-form program whose host more or less spoke for the other side. Weirdly enough, up through the mid-eighties it was usually the U.S. right that benefited most from the Doctrine. Pioneer talk syndicator Ed McLaughlin, who managed San Francisco's KGO in the 1960s, recalls that "I had more liberals on the air than I had conservatives or even moderates for that matter, and I had a hell of a time finding the other voice."

The Fairness Doctrine's repeal was part of the sweeping deregulations of the Reagan era, which aimed to liberate all sorts of industries from government interference and allow them to compete freely in the marketplace. The old, Rooseveltian logic of the Doctrine had been that since the airwaves belonged to everyone, a license to profit from those airwaves conferred on the broadcast industry some special obligation to serve the public interest. Commercial radio broadcasting was not, in other words, originally conceived as just another for-profit industry; it was supposed to meet a higher standard of social responsibility. After 1987, though, just another industry is pretty much what radio became, and its only real responsibility now is to attract and retain listeners in order to generate revenue. In other words, the sort of distinction explicitly drawn by FCC Chairman Newton Minow in the 1960s—namely, that between "the public interest" and "merely what interests the public"—no longer exists.

More or less on the heels of the Fairness Doctrine's repeal came the West Coast and then national syndication of *The Rush Limbaugh Show* through Mr. McLaughlin's EFM Media. Limbaugh is the third great progenitor of today's political talk radio partly because he's a host of extraordinary, once-in-a-generation talent and charisma—bright, loquacious, witty, complexly authoritative—whose show's blend of news, entertainment, and partisan analysis became the model for legions of imitators. But he was also the first great promulgator of the Mainstream Media's Liberal Bias idea. This turned out to be a brilliantly effective rhetorical move, since the MMLB concept functioned simultaneously as a standard around which Rush's audience could rally, as an articulation of the need for right-wing (i.e., unbiased) media, and as a mechanism by which any criticism or refutation of conservative ideas could be dismissed (either as biased or as the product of indoctrination by biased media). Boiled way down, the MMLB thesis is able both to exploit and to perpetuate many conservatives' dissatisfaction with extant media sources—and it's this dissatisfaction that cements political talk radio's large and loyal audience.

Source: Excerpted from David Foster Wallace, "Host: The Origins of Talk Radio," *Atlantic,* April 2005, 66–68.

● The nation's top Spanish-language radio personality, Renán Almendárez Coello, known on-air as El Cucuy ("bogeyman" in English), moved from Univision to the rival Spanish Broadcasting System in 2004. His humorous morning drive-time show originates from KLAX-FM (97.9 La Raza) in Los Angeles and for several years has beaten all other LA Spanish- and English-language radio shows. His program is also syndicated to several other U.S. markets.

featured a seven-minute version for FM and a three-minute Top 40 AM version. The same year, some FM stations played Arlo Guthrie's "Alice's Restaurant," an eighteen-minute satiric antiwar folk ballad. FM offered a cultural space for hard-edged political folk and for rock music that commented on the Civil Rights movement and protested America's involvement in the Vietnam War. By the 1970s, progressive rock had been copied, tamed, and absorbed by mainstream radio under the format label **album-oriented rock (AOR)**. By 1972, AOR-driven album sales already accounted for more than 85 percent of the retail record business. By the 1980s, as first-generation rock and rollers aged and became more affluent, AOR had become less political and played mostly white post-Beatles music featuring such groups as Pink Floyd, Led Zeppelin, Cream, and Queen.

A number of critics have denounced AOR for limiting the definition of rock music. They argue that the strictly controlled AOR format displaced progressive rock by aiming "programming at an extremely specific, limited listenership," mostly white males in the thirteen to twenty-five age range. AOR programming guidelines initially ignored most black and female performers, who program directors claimed held little appeal for AOR's target audience. By discouraging certain kinds of music, it was claimed that AOR formats encouraged a type of "institutionalized racism and sexism." These guidelines were later adopted by MTV in its formative years, making it harder for black and female artists to crack the video scene in the early 1980s.[10]

Today, there are several spin-offs from AOR. *Classic rock* serves up rock oldies from the mid-1960s through the 1980s to the baby-boom generation and is aimed primarily at listeners who have outgrown the conventional Top 40. The *oldies* format serves adults who grew up on 1950s and early 1960s rock and roll. Begun in California in the mid-1960s, oldies formats recall the integrationist impulse of early rock as well as emphasizing soul and Motown music from the 1960s. Listening habits and record research indicate that most people identify closely with the music they listened to as adolescents and young adults. This tendency partially explains why oldies and classic rock stations combined have surpassed Top 40 stations today. It also helps to explain the recent nostalgia for music from the 1980s and early 1990s. The *alternative music* format recaptures some of the experimental approach of the FM stations of the 1960s, albeit with much more controlled playlists, and has helped to introduce artists such as The Strokes and Panic! At the Disco.

Radio Ownership since 1996

In recent years, the rules concerning ownership of the public airwaves have changed substantially. With the passage of the **Telecommunications Act of 1996**, the FCC eliminated most ownership restrictions on radio. As a result, in 1996 alone some twenty-one hundred stations switched owners, as $15 billion changed hands. Since 1996, the number of radio station owners has declined by 34 percent.[11]

The FCC once tried to encourage diversity in broadcast ownership. From the 1950s through the 1980s, a media company could not own more than seven AM, seven FM, and seven TV stations nationally, and only one radio station per market. Just prior to the 1996 act, the ownership rules were relaxed to allow any single person or company to own up to twenty AM, twenty FM, and twelve television stations nationwide, and only two could be in the same market. But today the FCC embraces the consolidation schemes pushed by the powerful National Association of Broadcasters lobbyists in Washington, D.C., under which fewer and fewer owners control more and more of the airwaves.

The 1996 act allows individuals and companies to acquire as many radio stations as they want, with relaxed restrictions on the number of stations a single broadcaster may own in the same city: The larger the market or area, the more stations a company may own within that market. For example, in areas where forty-five or more stations are available to listeners, a broadcaster may own up to eight stations, but not more than five of one type (AM or FM). In areas with fourteen or fewer stations, a broadcaster may own up to five stations (three of any one type). In very small markets with a handful of stations, a broadcast company may not own more than half the stations.

The consequences of the 1996 Telecommunications Act on radio ownership have been significant (see Table 4.1 on page 146). Consider the cases of Clear Channel Communications and CBS Radio (formerly Viacom), which are the two largest radio chain owners in terms of total revenue. Clear Channel Communications was formed in 1972 with one San Antonio station. In 1998, it swallowed up Jacor Communications, the fifth-largest radio chain, and became the nation's second-largest group, with 454 stations in 101 cities. In 1999, Clear Channel gobbled up another growing conglomerate, AMFM (formerly Chancellor Media Corporation), which had 463 stations and an estimated $1.6 billion in revenue. The deal broadened Clear Channel's operation to 874 stations in 187 U.S. markets, providing access to more than 110 million listeners. By 2006, Clear Channel owned 1,190 radio stations, 40 television stations, more than 820,000 billboard and outdoor displays, and an interest in more than 240 stations internationally. With recent mergers, Clear Channel also distributes many of the leading syndicated programs, including *Dr. Laura, Rush Limbaugh, The Jim Rome Show, Carson Daly Most Requested,* and *The Bob & Tom Show.*

CBS Radio, formerly Infinity Broadcasting, was created when media giant Viacom split into two companies in late 2005. CBS Radio is the second leading radio conglomerate in terms of revenue, with 179 stations. It is also the leading outdoor advertising company in the nation. Whereas Clear Channel's stations are mostly in small and medium-sized markets, CBS Radio's stations dominate the nation's top markets, with 91 percent of its stations located in the fifty largest markets. CBS

● As a response to the dominance of politically conservative talk radio in the United States, in 2004 investors launched Air America Radio, a liberal talk radio network. Pictured above is one of the hosts, Al Franken. After a rocky start (rumors of bankruptcy continued in 2006), Air America seems to be gaining listeners in nearly every major market. Even the top radio conglomerate, Clear Channel, has noticed the economic possibilities of Air America's format, converting Columbus, Detroit, Cincinnati, Washington, D.C., and San Antonio stations to the "progressive talk" radio format.

" Radio affects most people intimately, person-to-person, offering a world of unspoken communication between writer-speaker and listener. That is the immediate aspect of radio. A private experience.**"**

–Marshall McLuhan, *Understanding Media,* 1964

● Table 4.1 Number of Stations Owned by Top Broadcasting Companies, 2006

Rank	Owner	Number of Stations
1	Clear Channel Communications	1,190
2	Cumulus Broadcasting Inc.	303
3	Citadel Broadcasting Corp.	249
4	CBS Radio (formerly Viacom's Infinity Broadcasting)	178
5	Educational Media Foundation	143
6	American Family Association Inc.	120
7	Salem Communications Corporation	104
8	Entercom	103
9	Saga Communications Inc.	86
10	Cox Broadcasting	78
11	Regent Communications, Inc.	74
12	Univision Communications Inc.	72
13	Radio One Inc.	69
14	NextMedia Group	59
15	NRG Media LLC	59
16	Entravision Holdings LLC	52
17	Nassau Broadcasting Partners LP	52
18	Family Stations Inc.	49
19	Three Eagles Communications Inc.	46
20	ABC/Disney	45

Source: BIA Financial Network Inc., MEDIA Access Pro.

Radio also operates the Westwood One radio network, the nation's leading programming and radio news syndicator.

Combined, Clear Channel and CBS own nearly fourteen hundred radio stations—about 14 percent of all commercial U.S. stations—and control more than 35 percent of the entire radio industry's $20 billion revenue (see Figure 4.5). Competing major radio groups that have grown in the recent radio industry consolidations include Cox, Entercom, ABC Radio, Citadel, and Radio One. As a result of the consolidations permitted by deregulation, in most American cities just two corporations dominate the radio market.

A smaller but perhaps the most dominant radio conglomerate in a single format area is Univision. The company is the United States' largest Spanish-language television broadcaster and owner of the top two Spanish-language cable networks (Galavisión and Telefutura). With the $3 billion takeover of Hispanic Broadcasting in 2003, Univision is also the top Spanish-language radio broadcaster in the United States and gets the privilege of playing its own music, as Univision is the top Spanish-language recording company as well, controlling Univision Records, Fonovisa Records (featuring top acts Los Temerarios, Marco Antonio Solis, and Los Tigres del Norte), and 50 percent of Mexico-based Disa Records. About 35 percent of the Top 100 Latin albums sold in the United States are by Univision Music Group artists.

Figure 4.5
Media Ownership: Principal Operations for Clear Channel Communications

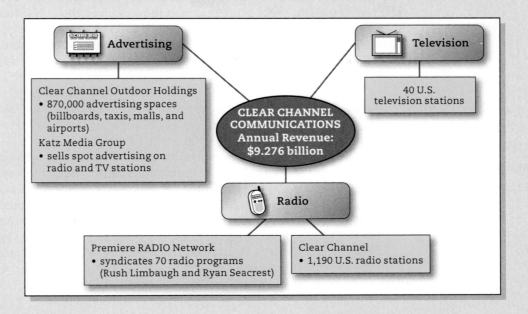

With the deregulation of the radio industry under the Clinton administration in 1996, San Antonio–based Clear Channel went from a small-time owner of 40-plus radio stations to a big-time owner of 1,200 stations. This kind of corporate size allows Clear Channel to influence popular music and radio formats, singling out certain artists for frequent play (and sometimes ignoring other artists for their politics). It also allows them to automate many of their operations and run canned-DJ chatter and pre-packaged music programs nationally with minimal local flavor or input from the communities they serve.

Discuss or examine how in today's cross platform business environment Clear Channel's various advertising ventures listed in the chart might serve their radio interests and operations. You might also do a LexisNexis search to find out how Clear Channel–owned stations have fared with payola and other recent music-radio industry scandals.

Nonprofit Radio and NPR

Although commercial radio (particularly those stations owned by huge radio conglomerates) dominates the radio spectrum, nonprofit radio maintains a voice. But the road to viability for nonprofit radio in the United States has not been easy. In the 1930s, the Wagner-Hatfield Amendment to the 1934 Communications Act intended to set aside 25 percent of radio for a wide variety of nonprofit stations. When the amendment was defeated in 1935, the future of educational and noncommercial radio looked bleak. Many nonprofits had sold out to for-profit owners during the Depression. The stations that remained were often banished from the air during the evening hours or assigned weak signals by federal regulators who favored commercial owners and their lobbying agents. Still, nonprofit public radio survived. More than 1,700 such stations now operate, many of them low-wattage stations on college campuses.

During the 1960s, nonprofit broadcasting found a Congress sympathetic to an old idea: using radio and television as educational tools. As a result, **National Public Radio (NPR)** and the **Public Broadcasting Service (PBS)** were created as the first noncommercial networks. Under the auspices of the **Public Broadcasting Act of 1967** and the **Corporation for Public Broadcasting (CPB)**, NPR and PBS were mandated to provide alternatives to commercial broadcasting. Now, NPR's popular news

> **❝** Although noncommercial radio seems to have turned the corner of public awareness, it has not yet overcome decades of disorganization and neglect and abuse by the federal government.**❞**
>
> —Peter Fornatale and Joshua Mills,
> *Radio in the Television Age,*
> 1980

and interview programs, *Morning Edition* and *All Things Considered,* draw three to four million listeners per day. Over the years, however, more time and attention have been devoted to public television than to public radio. When government funding tightened in the late 1980s and 1990s, television received the lion's share. In 1994, a conservative majority in Congress cut financial support and threatened to scrap the CPB, the funding authority for public broadcasting. Consequently, stations became more reliant than ever on private donations and corporate sponsorship. While depending on handouts, especially from big business, public broadcasters steered clear of some controversial subjects, especially those that critically examined corporations. (See "Media Literacy and the Critical Process: Comparing Commercial and Noncommercial Radio" on opposite page.)

> **66** We have a huge responsibility to keep the airwaves open for what I think is the majority — representing the voices that are locked out of the mainstream media. **99**
>
> —Amy Goodman, co-host of radio's *Democracy Now!* 2001

Like commercial stations, nonprofit radio has also adopted the format style. Unlike commercial radio, however, the dominant style in public radio is a loose variety format whereby a station may actually switch from jazz, classical music, and alternative rock to news and talk during different parts of the day. Some college stations, too small to affiliate, have kept alive the spirit of early 1950s radio, when deejays chose the music. Noncommercial radio still remains the place for both tradition and experimentation, for programs that do not draw enough listeners for commercial success.

Although the proposed Wagner-Hatfield Amendment failed to redistribute radio resources in the mid-1930s, public and nonprofit radio have managed to maintain a presence on the radio dial. Two government rulings, both in 1948, aided nonprofit radio. First, the government began authorizing noncommercial licenses to stations not affiliated with labor, religion, education, or a civic group. The first license went to Lewis Kimball Hill, a radio reporter and pacifist during World War II who started the **Pacifica Foundation** to run experimental public stations. Pacifica stations, like Hill himself, have often challenged the status quo in radio as well as in government. Most notably, in the 1950s they aired the poetry, prose, and music of performers— considered radical, left-wing, or communist—who were blacklisted by television and seldom acknowledged by AM stations. Over the years, Pacifica has also been fined and reprimanded by the FCC and Congress for airing programs that critics considered inappropriate for public airwaves. By 2006, Pacifica had about seventy-eight affiliate stations.

Second, the FCC approved 10-watt FM stations, beginning in 1948. Prior to this time, radio stations had to have at least 250 watts to get licensed. A 10-watt station with a broadcast range of only about seven miles took very little capital to operate, so more people could participate in the new FM phenomenon. These stations not only promoted Edwin Armstrong's invention but also became training sites for students interested in broadcasting. Although the FCC stopped licensing new 10-watt stations in 1978 (and didn't resume until a new class of low-power FM stations was approved in 2000), and although low-power stations aren't eligible for funding from the CPB, one hundred longtime 10-watters are still in operation.

Alternative Voices

As large corporations gained control of America's radio airwaves, activists in hundreds of communities across the United States in the 1990s protested the exclusivity of radio broadcasting by starting up their own noncommercial "pirate" radio stations. Broadcasting over a radius of just a few miles with low-power FM signals of 1 to 10 watts, the pirate radio stations challenged corporate broadcasters' dominance of public airwaves. The National Association of Broadcasters (NAB) and other indus-

Comparing Commercial and Noncommercial Radio

After the arrival and growth of commercial TV, the Corporation for Public Broadcasting (CPB) was created in 1967 as the funding agent for public broadcasting—an alternative to commercial TV and radio for educational and cultural programming that could not be easily sustained by commercial broadcasters in search of large general audiences. As a result, NPR (National Public Radio) developed to provide national programming to public stations to supplement local programming efforts. Today, NPR affiliates get as little as 2 percent of their funding from the government. Most money for public radio comes instead from corporate sponsorships, individual grants, and private donations.

Description. Listen to a typical morning or late afternoon hour of a popular local commercial talk-news radio and a typical hour of your local NPR station, from the same time period over a two-to-three-day period. Keep a log on what topics are covered and what news stories are reported. For the commercial station, log what commercials are carried and how much time in an hour is devoted to ads. For the noncommercial station, note how much time is devoted to recognizing the station's sources of funding support and who the supporters are.

Analysis. Look for patterns. What kinds of stories are covered? What kinds of topics are discussed? Create a chart to categorize the stories. To cover events and issues, do the stations use actual reporters at the scene? How much time is given to reporting versus how much time is used for opinion? How many sources are cited in each story? What kinds of interview sources are used? Are they expert sources or regular person-on-the street interviews? How many sources are men and how many are women?

Interpretation. What do these patterns mean? Is there a balance between reporting and opinion? Do you detect any bias and, if so, how did you determine this? Are the stations serving as watchdogs to ensure that democracy's best interests are being served? What effect, if any, do you think the advertisers/supporters have on the programming? What arguments might you make about commercial and noncommercial radio based on your findings?

Evaluation. Which station seems to be doing a better job serving their local audience? Why? Do you buy the 1930s argument that noncommercial stations serve narrow, special interests while commercial stations serve capitalism and the public interest? Why or why not? From which station did you learn the most, and which station did you find most entertaining? Explain. What did you like and dislike about each station?

Engagement. Contact the local general manager, program director, or news director at the stations you analyzed. Ask them what their goals are for a typical hour of programming and what audience they are trying to reach. Incorporate their comments into a report of your findings. Finally, offer suggestions on how to make the programming at each station better.

try groups pressed to have the pirate broadcasters closed down, citing their illegality and their potential to create interference with existing stations. Between 1995 and 2000, more than five hundred illegal micropower radio stations were shut down. Still, an estimated one hundred to one thousand pirate stations are in operation in the United States, in both large urban areas and small rural towns.

The major complaint of pirate radio station operators was that the FCC had long ago ceased licensing low-power community radio stations. That problem was resolved in 2000 when the FCC, responding to tens of thousands of inquiries about the development of a new local radio broadcasting service, approved a new noncommercial **low power FM (LPFM)** class of stations in order to give voice to local groups lacking

● Jon Fasselius, general manager of KULT-FM, an alternative music station and one of the noncommercial 100-watt low power FM (LPFM) stations licensed by the FCC in the early 2000s. The station was the first LPFM to be licensed in Iowa and is operated solely by student volunteers at the University of Northern Iowa in Cedar Falls, Iowa.

66 Just as TiVo ensured that there'd always be something to watch when you get home, [podcasting and] podcasters fill your computer with interesting music and radio-style talk shows from around the world. Unlike TiVo, though, podcast subscriptions . . . are still free, and anyone with an Internet connection can create a show. 99

—David Battino, *Electronic Musician*, 2005

access to the public airwaves. The LPFM service, which licenses 10- and 100-watt stations, planned to create one thousand new FM stations in the United States. LPFM station licensees included mostly religious groups but also high schools, colleges and universities, Native American tribes, labor groups, and museums.

The technical plans for LPFM located the stations in unused frequencies on the FM dial. Still, the NAB, the powerful Washington-based lobbying group representing commercial broadcasters, and National Public Radio fought to delay and limit the number of LPFM stations, arguing that such stations would cause interference with existing full-power FM stations. Then FCC chairman William E. Kennard, who fostered the LPFM initiative, responded: "This is about the haves—the broadcast industry—trying to prevent many have-nots—small community and educational organizations—from having just a little piece of the pie. Just a little piece of the airwaves which belong to all of the people."[12] By 2006, about 750 LPFM stations were broadcasting, and another 313 organizations had gained permission to build LPFM stations.

Radio Goes Digital

Three alternative radio technologies also helped to bring more diverse sounds to listeners. First, **Internet radio** emerged in the 1990s, with the popularity of the Web. Internet radio stations come in two types: An existing station may "stream" a simulcast version of its on-air signal over the Web, or a station may be created exclusively for the Internet. Some of the most popular Internet radio stations are those that carry music formats unavailable on local radio, such as jazz, blues, and New Age music. But a decision by the Librarian of Congress in 2002 that established music royalty rates for Internet radio had an enormous chilling effect on Webcasters, which had grown to more than forty thousand stations. The ruling would require that commercial Webcasters pay a royalty of 0.07 cents to the recording industry for each song played (and 0.02 cents per song for nonprofit Webcasters), a fee that corporate Webcasters like Yahoo! could afford but that would bankrupt low-revenue Webcasters on sites like Live365.com. (Interestingly, AM and FM radio broadcasters don't pay music performance fees, since airplay alone is considered to be of such high promotional value to the music industry.) Some members of Congress, fearing that most Webcasters would be forced off the Internet by thousands of dollars in royalty payments, responded with a bill that enabled small and nonprofit Internet radio stations to negotiate a smaller flat rate.

A second alternative radio technology added a third band—**satellite radio**—to AM and FM. (See "Tracking Technology—Satellite Radio: Defying Gravity" on opposite page.) The two similar services, XM and Sirius, completed their national introduction by 2002 and offer more than one hundred digital music, news, and talk channels to the continental United States via satellite, at monthly prices starting at $12.95 and satellite radio receivers costing from $15 to $2,000. Programming includes a range of music channels, from rock to reggae, to Spanish Top 40 and opera, as well as channels dedicated to NASCAR, NPR, cooking, and comedy. Another feature of satellite radio's programming is the hiring of popular personalities to host their own shows or have their own channels including Howard Stern, Martha Stewart, Oprah Winfrey, and Bob Dylan. In 2002, U.S. automakers (who are investors in the two competing satellite radio companies) began equipping most new cars with an XM or SAT satellite band, in addition to AM and FM, helping to ensure the adoption of satellite radio.

Developed in 2004, the third alternative to broadcast radio is **podcasting**—a converged media term that marries "iPod" and "broadcasting." Podcasting refers to the practice of making audio files available on the Internet so listeners can download them onto their computers. There they transfer them to portable music players, like Apple's iPod, or listen to the files on the computer. Popularized by former MTV VJ

TRACKING TECHNOLOGY

Satellite Radio: Defying Gravity

By Katy Bachman

Thanks in large part to Howard Stern's P.T. Barnum–like exit from traditional radio to Sirius Satellite Radio, awareness of the medium is at an all-time high. Riding the buzz, which at times seems almost deafening, XM Satellite Radio and Sirius now count more than 9 million subscribers combined. Sirius grew faster in fourth-quarter 2005 than XM, tripling its subscribers last year to 3.3 million. XM nearly doubled its subscriber base to 6 million. While still only a fraction of traditional radio's 230 million weekly listeners, satellite is now considered a permanent part of the media landscape and a legitimate rival to terrestrial radio.

Perhaps even more telling than the public relations blitz was the response from the marketplace. Suddenly, everyone is trying to get into the subscription audio business or counter satellite radio's irresistible draw of commercial-free music, from such cell phone subscription-based radio services as Motorola's iRadio to traditional radio broadcasters that are rolling out hundreds of commercial-free digital side channels.

Satellite radio executives do not appear to be worried. After all, competition is a sure sign that their model has been validated. "It's flattering," XM executive VP of programming Eric Logan says.

Broadcasters continue to insist satellite radio cannot work. The format "has done a brilliant job marketing themselves, but no one has ever made money in pay radio, and they have a long way to go," Emmis Communications chairman/CEO Jeff Smulyan says.

But even after spending billions of dollars on programming deals—including Sirius' $500 million, five-year pact with Stern or XM's $650 million, 10-year deal for Major League Baseball—satellite services insist they are poised to turn the corner in 2006. XM forecasts it will begin making money by the second half of this year. Sirius says its first quarter of positive cash flow could come as early as fourth-quarter 2006.

This year, XM and Sirius expect to add more than 3 million subscribers apiece, bringing the total number to more than 15 million. XM forecasts it will have 20 million subscribers by 2010. And by 2014, Kagan Research is projecting that the two services will count 46.8 million subscribers and total revenue of $7.6 billion. Not too shabby for services that even a year ago had uncertain futures.

Already, satellite radio has begun nibbling into terrestrial's listenership and its advertising revenue. There is no

● The latest portable audio players are capable of streaming satellite radio as well as storing and playing both radio programs and MP3s.

question the number of radio choices has affected the amount of time consumers spend with traditional radio, dipping about 5% during the past five years, on average about 1% per year, according to Arbitron.

"Satellite radio isn't going to go away. It's the same thing when cable came on. People want choices . . . whether that's terrestrial radio, streaming or satellite radio," says Agnes Lukasewych, VP/account director for radio broadcast at MPG. "Advertising has to follow the consumer throughout the day."

A satellite radio buy fits into a growing trend among advertisers to aggregate niche players to reach a mass audience. Although satellite is often an add-on to radio or other media buys, it is becoming an increasingly attractive one.

Just because the audience is small does not mean it does not have value for an advertiser. Traditional radio and cable have built a good business around niche programming. Take sports outlets, for example. Often mediocre performers in the ratings, the stations are lucrative revenue generators. CBS Radio sports/talk WFAN-AM New York is one of the top five billing stations in the nation.

"One should not forget the early lesson of MTV. The network's reach wasn't as big as network TV until one day advertisers figured out that MTV might have the right audience," Sirius' Greenstein explains. "Certain channels may be exactly right for some advertisers." In his first week, Stern attracted advertisers "exactly right" for his audience, such as Heineken, Sony movies, Vermont Teddy Bear and several dot-coms.

Source: Excerpted from Katy Bachman, "Satellite Radio: Defying Gravity," *Billboard Radio Monitor,* February 3, 2006.

Adam Curry, podcasting technology allows anyone to become his or her own DJ, VJ, or "radio" talk show host. As this new distribution method became more popular, mainstream media chased the trend, creating commercial podcasts to promote and extend coverage of existing media, such as news or reality TV programs. But for most users what makes podcasting a truly alternative media form, according to Paul Lehrman of *Mix* magazine, "is that the content is made to be given away for free — almost no one charges for a podcast, and no one violates copyright by listening to it. . . . Most podcasts are spoken word — oriented like the early days of radio, when people actually listened to it."[13]

Radio and the Democracy of the Airwaves

The history of radio is also the history of broadcasting. In the United States, radio began as a crude but tremendously thrilling wireless communication tool of hobbyists and engineering students. As early inventors and entrepreneurs reconsidered radio as not just a wireless telegraph but also a medium for mass communication, broadcasting was born. The U.S. government also envisioned radio as a way for the country to gain global communication dominance. It sanctioned RCA as a private monopoly, one that soon gained control of radio technology manufacturing.

In the decades before television, radio broadcasting experienced a golden age of programming, with high-quality variety, quiz, drama, comedy, and music shows carried on national networks like NBC and CBS. As network television overtook radio as the new American pastime, radio evolved into a portable medium for music. Format radio programming, which played Top 40 hits on an endless rotation, energized rock and roll in the 1950s and helped cultivate teen culture. In the 1990s, radio in the United States changed dramatically as government deregulation permitted unprecedented consolidation in ownership, with just a few corporations wielding great influence over the sound of radio.

Although the big radio chains control the largest share of radio's listeners, some critics charge that they have gotten even greedier. Along with deregulation of ownership, the 1996 Telecommunications Act also relaxed limits on radio advertising time, leading some formats, especially news/talk, to run up to thirty minutes of commercials each hour. Digital technology has aided the drive to squeeze more ads into each hour of radio. A small audio-processing device called Cash briefly delays live radio programs by a minute or two, shortens pauses between words, and clips long vowels before replaying the processed signal on air. The resulting digital compression speeds up the pace of the show and saves time for the insertion of up to four extra minutes of ads each hour. Listeners generally don't notice the tighter pace of the program, but they do notice the extra commercials. In fact, thousands of Rush Limbaugh's listeners complained about the additional commercials on his program. WABC in New York suspended the use of the technology for Limbaugh's show in that market, although many other stations continue to use it.[14]

Given broadcasters' reluctance to raise questions about these economic arrangements, public debate regarding radio as a special national resource has remained minuscule. Looking to the future, and with instances like the corporate radio response to the Minot train disaster in mind, a big question remains to be answered: With a few large broadcast companies now permitted to dominate radio ownership nationwide, will this consolidation of power restrict the number and kinds of voices permitted to speak over public airwaves? To ensure that mass media industries continue to serve democracy and local communities, the public needs to play a role in developing the answer to this question.

www.

For review questions and activities for Chapter 4, go to the interactive *Media and Culture* Online Study Guide at *bedfordstmartins.com/ mediaculture*

REVIEW QUESTIONS

Early Technology and the Development of Broadcasting

1. Why was the development of the telegraph important in media history? What were some of the disadvantages of telegraph technology?

2. How is the concept of the wireless different from that of radio?

3. What was Guglielmo Marconi's role in the development of the wireless?

4. What were Lee De Forest's contributions to radio?

5. Why was the RCA monopoly formed?

6. How did broadcasting, unlike print media, come to be federally regulated?

The Evolution of Commercial Radio

7. What was AT&T's role in the early days of radio?

8. How did the radio networks develop? What were the contributions of David Sarnoff and William Paley to network radio?

9. Why did the government-sanctioned RCA monopoly end?

10. What is the significance of the Federal Communications Act of 1934?

Radio Reinvents Itself

11. How did radio adapt to the arrival of television?

12. What was Edwin Armstrong's role in the advancement of radio technology? Why did RCA hamper Armstrong's work?

13. How did music on radio change in the 1950s?

14. What was format radio, and why was it important to the survival of radio?

The Sounds of Radio Today

15. Why are there so many radio formats today?

16. Why did Top 40 radio diminish as a format in the 1980s and 1990s?

17. What is the state of nonprofit radio today?

18. What arguments do pirate radio operators use to justify the existence of their stations?

19. What are the reasons existing full-power radio broadcasters sought to delay and limit the emergence of low-power FM stations?

20. What are the current ownership rules governing American radio?

21. How do Internet radio and satellite radio present an alternative to broadcast radio?

22. What has been the main effect of the Telecommunications Act of 1996 on radio station ownership?

Radio and the Democracy of the Airwaves

23. Throughout the history of radio, why did the government encourage monopoly or oligopoly ownership of radio broadcasting?

QUESTIONING THE MEDIA

1. Describe your earliest memories of listening to radio. Do you remember a favorite song? How old were you? Do you remember the station's call letters? Why did you listen?

2. Count the number and types of radio stations in your area today. What formats do they use? Do a little research and compare today's situation with the number and types of stations available in the 1930s and the 1950s. Describe the changes that have occurred.

3. If you could own and manage a commercial radio station, what format would you choose and why?

4. If you ran a noncommercial radio station in your area, what services would you provide that are not being met by commercial format radio?

5. How might radio be used to improve social and political discussions in the United States?

6. If you were the head of a large radio group, what arguments would you make in response to charges that your company limited the number of voices in the local media?

SEARCHING THE INTERNET

http://www.radio-locator.com

One of the most comprehensive listings of U.S. and worldwide radio station Web pages, including those stations that broadcast their audio signal on the Internet.

http://www.fcc.gov

A comprehensive government site, with sections on radio and the full text of the Telecommunications Act of 1996.

http://www.pri.org

PRI is a top provider of content for more than six hundred public radio stations, with programs such as Garrison Keillor's *A Prairie Home Companion,* Ira Glass's *This American Life,* and *World Café.*

http://www.npr.org

NPR's site includes audio files of special reports and hourly news updates, along with guides to other NPR programming.

http://www.bbc.co.uk/radio

BBC Radio's home page, featuring eleven unique noncommercial radio channels, all with program archives.

http://www.xmradio.com and http://www.sirius.com

The Web sites for the two competing U.S. satellite radio services, XM and Sirius.

KEY TERMS

telegraph, 119
Morse code, 119
electromagnetic waves, 120
radio waves, 120
wireless telegraphy, 121
wireless telephony, 122
broadcasting, 123
narrowcasting, 123
Radio Act of 1912, 124
Radio Corporation of America (RCA), 124
network, 127
option time, 129
Radio Act of 1927, 131
Federal Communications Act of 1934, 131

Federal Radio Commission (FRC), 131
Federal Communications Commission (FCC), 131
transistors, 135
FM, 135
AM, 135
format radio, 137
rotation, 137
payola, 138
pay-for-play, 139
drive time, 140
news/talk format, 141
adult contemporary (AC), 141
contemporary hit radio (CHR), 142
country, 142

urban, 142
album-oriented rock (AOR), 144
Telecommunications Act of 1996, 144
National Public Radio (NPR), 147
Public Broadcasting Service (PBS), 147
Public Broadcasting Act of 1967, 147
Corporation for Public Broadcasting (CPB), 147
Pacifica Foundation, 148
low power FM (LPFM), 149
Internet radio, 150
satellite radio, 150
podcasting, 150

In Brief

Think: Take two minutes to write down answers to the following questions about your radio-listening habits: How much radio do you listen to? When do you listen? What attracts you to a particular station?

Pair: Turn to a neighbor and compare notes. Which radio formats (if any) do you agree on? What do you think the stations are doing that is "right"? What aspects of radio programming bother you?

Share: Open up the discussion to the entire class. If you could envision the perfect radio station with the perfect format, what would it be? How would it be funded? Whom would it serve? What should be the purpose of this radio station in the community?

In Depth

This exercise examines radio-group ownership and format specialization. Assign each radio station in your market to individuals or small groups in the class. Listen to the same hour (e.g., 4:00 to 5:00 P.M.) during the day for each station.

Description. Use a chart and break down the hour into a program log, describing what you hear, including music, news, deejay chatter, ads, community announcements, station promotions, and contests. Describe the style of these broadcasts, as well as the time devoted to each category. Who is the target audience? Who owns the station? Do the ad and promotion styles match the general flavor of the station?

Analysis. Compare program logs and other station information with classmates. What patterns emerge? Do the stations owned by the same radio group sound similar in certain ways (e.g., advertisers, newscasters, promotions)? Are there any locally owned stations, and do they program differently? Which (if any) stations provide the best local news, events, and weather information? Which (if any) stations feature local artists? What did you like best of what you heard? What did you like least?

Interpretation. According to FCC rules, radio stations are trustees of public airwaves. Basing your opinion on the limited hours you listened, do you think these stations were doing a responsible job of serving the public? If some radio stations in a single market have similar formats, is that bad? Is there enough station differentiation in your market? What audience segments are not targeted by the radio stations in your market? Why not?

Evaluation. Does the radio industry give listeners what they want, or does it give listeners what the industry wants? Do you think radio companies are being responsible stewards of the public airwaves? What are some changes you'd like to see in radio?

Engagement. Listeners have the right to provide written comments about a station's programming to both radio stations and the FCC. Commercial stations are required to keep letters and e-mails received from the public in their public file, which must be open for inspection at every station by any citizen during regular business hours. Listeners also have the right to comment on a radio (or TV) station's license renewal process (which usually happens every eight years). Citizens may file a petition to deny a license, an informal objection, or positive comments with the FCC. For details on how to do this, see "The Public and Broadcasting" document at www.fcc.gov.

television

and the power of visual culture

Law & Order: Criminal Intent cocreators Dick Wolf and Rene Balcher, the program's head writer, modeled the odd, smart, cerebral, jumpy, streetwise New York detective Robert Goren (played by Vincent D'Onofrio) after nineteenth-century sleuth Sherlock Holmes. Such attention to character offers a twenty-first-century clue about why prime-time television — experimenting in the last few years with a plethora of instant and cheap "reality shows" — won't kill off traditional forms of dramatic storytelling.

NBC's *Criminal Intent* and *Law & Order: Special Victims Unit* are successful spinoffs to Wolf's long-running original *Law & Order,* which premiered in 1990 (and was still producing new episodes for NBC in 2006–07). The storytelling on the *Law & Order* shows — and its CBS counterpart *CSI* (and its franchise) — stand up much better than reality programs like *Survivor, The Apprentice,* and *American Idol* in the lucrative rerun syndication market for local TV stations and cable channels. Since most *Law & Order* and *CSI*

episodes are self-contained stories (i.e., they don't require us to follow the story over weeks like a soap opera or reality series), they can be shown as reruns five days a week or on weekends—out of order. In addition, unlike most reality programs, traditional network dramas require talented writers, editors, and actors to sustain their stories over time. While reality shows like *Survivor* and *American Idol* appear more popular in their prime-time runs on network television, a good dramatic series has a longer shelf life. As Wolf said in 2006 about the enduring power of his three shows (controlled by him and his syndicator, NBC Universal), "The three shows have got 600 combined episodes. They have turned TNT into the No. 1 network on cable and USA into the No. 2 network on cable."[1]

Episodes of *Law & Order* and *CSI*, as well as other dramas such as *Lost, 24, Grey's Anatomy,* and *Desperate Housewives,* are also among the newest offerings of the latest technology affecting traditional television. Multiple forms of non-television delivery systems are now available for downloading TV programs—on video iPods and cell phones—for fees ranging from 99 cents to $1.99 per episode. In addition, cable TV giants like Comcast and Time Warner are making traditional network programs available as part of their video-on-demand (VOD) services, which allow customers to buy TV shows and watch them when they want—minus commercials. Paul Saffo, director of the Institute for the Future, argued in 2005: "No old media form ever disappears. They just get reinvented into a new purpose. TV is about to go through a profound reinvention."[2]

Not only is TV being reinvented but its audience, although fragmented, is also growing, given all the new ways there are to watch television. Just a few years ago, televisions glimmered in the average U.S. household just over seven hours a day, but by late 2006 that figure grew to eight hours per day. And with the growth of DVRs (digital video recorders) like TiVo, which were in 13 percent of U.S. homes by late 2006, television viewing was up almost 5 percent in these homes. Forecasters predict that 25 percent of homes will have DVR technology by 2010. DVRs not only allow viewers to store regular TV programs in computer memories but also can pause programs in "real time," record entire TV series—like *Criminal Intent* on cable reruns—and skip through commercials, all with the press of a button. So while new technology is changing television delivery, the networks still rely on good old storytelling—despite the crop of reality programs that have dominated the TV landscape in the last decade—to keep viewers watching and earn money through syndication.

oday network television is surviving and mostly prospering—not only with dramatic series like *Law & Order* but by recycling old program ideas like the quiz show, by swiping concepts from European programmers (like *American Idol*), or just by stealing shows from each other. There is a long and storied history to all these techniques. After all, in the beginning, network television "borrowed" most of its best program ideas from radio. Throughout the 1950s, television snatched radio's national sponsors, program ideas, and even its **prime-time** audience. Old radio scripts began reappearing in TV form. In 1949, for instance, *The Lone Ranger* rode over to television from radio, where the program had originated in 1933. *Amos 'n' Andy,* a fixture on network radio since 1928, became the first TV series to have an entirely black cast in 1951. Jack Benny, Red Skelton, and George Burns and Gracie Allen, among the most prominent comedians of their day, all left radio for television. Symbolic of the times, the radio news program *Hear It Now* turned into TV's *See It Now,* and *Candid Microphone* became *Candid Camera.*

Since replacing radio in the 1950s as our most popular medium, television has sparked repeated arguments about its social and cultural impact. During the 1990s, for example, teachers, clergy, journalists, and others waged a public assault on TV's negative impact on children. A 1995 *New York Times* poll suggested that most Americans blamed television as the biggest single factor underlying teenage sex and violence (although TV viewing during teenage years actually decreases).[3] During the 2000 and 2004 presidential election campaigns, television was targeted once again for reinforcing an outmoded two-party political system driven by big-money TV ads.

But there is another side to this story. In times of crisis, our fragmented and pluralistic society has turned to television as a touchstone, as common ground. We did this during the Army–McCarthy hearings on communism in the 1950s, during the exposure of civil rights violations in the South and in the aftermath of the Kennedy and King assassinations in the 1960s, and during the political turmoil of Watergate in the 1970s. In 1995, when 168 people died in the bombing of the Oklahoma City federal building, we looked to television to make sense of senselessness. In September 2001—in shock and horror—we all turned to television to learn that nearly 3,000 people had been killed in terrorist attacks on the World Trade Center and the Pentagon and in a plane crash in Pennsylvania. In 2003, we watched the beginning of the Iraq War. And in 2005, we watched the coverage of Hurricane Katrina and saw haunting images of people drowned in flooding or displaced forever from the homes they grew up in. For better or worse, television has woven itself into the cultural fabric of daily life.

In this age of increasing market specialization, television is still the one mass medium that delivers content millions can share simultaneously—everything from the Super Bowl to a network game show to the coverage of natural disasters. In this chapter, we will examine television's impact: the cultural, social, and economic factors surrounding the most influential media innovation since the printing press. We will begin by reviewing the early experiments with TV technology that led to the medium's development. We will then focus on the TV boom in the 1950s, including the downfall of sponsor-controlled content and the impact of the quiz-show scandals. Most of TV's major programming trends developed during this period, and we will investigate the most significant ones, including news, comedy, and drama. We will trace the audience decline that has affected the major networks and explore television as a prime-time money factory, examining various developments and costs in the production, distribution, and syndication of programs. Finally, we will look at television's impact on democracy.

> " *Criminal Intent* is not one of those tedious howdunits, along the lines of *CSI,* . . . and its countless imitators, but rather a whydunit. "
>
> —Alex Strachan, Montreal *Gazette,* November 2005

> " Television is the medium from which most of us receive our news, sports, entertainment, cues for civic discourse, and, most of all, our marching orders as consumers. "
>
> —Frank Rich, *New York Times,* 1998

The Origins and Early Development of Television

In 1948, only 1 percent of America's households had a television set; by 1953, more than 50 percent had one; and by the early 1960s, more than 90 percent of all homes had a TV set. With television on the rise throughout the 1950s, many feared that radio—as well as books, magazines, and movies—would become irrelevant and unnecessary. What happened, of course, is that both radio and print media adapted to this new technology. In fact, today more radio stations are operating and more books and magazines are published than ever before; only ticket sales for movies have flattened and declined slightly since the 1960s.

Early TV Technology

Although television achieved mass media status in the 1950s, inventors from a number of nations had been toying with the idea of televised images for nearly a hundred years. Isolating TV and radio waves—part of the electromagnetic spectrum—required two ingredients: a photoelectric sensing material and a technique for encoding pictures for transmission via radio waves. Inventors needed a medium like film so that when light struck it, an electric current could be generated. In the late 1800s, the invention of the *cathode ray tube,* the forerunner of the TV picture tube, combined principles of the camera and electricity. Because television images could not physically float through the air, technicians and inventors developed a method of encoding them at a transmission point (a TV station) and decoding them at the reception point (a TV set). In the 1880s, German inventor Paul Nipkow developed the *scanning disk,* a large flat metal disk with a series of small perforations organized in a spiral pattern. As the disk rotated, it separated pictures into pinpoints of light that could be transmitted as a series of electronic lines. As the disk spun, each small hole scanned one line of a scene to be televised. For years, Nipkow's disk served as the foundation for experiments regarding the transmission of visual images.

● At the 1939 World's Fair in New York, the "guts" of a TV set featured a sealed glass device called a *cathode ray tube.* Such picture tubes were the technical standard in television for more than fifty years. Late in 1996, the FCC approved a new standard—digital, high-definition television.

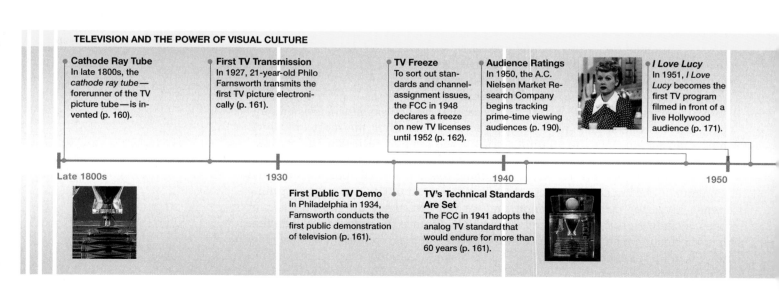

TELEVISION AND THE POWER OF VISUAL CULTURE

Cathode Ray Tube
In late 1800s, the *cathode ray tube*—forerunner of the TV picture tube—is invented (p. 160).

First TV Transmission
In 1927, 21-year-old Philo Farnsworth transmits the first TV picture electronically (p. 161).

TV Freeze
To sort out standards and channel-assignment issues, the FCC in 1948 declares a freeze on new TV licenses until 1952 (p. 162).

Audience Ratings
In 1950, the A.C. Nielsen Market Research Company begins tracking prime-time viewing audiences (p. 190).

I Love Lucy
In 1951, *I Love Lucy* becomes the first TV program filmed in front of a live Hollywood audience (p. 171).

Late 1800s   1930   1940   1950

First Public TV Demo
In Philadelphia in 1934, Farnsworth conducts the first public demonstration of television (p. 161).

TV's Technical Standards Are Set
The FCC in 1941 adopts the analog TV standard that would endure for more than 60 years (p. 161).

In 1907, Russian physicist Boris Rosing improved the mechanical scanning device, but it was his lab assistant, Vladimir Zworykin, and an Idaho teenager, Philo Farnsworth, who independently pioneered an electronic TV system. Zworykin left Russia for America in 1919 and went to work for Westinghouse, where he developed the *iconoscope,* the first TV camera tube to convert light rays into electrical signals. By breaking down and converting these signals into radio waves, transmitting them through the air, and reconstructing them in a receiver set, inventors made television a possibility by 1923.

By age sixteen, Farnsworth had figured out that mechanical scanning systems would not work for sending pictures through the air over long distances. On September 7, 1927, at age twenty-one, Farnsworth transmitted the first TV picture electronically by rotating a straight line scratched on a square of painted glass by 90°. Finally, in 1930, he patented the first electronic television. RCA, then the world leader in broadcasting technology, challenged Farnsworth in a major patents battle. He had to rely on his high school science teacher to produce his original drawings from 1922. After its court defeat, RCA had to negotiate to use Farnsworth's patents. He later licensed these patents to RCA and AT&T for use in the commercial development of television. Farnsworth conducted the first public demonstration of television at the Franklin Institute in Philadelphia in 1934—five years *before* RCA's famous public demo at the 1939 World's Fair.

> **❝ 'There's nothing on it worthwhile, and we're not going to watch it in this household, and I don't want it in your intellectual diet.'❞**
>
> –Kent Farnsworth, recalling his father's attitude toward TV when Kent was growing up

Setting Technical Standards

In the late 1930s, the National Television Systems Committee (NTSC), a group representing major electronics firms, began meeting to outline industry-wide manufacturing and technical standards. As a result of these meetings, in 1941 the Federal Communications Commission (FCC) adopted a 525-line image, scanned electronically at thirty frames per second (fps); this still is the standard for all TV sets produced in the United States until the new digital standard phases out old sets (see "Tracking Technology: Digital TV and the End of Analog" on page 164). About thirty countries, including Japan, Canada, Mexico, Saudi Arabia, and most Latin American nations, adopted the NTSC system. Great Britain and the former Soviet Union, however, waited for the technology to improve and eventually adopted a slightly superior 625-line, 25-fps system, used for decades throughout most of Europe and Asia. A third standard operated in France, Belgium, Algeria, and a few other countries.

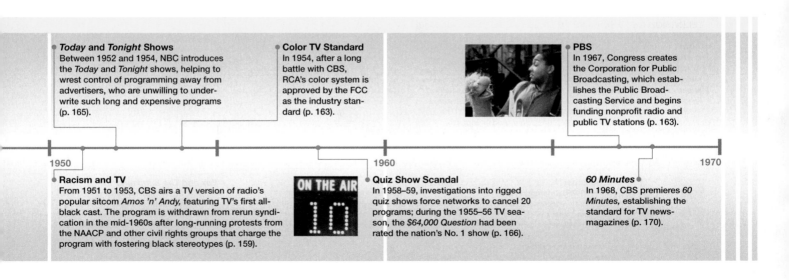

Today and Tonight Shows
Between 1952 and 1954, NBC introduces the *Today* and *Tonight* shows, helping to wrest control of programming away from advertisers, who are unwilling to underwrite such long and expensive programs (p. 165).

Color TV Standard
In 1954, after a long battle with CBS, RCA's color system is approved by the FCC as the industry standard (p. 163).

PBS
In 1967, Congress creates the Corporation for Public Broadcasting, which establishes the Public Broadcasting Service and begins funding nonprofit radio and public TV stations (p. 163).

1950   1960   1970

Racism and TV
From 1951 to 1953, CBS airs a TV version of radio's popular sitcom *Amos 'n' Andy,* featuring TV's first all-black cast. The program is withdrawn from rerun syndication in the mid-1960s after long-running protests from the NAACP and other civil rights groups that charge the program with fostering black stereotypes (p. 159).

ON THE AIR
10

Quiz Show Scandal
In 1958–59, investigations into rigged quiz shows force networks to cancel 20 programs; during the 1955–56 TV season, the *$64,000 Question* had been rated the nation's No. 1 show (p. 166).

60 Minutes
In 1968, CBS premieres *60 Minutes,* establishing the standard for TV newsmagazines (p. 170).

Fiddling with Frequencies and Freezing TV Licenses

A fundamental difference between broadcast television and cable is that traditional TV signals travel through the airwaves via the same electromagnetic spectrum that carries radio signals. This meant that the number of TV stations a city or market could support in television's early days (and today in some sparsely populated areas) was limited because airwave frequencies would interfere with one another. So a TV market could have a channel 2 and a channel 4 but not a channel 3, or a channel 5 and a channel 7 but not a channel 6. Cable systems don't have this problem because they download both regular wireless TV signals and satellite cable services and reassign them new channel allocations in a wired system. Frequency congestion and limited space problems are cleared up when over-the-air TV signals get assigned to their own cable channels.

In the 1940s, the FCC began assigning certain channels in specific geographic areas to make sure there was no interference. (One effect of this was that for years New Jersey had no TV stations because those signals would have interfered with the New York stations.) The FCC also set aside thirteen channels (1–13) on a **VHF** (very high frequency) band for black-and-white television. At this time, though, most electronics firms were converting to wartime production, so commercial TV development was limited: Only ten stations were operating when Pearl Harbor was attacked in December 1941. However, by 1948, the FCC had issued nearly a hundred television licenses. Due to growing concern about the allocation of a finite number of channels and with growing frequency-interference problems as existing channels "overlapped," the FCC declared a freeze on new licenses from 1948 to 1952.

The Korean War prolonged the freeze. During this time, cities such as New York, Chicago, and Los Angeles had several TV stations, whereas other areas, including Little Rock, Arkansas, and Portland, Oregon, had none. Cities with TV stations saw a 20 to 40 percent drop in movie attendance during this period; more than sixty movie theaters closed in the Chicago area alone. But in non-TV cities, movie audiences increased. Taxi receipts and nightclub attendance also fell in TV cities, as did library book circulation. At the same time, radio listening declined; for example, Bob Hope's network radio show lost half its national audience between 1949 and 1951. By 1951, sales of television sets had surpassed sales of radio receivers.

After a second NTSC conference in 1952 sorted out technical problems, the FCC

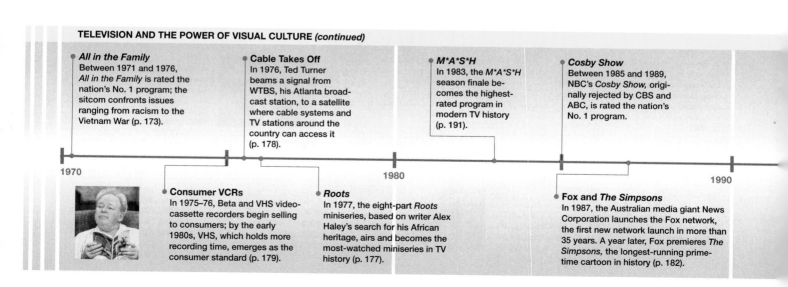

TELEVISION AND THE POWER OF VISUAL CULTURE *(continued)*

All in the Family
Between 1971 and 1976, *All in the Family* is rated the nation's No. 1 program; the sitcom confronts issues ranging from racism to the Vietnam War (p. 173).

Cable Takes Off
In 1976, Ted Turner beams a signal from WTBS, his Atlanta broadcast station, to a satellite where cable systems and TV stations around the country can access it (p. 178).

*M*A*S*H*
In 1983, the *M*A*S*H* season finale becomes the highest-rated program in modern TV history (p. 191).

Cosby Show
Between 1985 and 1989, NBC's *Cosby Show*, originally rejected by CBS and ABC, is rated the nation's No. 1 program.

1970

1980

1990

Consumer VCRs
In 1975–76, Beta and VHS videocassette recorders begin selling to consumers; by the early 1980s, VHS, which holds more recording time, emerges as the consumer standard (p. 179).

Roots
In 1977, the eight-part *Roots* miniseries, based on writer Alex Haley's search for his African heritage, airs and becomes the most-watched miniseries in TV history (p. 177).

Fox and *The Simpsons*
In 1987, the Australian media giant News Corporation launches the Fox network, the first new network launch in more than 35 years. A year later, Fox premieres *The Simpsons*, the longest-running prime-time cartoon in history (p. 182).

ended the licensing freeze and issued a major report finalizing technical standards, many still in use today. Among its actions, the FCC set aside seventy new channels (14–83) on a **UHF** (ultrahigh frequency) band, although few manufacturers in the 1950s made TV sets equipped with UHF reception. As a result, UHF license holders struggled for years, until a 1964 law finally required manufacturers to equip sets with UHF reception. With the expansion of UHF slowed by technical snags, the FCC eventually "took back" channels 70–83 and reassigned those frequencies (plus VHF's channel 1) to other communication services, including new radio allocations and cellular phones. During this period, most major cities were assigned four to five VHF signals and maybe another five to six UHF signals.

In all the TV markets across the country, nearly 250 channels were initially set aside for educational or nonprofit status, most of them on the newly created UHF band. Commercial interests, as they did in radio, had gobbled up most of the early VHF assignments with the FCC's blessing. But the FCC did not establish a method for financing nonprofit stations, and a long economic struggle followed for many of the educational TV stations. Even with the creation of the Corporation for Public Broadcasting (CPB) in 1967, which funneled federal funds to nonprofit radio and public TV stations, the loose, decentralized network of stations that share Public Broadcasting Service (PBS) programming have had to beg listeners and corporate underwriters for most of their financial support. This has been especially true since the 1990s, when Congress reduced CPB's funding to public TV to about 15 percent of its actual costs.

Another outcome of the freeze featured deliberations about the standards for a color TV system. In 1952, the FCC tentatively approved the experimental CBS system. Because its signal could not be received by black-and-white sets, however, the system was incompatible with those that most Americans owned. In 1954, RCA's color system, which could also receive black-and-white images, usurped CBS to become the color standard. Although NBC began broadcasting a few shows in color in the mid-1950s, it wasn't until 1966 that all three networks broadcast their entire evening lineups in color.

Almost thirteen hundred communities received TV channel allocations from the FCC after the freeze ended. Because broadcast signals could interfere with one another, the FCC created a national map and tried to distribute all available channels evenly throughout the country. By the mid-1950s, there were more than four hundred television stations in operation, a 400 percent surge since the pre-freeze era.

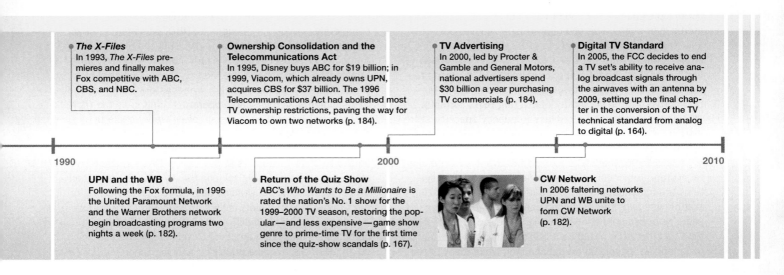

The X-Files
In 1993, *The X-Files* premieres and finally makes Fox competitive with ABC, CBS, and NBC.

Ownership Consolidation and the Telecommunications Act
In 1995, Disney buys ABC for $19 billion; in 1999, Viacom, which already owns UPN, acquires CBS for $37 billion. The 1996 Telecommunications Act had abolished most TV ownership restrictions, paving the way for Viacom to own two networks (p. 184).

TV Advertising
In 2000, led by Procter & Gamble and General Motors, national advertisers spend $30 billion a year purchasing TV commercials (p. 184).

Digital TV Standard
In 2005, the FCC decides to end a TV set's ability to receive analog broadcast signals through the airwaves with an antenna by 2009, setting up the final chapter in the conversion of the TV technical standard from analog to digital (p. 164).

1990   2000   2010

UPN and the WB
Following the Fox formula, in 1995 the United Paramount Network and the Warner Brothers network begin broadcasting programs two nights a week (p. 182).

Return of the Quiz Show
ABC's *Who Wants to Be a Millionaire* is rated the nation's No. 1 show for the 1999–2000 TV season, restoring the popular—and less expensive—game show genre to prime-time TV for the first time since the quiz-show scandals (p. 167).

CW Network
In 2006 faltering networks UPN and WB unite to form CW Network (p. 182).

Digital TV and the End of Analog

In 2005, Congress ruled that 2009 would bring an end to a TV set's ability to receive analog broadcast signals through the airwaves with an antenna. So unless homes have cable or satellite service (or buy a digital converter), about 15 to 20 percent of the 265 million existing analog TV sets now in use in the United States won't work after 2009.

The story behind the analog-to-digital conversion began in late 1996, when the FCC initiated the first fundamental changes in TV technology in more than fifty years.[1] Since the early 1960s, TV engineers had been searching to improve the clarity and resolution of the standard NTSC 525-line TV image established in the 1940s. Most experiments focused on improving existing **analog** transmission, in which images are sent as continuous signals through the airwaves on specific frequencies. By the 1980s, Japanese firms had developed high-definition television (HDTV) for their own markets; with 1,100-plus lines of resolution, HDTV was the far superior analog alternative to the old NTSC standard, which had only 525 lines of resolution. Some version of this early HDTV experiment seemed certain to become the new U.S. television standard.

In the late 1980s, however, HDTV ran into the digital revolution. After seeing an impressive Sony HDTV demonstration in 1987, the FCC set up a race among various companies to develop a new American standard that used **digital** technology, which converts images and text to computerized signals. Sony and other Japanese firms then created a hybrid of analog and digital HDTV innovations. To beat the Japanese challenge, in 1988 a consortium of broadcasters, electronics and computer manufacturers, and researchers from Europe and America—known as the Grand Alliance—began developing an all-digital system that surpassed the versatility of existing HDTV formats. The digital standard required less frequency space to store more images, channels, and computer data than analog or hybrid HDTV systems.

In late 1996, the FCC approved the Grand Alliance digital system. Under this plan, since analog and digital systems are incompatible without a converter, each existing station was allocated a second channel for roughly ten years as consumers convert to digital sets. During that time, each station would continue to broadcast programs using analog signals on its old channel, while many of the same programs would begin transmitting on a newly allo-

cated digital channel. Because of the expense of digital conversion (roughly $1 million), by 2004 only about half of the nation's 1,300 commercial broadcast stations had begun digital transmissions. At the end of the adjustment period (2009), local stations are supposed to surrender their old analog frequencies to the FCC, which will then auction them off—to various competing companies for use by cell phones or public safety communications—formally ending analog broadcasting.

Analysts expect the pace of digital TV to pick up, although by 2006 only 15 percent of U.S. households received digital signals. It is not likely Americans will quickly throw out their more than 265 million analog TV sets (which have about a ten-year life span) when the current analog broadcast system changes over to digital. Instead, most people without cable or satellite service will probably purchase set-top tuner/converters to pick up the digital signals. These converters sold for about $700 in 2005 but analysts predict a cost of only $50 by 2009. In 2005–06, Congress offered to help subsidize converters by setting aside $1.5 billion to pay for up to two $40 vouchers per household.

With the conversion under way, in the 2001–02 TV season the major TV networks began carrying partial digital schedules, with the expensive high-definition broadcasts typically underwritten by the digital setmakers. By 2002, though, the best medium for digital television was direct broadcast satellite systems like DirecTV, which offered a completely high-definition signal of HBO, plus another channel of special events in digital HDTV. Still, the majority of American TV households, the nearly 70 percent that watch broadcast TV via cable, were missing the crisp digital pictures. That is because although broadcasters were required to send digital signals, cable operators, limited by the technical capacities of their systems, often were unable to carry the broadcasters' digital programs. Interestingly enough, it is DVDs and not digital broadcasts that have helped to push consumers to buy digital TV sets, since DVD movies look better on digital monitors. By 2006, more than 60 percent of U.S. households had a DVD player, helping to pave the way to complete TV's digital revolution. Additionally, the cost of a good digital set—like that of computers—has been dropping by half every two years or so. In 1999 the average price of a fully digital projection TV was $8,000, but by 2006 that price was less than $2,000.

Today, about seventeen hundred TV stations are in operation, including more than three hundred nonprofit stations.

Sponsorship and Scandal — TV Grows Up

Although television was considered a novelty in the late 1940s and early 1950s, by the close of the 1950s the new technology had become a dominant mass medium and cultural force with more than 90 percent of U.S. households owning at least one set. Partly, television's new standing came as it moved away from the influence of radio and established a separate identity. Two important contributors to this identity were (1) a major change in the advertising and sponsorship structure of television, and, more significant, (2) a major cultural scandal.

The Rise and Fall of Sponsorship

Like radio in the 1930s and 1940s, early television programs were often conceived, produced, and supported by a single sponsor. Many of the top-rated programs in the 1950s even included the sponsor's name in the title: *Buick Circus Hour, Camel News Caravan, Colgate Comedy Hour,* and *Goodyear TV Playhouse.* Today no regular program on network television is named after and controlled by a single sponsor.

Throughout the early 1950s, the broadcast networks became increasingly unhappy with the control sponsors exerted over program content, and they took steps to change things. With the growing popularity of television came opportunities to alter prior financial arrangements, especially given the high cost of producing programs on a weekly basis. In 1952, for example, a single one-hour TV show cost a sponsor about $35,000, a figure that rose to $90,000 by the end of the decade. These weekly costs became increasingly difficult for sponsors to bear.

David Sarnoff, then head of RCA/NBC, and William Paley, head of CBS, saw the opportunity to diminish the role of sponsors. Enter Sylvester "Pat" Weaver (father of actress Sigourney Weaver), who was appointed president of NBC by Sarnoff in 1953. A former advertising executive, Weaver was used to controlling radio content for his clients. When he made the switch to television, Weaver sought to retain that control — by forcing advertisers out of the content game. By increasing program length from fifteen minutes (standard for radio programs) to thirty minutes and longer, Weaver substantially raised program costs for advertisers. In addition, two new programming changes made significant inroads in helping the networks gain control of content.

The first strategy featured the concept of a "magazine" program that included multiple segments — news, talk, comedy, music, and the like — similar to the content variety found in a general-interest or newsmagazine of the day, such as *Life* or *Time.* In January 1952, NBC introduced the *Today* show, which started

● Following in the tradition of *The Tonight Show, Late Night with Conan O'Brien* — which airs right after Jay Leno's *Tonight Show* — is a talk-comedy program that is especially popular among college students. A former Emmy-winning writer on *Saturday Night Live* and *The Simpsons,* the Harvard-educated O'Brien (*right,* with actor Mike Myers) inherited *Late Night* when David Letterman went to CBS in 1993 to compete head-to-head against Leno.

as a three-hour morning talk-news program. Then in September 1954, NBC premiered the ninety-minute *Tonight Show*. Because both shows ran daily rather than weekly, studio production costs managed by a single sponsor were prohibitive. Rather than selling the whole concept to one sponsor, NBC sold spot ads within the shows: Advertisers paid the network for thirty- or sixty-second time slots. The network, not the sponsor, now owned the programs or bought them from independent producers. Fifty years later, the *Today* and *Tonight* shows remain fixtures on NBC.

The second strategy, known originally as the "spectacular," is today recognized by a more modest term, the *television special*. At NBC, Weaver bought special programs, like Laurence Olivier's filmed version of *Richard III* and the Broadway production of *Peter Pan*, again selling spot ads to multiple sponsors. The 1955 TV version of *Peter Pan* was a particular success, watched by some sixty-five million viewers (compare the final episode of NBC's *Friends*, watched by about fifty million viewers in spring 2004). More typical specials featured music-variety shows hosted by top singers such as Judy Garland and Frank Sinatra. The combination of these programming strategies—and one juicy television scandal—ended sponsors' control over television content.

The Quiz-Show Scandals Seal Sponsorship's Fate

Corporate backers of quiz shows drove the final nail into the coffin of sponsor-controlled TV content. In the mid-1950s, the networks revived the radio quiz-show genre. CBS aired the *$64,000 Question*, originally radio's more modest *$64 Question*—symbolic of how much television had raised the economic stakes. Sponsored by Revlon, which bought a half-hour block of evening prime time from the network in 1955, the program ranked as the most popular TV show in America during its first year. As one historian has suggested: "It is impossible to explain fully the popular appeal of the *$64,000 Question*. Be it the lure of sudden wealth, the challenge to answer

● Quizmaster Jack Barry questions contestants on *Twenty-One* (NBC, 1956–58), the popular game show that was struck by scandal in 1958.

esoteric questions, happiness at seeing other people achieving financial success, whatever the program touched in the American psyche at mid-century, this was stunning TV."[4] By the end of the 1957–58 season, twenty-two quiz shows aired on network television.

Revlon followed its success with the $64,000 *Challenge* in 1956. At one point, Revlon's two shows were running first and second in the national ratings, and its name recognition was so enhanced that the company periodically ran out of products. In fact, the company's cosmetic sales skyrocketed from $1.2 million before its sponsorship of the quiz shows to nearly $10 million by 1959.

Compared with dramas and situation comedies (which we'll look at shortly), quiz shows were (and are today) cheap to produce, with inexpensive sets and mostly nonactors as guests. In addition, these programs offered the corporate sponsor the opportunity to have its name displayed on the set throughout the program. The problem was that most of these shows were rigged. To heighten the drama and get rid of guests whom the sponsors or producers did not find appealing, key contestants were rehearsed and given the answers. The most notorious rigging occurred on *Twenty-One,* a quiz show owned by Geritol (whose profits climbed by $4 million one year after deciding to sponsor the program in 1956). The subject of Robert Redford's 1994 film *Quiz Show,* Charles Van Doren was *Twenty-One's* most infamous contestant. A Columbia University English professor from a famous literary family, Van Doren won $129,000 in 1957 during his fifteen-week run on the program; his fame then landed him a job on NBC's *Today* show. In 1958, after a series of contestants accused the morning show *Dotto* of being fixed, the networks quickly dropped twenty quiz shows. Following further rumors, a *TV Guide* story, a New York grand jury probe, and a congressional investigation in 1959 (during which Van Doren admitted to cheating), big-money prime-time quiz shows ended—until ABC revived the format forty years later with *Who Wants to Be a Millionaire.*

Although often little more than a compelling footnote in many accounts of television's history, the impact of the quiz-show scandals was enormous. First, the pressure on TV executives to rig the programs and the subsequent fraud effectively put an end to any role sponsors might have had in creating television content. Second, although many Americans had believed in the democratic possibilities of television—bringing inexpensive information and entertainment into every household—this belief was undermined by the sponsors and TV executives who participated in the quiz-show fraud. During the 1950s, many people trusted that the novelty of new TV images was more honest than words. But the scandals provided the first dramatic indication that TV images could be manipulated. Our contemporary cynicism about electronic culture began in this time, and by the end of the decade, many middle-class parents were even refusing to allow their children to watch television.

The third, and most important, impact of the quiz-show scandals was that they magnified the separation between the privileged few and the general public, a division between high and low that would affect print and visual culture for at least the next forty years. That Charles Van Doren had come from a family of Ivy League intellectuals and "sold his soul" for fame and money drove a wedge between intellectuals and the popular new medium. At the time, many well-educated people aimed a wary skepticism toward television. This was best captured in the famous 1961 speech by FCC commissioner Newton Minow, who labeled game shows, westerns, cartoons, and other popular genres part of commercial television's "vast wasteland." Critics have used the wasteland metaphor ever since to admonish the TV industry for failing to live up to its potential. After the quiz-show scandal, non-network, independently produced programs like *Jeopardy* and *Wheel of Fortune,* now called *game shows,* made a strong comeback in syndicated late-afternoon time slots. Then cable services

> **"**I was fascinated by the seduction of [Charles] Van Doren, by the Faustian bargain that lured entirely good and honest people into careers of deception.**"**
>
> —Robert Redford, director, *Quiz Show,* 1995

like ESPN and Comedy Central experimented with less serious game programs in evening hours. The major broadcast networks, however, remained reluctant to put game shows on again in prime time. Finally, in 1999, ABC gambled that the nation was ready once again for a quiz show in prime time. The network, at least for a couple of years, had success with *Who Wants to Be a Millionaire*.

Major Programming Trends in the TV Age

The disappearance of quiz shows marked the end of most prime-time network programs originating from New York. From 1955 through 1957, the three major networks gradually moved their entertainment divisions to Los Angeles because of its proximity to Hollywood production studios. Network news operations, however, remained in New York. Symbolically, these cities came to represent the two major branches of TV programming: *entertainment* and *information*. Although there is considerable blurring between these categories today, at one time the two were more distinct.

TV Information: Our Daily News Culture

In television journalism, local broadcast stations, TV newsmagazines, and cable's CNN and Fox News have all made key contributions and generated their own controversies. But in this section our focus is on the traditional network evening news and the changes in TV news viewing ushered in by cable TV services. Interestingly, since the 1960s, broadcast journalism has consistently topped print news in national research polls that ask which news medium is most trustworthy. This fact alone makes the evening news a force to be reckoned with in our information culture.

NBC News

Featuring in the beginning a panel of reporters interrogating political figures, NBC's weekly *Meet the Press* (1947–) remains the oldest show on television. Daily evening newscasts, though, began on NBC in February 1948 with the *Camel Newsreel Theater.* Originally a ten-minute Fox Movietone newsreel that was also shown in theaters, this filmed news service was converted to a live broadcast one year later. Renamed the *Camel News Caravan* and anchored by John Cameron Swayze (who later became the major spokesperson for Timex watches), the NBC newscast showed Swayze reading short news items in a converted radio studio. Toward the end of the fifteen-minute show he would announce grandly, "Now let's go hopscotching the world for headlines!" and read a list of very brief reports, which were occasionally accompanied by whatever filmed newsreel footage the network could get that day.

Camel News, sponsored by a cigarette company, was succeeded by the *Huntley-Brinkley Report* in 1956. With Chet Huntley in New York and David Brinkley in Washington, this coanchored NBC program became the most popular TV evening news show. To provide a touch of intimacy, the coanchors would sign off their broadcasts saying, "Good night, Chet."/"Good night, David." Chet and David, who were not close friends, served as the model for hundreds of local news broadcasts that eventually developed dual anchors to present the news. After Huntley retired in 1970, the program was renamed *NBC Nightly News* and struggled to compete with CBS's emerging star anchor, Walter Cronkite. A series of anchors and coanchors followed before Tom Brokaw settled in as NBC's sole anchor in September 1983. Brian Williams took over for Brokaw following the 2004 presidential election.

CBS News

A second regular evening news show, *The CBS-TV News* with Douglas Edwards, premiered on CBS in May 1948. In 1956, the CBS program became the first news show videotaped for rebroadcast on **affiliate stations** (independently owned stations that sign contracts with a network and carry its programs) in western time zones. (Ampex had just developed the first workable videotape recorder.) Walter Cronkite succeeded Edwards in 1962, starting a nineteen-year run as anchor of the renamed *CBS Evening News*. Formerly a World War II correspondent for a print wire service, Cronkite in 1963 anchored the first thirty-minute network newscast, which featured a live ocean-side interview with President John Kennedy twelve weeks before his assassination. In 1968, Cronkite went to Vietnam to cover firsthand America's involvement in that civil war. Putting aside his role as a neutral news anchor, he concluded on the air that the American public had been misled about Vietnam and that U.S. participation in the war was a mistake. With such a centrist news personality now echoing the protest movement, public opinion against U.S. intervention mounted. In fact, partly because of the influence of Cronkite's criticisms, President Lyndon Johnson decided not to seek reelection in 1968.

Retiring from his anchor position in 1981, Cronkite was succeeded by Dan Rather, a former White House correspondent who had starred on CBS's respected TV news program *60 Minutes* since 1975. Despite a $22 million, ten-year contract, Rather could not sustain the program as the highest-rated evening newscast. However, to woo viewers and exude warmth, he tried wearing colorful sweater vests and briefly signed off with the slogan "Courage." But neither effort succeeded in increasing the size of his audience. In 1993, the network paired Rather with former *Today* show host Connie Chung. Unlike CNN and many local news stations, which routinely use male and female news teams, women anchors on the networks have long been relegated to substitute or weekend duty. Ratings continued to sag, however, and CBS terminated Chung after just a few months. Rather resigned in 2005, replaced by veteran CBS newsman Bob Schieffer. Then in 2006, CBS hired Katie Couric from NBC's popular *Today Show* as the main news anchor.

ABC News

Over the years, the ABC network tried many anchors and formats as it attempted to compete with NBC in the 1960s and CBS in the 1970s. After premiering a daily program in 1948, which folded when few affiliates chose to carry it, ABC launched a daily news show in 1953, anchored by John Daly, the head of ABC News and the host of CBS's evening game show *What's My Line?* After Daly left in 1960, a series of personalities anchored the show, including John Cameron Swayze and, in 1965, a twenty-six-year-old Canadian, Peter Jennings. Another series of rotating anchors ensued, including Harry Reasoner and Howard K. Smith. Then, in 1976, the network hired Barbara Walters away from NBC's *Today* show, gave her a $1 million annual contract, and made her the first woman to regularly coanchor a network newscast. With Walters and Reasoner together, viewer ratings rose slightly, but the network was still behind CBS and NBC. In 1977, ABC sports director Roone Arledge took over as head of the newly combined ABC News and Sports division. In 1978, he launched *ABC World News Tonight*, featuring four anchors: Frank Reynolds in Washington, Jennings in London, Walters in New York, and Max Robinson in Chicago. Robinson was the first black reporter to coanchor a network news program. Walters left her anchor position in the early 1980s to focus on celebrity and political interviews. In 1983, ABC chose Jennings to return as the sole anchor. By the late 1980s, the ABC evening news had become the most-watched newscast until, in 1996, it was dethroned by Brokaw's

● Walter Cronkite, the most respected and popular network newsman in TV history, anchored the *CBS Evening News* from 1963 to 1981. Cronkite ended his newscasts with his famous signature line, "And that's the way it is," followed by the day's date. (When the popular anchor took a stand against the Vietnam War, it influenced President Lyndon Johnson's decision not to run again for president in 1968.)

NBC Nightly News. In August 2005, Jennings succumbed to lung cancer after taking a leave of absence to fight the disease. He was replaced briefly by co-anchors Elizabeth Vargas and Bob Woodruff, who late in 2005 was seriously wounded covering Iraq. In 2006 Charles Gibson—from ABC's *Good Morning America* program—became the anchor of ABC's evening news.

Contemporary Trends in Network and Cable News

Audiences watching the network news contributed to the demise of many afternoon daily newspapers (which have virtually disappeared in most large U.S. cities). By the 1980s, though, network audiences also began to decline. Facing competition from VCRs and cable, especially CNN, network advertising revenues flattened out. In response, the networks cut back staffs in the late 1980s and early 1990s, eliminating many national and foreign reporter posts. Unfortunately, these cutbacks would later hamper their ability to cover global stories and international terrorism adequately in the aftermath of 9/11.

In an effort to duplicate the financial success of *60 Minutes,* the most profitable show in TV history, the Big Three networks began developing relatively inexpensive **TV newsmagazines**. This format, pioneered in 1968 by *60 Minutes,* usually featured three stories per episode (rather than one topic per hour—as was the custom on Edward R. Murrow's *See It Now* [CBS 1951–59]), alternating hard-hitting investigations of corruption or political intrigue with "softer" features on Hollywood celebrities, cultural trends, and assorted dignitaries. Copying this formula, ABC's *20/20* and *Primetime Live* became moneymakers, and *20/20* aired three or four evenings a week by 2000. NBC's newsmagazine *Dateline* was appearing up to five nights a week by 2000— airing so often that critics accused NBC of trivializing the formula. From fall 2002, the program aired only two to three nights per week. Building on the success of *60 Minutes,* CBS launched *60 Minutes II* in January 1999 to compete with *Dateline* and other weeknight newsmagazines. (The new version helped break the Iraqi prisoner abuse scandal in spring 2004 but was cancelled in 2005.) In addition, independent producers developed a number of syndicated non-network newsmagazines for the local late-afternoon and late-night markets. These featured more than twenty breezy-sometimes-sleazy syndicated tabloids, including *Entertainment Tonight* and *A Current Affair.*

By 2000 the Fox network had started its own twenty-four-hour news service on cable, and NBC, which already operated one cable news channel (CNBC), had teamed up with Microsoft to launch MSNBC, the first news channel available simultaneously on cable and the Web. Both cable and the Internet, offering twenty-four-hour access to wire services and instant access to news about specific topics, continue the slow erosion of the traditional network news audience. Two important variations on the news have surfaced in these programs. First, daily opinion programs such as MSNBC's *Hardball,* starring Chris Matthews, and Fox News's *The O'Reilly Factor,* starring Bill O'Reilly, proliferated on cable. Usually touting speculation and conjecture over traditional reporting based on verifying facts, these programs emerged primarily because of their inexpensive costs compared to traditional news: It is much cheaper to anchor a program around a single "talking head" personality and a few guests than to dispatch expensive equipment and field reporters to cover stories from multiple locations. Second, the demands of filling up time inexpensively during a twenty-four-hour daily news operation have led to more viewer participation via studio audiences asking questions and call-in phone lines. CNN's long-running *Larry King Live* program allows selected viewers to participate in the news while at the same time keeping program costs down. We will return to these developments in Chapter 14.

TV Entertainment: Our Comic and Dramatic Culture

Even during the quiz-show boom of the mid and late 1950s, the primary staples of television entertainment were comedy and drama, both significantly influenced by New York radio, vaudeville, and theater. This period is often referred to as the "golden age" of television. While news divisions remained anchored in New York, the networks began to shift their entertainment divisions to Los Angeles, partly due to the success of the pioneering series *I Love Lucy* (1951–57). *Lucy's* owners and costars, Desi Arnaz and Lucille Ball, began filming the top-rated situation comedy in California near their home, although CBS originally wanted them to shoot live in New York. Instead, in 1951, *Lucy* became the first TV program filmed in front of a live Hollywood audience. This was before the days of videotape, when the only way to preserve a live broadcast, other than by filming it like a movie, was through a technique called **kinescope**. In this process, a film camera recorded a live TV show off a studio monitor. The quality of the kinescope was poor, and most series that were saved in this way have not survived. *I Love Lucy, Alfred Hitchcock Presents,* and the original *Dragnet* are among a handful of series from the 1950s that endured because they were originally shot and preserved on film, like movies.

Televised Comedy: From Sketches to Sitcoms

Television comedy then (as now) came in three varieties: the sketch comedy (the forerunner of programs such as *Saturday Night Live*), the situation comedy (or sitcom), and the domestic comedy. These comedy variations come from a rich history in popular culture that includes vaudeville stage comedy from the late 1800s, stand-up comedy routines that began in vaudeville and ended up in the comedy nightclubs that emerged in major cities after World War II, and the radio comedy programs that television would steal heavily from in its early days.

Sketch Comedy. Identified on occasion as *vaudeo,* or the marriage of vaudeville and video, **sketch comedy** was a key element in early vaudeville-like TV variety shows. These programs included singers, dancers, acrobats, animal acts, and ventriloquists as well as comedy skits. The shows "resurrected the essentials of stage variety entertainment" and played to noisy studio audiences.[5] Vaudeville performers dominated television's early history. Stars of sketch comedy included Milton Berle, TV's first major celebrity, in *Texaco Star Theater* (1948–67); Red Skelton in the *Red Skelton Show* (1951–71); and Sid Caesar, Imogene

● *Your Show of Shows* (NBC, 1950–54), starring Sid Caesar and Imogene Coca, was one of the most ambitious and influential comedy programs in TV history. Each week it featured 90 minutes of original, high-quality, live sketch comedy. A major influence on programs like *Saturday Night Live* (NBC, 1975–), *Your Show of Shows* also jump-started the careers of a number of comedy writers, including Neil Simon, Mel Brooks, and Woody Allen.

Table 5.1 Selected Situation and Domestic Comedies Rated in the Top 10 Shows

The most durable genre in the history of television has been the half-hour comedy. It is the only genre that has been represented in the Nielsen rating Top 10 lists every year since 1949. Below is a selection of top-rated comedies at five-year intervals, spanning fifty years.

1955–56

I Love Lucy (#2)
Jack Benny Show (#5)
December Bride (#6)

1960–61

Andy Griffith Show (#4)
The Real McCoys (#8)
Jack Benny Show (#10)

1965–66

Gomer Pyle, U.S.M.C. (#2)
The Lucy Show (#3)
Andy Griffith Show,
    Bewitched, Beverly Hillbillies (tie #7)
Hogan's Heroes (#9)

1970–71

Here's Lucy (#3)

1975–76

All in the Family (#1)
Laverne & Shirley (#3)

1975–76 (column 2)

Maude (#4)
Phyllis (#6)
Sanford and Son, Rhoda (tie #7)

1980–81

*M*A*S*H* (#4)
The Jeffersons (#6)
Alice (#7)
House Calls, Three's Company
    (tie #8)

1985–86

Cosby Show (#1)
Family Ties (#2)
Cheers (#5)
Golden Girls (#7)
Who's the Boss? (#10)

1990–91

Cheers (#1)
Roseanne (#3)
A Different World (#4)
Cosby Show (#5)
Murphy Brown (#6)

1990–91 (column 3)

Empty Nest (#7)
Golden Girls, Designing
    Women (tie #10)

1995–96

Seinfeld (#2)
Friends (#3)
Caroline in the City (#4)
The Single Guy (#6)
Home Improvement (#7)
Boston Common (#8)

2000–01

Friends (#3)
Everybody Loves Raymond
    (#4)
Will & Grace (#10)

2005–06

For the first time in TV history, a half-hour comedy series did not rate among the season's top ten programs.

Sources: Tim Brooks and Earle Marsh, *The Complete Directory to Prime Time Network and Cable TV Shows,* 7th ed. (New York: Ballantine, 1999); *Times Almanac 1999* (Boston: Information Please LLC, 1998), 716; and A. C. Nielsen Media Research, 2005–06.

Coca, and Carl Reiner in *Your Show of Shows* (1950–54), for which playwright Neil Simon, filmmakers Mel Brooks and Woody Allen, and writer Larry Gelbart (*M*A*S*H*) all served for a time as sketch writers.

Sketch comedy had major drawbacks, though. Because skits were an integral part of the hour-long variety series, these programs were more expensive to produce than half-hour sitcoms. Skits on weekly variety shows, such as the *Perry Como Show* (1948–63), the *Dinah Shore Chevy Show* (1956–63), and the *Carol Burnett Show* (1967–79), also used up new routines very quickly. The ventriloquist Edgar Bergen (the father of actress Candice Bergen) once commented that "no comedian should be on TV once a week; he shouldn't be on more than once a month."[6]

With original skits and new sets required each week, production costs mounted, and the vaudeville-influenced variety series faded. The last successful program of this music-comedy type, *Barbara Mandrell & the Mandrell Sisters,* ended its two-year NBC run in 1982 due to the demanding schedule of doing music and comedy on a weekly basis. In this instance, it was Mandrell, not low ratings, who stopped production of the show. Echoing Bergen, Mandrell explained that musical numbers and sketch comedy, which could be used over and over for different audiences on the nightclub circuit, lasted only one week on television. Since the early 1980s, network variety shows have appeared only as yearly specials.

Situation Comedy. Over the years, the major staple on television has been the half-hour comedy series, the only genre represented in the Top 10–rated programs *every* year between 1949 and 2006, when the rise of dramas and reality shows made up the Top 10 programs. (See Table 5.1.) One type of comedy series, the **situation comedy**, features a recurring cast. The story establishes a situation, complicates it, develops increasing confusion among its characters, and then usually alleviates the complications.[7] *I Love Lucy* from the 1950s, the *Beverly Hillbillies* from the 1960s, *Happy Days* from the 1970s, *Night Court* from the 1980s, *Seinfeld* from the 1990s, and *Will & Grace, The Office,* and HBO's *Curb Your Enthusiasm* from the 2000s are all part of this long tradition.

In most situation comedies, character development is downplayed in favor of zany plot twists and disruptions. Characters are usually static and predictable; they generally do not develop much during the course of a series. Such characters "are never troubled in profound ways." Stress, more often the result of external confusion rather than emotional anxiety, "is always funny."[8] While watching situation-driven comedies, many viewers usually think of themselves as slightly superior to the characters who inhabit the sitcom world. Much like viewers who are attracted to soap operas, sitcom fans feel just a little bit smarter than the characters whose lives seem wacky and out of control.

Domestic Comedy. One spin-off of the sitcom form is the **domestic comedy**, in which characters and settings are usually more important than complicated predicaments. Although any given show might offer a wacky situation as part of a subplot, more typically the main narrative features a personal problem or family crisis that characters have to solve. There is a greater emphasis on character development than on reestablishing the order that has been disrupted by confusion. Domestic comedies take place primarily at home (*Leave It to Beaver; Everybody Loves Raymond*), at the workplace (*Just Shoot Me; Spin City*), or at both (*Frasier; Friends*).

Although funny things happen in domestic comedies, the main emphasis is on how the characters react to one another. Family and workplace bonds are tested and strengthened by the end of the show. Generally, viewers identify more closely with the major characters in domestic comedies. One example illustrates the difference between a sitcom and its domestic counterpart. In an early episode of the sitcom *Happy Days* (1974–84), the main characters were accidentally locked in a vault over a weekend. The plot turned on how they were going to free themselves, which they did after assorted goofy adventures. Contrast this with an episode from the domestic comedy *All in the Family* (1971–83), in which archconservative Archie and his ultraliberal son-in-law Mike are accidentally locked in the basement. The physical predicament became a subplot as the main "action" shifted to the characters themselves, who reflected on their generational and political differences.

Today, many programs are a mix of both situation and domestic comedy. For example, an episode of *Friends* (1994–2004) might offer a character-driven plot about the generation gap and a minor subplot about a pet monkey gone berserk. Domestic comedies also mix dramatic and comedic elements. An episode of *Roseanne* (1988–97), too, might juxtapose a dramatic scene in which a main character has a heart attack with another in which the Conner family intentionally offends their stuffy neighbors by decorating their home in a "white trash" holiday motif. This blurring of serious and comic themes marks a contemporary hybrid, sometimes labeled

Comedies often are among the most popular shows on television. *I Love Lucy* (*top*) was the top ranked show from 1952 to 1955 and was a model for other shows such as *Dick Van Dyke, Laverne & Shirley, Roseanne,* and *Will & Grace*. Similarly, *All in the Family* (*middle*) was the No. 1 rated sitcom five years running between 1971 and 1976 and also explored issues of class, race, gender, and ethnicity, which—until the success of this program—had been considered taboo topics for U.S. comedy programs. But for the first time in the 2005–06 season, no comedy ranked in the top 10 programs. Despite its Emmy nomination for Best Comedy Series, the once popular *Scrubs* (*bottom*) struggled in the general audience rating.

dramedy, which has included such series as the *Wonder Years* (1988–93), *Northern Exposure* (1990–95), *Ally McBeal* (1997–2002), HBO's *Sex and the City* (1999–2004), and *Desperate Housewives* (2005–).

Televised Drama: Anthologies vs. Episodes

Because the production of TV entertainment was centered in New York in its early days, many of its ideas, sets, technicians, actors, and directors came from New York theater. Young stage actors—including Anne Bancroft, Ossie Davis, James Dean, Grace Kelly, Paul Newman, Sidney Poitier, Robert Redford, and Joanne Woodward— began their professional careers in early television, often because they could not find stage work in New York. The TV dramas that grew from these early influences fit roughly into two categories: the anthology drama and the episodic series.

Anthology Drama. In the early 1950s, television—like cable in the early 1980s— served a more elite and wealthier audience. **Anthology drama**, which brought live dramatic theater to television, entertained and often challenged that audience. Influenced by stage plays, anthologies offered new teleplays, casts, directors, writers, and sets from one week to the next. Because movie studios owned the rights to major stage plays of the day, anthology television was often based on original material. In fact, this genre launched the careers of such writers as Rod Serling (*Requiem for a Heavyweight*), William Gibson (*The Miracle Worker*), Reginald Rose (*Twelve Angry Men*), and Paddy Chayefsky (*Marty*). The teleplays of these writers were often later made into movies. Chayefsky, in fact, would go on to write the screenplay for the 1976 film *Network,* a biting condemnation of television.

In the 1952–53 season alone, there were eighteen anthology dramas competing on the networks. Programs such as *Kraft Television Theater* (1947–58 and actually created to introduce Kraft's Cheez Whiz product), *Studio One* (1948–58), *Alfred Hitchcock Presents* (1955–65), *Playhouse 90* (1956–60), and the *Twilight Zone* (1959–64) mounted original plays each week. However, the demands on the schedule were such that many of these programs took more than a week to produce and had to alternate bi-weekly with other anthologies or with variety or news programs.

The commercial networks eventually stopped producing anthologies for economic and political reasons. First, although anthologies were popular, advertisers disliked them. Anthologies often presented stories that confronted complex human problems that were not easily resolved. Chayefsky had referred to these dramas as the "marvelous world of the ordinary."[9] The commercials that interrupted the drama, however, told upbeat stories in which problems were easily solved by purchasing a product: "a new pill, deodorant, toothpaste, shampoo, shaving lotion, hair tonic, car, girdle, coffee, muffin recipe, or floor wax."[10] By probing the psychology of the human condition, complicated anthologies made the simplicity of the commercial pitch ring false. Another aspect of the sponsors' dilemma was that these dramas often cast "non-beautiful heroes and heroines,"[11] unlike the stars of the commercials.

By 1954, sponsors and ad agencies were demanding more input into script revisions. For instance, Reginald Rose's teleplay *Thunder on Sycamore Street* was based on a real incident in which a black family moved into an all-white neighborhood and felt pressured to leave. CBS, pressured by advertisers who wanted to avoid public controversy, asked that the black family be changed to "something else." To make the teleplay more commercially palatable, Rose rewrote the script, abandoning the black family in favor of a white ex-convict. Faced with increasing creative battles with the writers and producers of these dramas, sponsors began to move toward less controversial programming, such as quiz shows and sitcoms.

A second reason for the demise of anthology dramas was that early on they were largely supported by a more affluent audience. The people who could afford TV sets in the early 1950s could also afford tickets to a play. For these viewers, the anthology drama was a welcome extension of their cultural tastes and simply brought theater directly into their homes. In 1950, fewer than 10 percent of American households had TV sets, with the heaviest concentration of ownership in New York. By 1956, however, 71 percent of all U.S. households had sets. As the production of TV sets rose during the post–World War II manufacturing boom, prices dropped as well. Working- and middle-class families were increasingly able to afford television. Anthology dramas were not as popular in this expanded market as they were with upscale theatergoers. When the networks began relocating their creative headquarters to Hollywood, such a geographical move also reduced theatrical influences. As a result, by the end of the decade, westerns, which were inexpensively produced by film studios on location near Los Angeles, had become the dominant TV genre.

> " Aristotle once said that a play should have a beginning, a middle, and an end. But what did he know? Today, a play must have a first half, a second half, and a station break. "
>
> —Alfred Hitchcock, director

Third, commercial networks stopped producing anthology dramas because they were expensive to produce—double the price of most other TV genres in the 1950s. Each week meant a completely new story line, as well as new writers, casts, and expensive sets. Sponsors and networks came to realize that it would be cheaper to use the same cast and set each week, and it would also be easier to build audience allegiance with an ongoing program. In an anthology series of individual plays, there were no continuing characters with whom viewers could identify over time.

In addition, anthologies that dealt seriously with the changing social landscape were sometimes labeled "politically controversial." This was especially true during the witch-hunts provoked by Senator Joseph McCarthy and his followers to rid media industries and government agencies (including the army) of left-wing influences. (See Chapter 16 on blacklisting.) Ultimately, sponsors and networks came to prefer less controversial programming such as quiz shows and westerns over anthologies. By the early 1960s, this dramatic form had virtually disappeared from network television, although its legacy continues on American public television, especially with the imported British program *Masterpiece Theatre* (1971–).

Episodic Series. Abandoning anthologies, producers and writers increasingly developed **episodic series**, first used in radio in 1929, because they seemed best suited for the weekly grind of televised drama. In this format, main characters continue from week to week, sets and locales remain the same, and technical crews stay with the program. Story concepts in episodic series are broad enough to accommodate new adventures each week, creating an atmosphere in which there are ongoing characters with whom viewers can regularly identify.

The episodic series comes in two general types: chapter shows and serial programs. **Chapter shows** employ self-contained stories that feature a problem, a series of conflicts, and a resolution. This structure can be used in a wide range of dramatic genres, including adult westerns like *Gunsmoke* (1955–75); medical dramas like *Marcus Welby, M.D.* (1969–76) and *Grey's Anatomy* (2005–); police/detective shows like *Dragnet* (1951–59, 1967–70) and *CSI: Crime Scene Investigation* (2000–); family dramas like *The Waltons* (1972–81) and *Little House on the Prairie* (1974–82); and fantasy/science fiction like *Star Trek* (1966–69) and some episodes of *The X-Files* (1993–2002).

Culturally, television dramas function as a window into the hopes and fears of the American psyche. In the 1970s, for instance, police/detective dramas became a chapter staple, mirroring the anxieties of many Americans regarding the urban unrest of the late 1960s. The 1970s brought more urban problems, which were precipitated by the loss of factory jobs and the decline of manufacturing. Americans' popular entertainment reflected the idea of heroic police and tenacious detectives protecting a nation from menacing forces that were undermining the economy and the cities. During this period, such shows as *The F.B.I.* (1965–74), *Ironside* (1967–75), *Mannix* (1967–75), *Hawaii Five-O* (1968–80), the *Mod Squad* (1968–73), *Kojak* (1973–75), and the *Rockford Files* (1974–80) all ranked among the nation's top-rated programs.

A spin-off of the police drama has been the law-enforcement documentary-like program, sometimes called *cop docs*. Series like Fox's *Cops* (1989–) are cheap to produce, with low overhead and a big return on a minimal investment. Cop docs, like many contemporary daytime talk shows, generally focus their stories on emotional situations and individual pathology rather than on a critical examination of the underlying social conditions that make crime and its related problems possible.

Prior to the rise of the cop was the reign of the cowboy, which marked an earlier period of change in America. The western served as one of the most popular chapter genres in television's early history. When movie studios such as Warner Brothers began dabbling in television in the 1950s, they produced a number of well-received series for ABC, such as *Cheyenne* (1955–63) and *Maverick* (1957–63). The popular western, with its themes of civilization confronting the frontier, apparently provided a symbol for many Middle Americans relocating to the suburbs—between the country and the city. Thirty prime-time westerns aired in the 1958–59 season alone. From this point through 1961, *Gunsmoke* (1955–75; TV's longest-running chapter series), *Wagon Train* (1957–65), and *Have Gun Will Travel* (1957–63) were the three most popular programs in America.

In contrast to chapter shows like westerns and police dramas, **serial programs** are open-ended episodic shows. That is, in these series most story lines continue from episode to episode. Cheaper to produce, usually employing just a few indoor

> **66** The show's original spirit has become kind of the spirit of the country— if not the world. . . . With the Berlin Wall down, with the global nuclear threat gone, with Russia trying to be a market economy, there is a growing paranoia because . . . there are no easy villains anymore.**99**
>
> –Chris Carter,
> *The X-Files* creator, 1998

sets, and running five days a week, daytime *soap operas* are among the longest-running serial programs in the history of television. Acquiring their name from soap-product ads that sponsored these programs in the days of fifteen-minute radio drama, popular soaps include *Guiding Light* (1952–), *As the World Turns* (1956–), *General Hospital* (1963–), *Days of Our Lives* (1965–), and *One Life to Live* (1968–).

With their cliff-hanging story lines and intimate close-up shots, which are well suited to television (a personal medium located in our living rooms and bed-rooms), soap operas have been good at creating audience allegiance. Soaps also probably do the best job of any genre at imitating the actual open-ended rhythms of daily life.

The success of the daytime soap formula opened a door to prime time. Although the first popular prime-time serial, *Peyton Place* (1964–69), ran two or three nights a week, producers later shied away from such programs because they had less value as syndicated reruns. Most reruns of old network shows are **stripped**—that is, shown five days a week in almost any order, not requiring viewers to watch them on a daily basis. Serials, however, require that audiences watch every day so that they don't lose track of the multiple story lines.

In the 1970s, however, with the popularity of the network *miniseries*—a serial that runs over a two-day to two-week period, usually on consecutive nights—producers and the networks began to look at the evening serial differently. The twelve-part *Rich Man, Poor Man,* adapted from an Irwin Shaw novel, ranked number three in national ratings in 1976. The next year, the eight-part *Roots* miniseries, based on writer Alex Haley's search for his African heritage, became the most-watched miniseries in TV history.

These miniseries demonstrated to the networks that viewers would watch a compelling, ongoing story in prime time. The success of these programs spawned such soap-opera-style series as *Dallas* (1978–91), *Dynasty* (1981–89), *Knots Landing* (1979–92), and *Falcon Crest* (1981–90), which in the 1984–85 season all ranked among America's Top 10 most-viewed programs. In fact, as the top-rated shows in America in the early 1980s, *Dallas* and *Dynasty* both celebrated and criticized the excesses of the rich and spoiled. These shows reached their popular peak during the early years of the Reagan administration, a time when the economic disparity between rich and poor Americans began and continued to widen dramatically.

Another type of contemporary serial is a *hybrid* form that developed in the early 1980s with the appearance of *Hill Street Blues* (1981–87). Mixing comic situations and grim plots, this multiple-cast show looked

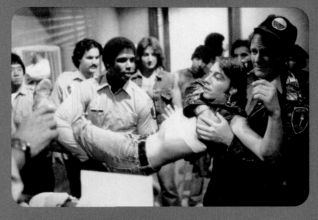

Hill Street Blues (*top*, 1981–87) began the hybrid form of dramas with its mix of comic and serious plot lines. Among the most popular dramas in TV history, *ER* (*middle*) premiered in 1994 and was the No. 1 rated program for several years. *ER* made history in 1998 when NBC agreed to pay the program's producers a record $13 million per episode. In 2005–06, *Grey's Anatomy* (*bottom*) emerged as the *ER* for a new generation, finishing No. 5 in the overall ratings and receiving 11 Emmy nominations.

like an open-ended soap opera. On occasion, as in real life, crimes were not solved and recurring characters died. As a hybrid form, *Hill Street Blues* combined elements of both chapter and serial television. Juggling multiple story lines, *Hill Street* featured some self-contained plots that were brought to resolution in a single episode as well as other plot lines that continued from week to week. This technique was copied by several successful dramatic hybrids, including *The X-Files* (1993–2002), *Law and Order* (1990–), *NYPD Blue* (1993–2005), *ER* (1994–), *Buffy the Vampire Slayer* (1997–2003), *The West Wing* (1999–2006), *Alias* (2001–2006), and *Grey's Anatomy* (2004–).

The Decline of the Network Era

Most historians mark the period from the late 1950s, when the networks gained control over TV's content, to the end of the 1970s as the **network era**. Except for British and American anthology dramas on PBS, this was a time when CBS, NBC, and ABC dictated virtually every trend in prime-time programming (see Figure 5.1). This network dominance was significant because it offered America's rich and diverse ethnic population a cultural center and common topics for daily conversation. Television is often credited, for example, with helping to heal the collective national consciousness after the assassination of President Kennedy in 1963 by creating time and space for shared mourning. During this period of supremacy, the networks collectively accounted for more than 95 percent of all prime-time TV viewing. By 2005, however, this figure had dropped to below 45 percent. So what happened? To understand the decline of the network era, we will look at three factors: technological changes, government regulations, and the development of new networks.

New Technologies Reduce Network Control

Two major technological developments contributed significantly to the erosion of network dominance: the arrival of communication satellite services for cable television and the home video market. Prior to the early 1970s, broadcast lobbyists and local stations, fearing that competition would lead to the loss of advertising revenue, effectively limited the growth of cable television, which had been around since the late 1940s. But a series of moves by the FCC sprung cable loose in 1972. That same year, when Time Inc. launched HBO into satellite orbit, serving movies to hotels and motels, the first crack in the network dam appeared. In 1975, HBO became available to individual cable markets throughout the country, offering the "Thrilla from Manila"—the heavyweight boxing match between Muhammad Ali and Joe Frazier via satellite from the Philippines.

Then, in December 1976, Ted Turner beamed, or uplinked, the signal from WTBS, his Atlanta-based **independent station** (not affiliated with a network), to a satellite where cable systems and broadcast stations around the country could access, or downlink, it. To encourage interest, the signal was initially provided free, supported only by the ads Turner sold during WTBS programs. But as Turner expanded services, creating new channels like CNN, he also earned revenue by charging monthly fees for his cable services. In its early days, WTBS delivered a steady stream of old TV reruns, wrestling, and live sports from the Atlanta Hawks and the Atlanta Braves (both owned by Turner). Turner and a number of investors would eventually buy the MGM film library to provide additional movie programming. In the mid-1970s, only about 15 percent of American households received cable. As this figure grew steadily (and flattened out at about 70 percent in the early 2000s), the TV networks, for the first time, began to face serious competition.

Figure 5.1
The Fall Prime-Time Schedule toward the End of the Network Era, 1978–79

	7	7:30	8	8:30	9	9:30	10	10:30	11 PM	
SUN	THE HARDY BOYS MYSTERIES 3		BATTLESTAR GALACTICA		MOVIE					ABC
	60 MINUTES 11		MARY		ALL IN THE FAMILY 9	ALICE 3	KAZ			CBS
	THE WONDERFUL WORLD OF DISNEY 25		THE BIG EVENT (I)				LIFELINE 2			NBC
MON			WELCOME BACK, KOTTER 4	OPERATION PETTICOAT 2	NFL MONDAY NIGHT FOOTBALL 9					ABC
			WKRP IN CINCINNATI	PEOPLE	M*A*S*H 7	ONE DAY AT A TIME 4	LOU GRANT 2			CBS
			LITTLE HOUSE ON THE PRAIRIE 5		MOVIE					NBC
TUE			HAPPY DAYS 6	LAVERNE AND SHIRLEY 4	THREE'S COMPANY 3	TAXI	STARSKY AND HUTCH 4			ABC
			THE PAPER CHASE		MOVIE					CBS
			GRANDPA GOES TO WASHINGTON		THE BIG EVENT (II) 2					NBC
WED			EIGHT IS ENOUGH 3		CHARLIE'S ANGELS 3		VEGA$			ABC
			THE JEFFERSONS 5	IN THE BEGINNING	MOVIE					CBS
			DICK CLARK'S LIVE WEDNESDAY		MOVIE					NBC
THU			MORK & MINDY	WHAT'S HAPPENING!! 3	BARNEY MILLER 5	SOAP 2	FAMILY 4			ABC
			THE WALTONS 7		HAWAII FIVE-0 11		BARNABY JONES 7			CBS
			PROJECT U.F.O. 2		QUINCY 3		W.E.B.			NBC
FRI			DONNY AND MARIE 4		MOVIE					ABC
			WONDER WOMAN 3		THE INCREDIBLE HULK 2		FLYING HIGH			CBS
			THE WAVERLY WONDERS	WHO'S WATCHING THE KIDS	THE ROCKFORD FILES 5		THE EDDIE CAPRA MYSTERIES			NBC
SAT			CARTER COUNTRY 2	APPLE PIE	THE LOVE BOAT 2		FANTASY ISLAND 2			ABC
			RHODA 5	GOOD TIMES 6	THE AMERICAN GIRLS		DALLAS 2			CBS
			CHiPS 2		SPECIALS		SWORD OF JUSTICE			NBC

1978–1979

Source: Alex McNeil, *Total Television: A Comprehensive Guide to Programming from 1948 to the Present,* 3rd ed. (New York: Penguin, 1991), 938.

The second technological breakthrough also came in 1975–76 with the consumer marketing of **videocassette recorders (VCRs)**, which enabled viewers to tape-record TV programs and play them back later on the TV. Earlier in the 1970s, Japan's Sony Corporation had introduced the TV industry to a three-quarter-inch-wide videocassette format that quickly revolutionized television news; until that time, TV news crews had relied solely on shooting film, which often took hours to develop and edit. Then, in 1975, Sony introduced a home version, *Betamax* (Beta for short), a half-inch format that enabled viewers to tape programs off the air for the first time. The next year, JVC in Japan introduced a slightly larger half-inch consumer format, *VHS* (Video Home System), which was incompatible with Beta. This triggered a marketing war, which helped drive the costs down and put VCRs in more homes.

Beta, though a smaller format and technically superior to VHS, ultimately lost the marketplace battle because of a cultural miscalculation by designers. Early Betamax tapes accommodated only about an hour and a half of programming. However, most American consumers used tapes primarily to record movies, usually two hours in length. This meant that two tapes, which cost around fifteen dollars apiece in the late 1970s, were necessary. When JVC developed the slightly larger VHS format, one standard tape accommodated two hours of programs, enough for an entire movie — or four sitcoms or soap operas. Even with technical improvements that compressed more programming onto a single tape, Betamax could never match the recording time or appeal of the longer VHS tapes.

The VCR also got a big boost from a failed suit brought against Sony by Disney and MCA (now GE-owned NBC Universal) in 1976: The two film studios alleged that home taping violated their movie copyrights. In 1979, a federal court ruled in favor of Sony and permitted home taping for personal use. In response, the defeated but industrious movie studios quickly set up videotaping facilities so that they could rent and sell movies via video stores, which exploded onto the scene in the early 1980s. By the mid-1980s, VHS had pretty much won the war for the video consumer market, and Sony concentrated on developing *Betacam,* a high-quality half-inch industrial format that in the late 1980s began replacing the bulkier three-quarter-inch format in TV newsrooms. Today, of course, the DVD format has replaced VHS, which as of 2006 was no longer produced.

The impact of videocassettes on the networks was enormous. By 1997, nearly 90 percent of American homes were equipped with VCRs that were used for two major purposes: time shifting and movie rentals. **Time shifting** occurs when viewers tape shows and watch them later, when it is more convenient. Before VCRs, advertisers and networks worried that consumers used TV ad time to fix a snack or go to the bathroom. With VCRs (and DVRs today), advertisers and networks had bigger things to worry about. For example, when consumers recorded TV programs for viewing at more convenient times, they produced more complex audience measurement problems. Along with the remote control, which enabled viewers to mute the sound during ads, time shifting made it possible to avoid ads altogether. In addition, by the mid-1990s, more than half of all households in America watched a rented movie during prime time at least once a week. VCRs and movie rentals shook the TV industry; when viewers watch videotapes—or DVDs, they aren't watching network shows or network ads.

At the outset of the twenty-first century, new technology brings even greater challenges to traditional network control of viewers' television-watching habits and also gives potential advertisers more information about consumer preferences than ever before. By late 2006, 13 percent of U.S. homes had **DVRs (digital video recorders),** enabling users to find and record specific shows onto the computer memory of the DVR, as opposed to storage on bulky tapes. Perhaps more important, the technology can seek out specific shows or even types of shows that appear on any channel connected to the DVR; for example, with one command a user can store or record all prime-time and syndicated versions of *Seinfeld* or *CSI* the household receives. The newest versions of DVRs are also recordable—like VHS—and allow users to make DVD collections of their favorite shows. Some critics argue that DVRs will completely shatter our current notion of prime-time television because viewers will be able to watch whatever show they like at any time.

While offering greater flexibility for viewers, DVRs also watch the watchers, providing advertisers with information about what is viewed in each household and altering the ways in which TV ratings are compiled and advertising dollars are divided. DVR technology is even capable of allowing advertisers to target viewers with specific ads when they play back their saved programs.

Government Regulations Temporarily Restrict Network Control

By the late 1960s, a progressive and active FCC, increasingly concerned about the monopoly-like impact of the three networks, passed a series of regulations that began undercutting their power. The first, the passage of the Prime Time Access Rule (PTAR) in April 1970, took the 7:30 to 8:00 P.M. slot (6:30 to 7:00 P.M. Central) away from the networks and gave it exclusively to local stations in the nation's fifty largest TV markets. With this move, the FCC hoped to encourage local news and public-affairs programs. However, most stations simply acquired syndicated quiz shows (*The Joker's Wild; Wheel of Fortune*) or **infotainment** programs (*P.M. Magazine; Entertainment Tonight*). These latter shows packaged human-interest and celebrity stories in TV news style, during which local affiliates sold lucrative regional ads.

In a second move, in 1970 the FCC created the Financial Interest and Syndication Rules—called **fin-syn**—which "constituted the most damaging attack against the

Figure 5.2
Top 12 TV Station Groups by $ Revenue and % of U.S. Households Reached

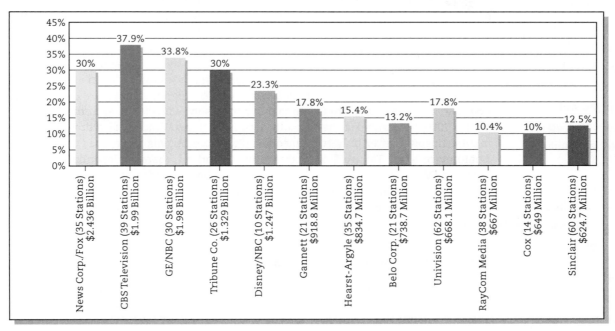

Source: "Special Report: This Time They Like What They See," *Broadcasting & Cable,* January 23, 2006, p. 34. Station groups are ranked according to 2004 revenue and TV households they reach as calculated by FCC ownership rules, which discount the reach of UHF TV stations (channel 14 and above) by half. Federal rules limit TV station group reach to no more than 39 percent of U.S. television households.

network TV monopoly in FCC history."[12] Throughout the 1960s, the networks had run their own syndication companies. They sometimes demanded as much as 50 percent of the profits that producers earned from airing older shows as reruns in local TV markets. This was the case even though those shows were no longer on the networks and most of them had been developed not by the networks but by independent companies. The networks claimed that since popular TV series had gained a national audience because of their reach, production companies owed the networks compensation even after shows completed their prime-time runs. The FCC banned the networks from reaping such profits from program syndication.

A third and separate action was instituted by the Department of Justice in 1975. Reacting to a number of legal claims against monopolistic practices, the Justice Department limited the networks' own production of non-news shows to a few hours a week. Initially, the limit was three hours of prime-time entertainment programs per week, but this was raised to five hours by the late 1980s. In addition, ABC, CBS, and NBC were limited to producing eight hours per week of in-house entertainment or non-news programs outside prime time, most of which was devoted to soap operas (economical to produce and popular with advertisers). This meant that the networks were forced to continue licensing most of their prime-time programs from independent producers and film studios. Given that the networks could produce their own TV newsmagazines and select which programs to license, however, they still retained a great deal of power over the content of prime-time television.

With increasing competition from cable and home video in the 1990s, the FCC gradually phased out the ban limiting network production. In addition, beginning in 1995, the networks were once again allowed to syndicate and profit from rerun programs, but only the ones they had produced in-house. The elimination of fin-syn and other rules opened the door for megamerger deals. For example, Disney, which bought ABC in 1995, has been able to use its vast movie production resources to develop more entertainment programming for its ABC network. This has reduced the opportunities for independent producers to create new shows and compete for prime-time slots on ABC. In fact, in fall 2000, ABC introduced only four new TV shows in prime time—the lowest number of new shows ever by a major network. Relying on multiple nights of its own *Who Wants to Be a Millionaire*, *20/20*, and cheap "reality" shows like *The Bachelor*, ABC ignored many new series possibilities from independent sources. Just as networks may now favor running programs that they own, shows now also have a much shorter time to prove themselves. To cite an extreme example, in May 2000 ABC canceled the critically acclaimed show *Wonderland*, a drama set in a mental hospital, after only two episodes. (For more on this topic, see "Case Study: Anatomy of a TV 'Failure'" on opposite page.) Indeed, many independent companies and TV critics fear the triumph of the oligopoly with Disney, CBS (formerly Viacom), News Corporation, and General Electric—the corporations that now own the networks—increasingly dictating the terms for broadcast television (see Figure 5.2 on page 181).

Emerging Networks Target the Youth Market

In addition to the number of cable services now available to consumers, the networks, which have lost about half of their audience since the 1980s, faced further challenges from the emergence of new networks. Rupert Murdoch, who heads the multinational company News Corporation, launched the Fox network in April 1987 after purchasing several TV stations and buying a major Hollywood film studio, Twentieth Century Fox (see Figure 5.3 on page 184). Not since 1955, when the Dumont network collapsed, had there been an attempt to challenge the Big Three networks.

At first, Fox lost money because it had fewer than a hundred affiliated stations to carry its programs around the country. This was less than half the two-hundred-plus affiliates each that were contracted to ABC, CBS, and NBC. Originally presenting programs just two nights a week, the Fox network began targeting both young and black audiences with shows like *The Simpsons*, *Beverly Hills 90210*, *In Living Color*, *Martin*, *Roc*, and *Melrose Place*. By 1994, after outbidding CBS for a portion of pro-football broadcasts, Fox was competing every night of the week. It had managed to lure more than sixty affiliates away from the other networks or from independent status. Some of these stations were in major markets where traditional networks suddenly found themselves without affiliates. By the early 1990s, Fox was making money. By the mid-1990s, the new network's total number of affiliates rivaled that of the Big Three.

Fox's success continued the erosion of network power and spurred others who were interested in starting new networks. Paramount, which had recently been acquired by Viacom, and Time Warner, the world's largest media company, both launched networks in January 1995: UPN and the WB. Using the strategy initiated by Fox, the new networks offered original programs two nights a week in 1995, added a third night in 1996, and by 2000 they programmed every night except Saturday (the evening that generally draws the lowest audience ratings). Backed by multinational financing, these companies slowly began going after independent outlets and luring other stations away from their old network affiliations. However, their main strategy targeted minority or young viewers with such programs as *Moesha*, *Buffy the Vampire Slayer*, *Angel*, *Felicity*, *Dawson's Creek*, *Charmed*, *Smallville*, *Girlfriends*, and *Gilmore Girls*. But after some success in the late 1990s, by 2005–06 *not one* WP or UPN show ranked among the top 100 programs according to audience ratings. After losing $1 billion each, CBS and Time Warner decided to merge the most popular shows into one network—now called CW—beginning in fall 2006.

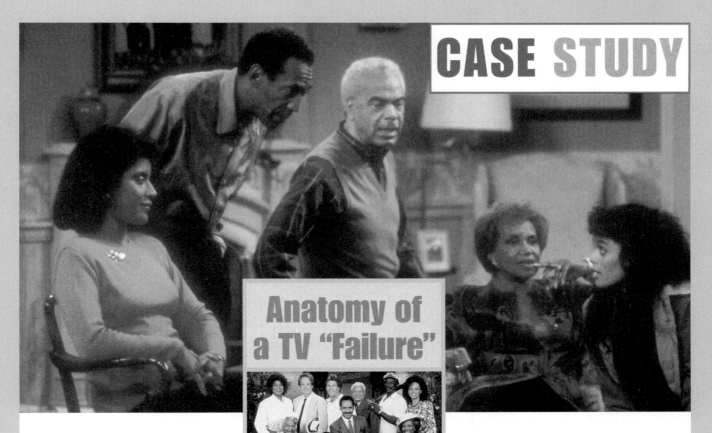

Anatomy of a TV "Failure"

Television shows die early deaths for many reasons. And some, like David Lynch's 1999 TV pilot for ABC, which eventually became the critically acclaimed film *Mulholland Drive,* are stillborn. Lynch is best known for the frightening film noir *Blue Velvet* (1986) and the weird, wacky cult TV hit *Twin Peaks* (ABC, 1990–92). His 1999 TV pilot for ABC, which explored the tension between innocence and evil along with the seamy underbelly of Hollywood, spooked some TV executives whose corporate parent just happened to be the Hollywood film studio Disney. Even after Lynch shortened the pilot by forty minutes and cut out a scene in which a scary tramp covered in moss and dirt frightens a man to death, ABC dumped the show and its $7 million investment.[1]

Although TV executives killing pilots never seen by audiences is one way TV shows die, other factors doom a show once it hits the air. Two of the most common are tough, competitive time slots and poor lead-in shows that fail to attract a big enough following. Then there's also the story of *Frank's Place* (1987–88), a critically acclaimed entry in the fall 1987 television lineup.

This series starred Tim Reid as a displaced history professor from Boston who inherited his estranged father's modest restaurant in a working-class area of New Orleans. The winner of three Emmys, *Frank's Place* was canceled by CBS just as it was set to produce new episodes for the 1988–89 TV season.

In fact, most new TV series fail. Even such successful series as *All in the Family, M*A*S*H, Hill Street Blues, Cheers,* and *60 Minutes* started out slowly, some at the bottom of the ratings. But they all got a second chance. Why not *Frank's Place*—especially after a strong premiere? In the first place, the show lacked a patient executive champion at the network level who would allow *Frank's Place* to "find" its audience gradually in a fixed time slot. During the show's first year, CBS programmers moved it to six different time slots on four different nights. In fact, the program moved so often that its coproducers, Reid and Hugh Wilson, said that their own mothers could no longer find it.[2] A second problem involved audience expectations. Instead of viewing *Frank's Place* as a series of short stories, as "individual little movies," viewers perhaps wanted a more traditional comedy. Intrinsic to this problem were the following questions: Was *Frank's Place* too much about black culture to develop an audience among mainstream America? Though it was primarily a comedy, was it also viewed as too serious because it tackled such issues as drugs, homelessness, corporate greed, alienation, and religion? No regular network series featuring a majority black cast had ever succeeded in prime time, although by 1993 there were nine sitcoms on television with predominantly black casts.

In one of the show's early episodes, the older bartender, Tiger, tells a disconsolate Frank, who's not a great businessman, "White folks don't come down here much at night." Like the bar's clientele, not enough TV viewers, white or black, were even aware of the program. Unlike the *Cosby Show,* essentially a show about social class, *Frank's Place* was about race as well as social class. Safer and less threatening, *Cosby* became one of the most popular shows in the history of television. *Frank's Place,* however, while it lasted, allowed mainstream America to see the viewpoints of characters who lived in a black working-class section of New Orleans—in the margins of America, a place where network prime-time television (as David Lynch also found out) has never been very comfortable.

Figure 5.3
Media Ownership: Principal U.S. Operations of News Corporation

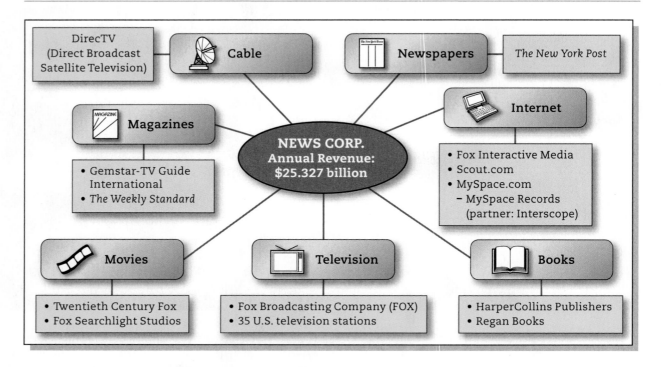

In 2006, News Corporation was the world's third-largest media conglomerate (behind Time Warner and Disney), with major holdings in film, television, and publishing. News Corporation produces and distributes movies through its filmed entertainment units while its television properties include the Fox Broadcasting network (with more than 200 U.S. affiliate stations), and it owns 35 TV stations in addition to a number of cable networks (such as Fox News, Fox Sports, and F/X). Its publishing business includes HarperCollins and many newspapers and magazines (mostly in Australia and the UK). Run by its founder and now CEO, Rupert Murdoch, News Corporation has also expanded into satellite television service and bought Internet ventures for its Interactive Media division. What advantages could be gained for the company by spreading into other media platforms?

The Economics of Television

Despite their declining reach, the traditional networks have remained attractive investments in the business world. In 1985, General Electric, which once helped start RCA/NBC, bought back NBC. In 1995, Disney bought ABC for $19 billion; in 1999, Viacom acquired CBS for $37 billion (Viacom and CBS split in 2005).

Even though their audiences and profits may have declined, the networks continue to attract larger audiences than their cable or online competitors. But the business of television is not just about larger audiences. To understand the TV business today, we need to examine the production, distribution, and syndication of programming, as well as the implications for audience share. At stake is $60 billion in advertising revenues each year. In fact, it would not be much of a stretch to define TV programming as a system that delivers viewers to merchandise displayed in blocks of ads. By the early 2000s, national advertisers alone, led by Procter & Gamble and General Motors, spent more than $30 billion a year in TV advertising.

Prime-Time Production

The key to the television industry's appeal resides in its ability to offer programs that American households will habitually watch on a weekly basis. The networks, producers, and film studios spend fortunes creating programs that they hope will keep us coming back. In 1988, while film studios produced a large chunk of network television, more than half of the prime-time schedule was created by independent producers. These companies, such as Carsey-Werner (the *Cosby Show; A Different World; Roseanne; Third Rock from the Sun; That '70s Show*), license, or "rent," each episode to a network for two broadcasts, one in the fall or winter and one in the spring or summer. (Usually about twenty-two new series episodes are produced in a TV season.)

Production costs in television generally fall into two categories: below-the-line and above-the-line. *Below-the-line* costs, which account for roughly 40 percent of a new program's production budget, include the technical, or "hardware," side of production: equipment, special effects, cameras and crews, sets and designers, carpenters, electricians, art directors, wardrobe, lighting, and transportation. More demanding are the *above-the-line,* or "software," costs, which include the creative talent: actors, writers, producers, editors, and directors. These costs account for about 60 percent of a program's budget, except in the case of successful long-running series (like *Friends* or *ER*), in which salary demands by actors drive up above-the-line costs.

> **❝** You can have the most brilliant people in the world running networks, but it's almost a scientific impossibility for bureaucracies to be inventive. They cannot. It's against their nature.**❞**
>
> – Robert Greenwald, independent television producer, *New York Times*, 2000

Risky Business: Deficit Financing and the Independents

Because of their high cost, many prime-time programs today are developed by independent production companies that are owned or backed by a major film studio such as Sony or Disney. These film studios serve as a bank, offering enough capital to carry producers through one or more seasons. In television, after a network agrees to carry a program, keeping it on the air is done through **deficit financing**. This means that the production company leases the show to a network for a license fee that is actually less than the cost of production. (The company hopes to recoup this loss later in lucrative rerun syndication.) Typically, the networks might lease an episode of a new half-hour sitcom for about $600,000 for two airings. Each episode, however, costs the producers about $800,000 to make, in which case they lose about $200,000 per episode. After two years of production (about forty-four episodes), an average show builds up a deficit in the millions. This is where film studios have been playing an increasingly crucial role: They finance the deficit and hope to make profits on lucrative syndicated shows like *Friends, Seinfeld, The Simpsons,* or *Everybody Loves Raymond*.

The key to erasing the losses generated by deficit financing is **rerun syndication**. In this process, programs that stay in a network's lineup long enough to build up sufficient episodes (usually four seasons' worth) are sold, or *syndicated,* to hundreds of TV stations in the United States and overseas. With a successful program, the profits can be enormous. For instance, the early rerun cycle of *Friends* earned more than $4 million an episode from syndication in more than 250 markets, totaling $944 million. Because the show had already been produced and the original production costs were covered, the syndication market at home and abroad became almost pure profit for the producers and their backers. It is for this reason that the practice of deficit financing endures. Although investors rarely hit the jackpot, when they do, it can more than cover a lot of losses.

Network Cost-Saving Strategies

Although the networks still purchase or license many prime-time TV programs, they create more of their own prime-time fare thanks to the relaxation of FCC rules in the

TV and the State of Storytelling

The rise of the so-called reality program over the past decade has more to do with the cheaper costs of this TV genre than with the wild popularity of these programs. In fact, in the history of television and viewer numbers, traditional sitcoms and dramas—and even prime-time news programs like *60 Minutes* and *20/20*—have been far more popular than even successful reality programs like *The Apprentice* or *American Idol*. When the major networks and the big film studios that create most national broadcast television cut costs by reducing writing and production staffs and hiring "regular people" instead of trained actors, do they weaken the craft of weekly storytelling for the short-term gratification of commercial savings? In this exercise, let's compare the storytelling competence of a reality program with a more traditional comedy or dramatic genre.

Description. Pick a current reality program and a current sitcom or drama. Choose programs that either started in the last year or two or that have been on television for roughly the same period of time. Now develop a "viewing sheet" that allows you to take notes as you watch the two programs over a three-to-four week period. Keep track of main characters, plot lines, settings, conflicts, and resolutions. Also track the main problems that are posed in the programs and how they are worked out in each episode. Research LexisNexis or other current news search engines to compare the basic production costs of each program.

Analysis. Look for patterns and differences in the way stories are told in the two programs. At a general level, what are the conflicts about (for example, men versus women, managers versus employees, tradition versus change, individuals versus institutions, honesty versus dishonesty, authenticity versus artificiality, any others?). How complicated or simple are the tensions in the two programs, and how are problems resolved? Are there noticeable differences between "the look" of each program—does one look more cheaply produced than the other?

Interpretation. What do some of the patterns mean? What seems to be the point of each program? What are they each trying to say about relationships, values, masculinity or femininity, power, social class, and so on?

Evaluation. What are the strengths and weaknesses of each program? Which program would you judge as better at telling a compelling story that you want to watch each week? How could each program improve its storytelling?

Engagement. Either through classified ads or personal contacts, find other viewers of these programs. Ask them follow-up questions about these programs—about what they like or don't like about the programs, about what they might change, about what the programs' creators might do differently. Then report your findings to the programs' producers, either through a letter, phone call, or e-mail. Try to elicit responses from the producers about the status of their programs. How did they respond to your findings?

mid-1990s. The production of TV newsmagazines and reality programs, for instance, became one major way for networks to save money and control content. Programs such as Fox's *American Idol* or NBC's *Dateline* require only about half the outlay (between $600,000 and $800,000 per episode) demanded by an hour's worth of drama. In addition, the networks, by producing projects in-house, avoid paying license fees to independent producers.

Over the years, CBS's highly rated program *60 Minutes* has been a money machine. By 1980, a commercial minute on *60 Minutes*, the nation's highest-rated program that year, sold for a then record $230,000. By the late 1990s, *60 Minutes* commanded more than $400,000 per minute for its seven to eight minutes of national ad slots. (By comparison, a low-rated program brought in only a quarter of this amount per minute.) This meant that *60 Minutes* generally earned back its production costs and fees to local stations for carrying the program after selling just a couple of minutes of ad time. Even newsmagazines with low ratings still recoup their lower production costs fairly easily. Don Hewitt, the creator of *60 Minutes*, estimated that in its first twenty-five years on the air, his program grossed well over $1 billion for CBS.[13]

Prime-Time Distribution

The networks have always been the main distributors of prime-time TV programs to their affiliate stations around the country. By 2006, ABC, CBS, NBC, Fox, and the new CW alliance were each allied with 200–250 stations. The networks pay a fee to affiliate stations to carry network programs; in return, networks sell the bulk of advertising time and recoup their investments in these programs. In this arrangement, local stations receive national programs that attract large local audiences. In addition, some local ad spaces are allocated during prime time so that stations can sell their own time during these slots.

A common misconception is that TV networks own their affiliated stations. This is not usually true. Although networks own stations in major markets like New York, Los Angeles, and Chicago, throughout most of the country networks merely sign short-term contracts to rent time on local stations. For example, WDIV (Channel 4) in Detroit has a contract to carry NBC programs but is owned by the Washington Post/Newsweek Company, based in Washington, D.C. Years ago, the FCC placed restrictions on network-owned-and-operated stations, called **O & Os**. Originally, networks and other companies were limited to owning five VHF and two UHF stations, but the limit was raised to twelve total stations during the 1980s. Hoping to ensure more diversity in ownership, the FCC during this time also mandated that an owner's combined TV stations could reach no more than 25 percent of the nation's then 90-million-plus TV households. Then, in 1996, the sweeping Telecommunications Act (which is discussed in more depth in Chapter 6) abolished most ownership restrictions. By 2006, one owner was permitted to reach up to 39 percent of the nation's 120 million TV households.

Although a local affiliate typically carries network programs, the station may preempt a network's offering by substituting other programs. According to *clearance rules,* established in the 1940s by the Justice Department and the FCC, all local affiliates are ultimately responsible for the content of their channels and must clear, or approve, all network programming.

Over the years, some of the circumstances in which local affiliates have rejected the network's programming have been controversial. For example, in 1956 Nat King Cole (singer Natalie Cole's father) was one of the first African American performers to host a network variety program. As a result of pressure applied by several white southern organizations, though, the program had trouble attracting a national sponsor. When some southern and northern affiliates refused to carry the program, NBC canceled it in 1957. More recently, in May 2004 the Maryland-based Sinclair Broadcast Group, which at the time owned sixty-two

● Winner of Fox's *American Idol* competition in 2006, singer Taylor Hicks immediately signed an endorsement deal with Ford trucks, a major advertiser on *Idol*. Popular "reality shows" like *Idol* are favored by TV network executives because they are much cheaper to produce than a drama or comedy series.

> ❝ **For the networks, the hit show is the hub in a growing wheel of interests: promotion platforms for related businesses; sales of replays on cable television or even Internet sites; and the creation of direct links between advertisers and viewers.** ❞
>
> –Bill Carter,
> *New York Times,* 1999

stations in thirty-nine TV markets, barred its seven ABC-affiliated stations from airing a special episode of ABC's *Nightline*. In a tribute to the more than seven hundred U.S. men and women who had died in the Iraq war at the time, the program's anchor Ted Koppel read the names and displayed images of every soldier. Sinclair's management, however, in refusing to clear the program, argued that broadcasting the obituaries constituted an antiwar position, offering "political statements . . . disguised as news content." At the time, 98 percent of all Sinclair's presidential campaign contributions had gone to the Republican Party and George W. Bush, who had supported the further deregulation of the TV industry that had allowed Sinclair to acquire so many stations.

Syndication Keeps Shows Going and Going . . .

Syndication, selling TV stations the exclusive rights to air TV shows, is a critical component of the distribution process. Early each year, executives from thousands of local TV stations and cable firms gather at the world's main "TV supermarket" convention, the National Association of Television Program Executives (NATPE), to buy or barter for programs that are up for syndication. In so doing, they acquire the exclusive local market rights, usually for two- or three-year periods, to game shows, talk shows, and **evergreens**—popular old network reruns such as the *Andy Griffith Show* or *I Love Lucy*. In such a competitive arena, most TV managers become less concerned with the quality of programs and more concerned with keeping costs low, delivering viewers to advertisers, and drawing higher ratings than their competitors.

Although the networks have long dominated the selection and distribution of prime-time television, syndicators have played a large role in the hours outside prime time. The distribution/syndication company King World, for example, began in 1972 after the fin-syn rules prevented the networks from participating in syndication. Starting out by distributing *Little Rascals* film shorts from the 1930s, King World barely survived its first year. By the end of the 1980s, however, it had become the distributor of the top shows in syndication—*Wheel of Fortune, Jeopardy,* and the *Oprah Winfrey Show*—and grossed nearly $400 million per year. With the suspension of fin-syn and the networks once again allowed to syndicate programming, CBS-Viacom in 1999 bought King World for $5 billion.

In addition to companies like Viacom and King World, major syndicators of TV programming include film studios such as Twentieth Century Fox, Disney-Touchstone, and Time Warner, all of which are also involved in the production of TV shows. Networks usually select and distribute about three hours of programming each night (four on Sunday) during prime time and another three to four hours of daytime programming, but this still leaves a substantial number of hours to fill a local affiliate's schedule. Because it is often cheaper to buy syndicated programs than to produce local programs (other than news), many station managers take the most profitable path rather than create topical shows that focus on issues that affect their own communities.

Off-Network and First-Run Syndication

For local affiliate stations, syndicated programs are often used or slotted in what is known as **fringe time**. This includes programming immediately before the evening's prime-time schedule, called *early fringe,* and the time following the local evening news or the network's late-night talk shows, called late *fringe.* Syndication to fill these slots comes in two forms. First, there is **off-network syndication**, in which older programs, no longer running during network prime time, are made available

> **66** When I heard that our big relaunch was facing Regis, I knew it was over. . . . The sad part is that a show like *Millionaire* makes every network think there is a quick, cheap fix to their schedules. . . . They become less interested in supporting harder-to-sell quality shows when they think there is a golden calf out there that can solve all their problems. **99**
>
> —Judd Apatow, executive producer of acclaimed but canceled *Freaks and Geeks*, 2000

for reruns to local stations, cable operators, online services, and foreign markets. A local station may purchase old *Cosby Show* or *Simpsons* episodes as a lead-in to boost the ratings for its late-afternoon news, or it may purchase *Friends* or *Everybody Loves Raymond* to boost its ratings after the late-evening news.

A second type of syndication used to fill fringe time is **first-run syndication**, which is any program that is specifically produced for sale into syndication markets. Quiz programs such as *Wheel of Fortune* and daytime talk or advice shows like *The Oprah Winfrey Show* are made for syndication. The producers of these programs sell them directly to local markets around the country and the world. When the FCC established the Prime Time Access Rule in 1970 to turn more prime time over to local stations, it created an immediate market for new non-network programs.

Barter vs. Cash Deals

Most financing of television syndication is based on either cash or barter. In a *cash deal*, the distributor of a program offers a series for syndication to the highest bidder in a market—typically a station trying to fill a particular time slot. Due to exclusive contractual arrangements, programs air on only one broadcast outlet per market. For example, CBS and its syndicator King World, which distributes *CSI*, offer early episodes in hundreds of television markets around the country. Whichever local station bids the most in a particular market gets the rights to that program, usually for a contract period of two or three years. A small-market station in Fargo, North Dakota, might pay a few thousand dollars to air a week's worth of episodes; in contrast, some Top 10 markets pay well over $250,000 a week for *CSI* reruns.

One common variation of a cash deal is called *cash-plus*. For shows that are successful in syndication, distributors may retain some time to sell national commercial spots. When *CSI* went into syndication, for example, CBS, in addition to receiving cash for the show from various local outlets and cable's Spike TV network, also sells two to three minutes of ad time to national advertisers. When local stations receive the programs, they already contain national ads. Some syndicators use cash-plus deals to keep down the cost per episode; in other words, stations pay less per episode in exchange for giving up ad slots to a syndicator's national advertisers.

● A scene from *CSI: Crime Scene Investigation,* which premiered on CBS in 2000. This popular, episodic cop-and-crime drama carries forward a tradition of "realistic" police shows, which have included *Hill Street Blues* (NBC, 1981–87) and *NYPD Blue* (ABC, 1993–2005). For the 2005–06 season, *CSI* finished third in audience ratings, and is also shown in syndication on the cable channel Spike TV.

Although syndicators prefer cash deals, *barter deals* are usually arranged for new, untested programs or older programs. In a straight barter deal, no money changes hands between the local station and the syndicator. Instead, a syndicator offers a program to a local TV station in exchange for a split of the advertising revenue. The program's syndicator will try to make an arrangement with the station that attracts the largest number of local viewers, though this is not always possible. The syndicator then sells some ads at the national level, charging advertisers more money if the program has been sold into a large number of markets. Many TV talk shows begin as barter deals. For example, in a 7/5 barter deal, during each airing the show's producers and syndicator retain seven minutes of ad time to sell national spots and leave stations with five minutes of ad time to sell local spots. As programs become more profitable, their syndicators repackage the shows as cash-plus deals.

● *Everybody Loves Raymond* (NBC, 1996–2005), one of the most popular programs in TV history, has made hundreds of millions of dollars in off-network syndication. An episodic chapter show, *Everybody Loves Raymond* does well in syndication because the 210 episodes can be aired five days a week and, unlike a serial program, out of order.

Measuring Television by Ratings and Shares

Although the networks wrested control of content from sponsors in the 1950s, advertising still drives the business. TV shows live or die based primarily on whether advertisers are satisfied with the quantity and quality of the viewing audience.

Since 1950, the major organization tracking prime-time viewing has been the A. C. Nielsen Market Research Company, which estimates what viewers are watching in the nation's major markets. During the 1950s and 1960s, before ratings were fine-tuned statistically, firms like Nielsen estimated only the mass numbers of households tuned to particular programs. By the 1970s, ratings services provided advertisers, networks, and local stations with much more detail about those viewers—from race and gender to age, occupation, and educational background.

In TV measurement a **rating** is a statistical estimate expressed as a percentage of households tuned to a program in the local or national market being sampled (see Table 5.2). By 2006, one Nielsen national ratings point represented about 1.2 million television households. Another audience measure is the **share**, a statistical estimate of the percentage of homes tuned to a program compared with those actually using their sets at the time of a sample. Let's say, for instance, that on a typical night, of the 5,000 metered homes sample-wired by Nielsen in 210 U.S. cities, 4,000 of those households have their TV sets tuned in to assorted networks, pay channels, and cable channels. Of those 4,000, about 1,000 are tuned to a *CSI* episode on CBS. The rating estimate for that show is 5,000 (number of sets monitored) divided by 1,000 (number of households watching *CSI*), which equals 20 percent. The share estimate is 4,000 (sets actually in use) divided by 1,000, which equals 25 percent.

Over the years share measurements became increasingly important because they tell advertising and TV executives approximately the number of viewers and the percentage of sets in use tuned to their programs in a competitive market. Shares are also good measures during fringe time, when most sets may be turned off. For example, on a given night, only 1,000 of the 5,000 sets may still be on for late-night viewing. If 500 of that 1,000 are tuned to the *Late Show*, its rating would be only 10 percent (5,000 divided by 500), but its share of the audience still tuned in would be 50 percent (1,000 divided by 500).

In the early 1970s, during the height of the network era, a prime-time series with a rating of 17 or 18 and a share of between 28 and 30 was generally a success. By the early 2000s, though, with increasing competition from cable and DVDs, the threshold for success had dropped to a rating of 8 or 9 and a share of under 13 or 14. With TV programs now available on iPods and cable's on-demand services, these thresholds will continue to shrink. Yet while Americans still watch television shows, delivery options have increased beyond traditional prime-time networks. For example, to account for the rise of DVRs, Nielsen in 2006 began offering three versions of its ratings: "live . . . ; live plus 24 hours, counting how many people who own DVRs played back shows within a day of recording them; and live plus seven days. . . ."[14]

The historical importance of ratings and shares to the survival of specific TV programs cannot be overestimated. (See "Case Study: Anatomy of a TV 'Failure'" on page 183.) Simply stated, audience measurement tells advertisers roughly how many people are watching. Even more important, it tells them what kind of people are watching. Prime-time advertisers are mainly interested in securing affluent eighteen- to forty-nine-year-old viewers, who account for most consumer spending. If a show is attracting viewers from that group, advertisers then decide if they want to buy time during that particular program and pay the network its asking price. In fact, television operates as an industry in which networks, producers, and distributors target, guarantee, and "sell" viewers in blocks to advertisers. Typically, as many as nine of ten new shows introduced each fall either do not attain the required ratings or fail to reach enough of the "right" viewers. The result is cancellation within the year. Unfortunately, over the years many popular programs also have been canceled because advertisers considered their audiences too young, too old, or too poor. Today, however, with the fragmentation of media audiences and the decline in viewership, targeting smaller niche markets and consumers has become advertisers' main game.

> " By 1960 television had become a mature and streamlined business, a great 'cash cow.' The focus now shifted from invention to convention, from carving out an acceptable social role for itself to counting the rewards of investment, planning, and monopoly. "
>
> —J. Fred MacDonald,
> *One Nation under Television,*
> 1994

● Table 5.2 The Top 10 Highest-Rated TV Series, Individual Programs (since 1960)

Program	Network	Date	Rating
1. M*A*S*H (final episode)	CBS	2/28/83	60.2
2. *Dallas* ("Who Shot J.R.?" episode)	CBS	11/21/80	53.3
3. *The Fugitive* (final episode)	ABC	8/29/67	45.9
4. *Cheers* (final episode)	NBC	5/20/93	45.5
5. *Ed Sullivan Show* (Beatles' first U.S. TV appearance)	CBS	2/9/64	45.3
6. *Beverly Hillbillies*	CBS	1/8/64	44.0
7. *Ed Sullivan Show* (Beatles' second U.S. TV appearance)	CBS	2/16/64	43.8
8. *Beverly Hillbillies*	CBS	1/15/64	42.8
9. *Beverly Hillbillies*	CBS	2/26/64	42.4
10. *Beverly Hillbillies*	CBS	3/25/64	42.2

Note: The *Seinfeld* finale, which aired in May 1998, drew a rating of 41-plus and a total viewership of 76 million; in contrast, the final episode of *Friends* in May 2004 had a 25 rating and drew about 52 million viewers. (The M*A*S*H finale in 1983 had more than 100 million viewers.)

Sources: The World Almanac and Book of Facts 1997 (Mahwah, N.J.: World Almanac Books, 1996), 296; Corbett Steinberg, *TV Facts* (New York: Facts on File Publications, 1985); A. C. Nielsen Media Research.

Alternative Voices

Even though the major networks and their big-city affiliates have dominated mainstream television, alternative programming does exist—particularly at the small, low-power stations or on cable's public-access channels. The king of "alt-TV" is probably Paper Tiger Television (PTTV), a loose and changing group of about one hundred producers, activists, artists, technicians, scholars, and "people-off-the-street" who have created more than 320 programs since 1981. For more than fifteen years, PTTV has run a weekly half-hour commentary program on contemporary culture on Manhattan Cable. PTTV's focus has been providing programs on issues that have either been ignored by mainstream television or oversimplified by traditional news outlets. These mini–TV documentaries, often combining irreverent humor and detailed analysis, specialize in exploring the connections among production, audience, and sponsors: "Paper Tiger . . . aims to disrupt the TV beliefs of its viewers."[15]

PTTV's alternative catalogue includes "Torn between Colors," a 1990 student production featuring African American and Latino high school teens who examine the media coverage of several high-profile crimes in New York. In their video (as in many PTTV productions), the students look at the role of language and image in shaping public opinion, using the medium of television to exert some control over their own lives and how they are portrayed. In 2001, "Who's Paying the Price?" examined the effects of 9/11 on working people of New York City. Focusing on laid-off Marriott Hotel workers from the destroyed Twin Towers, this documentary investigated "the contradictory glorification of workers in the immediate aftermath of the attacks and the near complete disregard of their needs in the ensuing national and local 'economic stimulus' packages." In 2004, PTTV added "Class Dismissed," a "critical look at how U.S. history is taught in high school, at the myths that reduce the complexity of history to simple sound bites, and the information that never seems to make it on the textbook pages." (See www.papertiger.org.)

 ## The Public, Television, and Democracy

At the outset of the new century, the dominant mass medium of the last half of the twentieth century has undergone significant transformations. In the 1950s, television's appearance significantly changed the media landscape—particularly the radio and magazine industries, both of which cultivated specialized audiences and markets to survive. But at the end of its dominant reign—with the coming of cable, the Internet, and even newer digital technologies—television changed too. While it still remains the main storytelling medium of our time, the news, comedy, and drama of television are increasingly controlled by larger and larger companies, most of which also own movie and recording studios and other media businesses. As in the sound recording business, it has become more difficult for independent producers to make their mark in network television as the major companies—like Disney (ABC), Viacom-Paramount (CBS), GE (NBC), and News Corporation (Fox)—have seized control of programming. The TV executives ruling over this concentration of storytelling power, however, have not figured out how to bring back viewers increasingly drawn to the more interactive and specialized terrain of cable and the Internet. Since the 1980s, the original Big Three networks have lost more than half their audience. And their main "new" idea is to recycle "reality" programs that lack the storytelling power of a well-crafted drama or a smart comedy.

As the television industry works to reimagine itself in the new century, it is important to remember that in the 1950s, television carried the antielitist promise that its technology could bypass traditional print literacy and reach all segments of society. In such a heterogeneous and diverse nation, the concept of a visual, affordable mass medium, giving citizens entertainment and information that they could all talk about the next day, held great appeal. However, since its creation, commercial television has tended to serve the interests of profit more than those of democracy. And networks have proved time and again that they are more interested in delivering audiences to advertisers than in providing educational and provocative programming to citizens and viewers.

Public television (PBS), which first aired in the late 1960s, has often filled the role of programming for viewers who are "less attractive" to commercial networks and advertisers. Besides providing programs for the over-fifty viewer, public television has played a key role in programming for audiences under age twelve—another demographic not valued by most advertisers and often neglected by the networks. Over the years, such children's series as *Mister Rogers' Neighborhood* (1967–2001), *Sesame Street* (1969–), and *Barney* (1991–) have been fixtures on PBS. With the exception of CBS's long-running *Captain Kangaroo* (1955–84), the major networks have pretty much abdicated the responsibility of developing educational series aimed at children under age twelve. In 1996, though, Congress did pass a law ordering the networks to offer three hours of children's educational programming per week. But the networks sidestepped this congressional mandate by claiming that many of their routine sitcoms, cartoons, and dramatic shows are educational.

By the early 2000s, the future of PBS and noncommercial television remained cloudy. Ever since the late 1960s, when the Nixon administration began threatening funding cuts for any programming critical of status quo politics and values, our noncommercial system has occasionally been held hostage. Because the government never required wealthy commercial broadcasters to subsidize public television (as many other democracies do), politics has played an increasing role in the fate of PBS. As federal funding levels dropped in the 1980s, PBS depended more and more on corporate underwriting. In 2005, corporate sponsors funded more than 20 percent of all public television. While this development has supported many PBS programs, it has had a chilling effect on PBS's traditional independence from corporate America. As a result, PBS has sometimes rejected controversial programming and hard-hitting documentaries, such as *Deadly Deception,* the 1991 Oscar-winning film that criticized General Electric (which owns NBC) and the nuclear power industry.

In another example, in January 1998 PBS decided to "bury" *Surviving the Bottom Line,* a probing documentary

● The most influential children's show in TV history, *Sesame Street* (PBS, 1969–) has been teaching young children their letters and numbers for more than thirty years. The program has also helped break down ethnic, racial, and class barriers by introducing TV audiences to a rich and diverse cast of puppets and people.

● Public television's Fred Rogers, creator of *Mr. Rogers' Neighborhood,* died on February 27, 2003. Between 1968 and 2000, Rogers produced more than 1,700 episodes of the program, 300 of which are still syndicated by PBS. Known for his welcoming song lyrics, "It's a beautiful day in the neighborhood . . . ," Mr. Rogers talked easily to children—even about difficult subjects like death and divorce. Perhaps *Mr. Rogers' Neighborhood*'s greatest achievement was its enduring success and popularity as a low-tech production—primitive puppet shows and cardboard cutout sets—in the high-tech world of television.

● The first televised presidential debates took place in 1960, pitting Massachusetts senator John F. Kennedy against Vice President Richard Nixon. Don Hewitt, who later created the long-running TV news-magazine *60 Minutes,* directed the first debate and has argued that the TV makeup that Nixon turned down would have helped create a better appearance alongside that of his tanned opponent. In fact, one study at the time reported that a majority of radio listeners thought Nixon won the first debate while the majority of TV viewers believed Kennedy won.

❝ Those who complain about a lack of community among television viewers might pay attention to the vitality and interaction of TV sports watchers wherever they assemble.**❞**

–Barbra Morris, University of Michigan, 1997

produced by the journalist Hedrick Smith, by airing it on successive Friday evenings, which typically draw a smaller TV audience. This pre-Enron film offered "a provocative attack on the kind of Wall Street thinking that places short-term shareholder interests above the welfare of communities." Longtime PBS journalist (and former press secretary to President Johnson) Bill Moyers sharply criticized PBS's scheduling decision, which, he argued, placed the "life of business" before the "business of life."[16]

In addition to problems faced by our public broadcasting system, the original ideal of "universal" television programming serving as our cultural yardstick has also been undercut. The development of cable, the VCR and DVD, new networks, DVRs, iPods, and Internet services has fragmented us by appealing to our individual and special needs. As new technological changes and individualized online services provide more specialized and individual choices, they also alter television's role as a national touchstone and the idea that we are all citizens who are part of a larger nation with a shared stake in the future.

But at the same time—supplementing PBS's role—diverse cable channels such as Nickelodeon and the Cartoon Network do appeal to one end of the age spectrum, while Lifetime, C-Span's Book TV, the History Channel, and Bravo serve the other end; each has built up loyal audiences that were not the main demographic target during the network era. To reinvigorate the ideal of television as a prevailing cultural center, local cable-access channels and electronic "town hall" meetings—in which citizens participate directly in the programming process—have begun tentatively to restore the idea of a shared national culture. And certainly the coverage of the aftermath of 9/11, the 2003 *Columbia* space-shuttle tragedy, the war in Iraq, and the 2005 coverage of Hurricane Katrina demonstrated television's continuing ability to serve as a touchstone for important national events. Such developments at both the local and national levels offer a counter to the economic situation in television today in which a few large multinational companies are controlling the bulk of national and international TV programming. Although we certainly have a greater variety of consumer choices today, we still have very little say in what programs (or products) we might like to see.

The future of television is uncertain. Like the other print and broadcast media that it changed, television has also changed. Technologically, digital advances have already made flat-screen, wall-mounted television sets a reality. However, with iPods, cell phones, and Internet services now offering our favorite TV shows via computer screen, we may no longer need a traditional TV set. In the digital age, distinctions between computer and TV screens might eventually break down. Most television programs are created by a handful of companies, but the networks still rely—at least in part—on independent producers to supply them with the next new idea or story. Although the 1990s and early 2000s featured talk shows, wrestling, reality-based programs, and newsmagazines as hot trends (like quiz shows and westerns before them), these genres, too, will surely fade.

The mainstream allure of television is both its strength and its weakness. As a plus, television offers coverage of special moments—inaugurations, successes and failures in space, football and Super Bowls, *Roots*, the Olympics, impeachment hearings, 9/11, and hurricanes—that bring large heterogeneous groups together for the common experiences of sharing information, celebrating triumphs, and mourning loss. One drawback, though, is that television does not easily explore or adapt to territory outside that common ground. When television aims for the great American middle, it can often mute points of view that are at the edges. As cultural activists and TV critics, we need to support the idea that many voices and views should have a place in the media market and on the screen.

www.

For review questions and activities for Chapter 5, go to the interactive *Media and Culture* Online Study Guide at *bedfordstmartins.com/ mediaculture*

REVIEW QUESTIONS

The Origins and Early Development of Television

1. What were the major technical standards established for television in the 1940s?

2. Why did the FCC freeze the allocation of TV licenses between 1948 and 1952?

3. How did the sponsorship of network programs change during the 1950s?

4. Why did it take forty years for the networks to put a quiz show—*Who Wants to Be a Millionaire*—back on the air in prime time?

Major Programming Trends in the TV Age

5. How did news develop at the networks in the late 1940s and 1950s?

6. What are the differences among sketch, situation, and domestic comedy on television?

7. Why did the anthology drama fade as a network programming staple?

8. What are the types of episodic TV series? Why did they survive as a TV staple?

The Decline of the Network Era

9. What were the technological changes that contributed to the decline of network control over television?

10. What rules and regulations did the government impose to restrict the networks' power?

11. How have new networks managed to grow over the last decade?

The Economics of Television

12. Why has it become more difficult for producers to independently create programs for television?

13. What are the differences between off-network and first-run syndication?

14. Why do syndicated American television shows have advantages in the global marketplace?

15. What is the difference between a rating and a share in audience measurement?

The Public, Television, and Democracy

16. How has television served as a national cultural center or reference point over the years?

17. What problems does traditional network television face in the mid 2000s?

QUESTIONING THE MEDIA

1. Describe your earliest memories of watching television. What was your favorite show? Which shows did your family watch together? Were there shows that you were not allowed to watch? Which ones and why?

2. How much television do you watch today? Which programs do you try to watch regularly? What attracts you to your favorite program(s)?

3. If you were a network television executive, what changes would you try to make in the programs that America watches?

4. If you ran a public television station, what programming would you provide that isn't currently being supplied by commercial television? How would you finance such programming?

5. How could television be used to improve social and political life in the United States?

SEARCHING THE INTERNET

http://www.nab.org

Official Web site for the National Association of Broadcasters, the main trade association and lobbying body for the broadcast industry.

http://www.cpb.org

This Corporation for Public Broadcasting site provides information on PBS programs, member stations, and those who use public TV for education.

http://www.mtr.org

The site for New York's Museum of Television and Radio where the general public can go to view historical collections of old TV programs and TV commercials.

http://www.nbc.com

http://www.abc.com

http://www.cbs.com

http://www.fox.com

http://www.cwtv.com

http://www.univision.com

These are the official national network Web sites. They contain information about their programs as well as listings of the local affiliates.

Media Literacy
and the Critical Process

In Brief

Do you think television plays a greater role in uniting us as a culture or in separating us as individuals? Make two lists of examples on the board (or in groups) that support your point and discuss them in class.

In Depth

Pick a fairly recent TV program that failed to survive on television for more than a year. Roughly following the steps in the critical process, write a four- to five-page examination of the reasons for your program's demise. (See the case study on page 183.)

Description. Do as much research as you can on the program (use the LexisNexis database to check old reviews). In your paper, give a brief description of the program—its story line and major characters. Also, describe the history of the program: when it aired, for how long, ratings information, and so forth. Discuss why you picked this program.

Analysis. After weeding through your research, identify specific problems that may have contributed to your program's failure to stay on the air. Discuss whether these were problems with the program itself or problems with the industry in general.

Interpretation. What does this all mean? Why do you think the program failed? What's your interpretation of all the information you've examined?

Evaluation. Try to go beyond conventional "TV executive" thinking here to offer some fresh insights. Was your program a good one that deserved better? What made it good? Was it a weak program that deserved to fail? What made it weak? Or was it a mixture?

Engagement. Write a letter to one or more network executives. Ask them what qualities they look for in a successful program. Ask them if they bear a responsibility to improve the cultural landscape.

KEY TERMS

prime time, 159
VHF, 162
UHF, 163
analog, 164
digital, 164
affiliate stations, 169
TV newsmagazines, 170
kinescope, 171
sketch comedy, 171
situation comedy, 173
domestic comedy, 173

anthology drama, 174
episodic series, 175
chapter shows, 176
serial programs, 176
stripped [syndicated reruns], 177
network era, 178
independent station, 178
videocassette recorders (VCRs), 179
time shifting, 180
DVRs (digital video recorders), 180
infotainment, 180

fin-syn, 180
deficit financing, 185
rerun syndication, 185
O & Os, 187
evergreens, 188
fringe time, 188
off-network syndication, 188
first-run syndication, 189
rating, 190
share, 190

cable

and the specialization of television

On May 9, 2006, Brian Williams, the top-rated television anchor of *NBC Nightly News,* launched into this story on his news broadcast: "Now to an item having to do with the deja vu at the CIA. If you watch this president closely, and if you were watching on Monday when President Bush nominated General Michael Hayden to run the CIA in place of Porter Goss, something the president said might have sounded familiar. Here is President Bush now from the Oval Office Monday morning." The story cut to a video clip of the president:

BUSH: He's the right man to lead the CIA at this critical moment in our nation's history.

Williams continued with another video clip of the president. "And here is the president back on August 10th 2004, back when he appointed Porter Goss, who's now out of a job."

BUSH: He's the right man to lead this important agency at this critical moment in our nation's history.

Williams concluded by noting "Full disclosure here—it wasn't

our discovery. The strange coincidence was actually uncovered by the crack staff at Comedy Central, the folks who bring you *The Daily Show with Jon Stewart*." The night before, on *The Daily Show,* Stewart juxtaposed the same two clips for his viewers, albeit with a slightly different presentation. After the exposé, Stewart rolled his eyes and did a small dance at his seat, then faced the camera and said, "Ahh, I luvva da TiVo!" That *The Daily Show* scooped the venerable *NBC Nightly News* and other traditional broadcast news programs is increasing evidence of the impact of Stewart's "fake news" product in the real world.

The Daily Show was launched in 1996 with Craig Kilborn as anchor. Stewart—formerly on MTV—took over in 1999 as news anchor, and a good satirical show got even better. In each program, Stewart and a team of correspondents, including Ed Helms, Samantha Bee, and Rob Corddry comment on the day's stories employing actual news footage, taped field pieces, and in-studio guests. A continuing gag features team members as expert "senior correspondents," presumably re-

porting live from news events around the world, when they are clearly in-studio in front of a blue-screen.

Through satire and sharp-witted lampoon of politics, the "fake news" on *The Daily Show* has become an effective critic of television and cable news, and the program has won Emmy and Peabody awards. And, although the program's audience is only about one million viewers, its influence is growing, particularly with young people. According to the Pew Research Center in 2004, more than one in five people age 18–29 say they "regularly learn[ed] about the campaign and the candidates from comedy shows like *Saturday Night Live* and *The Daily Show,* twice as many as said this four years ago."[1] That's about the same proportion of young adults who learn about the campaign and candidates from traditional network news shows.

In fall 2005, former *Daily Show* correspondent Stephen Colbert began a spin-off program, *The Colbert Report,* a half-hour comedy following the *Daily Show* in which Colbert plays a conservative opinion program host, not

unlike Fox News Channel's Bill O'Reilly. Colbert has also become a figure with large impact. In April 2006, Colbert was the main speaker at the White House Correspondents Association dinner. Just steps away from President Bush, Colbert delivered a sharp, heavily ironic address that skewered both the president and the White House press. Colbert's address was watched by relatively few on C-Span but became a viral video on the Internet and generated a debate over whether Colbert wasn't funny (the president and his wife weren't laughing by the end) or whether his humor was too painfully on-target for the Washington crowd.

The Daily Show with Jon Stewart and *The Colbert Report* are two top programs on the Comedy Central cable network, which is available in more than eighty-eight million homes nationwide. Comedy Central is one of Viacom's many cable channels, and is part of the media conglomerate's lock on the young adult cable television market, with other holdings including MTV, VH1, BET, TV Land, Spike TV, CMT, and LOGO, a new channel that is targeted to LGBT audiences.

although cable television is almost as old as broadcast television, broadcasters worked hard to stunt its growth throughout its first twenty-five years. Since the mid-1970s, however, when both HBO (Time Warner's premium movie service) and WTBS (Ted Turner's Atlanta TV station) became available to cable companies across the nation, cable television's growth has been rapid. In 1977, only 14 percent of all American homes received cable. By 1985, that number had climbed to 46 percent. In 1999, cable penetration hit about 70 percent, but it fell to 59 percent by 2006 as **direct broadcast satellite (DBS)** services like DirecTV captured a bigger piece of the market.

The cable industry's emergence from the shadow of broadcast television and its rapid rise to prominence were due partly to the shortcomings of broadcast television. For example, cable generally improved signal reception in most communities. In addition, whereas prime-time broadcast television has traditionally tried to reach the largest possible audiences, cable channels—like magazines and radio—focused more on providing specialized services for smaller audiences that broadcasters often ignored. Furthermore, through its greater channel capacity, cable has provided more access. In many communities, various public, government, and educational channels have made it possible for anyone to air a point of view or produce a TV program. When it has lived up to its potential, cable has offered the public greater opportunities to more fully participate in the democratic promises of television.

We will begin this chapter by examining cable's technological development and traditional broadcasters' attempts to restrict its growth. We will discuss the impact of the various rules and regulations aimed at the cable industry, including the Telecommunications Act of 1996, which was the first major revision of communications law since 1934. We will then turn to various programming strategies, including basic service, premium cable, pay-per-view, video-on-demand, and cable music services, as well as the innovative contributions of CNN, MTV, and HBO. We will also explore the impact of direct broadcast satellite services on cable. Finally, we will look at business and ownership patterns, particularly the influence of the largest cable operators, Comcast Corporation and Time Warner Cable, and investigate cable's role in a democratic society.

> **“** New viewers are not coming to network television. How do you build for the future? If I was a young executive, I don't know if I would come into the network business. I'd probably rather program Comedy Central. **”**
>
> –Leslie Moonves, president of CBS Television, 1998

Technology and the Development of Cable

Unlike recording, radio, and broadcast television, cable television's earliest technical breakthroughs came from a fairly anonymous and practical group of people. Originating in rural and small-town communities in the late 1940s, cable sprang from obstacles that appliance store owners faced in selling TV sets to people who lived in remote areas. To increase sales in places where hills and mountains blocked broadcast signals, TV dealers and electronics firms built antenna relay towers on the outskirts of their communities to pick up blocked signals. They strung wire from utility poles and then ran cables from the towers into individual homes. This created a market for their products by ensuring clear TV reception for viewers.

Although today's technology is more advanced, cable TV continues to operate in pretty much the same way. The key technical distinction between cable and broadcasting remains: In cable, programs reach TV sets through signals transmitted via wire; in broadcasting, signals are transmitted over the air. The advantage of cable is that whereas the airwaves in any given community can accommodate fifteen or so VHF and UHF channels without electrical interference, cable wires can transmit hundreds of channels with no interference.

> **“** If Mark Twain were back today, he'd be on Comedy Central. **”**
>
> –Bill Moyers, talking to Jon Stewart on *The Daily Show*.

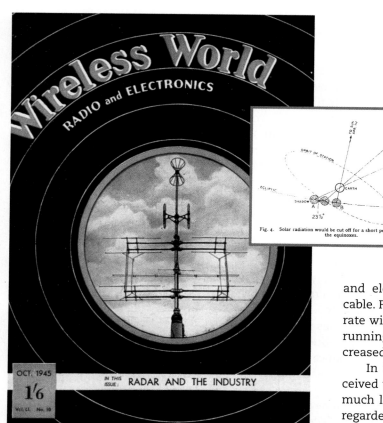

● Writer Arthur C. Clarke published a paper, "Extra-Terrestrial Relays: Can Rocket Stations Give World-wide Radio Coverage?" in the October 1945 issue of *Wireless World Magazine,* envisioning a global communications network based on three satellites in geosynchronous orbit. He wrote, "A true broadcast service . . . over the whole globe would be invaluable, not to say indispensable, in a world society."

CATV—Community Antenna Television

The first small cable systems—called **CATV**, or community antenna television—originated in Oregon, Pennsylvania, and Manhattan (New York City), where mountains or tall buildings blocked TV signals. The early systems served roughly 10 percent of the country and, because of early technical and regulatory limits, contained only twelve channels. Even at this early stage, though, TV sales personnel, broadcasters, and electronics firms recognized the two big advantages of cable. First, by routing and reamplifying each channel in a separate wire, cable eliminated over-the-air interference. Second, by running signals through coaxial cable, channel capacity was increased.

In the early days, small communities with CATV often received twice as many channels as were available over the air in much larger cities. Because broadcast channels were generally regarded as a limited natural resource, CATV foreshadowed later developments in which cable-channel capacity grew dramatically and the need to operate a broadcast frequency diminished. In combination, the two early technological advantages of cable would soon propel the new cable industry into competition with conventional broadcast television. Unlike radio, which was intended to free mass communication from unwieldy wires, early cable technology sought to restore wires to improve the potential of television.

The Wires and Satellites behind Cable Television

The idea for using space satellites for receiving and transmitting communication signals was literally right out of science fiction: In 1945, Arthur C. Clarke (who would later author dozens of sci-fi books, including *2001: A Space Odyssey*) published the original theory for a global communication system based on three satellites equally

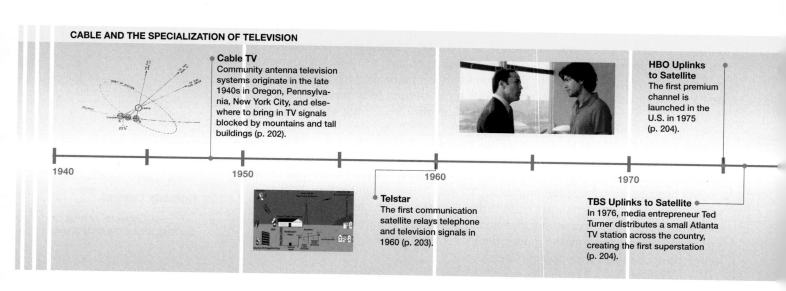

CABLE AND THE SPECIALIZATION OF TELEVISION

Cable TV
Community antenna television systems originate in the late 1940s in Oregon, Pennsylvania, New York City, and elsewhere to bring in TV signals blocked by mountains and tall buildings (p. 202).

HBO Uplinks to Satellite
The first premium channel is launched in the U.S. in 1975 (p. 204).

1940   1950   1960   1970

Telstar
The first communication satellite relays telephone and television signals in 1960 (p. 203).

TBS Uplinks to Satellite
In 1976, media entrepreneur Ted Turner distributes a small Atlanta TV station across the country, creating the first superstation (p. 204).

spaced from each other, rotating with the earth's orbit. In the mid-1950s, these theories became reality, as the Soviet Union and then the United States successfully sent satellites into orbit around the earth.

In 1960, AT&T launched Telstar, the first communication satellite capable of receiving, amplifying, and returning signals. Telstar received transmissions from the ground, beamed from an *uplink* facility, and retransmitted the signals to a receiving dish called a *downlink*. An active satellite, Telstar was able to process and relay telephone and occasional television signals between the United States and Europe. By the mid-1960s, scientists figured out how to lock a communication satellite into **geosynchronous orbit**. Hovering 22,300 miles from the equator, satellites could travel at more than 6,800 mph and circle the earth at the same speed the earth revolves on its axis. For cable television, the breakthrough was the launch of domestic communication satellites, first with Canada's *Anik* satellite in 1972, followed by the United States' *Westar* in 1974.

The first satellites were capable of operating for seven or eight years and had twelve or twenty-four **transponders**, the relay points on a satellite that perform the receive-and-transmit functions. By the mid-1990s, the newest satellites had forty-eight transponders and lifetimes of more than fifteen years. Cable program services such as MSNBC or the Discovery Network rent these transponders from satellite companies for million-dollar monthly fees. One conventional transponder can process one color TV signal or about three thousand simultaneous long-distance phone calls. In recent years, companies have begun using digital compression, a way of increasing the number of signals transmitted simultaneously without disturbing image quality. This process has enabled one transponder to handle four to six TV signals.

With cable, TV signals are processed at a computerized nerve center, or *headend,* which operates various large satellite dishes that receive and process long-distance signals from, say, CNN in Atlanta or MTV in New York. In addition, the headend house's receiving equipment can pick up an area's local broadcast signals or a nearby city's PBS station. The headend relays each premium channel, local network affiliate, independent station, and public TV signal along its own separate line. These lines are made up of *coaxial cable, fiber optics,* or a combination of both. Until the 1980s, when scientists developed fiber-optic technology—sending coded information along beams of laser light—most cable systems transmitted electronic TV signals via coaxial cable, a solid core of copper-clad aluminum wire encircled by an outer axis of braided wires. These bundles of thin wire could accommodate fifty or more separate channels, or lines, running side by side with virtually no interference.

> **"** Much of the excitement and enjoyment of the early years, you see, was that everyone thought we were crazy—but we knew we weren't. **"**
>
> —Arthur C. Clarke, futurist and renowned science-fiction writer who laid down the principles (in 1945) for satellite communication

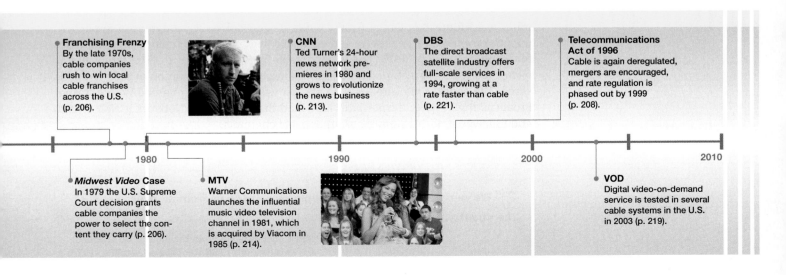

Franchising Frenzy
By the late 1970s, cable companies rush to win local cable franchises across the U.S. (p. 206).

CNN
Ted Turner's 24-hour news network premieres in 1980 and grows to revolutionize the news business (p. 213).

DBS
The direct broadcast satellite industry offers full-scale services in 1994, growing at a rate faster than cable (p. 221).

Telecommunications Act of 1996
Cable is again deregulated, mergers are encouraged, and rate regulation is phased out by 1999 (p. 208).

1980   1990   2000   2010

***Midwest Video* Case**
In 1979 the U.S. Supreme Court decision grants cable companies the power to select the content they carry (p. 206).

MTV
Warner Communications launches the influential music video television channel in 1981, which is acquired by Viacom in 1985 (p. 214).

VOD
Digital video-on-demand service is tested in several cable systems in the U.S. in 2003 (p. 219).

Figure 6.1
A Basic Cable Television System

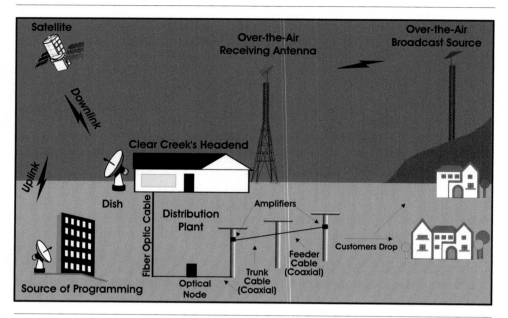

Source: Clear Creek Telephone & TeleVision, www.ccmtc.com/catvhis.htm.

After "downlinking" various channels from satellites and pulling in nearby stations from the airwaves, headend computers relay them in the same way that telephone calls and electric power reach individual households. Most TV channels are relayed from the headend through *trunk* and *feeder cables* attached to existing utility poles. Cable companies rent space on these poles from phone and electric companies. Signals are then transmitted to *drop* or *tap lines* that run from the utility poles into subscribers' homes. TV signals either move from drop lines to cable-ready TV sets or pass through a cable converter box, which enables older TV sets to receive each channel. The newest set-top cable converter boxes can also bring digital channels and on-demand services to subscribers. (See Figure 6.1.)

Advances in satellite technology in the 1970s dramatically changed the fortunes of cable by creating a reliable system for the distribution of programming to cable companies across the nation. In a few short years throughout the late 1970s and 1980s, cable television became popularized as dozens of new cable channels were launched.

The first cable network to use satellites for regular transmission of TV programming was Home Box Office (HBO), which began delivering programming such as uncut, commercial-free movies and exclusive live coverage of major boxing matches for a monthly fee in 1975. The second cable network began in 1976, when media owner Ted Turner distributed his small Atlanta broadcast TV station to cable systems across the country via satellite. The station was eventually renamed WTBS (Turner Broadcasting Service). Turner later launched the Cable News Network (CNN) in 1980 and followed it with a number of other cable channels.

> **❝ We're up on the bird. Now people can watch us from all over the country. ❞**
>
> —Ted Turner, walking down the halls of his television station, after TBS went live on satellite, 1976

Cable Threatens Broadcasting

Though the technology for cable existed as early as the late 1940s, cable's growth was effectively short-circuited by conventional broadcasters. For nearly thirty years, local broadcasters, the networks, and television's professional organization—the National Association of Broadcasters (NAB)—successfully lobbied to curb cable development in most cities. Throughout the 1950s and 1960s, the Federal Communications Commission (FCC) operated on behalf of the broadcast industry to ensure that cable would not compete with conventional television. Local broadcasters worried that if towns could bring in distant signals from more glamorous cities like Chicago or New York, viewers would reject their local stations—and their local advertisers—in favor of big-city signals. Early FCC rules therefore blocked cable companies from bringing distant TV stations into cities and towns with local channels.

There was one exception to these lobbying efforts: CATV service for sparsely populated communities. Because CATV generally served towns that had no TV stations of their own, the broadcast industry welcomed the distribution of distant signals to these areas via cable. After all, relaying a commercial signal to rural areas increased the audience reach and potential ad revenue of a broadcast station.

Balancing Cable's Growth against Broadcasters' Interests

By the early 1970s, particularly with the advent of communication satellites, it was clear that cable's growth could no longer be limited to small, isolated communities. With cable's capacity for more channels and better reception, the FCC began to seriously examine industry issues. In 1972, the commission updated or enacted two rules with long-term effects on cable's expansion.

First, the FCC reaffirmed **must-carry rules**, first established in 1965, which required all cable operators to assign channels to and carry all local TV broadcasts on their systems. This rule ensured that local network affiliates, independent stations (those not carrying network programs), and public television channels would benefit from cable's clearer reception. The FCC guidelines also allowed additional noncommercial channels to be introduced into bigger TV markets, but the guidelines limited the number of distant commercial TV signals to two or three independent stations per cable system. In addition, the guidelines prohibited cable companies from bringing in a network affiliate from another city when a local station already carried that network's programming. This ensured that a network affiliate in one market would not have to compete for viewers against a similar affiliate imported from another market.

Second, the 1972 FCC rules required cable systems to carry their own original programming by mandating **access channels** in the nation's top one hundred TV markets. In other words, operators of cable systems were compelled to provide and fund a tier of nonbroadcast channels dedicated to local education, government, and the public. The FCC required large-market cable operators to assign separate channels for each access service, whereas cable operators in smaller markets (and with fewer channels) could require education, government, and the public to share one channel. In addition to free public-access channels, the FCC called for **leased channels**. Citizens could buy time on these channels and produce longer programs or present controversial views.

Cable's Role: Common Carrier or Electronic Publisher?

Despite the 1972 ruling requiring cable firms to provide local-access channels and a selection of leased channels to local bidders, the cable industry had long preferred to view its content (the programming provided on its cable systems) as similar to that provided by **electronic publishers**, with the same "publishing" freedoms and legal protections that broadcast and print media enjoy in selecting content. That meant that the cable companies felt entitled to pick and choose which channels to carry. The FCC argued the opposite: that cable systems should be **common carriers**— services that do not get involved in channel content. Like telephone operators, who do not question the topics of personal conversations ("Hi, I'm the phone company, and what are you going to be talking about today?"), the FCC argued that cable companies should offer part of their services on a first-come, first-served basis to whoever can pay the rate. In 1979, the debate over this issue ended in the landmark *Midwest Video* case, when the U.S. Supreme Court upheld the rights of cable companies to dictate their content and defined the industry as a form of "electronic publishing."[2] Although the FCC could no longer mandate channels, the Court said that it was still okay for communities to "request" access channels as part of contract negotiations in the franchising process. Access channels are no longer a requirement, but most cable companies continue to offer them in order to remain on good terms with their communities.

Franchising Frenzy

By the end of the 1970s, particularly after the *Midwest Video* decision, the future of cable programming was clear, and competition over obtaining franchises to supply local cable service had become intense. Essentially, a cable franchise was a mini-monopoly awarded by a local community to the most attractive bidder, usually for a fifteen-year period. Although a few large cities permitted two companies to build different parts of their cable systems, in most cases communities granted franchises to only one company. Cities and states used the same logic that had been used in granting monopoly status to AT&T for more than a hundred years: They did not want more than one operator trampling over private property to string wire from utility poles or to bury cables underground.

The period from the late 1970s through the early 1990s constituted a unique, if turbulent, era in media history, for it was during this time that most of the nation's

Figure 6.2
U.S. Cable Systems, 1970–2010

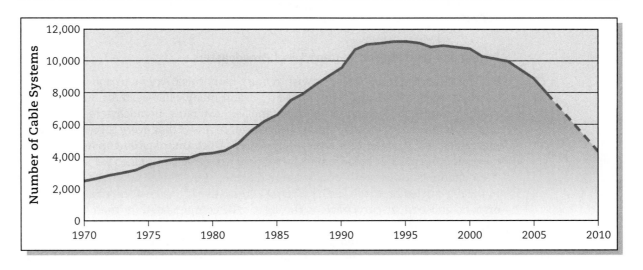

Source: National Cable & Telecommunications Association (NCTA), www.ncta.com.

cable systems were built (see Figure 6.2). During the franchising process, a city (or state) would outline its cable system needs and request bids from cable companies. Then a number of companies—none of which could also own broadcast stations or newspapers in the community—competed for the right to install and manage the cable system. In the bid, a company would make a list of promises to the city, including information about construction schedules, system design, subscription rates, channel capacity, types of programming, financial backing, deadlines, and a *franchise fee*: the money the cable company would pay the city annually for the right to operate the local cable system.

Few rules or laws existed to regulate the process of franchise negotiations. During the franchising process, competing cable companies made attractive offers and promises to gain monopoly rights in certain areas. In the early 1980s, for example, Sammon Communication bid for the Fort Worth, Texas, franchise by offering that city a multi-million-dollar community-access package that included three mobile television vans (for producing community programs), $50,000 for student internship training programs, $175,000 as an annual budget for access channels, and $100,000 to modernize educational buildings and studios. Such offers were typical in large cable markets.

From the late 1970s through the 1980s, lots of wheeling and dealing transpired, along with occasional corruption. Cable companies sometimes offered far more than they could deliver, and some cities and suburbs occasionally made unfair demands on the franchise awardees. Often, battles over broken promises, unreasonable contracts, or escalating rates ended up in court.

New Rules Aid Cable's Growth

From the very beginning of cable, no one seemed to know who held legal jurisdiction over wired television. Because the 1934 Communications Act had not anticipated cable, its regulatory status was problematic during its early years. However, once cable began importing distant signals into bigger television markets, the FCC's interest perked up. By the mid-1980s, Congress, the FCC, and courts had repealed most early cable regulations, stimulating growth in the medium that had begun to acquaint the world with innovative programming like that carried on MTV and CNN, but also triggering regular rate increases for cable customers.

Paying and Deal Making to Carry Local Broadcasters

In 1992, a new cable act added a twist to must-carry rules. After a period in the 1980s in which must-carry rules were phased out and many cable systems subsequently dropped weaker independent stations and PBS affiliates, broadcasters lobbied for new leverage with cable operators. The 1992 act required that every three years commercial broadcasters opt for either must-carry or **retransmission consent**. The latter option meant that broadcasters could now ask cable companies for fees to carry their channels. However, if broadcasters did this, they waived the right to be automatically carried on these cable systems. Alternatively, local commercial broadcasters who chose must-carry gave up the right to be compensated for their channel but were guaranteed a channel assignment on their local cable system. By June 1993, each of the eleven-hundred-plus commercial U.S. TV stations (noncommercial stations could choose only must-carry) had to inform all cable system operators in their broadcast range whether they were opting for must-carry or retransmission. At the time, only low-rated independent stations on the fringes of a market opted for must-carry.

In 1993, the stations that chose retransmission consent did so because they correctly believed cable companies would not risk alienating customers by dropping the popular broadcast stations that carried network programs. In general, a broadcast station wanted either money from cable companies for carrying its signal or the right to advertise on more cable channels. A few large broadcast stations owned by powerful media conglomerates, such as Disney (which has at least ten owned-and-operated stations), struck deals with cable companies that owned a large number of systems. For example, rather than ask for money, Disney requested that cable systems carry its new ESPN2 sports channel, which debuted in 1993. Disney's strategy successfully leveraged ESPN2—and later ESPN News and ESPN Classic—onto the lineups of major cable systems around the country. Similar tactics have been used by other broadcasters to launch cable channels such as FX and MSNBC.

The Telecommunications Act of 1996

After sixty-two years, Congress finally rewrote the nation's communications laws in the **Telecommunications Act of 1996**, bringing cable fully under the federal rules that had long governed the telephone, radio, and TV industries. In its most significant move, Congress used the Telecommunications Act to knock down regulatory barriers, allowing regional phone companies, long-distance carriers, and cable companies to enter one another's markets. For the first time, owners could operate TV or radio stations in the same market where they owned a cable system. Just as the Telecommunications Act allows cable companies to offer telephone services, it also permits phone companies to use fiber-optic wires to offer Internet services and to buy or construct cable systems in communities where there are fewer than fifty thousand residents. Before passage of the 1996 legislation, the phone and cable in-

> 66 If this [telecommunications] bill is a blueprint, it's written in washable ink. Congress is putting out a picture of how things will evolve. But technology is transforming the industry in ways that we don't yet understand. 99
>
> —Mark Rotenberg, Electronic Privacy Information Center, 1996

dustries had long benefited from their regional and national monopoly status. Congress hoped that the new rules would spur competition and lower both phone and cable rates, although this did not usually happen.

While broadcasters fought steadily for must-carry rules over the years, cable companies continued to argue that these rules violated their free-speech rights by dictating what signals must be included among their cable offerings. The Telecommunications Act appeared to settle the issue by reaffirming broadcasters' need for must-carry rules. However, cable companies with limited channel capacity still objected to having to carry low-rated stations; operators could make more money carrying satellite-delivered movie services and specialty channels on topics such as history or health. The nation's cable companies continued to periodically ask the courts to repeal must-carry rules and free the cable companies to carry whatever channels best served their commercial interests. In 1997, however, broadcasting won a final victory when the Supreme Court upheld the constitutionality of must-carry rules, ensuring that most broadcasters would be carried by their local cable companies.

So far, the 1996 act has had mixed impact on cable customers. Cable companies argued that it would lead to more competition and innovations in programming, services, and technology. The cable industry has delivered on the technology, investing more than $100 billion in technological infrastructure between 1996 and 2006. This has enabled cable companies to offer what they call the "triple play"—digital cable television, broadband Internet, and telephone service, all bundled through the same household cable connection. By 2006, U.S. cable companies had signed more than thirty million households to digital programming packages; about twenty-eight million households had cable Internet service, and nearly six million households received their telephone service via cable.[3]

But the 1996 act has not resulted in extensive competition in cable. About 92 percent of U.S. cable subscribers live in communities that still have no viable competition to the local cable company. In these areas, cable rates have risen faster than the rate of inflation. In the few communities with multiple cable providers, the competition makes a difference—monthly rates are up to 16 percent lower, according to an FCC study.[4] But, where there is no competition, cable rates are determined by local cable companies, and the FCC has no authority to enforce rate freezes or cuts because the 1996 act required the FCC to end rate regulation in 1999.

> **❝ Cable companies have monopoly power, and this shows in the prices they charge.❞**
> –The Consumers Union, 2003

Cable Comes of Age

Although its audience and advertising revenues remain smaller than those of the major TV networks, cable has emerged as a serious challenger to—and partner of—broadcasting. As the broadcast audience continued to erode throughout the 1990s and 2000s, the major networks developed or acquired several cable channels in order to capture some of the migrating viewers. NBC, for example, operated cable news services CNBC and MSNBC (with Microsoft) and entertainment channel Bravo. ABC owned ESPN and its many channels, along with portions of Lifetime, A&E, History, and E! CBS was the slowest to develop cable outlets, and even its once successful TNN (The National Network, now Spike TV) and CMT (Country Music Television) channels are now owned by Viacom (although in 2006 CBS's largest shareholder was Sumner Redstone, chairman of Viacom). Disney's purchase of ABC in 1995 and Viacom's purchase of CBS in 1999 paired the networks' cable channels with the more extensive cable properties of their corporate parents (in 2006, Viacom and CBS split into separate companies). The shifting balance of power between broadcasting and

Figure 6.3
The Top Cable Networks, 2006 (Ranked by Number of Subscribers)

Note: Figures may include noncable affiliates and/or subscribers. Broadcast viewership is not included.
Source: National Cable & Telecommunications Association, www.ncta.com, May 2006.

cable in the 1990s was even apparent in how the industry covered itself. *Broadcasting,* the trade magazine for television and an opponent of cable's early growth, became *Broadcasting & Cable* in 1993.

During the old network era in television, ABC, CBS, and NBC accounted for more than 95 percent of prime-time viewing; independent stations and public television accounted for the rest. By the summer of 1997, basic cable channels had captured a larger prime-time audience than the broadcast networks, the first time that had ever happened. The networks have responded to cable's increased investment in original series by increasing the profile of their summer offerings (summer traditionally being a "lull" time for programming), but this strategy has been only partially successful. The decline in the networks' viewer base appeared to be healthy for both competition and democracy. Yet with recent consolidations in media ownership, the companies that own the broadcast networks are often the same as those that control many of the leading cable channels. Thus the appearance of competition may at times be illusory.

In the new cable era, a redefined concept of **narrowcasting**—providing specialized programming for diverse and fragmented groups—has cut into broadcasting's large mass audience. For the advertising industry, cable programs provide access to specific target audiences that cannot be guaranteed in broadcasting (see, for example, "Case Study—The United Segments of America: Niche Marketing in Cable" on page 212). For example, a golf-equipment manufacturer can buy ads on the Golf Channel and reach only golf enthusiasts. Because the audience is small and specialized, ads are a fraction of the cost of a network ad; they reach only the targeted viewers and not the larger general public. As cable channels have become more and more like specialized magazines or radio formats (see Figure 6.3), they have siphoned off network viewers. As a consequence, the networks' role as the chief programmer of the shared culture has eroded.

Cable consumers usually choose programming from a two-tiered structure: Basic cable services are part of one monthly fee, and premium cable services are available individually to customers at an extra monthly or per-use fee. (See "Tracking Technology: Cable TV a la Carte" on page 220.) These services are the production arm of the cable industry, supplying programming to the nation's nearly ten thousand cable operators, which function as program distributors to cable households.

Basic Cable Services

A typical **basic cable** system today includes a thirty-six- to seventy-two-channel lineup composed of local broadcast signals, nonbroadcast access channels (for local government, education, and general public use), one or more regional PBS stations, and a variety of services retrieved from national communication satellites. These basic cable channels include ESPN, CNN, MTV, VH1, the USA Network, Bravo, Nickelodeon, Lifetime, ABC Family, Comedy Central, CNBC, C-Span and C-Span2, Black Entertainment Television, Telemundo, the Weather Channel, a home-shopping service, **superstations** (independent TV stations linked to a satellite) such as WGN (Chicago) or WPIX (New York), and ten to thirty additional channels, depending on a cable system's capacity and regional interests.

Typically, local cable companies pay each of these satellite-delivered services between five cents (for low-cost, low-demand channels like C-Span) and more than $2.60 (for high-cost, high-demand channels like ESPN) a month per subscriber. That fee is passed along to consumers as part of their basic monthly cable rate. Unlike local broadcasters, which make money almost exclusively through advertising, cable companies earn revenue in a variety of ways: through monthly subscriptions for basic service, local ad sales, pay-per-view programming, and premium movie channels. Most basic cable channels, such as ESPN or A&E, block out time for inexpensive local and regional ads. These local ads are cheaply produced compared with national network ads and reach a smaller audience than do broadcast commercials. Cable, in fact, has permitted many small local companies—from restaurants to clothing stores—that might not otherwise be able to afford TV spots to use television as a means of advertising.

The 1990s witnessed a proliferation of new basic cable channels, increasingly specialized for smaller but more definable audiences. These include the popular Sci-Fi Channel (owned by the USA Network), the Cartoon Network (owned by Time Warner), Comedy Central (owned by Time Warner and Viacom), and FX (owned by News Corporation). Newer services featured channels devoted to history, health and fitness, books, games, parenting, pets, and therapy.

> **" If Desert Storm fixed CNN's reputation, and O.J. did the same for Court TV, then the blizzard of '96 has put the Weather Channel solidly on the map. "**
> —*Newsweek*, January 1996

The United Segments of America: Niche Marketing in Cable

Individually, most cable television programs don't generate very impressive audience numbers. A top network television program like *Grey's Anatomy* on ABC delivers more than 20 million television viewers for an episode. A top cable television program like *SpongeBob SquarePants* on Nickelodeon delivers about four million viewers.

Yet, taken together, cable television now edges out the traditional television networks (ABC, CBS, NBC, Fox, CW, and PAX) in total audience. Moreover, a number of top advertisers such as General Motors are putting the majority of their television advertising budget in cable, not broadcast network television. The key to cable's success is its ability to attract highly specific audiences. The profiles of cable viewers provided by the CableTelevision Advertising Bureau read much like profiles of magazine audiences; like magazines, cable channels target precise audience segments.

For example, Bravo, home of *Project Runway* and *Inside the Actors Studio,* bills itself as the best cable network to reach adult viewers, ages 25–54, who have a household income greater than $150,000 and who hold top management positions and have a graduate degree. Also, the Food Network is a top choice for reaching what it calls "upscale" women in this age bracket. These viewers are likely to be working women with a household income of $75,000 or more and have a Visa or MasterCard Gold card. Even news channels have niche audiences—Fox News Channel is known for being politically to the right of CNN and draws more male viewers, whereas CNN draws slightly more female viewers.

MTV offers itself to advertisers as the one channel that "owns the young adult demographic." MTV says that it is the "best way to connect" with the 12–34 age group, which at 91 million strong and growing represents 33 percent of the population and more than $250 billion in spending power. The median age of MTV's viewers is 20.4.

Similarly, Black Entertainment Television (BET) markets itself as the best way to reach African Americans, who spend more than $500 billion on consumer products annually. BET's main focus, especially in prime time, is the demographic of African Americans ages 18–34.

Where do you find the older demographics? Flip between The History Channel and The Weather Channel (median age 46) and A&E (median age 47).

To reach children, advertisers can look to the Cartoon Network, where the audience is composed of 70 percent kids and teens. However, Nickelodeon is the king of this demographic, delivering more children under 12 than any other basic cable network. Its shows *SpongeBob Squarepants* and *Fairly Odd Parents* are the two leading children's programs on cable. Overall, 62 percent of Nickelodeon's audience is ages 2–11, 12 percent ages 12–17, and 26 percent adults 18 and above. Even more specifically, Nickelodeon claims to deliver more women ages 18–49 who have children under 12 years of age than any other basic cable network (apparently, the moms are watching with their children).

For women, Lifetime (with an audience of 76 percent women) is the top cable network, with Oxygen, SoapNet, and HGTV competing for the same audience. For men, ESPN (with an audience of 75 percent men) is the leader, and it claims more high-income male viewers than any other ad-supported network. Other cable networks that skew heavily male include the Speed Channel (85 percent men); OLN, the Outdoor Life Network, which became Versus in Fall 2006 (78 percent men); the Golf Channel (74.5 percent men); ESPN2 (72.3 percent men); and Comedy Central (its hit series *South Park* "out-delivers all cable programs among men 12–34").

Battling with national cable networks are regional cable services, which target audiences geographically. More than ninety regional channels exist in the United States, and nearly all of them are located in large metropolitan areas that can support such specialized programming. Many of the regional channels are news/talk formats modeled on CNN, but with coverage limited to a single media market. New York, for example, has New York 1 News, a twenty-four-hour service that began in 1992. The New York region also has News 12 cable channels, which cover local markets outside the city. Similar services include NorthWest Cable News (Seattle), News Channel 8 (Washington, D.C.), and ChicagoLand Television News. Regional sports channels—many of them affiliates of the national Fox Sports Network—also thrive in many of the same top television markets and regions that are home to multiple professional sports teams.

In 1992, eighty-seven cable networks were in business. By 2006, that number had grown to more than 530 networks serving cable and satellite television.[5] Cable system capacities continued to increase due to (1) the rebuilding of cable systems with high-bandwidth fiber-optic cable, and (2) the advent of digital cable services in the late 1990s, which have enabled cable companies to expand their offerings beyond the basic analog cable channels. Digital cable typically uses set-top cable boxes to offer interactive on-screen program guides and dozens of additional premium, pay-per-view, and audio music channels, increasing total cable capacities to between 150 and 200 channels. By 2006, about thirty million U.S. households subscribed to digital cable services.[6]

The general success rate of new channels has been about 10 to 15 percent, which means that about 85 to 90 percent of new cable channels fail or are bought out by another cable service. The most difficult challenge new channels face is getting onto enough cable systems—many with limited channel capacity—to become profitable. Although several basic cable channels, such as the Discovery Channel and ESPN (both with about ninety million cable subscribers), have been extremely successful, two basic channels—CNN and MTV—have made their mark both on American society and on global culture.

CNN's Window to the World

When it premiered in 1980, many people viewed Cable News Network (CNN), the first 24/7 cable TV news channel, as a joke—the "Chicken Noodle Network." CNN was the brainchild of Ted Turner, who had already revolutionized cable by uplinking his small independent Atlanta station WTBS (Turner Broadcast Service) to a satellite, creating the first superstation. It wasn't until Turner launched Headline News in 1982, and turned a profit with both operations in 1985, that the traditional networks began to take notice of cable news.

In 1991, CNN emerged as a serious news competitor to ABC, CBS, and NBC during the Gulf War when two of its reporters were able to maintain a live phone link from a downtown Baghdad hotel during the initial U.S. bombing of the Iraqi capital. Even Iraq's military leaders watched the channel. CNN's ratings soared—from an audience of fewer than one million households before the crisis to as many as ten million homes after the war began. About two hundred local broadcast stations with CNN agreements, including many network affiliates that ordinarily carried network news, switched to CNN for coverage of the crisis.

Beyond its financial success, CNN changed the way people watch news. Before CNN launched in 1980, and before the Internet, there were just two news cycles a day: in the morning, when people read the newspaper or tuned in to a radio or TV news show; and in the evening, when people listened to radio news on the way home or watched the evening network news on television. But CNN liberated viewers by offering a constant window into news happenings around the world. The

● Launched in 1985 to feature programming on scientific discoveries and achievements, the Discovery Channel has become cable television's most popular channel. The channel's parent corporation, Discovery Communications, Inc. of Silver Spring, Maryland, has grown into a major media corporation, whose holdings now include the Travel Channel, Animal Planet, TLC, BBC America, FitTV, a number of digital cable channels, and Discovery Channel retail stores. (Pictured above is one of the most popular Discovery Channel shows, Mythbusters.)

After an early career that included stints with the school news service Channel One and ABC reality show *The Mole,* Anderson Cooper joined CNN in 2001. He became one of their top newscasters in 2003, anchoring the news program *Anderson Cooper 360°.* Cooper is best known for his live reports from news locations around the world.

network mastered continuous coverage of breaking news events, such as natural disasters and wars, and aimed to put news first, creating a reporting style that refused to transform news anchors into celebrities. Because it wasn't forced to compress the day's news into a half-hour show, it was also able to deliver more timely news in greater detail and feature live, unedited coverage of news conferences, press briefings, and special events. Moreover, with a commitment to maintaining international bureaus (while other networks were shutting them down), CNN made a big impact on international news coverage. Today, CNN appears in more than two hundred countries and territories around the globe; more than one billion people have access to a CNN service.

The success of CNN proved that there is both a need and a lucrative market for twenty-four-hour news. Spawning a host of competitors in the United States and worldwide, CNN now battles for viewers with other twenty-four-hour news providers, including FoxNews Channel, MSNBC, CNBC, EuroNews, Sky Broadcasting, and countless Web sites. Ironically, in the same manner that CNN rose to prominence during the Gulf War in 1991, its main rival, FoxNews, surpassed CNN's ratings in 2002, as international terrorism and the buildup to a second U.S.-Iraq war were main news events. Despite being beaten in the ratings by FoxNews commentary shows like *The O'Reilly Factor* and *Hannity & Colmes,* CNN still garnered higher advertising rates on the strength of its worldwide news reputation.

"I Want My MTV"

The second basic cable service to dramatically change the world's cultural landscape is MTV (the Music Television Network). Launched in 1981 by Warner Communications and purchased by Viacom in 1985, MTV and its global offspring—including MTV Europe, MTV Brasil, MTV Latin America, MTV Russia, MTV Australia, MTV Africa, and MTV Asia—reach more than 440 million homes worldwide. Its international appeal is so great that when Poland became free of Soviet control in the late 1980s, its national television operation immediately began broadcasting MTV. By the late 1990s, more than a quarter of MTV's revenue came from international sources.

Although today MTV exerts a powerful influence on global culture, it was slow to develop in at least one significant way. In its formative years, MTV gave little airtime to African American artists. This history recalls the 1950s and the problems black rock and rollers faced in getting mainstream radio play. In the early 1980s, however, MTV's reluctance to play music videos by black artists was related not to racial tensions but to the economics of the cable system. At that time, most cable companies were operating primarily in affluent white communities in U.S. suburbs. These were the areas that could most easily afford cable. Because rock had been dominated by white male groups throughout the 1970s, MTV determined that white suburban teens probably wanted to see similar groups in their music videos. It took Michael Jackson's *Thriller* album in 1982 to break down music video's early color barrier. The album's large crossover appeal, coupled with the expansion of cable into more urban areas, opened the door to far more diverse videos. With hip-hop's rise in popularity throughout the 1980s and 1990s among both black and white audiences, MTV began to add more hip-hop, soul, and R&B videos to the rotation, as well as programs like *Yo! MTV Raps* and *Jams Countdown*. Through its daily programming, MTV helped sell African American hip-hop culture—with its hip-hop beats, baggy clothes, urban sensibility, and street language—to suburban America and the world at large.

Throughout the 1980s, MTV sought more and more control over music video distribution and exhibition, employing two monopoly tactics to ensure dominance. First, MTV paid record companies for exclusive rights to the most popular music videos (for periods ranging from thirty days to one year), thereby preventing access by other music video services. Although this was a form of payola, federal laws prohibiting this practice applied only to broadcasting, not to cable.

Second, MTV signed agreements with the major cable companies to ensure that it would become the music video network in all the main cable markets. Those cable companies with limited channel capacity were often reluctant to carry more than one music channel. Competing services, like Ted Turner's attempted music video channel in 1984, were quickly countered by MTV's launch of VH1, which was geared toward the baby-boom generation and the parents of the MTV crowd and became part of a bundled MTV-VH1 package sold to cable operators.

The music video channel Fuse, owned by Cablevision Systems (which also owns national channels such as AMC and the Independent Film Channel), has presented MTV with its most spirited challenge in recent years. The channel targets the twelve- to thirty-four-year-old audience with music videos and live music performances and an underdog image that tries to out-cool MTV. Fuse reached more than thirty-eight million households by 2006.

The major recording labels, spending as much as $50 million a year to produce videos in the 1990s, have grown dependent on MTV's power to certify a hit recording. These companies have also criticized the small group of MTV executives who wade through the hundreds of new videos released each week and judge which 10 to 15 percent are fit for MTV play. The recording companies want to see more of their

● Fans in the studio of MTV's popular afternoon request show *Total Request Live* cheer for singer Beyoncé. *TRL*'s live broadcasts draw large crowds each day to its Times Square studios in New York City.

products on MTV's regular music rotation, which usually accommodates about sixty recordings per week.

MTV began to stray from a rotation of music videos in the early 1990s to more original programming, including the reality-based soap opera *The Real World*, the cartoon *Beavis and Butt-head*, and the dating show *Singled Out*. The shift was an effort to provide advertisers with more regular audiences during specific viewing times, but it ended up infuriating record labels and many MTV viewers by further narrowing the channel's video playlists. MTV responded in 1996 by creating another channel, MTV2, which is designed to present music videos like MTV originally did. By 2006, MTV2 was on cable systems that reached about fifty-nine million subscribers.

At the same time, MTV continued to branch out into a more structured format. Some new programs featured music, such as *Total Request Live (TRL)*, added to MTV's weekday schedule in 1998. The show's various hosts introduce popular music videos determined by viewers' votes and interview artists and other pop culture celebrities like actors. The *MTV Music Video Awards* have also become a significant MTV staple, rivaling the Grammy Awards as a television event. But the biggest portion of MTV's schedule has been reality series. *Real World*, which first aired in 1992 and helped to inspire a craze of reality television on network TV in the early 2000s, has been the model for a number of other MTV youth-oriented reality programs, including *Road Rules, Laguna Beach, Pimp My Ride, MADE*, and *My Super Sweet 16*.

As a subsidiary of Viacom, one of the world's largest media conglomerates, MTV actually draws more fire for its cultural than for its economic impact. Many critics worry that its influence has eroded local culture-specific traits among the world's young people and has substituted an overabundance of U.S. culture in its place. Others argue that MTV has contributed to the decline of conversation and civil discourse through its often sexually suggestive and rapid-fire style. Defenders of the network, however, point out that MTV and cable have created a global village, giving the world a common language. They also applaud a variety of MTV's special programs on issues ranging from drug addiction to racism and social activism. The visual style of MTV—from shaky camera footage and quick cuts to bright colors and dazzling visual innovations—has also had, and continues to have, an influence on the media landscape. Touching everything from movies to TV drama and commercials, the MTV style is one that constantly breaks rules and establishes new conventions. Besides turning to MTV for visual inspiration, Hollywood now looks to the channel as a farm league of sorts for its hot new directors; indeed, a well-produced music video is considered an ideal audition reel. For many critics, however, MTV has become a virus, with its ceaseless succession of disconnected three-minute mini-musicals and compressed narratives infecting most major sound and visual media with plenty of style but little substance.

Beyond the world of music, one of MTV's major programming innovations has been the Nickelodeon channel.[7] In an era in which the major networks have largely abandoned children's programming because it wasn't lucrative enough, competitors such as PBS and Nickelodeon have tried to fill the gap. As Nickelodeon and MTV kids reach adulthood, they no longer view broadcast programs as superior to cable, since they've spent most of their childhood watching cable networks.

Premium Cable Services

Besides basic programming, cable offers a wide range of special channels, known as **premium channels**, and other services. These include

> **❝**I may have destroyed world culture, but MTV wouldn't exist today if it wasn't for me.**❞**
>
> —Advertising art director George Lois, who coined the phrase "I want my MTV," 2003

> **❝**MTV is popular fascism at its worst. MTV just doesn't care (and never has) about anything related to a big thing called talent!**❞**
>
> —statement posted at http://www.egroups.com/group/Anti-MTV, an anti-MTV discussion site, 2000

movie channels, such as HBO and Showtime; pay-per-view (PPV) programs; video-on-demand (VOD); and interactive (two-way) services that enable consumers to use their televisions to bank, shop, play games, and access the Internet. Subscribers to such services pay extra fees in addition to the fee for basic cable. In the early days of cable, there was only a single monthly charge; but with HBO providing movies, a new source of revenue—the premium, or deluxe, tier—was added to the subscription mix. In fact, luring customers to premium channels has plenty of incentives for cable companies: The cost to them is four to six dollars per month per subscriber to carry a premium channel, but they then charge customers ten dollars or more per month and reap a nice profit.

● Music video network Fuse's *Daily Download* program—like its dominant competitor, MTV's *Total Request Live*—features a live New York City studio audience, a music video countdown, and performances by artists such as Usher (*pictured*). *Daily Download* also offers free music downloads on the show's Web site.

The HBO Alternative

By far the oldest and most influential premium channel is Home Box Office (HBO), a subsidiary of Time Warner, one of the nation's largest owners of cable companies. Although HBO reaches less than one-third the audience of a popular basic channel, it has remained the dominant premium channel, selling monthly subscriptions to more than 27 million homes by 2006. HBO and Cinemax, the second-highest rated premium channel, bring a combined total of about 39 million premium subscribers to parent corporation Time Warner. Competing premium channels include Liberty Media's Encore, STARZ!, and MOVIEplex channels, which combined had about 41 million subscribers in 2006; and CBS's Showtime, the Movie Channel, and Flix, which had 39.5 million combined subscribers. New premium film channels such as the Sundance Channel (operated by Showtime and owned by actor Robert Redford,

Universal Studios, and Showtime) and the Independent Film Channel emerged with the growing market of independent films in the mid-1990s.

The movie business initially feared that HBO would be a detriment to film attendance in theaters. Eventually, though, HBO and the other premium channels brought a lucrative source of income to the movie studios, which earn roughly a 15 percent share of premium cable's profits. With premium cable channels locking up the rights to feature-length movies after their initial theater runs, film companies recognized that they could recoup losses from a weak theater run by extending a film's life. This could be done not just via television or neighborhood second-run theaters but through lucrative arrangements with premium cable. Today, HBO runs more than ninety theatrical motion pictures a month.

In the early 1980s, when there was little competition, HBO dictated to movie studios which films it wanted and how much it was willing to pay. HBO and other premium channels ran into trouble, however, as videotapes became the preferred method of viewing movies after their theater runs. Both VCRs and PPV (pay-per-view) options brought competition to the movie channels. In the mid-1980s, film studios started releasing movies to PPV and to video stores before offering them to movie channels. The new competition forced the movie channels to expand their services. HBO, for example, began developing its own programming—from children's shows like *Fraggle Rock* to comedies like the *Larry Sanders Show*, an Emmy-winning satire of late-night talk shows. HBO's successes in original programming continue today with critical praise for programs like *The Sopranos*, *Deadwood*, *Entourage*, and *Curb Your Enthusiasm*.

What film studios clearly did not like was HBO's production of its own feature-length films. In 1982, HBO entered into an arrangement with CBS and Columbia Pictures (later bought by Sony) to form a new production house, TriStar Pictures. Many in the movie industry charged that HBO's movie productions constituted vertical integration, with involvement in production, distribution, and exhibition. They argued that when Time Inc. (before its merger with Warner) began making movies through HBO and TriStar, the media conglomerate was permitted to do something that film studios could not do. A Supreme Court decision in 1948 had broken up the film industry's vertical structure by forcing the major studios to sell their theaters, the exhibition part of their operations. Time Inc., on the other hand, was the second-largest owner of cable systems—the movie studio equivalent of owning theaters. Because so many cable companies and services existed, though, the government did not seriously challenge HBO's role in movie production.

Pay-per-View, Video-on-Demand, and Interactive Cable

Beginning in 1985, cable companies began introducing new viewing options for their customers. **Pay-per-view (PPV)** channels came first, offering recently released movies or special one-time sporting events (such as a championship boxing match) to subscribers who paid a designated charge to their cable company, allowing them to view the program at its designated time slot. Even though numerous industry analysts predicted that PPV would overtake the video rental market, there weren't enough PPV choices available, and it became evident by the late 1990s that consumers preferred the variety and flexibility of rented videos and DVDs, even if they had to drive to the store to get them and pay late fees.

U.S. cable companies introduced a new and improved pay-per-view option to their digital customers in the early 2000s. Pioneered in Japan in the early 1990s and called **video-on-demand (VOD)**, this digital cable service enabled customers to choose among hundreds of titles, then download a selection from the cable operator's server onto their cable TV box hard drive for one to four dollars and watch the movie the same way they would watch a video, pausing and fast-forwarding when desired. The company iN DEMAND, the largest PPV provider, is also the leading provider of VOD services, although premium cable channels such as HBO, Cinemax, Showtime, and the Movie Channel, and basic cable networks like HGTV and the Food Network have begun to release their program libraries through VOD channels. The largest cable companies and DBS services also offer digital video recorders (DVRs) to their customers, a high-end, programmable alternative to VCRs that competes with TiVo and Replay services. The rapid growth of VOD services is moving video fans closer to the day when ordering a movie off television will be preferable to driving to the local video store.

Another type of cable service feature, developed throughout the 1990s, is **interactive**, or two-way, **cable television**. When equipped with two-way technology, such systems enable users to send signals upstream or back to the headend. (Most systems are one-way and can send signals only downstream to subscribers' homes.) Interactive cable can connect households to their banks, where customers can pay bills or transfer money. Some cable services also permit police burglary units and fire stations to monitor homes and apartments. Like the bulk of cable programming, the most frequent type of two-way service involves entertainment. In 1991, Interactive Network began offering video games to cable consumers, including play-along versions of *Wheel of Fortune* and *Jeopardy*. It also provided services that allowed viewers to guess the next play during a football game. The limiting factor for interactive services, though, is bandwidth. Because interactive services require more space to send two-way information on cable (in contrast to the one-way communication of regular cable TV channels), most cable operators are unwilling to offer this feature at the expense of lucrative one-way channels.

Cable Music Services

In addition to movies and videos on request, many cable systems now offer CD-quality premium audio services. Routed through a consumer's stereo equipment, **cable music** companies like Music Choice and DMX Music provide twenty-four-hour

> 66 [HBO is] a network that hires people that they like and says that's the end of their job. 'We like you; do what you think you should do,' and it leads to much more distinctive programming. 99
> –Jerry Seinfeld, 2004

> 66 Murdoch's DirecTV is really the six-hundred-pound gorilla people are looking at. If Murdoch brings out [interactive television] and has success with it, that will force cable to follow. 99
> –Phillip Swann, president and publisher of TVPRedictions.com

Cable TV a la Carte

By Leslie Cauley

Cable TV companies have long said the "expanded-basic" package of channels that most viewers choose is a bargain. For about $41 a month, they note, you can see scores of channels, including CNN and ESPN.

Most of us, though, typically watch only 15 to 17 channels a month, according to industry estimates. Yet expanded basic continues to swell like a hot-air balloon—and so has its price. A few years ago, expanded basic offered about 35 channels; today, 200 to 300 channels are common. The price of expanded basic has jumped more than 40% in five years. In that time, overall prices for goods and services are up just 12%.

Now, thanks to new technology, shifting sentiment in Washington and deep-pocketed rivals such as AT&T and Verizon, the expanded-basic balloon might be about to pop. On the horizon: a la carte programming, which would let people buy only the channels they want and include special-interest packages for sports, news, hobbies and more.

Within five years, the cable industry's system of bundled channels, ever-rising prices and near-monopolistic control will fade into history, predicts Ford Cavallari, a media analyst at Adventis. Satellite TV operators, which have also come to depend on various versions of expanded basic, could also be affected. Together, the cable and satellite TV industries serve more than 100 million U.S. customers. All could face a new frontier of viewing options under an a la carte system.

Not everyone wants to change the system. Programmers that supply channels to cable companies are reluctant to do anything that might siphon off customers from the Big Bundle, industry slang for expanded basic.

A la carte gives consumers an escape hatch from expanded basic. That's why programmers don't like it. To protect themselves, they bar cable and satellite TV companies from selling their channels a la carte or in special-interest tiers.

Last fall [2005], he notes, Disney started offering commercial-free Internet downloads of *Lost, Desperate Housewives* and other ABC shows for $1.99 per episode. NBC (owned by General Electric) and CBS are doing the same with some of their shows, at 99 cents an episode.

These offerings, Cavallari says, are essentially a la carte content. As the market for on-demand TV catches fire, he predicts, "It will become harder for programmers to argue that you have to keep the (expanded-basic) business model propped up forever."

Charles Dolan, chairman of Cablevision, which owns cable networks and programming, is one of the few cable operators to openly favor an a la carte system. "Fundamentally, (a la carte) would be better for the consumer," Dolan says. "And if you do something that is better for the consumer, financially and economically it's going to be better for the industry."

Charlie Ergen, CEO of EchoStar, the USA's No. 2 satellite operator, is also a booster of a la carte. "We just think it's good business to give customers what they want," Ergen says. "And what they want is a la carte programming."

A recent USA TODAY/CNN/Gallup Poll of U.S. viewers supports that argument. Of those surveyed, 54% said they would prefer to buy channels individually; 43% said they'd rather pay a flat fee for a fixed number of channels. The results challenge what the U.S. cable industry has been saying for decades: that most customers in the USA don't want a la carte programming.

[Expanded basic is] also lucrative for cable companies. With expanded basic, companies don't have to worry about selling channels on their merits; they can just jam them into the bundle. In that one-size-fits-all system, programmers get paid even if no one tunes in.

"The main reason Disney and the others don't want to sell a la carte is because when you give customers the choice, they buy less channels," Ergen says. "Less channels mean you make less money."

Basic Cable Menu

☐ Discovery Channel
☑ MTV
☐ CNN
☑ Comedy Central
☐ VH1
☑ Bravo
☑ ESPN2

Source: Leslie Cauley, "How We Pay for Cable May Be about to Change," *USA TODAY,* March 2, 2006, p. 1A.

music channels uninterrupted by ads. Originally known as Digital Cable Radio in the 1980s, Music Choice was the first digital audio service. By 2006, Music Choice reached more than thirty-nine million households and offered more than fifty music channels, ranging from reggae to gospel. Such satellite-delivered channels are another example of media convergence; they link cable, sound recordings, and home stereo units for a monthly fee of about nine dollars, less than the price of a new CD.

For the home market, audio developments such as live-streaming Internet radio stations and downloadable digital music files, as well as satellite radio services like Sirius and XM, threatened premium cable music services. But digital cable and direct broadcast satellite television, with their large channel capacity, helped to reinvigorate cable music services, as they were frequently bundled with digital programming packages.

> **"** It is not conceivable to me that the revolution we're now going through—which is in my view even deeper, and faster, than the Industrial Revolution—is going to occur smoothly. It cannot. **"**
>
> —Alvin Toffler, futurist, 1993

Direct Broadcast Satellites: Cable without Wires

Because of its dependence on communication satellites, cable TV has always been on the cutting edge of technological developments. Now many of those advances are posing an economic threat to cable in the same ways that cable challenged traditional broadcasting in the 1970s. Of all the emerging technologies, including the Internet, direct broadcast satellites (DBS) present the biggest challenge to the existing cable and television industries.

The earliest earth-station antennas, or dishes—set up in the mid-1970s to receive cable programming—were large, measuring twenty to forty feet in diameter, and expensive (with FCC license fees adding to their high cost). From the beginning, however, engineers worked to reduce the size and cost of the receiving dishes in order to develop a consumer model. In regions and countries with rugged terrain, the installation of cable wiring was not always easy or possible.

To protect the fledgling cable business throughout the 1970s and 1980s, the FCC restricted the development of DBS companies, which get their programming from the same satellite channels (such as CNN, MTV, ESPN, and HBO) that supply the regular cable industry. In the United States, rural residents bypassed FCC restrictions by investing in seven- to ten-foot receiving dishes and downlinking, for free, the same channels that cable companies were supplying to wired communities. These home-satellite dishes, like early cable systems, appeared mostly in sprawling but sparsely populated areas that were too costly for cable companies to wire. Receiving dishes, visible from many interstate highways, began springing up on farms by the late 1970s. Initially, households could pick up channels once they had invested $2,000 to $3,000 in a large receiving dish. Not surprisingly, satellite programmers launched a flurry of legal challenges against farmers and small-town residents who were receiving their signals. Rural communities countered that they had the rights to the airspace above their own property; the satellite firms contended that their signals were being stolen. With the law being unclear, a number of cable channels began scrambling their signals. As a result, most satellite users had to buy or rent descramblers and subscribe to services, as cable customers did.

From home satellites, the DBS business developed. Signal scrambling spawned companies that provided both receiving dishes and satellite program services for a monthly fee. In 1978, Japanese companies, which had been experimenting with "wireless cable" alternatives for a number of years, launched the first DBS system in

Florida. With gradual improvements in satellite technology, the diameters of satellite receiving dishes decreased from more than twenty feet to three feet in a few years. By 1994, full-scale DBS service was available, and consumers could order satellite dishes the size of a large pizza.

Today, the two leading DBS companies—DirecTV and EchoStar (known as the DISH Network)—offer consumers most of the channels and tiers of service that cable companies carry, often at a slightly lower monthly cost (plus the initial investment of zero to three hundred dollars for purchasing and installing the small-dish antenna system). In addition, DBS systems carry between 350 and 500 basic, premium, and pay-per-view channels, which can be purchased by customers in various packages. Thus DBS presents far more options than what is available on most conventional cable systems, which are limited by channel capacity. Buoyed by high consumer interest and competing in large cities as well as rural areas, DBS firms are challenging the long-standing monopoly status of most cable systems, offering distinct advantages—and disadvantages—compared with cable.

On the upside, DBS's digital technology is superior to standard cable and broadcast signals, providing digital-quality pictures and CD-quality sound. Another big drawing card for DBS is the ability to offer sports packages that give subscribers nationwide access to all the games of professional sports leagues—including football, baseball, soccer, and men's and women's basketball—that aren't carried locally on broadcast networks or basic cable channels.

On the downside, along with the initial start-up cost for consumers, DBS systems don't have the same ability as cable to bundle high-speed Internet and telephone service with their video programming. Another disadvantage of DBS systems was remedied in 1999, when Congress passed legislation allowing DBS to carry local broadcast channels. Until that time, DBS did not pick up an area's local broadcast signals, which were not uplinked to satellites. This meant that most subscribers had to use a local cable company, an outside TV antenna, or rabbit-ear antennas on their TV set to get the local PBS, independent, and broadcast network programming. The gradual addition of local broadcast signals to DBS's offerings across the United States since then has been a great catalyst for new DBS subscribers. DirecTV, the top DBS company, holds about 55 percent of the DBS market, with more than fifteen million customers; EchoStar, at No. 2, has twelve million subscribers, about 45 percent of the market. DBS's threat to cable has increased in the past few years, particularly with its ability to offer local broadcast signals via satellite. DBS's share of the multichannel video market has grown from 13.8 percent in 2000 to about 30 percent in 2006. Yet cable is responding, using digital compression technology to build systems that carry up to five hundred channels, too. Cable's addition of VOD, interactive video, high-speed Internet connections, and telephone service is also an advantage over DBS. But even here, DBS is battling back with offers of satellite-based broadband Internet connections, with comparable connection speeds and pricing.

Ownership and Business Issues in Cable and DBS

Although there are about 7,900 cable systems in the United States, most of these systems are controlled by **multiple-system operators (MSOs)**, a shrinking number of large corporations that each own many cable systems. Consolidation has happened quickly. For example, by 1998, the Top 12 MSOs controlled the lines into 70 percent of all households wired for cable. By 2005, the Top 5 MSOs served almost 70 percent of all U.S. cable subscribers (see Figure 6.4). Once again, the economic trend points to an industry moving toward oligopoly, with a handful of megamedia firms controlling programming for future generations. Like the Internet, however, cable and DBS hold the promise of offering more specialized services through which the diverse needs of individuals and communities might be met.

The Major Cable and DBS Corporations

For much of the 1980s and 1990s, two large companies—TCI (Tele-Communications, Inc.) and Time Warner Cable—dominated the acquisition of smaller cable companies and the accumulation of cable subscribers. But, by the late 1990s, cable became a coveted investment, not so much for its ability to carry television programming but for its infrastructure of households connected with high-bandwidth wires.

With increasing competition and declining long-distance revenues, AT&T, the nation's leading long-distance phone company, developed a new business plan in the 1990s to buy its way into the lucrative emerging broadband cable and Internet business. In 1998, AT&T purchased TCI, the leading cable MSO at the time with 13.1 million households, and renamed the cable division AT&T Broadband & Internet Services (BIS). In 2000, AT&T struck again, acquiring MediaOne, the third-largest cable firm, and boosting its direct subscriber base to 16 million.[8]

Ultimately, AT&T's appetite for acquisitions gave it a bad case of debt, and its stock lost half of its value in 2000. In late 2000, AT&T made a surprise announcement to voluntarily break the company into four components—consumer long distance, business services, wireless, and broadband services. AT&T also spun off its cable programming subsidiary, Liberty Media. In late 2001, only three years after it ventured

Figure 6.4
Top 10 U.S. Cable and DBS Operators, 2006

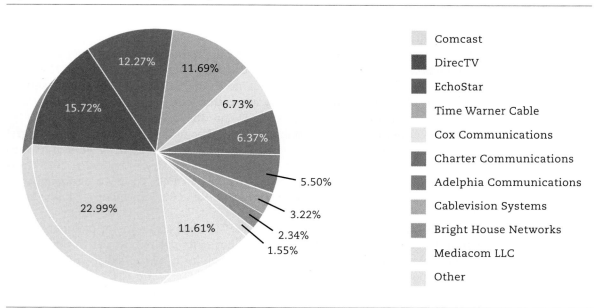

Comcast
DirecTV
EchoStar
Time Warner Cable
Cox Communications
Charter Communications
Adelphia Communications
Cablevision Systems
Bright House Networks
Mediacom LLC
Other

Source: Federal Communications Commission, *Twelfth Annual Report, Assessment of the Status of Competition in the Market for the Delivery of Video Programming,* March 3, 2006. Figures are a percentage of the total MVPD market of 94.23 million subscribers. The figure does not reflect the 2005 Comcast-Time Warner offer to purchase Adelphia.

A Democracy of Channels?

For a new basic cable programming service to have a chance of financial viability, it needs to reach at least 50 percent of the cable audience. But what companies have the opportunity to create a successful cable channel?

Description. Take note of the Top 20 cable networks, ranked by number of subscribers (see Figure 6.3 on page 210 and also the Web site for the National Cable & Telecommunications Association, http://www.ncta .com).

Analysis. Compare ownership among the top networks. There should be clear patterns. For example, Time Warner owns TBS, TNT, and CNN, among several other cable networks.

Interpretation. What do the patterns mean? As noted on page 000, cable television programming companies have leveraged retransmission consent regulations to get cable systems to adopt their new channel offerings. Thus, Disney owns not only ESPN but also highly rated ESPN2, ESPN News, and ESPN Classic. Other media corporations have been able to purchase larger shares of the cable audience. For ex-

ample, Viacom owns MTV Networks (which operates MTV, Nickelodeon/Nick at Nite, VH1, and other channels) and gained TNN and CMT through its acquisition of CBS.

Evaluation. Does the fact that a handful of large media corporations control many of cable's most popular networks reduce cable's promise of a multiplicity of networks representing a wide range of voices? Are networks such as CNBC and MSNBC just an extension of NBC? Or does ownership not matter; do all of the top cable networks serve as independent, unique voices? How is the quality of programming affected?

Engagement. Talk to your local cable operator(s) and find out when channel capacity will increase, or when there will be a review of the cable channel lineup. Find out what it takes to add a cable network to the system. Few people ever bother to write their cable operator requesting a network, so if there is a network that would bring a valuable perspective to the community, consider developing a petition or letter-writing campaign to persuasively argue for it.

into the cable and broadband industry, AT&T got out of the business by merging its cable division in a $72 billion deal with Comcast, then the third-largest MSO. The new Comcast Corporation instantly became the cable industry behemoth, serving more than 21 million households—twice as many as the next largest MSO. Comcast's properties also include interests in E! Entertainment and the Golf Channel.

Time Warner Cable, the second-largest MSO, is a division of the world's largest media company, Time Warner, a company that became even larger when it merged with America Online (the nation's largest Internet service provider) in 2000. Time Warner Cable had 1.9 million subscribers in 1982. In 1995, Time Warner bought Cablevision Industries—the eighth-largest MSO. By 2006, Time Warner had almost 11 million cable subscribers.

Beyond its cable-subscriber base, Time Warner is also a major provider of programming services. In 1995, Time Warner buoyed its position as the world's largest media corporation by offering $6.5 billion to acquire Turner Broadcasting, which included superstation WTBS, CNN, Headline News, TNT, and CNN Radio. Although some FCC staffers raised concerns about sanctioning the extended economic power of Time Warner, the commission formally approved the deal in the fall of 1996. Time Warner—with its magazine, movie, publishing, television, and music divisions—

also produces content for its cable services. In addition to acquiring Turner and co-owning the CW television network, Time Warner is the parent company of Cinemax and HBO, and it holds interests in Court TV.

In the 2000s, the two rival DBS companies DirecTV and EchoStar vaulted onto the list of major players in the industry-defined multichannel video programming distributor (MVPD) market. DirecTV was established in 1977 and its DBS system debuted in 1994. The News Corporation, owner of several media properties including the Fox television network and Twentieth Century Fox movie studios, acquired DirecTV in 2003. Independently owned EchoStar Communications Corporation was founded in 1980 as a distributor of big-dish television systems, but it later refocused on the emerging DBS market and launched its DISH Network service in 1995. Each of the two DBS companies operates between eight and ten satellites to deliver its service to customers in the continental United States.

A number of cable critics worry that the trend toward fewer owners will limit the number of viewpoints, options, and innovations available on cable. (See "Media Literacy and the Critical Process: A Democracy of Channels?" on opposite page.) The response from the cable industry is that given the tremendous capital investment it takes to run cable, DBS, and other media enterprises, media conglomerates are necessary to buy up struggling companies and keep them afloat. This argument suggests that

Figure 6.5
Media Ownership: Principal U.S. Operations for Viacom, Inc.

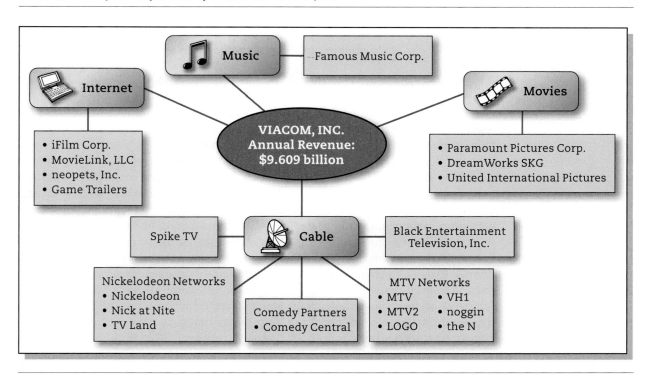

After spinning off its broadcasting holdings (including CBS Television, CBS Radio, The CW network, Showtime, and Simon & Schuster publishers) into a separate CBS Corporation, Viacom emerged in 2006 a smaller but still enormous media corporation. Viacom's current holdings include Paramount Studios, MTV Networks, and BET Networks. Recent acquisitions include DreamWorks Studios, YouTube rivals atomfilms.com and ifilm.com, and the Neopets.com virtual pet Web site. Although Viacom and CBS split, Sumner Redstone is still the chairman and majority shareholder of both corporations. What advantages could there be to splitting off the broadcast portion of Viacom's holdings?

● The message televised on Time Warner Cable on May 2, 2000, the day after Disney-owned ABC pulled its programming off the cable network because of a contract dispute.

without today's MSOs, many smaller cable ventures in programming would not be possible.

Concerns have surfaced, though, that cable and telephone services will merge into giant communications overlords, fixing prices without the benefit of competition. These concerns raise an important question: In an economic climate in which fewer owners control the circulation of communication, what happens to new ideas or controversial views that may not always be profitable to circulate? Will crushing debt and declining stocks be enough to check these companies?

There is already evidence that large MSOs can wield their monopoly power unfairly. In May 2000, a business dispute between Disney and Time Warner erupted into a public spectacle as Time Warner dropped the ABC television network from 3.4 million of its cable customers in New York, Houston, Raleigh, and elsewhere for more than thirty hours. The conflict was over the renewal of the retransmission consent agreement for ABC on many Time Warner cable systems. Disney proposed that Time Warner expand carriage of existing channels and introduce its new SoapNet and Toon Disney channels, among other things, in return for allowing Time Warner to carry ABC on its cable systems. Talks broke down, Time Warner refused to grant Disney a contract extension, and Time Warner customers in affected areas saw only blue screens with messages such as: "Disney has taken ABC away from you." A similar dispute occurred in 2004, as EchoStar and Viacom deadlocked in rate negotiations for putting CBS and Viacom's cable channels on EchoStar's DISH Network. Nine million DISH customers lost CBS, MTV, Nickelodeon, and other Viacom networks for thirty-six hours before an agreement was reached. (See Figure 6.5 on page 225.) In 2006, EchoStar's dispute with Lifetime Entertainment over carriage fees resulted in the removal of the Lifetime and Lifetime movie channels from the DISH Network. After protests by women's groups in several cities, the two parties reached an agreement, restoring the two channels after a month's absence.

The Business of Cable

In 1970, there were about 2,500 small cable systems operating in the United States; by 2006, about 7,900 systems were running. In 1976, there were two basic satellite-delivered services, two premium services, and no such thing as pay-per-view. Thirty years later, more than 530 channels were competing for channel space. Since 1980, basic cable rates have grown from about $7 per month to more than $41. Monthly prices for premium services, however, have essentially remained the same—less than $9 a month per channel in 1980, and only a dollar or two more today. By 2006, total revenues from cable subscriptions and advertising exceeded $94 billion a year.

The cable industry employed about 23,000 people in 1978 and more than 137,000 by 2006. The cable workforce serves the production, distribution, and exhibition sectors of the industry. The production end includes the hundreds of providers who either make original programs or purchase older TV programming for national and global distribution. At the local level, production also includes staffers, volunteers, and student interns who create programming on access channels. The distribution sector includes the delivery systems and PPV services that transmit programming via satellite, then via coaxial or fiber-optic cable. The exhibition branch of the industry encompasses thousands of local cable systems, which require programming, sales, technical, and administrative divisions to operate.

Alternative Voices

After suffering through years of rising rates and limited expansion of service, some of the smallest cities in America have decided to challenge the private monopolies of cable giants by building competing, publicly owned cable systems. So far, the municipally owned cable systems number only in the hundreds and can be found in places like Glasgow, Kentucky; Kutztown, Pennsylvania; Cedar Falls, Iowa; and Provo, Utah. In most cases, they're operated by the community-owned, nonprofit electric utilities. There are more than two thousand such municipal utilities across the United States, serving about 14 percent of Americans and creating the potential for more municipal utilities to expand into communications services. As nonprofit entities, the municipal operations are less expensive for cable subscribers, too.

Cities with public cable systems argue that with no competition, the private cable corporations have been slow to replace older coaxial cables with high-speed fiber-optic networks. Moreover, the lower population densities of small towns and rural areas mean that these towns are often the last places to get innovative cable services. The first town to take on an existing private cable provider was Glasgow, Kentucky, which built its own municipal cable system in 1989. The town of fourteen thousand now has seven thousand municipal cable customers. William J. Ray, the town's Electric Plant Board superintendent and the visionary behind the municipal communications service, argues that this is not a new idea:

> Cities have long been turning a limited number of formerly private businesses into public-works projects. This happens only when the people making up a local government believe that the service has become so essential to the citizens that it is better if it is operated by the government. In colonial America, it was all about drinking water. . . . In the twentieth century, the issue was electric power and natural gas service. Now, we are facing the same transformation in broadband networks.[9]

For the customer, competition in the local cable market is beneficial. For example, in 1994 in Cedar Falls, Iowa, voters approved the creation of a new municipal broadband fiber-optic cable network, capable of carrying cable and Internet service. With the new challenges of competition, commercial provider TCI then decided to upgrade its own cable system in the city. The benefits of competition in Cedar Falls angered the nearby residents of Waterloo, Iowa, who were served only by TCI. In Waterloo, TCI offered only thirty-six channels for the same monthly fee that brought seventy-six channels to TCI customers in Cedar Falls. Only by threatening to build their own municipal cable system did Waterloo city officials get TCI to rebuild the Waterloo cable system and add more channels.

More than a quarter of the country's two thousand municipal utilities offer broadband, including cable, high-speed Internet, and telephone services. How will commercial cable operators fend off this unprecedented competition? William Ray of Glasgow, Kentucky, has the answer: "If cable operators are afraid of cities competing with them, there is a defense that is impregnable—they can charge reasonable rates, offer consummate customer service, improve their product, and conduct their business as if they were a guest that owes their existence to the benevolence of the city that has invited them in."[10]

★ Cable, DBS, and Implications for Democracy

When cable emerged to challenge traditional broadcasting in the 1970s, expectations were high, not unlike today's expectations for the Internet. When cable communication mushroomed in the 1980s, network supremacy over television ended. Offering more than new competition, cable's increased channel capacity provided the promise of access. With more channels, it was believed that access on cable would create vibrant debates, allowing ordinary citizens a voice via television. Access channels have, in fact, provided some opportunities for citizens to participate in democracy and even create their own programs. But by the late 1990s, major cities like Kansas City decided that public-access channels need not even be a requirement for cable franchises. For the most part, cable and DBS have come to follow the one-way broadcast model: Their operators choose the programming from a few service providers, with little input from citizens and consumers.

Most cable channels have become heavily dependent on recycling old television shows and movies to fill up their program schedules. In some ways, this has been beneficial. Cable, particularly through programming like Nickelodeon's Nick at Nite and TV Land, has become a repository for TV shows that are passed along from generation to generation. Ultimately, however, except for C-Span, local access channels, and some interactive services, cable still has not developed its potential to become a clear alternative to traditional broadcasting services. In fact, given that the television networks and many leading cable channels are owned by the same media conglomerates, cable has evolved into something of an ancillary service to the networks.

In the broadest sense, the development of cable has always posed a contradiction. On the one hand, cable has dramatically increased the number of channels and offered previously unserved groups the opportunity to address their particular issues on television. On the other hand, cable has undermined the network era during which television worked as a kind of social adhesive, giving most of the population a common bond, a set of shared programs.

In discussions about video programming technologies and policies, it's important to remember that not everyone has access to cable or satellite television. By 2006, 14 percent of U.S. households still relied on over-the-air broadcasts for their television programming. Although some people choose to limit their television options, others simply cannot afford the cost. So, as we ask ourselves how we can employ cable, DBS, and related technologies to serve social agendas while continuing to meet business and consumer needs, we need to remember to include in the discussion those who are disconnected from these communication systems.

www.

For review questions and activities for Chapter 6, go to the interactive *Media and Culture* Online Study Guide at *bedfordstmartins.com/ mediaculture*

REVIEW QUESTIONS

Technology and the Development of Cable

1. What is CATV, and what were its advantages over broadcast television?

2. How did satellite distribution change the cable industry?

Cable Threatens Broadcasting

3. How did cable pose a challenge to broadcasting, and how did the FCC respond to cable's early development?

4. What is the cable franchising process, and how did it work in the 1980s?

5. Why aren't cable companies treated more like a utility company and a common carrier?

6. How did the Telecommunications Act of 1996 change the economic shape and future of the cable industry?

Cable Comes of Age

7. What are the differences between basic cable service and premium services?

8. How have CNN and MTV influenced culture worldwide?

9. How and why did HBO develop? How has HBO threatened the film industry?

10. What is video-on-demand, and how does it differ from pay-per-view services?

Direct Broadcast Satellites: Cable without Wires

11. What is DBS? How well does it compete with the cable industry?

Ownership and Business Issues in Cable and DBS

12. Who are the biggest players in the cable and DBS business, and what has driven their recently acquired cable empires?

13. What are the three basic divisions in the organization of the cable business?

14. What are the main reasons some municipalities are building their own cable systems?

Cable, DBS, and Implications for Democracy

15. In terms of fostering democracy, what are the main advantages of cable and DBS over traditional broadcasting?

QUESTIONING THE MEDIA

1. How many cable channels do you watch regularly? What programs do you watch? What attracts you to a certain channel?

2. If you controlled a cable public-access channel in your community, what would be your channel's goal? What could we do to make public-, government-, or educational-access programming more appealing? Should we?

3. Do you think the must-carry rules violate a cable company's First Amendment rights? Why or why not?

4. CNN and MTV have changed our society as well as the global culture. Have these changes been positive or negative? Explain.

5. Do you think DBS is an equal competitor to cable? Why or why not?

6. Some critics argue that citizens no longer participate in traditional neighborhoods and that cable has played a role in fragmenting society, keeping us in our homes. Do you agree or disagree? What has cable done well, and in what ways has it adversely affected society?

SEARCHING THE INTERNET

http://www.ncta.com

The site for the cable industry's major trade association, the National Cable & Telecommunications Association, details cable history, the latest developments in cable technology, and industry news.

http://www.cablecenter.org

A site funded by the cable industry, offering an excellent history of cable's development in the United States.

http://www.broadcastingcable.com

The online version of *Broadcasting & Cable,* a weekly magazine geared toward executives and managers of the television, radio, and cable industries.

http://www.mtv.com

MTV Online offers a comprehensive database of music videos, show information, music news, tips on where to find local bands, music reviews, and chat rooms.

http://www.cnn.com

One of the most sophisticated sites on the Web, CNN.com offers constantly updated news stories as well as news archives, free video, on-air transcripts, and other services.

http://www.sbca.com

The Satellite Broadcasting and Communication Association of America site, representing DBS and other segments of the satellite industry.

Media Literacy
and the Critical Process

In Brief

Working alone or in a group, propose a new cable channel that will do two things: (1) find a unique market niche, and (2) be successful, meaning it should satisfy the demands of the television industry by drawing an audience that appeals to advertisers. Keep in mind that only 10 to 15 percent of new cable channels succeed. Lists of existing and planned cable channels are available online at the National Cable & Telecommunications Association's Web site at www.ncta.com.

Consider the following while creating your proposal: What kinds of programs would run each day? What audience would the channel try to reach? Why would this market be attractive to advertisers?

In Depth

Divide the class into groups of four to six. Each group should prepare an editorial for presentation on public-access cable. The editorial should be roughly four to five minutes in length (750–1,000 words) and should address a controversial or important public issue, such as equal access to the information highway, the state of media education, the impact of talk radio and television talk shows, or the advantages of wealth in the legal process.

Description. As a group, draft the editorial. Describe the issue in a compelling manner. Consult with your instructor for topic ideas and writing strategies. Rewrite the final copy of the editorial.

Analysis. Next, divide each group into two subgroups. One subgroup should approach (by phone, mail, e-mail, or face-to-face meeting) a local cable-access channel and request time to read the editorial. The other subgroup should approach a local commercial television station with the same editorial. Tell the

station manager or news director that you would like to get your idea onto the public airwaves. Note the patterns in how your proposal is received by each medium, particularly in terms of how seriously they took your request, their timeliness in response, and the conditions they required to air your editorial.

Interpretation. Designate a time for your entire group to meet and write a report about how your editorial was treated by the media you approached. Address the following questions in your report:

- How easy or difficult was it to get access to traditional broadcasting as opposed to cable? How was your group treated?
- Based on your experience, do broadcast airwaves and cable services "belong" to the public? How democratic is the process of gaining cable access?

Evaluation. During class, the various groups should share and compare reports and experiences. If you were permitted to cablecast or broadcast your editorial, share it with the class. Given this experience, do cable-access channels offer reasonable access to the public? Are there certain topics that shouldn't be given such editorial airtime on broadcast or cable television? If so, why?

Engagement. The groups should carefully document their activities. If you are not satisfied with the response of the cable-access channel operators and/or the television broadcasters, write a letter (individually or as a group) to the editor of a local newspaper that critically comments on the accessibility of the local cable and television media to citizens who wish to address public issues. If the cable and broadcast television outlets are amenable to carrying your editorial, then you may wish to use the letter to publicly recognize their open access as a forum for citizens.

KEY TERMS

direct broadcast satellites (DBS), 201
CATV, 202
geosynchronous orbit, 203
transponders, 203
must-carry rules, 205
access channels, 206
leased channels, 206

electronic publishers, 206
common carriers, 206
retransmission consent, 208
Telecommunications Act of 1996, 208
narrowcasting, 211
basic cable, 211
superstations, 211

premium channels, 216
pay-per-view (PPV), 219
video-on-demand (VOD), 219
interactive cable television, 219
cable music, 219
multiple-system operators
   (MSOs), 222

movies

and the impact of images

In a pivotal scene in *Star Wars: Episode III — Revenge of the Sith* (2005), Senator Padmé Amidala (Natalie Portman) witnesses the power-hungry Supreme Chancellor's decree of the first Galactic Empire, to the cheers of the Senate. She responds, "This is how liberty dies. With thunderous applause." This is how *Star Wars* ends as well, to the thunderous applause of millions of fans. Or, rather, how *Star Wars* begins, since episode 3 sets up the story line of the original *Star Wars* from 1977 (the original three films were actually episodes 4, 5, and 6).

The enormous success of the 1977 *Star Wars,* produced, written, and directed by George Lucas, changed the culture of the movie industry. As film critic Roger Ebert explained: "*Star Wars* effectively brought to an end the golden era of early-1970s personal filmmaking and focused the industry on big-budget special-effects blockbusters, blasting off a trend we are still living through. . . . In one way or another all the big studios have been trying to make another *Star Wars* ever since."

A *Star Wars* fan dressed as a Storm Trooper shops for *Star Wars: Revenge of the Sith* merchandise at a Toys "R" Us in New York City.

The release of *Revenge of the Sith* had all of the now-typical blockbuster characteristics of a summer or winter holiday release date: a targeted youth audience, massive promotion, and lucrative merchandising tie-ins.

The blockbuster mentality spawned by *Star Wars* formed a new primary audience for Hollywood—teenagers. Repeat attendance and positive buzz among young people made the first *Star Wars* the most successful movie of its generation, and started the initial trilogy that included *The Empire Strikes Back* (1980) and *Return of the Jedi* (1983). The youth-oriented focus begun by *Star Wars* is still evident in Hollywood today, with the largest segment of the U.S. movie audience—the twelve- to twenty-four-year-old age group—accounting for 38 percent of theater attendance.

Another part of the blockbuster mentality created by *Star Wars* and mimicked by other films is the way in which movies are made into big-budget summer releases with merchandising tie-ins

and high potential for international distribution. Lucas, who also created the popular *Indiana Jones* film series, argues that selling licensing rights is one of the ways he supports his independent filmmaking. Prior to the release of *Sith,* the first five *Star Wars* films had generated an unprecedented $9 billion in merchandising—far more than the record-breaking $3.4 billion worldwide box-office revenues— as *Star Wars* images appeared on an astonishing array of products, from Lego's X-Wing fighter kits to Darth Vader toothbrushes.

Star Wars has impacted not only the cultural side of moviemaking but also the technical form. In the first *Star Wars* trilogy produced in the 1970s and 1980s, Lucas developed technologies now commonplace in moviemaking— digital animation, special effects, and computer-based film editing. With the second trilogy, beginning with *Star Wars: Episode I— The Phantom Menace* (1999), Lucas again broke new ground in the film industry—this time becoming a force in the emerging era of digital filmmaking. Several

scenes of the movie were not shot on film but on digital video, easing integration with digital special effects. The two subsequent movies, *Star Wars: Episode II—Attack of the Clones* (2002) and *Revenge of the Sith* were shot entirely in the digital format.

The Phantom Menace also used digital exhibition—becoming the first full-length motion picture from a major studio to use digital projectors, replacing standard film projectors. Changing exhibition technology will eventually move motion pictures away from bulky and expensive film reels toward a digital distribution system via satellite or optical disks. Digital film distribution also threatens to bypass theaters, as films are delivered directly to a viewer's computer or digital television set-top box.

dating back to the late 1800s, American films have had a substantial social and cultural impact on society. Blockbuster movies such as *Star Wars, E.T., Jurassic Park, Titanic, Lord of the Rings,* and *Spider-Man* represent what Hollywood has become—America's storyteller. Telling cinematic tales that in 1909 drew us to a nickelodeon theater and last weekend to our local video store, Hollywood movies have long acted as contemporary mythmakers. At their best, they tell communal stories that evoke and symbolize our most enduring values and our secret desires. The most popular films often make the world seem clearer, more manageable, and more understandable.

Throughout the twentieth century, films helped moviegoers sort through experiences that either affirmed or deviated from their own values. Some movies allowed audiences to survey "the boundary between the permitted and the forbidden" and to experience, in a controlled way, "the possibility of stepping across this boundary."[1] Popular movies today such as *Silence of the Lambs, Kill Bill* (vols. 1 and 2), and *Sin City* examined the distinctions between the normal and the abnormal—a moral border repeatedly fought over by religious leaders, politicians, and entrepreneurs as well as by teachers, parents, and the mass media.

Although the development and production time for films can often be two or more years, the movie industry as a whole must often react quickly to social events and cultural shifts. This was never more apparent than after the terrorist attacks of September 11, 2001. Hollywood studios suspended production or delayed the release of several movies with terrorism themes. Marketing campaigns were changed, and scenes with images of the World Trade Center towers were altered. By 2006, Holly-

> **"** The movie is not only a supreme expression of mechanism, but paradoxically it offers as product the most magical of consumer commodities, namely dreams. **"**
>
> –Marshall McLuhan, *Understanding Media,* 1964

● **Table 7.1 The Top 10 Box-Office Champions, 2006***

Rank	Title/Date	Domestic Gross** (millions)
1	*Titanic* (1997)	$601
2	*Star Wars* (1977)	461
3	*Shrek 2* (2004)	437
4	*E.T.: The Extra-Terrestrial* (1982)	435
5	*Star Wars: Episode I: The Phantom Menace* (1999)	431
6	*Pirates of the Caribbean: Dead Man's Chest* (2006)	421
7	*Spider-Man* (2002)	408
8	*Star Wars: Episode III—Revenge of the Sith* (2005)	380
9	*The Lord of the Rings: The Return of the King* (2003)	377
10	*Spider-Man 2* (2004)	373

Source: "All Time Top 100 Grossing Films," October 4, 2006, http://www.movieweb.com/movies/box_office/alltime.php. © 2006 MovieWeb. All Rights Reserved.

*Most rankings of the Top 10 most popular films are based on American box-office receipts. If these were adjusted for inflation, *Gone with the Wind* (1939) would become No. 1 in U.S. theater revenue.

**Gross is shown in absolute dollars based on box-office sales in the United States and Canada.

● Breaking multiple box office records its opening weekend, *Pirates of the Caribbean: Dead Man's Chest* quickly made it onto the list of Top Ten Box Office champions. The movie is the second installment of the trilogy starring Johnny Depp, Orlando Bloom, and Kiera Knightley.

wood finally felt comfortable enough to tackle 9/11 visually, with *United 93* (about the hijacked plane that crashed in Pennsylvania) and Oliver Stone's *World Trade Center* (which centered on the heroic efforts of two police officers).

Over and above their immense economic impact (see Table 7.1 on page 235), movies have always worked on several social and cultural levels. While they distract us from our daily struggles, at the same time they encourage us to take part in rethinking contemporary ideas. We continue to be attracted to the stories that movies tell.

In this chapter, we will examine the rich legacy and current standing of Hollywood as a national and international mythmaker. We will begin by considering film's early technology and the evolution of film as a mass medium. We will look at the arrival of silent feature films, the emergence of Hollywood, and the development of the studio system with regard to production, distribution, and exhibition. We will then explore the coming of sound and the power of movie storytelling. In the context of

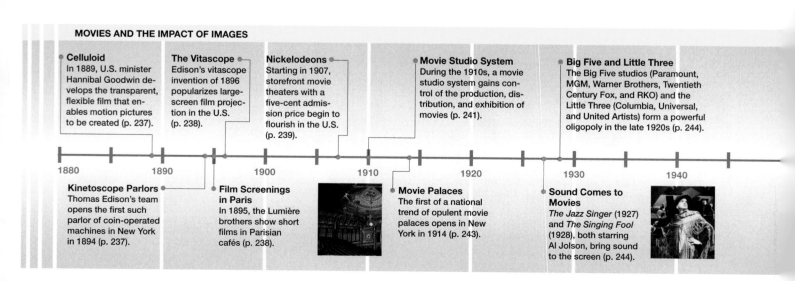

MOVIES AND THE IMPACT OF IMAGES

Celluloid
In 1889, U.S. minister Hannibal Goodwin develops the transparent, flexible film that enables motion pictures to be created (p. 237).

The Vitascope
Edison's vitascope invention of 1896 popularizes large-screen film projection in the U.S. (p. 238).

Nickelodeons
Starting in 1907, storefront movie theaters with a five-cent admission price begin to flourish in the U.S. (p. 239).

Movie Studio System
During the 1910s, a movie studio system gains control of the production, distribution, and exhibition of movies (p. 241).

Big Five and Little Three
The Big Five studios (Paramount, MGM, Warner Brothers, Twentieth Century Fox, and RKO) and the Little Three (Columbia, Universal, and United Artists) form a powerful oligopoly in the late 1920s (p. 244).

1880   1890   1900   1910   1920   1930   1940

Kinetoscope Parlors
Thomas Edison's team opens the first such parlor of coin-operated machines in New York in 1894 (p. 237).

Film Screenings in Paris
In 1895, the Lumière brothers show short films in Parisian cafés (p. 238).

Movie Palaces
The first of a national trend of opulent movie palaces opens in New York in 1914 (p. 243).

Sound Comes to Movies
The Jazz Singer (1927) and *The Singing Fool* (1928), both starring Al Jolson, bring sound to the screen (p. 244).

Hollywood moviemaking, we will consider major film genres, directors, and alternatives to Hollywood's style, including foreign films and documentaries. Finally, we will look at the movie business today—its major players, economic clout, technological advances, and implications for democracy.

Early Technology and the Evolution of Movies

History often credits a handful of enterprising individuals with developing new technologies and new categories of mass media. Such innovations, however, are usually the result of extended and simultaneous investigations by a wide variety of people. In addition, the media innovations of both known and unknown inventors are propelled by economic and social forces as well as by individual abilities.[2]

The Development of Film

Solving the puzzle of making a picture move depended both on advances in photography and on the development of a flexible film stock to replace the heavy metal-and-glass plates used to make individual pictures in the 1800s. In 1889, an American minister, Hannibal Goodwin, developed a transparent and pliable film—called **celluloid**—that could hold a coating, or film, of chemicals sensitive to light. This breakthrough solved a major problem: It enabled a strip of film to move through a camera and be photographed in rapid succession, producing a series of pictures. In the 1890s, George Eastman (later of Eastman Kodak) bought Goodwin's patents, improved the ideas, and manufactured the first film used for motion pictures.

As with the development of sound recording, Thomas Edison takes center stage in most accounts of the invention of motion pictures. In the late 1800s, Edison initially planned to merge phonograph technology and moving images to create talking pictures (which would not happen in feature films until 1927). Because there was no breakthrough, however, Edison lost interest. But he directed an assistant, William Kennedy Dickson, to combine advances in Europe with the new celluloid to create an early movie camera, called the **kinetograph**, and a viewing system, called the **kinetoscope**. This small projection system housed fifty feet of film that revolved on spools (similar to a library microfilm reader). It was a kind of peep show in which

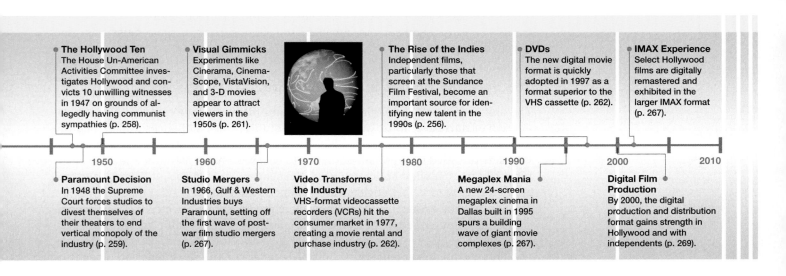

The Hollywood Ten
The House Un-American Activities Committee investigates Hollywood and convicts 10 unwilling witnesses in 1947 on grounds of allegedly having communist sympathies (p. 258).

Visual Gimmicks
Experiments like Cinerama, Cinema-Scope, VistaVision, and 3-D movies appear to attract viewers in the 1950s (p. 261).

The Rise of the Indies
Independent films, particularly those that screen at the Sundance Film Festival, become an important source for identifying new talent in the 1990s (p. 256).

DVDs
The new digital movie format is quickly adopted in 1997 as a format superior to the VHS cassette (p. 262).

IMAX Experience
Select Hollywood films are digitally remastered and exhibited in the larger IMAX format (p. 267).

1950   1960   1970   1980   1990   2000   2010

Paramount Decision
In 1948 the Supreme Court forces studios to divest themselves of their theaters to end vertical monopoly of the industry (p. 259).

Studio Mergers
In 1966, Gulf & Western Industries buys Paramount, setting off the first wave of postwar film studio mergers (p. 267).

Video Transforms the Industry
VHS-format videocassette recorders (VCRs) hit the consumer market in 1977, creating a movie rental and purchase industry (p. 262).

Megaplex Mania
A new 24-screen megaplex cinema in Dallas built in 1995 spurs a building wave of giant movie complexes (p. 267).

Digital Film Production
By 2000, the digital production and distribution format gains strength in Hollywood and with independents (p. 269).

● Before the arrival of feature-length movies, audiences in the late 1890s were fascinated by the novelty of any moving image. This Edison kinetoscope reel from 1894 featured one of the first close-up shots ever recorded on film—a man sneezing.

viewers looked through a hole and saw images moving on a tiny plate. In 1894, a kinetoscope parlor, featuring two rows of coin-operated machines, opened in New York.

From the start, Edison envisioned movies only as a passing fad or an arcade novelty. Meanwhile, in France, Louis and Auguste Lumière, who ran a photographic equipment factory, were hard at work. The brothers developed a projection system so that more than one person at a time could see the moving images on a 9- by 6-foot projection screen. In a Paris café on December 28, 1895, they projected ten short movies, for viewers who paid one franc each, on such subjects as a man falling off a horse and a child trying to grab a fish from a bowl. Within three weeks, twenty-five hundred people were coming each night to see how, according to one Paris paper, film "perpetuates the image of movement."

With innovators around the world dabbling in moving pictures, Edison's lab and kinetoscope company renewed its interest. Edison patented several inventions and manufactured a new large-screen system called the **vitascope**, which enabled filmstrips of longer lengths to be projected without interruption. Unlike the kinetoscope, vitascope projection improved viewing for large audiences, hinting at the potential of movies as a future mass medium.

Staged at a music hall in New York in April 1896, Edison's first public showing of the vitascope featured shots from a boxing match and waves rolling onto a beach. The *New York Times* described the exhibition as "wonderfully real and singularly exhilarating." Some members of the audience were so taken with the realism of the film images that they stepped back from the screen's crashing waves to avoid getting their feet wet.

Early movie demonstrations such as these marked the beginning of the film industry. At this point, movies consisted of movement recorded by a single continuous camera shot. Early filmmakers had not yet figured out how to move the camera around or how to edit film shots together. Nonetheless, various innovators were beginning to see the commercial possibilities of film. By 1900, short movies had become a part of amusement arcades, traveling carnivals, wax museums, and vaudeville theater.

The Power of Stories in the Silent Era

The shift from early development to the mass medium stage came with the introduction of **narrative films**: movies that tell stories. Once audiences understood the illusion of moving images, they quickly tired of waves breaking on beaches or vaudeville acts recorded by immobile cameras. To become a mass medium, the early silent films had to offer what books achieved: the suspension of disbelief. They had to create narrative worlds that engaged an audience's imagination.

Some of the earliest narrative films were produced and directed by French magician and inventor Georges Méliès, who opened the first public movie theater in France in 1896. Méliès may have been the first director to realize that a movie was not simply a means of recording reality. He understood that a movie could be artificially planned and controlled like a staged play. By the late 1800s, Méliès was producing fairy tales and science-fiction stories—including *Joan of Arc, Red Riding Hood, Cinderella,* and *A Trip to the Moon.* These film shorts lasted less than ten minutes each. By the early 1900s, he had discovered camera tricks and techniques, such as slow motion and cartoon animation, that became key ingredients in future narrative film-making.

The first American filmmaker to adapt Méliès's innovations to narrative film was Edwin S. Porter. A cameraman who had studied Méliès's work in an Edison lab, Porter mastered the technique of editing diverse shots together to tell a coherent story. Early filmmakers plotted and recorded action in a long, continuous filmed sequence. But Porter shot narrative scenes out of order (for instance, some in a studio and some outdoors) and reassembled them in the editing process to make a story. In 1902, he made what is regarded as America's first narrative film, *The Life of an American Fireman.*

● Italian-born Rudolph Valentino came to the United States in 1913, when he was eighteen. After finding his way to California, he quickly emerged as a star in the 1920s, appearing in fourteen major films in only seven years. His sexy and passionate portrayal of Sheik Ahmed (opposite Agnes Ayres in *The Sheik,* 1921) earned him the nickname "Great Lover." Famous for his good looks and comic timing in silent films, he was also partially responsible for the popularity of the tango in the 1920s. Valentino died in 1926 at the age of 31.

Porter also pioneered other innovations in filmmaking. First, he moved the camera and varied its distance from subjects and objects. *American Fireman,* for example, contained the first close-up shot in U.S. narrative film history—a ringing fire alarm. Until then, early moviemakers thought that close-ups cheated the audience of the opportunity to see an entire scene. Second, Porter's most important film, *The Great Train Robbery,* introduced the western as well as chase scenes. In this eleven-minute movie, Porter demonstrated the art of film suspense by alternating shots of the robbers with those of a posse in hot pursuit.

The Arrival of Nickelodeons

Another major development in the evolution of film as a mass medium was the arrival of movie theaters. They were called **nickelodeons**, a term that combines the admission price with the Greek word for "theater." According to media historian Douglas Gomery, these small and uncomfortable makeshift theaters were often converted cigar stores, pawnshops, or restaurants redecorated to mimic vaudeville theaters: "In front, large, hand-painted posters announced the movies for the day. Inside, the screening of news, documentary, comedy, fantasy, and dramatic shorts lasted about one hour."[3] Because they showed silent narrative film shorts that usually transcended language barriers, nickelodeons flourished during the great European immigration at the turn of the twentieth century. These theaters filled a need for many newly arrived people struggling to learn English and seeking an inexpensive escape from the hard life of the city. Often managed by immigrants, nickelodeons required a minimal investment: just a secondhand projector and a large white sheet. Usually a piano player added live music, and sometimes theater operators used sound effects to simulate gunshots or loud crashes.

Although vaudeville theaters continued to feature movies, by 1908 nickelodeons had displaced the vaudeville circuit as the main showplace for films. Because they were less expensive than vaudeville shows and drew fewer well-to-do audiences, nickelodeons were labeled "democracy's theater." Between 1907 and 1909, the number of nickelodeons grew from five thousand to ten thousand. The craze had peaked by 1910, when entrepreneurs began to seek more affluent spectators, attracting them with larger and more lavish movie theaters.

The Power of the Studio System

By the late 1910s, the movie industry had three basic economic divisions—production, distribution, and exhibition. In its early phase, control of *production* meant control over camera and projector technology. But as narrative films became central to attracting consumers, production came to mean controlling the making of movies, from writing a script and hiring actors to raising money and filming the story. This is still the case today. *Distribution* constitutes the individuals or companies that deliver films into theaters in various regional, national, and international markets. Finally, *exhibition* refers to the places where films are displayed—the theaters themselves and the people and companies that own them. Much of film history, as well as the current state of moviemaking, has been significantly affected by the power struggles of film studios vying to dominate one or all of these industry divisions.

Among the first to try his hand at dominating the movie business, Thomas Edison had been observing the growing popularity of film. In 1908 he formed the Motion Picture Patents Company, a cartel of major U.S. and French film producers. Known as the *Trust*, Edison's company pooled patents in an effort to control film's major technology and, by default, the production of most movies. In addition, the Trust acquired most major film distributorships and signed an exclusive deal with George Eastman, who agreed to supply movie film only to Trust-approved companies.

However, some independent producers refused to bow to the Trust's terms. There was too much demand for films, too much money to be made, and too many ways to avoid the Trust's scrutiny. Some producers began to relocate from the early centers of film production in New York and New Jersey to Cuba and Florida. Ultimately, though, Hollywood became a movie magnet and the film capital of the world. Southern California offered cheap labor, diverse scenery for outdoor shooting, barns that could be converted into studios, and a mild climate suitable for year-round production. Geographically far from the Trust, independent companies could also easily slip over the border into Mexico to escape legal prosecution for patent violations.

Two Hungarian immigrants, Adolph Zukor, who would eventually run Paramount Pictures, and William Fox, who would found the Fox Film Corporation (which later became Twentieth Century Fox), played a role in the collapse of Edison's Trust. Zukor's early companies figured out ways to bypass the Trust, and a suit by Fox, a nickelodeon operator turned film distributor, resulted in the Trust's breakup for restraint of trade violations in 1917.

Ironically, although the Trust's monopoly efforts failed, entrepreneurs like Zukor developed other tactics for controlling the industry. The new strategies, many of which are still used today, were more ambitious than just monopolizing patents and technology. They aimed at dominating the movie business at all three essential levels—production, distribution, and exhibition—in a **vertical integration** of power and control. The new tactics ultimately spawned a system that turned the film industry into an **oligopoly**, in which a few firms controlled the bulk of the business.

> **"** The American cinema is a classical art, but why not then admire in it what is most admirable, i.e., not only the talent of this or that filmmaker, but the genius of the system. **"**
>
> –André Bazin, film theorist, 1957

● With legions of fans, Mary Pickford became the first woman ever to make a salary of $1 million in a year and gained freedom to take artistic risks with her roles. She launched United Artists, a film distributing company, with Douglas Fairbanks and Charlie Chaplin. No woman since has been as powerful a player in the movie industry.

Controlling Production

When films were just novelties, producers and distributors had not yet recognized that fans would not only seek particular film stories—like dramas, westerns, and romances—but also particular film actors. This behavior was not unlike what later happened in the 1950s, when radio station managers noticed that teenagers listened to favorite performers again and again. Initially, film companies were reluctant to identify their anonymous actors for fear that their popularity would raise the typical five-to-fifteen dollar actor salary. Eventually, though, the industry understood how important the actors' identity would be to a film's success.

Responding to discerning audiences and competing against Edison's Trust, Adolph Zukor hired a number of popular actors and formed the Famous Players Company in 1912. His idea was to control movie production not through patents but through exclusive contracts with these actors. One Famous Players performer was Mary Pickford. Known as "America's Sweetheart" for her portrayal of spunky and innocent heroines, Pickford was "unspoiled" by a theater background and more suited to the more subtle, more intimate new medium. She became so popular that audiences waited in line to see her movies, and producers had to pay her increasingly larger salaries to keep her services.

An astute businesswoman, Mary Pickford was the key figure in elevating the financial status and professional role of film actors. Whereas in 1910 Pickford made about $100 a week, by 1914 she earned $1,000 a week. By 1917, Zukor was paying Pickford a weekly salary of $15,000. Having appeared in nearly two hundred films, Pickford was so influential that in 1919 she broke from Zukor to form her own company, United Artists. Joining her were actor Douglas Fairbanks (her future husband), comedian-director Charlie Chaplin, and director D. W. Griffith.

By the beginning of the 1920s, film production had evolved into the **studio system**. Pioneered by director Thomas Ince and his Hollywood company, Triangle, this system constituted a sort of assembly-line process for moviemaking. It organized a staff of the best technicians and directors schooled in the latest film techniques. According to the system, not only stars but also directors, editors, writers, and others worked under exclusive contracts for the major studios. Indeed, those who weren't under contract with some movie company probably weren't working at all. Ince also developed the notion of the studio head; he gave up directing in 1915 and appointed producers to handle hiring, logistics, and finances so that he could more easily supervise many pictures at one time.

> **❝ No, I really cannot afford to work for only $10,000 a week. ❞**
>
> –Mary Pickford
> to Adolph Zukor, 1915

Although United Artists represented a brief triumph of autonomy for a few powerful actors, by the 1920s the studio system firmly controlled creative talent in the industry. The system was so efficient that each major studio was producing a feature film every week. Pooling talent, rather than patents, was a more ingenious approach for movie studios aiming to dominate film production.

Controlling Distribution

One of the early forms of movie distribution, *film exchanges* appeared around 1904 as movie companies provided vaudeville theaters with films and projectors. In exchange for their short films, shown between live acts, movie producers received a small percentage of the vaudeville ticket-gate receipts. Gradually, as the number of production companies and the popularity of narrative films grew, demand for a distribution system serving national and international markets increased as well. Because few regulations existed in these early days, movies were often stolen or copied. Edison's Trust represented, in part, an attempt to prevent film pirating and to manage the industry by withholding equipment from companies not willing to pay the Trust's patent-use fees.

However, emerging film companies and other independent firms looked to distribution strategies to gain a foothold in the fledgling industry. Early independents like Adolph Zukor, who opposed the Trust, developed several distribution techniques, including **block booking**. Under this system, to gain access to popular films exhibitors had to agree to rent new or marginal films with no stars. Zukor would pressure theater operators into taking a hundred movies at a time to get the few Pickford titles they wanted. Such contracts enabled studios to test-market a new star without taking much financial risk. Although this practice was eventually outlawed as monopolistic, rising film studios used the tactic effectively to guarantee the success of their films in a competitive marketplace.

Another distribution strategy involved the marketing of American films in Europe. When World War I disrupted European film production, only U.S. studios were able to meet the demand. The war thus marked a turning point, making the United States the leader in the commercial movie business. Europe never regained its edge. After the war, no other film industry could compete economically with Hollywood. By the mid-1920s, foreign revenue from U.S. films totaled $100 million. Today, in any given week, when the industry trade magazine *Variety* ranks the top-grossing films in foreign countries, U.S. movies (especially easily translatable action/adventure features) continue to dominate the list. For example, 2006's *The Da Vinci Code* emerged as a top box-office draw in Spain, Italy, Japan, France, and the United Kingdom.

Controlling Exhibition

When industrious theater owners began forming film cooperatives to compete with block-booking tactics, producers like Zukor conspired to dominate exhibition. By 1921, Zukor's company owned three hundred theaters, solidifying its ability to show the movies it created. In 1925, a business merger between Paramount and Publix (the country's largest theater chain at the time, with more than five hundred screens) gave Zukor enormous influence over movie exhibition.

Zukor and the heads of several major studios understood that they did not have to own all theaters to ensure that their movies were shown. Over time, the five major studios (which would eventually include MGM, RKO, Warner Brothers, Twentieth Century Fox, and Paramount) merely needed to own about 15 percent of the nation's twenty thousand movie houses. They needed only the first-run theaters, which premiered new films in major downtown areas in front of the largest audiences.

> **"** It's still a business where the hits make up for all the losses along the way. *Star Wars* accentuated that. Everyone wants to reproduce that success, even just once. This tells you about the strength of this kind of franchise. **"**
>
> —Jill Krutick, analyst, Smith Barney, 1997

Throughout the 1940s, ticket sales from these venues generated 85 to 95 percent of all film revenue.

Movie Palaces

Entrepreneurs ultimately realized that drawing the middle and upper-middle classes to movies required something more attractive than a sheet hung in an abandoned pawnshop. To provide a more hospitable moviegoing environment, exhibitors converted vaudeville theaters into full-time use as single-screen movie theaters. In 1914, the 3,000-seat Strand Theatre, the first **movie palace**, opened in New York. With elaborate architecture, movie palaces lured spectators who enjoyed entertainment amid the elegant décor usually reserved for high-society opera, ballet, symphony, and live theater.

To work their magic on the outside, these theaters often evoked the grandeur of palaces, with massive electric-light displays that announced their presence from blocks away. Linking the moviegoing experience with the trappings of royalty created a powerful attraction. Inside the theater, customers meandered through lavish lobbies, plush promenades, and fancy waiting rooms. Movie exhibitors treated "the movie patron like a king or queen," with ushers, doormen, and services ranging from free child care to "smoking rooms and painting galleries."[4] Taking advantage of new air-cooling systems developed by Chicago's meatpacking industry, movie palaces also featured the first mechanically air-cooled theaters. This perquisite alone transformed summer moviegoing in Chicago into peak viewing time. Doctors even advised pregnant women to escape the heat by spending their afternoons at the movies.

● With its Chinese-inspired design, Seattle's 5th Avenue Theatre opened in 1926 as a venue for vaudeville and silent movies. The theater was modeled after Imperial China's Forbidden City, the Temple of Heavenly Peace, and the Summer Palace. A large coiled dragon holds the centerpiece chandelier in its teeth. The 2,100-plus-seat theater closed in 1978 and was restored during the 1980s, and it is now home to a theater company.

Mid-City Theaters

Another major innovation in exhibition was the development of mid-city movie theaters. The first wave of middle-class people moved from urban centers to city outskirts in the 1920s, and mass-transit systems emerged to shuttle these suburbanites to and from work. Movie theaters soon followed, as exhibitors in Chicago began to locate theaters at major transportation intersections in outlying business areas rather than downtown. (For another view of exhibition, see "Case Study: Breaking through Hollywood's Race Barrier" on opposite page.) This idea continues today, as **multiplexes** featuring multiple screens lure middle-class crowds to interstate crossroads.

Throughout the 1920s, movie attendance climbed steadily. But the Depression hit the industry hard, and many customers turned to radio, a cheaper form of entertainment. To compete, theaters began holding contests and prize giveaways. They also offered double features — two movies for the price of one — and started selling candy, soda, and eventually popcorn (which, thanks to the movies, turned corn into a major farm crop in the late 1930s). With jobs restored during World War II, movie attendance surged during the 1940s. In 1946 — the industry's all-time peak attendance year — 100 million people (out of a U.S. population of 141 million at that time) went to the movies *each week*.

By the late 1920s, the major studios had clearly established vertical integration in the industry. What had once been a fairly easy and cheap business to enter now was complex and capital-intensive. What had been many small competitive firms in the early 1900s now became a few powerful studios, including the **Big Five** — Paramount, MGM, Warner Brothers, Twentieth Century Fox, and RKO — and the **Little Three** (which did not own theaters) — Columbia, Universal, and United Artists. Together these eight companies formed a powerful oligopoly, which made it increasingly difficult for independent companies to make, distribute, and exhibit commercial films.

● Since 1995, Magic Johnson has partnered with Loews Cineplex Entertainment (now part of AMC) to open Magic Johnson Theatres in urban neighborhoods in Los Angeles, Houston, Atlanta, Cleveland, and New York.

The Triumph of Hollywood Storytelling

Whereas early filmmakers like Edwin S. Porter and D. W. Griffith demonstrated the appeal of the film narrative, early stars like Mary Pickford and Charlie Chaplin revealed the audience's attraction to movie actors. Meanwhile, the studios searched for the next technical innovation to enliven the industry and further enhance film's storytelling capabilities. They found it by adding sound to moving images.

The "Sound" of Movies

With the studio system and Hollywood's worldwide dominance firmly in place, the next big challenge involved bringing sound to moving pictures. Various attempts at **talkies** had failed since Edison first tried to link phonograph and moving picture technologies in the 1890s. During the 1910s, however, technical breakthroughs at AT&T's research arm, Bell Labs, produced prototypes of loudspeakers and sound amplifiers. By the end of the decade, the idea of projecting clear sounds throughout

CASE STUDY

Breaking through Hollywood's Race Barrier

Despite inequities and discrimination, a thriving black cinema existed in New York's Harlem district during the 1930s and 1940s. Usually bankrolled by white business executives who were capitalizing on the black-only theaters fostered by segregation, independent films featuring black casts were supported by African American moviegoers, even during the Depression. But it was a popular Hollywood film, *Imitation of Life* (1934), that emerged as the highest-grossing film in black theaters during the mid-1930s. The film told the story of a friendship between a white woman and a black woman whose young daughter denied her heritage and passed for white, breaking her mother's heart.

Despite African Americans' long support of the film industry, their moviegoing experience has not been the same as that of whites. From the late 1800s until the passage of civil rights legislation in the mid-1960s, many theater owners discriminated against black patrons. In large cities, blacks often had to attend separate theaters where new movies might not appear until a year or two after white theaters had shown them. In smaller towns and in the South, blacks were often able to patronize local theaters only after midnight. In addition, some theater managers required black patrons to sit in less desirable areas of the theater.[1]

Changes took place during and after World War II, however. When the "white flight" from central cities began during the suburbanization of the 1950s, many downtown and neighborhood theaters began catering to black customers in order to keep from going out of business. By the late 1960s and early 1970s, these theaters had become major venues for popular commercial films, even featuring a few movies about African Americans, including *Guess Who's Coming to Dinner?* (1967), *In the Heat of the Night* (1967), *The Learning Tree* (1969), and *Sounder* (1972).

Based on the popularity of these films, black photographer-turned-filmmaker Gordon Parks, who directed *The*

● Spike Lee

Learning Tree (adapted from his own novel), went on to make commercial action/adventure films, including *Shaft* (1971, remade by John Singleton in 2000). Popular in urban theaters, especially among black teenagers, the movies produced by Parks and his son—Gordon Parks Jr. (*Super Fly,* 1972)—spawned a number of commercial imitators, labeled blaxploitation movies. These films were the subject of heated cultural debates in the 1970s; like some rap songs today, they were both praised for their realistic depictions of black urban life and criticized for glorifying violence. Nevertheless, these films reinvigorated urban movie attendance, reaching an audience that had not been well served by the film industry until the 1960s.

Although opportunities for black film directors expanded in the 1980s, during the 1990s mainstream Hollywood was still a formidable place for outsiders to crack. Even acclaimed director Spike Lee has had difficulty in getting large budgets from the studios. For example, in making *Get on the Bus* (1996), Lee asked a number of wealthy black men to bankroll $2 million for the film (made for one-tenth the cost of the average Hollywood movie at the time). The film depicted the October 1995 Million Man March on Washington, D.C., celebrating the kind of black self-reliance that Lee's own moviemaking has long illustrated.

● Gordon Parks

large movie palaces was technically possible, although the cost of outfitting theaters with the necessary equipment remained high.

Experiments with ten-minute sound shorts continued during the 1920s. The four Warner brothers (Harry, Abe, Jack, and Sam), who ran a minor studio at the time, experimented with sound as a novelty, although they did not believe such films would replace silent movies. So Warner Brothers made short sound versions of vaudeville acts, featuring singers and comedians. The studio packaged them as a novelty along with silent feature films. Over time, Warner Brothers began outfitting theaters with the necessary sound equipment.

In 1927, Warner Brothers produced a feature-length film, *The Jazz Singer,* starring Al Jolson, a charismatic and popular vaudeville singer who wore blackface makeup as part of his act. An experiment, *The Jazz Singer* was basically a silent film interspersed with musical numbers and brief dialogue. At first, there was only modest interest in the movie, which featured just 354 spoken words. But the film grew in popularity as it toured the Midwest, where audiences stood and cheered the short bursts of dialogue. The breakthrough film, however, was Warner Brothers' 1928 release *The Singing Fool,* which also starred Jolson. Costing $200,000 to make, the film took in $5 million and "proved to all doubters that talkies were here to stay."[5]

By the mid-1920s, Bell Labs had developed the system used by Warner Brothers that coordinated sound on records with a film projector. Warner Brothers, however, was not the only studio forging into the technology of sound. In April 1927, five months before *The Jazz Singer* opened, the Fox studio premiered sound-film **newsreels**. Fox's newsreel company, Movietone, captured the first film footage, with sound, of the takeoff and return of Charles Lindbergh, who piloted the first solo, nonstop flight across the Atlantic Ocean in May 1927. Fox's Movietone system actually photographed sound directly onto the film, running it on a narrow filmstrip that ran alongside the larger, image portion of the film. Superior to the sound-on-record system, the Movietone method eventually became film's standard sound system.

● Al Jolson in *The Singing Fool* (1928). The film was the box-office champ for more than ten years until 1939, when it was dethroned by *Gone with the Wind.*

Meanwhile, Fox was sending camera crews around the world in search of talking news. By 1928, the success of newsreels, as popular as most silent features of the day, led to the full conversion to talking pictures. Boosted by the innovation of sound, annual movie attendance in the United States rose from 60 million a week in 1927 to 90 million a week in 1929. By 1931, nearly 85 percent of America's twenty thousand theaters accommodated sound pictures, and by 1935, the world had adopted talking films as the commercial standard.

Classic Hollywood Cinema

By the time sound came to movies, Hollywood dictated not only the business but the style of most moviemaking worldwide. That style, or model, for storytelling developed with the studio system and continues to dominate American filmmaking today. The model serves up three ingredients that give Hollywood movies their distinctive flavor: the narrative, the genre, and the author (or director). The right blend of these ingredients—combined with timing, marketing, and luck—have led to **blockbuster** movie hits from *Gone with the Wind* to *Pirates of the Caribbean: Dead Man's Chest*. Major studios have historically relied on blockbusters to underwrite the 80 to 90 percent of films that fail at the box office.

Hollywood Narratives

American filmmakers from D. W. Griffith to Steven Spielberg have understood the allure of *narrative,* which always includes two basic components: the story (what happens to whom) and the discourse (how the story is told). Most movies, like most TV shows and novels, feature a number of stories that play out within the larger narrative of the entire film. For example, in director Bryan Singer's *Superman Returns* (2006), Superman (Brandon Routh) returns as mild-mannered Clark Kent to work for the *Daily Planet* after a mysterious five-year absence and finds that his love, star reporter Lois Lane (Kate Bosworth), is engaged and has a young son. Meanwhile, Superman's nemesis Lex Luthor (Kevin Spacey) is out of prison and hatching an evil plan. The intertwining stories—Superman's challenge to win back Lois, his fight against Lex Luthor, and his mysterious disappearance—offer yet another narrative film based on the indestructible comic book hero.

Within Hollywood's classic narratives, filmgoers find an amazing array of intriguing cultural variations. *Superman Returns* features the familiar narrative *conventions* of heroes, villains, conflicts, and resolutions. However, the film *differentiates* itself through enhanced *inventions*: images were shot with an entirely new digital camera system, and the film was digitally remastered for an IMAX 3D Experience release. This combination of convention and invention—standardized Hollywood stories and differentiated special effects—provides a powerful economic package that satisfies most audiences' appetites for both the familiar and the distinctive.

Hollywood Genres

In general, Hollywood narratives fit a **genre**, or category, in which conventions regarding similar characters, scenes, structures, and themes recur in combination. Grouping films by category enables the industry to achieve two related economic goals: *product standardization* and *product differentiation*. By making films that fall into popular genres, the movie industry provides familiar models that can be imitated. It is much easier for a studio to promote a film that already fits into a preexisting category with which viewers are familiar. Among the most familiar genres are comedy, drama, romance, action/adventure, mystery/suspense, fantasy/science fiction, musical, horror, gangster, western, and film noir. (See Table 7.2 on pages 248–49.)

An enduring genre such as the western typically features "good" cowboys battling "evil" bad guys or resolves tension between the natural forces of the wilderness and the civilizing influence of a town. Romances present narratives in which women play more central roles and conflicts are mediated by the ideal of love. Another popular genre, mystery/suspense, usually casts "the city" as a corrupting place that needs to be overcome by the moral courage of a heroic detective. In these movies, the hero searches for clues of criminal violation, then confronts villains, victims, and bystanders, and finally explains and resolves the violation or transgression.[6]

Besides variations of dramas and comedies, which dominate film's long narrative history, another significant genre, the movie musical, added the innovation of on-screen music. The genre's popularity peaked in the 1940s and 1950s. Later musi-

> 66 I think that American movies, to be honest, are just simple. You blow things up, you shoot people, you have sex and you have a movie. And I think it appeals to just the more base emotions of people anywhere. 99
>
> —Anthony Kaufmann, film journalist, 2004

> 66 We tell ourselves stories in order to live. 99
>
> —Joan Didion, *The White Album*, 1979

> 66 The thing of a musical is that you take a simple story, and tell it in a complicated way. 99
>
> —Baz Luhrmann, at the 2002 Academy Awards, on *Moulin Rouge!*

● *Citizen Kane*

● *Brokeback Mountain*

Movies, especially contemporary films, are difficult to categorize because they often combine characteristics from different genres. For example, in 2006, the film *Pirates of the Caribbean: Dead Man's Chest* combined aspects of action/adventure, comedy, and romance. Shown below are the categories that are generally used by video stores to sort movies. Films from different decades represent the most familiar major genres.

Comedy

The Gold Rush (1925)	*A Fish Called Wanda* (1988)
Horse Feathers (1932)	*The Birdcage* (1995)
Arsenic and Old Lace (1944)	*American Beauty* (1999)*
Some Like It Hot (1959)	*High Fidelity* (2000)
Dr. Strangelove (1964)	*Shrek 2* (2004)
Annie Hall (1977)*	*Meet the Fockers* (2004)

Drama

Grand Hotel (1932)	*Fried Green Tomatoes* (1991)
Gone with the Wind (1939)	*Good Will Hunting* (1997)
Citizen Kane (1941)	*Saving Private Ryan* (1998)
On the Waterfront (1954)*	*A Beautiful Mind* (2001)
A Man for All Seasons (1966)*	*Mystic River* (2003)
One Flew over the Cuckoo's Nest (1975)*	*Million Dollar Baby* (2004)*
Raging Bull (1980)	*Crash* (2005)*
Do the Right Thing (1989)	

Romance

It Happened One Night (1934)*	*Tootsie* (1984)
Casablanca (1943)*	*Beauty and the Beast* (1993)
Adam's Rib (1949)	*Titanic* (1997)*
Sabrina (1954)	*Shakespeare in Love* (1998)*
Dr. Zhivago (1965)	*My Big Fat Greek Wedding* (2002)
The Graduate (1967)	*Brokeback Mountain* (2005)
The Goodbye Girl (1977)	*The Break Up* (2006)

Action/Adventure

The Adventures of Robin Hood (1938)	*Die Hard* (1988)
Sands of Iwo Jima (1949)	*Thelma & Louise* (1991)
Ben Hur (1959)*	*Mission Impossible II* (2000)
The Great Escape (1963)	*Kill Bill–Vol. 1* (2003)
The Sting (1973)*	*Mission: Impossible III* (2006)

Mystery/Suspense

The Lady Vanishes (1938)	*Witness* (1985)
Rebecca (1940)*	*Silence of the Lambs* (1991)*
North by Northwest (1959)	*Seven* (1996)
Psycho (1960)	*The Sixth Sense* (1999)
Chinatown (1974)	*The Bourne Supremacy* (2004)

Westerns

Cimarron (1931)*	*The Outlaw Josey Wales* (1976)
Stagecoach (1939)	*Silverado* (1985)
The Searchers (1956)	*Unforgiven* (1992)*
Butch Cassidy and the Sundance Kid (1969)	*Maverick* (1994)
Little Big Man (1970)	*The Missing* (2003)

(continued on next page)

● **Table 7.2 Hollywood Genres** *(continued)*

Gangster

Public Enemy (1931)	*Goodfellas* (1990)
Scarface (1932)	*Boyz N the Hood* (1991)
High Sierra (1941)	*Menace II Society* (1993)
Bonnie and Clyde (1967)	*Donnie Brasco* (1997)
The Godfather (1972)*	*Ocean's Twelve* (2004)
The Godfather, Part II (1974)*	*The Departed* (2006)*
Scarface (1983)	

Horror

Phantom of the Opera (1925)	*Nightmare on Elm Street* (1985)
Dracula (1931)	*Mary Shelley's Frankenstein* (1994)
Bride of Frankenstein (1935)	*Scream* (1996)
The Wolf Man (1941)	*The Blair Witch Project* (1999)
The Blob (1958)	*The Ring* (2002)
The Birds (1963)	*Van Helsing* (2004)
The Exorcist (1973)	*The Omen* (2006)

Fantasy/Science Fiction

Metropolis (1926)	*Terminator 2: Judgment Day* (1991)
The Wizard of Oz (1939)	*Independence Day* (1996)
Invasion of the Body Snatchers (1956)	*The Matrix* (1999)
2001: A Space Odyssey (1968)	*The Lord of the Rings: The Return*
Star Wars (1977)	*of the King* (2003)*
Blade Runner (1982)	*Star Wars: Episode III—Revenge*
The Princess Bride (1987)	*of the Sith* (2005)

Musicals

Broadway Melody (1929)*	*Jesus Christ Superstar* (1973)
Top Hat (1935)	*Annie* (1982)
Meet Me in St. Louis (1944)	*Evita* (1997)
An American in Paris (1951)*	*Moulin Rouge!* (2001)
West Side Story (1961)*	*Chicago* (2002)*
The Sound of Music (1965)*	

Film Noir

Double Indemnity (1944)	*Border Incident* (1949)
Detour (1945)	*Sunset Boulevard* (1950)
The Postman Always Rings Twice (1946)	*Se7en* (1995)
The Strange Love of Martha Ivers (1946)	*L.A. Confidential* (1997)
The Big Sleep (1946)	*The Man Who Wasn't There* (2001)
Key Largo (1948)	*Black Dahlia* (2006)
They Live by Night (1948)	

*Won the Academy Award for that year's best picture.

● *The Godfather*

● *Se7en*

cals such as *Jesus Christ Superstar* (1973) and *Hair* (1979) were early influences on the music-video era, but the genre was ultimately overwhelmed by MTV. Disney sustained the musical genre with its string of hybrid animation-musicals, such as *Beauty and the Beast* (1991) and *The Lion King* (1994), both of which later resurfaced as successful Broadway shows. Because most Hollywood narratives try to create believable worlds, the artificial style of musicals is sometimes a disruption of what many viewers expect. Nevertheless, live action musicals showed new life in the early

● A classic film noir, *Sunset Boulevard* (1950) explores the dark forces behind the Hollywood dream factory. Here, Norma Desmond is a faded silent-film star (played by Gloria Swanson, a real-life faded silent-film star) who takes in struggling Hollywood writer Joe Gillis (played by William Holden). The limousine driver is Max Von Mayerling, Desmond's former husband (played by Eric Von Stroheim, himself a silent-film director who found little directorial work after the advent of talkies). In film noir style, the movie ends in madness and death.

2000s, with Baz Luhrmann's acclaimed *Moulin Rouge!* (2001) and Rob Marshall's *Chicago* (2002), an Academy Award Best Picture winner. Still, no live-action musicals rank among the top fifty highest-grossing films of all time.

Another fascinating genre is the horror film, which in 2006 counted only one movie among the top fifty highest-grossing films of all time: *Signs,* from 2002. In fact, from *Psycho* (the original 1960 version) to *The Grudge 2* (2006), this lightly regarded genre has earned only one Oscar for best picture: *Silence of the Lambs,* a mystery/suspense-horror hybrid from 1991. Yet these movies are extremely popular with teenagers, among the largest theatergoing audience, who are in search of cultural choices distinct from those of their parents. Critics suggest that the teen appeal of such horror movies as *Snakes on a Plane* (2006) is similar to the allure of gangster rap or heavy-metal music. That is, the horror genre is a cultural form that often carries anti-adult messages or does not appeal to most adults. In other words, this genre repels parents while simultaneously attracting their children.

An interesting and relatively new genre is *film noir* (French for "black film"), which developed in the United States after World War II and continues to influence movies today. Using low-lighting techniques, few daytime scenes, and bleak urban settings that generate a chilling mood, films in this genre (such as *The Big Sleep,* 1946, and *Sunset Boulevard,* 1950) explore unstable characters and the sinister side of human nature. These films also often resist the conventional closure of the classic narrative. Although the French critics who first identified noir as a genre place these films in the 1940s, their influence resonates in contemporary films—sometimes called *neo-noir*—including *Raging Bull, Pulp Fiction, The Usual Suspects, Se7en, L.A. Confidential,* and *Memento.*

Hollywood "Authors"

Film has generally been called a director's medium. Although commercial filmmaking requires hundreds of people to perform complicated tasks, from scriptwriting and casting to set design and editing, the director serves as the main "author" of a film. Certainly the names Steven Spielberg (*E.T.; Schindler's List; Jurassic Park; Munich*) and Spike Lee (*Do the Right Thing; Malcolm X; Get on the Bus; Inside Man*) attract many moviegoers to a film today.

D. W. Griffith, among the first "star" directors, paved the way for future filmmakers. Griffith refined many of the narrative techniques that are still in use today, including varied camera distances, close-up shots, multiple story lines, fast-paced editing, and symbolic imagery. His major work, *The Birth of a Nation* (1915), was a controversial three-hour Civil War epic. Although considered a technical masterpiece, the film glorified the Ku Klux Klan and stereotyped southern blacks. It is nevertheless the movie that triggered Hollywood's ongoing fascination with long narrative films. By 1915, more than 20 percent of films were feature-length (around two hours), and *The Birth of a Nation*, which cost filmgoers a record two-dollar admission, ran for a year on Broadway.

Successful directors, in general, develop a particular cinematic style or an interest in particular topics that differentiates their narratives from those of other directors. Alfred Hitchcock, for instance, redefined the suspense drama through editing techniques that heightened tension (*North by Northwest*, 1959; *Psycho*, 1960); and Frank Capra championed romantic characters who stood up for the common person (*Mr. Smith Goes to Washington*, 1939; *It's a Wonderful Life*, 1946).

The contemporary status of directors probably stems from two breakthrough films: Dennis Hopper's *Easy Rider* (1969) and George Lucas's *American Graffiti* (1973), which became surprise box-office hits. Their inexpensive budgets, rock-and-roll soundtracks, and big payoffs created opportunities for a new generation of directors. The success of these films exposed cracks in the Hollywood system, which was losing money in the late 1960s and early 1970s. Studio executives seemed at a loss to explain and predict the tastes of a new generation of moviegoers. Yet Hopper and Lucas had tapped into the anxieties of the postwar baby-boom generation in its search for self-realization, its longing for an innocent past, and its efforts to cope with the social turbulence of the late 1960s.

Trained in California or New York film schools and products of the 1960s, Francis Ford Coppola (*The Godfather*), Brian De Palma (*Carrie*), William Friedkin (*The Exorcist*), George Lucas (*Star Wars*), Martin Scorsese (*Taxi Driver; Raging Bull*), and Steven Spielberg (*Jaws; Raiders of the Lost Ark*) represented a new wave of Hollywood directors. Combining news or documentary techniques and Hollywood narratives, they demonstrated not only how mass media borders had become blurred but also how movies had become more dependent on audiences that were used to television and rock and roll. These films signaled the start of a period that Scorsese has called "the deification of the director." A handful of successful men gained the kind of economic clout and celebrity standing that had belonged almost exclusively to top movie stars, and a few of these directors were transformed into big-time Hollywood producers.

> ❝ There are women in the Senate, women heading studios, and busloads of young women emerging from film school. So why are 96 percent of films directed by men? ❞
>
> –Michelle Goldberg, Salon.com, 2002

● Sofia Coppola, a leading female director in Hollywood, has written and directed *The Virgin Suicides* (1999), *Lost in Translation* (2003), and *Marie-Antoinette* (2006).

> ❝ Growing up in this country, the rich culture I saw in my neighborhood, in my family—I didn't see that on television or on the movie screen. It was always my ambition that if I was successful I would try to portray a truthful portrait of African Americans in this country, negative and positive. ❞
>
> –Spike Lee, filmmaker, 1996

A budget of $10 million made the 2002 remake of *Devdas* the most expensive Indian film to date. The musical featured Aishwarya Rai, one of Bollywood's most popular stars.

Although the status of directors grew in the 1960s and 1970s, recognition for women directors of Hollywood features remained rare.[7] In the history of the Academy Awards, only three women have received an Academy Award nomination for directing a feature film: Lina Wertmuller in 1976 for *Seven Beauties*, Jane Campion in 1993 for *The Piano*, and Sofia Coppola in 2004 for *Lost in Translation*. It's worth noting that both Wertmuller and Campion are from outside the United States, where women directors often receive more funding opportunities for film development. When women in the United States do get an opportunity, it is often because their prominent standing as popular actors has given them the power to produce or direct. Barbra Streisand, Jodie Foster, Penny Marshall, and Sally Field all fall into this category. Other women have come to direct films via their script-writing successes. Respected essayist Nora Ephron, for example, wrote *Silkwood* in 1983, wrote and produced *When Harry Met Sally* in 1989, and then went on to direct *Sleepless in Seattle* and *You've Got Mail* in 1993 and 1998, each grossing more than $100 million.

Although women have made strong contributions in commercial movies as actors, editors, writers, artists, and designers, critics generally attribute their lack of power to the long history of male executives being atop the studio system. With the exception of Mary Pickford, the early studio moguls who ran Hollywood were men. Even by the late 1990s, among the major studio executives, only a few women held top posts. Independent filmmaker Julie Dash (*Daughters of the Dust*, 1992) has argued that women's best chances of controlling the movie process, apart from acting, remain outside the Hollywood system. But some women directors are proving otherwise. Beeban Kidron (*Bridget Jones: The Edge of Reason*, 2004), Catherine Hardwicke (*Lords of Dogtown*, 2005), Nancy Meyers (*Something's Gotta Give*, 2003), and Niki Caro (*North Country*, 2005) have gotten past the barrier of their second and third films, proving themselves as trusted studio auteurs.

Outside the Hollywood System

The contemporary film industry tends to focus on feature-length movies that command popular attention and most of the money. However, shorter narrative films and documentaries dominated cinema's first twenty years and continue to account for most of the movies made today. In addition, movie history has a long tradition in experimental, or avant-garde, films. These types of film, often produced outside the United States, provide opportunities for new filmmakers, both women and men. In the following sections, we will look at three alternatives to Hollywood: foreign films, documentaries, and independent films.

> **❝ Even bad or mediocre foreign movies have important things to teach us. Consider them cultural CARE packages, precious news bulletins, breaths of air (fresh or stale) from diverse corners of the globe. ❞**
>
> –Jonathan Rosenbaum, *Movie Wars*, 2000

Foreign Films

For generations, Hollywood has dominated the international movie scene. In many countries, American films have captured up to 90 percent of the market. In striking contrast, foreign films comprise only a tiny fraction—1.6 percent—of motion pictures seen in the United States today. Despite Hollywood's domination of global film distribution, other countries have a rich history in producing both successful and provocative short-subject and feature films. For example, German expressionism (1919–24), Soviet realism (1924–30), Italian neorealism (1942–51), French new-wave cinema (1959–60), and post–World War II Japanese cinema have all demonstrated alternatives to the Hollywood approach. Today, the largest film industry is in India, out of "Bollywood" (a play on words combining Bombay [now Mumbai] and Hollywood) where 1,000 films a year are produced—mostly romance or adventure musicals in a distinct style, but with Western influences.[8] In comparison, Hollywood moviemakers release 450 to 500 films a year.

Americans showed early interest in British and French short films and in experimental films such as Germany's *The Cabinet of Dr. Caligari* (1919). The studio moguls, however, held tight rein over the entry of foreign titles into the United States. Foreign-language movies did reasonably well throughout the 1920s, especially in ethnic neighborhood theaters in large American cities. For a time, Hollywood studios even dubbed some popular American movies into Spanish, Italian, French, and German for these theaters. But the Depression brought cutbacks, and by the 1930s the daughters and sons of turn-of-the-century immigrants—many of whom were trying to assimilate into mainstream American culture—preferred their Hollywood movies in English.[9]

Postwar prosperity and a rising globalism in the 1950s and 1960s saw a rebirth of interest in foreign-language films by such prominent directors as Sweden's Ingmar Bergman (*Wild Strawberries*, 1957), Italy's Federico Fellini (*La Dolce Vita*, 1960), France's François Truffaut (*Jules and Jim*, 1961), Japan's Akira Kurosawa (*Seven Samurai*, 1954), and India's Satyajit Ray (*Apu Trilogy*, 1955–59). In the 1950s, the gradual breakup of the studios' hold over theater exhibition stimulated the rise of art-house theaters, many specializing in foreign titles. Catering to academic audiences, art houses made a statement against Hollywood commercialism as they sought alternative movies.

Art houses numbered close to a thousand during their peak years in the late 1960s. By the late 1970s, though, the home-video market had emerged, and audiences began staying home to watch both foreign and domestic films. New multiplex theater owners also rejected the smaller profit margins of most foreign titles, which lacked the promotional hype of U.S. films. In addition, many viewers complained that English subtitles distracted them from devoting their attention to the visual images. As a result, between 1966 and 1990 the number of foreign films released annually in the United States dropped by two-thirds, from nearly three hundred to about one hundred titles per year.

With the growth of superstore video chains like Blockbuster in the 1990s, however, more shelf space opened up for diverse kinds of movies, including a larger

● The South African film *Tsotsi* won the 2006 Oscar for Best Foreign Language Film of the Year. The film chronicles a week in the life of a gang leader in Johannesburg, South Africa.

selection of foreign-language titles. The successes of *Amélie* (France, 2001), *Respiro* (Italy, 2002), and *Tsotsi* (South Africa, 2005) illustrate that U.S. audiences are willing to watch subtitled films with non-Hollywood perspectives. Nevertheless, fewer than 2 percent of the nation's movie screens regularly show foreign-language films. Foreign films are even losing ground at these "alternative" screening sites, as they compete with the expanding independent American film market for screen space. (For a broader perspective on foreign film, see "The Global Village—Beyond Hollywood: Asian Cinema" on opposite page.)

The Documentary Tradition

Both TV news and nonfiction films trace their roots to the movie industry's *interest films* and newsreels of the late 1890s. In Britain, interest films contained compiled footage of regional wars, political leaders, industrial workers, and agricultural scenes. These films accompanied fiction shorts as part of the early moviegoing experience. Pioneered in France and England, *newsreels* consisted of weekly ten-minute magazine-style compilations of filmed news events from around the world organized in a sequence of short reports. A number of international news services began supplying theaters and movie studios with newsreels, and by 1911 they had become a regular part of the moviegoing menu.

Early filmmakers also produced *travelogues,* which recorded daily life in various communities around the world. Travel films reached documentary status in Robert Flaherty's classic *Nanook of the North* (1922), which tracked a resourceful Inuit family in the harsh Hudson Bay region of Canada. Flaherty edited his fifty-five-minute film to both tell and interpret the story of his subject. Flaherty's second film, *Moana* (1925), a Paramount-funded study of the lush South Pacific islands and a direct contrast to *Nanook,* inspired the term **documentary** in a 1926 film review by John Grierson, a Scottish film producer. Grierson defined Flaherty's work and the documentary form as "the creative treatment of actuality," or a genre that interprets reality by recording real people and settings.

Over time, the documentary developed an identity apart from its commercial presentation. As an educational, noncommercial form, the documentary usually required the backing of industry, government, or philanthropy to cover costs. In support of a clear alternative to Hollywood cinema, various governments began creating special units, such as Canada's National Film Board, to sponsor documentaries. In the United States, art and film received considerable support from the Roosevelt administration during the Depression. Such funding produced Pare Lorentz's *The Plow That Broke the Plains* (1936), which recounted the ecological abuse and erosion of the Great Plains in the 1930s. During World War II, the government continued to turn to filmmakers and to Hollywood to "sell" patriotism. Director Frank Capra produced the seven-part *Why We Fight* documentary series as propaganda to inspire support for the war effort against Germany and Japan.

By the late 1950s and early 1960s, the development of portable cameras had led to **cinema verité** (a French term for "truth film"). This documentary style allowed filmmakers to go where cameras could not go before and record fragments of everyday life more unobtrusively. Directly opposed to packaged, high-gloss Hollywood features, verité aimed to track reality, employing a rough, grainy look and shaky, handheld camerawork.

Among the key innovators in cinema verité were Drew and Associates, led by Robert Drew, a former *Life* magazine photographer. Through his connection to Time

"I would be just as offended if they refused to release a film that was in favor of George Bush and his policies."

—Michael Moore, filmmaker, 2004, on the Miramax decision not to release his film, *Fahrenheit 9/11,* in the United States

● After targeting GM (*Roger and Me*), the gun lobby (*Bowling for Columbine*), and the Bush administration (*Fahrenheit 9/11*), muckraking director Michael Moore set his sights on the health-care industry with *Sicko.*

THE GLOBAL VILLAGE

Beyond Hollywood: Asian Cinema

Asian nations easily outstrip Hollywood in quantity of films produced. India alone produces about a thousand movies a year. But from India to South Korea (which produces about eighty to ninety films a year), Asian films are increasingly challenging Hollywood in quality, and have become more influential as Asian directors, actors, and film styles are exported to Hollywood and the rest of the world.

● The 2005 award-winning Bollywood film *Water* was written and directed by Deepa Mehta.

India

Part musical, part action, part romance, and part suspense, the epic films of Bollywood typically have fantastic sets, hordes of extras, plenty of wet saris, and symbolic fountain bursts (as a substitute for kissing and sex, which are prohibited from being shown). Indian movie fans pay from 75 cents to $5 to see these films, and they feel short-changed if a Bollywood film is shorter than three hours.

With many films produced in less than a week, however, most of the Bollywood fare is cheaply produced and badly acted. But these production aesthetics are changing, as bigger budget releases target middle and upper classes in India, the twenty-five million Indians living abroad, and Western audiences. Hollywood has also taken notice as Bollywood directors, producers, and actors have come to town. Indian director Shekhar Kapur, for example, directed *Elizabeth* (1998), a stunning epic nominated for seven Oscars, and its sequel *The Golden Age* (2007). British director Gurinder Chadha (*Bend It Like Beckham*, 2002) brought the Bollywood musical style to *Bride and Prejudice* (2004), an adaptation of Jane Austen's classic novel.

China

Since the late 1980s, Chinese cinema has developed an international reputation. Leading this generation of directors are Zhang Yimou (*Raise the Red Lantern*, 1991; *Happy Times*, 2000; *House of Flying Daggers*, 2004) and Kaige Chen (*Farewell My Concubine*, 1993; *The Emperor and the Assassin*, 1999; *Together*, 2002), whose work has spanned genres such as historical epics, love stories, contemporary tales of city life, and action fantasy. They have also helped to make international stars out of Gong Li (*Memoirs of a Geisha*, 2005; *Miami Vice*, 2006) and Ziyi Zhang (*Crouching Tiger, Hidden Dragon*, 2000; *Memoirs of a Geisha*, 2005).

Hong Kong

Hong Kong films were the most talked about — and the most influential — film genre in cinema throughout the late 1980s and 1990s (Hong Kong became part of mainland China in 1997). The style of highly choreographed action with often breathtaking, ballet-like violence became hugely popular around the world, reaching American audiences and in some cases even outselling Hollywood blockbusters. Hong Kong directors like John Woo, Ringo Lam, and Jackie Chan (who also acts in his movies) have directed Hollywood action films; and Hong Kong stars like Jet Li (*Lethal Weapon 4*, 1998; *Romeo Must Die*, 2000), Chow Yun-Fat (*The Replacement Killers*, 1998; *Bulletproof Monk*, 2003), and Malaysia's Michelle Yeoh (*Tomorrow Never Dies*, 1997; *Memoirs of a Geisha*, 2005) are landing leading roles in American movies.

Japan

Americans may be most familiar with low-budget monster movies like *Godzilla*, but the widely heralded films of the late director Akira Kurosawa have had an even greater impact: His *Seven Samurai* (1954) was remade by Hollywood as *The Magnificent Seven* (1960), and *The Hidden Fortress* (1958) was George Lucas's inspiration for *Star Wars*. New forces in Japanese cinema include Hayao Miyazaki (*Spirited Away*, 2001; *Howl's Moving Castle*, 2005), the country's top director of anime movies. Japanese live-action thrillers like *Ringu* (1998) and *Ju-on: The Grudge* (2003) were remade into successful American horror films, *The Ring* (2002) and *The Grudge* (2004). The Hollywood sequel, *The Ring Two* (2005), was directed by Hideo Nakata, director of the original *Ringu*.

South Korea

The end of military regimes in the late 1980s and corporate investment in the film business in the 1990s created a new era in Korean moviemaking. Since 2001, Korean films have overtaken Hollywood offerings in popularity at Korean theaters. Leading directors include Kim Jee-woon (*A Tale of Two Sisters*, 2003), Lee Chang-dong (winner of the Best Director award at Venice for *Oasis*, 2002), and Park Chan-wook, whose Revenge Trilogy films (*Sympathy for Mr. Vengeance*, 2002; *Old Boy*, 2003; and *Lady Vengeance*, 2005) have won international acclaim, including the Grand Prix at Cannes in 2004 for *Old Boy*. Korean films are hot properties in Hollywood, as major U.S. studios have bought the rights to a number of hits including Kim's *A Tale of Two Sisters*, and Park's *Old Boy*.

● Among the most financially successful documentaries of all time, *An Inconvenient Truth* premiered in 2006 with former Vice President Al Gore offering this introduction, "I am Al Gore, I used to be the next president of the United States of America," and then making his case for global warming. One critic called this 95-minute independent film "a call to action laying out the case that Earth is growing dangerously warmer as a result of man-made influences."

Inc. (which owned *Life*) and its chain of TV stations, Drew shot the groundbreaking documentary *Primary*, which followed the 1960 Democratic presidential primary race between Hubert Humphrey and John F. Kennedy.

Another leading American practitioner of cinema verité is Frederick Wiseman, whose documentaries for public television focus on the misuses of power in American institutions. Unlike traditional TV news, in which the reporter's voice-over narration organizes the story, Wiseman used careful and clever editing to make his point without a reporter's comments. His work includes *Titicut Follies* (1967), which until 1993 was banned from public viewing in Massachusetts for its piercing look at a state-run mental health facility. Wiseman's films indirectly reveal institutional abuse and waste, and he and the verité tradition have been praised for bringing such issues to light. They have also been criticized, though, for offering few solutions to the institutional problems they expose.

The documentary form, both inside and outside the United States, extends from turn-of-the-century film shorts to Dziga Vertov's *Man with a Movie Camera* (1927), which demonstrated Soviet-sponsored innovations in film editing. In later eras, the documentary tradition included the French film *Night and Fog* (1955), which reported the atrocities of the Nazi death camps during World War II, and *Hoop Dreams* (1994), a three-hour examination of the rituals of college basketball recruiting in the United States.

Perhaps the major contribution of documentaries has been their willingness to tackle controversial or unpopular subject matter. For example, Michael Moore's *Roger and Me* (1989) presented a comic and controversial look at the complex relationship between the city of Flint, Michigan, and General Motors. More recently, Moore again created controversy with the Oscar-winning *Bowling for Columbine* (2002), which explored the predilection for violence with guns in the United States, and *Fahrenheit 9/11* (2004; a play on the title of the Ray Bradbury novel *Fahrenheit 451*), a critique of the Bush administration's Middle East policies and its war in Iraq. The film was so potent that its distributor, Disney (parent corporation of Miramax), refused to bring it to U.S. screens, even though the film won the Palme d'Or at the Cannes Film Festival in 2004—the first documentary to win the honor in almost fifty years. According to Michael Moore, former Disney CEO Michael Eisner backed out of the distribution agreement because he did not want to anger Jeb Bush, the president's brother and governor of Florida, a state where Disney receives millions of dollars in incentives and tax breaks. The film was eventually released by Lion's Gate, a Canadian independent distributor. Another 2004 documentary, *Super Size Me* (2004), followed the filmmaker Morgan Spurlock over a month of eating nothing but McDonald's fast food in an irreverent analysis of obesity in the United States. *Fahrenheit 9/11* and *Super Size Me* were part of a resurgence in high-profile documentary filmmaking, which included *Spellbound* (2002), Errol Morris's *The Fog of War* (2003), *March of the Penguins* (2005), and *An Inconvenient Truth* (2006).

The Rise of Independent Films

The success of documentary films like *Super Size Me* and *Fahrenheit 9/11* dovetails with the rise of **indies**, or independently produced films. As opposed to directors

> **❝** After the success of *The Blair Witch Project* . . . it seemed that anyone with a dream, a camera and an Internet account could get a film made—or, at least, market it cheaply once it was made. **❞**
>
> –Abby Ellin,
> *New York Times*, 2000

● *The Passion of the Christ* (2004) remains the most successful independent film in history. Controversial because of its graphic violence and depiction of the role of Jews in Jesus' crucifixion and death, the film was rejected by Hollywood but became a blockbuster with the vigorous support of Christian groups. A tamer version of the film, *The Passion Recut*, was released a year later.

working in the Hollywood system, independent filmmakers typically operate on a shoestring budget and show their movies in thousands of campus auditoriums and at hundreds of small film festivals. The decreasing costs of portable technology, including smaller cameras and digital computer editing, has kept many documentarists and other independent filmmakers in business. They make movies inexpensively, relying on real-life situations, stage actors and nonactors, crews made up of friends and students, and local settings outside the studio environment. Successful independents like Kevin Smith (*Clerks, Dogma*), Todd Haynes (*Velvet Goldmine; Far from Heaven*), and Mira Nair (*Salaam Bombay; Monsoon Wedding*) continue to find substantial audiences in college and art-house theaters and through online mail-order DVD services like Netflix that promote work produced outside the studio system.

The rise of independent film festivals in the 1990s—especially the Sundance Film Festival held every January in Park City, Utah—has helped Hollywood rediscover low-cost independent films as an alternative to traditional movies with *Titanic*-size budgets. Films such as *Sex, Lies, and Videotape* (1989), *El Mariachi* (1993), *Shine* (1996), *The Full Monty* (1997), *The Blair Witch Project* (1999), and *Hustle & Flow* (2005) were all able to generate industry buzz and major studio distribution deals through Sundance screenings and became star vehicles for several directors and actors. As with the recording industry, the major studios have recognized that in the 1990s, indies became a strong venue for discovering new talent. The studios have responded either by purchasing successful independent film companies (e.g., Disney's purchase of Miramax) or by developing in-house indie divisions (e.g., Sony's Sony Pictures Classics).

In 2004, Mel Gibson's *The Passion of the Christ* became, by far, the most successful independent film to date. Hollywood studios were not interested in the movie, which was expected to appeal only to a small conservative Christian niche audience. But controversy over the film's depiction of Jews, the graphic portrayal of Christ's crucifixion, and Gibson's own religious beliefs created mainstream debate and widespread interest in the film. The movie earned more than $370 million in U.S. box-office revenues.

The Transformation of the Hollywood System

Beginning in 1946 and continuing over the next seventeen years, the movie industry lost much of its theatergoing audience. In 1951 alone, more than fifty theaters shut down in New York City. The ninety million people going to movies weekly in 1946 had fallen to less than twenty-five million by 1963. It seemed that the movie industry was in deep trouble, especially in light of television's ascent. Critics and observers began talking about the death of Hollywood. Although Hollywood had diminished as the geographic heart of the industry, a number of dramatic changes altered and eventually strengthened many aspects of the commercial movie business.

By the mid-1950s, significant cultural and social changes—such as suburbanization and the widespread availability of television—had begun to reshape the moviegoing experience. Fifty years later, millions of moviegoers flocked to brand-new **megaplexes** (facilities with fourteen or more screens), but admissions declined steadily after a peak of 1.64 billion tickets sold in 2002. Theaters, as well, have been dramatically downsized from the five-thousand-seat movie palaces that reigned in the 1940s. But despite major social transformations, the commercial film industry remains controlled, as it was earlier, by a few powerful companies. Next, we will review the film industry's adjustments to changing conditions, particularly the impact of political and legal challenges, suburbanization, television, and other technological changes such as cable, VCRs, and DVDs.

The Hollywood Ten

In 1947, in the wake of the unfolding Cold War with the Soviet Union, conservative members of Congress began investigating Hollywood for alleged subversive and communist ties. That year, the aggressive witch-hunts for political radicals in the film industry by the House Un-American Activities Committee (HUAC) led to the famous **Hollywood Ten** hearings and subsequent trial. At the time, Congressman J. Parnell Thomas of New Jersey chaired HUAC, which included future president Richard M. Nixon, then a congressman from California.

During the investigations, HUAC coerced prominent people from the film industry to declare their patriotism and to list those suspected of politically unfriendly tendencies. Upset over labor union strikes and outspoken writers, many film executives were eager to testify. During the hearings, Jack L. Warner, of Warner Brothers, suggested that whenever film writers made fun of rich men or America's political system, they were engaging in communist propaganda. He reported that movies sympathetic to "Indians and the colored folks" were also suspect.[10] Film producer Sam Wood, who had directed Marx Brothers comedies in the mid-1930s, testified that communist writers could be spotted because they portrayed bankers and senators as villainous characters. Whether they believed it was their patriotic duty or they were afraid of losing their jobs, many film executives and prominent actors "named names" in 1947.

Eventually, HUAC subpoenaed ten unwilling witnesses who were questioned about their membership in various organizations. The so-called Hollywood Ten—nine screenwriters and one director—refused to discuss their memberships or to identify communist sympathizers. Charged with contempt of Congress in November 1947, they were eventually sent to prison. Ironically, two Hollywood Ten members went to the same prison as HUAC chairman Thomas, who would later be convicted of conspiracy to defraud the government in a phony payroll scheme. Although jailing the Hollywood Ten clearly violated their free-speech rights, in the atmosphere of the Cold War many seemingly well-intentioned people worried that "the American way" could be sabotaged via unfriendly messages planted in films. Upon release from jail, the Hollywood Ten found themselves *blacklisted,* or boycotted, by the major studios, and their careers in the film industry were all but ruined. The national fervor over communism continued to plague Hollywood well into the 1950s.

The Paramount Decision

Coinciding with the political investigations, the government increased its scrutiny of the industry's aggressive business practices. By the mid-1940s, the Justice Department demanded that the five major film companies—Paramount, Warner Brothers, Twentieth Century Fox, MGM, and RKO—end vertical integration. In 1948, after a series of court appeals, the Supreme Court ruled against the film industry in what is commonly known as the **Paramount decision**, forcing the studios to gradually divest themselves of their theaters.

Although the government had hoped to increase competition, the Paramount case never really changed the oligopoly structure of the commercial film industry. Initially, the 1948 decision did create opportunities in the exhibition part of the industry. In addition to art houses showing documentaries or foreign films, thousands of drive-in theaters sprang up in farmers' fields, welcoming new suburbanites who had left the city and embraced the automobile. Although drive-ins had been around since the 1930s, by the end of the 1950s more than four thousand existed. The Paramount decision encouraged other new indoor theater openings as well, but the major studios continued to dominate distribution. By producing the most polished and popular films, they still controlled consumer demand and orchestrated where the movies would play.

Moving to the Suburbs

Common sense might suggest that television alone precipitated the decline in post–World War II movie attendance, but the most dramatic drop actually occurred in the late 1940s—*before* most Americans even owned TV sets.[11] In fact, with the FCC freeze on TV licenses between 1948 and 1952, most communities did not have TV stations up and running until 1954. By then, the theatergoing audience had already dropped by half.

The transformation of a wartime economy and an unprecedented surge in consumer production had a significant impact on moviegoing. With industries turning from armaments to appliances, Americans started cashing in their savings bonds for household goods and new cars. Discretionary income that formerly went to movie tickets now went to acquiring consumer products. And the biggest product of all was a new house in the suburbs, far from the downtown theaters where movies still premiered. Relying on government help through Veterans Administration loans, people

● *Rebel without a Cause* (1955), starring James Dean and Natalie Wood, was marketed in movie posters as "Warner Bros. Challenging Drama of Today's Teenage Violence!" James Dean's memorable portrayal of a troubled youth forever fixed his place in movie history. He was killed in a car crash a month before the movie opened.

left the cities in record numbers to buy affordable houses in suburban areas where tax bases were lower. Home ownership in the United States doubled between 1945 and 1950, while the moviegoing public decreased just as quickly. According to census data, new housing starts, which had held steady at about 100,000 a year since the late 1920s, leaped to more than 930,000 in 1946 and peaked at 1,700,000 in 1950.

After World War II, the average age for couples entering marriage dropped from twenty-four to nineteen. Unlike their parents, many postwar couples had their first children before they turned twenty-one. The combination of social and economic changes meant there were significantly fewer couples dating at the movies. The suburban move altered spending patterns and had a far more profound impact on movie attendance than did television in the early 1950s. In terms of income, there was little left over for movies after mortgage and car payments. When television exploded in the late 1950s, there was even less discretionary income—and less reason to go to the movies.

Television Changes Hollywood

In the late 1940s, radio's popularity had a stronger impact than television on film's apparent decline. Not only were 1948 and 1949 high points in radio listenership, but with the shift to the suburbs, radio entertainment offered Americans an inexpensive alternative to the movies (as it had in the 1930s). As a result, many people stayed home and listened to radio programs until TV assumed this social function in the mid-1950s. Moviegoing was already in steep decline by the time television further eroded the annual number of movie tickets sold, which had peaked at four billion in 1946 but declined and then leveled off at around one billion by 1963.

By the mid-1950s, television had displaced both radio and movies as the medium of national entertainment. With growing legions of people gathering around their living-room TV sets, movie content slowly shifted toward more serious subjects. Although this shift may at first have been a response to the war and an acknowledgment of life's complexity, later movies started to focus on subject matter that television did not encourage. The shift in content began with the rise of film noir in the 1940s but continued into the 1950s as commercial movies, for the first time, explored larger social problems such as alcoholism (*The Lost Weekend*, 1945), anti-Semitism (*Gentleman's Agreement*, 1947), mental illness (*The Snake Pit*, 1948), racism (*Pinky*, 1949), adult–teen relationships (*Rebel without a Cause*, 1955), and drug abuse (*The Man with the Golden Arm*, 1955).

● *Who's Afraid of Virginia Woolf?*

Directors even explored sexual relationships that were formerly off-limits to film (in movies such as *Peyton Place*, 1957; *Butterfield 8*, 1960; and *Lolita*, 1962) and certainly off-limits to viewers of wholesome family television. Filmmakers also challenged the industry's own prohibitive Motion Picture Production Code (see Chapter 16), which had placed restrictions on film content to quiet public and political concerns about the movie business. Like sound recording executives in the early 1990s, movie administrators who worried about government regulation and public boycotts began planning a self-imposed ratings system. The explicit language and situations of *Who's Afraid of Virginia Woolf?* (*above*; 1966), based on an Edward Albee play, led to the formation of the current ratings system in 1967. Nevertheless, filmmakers continued to make movies considered inappropriate for television as a way of holding on to under-thirty audiences, which had become the dominant group of theatergoers. By the 1980s and 1990s, however, with the baby-boom generation growing older and starting families, commercial opportunities emerged for popular feature-length cartoons and family movies, making Disney the most successful contemporary studio.

In terms of technology, Hollywood tried a number of approaches in an effort to appeal to the new TV generation. Technicolor, invented by an MIT scientist in 1917, had gradually improved, and it offered images that far surpassed those on a fuzzy black-and-white TV. Color advancement, though, was not enough for studio chiefs, who were increasingly alarmed by TV's popularity. Just as radio in the 1950s worked to improve sound to maintain an advantage over television, the film industry introduced a host of gimmicks to draw attention to the superiority of movie narratives.

In the early to mid-1950s, Cinerama, CinemaScope, and VistaVision all arrived in movie theaters, featuring striking wide-screen images, multiple synchronized projectors, and stereophonic sound. Then 3-D (three-dimensional) movies appeared, including Warner Brothers' horror film *House of Wax*, wildly popular in its first few weeks in theaters. But, like other experiments, 3-D required a large investment in new projection technology, plus special glasses distributed to all moviegoers. In addition, 3-D suffered from out-of-focus images; it wore off quickly as a novelty. Panavision, which used special Eastman color film and camera lenses that decreased the fuzziness of images, finally became the wide-screen standard throughout the industry. The new gimmicks, however, generally failed to address the movies' primary problem: the middle-class flight to the suburbs, away from downtown theaters.

Hollywood Adapts to Home Entertainment

Just as nickelodeons, movie palaces, and drive-ins transformed movie exhibition in earlier times, the videocassette transformed contemporary movie exhibition. Despite the scope of Technicolor and wide-screen cinema, and despite theaters experimenting with five-story IMAX megascreens and surround sound, most people still prefer the convenience of watching movies at home. In fact, more than 50 percent of domestic revenue for Hollywood studios comes from the video/DVD rental and sales markets. Aside from videocassettes, pay-per-view and premium cable have also stolen parts of the theatergoing crowd, leaving box-office receipts accounting for just 20 percent of total film revenue. With the advent of videocassettes, DVDs, and cable, viewers are no longer required to catch a film in limited theatrical release — they can always view it later on. To keep their edge, TV manufacturers have introduced stereo sets and produced larger TV screens. New digital screens permit image projection the size of a living room wall, more closely replicating a theater experience. As television monitors adopt the 16 : 9 aspect ratio that mimics the film screen (wider than the standard 4 : 3 dimension of television screens), the home video experience feels even more like going to a movie theater.

Even though theater crowds have dwindled over the years, watching movies is a bigger business than ever. Film studios initially feared the coming of television in the 1950s — to the point of banning film actors from performing on the small screen — but television has, ironically, become a major second-run venue for many movies. In similar fashion, the movie industry tried to stall the arrival of the VCR in the 1970s — even filing suits to prohibit consumers from copying movies from television. But home cassette and DVD rentals and purchases have turned into a bonanza for the movie business, extending the profitability of a movie product. For example, *Napoleon Dynamite* (2004) earned $44.5 million in domestic box-office receipts, but earned more than twice that amount from its DVD. "Nowadays," says talent agent John Lesher, "the movies are commercials for the DVDs."[12]

Figure 7.1
DVD Profits and Sales

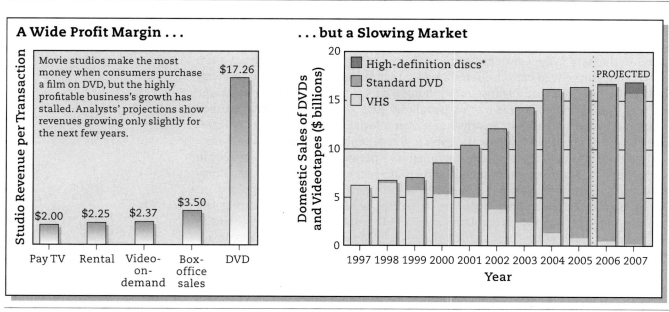

Source: "A Star May Be Fading: As DVD Sales Slow, the Hunt Is on for a New Cash Cow," *New York Times*, June 13, 2006, p. C1.

By 2006, 90 percent of U.S. homes had VCRs and more than 76 percent had DVD players, but Americans rent and watch far more DVDs than videos, making DVDs the leading recorded video format. The 1997 introduction of the DVD helped reinvigorate the flat sales of the home video market as people began to acquire new movie collections on DVD. The growing popularity of DVDs has also made sales of recorded movies outweigh rentals. Yet, the home video retail market maintains an edge over pay-per-view and premium cable channels by offering large libraries of titles. Blockbuster dominates this industry, with more than 5,600 stores in the United States (and 3,300 more stores outside the United States). Its nearest competitor, Movie Gallery/Hollywood Video, has about 4,700 stores. However, the total number of video/DVD stores has decreased in recent years due to competition from general retailers—Wal-Mart is now the number-one seller of videos and DVDs. Online movie rental companies like Netflix have also claimed part of the DVD rental market and have influenced Blockbuster to introduce a similar rental program. But, by 2006, as DVDs saturated the market, DVD sales had begun to slow, leading Hollywood to stake its future on a new format—HD DVD.[13] (See Figure 7.1.)

> **❝When downloading movies becomes an everyday activity, will it be of much use to have a large mail-order DVD rental business like that of Netflix?❞**
>
> —Daniel Akst, *New York Times*, 2005

The Economics of the Movie Business

Despite the development of made-for-TV movies as well as the rise of the network era, cable television, pay-per-view, and home video, the movie business has continued to thrive. In fact, since 1963 Americans have purchased roughly 1 billion movie tickets each year; in 2005 1.4 billion tickets were sold.[14] With first-run movie tickets in some areas rising gradually to more than $10 by 2006, gross revenues from box-office sales had climbed to $8.99 billion, up from $3.8 billion annually in the mid-1980s, as shown in Figure 7.2, but down from a record $9.53 billion in 2004. In addition, video rentals and sales produced another $22 billion a year, more than doubling box-office receipts. To survive and flourish, the movie industry not only followed middle-class migration to the shopping malls but also moved right into suburban homes. In

Figure 7.2
Gross Revenues from Box-Office Sales, 1984–2005

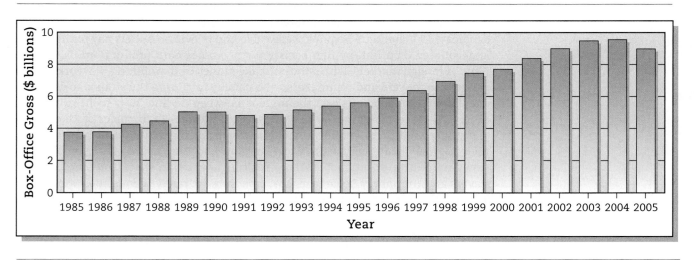

Source: Motion Picture Association of America, *U.S. Market Statistics,* 2005, http://www.mpaa.org. See footnote 14 on this page and in the Notes section at the back of the book.

other words, more people now watch commercial films on home video and DVD players in one month than attend movie theaters for the entire year.

Production, Distribution, and Exhibition Today

It took until the 1970s for the movie industry to determine where the moviegoers had gone and how to catch up with them. Among the major "stars" in this effort were multiscreen movie complexes, called *multiplexes,* located either in shopping malls or at the crossroads of major highways. Throughout the 1970s, attendance by young moviegoers at the new multiplexes made megahits of *The Godfather* (1972), *The Exorcist* (1973), *Jaws* (1975), *Rocky* (1976), and *Star Wars* (1977). During this period, *Jaws* and *Star Wars* became the first movies to gross more than $100 million at the U.S. box office in a single year.

In trying to copy the success of these blockbuster hits, the major studios set in place economic strategies for future decades. With 80 to 90 percent of newly released movies failing to make money at the box office, the studios hoped for at least one major hit each year to offset losses on other films. By the 1980s, though, studios were already recouping box-office losses through the lucrative video (and later the DVD) market, as well as through foreign markets. For example, Steven Spielberg's critically acclaimed *Munich* (2006) earned $47.5 million in U.S. box-office receipts (far less than its estimated $75 million budget), but it went on to earn an additional $80 million in international markets and recorded an overall box-office profit. (See "Media Literacy and the Critical Process: The Blockbuster Mentality" on opposite page.)

At the same time, movie studios were also confronting the high costs of making films. By 2005, a major studio film, on average, cost $60 million to produce. In that same year, marketing, advertising, and print costs averaged about $36.2 million per film, bringing the total average cost for major studio motion pictures to $96.2 million, compared to $82.1 million in 2000.[15]

With climbing film costs, creating revenue from a movie is a formidable task. Studios make money on movies from six major sources. First, the studios get a portion of the theater box-office revenue—about 40 percent of the box-office take goes to the producing studio, with 60 percent going to the theaters. Overall, box-office receipts provide studios with approximately 20 percent of a movie's domestic revenue. Second, about four months after the theatrical release, come the DVD/video sales and rentals "windows," which account for about 60 percent of all domestic-film income for major studios. Third, the film is later released to various cable and television outlets, including pay-per-view channels, video-on-demand channels, premium cable channels (such as HBO), network and basic cable channels, and, finally, the syndicated TV market. The price these cable and television outlets pay to the studios is negotiated on a film-by-film basis. Fourth, studios earn profits from distributing films in foreign markets. Fifth, studios make money by distributing the work of independent producers and filmmakers, who usually must hire the studios to gain wide circulation. Independents pay the studios between 30 and 50 percent of the box-office and video rental money they make from movies. Sixth, major studios are increasingly gaining revenue from merchandise licensing and product placements in their movies. In the earlier days of television and film, characters generally used generic products, or product labels weren't highlighted in shots. For example, Bette Davis's and Humphrey Bogart's cigarette packs were rarely seen in their movies. But with soaring film production costs, product placements are adding extra revenues while lending an element of authenticity to the staging. Famous product placements in movies include Reese's Pieces in *E.T.: The Extra-Terrestrial* (1982), Pepsi-Cola in *Back to the Future II* (1989), Dunkin' Donuts in *Good Will Hunting* (1997), and Samsung wireless phones in *The Matrix: Reloaded* (2003). The high profile of AOL in *You've Got Mail*

> **"** Hollywood may be the only industry that makes more money dumping failed products abroad than it does marketing successful ones at home. **"**
>
> —David Kipen, author of *Screenwriting for a Global Market,* 2004

Media Literacy and the Critical Process

The Blockbuster Mentality

In the beginning of this chapter, we quoted film critic Roger Ebert, who noted Hollywood's shift toward a blockbuster mentality after the success of films like *Star Wars*. How pervasive is this blockbuster mentality, whose characteristics include young adults as the target audience, action-packed big-budget releases, heavy merchandising tie-ins, and the possibility of sequels?

Description. Consider a list of the top twenty-five all-time highest-grossing movies in the United States, such as the one on the Internet Movie Database, http://us.imdb.com/boxoffice/alltimegross.

Analysis. Note patterns in the list. For example, of these twenty-five top-grossing films, twenty-two target young audiences (*Forrest Gump*, *The Sixth Sense*, and *The Passion of the Christ* are the only exceptions). Three-quarters of these top-grossing films feature animated or digitally composited characters (e.g., *Lion King*; *Shrek*; *Jurassic Park* dinosaurs) or extensive special effects (*The Lord of the Rings*; *Spider-Man*). Two-thirds also either spawned or are a part of a series, like *The Lord of the Rings*, *Batman*, and *Harry Potter*. More than half of the films fit into the action movie genre. Nearly all of the top twenty-five had intense merchandising campaigns that featured action figures, fast-food tie-ins, and an incredible variety of products for sale. That is, nearly all weren't "surprise" hits.

Interpretation. What do the patterns mean? It's clear, economically, why Hollywood likes to have successful blockbuster movie franchises. But what kinds of films get left out of the mix? Hits like *Forrest Gump*

and *The Sixth Sense*, which may have had big-budget releases but lack some of the other attributes of blockbusters, are clearly anomalies of the blockbuster mentality, although they illustrate that strong characters and compelling stories can carry a film to great commercial success.

Evaluation. It is likely that we will continue to see an increase in youth-oriented, animated/action movie franchises that are heavily merchandised and intended for wide international distribution. Indeed, Hollywood does not have a lot of motivation to put out other kinds of movies that don't fit these categories. Is this a good thing? Can you think of a film that you thought was excellent and that would have likely been a bigger hit with better promotion and wider distribution? Do you think independent successes like *My Big Fat Greek Wedding*—produced for $5 million and now in the top fifty of highest-grossing films—and *The Passion of the Christ* may mark a change in Hollywood storytelling?

Engagement. Watch independent and foreign films and see what you're missing. Visit the Independent Film section in the Independent Movie Database (http://indie.imdb.com/index.indie) or ForeignFilms.com (http://www.foreignfilms.com) and browse through the many films listed. See if your video store carries any of these titles, and request them if they don't. Make a similar request to your local theater chain. Write your cable company and request to have the Sundance Channel and the Independent Film Channel on your cable lineup. Organize an independent film night on your college campus, and bring these films to a crowd.

(1998) netted between $3 and $6 million for Warner Brothers—the largest product placement deal yet.

Generally, major stars and directors receive separate fees and percentages totaling more than $30 million over and above the production costs for a blockbuster-type movie. Lesser-known actors and directors, assistant producers, screenplay writers, costume and set designers, film editors, music composers, and the cinematographers who physically shoot the movie, however, are paid a flat fee for their work and do not usually share in the net profits from a movie (although DreamWorks, Disney,

Warner Brothers, and Columbia Pictures now write contracts that give cartoon animators and screenwriters a share of a film's profits).

Film exhibition, like distribution, is now controlled by a handful of theater chains. Several major consolidations and extensive theater expansion projects have left the top seven companies operating more than 50 percent of U.S. screens. The major chains—Regal Cinemas, AMC Entertainment, Cinemark USA, Carmike Cinemas, National Amusements, Century Theatres, and Cineplex Entertainment—own thousands of screens each in suburban malls and at highway crossroads, and most have expanded into international markets as well (see Figure 7.3). Because distributors require access to movie screens, they do business with those chains that control the most screens. In a multiplex, an exhibitor can project a potential hit on two or three screens at the same time; films that do not debut well are relegated to the smallest theaters or bumped quickly for a new release.

The strategy of the leading theater chains during the 1990s was to build more megaplexes (facilities with fourteen or more screens), but with upscale concession services and luxurious screening rooms with stadium-style seating and digital sound to make moviegoing a special event. Still, going out to the movies appeals mainly to a specific market of people. Moviegoers between ages twelve and twenty-nine account for about 50 percent of movie theater attendance.

In the past decade, the movie exhibition industry has been tapping into markets that are generally underserved. Notable is the partnership formed between Earvin "Magic" Johnson (formerly of the NBA's Los Angeles Lakers) and what is now AMC Entertainment in the 1990s to build Magic Johnson Theatres in urban minority communities in Los Angeles, Atlanta, Houston, and elsewhere. By building near existing

Figure 7.3
Top Movie Theater Chains in North America

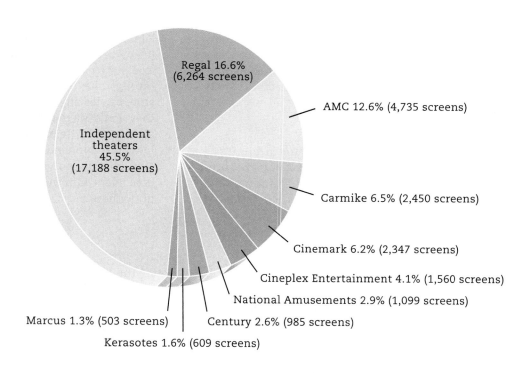

Source: National Association of Theatre Owners, 2006.

shopping areas and hiring from the surrounding community, these state-of-the-art multiplexes provide employment opportunities and foster local economic growth as well as offer entertainment.

Even with record box-office revenues, the major movie theater chains entered the 2000s in miserable financial shape. After several years of fast-paced building and renovations, beginning with a twenty-four-screen AMC megaplex in Dallas in 1995, the major chains had built an excess of screens and accrued an enormous debt. Although the attractive new megaplexes have pleased moviegoers, they have been expensive to build. In 2000, the cost to construct new theaters jumped to $1 million per screen, up from $500,000 per screen just five years earlier. To further combat the home theater market, movie theater chains continued to add IMAX screens to their megaplexes in order to exhibit blockbusters digitally remastered in the big-screen IMAX format.[16] But after closing hundreds of underperforming theaters and with a record finish to the box office in 2001, the movie exhibition business began to recover in 2002 and had grown to a record number (37,740) of indoor screens by 2005.

The Major Players

The American commercial film business and the classic Hollywood narrative remain dominant into the twenty-first century. The industry is ruled primarily by six companies: Warner Brothers, Paramount, Twentieth Century Fox, Universal, Columbia Pictures, and Disney. Except for Disney, all these companies are owned by large parent conglomerates (see Figure 7.4 on page 268). One studio, DreamWorks SKG, created in 1994 by Steven Spielberg, former Disney executive Jeffrey Katzenberg, and sound recording tycoon David Geffen, began to rival the production capabilities of the majors with films like *Shrek 2, Madagascar,* and *Anchorman.* Nevertheless, even DreamWorks could not sustain the high costs of distribution as an independent studio, and after an eleven-year run, sold themselves to Paramount (Viacom) in 2005. The six major studios account for more than 90 percent of the revenue generated by commercial films. They also control more than half the movie market in Europe and Asia, with nearly a third of the industry's annual box-office profits coming from overseas.

In the 1980s, to offset losses resulting from box-office failures, the movie industry began to diversify, expanding into other product lines and other mass media. This expansion included television programming, print media, sound recordings, and home videos/DVDs as well as cable and computers, electronic hardware and software, videocassettes, and theme parks such as Universal Studios. Indicative of the effectiveness of this strategy is the fact that in 1980 more than 80 percent of movie studio revenue came from box-office receipts; today, in contrast, about 20 percent comes from that source.

To maintain the industry's economic stability, management strategies today rely on both heavy advance promotion (which can double the cost of a commercial film) and **synergy**—the promotion and sale of a product throughout the various subsidiaries of the media conglomerate. Companies promote not only the new movie itself but also its book form, soundtrack, calendars, T-shirts, Web site, toy action figures, and "the-making-of" story for distribution on television, cable, and home video. The Disney studio, in particular, has been successful with its multiple packaging of youth-targeted movies, which includes comic books, toys, cable specials, fast-food tie-ins, and new theme-park attractions. Since the 1950s, this synergy has been the biggest change in the film industry and a key element in the flood of corporate mergers.

The first company to change hands in the atmosphere of postwar business mergers was Paramount, which was sold to Gulf & Western Industries in 1966. (Paramount is now owned by Viacom, which originally made its mark by syndicating TV shows.) The next year Transamerica, an insurance and financial services company,

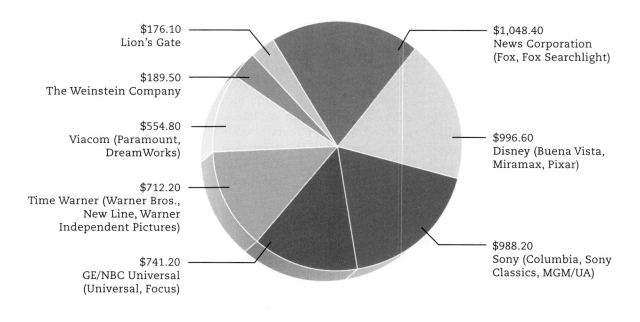

$176.10
Lion's Gate

$189.50
The Weinstein Company

$554.80
Viacom (Paramount,
DreamWorks)

$712.20
Time Warner (Warner Bros.,
New Line, Warner
Independent Pictures)

$741.20
GE/NBC Universal
(Universal, Focus)

$1,048.40
News Corporation
(Fox, Fox Searchlight)

$996.60
Disney (Buena Vista,
Miramax, Pixar)

$988.20
Sony (Columbia, Sony
Classics, MGM/UA)

Note: Based on gross box-office revenue in millions of dollars, for the period January 3, 2006–August 6, 2006. Includes only studios with at least 1 percent share of the domestic theatrical market.

bought United Artists (which merged with MGM in 1981). The biggest mergers, how-ever, have involved the internationalization of the American film business. This began in 1985, when the Australian media conglomerate News Corporation paid nearly $1 billion for Twentieth Century Fox. Along with News Corporation, the new players in Hollywood have been large Japanese electronics firms. First purchased by Coca-Cola in 1980, Columbia Pictures was absorbed by Sony for more than $4 billion in 1989. In the deal, Sony acquired a library of twenty-seven hundred films and twenty-three thousand TV episodes. Universal has changed hands multiple times. In 1990, Matsushita acquired MCA/Universal, and in 1995 sold the majority of its Uni-versal stock to Seagram, the Canadian beverage company. Vivendi, a French utility, acquired Universal in 2000 but suffered through mismanagement and unloaded Uni-versal in 2003 to General Electric, owner of NBC, which had been the only major U.S. television network without an affiliated movie studio. In 2005, Sony bought the neg-lected MGM/UA, mainly for its library of four thousand films. In 2006, Disney followed by buying its computer animation partner Pixar (see Figure 7.5), and Viacom bought the struggling studio, DreamWorks.

Investment in American popular culture by the international electronics indus-try is particularly significant. This business strategy represents a new, high-tech kind of vertical integration — an attempt to control both the production of electronic equipment that consumers buy for their homes and the production/distribution of the content that runs on that equipment. Companies such as Sony in Japan or Philips in the Netherlands have sought to increase markets for their electronics hardware by buying "software," especially movies, recordings, and TV shows.

Even as foreign investment in the U.S. commercial film industry has increased, government policies in many nations have attempted to limit the influence of Amer-

Figure 7.5
Media Ownership: Principal U.S. Operations for the Walt Disney Company

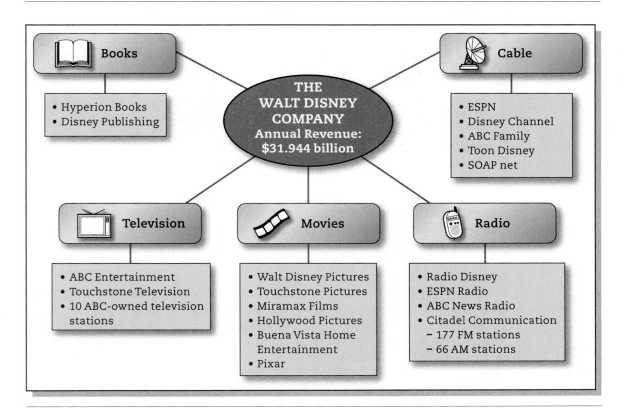

Books
- Hyperion Books
- Disney Publishing

THE WALT DISNEY COMPANY
Annual Revenue: $31.944 billion

Cable
- ESPN
- Disney Channel
- ABC Family
- Toon Disney
- SOAP net

Television
- ABC Entertainment
- Touchstone Television
- 10 ABC-owned television stations

Movies
- Walt Disney Pictures
- Touchstone Pictures
- Miramax Films
- Hollywood Pictures
- Buena Vista Home Entertainment
- Pixar

Radio
- Radio Disney
- ESPN Radio
- ABC News Radio
- Citadel Communication
  - 177 FM stations
  - 66 AM stations

Founded in 1923 as the Disney Brothers Cartoon Studios, the Walt Disney Company is now the second-largest media conglomerate, with more than $31 billion in annual revenue. The company is responsible for such varied operations as the ABC Television Network, the X Games, Touchstone Pictures, Disneyland and Disneyworld, and consumer products like Power Rangers, Baby Einstein, the Disney Princess line, and Mickey Mouse licensed merchandise. With its holdings in movies, television, cable, and its merchandising power, synergistic campaigns can easily take place among Disney companies; can you think of a specific example?

ican films. Restrictions on importing U.S. films and TV programs are intended to promote the domestic film/TV industries in various countries and blunt the impact of U.S. popular culture. In 1989, for example, twelve European countries began placing a 50 percent quota on the amount of time they would allocate for the exhibition of American films and TV shows. With the expansion of cable and satellite-delivered television and movies, however, many countries still depend on inexpensive and abundant U.S. products to fill up channels.

Alternative Voices

The digital revolution in movie production is also a revolution in the cost and accessibility of high-quality production equipment. The revolution is really about a shift from celluloid film to **digital video**, as movie directors replace expensive and bulky 16-mm and 35-mm film cameras

● The aesthetic of cell animation (based on drawings) lost popularity with audiences in the mid-1990s. To hold its reign over the animation market, Disney distributed the films of leading computer animator Pixar and eventually bought the company in 2006. The Disney-Pixar production *Cars* was the most successful animated movie of 2006, with more than $240 million in domestic box office revenues.

with less expensive, lightweight digital video cameras. For moviemakers, digital video also means seeing camerawork instantly instead of waiting for film to be developed, and being able to capture additional footage without concern for the high cost of film stock and processing.

By 2002, a number of major directors began testing the digital video format, including Steven Soderbergh, Spike Lee, Francis Ford Coppola, and Gus Van Sant. George Lucas, an early supporter of digital video with *The Phantom Menace* (1999), went entirely digital for the remaining *Star Wars* episodes, but British director Mike Figgis reached the milestone of the first fully digital release from a major studio with *Time Code* (2000). The impact of the digital format on major movie productions is significant. Lucas estimates that in processing and distribution, digital video will ultimately pare as much as $15 million from the cost of a major motion picture.

But the greatest impact of digital technology is on independent filmmakers. The high cost of film has long acted as a gatekeeper to would-be directors, and only those with generous benefactors or investors have been able to work with the medium. Low-cost digital video opens up the creative process to countless new artists. With digital video camera equipment and computer-based desktop editors, short movies can now be made for just a few thousand dollars, a fraction of what the cost would be on film. For example, the indie hit, *The Blair Witch Project* (1999), was made for about $40,000 with mostly digital equipment and went on to gross more that $141 million in theaters. By 2006, independent filmmakers using digital cameras had clearly shifted from the novelty to the norm, and many directors at venues like the Sundance Film Festival had already upgraded to high definition digital cameras, which rival film's visual quality.

Because digital production puts movies in the same format as DVDs and the Internet, independent filmmakers have new distribution venues beyond the short runs of film festivals. For example, AtomFilms.com, IFILM.com, and YouTube.com have grown into leading Internet sites for the screening and distribution of short films, providing filmmakers with their most valuable asset—an audience.

 ## ★ Popular Movies and Implications for Democracy

Although alternative films may be hard to find, most other movies are readily available today—at the mall, on broadcast and cable television, in campus auditoriums, on DVD, on pay-per-view, and in neighborhood theaters. However flawed, most of these are Hollywood films: the common currency in a global market.

At the cultural level, commercial U.S. films function as **consensus narratives**, a term that describes cultural products that become popular and command wide attention. For all their limitations, classic Hollywood movies, as consensus narratives, provide shared cultural experiences, operating across different times and cultures. In this sense, movies are part of a long narrative tradition, encompassing "the oral-formulaic of Homer's day, the theater of Sophocles, the Elizabethan theater, the English novel from Defoe to Dickens, . . . the silent film, the sound film, and television during the Network Era."[17] Consensus narratives—whether they are dramas, romances, westerns, or mysteries—speak to central myths and values in an accessible language that often bridges global boundaries.

At the international level, countries continue to struggle with questions about the influence of American films on local customs and culture. Like other media industries, the long reach of Hollywood movies is one of the key contradictions of contemporary life: Do such films contribute to a global village in which people throughout the world share a universal culture that breaks down barriers? Or does an American-based common culture stifle the development of local cultures worldwide and diversity in moviemaking? Clearly, the steady production of profitable action/adventure movies—whether they originate in the United States, Africa, France, or China—continues not only because these movies appeal to teens and young adults but also because they translate easily into other languages.

With the rise of international media conglomerates, it has become more difficult to awaken public debate over issues of movie diversity and America's domination of the film business. In addition, technological innovations—whether they affect radio, television, film, cable, or the Internet—tend to outpace questions of legislation and regulation. Consequently, issues concerning greater competition and a better variety of movies sometimes fall by the wayside. As critical consumers, those of us who enjoy movies and recognize their cultural significance must raise these broader issues in public forums as well as in our personal conversations.

www.

For review questions and activities for Chapter 7, go to the interactive *Media and Culture* Online Study Guide at *bedfordstmartins.com/ mediaculture*

REVIEW QUESTIONS

Early Technology and the Evolution of Movies

1. How did film go from the novelty stage to the mass medium stage?

2. Why were early silent films popular?

3. What contribution did nickelodeons make to film history?

The Power of the Studio System

4. Why did Hollywood end up as the center of film production?

5. Why did Thomas Edison and the patents Trust fail to shape and control the film industry, and why did Adolph Zukor of Paramount succeed?

6. How does vertical integration work in the film business?

The Triumph of Hollywood Storytelling

7. Why did a certain structure of film—called classic Hollywood narrative—become so dominant in moviemaking?

8. Why are genres and directors important to the film industry?

9. Why are documentaries an important alternative to traditional Hollywood filmmaking? What contributions have they made to the film industry?

The Transformation of the Hollywood System

10. What political and cultural forces changed the Hollywood system in the 1950s?

11. Explain how home entertainment changed the film industry.

12. How has the movie industry used television to its advantage?

The Economics of the Movie Business

13. What are the various ways in which major movie studios make money from the film business?

14. How do a few large film studios manage to control more than 90 percent of the commercial industry?

15. Why do U.S. movies remain popular worldwide while other countries have great difficulty getting their films into the United States?

16. What is the current economic health of the movie industry, compared to previous eras?

Popular Movies and Implications for Democracy

17. Do films contribute to a global village in which people throughout the world share a universal culture? Or do U.S.-based films overwhelm the development of other cultures worldwide? Discuss.

QUESTIONING THE MEDIA

1. Describe your earliest memory of going to a movie. Do some research and compare this with a parent's or grandparent's earliest memory. Compare the different experiences.

2. Do you remember seeing a movie you were not allowed to see? Discuss the experience.

3. How often do you go to movie theaters today? How often do you rent movies on video or DVD? Which experience do you prefer and why?

4. If you were a Hollywood film producer or executive, what kinds of films would you like to see made? What changes would you make in what we see at the movies?

5. Look at the international film box-office statistics in the latest issue of *Variety* magazine. Note which films are the most popular worldwide. What do you think about the significant role U.S. movies play in global culture? Should their role be less significant? Explain your answer.

SEARCHING THE INTERNET

http://us.imdb.com

The Internet Movie Database is a powerful, searchable movie database of hundreds of thousands of film titles.

http://www.rottentomatoes.com

An extensive movie review Web site that gives "fresh" or "rotten" tomato ratings to current releases and maintains a database of more than 170,000 reviews.

http://www.foreignfilms.com

A comprehensive Web site featuring news and information about classic foreign titles and the latest art-house releases.

http://www.aint-it-cool-news.com

Movie reviews and humorous, critical industry-insider accounts written by Texas-based Harry Knowles.

http://movieweb.com

Movieweb contains listings of theatrical release dates, as well as weekly box-office rankings.

http://www.indiewire.com

News about independent films and do-it-yourself moviemaking information.

http://www.sundance.org

Information on the Sundance Film Festival, and a searchable database of independent films.

http://www.brandhype.org

A critical Web resource that documents product placement in the movies.

Media Literacy
and the Critical Process

In Brief

In class, make a tally of who prefers to attend movies in the theater and who prefers to watch movies at home on DVD or video. Discuss the advantages and disadvantages of both viewing habits. Discuss whether theatergoing will become obsolete in the next decade, given that increasingly more revenue is earned through video release than through box-office receipts.

What could be done to enhance moviegoing in theaters? Make a list. How might your ideas be reasonably financed? Would there be a payoff for theater owners?

In Depth

Pick a current popular film you have seen or one the class has seen together. Write a three- to four-page (750–1,000 word) movie critique either defending or attacking the movie as a form of popular culture (see Chapter 1). Include plenty of examples to support your argument, and focus on three or four significant points. Follow the five stages of the critical process to organize your critique:

Description. In preparing to write your paper, describe important plot, theme, or character points that are relevant to your argument. (This is essentially the note-taking part of your paper.)

Analysis. Analyze the particular patterns (the three or four significant points) that emerge from your Description step and that you have chosen to examine.

Interpretation. Interpret what all of this information might mean based on the evidence you provide.

Evaluation. Discuss the limits of your critique and offer evaluations of the film industry based on your evidence and your interpretations. Evaluate the movie by judging whether it works as high art or as popular culture.

Engagement. Does your critique of the movie differ substantially from published reviews in local or national newspapers and magazines, or a Web page (try Movie Review Query Engine, http://www.mrqe.com)? Use the evidence from your critique to present your interpretation of the film in a written response to a published review.

KEY TERMS

celluloid, 237
kinetograph, 237
kinetoscope, 237
vitascope, 238
narrative films, 238
nickelodeons, 239
vertical integration, 240
oligopoly, 240
studio system, 241

block booking, 242
movie palace, 243
multiplexes, 244
Big Five/Little Three, 244
talkies, 244
newsreels, 246
blockbuster, 247
genre, 247
documentary, 254

cinema verité, 254
indies, 256
megaplexes, 258
Hollywood Ten, 258
Paramount decision, 259
synergy, 267
digital video, 269
consensus narratives, 270

newspapers

and the rise of modern journalism

In 1887, a young reporter left her job at the *Pittsburgh Dispatch* to seek her fortune in New York City. Only twenty-three years old, Elizabeth "Pink" Cochrane had grown tired of writing for the society pages and answering letters to the editor. She wanted to be on the front page. But at that time, it was considered "unladylike" for women journalists to use their real names, so the *Dispatch* editors, borrowing from a Stephen Foster song, had dubbed her "Nellie Bly."

After four months of persistent job-hunting and freelance writing, Nellie Bly earned a tryout at Joseph Pulitzer's *New York World,* the nation's biggest paper. Her assignment: to investigate the deplorable conditions at the Women's Lunatic Asylum on Blackwell's Island. Her method: to get herself declared mad and committed to the asylum. After practicing the look of a disheveled lunatic in front of mirrors, wandering city streets unwashed and seemingly dazed, and terrifying her fellow boarders in a New York rooming house by acting crazy, she succeeded in convincing doctors and officials to commit her. Other New York

newspapers even reported her incarceration, speculating on the identity of this "mysterious waif," this "pretty crazy girl" with the "wild, hunted look in her eyes."[1]

Ten days later, an attorney from the *World* went in to get her out. Her two-part story appeared in October 1887 and caused a sensation. She was the first reporter to pull off such a stunt. In the days before so-called objective journalism, Nellie Bly's dramatic first-person accounts documented harsh cold baths ("three buckets of water over my head—ice cold water—into my eyes, my ears, my nose and my mouth"); attendants who abused and taunted patients; and newly arrived immigrant women, completely sane, who were committed to this "rat trap" simply because no one could understand them. After the series, Bly was famous. Pulitzer gave her a permanent job, and the city of New York committed $1 million toward upgrading the conditions of its asylums.

Within a year, Nellie Bly had exposed a variety of shady scam artists, corrupt politicians and lobbyists, and unscrupulous business practices. Posing as an unwed mother with an unwanted child, she uncovered an outfit trafficking in newborn babies. Disguised as a sinner in need of reform, she revealed the appalling conditions at a home for "unfortunate women." And after stealing fifty dollars from another woman's purse, she got herself arrested and then reported on how women were treated in New York jails.

A lifetime champion of women and the poor, Nellie Bly pioneered what was then called *detective* or *stunt* journalism. Her work inspired the twentieth-century practice of investigative journalism—from Ida Tarbell's exposés of oil corporations in the early 1900s to the 2006 Pulitzer Prize for investigative reporting—awarded to the *Washington Post* for its probe of lobbyist Jack Abramoff, exposing Congressional corruption and spurring lobby reform.

But such journalism can also be dangerous work. Working for Dublin's *Sunday Independent*, Veronica Guerin was the first reporter to cover in depth Ireland's escalating organized crime and drug problem. In 1995, a man forced his way into her home and shot her in the thigh. After the assault, she wrote about the incident, vowing to continue her reporting despite her fears. She was also punched in the face by the suspected head of Ireland's gang scene, who threatened to hurt Guerin's son and kill her if she wrote about him. She kept writing. In December 1995, she flew to New York to receive the International Press Freedom Award from the Committee to Protect Journalists.

When Guerin returned to Dublin, in her stories she began naming names of gang members suspected of masterminding drug-related crimes and a string of eleven unsolved contract murders. Then, in June 1996, while stopped in her car at a Dublin intersection, she was shot five times by two hired killers on a motorcycle. She had become contract murder victim number twelve. Ireland mourned Veronica Guerin's death for days. After her funeral, the government invoked her name, passing laws that allowed judges to deny bail to dangerous suspects and creating a bureau to confiscate money and property from suspected drug criminals and gang members.

a long with their investigative role, newspapers play many parts in contemporary culture. As chroniclers of daily life, newspapers both inform and entertain. They give assurances that communities are safe and nations are secure. Newspapers help readers make choices about everything from the kind of food to eat to the kind of leaders to elect. Comic strips and political cartoons find humor in everyday events. Opinion pages organize public debates and offer differing points of view. Syndicated columnists offer everything from advice on raising children to opinion on the U.S. role as economic and military superpower.

Despite the importance of newspapers in daily life, in today's digital age the industry is losing both papers and readers at an alarming rate. Newspapers still garner a substantial portion of the nation's advertising dollars, but the loss of papers and readers raises significant concerns in a nation where daily news has historically functioned as a watchdog over democratic life. To provide some background for the current declines, we will trace the history of newspapers through a number of influential periods and styles. We will explore the eras of the early political-commercial press, the penny press, and yellow journalism. Turning to the modern era, we will examine the influence of the *New York Times* and twentieth-century journalism's embrace of objectivity. During this era, interpretive journalism emerged in the 1920s and 1930s to improve news practices, and the revival of literary journalism followed in the 1960s. We will also look at the evolution of contemporary newspapers and examine different ways of categorizing them. Finally, we will review issues of chain ownership, new technology, and the crucial role of newspapers in our democracy.

> **"** There's almost no media experience sweeter . . . than poring over a good newspaper. In the quiet morning, with a cup of coffee — so long as you haven't turned on the TV, listened to the radio, or checked in online — it's as comfortable and personal as information gets. **"**
>
> —Jon Katz,
> *Wired* magazine, 1994

The Evolution of American Newspapers

The idea of news is as old as language itself. The earliest news was passed along orally from family to family, from tribe to tribe, by community leaders and oral historians. The first written news accounts, or *news sheets,* were probably posted items distributed by local rulers and governments. The earliest known news sheet, *Acta Diurna* (Latin for "daily events"), was developed by Julius Caesar and posted in Rome in 59 B.C. Even in its oral and early written stages, news informed people on the state of their relations with neighboring tribes and towns. The development of the printing press in the fifteenth century greatly accelerated a society's ability to send and receive information. Throughout history, news has satisfied our need to know things we cannot experience personally. Newspapers today continue to document daily life and bear witness to both ordinary and extraordinary events.

Colonial Newspapers and the Partisan Press

The first newspaper produced in North America was *Publick Occurrences, Both Foreign and Domestick,* published on September 25, 1690, by Boston printer Benjamin Harris. The colonial government objected to Harris's negative tone regarding British rule, and local ministers were offended by a report that the king of France had had an affair with his son's wife. The newspaper was banned after one issue.

In 1704, the first regularly published newspaper appeared in the American colonies—the *Boston News-Letter,* published by John Campbell. Considered dull, it reported on mundane events that had taken place in Europe months earlier. Because European news took weeks to travel by ship, these early colonial papers were not very timely. In their more spirited sections, however, the papers did report local illnesses, public floggings, and even suicides. In 1721, also in Boston, James Franklin,

> **"** Oral news systems must have arrived early in the development of language, some tens or even hundreds of thousands of years ago. . . . And the dissemination of news accomplishes some of the basic purposes of language: informing others, entertaining others, protecting the tribe. **"**
>
> —Mitchell Stephens,
> *A History of News,* 1988

During the colonial period, New York printer John Peter Zenger was arrested for libel. He eventually won his case, which established the precedent that today allows U.S. journalists and citizens to criticize public officials. In this 1734 issue, Zenger's *New-York Weekly Journal* reported his own arrest and the burning of the paper by the city's "Common Hangman."

the older brother of Benjamin Franklin, started the *New England Courant*. The *Courant* established a tradition of running stories that interested ordinary readers rather than printing articles that appealed primarily to business and colonial leaders. In 1729, Benjamin Franklin, at age twenty-four, took over the *Pennsylvania Gazette,* which historians rate among the best of the colonial papers. Although a number of colonial papers operated solely on subsidies from political parties, the *Gazette* also made money by advertising products.

Another important colonial paper was the *New-York Weekly Journal,* which appeared in 1733. John Peter Zenger had been installed as the printer of the *Journal* by the Popular Party, a political group that opposed British rule and ran articles that criticized the royal governor of New York. After a Popular Party judge was dismissed from office, the *Journal* escalated its attack on the governor. When Zenger shielded the writers of the critical articles, he was arrested in 1734 for *seditious libel*—defaming a public official's character in print. Championed by famed Philadelphia lawyer Andrew Hamilton, Zenger ultimately won his case in 1735. A sympathetic jury, in revolt against the colonial government, ruled that newspapers had the right to criticize government leaders as long as the reports were true. After the Zenger case, the British never prosecuted another colonial printer. Although the case did not substantially change sedition laws at the time, the Zenger decision would later provide a key foundation for the First Amendment to the Constitution—the right of a democratic press to criticize public officials.

By 1765, about thirty newspapers operated in the American colonies. The first *daily* paper began in 1784. These papers were of two general types: political or commercial. The development of both types was shaped in large part by social, cultural, and political responses to British rule and by its eventual overthrow. The gradual rise of political parties and the spread of commerce also played a significant role in the development of these early papers. Although the political and commercial papers carried both party news and business news, they had different agendas. Political papers, known as **partisan press**, generally pushed the plan of the particular political group that subsidized the paper. The commercial press, on the other hand, served the leaders of commerce, who were interested in economic issues. Both types of

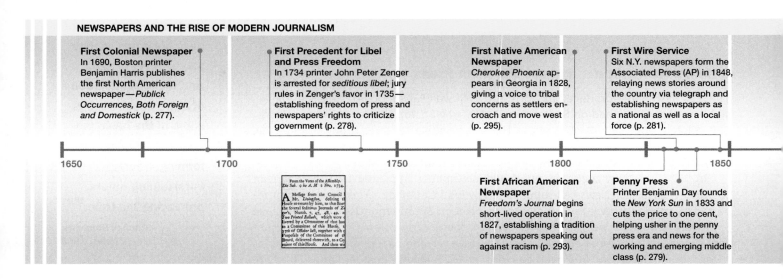

NEWSPAPERS AND THE RISE OF MODERN JOURNALISM

First Colonial Newspaper
In 1690, Boston printer Benjamin Harris publishes the first North American newspaper—*Publick Occurrences, Both Foreign and Domestick* (p. 277).

First Precedent for Libel and Press Freedom
In 1734 printer John Peter Zenger is arrested for *seditious libel*; jury rules in Zenger's favor in 1735—establishing freedom of press and newspapers' rights to criticize government (p. 278).

First Native American Newspaper
Cherokee Phoenix appears in Georgia in 1828, giving a voice to tribal concerns as settlers encroach and move west (p. 295).

First Wire Service
Six N.Y. newspapers form the Associated Press (AP) in 1848, relaying news stories around the country via telegraph and establishing newspapers as a national as well as a local force (p. 281).

1650   1700   1750   1800   1850

First African American Newspaper
Freedom's Journal begins short-lived operation in 1827, establishing a tradition of newspapers speaking out against racism (p. 293).

Penny Press
Printer Benjamin Day founds the *New York Sun* in 1833 and cuts the price to one cent, helping usher in the penny press era and news for the working and emerging middle class (p. 279).

journalism left a legacy. The partisan press gave us the editorial pages, and the early commercial press was the forerunner of the business section in modern papers.

From the early 1700s to the early 1800s, even the largest of these papers rarely reached a circulation of 1,500. Readership was confined primarily to educated or wealthy men who controlled local politics and commerce. During this time, though, a few pioneering women operated newspapers, including Elizabeth Timothy, the first American woman newspaper publisher and a mother of eight children. After her husband died of smallpox in 1738, Timothy took over the *South Carolina Gazette*, established in 1734 by Benjamin Franklin and the Timothy family. Also during this period, Anna Maul Zenger ran the *New-York Weekly Journal* throughout her husband's trial and after his death in 1746.[2] In general, though, the interests of women readers were not well addressed by either the political or the commercial press. By the 1830s, however, the Industrial Revolution and the rise of the middle classes had spurred the growth of literacy and set the stage for a more popular and inclusive press.

The Penny Press Era: Newspapers Become Mass Media

By the late 1820s, the average newspaper cost six cents a copy and was sold not through street sales but through yearly subscriptions priced at ten to twelve dollars. Because that price represented more than a week's salary for most skilled workers, newspaper readers were mostly affluent. The Industrial Revolution, however, spawned the conversion from expensive handmade to inexpensive machine-made paper. And when cheaper paper combined with increased literacy, **penny papers** soon began competing with conventional six-cent papers. In the 1820s, breakthroughs in technology, particularly steam-powered presses replacing mechanical presses, permitted publishers to produce as many as 4,000 newspapers an hour. Subscriptions remained the preferred sales tool of many penny papers, although they began relying increasingly on daily street sales.

In 1833, printer Benjamin Day founded the *New York Sun*. After cutting the price to one penny, he also eliminated subscriptions. The *Sun* (whose slogan was "It shines for all") highlighted local events, scandals, and police reports. It also ran serialized stories, making legends of frontiersmen Davy Crockett and Daniel Boone and blazing the trail for the media's twentieth-century enthusiasm for celebrity news. In the tradition of today's tabloids, the *Sun* fabricated stories, including the famous moon hoax, which reported "scientific" evidence of life on the moon. Within six months, the *Sun*'s lower price had generated a circulation of eight thousand, twice that of its nearest competitor.

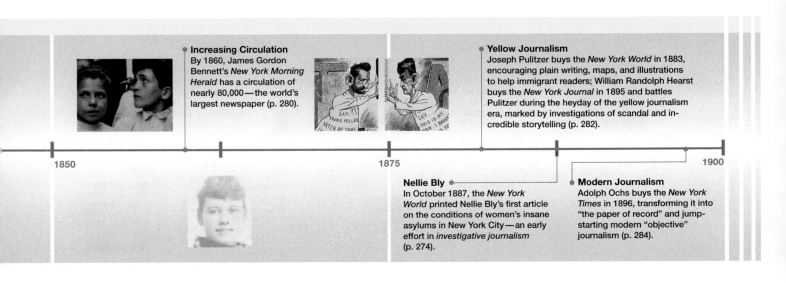

Increasing Circulation
By 1860, James Gordon Bennett's *New York Morning Herald* has a circulation of nearly 80,000—the world's largest newspaper (p. 280).

Yellow Journalism
Joseph Pulitzer buys the *New York World* in 1883, encouraging plain writing, maps, and illustrations to help immigrant readers; William Randolph Hearst buys the *New York Journal* in 1895 and battles Pulitzer during the heyday of the yellow journalism era, marked by investigations of scandal and incredible storytelling (p. 282).

1850   1875   1900

Nellie Bly
In October 1887, the *New York World* printed Nellie Bly's first article on the conditions of women's insane asylums in New York City—an early effort in *investigative journalism* (p. 274).

Modern Journalism
Adolph Ochs buys the *New York Times* in 1896, transforming it into "the paper of record" and jumpstarting modern "objective" journalism (p. 284).

● Newsboys sold Hearst and Pulitzer papers on the streets of New York in the 1890s. With more than a dozen dailies competing, street tactics were ferocious, and publishers often made young "newsies" buy the papers they could not sell.

The *Sun*'s success initiated a wave of penny papers that favored **human-interest stories**: news accounts that focus on the daily trials and triumphs of the human condition, often featuring ordinary individuals facing extraordinary challenges. These kinds of stories reveal journalism's ties to literary traditions (which today can be found in the horror or gangster news story genres of drug and crime coverage).

The penny press era also featured James Gordon Bennett's *New York Morning Herald,* founded in 1835. Bennett, considered the first U.S. press baron, aimed to free his newspaper from political parties. He wanted to establish an independent paper serving middle- and working-class readers as well as his own business ambitions. The *Herald* carried political essays and scandals, business stories, a letters section, fash-

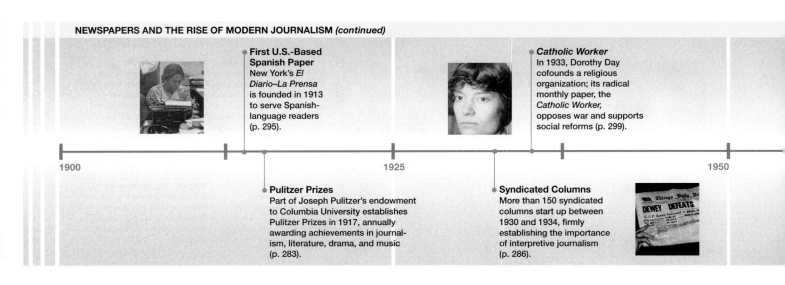

NEWSPAPERS AND THE RISE OF MODERN JOURNALISM *(continued)*

● **First U.S.-Based Spanish Paper**
New York's *El Diario–La Prensa* is founded in 1913 to serve Spanish-language readers (p. 295).

● *Catholic Worker*
In 1933, Dorothy Day cofounds a religious organization; its radical monthly paper, the *Catholic Worker,* opposes war and supports social reforms (p. 299).

1900

1925

1950

● **Pulitzer Prizes**
Part of Joseph Pulitzer's endowment to Columbia University establishes Pulitzer Prizes in 1917, annually awarding achievements in journalism, literature, drama, and music (p. 283).

● **Syndicated Columns**
More than 150 syndicated columns start up between 1930 and 1934, firmly establishing the importance of interpretive journalism (p. 286).

ion notes, moral reflections, religious news, society gossip, colloquial tales and jokes, sports stories, and later, reports from correspondents sent to cover the Civil War. In an era before modern "objective" journalism, Bennett's paper sponsored balloon races, financed safaris, and overplayed crime stories. After his first visit to America in the early 1840s, British writer Charles Dickens used the Herald as a model for the sleazy *Rowdy Journal*, the fictional newspaper in his novel *Martin Chuzzlewit*. By 1860, the *Herald* reached nearly eighty thousand readers, making it the world's largest daily paper at the time.

The penny papers were innovative. For example, they were the first to assign reporters to cover crime. In New York, where the penny press competition was fierce, readers enthusiastically embraced the reporting of local news and crime. By gradually separating daily front-page reporting from overt political viewpoints on an editorial page, New York's penny papers shifted their economic base from political party subsidies to the market—to advertising revenue, classified ads, and street sales. Although many partisan papers took a moral stand against advertising certain questionable products, the penny press became more neutral toward advertisers and printed virtually any ad. In fact, many penny papers regarded advertising as a kind of consumer news. The rise in ad revenues and circulation accelerated the growth of the newspaper industry. In 1830, 650 weekly and 65 daily papers operated in the United States, reaching 80,000 readers. By 1840, a total of 1,140 weeklies and 140 dailies attracted 300,000 readers.

In 1848, six New York newspapers formed a cooperative arrangement and founded the Associated Press (AP), the first major news wire service. **Wire services** began as commercial organizations that relayed news stories and information around the country and the world using telegraph lines and, later, radio waves and digital transmissions. In the case of the AP, the New York papers provided access to both their own stories and those from other newspapers. In the 1850s, papers started sending reporters to cover Washington, D.C., and in the early 1860s more than a hundred reporters from northern papers went south to cover the Civil War, relaying their reports back to their home papers via telegraph and wire services. The news wire companies enabled news to travel rapidly from coast to coast and set the stage for modern journalism.

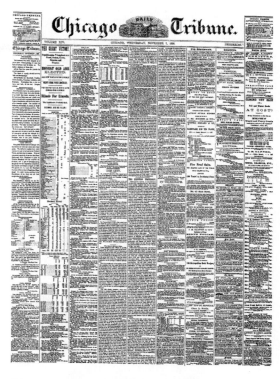

● Launched in June 1847, the Midwest's first great newspaper was probably the *Chicago Tribune*. In October 1871, the Great Chicago Fire destroyed most of the city and the *Tribune*'s original wooden building. But the *Tribune* missed only two days, reappearing with an editorial proclaiming "Chicago Shall Rise Again." The paper's editor, Joseph Medill, was elected mayor and led the city's comeback and reconstruction. In 1924 the *Tribune* launched Chicago's WGN Radio, its call letters reflecting the *Tribune* slogan, "World's Greatest Newspaper." The headline from the paper above announces Abraham Lincoln's election to president in 1860.

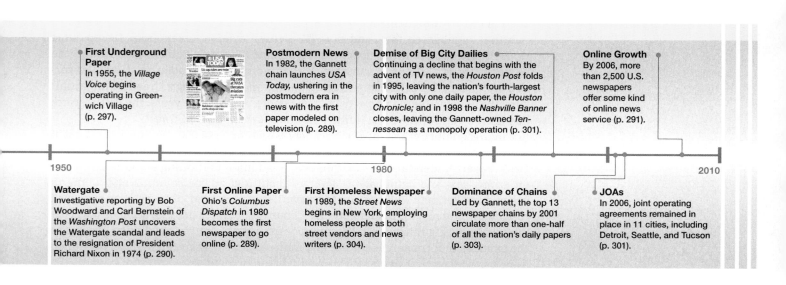

First Underground Paper
In 1955, the *Village Voice* begins operating in Greenwich Village (p. 297).

Postmodern News
In 1982, the Gannett chain launches *USA Today*, ushering in the postmodern era in news with the first paper modeled on television (p. 289).

Demise of Big City Dailies
Continuing a decline that begins with the advent of TV news, the *Houston Post* folds in 1995, leaving the nation's fourth-largest city with only one daily paper, the *Houston Chronicle*; and in 1998 the *Nashville Banner* closes, leaving the Gannett-owned *Tennessean* as a monopoly operation (p. 301).

Online Growth
By 2006, more than 2,500 U.S. newspapers offer some kind of online news service (p. 291).

1950 — 1980 — 2010

Watergate
Investigative reporting by Bob Woodward and Carl Bernstein of the *Washington Post* uncovers the Watergate scandal and leads to the resignation of President Richard Nixon in 1974 (p. 290).

First Online Paper
Ohio's *Columbus Dispatch* in 1980 becomes the first newspaper to go online (p. 289).

First Homeless Newspaper
In 1989, the *Street News* begins in New York, employing homeless people as both street vendors and news writers (p. 304).

Dominance of Chains
Led by Gannett, the top 13 newspaper chains by 2001 circulate more than one-half of all the nation's daily papers (p. 303).

JOAs
In 2006, joint operating agreements remained in place in 11 cities, including Detroit, Seattle, and Tucson (p. 301).

The combination of marketing news as a national and global product and using modern technology to dramatically cut costs gradually elevated newspapers to the status of a mass medium. By also adapting news content, penny papers captured the middle- and working-class readers who could now afford the paper and also had more leisure time to read it. As newspapers sought to sustain their mass appeal, news and "factual" reports about crimes and other items of human interest eventually superseded the importance of partisan articles about politics and commerce.

The Age of Yellow Journalism: Sensationalism and Investigation

The rise of competitive dailies and the penny press triggered the next significant period in American journalism. Labeled the era of **yellow journalism**, this late 1800s development emphasized profitable papers that carried exciting human-interest stories, crime news, large headlines, and more readable copy. This period is generally regarded as the age of sensationalism, the direct forerunner of today's tabloid papers, reality TV, and TV magazine shows like *Access Hollywood*. The era of yellow journalism featured two major characteristics. First were the overly dramatic—or sensational—stories about crimes, celebrities, disasters, scandals, and intrigue. The second, and sometimes forgotten, legacy is that the yellow press provided the roots for investigative journalism: news reports that hunted out and exposed corruption, particularly in business and government. Reporting increasingly became a crusading force for common people, with the press assuming a watchdog role on behalf of the public.

During this period, a newspaper circulation war pitted William Randolph Hearst's *New York Journal* against Joseph Pulitzer's *New York World*. A key player in the war was the first popular cartoon strip, *The Yellow Kid*, created in 1895 by artist R. F. Outcault, who once worked for Thomas Edison. The phrase *yellow journalism* has since become associated with the cartoon strip, which shuttled between the Hearst and Pulitzer papers during their furious battle for readers in the mid- to late 1890s.

Pulitzer and the *New York World*

After a brief venture into St. Louis politics, Joseph Pulitzer, a Jewish-Hungarian immigrant, began his career in newspaper publishing in the early 1870s as part owner of the *St. Louis Post*. He then bought the bankrupt *St. Louis Dispatch* for $2,500 at an auction in 1878 and merged it with the *Post*. The *Post-Dispatch* became known for stories that highlighted "sex and sin" ("A Denver Maiden Taken from Disreputable House") and satires of the upper class ("St. Louis Swells"). Pulitzer also viewed the *Post-Dispatch* as a "national conscience" that promoted the public good. Pulitzer carried on the legacies of Bennett: making money and developing a "free and impartial" paper that would "serve no party but the people." Within five years, the *Post-Dispatch* had become one of the most influential newspapers in the Midwest.

In 1883, Pulitzer bought the *New York World* for $346,000. He encouraged plain writing and the inclusion of maps and illustrations to help immigrant and working-class readers understand the written text. In addition to running sensational stories on crime, sex, and cannibalism, Pulitzer instituted advice columns and women's pages. Like Bennett, Pulitzer treated advertising as a kind of news that displayed consumer products for readers. In fact, department stores became a major advertising source during this period. The revenue from these stores contributed directly to the expansion of consumer culture and indirectly to the acknowledgment of women as newspaper readers and to their eventual employment as reporters.

● The *World* (top) and the *New York Journal* (bottom) cover the same story in May 1898.

The *World* reflected the contradictory spirit of the yellow press. It crusaded for improved urban housing, better conditions for women, and equitable labor laws. It campaigned against monopoly practices by AT&T, Standard Oil, and Equitable Insurance. Such popular crusades helped lay the groundwork for tightening federal antitrust laws in the early 1910s. At the same time, Pulitzer's paper manufactured news events and staged stunts, such as sending star reporter Nellie Bly around the world in seventy-two days to beat the fictional "record" in the popular 1873 Jules Verne novel *Around the World in Eighty Days.*

Pulitzer created a lasting legacy by leaving $2 million to establish the graduate school of journalism at Columbia University in 1912. In 1917, part of Pulitzer's Columbia endowment launched the Pulitzer Prizes, the prestigious awards given each year for achievements in journalism, literature, drama, and music.

Hearst and the *New York Journal*

By 1887, the *World*'s Sunday circulation had soared to more than 250,000, the largest in the world. Eight years later, however, the paper faced its fiercest competition when William Randolph Hearst bought the *New York Journal*. Before moving to New York, Hearst had taken the reins of the *San Francisco Examiner* from his father, George Hearst, who had purchased the paper to further a political career. In 1887, when George was elected to the U.S. Senate, he turned the paper over to his twenty-four-year-old son, who had recently been expelled from Harvard for a practical joke he played on his professors. In 1895, with an inheritance from his father, Hearst bought the ailing *New York Journal* (a penny paper founded by Pulitzer's brother Albert) and then raided Joseph Pulitzer's paper for editors, writers, and cartoonists.

Taking his cue from Bennett and Pulitzer, Hearst focused on lurid, sensational stories and appealed (and pandered) to immigrant readers by using large headlines and bold layout designs. To boost circulation, the *Journal* invented interviews, faked pictures, and encouraged conflicts that might result in a story. One account of Hearst's tabloid legacy describes "tales about two-headed virgins" and "prehistoric creatures roaming the plains of Wyoming."[3] In promoting journalism as storytelling, Hearst reportedly said, "The modern editor of the popular journal does not care for facts. The editor wants novelty. The editor has no objection to facts if they are also novel. But he would prefer a novelty that is not a fact to a fact that is not a novelty."[4]

Hearst is remembered as an unscrupulous publisher who once hired gangsters to distribute his newspapers. He was also, however, considered a champion of the underdog, and his paper's readership soared among the working and middle classes. In 1896, the *Journal*'s daily circulation reached 450,000, and by 1897 the Sunday edition of the paper rivaled the 600,000 circulation of the *World*. By the 1930s, Hearst's holdings

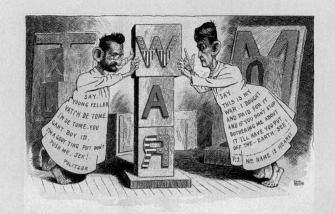

● Generally considered America's first comic-strip character, the Yellow Kid was created in the mid-1890s by cartoonist Richard Outcault. The cartoon was so popular that newspaper barons Joseph Pulitzer and William Randolph Hearst fought over Outcault's services, giving yellow journalism its name.

66 **There is room in this great and growing city for a journal that is not only cheap but bright, not only bright but large . . . that will expose all fraud and sham, fight all public evils and abuses — that will serve and battle for the people.** 99

–Joseph Pulitzer, publisher,
New York World, 1883

included more than forty daily and Sunday papers, thirteen magazines (including *Good Housekeeping* and *Cosmopolitan*), eight radio stations, and two film companies. In addition, he controlled King Features Syndicate, which sold and distributed articles, comics, and features to many of the nation's 2,500 dailies. Hearst, the model for Charles Foster Kane, the ruthless and lonely publisher in Orson Welles's classic 1940 film *Citizen Kane,* operated the largest media business in the world—the Time Warner of its day.

Competing Models of Modern Print Journalism

Over the years, the methods that journalists have used to convey information have varied. The early commercial and partisan presses were, to some extent, covering important events impartially. These papers often carried verbatim reports of presidential addresses, murder trials, or the annual statements of the U.S. Treasury. In the late 1800s, as newspapers pushed for greater circulation, newspaper reporting changed. Two distinct types of journalism were competing for readers: The penny papers and the yellow press focused on a story-driven model, dramatizing important events; the six-cent papers emphasized "the facts," an approach that appeared to package information more impartially.[5] Over the years, journalism has continued to try different ways to convey stories and information. Overriding these efforts has been the notion of whether, in journalism, there is an ideal, attainable objective model or whether the quest to be objective actually conflicts with the traditional role of journalists to raise important questions about the abuses of power in a democratic society.

● This 1936 scene reveals the newsroom of Harlem's *Amsterdam News,* one of the nation's leading African American newspapers. Ironically, the Civil Rights movement and affirmative action policies in the 1960s "helped" drain talented reporters from the black press by encouraging them to work for mainstream white newspapers.

"Objectivity" in Modern Journalism

As the consumer marketplace expanded during the Industrial Revolution, facts and news became marketable products that could be sold to consumers. Throughout the mid-1800s, the more a newspaper appeared not to take sides, the more its readership base could be extended (although editorial pages were often rabidly supportive of particular political candidates). In addition, wire service organizations were serving a variety of newspaper clients in different regions of the country. To satisfy all their clients and the wide range of political views, newspapers began at least to look more impartial.

Ochs and the *New York Times*

The ideal of an impartial, or purely informational, news model was reinvented by Adolph Ochs, who bought the *New York Times* in 1896. The son of immigrant German Jews, Ochs grew up in Ohio and Tennessee, where at age twenty-one he took over the *Chattanooga Times* in 1878. Known more for his business and organizational ability

● Table 8.1 The Nation's 10 Largest Daily Newspapers

Newspaper	2006 Average Weekday Circulation*	Newspaper	2006 Average Weekday Circulation*
USA Today	2,272,815	(New York) Daily News	708,477
Wall Street Journal	2,049,786	New York Post	673,379
New York Times	1,142,464	Chicago Tribune	579,079
Los Angeles Times	851,832	Houston Chronicle	513,387
Washington Post	724,242	Arizona Republic	438,722

Source: Audit Bureau of Circulations; Los Angeles Times, May 9, 2006.
*Average for six months ending March 31, 2006.

than for his writing and editing skills, he transformed the Tennessee paper. Ochs then moved to New York and invested $75,000 in the struggling *Times*. Through wise hiring, Ochs's staff of editors rebuilt the paper around substantial news coverage and provocative editorial pages. To distance themselves from the yellow press, the editors also downplayed sensational stories, favoring the documentation of major events or issues.

Such distancing was partly a marketing strategy to counter the large circulations of the Hearst and Pulitzer papers. Ochs offered a distinct contrast to the more sensational newspapers: an informational paper that provided stock and real estate reports to businesses, court reports to legal professionals, treaty summaries to political leaders, and theater and book reviews to intellectuals. Ochs's promotional gimmicks took direct aim at yellow journalism, advertising the *Times* under the motto "It does not soil the breakfast cloth." This strategy was similar to TV marketing today that targets upscale viewers who control a disproportionate share of consumer dollars.

With the Hearst and Pulitzer papers capturing the bulk of working- and middle-class readers, managers at the *Times* at first decided to associate their straightforward reporting with more affluent readers and high social status. In 1898, however, Ochs lowered the paper's price to a penny. He believed that people bought the *World* and the *Journal* primarily because they were cheap, not because of their stories. As a result, the *Times* began attracting middle-class readers who gravitated to the paper as a status marker for the educated and well informed. Between 1898 and 1899, its circulation rose from 25,000 to 75,000. By 1921, the *Times* had a daily circulation of 330,000 and 500,000 on Sunday. (For contemporary circulation figures, see Table 8.1.)

"Just the Facts, Please"

Early in the twentieth century, with reporters adopting a more "scientific" attitude to news- and fact-gathering, the ideal of objectivity began to anchor journalism. In **objective journalism**, which distinguishes factual reports from opinion columns, modern reporters strive to maintain a neutral attitude toward the issue or event they cover; they also search out competing points of view among the sources for a story. The writing and representation of this kind of reporting is often designated as the **inverted-pyramid style**. Civil War correspondents developed this style by imitating the terse, compact press releases that came from President Lincoln's secretary of war, Edwin M. Stanton.[6] Often stripped of adverbs and adjectives, inverted-pyramid reports began—as they do today—with the most dramatic or newsworthy information. They answer *who, what, where, when* (and, less frequently, *why* or *how*) questions

● By the 1920s, the *New York Times* had established itself as the official paper of record, available in the nation's libraries and setting the standard that other newspapers emulated. The *Times* became the first modern newspaper, gathering information and presenting news in a straightforward way — without the opinion of the reporter. This continued when the *Times* went online. This style of writing on the Internet, where reporters present a short overview on the paper's first Web page with links to other pages, continues to copy the inverted pyramid model that served print journalism throughout the twentieth century. As with print, though, the majority of readers do not read past the first "page" of an article.

at the top of the story and then narrow down to less significant details. If wars or natural disasters disrupted the telegraph transmissions of these dispatches, the information the reporter chose to lead with in the story often had the best chance of getting through.

For much of the twentieth century, the inverted-pyramid style served as an efficient way to arrange a timely story. As one news critic pointed out, the wire services that used the inverted-pyramid style when distributing stories to newspapers nationwide "had to deal with large numbers of newspapers with widely different political and regional interests. The news had to be 'objective' . . . to be accepted by such a heterogeneous group."[7] Among other things, the importance of objectivity and the reliance on the inverted pyramid signaled journalism's break from the partisan tradition. Although difficult to achieve, the notion of objectivity nonetheless became (and in many ways remains) the guiding ideal of the modern press.

Despite the success of the *New York Times* and other modern papers, the more factual inverted-pyramid approach toward news has come under increasing scrutiny. As news critic Roy Peter Clark has noted: "Some reporters let the pyramid control the content so that the news comes out homogenized. Traffic fatalities, three-alarm fires, and new city ordinances all begin to look alike. In extreme cases, reporters have been known to keep files of story forms. Fill in the blanks. Stick it in the paper."[8] Although the inverted-pyramid style has for years solved deadline problems for reporters and enabled editors to cut a story from the bottom to fit available space, it has also discouraged many readers from continuing beyond the key details in the opening paragraphs. Studies have demonstrated that the majority of readers do not follow a front-page story when it continues, or "jumps," inside the paper.

Interpretive Journalism Provides Explanation

By the 1920s, the more factual or "information" model of news with the reporter as a "detached observer" had become the standard for most mainstream journalism. There was still a sense, however, especially after the trauma of World War I, that the impartial approach to reporting was insufficient for explaining complex national and global conditions. It was partly as a result of "drab, factual, objective reporting," one news scholar contended, that "the American people were utterly amazed when war broke out in August 1914, as they had no understanding of the foreign scene to prepare them for it."[9]

The Limits of Objectivity in Journalism

Modern journalism had undermined an early role of the partisan press — that of offering analysis and opinion. But with the world becoming more complex in the modern age, some papers began to reexplore the analytical function of news. The result was the rise of **interpretive journalism**, which tries to explain key issues or events and place them in a broader historical or social context. According to one historian, this approach, especially in the 1930s and 1940s, was a viable way for journalism to address "the New Deal years, the rise of modern scientific technology, the increasing interdependence of economic groups at home, and the shrinking of the world into one vast arena for power politics."[10] In other words, journalism took an analytic turn in a world grown more interconnected and complicated.

Noting that objectivity and factuality *should* serve as the foundation for journalism, by the 1920s editor and columnist Walter Lippmann insisted that the press should do more. He ranked three press responsibilities: (1) "to make a current record," (2) "to make a running analysis of it," and (3) "on the basis of both, to suggest plans."[11] Indeed, reporters and readers alike have historically distinguished between informational reports and editorials, or interpretive pieces, that offer particular viewpoints or deeper analyses of the issues. The boundary between information and interpretation can be somewhat ambiguous. For this reason, American papers have traditionally placed news analysis in separate columns and opinion articles on certain pages so that readers do not confuse them with "straight news."

In the 1930s, the Depression and the Nazi threat to global stability helped news analysis take root in newsmagazines and radio commentary. First developed in the partisan era, editorial pages also made a strong comeback. More significant, however, was the growth of the political column. Although literary and humor columns existed prior to World War I, the political column was a new form. More than 150 syndicated columns developed between 1930 and 1934 alone. Moving beyond the informational and storytelling functions of news, journalists and newspapers began to extend their role as analysts.

The Press-Radio War

With the rise of radio in the 1930s, the newspaper industry became increasingly annoyed by broadcasters who took their news directly from papers and wire services. As a result, a major battle developed between radio journalism and the established power of print. Although they would eventually lose most of these cases in court, mainstream newspapers attempted to copyright facts reported in the news and even sued radio stations, which routinely used newspapers as their main sources (a common practice to this day). Editors and newspaper lobbyists argued that radio should be permitted to do only commentary. By conceding this interpretive role to radio, the print press tried to protect its dominion over "the facts." It was amid the press-radio war that radio analysis began to flourish as a form of interpretive news. Lowell Thomas delivered the first daily network analysis for CBS on September 29, 1930, attacking Hitler's rise to power in Germany. By 1941, twenty regular network commentators were explaining their version of the world to millions of listeners.

In the 1930s, many print journalists and some editors believed that interpretive stories, rather than objective reports, could better compete with radio. They realized that interpretation was a way to counter radio's (and later television's) superior ability to report breaking news quickly. In 1933, the American Society of Newspaper Editors (ASNE) supported the idea of interpretive journalism, resolving to "devote a larger amount of attention and space to analytical and interpretative news and to presenting a background of information which will enable the average reader more adequately to understand the movement and the significance of events."[12] Newspapers, however, did not embrace probing analysis during the 1930s. Even Walter Lippmann believed that interpretation was misdirected without the foundation of facts and a "current record." As he put it, "the really important thing is to try and make opinion increasingly responsible to the facts."[13]

In Europe, interpretive news and partisan papers have long been the norm, but in U.S. dailies explicit interpretation remains relegated to a few editorial and opinion pages in most papers. After World War II, interpretive journalism diminished substantially. It wasn't until the 1950s—with the Korean War, the development of atomic power, tensions with the Soviet Union, and the anticommunist movement—that news analysis resurfaced in a new form on television. Interpretive journalism in newspapers grew at the same time, especially in such areas as the environment, science, agriculture, sports, health, politics, and business.

Literary Forms of Journalism

By the late 1960s, many people were criticizing America's major social institutions. Political assassinations, civil rights protests, the Vietnam War, the drug culture, and the women's movement were not easily explained. Faced with so much change and turmoil, many individuals began to lose faith in the ability of institutions to oversee and ensure the social order. Members of protest movements as well as many middle- and working-class Americans began to suspect the privileges and power of traditional authority. As a result, key institutions—including journalism—lost much of the credibility they had previously commanded.

The Attack on Objectivity

Former *New York Times* columnist Tom Wicker has argued that in the early 1960s an objective approach to news remained the dominant model. According to Wicker, the "press had so wrapped itself in the paper chains of 'objective journalism' that it had little ability to report anything beyond the bare and undeniable facts."[14] Through the 1960s, attacks on the detachment of reporters escalated. News critic Jack Newfield indicted journalistic impartiality as "a figleaf for covert prejudice": "Objectivity is believing people with power and printing their press releases. Objectivity is not shouting 'liar' in a crowded country."[15] Consequently, the objective ideal became suspect along with the authority of experts and professionals in various fields.

A number of reporters responded to the criticism by rethinking the framework of conventional journalism. To improve on the older approach, they adopted a variety of alternative techniques. One of these was **advocacy journalism**, an approach in which the reporter actively promotes a particular cause or viewpoint. Following this approach, some women reporters, for instance, displayed feminist points of view in their writing; they argued that merely recording events in a neutral way failed to confront the unequal arrangement of jobs and power in many institutions. **Precision journalism**, another technique, attempted to push news more in the direction of science. Precision journalists argued that only by applying rigorous social science methods, such as using poll surveys and questionnaires, could they achieve a valid portrait of social reality.

Throughout the 1990s, major daily papers increasingly invested in training journalists in survey techniques and in hiring pollsters to do periodic research on key trends in their regions. However, critics charged that by the 2000 presidential campaign, many newspapers and TV stations had become too reliant on tracking polls. This reduced campaign coverage to "race-horse" journalism, telling "who's ahead" and "who's behind" stories rather than promoting substantial debates on serious issue differences among major contenders and third-party candidates (who were often ignored in poll journalism).

Journalism as an Art Form

Throughout the twentieth century's modern period, the story dimension of news reports—clouded by the abuses of yellow journalism—was downplayed to favor such conventions as the inverted pyramid and the separation of fact from opinion. Dissatisfied with these approaches, some reporters began reexploring and promoting journalism's ties to storytelling. This model of reporting, **literary journalism**—sometimes dubbed *new journalism*—adapted fictional storytelling techniques to nonfictional material and in-depth reporting. In the United States, literary journalism's roots are evident in such novelists as Mark Twain, Stephen Crane, and Theodore Dreiser, all of whom started out as reporters in the nineteenth century. In the late 1930s and 1940s, new journalism surfaced in literary reports: Journalists began to demonstrate how writing about real events could achieve an artistry often associated only with good fiction.

A leading practitioner, Tom Wolfe, argued that new journalism mixed the *content* of reporting with the *form* of fiction to create "both the kind of objective reality of journalism" and "the subjective reality" of the novel.[16] Writers such as Wolfe (*The Electric Kool-Aid Acid Test*), Truman Capote (*In Cold Blood*), Joan Didion (*The White Album*), Norman Mailer (*Armies of the Night*), and Hunter Thompson (*Hell's Angels*) turned to new journalism in the 1960s to overcome flaws they perceived in routine reporting. Their often self-conscious treatment of social problems gave their writing a perspective that conventional journalism did not offer.

● Hunter Thompson, the most outrageous practitioner of the new journalism, was a harsh critic of mainstream news and the ideal of objectivity. He was also the inspiration for the Uncle Duke character in the comic strip *Doonesbury* and for two Hollywood movies — *Where the Buffalo Roam* (1980) and *Fear and Loathing in Las Vegas* (1998). A longtime correspondent for *Rolling Stone*, he once called journalism "a cheap catch-all for . . . misfits — a false doorway to the backside of life." Much of his work, sometimes called gonzo journalism, tested the boundary between the objective and subjective. In 2005 at age sixty-seven, Thompson committed suicide.

The dilemmas and turmoil of the 1960s, according to critics, demanded a new journalistic form that could deal more effectively with social contradictions. After the tide of intense social upheaval ebbed, however, the new journalism subsided as well. In retrospect, literary reporting has often been criticized for being influenced by television or for blurring the lines between fact and fiction. Nevertheless, the legacy of literary journalism continues. Not only did it influence magazines like *Mother Jones* and *Rolling Stone,* but it also affected the lifestyle and sports sections of most daily newspapers by emphasizing longer feature stories on cultural trends and social issues. These reports reject the inverted-pyramid format by inviting readers into the stories through a more literary style that tries to set the scene using detailed description or dialogue. Today, writers such as Anna Quindlen (*Living Out Loud*) and John McPhee (*Annals of the Former World*) keep this tradition alive. (See Table 8.2 on page 290 for top works in American journalism.)

Contemporary Journalism in the TV and Online Age

If Adolph Ochs and the *New York Times* planted the seeds of modern journalism in the late 1890s, a postmodern brand of journalism arose from two developments in the early 1980s. First, the *Columbus Dispatch* in 1980 became the first paper to go online. By 2006, more than 2,500 U.S. papers were offering some kind of computerized news service. Second, the arrival of the colorful *USA Today* in 1982 radically changed the look of most major U.S. dailies. This new paper incorporated features closely associated with postmodern forms, including an emphasis on visual style over substantive news or analysis and the use of brief news items that appealed to readers' short attention spans. Now the most widely circulated paper in the nation, *USA Today* represents the only successful launch of a new major U.S. daily newspaper in the last several decades. Showing its marketing savvy, *USA Today* was the first paper to openly acknowledge television's central role in mass culture: The paper designed its vending boxes to look like color TV sets. Today, even the writing style of *USA Today* news mimics TV news by casting many of its reports in the immediacy of the present tense rather than the past tense (which was the print news norm throughout the twentieth century).

Writing for *Rolling Stone* in March 1992, media critic Jon Katz argued that the authority of modern newspapers suffered in the wake of a variety of "new news" forms

● Table 8.2 Exceptional Works of American Journalism

Working under the aegis of New York University's journalism department, thirty-six judges compiled a list of the Top 100 works of American journalism in the twentieth century. The list takes into account not just the newsworthiness of the event but the craft of the writing and reporting. What do you think of the Top 10 works listed below? What are some problems associated with making a list like this? Do you think newswriting should be judged in the same way we judge novels or movies?

Journalists	Title or Subject	Publisher	Year
1. John Hersey	"Hiroshima"	*New Yorker*	1946
2. Rachel Carson	*Silent Spring*	Houghton Mifflin	1962
3. Bob Woodward/ Carl Bernstein	Watergate investigation	*Washington Post*	1972–73
4. Edward R. Murrow	Battle of Britain	CBS Radio	1940
5. Ida Tarbell	"The History of the Standard Oil Company"	*McClure's Magazine*	1902–04
6. Lincoln Steffens	"The Shame of the Cities"	*McClure's Magazine*	1902–04
7. John Reed	*Ten Days That Shook the World*	Random House	1919
8. H. L. Mencken	Coverage of the Scopes "monkey" trial	*Baltimore Sun*	1925
9. Ernie Pyle	Reports from Europe and the Pacific during World War II	Scripps-Howard newspapers	1940–45
10. Edward R. Murrow/ Fred Friendly	Investigation of Senator Joseph McCarthy	CBS Television	1954

Source: New York University, Department of Journalism, New York, N.Y., 1999.

---

66 **Critics [in the 1960s] claimed that urban planning created slums, that school made people stupid, that medicine caused disease, that psychiatry invented mental illness, and that the courts promoted injustice. . . . And objectivity in journalism, regarded as an antidote to bias, came to be looked upon as the most insidious bias of all. For 'objective' reporting reproduced a vision of social reality which refused to examine the basic structures of power and privilege.** 99

—Michael Schudson,
Discovering the News, 1978

that combined immediacy, information, entertainment, persuasion, and analysis. Katz claimed that the news supremacy of most prominent daily papers, such as the *New York Times* and the *Washington Post,* was being challenged by "news" coming from talk shows, television sitcoms, popular films, and even rap music. In other words, we were passing from a society in which the transmission of knowledge depended mainly on books, newspapers, and magazines to a society dominated by a mix of print, visual, electronic, and digital information. In the process, the new forms of news began taking over the roles of traditional journalism, setting the nation's cultural, social, and political agendas. For instance, Matt Drudge, conservative Internet news source and gossip behind *The Drudge Report,* hijacked the national agenda in January 1998 and launched the Clinton-Lewinsky scandal when he posted a story claiming that *Newsweek* had backed off, or "spiked," a story about President Clinton having an affair with a White House intern. Although Drudge's report was essentially accurate, *Newsweek* delayed the story because its editors thought they needed more confirming sources before they could responsibly publish the allegations. Drudge effectively "outed" the *Newsweek* story prematurely, though critics debate whether his actions were legitimate or irresponsible.

Today, a fundamental tension exists between print and electronic conceptions of news. With news-reading habits among young people in decline, TV magazine programs, Internet sites, talk shows, sitcoms, movies, and popular music are sparking public conversation more often than are traditional newspapers. Add to this the speed at which personal computers can now transmit data. As Jon Katz wrote in *Wired*: "When in January 1994 a RadioMail subscriber used his wireless modem to flash news of the LA earthquake to the Net well before CNN or the Associated Press could report it, a new news medium was born."[17] With radio, television, film, music, and Internet bloggers all competing with newspapers, their traditional roles are being challenged and changed. With more than 2,500 U.S. newspapers online by 2006, more and more readers began their day by logging on to the Internet to scan the wide variety of papers available.

Categorizing News and U.S. Newspapers

In a visual and digital age, printed newspapers may have to fight harder to keep their readers, but they have not been abandoned. By 2006, the nation's 1,450 daily papers sold 54 million papers each weekday. This, however, is down from 2,600 dailies in 1910, the high-water mark for daily newspapers in the United States; and as late as 1992, weekday circulation had been over 60 million.[18]

In the news industry today, there are several kinds of papers. *National newspapers* (such as the *Wall Street Journal,* the *New York Times,* the *Christian Science Monitor,* and *USA Today*) serve a broad readership across the country. Other papers primarily serve specific geographic regions. Roughly 100 *metropolitan dailies* have a circulation of 100,000 or more. About 35 of these papers had a circulation of more than 250,000 in 2006. In addition, approximately 110 daily newspapers are classified as medium dailies, with 50,000 to 100,000 in circulation. By far the largest number of U.S. dailies—about 1,250 papers—fall into the small daily category, with circulations under 50,000. Whereas dailies serve urban and suburban centers, more than 8,000 nondaily and *weekly newspapers* (down from 14,000 in 1910) serve smaller communities and average just over 5,000 copies per issue.[19]

● Often called the first postmodern newspaper, *USA Today* began in 1982—the first daily newspaper to intentionally copy television, both in the TV-like look of its street vendor boxes and in its brief, compact stories.

Consensus vs. Conflict: Newspapers Play Different Roles

Smaller nondaily papers tend to promote social and economic harmony in their communities. Besides providing community calendars and meeting notices, nondaily papers focus on **consensus-oriented journalism**, carrying articles on local schools, social events, town government, property crimes, and zoning issues. Recalling the partisan spirit of an earlier era, small newspapers are often owned by business leaders who may also serve in local politics. Because consensus-oriented papers have a small advertising base, they are generally careful not to offend local advertisers, who provide the financial underpinnings for many of these papers. At their best, these small-town papers foster a sense of community; at their worst, they overlook or downplay discord and problems.

In contrast, national and metro dailies practice **conflict-oriented journalism** in which front-page news is often defined primarily as events, issues, or experiences that deviate from social norms. Under this news orientation, journalists see their role not merely as neutral fact-gatherers but as observers who monitor their city's institutions and problems. They often maintain an adversarial relationship with local politicians and public officials. These papers offer competing perspectives on

**Media Literacy
and the Critical Process**

Covering Business and Economic News

In 2001–2002 the collapse of Houston-based giant energy company Enron, the largest corporation ever to go bankrupt, put the spotlight on corporate corruption and journalism's coverage of this and similar issues. The 2006 trials of the top Enron executive kept this story in the news. Over the years, critics have claimed that business news pages tend to favor issues related to management and downplay the role of everyday employees. Critics also charge that business news pages favor more positive business stories—such as manager promotions—and minimize negative business news (unlike the front pages, which usually emphasize routine crime news). In the wake of Enron and other corporate scandals, check the business coverage in your local daily paper to see if these charges still seem accurate.

Description. Check a week's worth of business news reporting in your local paper. Examine both the business pages and the front and local sections for these stories. Devise a chart and create categories for sorting stories (e.g., promotion news, scandal stories, earnings reports, media-related news, etc.), and gauge whether these stories are positive or negative. If possible, compare this coverage to a week's worth of news from before the Enron scandal—during the business boom years of the 1990s. Or compare your local paper to business coverage in one of the nation's major dailies and how it covered the 2006 Enron trials compared to the *New York Times*. Or note how much coverage your paper devotes to media-related business stories.

Analysis. Look for patterns in the coverage. How many stories are positive? How many are negative?

Do the stories show any kind of gender favoritism (such as more men covered than women) or class bias (management favored over workers)? Compared to the local paper, are there differences in the frequency and kinds of coverage offered in the national newspaper? Does your paper routinely cover the business of the parent company that owns the local paper? Does it cover national business stories? How many stories are there on the business of newspapers and media in general?

Interpretation. What do some of the patterns mean? Did you find examples where the coverage of business seems comprehensive and fair? If business news gets more positive coverage than political news, what might this mean? If managers get more coverage than employees, what does this mean, particularly given that there are many more regular employees than managers at most businesses? What might it mean if men are more prominently featured than women in business stories? Considering the central role of media and news businesses in everyday life, what does it mean if these businesses are not being covered adequately by local and national news operations?

Evaluation. Determine which papers and stories you would judge as good and which ones you would judge as weaker models for how business should be covered. Are some elements missing from coverage that should be included? If so, make suggestions.

Engagement. Either write a letter to the editor reporting your findings or make an appointment with the editor to discuss what you discovered. Make a recommendation on how to improve coverage.

such issues as education, government, poverty, crime, and the economy; and their publishers, editors, or reporters avoid playing major, overt roles in community politics. In theory, modern newspapers believe their role in large cities is to keep a wary eye fixed on local and state intrigue and events—mostly from the day before.

In telling stories about complex and controversial topics, conflict-oriented journalists often turn such topics into two-dimensional stories, pitting one idea or person against another. This convention, often called "telling both sides of a story," allows a reporter to take the position of a detached observer. Although this practice offers the appearance of balance, it usually functions to generate conflict and sustain a lively news story; sometimes reporters ignore the idea that there may be more than two sides to a story. But faced with deadline pressures, reporters often do not have the time—or the space—to develop a multifaceted and complex report or series of reports. (See "Media Literacy and the Critical Process: Covering Business and Economic News" on opposite page.)

Ethnic, Minority, and Oppositional Newspapers

Historically, small-town weeklies and daily newspapers have served predominantly white, mainstream readers. Exceptions to this include the various minority, foreign-language, and alternative papers, which have played a prominent role for Mexican and Cuban immigrants, Korean Americans, disabled veterans, retired workers, gay and lesbian communities, and the homeless. Most of these weekly and monthly newspapers serve some of the same functions for their constituencies as the "majority" papers. Minority papers, however, are often published outside the social mainstream. Consequently, they provide viewpoints that are different from the mostly middle- and upper-class white attitudes that have shaped the media throughout much of America's history.

The Immigrant and Ethnic Press

Since Benjamin Franklin launched the short-lived German-language *Philadelphische Zeitung* in 1732, newspapers aimed at ethnic groups have played a major role in initiating immigrants into American society. During the nineteenth century, Swedish- and Norwegian-language papers informed various immigrant communities in the Midwest. The early twentieth century gave rise to papers written in German, Yiddish, Russian, and Polish, which assisted the massive influx of European immigrants. In the 1980s, hundreds of small papers developed to serve immigrants from Cuba, Haiti, Pakistan, Laos, Cambodia, and China. More than fifty small U.S. papers are now printed in Vietnamese. Throughout the 1990s and into the twenty-first century, several hundred foreign-language daily and nondaily presses existed in at least forty different languages. Many are financially healthy today, supported by classified ads, local businesses, and increased ad revenue from long-distance phone companies and online computer services, which see the ethnic press as an ideal place to reach those customers most likely to use international phone services or the Internet.[20]

Ethnic papers help readers both adjust to foreign surroundings and retain ties to their traditional heritage. In addition, these papers often cover major stories that are downplayed in the mainstream press. For example, in the aftermath of 9/11, airport security teams detained thousands of Middle Eastern–looking men. The *Weekly Bangla Patrika*, a Long Island, New York, paper with a circulation of twelve thousand, not only reported in detail on the one hundred people the Bangladeshi community lost in the World Trade Center attacks, but it also took the lead in reporting on how it feels to be innocent yet targeted in ethnic profiling at New York's major area airports.[21]

African American Newspapers

Between 1827 and the end of the Civil War in 1865, forty newspapers directed at black readers and opposed to slavery struggled for survival. These papers faced not only higher rates of illiteracy among black slaves and citizens but also hostility from white society and the majority press of the day. The first black newspaper, *Freedom's Journal,* operated from 1827 to 1829 and opposed the racism of

● In 1847 Frederick Douglass helped found the *North Star*, printed in the basement of the Memorial African Methodist Episcopal Zion Church, a gathering spot for abolitionists and "underground" activities in Rochester, New York. At the time, the white-owned *New York Herald* urged Rochester's citizens to throw the paper's printing press into Lake Ontario. Under Douglass's leadership, the paper published as a weekly until 1860, addressing problems facing blacks around the country and offering a forum for Douglass to debate his fellow black activists.

many New York newspapers. In addition, it offered a voice for a number of antislavery societies. Other notable papers included the *Alienated American* (1852–56) and the *New Orleans Daily Creole,* which began its short life in 1856 as the first black-owned daily in the South. The most influential oppositional newspaper at the time was Frederick Douglass's *North Star,* a weekly antislavery newspaper in Rochester, New York, that began in 1847 and reached a circulation of three thousand. Douglass, a former slave, wrote essays on slavery and on a variety of national and international topics.

Since 1827, more than three thousand newspapers have been edited and owned by blacks. These papers, with an average life span of nine years, took stands against race baiting, lynching, and the Ku Klux Klan. They promoted racial pride long before the Civil Rights movement of the 1950s and 1960s. The most widely circulated black-owned paper was Robert C. Vann's weekly *Pittsburgh Courier,* founded in 1910. Its circulation peaked at 350,000 in 1947—the year professional baseball was integrated by Jackie Robinson, thanks in part to relentless editorials in the *Courier* that denounced the color barrier in pro sports. As they have throughout their history, these papers offer oppositional viewpoints to the mainstream press and record the daily activities of black communities by listing weddings, births, deaths, graduations, meetings, and church functions. More than 125 African American papers survive today and remain influential, including Baltimore's *Afro-American,* New York's *Amsterdam News,* and Chicago's *Defender,* which celebrated its one hundredth anniversary in 2005.

The circulation rates of most black papers have dropped sharply, however, particularly since the 1960s. The local and national editions of the *Pittsburgh Courier,* for instance, had a combined circulation of only twenty thousand by the early 1980s.[22] Several factors contributed to these declines. First, television and specialized black radio stations tapped into the limited pool of money that businesses allocated for advertising. Second, some advertisers, to avoid controversy, withdrew their support when the black press started giving favorable coverage to the Civil Rights movement in the 1960s. Third, the loss of industrial urban jobs in the 1970s and 1980s not only

Ethnic and foreign-language newspapers serve an important function, providing news and a sense of community to populations not targeted by mainstream papers. Clockwise, from top left: *Al-Ahram* (Arabic), *El Diario* (Spanish), the *World Journal* (Chinese), and the *Forward* (Yiddish).

diminished readership but also hurt small neighborhood businesses, which could no longer afford to advertise in both the mainstream and the black press. Finally, after the enactment of civil rights and affirmative action laws, black papers were raided by mainstream papers seeking to integrate their newsrooms with good black journalists. Black papers could seldom match the offers from large white-owned dailies.

As civil rights legislation brought improved economic conditions for many working- and middle-class African Americans, the mainstream press began to court them as a consumer group, devoting weekly special sections to black issues and finding advertisers to support those sections. In siphoning off both ads and talent, a more integrated mainstream press diminished the status of many black papers—an ironic effect of the 1960s civil rights laws. By 2006, while one-third of the overall U.S. population was classified as part of a minority group, only 13.9 percent of the newsroom staffs at the nation's 1,400-plus daily papers were African American, Hispanic, Asian American, or Native American.[23]

Spanish-Language Newspapers

Bilingual and Spanish-language newspapers have long served a variety of Cuban, Mexican, Puerto Rican, and other Latino readerships. New York's *El Diario–La Prensa* has been serving Spanish-language readers since 1913. Los Angeles boasts *La Opinión,* founded in 1926 and the nation's largest Spanish-language daily, with 125,000 in circulation in 2006. These two papers merged their business operations in 2004.[24] Other prominent publications are in Miami (*La Voz* and *Diario Las Americas*), Houston (*La Información*), Chicago (*El Mañana Daily News* and *La Raza*), San Diego (*El Sol*), and New York (*Hoy, El Noticias del Mundo*). *Hoy,* owned by the *Chicago Tribune,* created an L.A. version in 2004 to compete with *La Opinión.* By the early 2000s, more than 1,500 daily and non-daily Spanish-language papers operated in the United States, reaching more than fifteen million readers nationwide, an increase of three million since 1984.[25]

Until the late 1960s, Hispanic issues and culture were virtually ignored by mainstream newspapers. But with the influx of Mexican, Haitian, Puerto Rican, and Cuban immigrants throughout the 1980s and 1990s, many mainstream papers began to feature weekly Spanish-language supplements. The first was the *Miami Herald*'s section, "El Nuevo Herald," introduced in 1976. Other mainstream papers also joined in, but many were folding their supplements by the mid-1990s. In 1995, the *Los Angeles Times* discontinued its supplement, "Nuestro Tiempo," and the *Miami Herald* trimmed budgets and staff for "El Nuevo Herald." Spanish-language radio and television had beaten the papers to these potential customers and to advertisers. By the early 2000s, Spanish-language radio formats were thriving in many urban areas and taking advertisers with them. While many of the nation's mainstream papers were cutting their Spanish-language sections, TV advertising aimed at Hispanic markets jumped 25 percent, and the number of Hispanics in U.S. TV newsrooms made up about 6 percent of those staffs.[26] However, on the print side in 2006, Hispanic journalists accounted for about 4.51 percent of the newsroom workforce at U.S. daily papers (compared to 5.56 percent for African Americans).[27]

Native American Newspapers

In mainstream journalism by 2006, Native American reporters and editors represented barely one-half of 1 percent of the 54,800 journalists working for the nation's daily papers.[28] (In 2000, the total Native American population was about 1 percent of the U.S. population.) As a result, much of the significant coverage of American Indian issues tends to come from other sources. An activist Native American press has provided oppositional voices to mainstream American media since 1828, when the *Cherokee Phoenix* appeared in Georgia. Another prominent early paper was the *Cherokee Rose Bud,* founded in 1848 by tribal women in the Oklahoma territory. The Native American Press Association has documented more than 350 different Native American papers, most of them printed in English but a few in tribal languages. Two national papers include *Akwesasne Notes*, a radical paper from the Mohawk nation published a few times a year, and *Wassaja*, a bimonthly paper of the American Indian Historical Society that promotes tribal pride and education.

To counter the neglect of their culture's viewpoints by the mainstream press, Native American newspapers have helped educate various tribes about their heritage and build community solidarity. These papers also have developed stories on both the problems and progress among those Indian tribes that have opened gambling resorts over the past decade. Overall, these smaller papers provide a forum for debates on tribal conflicts and concerns that are generally overlooked in major papers, and they often signal the mainstream press on issues—such as gambling or hunting and fishing—that have significance for the larger culture.

The Underground Press

Another important historical development in the mid to late 1960s involved the explosion of alternative newspapers. Labeled the *underground press* at the time, these papers questioned mainstream political policies and conventional values. Generally running on shoestring budgets, they often voiced radical viewpoints and were erratic in meeting publication schedules. Springing up on college campuses and in major cities, underground papers were inspired by the writings of socialists and intellectuals from the 1930s and 1940s and, in their own time, by a new wave of thinkers and artists. Particularly inspirational were poets and writers (such as Allen Ginsberg, Jack Kerouac, LeRoi Jones, and Eldridge Cleaver) and "protest" musicians (including Bob Dylan, Pete Seeger, and Joan Baez). In criticizing social institutions, alternative papers questioned the official reports distributed by public relations agents, government spokespeople, and the conventional press (see "Case Study—Alternative Journalism: Dorothy Day and I. F. Stone" on page 299).

Figure 8.1
Selected Alternative Newspapers in the United States

Source: Association of Alternative Newsweeklies, www.aan.org.

During the 1960s, underground papers played a unique role in documenting social tension by including the voices of students, women, blacks, Native Americans, gay men and lesbians, and others whose opinions were often excluded from the mainstream press. The first and most enduring underground paper, the *Village Voice,* was founded in Greenwich Village in 1955. Today its circulation is 250,000. Among campus underground papers, the *Berkeley Barb* was the most influential, developing amid the free-speech movement in the mid-1960s. Despite their irreverent and often vulgar tone, many underground papers turned a spotlight on racial and gender inequities and, on occasion, influenced mainstream journalism to examine social issues. Like the black press, though, many early underground papers folded after the 1960s. Given their radical outlook, it was difficult for them to generate sponsors or appeal to advertisers. In addition, like the black press, the underground press was raided by mainstream papers, which began expanding their own coverage of culture by hiring the underground's best writers. Still, today more than 120 papers are members of the Association of Alternative Newsweeklies (see Figure 8.1).

Newspaper Operations:
Economic Demands vs. Editorial Duties

Today a weekly paper might employ only two or three people, whereas a major metro daily might have more than two thousand staffers. In either situation, however, most newspapers distinguish business operations from editorial or news functions. Journalists' and readers' praise or criticism usually rests on the quality of a paper's news and editorial components, but the business and advertising divisions drive today's industry.

Business and Advertising Decisions

Most major daily papers devote one-half to two-thirds of their pages to advertisements. Accounting for about 18 to 19 percent of all ad dollars spent annually in the United States, newspapers carry everything from expensive full-page spreads for department stores to classifieds, which consumers can purchase for a few dollars to advertise everything from used cars to furniture. In most cases, ads are positioned in the paper first. The space left over after ads are placed is called the **newshole**, which accounts for the remaining 35 to 50 percent of the content of daily newspapers—everything from front-page news reports to horoscopes and advice columns.

In addition to managing a paper's finances, business operations generally include departments of advertising, circulation, and promotion. Advertising staffs sell space to various companies and classified spots to individuals and small businesses. Circulation departments oversee distribution through street-corner boxes and newsstand sales, neighborhood paper routes, mail subscriptions, and, most recently, the Internet (although many papers now have separate Internet divisions). Promotion departments seek new readers and advertisers, paying particular attention to younger, hard-to-reach readers. Mechanical departments, supervised by a production manager,

> **❝** My main concern is that, however we distribute our work, we have to generate the money to pay for it. The advertising model looks appealing now, but do we want our future to depend on that single source of revenue: What happens if advertising goes flat? What happens when somebody develops software to filter out advertising—TiVO for the Web?**❞**
>
> –Bill Keller, executive editor of the *New York Times,* on advertising being the only revenue for online newspapers

generally run the technical and computerized processes of assembling the pages of the paper and operating the printing presses.

News and Editorial Responsibilities

On the news and editorial side, the chain of command at most larger papers starts at the top, with the publisher and owner, and then moves to the editor in chief and managing editor, the persons in charge of the daily news-gathering and writing processes. Under the main editors, assistant editors and news managers run different news divisions, including features, sports, photos, local news, state news, and wire service reports that contain much of the day's national and international news. In addition, copy editors check each story for accuracy, style, and grammar and write the headlines for each report.

Reporters work for editors and are generally grouped into two broad categories: *general assignment reporters,* who handle all sorts of stories that might emerge—or "break"—in a given day, and *specialty reporters,* who are assigned to particular beats (police, courts, schools, government) or topics (education, religion, health, environment, technology). On large dailies, *bureau reporters* file reports every day from other major cities—such as Washington or their state's capital. Daily papers also feature columnists and critics; these reporters have usually worked their way up the hierarchy and may review or analyze everything from fashion to foreign policy. By the early 2000s, many newspapers employed a separate staff for their online operations, even though the vast majority of these operations were losing money.

Wire Services and Feature Syndication

Major daily papers might have between one hundred and two hundred local reporters and writers, but they still cannot cover the world or produce enough material to fill up the newshole each day. For this reason, newspapers rely on wire services and syndicated feature services to supplement local coverage. A few major dailies, such as the *New York Times,* run their own wire services, selling their reprinted stories

● Political cartoons are often syndicated features in newspapers.

CASE STUDY

Alternative Journalism: Dorothy Day and I. F. Stone

Over the years, a number of unconventional reporters have struggled against the status quo to find a place for unheard voices and alternative ways to practice their craft. For example, Ida Wells fearlessly investigated violence against blacks for the *Memphis Free Speech* in the late 1800s. Newspaper lore also offers a rich history of alternative journalists and their publications, such as Dorothy Day's *Catholic Worker* and *I. F. Stone's Weekly.*

In 1933, Dorothy Day (1897–1980) cofounded a radical religious organization with a monthly newspaper, the *Catholic Worker,* that opposed war and supported social reforms. Like many young intellectual writers during World War I, Day was a pacifist; she also joined the Socialist Party. Quitting college at age eighteen to work as an activist reporter for socialist newspapers, Day participated in the ongoing suffrage movement to give women the right to vote. Throughout the 1930s, her Catholic Worker organization invested in thirty hospices for the poor and homeless, providing food and shelter for five thousand people a day. This legacy endures today with the organization continuing to fund soup kitchens and homeless shelters throughout the country.

For more than seventy years, the *Worker* has consistently advocated personal activism to further social justice, opposing anti-Semitism, Japanese American internment camps during World War II, nuclear weapons, the Korean War, military drafts, and the communist witch-hunts of the 1950s. The *Worker*'s circulation peaked in 1938 at 190,000, then fell dramatically during World War II, when Day's pacifism was at odds with much of America. Today *Catholic Worker* has a circulation of 80,000.

I. F. Stone (1907–1989) shared Dorothy Day's passion for social activism. He also started early, publishing his own monthly paper at the age of fourteen and becoming a full-time reporter by age twenty. He worked as a Washington political writer for the *Nation* in the early 1940s and later for the *New York Daily Compass.* Throughout his career, Stone challenged the conventions and privileges of both politics and journalism. In 1941, for example, he resigned from the National Press Club when it refused to serve his guest, the nation's first African American federal judge. In the early 1950s, he actively opposed Joseph McCarthy's rabid search to rid government and the media of alleged communists.

When the *Daily Compass* failed in 1952, the radical Stone was unable to find a newspaper job and decided to create his own newsletter, *I. F. Stone's Weekly,* which he published for nineteen years. Practicing interpretive and investigative reporting, Stone became as adept as any major journalist at tracking down government records to discover contradictions, inaccuracies, and lies. Over the years, Stone questioned decisions by the Supreme Court, investigated the substandard living conditions of many African Americans, and criticized political corruption. He guided the *Weekly* to a circulation that reached 70,000 during the 1960s, when he probed American investments of money and military might in Vietnam.

I. F. Stone and Dorothy Day embodied a spirit of independent reporting that has been threatened by the decline in newspaper readership and the rise of chain ownership. Stone, who believed that alternative ideas were crucial to maintaining a healthy democracy, once wrote that "there must be free play for so-called 'subversive' ideas — every idea 'subverts' the old to make way for the new. To shut off 'subversion' is to shut off peaceful progress and to invite revolution and war."[1]

to other papers. Other agencies, such as the Associated Press and United Press International (UPI), have hundreds of staffers stationed throughout major U.S. cities and the world capitals. They submit stories and photos each day for distribution to newspapers across the country. Some U.S. papers also subscribe to foreign wire services, such as Agence France-Presse in Paris or Reuters in London. Daily papers generally pay monthly fees for access to all wire stories, which are relayed by computer, satellite, and Teletype machines. Although they use only a fraction of what is available over the wires, editors carefully monitor wire services each day for important stories and ideas for local angles. Wire services have greatly expanded the national and international scope of news, but editors often must put their trust in a handful of powerful wire firms when they select a newsworthy issue or event for reprinting.

In addition, **feature syndicates**, such as United Features and Tribune Media Services, are commercial outlets that contract with newspapers to provide work from the nation's best political writers, editorial cartoonists, comic-strip artists, and self-help columnists. These companies serve as brokers, distributing horoscopes and crossword puzzles as well as the columns and comic strips that appeal to a wide audience. When a paper bids on and acquires the rights to a cartoonist or columnist, it signs exclusivity agreements with a syndicate to ensure that it is the only paper in the region to carry, say, *Dilbert*, Ellen Goodman, Molly Ivins, Bob Herbert, George Will, or "Dear Abby." Feature syndicates, like wire services, wield great influence in determining which writers and cartoonists gain national prominence.

Ownership, Economics, Technology, and Innovation

A number of tough issues face the newspaper industry as it adapts to changes in economics and technology. For publishers and journalists, no issues are more worrisome than the decline in newspaper readership and the failure of many papers to attract younger readers. Other problems persist as well, including the inability of most cities to support competing newspapers and the capability of online computer services and telephone and cable companies to vie with newspapers for lucrative classified advertising. Finally, the newspaper industry struggles to find its place on the Internet, trying to predict the future of printed and digital versions of the news.

Circulation Suffers as Readership Declines

Newspaper owners struggle daily with readership concerns. Between 1970 and 1990, yearly circulation flattened out at just over 60 million copies per day. By 2005, though, only 54 million copies circulated each weekday and 57 million on Sunday, down also from 62 million in the early 1990s. Although the population increased during that period, the percentage of adults who read the paper at least once a day dropped from 78 percent in 1970 to 51.6 percent by 2005 (59.6 on Sunday). This decline in readership actually began during the Depression and the rise of radio. Between 1931 and 1939, 600 newspapers ceased operation. Between 1950 and 2006, the number of daily papers in the United States dropped from 1,772 to 1,450.[29]

The biggest circulation crisis for newspapers occurred from the late 1960s through the 1970s. Both the rise in network television viewing and the competition from suburban weeklies intensified the decline in daily readership. In addition, with an increasing number of women working full-time outside the home throughout the 1970s, newspapers could no longer consistently count on one of their core readership groups. (In fact, by 2000 women made up only 45 percent of all daily newspaper readers.) Circulation dropped by more than 20 percent in the nation's twenty largest cities (even though the population declined by only 6 percent in those areas).[30]

Although some newspapers experienced circulation gains in the 1980s and mid-1990s, especially in more affluent suburban communities, readership in the United States generally declined or flattened out during this period. Increases at many suburban weekly papers actually siphoned off readers of large city dailies. By comparison, many other countries did not experience readership declines. For example, for every 1,000 people, Sweden sells 500 papers per day. In the United States that figure is fewer than 250 copies sold daily for every 1,000 people.[31] Countries such as Norway, Finland, Japan, South Korea, and Germany also have higher rates of readership.

Joint Operating Agreements and Declining Competition

In the past, antimonopoly rules prevented a single owner from controlling all the newspapers in a city or town. Today, however, such rules have little impact because most communities are now served by just one paper. In addition, before the 1996 Telecommunications Act, the FCC prohibited newspaper owners from purchasing broadcast or cable outlets in the same markets where they published newspapers. Such restrictions once encouraged more voices in the media marketplace.

Although regulation has lessened, in general the government continues to monitor the declining number of newspapers in various American cities as well as mergers in cities where competition among papers might be endangered. The Justice Department has allowed a number of mergers over the years, but it was not until 1970 that Congress passed the Newspaper Preservation Act, which enabled failing papers to continue operating through a **joint operating agreement (JOA)**. Under a JOA, two competing papers keep separate news divisions while merging business and production operations for a period of years.

In 2006, JOAs were still in place in eleven cities, including Cincinnati, Seattle, and Tucson. Although JOAs and mergers encourage monopolistic tendencies, they have sometimes been the only way to maintain competition between newspapers in the Information Age. In the mid-1920s, about five hundred American cities had two or more newspapers with separate owners. By 2000, fewer than twenty cities had independent, competing papers. In 1995, the *Houston Post* folded, leaving the nation's fourth-largest city with only one daily paper, the *Houston Chronicle*. In 1998, the *Nashville Banner* closed, leaving the Gannett-owned *Tennessean* as the main daily print game in town. When the Cincinnati JOA expires in 2007, the *Post* is expected to close, leaving only the Gannett-owned *Enquirer*.

Until 1989, Detroit was one of the most competitive newspaper cities in the nation. The *Detroit News* and the *Detroit Free Press* both ranked among the ten most widely circulated papers in the country and sold their weekday editions for just fifteen cents a copy. But managers at the two papers began exploring joint ways to stabilize revenue declines. Claiming that in Detroit's depressed economy the death of one newspaper might result in substantial job losses, the papers asked for a JOA, which the government authorized in 1989. In the largest JOA to date, the *News*, then owned by Gannett, and the *Free Press*, then owned by Knight Ridder, began sharing business and production operations, although the companies remained independently owned and staffed separate news and editorial departments.

On Saturday and Sunday, the two papers circulated one edition, which featured special sections from both papers. In 1995, a prolonged and bitter strike by several unions sharply reduced circulation, especially at the *News*, which had become an afternoon daily under the terms of the JOA. One of the unions' concerns involved reduced competition under the JOA, which had allowed managers at both papers to cut costs and jobs to sustain high profits for stockholders. Before the 1995 strike,

> **"** Teens have a greater interest in news than the generations before them. Newspapers have a great future as news organizations on the Web and perhaps elsewhere. Sadly, today in America when a newspaper reader dies, he or she is not replaced by a new reader. **"**
>
> –Jeffrey Cole, director, Center for the Digital Future, USC Annenberg School, 2006

Gannett and Knight Ridder—accused of trying to break the labor unions in Detroit—had both reported profit margins of well over 15 percent on all their newspaper holdings.[32] In 2005, Gannett sold the *News* to MediaNews Group and bought the *Free Press*. While both were ranked in the Top 10 circulated papers in the 1980s, neither paper was ranked in the Top 15 in 2006.

Newspaper Chains Consolidate Ownership

Another key economic change in the newspaper industry has been the influence of **newspaper chains**, companies that own several papers throughout the country. Edward Wyllis Scripps founded the first newspaper chain in the 1890s. By the 1920s, there were about 30 chains in the United States, each one owning an average of five papers. The emergence of chains paralleled the major business trend during the twentieth century: the movement toward oligopolies in which fewer and fewer cor-

Figure 8.2
Media Ownership: Principal U.S. Operations of Gannett Company, Inc.

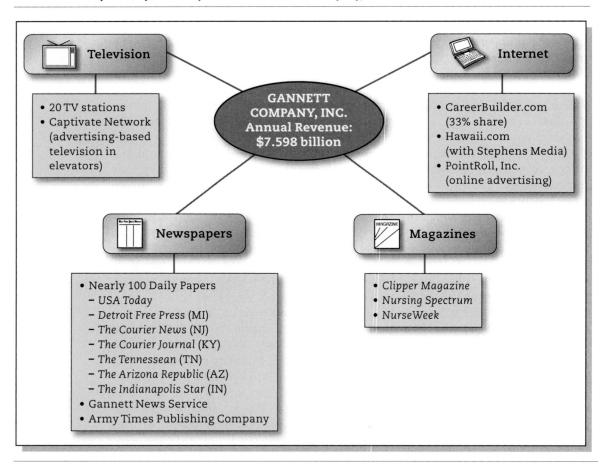

Gannett is the nation's largest newspaper publisher, and its flagship paper *USA Today* is the most widely circulated U.S. paper. Gannett's 90-plus U.S. dailies had a combined circulation of about 7.3 million in 2005. The company also owns 1,000 non-daily publications and a weekend newspaper insert magazine, *USA Weekend*. A major player on the Internet, Gannett operates more than 130 Web sites. Although newspapers generate 80% of Gannett's sales, the company also owns 20-plus TV stations and operates commercial printing, newswire, and data services.

To get an idea of the future of this newspaper conglomerate, do online research to find (1) how profitable Gannett newspapers are and (2) how Gannett executives plan to handle the transition from newspaper to Internet advertising.

porations control each industry. By the 1980s, more than 130 chains owned an average of nine papers each, with the 12 largest chains accounting for 40 percent of the total circulation in the United States. By the early 2000s the top 13 chains circulated more than one-half of all the nation's daily papers. Gannett, for example, the nation's largest chain, owns about 90 daily papers (and 500 more nondailies), ranging from small suburban papers to the *Cincinnati Enquirer,* the Nashville *Tennessean,* and *USA Today* (see Figure 8.2).

A disturbing trend in the 1990s found daily newspapers changing hands at a much faster rate than in previous years. For example, between 1993 and 1996, more than 250 of the nation's 1,500-plus daily papers were sold—usually to distant chains not headquartered in the community where the paper operates.[33] News critics fear that having only a few chain owners will make it more difficult for multiple viewpoints to be expressed in the news media. They are also concerned about whether out-of-town owners and newly installed editors will put the special needs of their communities below corporate interests and the bottom line. Increasingly, chains favor editors who are bottom line–oriented business managers over independent or progressive editors who seek to increase the newshole and the number of reporters and enterprising reports and series.

By 2006 investors voted to sell Knight Ridder—the nation's second leading newspaper chain with 32 daily papers—to the McClatchy Company for $4.5 billion. The Knight Ridder sale came even though that chain's papers averaged more than 16 percent profit in 2005, near the industry average. However, with the rise of online news, the loss of younger readers, cutbacks in reporting and editing jobs, and Internet competition for ad revenue, some investors were betting against a future for traditional newspapers. Furthermore, many newspaper companies, instead of investing in investigative reporting to spur readership, have directed much of their profits to buying radio and TV properties. Other companies, like the Sacramento-based McClatchy, see newspapers as monopoly opportunities—publishing in cities with high consumer recognition and with local news gathering operations that are unrivaled by broadcasters and still in demand by readers. Still, McClatchy kept only 21 of its 32 papers, selling four to the Denver-based NewsMedia Group, including the *San Jose Mercury News* and *St. Paul Pioneer Press,* which "only" had profit margins of 8 and 10 percent, respectively, in 2005. McClatchy also sold Knight Ridder's two former Philadelphia papers to a local investment group for $565 million.[34]

Incorporating Electronic and Digital Technology to Survive

Modern computer technology began radically revolutionizing newsrooms in the 1970s. VDTs (video display terminals), for instance, displaced typewriters, enabling reporters to change or share stories easily; editors could also measure headlines or design pages on their personal computer screens. As dramatic as this change was, however, it did not pose the challenges of the Internet and digital news, which brought a brand of competition that newspapers had never seen.

The 1996 Telecommunications Act spurred alliances among cable television and telephone companies in their quest to deliver digital data into homes via cable, copper, and fiber-optic wires. Hundreds of newspapers responded by developing online versions of their paper product. Most newspaper editors believe they can provide better electronic versions of local community news and services than can cable or phone systems, which offer mostly national services. Many newspapers now face competition with online computer services, cable companies, and phone services in the battle for lucrative local classified advertisements.

Because of their local monopoly status, many newspapers were slower than other media to confront the challenges of the electronic and digital revolution. Into the early part of the twenty-first century, however, newspapers were still the

Figure 8.3
Newspapers' Slice of the U.S. Advertising Pie, 2005

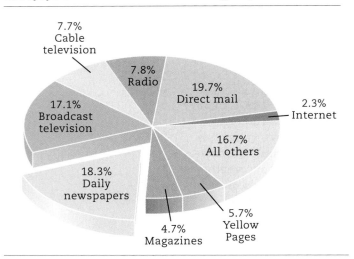

7.7%
Cable
television

7.8%
Radio

19.7%
Direct mail

2.3%
Internet

17.1%
Broadcast
television

16.7%
All others

18.3%
Daily
newspapers

5.7%
Yellow
Pages

4.7%
Magazines

Source: Newspaper Association of America, Total U.S. Advertising Volume, www.naa.org, 2006.

media leader in collecting advertising revenue. The nation's newspapers annually attract about 18–19 percent of all ad revenues spent in the United States, which is down from a 27 percent share in the late 1980s (see Figure 8.3).

Although some observers think newspapers are on the verge of extinction as the digital age eclipses the print era, the industry is no dinosaur. In fact, the history of communication demonstrates that older mass media have always adapted. Actually, with more than 1,500 North American daily papers online in 2006, newspapers are tackling one of the industry's major economic headaches: the cost of newsprint. After salaries, purchasing newsprint from paper manufacturers is the industry's largest expense, typically accounting for more than 25 percent of a newspaper's total cost.

In addition, online newspapers are truly taking advantage of the flexibility the Internet offers (for a different view, see "Tracking Technology: Publishers Face the Risky Economics of Charging Online" on opposite page). Because space is not an issue, newspapers can post stories and reader letters online that they weren't able to print in the paper edition. They can also run longer stories with more in-depth coverage, as well as offer immediate updates to breaking news. Also, most stories appear online before traditional print venues and are posted and updated several times a day. Online newspapers are also making themselves an invaluable resource to readers by offering hyperlinks to Web sites related to stories and by linking news reports to an archive of related articles. Free of charge or for a modest fee, a reader can search the newspaper's database from home and investigate the entire sequence and history of an ongoing story, such as the outcome of a trial over the course of several months. Taking advantage of the multimedia capabilities of the Internet, online newspapers offer readers the ability to download audio and video files—everything from presidential news conferences to sports highlights. Today's online newspapers offer readers a dynamic rather than a static resource—one that does more than line the bottom of a birdcage a day after publication.

Alternative Voices

With most news organizations moving into the digital age and online editions, traditional printed newspapers found a new outlet in the 1980s: the development of *street papers.* Originally an idea for employing homeless people—both as street vendors and as news writers—the first such paper, *Street News,* emerged in New York in 1989. A number of urban imitators soon followed, including *Spare Change* in Boston and Toronto, *Street Sheet* in San Francisco, *Homeless Gazette News* in Dallas, and *Hard Times* in Los Angeles. These papers typically sell for fifty cents to three dollars, and the proceeds mostly go to the homeless. They cover such topics as the political and economic factors that contribute to homelessness, including the availability of inexpensive drugs like crack cocaine, the loss of urban manufacturing jobs, the downsizing of mental hospitals, and the gentrification of downtown areas. Featuring stories by and about the homeless, these papers often serve as a voice for the disenfranchised.

By the early 2000s, fifty U.S. street papers were available, as well as another eighty worldwide. But in addition to sporadic publishing schedules and financial woes, many street papers face bureaucratic obstacles that curtail distribution. For

TRACKING TECHNOLOGY

Publishers Face the Risky Economics of Charging Online

By Katharine Q. Seelye

Consumers are willing to spend millions of dollars on the Web when it comes to music services like iTunes and gaming sites like Xbox Live. But when it comes to online news, they are happy to read it but loath to pay for it.

Newspaper Web sites have been so popular that at some newspapers, including the *New York Times,* the number of people who read the paper online now surpasses the number who buy the print edition.

This migration of readers is beginning to transform the newspaper industry. Advertising revenue from online sites is booming and, while it accounts for only 2 percent or 3 percent of most newspapers' overall revenues, it is the fastest-growing source of revenue. And newspaper executives are watching anxiously as the number of online readers grows while the number of print readers declines.

"For some publishers, it really sticks in the craw that they are giving away their content for free," said Colby Atwood, vice president of Borrell Associates Inc., a media research firm. The giveaway means less support for expensive news-gathering operations and the potential erosion of advertising revenue from the print side, which is much more profitable.

As a result, nearly a decade after newspapers began building and showcasing their Web sites, one of the most vexing questions in newspaper economics endures: should publishers charge for Web news, knowing that they may drive readers away and into the arms of the competition?

Of the nation's 1,456 daily newspapers, only one national paper, the *Wall Street Journal,* which is published by Dow Jones & Company, and about 40 small dailies charge readers to use their Web sites. Other papers charge for either online access to portions of their content or offer online subscribers additional features.

"A big part of the motivation for newspapers to charge for their online content is not the revenue it will generate, but the revenue it will save, by slowing the erosion of their print subscriptions," Mr. Atwood said. "We're in the midst of a long and painful transition."

The difficulty comes in determining what readers will pay for on the Web. Most executives agree that national news can be found in so many places that it would be self-defeating to try to charge for it. But they are finding that readers will pay for sports, if the Web offers more than the printed page. The *Milwaukee Journal Sentinel* provides in-depth coverage of the Green Bay Packers, along with blogs, fan photos and audio reports, in "Packer Insider" for $34.95 a year.

But for the most part, publishers make money on Web sites by selling space to advertisers, and that is a booming

business. Mr. Atwood at Borrell said a preliminary analysis of online revenues for about 700 daily newspaper Web sites showed an average increase of 45 percent from 2003 to 2004.

Perhaps the biggest obstacle for newspapers is that online readers have been conditioned to expect free news. "Most newspapers believe that if they charged for the Web, the number of users would decline to such an extent that their advertising revenues would decline more than they get from charging users," said Gary B. Pruitt, chairman and chief executive of the McClatchy Company, which publishes the *Sacramento Bee,* the *Star Tribune in Minneapolis* and other papers, which do not charge for their Web sites.

Mr. Jaroslovsky, the former editor of the *Wall Street Journal Online,* said that some publishers were regretting not having charged for the Web back in the 1990s when it was developing, because doing so now will be a bigger shock to their readers. Also, he said, the stakes are higher.

"When we did this, we were at the beginning of an investment curve and the amount of money at stake was not as great," he said. "Today, if you make a wrong decision, there's a chance it will be not only embarrassing, but very costly."

Source: Katharine Q. Seelye, "Publishers Face the Risky Economics of Charging Online," *New York Times,* March 14, 2005, p. C1.

example, a New York Transit Authority regulation in the mid-1990s prohibited street vendors from selling papers on commuter trains, and in 1998 the Dallas public library system, a major gathering place for the homeless, declared a "temporary moratorium" on displaying free publications and street papers.

Oddly enough, in 1998 street papers in Los Angeles even found themselves competing against a glossy international general-interest publication, the *Big Issue*. Started in London in 1991 as a simple street paper and boasting a weekly circulation of more than 250,000, mostly in England, the *Big Issue* launched an L.A. version in April 1998. Although the L.A. venture eventually failed, other versions, including Australian editions in Melbourne, Sydney, Brisbane, and Geelong, have been successful. (In fact, the color photos, celebrity profiles, and mainstream ads of the *Big Issue* remain the formula for contemporary street papers.) Unlike other street papers, the *Big Issue*'s content is written by professionals, while homeless vendors sell the paper and keep part of the sale price. This has left many street-paper publishers questioning the value of generating money for the homeless without providing them with new skills.[35]

Newspapers and Democracy

Of all mass media, newspapers have played the longest and strongest role in sustaining democracy. As a venue for the expression of ideas and the distribution of information, newspapers keep readers abreast of issues and events in their community, their nation, and their world. Over the years, newspapers have fought heroic battles in places that had little tolerance for differing points of view. During a ten-year period—from 1996 through 2006—338 reporters from around the world were killed trying to do their jobs. Of the 338, the international Committee to Protect Journalists reported that 238 were murdered.[36] Many of the more recent deaths reported by the CPJ have come from the war in Iraq, which began in 2003. By mid-2006, more than 70 reporters had died in Iraq as had another 30 media workers and support staff. As the *New York Times* and the Freedom Forum reported in May 2006, "That number is more than the 63 killed in Vietnam, the 17 killed in Korea, and even the 69 killed in World War II."[37]

Although we need heroic reporters to go where we cannot and newspapers remain a strong medium of communication, critics have raised a number of concerns about their future. For instance, some charge that newspapers have become so formulaic in their design and reporting styles that they may actually discourage new approaches to telling stories and reporting news. Another criticism is that many one-newspaper cities cover only issues and events of interest to middle- and upper-middle-class readers, thereby underreporting the experiences and events that affect poorer and working-class citizens. In addition, given the rise of newspaper chains, the likelihood of including new opinions, ideas, and information in mainstream daily papers may be diminishing. Although wealthy and powerful chains may keep smaller struggling papers solvent, such chains sometimes have little commitment to local communities beyond profits. Moreover, chain ownership tends to discourage watchdog journalism and the crusading traditions of newspapers. Like other business managers, many news executives prefer not to offend investors or outrage potential advertisers by running too many investigative re-

In 2004, newspapers were hesitant to declare a winner of the close presidential election. In 2000 they had followed the lead of cable and TV news programs, which made a premature call. Although George W. Bush eventually won the controversial 2000 election, the media bungling brought back memories of the pre-TV 1948 election, in which the *Chicago Tribune* miscalled the race between President Truman and his Republican challenger, Thomas E. Dewey.

ports, especially business probes. Indeed, reporters have generally undercovered the business and ownership arrangements in their own industry.

Critics today have raised important questions about the transformation from a modern print to a postmodern digital culture. For example, does such a transformation represent a cheapening of public discourse? Do "new news" forums and non-print media offer opportunities to improve democracy by permitting public conversations that are not dependent on major newspapers? Also, what is the role of large corporations in this transformation? Do they allow enough different voices and viewpoints into the market? Do corporate owners prevent their newspaper divisions from reporting fully on the business aspects of journalism? (We will return to these questions and the public journalism movement in Chapter 14.)

By the late 1990s, the social definition and role of a reporter seemed in question. In reporting the latest White House gossip, weekly supermarket tabloids had a readership three and four times larger than that of the *New York Times,* which began to pursue stories that first appeared in tabloids. Talk-show hosts were also performing news functions by bringing to light controversial issues. Giving third-party candidates like Ross Perot a platform, Larry King's talk show on CNN played a journalistic role in the 1992 and more recent presidential campaigns. By 2004, the twenty-four-hour cable news prime-time talk shows had become major venues for political discussion and national debate. The early 2000s also saw furious competition for younger readers raised on moving images in a highly visual culture. Because most major newspapers are now available via interactive computer services, the old battle lines between print and electronic culture need to be redrawn and remapped. For better or worse, journalism today encompasses a host of resources that perform news and entertainment functions. Newspapers are working to keep up as they compete in a world overloaded with information. The best of them continue to sustain journalism's democratic traditions: They make sense of important events, watch over our central institutions, and go where we often cannot.

www.

For review questions and activities for Chapter 8, go to the interactive *Media and Culture* Online Study Guide at *bedfordstmartins.com/ mediaculture*

REVIEW QUESTIONS

The Evolution of American Newspapers

1. What are the limitations of a press that serves only partisan interests? Why did the earliest papers appeal mainly to more privileged readers?

2. How did newspapers emerge as a mass medium during the penny press era? How did content changes make this happen?

3. What are the two main features of yellow journalism? How have Joseph Pulitzer and William Randolph Hearst contributed to newspaper history?

Competing Models of Modern Print Journalism

4. Why did objective journalism develop? What are its characteristics? What are its strengths and limitations?

5. Why did interpretive forms of journalism develop in the modern era? What are the limits of objectivity?

6. How would you define literary journalism? Why did it emerge in such an intense way in the 1960s? How is literary journalism an attack on objective news?

Categorizing News and U.S. Newspapers

7. What is the difference between consensus- and conflict-oriented newspapers?

8. What role have ethnic, minority, and oppositional newspapers played in the United States?

9. Why have African American newspapers struggled to maintain their circulation levels over the past two decades?

Newspaper Operations: Economic Demands vs. Editorial Duties

10. Explain the distinction between the business and news operations of a newspaper.

11. Define *wire service* and *syndication*.

Ownership, Economics, Technology, and Innovation

12. What are the major reasons for the decline in newspaper circulation figures?

13. What is the impact of a JOA (joint operating agreement) on the business and editorial divisions of competing newspapers?

14. Why did newspaper chains become an economic trend in the twentieth century?

15. What major challenges does new technology pose to the newspaper industry?

Newspapers and Democracy

16. What is a newspaper's role in a democracy?

17. How has the definition of a reporter changed in recent years?

QUESTIONING THE MEDIA

1. What kinds of stories, topics, or issues are not being covered well by mainstream papers?

2. Why do you think people aren't reading daily newspapers as frequently as they once did? What can newspapers do to increase circulation?

3. Discuss whether newspaper chains are ultimately good or bad for the future of journalism.

4. Are Larry King and Oprah Winfrey practicing a form of journalism on their talk shows? Explain your answer.

5. Do newspapers today play a vigorous role as watchdogs of our powerful institutions? Why or why not?

6. Will twenty-four-hour cable TV news and Internet news services eventually replace newspapers? Explain your response.

SEARCHING THE INTERNET

http://www.mediainfo.com

The official Web site of *Editor & Publisher,* the newspaper industry's top trade journal. This site offers statistics on the industry, links to national and international newspaper sites, library and research services, and major stories on the newspaper business.

http://www.naa.org

The site for the Newspaper Association of America, the Newspaper industry's main trade organization, offers information on advertising, circulation, readership, and diversity issues.

http://www.nytimes.com

The site for the nation's most influential newspaper, the *New York Times,* not only offers a Web version of its daily newspaper but also updates major stories throughout the day.

http://www.wsj.com

The site for the nation's most widely circulated daily newspaper, the *Wall Street Journal.* Although parts of the site are by paid subscription only, free services allow readers to access current articles on a range of topics including the economy, financial markets, and politics.

http://www.usatoday.com

The colorful site for the Web version of the nation's newest national paper, *USA Today,* founded in 1982, offers online counterparts to its four main print sections as well as a version of its famous full-color weather map.

http://www.washingtonpost.com

The site for one of the nation's most influential papers, the *Washington Post,* whose publisher also owns *Newsweek* magazine.

Media Literacy
and the Critical Process

In Brief

In class, make several lists on the board regarding what sections of the newspaper you and your classmates read first, second, and/or not at all. Why do you make these choices? What do you think draws you to these particular sections? In terms of the whole class, which sections are people more likely to read first? Can you make any generalizations about your own newspaper-reading behavior and the newspaper-reading habits of your classmates?

In Depth

The purpose of this project is to sharpen your critical approach to news. Work with a partner or in a small group. Over a period of three weekdays, study the *New York Times, USA Today,* and one local daily paper. Devise a chart and a descriptive scheme so that you can compare how each of the three papers covers international news. You should consider international news to be any news story that is predominantly about a country or about another nation's relationship with the United States. Exclude the sports section of the papers. Follow these steps as you work on your project:

Description. Count the total number of international news stories in each paper. Which foreign cities are covered? Which countries? What are the subjects of these stories (civil wars, anti-Americanism, natural disasters, travelogue profiles, etc.)?

Prepare a descriptive chart to show the differences among the three papers.

Analysis. Using your chart as a guide, write two or three paragraphs discussing patterns that emerge. What locales get the most attention? What kinds of stories appear most frequently? In other words, what kind of issue or event makes another country newsworthy? Do not try to summarize your chart here. Instead, focus on three or four intriguing patterns that you noticed.

Interpretation. Write a two- or three-paragraph critical interpretation of your findings. What does your analysis mean? Why do some countries appear more frequently than others? Why do certain kinds of stories seem to get featured?

Evaluation. Discuss the limitations of your study. Which paper seemed to do the best job of covering the rest of the world? Why? Do you think newspapers give us enough information about other people's cultures and experiences?

Engagement. Either individually or with a group of students, write a letter or e-mail to your local editor. Report your findings. In the note, discuss the strengths and weaknesses of the local coverage of international news and other cultures. Mention what the paper does well in this area and suggest what the paper might do better. What kind of response did you get?

KEY TERMS

partisan press, 278
penny papers, 279
human-interest stories, 280
wire services, 281
yellow journalism, 282
objective journalism, 285

inverted-pyramid style, 285
interpretive journalism, 286
advocacy journalism, 288
precision journalism, 288
literary journalism, 288
consensus-oriented journalism, 291

conflict-oriented journalism, 291
newshole, 297
feature syndicates, 300
joint operating agreement (JOA), 301
newspaper chains, 302

magazines

in the age of specialization

Nearly all consumer magazines depend on advertising. In fact, the U.S. consumer economy, for better or worse, owes part of its great growth to the consumer magazine industry, which has both chronicled and advertised consumable lifestyles and products for more than a century. Throughout that time, magazine pages have generally maintained an even balance of about 50 percent editorial content and 50 percent ad copy.

But now, for fashion magazines in particular, the line between editorial content and advertising is be-coming increasingly less important. In a 2005 interview, Cathie Black, president of Hearst Magazines (home of magazines such as *Seventeen*, *Cosmo Girl*, *Marie Claire*, and *Cosmopolitan*), said, "I think over, say, the last five-year period and certainly going forward, maybe a columnist today might write 400 words, as opposed to a 2,000-word piece about 10 years ago. But you want that interactivity. You want those pages to come alive, to show them how to buy products."

Some new magazines have gone even further than using shorter

THE MAGAZINE ABOUT SHOPPING

www.luckymag.com

Lucky.

AUGUST 2006

20
utterly sexy
dresses

Beauty
Secrets
The ultimate
list of must-
have items

ONE-STEP
INSTANT
GLAMOUR
PAGE 176

**Denim
special!**
The best,
newest
mo
flatte
jeans

829

brilliant
ways to
update
your look

Free
Win clothes,
jewelry, gadgets,
and more
LUCKY BREAKS
PAGE 199

AMY SMART
Laid-back,
totally chic

$2.99 USA $3.99 CANADA+FOREIGN

08>

084 51

0 753364 8

chunks of editorial material to engage readers and "show them how to buy products." For these new "shopper" magazines, the whole point is buying products. The magazines feature traditional display ads and editorial content that is also an advertisement.

Leading the pack of shopper magazines is *Lucky*, started in 2000 by Condé Nast, a top magazine publisher. *Lucky* describes itself as "America's ultimate shopping magazine: 100% shopping—and nothing else. The best to buy in fashion, beauty and living. The voice of a friend you love to take shopping. Choices, not dictates. Price points ranging from high to low. Buying info for every item featured."

A typical issue of *Lucky* is built around a theme, such as handbags, jewelry, shoes, or hair. As a glance at the magazine might suggest, *Lucky*'s typical reader is a woman (who likes to shop), with a median age of 29.8 and a median household income of $67,666 (to help pay for all of that shopping). With a circulation of

more than 1 million, *Lucky* is now one of the nation's Top 100 magazines. Given *Lucky*'s success, in 2005 Condé Nast premiered *Domino* magazine, for the woman who "wants to have fun on the never-ending search for items for her home." *Domino* is happy to assist in that never-ending journey, particularly for targeted women with a median age of 34.2 and a median household income of $78,170. *Domino* has a circulation of over 500,000.

Shopper magazines for men have not fared as well. In 2004, Condé Nast created a "buyer's guide for men" called *Cargo*—like *Lucky*, but with a heavy whiff of testosterone-rich upper-middle-class aspiration. *Cargo*'s target readers were men 25 to 45, with an interest in men's fashion and gadgets, gear, electronics, liquor, and automobiles. Where a *Lucky* cover might profess "Totally chic workout stuff (really!)," *Cargo* suggests "Five Tech Toys We Gotta Have." But, the guys weren't buying it, and in 2006 Condé Nast shut down *Cargo.*

With their breakdown of the firewall between editorial and advertising copy, shopper magazines read almost like glossy specialty store catalogues (sometimes called "magalogs") such as those from J. Crew (fashion), Williams-Sonoma (cooking), and Ikea (furnishings), which mix narratives and beautiful photos or illustrations with the items they are trying to sell.

But shopper magazines are just one segment of a thriving magazine marketplace. At the other end of the spectrum are those magazines that shun ad copy in order to preserve editorial independence. In the world of consumer buyer's guides, for example, *Consumer Reports* (with a circulation larger than *Lucky* and *Domino* combined) accepts no advertising so that it can maintain its integrity as a consumer product testing center. *Cook's Illustrated* magazine operates the same way, accepting no advertising so that it can be an unbiased evaluator of recipes, pantry foods, kitchen equipment, and cookware.

When television was on the rise in the early 1950s, many critics predicted the collapse of the magazine industry. But, like radio, the magazine industry showed remarkable resilience in adapting to a changing media landscape. In fact, between 350 and 500 new consumer magazines, like *Domino*, are launched annually.

Magazines adapted readily to the TV era. The introduction in 1953 of an inconspicuous publication—*TV Guide*—was a significant turning point in modern magazine history because *TV Guide* capitalized instantly on TV's popularity. *TV Guide* was also an early example of media convergence: one medium devoting its content to another medium. It demonstrated one way the magazine industry could survive television, which would soon digest ever-larger portions of the national advertising pie.

Traditional national magazines discovered they would have to retool rapidly; television was snatching away sponsors and displacing general-circulation magazines as the dominant family medium. As a result, many magazines started developing market niches, appealing to advertisers who wanted to reach specific audiences defined by gender, age, race, class, or social and cultural interests.

Since the 1740s, magazines have played a key role in our social and cultural lives. More than newspapers, which have been mainly local and regional in scope, magazines became America's earliest national mass medium. They created some of the first spaces for discussing the broad issues of the age, including public education, the abolition of slavery, women's suffrage, literacy, and the Civil War. Early publications provided a political forum for debates among the colonial elite. In addition, many leading literary figures used magazines to gain public exposure for their essays and fiction.

In the nineteenth century, magazines became an important educational forum for women, who were barred from higher education and from active participation in the nation's political life. At the turn of the twentieth century, magazines contained probing reports that would influence a century of investigative print and broadcast journalism. From an economic perspective, magazines helped reorient households toward advertised products, hastening the rise of a consumer society. From a cultural perspective, magazines pioneered the use of engraving and photography, providing the earliest hints of the visual culture to come.

Today—despite movies, radio, television, and cable—magazines still give us voices that are not readily heard in mainstream electronic culture. Certainly, newsmagazines such as *Time* and *Newsweek* play a pivotal role in determining what consumers think about. But outside the mainstream, specialized magazines cover everything from radical politics to unusual hobbies. These publications bring information and viewpoints to readers who are not being served by the major media channels.

More than twenty-two thousand commercial, alternative, and noncommercial publications and newsletters are published in the United States annually. Like newspapers and television, magazines continue to both reflect and construct portraits of American life. They are catalogues for daily events and experiences. They show us the latest products, putting our consumer culture on continuous display. Just as we delve into other forms of culture, we read and view our favorite magazines to learn something about our community, our nation, our world, and ourselves.

In this chapter we will investigate the history and health of the magazine industry, highlighting the colonial and early American eras, the arrival of national magazines, and the development of engraving and photography. Turning to the modern American magazine, we will also focus on the age of muckraking and the rise of general-interest publications and consumer magazines. We will then look at the decline of mass market magazines and TV's impact on the older print medium. We will see how magazines have specialized in order to survive in a fragmented market and adapt in the Information Age. Finally, we will investigate the organization and economics of magazines and their function in a democracy.

> **"** No matter how Net-savvy they might be, readers just want paper. That's good news for [magazine] publishers.**"**
>
> *– Minneapolis Star Tribune*, **2001**

The Early History of Magazines

The first magazines probably developed in seventeenth-century France from book-seller catalogues and notices that book publishers inserted in newspapers. The word *magazine* derives from the French term *magasin,* meaning "storehouse." The earliest magazines were indeed storehouses of contemporary writing and reports taken mostly from newspapers. Today, the word **magazine** broadly refers to collections of articles, stories, and advertisements appearing in nondaily (such as weekly or monthly) periodicals that are published in tabloid style rather than newspaper style.

The first political magazine, called the *Review,* appeared in London in 1704. Edited by political activist and novelist Daniel Defoe (author of *Robinson Crusoe*), the *Review* was printed sporadically until 1713. Like the *Nation, National Review,* and the *Progressive* in the United States today, early European magazines were channels for political commentary and argument. These periodicals looked like newspapers but appeared less frequently and were oriented more toward broad domestic and political issues than toward recent news.

In the eighteenth century, regularly published magazines or pamphlets, such as the *Tatler* and the *Spectator,* also appeared in England. They offered poetry, politics, and philosophy for London's elite, and they served readerships of a few thousand. The first publication to use the term *magazine* was *Gentleman's Magazine,* which appeared in London in 1731 and consisted of reprinted articles from newspapers, books, and political pamphlets. Later the magazine began publishing original work by such writers as Defoe, Samuel Johnson, and Alexander Pope.

Colonial Magazines

With neither a substantial middle class nor advanced printing technology, magazines developed slowly in the United States. Like partisan newspapers, magazines served politicians, the educated, and the merchant classes, interpreting their political, commercial, and cultural world. Paid circulations were slight—between one hundred and fifteen hundred. In the late 1700s, reading magazines was not a habit among the working classes; most adults were illiterate. However, early magazines did document a new nation coming to terms with issues of taxation, state versus federal power, Indian treaties, public education, and the end of colonialism. George

MAGAZINES IN THE AGE OF SPECIALIZATION

National Magazines
The *Saturday Evening Post* is launched in 1821, becoming the first major magazine to appeal directly to women. It becomes the longest-running magazine in U.S. history (p. 316).

Postal Act of 1879
Both postal rates and rail transportation costs plummet, allowing magazine distribution to thrive (p. 317).

1700   1800   1850   1900

Colonial Magazines
First appearing in Philadelphia and Boston in 1741, these generally unsuccessful magazines reprint material from local newspapers (p. 315).

Engravings and Illustrations
By the 1850s, elaborate pictures and photographs begin to fill the pages of magazines (p. 317).

Washington, Alexander Hamilton, and John Hancock all wrote for magazines, and Paul Revere worked as a magazine illustrator for a time.

The first colonial magazines appeared in Philadelphia in 1741, about fifty years after the first newspapers. Andrew Bradford started it all with *American Magazine, or A Monthly View of the Political State of the British Colonies*. Three days later, Ben Franklin's *General Magazine and Historical Chronicle* appeared. Bradford's magazine lasted only three months and three issues. It faced circulation and postal obstacles that Franklin, who had replaced Bradford as Philadelphia's postmaster, put in its way. For instance, Franklin mailed his magazine without paying the high postal rates that he subsequently charged others. Franklin's magazine primarily duplicated what was already available in local papers. After six months he, too, stopped publication.

Following the Philadelphia experiments, magazines emerged in other colonies as well. Several magazines were produced in Boston beginning in the 1740s. The most successful publications simply reprinted articles from leading London periodicals, keeping readers abreast of European events. Magazines such as the *Independent Reflector* also sprang up in New York, featuring poetry as well as cultural and political essays. The *Pennsylvania Magazine*, edited by activist Thomas Paine, helped rally the colonies against British rule. While editing the magazine, Paine worked on his famous 1776 pamphlet *Common Sense*, which made the intellectual case for American independence. By 1776, about a hundred colonial magazines had appeared and disappeared. Although historians consider them dull and uninspired, these magazines did launch a new medium that ultimately caught on after the Revolution.

The Development of the Early U.S. Magazines

The early growth of magazines in the United States was steady but slow. Delivery costs remained high, and some postal carriers even refused to carry magazines because they added so much weight to a load. Only twelve magazines operated in 1800. By 1825, about a hundred magazines existed, although another five hundred or so had failed in the same period. By the early 1800s, most communities had their own weekly magazines, but much of the material was still reprinted from other sources. These magazines featured essays on local issues, government activities, and political intrigue. They sold some advertising but were usually in precarious financial straits because of their small circulations.

The idea of specialized magazines devoted to certain categories of readers developed throughout the nineteenth century. Many early periodicals, for instance,

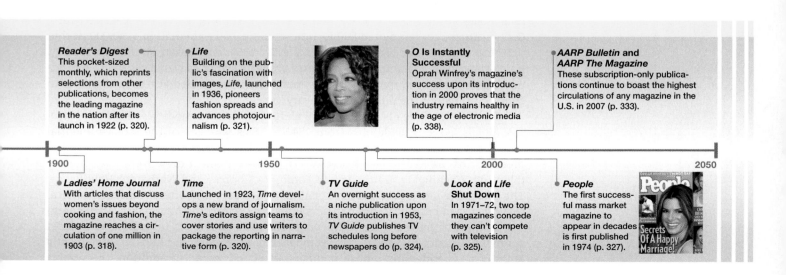

Reader's Digest This pocket-sized monthly, which reprints selections from other publications, becomes the leading magazine in the nation after its launch in 1922 (p. 320).

Life Building on the public's fascination with images, *Life*, launched in 1936, pioneers fashion spreads and advances photojournalism (p. 321).

O Is Instantly Successful Oprah Winfrey's magazine's success upon its introduction in 2000 proves that the industry remains healthy in the age of electronic media (p. 338).

AARP Bulletin and **AARP The Magazine** These subscription-only publications continue to boast the highest circulations of any magazine in the U.S. in 2007 (p. 333).

1900   1950   2000   2050

Ladies' Home Journal With articles that discuss women's issues beyond cooking and fashion, the magazine reaches a circulation of one million in 1903 (p. 318).

Time Launched in 1923, *Time* develops a new brand of journalism. *Time*'s editors assign teams to cover stories and use writers to package the reporting in narrative form (p. 320).

TV Guide An overnight success as a niche publication upon its introduction in 1953, *TV Guide* publishes TV schedules long before newspapers do (p. 324).

Look and **Life Shut Down** In 1971–72, two top magazines concede they can't compete with television (p. 325).

People The first successful mass market magazine to appear in decades is first published in 1974 (p. 327).

were overtly religious. Published by various denominations, religious magazines boasted the largest readerships in their day. The Methodist *Christian Journal and Advocate,* for example, claimed twenty-five thousand subscribers by 1826. Literary magazines also emerged. The *North American Review,* for example, established the work of important writers such as Ralph Waldo Emerson, Henry David Thoreau, and Mark Twain. Besides religion and literature, magazines addressed various professions, lifestyles, and topics, including agriculture (*American Farmer*), education (*American Journal of Education*), law (*American Law Journal*), medicine (*Medical Repository*), and science (*American Journal of Science*). Such specialization spawned the modern trend of reaching readers who share a profession, a set of beliefs, cultural tastes, or a social identity.

In 1821, two young Philadelphia printers, Charles Alexander and Samuel Coate Atkinson, launched the *Saturday Evening Post,* which became the longest-running magazine in U.S. history. The printers operated their venture from the same printing plant that formerly published Franklin's newspaper, the *Pennsylvania Gazette.* Like most magazines of the day, the early *Post* included a few original essays by its own editors but "borrowed" many pieces from other sources. Eventually the *Post* developed into one of the leading magazines of the nineteenth century, featuring news, poetry, essays, and play reviews. Its editors published the writings of such prominent popular authors as Nathaniel Hawthorne and Harriet Beecher Stowe. It was the first major magazine to appeal directly to women, starting the "Lady's Friend," a column that addressed women's issues. During the 1800s, the weekly *Post* became the first important general-interest magazine aimed at a national audience.

The Arrival of National Magazines

With increases in literacy and public education, and with developments in faster printing technology in the mid-1880s, a market was created for more magazines like the *Post.* Improvements in rail transportation also made it possible to ship magazines and other consumer products easily from city to city. Whereas in 1825 a hundred magazines struggled for survival, by 1850 nearly six hundred magazines were being produced. During this twenty-five-year period, publishers launched as many as five thousand magazines, although most of them lasted less than a year.

Besides the *Saturday Evening Post,* the most influential general magazines of the day were targeted at women. In 1828, Sarah Josepha Hale started the first women's magazine, *Ladies' Magazine.* It advocated women's rights and schools to train women as teachers. (Hale did not believe men and women should be educated together.) After nine years and marginal success, Hale merged her magazine with its main rival, *Godey's Lady's Book* (1830–98), which she edited for the next forty years. By 1850, *Godey's,* known for its colored fashion illustrations, had a circulation of 40,000, at that time the biggest ever for a U.S. magazine. By 1860, circulation swelled to 150,000. Hale's magazine, a champion of women's property rights, played a central role in educating working- and middle-class women, who were denied access to higher education throughout the nineteenth century.

Other magazines also marked the shift to national periodicals. *Graham's Magazine,* published in Philadelphia from 1840 to 1858, was one of the most influential and entertaining magazines in the country. Also important at the time was the precursor of the *New Yorker, Knickerbocker* (1833–64), which drew from such literary talent as Washington Irving, James Fenimore Cooper, and Nathaniel Hawthorne. The magazine introduced the "Editor's Table," a breezy and often humorous column that discussed current topics and was later imitated by the *New Yorker.* Also emerging during this period was the *Nation,* founded in 1865 by E. L. Godkin. The oldest surviving American political opinion magazine, the *Nation* continues to serve mostly an educated readership whose politics are left of center. In addition, the weekly

Youth's Companion (1826–1929) became one of the first successful magazines for younger readers. It, too, sought to extend the reach of magazines beyond local boundaries.

Pictorial Pioneers

Like the first newspapers, many early magazines were dull and gray in appearance, totally dependent on the printed word. By the mid-1850s, though, drawings, engravings, woodcuts, and other forms of illustration had become major features of magazines. During this time, *Godey's Lady's Book* employed up to 150 women to color-tint its magazine illustrations and stencil drawings. *Harper's New Monthly Magazine*, founded in 1850, published the work of top American and British writers but also offered extensive woodcut illustrations with each issue. During the Civil War, many readers relied on *Harper's* for its elaborate battlefield sketches. Publications like *Harper's* married visual language to the printed word, helping to transform magazines into a popular national mass medium.

Bringing photographs to magazines took a bit longer. Mathew Brady and his employees, whose thirty-five hundred photos documented the Civil War, had popularized photography by the 1860s. But it was not until the 1890s that newspapers and magazines had the technology to adapt photos to print media.

● Launched in 1886 as a magazine for "first-class families," *Cosmopolitan* began as a literary publication, offering both general-interest and fiction articles. It was not until the 1960s that *Cosmopolitan* began to focus on young, career-oriented women. *McClure's Magazine* inaugurated the era of muckraking in 1902 with Ida Tarbell's investigative series on the Standard Oil Company monopoly.

The Development of Modern American Magazines

In 1870, about twelve hundred magazines were produced in the United States. By 1890, that number reached forty-five hundred; by 1905, more than six thousand existed, most of them intended for local and regional audiences. The rate of failure, however, was high. Although publishers launched approximately seventy-five hundred magazines between 1895 and 1905, more than half of them died or merged with other magazines.[1] Part of this surge in titles and readership was facilitated by the Postal Act of 1879, which assigned magazines lower postage rates and put them on an equal footing with newspapers delivered by mail.

While lower postal rates and better rail transportation were reducing magazines' distribution costs, advances in modern technology were lowering production costs. By the end of the nineteenth century, advances in mass-production printing, conveyor systems, assembly lines, and faster presses made large-circulation national magazines possible.[2] These technological improvements slashed magazine prices, which ran about thirty-five cents a copy in the late 1880s. As prices dropped to fifteen and then to ten cents, the working classes were gradually able to purchase national publications. By 1905, there were about twenty-five national magazines, available from coast to coast and serving millions of readers.[3]

As magazine circulation started to skyrocket, publishers began deriving higher ad revenues from companies eager to sell their wares in the expanding market. Ad pages in national magazines soared. *Harper's*, for instance, devoted only seven pages to ads in the mid-1880s, nearly fifty pages in 1890, and more than ninety pages in 1900.[4] By the turn of the century, advertisers increasingly used national magazines to capture consumers' attention and build a national marketplace. In addition, the dramatic growth of drugstores and dime stores, supermarkets, and department stores offered new venues and shelf space for selling consumer goods, including magazines. As jobs and the population began shifting from farms and small towns to urban areas, magazines helped readers to imagine themselves as part of a nation rather than as individuals with only local or regional identities.

One magazine that took advantage of these changes was *Ladies' Home Journal*, begun in 1883 by Cyrus Curtis. Prior to *LHJ*, many women's magazines had been called cookie-and-pattern publications because they narrowly confined women's concerns to baking and sewing. *LHJ* broadened the scope of magazines as its editors and advertisers realized that women consumers constituted a growing and lucrative market. Publishing popular fiction and sheet music as well as the latest consumer ads, *LHJ* had a circulation of half a million by the early 1890s—the highest of any magazine in the country. In 1903, it became the first magazine to reach a circulation of one million.

Social Reform and the Muckrakers

The economics behind the rise of popular magazines was simple: A commercial publisher could dramatically expand circulation by dropping the price of an issue below the actual production cost for a single copy. The publisher recouped the loss through ad revenue, guaranteeing large readerships to advertisers who were willing to pay more to reach more readers. Throughout the twentieth century, many commercial magazines adopted this principle. However, simply lowering costs from twenty-five or thirty-five cents to a dime wasn't enough. Like the penny press, magazines had to change content as well.

Besides being attracted to the ten-cent price tag, readers were drawn to the issues that magazines addressed. While printing the fiction and essays of good writers of the day, magazines also engaged in one aspect of yellow journalism—crusading for social reform on behalf of the public good. In the early 1890s, for example, Curtis's *LHJ* and its editor, Edward Bok, led the fight against unregulated patent medicines (which often contained nearly 50 percent alcohol). Other magazines joined the fight against phony medicines, poor living and working conditions, and unsanitary practices in various food industries.

The rise in magazine circulation coincided with the search for better jobs. In the move from farms to factories, hundreds of thousands of Americans and new immigrants poured into cities. Thus, the nation that journalists and magazines wrote about had grown increasingly complex by the turn of the century. Some reporters became dissatisfied with conventional journalism and turned from newspapers to magazines, where they were able to write in greater depth about broader issues. They wrote both factual and fictional accounts on such topics as corruption in big business and government, urban problems faced by immigrants, labor conflicts, and race relations. Angry with so much negative reporting, President Theodore Roosevelt in 1906 dubbed these reporters *muckrakers*, because they were willing to crawl in society's muck to uncover a story. **Muckraking** was a label that Roosevelt used with disdain, but it was worn with pride by reporters such as Ray Stannard Baker, Frank Norris, Lincoln Steffens, and Ida Tarbell.

In 1902, *McClure's Magazine* (1893–1933) touched off this investigative era in magazine reporting with a series of probing stories on business monopolies, life insurance frauds, political dishonesty in city governments, and the problems of working people. The muckrakers distrusted established institutions and undertook to protect ordinary citizens from corruption. First serialized in *McClure's,* Ida Tarbell's *The History of the Standard Oil Company* took on John D. Rockefeller's big oil monopoly. Lincoln Steffens's "Shame of the Cities" series tackled urban problems. Steffens said of his own investigations, "When I set out to describe the corrupt systems of certain typical cities, I meant to show simply how the people were deceived and betrayed."[5]

In 1906, *Cosmopolitan* (1886–), recently purchased by William Randolph Hearst, joined the muckraking parade with a series called "The Treason of the Senate." *Collier's* (1888–1957) developed "The Great American Fraud" series, focusing on patent

> **"**Dig and dig some more. Do your job, pile up the proof, believe that if you can simply speak the truth, people—maybe lots of people—will see it your way. That's the creed of the muckraker.**"**
>
> –Kenneth Klee,
> *Book Magazine,* 2001

A NAUSEATING JOB, BUT IT MUST BE DONE

(President Roosevelt takes hold of the investigating muck-rake himself in the packing-house scandal.)

From the *Saturday Globe* (Utica)

medicines (whose ads accounted for 30 percent of the profits made by the American press by the 1890s). Influenced by Upton Sinclair's novel *The Jungle,* a fictional account of Chicago's meatpacking industry, and by the muckraking reports of *Collier's* and *LHJ,* Congress passed the Pure Food and Drug Act in 1906.

The Rise of General-Interest Magazines

The heyday of the muckraking era lasted into the mid-1910s. Then national social crusades and reforms became less significant, as America and journalism were gradually drawn into the first major international war. After World War I the prominent publications were **general-interest magazines,** which offered occasional investigative articles but covered a wide variety of topics aimed at a broad national audience. A key to these magazines, predominant from the 1920s into the 1950s, was the pioneering influence of **photojournalism**—the use of photos to document the rhythms of daily life (see "Case Study: The Evolution of Photojournalism" on pages 322–23). With their high-quality photos, national picture magazines gave the industry at least one advantage over radio, which was developing into the most popular medium of the day.

Saturday Evening Post

The first widely popular general-interest magazine was the *Saturday Evening Post.* When Cyrus Curtis bought the *Post* in 1897 for $1,000, it had a circulation of approximately ten thousand. Curtis's strategy for reinvigorating the magazine included printing popular fiction and romanticizing American virtues through words and pictures (a *Post* tradition best depicted in the three-hundred-plus cover illustrations by

Norman Rockwell). Curtis also featured articles that celebrated the business boom of the 1920s. This reversed the journalistic direction of the muckraking era, in which business corruption was often the focus. By the 1920s, the *Post* had reached 2 million in circulation, the first magazine to hit that mark. By 1920, about fifty-five magazines fit the general-interest category; by 1946, more than a hundred such magazines competed with radio networks for the national audience.

Reader's Digest

The most widely circulated general-interest magazine during this period was *Reader's Digest*. Started in 1922 by Dewitt Wallace and Lila Acheson Wallace for $5,000 in a Greenwich Village basement, *Reader's Digest* championed one of the earliest functions of magazines: printing condensed versions of selected articles from other magazines. In the magazine's early years, the Wallaces refused to accept ads and sold the *Digest* only through subscriptions. The *Digest*'s circulation was just over 100,000 by the late 1920s, when it began to appear on newsstands. With its inexpensive production costs and low price, the magazine's circulation climbed to 1 million in 1935 during the depths of the Great Depression. By 1946, *Reader's Digest* was the nation's most popular magazine, with a circulation of 9 million. Its pocket-size format made it popular both at home and for travel. By 1963, the *Digest* had a circulation of more than 14 million, 5 million more than its nearest rival, *TV Guide*.

For years the *Digest* selected articles based on three criteria: "applicability" (articles relevant to readers' daily lives); "lasting interest" (articles that could still be read the next year); and "constructiveness" (articles that had an optimistic, upbeat outlook on life).[6] Although over the years *Reader's Digest* has been both chastised and praised for its conservative viewpoints and occasionally pious moral tone, by the mid-1980s it had become the most popular magazine in the world. At its peak, it reached a circulation of 20 million in America and another 10 to 12 million in 160 other countries. (See Table 9.1 for the circulation figures of the Top 10 U.S. magazines.)

Time

During the general-interest era, national newsmagazines such as *Time* were also major commercial successes. Begun in 1923 by Henry Luce and Britton Hadden, *Time* developed a magazine brand of interpretive journalism, assigning reporter-researcher teams to cover stories over a period of several weeks. A rewrite editor would then put the whole project together in narrative form and provide an interpretive point of view. Luce believed that journalistic objectivity was a myth and sought instead to be fair. Critics, however, charged that *Time* became increasingly conservative politically as the magazine grew more successful in the 1940s and 1950s. *Time* had a circulation of 200,000 by 1930, increasing to more than 3 million by the mid-1960s.

● **Table 9.1 The Top 10 Magazines (ranked by paid U.S. circulation and single-copy sales, 1972 vs. 2006)**

1972		2006	
Rank/Publication	Circulation	Rank/Publication	Circulation
1 Reader's Digest	17,825,661	1 AARP The Magazine	22,675,583
2 TV Guide	16,410,858	2 AARP Bulletin	22,075,011
3 Woman's Day	8,191,731	3 Reader's Digest	10,111,773
4 Better Homes and Gardens	7,996,050	4 TV Guide	8,211,581
5 Family Circle	7,889,587	5 Better Homes and Gardens	7,620,932
6 McCall's	7,516,960	6 National Geographic	5,403,934
7 National Geographic	7,260,179	7 Good Housekeeping	4,634,763
8 Ladies' Home Journal	7,014,251	8 Family Circle	4,296,370
9 Playboy	6,400,573	9 Ladies' Home Journal	4,122,460
10 Good Housekeeping	5,801,446	10 Woman's Day	4,048,799

Source: Magazine Publishers of America, http://www.magazine.org.

Time's success encouraged prominent imitators, including *Newsweek* (1933–) and *U.S. News & World Report* (1948–). When the major weekly general-interest magazines *Life* and *Look* failed in the early 1970s, newsmagazines took over photojournalism's role in news reporting, visually documenting both national and international events. By 2006, the three major newsmagazines had circulations ranging from *Time*'s 4 million to *Newsweek*'s 3.1 million and *U.S. News*'s 2 million.

Life

Despite the commercial success of *Reader's Digest* and *Time*, these two magazines did not come to symbolize general-interest publications during the 1930s. That honor belongs to the oversized pictorial weeklies *Look* and, especially, *Life*. More than any other magazine of its day, *Life* developed an effective strategy for competing with popular radio by advancing photojournalism. Launched as a weekly by Henry Luce in 1936, *Life* combined the public's fascination with images (invigorated by the movie industry), radio journalism, and the popularity of advertising and fashion photography. By the end of the 1930s, *Life* had a **pass-along readership**—that is, the total number of people who come into contact with a single copy of a magazine—of more than 17 million, rivaling the ratings of popular national radio programs.

Life's first editor, Wilson Hicks, formerly a picture editor for the Associated Press, built a staff of renowned photographer-reporters who chronicled the world's ordinary and extraordinary events from the late 1930s through the 1960s. Among them were Margaret Bourke-White, the first woman war correspondent to fly combat missions during World War II, and Gordon Parks, who later became Hollywood's first African American director of major feature films. *Life*—child of the turn-of-the-century pictorial magazines and parent to *People, Us,* and *Entertainment Weekly*—used an oversized format featuring ninety-six pages of pictures with a minimum of written text.

> **❝** Ford gave Everyman a car he could drive, [and] Wallace gave Everyman some literature he could read; both turned the trick with mass production. **❞**
>
> —John Bainbridge, magazine historian, 1945

The Evolution of Photojournalism

By Christopher R. Harris

What we now recognize as photojournalism started with the assignment of photographer Roger Fenton, of the *Sunday Times of London,* to document the Crimean War in 1856. Technical limitations did not allow *direct* reproduction of photodocumentary images in the publications of the day, however. Woodcut artists had to interpret the photographic images as black-and-white-toned woodblocks that could be reproduced by the presses of the period. Images interpreted by artists therefore lost the inherent qualities of photographic visual documentation: an on-site visual representation of facts for those who weren't present.

Woodcuts remained the basic method of press reproduction until 1880, when *New York Daily Graphic* photographer Stephen Horgan invented half-tone reproduction using a dot-pattern screen. This screen enabled metallic plates to directly represent photographic images in the printing process; now periodicals could bring exciting visual reportage to their pages.

In the mid-1890s, Jimmy Hare became the first photographer recognized as a photojournalist in the United States. Taken for *Collier's Weekly,* Hare's photoreportage on the sinking of the battleship *Maine* in 1898 near Havana, Cuba, established his reputation as a newsman traveling the world to bring back images of news events. Hare's images fed into growing popular support for Cuban independence from Spain and eventual U.S. involvement in the Spanish-American War.

In 1888, George Eastman opened photography to the working and middle classes when he introduced the first flexible-film camera from Kodak, his company in Rochester, New York. Gone were the bulky equipment and fragile photographic plates of the past. Now families and journalists could more easily and affordably document gatherings and events.

As photography became easier and more widespread, photojournalism began to take on an increasingly important social role. At the turn of the century, the documentary photography of Jacob Riis and Lewis Hine captured the harsh working and living conditions of the nation's many child laborers, including crowded ghettos and unsafe mills and factories. Reaction to these shockingly honest photographs resulted in public outcry and new laws against the exploitation of children. Pho-

● Jacob Riis, *The Tramp,* c. 1890. Riis, who emigrated from Denmark in 1870, lived in poverty in New York for several years before becoming a photojournalist. He spent much of his later life chronicling the lives of the poor in New York City. Courtesy: The Jacob A. Riis Collection, Museum of the City of New York.

tographs also brought the horrors of World War I to people far from the battlefields.

In 1923, visionaries Henry Luce and Britton Hadden published *Time,* the first modern photographic newsweekly; *Life* and *Fortune* soon followed. From coverage of the Roaring Twenties to the Great Depression, these magazines used images that changed the way people viewed the world.

Life, with its spacious 10- by 13-inch format and large photographs, became one of the most influential magazines in America, printing what are now classic images from World War II and the Korean War. Often, *Life* offered images that were unavailable anywhere else: Margaret Bourke-White's photographic proof of the unspeakably horrific concentration camps; W. Eugene Smith's gentle portraits of the humanitarian Albert Schweitzer in Africa; David Duncan's gritty images of the faces of U.S. troops fighting in Korea.

Television photojournalism made its quantum leap into the public mind as it documented the assassination of President Kennedy in 1963. In televised images that were broadcast and rebroadcast, the public witnessed the actual assassination and the confusing aftermath, including live coverage of the murder of alleged assassin Lee Harvey Oswald and of President Kennedy's funeral procession.

Photojournalism also provided visual documentation of the turbulent 1960s, including aggressive photographic coverage of the Vietnam War—its protesters and supporters. Pulitzer Prize–winning photographer Eddie Adams shook the emotions of the American public with his photographs of a South Vietnamese colonel's summary execution of a suspected Vietcong terrorist. Closer to home, shocking images of the Civil Rights movement culminated in pictures of Birmingham police and police dogs attacking civil rights protesters.

In the 1970s, new computer technologies emerged that were embraced by print and television media worldwide. By the late 1980s, computers could transform images into digital form, easily manipulated by sophisticated software programs. In addition, any photographer can now transmit images around the world almost instantaneously by using digital transmission, and the Internet allows publication of virtually any image, without censorship. In 1999, a reporter in war-torn Kosovo could take a picture and within minutes send that picture to news offices in Tokyo, Berlin, and New York; moments later, the images could be posted on the Internet or used in a late-breaking TV story.

Digital technology is likely to revolutionize photojournalism, perhaps even more than the advent of roll film did in the late nineteenth century. Because of rapid delivery times, competition among print publications, television networks, and online news providers is heightened, as each can run late-breaking images transmitted from anywhere in the world.

There is a dark side to digital technology as well. Because of the absence of physical film, there is a resulting loss of proof, or veracity, of the authenticity of images. Original film has qualities that make it easy to determine whether it has been tampered with. Digital images, by con-

● John Dominis is best known for his pictures of celebrities and athletes, and his work was often published in *Life* magazine in the 1960s. In the above image, *Stringer* (1964), he chronicled one of the poorest sections in America through the life of an unemployed miner and his family who were living in poverty in Appalachia.

trast, can be easily altered, but such alteration can be very difficult to detect.

A relatively recent example of image-tampering involved a publicity photo of Katie Couric promoted a few weeks before her debut as a CBS weeknight anchor. CBS had doctored the image, which appeared on the CBS Web site, in order to make Couric's entire body drastically thinner and, perhaps in their mind, more attractive. Accusations of foul play from the public and the media forced CBS to remove the picture, and side-by-side versions of the picture, before and after, showed the severity of the tampering. This event gives a small indication of the dangers of altering photographs.

Photojournalists and news sources are now confronted with unprecedented concerns over truth-telling. In the past, trust in documentary photojournalism rested solely on the verifiability of images as they were used in the media. Just as we must evaluate the words we read, at the start of a new century we must also view with a more critical eye these images that mean so much to so many.

Christopher R. Harris is a professor in the Department of Electronic Media Communication at Middle Tennessee State University.

● Photographers for *Life* magazine captured important historical events as well as all aspects of American culture. The image (*above, left*) of Ella Watson was the "first professional photograph" taken by Gordon Parks and is widely considered his signature image. Watson was a cleaning woman in a government building who spoke to Parks about the racial injustice she faced in 1940s Washington, D.C. Photographer Milton Greene was known for his fashion industry images and work with mid-twentieth century Hollywood stars. Greene worked extensively with Marilyn Monroe (*above, right*).

The Fall of General-Interest Magazines

In 1970, *Life*'s circulation peaked at 8.5 million, with an estimated pass-along readership of nearly 50 million. *Life*'s chief competitor, *Look*, founded by Gardner Cowles in 1937, reached 2 million in circulation by 1945 and 4 million by 1955. It climbed to almost 8 million in 1971. Dramatically, though, both magazines suspended publication. The demise of these popular periodicals at the peak of their circulations seems inexplicable, but their fall illustrates a key economic shift in media history as well as a crucial moment in the conversion to an electronically oriented culture.

TV Guide Is Born

While *Life* and *Look* were just beginning to make sense of the impact of television on their audiences, *TV Guide* appeared in 1953. Taking its cue from the pocket-size format of *Reader's Digest* and the supermarket sales strategy used by women's magazines, *TV Guide*, started by Walter Annenberg's Triangle Publications, soon rivaled the success of *Reader's Digest* by specializing in TV listings and addressing the nation's growing fascination with television. The first issue sold a record 1.5 million copies in ten urban markets. The next year, *TV Guide* featured twenty-seven regional editions, tailoring its listings to TV channels in specific areas of the country. Because many newspapers were not yet listing TV programs, *TV Guide*'s circulation soared to 2.2 million in its second year. In 1962, the magazine became the first weekly to reach a circulation of 8 million with its seventy regional editions.

    TV Guide would rank among the nation's most popular magazines from the late 1950s into the twenty-first century. However, with increased competition from newspaper TV supplements and thousands of new magazines, *TV Guide*'s prominence and circulation began flattening out in the 1980s. Then, in 1988, media baron Rupert Murdoch acquired Triangle Publications for $3 billion. Out of this magazine group (which included *Seventeen* and the *Daily Racing Form*), Murdoch kept only *TV*

Guide. Murdoch's News Corporation already owned the new Fox network, and buying *TV Guide* ensured that the fledgling network would have its programs listed. Prior to this move, many predicted that no one would be able to start a new network because ABC, CBS, and NBC exercised so much control over television. By the mid-1990s, however, Fox was using *TV Guide* to promote the network's programming in the magazine's 100-plus regional editions. The other networks occasionally complained that their programs were not treated as well and even threatened to pull their ads.

The *TV Guide* story illustrates a number of key trends in the magazine business. First, in exploiting Americans' shared interest in television, *TV Guide* emerged as a wildly successful magazine just as general magazines began their economic decline. Second, *TV Guide* demonstrated the growing sales power of the nation's checkout lines, which also sustained the high circulation rates of women's magazines and supermarket tabloids. Third, News Corporation's ownership of *TV Guide* underscored the fact that magazines were facing the same challenges as other mass media: Large media companies were strategically buying up smaller media outlets and applying the economic synergy of using one medium to promote another.

After the Fox network became firmly established, Murdoch's News Corporation looked for ways to expand the publication's reach and prevent it from becoming obsolete in the new electronic media environment. In 1999, Murdoch struck a deal with cable television's Prevue Channel. The deal combined *TV Guide*'s print listings with the Prevue Channel's program listings to create the TV Guide Channel. In 2000, the *TV Guide* franchise morphed again when Gemstar International acquired TV Guide, Inc. in a $7 billion merger. Because Gemstar controlled all the patents that make digital TV guides possible, the new company—Gemstar–TV Guide International, Inc. (News Corporation has a 40 percent share)—quickly became the leading on-screen guide for program information on cable and satellite TV systems. Although the TV Guide Channel has prospered, *TV Guide* magazine has not. In 2005, as the magazine's circulation continued to decline, Gemstar radically redesigned *TV Guide* as a full-sized single-edition national magazine, dropping its smaller digest format and its 140 local editions. The new magazine focuses on entertainment and lifestyle news and carries only limited listings of cable and network TV schedules.

The rise of *TV Guide* in the 1950s as a specialized service paralleled the decline of the weekly general-interest magazines that had dominated the industry for thirty years. By 1957, both *Collier's* (founded in 1888) and *Woman's Home Companion* (founded in 1873) had folded. Each magazine had a national circulation of more than 4 million the year it died. No magazine with this kind of circulation had ever shut down before. Together, the two publications brought in advertising revenues of more than $26 million in 1956. Although some critics blamed poor management, both magazines were victims of changing consumer tastes, rising postal costs, falling ad revenues—and television, which began usurping the role of magazines as the preferred family medium.

Life and *Look* Expire

Although *Reader's Digest* and women's supermarket magazines were not greatly affected by television, other general-interest magazines were. The weekly *Saturday Evening Post* folded in 1969, *Look* in 1971, and *Life* in 1972. At the time, all three magazines were rated in the Top 10 in terms of paid circulation; each had a readership that exceeded 6 million per issue. To maintain these figures, however, their publishers were selling the magazines for far less than the cost of production. For example, by the early 1970s a subscription to *Life* cost a consumer twelve cents an issue, yet it cost the publisher more than forty cents per copy to make and mail a single issue.

Eventually, the national advertising revenue pie that helped make up the cost differences for *Life* and *Look* had to be shared with network television—and maga-

IN A HAREM

BEACH EXERCISE

SCIENTIFIC G-MEN

YOUR FUTURE

OIL WELL FIRE

10¢

JULY 19, 1938

Look

MARLENE DIETRICH'S TROUBLES EXPOSED!

zines' slices were getting smaller. *Life*'s high pass-along readership meant that it had a larger audience than many prime-time TV shows. But it cost more in 1971 to reach that general audience with a single full-page ad in *Life* than it did to buy a minute of time during evening television. National advertisers were often forced to choose between the two, and in the late 1960s and early 1970s television seemed a slightly better buy to many general advertisers looking for the biggest audience.

The failure of prominent general magazines was complicated by other problems as well. Essentially, both distribution and production costs (especially paper) were rising, whereas national magazine ad sales had flattened out. Also, the *Saturday Evening Post, Life,* and *Look* still relied more on subscriptions than on supermarket and newsstand sales. Dramatic increases in postal rates, however, had a particularly negative effect on oversized publications (those larger than the 8- by 10.5-inch standard for most magazines). In the 1970s, postal rates increased by more than 400 percent for these magazines. The *Post* and *Life* cut their circulations drastically to save money. The *Post* went from producing 6.8 million to 3 million copies per issue; *Life*, which lost $30 million between 1968 and 1972, cut circulation from 8.5 million to 7 million. The economic rationale here was that limiting the number of copies would reduce production and postal costs, enabling the magazines to lower their ad rates to compete with network television. But, in fact, with decreased circulation, these magazines became less attractive than television for advertisers trying to reach the largest general audience.

The general magazines that survived the competition for national ad dollars tended to be women's magazines, such as *Good Housekeeping, Better Homes and Gardens, Redbook, Ladies' Home Journal,* and *Woman's Day.* These publications were in smaller formats and depended primarily on supermarket sales rather than on expensive mail-delivered subscriptions. However, the most popular magazines, *TV Guide* and *Reader's Digest,* benefited not only from supermarket sales but also from their larger circulation (twice that of *Life*), their pocket size, and their small photo budget. Although the *Saturday Evening Post* and *Life* later returned as downsized monthlies, their failure as oversized weeklies ushered in a new era of specialization.

People Puts *Life* Back into Magazines

In March 1974, Time Inc. launched *People*, the first successful mass market magazine to appear in decades. With an abundance of celebrity profiles and human-interest stories, *People* showed a profit in two years and reached a circulation of more than 2 million within five years. *People* now ranks first in revenue from advertising and circulation sales—more than $1.2 billion a year.

The success of *People* is instructive, particularly because only two years earlier television had helped kill *Life* by draining away national ad dollars. Instead of using a bulky oversized format and relying on subscriptions, *People* downsized and generated most of its circulation revenue from newsstand and supermarket sales. For content, it took its cue from our culture's fascination with celebrities. Supported by plenty of photos, its articles were short, with about one-third as many words as those of a typical newsmagazine.

Time Inc. used *People* as the model for reviving *Life* in 1978 as a standard-size supermarket monthly. In this format, *Life* had modest success, but parent company

● With large pages, beautiful photographs, and compelling stories on celebrities like Marlene Dietrich, *Look* entertained millions of readers from 1939 to 1971, emphasizing photojournalism to compete with radio. By the late 1960s, however, TV lured away national advertisers, postal rates increased, and production costs rose, forcing *Look* to fold despite a readership of more than eight million.

OPRAH WINFREY: I'M NOT GAY
JULY 31, 2004

People

CHRISTIE BRINKLEY'S SHOCKING SPLIT: HUSBAND CHEATS WITH TEEN

AVRIL LAVIGNE'S Un-Punk Wedding

Sandra & Jesse's First Anniversary

Secrets Of A Happy Marriage!

Surprise gifts, sweet messages, nonstop PDA. And? She 'makes me feel like I'm Superman,' says Jesse

● Although *People* magazine doesn't have the widest circulation, it is the most profitable of all U.S. magazines. In combined subscription and single-copy sales, *People* generates more than a half-billion dollars a year for Time Warner.

Time Warner ended its run in 2000 due to low profit margins. *Life* was again resuscitated in 2004 as a weekend magazine insert for newspapers in markets across the nation.

Although *People* has not achieved the broad popularity that *Life* once commanded, it does seem to defy the contemporary trend of specialized magazines aimed at narrow but well-defined audiences, such as *Tennis World*, *Game Informer*, and *Hispanic Business*. One argument suggests that *People* is not, in fact, a mass market magazine but a specialized publication targeting people with particular cultural interests: a fascination with music, TV, and movie stars. If *People* is viewed as a specialty magazine, its financial success makes much more sense in a world dominated by electronic mass media.

The Domination of Specialization

The general trend away from mass market publications and toward specialty magazines coincided with radio's move to specialized formats in the 1950s. With the rise of television in that decade, magazines ultimately reacted the same way radio did: They adapted, trading the mass audience for smaller, discrete audiences that could be guaranteed to advertisers. Two major marketing innovations also helped ease the industry into a new era: the development of regional and demographic editions.

Regional Editions

As television advertising siphoned off national ad revenues, magazines began introducing **regional editions**: national magazines whose content is tailored to the interests of different geographic areas. For example, *Reader's Digest* for years had been printing different language editions for international markets.

Other magazines adapted this idea to advertising variations and inserts. Often called **split-run editions**, these national magazines tailor ads to different geographic areas. Most editions of *Time*, *Newsweek*, and *Sports Illustrated*, for example, contain a number of pages of regional ads. The editorial content remains the same, but the magazine includes a few pages of ads purchased by local or regional companies in various areas of the country. By the end of the 1960s, nearly 250 magazines featured split-run editions. This strategy has been enhanced by the growth of regional printing centers, which enable publishers to download national magazines from communications satellites for printing near their distribution points. The local ads are inserted at the various regional production sites.

Demographic Editions

Another variation of specialization includes **demographic editions**, which target particular groups of consumers. In this strategy, market researchers identify subscribers primarily by occupation, class, and zip-code address. In an experiment conducted in 1963, *Time* pioneered demographic editions by carrying advertising from a drug company that was inserted into copies of its magazine. These editions were then sent to only 60,000 doctors chosen from *Time*'s subscription rolls. By the 1980s, aided by developments in computer technology, *Time* had also developed special editions for top management, high-income zip-code areas, and ultrahigh-income professional/managerial households. Certain high-income zip-code editions, for instance, would include ads for more expensive consumer products. *Sports Illustrated* uses demographic editions to offer advertisers its most affluent subscribers, and also its "adventure" readers who regularly participate in outdoor individual sports.

The economic strategy behind regional and demographic editions guaranteed advertisers a particular magazine audience at lower rates. Because these ads would run only in special editions, advertisers had to purchase only part of the total audience. Not only is this less expensive than buying access to a publication's entire readership, but it also links a national magazine with local retailers. The magazine can then compete with advertising in regional television or cable markets and in newspaper supplements. Because of the flexibility of special editions, new sources of income opened up for national magazines. Ultimately, these marketing strategies permitted the massive growth of magazines in the face of predictions that television would cripple the magazine industry.

> **"Demographics should be the province of marketers and advertisers, not magazine editors."**
>
> —Matt Goldberg, former editor of the defunct magazine *Swing*, 1998

Magazine Types: *Playboy* to *AARP The Magazine*

Although regional and demographic editions provided specific strategies for financial survival, the magazine industry ultimately prospered by fragmenting into a wide range of choices and categories. Given their current variety, magazines are not easily classified by type, but one method has been to divide them by advertiser type: consumer magazines *(Newsweek; Maxim)*, which carry a host of general consumer product ads; business or trade magazines *(Advertising Age; Progressive Grocer)*, which include ads for products and services for various occupational groups; or farm magazines *(Dairy Herd Management; Dakota Farmer)*, which contain ads for agricultural products and farming lifestyles. Grouping by advertisers further distinguishes commercial magazines from noncommercial magazine-like periodicals. The noncommercial category includes everything from activist newsletters and scholarly journals to business newsletters created by companies for distribution to employees. Magazines such as *Ms.* and *Consumer Reports*, which rely solely on subscription and newsstand sales, also accept no advertising.

As we have seen, during the 1950s radio, film, and magazines arrived at a crossroads as they encountered television. In their own ways, all three media shifted to specialization. Radio developed formats for older and younger audiences, for rock fans and classical fans. At the movies, filmmakers focused on more adult subject matter that was off-limits to television's image as a family medium. The depiction of language, violence, and sexuality all changed as movies sought an identity apart from television.

Magazines also used such strategies as they searched for niche audiences that were not being served by the new medium. In the magazine industry, publications targeted older and younger readers, tennis buffs, and quilting enthusiasts. Magazine content changed, too. *Playboy*, started in 1953 by Hugh Hefner, undermined the conventional values of pre–World War II America and emphasized subject matter that was taboo on television in the 1950s. Scraping together $7,000, Hefner published his first issue, which contained a nude calendar reprint of actress Marilyn Monroe together with an attack on

> **"The idea was there of a magazine that would paint the picture of a more entertaining, romantic life for a generation of men who had come back from World War II, were going to college in record numbers, and started to envision the possibilities of a life that was different and richer than what their fathers had lived."**
>
> —Christie Hefner, *Playboy* editor in chief, 2003

alimony payments and gold-digging women. With the financial success of that first issue, which sold more than 50,000 copies, Hefner was in business.

Circulation gradually climbed, and Hefner introduced advertising in 1956. *Playboy*'s circulation peaked in the 1960s, at more than 7 million, but fell gradually throughout the 1970s as the magazine faced competition from imitators and video, as well as criticism for "packaging" women for the enjoyment of men. Throughout the 1970s and 1980s, government commissions and religious groups succeeded in eliminating the sale of *Playboy* and similar magazines at military bases and in many local retail chains.

Playboy's early financial success demonstrated to the magazine industry that specialty magazines aimed at men could achieve large circulation figures. Women's publications sold in supermarkets had long demonstrated that gender-based magazines were highly marketable and that women wielded enormous economic clout. *Better Homes and Gardens, Good Housekeeping, Ladies' Home Journal, Family Circle,* and *Woman's Day* have all ranked among the Top 12 for years, with circulations ranging from 4 million to 7.6 million by 2006. But these numbers are the exception rather

> **" It was a response to Puritan repression. "**
>
> –Hugh Hefner, 2003, on launching *Playboy*

● **Table 9.2 Number of New Consumer Magazine Launches by Interest Category, 2005**

Category	Number	Category	Number	Category	Number
Metropolitan/ Regional/State	57	Fashion/Beauty/ Grooming	7	Gay/Lesbian	3
Crafts, Games, Hobbies & Models	34	Men's	6	Health	3
Black/Ethnic	30	Political/Social Topics	6	Horses/Riding/ Breeding	3
Special Interest	21	Travel	6	Military/Naval	3
Home Service/Home	19	TV/Radio/ Communications/ Electronics	6	Babies	2
Sex	18	Computers	5	Fishing/Hunting	2
Automotive	13	Fitness	5	Literary Reviews/ Writing	2
Sports	13	Gaming	5	Media Personalities	2
Music	10	Arts/Antiques	4	Teen	2
Epicurean	9	Business/Finance	4	Boating/Yachting	1
Pop Culture	9	Children's	4	Bridal	1
Women's	8	Motorcycles	4	Dressmaking/ Needlework	1
Comic/Comic Technique	7	Religious/ Denominational	4	Science/Technology	1
Entertainment/ Performing Arts	7	Camping/Outdoor Recreation	3		
				TOTAL	**350**

Source: Magazine Publishers of America, http://www.magazine.org, 2006.

Note: This list represents only weekly, bimonthly, monthly, and quarterly titles that meet MPA criteria.

than the norm. Of the eighteen thousand or so consumer magazines published in the United States today, fewer than ninety have a circulation of more than 1 million. Most contemporary magazines and newsletters aim at smaller communities of readers who share values, interests, or social identity—from Asian Americans to disabled veterans and politically conservative students. Indeed, in 2006 the Magazine Publishers of America trade organization listed more than forty special categories of consumer magazines, illustrating the fragmentation of the industry. These include magazines organized around sports and leisure activities, travel and geography, lifestyle and age, and race and ethnicity (see Table 9.2).

Leisure, Sports, and Music Magazines

The television age spawned not only *TV Guide* but also a number of specialized leisure magazines. For example, *Soap Opera Digest* updates viewers on the latest plot twists and their favorite characters. In the age of specialization, magazine executives have developed multiple magazines for fans of soap operas, running, tennis, golf, hunting, quilting, antiquing, surfing, and video game playing, to name only a few. Within categories, magazines specialize further, targeting older or younger runners, men or women golfers, duck hunters or bird-watchers, and midwestern or southern antique collectors.

The most popular sports and leisure magazine is *Sports Illustrated*, which took its name from a failed 1935 publication. Launched in 1954 by Henry Luce's Time Inc., *Sports Illustrated* was initially aimed at well-educated, middle-class men. It has become the most successful general sports magazine in history, covering everything from major-league sports and mountain climbing to fox hunts and snorkeling. Although frequently criticized for its popular but exploitative yearly swimsuit editions, *Sports Illustrated* over the years has done major investigative pieces—for example, on racketeering in boxing and on land conservation. Its circulation climbed from more than half a million in its first year to 2 million by 1980 and more than 3.1 million by 2006.

Another popular magazine type that fits loosely into the leisure category includes magazines devoted to music—everything from rap's *The Source* to country's *Country Weekly*. The all-time circulation champ in this category is *Rolling Stone*, started in 1967 as an irreverent, left-wing political and cultural magazine by twenty-one-year-old Jann Wenner. Once considered an alternative magazine, by 1982 *Rolling Stone* had paddled into the mainstream with a circulation approaching 800,000—with half of its ninety-six-plus pages devoted to high-gloss fashion and consumer ads. By 2006 *Rolling Stone*, still famous for its personality profiles and occasionally radical feature articles on economics or politics, had a circulation of more than 1.3 million. Many fans of the early *Rolling Stone*, however, disappointed with its move to increase circulation and reflect mainstream consumer values, turned to less high-gloss alternatives such as *Spin* and *Blender*.

Travel and Geography Magazines

In 1992 and 1993, capitalizing on the increasing longevity of the American population and retirees interested in travel, publishers introduced

● Drawing on the built-in audience of Oprah Winfrey's millions of fans, *O: The Oprah Magazine* has quickly become one of the top-selling magazines in the country since its launch in 2000.

● One growing segment of the magazine industry is publications devoted to video and computer games (of course, this growth parallels the expanding popularity of the games themselves). *Game Informer* magazine covers all areas of the gaming industry from previews of upcoming games and reviews to providing code information and a Web site with forums.

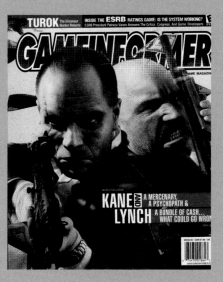

Media Literacy
and the Critical Process

Uncovering American Beauty

How does the leading fashion magazine in the United States define "beauty"? One way to explore this question is by critically analyzing the covers of *Cosmopolitan*.

Description. If you review a number of *Cosmopolitan* covers, you'll notice that they typically feature a body shot of a female model, surrounded by blaring headlines—often using words like *Hot* and *Sex* to lure readers inside the magazine. The cover model is dressed provocatively and is positioned against a solid color background. She looks confident. Everything about the cover is loud and brassy.

Analysis. What are some *significant* patterns here? If you look at issue after issue, all of these models look incredibly alike: They're tall, they've got a sassy expression, they've got long hair, and they're white. It's as if they are all the same person, recast with every issue. In fact, with a little more research, you would discover that *Cosmopolitan* has used only three black models and three Hispanic models since 1990 (Naomi Campbell in 1990; Halle Berry in 2002; Cameron Diaz, Eva Longoria, and Jennifer Lopez in 2005; and Beyoncé in 2006) and only six black models since the magazine began using cover photos in 1964.[1]

Interpretation. What does this mean? Do *Cosmopolitan*'s covers even come close to reflecting the racial composition of the United States, which is 30 percent nonwhite? Does the magazine narrowly define beauty as almost exclusively white? All of the models, it seems, appeal to the fashion and advertising industries' narrow mainstream standard of beauty.

Evaluation. Perhaps *Cosmo*'s lack of diversity on its covers is due to a lack of diversity within the magazine's staff. The magazine industry as a whole is only 6.1 percent nonwhite. Perhaps this broad-circulation magazine is scared of alienating its audience of Middle Americans by featuring a cover girl who does not look like them. Either way, *Cosmo* seems to be increasingly out of touch. There could also be a generation gap. Teen magazines are increasingly presenting more diverse notions of beauty; magazines like *Teen Vogue* more frequently feature nonwhite cover models. Judge the magazine. How is it doing, and how could it do better?

Engagement. Contact *Cosmo*'s editor in chief, Kate White, and request greater representation of ethnic minorities on the magazine's covers. You can contact her and the editorial department via e-mail (cosmo_letters@hearst.com), telephone (212-649-3570), or U.S. mail: Kate White, Editor, Cosmopolitan, 224 West 57th Street, New York, NY 10019. Also, track representation issues with other fashion magazines.

---

thirty new travel magazines. Periodicals such as *Discover, Smithsonian, AAA Going Places, Travel & Leisure,* and *Condé Nast Traveler* have all ranked among the nation's Top 200 magazines. Some accompany subscriptions to museum organizations or travel clubs, like the American Automobile Association (AAA). Others are devoted to exploring distant cultures or planning trips to various locales.

The undisputed champion in this category is *National Geographic*. Boston lawyer Gardiner Green Hubbard and his famous son-in-law, Alexander Graham Bell, founded the magazine in 1888 along with the nonprofit National Geographic Society. From the outset, *National Geographic* relied for its content on a number of distinguished mapmakers, naturalists, explorers, geologists, and geographers. Bell, who became the society's director in 1889, referred to the magazine as "a vehicle for carrying the living, breathing human-interest truth about this great world of ours to the people."[7] Promoted as "humanized geography," *National Geographic* helped pioneer color photography in 1910. It was the first publication to publish both undersea and aerial color photographs. It remains one of the few magazines that subscribers save from year to year and also pass along from generation to generation. In addition, many of *National Geographic*'s nature and culture specials on television, which began in 1965, rank among the most popular programs in the history of public television. *National Geographic*'s popularity grew slowly and steadily throughout the twentieth century, reaching 1 million in circulation in 1935 and 10 million in the 1970s. In the late 1990s, its circulation of paid subscriptions slipped to under 9 million, prompting the staid National Geographic Society to diversify and lend its name to for-profit ventures such as CD-ROMs, television miniseries, a cable channel, and a line of road maps and atlases. The other media ventures provided new revenue as circulation for the magazine continued to slide, falling to 5.4 million by 2006.

Magazines for the Ages

For years, magazines have targeted readers by economic class and lifestyle, usually distinguishing the mass appeal of *People* and *Reader's Digest* from the more sophisticated appeal of, say, the *New Yorker* or the *Economist*. In the age of specialization, however, magazines have further delineated readers along ever-narrowing age lines, appealing more and more to very young and to older readers, groups that have often been ignored by mainstream television.

The first children's magazines appeared in New England in the late 1700s. Ever since, magazines such as *Youth's Companion, Boy's Life* (the Boy Scouts' national publication since 1912), *Highlights for Children,* and *Ranger Rick* have successfully targeted preschool and elementary-school children. The ad-free *Highlights for Children,* which can be obtained only through subscription, led the top children's magazine category in 2005, with a circulation of more than 2 million.

In the popular arena, the leading female teen magazines have shown substantial growth; the top magazine for thirteen- to nineteen-year-olds is *Seventeen*, with a circulation of 2 million in 2006. Several established magazines responded to the growing popularity of the teen market by introducing specialized editions, such as *Teen Vogue, Teen People,* and *Cosmo Girl!* Targeting young men in their twenties, *Maxim,* launched in 1997, was one of the fastest-growing magazines of the late 1990s, leveling off with a circulation of 2.5 million by 2005. *Maxim*'s covers boast the magazine's obsession with "sex, sports, beer, gadgets, clothes, fitness," a content mix that helped it eclipse rivals like *GQ* and *Esquire*, and inspired other "lad" magazines like *FHM* and *Stuff*. To extend its franchises, *Maxim*'s publisher will be partner in the Maxim Hotel and Casino that is scheduled to open on the Las Vegas strip in 2010.

Especially in the beauty and fashion segments, marketing magazines toward age groups continues through the lifespan. For example, women ages eighteen to forty-nine are targeted with titles such as *Cosmopolitan, Vogue, Glamour, Elle, Harper's Bazaar, Self,* and *Allure*. (For more on women's fashion magazines, see "Media Literacy and the Critical Process: Uncovering American Beauty" on opposite page.)

In targeting audiences by age, the most dramatic success has come from magazines aimed at readers over age fifty, America's fastest-growing age segment. These publications have tried to meet the cultural interests of older Americans, who historically have not been prominently featured in mainstream consumer culture. The American Association of Retired Persons (AARP) and its magazine, *AARP The Magazine* (formerly *Modern Maturity*), were founded in 1958 by retired California teacher Ethel Percy Andrus, who eleven years earlier had established the National Retired Teachers Association (NRTA). For years, both groups published newsletters—which they later merged into the *AARP Bulletin* —keeping older citizens current on politics, health, and culture.

Subscriptions to the bimonthly *AARP The Magazine* and the monthly *AARP Bulletin* have always carried a modest membership fee ($12.50 in 2006). By the early 1980s, *AARP The Magazine*'s circulation approached 7 million. However, with the AARP signing up thirty thousand new members each week by the late 1980s, both

> **"** Every magazine has its own architecture. *National Geographic* is a Greek revival temple. *TV Guide* is a fruit stand. The *New Yorker* is a men's hat store. The *Atlantic* is a church (Congregational). **"**
>
> —Roger Rosenblatt, *New Republic*, 1989

> **"** The seniors' group is using its magazine to assure us getting older is, uh, sexy and, oh yeah, fun. The seniors group's magazine is trying to appeal to varying generations of (ssshhh) older people. **"**
>
> —Bob Baker, *Los Angeles Times* staff writer

● Many magazines circulate worldwide, producing international editions in several languages. Here, a Beijing woman stands amid hundreds of magazine titles from around the globe.

AARP *The Magazine* and the newsletter overtook *TV Guide* and *Reader's Digest* as the top circulated magazines. By 2006, both had circulations of about 22 million, far surpassing the circulations of all other magazines. Article topics in the magazine cover a range of lifestyle, travel, money, health, and entertainment issues, such as the effects of Viagra on relationships, secrets for spectacular vacations, and how poker can give you a sharper mind. Not available at newsstands, AARP *The Magazine* also did not carry advertising during its first ten years. The conventional wisdom in many ad agencies, dominated by staffers under age fifty, suggested that people over fifty were loyal to certain brand names and were difficult to influence through ads. Research demonstrated, however, that many in this group are more affluent than eighteen- to forty-nine-year-olds and have consumer interests increasingly in line with the thirty-nine to forty-nine age bracket. Today, AARP *The Magazine* still carries few consumer ads, relying mostly on inexpensive subscriptions, the growth of its target age group, and its readers' continuing interest in the printed word.

Elite Magazines and Cultural Minorities

In his important 1964 study, *Magazines in the Twentieth Century*, historian Theodore Peterson devoted a chapter to cultural minorities. In the mid-1960s, though, the term *cultural minorities* referred to elite readers who were served mainly by non–mass market political and literary magazines such as *Atlantic Monthly, Kenyon Review,* the *Nation, National Review,* the *New Republic,* the *New Yorker, Partisan Review,* and

Poetry. In general, these political and literary magazines appealed to formally educated readers who shared political ideas, aesthetic concerns, or social values. To their credit, the editors and publishers of these magazines have often struggled financially to maintain the integrity of their magazines in an industry dominated by advertising and mass market publications.

The *New Yorker*

The most widely circulated "elite" magazine in the twentieth century was the *New Yorker.* Launched in 1925 by Harold Ross, the *New Yorker* became the first city magazine aimed at a national upscale audience. In some ways, the *New Yorker* was the magazine equivalent of the *New York Times,* cultivating an affluent and educated audience and excluding general readers. Snubbing the Midwest, Ross once claimed, "The *New Yorker* will be the magazine which is not edited for the old lady in Dubuque. It will not be concerned in what she is thinking about."[8] Over the years, the *New Yorker* featured many of the twentieth century's most prominent biographers, writers, reporters, and humorists, including A. J. Liebling, Dorothy Parker, Lillian Ross, John Updike, E. B. White, and Garrison Keillor, as well as James Thurber's cartoons and Ogden Nash's poetry. It introduced some of the finest literary journalism of the twentieth century, devoting an entire issue to John Hersey's *Hiroshima* and serializing Truman Capote's *In Cold Blood.*

By the mid-1960s, the *New Yorker's* circulation hovered around 500,000. Just as the *New York Times* became known as the nation's best newspaper, the *New Yorker* made promotional claims as the country's best magazine. By the 1960s, the magazine even had a hundred subscribers in Dubuque, Iowa, including a number of "old ladies." In 1985, the *New Yorker* was acquired for $168 million by Advance Publications, the Newhouse newspaper publishing conglomerate. By 2006, the magazine's circulation had reached 1 million and was experiencing its most profitable period since Advance purchased it.

Redefining Cultural Minorities

By the 1980s and 1990s, the term *cultural minority* had taken on different connotations. It referred to distinctions regarding gender, age, race, ethnicity, and sexual orientation. Since the late 1960s, with attention drawn to many discriminatory practices, a number of magazines have developed to address concerns that were often ignored by mainstream magazines. Historically, one key magazine has been the *Advocate,* which began in 1967 as a twelve-page newsletter addressing issues about homosexuality. By the mid-1980s, the magazine had a circulation of nearly 90,000, and by 2006, it had reached 120,000. Late in 2005, PlanetOut bought both *The Advocate* and *Out,* another gay-oriented magazine with 130,000 circulation, for $31 million. Each year, about three new gay/lesbian magazines are launched in the United States.

PRICE $3.99   THE NEW YORKER   JULY 31, 2006

● Famous for its inventive cartoons, well-crafted prose, and whimsical covers, the *New Yorker* first appeared in 1925. Originally planned as a local publication, the *New Yorker* developed into one of the nation's most influential magazines over the years, shaping public opinion on everything from national politics to popular culture.

The *Advocate* has published some of the best journalism on AIDS, antigay violence, and policy issues affecting gay communities. In some instances, its reporting has led to increased coverage of important issues by the mainstream press.

In general, the term *cultural minority* has been more closely associated with racial and ethnic groups that have often been misrepresented or underrepresented in America's popular media. To counter white mainstream conceptions, African American magazines, for example, date to antislavery publications such as the *Emancipator, Liberator,* and *Reformer* during the pre–Civil War era. In the modern age, the major magazine publisher for African Americans has been John H. Johnson, a former Chicago insurance salesman who started *Negro Digest* in 1942 on $500 borrowed against his mother's furniture. By 1945, with a circulation of more than 100,000, the *Digest*'s profits enabled Johnson and a small group of editors to start *Ebony,* a picture-text magazine modeled on *Life* but serving chiefly black readers. The Johnson Publishing Company has since successfully introduced *Jet,* a pocket-size supermarket magazine that originally contained shorter pieces left over from *Ebony.* In 2006, *Jet*'s circulation was close to 1 million.

Johnson's publications were among the first places where people could see black images on a weekly basis in American popular culture. Originally criticized for favoring light-skinned over dark-skinned black faces, *Ebony* has developed over the years into the leading popular magazine forum for black politics and social life in the United States. In fact, Johnson's publications were among the first forums to help clarify what it meant to be black and middle-class in America after World War II. By 2006, *Ebony* had more than 1.4 million paid subscribers. In 1970, the first successful magazine aimed at black middle-class women, *Essence,* was started by Edward Lewis and enjoyed a circulation of 1 million in 2006.

With increases in Hispanic populations and immigration, magazines appealing to Spanish-speaking readers have developed rapidly since the 1980s. In 1983, the De Armas Spanish Magazine Network began distributing Spanish-language versions of mainstream American magazines, including *Cosmopolitan en Español, Harper's Bazaar en Español,* and *Ring,* the prominent boxing magazine. By the late 1990s, a new wave of magazines was released, some in Spanish, some in English, and some in a combination of both languages to reflect the bilingual lives of many Americans of Hispanic descent. The involvement of major media corporations signaled that the Hispanic magazine audience had arrived for major advertisers: The bilingual *Latina* magazine was started with the help of Essence Communications in 1996, media giant Time Warner launched *People en Español* nationally in 1997, and Condé Nast and Ideas Publishing Group introduced *Glamour en Español* in 1998. *People en Español, Latina,* and *Glamour en Español* rank as the Top 3 Hispanic magazines by ad revenue. Other top Hispanic magazines include *Reader's Digest Selecciones, Vogue en Español, Hispanic Business, Vanidades,* and *TV y Novelas.* Recent magazine launches include *ESPN Deportes* and *Sports Illustrated en Español.* The new magazines are targeted at the most upwardly mobile segments of the growing American Latino population, which numbered more than 42 million—about 14 percent of the U.S. population—by 2006.

Supermarket Tabloids

Partly due to the bad reputation of **supermarket tabloids**, neither the newspaper nor the magazine industry likes to claim them as part of its domain. With headlines like "J. Lo Meltdown!" "Plastic Surgery Disaster!" "Ashton and Demi's Secret Life Exposed!" and "Al Qaeda Breeding Killer Mosquitos," tabloids push the limits of both decency and credibility. Although they are published on newsprint, the Audit Bureau of Circulations, which checks newspaper and magazine circulation figures to determine advertising rates, counts weekly tabloids as magazines. Tabloid history can be traced to newspapers' use of graphics and pictorial layouts in the 1860s and 1870s, but the modern U.S. tabloid dates from the founding of the *National Enquirer* by William Randolph Hearst in 1926. The *Enquirer* struggled until it was purchased in 1952 by Generoso Pope, who had worked in the cement business and for his father's New York–based Italian-language newspaper, *Il Progresso*. Also a former intelligence officer for the CIA's psychological warfare unit, Pope intended to use the paper to "fight for the rights of man" and "human decency and dignity."[9] In the interest of profit, though, he settled on the "gore formula" to transform the paper's anemic weekly circulation of 7,000: "I noticed how auto accidents drew crowds and I decided that if it was blood that interested people, I'd give it to them."[10]

By the mid-1960s, Pope had built the *Enquirer's* circulation to 1 million through the use of bizarre human-interest stories, gruesome murder tales, violent accident accounts, unexplained phenomena stories, and malicious celebrity gossip. Later, the *Enquirer* incorporated some of yellow journalism's crusading traditions, reporting government cover-ups and stories of bureaucratic waste. By 1974, the magazine's weekly circulation topped 4 million, where it remained for several years. In 1977, its edition covering the death of Elvis Presley included a controversial picture of Presley in his open coffin and sold more than 6.6 million copies, still a tabloid record.

In 1974, Rupert Murdoch's News Corporation launched the *Star,* built on the "circus-poster layout, garish headlines, and steamy prose" traditions of Great Britain's tabloid press. Among the *Star's* announced objectives: to "not be politically committed, not be a killjoy, not be bullied, not be boring."[11] The *Star* and a third major tabloid player, the *Globe* (founded in 1954), cut into the *Enquirer's* circulation and set the tone for current trends in tabloid content, including stories on medical cures, astrological predictions, alien mutants, celebrity gossip, and the occult.

During the 1990s, the circulation of the three largest tabloids fell precipitously. Not only did imitators like the *National Examiner,* the *Sun,* and the *Weekly World News* offer competition, but *People, Us,* new entertainment magazines, newsmagazines, and talk shows also began claiming part of the tabloid audience.[12] At the same time, occasional investigative and political stories started appearing in tabloids and influencing coverage by major newspapers and newsmagazines. Tabloid editors, however, have tried to avoid most political stories: Circulation apparently declines when political intrigue graces their front pages.[13] Although their popularity peaked in the 1980s, tabloids continue to specialize in reaching audiences not served by mainstream media.

● Launched in 1996, *Latina* has become the largest magazine targeted to Hispanic women in the United States. It counts a readership of two million bilingual, bicultural women and is also the top Hispanic magazine in advertising pages.

Web Magazines and Media Convergence

By 2006, the three most popular Internet magazines—in terms of hits—were *Entrepreneur, Forbes,* and *Sports Illustrated,* with entrepreneur.com scoring "6 million unique visitors" in February 2006.[14] The Internet's flexibility and vast, inexpensive distribution capabilities make it an attractive area of investment for companies and individuals looking to create a successful magazine or to broaden the reach of print versions. Just like newspapers, magazines can solve space limitation problems by using the Internet to offer increased content, including promotions that encourage readers to subscribe or buy the printed magazine at the newsstand. For example, Condé Nast, owned by Advance Publications and in 2006 the No. 2 magazine publisher after Time Warner, views the Internet as a way to take their printed versions and "extend the experience into the Web." By 2006, Condé Nast, which publishes *Vanity Fair, Vogue, GQ, Glamour, Jane,* and three bridal magazines, planned to expand its online presence by creating for each of its twenty-nine traditional magazines a Web site that allows readers to talk with editors and each other in forums and that includes video. *Jane* editor Brandon Holley even engaged film/video students to come to the magazine's offices and make videos of *Jane* workers: "Our beauty editor will show people how to cover up a zit on a fellow staffer."[15]

A few Web sites, such as Web MD, BabyCenter, and AlwaysOn, have moved from the Internet to glossy paper as they introduced a print magazine in order to expand their readership. But more typically magazines are working in the other direction. Hachette Filipacchi Media closed down publication of its new *Elle Girl* magazine in 2006, keeping only its free online version. The company said it would be less expensive to recruit new generations of teen readers on the Web.

The Internet also offers a solution to some of the distribution problems associated with magazines. With production costs much lower than those of glossy print publications, and with the potential for an interactive interface and widespread distribution, the Web provides an alternate route to maintaining our culture's connection to words, analysis, and ideas. **Webzines** such as *Salon* and *Slate*, which are magazines that appear exclusively on the Web, have made the Web a legitimate site for breaking news and discussing culture and politics. Although some Webzines, such as Microsoft's *Slate*, have big corporate backers, most original Webzines have more modest beginnings and arise out of an interest in creating a cultural or political forum. For example, *Salon* magazine was founded in 1995 by five former reporters from the *San Francisco Examiner* who wanted to break from the traditions of newspaper publishing and build "a different kind of newsroom" to create well-developed stories and commentary. With the help of positive word-of-mouth comments, *Salon* became the leading Webzine, claiming 2.4 million unique visitors by 2006. Yet stand-alone, advertising-supported Webzines have yet to find great financial success. As *Slate* discovered in 1999, Web readers aren't likely to pay for subscriptions. Some Webzines continue to struggle in the slow transition from print-oriented advertising to Internet-based ads.

In the meantime, new titles continue to be launched in the magazine industry, often with brand-extending synergies in mind. For example, in the late 1990s cable network ESPN started *ESPN the Magazine*, and A&E introduced *Biography* magazine, based on its successful program franchise. Oprah Winfrey's talk show and Web site helped to drive millions of subscribers to *O: The Oprah Magazine* in 2000. More recently, Reader's Digest Association launched *Everyday with Rachael Ray*, capitalizing on the Food Network's celebrity chef, while Modern Media used a well-known book series as the inspiration for *Chicken Soup for the Soul Magazine*, which promises to be "a magazine that reaffirms our faith in the basic goodness of the human condition."

> **"** . . . inevitably, fashion advertisers that prop up the glossies will, like everyone else, increasingly migrate to Web and mobile interactive advertising. **"**
>
> *– Advertising Age, 2006*

The Organization and Economics of Magazines

Given the great diversity in magazine content and ownership, it is hard to offer a common profile of a successful magazine. Unlike a broadcast station or a daily newspaper, a small newsletter or magazine can begin cheaply via the computer-driven technology of **desktop publishing**, which enables one aspiring publisher-editor to write, design, lay out, and even print a modest publication. Such self-published magazines—sometimes called **zines** (pronounced "zeens")—are also mushrooming on the Internet.

Departments and Duties

Throughout the 1990s, electronic alternatives did not slow the growth of printed magazines. Despite the rise of inexpensive desktop publishing, most large commercial magazines still operate several departments, which employ hundreds of people.

Production and Technology

The magazine unit most concerned with merging old and new ideas is the production and technology department, which maintains the computer and printing hardware necessary for mass market production. Because magazines are usually printed weekly, monthly, or bimonthly, it is not economically practical for most magazine publishers to maintain expensive print facilities. As with *USA Today,* many national magazines are now able to digitally transport magazine copy via satellite to various regional printing sites for the insertion of local ads and for faster distribution.

To attract advertisers and audiences over the years, magazines have deployed other technological innovations: from *National Geographic*'s pioneering 3-D color holograph cover to digitized full-color versions of magazines on the Internet. Today they have developed special inserts, called *selective edits,* for specific customers. For example, *Sports Illustrated* identified 500,000 serious golfers among its readers and began a "Golf Plus" insert for those copies sent to golfing enthusiasts.[16]

Editorial Content

The lifeblood of a magazine is the editorial department, which produces its content, excluding advertisements. Like newspapers, most magazines have a chain of command that begins with the publisher and extends to the editor in chief, the managing editor, and a variety of subeditors. These subeditors oversee such editorial functions as photography, illustrations, reporting and writing, copyediting, and layout and design. Writing staffs for magazines generally include contributing writers, who are specialists in certain fields. Magazines also hire professional, nonstaff *freelance writers,* who are assigned to cover particular stories or a region of the country. Many magazines, especially those with small budgets, also rely on well-written unsolicited manuscripts to fill their pages. Most commercial magazines, however, reject more than 95 percent of unsolicited pieces.

Advertising and Sales

The advertising and sales department of a magazine secures clients, arranges promotions, and places ads. Industrywide, this unit has pioneered innovations such as the scent strip in perfume ads, pop-up ads, and ads on computer microchips that emit sounds when a page is turned. Besides stuffing magazines with the ever-present subscription renewal postcards, this department also conducts market research to study trends and changes in magazine-reading habits.

Magazines generate about half their annual revenue from selling ads, with the remaining money coming from single-copy and subscription sales. (Another source of magazine revenue—but one that the magazine industry rarely wishes to discuss with the general public—is the sale of subscription lists to advertisers and marketers.) Like radio and TV stations, consumer magazines offer advertisers rate cards, which list what a magazine charges for an ad. For example, a top-rated consumer magazine might charge $140,000 for a full-page color ad and $30,000 for a one-third page, black-and-white ad. However, in today's competitive world most rate cards are not very meaningful: Almost all magazines offer 25 to 50 percent rate discounts to advertisers.[17]

Although fashion and general-interest magazines carry a higher percentage of ads than do political-literary magazines, the average magazine contains about 50 percent ad copy and 50 percent editorial material. This figure has remained fairly constant over the past twenty-five years.

A few contemporary magazines, such as *Highlights for Children,* have decided not to carry ads and rely solely on subscriptions and newsstand sales instead. To protect the integrity of its various tests and product comparisons, for instance, *Consumer Reports* carries no advertising. To strengthen its editorial independence, *Ms.* magazine abandoned ads in 1990 after years of pressure from the food, cosmetics, and fashion industries to feature recipes and more complementary copy. Some advertisers and companies have canceled ads when a magazine featured an unflattering or critical article about a company or industry.[18] In some instances, this practice has put enor-

> **❝ So that's the creative challenge, especially when you work for a bridal magazine, is how do we keep this material fresh? How do we keep it relevant? How do we, you know, get the reader excited, keep ourselves excited?❞**
>
> —Diane Forden, editor in chief,
> *Bridal Guide* magazine, 2004

EXAMINING ETHICS

Ms. Magazine's Latest Challenge

In spring 1972, *Ms.* magazine jolted the U.S. magazine industry with the first issue of a magazine that took the feminist movement seriously. The magazine had its detractors, including network news anchor Harry Reasoner, who quipped, "I'll give it six months before they run out of things to say."

It turned out that *Ms.* had a lot of things to say. The magazine became a leading and award-winning voice on issues such as abortion, the Equal Rights Amendment, domestic violence, pornography, and date rape.

In 1990, *Ms.* magazine cofounder Gloria Steinem, surveying the state of women's magazines and the influence advertisers have over journalism, asked, "Can't we do better than this?" That was the beginning of another bold move for *Ms.* magazine, which subsequently stopped carrying advertisements (except for nonprofit and cause-related organizations).

Although its rejection of advertisers has enabled *Ms.* to be uniquely outspoken and independent in U.S. journalism, it has also made the magazine financially unstable at times, as it has had more than a half-dozen owners. In 2001, the Los Angeles–based Feminist Majority Foundation assumed ownership of the magazine and changed *Ms.* to a quarterly publication schedule.

The challenge for *Ms.* now is to engage a new generation of readers who may not have even been around in 1972. As the *Los Angeles Times* put it, "The new *Ms.* has a mandate to remind American women that feminism isn't dead, isn't irrelevant, and isn't lame just because your mother was into it."[1]

"I want twenty-year-olds to read this magazine."

—*Ms.* editor in chief, Elaine Lafferty, 2003

Table 9.3 Major Magazine Chains (selected holdings as of 2006)

Advance Publications (Staten Island, NY)

Condé Nast Group

Allure	Lucky
Architectural Digest	Modern Bride
Bon Appétit	New Yorker
Bride's	Parade
Condé Nast Traveler	Self
Domino	Teen Vogue
Glamour	Vanity Fair
Gourmet	Vogue
GQ	W
House & Garden	Wired

Hachette Filipacchi, a subsidiary of Lagardère Groupe (Paris)

Car and Driver	Metropolitan Home
Cycle World	Premiere
Elle	Road & Track
Elle Decor	Woman's Day

Hearst Corporation (New York, NY)

Cosmopolitan	Marie Claire
Country Living	O: The Oprah Magazine
Esquire	Popular Mechanics
Good Housekeeping	Redbook
Harper's Bazaar	Seventeen
House Beautiful	Town & Country

Meredith Corporation (Des Moines, IA)

American Baby	Child
Better Homes and Gardens	Country Home

(Continued on next page)

mous pressure on editors not to offend advertisers. The cozy relationships between some advertisers and magazines have led to a dramatic decline in investigative reporting, once central to popular magazines during the muckraking era (see "Examining Ethics: *Ms.* Magazine's Latest Challenge" on page 341).

Circulation and Distribution

The circulation and distribution department of a magazine monitors single-copy and subscription sales. Subscriptions, which dominated the industry's infancy, have made a strong comeback. For example, toward the end of the general-interest era in 1950, single-copy sales at supermarkets and newsstands accounted for about 43 percent of magazine sales and subscriptions constituted 57 percent. By 2005, single-copy sales had fallen to 13 percent, whereas subscriptions had risen to 87 percent. One tactic used by circulation departments is to encourage consumers to renew well in advance of their actual renewal dates. Magazines can thus invest and earn interest on early renewal money as a hedge against consumers who drop their subscriptions each year. Another strategy is "evergreen" subscriptions, those that automatically

Meredith Corporation (Des Moines, IA) *continued*

Do It Yourself	*Ladies' Home Journal*
Family Circle	*Parents*
Fitness	*Successful Farming*

PRIMEDIA (New York, NY)

America's Civil War	*Snowboarder*
American History	*Soap Opera Digest*
Canoe & Kayak	*Soap Opera Weekly*
Guns & Ammo	*Surfing*
Hot Rod	*Truckin'*
Motor Trend	*Turbo & High-Tech Performance*
New York Magazine	*Walleye In-Sider*

Rodale Press (Emmaus, PA)

Backpacker	*Mountain Bike*
Bicycling	*Prevention*
Men's Health	*Runner's World*

Time Inc. (New York, NY)

Cooking Light	*Progressive Farmer*
Entertainment Weekly	*Southern Living*
FORTUNE	*Sports Illustrated*
Health	*Sports Illustrated for Kids*
Money	*Sunset*
Parenting	*This Old House*
People	*Time*

Sources: Hoover's Online, www.hoovers.com; *Advertising Age*, Ad Age DataCenter, http://www.adage.com/datacenter.cms.

renew on a credit card account unless subscribers request that the automatic renewal be stopped.

Magazines circulate in two basic ways: paid or controlled. *Paid circulation* means that consumers either pay for a regular subscription to the magazine or buy individual copies at a newsstand or supermarket. Most consumer magazines depend on paid circulation as well as advertising. *Controlled circulation* provides readers with the magazine at no charge and generally targets captive audiences such as airline passengers or association members. Many business or technical magazines and newsletters, which depend on advertising or corporate sponsorship, are distributed free to members or loyal customers. Major magazine publishing company Hachette Filipacchi developed new titles in the 1990s by producing custom-controlled circulation magazines for specific organizations, such as *Trump Style* for guests of Donald Trump's casinos.[19]

Studies by the Magazine Publishers of America suggest that more than 80 percent of all American households either subscribe to a magazine or purchase one on a regular basis. The average household typically purchases at least six different titles during a given year. Although the magazine industry was generally regarded as economically healthy throughout the 1980s, some signs worry editors and publishers.

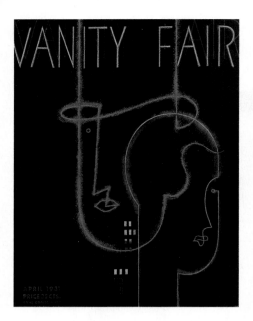

Originally launched in the United States in 1914 by Condé Nast, *Vanity Fair* featured top writers such as Dorothy Parker and P. G. Wodehouse. In 1922, it helped to identify the "flapper" style emerging among young women. The magazine folded in 1936 but was revived in its current form by Condé Nast in 1983. It is now known for its mix of social and political commentary, celebrity profiles, fiction, fashion, and arts coverage. Today's contributors include photographer Annie Leibovitz and writers James Wolcott and Christopher Hitchens.

> **"** If you don't acknowledge your magazine's advertisers, you don't have a magazine. **"**
>
> –Anna Wintour, editor of *Vogue*, 2000

For instance, in 1990, for the first time since the Great Depression, the number of consumer magazine titles declined. In addition, a decline in operating pretax profit margins for magazines, which began in the early 1990s, plagued the industry. In part, the decline was attributed to the proliferation of specialized cable television channels and new Internet services that competed for the same advertisers. The magazine industry boomed through the late 1990s, but by 2001 and on, as the U.S. economy slowed, the magazine industry has felt the pinch of declining ad sales.

Major Magazine Chains

In terms of ownership, the commercial magazine industry most closely resembles the cable television business, which actually patterned its specialized channels on the consumer magazine market. About seventeen thousand commercial magazine titles appear each year—many of them independently owned—compared to roughly ten thousand cable systems that now operate in the United States. Also, as in the cable industry, large companies or chains increasingly dominate the magazine business. This raises yet unanswered questions about the impact of a handful of powerful magazine owners on the ideas that circulate in the commercial marketplace.

Time Warner, the world's largest media conglomerate and the nation's largest Internet service provider, also runs a magazine subsidiary, Time Inc., a top player among magazine-chain operators with about thirty major titles. (See Table 9.3 on pages 342–43.) Cross-division synergies at Time Warner have been particularly helpful to its magazines. For example, pop-up boxes on AOL generated 1.1 million subscriptions for Time Inc. magazines in less than a year.

Other important commercial players include Mortimer Zuckerman, who owns the *Atlantic Monthly* and *U.S. News & World Report,* and the Meredith Corporation, which specializes in women's and home-related magazines. The Hearst Corporation, the leading magazine chain early in the twentieth century, still remains a formidable publisher. New York City–based PRIMEDIA (formerly K-III Communications, and owned by investment firm Kohlberg Kravis Roberts) publishes more than ninety magazine titles, ranging from *Lowrider* to *Dressage Today*, and also controls the school-based Channel One news.

Long a force in upscale consumer magazines, Condé Nast is a division of Advance Publications, which operates the Newhouse newspaper chain (see Figure 9.1). The Condé Nast group controls several key magazines, including *Vanity Fair, GQ*, and *Vogue*. Advance Publications also owns *Parade* magazine, the popular Sunday newspaper supplement that goes to 33.9 million homes each week. Because Sunday supplements come with newspaper subscriptions, they are not counted among most official magazine tallies. Nevertheless, *Parade* and its closest rival, *USA Weekend* (23.3 million weekly circulation), reach far more readers than the leading popular magazines.

International companies like Paris-based Hachette Filipacchi are also major players in the U.S. magazine industry. Hachette owns more than two hundred magazine titles worldwide, including about twenty in the United States. Its holdings include *Elle, Woman's Day, Premiere,* and *Car and Driver.* Germany's Bertelsmann is a

Figure 9.1
Media Ownership: Principal Operations for Advance Publications

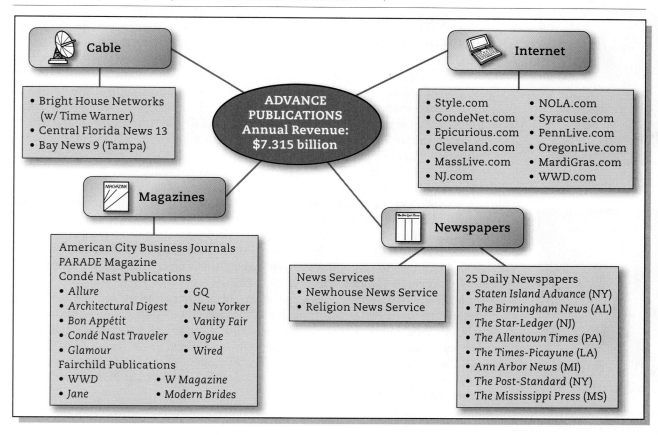

Advance Publications, Inc. is a rarity among media conglomerates because it is privately owned. Since the 1920s, the Newhouse family (namesakes of the School of Public Communications at Syracuse University) has quietly amassed media properties that now include Condé Nast Publications, Parade Publications, Fairchild Publications, American City Business Journals, the Golf Digest Companies, newspapers in more than twenty U.S. cities, and Bright House, a leading cable television system operator. What effect, if any, could one family's private ownership of these media outlets have on their content?

dominant European publisher, with titles like *Stern* and *Brigitte* (Germany), *Voici* and *Gala* (France), and *Muy Interesante* (Spain).

In addition, a number of American magazines have carved out market niches worldwide. *Reader's Digest, Cosmopolitan, Newsweek,* and *Time,* for example, all produce international editions in several languages. In general, though, most American magazines are local, regional, or specialized and therefore less exportable than this country's movies and television. Of the nearly nineteen thousand titles, only about two hundred magazines from the United States circulate routinely in the world market. Such magazines, however, like exported American TV shows and films, still play a key role in determining the look of global culture.

Alternative Voices

With fewer than ninety of the almost nineteen thousand American commercial, trade, and farm magazines reaching circulations that top 1 million, the great bulk of

● Although their magazines have seldom been profitable, editors William F. Buckley (*top*) and Victor Navasky (*bottom*) have played an influential role in American political thought. Buckley founded the conservative magazine *National Review* in 1955.

From 1978 to 2005, Navasky was the editor, and later publisher, of the *Nation*—a liberal magazine—before becoming chairman of the *Columbia Journalism Review*. Despite relatively small circulations, leading political magazines are influential because they tend to be read by politicians and other key decision makers.

alternative publications struggle to satisfy small but loyal groups of readers. Of these more modest periodicals, alternative magazines number more than two thousand, with many failing and others starting up from month to month.

Alternative magazines have historically defined themselves in terms of politics—published either by the Left (e.g., the *Progressive; In These Times;* the *Nation*) or the Right (e.g., *National Review; American Spectator; Insight*). However, what constitutes an alternative magazine has broadened far beyond politics to include just about any publication considered "outside the mainstream," ranging from politics to punk-zines—the magazine answer to punk rock. The *Utne Reader,* widely regarded as "the *Reader's Digest* of alternative magazines," has defined *alternative* as any sort of "thinking that doesn't reinvent the status quo, that broadens issues you might see on TV or in the daily paper."

Occasionally, alternative magazines have become marginally mainstream. For example, during the conservative Reagan era in the 1980s, William F. Buckley's *National Review* saw its circulation swell to more than 100,000—enormous by alternative standards. In the late 1980s, the *Review* even ran slick TV ads featuring actors such as Charlton Heston and Tom Selleck and former actor and president Ronald Reagan. On the Left, *Mother Jones* (named after labor organizer Mary Harris Jones), which continues to champion the muckraking tradition of investigative journalism, had a circulation of more than 240,000 in 2006.

Most alternative magazines, however, are content to swim outside the mainstream. These are the small magazines that typically include diverse political, cultural, religious, international, environmental, and humorous alternative publications such as *Against the Current; Punk Planet; Christianity and Crisis; Jewish Currents; Asia Book Club Review; Whole Earth Review; Yellow Silk: Journal of Erotic Arts; Hysteria: Women, Humor and Social Change*; and the *Journal of Polymorphous Perversity* ("a social scientist's answer to *Mad* magazine").

Magazines in a Democratic Society

Like other mass media whose product lines have proliferated, magazines are a major part of the cluttered media landscape. To keep pace, the magazine has become fast-paced and high-risk. Of the eight hundred to one thousand new magazines that start up each year, fewer than two hundred will survive longer than a year.

As an industry, magazine publishing—like advertising and public relations—has played a central role in transforming the United States from a producer to a consumer society. Since the 1950s, though, magazines have not been the powerful national voice they once were, uniting separate communities around important issues such as abolition and suffrage. Today, with so many specialized magazines appealing to distinct groups of consumers, magazines play a much-diminished role in creating a sense of national identity.

On the positive side, magazine ownership is more diversified than ownership in other mass media. More magazine voices circulate in the marketplace than do broadcast or cable television channels. Moreover, many new magazines still play an important role in uniting dispersed groups of readers, often giving cultural minorities or newly arrived immigrants a sense of membership in a broader community.

Contemporary commercial magazines provide essential information about politics, society, and culture, thus helping us think about ourselves as participants in a democracy. Unfortunately, however, these magazines have often identified their readers as consumers first and as citizens only secondarily. With magazines' growing dependence on advertising, controversial content sometimes has difficulty finding its way into print. More and more, magazines define their readers merely as viewers of displayed products and purchasers of material goods.

At the same time, magazines arguably have had more freedom than other media to encourage and participate in democratic debates. In addition, because magazines are distributed weekly, monthly, or bimonthly, they are less restricted by the deadline pressures of daily newspapers or evening broadcasts. Good magazines can usually offer more analysis of and insight into society than other media outlets can. In the midst of today's swirl of images, magazines and their advertisements certainly contribute to the commotion. But good magazines also maintain our connection to words, sustaining their vital role in an increasingly electronic and digital culture.

www.

For review questions and activities for Chapter 9, go to the interactive *Media and Culture* Online Study Guide at *bedfordstmartins.com/mediaculture*

REVIEW QUESTIONS

The Early History of Magazines

1. Why did magazines develop later than newspapers in the American colonies?

2. Why did most of the earliest magazines have so much trouble staying financially solvent?

3. How did magazines become national in scope?

The Development of Modern American Magazines

4. What role did magazines play in social reform at the turn of the twentieth century?

5. When and why did general-interest magazines become so popular?

6. Why did some of the major general-interest magazines fail in the twentieth century?

The Domination of Specialization

7. What triggered the move toward magazine specialization?

8. What are the differences between regional and demographic editions?

9. What are the most useful ways to categorize the magazine industry? Why?

The Organization and Economics of Magazines

10. What are the four main departments at a typical consumer magazine?

11. What are the major magazine chains, and what is their impact on the mass media industry in general?

Magazines in a Democratic Society

12. How do magazines serve a democratic society?

QUESTIONING THE MEDIA

1. What are your earliest recollections of magazines? Which magazines do you read regularly today? Why?

2. What role did magazines play in America's political and social shift from being colonies of Great Britain to becoming an independent nation?

3. Why is the muckraking spirit—so important in popular magazines at the turn of the twentieth century—generally missing from magazines today?

4. If you were the marketing director of your favorite magazine, how would you increase circulation?

5. Think of stories, ideas, and images (illustrations and photos) that do not appear in mainstream maga-

zines. Why do you think this is so? (Use the Internet, LexisNexis, or the library to compare your list with Project Censored, an annual list of the year's most underreported stories.)

6. Discuss whether your favorite magazines define you primarily as a consumer or as a citizen. Do you think magazines have a responsibility to educate their readers as both? What can they do to promote responsible citizenship?

7. Do you think cable television, the Internet, and other technology will eventually displace magazines? Why or why not?

SEARCHING THE INTERNET

http://www.newpages.com/npguides/altmags.htm

The NewPages Guide to Alternative Periodicals lists (and links to) hundreds of alternative magazines published in the United States and throughout the world.

http://www.magazine.org

The site of the Magazine Publishers of America, the industry association for consumer magazines, loaded with magazine facts and data.

http://www.aarp.org

The American Association of Retired Persons (AARP) is a nonprofit association founded in 1958 and dedicated to aging issues. The site includes links to AARP's *Bulletin* and AARP *The Magazine*.

http://www.mrmagazine.com

The Web site of a leading magazine expert, Samir Husni, a University of Mississippi journalism professor also known as "Mr. Magazine." An excellent resource for tracking new magazine titles.

http://www.oprah.com

The popular site for Oprah Winfrey's synergistic media empire, including links to *O: The Oprah Magazine*.

http://www.condenast.com

Home to Condé Nast Publications, one of the leading magazine publishers. Includes links to the media kits for the company's publications.

Media Literacy
and the Critical Process

In Brief

Using a few sample magazines in class, consider the following issues related to magazine advertisements:

- Are ads placed in proximity to editorial content of a related topic (e.g., suntan lotion or sunglasses ads next to an article about beach vacations)?
- How aesthetically similar are the ads and editorial content (e.g., the style of a magazine's photo shoot and its fashion ads)?
- Are there ads that seem to be at odds with the editorial content (e.g., cigarette ads in a youth-oriented magazine)?
- Do ad pages outnumber editorial content pages?
- Do ad pages make it hard to find the magazine's table of contents?

Discuss the following questions: Do ads add a positive experience to magazine reading? Do they seem to influence magazine content? Can a magazine's credibility be damaged by too much adherence to advertiser values? Are there some magazines that are purchased largely for the ads?

In Depth

The purpose of this project is to appreciate the ideological diversity of weekly newsmagazines. Work with a partner or in small groups. (This project could also be converted into a formal argument paper.)

Description. Take a recent issue of the mainstream newsweekly *Time* (circulation 4 million) and review all the articles, including the various topics covered, the writing style and tone, the level of analysis within the articles, and the information sources employed. Next, take a recent issue of the conservative magazine the *Weekly Standard* (circulation about

65,000) and the progressive magazine the *Nation* (circulation about 184,000). (Other political magazines may be substituted.) In the same manner, review all the articles. To add another dimension to your research, review the ads in each magazine.

Analysis. Devise a chart to organize your findings according to (a) the stories covered and (b) the *way* the stories are covered. What patterns emerge? How do the publications differ? What do you notice about the advertisers in each magazine?

Interpretation. The *Weekly Standard* and the *Nation* represent competing visions of society. To what extent are their viewpoints also reflected in the mainstream media? Why do you think certain topics covered in these magazines are included/excluded from mainstream magazines like *Time*?

Evaluation. What value do magazines like the *Weekly Standard* and the *Nation* add to the debate on various social issues? Are there other mass media (television, radio, etc.) that cover the same issues from their political perspective regularly? Should their views be reflected more in the mainstream media? What would this public dialogue look like? If people are reading only mainstream media, what are they missing?

Engagement. Keep track of what may be missing in the mainstream media sphere by reading magazines that offer alternatives, and make sure you read articles that you don't agree with. Try dipping into the following conservative publications: the *National Review*, the *Weekly Standard*, and the *American Conservative*. Likewise, sample the stories from the *Nation*, the *Progressive*, and *Mother Jones*. Begin to question your own ideology. Where do you stand on these important issues? Finally, impress your friends with your knowledge and inspire them to start reading more.

KEY TERMS

books
and the power of print

The two major publishing phenomena of the past decade are the Harry Potter series and *The Da Vinci Code*. In fact, by 2006 a few critics even predicted that *The Da Vinci Code*, written by Dan Brown in 2003, would some day rank second only to the Bible as the most popular single book of all time. *The Da Vinci Code*—made into a 2006 blockbuster film by director Ron Howard—offers a juicy conspiracy theory about a marriage between Jesus and Mary Magdalene that produced offspring and a royal bloodline that extends to today. In the novel, conservative Catholic Church authorities try to cover up this tale—even condoning murder to do so (committed mostly by a spiritually impaired albino who beats himself after each murder). By 2006, 40 million–plus copies of the *Code* were in circulation, but the fictional thriller faced criticism about the liberties Brown took with actual history and the Bible. By comparison, by 2006 the first six books in J. K. Rowling's Harry Potter series had sold 300 million copies worldwide (book 6 alone sold 10 million copies in twenty-four hours after its 2005 release). These books also faced criticism

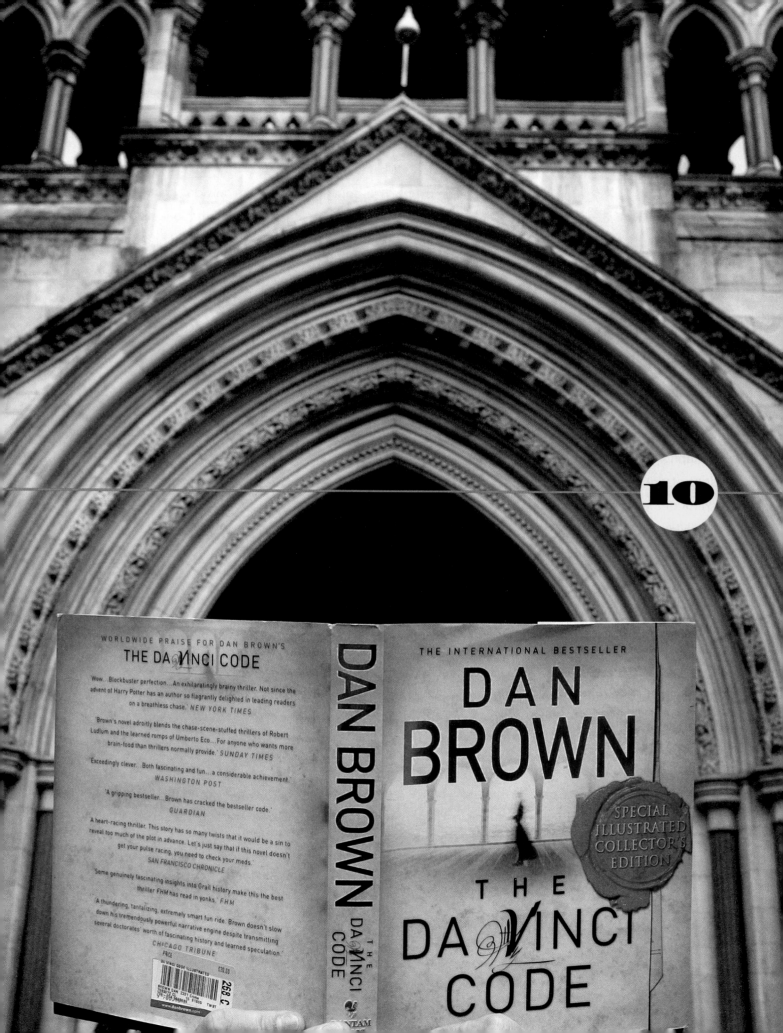

WORLDWIDE PRAISE FOR DAN BROWN'S

THE DA VINCI CODE

'Wow...Blockbuster perfection...An exhilaratingly brainy thriller. Not since the advent of Harry Potter has an author so flagrantly delighted in leading readers on a breathless chase.' *NEW YORK TIMES*

'Brown's novel adroitly blends the chase-scene-stuffed thrillers of Robert Ludlum and the learned romps of Umberto Eco...For anyone who wants more brain-food than thrillers normally provide.' *SUNDAY TIMES*

'Exceedingly clever...Both fascinating and fun...a considerable achievement.' *WASHINGTON POST*

'A gripping bestseller...Brown has cracked the bestseller code.' *GUARDIAN*

'A heart-racing thriller. This story has so many twists that it would be a sin to reveal too much of the plot in advance. Let's just say that if this novel doesn't get your pulse racing, you need to check your meds.' *SAN FRANCISCO CHRONICLE*

'Some genuinely fascinating insights into Grail history make this the best thriller FHM has read in yonks.' *FHM*

'A thundering, tantalizing, extremely smart fun ride. Brown doesn't slow down his tremendously powerful narrative engine despite transmitting several doctorates' worth of fascinating history and learned speculation.' *CHICAGO TRIBUNE*

THE INTERNATIONAL BESTSELLER

DAN BROWN

SPECIAL ILLUSTRATED COLLECTOR'S EDITION

DAN BROWN

THE DA VINCI CODE

THE DA VINCI CODE

from some conservative religious critics—and were even banned in some schools—for "endorsing" magic and witchcraft.

Literary critics also attacked the Potter series. Harold Bloom, a Yale literature professor, accused the books of "making no demands" on its readers and "dumbing down" the children's literature tradition of J.R.R. Tolkien and C. S. Lewis. He claimed, "Rowling's mind is so governed by clichés and dead metaphors that she has no other style of writing."[1] Jack Zipes, editor of the *Norton Anthology of Children's Literature*, said the Potter books are "conventional and mediocre" (although he did try to include a selection in the anthology).[2] And as for *The Da Vinci Code*, the London *Times* said Dan Brown's book was "written in peanut butter prose, with a plot so clunky that the book rattles."[3] Anthony Lane, film critic for the *New Yorker*, said he "never managed to crawl past page 100" and criticized this

random sentence: "Prominent New York editor Jonas Faukman tugged nervously at his goatee." Lane added, "What is more, he does so over 'a half-eaten power lunch,' one of the saddest phrases I have ever heard."[4]

In spite of the religious critics demanding boycotts and literary snipers making demands, these books have millions of devoted fans. Why? For the Potter series, many children report that they enjoy that the protagonists live in two worlds—a "normal" one dealing with parents, teachers, and friends, and a wizard world full of magic tricks, wild creatures, and exotic adventures. The books are comforting because young readers can identify with the main characters as children and later as teenagers, and, on another level, can escape into the adventures of the fantastic worlds that books can create.

In the case of *The Da Vinci Code*, some critics argue that the book, although not great literature, of-

fers a clever plot and a major conspiracy theory that hooks the reader. Also, the book's appearance in 2003 coincided with the nationwide scandals over the revelation that priests had been accused of (and had committed) child abuse, which Catholic Church authorities had long downplayed and covered up in many dioceses. The lure of the book had much to do with extending the real world problems of a big institutional religious power like the Church into the fictional world of conspiracies and cover-ups. In addition, both the Potter books and the Brown novel have been translated into wildly popular visual media, which almost always invite attacks from critics in our culture who associate "Art" with serious print literature. Of course, powerful best-sellers such as the Bible, the Harry Potter series, and *The Da Vinci Code* share common threads, especially regarding our collective fascination with worlds beyond our own—with magic, fantasy, mystery, and the supernatural.

O ver the past two decades, the interdependence between print and visual forms of popular media has become commonplace. Apart from economics, however, a cultural gulf between the two genres remains. Public debate continues to pit the "superior" quality of print media—usually represented by serious books—against the "inferior" fluff of television. Even within print culture itself, a mini-version of the high-low cultural gulf is apparent. It pits high-quality literature against such popular forms as *The Da Vinci Code*, a supermarket romance novel, or a children's fantasy like a Harry Potter book.

As individuals and as a society, we continue to create classifications that distinguish good from bad, organizing the world through black-and-white categories. We also make critical judgments about what culture best entertains, informs, and serves a democracy. Because lines between print and electronic culture have become blurred, we need to look at the developments that have made these media more interdependent. On one hand, publishers and video-stocked libraries use talk shows, TV advertising, and public-service announcements to promote reading. On the other hand, the networks follow made-for-TV movies, special miniseries, and even NBA games with promotions for books and libraries.

In the 1950s and 1960s, cultural forecasters thought that the popularity of television might spell the demise of a healthy book industry. It did not happen. In 1950, more than 11,000 new book titles were introduced, and by 2005 publishers were producing over fourteen times that number—more than 172,000 titles per year (see Table 10.1). Despite the absorption of small publishing houses by big media corporations, more than twenty thousand different publishers—mostly small independents—issue at least one title a year. Still, economic trends in the book industry are similar to those in other media industries: Several large publishing firms—owned by large media conglomerates like News Corporation and Bertelsmann—distribution

> 66 In fifty years today's children will not remember who survived *Survivor* . . . but they will remember Harry [Potter]. 99
>
> —Anna Quindlen,
> *Newsweek*, July 2000

> 66 A good book is the best of friends, the same today and forever. 99
>
> —Martin Farquhar Tupper,
> *Proverbial Philosophy*, 1838

● **Table 10.1 Annual Numbers of New Book Titles Published, Selected Years**

Year	Number of Titles	Year	Number of Titles
1778	461	1935	8,766 (Great Depression)
1798	1,808	1940	11,328
1880	2,076	1945	6,548 (World War II)
1890	4,559	1950	11,022
1900	6,356	1960	15,012
1910	13,470 (peak until after World War II)	1970	36,071
		1980	42,377
1915	8,202	1990	46,473
1919	5,714 (low point as a result of World War I)	1996	68,175
		2001	114,487*
1925	8,173	2004	190,000
1930	10,027	2005	172,000

Sources: Figures through 1945 from John Tebbel, *A History of Book Publishing in the United States*, 4 vols. (New York: R. R. Bowker, 1978); figures after 1945 from various editions of *The Bowker Annual Library and Book Trade Almanac* (Information Today, Inc.) and Bowker press releases; see "U.S. Book Production Plummets 18K in 2005," www.bowker.com/press/bowker/2006_0509bowker.htm.

*A change in the *Bowker Annual*'s methodology in 1997 resulted in a more accurate count of annual book title production in the United States, and this accounts for the statistical jump since 1996.

companies, and bookstore chains control the commercial end of the business and claim the bulk of the profits.

The bottom line is that the book industry has met the social and cultural challenges of television. Books have managed to maintain a distinct cultural identity, partly because of the book industry's willingness to capitalize on TV's reach, and vice versa. For example, when talk show host Oprah Winfrey chooses a book for her club, it often instantly appears on best-seller lists. In September 2005, when she announced her new choice, *A Million Little Pieces*, a memoir by James Frey, publisher Vintage printed 600,000 copies to keep up with the expected demand. Later, when parts of Frey's books were revealed as fabrication, Winfrey confronted him on another episode of her show.

Our oldest mass medium is still our most influential and our most diverse. The portability and compactness of books make them a preferred medium in many situations, including relaxing at the beach or in the park, resting in bed, and traveling to work on buses or commuter trains. Most important, books and print culture enable individuals and nations to store knowledge from the past. In their key social role, books are still the main repository of history and everyday experience, passing along stories, knowledge, and wisdom from generation to generation.

In this chapter, we will trace the history of the book from its earliest roots in Egyptian papyrus plants to its evolution as a paperback, a CD-ROM, and a downloadable electronic file. After examining the development of the printing press, we will investigate the rise of the book industry. We will look first at publishing in Europe and colonial America and later at the development of publishing houses in the nineteenth and twentieth centuries. As part of this discussion, we will review the various types of books and the economic issues facing the book industry, particularly the growth of book clubs, bookstore chains, and publishing conglomerates. Finally, we will consider trends in the industry, including books on tape, electronic books, and book preservation. Influencing everything from educational curricula to popular movies, books continue to play a pivotal role in media culture and democratic life.

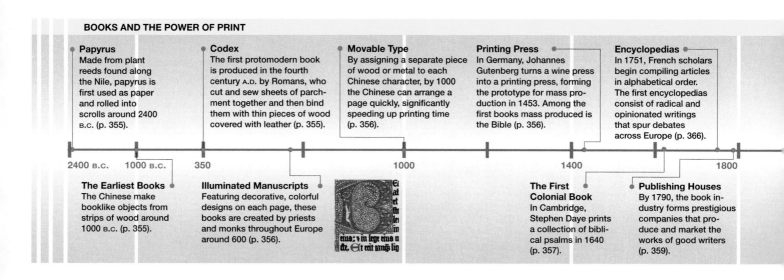

BOOKS AND THE POWER OF PRINT

Papyrus
Made from plant reeds found along the Nile, papyrus is first used as paper and rolled into scrolls around 2400 B.C. (p. 355).

Codex
The first protomodern book is produced in the fourth century A.D. by Romans, who cut and sew sheets of parchment together and then bind them with thin pieces of wood covered with leather (p. 355).

Movable Type
By assigning a separate piece of wood or metal to each Chinese character, by 1000 the Chinese can arrange a page quickly, significantly speeding up printing time (p. 356).

Printing Press
In Germany, Johannes Gutenberg turns a wine press into a printing press, forming the prototype for mass production in 1453. Among the first books mass produced is the Bible (p. 356).

Encyclopedias
In 1751, French scholars begin compiling articles in alphabetical order. The first encyclopedias consist of radical and opinionated writings that spur debates across Europe (p. 366).

2400 B.C.   1000 B.C.   350   1000   1400   1800

The Earliest Books
The Chinese make booklike objects from strips of wood around 1000 B.C. (p. 355).

Illuminated Manuscripts
Featuring decorative, colorful designs on each page, these books are created by priests and monks throughout Europe around 600 (p. 356).

The First Colonial Book
In Cambridge, Stephen Daye prints a collection of biblical psalms in 1640 (p. 357).

Publishing Houses
By 1790, the book industry forms prestigious companies that produce and market the works of good writers (p. 359).

The History of Books from Papyrus to Paperbacks

Ever since the ancient Babylonians and Egyptians began experimenting with alphabets some five thousand years ago, people have found ways to preserve their written symbols. Initially, pictorial symbols and letters appeared on wood strips or clay tablets, tied or stacked together to form the first "books." As early as 2400 B.C., the Egyptians wrote on **papyrus** (from which the word *paper* is derived) made from plant reeds found along the Nile River. They rolled these writings in scrolls, much as builders do today with blueprints. This method was adopted by the Greeks in 650 B.C. and by the Romans (who imported the papyrus from Egypt) from 300 to 100 B.C.

Around 1000 B.C., the Chinese made booklike objects from strips of wood and bamboo tied together in bundles. About the time the Egyptians started using papyrus, the Babylonians began pressing symbols and marks into small tablets of clay. These stacked tablets recorded business transactions, government records, favorite stories, and local history. Gradually, **parchment**—treated animal skin—replaced papyrus. Parchment was stronger, smoother, more durable, and less expensive because it did not have to be imported from Egypt.

Although the Chinese began making paper in A.D. 105, paper made by hand from cotton and linen did not replace parchment in Europe until the thirteenth century. Paper was not as strong as parchment, but it was cheaper. The first protomodern book was probably produced in the fourth century by the Romans, who created the **codex**, a type of book cut into sheets of parchment and sewn together along the edge, then bound with thin pieces of wood and covered with leather. Whereas scrolls had to be wound, unwound, and rewound, codices could be opened to any page, and their configuration allowed writing on both sides of a page.

Manuscript Culture

During the Middle Ages (A.D. 400 to 1500), the Christian clergy strongly influenced what has become known as **manuscript culture**, a period in which books were painstakingly lettered, decorated, and bound by hand. During this time, priests and monks advanced the art of bookmaking; in many ways, they may be considered the earliest professional editors. Known as *scribes*, they "wrote" most of the books of this period, making copies of existing philosophical tracts and religious books, especially

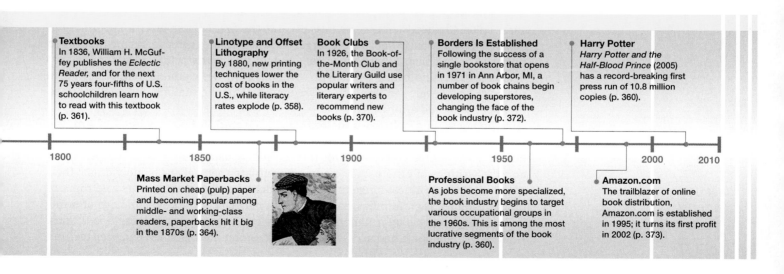

Textbooks
In 1836, William H. McGuffey publishes the *Eclectic Reader,* and for the next 75 years four-fifths of U.S. schoolchildren learn how to read with this textbook (p. 361).

Linotype and Offset Lithography
By 1880, new printing techniques lower the cost of books in the U.S., while literacy rates explode (p. 358).

Book Clubs
In 1926, the Book-of-the-Month Club and the Literary Guild use popular writers and literary experts to recommend new books (p. 370).

Borders Is Established
Following the success of a single bookstore that opens in 1971 in Ann Arbor, MI, a number of book chains begin developing superstores, changing the face of the book industry (p. 372).

Harry Potter
Harry Potter and the Half-Blood Prince (2005) has a record-breaking first press run of 10.8 million copies (p. 360).

1800   1850   1900   1950   2000   2010

Mass Market Paperbacks
Printed on cheap (pulp) paper and becoming popular among middle- and working-class readers, paperbacks hit it big in the 1870s (p. 364).

Professional Books
As jobs become more specialized, the book industry begins to target various occupational groups in the 1960s. This is among the most lucrative segments of the book industry (p. 360).

Amazon.com
The trailblazer of online book distribution, Amazon.com is established in 1995; it turns its first profit in 2002 (p. 373).

versions of the Bible. Through tedious and painstaking work, scribes became the chief caretakers of recorded history and culture.

Many works from the Middle Ages were **illuminated manuscripts**. These books featured decorative, colorful designs and illustrations on each page. Their covers were made from leather, and some were inscribed with precious gems or gold and silver trim. During this period, scribes developed rules of punctuation and made distinctions between small and capital letters; they also put space between words, which made reading easier. Older Roman writing had used all capital letters, and words ran together on a page, making reading a torturous experience.

The oldest printed book still in existence is China's *Diamond Sutra* by Wang Chieh, from A.D. 868. It consists of seven sheets pasted together and rolled up in a scroll. To make copies of pages, early Chinese printers developed **block printing**, a technique using sheets of paper applied to a block of inked wood with raised surfaces in hand-carved letters and sketches. This constituted the basic technique used in printing newspapers, magazines, and books throughout much of modern history. Although hand-carving each block, or "page," was time-consuming, this printing breakthrough enabled multiple copies to be produced and then bound together. In 1295, explorer Marco Polo introduced these techniques to Europe after his excursion to China. The first handmade printed books appeared in Europe during the 1400s, and demand for them began to grow among the literate middle-class populace emerging in large European cities.

The Gutenberg Revolution

The next step in printing was the radical development of movable type, first invented in China around the year 1000. Movable type featured Chinese characters made from reusable pieces of wood or metal. Printers arranged or moved letters into various word combinations, greatly speeding up the time it took to make a page. This process, also used in Korea as early as the thirteenth century, developed independently in Europe in the 1400s. Then, in Germany, between 1453 and 1456, Johannes Gutenberg used movable type to develop a **printing press**, which he adapted from a wine press. Gutenberg's staff of printers produced the first so-called modern books, including two hundred copies of a Latin Bible, twenty-one copies of which still exist. The Bible required six presses, many printers, and several months to produce. It was printed on fine handmade paper, a treated animal skin called **vellum**. The pages were hand-decorated, and the use of woodcuts made illustrations possible.

Essentially, Gutenberg and his printing assistants had not only found a way to carry knowledge across geographic borders but had also formed the prototype for mass production. Printing presses spread rapidly across Europe in the late 1400s and early 1500s. Chaucer's *Canterbury Tales* became the first English work to be printed in book form. Many early books were large, elaborate, and expensive, taking months to illustrate and publish. They were usually purchased by aristocrats, royal families, religious leaders, and ruling politicians. Printers, however, gradually reduced the size of books and developed less expensive grades of paper, making books cheaper so more people could afford them.

The social and cultural transformations ushered in by the spread of printing presses and books cannot be overestimated. As historian Elizabeth Eisenstein has noted, when people could learn for themselves by using maps, dictionaries, Bibles, and the writings of others, they could differentiate themselves as individuals; their social identities were no longer solely dependent on what their leaders told them or on the habits of their families, communities, or social class. The technology of printing presses permitted information and knowledge to spread outside local jurisdictions. Gradually, individuals had access to ideas far beyond their isolated experiences, and

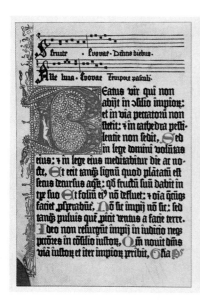

● Probably the most revolutionary development in media history, the printing press and the mass production of books paved the way for both a consumer market and the democratic spread of knowledge. This page from the *Psalter*, or *Book of Psalms* (*left*), was printed by Gutenberg's partner, Johann Fust, in 1457. Beside it is a re-creation of a plate that could have been used to print it.

this permitted them to challenge the traditional wisdom and customs of their tribes and leaders.[5]

Book Production in the United States

In colonial America, English locksmith Stephen Daye set up a print shop in the late 1630s in Cambridge, Massachusetts. In 1640, Daye and his son Matthew printed the first colonial book, *The Whole Booke of Psalms* (known today as *The Bay Psalm Book*). This collection of biblical psalms sold out its printing of 1,750 copies even though fewer than 3,500 families lived in the colonies at the time. By the mid-1760s, all thirteen colonies had printing shops.

In 1744, Benjamin Franklin imported *Pamela; or, Virtue Rewarded,* the first novel reprinted and sold in colonial America. *Pamela* had been written four years earlier by Britain's Samuel Richardson, who helped pioneer the novel as a literary form. *Pamela* and Richardson's second novel, *Clarissa; or, The History of a Young Lady* (1747), connected with the newly emerging and literate middle classes, especially with women, who were just starting to gain a social identity as individuals apart from the men they were married to or worked for. Richardson's novels, overly long and sentimental by current standards, were among the earliest mass media works to portray women in subordinate roles. Richardson also, however, depicted women triumphing over tragedy, so he is credited as one of the first popular writers to take the domestic life of women seriously.

By the early 1800s, the demand for books among both literate women and men was growing. Machine-made paper supplanted more expensive handmade varieties in the 1830s. The use of cloth rather than leather covers also helped reduce book prices. By the early 1830s, **paperback books** made with cheaper paper covers had been introduced in the United States from Europe. In 1860, Erastus and Irwin Beadle pioneered paperback **dime novels** (sold for five or ten cents). Magazine editor–writer Ann Stephens authored the Beadles' first dime novel, *Malaeska: The Indian Wife of the White Hunter,* which was actually a reprint of a serialized magazine story she had written in 1839 for the *Ladies' Companion.*[6] By 1870, dime novels had sold 7 million copies. By 1885, one-third of all books published in the United States were popular

> ❝ **For books, issuing from those primal founts of heresy and rebellion, the printing presses have done more to shape the course of human affairs than any other product of the human mind because they are the carriers of ideas and it is ideas that change the world.** ❞
>
> –John Tebbel, *A History of Book Publishing in the United States,* 1972

● The weekly paperback series *Tip Top Weekly,* which was published between 1896 and 1912, featured stories of the most popular dime novel hero of the day, the fictional Yale football star and heroic adventurer Frank Merriwell. This issue, from 1901, followed Frank's exploits in the wilds of the Florida Everglades.

paperbacks and dime novels, sometimes identified as **pulp fiction**, a reference to the cheap, machine-made pulp paper they were printed on.

The printing process also became quicker and more mechanized. The introduction of **linotype** machines in the mid-1880s finally enabled printers to set type mechanically using a typewriter-style keyboard. The introduction of steam-powered machines and high-speed rotary presses also permitted the production of more books at lower costs. Another printing development in the early 1900s, **offset lithography**, allowed books to be printed from photographic plates rather than metal casts. Reducing the cost of color and illustrations, offset printing accelerated production and eventually led to computerized typesetting.

The early history of publishing demonstrated that books could widely disseminate and preserve culture and knowledge over time. Even if a paperback fell apart, another version usually existed in a public library or a personal book collection. Oral culture depended on information and values passed down through the wisdom and memories of a community's elders or tribal storytellers, and sometimes these rich traditions were lost. Print culture and the book, however, gave future generations different and often more enduring records of particular authors' words at particular periods in history.

Modern Publishing and the Book Industry

Throughout the 1800s, the rapid spread of knowledge and literacy as well as the Industrial Revolution spurred the emergence of the middle class. New professions developed in areas such as the social sciences, business management, and journalism. The demand for books also promoted the development of a class of publishing professionals, who capitalized on increased middle-class literacy and widespread compulsory education. Many of these early publishers were less interested in applying skillful marketing strategies than in finding quality authors. But with the growth of advertising and the rise of a market economy in the latter half of the nineteenth century, publishing gradually became more competitive and more concerned with the sales value of titles and authors.

The Formation of Publishing Houses

The modern book industry developed gradually in the 1800s with the formation of the early prestigious **publishing houses**: companies that tried to identify and produce the works of good writers.[7] These companies professionalized the book industry by dividing into discrete tasks the jobs of acquiring, publishing, and marketing books. Among the oldest American houses established in the 1800s (all are now part of media conglomerates) were J. B. Lippincott (1792); Harper & Bros. (1817), which became Harper & Row in 1962 and HarperCollins in 1990; Houghton Mifflin (1832); Little, Brown (1837); G. P. Putnam (1838); Scribner's (1842); E. P. Dutton (1852); Rand McNally (1856); and Macmillan (1869).

Between 1880 and 1920, as the center of social and economic life shifted from rural farm production to an industrialized urban culture, the demand for books and bookstores grew. Helped by the influx of European immigrants, the book industry acclimated newcomers to the English language and to American culture. In fact, 1910 marked a peak year in the number of new titles produced—13,470—a record that would not be challenged until the 1950s.

The turn of the twentieth century also marked the next wave of prominent publishing houses, as entrepreneurs began to better understand the marketing potential of books. These houses included Doubleday (1897), McGraw-Hill (1909), Prentice-Hall (1913), Alfred A. Knopf (1914), Simon & Schuster (1924), and Random House (1925). After World War II, Doubleday became the world's largest publishing firm for a time. Unlike radio and magazines, however, book publishing sputtered from 1910 into the 1950s. Book industry profits were adversely affected by the two world wars and the Great Depression. Radio and magazines fared better because they were generally less expensive and could more immediately cover topical issues during times of crisis.

Types of Books

The divisions of the modern book industry, a $36 billion business in the United States in 2005, come from economic and structural categories developed by publishers and by trade organizations such as the Association of American Publishers (AAP), Book Industry Study Group (BISG), and the American Booksellers Association (ABA). The categories include trade books (both adult and juvenile); professional books; elementary, high school (called "el-hi"), and college textbooks; mass market paperbacks; religious books; reference works; and university press books. An additional category—comic books—also exists but is not acknowledged by most conventional publishers (see "Case Study—Comic Books: Alternative Themes, but Superheroes Prevail" on pages 362–63).

Trade Books

One of the most lucrative parts of the industry, **trade books** include hardbound and paperback books aimed at general readers and sold at various retail outlets (see

“ He was a genius at devising ways to put books into the hands of the unbookish. ”

—Edna Ferber, writer, commenting on Nelson Doubleday, publisher

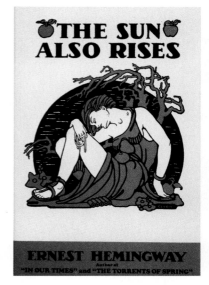

● Scribner's—known more for its magazines in the late 1800s than for its books—became the most prestigious literary house of the 1920s and 1930s, publishing the first novels of F. Scott Fitzgerald (*This Side of Paradise*, 1920) and Ernest Hemingway (*The Sun Also Rises*, 1926).

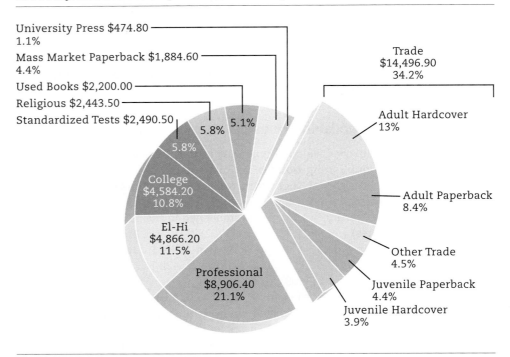

Figure 10.1
2006 Projected Book Sales (in Millions of Dollars)

University Press $474.80
1.1%

Mass Market Paperback $1,884.60
4.4%

Used Books $2,200.00

Religious $2,443.50

Standardized Tests $2,490.50

5.8%

5.1%

5.8%

College
$4,584.20
10.8%

El-Hi
$4,866.20
11.5%

Professional
$8,906.40
21.1%

Trade
$14,496.90
34.2%

Adult Hardcover
13%

Adult Paperback
8.4%

Other Trade
4.5%

Juvenile Paperback
4.4%

Juvenile Hardcover
3.9%

Figure 10.1). The industry distinguishes between adult and juvenile trade divisions. Adult trade books include hardbound fiction; current nonfiction and biographies; literary classics; books on hobbies, art, and travel; popular science, technology, and computer publications; self-help books; and cookbooks. (*Betty Crocker's Cookbook,* first published in 1950, has sold more than 22 million copies in hardcover trade editions.) Like most of the book industry, fiction and nonfiction trade books have experienced long-term growth in the electronic age.

Juvenile book categories range from preschool picture books to young-adult or young-reader books, such as HarperCollins's Lemony Snicket series, Pocket Books' Fear Street series, and Scholastic's Harry Potter series. In fact, the Harry Potter series alone provided an enormous boost to the segment, helping create record-breaking first-press runs for each release: 5 million for *Harry Potter and the Order of the Phoenix* (2003) and a record 10.8 million for *Harry Potter and the Half-Blood Prince* (2005).

Professional Books

The counterpart to trade publications in the magazine industry, **professional books** target various occupational groups and are not intended for the general consumer market. This area of publishing mirrors the growth of professional and technical specialties that has characterized the job market, particularly since the 1960s. Traditionally, the industry has subdivided professional books into the areas of law, business, medicine, and technical-scientific works. These books are sold mostly through mail order, the Internet, or by sales representatives knowledgeable about various subject areas. This segment of the book industry has found profitable market niches by capitalizing on the expansion of job specialization.

Textbooks

The most widely read secular book in North American history was a textbook first written by William Holmes McGuffey, a Presbyterian minister and college professor. From 1836 to 1920 more than 100 million copies of his *Eclectic Reader* were sold. Through stories, poems, and illustrations, these readers taught nineteenth-century schoolchildren to spell and read simultaneously—and to respect the nation's political and economic systems. Ever since the McGuffey reader, **textbooks** have served a nation intent on improving literacy rates and public education. Elementary school textbooks found a solid market niche in the nineteenth century, but college textbooks boomed in the 1950s, when the GI Bill enabled hundreds of thousands of working- and middle-class men returning from World War II to attend college. The demand for textbooks further accelerated in the 1960s, as opportunities for women and minorities expanded.

Textbooks are divided into elementary–high school, known as *el-hi*; vocational education; and college texts. In most states, local school districts determine which el-hi textbooks are appropriate for their students. Texas and California, however, use statewide adoption policies that control text selections. In such situations, only a small number of texts are mandated by the state. If individual schools choose to use books other than those mandated, they are not reimbursed by the state for their purchases. Some teachers and publishers have argued that such sweeping authority undermines the local autonomy of districts, which have varied educational needs and problems. The statewide system of adoptions also enables a few states, which are courted heavily by publishers, to virtually determine the content of the texts sold to every state in the nation. In addition, when publishers aim textbooks at a broad nationwide audience, they tend to water down the content by eliminating regional material or controversial ideas that might offend a group of adopters or a local selection committee.

● First published in 1836, McGuffey readers helped enable the nineteenth-century U.S. literacy movement and the wave of western expansion. After the Civil War they were the standard textbooks in 37 states. With 130 million copies published since the first edition, the readers are still in print and in use, with the latest revised version published in the late 1990s.

Figure 10.2
Where the New Textbook Dollar Goes*

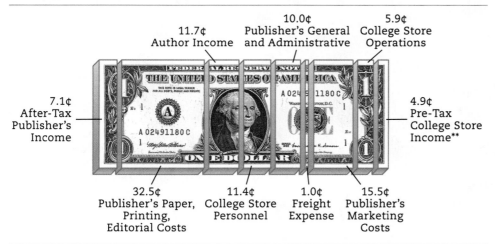

11.7¢
Author Income

10.0¢
Publisher's General
and Administrative

5.9¢
College Store
Operations

7.1¢
After-Tax
Publisher's
Income

4.9¢
Pre-Tax
College Store
Income**

32.5¢
Publisher's Paper,
Printing,
Editorial Costs

11.4¢
College Store
Personnel

1.0¢
Freight
Expense

15.5¢
Publisher's
Marketing
Costs

Source: © 2006 by the National Association of College Stores, www.nacs.org/common/research/textbook$.pdf.

*The statistics in this illustration reflect the most current 2004–2005 financial data gathered by the National Association of College Stores and financial data provided by the Association of American Publishers.

***Note:* The amount of federal, state, and/or local tax, and therefore the amount and use of any after-tax profit, is determined by the store's ownership, and depends on whether the college store is owned by an institution of higher education, a contract management company, a cooperative, a foundation, or by private individuals.

These numbers are averages and do not represent a particular publisher or store.

Comic Books: Alternative Themes, but Superheroes Prevail

By Mark C. Rogers

At the precarious edge of the book industry are comic books, which are sometimes called *graphic novels* or simply *comix*. A medium that neither conventional book nor magazine publishers will claim as their own, comics have long integrated print and visual culture. They remain a paradoxical medium, existing as both collectibles and consumables.

They are perhaps the medium most open to independent producers—anyone with a pencil and access to a Xerox machine can produce mini-comics. Nevertheless, two companies—Marvel and DC—have dominated the commercial industry for more than thirty years, publishing the routine superhero stories that have been so marketable.

Comics are a relatively young mass medium, first appearing in their present format in the 1920s in Japan and in the 1930s in the United States. They began as simple reprints of newspaper comic strips, but by the mid-1930s most comic books featured original material. Comics have always been published in a variety of genres, but their signature contribution to American culture has been the superhero. In 1938, Jerry Siegel and Joe Shuster created Superman for DC comics. Bob Kane's Batman character arrived the following year. In 1941, Marvel comics introduced Captain America to fight Nazis, and except for a brief period in the 1950s, the superhero genre has dominated the history of comics.

After World War II, comic books moved away from superheroes and began experimenting with other genres, most notably crime and horror (e.g., *Tales from the Crypt*). With the end of the war, the reading public was ready for more moral ambiguity than was possible in the simple good-versus-evil world of the superhero. Comics became increasingly graphic and lurid as they tried to compete with other mass media, especially television and mass-market paperbacks.

In the early 1950s, the popularity of crime and horror comics led to a moral panic about their effects on society. Frederic Wertham, a prominent psychiatrist, campaigned against them, claiming they led to juvenile delinquency. Wertham was joined by many religious and parent groups, and Senate hearings were held on the issue in 1954. In October 1954, the Comics Magazine Association of America adopted a code of acceptable conduct for publishers of comic books. One of the most restrictive examples of industry self-censorship in mass-media history, the code kept the government from legislating its own code or restricting the sale of comic books to minors.

The code had both immediate and long-term effects on comics. In the short run, the number of comics sold in the United States declined sharply. Comic books lost many of their adult readers because the code confined comics' topics to those suitable for children. Consequently, comics have rarely been taken seriously as a mass medium or as an art form; they remain stigmatized as the lowest of low culture—a sort of literature for the subliterate. In the 1960s, Marvel and DC led the way as superhero comics regained their dominance. This period also gave rise to underground comics, which featured more explicit sexual, violent, and drug themes—for example, R. Crumb's *Mr. Natural* and Bill Griffith's *Zippy the Pinhead.* These alternative comics, like underground newspapers, originated in the 1960s counterculture and challenged the major institutions of the time. Instead of relying on newsstand sales, underground comics were sold through record stores, at alternative bookstores, and in a growing number of comic-book specialty shops.

In the 1970s, responding in part to the challenge of the underground form, "legitimate" comics began to increase the political content and relevance of their story lines. In 1974, a new method of distributing comics—direct sales—developed, catering to the increasing number of comic-book stores. This direct-sales method involved selling comics on a nonreturnable basis but with a higher discount than was available to newsstand distributors, who bought comics only on the condition that they could return unsold copies. The percentage of comics sold through specialty shops increased gradually, and by the early 1990s more than 80 percent of all comics were sold through direct sales.

The shift from newsstand to direct sales enabled comics to once again approach adult themes and also created an explosion in the number of comics available and in the number of companies publishing comics. Comic books peaked in 1993, generating more than $850 million in sales. That year the industry sold about 45 million comic books per month, but it then began a steady decline that led Marvel to declare bankruptcy in the late 1990s. After comic-book sales fell to $250 million in 2000 and Marvel reorganized, the industry rebounded. By 2005, sales reached $400 million with an additional $150 million generated through statue and action figure sales. Today, the industry releases 70 to 80 million comics a year. Marvel and DC control more than 75 percent of comic-book sales, but challengers like Dark House and Image plus another 150 small firms keep the industry vital by pro-

viding innovation and identifying new talent.

In the wake of the 1980s success of *Teenage Mutant Ninja Turtles* (who began life in an alternative comic book), many independent companies have been purchased by or have entered into alliances with larger media firms that want to exploit particular characters or superheroes. DC, for example, is owned by Time Warner, which has used the DC characters, especially Superman and Batman, to build successful film and television properties. Marvel also got into the licensing act with film versions of Spiderman and X-Men.

In 1992, comics' flexibility was demonstrated in *Maus: A Survivor's Tale* by Art Spiegelman, cofounder and editor of *Raw* (an alternative magazine for comics and graphic art). The first comic-style book to win a Pulitzer Prize, Spiegelman's two-book fable merged print and visual styles to recount his complex relationship with his father, a Holocaust survivor.

Although electronic comics may prove a way for comics to continue to flourish—as suggested by underground comic author Scott McCloud in his manifesto *Reinventing Comics* posted at www.scottmccloud.com—comics may also be making a resurgence through traditional book publishers. For example, Pantheon, a division of Random House, first published *Maus* as a hardback in 1996 and has since created a graphic novels imprint featuring newer artists who focus on diverse themes including Chris Ware (*Jimmy Corrigan*), Charles Burns (*Black Hole*), and Marjane Satrapi (*Persepolis*).

As other writers and artists continue to adapt the form to both fictional and nonfictional stories, comics endure as part of popular and alternative culture.

Mark C. Rogers teaches communication at Walsh University. He wrote his doctoral dissertation on the comic-book industry.

Unlike el-hi texts, which are subsidized by various states and school districts, hardbound and softcover college texts are paid for by individual students (and parents). At some time during most students' experience, in fact, disputes erupt on campuses about the increasing cost of textbooks, the mark-up on used books, and the profit margins of local college bookstores, which in many cases face no on-campus competition. According to a 2005 survey, the average college student spends $832 on textbooks and supplies each year.[8] (See Figure 10.2 on page 361.)

Today, more than 4,800 college bookstores in the United States sell both texts and trade books. In the late 1990s several new online booksellers, modeled on Amazon.com but specializing in college textbooks, promoted themselves as an alternative to local college bookstores. By 2005, big e-commerce sites like Amazon.com, BarnesandNoble.com, and eBay.com, along with start-ups like ecampus.com, accounted for about 16 percent of the total college textbook market.[9] Some enterprising students have developed swap sites on the Web to trade and resell books. Meanwhile, many traditional college stores have developed "clicks and mortar" strategies with their own Web sites—enabling students to purchase texts online and pick them up at the local store.

Mass Market Paperbacks

Unlike larger trade paperbacks, which are sold mostly in bookstores, **mass market paperbacks** are sold off racks in drugstores, supermarkets, and airports as well as in bookstores. Mass market paperbacks—often the work of blockbuster authors such as Stephen King, Danielle Steel, Patricia Cornwell, and John Grisham—represent the largest segment of the industry in terms of units sold, but because the books are low-priced (under $10), they generate less revenue than trade books. Moreover, mass market paperbacks have had declining sales in recent years, as big bookstore chains display and heavily promote the more expensive and higher quality (in terms of paper and packaging) paperback and hardbound trade books.

Paperbacks did not hit it big until the 1870s, when they became popular among middle- and working-class readers. This phenomenon sparked fear and outrage among those in the professional and educated classes, many of whom thought that reading cheap westerns and crime novels might ruin civilization. Some of the earliest paperbacks ripped off foreign writers, who were unprotected by copyright law and did not receive royalties for the books they sold in the United States. This changed with the International Copyright Law of 1891, which mandated that all authors' works could be reproduced only with their permission.

The popularity of paperbacks hit a major peak in 1939 with the establishment of Pocket Books under the leadership of Robert de Graff. Revolutionizing the paperback industry, Pocket Books lowered the standard book price of fifty or seventy-five cents to twenty-five cents. To accomplish this, de Graff cut bookstore discounts from 30 to 20 percent. The book distributor's share fell from 46 to 36 percent of the cover price, and author royalty rates went from 10 to 4 percent. In its first three weeks, Pocket Books sold 100,000 books in New York City alone. Among its first titles was *Wake Up and Live* by Dorothea Brande, a 1936 best-seller on self-improvement that ignited an early wave of self-help books. In testing the market with both nonfiction and fiction, Pocket Books also published paperbacks of *The Murder of Roger Ackroyd* by Agatha Christie; *Enough Rope,* a collection of poems by Dorothy Parker; *Five Great Tragedies* by Shakespeare; and *Bambi* by Felix Salten, which became a children's classic three years before Walt Disney released the film version. Pocket Books' success spawned a series of imitators, including Dell, Fawcett, and Bantam Books.[10]

A major innovation of paperback publishers was the **instant book**, a marketing strategy that involves publishing a topical book quickly after a major event occurs. Pocket Books produced the first instant book, *Franklin Delano Roosevelt: A Memorial,* six days after FDR's death in 1945. Similar to made-for-TV movies that capitalize on contemporary events, instant books enable the industry to better compete with journalism and magazines. Such books, however, like their TV counterparts, have been accused of offering shoddy writing and exploiting tragedies for quick profits.

Bantam began dominating this field in 1964 with *The Report of the Warren Commission on the Assassination of President Kennedy*, the first Bantam "extra" edition. (*Extra* is a term borrowed from daily newspapers, which produced extra editions to tell important breaking news stories in the pre-TV era.) After receiving the 385,000-word report on a Friday afternoon, Bantam staffers immediately began editing the Warren Report; the book was produced within a week. The publisher, in a joint venture with the *New York Times,* ultimately sold 1.6 million copies.

Today, instant books continue to capitalize on a variety of contemporary events, from President Bush's address about the terrorist attacks of September 11, 2001, former president Ronald Reagan's death in 2004, and Hurricane Katrina in 2005. Although instant books make fast money for their publishers, they often sacrifice the kind of in-depth analysis and historical perspective that the book medium has generally brought to important social events.

Religious Books

The best-selling book of all time is the Bible, in all its diverse versions. Over the years the success of Bible sales spawned a large industry for **religious books**, now divided into four categories: Bibles, hymnals, and other materials related to religious observances; spiritual or inspirational books aimed at lay readers; professional publications focusing on the work of clergy and theologians; and religious education textbooks.

After World War II, sales of religious books soared. Historians attribute the sales boom to economic growth and a nation seeking peace and security while facing the threat of "godless communism" and the Soviet Union.[11] By the 1960s, though, the scene had changed dramatically. The impact of the civil rights struggle, the Vietnam War, the sexual revolution, and the youth rebellion against authority led to declines in formal church membership. Not surprisingly, sales of some types of religious books dropped as well. To compete, many religious-book publishers extended their offerings to include serious secular titles on such topics as war and peace, race, poverty, gender, and civic responsibility.

Throughout this period of change, the publication of fundamentalist and evangelical literature remained steady. It then expanded rapidly during the 1980s, when the Republican Party began making political overtures to conservative groups and prominent TV evangelists. The popularity of conservative and tradition-bound publications stabilized religious publishing during turbulent social times. In 2005 and 2006, religious books again emerged as an impressive growth category in the book publishing industry. Industry analysts predict that by 2010, the sale of religious books will increase by 50 percent.

> 66 Religion is just so much a part of the cultural conversation these days because of global terrorism and radical Islam. People want to understand those things. 99
>
> –Lynn Garrett, religion editor at *Publishers Weekly,* 2004

Reference Books

Another major division of the book industry—**reference books**—includes dictionaries, encyclopedias, atlases, and a number of substantial volumes directly related to particular professions or trades, such as legal casebooks and medical manuals. The idea of developing encyclopedic writings to document the extent of human knowledge is attributed to Aristotle. Pliny the Elder (A.D. 23–79) wrote the oldest reference work still in existence, *Historia Naturalis,* detailing in Latin thousands of facts about animals, minerals, and plants. But it wasn't until the early 1700s that the compilers of reference works began organizing articles in alphabetical order and relying on specialists to contribute essays in their areas of interest. Between 1751 and 1771, a group of French scholars produced a twenty-eight-volume set of encyclopedias. The circulation of these volumes, full of new and often radical ideas, encouraged support for the French Revolution against aristocratic rule later in that century.

The oldest English-language encyclopedia still in production, the *Encyclopaedia Britannica* (*EB*), was first published in Scotland in 1768. Significant U.S. encyclopedias followed, including *Encyclopedia Americana* (1829), *The World Book Encyclopedia* (1917), and *Compton's Pictured Encyclopedia* (1922), bought by *EB* in 1961. *EB* produced its first U.S. edition in 1908. Purchased by Sears in 1920 and later by a U.S. ad agency, *EB* was eventually run as a nonprofit venture for the University of Chicago. *EB* contributed more than $125 million to the university over the years. However, its sales fell from 117,000 sets in 1990 to 51,000 in 1994 due to competition from electronic encyclopedias (which many critics considered inferior in quality) bundled with many home computers. In 1996, the company was forced to reorganize and disband its famous door-to-door sales force. *EB,* Microsoft's *Encarta,* and *World Book* are now the leading CD and DVD encyclopedias, and all three encyclopedias are also offered on the Web but require paid subscriptions for full access. Today, even the online versions struggle

● The New York Public Library's reference room, where computers and printers have displaced books as the main reference tool.

as young researchers increasingly rely on search engines such as Google or sources like Wikipedia to find information.

Dictionaries have also accounted for a large portion of reference sales. Like encyclopedias, the earliest dictionaries were produced by Greek and Roman writers attempting to document specialized and rare words. During the manuscript period in the Middle Ages, however, European scribes and monks began creating glossaries and dictionaries to help people understand Latin. In 1604, a British schoolmaster prepared a three-thousand-word English dictionary. A sixty-thousand-word English dictionary was produced in 1721, followed by Samuel Johnson's *Dictionary of the English Language* in 1755. Describing rather than prescribing word usage, Johnson was among the first to understand that language changes—that words and usage cannot be fixed for all time. Johnson's dictionary served as the model and standard for English dictionaries into the mid-1800s. In the United States in 1828, Noah Webster, using Johnson's work as a model, published the seventy-thousand-word, two-volume *American Dictionary of the English Language,* differentiating between British and American usages and simplifying spelling (for example, *colour* became *color* and *musick* became *music*).

Other reference works include the atlases and almanacs that have become so popular in schools, homes, offices, and libraries. Media trade organizations publish their own reference works, such as *Editor & Publisher International Year Book* and *Broadcasting & Cable Yearbook.* Each year, Information Today, Inc., publishes *Books in Print*, which lists all new and available book titles. *The Bowker Annual Library and Book Trade Almanac* reprints articles and compiles statistics on the book industry.

> **"** These are lonely days for encyclopedias. At libraries, the volumes sit ignored for days on end as information-seeking patrons tap busily away at nearby computers. **"**
>
> –May Wong, Associated Press, 2004

University Press Books

The smallest unit in the book industry is the nonprofit **university press** sector, which publishes scholarly works for small groups of readers interested in specialized areas. Professors often try to secure book contracts from reputable university presses to increase their chances for tenure, a lifetime teaching contract. Some university presses are very small, producing as few as ten books a year. The largest, the University of Chicago Press, regularly publishes more than two hundred titles a year. Among the oldest and most prestigious of these presses in the United States are Yale University Press, established in 1908, and Harvard University Press, formally founded in 1913 but claiming roots that go back to 1640, when Stephen Daye published the first colonial book in a small shop located behind the house of Harvard's president.

University presses traditionally have not faced pressure to produce commercially viable books, so they can encourage obscure topics or innovative thinkers. Large commercial trade houses are often criticized for encouraging only blockbuster books, but university presses often suffer an opposite criticism—that they produce subsidized books that only a handful of scholars read. Nonetheless, many scholars believe that university presses need to protect narrowly focused, specialized, noncommercial publications. Others argue that it is time to declare "an end to scholarly publications as a series of guarded conversations between professors."[12]

University press books typically sell fewer than a thousand copies each, most of which are sold to libraries. Although they bring academic institutions a certain prestige, university presses routinely lose money. Even academic books written in accessible language rarely attract the interest of the general public because university presses have little money for marketing and promotion. Increasingly, administrators are reducing subsidies, requiring presses to show more profit. This has led to a

> **"** The [university] presses are meant to be one of the few alternative sources of scholarship and information available in the United States. . . . Does the bargain involved in publishing commercial titles compromise that role? **"**
>
> –André Schiffrin, *Chronicle of Higher Education*, 1999

decrease in the number of books university presses can publish. To offset costs and increase revenue, some presses are trying to form alliances with commercial houses to help promote and produce academic books that have wider appeal.

The Organization and Ownership of the Book Industry

Compared with the revenues earned by other mass media industries, the steady growth of book publishing has been relatively modest. From the mid-1980s to 2006, total revenues went from $9 billion to $36 billion. Within the industry, the concept of who or what constitutes a publisher varies widely. A publisher may be a large company that is a subsidiary of a global media conglomerate and occupies an entire office building, or a publisher may be a one-person home office operation using a desktop computer. Unlike commercial television and film, small book publishers can start up relatively easily because of advances in personal computer technology.

The Structure of Book Publishing

Medium-size and large publishing houses employ hundreds of people and share certain similarities. Most of the thousands of small houses, however, have staffs of fewer than twenty. In the larger houses, divisions usually include acquisitions and development; copyediting, design, and production; marketing and sales; and admin-

● Readers of *Harry Potter and the Half-Blood Prince* in New Delhi, India, hours after the book's release in 2005.

istration and business. Unlike daily newspapers but similar to magazines, most publishing houses contract independent printers to produce their books.

Most publishers employ **acquisitions editors** to seek out and sign authors to contracts. In the trade fiction area, this might mean discovering talented writers by working with book agents or reading unsolicited manuscripts. In nonfiction, editors might examine manuscripts and letters of inquiry or actively match a known writer to a project (such as a celebrity biography). Acquisitions editors also handle **subsidiary rights** for an author—that is, selling the rights to a book for use in other media, such as a mass market paperback or as the basis for a screenplay.

As part of their contracts, writers sometimes receive advance money, which is actually an early payment against royalties to be earned later. New authors may receive little or no advance from a publisher, but commercially successful authors can receive millions. For example, *Interview with a Vampire* author Anne Rice hauled in a $17 million advance from Knopf for three more vampire novels. First-time authors who are nationally recognized, such as political leaders, sports figures, or movie stars, can also command large advances from publishers who are banking on the well-known person's commercial potential. Retired general and former secretary of state Colin Powell, who directed military operations during the Gulf War and was the first African American to head the Joint Chiefs of Staff, received a $6.5 million advance from Random House for his autobiography. In 2006, former longtime chairman of the Federal Reserve Alan Greenspan received $8.5 million for his memoir. (See Table 10.2.) Typically, an author's royalty is between 5 and 15 percent of the net price of the book. But before a royalty check is paid, advance money is subtracted from royalties earned during the sale of the book (see Table 10.3 on page 370).

After a contract is signed, the acquisitions editor guides the manuscript through several stages. In educational publishing, a major text may also be turned over to a **developmental editor**, who provides the author with feedback, makes suggestions for improvements, and obtains advice from knowledgeable members of the academic community. If a book is illustrated, editors work closely with photo researchers to select photographs and pieces of art. Then copyediting, design, and production staff enter the picture. While **copy editors** attend to specific problems in writing or length, production and **design managers** work on the look of the book, making decisions about type style, paper, cover design, and layout.

> **66** We've seen plenty of sparkly, fabulous people with so-so ideas. The best possible combination is a fresh idea and a sparkly author. **99**
>
> – Barb Burg, executive director of publicity and public relations, Bantam Dell, 2005

● **Table 10.2 Notable Nonfiction Book Advances**

Author	Deal Struck	Publisher	Title	Reported Amount, Millions
Bill Clinton	2001	Alfred A. Knopf	*My Life*	$10.0
Pope John Paul II	1994	Alfred A. Knopf	*Crossing the Threshold of Hope*	8.5
Ronald Reagan	1989	Simon & Schuster	*An American Life*	8.5
Hillary Clinton	2000	Simon & Schuster	*Living History*	8.0
John F. Welch Jr.	2000	Warner Books	*Straight from the Gut*	7.1
Robert E. Rubin	2000	Random House	*In an Uncertain World*	3.3
Rudolph Giuliani	2001	Miramax Books	*Leadership*	3.0
Nancy Reagan	1989	Random House	*My Turn*	2.0

Source: Edward Wyatt, "Greenspan's Book Deal Is Said to Be among the Richest," *New York Times*, March 8, 2006, p. C1, 8.

● **Table 10.3 How Most Trade Books Lose Money**

Publishing is hit-driven; most books lose money. Here is a hardcover priced at $25 ($11.75 goes to the publisher) with initial sales of 24,000, of which retailers send back 36%.

Net Sales (after returns)	$180,000
Printing	-84,000
Author's royalty (at 10% of net sales)	-18,000
Unearned royalty (from $25,000 advance)	-7,000
Write-offs from returned books (at $3 each)	-26,000
Direct marketing	-25,000
Overhead (shipping, warehousing, sales commission, etc.)	-54,000
Net Loss	-$34,000

Source: Albert N. Greco, Fordham University.

Simultaneously, plans are under way to market and sell the book. Decisions generally need to be made concerning the number of copies to print, how to reach potential readers, and costs for promotion and advertising. For trade books and some scholarly books, publishing houses may send advance copies of a book to appropriate magazines and newspapers with the hope of receiving favorable reviews that can be used in promotional material. Prominent trade writers typically sign autographs at selected bookstores and travel the radio and TV talk-show circuit to promote their new books. Unlike trade publishers, college textbook firms rarely sell directly to bookstores. Instead, they contact instructors through either direct-mail brochures or sales representatives assigned to various geographic regions.

Large trade houses spend millions of dollars promoting new books. To help create a best-seller, trade houses often distribute large cardboard bins, called *dumps*, to thousands of stores to display a book in bulk quantity. Like food merchants who buy eye-level shelf placement for their products in supermarkets, large trade houses buy shelf space from major chains to ensure prominent locations in bookstores. For example, to have copies of one title placed in a front-of-the-store dump bin or table at all the Borders bookstore locations costs about $10,000 for two weeks.[13] Publishers also buy ad space on buses and billboards and in newspapers and magazines. Some trade houses now routinely purchase ads on television, radio, and the Web.

The final part of the publishing process involves the business and order fulfillment stages—getting books to market and shipping and invoicing orders to thousands of commercial outlets and college bookstores. Warehouse inventories are monitored to ensure that enough copies of a book will be available to meet demand. Anticipating such demand, though, is a tricky business. No publisher wants to get stuck with books it cannot sell or be caught short if a book becomes more popular than originally predicted. Publishers must absorb the cost of returned books. Independent bookstores, which tend to order more carefully, return about 20 percent of books ordered; in contrast, mass merchandisers such as Wal-Mart and Costco, which routinely overstock popular titles, often return up to 40 percent. Returns this high can seriously impact a publisher's bottom line.

Book Clubs and Mail Order

In terms of selling books, two alternative strategies have worked for a number of years—book clubs and mail order. Book clubs, similar to music clubs, entice new members with offers such as five books for one dollar, then require regular purchases from their list of recommended titles. Mail-order services typically market specialized titles directly to readers. Both sales strategies have in many cases sustained publishers during the changeover from a print-based to an electronically influenced culture. The two tactics also helped the industry in earlier times when bookstores were not as numerous as they are today. Modeled on the turn-of-the-century catalogue sales techniques used by retailers such as Sears, direct-mail services brought books to rural and small-town areas that had no bookstores.

The Book-of-the-Month Club and the Literary Guild both started in 1926. Using popular writers and literary experts to recommend new books, the clubs were successful immediately. Book clubs have long served as editors for their customers, screening thousands of titles and recommending key books in particular genres. Occasionally, though, important books have been overlooked by clubs, including Steinbeck's *The Grapes of Wrath* and Hemingway's *The Sun Also Rises*.

During the 1980s, as book clubs experienced declining sales, they became more susceptible to pressure from major publishers. Indeed, the outside experts for the clubs began complaining not only that their recommendations were frequently bypassed by club editors but also that the clubs were stressing commercially viable authors without regard to literary merit.

Besides screening new books for consumers, clubs have offered incentives, such as free books and occasional price reductions, to compete with bookstores. Book clubs offer the same advantages as a cable home-shopping network: You can order from the comfort of your home and avoid "mall madness" or the congestion of downtown shopping. While Time Warner operates the Book-of-the-Month Club (the largest single club, with more than one million members), Doubleday remains the most active publisher in the book club business. In the late 1990s, Doubleday owned and operated both the Literary Guild and Doubleday Book Club as well as several specialty clubs, including the Mystery Guild, the Military Book Club, the Science Fiction Book Club, and the Black Expressions Book Club for African American literature.

In 2000, the Book-of-the-Month Club, the Literary Guild, and Doubleday combined their online efforts with a partnership called Bookspan (really a partnership between their owners—Bertelsmann and Time Warner). The alliance offers such benefits as discussion forums, live chats with authors, bulletin boards, reviews, and book excerpts from upcoming selections.[14] This strategy was intended to make book clubs more competitive with online booksellers, which had been making significant inroads into book club sales.

Mail-order bookselling is used primarily by trade, professional, and university press publishers. The mail-order strategy offers many of the benefits of book clubs in terms of immediately notifying readers about new book titles. Mail-order bookselling was pioneered in the 1950s by magazine publishers. They created special sets of books, such as Time-Life Books, focusing on science, nature, household maintenance, cooking, and so forth. These series usually offered one book at a time (unlike encyclopedias) and sustained sales through direct-mail flyers and other advertising. To enhance their perceived value, most of these sets could be obtained only through the mail. Although such sets are more costly due to advertising and postal charges, mail-order books still appeal to customers who prefer mail to the hassle of shopping. Others like the privacy of mail order (particularly if they are ordering sexually explicit books or magazines). In 2005, book-club and mail-order sales declined by 9 percent.

Bookstores

Although the book industry remains the most diverse of all mass media, the same trend toward large chain ownership prevails. About twenty-five thousand outlets sell books in the United States, including traditional bookstores, department stores, drugstores, used-book stores, and toy stores (see Table 10.4). Book sales, however, are dominated by two large chains: Borders-Walden and Barnes & Noble, which includes B. Dalton stores. These chains operate hundreds of stores each and account for about one-quarter of all book sales.

Shopping-mall bookstores have boosted book sales since the late 1960s. But the trend currently reinvigorating the business began in the 1980s with the development of superstores. The idea was to adapt to the book trade the large retail store concept, such as Home Depot in home improvement or Wal-Mart in general retail. Following the success of a single Borders store in Ann Arbor, Michigan, a number of book chains began developing **book superstores** that catered to suburban areas and to avid readers. A typical superstore now stocks more than 150,000 titles, compared with the 20,000 or 40,000 titles found in older B. Dalton or Waldenbooks stores. As superstores expanded, they also started to sell recorded music and feature coffee shops, restaurants, and live performances. By 2005, Borders had grown from only 14 superstores in 1991 to more than 460 superstores in addition to 650 Waldenbooks stores. With 37 new stores in places like Australia, New Zealand, Singapore, and the United Kingdom, Borders was also growing abroad. Similarly, Barnes & Noble was operating more than 670 superstores and 150 smaller B. Dalton bookstores.

● **Table 10.4 Bookstores in the United States, 2005**

Category of Store	Number	Category of Store	Number
Antiquarian general	1,103	Mail-order general	204
Antiquarian mail order	414	Mail-order specialized	524
Antiquarian specialized	201	Metaphysics, New Age, and occult	206
Art supply store	84	Museum store and art gallery	539
College general	3,226	Nature and natural history	158
College specialized	122	Newsdealer	65
Comics	210	Office supply	24
Computer software	1,347	Other§	2,330
Cooking	276	Paperback‡	180
Department store	1,673	Religious*	2,812
Educational*	188	Self-help/Development	27
Federal sites†	249	Stationer	7
Foreign language*	34	Toy store	41
General	5,238	Used*	503
Gift shop	153	Total	22,321
Juvenile*	183		

Source: The Bowker Annual Library and Book Trade Almanac, 2005 (Medford, N.J.: Information Today, Inc.).

*Includes mail-order shops for this topic, which are not counted elsewhere in this survey.

†National historic sites, national monuments, and national parks.

§Stores specializing in subjects or services other than those covered in this survey.

‡Includes mail order. Excludes used-paperback bookstores, stationers, drugstores, or wholesalers handling paperbacks.

The rise of book superstores severely cut into independent bookstores' business, which dropped from a 31 percent market share in 1991 to about 15 percent today. Yet independents have successfully maintained their market share for several years, suggesting that their business has stabilized. Despite the control that chains have over commercial trade books (73 percent of trade and mass market sales in 2005), the majority of bookstores today remain small and independent. For example, hundreds of used- and rare-book stores operate nationwide. But while there were 5,100 independent bookstores in 1991, there are just 900-plus stores today.[15] To oppose chains, many independents have formed regional or statewide groups to plan survival tactics. For instance, independents in Madison, Wisconsin, once countered the arrival of a new Borders superstore by redecorating, extending hours and services, creating newsletters, and offering musical and children's performances.

> **" Many independents have perished in a life-or-death struggle with the 'Killer B's' — Barnes & Noble and Borders. "**
>
> —Jon Ortiz, *Sacramento Bee*, 2005

Online Bookstores

In just a few years, online booksellers have created an entirely new book distribution system on the Internet. The trailblazer is Amazon.com, established in 1995 by then-thirty-year-old Jeff Bezos, who left Wall Street to start a Web-based business. Bezos realized books were an untapped and ideal market for the Internet, with more than three million publications in print and plenty of distributors to fulfill orders. He moved to Seattle and started Amazon.com, so named because search engines like Yahoo! listed categories in alphabetical order, putting Amazon near the top of the list.

In 1997, Barnes & Noble, the leading retail store bookseller, launched its heavily invested and carefully researched bn.com Web site (of which publishing giant Bertelsmann bought 50 percent in the following year after it canceled plans to start its own online store). The Web site's success, however, remains dwarfed by Amazon. In 1999, the American Booksellers Association also launched BookSense.com to help more than one thousand independent bookstores create an online presence. By 2003, online booksellers controlled about 8.1 percent of the retail book market, and their share of the market was estimated to be nearly 15 percent of consumer book sales by 2006.[16] The strength of online sellers lies in their convenience, low prices, and especially their ability to offer backlist titles and the works of less famous authors that even 150,000-volume superstores don't carry on their shelves. Online customers are also drawn to the interactive nature of these sites, which allow them to post their own book reviews, read those of fellow customers, and receive book recommendations based upon book searches and past purchases. The chief business strategy of online booksellers is to buy exclusive listings with the most popular Internet portals. For example, bn.com signed a multimillion-dollar deal with Microsoft to be the "buy books" button on MSN.com, and it is the exclusive bookseller on AOL. Similarly, Amazon.com has marketing agreements with Yahoo!, and in 2001 it took over operation of Borders.com after Borders failed to gain a strong Web presence.

● Employees filling holiday orders in Amazon.com's Seattle distribution warehouse.

Ownership Patterns

Like most mass media, commercial publishing is dominated by a handful of major corporations with ties to international media conglomerates such as Viacom (which now owns Simon & Schuster), Time Warner, News Corporation, and Bertelsmann, which began by publishing German Bibles in the 1700s (see Figure 10.3 on page 375).

Media Literacy and the Critical Process

How Do You Find Out about Books?

Every year, the book industry publishes 100,000+ titles in North America. Some could be life-changing, inspiring, and unbelievably fascinating, but you might never know about them because somehow the book industry failed to reach you. How do you discover books? And if you knew about more great reading material, would you read more often?

Description. Interview ten of your friends about their relationship with books. First, ask them whether they read books at all, and why or why not. Second, ask them how they choose the books they read. Third, ask them what books were transformative for them, and whether they would read more books if they knew about recommended titles.

Analysis. What important patterns emerge? For example, how many of your participants said "word of mouth"? How many browsed the shelves of libraries or bookstores; read about books in fashion, sports, or other magazines; heard about books on TV; saw a movie and read the book it was based on (or heard about the movie, read the book, then saw the movie); read book reviews in the newspaper; actively sought out books on the Internet by reading recommended listings (perhaps on Amazon); participated in a book club or reading group; or never read books at all? Discuss the most significant patterns.

Interpretation. What can you glean from this information? Is it difficult to learn about book titles you'd be interested in reading? Why do some people read more than others?

Evaluation. Do you think the publishing industry is doing a good job educating U.S. citizens about books? How does publicity for books compare to other mass media products (films, television, recordings)? Is publicizing books a good or a bad thing? Discuss.

Engagement. One of the best places to find out about past and present titles is BookBrowser. Go to the Barnes & Noble Web site (http://www.bn.com) and choose the "Browse" button to access titles and reviews by subject, author, store recommendations, book awards, great new writers (and its archive), first chapters and excerpts, various best-seller lists, language, and so on, which are listed in "best-selling" order. You may also want to start reading the *New York Times Book Review*, which can be found online at http://www.nytimes.com/pages/books/index.html. Choose some titles. Begin a book club. Read.

Since the 1960s and 1970s—when CBS acquired Holt, Rinehart & Winston; Popular Library; and Fawcett—mergers and consolidations have driven the book industry. Germany's Bertelsmann purchased Dell in the late 1970s for $35 million and in the 1980s bought Doubleday for $475 million. In 1998, Bertelsmann shook up the book industry by adding Random House, the largest U.S. book publisher, to its fold. With the $1.4 billion purchase of Random House from Advance Publications, Bertelsmann gained control of about one-third of the U.S. trade book market (about 10 percent of the total U.S. book market) and became the world's largest publisher of English-language books.[17] Bertelsmann's book companies include the Bantam Dell Publishing Group, the Doubleday Broadway Publishing Group, the Ballantine Publishing Group, the Knopf Publishing Group, the Random House Trade Publishing Group, and the Random House imprints of Modern Library and Fodor's Travel Publications, among others (see Figure 10.4 on page 376).

A number of concerns have surfaced regarding conglomerates' control over the publishing industry. The distinctive styles of older houses and their associations with certain literary figures and book types no longer characterize the industry. Of special concern has been the financial struggle of independent publishers and book-sellers, who are often undercut in price and promotion by large corporations and bookstore chains. Large houses also tend to favor blockbusters or best-sellers and do not aggressively pursue more modest or unconventional books.

From the corporate point of view, book industry executives argue that large companies can financially support a number of smaller struggling firms and that the editorial ideas of these firms can remain independent from the parent corporation. Executives also tout the advantages of *synergy:* the involvement of several media subsidiaries under one corporate umbrella, all working to develop different versions of a similar product. One writer commented on these synergistic possibilities when Time and Warner merged in 1989: "Theoretically, this unprecedented corporate fusion makes it possible for a title to be published in hardcover by Little, Brown (a division of Time Inc.), featured as a Book-of-the-Month Club main selection, reviewed by *Time* magazine, issued in paperback by Warner Books, made into a major motion picture, and turned into a TV series by Warner television."[18] Still, authors and critics worry that book ideas that lack such multimedia—or synergistic—potential may be rejected in the trend toward large corporate control.

On one level, the industry appears healthy, with thousands of independent presses still able to make books using inexpensive production techniques and desktop computer publishing. Many independents, however, struggle against the few large conglomerates that define the direction of much of the industry.

Trends in Book Publishing

A number of technological changes in the publishing industry demonstrate the blurring of print and electronic cultures. The book industry has adapted successfully in the digital age by using computer technology to effectively lower costs: Everything from an author's word-processing program to printing and distribution is digitized.[19]

Figure 10.3
Five Largest Trade Book Publishers (revenue in $millions)

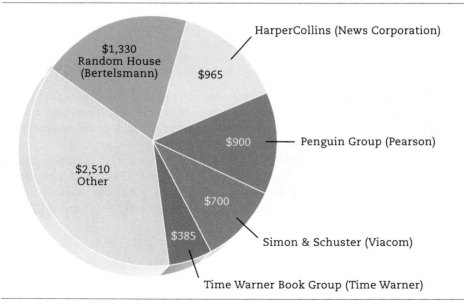

Source: Publishers Weekly, April 25, 2005.

Note: Based on 2004 North American sales revenue in $millions.

Figure 10.4

Media Ownership: Principal U.S. Operations for Bertelsmann AG

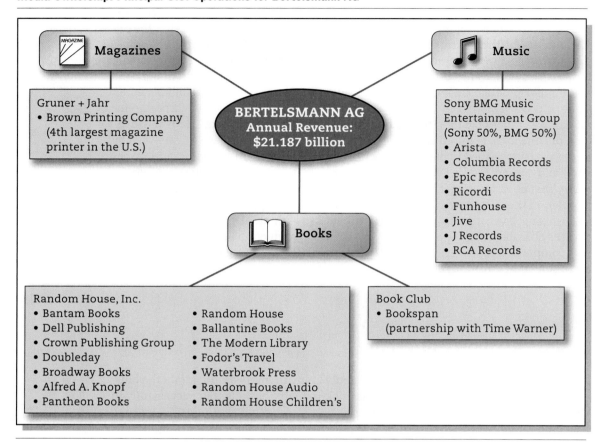

Among the world's top-grossing media conglomerates, Bertelsmann has holdings in publishing, music, and broadcasting in nearly 60 countries. Founded in Germany in 1835, Bertelsmann today owns the No. 1 trade book publisher, U.S.-based Random House, and 50% of the world's No. 2 music company, Sony BMG. In 2006, it also owned 90% of RTL Group, Europe's No. 1 TV broadcaster. Bertelsmann also owns several book and music clubs, and "e-tail" (or e-commerce) and Internet services.

Do a LexisNexis search to find out how Bertelsmann executives—and media critics—think about the significance of large companies that own media and produce popular culture worldwide.

Leading distributors, publishers, and bookstores have all begun using digital technology to print books on demand, reviving books that would otherwise go out of print and avoiding the inconveniences of carrying unsold books or being unable to respond to limited demand for a book.

Because e-books make possible such low publishing and distribution costs, **e-publishing** has also enabled authors to sidestep traditional publishers. A new breed of large Internet-based publishing houses, such as Xlibris, iUniverse, BookSurg, and AuthorHouse, design and distribute books for a comparatively small price ($99 to

> **❝** Traditional publishers are cautiously preparing for an uncharted future, digitizing thousands of old backlist titles in preparation for an e–new world where books can live forever because they will never go out of print. **❞**
>
> –Doreen Carvajal, *New York Times,* 1999

$1,600, depending on the level of services) for aspiring authors who want to self-publish a title. The companies then distribute the books in both print and e-book formats through Internet sellers. Although sales are typically low for such books, the low overhead costs allow higher royalty rates for the authors and lower retail prices for readers.

But the optimistic vision of an enormous market for **e-books** — electronic books that can be downloaded to portable e-book reading devices — did not materialize, despite predictions that e-books would garner at least 10 percent of publishing sales by 2005. Readers never warmed up to sitting down with a cup of tea and a lightweight LED monitor. After the publishing and technology industries invested hundreds of millions of dollars in the future of digital books, by 2003 their hopes fizzled, as Gemstar–TV Guide International announced it would stop production of its RCA eBook reader, and Barnes & Noble followed by ending e-book sales on its Web site. In 2006, Sony took a stab at the e-book industry with the introduction of its Sony Reader, a ten-ounce device with a six-inch screen and sharp, paper-like display. (For more on e-books, see "Examining Ethics: Digital Publishing Scrambles the Rules" on page 380.)

The publishing industry sees a future for e-books, but that market will develop slowly as engineers try to figure out how to make digital images feel like books. Until that time, the Internet offers new print-on-demand services like Blurb.com, which provides free custom publishing software to an aspiring author. The company will then produce and sell that person's work as a traditional book, offering it for sale "printed on coated paper, bound with a linen fabric hard cover, and then wrapped with a dust jacket," and available to individual buyers.[20]

Influences of Television and Film

Through their vast television exposure, books by TV anchors and actors such as Tom Brokaw, Tim Russert, and Jerry Seinfeld have sold millions of copies — enormous sales in a business where 100,000 in sales constitutes remarkable success. In national polls conducted in the 1980s and 1990s, nearly 30 percent of respondents said they had read a book after seeing the story or a promotion on television.

Even before the development of Oprah's Book Club in 1996, Oprah Winfrey's afternoon talk show had become a major power broker in selling books. In 1993, for example, Holocaust survivor and Nobel Prize recipient Elie Wiesel appeared on *Oprah.* Afterward, his 1960 memoir, *Night,* which had been issued as a Bantam paperback in 1982, returned to the best-seller lists. In 1996, novelist Toni Morrison's nineteen-year-old book *Song of Solomon* became a paperback best-seller after Morrison appeared on *Oprah.* In 1998, Winfrey, as actor and producer, brought another of Morrison's novels — the Pulitzer Prize–winning *Beloved* — to movie screens. The film version inspired new interest in the book, putting *Beloved* on the best-seller lists. The success of Oprah's Book Club extended far beyond anyone's expectations. Each selection became an immediate best-seller, generating tremendous excitement within the book industry. Winfrey briefly ended the book club in 2002 but then revived it in 2003, continuing to influence which books make it to the best-seller lists, including *Night* again in 2006.

Television and film continue to get many of their story ideas from books. Michael Crichton's *Jurassic Park* and Laura Hillenbrand's *Seabiscuit* became major motion pictures. Even nineteenth-century novels still translate to the screen. For example, the popular 1994 film version of *Little Women,* written in 1868 by Louisa May Alcott, sent the Random House reissue of the novel to the top of the juvenile best-seller list, and in 2005, a screen version of Jane Austen's 1813 novel *Pride and Prejudice* was released. Children's books also translate to the screen.

● Books like the *Lord of the Rings* trilogy and the *Harry Potter* series draw large movie audiences because of the built-in fan base for these popular stories. But comic books like *Spider-man, X-Men,* and *Superman* translate well too in terms of box-office success, bringing in legions of fans to see how Hollywood treats our favorite superheroes.

Scholastic's successful *Clifford* books about a lovable big red dog, first published by Norman Bridwell in 1963, became an animated television series from 2000–03, giving Scholastic a boost in book sales and paving the way for other TV tie-ins. The Dr. Seuss children's classic of 1957, *How the Grinch Stole Christmas,* has had even greater resonance, inspiring first a 1966 television special narrated by Boris Karloff and then a feature-length film starring Jim Carrey in 2000. In 2004 Carrey returned in a starring role in a children's book adaptation of *Lemony Snicket's A Series of Unfortunate Events.*

The most successful relationship between books and movies in the past few years emerged from the fantasy works of two British authors—J. K. Rowling's Harry Potter series and J.R.R. Tolkien's *The Lord of the Rings* trilogy (works ten years in the making, published in 1954 and 1955). The first four Harry Potter movies, have been popular hits, as has Peter Jackson's film trilogy of the *Rings* series. The triumph of these stories as books, films, and video games has inspired new reader interest in the seven fantasy novels known as *The Chronicles of Narnia,* authored by Tolkien's good friend C. S. Lewis and published between 1950 and 1956. Disney optioned the rights to the books and released the first installment, *The Chronicles of Narnia: The Lion, the Witch, and the Wardrobe,* late in 2005. By early 2006, the film had grossed nearly $300 million at U.S. theaters and increased sales of the book.

Blockbusters and Licenses

Since Harriet Beecher Stowe's abolitionist novel *Uncle Tom's Cabin* sold 15,000 copies in fifteen days back in 1852 (and 3 million total copies prior to the Civil War), many American publishers have stalked the best-seller. As in the movie business, large publishers are always searching for the blockbuster. To ensure popular success, publishers often pay rights to license popular film and television programs, especially in the juvenile book trade. For instance, the Disney Company's resurgence in animated films since the 1980s generated a wave of successful book titles based on its movies.

The drive to create blockbusters in the book industry also led to a number of overpriced book advances to media figures without much writing talent. Although Ellen DeGeneres, Jerry Seinfeld, and the professional wrestlers "The Rock" and "Mankind" had best-selling books, readers apparently do not find the written work of all entertainers to be compelling reading. Whoopi Goldberg received a whopping $6 million advance for a book that sold poorly in 1997, and Jay Leno's publisher took a beating after Leno's $7.7 million advance resulted in 400,000 returned unsold copies of his book.

Audio Books

Another major development in publishing has been the merger of sound recording with publishing. Audio books, talking books, or books on tape, generally feature actors or authors reading abridged versions of popular fiction and nonfiction trade books. Indispensable to many sightless readers and older readers whose vision is diminished, talking books are also popular among regular readers who do a lot of commuter driving or who want to listen to a book at home while doing something else. A 1999 study by the Audio Publishers Association reported that about 45 percent of all audio-book use took place in cars, and that listening while exercising is becoming an increasingly popular use. Recent award-winning audio books include *The Opposite of Fate* by Amy Tan (read by the author), *Last Car to Elysian Fields* by James Lee Burke (read by actor Will Patton), and the Harry Potter series (read by Jim Dale, who used more than a hundred different voices for all the characters). The number of audio books borrowed from libraries soared in the 1990s and early 2000s, and small bookstore chains such as Talking Book World developed to cater to the audio-book niche. Audio books also began to be released on CDs in the late 1990s, as CD players become more commonplace in car sound systems. By 2006, audio books were being

> **"** Almost a fifth of the decade's 100 best-sellers (1994–2004) had movie tie-ins. **"**
>
> —Ann Lloyd Merriman, book editor, *Richmond Times Dispatch*

heavily downloaded on iPods. The four hundred-plus new audio books available annually generate more than $800 million in sales.

Book Preservation

Another recent trend in the book industry involves the preservation of older books, especially those from the nineteenth century printed on acid-based paper. Ever since the conversion to machine-made publishing materials during the Industrial Revolution, paper had been produced by using chemicals that gradually deteriorate over time. At the turn of the twentieth century, research provided evidence that acid-based paper would eventually turn brittle and self-destruct. This research, initiated by libraries concerned with losing valuable older collections, was confirmed by further studies in the 1940s and 1950s. The paper industry, however, did not respond. In the 1970s, leading libraries began developing techniques to de-acidify book pages in an attempt to halt any further deterioration (although this process could not restore books to their original state). The professional conservators of the Book and Paper Group, the fastest growing division of the American Institute for the Conservation of Historic and Artistic Works, have worked for the last three decades to stabilize and restore older books and documents.

Despite evidence that alkaline-based paper was easier on machinery, produced a whiter paper, and caused less pollution, the paper industry did not change. But by the early 1990s, motivated almost entirely by economics rather than by the cultural value of books, the industry finally began producing paper that was acid-free. Libraries and book conservationists, however, still had to focus attention on older, at-risk books. Although clumsy, hard-to-read microfilm remained an option, some institutions began photocopying original books onto acid-free paper to make copies available to the public. Libraries then stored the originals, which were treated to halt further wear. Today, research libraries are building depositories for older books of permanent research value. Based on a model pioneered at Harvard, such depositories provide secure, climate-controlled storage that allow libraries to preserve low-use materials in off-site areas.

More recently, pioneering projects in digital technology by Xerox and Cornell University have produced electronic copies of books through computer scanning. Other companies, such as netLibrary, have eschewed scanning, which they say produces too many errors, and have enlisted armies of typists in China, India, and the Philippines to convert books into electronic form. The Colorado-based company, a division of the nonprofit Online Computer Library Center, digitizes about two hundred books a day. By 2006, netLibrary had more than a hundred thousand titles and, for a small fee, more than twelve thousand libraries subscribed to its service. Library patrons can "check out" the digitalized books over the Internet. Finally, the Google Library Project features partnerships with several major research libraries—including Harvard, Michigan, Oxford, and Stanford—to scan millions of books and make them available online. Google uses fully automated "robots" that safely, quickly, and accurately scan even fragile books face-up without damaging the binding. Several companies now provide this type of scanning for libraries that need to replace brittle or worn-out books.

Alternative Voices

Even though the book industry is dominated by large book conglomerates and superstores, there are still major efforts to make books freely available to everyone. The idea is not a new one. In the late nineteenth and early twentieth centuries, industrialist Andrew Carnegie used millions of dollars from his vast steel fortune to build more than twenty-five hundred libraries in the United States, Britain, Australia, and

● Many U.S. colleges and universities have instituted summer reading programs, which suggest a book to all first-year students for reading and discussion. A sampling of summer reading selections illustrates a wide range of themes, including Elie Wiesel's *Night* (Texas State–San Marcos); Tamim Ansary's *West of Kabul, East of New York* (Temple University); Barbara Ehrenreich's *Nickel and Dimed: On (Not) Getting By in America* (San Diego State University); Penny Le Couteur and Jay Burreson's *Napoleon's Buttons: 17 Molecules That Changed History* (Saint Louis University); and Mary Shelley's *Frankenstein* (Luther College).

EXAMINING ETHICS

Digital Publishing Scrambles the Rules

By Motoko Rich

When Mark Z. Danielewski's second novel, *Only Revolutions*, [was] published in September [2006], it include[d] hundreds of margin notes listing moments in history suggested online by fans of his work. Nearly 60 of his contributors have already received galleys of the experimental book, which they're commenting about in a private forum at Mr. Danielewski's Web site, www.onlyrevolutions.com.

Yochai Benkler, a Yale University law professor and author of the new book *The Wealth of Networks: How Social Production Transforms Markets and Freedom* (Yale University Press), has gone even farther: his entire book is available—free—as a download from his Web site. Between 15,000 and 20,000 people have accessed the book electronically, with some of them adding comments and links to the online version. Mr. Benkler said he saw the project as "simply an experiment of how books might be in the future."

That is one of the hottest debates in the book world right now, as publishers, editors and writers grapple with the Web's ability to connect readers and writers more quickly and intimately, new technologies that make it easier to search books electronically and the advent of digital devices that promise to do for books what the iPod has done for music: making them easily downloadable and completely portable. Not surprisingly, writers have greeted these measures with a mixture of enthusiasm and dread. The dread was perhaps most eloquently crystallized last month in Washington at BookExpo 2006, the publishing industry's annual convention, when the novelist John Updike forcefully decried a digital future composed of free downloads of books and the mixing and matching of "snippets" of text, calling it a "grisly scenario."

Hovering above the discussion of all these technologies is the fear that the publishing industry could be subject to the same upheaval that has plagued the music industry, where digitalization has started to displace the traditional artistic and economic model of the record album with 99-cent song downloads and personalized playlists. Total album sales are down 19 percent since 2001, while CD sales have dropped 16 percent during the same period, according to Nielsen BookScan.

For many authors, the question of how technology will shape book publishing inevitably leads to the question of how writers will be paid. Mr. Benkler, the Yale professor and author, argues that people will continue to pay for books if the price is low enough. "Even in music, price can compete with free," Mr. Benkler said. "The service has to be sufficiently better and the moral culture needs to be one where, as an act of respect, when the price is reasonable, you pay. It's not clear to me why, if people are willing to pay 99 cents for a song they won't be willing to pay $3 for

● One day, could book fairs like the one above feature only digital books?

a book." He argues that without the costs of paper and physical book production, publishers could afford to give authors a higher cut of the sale price as royalties.

In the context of history, the changes that today's technology will impose on literary society may not be as earth-shattering as some may think. In fact, books themselves are a relatively new construct, inheritors of a longstanding oral storytelling culture. Mass-produced books are an even newer phenomenon, enabled by the invention of the printing press that likely put legions of calligraphers and book-binders out of business.

Mr. Danielewski said that the physical book would persist as long as authors figure out ways to stretch the format in new ways. "*Only Revolutions*," he pointed out, tracks the experiences of two intersecting characters, whose narratives begin at different ends of the book, requiring readers to turn it upside down every eight pages to get both of their stories. "As excited as I am by technology, I'm ultimately creating a book that can't exist online," he said. "The experience of starting at either end of the book and feeling the space close between the characters until you're exactly at the halfway point is not something you could experience online. I think that's the bar that the Internet is driving towards: how to further emphasize what is different and exceptional about books."

Source: Motoko Rich, "Digital Publishing Scrambles the Rules," *New York Times*, June 5, 2006, p. E1.

New Zealand. Carnegie believed that libraries created great learning opportunities for citizens, and especially for immigrants like himself.

Indeed, public libraries may be some of the best venues for alternative voices—where a myriad of ideas exist side by side. Yet libraries can't (and don't) carry every book, and there are so many books out there with unique visions and information. One Internet source, Newpages.com, is working to bring a vast array of alternative and university presses, independent bookstores, and guides to literary and alternative magazines together. The site lists, for example, about four hundred independent publishers, mostly based in the United States and Canada, that range from Africa World Press (which publishes titles featuring Africa and African American interests) to Zoo Press (which publishes the poetry and essay collections of emerging writers).

Books and the Future of Democracy

As we enter the digital age, the book-reading habits of children and adults are a social concern. After all, books have played an important role not only in spreading the idea of democracy but also in connecting us to new ideas beyond our local experience. A 2004 National Endowment for the Arts (NEA) study, *Reading at Risk*, reported that reading literature had declined 10 percent among all age groups over the past decade, especially among eighteen to twenty-four year olds. Nineteen percent of seventeen year olds said they never or hardly ever read—up from just 9 percent in 1992. Four of ten college-aged people reported they read literature on a regular basis, compared to six of ten in 1982. Of seventeen thousand adults surveyed, nearly two-thirds of the men said they did not read literature at all (the study did not ask about biography and nonfiction). Among all adults surveyed, 96 percent favored watching TV, 60 percent preferred attending a movie, and 55 percent liked exercising—all activities ranking higher than reading literature. The NEA report noted that people who read literature at higher levels were also more active in civic and cultural life, performing volunteer and charity work, visiting art museums and culture programs, and attending sporting events.[21] (See Table 10.5.)

Yet other studies also suggest that reading habits are generally more evident among the young than among older people; 60 percent of all avid or regular book readers, for example, are under the age of forty. The Harry Potter phenomenon—now translated into sixty-two languages—has renewed reading among young people. One study in England reported that 60 percent of children surveyed said that the Potter books had improved their reading skills and 48 percent said the series is the main reason they read more. In the United States, an executive at Borders Books noted that in the 1980s less than 5 percent of their inventory was devoted to children's books, but in 2005 "10 to 15 percent" of their 150,000-plus books target young readers. Many of the nation's libraries have also reported higher circulation figures for children's literature. For example, in St. Petersburg, Florida, circulation for children's books has risen 10 percent since the end of the 1990s.[22]

Although our society is being dramatically influenced by electronic and digital culture, the impact of our oldest mass medium—the book—remains immense. Without the development of

● Table 10.5 Participation in Cultural and Social Activities		
	Percentage of U.S. Adult Population	
	Literary Readers	Non-Literary Readers
Perform Volunteer and Charity Work	43.0	17.0
Visit Art Museums	44.0	12.0
Attend Performing Arts Events	49.0	17.0
Attend Sporting Events	45.0	27.0

Source: National Endowment for the Arts, *Reading at Risk: A Survey of Literary Reading in America,* June 2004, xiii, http://www.nea.gov/pub/ReadingAtRisk.pdf.

printing presses and books, the idea of democracy would be hard to imagine. From the impact of Stowe's *Uncle Tom's Cabin,* which helped bring an end to slavery in the 1860s, to Rachel Carson's *Silent Spring,* which led to reforms in the pesticide industry in the 1960s, books have made a difference. They have told us things that we wanted — and needed — to know.

Over time, the wide circulation of books gave many ordinary people the same opportunities to learn that were once available to only a privileged few. However, as societies discovered the power associated with knowledge and the printed word, books were subjected to a variety of censors. Imposed by various rulers and groups intent on maintaining their authority, the censorship of books often prevented people from learning about the rituals and moral standards of other cultures. Political censors sought to banish "dangerous" books that promoted radical ideas or challenged conventional authority. Some versions of the Bible, Karl Marx's *Das Kapital* (1867), *The Autobiography of Malcolm X* (1965), and Salman Rushdie's *The Satanic Verses* (1989) have all been banned at one time or another. In fact, one of the triumphs of the Internet is that it allows the digital passage of banned books into nations where printed versions have been outlawed.

Beyond censorship issues, other concerns have surfaced regarding the limits that democratic societies place on books. For example, the economic clout of publishing houses run by large multinational corporations has made it more difficult for new authors and new ideas to gain a foothold in commercial publishing. Often, editors and executives prefer to invest in commercially successful writers or authors who have a built-in television, sports, or movie audience.

Another issue is whether the contemporary book industry, in its own way, has contributed to entertainment and information overload. For example, in his book *The Death of Literature,* Alvin Kernan argues that serious literary work has been increasingly overwhelmed by the triumph of consumerism. In other words, people accumulate craftily marketed celebrity biographies and popular fiction but seldom read serious works. Kernan's critique reflects the long-standing view that "superior" cultural taste is associated with reading literature. He contends that cultural standards have been undermined by marketing ploys that divert attention away from serious books and toward mass-produced works that are more easily consumed.[23]

Because democracies generally depend on literate populations to sift through cultural products and make informed decisions, the abundance of media products raises other important questions. Of particular concern is the apparent decline in juvenile reading levels as measured by standardized tests over the past few decades. Indeed, the increase in published book titles since the 1950s does not mean that we have become a more literate society. The adult illiteracy rate has remained fairly constant at about 10 percent over the years. And today children have multiple electronic and digital distractions and options competing for their leisure time.

Yet books and reading have survived the challenge of visual and digital culture. Developments such as word processing, audio books, children's pictorial literature, and online services have integrated aspects of print and electronic culture into our daily lives. Most of these new forms carry on the legacy of books: transcending borders to provide personal stories, world history, and general knowledge to all who can read.

Despite a commercial book industry that has increasingly developed its own star system of authors, about a thousand new publishers enter the business each year. Tensions persist, however, between businesspeople who publish books as a money-making enterprise and authors who try to write well and advance knowledge—or between authors who seek fame and fortune and editor-publishers who are interested in wisdom and the written word. Some argue that the industry balanced these conflicts better before corporate takeovers tipped the scales heavily toward high-profit motives. As our society's oldest media institution, the book industry bears the weight of these economic and cultural battles perhaps more than any other medium.

Given our increasing channels of specialized media, people can zero in on their own interests. Books, however, are one medium that takes us in other directions. Since the early days of the printing press, books have helped us to understand ideas and customs outside our own experiences. For democracy to work well, we must read. When we examine other cultures through books, we discover not only who we are and what we value but also who others are and what our common ties might be.

www.

For review questions and activities for Chapter 10, go to the interactive *Media and Culture* Online Study Guide at bedfordstmartins.com/mediaculture

REVIEW QUESTIONS

The History of Books from Papyrus to Paperbacks

1. What distinguishes the manuscript culture of the Middle Ages from both the oral and print eras in communication?

2. Why was the printing press such an important and revolutionary invention?

3. Why were books considered so dangerous to colonial rulers and other leaders during the early periods of American history?

Modern Publishing and the Book Industry

4. Why did publishing houses develop?

5. Why have instant books become important to the paperback market?

6. What are the major issues that affect textbook publishing?

7. Why have religious books been so successful historically?

8. What has hampered the sales of subscription reference encyclopedias?

The Organization and Ownership of the Book Industry

9. What are the general divisions within a typical publishing house?

10. Why have book clubs and mail-order strategies continued to flourish despite the rapid growth of mall stores and superstores?

11. Why have book superstores been so successful?

12. What are the strengths of online bookstores?

13. What are the current ownership patterns in the book industry? How are independent stores affected?

Trends in Book Publishing

14. What are the main ways in which digital technologies have changed the publishing industry?

15. Why did paper manufacturers convert to acid-free paper in the late 1980s and early 1990s?

Books and the Future of Democracy

16. What have book publishers and sellers done to keep pace with changes in technology and society?

17. What have been the major contributions of books to democratic life?

QUESTIONING THE MEDIA

1. What are your earliest recollections of books? Do you read for pleasure? If yes, what kind of books do you enjoy? Why?

2. What can the book industry do better to ensure that we are not overwhelmed by a visual and electronic culture?

3. If you were opening an independent bookstore in a town with a chain store, such as a Borders or a Barnes & Noble, how would you compete?

4. Imagine that you are on a committee that oversees book choices for a high school library in your town. What policies do you think should guide the committee's selection of controversial books?

5. Why do you think the availability of television and cable hasn't substantially decreased the number of new book titles available each year? What do books offer that television doesn't?

6. Would you read a book on an iPod? Why or why not?

SEARCHING THE INTERNET

http://www.bookweb.org

The Web home of the American Booksellers Association, the trade association representing independent bookstores in the United States.

http://www.publishersweekly.com/

The online version of *Publishers Weekly*, the book industry's trade magazine.

http://www.publishers.org/

Home site for the Association of American Publishers, the principal trade association of the book-publishing industry.

http://www.gutenberg.net

Founded in 1971, Project Gutenberg is a nonprofit database that makes hundreds of public domain literature titles (from Jane Austen to Leo Tolstoy) available to Internet users for free.

http://www.amazon.com

Established in 1995, this online bookseller claims to be the world's largest bookstore. Competing online bookstores include bn.com (Barnes & Noble).

http://bookbrowser.com

Barnes & Noble's recently acquired book exploration tool, this feature enables users to search titles under multiple categories, such as book awards, biography, or women's fiction.

http://www.nytimes.com/pages/books/index.html

This Web site features *New York Times* book reviews, bestseller lists, first chapters, art news, and book forums. (It's a free site, but registration is required.)

http://www.ala.org/bbooks

Part of the American Library Association's Web site, this page provides information about censorship and banned books.

Media Literacy
and the Critical Process

In Brief

This "think-pair-share" exercise focuses on the publishing and sales of college and university textbooks.

Think: On your own, write down:

- money you spent this semester on textbooks and cost of each book

- if you returned any books last semester, how much money you got back

- what your choices are for purchasing textbooks

Pair: With a partner, discuss your observations and consider these questions: Which types of books seem most expensive? Why do they cost so much? What do you typically do with textbooks at the end of a semester—keep them or sell them—and why? Who do you think is responsible for pricing books? Who do you think reaps the most profit from textbooks?

Share: As a class, consider the college textbook publishing business. If a book is more expensive, are you more or less likely to buy it? Should professors tie lectures closely to the texts, or should the required reading be done independently by the student? What are some of the factors in the production and distribution of textbooks that account for their cost?

In Depth

In small groups, investigate a college bookstore in your area. Compare it with other college bookstores in your state. Look at the National Association of College Stores Web site for information, www.nacs.org, and see Figure 10.2, "Where the New Textbook Dollar Goes" (page 361). Follow the five steps in the critical process:

Description. Describe each store and the variety of products sold. How does the bookstore make most of its money? Is it operated by the college or university, by a private franchise that contracts to manage the store for the college, or is it independently owned? Does it have any local competitors? How does it price its textbooks? What is the bookstore's policy on returning/reselling used texts? Is warehousing and handling used books expensive? What factors also affect the store's bottom line?

Analysis. Make a chart to organize your comparisons of the bookstores. What sort of patterns emerge? Are textbook sale and return policies and prices similar? Are supplies, computer products, trade books, and insignia merchandise important? Are local residents significant customers, too?

Interpretation. Critically interpret the findings. For example, does competition (or lack of it) have an impact on the pricing and strategies of the stores?

Evaluation. How would you evaluate the college bookstore industry based on your observations and experiences? Can you envision creative ways for existing or new bookstores to discount textbooks to students, yet still be reasonably profitable?

Engagement. You could directly lobby the university bookstore to reduce rates on textbooks. Alternatively, you could do what other students have already done—set up a book swap Web site. Low-tech variations of this could include an informal network of person-to-person book swaps, or establishing a designated book swap/sale day in a public location at the end or beginning of each semester.

KEY TERMS

advertising

and commercial culture

In his 1996 novel *Infinite Jest,* David Foster Wallace writes of a time in the not-so-distant future when entire calendar years will be sponsored by corporations. So a letter dated 17 November Y.D.A.U. means it was written in the Year of the Depend Adult Undergarment. Other twelve-month periods are renamed the Year of Dairy Products from the American Heartland, the Year of the Trial-Size Dove Bar, and the Year of the Whopper.

Wallace's jesting is not far from today's reality. College football bowl games are rarely named after regional flowers or agricul-

tural goods these days. Instead, we have the FedEx Orange Bowl, the Tostitos Fiesta Bowl, and the Chick-fil-A Peach Bowl, among others. The sites for sporting events, too, may be past the day when they would be named for an esteemed coach or player, or for the host city. Instead, naming goes to the highest bidder. Today, major-league baseball and NBA games can be found in places like Coors Field, the United Center, and Qualcomm Stadium. This trend backfired in 2001 and 2002 in the wake of a series of corporate scandals. In Houston and Nashville, for example, after both

↓

Enron and Adelphia Communications declared bankruptcy, the Astros' baseball team and the Titans' NFL franchise purged the corporate names from Enron Field and Adelphia Coliseum. Yet, in 2006, the New York pro-soccer team—the MetroStars—changed its name to the Red Bulls, a sponsoring energy drink that paid $100 million for team-naming rights.

The trend toward corporate sponsorship is catching on at colleges and universities, too. Louisville has the Papa John's Cardinal Stadium, and Ohio State has the Value City Arena. College athletes are billboards for products as well, with the ubiquitous Nike swoosh logo on the uniforms of nearly every NCAA Division I sports powerhouse.

Some people wonder if the commercialization of everyday life has gone too far. In 2000, babies became unwitting corporate icons for life when the now defunct Internet Underground Music Archive, in a national promotion, paid ten families $5,000 each for naming their newborns IUMA. The most recent trend in advertising space is human skin. In 2004 and 2005, several people turned to eBay online auctions to sell various parts of their bodies—foreheads, arms, and pregnant bellies—for the display of temporary or permanent ad tattoos. Prices for such ads varied widely. In 2005, twenty-year-old Andrew Fischer won a $37,375 auction bid for a thirty-day tattoo carrying the name of an anti-snoring remedy on his forehead. And a woman from Myrtle Beach, South Carolina, auctioned her pregnant belly (for $4,050) to carry a temporary tattoo for an online gambling Web site.

The relationship with advertising and its symbols around the world is more complicated than sponsorship agreements and sellouts to corporations. Millions of people happily purchase and don clothing decorated with Nike swooshes, soft drink logos, NFL sports team symbols, university names, Disney characters, or the clothing's designer name. Others delight in a McDonald's jingle or Budweiser's lizard ads or admire the daring design of Calvin Klein print ads. Advertising can be an annoying, even oppressive, intrusion into our lives, but it also seems to have become a "natural" part of our popular culture's landscape.

But some people are opposing the "naturalization" of advertising culture. Some teenagers reject brand-name culture to shop at thrift stores, while some college students oppose the commercialization of their sports teams. More significantly, in May 2006 health advocates and education activists forced a national voluntary agreement from the three largest soft-drink companies to serve only "bottled water, low-fat and nonfat milk and 100 percent fruit juice" in the commercial vending machines placed in school cafeterias. In removing "sweetened drinks like Coke, Pepsi, and iced teas" from schools, the big beverage conglomerates acknowledged the growing threat of state lawsuits aimed at the record 64 percent obesity and overweight rate among adults and adolescents.[1] The new beverage rules will be phased in slowly and completed by the 2010 school year. But even though schools "have been good places to create loyalty among the next generation of consumers," the policy is not "a big deal for the beverage industry" since schools generate "less than 1 percent" of such sales.[2]

today, ads are scattered everywhere—and they are multiplying. Chameleon-like, advertising adapts to most media forms. At local theaters and on home videos, advertisements now precede the latest Hollywood movies. Corporate sponsors spend millions for **product placement**: buying spaces for their particular goods to appear on a TV show or in a movie. Ads are part of a deejay's morning patter, and ads routinely interrupt our favorite TV and cable programs. By 2006, eighteen minutes of each hour of prime-time network television carried commercials, program promos, and public service announcements—an increase from the thirteen minutes an hour in 1992.

Ads take up more than half the space in most daily newspapers and consumer magazines. They are inserted into trade books and text-books. They clutter Web sites on the Internet. They fill our mailboxes

● Often the major public symbol and ad icon for women's golf, 17-year-old Michelle Wie has product endorsements with Sony's Cyber-shot camera and, of course, Nike despite the fact that she had not won a professional tournament by the end of 2006. Due to her age, one concern raised about her celebrity status has been that she is not having a normal teenage life, becoming too famous too fast and carrying too many adult expectations.

and wallpaper the buses we ride. Dotting the nation's highways, billboards promote fast-food and hotel chains while neon signs announce the names of stores along major streets and strip malls. According to the Food Marketing Institute, the typical supermarket's shelves are filled with thirty thousand to fifty thousand different brand-name packages, each functioning like miniature billboards. Consumers can also order products displayed on cable home-shopping networks and on the Internet twenty-four hours a day. By some research estimates, the average American comes into contact with two thousand forms of advertising each day.

Advertising comes in many forms, from classified ads to business-to-business ads, providing detailed information on specific products. In this chapter, however, we will concentrate on the more conspicuous advertisements that shape product images and brand-name identities. Because so much consumer advertising intrudes into daily life, ads are often viewed in a negative light. Although business managers agree that advertising is the foundation of a healthy media economy—far preferable to government-controlled media—citizens routinely complain about how many ads they are forced to endure. Accordingly, the national cynicism about advertising has caused advertisers to become more competitive. And ad agencies, in turn, create ads that not only seem natural but also stand out in some way. To get noticed, ads routinely include celebrities, humor, computer animation, music video devices, and Hollywood movie special effects.

Given the public's increasing sophistication regarding visual culture, companies work hard to get our attention. But consumers have found a variety of ways to dodge ads they dislike: remote controls, mute buttons, VCRs, and DVRs. Advertisers try to counter the new technology with computer tricks and technological wizardry of their own. To ensure that we pay attention, advertisers also spend enormous sums to associate their products with celebrities. For example, by his mid-twenties Tiger

Woods had become the leading sports spokesperson, providing endorsements for a growing list of companies, including Nike, American Express, Accenture, Electronic Arts video games, Golf Digest, All Star Café, Rolex, Wheaties, CBS SportsLine, ABC, ESPN, Warner Books, TLC Laser Eye Centers, Buick, and Asahi Beverages in Japan. Now the most recognizable sports figure on the planet, Woods amassed $90 million in 2006, far more than the $45 million that basketball star Michael Jordan made in his best year of endorsements.

The cultural and social impact of advertising has been extensive. By the late 1800s, advertising had begun transforming American society from its agrarian, small-town customs to today's urban, consumer-driven lifestyles. The same kind of social transformations occurred with the fall of the communist governments in Europe in the 1980s and 1990s. When Poland became free of Soviet influence in the late 1980s, TV ads and billboards proliferated—announcing Poland's leap into a market-driven economy. For generations, advertisers have informed society about "new and improved" products, both satisfying consumers' desires and creating needs we never knew we had. Advertising, finally, has taught us to imagine ourselves as consumers before thinking of ourselves as citizens.

Without consumer advertisements, mass communication industries would cease to function in their present forms. Advertising is the economic glue that holds most media industries together. Yet despite advertising's importance to the economy, many of us remain skeptical about its impact on American life. In this chapter, we will examine the historical development and role of advertising—an industry that helped transform a number of nations into consumer societies. We will look at the first U.S. ad agencies, early advertisements, and the emergence of packaging, trademarks, and brand-name recognition. Then we will consider the growth of advertising in the last century, scrutinizing the increasing influence of ad agencies and the shift to a more visually oriented culture. In keeping with our goal of developing critical skills, we will outline the key persuasive techniques used in consumer advertising. In addition, we will investigate ads as a form of commercial speech and discuss the measures aimed at regulating advertising. Finally, we will look at political advertising and its impact on democracy.

> **"** In a mobile society, commercial products with familiar [brand] names provide people with some sense of identity and continuity in their lives. **"**
>
> –Michael Schudson,
> *Advertising, the Uneasy Persuasion*, 1984

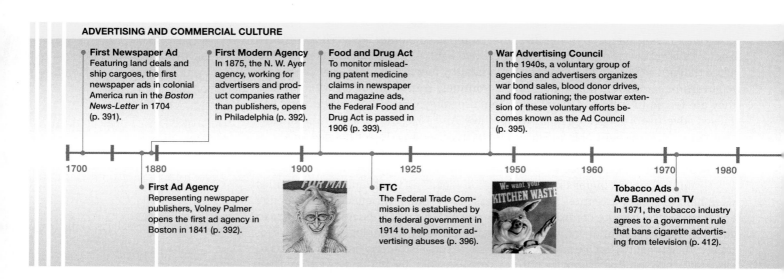

ADVERTISING AND COMMERCIAL CULTURE

First Newspaper Ad
Featuring land deals and ship cargoes, the first newspaper ads in colonial America run in the *Boston News-Letter* in 1704 (p. 391).

First Modern Agency
In 1875, the N. W. Ayer agency, working for advertisers and product companies rather than publishers, opens in Philadelphia (p. 392).

Food and Drug Act
To monitor misleading patent medicine claims in newspaper and magazine ads, the Federal Food and Drug Act is passed in 1906 (p. 393).

War Advertising Council
In the 1940s, a voluntary group of agencies and advertisers organizes war bond sales, blood donor drives, and food rationing; the postwar extension of these voluntary efforts becomes known as the Ad Council (p. 395).

1700   1880   1900   1925   1950   1960   1970   1980

First Ad Agency
Representing newspaper publishers, Volney Palmer opens the first ad agency in Boston in 1841 (p. 392).

FTC
The Federal Trade Commission is established by the federal government in 1914 to help monitor advertising abuses (p. 396).

Tobacco Ads Are Banned on TV
In 1971, the tobacco industry agrees to a government rule that bans cigarette advertising from television (p. 412).

Early Developments in American Advertising

Advertising has existed since 3000 B.C., when shop owners in ancient Babylon first began hanging outdoor signs carved in stone and wood so that customers could spot their stores. Merchants in early Egyptian society hired town criers to walk through the streets, announcing the arrival of ships and listing the goods on board. When archaeologists searched Pompeii, the ancient Italian city destroyed when Mount Vesuvius erupted in A.D. 79, they turned up advertising messages painted on walls. By 900 A.D., many European cities featured town criers who not only called out the news of the day but also directed customers to various stores.

The earliest media ads were in the form of handbills, posters, and broadsides (long newsprint-quality posters). English booksellers printed brochures and bills announcing new publications as early as the 1470s, when posters advertising religious books were tacked on church doors. In 1622, print ads imitating the oral style of criers began appearing in the first English newspapers. Announcing land deals and ship cargoes, the first newspaper ads in colonial America ran in the *Boston News-Letter* in 1704.

To distinguish themselves from the commercialism of newspapers, early magazines refused to carry advertisements. By the mid-1800s, though, most magazines contained ads and most publishers started magazines hoping to earn advertising dollars. About 80 percent of early advertisements covered three subjects: land sales, transportation announcements (stagecoach and ship schedules), and "runaways" (ads placed by farm and plantation owners whose slaves had fled).[3]

> **❝ You can tell the ideals of a nation by its advertisements. ❞**
> —Norman Douglas, *South Wind*, 1917

The First Advertising Agencies

Until the 1830s, little need existed for elaborate advertising. Prior to the full impact of manufacturing plants and the Industrial Revolution, few goods and products were even available for sale. Demand was also low because 90 percent of Americans lived in isolated areas and produced most of their own tools, clothes, and food. The minimal advertising that did exist usually featured local merchants selling goods and services in their own communities. National advertising, which initially focused on patent medicines, didn't start in earnest until the 1850s. At that point, railroads first linked towns from the East Coast to the Mississippi River and began carrying news-

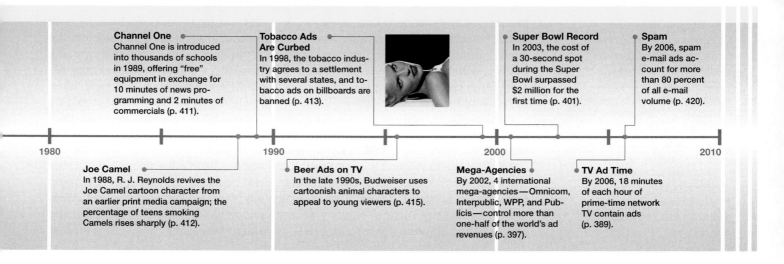

Channel One
Channel One is introduced into thousands of schools in 1989, offering "free" equipment in exchange for 10 minutes of news programming and 2 minutes of commercials (p. 411).

Tobacco Ads Are Curbed
In 1998, the tobacco industry agrees to a settlement with several states, and tobacco ads on billboards are banned (p. 413).

Super Bowl Record
In 2003, the cost of a 30-second spot during the Super Bowl surpassed $2 million for the first time (p. 401).

Spam
By 2006, spam e-mail ads account for more than 80 percent of all e-mail volume (p. 420).

1980   1990   2000   2010

Joe Camel
In 1988, R. J. Reynolds revives the Joe Camel cartoon character from an earlier print media campaign; the percentage of teens smoking Camels rises sharply (p. 412).

Beer Ads on TV
In the late 1990s, Budweiser uses cartoonish animal characters to appeal to young viewers (p. 415).

Mega-Agencies
By 2002, 4 international mega-agencies—Omnicom, Interpublic, WPP, and Publicis—control more than one-half of the world's ad revenues (p. 397).

TV Ad Time
By 2006, 18 minutes of each hour of prime-time network TV contain ads (p. 389).

papers, handbills, and broadsides—as well as national consumer goods—across the country.

The first American advertising agencies were really newspaper **space brokers**: individuals who purchased space in newspapers and sold it to various merchants. Newspapers, accustomed to a 25 percent nonpayment rate from advertisers, welcomed the space brokers, who paid up front. In return, brokers usually received discounts of 15 to 30 percent but sold the space to advertisers at the going rate. In 1841, Volney Palmer opened the first ad agency in Boston; for a 25 percent commission he worked for newspaper publishers and sold space to advertisers.

Advertising in the 1800s

The first so-called modern ad agency, N. W. Ayer, worked primarily for advertisers and product companies rather than for publishers. Opening in 1875 in Philadelphia, the agency helped create, write, produce, and place ads in selected newspapers and magazines. To this day, under a payment structure that began in the nineteenth century, the agency collects a fee from its advertising client for each ad placed; the fee covers the price that each media outlet charges for placement of the ad. Typically, the agency then keeps 15 percent of this fee for itself and passes on the rest to the appropriate mass media. For example, if a local TV station charges $1,000 for a thirty-second commercial, the ad agency tacks on 15 percent; it then charges the client $1,150, passes on $1,000 to the station, and pockets $150 for its services. The more ads an agency places, the larger the agency's revenue. Thus agencies have little incentive to buy fewer ads on behalf of their clients. Since the beginning of space brokerage in the 1840s, few have seriously challenged this odd relationship, which drives up costs, adds clutter to the media landscape, encourages cynicism among consumers, and does not always represent the best interests of the client.

Trademarks and Packaging

Some historians contend that the Industrial Revolution generated so many new products that national advertising was necessary to sell these goods quickly and keep factories humming. Now, though, other historians point to a more fundamental reason for advertising's development on a national scale: "the need to get control of the price the manufacturer charged for his goods."[4] During the mid-1800s, most manufacturers served retail store owners, who usually set their own prices by purchasing goods in large quantities. Over time, however, manufacturers came to realize that if their products were distinctive and became associated with quality, customers would ask for them by name; manufacturers would then be able to dictate prices without worrying about being undersold by generic products or bulk items. To achieve this end, manufacturers began to use advertising to establish the special identity of their products and to separate themselves from competitors. Like many ads today, nineteenth-century advertisements for patent medicines and cereals often created the impression of significant differences among products when in fact very few differences actually existed. But when consumers began demanding certain products—either because of quality or because of advertising—manufacturers seized control of pricing. With ads creating and maintaining brand-name recognition, retail stores had to stock the desired brands.

One of the first brand names, Smith Brothers, has been advertising cough drops since the early 1850s. Quaker Oats, the first cereal company to register a trademark, has used the image of William Penn, a Quaker who founded Pennsylvania in 1681, to project a company image of honesty, decency, and hard work since 1877. Other early and enduring brands include Campbell Soup, which came along in 1869, Levi Strauss

● Originally called the Joseph A. Campbell Preserve Company back in 1869, the Campbell Soup Co. introduced its classic red and white soup can labels in 1897 after an employee was inspired by the uniforms of the Cornell University football team. Today, the label looks different, but Campbell's red and white cans remain one of the most recognized brands in the country.

overalls in 1873, Ivory Soap in 1879, and Eastman Kodak film in 1888. Many of these companies packaged their products in small quantities, thereby distinguishing them from the generic products sold in large barrels and bins.

Packaging also enabled manufacturers to add preservatives and to claim less contamination and more freshness than might be found in loose food barrels at the local general store. For example, Quaker Oats developed the folding carton, which could be printed with color displays and recipes before it was filled with cereal. This marketing strategy represented "the beginning of the end of selling cereal to retailers in bulk."[5] Product differentiation associated with brand-name packaged goods represents the single biggest triumph of advertising. Studies suggest that although most ads are not very effective in the short run, over time they create demand by leading consumers to associate particular brands with quality.

Not surprisingly, building or sustaining brand-name recognition is the focus of many product-marketing campaigns. But the costs that packaging and advertising add to products generate many consumer complaints. The high price of many contemporary products results from advertising costs. For example, designer jeans that cost $100 (or more) today are made from the same inexpensive denim that has outfitted farmworkers since the 1800s. The difference now is that more than 90 percent of the jeans' costs go toward advertising and profit.

Patent Medicines and Department Stores

By the end of the 1800s, patent medicines and department stores dominated advertising copy, accounting for half of the revenues taken in by ad agencies. During this period, one-sixth of all print ads came from patent medicine and drug companies. Such ads ensured the financial survival of numerous magazines, as "the role of the publisher changed from being a seller of a product to consumers to being a gatherer of consumers for the advertisers."[6] Bearing names like Lydia Pinkham's Vegetable Compound, Dr. Lin's Chinese Blood Pills, and William Radam's Microbe Killer, patent medicines were often made with water and 15 to 40 percent concentrations of ethyl alcohol. One patent medicine—Mrs. Winslow's Soothing Syrup—actually contained morphine. The alcohol and other powerful drugs in these medicines went a long way toward explaining why people felt "better" after taking them; at the same time, they triggered lifelong addiction problems for many customers.

Many contemporary products, in fact, originated as medicines. Coca-Cola, for instance, was initially sold as a medicinal tonic and even contained traces of cocaine until 1903, when that drug was replaced by caffeine. Early Post and Kellogg's cereal ads promised to cure stomach and digestive problems. Many patent medicines made outrageous claims about what they could cure, leading ultimately to increased public cynicism. As a result, advertisers began to police their ranks and develop industry codes to restore customer confidence. Partly to monitor patent medicine claims, the Federal Food and Drug Act was passed in 1906.

Along with patent medicines, department store ads were also becoming prominent in newspapers and magazines. By the early 1890s, more than 20 percent of ad space was devoted to department stores and the product lines they carried. At the

● Unregulated patent medicines, such as the one represented in this 1880 ad for Pratts Healing Ointment, created a bonanza for nineteenth-century print media in search of advertising revenue. After several muckraking magazine reports about deceptive patent medicine claims, Congress created the Food and Drug Administration in 1906.

Rank	Advertiser	Headquarters	2005 Advertising Expenditures (in $billions)	% Change from 2004
1	Procter & Gamble Co.	Cincinnati	$4.60	-3.5
2	General Motors Corp.	Detroit	4.35	+7.1
3	Time Warner	New York	3.49	+2.7
4	Verizon Communications	New York	2.48	+4.9
5	AT&T	San Antonio	2.47	-26.0
6	Ford Motor Co.	Dearborn, Mich.	2.39	+0.6
7	Walt Disney Co.	Burbank, Calif.	2.27	-5.4
8	Johnson & Johnson	New Brunswick, N.J.	2.20	+3.6
9	GlaxoSmithKline	Brentford, Middlesex, U.K.	2.19	+18.1
10	DaimlerChrysler	Auburn Hills, Mich./Stuttgart, Germany	2.17	-12.9

Source: "Special Report: 100 Leading National Advertisers Supplement," *Advertising Age,* June 26, 2006, p. 8.

time, these stores were frequently reviled for undermining small shops and businesses, which depended on shopkeepers to direct people to store items. The more impersonal department stores allowed shoppers to browse and find brand-name goods themselves. Because these stores purchased merchandise in large quantities, they could generally sell the same products for less. With increased volume and less money spent on individualized service, department store chains, like Target and Wal-Mart today, undercut small local stores and put more of their profits into ads.

With the advent of the Industrial Revolution, "continuous-process machinery" kept company factories operating at peak efficiency, helping to produce an abundance of inexpensive packaged consumer goods.[7] The companies that produced those goods were some of the first to advertise, and they remain major advertisers today (although many of these brand names have been absorbed by larger conglomerates; see Table 11.1). They include Procter & Gamble, Colgate-Palmolive, Heinz, Borden, Pillsbury, Eastman Kodak, Carnation, and American Tobacco. A few firms, such as Hershey's Chocolate, chose not to advertise initially yet still rose to national prominence through word-of-mouth reputations. By the 1880s, however, the demand for newspaper advertising by product companies and retail stores had significantly changed the ratio of copy at most newspapers. Whereas in the mid-1880s papers featured 70 to 75 percent news and editorial material and only 25 to 30 percent advertisements, by the early 1900s more than half the space in daily papers was devoted to advertising. This trend continues today, with more than 60 percent of the space in large daily newspapers consumed by ads.

> **❝Consumption, Asthma, Bronchitis, Deafness, cured at HOME!❞**
>
> —Ad for Carbolate of Tar Inhalants, 1883

Promoting Social Change and Dictating Values

As U.S. advertising became more pervasive, it contributed to major social changes in the twentieth century. First, it significantly influenced the transition from a producer-directed to a consumer-driven society. By stimulating demand for new products, advertising helped manufacturers create new markets and recover product start-up costs quickly. From farms to cities, advertising spread the word—first in newspapers and magazines and later on radio and television. Second, advertising promoted technological advances by showing how new machines, such as vacuum cleaners, washing machines, and cars, could improve daily life. Third, advertising encouraged economic growth by increasing sales. To meet the demand generated by ads, manufacturers produced greater quantities, which reduced their costs per unit, although they did not always pass these savings along to consumers.

By the early 1900s, advertisers and ad agencies believed that women, who constituted 70 to 80 percent of newspaper and magazine readers, controlled most household purchasing decisions. (This is still a fundamental principle of advertising today.) Ironically, more than 99 percent of the copywriters and ad executives at that time were men, primarily from Chicago and New York. They emphasized stereotyped appeals to women, believing that simple ads with emotional and even irrational content worked best. Thus early ad copy featured personal tales of "heroic" cleaning products and household appliances. The intention was to help consumers feel good about defeating life's problems—an advertising strategy that endured throughout much of the twentieth century.

Although ad revenues fell during the Great Depression in the 1930s, World War II marked a rejuvenation for advertising. For the first time, the federal government bought large quantities of advertising space to promote U.S. involvement in a war. These purchases helped offset a decline in traditional advertising, as many industries had turned their attention and production facilities to the war effort. Also during the 1940s, the industry began to actively deflect criticism that advertising created consumer needs that ordinary citizens never knew they had. To promote a more positive image, the industry developed the War Advertising Council—a voluntary group of agencies and advertisers that organized war bond sales, blood donor drives, and the rationing of scarce goods.

The postwar extension of advertising's voluntary efforts became known as the Ad Council, praised over the years for its Smokey the Bear campaign ("Only you can prevent forest fires"), its fund-raising campaign for the United Negro College Fund ("A mind is a terrible thing to waste"), and its "crash dummy" spots for the Department of Transportation, which substantially increased seat belt use. Choosing a dozen worthy causes annually, the Ad Council continues to produce pro bono *public-service announcements* (PSAs) on a wide range of topics, including literacy, homelessness, drug addiction, antismoking, and AIDS education.

After the Great Depression and World War II, the advent of television dramatically altered advertising. With this new visual medium, ads increasingly intruded on daily life. Criticism of advertising grew as the industry appeared to be dictating American values as well as driving the economy. Critics discovered that some agencies used **subliminal advertising**. This term, coined in the 1950s, refers to hidden or disguised print and visual messages that allegedly register on the subconscious and fool people into buying products. Only a few examples of subliminal ads actually exist (for example, a "Drink Coca-Cola" ad embedded in a few frames of a movie, or hidden sexual activity drawn into liquor ads), and research has suggested that such ads are no more effective than regular ads.

● During World War II, the federal government engaged the advertising industry to create messages to support the U.S. war effort. Advertisers promoted the sale of war bonds, conservation of natural resources such as tin and gasoline, and even saving kitchen waste so it could be fed to farm animals.

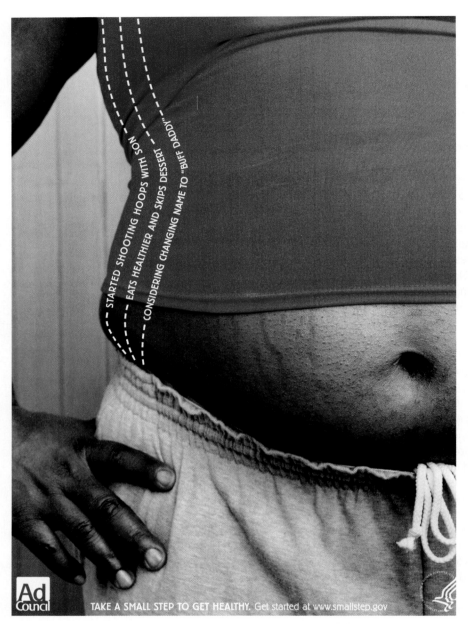

Ad Council

TAKE A SMALL STEP TO GET HEALTHY. Get started at www.smallstep.gov

STARTED SHOOTING HOOPS WITH SON
EATS HEALTHIER AND SKIPS DESSERT
CONSIDERING CHANGING NAME TO "BUFF DADDY"

● The Ad Council has been creating public service announcements (PSAs) since 1942. Supported by contributions from 375 individuals, corporations, and foundations, the Council's PSAs are produced pro bono by ad agencies. This recent PSA is part of the obesity prevention campaign.

Early Ad Regulation

During the early 1900s, the emerging clout of ad agencies and revelations of fraudulent advertising practices led to the formation of several watchdog organizations. Partly to keep tabs on deceptive advertising, advocates in the business community in 1913 created the nonprofit Better Business Bureau, which by the early 2000s had more than one hundred branch offices in the United States. At the same time, advertisers wanted a formal service that tracked newspaper readership, guaranteed accurate audience measures, and ensured that papers would not overcharge agencies and their clients. As a result, publishers formed the Audit Bureau of Circulation (ABC) in 1914. That same year, the government created the Federal Trade Commission (FTC), in part to help monitor advertising abuses. Thereafter, the industry urged self-regulatory measures in order to keep government interference at bay. The American Association of Advertising Agencies (AAAA), for example, established in 1917, tried to minimize government oversight by urging ad agencies to refrain from making misleading product claims.

The Shape of U.S. Advertising Today

Most of the history of modern advertising has been influenced by the print media and the facility of copywriters, who create the words in advertisements. Until the 1960s, the shape and pitch of most U.S. ads were determined by a **slogan**, the phrase that attempts to sell a product by capturing its essence in words. With slogans such as Clairol's "Does she or doesn't she?" and "Only her hairdresser knows for sure," the visual dimension of ads was merely a complement. Eventually, however, through the influence of movies, television, and European design, images asserted themselves and visual style began to dictate printed substance in U.S. advertising as mega-agencies dominated and boutique agencies emerged.

The Influence of Visual Design

Just as a postmodern design phase developed in art and architecture during the 1960s and 1970s, an era of stunning image fragments began to affect advertising at the same time. Part of this visual revolution was imported from non-U.S. schools of design; indeed, ad-rich magazines such as *Vogue* and *Vanity Fair* increasingly hired European designers as art directors. These directors tended to be less tied to U.S. word-driven radio advertising, because most European countries had government-sponsored radio systems with no ads.

By the early 1970s, agencies had developed teams of writers and artists: Images and words were granted equal status in the creative process. By the mid-1980s, the visual techniques of MTV, which initially modeled its videos on advertising, influenced many ads and most agencies. MTV promoted a particular visual aesthetic—rapid edits, creative camera angles, compressed narratives, and staged performances. Video-style ads soon saturated television and featured such prominent performers as Paula Abdul, Ray Charles, Michael Jackson, Elton John, and Madonna. The popularity of MTV's visual style also started a trend in the 1980s to license hit songs for commercial tie-ins. Warner Music, for example, aggressively pitched its music catalogue for use by advertisers. By the 2000s, a wide range of short, polished musical performances and familiar songs—including the work of Paul McCartney (Fidelity Investments), Gorillaz (iTunes), Taylor Hicks (Ford), The Concretes (Target), and even the Muppets (Diet Cherry Vanilla Dr. Pepper)—were routinely used in TV ads to encourage consumers not to click the remote control.

The Mega-Agency

Although more than thirteen thousand ad agencies currently operate in the United States, advertising revenue worldwide is dominated by **mega-agencies**, large ad firms that are formed by merging several individual agencies that maintain worldwide regional offices. In addition to providing both advertising and public relations services, these agencies usually operate their own in-house radio and TV production studios. By 2002, four mega-agencies controlled more than one-half of the world's ad revenues. These include Omnicom, Interpublic, WPP, and Publicis.[8] The London-based WPP Group, which had its beginnings as a British company named Wire & Plastic Products, grew quickly in the 1980s with the 1987 purchase of J. Walter Thompson, the largest U.S. ad firm at the time. WPP also bought Hill & Knowlton, one of the largest U.S. public relations agencies, and in 1989 acquired Ogilvy & Mather Worldwide, another significant U.S. agency. In 2000, WPP Group continued its growth and acquired Young & Rubicam, and four years later, Grey Global—both major U.S. ad firms. By 2005, WPP included more than seventy thousand employees with offices in 104 countries. Two other top ad giants are New York–based megafirms—the Omnicom Group and the Interpublic Group, each with dozens of advertising and marketing firms operating around the globe and each with more than forty-three thousand employees. The fourth mega-agency, the Paris-based Publicis Groupe, in 2002 acquired the number seven ranked U.S.-based Bcom3 Group (which includes both the Leo Burnett and the D'Arcy Masius Benton & Bowles agencies). Publicis, which also owns the top British agency, Saatchi & Saatchi, employed more than thirty-six thousand people worldwide in 2005 (see Figure 11.1 on page 398).

❝ Besides dominating commercial speech, a $500-billion-a-year industry, these four companies . . . — . . . Omnicom . . . Interpublic . . . WPP . . . and . . . Publicis—also hold incredible sway over the media. By deciding when and where to spend their clients' ad budgets, they can indirectly set network television schedules and starve magazines to death or help them flourish.**❞**

–Stuart Elliott, *New York Times*, March 2002

Figure 11.1
The World's Four Largest Advertising Agencies, 2006 (Income in Billions)

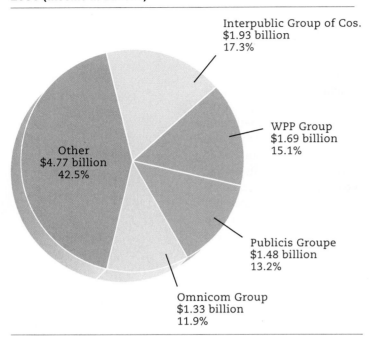

Interpublic Group of Cos.
$1.93 billion
17.3%

WPP Group
$1.69 billion
15.1%

Publicis Groupe
$1.48 billion
13.2%

Omnicom Group
$1.33 billion
11.9%

Other
$4.77 billion
42.5%

Source: "2006 FactPack," *Advertising Age,* February 27, 2006, p. 45.

*Note: Based on $11.20 billion U.S. revenue from agency advertising and media activities. Non-advertising revenue is excluded.

The mega-agency trend has stirred debate among consumer and media watchdog groups. Some consider large agencies a threat to the independence of smaller firms, which are slowly being bought out. An additional concern is that four firms now control more than half the distribution of advertising dollars globally. As a result, the cultural values represented by U.S. and European ads may undermine or overwhelm the values and products of developing countries.

The Boutique Agency

The visual revolutions in advertising during the 1960s elevated the standing of designers and graphic artists, who became closely identified with the look of particular ads. Breaking away from bigger agencies, many of these creative individuals formed small **boutique agencies** to devote their talents to a handful of select clients. Offering more personal services, the boutiques prospered, bolstered by innovative ad campaigns and increasing profits from TV accounts. By the 1980s, large agencies had bought up many of the boutiques. Nevertheless, they continued to operate as fairly independent subsidiaries within multinational corporate structures.

One boutique agency in Minneapolis, Peterson Milla Hooks, has made its name with a boldly graphic national branding ad campaign for Target department stores. The series of ads play on the red and white Target bull's-eye, which was recognized by 96 percent of U.S. consumers by 2004. Of course, the ads that feature the recognizable bull's-eye are always accompanied by the equally famous Target slogan, "Expect More. Pay Less."[9] Peterson Milla Hooks won Best of Show at the Obie Awards for the Target campaign in 2005. The agency employs only about thirty people and counts Mattel, Turner Classic Movies, and Radisson Hotels among its other clients.

The Structure of Ad Agencies

The nation's agencies, regardless of their size, generally divide the labor of creating and maintaining advertising campaigns among four departments: market research, creative development, media selection, and account services. A separate administrative unit, besides handling employee salaries, pays each media outlet that runs ads and collects an agency's fees. As previously mentioned, agencies typically take a 10 to 15 percent commission on total ad costs and then pay the media outlet. Expenses incurred for producing the ads are part of a separate negotiation between the agency and the advertiser. As a result of this commission arrangement, it generally costs most large-volume advertisers no more to use an agency than it does to use their own staff.

Market Research and VALS

Before an agency can pay bills or collect commissions, a great deal of planning and research takes place. Because computer technology now enables companies to gather intimate data about consumers, the **market research** department plays a significant role in any agency. This department assesses the behaviors and attitudes of consumers toward particular products long before any ads are created. It may study everything from possible names for a new product to the size of the copy for a print ad. Research is conducted not only on toothpastes and cereals but also on books, television comedies, and Hollywood action films. In trying to predict customers' buying habits, researchers also test new ideas and products on groups of consumers to get feedback before developing final ad strategies. In addition, some researchers contract with outside polling firms, which are better equipped to conduct regional and national studies of consumer preferences.

> " The best advertising artist of all time was Raphael. He had the best client — the papacy; the best art director — the College of Cardinals; and the best product — salvation. And we never disparage Raphael for working for a client or selling an idea. "
>
> – Mark Fenske, creative director, N. W. Ayer, 1996

As the economic stakes in advertising have grown, agencies have employed scientific methods to study consumer behavior. In 1932, Young & Rubicam first used statistical techniques developed by pollster George Gallup. By the 1980s, most large agencies retained psychologists and anthropologists to advise them on human nature and buying habits. The earliest type of market research, **demographics**, mainly studied and documented audience members' age, gender, occupation, ethnicity, education, and income. Early demographic analyses provided advertisers with data on people's behavior and social status but revealed less about feelings and attitudes. Today, demographic data are much more specific. They make it possible for not only advertisers but also Internet heavyweights like Amazon.com and phone giants like AT&T to locate consumers in particular geographic regions — usually by zip code. This enables advertisers and product companies to target ethnic neighborhoods or affluent suburbs for direct mail, point-of-purchase store displays, or specialized magazines and newspaper inserts.

By the 1960s and 1970s, television had greatly increased advertising revenues, allowing agencies to expand their research activities. Advertisers and agencies began using **psychographics**, a research approach that attempts to categorize consumers according to their attitudes, beliefs, interests, and motivations. Psychographic analysis often relies on **focus groups**, a small-group interview technique in which a moderator leads a discussion about a product or an issue, usually with six to twelve people. Because focus groups are small and less scientific than most demographic research, the findings from such groups may be suspect.

In 1978, the Stanford Research Institute (SRI), now called SRI Consulting Business Intelligence, instituted its **Values and Lifestyles (VALS)** strategy, which divides consumers into types (see Figure 11.2 on page 400). Using questionnaires, VALS researchers parceled the public into clusters and measured psychological factors, including how consumers think and feel about products. Many advertisers adopted VALS to help focus their sales pitch to get the most appropriate target audience for their dollars. VALS research assumed that not every product suited every consumer, encouraging advertisers to vary their sales slants to find specific market niches.

Over the years, the VALS psychological consumer segmentation system has been updated to reflect changes in consumer orientations. The most recent system classifies people by their primary consumer motivations: ideals, achievement, or self-expression. The ideals-oriented group, for instance, includes *thinkers* — "mature, satisfied, comfortable people who value order, knowledge, and responsibility." These consumers apparently like products that are functional, fairly priced, and durable. Also in this group, *believers* have "modest but sufficient" income and education; they are generally considered "conservative, conventional people with concrete beliefs based on traditional, established codes." VALS and similar research techniques

> " Alcohol marketers appear to believe that the prototypical college student is (1) male; (2) a nitwit; and (3) interested in nothing but booze and 'babes.' "
>
> – Michael F. Jacobson and Laurie Ann Mazur, *Marketing Madness*, 1995

Figure 11.2
VALS Types and Characteristics

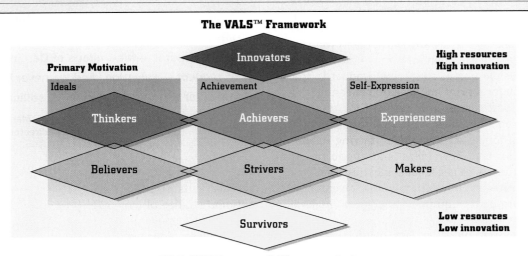

VALS™ Types and Characteristics

Innovators Innovators are successful, sophisticated, take-charge people with high self-esteem and abundant resources. They exhibit all three primary motivations in varying degrees. They are change leaders and are the most receptive to new ideas and technologies. They are very active consumers, and their purchases reflect cultivated tastes for upscale, niche products and services.

Thinkers Thinkers are motivated by ideals. They are mature, satisfied, comfortable, and reflective people who value order, knowledge, and responsibility. They tend to be well educated and actively seek out information in the decision-making process. They are well informed about world and national events and are alert to opportunities to broaden their knowledge.

Achievers Motivated by the desire for achievement, Achievers have goal-oriented lifestyles and a deep commitment to career and family. Their social lives reflect this focus and are structured around family, their place of worship, and work. Achievers live conventional lives, are politically conservative, and respect authority and the status quo. They value consensus, predictability, and stability over risk, intimacy, and self-discovery.

Experiencers Experiencers are motivated by self-expression. As young, enthusiastic, and impulsive consumers, Experiencers quickly become enthusiastic about new possibilities but are equally quick to cool. They seek variety and excitement, savoring the new, the offbeat, and the risky. Their energy finds an outlet in exercise, sports, outdoor recreation, and social activities.

Believers Like thinkers, Believers are motivated by ideals. They are conservative, conventional people with concrete beliefs based on traditional, established codes; family, religion, community, and the nation. Many Believers express moral codes that are deeply rooted and literally interpreted. They follow established routines, organized in large part around home, family, community, and social or religious organizations to which they belong.

Strivers Strivers are trendy and fun loving. Because they are motivated by achievement, Strivers are concerned about the opinions and approval of others. Money defines success for Strivers, who don't have enough of it to meet their desires. They favor stylish products that emulate the purchases of people with greater material wealth. Many see themselves as having a job rather than a career, and a lack of skills and focus often prevents them from moving ahead.

Makers Like Experiencers, Makers are motivated by self-expression. They express themselves and experience the world by working on it—building a house, raising children, fixing a car, or canning vegetables—and have enough skill and energy to carry out their projects successfully. Makers are practical people who have constructive skills and value self-sufficiency. They live within a traditional context of family, practical work, and physical recreation and have little interest in what lies outside that context.

Survivors Survivors live narrowly focused lives. With few resources with which to cope, they often believe that the world is changing too quickly. They are comfortable with the familiar and are primarily concerned with safety and security. Because they must focus on meeting needs rather than fulfilling desires, Survivors do not show a strong primary motivation.

Source: SRI Consulting Business Intelligence, 2006, http://www.sric-bi.com/VALS.

ultimately provide advertisers with microscopic details about which consumers are most likely to buy which products.

Agencies and clients—particularly auto manufacturers—have relied heavily on VALS to determine the best placement for TV and magazine ads. VALS data suggest, for example, that *achievers* and *experiencers* watch more sports and news programs; these groups prefer luxury cars or sport-utility vehicles. *Thinkers,* on the other hand, favor TV dramas and documentaries and like the functionality of minivans or the gas efficiency of hybrids. VALS researchers do not claim that most people fit neatly into a category. But many agencies believe that VALS research can give them an edge in markets where few differences in quality may actually exist among top-selling brands, whether they are headache medicines or designer jeans. Consumer groups, wary of such research, argue that too many ads promote only an image and provide little information about a product's price, its content, or the work conditions under which it was produced.

Creative Development

The creative aspects of the advertising business—teams of writers and artists— make up its nerve center. Many of these individuals regard ads as a commercial art form. For print and online ads, the creative department outlines the rough sketches for newspaper, magazine, direct-mail, and Web advertisements, developing the words and graphics. For radio, the creative side prepares a working script, generating ideas for everything from choosing the narrator's voice to determining background sound effects. For television, the creative department develops a **storyboard**, a sort of blueprint or roughly drawn comic-strip version of the potential ad.

Just as tension has always existed between network executives and the creative people who develop TV programs, advertising has its own version of this battle. Often the creative side of the business (the copywriters who create jingles and the graphic artists who design the look of an ad) finds itself in conflict with the research side (the marketers who collect the consumer data to target an ad campaign). In most cases, however, both sides share the responsibility for successful or failed ad campaigns. In the 1960s, for example, both Doyle Dane Bernbach (DDB) and Ogilvy & Mather downplayed research; they championed the art of persuasion and what "felt right." Yet DDB's simple ads for Volkswagen Beetles in the 1960s were based on weeks of intensive interviews with VW workers as well as on creative instincts. The campaign was remarkably successful in establishing the first niche for a foreign car manufacturer in the United States. Although sales of the VW "bug" had been growing before the ad campaign started, the successful ads helped Volkswagen preempt the Detroit auto industry's entry into the small-car field.

The cost of advertising, especially on network television, increases each year. The Super Bowl remains the most expensive program for purchasing television advertising, with thirty seconds of time costing about $2.5 million in 2006. Running a thirty-second ad during a national prime-time TV show can cost from $100,000 to more than $1 million, depending on the popularity and ratings of the program (see Figure 11.3 on page 402). Moreover, even with their greater emphasis on market research, both the creative and research sides of the business acknowledge that they cannot predict with any certainty which ads and which campaigns will succeed. They say ads work best by slowly creating brand-name identities—by associating certain products over time with quality and reliability in the minds of consumers. Some economists, however, believe that much of the money spent on advertising is ultimately wasted because it simply encourages consumers to change from one brand name to another. Such switching may lead to increased profits for a particular manufacturer, but it has little positive impact on the overall economy.

Figure 11.3
Prime Time Network TV Pricing

The average costs for a thirty-second commercial during popular prime-time programs on network television for a Tuesday and Sunday night.

TUESDAY	8 p.m. (ET)		9 p.m.		10 p.m.	
ABC	According to Jim $192,900	Rodney $132,600	Commander in Chief $182,580		Boston Legal $191,100	
CBS	NCIS $133,300		The Amazing Race $210,900		Close to Home $144,800	
NBC	The Biggest Loser $130,748		My Name Is Earl $189,536	The Office $217,000	Law & Order: SVU $191,776	
FOX	Bones/American Idol $101,328/$496,866		House/Bones $204,533/$210,000		No Fox programming	

SUNDAY	7 p.m. (ET)		8 p.m.		9 p.m.		10 p.m.	
ABC	America's Funniest Home Videos $86,302		Extreme Makeover: Home Edition $342,000		Desperate Housewives $439,499		Grey's Anatomy $352,569	
CBS	60 Minutes $109,980		Cold Case $130,978		CBS Sunday Movie $94,200			
NBC	Dateline $64,490		West Wing $120,000		Law & Order: Criminal Intent $141,870		Crossing Jordan $154,563	
FOX	Animation $79,300	King of the Hill $143,700	The Simpsons $340,700	War at Home $148,461	Family Guy $166,378	American Dad $218,000	No Fox programming	

Source: "2006 FactPack," Advertising Age, February 27, 2006, pp. 28–29.

Media Selection and Buying Ads

Another integral department in an ad agency, media selection, is staffed by **media buyers**: people who choose and purchase the types of media that are best suited to carry a client's ads and reach the targeted audience. For instance, a company like Procter & Gamble, one of the world's leading advertisers, displays its more than three hundred major brands—most of them household products like Crest toothpaste and Huggies diapers—on TV shows viewed primarily by women. To reach male viewers, however, media buyers encourage beer advertisers to spend their ad budgets on cable and network sports programming, evening talk radio, or sports magazines. Buyers pay particular attention to the relative strengths and weaknesses of print and electronic forms of advertising. For example, ad campaigns aimed at supermarket shoppers effectively use newspapers, direct mail, and magazine inserts, all of which encourage the tradition of coupon clipping; local news programs, which do not have many teenage viewers, might not be a good buy for a client selling pop music or snack food.

Along with the typical 10 to 15 percent commission, advertisers often add incentive clauses to their contracts with agencies, raising the fee if sales goals are met and lowering it if goals are missed. With incentive clauses, it is in the agencies' best interests to conduct repetitive **saturation advertising**, in which a variety of media are inundated with ads aimed at target audiences. The initial Miller Lite beer campaign ("Tastes great, less filling"), which used humor and retired athletes to reach its male audience, became one of the most successful saturation campaigns in media history. It ran from 1973 to 1991 and included television and radio spots, magazine and newspaper ads, and billboards and point-of-purchase store displays. The exces-

> **"Ads seem to work on the very advanced principle that a very small pellet or pattern in a noisy, redundant barrage of repetition will gradually assert itself."**
>
> –Marshall McLuhan, *Understanding Media,* 1964

Lemon.

Less flower. More power.

● The New York ad agency Doyle Dane Bernbach created a famous series of print and television ads for Volkswagen beginning in 1959, and helped to usher in an era of creative advertising that combined a single-point sales emphasis with bold design, humor, and honesty. Arnold Worldwide, a Boston agency, continued the highly creative approach with its clever, award-winning "Drivers Wanted" campaign for the New Beetle.

Drivers wanted.

sive repetition of the campaign helped light beer overcome a potential image problem, that of being viewed as watered-down beer unworthy of "real" men.

Account and Client Management

Ad agencies also include a department of client liaisons, or **account executives**: individuals responsible for bringing in new business and managing the accounts of established clients. This department oversees new ad campaigns in which several agencies bid for the business of a client. Account managers coordinate the presentation of a proposed campaign and various aspects of the bidding process, such as what a series of ads will cost a client. Account executives function as liaisons between the advertiser and the agency's creative team. Because most major companies maintain their own ad departments to handle everyday details, account executives also coordinate activities between their agency and a client's in-house personnel.

The advertising business is volatile, and account departments are especially vulnerable to upheavals. For instance, the esteemed ad firm Leo Burnett (creator of the Pillsbury Doughboy, the Marlboro Man, the Keebler Elves, and Kellogg's Tony the Tiger) had a particularly tough time between 2003 and 2004 when it lost its Philips Electronics account (worth $250 million), its Toys "R" Us account (worth $120 million), and its Delta Airlines and Polaroid accounts (worth $45 million combined). Clients routinely conduct **account reviews**, the process of evaluating and reinvigorating a product's image by reviewing an existing ad agency's campaign or by inviting several new agencies to submit new campaign strategies, which may result in the product company switching agencies.[10] One industry study conducted in the mid-1980s indicated that client accounts stayed with the same agency on average for about seven years, but since the late 1980s clients have changed agencies much more often. One exception is General Motors—the nation's No. 2 advertiser in 2005 ($2.9 billion)— "famous for being loyal to the agencies on its roster." Campbell-Ewald of Interpublic has held the Chevy account since 1914; Leo Burnett (Publicis)—Pontiac and Cadillac since the mid-1930s; and McCann Erickson (Interpublic)—Buick since 1958. But even GM, with sales falling, decided to review its old accounts in 2006.[11]

Persuasive Techniques in Contemporary Advertising

Ad agencies and product companies often argue that the main purpose of advertising is to inform consumers about available products in a straightforward way. In fact, many types of advertisements, like classified ads in newspapers, are devoted primarily to delivering price information. Most consumer ads, however, merely create a mood or tell stories about products without revealing much about prices. Because national advertisers generally choose to buy a one-page magazine ad or a thirty-second TV spot to deliver their pitch, consumers get little information about how a product was made or how it compares with similar brands. In managing space and time constraints, advertising agencies engage in a variety of persuasive techniques.

Conventional Persuasive Strategies

One of the most frequently used advertising approaches is the **famous-person testimonial**, whereby a product is endorsed by a well-known person, such as actor Ken Wantanabe touting the American Express credit card or actress Eva Longoria starring in Pepsi commercials. Another technique, the **plain-folks pitch**, associates a product with simplicity. Over the years, Volkswagen ("Drivers wanted"), General Electric ("We bring good things to life"), and Microsoft ("Where do you want to go today?") have each used slogans that stress how new technologies fit into the lives of ordinary people. By contrast, the **snob-appeal approach** attempts to persuade consumers that using a product will maintain or elevate their social status. Advertisers selling jewelry, perfume, clothing, and luxury automobiles often use snob appeal. For example, television ads for the upscale BMW 7 series aimed to make the car owners feel more special and "in charge" than ordinary folks: "Be the Centre. Be the Focus. Be the measure of all things. Listen to intuition. Find intelligent solutions. Live passionately. And in all things, keep the balance." In a related print ad, the tag line read, "No one ever said 'civilized' had to mean tame."

Another approach, the **bandwagon effect**, points out in exaggerated claims that *everyone* is using a particular product. Brands that refer to themselves as "America's favorite" or "the best" imply that consumers will be "left behind" if they ignore these products. A different technique, the **hidden-fear appeal**, plays on consumers' sense of insecurity. Deodorant, mouthwash, and shampoo ads frequently invoke anxiety, pointing out that only a specific product could relieve embarrassing personal hygiene problems and restore a person to social acceptability.

A final ad strategy, used more in local TV and radio campaigns than in national ones, has been labeled **irritation advertising**: creating product-name recognition by being annoying or obnoxious. Although both research and common sense suggest that irritating ads do not work very well, there have been exceptions. In the 1950s and 1960s, for instance, an aspirin company ran a TV ad illustrating a hammer pounding inside a person's brain. Critics and the product's own agency suggested that people bought the product, which sold well, to get relief from the ad as well as from their headaches. For years, Charmin tissue used the annoying Mr. Whipple, a fussy store clerk who commanded customers, "Please don't squeeze the Charmin." One study found that people hated the ad but bought the product anyway. On the regional level, irritation ads are often used by appliance discount stores or local car dealers, who dress in outrageous costumes and yell at the camera.

The Association Principle

Historically, American car advertisements have displayed automobiles in natural settings—on winding back roads that cut through rugged mountain passes or across shimmering wheat fields. These ads rarely contain images of cars on congested city streets or in other urban settings where most driving actually occurs. Instead, the car—an example of advanced technology— merges seamlessly into the natural world.

This type of advertising exemplifies the **association principle**, a persuasive technique used in most consumer ads. Employing this principle, an ad associates a product with some cultural value or image that has a positive connotation but may have little connection to the actual product. For example, many ads displayed visual symbols of American patriotism in the wake of the September 11, 2001, terrorist attacks in an attempt to associate products and companies with national pride. In trying "to convince us that there's an innate relationship between a brand name and an attitude,"[12] agencies and advertisers may associate products with nationalism, happy families, success at school or work, natural scenery, or humor.

Over the years, one of the more controversial uses of the association principle has been the linkage of products to stereotyped caricatures of women. In numerous instances, women have been portrayed either as sex objects or as clueless housewives who, during many a daytime TV commercial, needed the powerful offscreen voice of a male narrator to instruct them in their own kitchens (see "Case Study—Idiots and Objects: Stereotyping in Advertising" on page 407).

In our technology-dependent environment, shaped by corporate giants, many consumers have come to value products that claim associations with "the real" and "the natural"—possibly the most familiar adjectives associated with advertising. For example, Coke sells itself as "the real thing," and the cosmetics industry offers synthetic products that make us look "natural." The twin adjectives—*real* and *natural*— saturate American ads yet almost always describe processed or synthetic goods.

For years, Philip Morris's Marlboro brand used the association principle to link its cigarettes to nature and completely transform the product's initial image. In the 1920s, Marlboro began as a fashionable woman's cigarette. Back then, the company's ads equated smoking with emancipation and a sense of freedom, attempting to appeal to women who had just won the right to vote. Marlboro, though, did poorly as a women's product, and new campaigns in the 1950s and 1960s transformed the brand into a man's cigarette. In these campaigns, powerful images of active, rugged men

● Back in 2000, Nike agreed to extend a multi-year ad endorsement deal with Tiger Woods—a deal worth $105 million. Woods dresses up in Nike's gear even when he is selling products from other sponsors, including Tag Heuer watches, American Express, and Buick cars. In 2006, GM's Buick division resigned Woods to another five-year deal worth $40 million.

● In April 2006, a Dutch company, Hotels.nl, paid 1 euro (then about $1.23) per sheep to have each sheep wear a coat featuring the company's logo and Web address. Despite facing hefty fines and public criticism, the company said it plans on expanding its advertising on sheep and that its business has grown 15% since it started using these ads.

dominated the ads. Often, Marlboro associated its product with the image of a lone cowboy roping a calf, building a fence, or riding over a snow-covered landscape. Ironically, over the years two of the Marlboro Man models died of lung cancer associated with smoking. By 2006, the branding consultancy Interbrand called Marlboro the world's twelfth "most valuable brand name," having an estimated worth of $21 billion. (Coca-Cola and Microsoft were the top two rated brands; see Table 11.2 on page 408.)[13]

As a response to corporate mergers and public skepticism toward impersonal companies, a *disassociation corollary* has emerged as a recent trend in advertising. The nation's largest winery, Gallo, pioneered the idea in the 1980s by establishing a dummy corporation, Bartles & Jaymes, to sell jug wine and wine coolers, thereby avoiding the Gallo corporate image in ads and on its bottles. The ads featured Frank and Ed, two low-key, grandfatherly types, as "co-owners" and ad spokesmen. On the one hand, the ad was "a way to connect with younger consumers who yearn for products that are handmade, quirky, and authentic."[14] On the other hand, this technique, by concealing the Gallo tie-in, also allowed the wine giant to *disassociate* from the negative publicity of the 1970s—a period when labor leader Cesar Chavez organized migrant workers in a long boycott of Gallo after the company signed a contract with the Teamsters, which eventually won a workers' election that Chavez and his union—the United Farm Workers—opposed.

In the 1990s, the disassociation strategy was used by General Motors. Reeling from a declining corporate reputation, GM "disassociate[d] itself from its innovative offspring, the Saturn," and tried to package the Saturn as "a small-town enterprise, run by folks not terribly unlike Frank and Ed" who provide caring, personal service.[15] As an ad strategy, disassociation links new brands in a product line to eccentric or simple regional places rather than to images conjured up by multinational conglomerates.

Advertising as Myth

Another way to understand ads is to use **myth analysis**, which provides insights into how ads work at a general cultural level. According to myth analysis, most ads are narratives with stories to tell and social conflicts to resolve. The term "myth" is not used here in a pejorative sense, referring to an untrue story or outright falsehood. Rather, myths help us to define people, organizations, and social norms. Myths are the stories a society constructs in order to bring order to the conflicts and contradictions of everyday life.

Three common mythical elements are found in many types of ads:

1. Ads incorporate myths in ministry form, featuring characters, settings, and plots.
2. Most stories in ads involve conflicts, pitting one set of characters or social values against another.
3. Such conflicts are negotiated or resolved by the end of the ad, usually by applying or purchasing a product. In advertising, the product and those who use it often emerge as the heroes of the story.

Even though the stories ads tell are usually compressed into thirty seconds or onto a single page, they still include the traditional elements of narrative. For instance, many SUV ads tell us a ministry of drivers in their shiny new vehicles. The advertisements ask us to imagine ourselves out in the raw, untamed wilderness, in a quiet, natural place that only a Jeep or Hummer can take us. The images sometimes even locate the SUV in implausible locations, such as a mountain ledge with no road access. The conflict is generated by the audience's implicit understanding that the

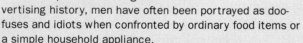

Idiots and Objects: Stereotyping in Advertising

Over the years, critics and consumers alike have complained about stereotyping in mainstream advertising. *Stereotyping* refers to the process of assigning people to abstract groups, whose members are assumed to act as a single entity — rather than as individuals with distinct identities — and to display shared characteristics, which often have negative connotations. Today, particularly in beer ads, men are often stereotyped as inept or stupid, incapable of negotiating a routine day or a normal conversation unless fortified — or dulled — by the heroic product. Throughout advertising history, men have often been portrayed as doofuses and idiots when confronted by ordinary food items or a simple household appliance.

On the other hand, in the early history of product ads on television, women were often stereotyped as naïve or emotional, needing the experienced voice of a rational male narrator to guide them around their own homes. Ads have also stereotyped women as brainless or helpless or offered them as a man's reward for drinking a particular beer, wearing cool jeans, or smoking the right cigarette. Worst of all, women, or even parts of women — with their heads cut from the frame — have been used as objects, merely associated with a particular product (e.g., a swimsuit model holding a new car muffler or wrapped around a bottle of Scotch). Influenced by the women's movement and critiques of advertising culture, such as Betty Friedan's *The Feminine Mystique* (1963), ads depicting women have changed. Although many sexist stereotypes still persist in advertising, women today are portrayed in a variety of social roles.

In addition to ads that have stereotyped men and women, there is also *invisible stereotyping.* This occurs when whole segments of the population are ignored — particularly African, Arab, Asian, Latin, and Native Americans. Advertising — especially in its early history — has often faced criticism that many segments of the varied and multicultural U.S. population have been missing or underrepresented in the ads and images that dominate the landscape. In the last several years, however, conscious of how diverse the United States has become, many companies have been doing a better job of representing various cultures in their product ads.

Ready-to-wear, Shoes, Leather Goods, Watches, Jewellery. Sold exclusively in Louis Vuitton stores. Tel. 020 7399 4050 www.vuitton.com

LOUIS VUITTON

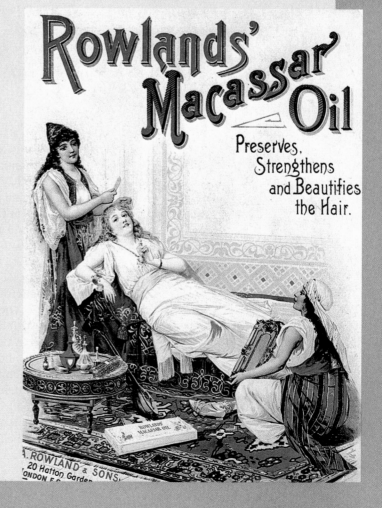

Rowlands' Macassar Oil

Preserves, Strengthens and Beautifies the Hair.

A. ROWLAND & SONS, 20 Hatton Garden, LONDON E.C.

● **Table 11.2 The Top 10 Global Brands**

Rank	Brand	2006 Brand Value (in $billions)	Country of Ownership	Description
1	COCA-COLA	67.00	U.S.	Flagging appetite for soda has cut demand for Coke, but the beverage giant has a raft of new products in the pipeline that could reverse its recent slide.
2	MICROSOFT	56.92	U.S.	Threats from Google and Apple haven't yet offset the power of its Windows and Office monopolies.
3	IBM	56.20	U.S.	Having off-loaded its low-profit PC business to Lenovo, IBM is marketing on the strategic level to corporate leaders.
4	GE	48.90	U.S.	The brand Edison built has extended its reach from ovens to credit cards, and the "Ecomagination" push is making GE look like a protector of the planet.
5	INTEL	32.31	U.S.	Profits and market share weren't the only things slammed by rival AMD. Intel's brand value tumbled 9%, as it lost business from high-profile customers.
6	NOKIA	30.13	Finland	Fashionable designs and low-cost models for the developing world enabled the mobile phone maker to regain ground against competitors.
7	TOYOTA	27.94	Japan	Toyota is closing in on GM to become the world's biggest automaker. A slated 10% increase in U.S. sales this year will help even more.
8	DISNEY	27.84	U.S.	New CEO Robert Iger expanded the brand by buying animation hit-maker Pixar and beefing up digital distribution of TV shows through the Internet and iPods.
9	McDONALD'S	27.50	U.S.	A new healthy-living marketing campaign—and the premium-priced sand-wiches and salads that came with it—have led to a fourth year of sales gains.
10	MERCEDES-BENZ	21.79	Germany	The new S-Class sedan and M-Class SUV are helping repair a tarnished quality reputation. High costs and weak margins will take longer to fix.

Source: "The 100 Top Brands," http://www.interbrand.com/best_brands_2006.asp.

Note: For an alternative list, see Millward Brown Optimor, a division of WPP, which includes Wal-Mart, China Mobile, and Google. Interbrand is a division of Omnicom.

SUVs take us out of a fast-paced, freeway-wrapped urban world with long commutes, traffic jams, and automobile exhaust. This implied conflict between the natural world and the manufactured world is apparently resolved by invoking the image of an SUV. Although SUVs typically pack our urban and suburban highways, inefficiently burn up gasoline on trips to strip malls, and create tons of air pollution particulates, the ads ignore those facts. Instead, they offer an alternative story about the wonders of nature, and the SUV literally becomes the vehicle that negotiates the conflict between city/suburban blight and the unspoiled wilderness.

Most advertisers do not expect consumers to accept without question the stories they tell or the associations they make in their ads; they do not "make the mistake of asking for belief."[16] Instead, ads are most effective when they create attitudes and reinforce values. Then they operate like popular fiction, encouraging us to suspend our disbelief. Although most of us realize that ads create a fictional world, we often get caught up in their stories and myths. Indeed, ads often work because the stories offer comfort about our deepest desires and conflicts—between men and women, nature and technology, tradition and change, the real and the artificial. Most contemporary consumer advertising does not provide much useful information about products. Instead, it tries to reassure us that through the use of familiar brand names, everyday tensions and problems can be managed (see "Media Literacy and the Critical Process: The Branded You" on page 411).

Commercial Speech and Regulating Advertising

In 1791, Congress passed and the states ratified the First Amendment to the U.S. Constitution, promising, among other guarantees, to "make no law . . . abridging the freedom of speech, or of the press." Over time, we have developed a shorthand label for the First Amendment, misnaming it the free-speech clause. The amendment ensures that citizens and reporters can generally say and write what they want, but it says nothing directly about speech that is not free. What, then, about **commercial speech**—any print or broadcast expression for which a fee is charged to organizations and individuals buying time or space in the mass media? Whereas freedom of speech refers to the right to express thoughts, beliefs, and opinions in the abstract marketplace of ideas, commercial speech supports the right to circulate goods, services, and images in the concrete marketplace of products. Although most people can buy some commercial speech inexpensively, such as a classified newspaper ad, only very wealthy citizens (like Ross Perot or Steve Forbes), established political parties, and multinational companies can routinely afford speech that reaches millions.

New forms of commercial speech and advertising continue to crowd the media landscape. Cable television offers several home-shopping networks, with nonstop banter about must-have goods. Late-night television is also filled with long-form spots advertising sex talk and fortune-telling to the lonely, the young, and the curious via pay telephone numbers that charge outrageous per-minute rates.

Infomercials represent another substantial growth area in cable and broadcast television. These thirty-minute, late-night and daytime programs usually feature fading TV and music celebrities who advertise a product or service in a format that looks like a laid-back talk show. Even on regular talk shows, guests generally appear when they have a book to sell or a movie to promote. Paid a fee by the program to boost ratings, such guests use their celebrity status and allotted time as a commercial forum to promote themselves as a cultural product they are selling.

Although the mass media have often not hesitated to carry product- and service-selling advertisements in publications and have embraced the concept of program-length infomercials and even twenty-four-hour cable shopping channels, they have also refused certain issue-based advertising that might upset their traditional advertisers. For example, although corporations have easy access in placing paid ads, many labor unions have had their print and broadcast ads rejected as "controversial." The nonprofit Adbusters Media Foundation, based in Vancouver, Canada, has also had difficulty getting networks to air its "uncommercials." One of its spots promotes the Friday after Thanksgiving (traditionally, the beginning of the holiday buying season) as "Buy Nothing Day."

> **"** There's no law that says we have to sell you time or space. We sell time for many many different things, but not controversial issues of social importance. **"**
>
> —Julie Hoover, vice president of advertising, ABC, 2004

Critical Issues in Advertising

In his 1957 book *The Hidden Persuaders,* Vance Packard expressed concern that advertising was manipulating helpless consumers, attacking our dignity, and invading "the privacy of our minds."[17] According to this view, the advertising industry was considered to be all-powerful. Although consumers have historically been regarded as dupes by many critics, research reveals that the consumer mind is not as easy to predict as some advertisers once thought. In the 1950s, for example, Ford could not successfully sell its midsize car, the Edsel, which was aimed at newly prosperous Ford customers looking to move up to the latest in push-button window wipers and antennas. After a splashy and expensive ad campaign, Ford sold only 63,000 Edsels in 1958 and just 2,000 in 1960, when the model was discontinued. Similarly, in the 1960s, the Scott paper company predicted that its disposable clothing line would challenge traditional apparel, but despite heavy advertising, throwaway apparel never caught on.

One of the most disastrous campaigns ever featured the now famous "This is not your father's Oldsmobile" spots that began running in 1989 and starred celebrities like former Beatles drummer Ringo Starr and his daughter. Oldsmobile (which became part of General Motors in 1903) and its agency, Leo Burnett, decided to market to a younger generation after sales declined from a high of 1.1 million vehicles in 1985 to only 715,000 in 1988. But the campaign backfired, apparently alienating its older loyal customers (who may have felt abandoned by Olds and its catchy new slogan) and failing to lure younger buyers (who probably still had trouble getting past the name "Olds"). In 2000, Oldsmobile sold only 260,000 cars, and GM phased out its Olds division by 2005.[18]

As these examples illustrate, most people are not easily persuaded by advertising. Over the years, studies have suggested that between 75 and 90 percent of new consumer products typically fail because they are not embraced by the buying public.[19] But despite public resistance to many new products and the cynical eye we cast on advertising, the ad industry has made contributions, including raising the American standard of living and financing most media industries. Yet serious concerns over the impact of advertising remain. Watchdog groups worry about the expansion of advertising's reach, and critics continue to condemn ads that stereotype or associate products with sex appeal, youth, and narrow definitions of beauty. Some of the most serious concerns involve children, teens, and health.

Children and Advertising

Children and teenagers, living in a culture dominated by TV ads, are often viewed as "consumer trainees." For years, groups such as Action for Children's Television (ACT) worked to limit advertising aimed at children. In the 1980s, ACT fought particularly hard to curb program-length commercials: thirty-minute cartoon programs (such as *G.I. Joe, My Little Pony and Friends, The Care Bear Family,* and *He-Man and the Masters of the Universe*) developed for television syndication primarily to promote a line of toys. This commercial tradition continued with programs such as *Pokémon* and *The Powerpuff Girls.*

In addition, parent groups have worried about the heavy promotion of products like sugar-coated cereals during children's programs. Pointing to European countries, where children's advertising is banned, these groups have pushed to limit advertising directed at children. Congress, faced with the protection that the First Amendment offers commercial speech, has responded weakly. The Children's Television Act of 1990 mandated that networks provide some educational and informational children's programming, but the act has been difficult to enforce and did little to restrict advertising aimed at kids. Because children and teenagers influence up to $500 billion a year in family spending—on everything from snacks to cars—they are increasingly targeted by advertisers.[20] A Stanford University study, however, found that a single thirty-second TV ad can influence the brand choices of children as young as age two. In addition, very young children cannot distinguish between a commercial and the TV program that the ad interrupts. Still, methods for marketing to children have become increasingly seductive. For example, producers of the 2006 blockbuster movie *Superman Returns* licensed the popular superhero's "S" shield for use on pajamas, cashmere sweaters, and costumes, and released a Man of Steel toy line through Mattel.[21]

Media Literacy
and the Critical Process

The Branded You

To what extent are you influenced by brands?

Description. Take a look around your home or dormitory room, and list all the branded products you've purchased, including food, electronics, clothes, shoes, toiletries, cleaning products, and so on.

Analysis. Now organize your branded items into categories. For example, how many of your clothes are branded with athletic or university logos? What patterns emerge and what kind of psychographic profile do these brands suggest about you?

Interpretation. Why did you buy each particular product? Was it because you thought it was of superior quality? Was it because it was cheaper? Was it because your parents used this product, so it was tried, trusted, and familiar? Was it because it made you feel a certain way about yourself and you wanted to project this image toward others? Have you ever purchased items without brands or removed logos once you bought the product? Why?

Evaluation. If you're more conscious of our branded environment (and your participation in it), what is your assessment of U.S. consumer culture? Is there too much conspicuous branding? What is good and bad about the ubiquity of brand names in our culture? How does branding relate to the common American ethic of individualism?

Engagement. Visit Adbusters.org and read about action projects that confront commercialism, including Buy Nothing Day, Media Carta, TV Turnoff, the Culturejammers Network, the Blackspot non-brand sneaker, and Unbrand America. Also visit the home page for advocacy organization Commercial Alert (http://www.commercialalert.org) to learn about the most recent commercial incursions into everyday life and what can be done about them. Or write a letter to a company about a product or ad that you think is a problem. How did the company respond?

Advertising in Schools

Among the most controversial developments in recent years was the introduction of Channel One into thousands of schools during the 1989–90 school year. The brainchild of Whittle Communications, Channel One offered "free" video and satellite equipment (tuned exclusively to Channel One) in exchange for a twelve-minute package of current events programming that included two minutes of commercials. If school districts decided to curtail or limit the program, Whittle could reclaim its "free" equipment. In 1994, Channel One was acquired by K-III Communications, which is now known as PRIMEDIA (also publisher of *Weekly Reader, Motor Trend,* and *Soap Opera Digest*). By 2005, Channel One reached a captive audience of eight million junior high and high school students in 12,000 U.S. schools each day.

Over the years, the National Dairy Council and other organizations have also used schools to promote products, providing free filmstrips, posters, magazines, folders, and study guides adorned with corporate logos. Teachers, especially in underfunded districts, have usually been grateful for the support. Channel One, however, has been viewed as a more intrusive threat, violating the implicit cultural border between an entertainment situation (watching commercial television) and a learning situation (going to school). One study showed that schools with a high concentration of low-income students were more than twice as likely as affluent schools to receive Channel One.[22] Some individual school districts have banned Channel One, as have the states of New York and California. These school systems have argued that Channel One provides students with only slight additional knowledge about current affairs; but students find the products advertised—sneakers, cereal, and soda, among others—more worthy of purchase because they are advertised in educational environments.[23] A 2006 study found that students remember "more of the advertising than they do the news stories shown on Channel One."[24]

Health and Advertising

Eating Disorders. Advertising has a powerful impact on the standards of youthful beauty in our culture. A long-standing trend in advertising is the association of certain products with ultra-thin female models, promoting a style of "attractiveness" that girls and women are invited to emulate. Even with the popularity today of resistance training and more shapely bodies, most fashion models remain much thinner than the norm. Some forms of fashion and cosmetics advertising actually pander to individuals' insecurities and low self-esteem. Such advertising suggests standards of style and behavior that may be not only unattainable but also harmful, leading to eating disorders such as anorexia and bulimia. Throughout history, however, many companies have capitalized on consumers' unhappiness and insecurity by promising the kind of body that is currently fashionable.

If advertising has been criticized for promoting skeleton-like beauty, it has also been blamed for the tripling of obesity rates in the United States since the 1980s, with a record 64 percent of Americans overweight or obese. Corn-syrup-laden soft drinks, fast food, junk food, and processed food are the staples of media advertising and are major contributors to the nationwide weight problem. More troubling is that an overweight and obese nation is good for business (creating a multibillion-dollar market for diet products, exercise equipment, self-help books, and larger clothing sizes), so media outlets see little reason to change current ad practices. The food and restaurant industry has denied any connection between its advertising and the rise of U.S. obesity rates; they have blamed individuals who make bad choices.

Tobacco. Along with criticism of promoting eating disorders, probably the most sustained criticism of advertising is its promotion of alcohol and tobacco consumption. Opponents of such advertising have become more vocal in the face of grim statistics. Each year, on average 400,000 Americans die from diseases related to nicotine addiction and poisoning; 100,000 die from alcohol-related diseases; and another 15,000 to 18,000 die in car crashes involving drunk drivers.

Tobacco ads disappeared from television in 1971, under pressure from Congress and the FCC, and the hard liquor industry voluntarily banned TV and radio ads for many decades. Still, staggering amounts of money are spent each year to promote tobacco. According to the Federal Trade Commission (FTC), by 1998, the year that the tobacco industry agreed to an enormous settlement with state attorneys general in the United States, tobacco companies spent a record $6.73 billion on advertising— even though no money went to television.

Over the years, numerous ad campaigns have appealed to teenage consumers of cigarettes. In 1988, for example, R. J. Reynolds, a subdivision of RJR Nabisco, revived its Joe Camel cartoon character from an earlier campaign, outfitting him with hipper clothes and sunglasses. Spending $75 million annually, the company put the new Joe on billboards and store posters and in sports stadiums and magazines. One study revealed that before 1988 fewer than 1 percent of teens under age eighteen smoked Camels. After the ad blitz, however, 33 percent of this age group preferred Camels.

In addition to young smokers, the tobacco industry has targeted other groups. In the 1960s, for instance, the advertising campaigns for Eve and Virginia Slims cigarettes (reminiscent of ads during the suffrage movement in the early 1900s) associated their products with women's liberation, equality, and slim fashion models. And

> **"** We have to sell cigarettes to your kids. We need half a million new smokers a year just to stay in business. So we advertise near schools, at candy counters. **"**
>
> –California anti-cigarette TV ad. Tobacco companies filed a federal suit against the ad and lost when the U.S. Supreme Court turned down their appeal in 2006.

in 1989, Reynolds introduced a cigarette called Uptown, targeting African American consumers. The ad campaign fizzled due to public protests by black leaders and government officials. When these leaders pointed to the high concentration of cigarette billboards in poor urban areas and the high mortality rates among black male smokers, the tobacco company withdrew the brand.

The government's position regarding the tobacco industry began to change in the mid-1990s, when new reports revealed that tobacco companies had known that nicotine was addictive as early as the 1950s and had withheld that information from the public. In 1998, after four states won settlements against the tobacco industry and the remaining states threatened to bring more expensive lawsuits against the companies, the tobacco industry agreed to an unprecedented $200 billion settlement that carried significant limits on advertising and marketing tobacco products. The agreement's provisions included banning cartoon characters in advertising, thus ending the use of the Joe Camel character; prohibiting the industry from targeting young people in ads and marketing, including free samples, tobacco-brand clothing, and other merchandise; and ending outdoor billboard and transit advertising. The agreement also banned tobacco-company sponsorship of concerts and athletic events, and it strictly limited other corporate sponsorships by tobacco companies. These agreements, however, do not apply to tobacco advertising abroad (see "The Global Village: Smoking Up the Global Market" on page 414). In 2005, tobacco companies spent $15.4 billion on U.S. advertisements—more than twenty times the amount spent on anti-tobacco ads.

Alcohol. Many of the same complaints regarding tobacco advertising are also being directed at alcohol ads. For

● These billboards along Sunset Boulevard in Los Angeles are symbolic of the pervasiveness of advertising. From towering billboards to people's T-shirts, sales pitches and product messages constantly bombard us. Leo Burnett's successful Marlboro Man images, which associate the cigarette with stoic masculinity and rugged individualism, are considered part of the most successful ad campaign in history. Since this photograph was taken, billboard advertising for cigarettes has become illegal.

● A 1998 settlement between the tobacco industry and the government now bans cigarette ads from billboards. (Cigarette ads on TV have been banned since the early 1970s.) The 1998 agreement also prohibits tobacco companies from using cartoon characters to appeal to young smokers. The tobacco industry also agreed in 1998 to pay state governments $246 billion to help with health costs long associated with smoking and lung cancer (although many states simply used this money to pay for several budget shortfalls during the economic recession in the early 2000s).

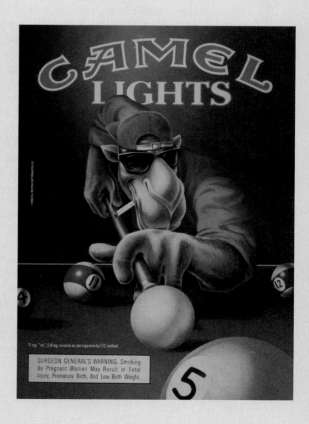

Smoking Up the Global Market

By 2000, the status of tobacco companies and their advertising in the United States had hit a low point. A $200 billion settlement between tobacco companies and state attorneys general ended tobacco advertising on billboards and severely limited the ways in which cigarette companies can promote their products in the United States. Advertising bans and antismoking public service announcements contributed to a growing disfavor about tobacco in America, with smoking rates dropping from a high of 42.5 percent of the population in 1965 to just 25 percent more than thirty years later.

As Western cultural attitudes have turned against tobacco, the large tobacco multinationals have shifted their global marketing focus, targeting Asia in particular. So while smoking has declined by 13 percent in developed countries over the last decade, it has increased by 20 percent in China, which now boasts an estimated 350 million smokers.[1] Underfunded government health programs and populations that generally admire American and European cultural products make Asian nations ill-equipped to deal with cigarette marketing efforts. For example, even though Vietnam strengthened its ban on print, broadcast, and billboard ads in 1994, nearly three-fourths of Vietnamese men smoke, the highest smoking rate for men in the world. In China, 63 percent of males over age eighteen now smoke; and across Asia in general, forty thousand to fifty thousand teens a day light up for the first time.

Advertising bans have actually forced tobacco companies to find alternative and, as it turns out, better ways to promote smoking. Philip Morris, the largest private tobacco company, and its global rival, British American Tobacco (BAT), practice "brand stretching," linking their logos to race-car events, soccer leagues, youth festivals, disco parties, rock concerts, TV shows, and popular cafés. The higher price for Western cigarettes in Asia has the effect of increasing their prestige, and it makes packs of Marlboros symbols of middle-class aspirations.

The unmistakable silhouette of the Marlboro Man is ubiquitous throughout developing countries, particularly in Asia. In Hanoi, Vietnam, almost every corner boasts a street vendor with a trolley cart, the bottom half of which carries the Marlboro logo or one of the other premium foreign brands. Vietnam's Ho Chi Minh City has two thousand such trolleys. Children in Malaysia are especially keen on Marlboro clothing, which, along with watches, binoculars, radios, knives, and backpacks, they can win by collecting a

certain number of empty Marlboro packages. (It is now illegal to sell tobacco-brand clothing and merchandise in the United States.)

Sporting-events have proved to be an especially successful brand-stretching technique with men, who smoke the majority of cigarettes in Asia. Many observers argue that much of the popularity of Marlboro cigarettes in China derives from Philip Morris's sponsorship of the Marlboro soccer league there. Throughout Asia, attractive young women wearing tight red Marlboro outfits cruise cities in

red Marlboro minivans, frequently stopping to distribute free cigarettes, even to minors.

Some critics suggest that the same marketing strategies will make their way into America and other Western countries, but that's unlikely. Tobacco companies are mainly interested in developing regions like Asia for two reasons. First, China alone accounts for nearly a third of the world's cigarette smoking, with people there consuming 1.9 trillion cigarettes in 2005. Because only one in twenty cigarettes now sold in China is a foreign brand, the potential market is staggering. Second, the majority of smokers in countries like China—whose government officially bans tobacco advertising—are unaware that smoking causes diseases like lung cancer. In fact, 3.5 million people—nearly 10,000 per day—now die from tobacco-related diseases.

example, one of the most popular beer ad campaigns of the late 1990s, featuring the trio of Budweiser frogs (which croak Bud-weis-errrr) and two envious lizards, has been accused of using cartoonish animal characters to appeal to young viewers. In fact, the Budweiser ads would be banned under the standards of the tobacco settlement, which prohibits the attribution of human characteristics to animals, plants, or other objects.

Alcohol ads have also targeted minority populations. Malt liquors, which contain higher concentrations of alcohol than beers do, have been touted in high-profile television ads for such labels as Colt 45, PowerMaster, and Magnum. There is also a trend toward marketing high-end liquors to African American and Hispanic male populations. In two separate 2006 marketing campaigns, Hennessey targeted African American populations in ads featuring musical icons Marvin Gaye and Miles Davis and the tagline "Never Blend In." Similarly, another ad campaign features actor-comedian John Leguizamo with the tagline "Pure Character," with the ads printed in English and Spanish.

College students, too, have been heavily targeted by alcohol ads, particularly by the beer industry. Although colleges and universities have outlawed "beer bashes" hosted and supplied directly by major brewers, both Coors and Miller, a unit of Philip Morris, still employ student representatives to help "create brand awareness." These students notify brewers of special events that might be sponsored by and linked to a specific beer label. The images and slogans in alcohol ads often associate the products with power, romance, sexual prowess, or athletic skill. In reality, though, alcohol is a chemical depressant; although it furnishes a temporary "high," it also diminishes athletic ability and sexual performance, triggers addiction in roughly 10 percent of the U.S. population, and factors in many spousal abuse cases. A national study released in 2006 demonstrated "that young people who see more ads for alcoholic beverages tend to drink more."[25]

Prescription Drugs. Another area of concern in health and advertising is the recent surge in prescription drug advertising. According to a study by the Kaiser Family Foundation, spending on direct-to-consumer advertising for prescription drugs increased ninefold, from $266 million in 1994 to $4 billion in 2004, largely due to growth in television advertising, which accounts for about two-thirds of such ads. The advertisements have made household words out of prescription drugs such as Nexium, Claritin, Paxil, Viagra, Celebrex, and Flonase. The ads have been effective for the pharmaceutical companies: A survey found that nearly one in three adults has talked to a doctor and one in eight has received a prescription in response to seeing an ad for a prescription drug.

● TBWA (now a unit of Omnicom) introduced Absolut Vodka's distinctive advertising campaign with a *New York Times* ad in 1980. The campaign marketed a little-known Swedish vodka as an exclusive lifestyle brand, an untraditional approach that parlayed it into one of the world's best-selling alcoholic spirits. The long-running ad campaign continues, with more than 1,450 ads to date, and maintains the brand's premium status by referencing fashion, artists, and contemporary music in the campaign.

ABSOLUT OBSESSION.

With the tremendous growth of prescription drug ads in television, newspapers, and magazines — affecting billions of dollars in prescription drug sales — there is the potential for false and misleading claims. But as spending on direct-to-consumer prescription drug advertisements has risen, federal enforcement is on the decline. A House Government Reform Committee report in 2004 found that responses by the Food and Drug Administration (FDA) to false and misleading advertisements were not timely, and that pharmaceutical companies who were repeat violators did not face tougher enforcement actions.

Watching over Advertising

Since 1998, Gary Ruskin and his small staff at Commercial Alert have been working to "keep commercial culture within its proper sphere." For example, in 2004 Sony announced it had made a $3.6 million deal with Major League Baseball to promote the company's upcoming movie *Spider-Man 2* by placing spiderweb patterns on first, second, and third bases, pitching-mound rubbers, and on-deck circles, along with stadium signage and movie trailers on scoreboards, in fifteen baseball stadiums for a weekend series in mid-June. In response to this plan, Commercial Alert notified the news media, sent letters of protest to baseball commissioner Bud Selig, and advised people to boycott Sony products. "How low will baseball sink?" Ruskin wrote in a news release sent around the country. "Next year, will they replace the bats with long Coke bottles, and the bases with big hamburger buns? . . . It's time for baseball fans to stand up to the greedy corporations that are insulting us and our national pastime." Major League Baseball ended up canceling the promotion after widespread fan outrage.

Commercial Alert, which was founded in part with longtime consumer advocate Ralph Nader, is a Portland, Oregon–based nonprofit organization and a lonely voice in checking the commercialization of U.S. culture. One of the watchdog group's main goals is to prevent commercial culture from exploiting children. Some of its activities have included challenges to specific marketing tactics, such as when the clothing retailer Limited Too enlisted with the Girl Scouts' "Fashion Adventure" project, which encouraged girls to shop, try on clothes, and model them in front of others. In constantly questioning the role of advertising in democracy, the organization has aimed to strengthen noncommercial culture and limit the amount of corporate influence on publicly elected government bodies.

Commercial Alert — along with other nonprofit watchdog and advocacy organizations like the Better Business Bureau and the National Consumers League — in many ways compensates for some of the shortcomings of the Federal Trade Commission (FTC) and other government agencies in monitoring false and deceptive ads and the excesses of commercialism.

Comparative Advertising

For years it was considered taboo for one advertiser to mention a competitor by name in its ads. Industry guidelines discouraged such advertising, and TV networks prohibited it. The government and networks feared that comparative ads would degenerate into unseemly name-calling, and advertisers believed they should not give

● From 1983 to 2000, former fashion photographer Oliviero Toscani developed one of the most talked-about ad campaigns of the late twentieth century. As creative director for clothing manufacturer Benetton, Toscani used "United Colors of Benetton" poster-style images featuring few words and no Benetton clothing. Instead, the ads carried frank, often controversial sociopolitical images such as a white infant nursing at a black woman's breast, a nun kissing a priest, Jewish and Arab boys embracing, dying AIDS patients, and U.S. death row prisoners.

UNITED COLORS OF BENETTON.

Less cars, more world. **Drivers wanted.®**

free time or space to competitors. This led to the development of so-called Brand X products, which identified a competing brand without using a real name. The FTC, however, began encouraging comparative advertising in 1971. The agency thought such ads would help consumers by providing more product information. Subsequently, various food industries started taste-test wars specifically targeting each other in their ads. Burger King took on McDonald's, and Pepsi challenged Coke. As comparative ads became the norm, Japanese and American auto manufacturers began to compare prices, gas mileage, safety records, and repair and recall rates in their ads.

In 2004, Budweiser and Miller beers battled each other in high-profile comparative advertising campaigns. Miller started the confrontation with an ad campaign that claimed they were running for "president of beers," a jab at Budweiser's slogan as the "King of Beers." The ads called Anheuser-Busch (Budweiser's brewer) un-American for refusing to debate them. Anheuser-Busch, the leading brewing company in the United States, used full-page national newspaper advertisements to tag Miller as "owned by South African Breweries," a reference to Miller's corporate owner since 2002, SABMiller of London, formerly South African Breweries. Miller responded with full-page ads that it was "American Born" and "American Brewed." The comparisons continued over carbohydrates, as Anheuser-Busch called Miller Lite the "Queen of Carbs" in another ad.

SABMiller ultimately responded by filing a lawsuit, which claimed "Evidently sensing a loss in marketshare, Anheuser-Busch has reacted in a mean-spirited, disparaging and ultimately illegal manner." However, a U.S. district court judge ruled that Anheuser-Busch was free to say in its advertising that "Miller was purchased by South African Breweries" and that "Miller is South African Owned," but could not say "Miller is owned by South African Breweries," because that was not the legal name of Miller's corporate owner.[26]

In 2005 the trade magazine *Advertising Age* issued this parable about comparative ads:

A Gillette razor ad suggesting its four blades are better than Schick's was taken off air by a Connecticut judge who felt its comparative claims went too far. Such outcomes are common in comparative advertising and have been considered one of the risks of taking direct shots at rivals. But this time, Gillette found itself, within days of the ruling, the recipient of class actions for deceptive advertising and shareholder value dilution in at least six states. Marketers should take note because class actions cut deep.[27]

Puffery and Deceptive Ads

Since the days when Lydia Pinkham's Vegetable Compound promised "a sure cure for all female weakness," false and misleading claims have haunted advertising. Over the years, the FTC has played an investigative role in substantiating the claims of various advertisers. A certain amount of *puffery*—ads featuring hyperbole and exaggeration—has usually been permitted, particularly when a product says it is "new and improved." However, when a product claims to be "the best," "the greatest," or "preferred by four out of five doctors," the FTC has often asked for supportive evidence.

Typical of deceptive advertising over the years were the Campbell Soup ads that used marbles in the bottom of a soup bowl to push more bulky ingredients—and less water—to the surface. In another instance, a 1990 Volvo commercial featured a monster truck driving over a line of cars and crushing all but the Volvo; the company later admitted that the Volvo had been specially reinforced and the other cars' support columns had been weakened. A more subtle form of deception featured the Klondike Lite ice-cream bar—"the 93 percent fat-free dessert with chocolate-flavored coating." The bars were indeed 93 percent fat-free, but only after the chocolate coating was removed.[28]

In 2003, the FTC brought enforcement actions against companies marketing the herbal weight-loss supplement ephedra. Ephedra has a long-standing connection to elevated blood pressure, strokes, and heart attacks, and has contributed to numerous deaths. Nevertheless, companies persisted in advertising ephedra as a safe and miraculous weight-loss supplement and, incredibly, as "a beneficial treatment for hypertension and coronary disease." According to the FTC during court testimony, one misleading ad said: "Teacher loses 70 pounds in only eight weeks. . . . This is how over one million people have safely lost millions of pounds! No calorie counting! No hunger! Guaranteed to work for you too!" As the director of the FTC's Bureau of Consumer Protection summed up, "There is no such thing as weight loss in a bottle. Claims that you'll lose substantial amounts of weight and still eat everything you want are simply false."[29] In 2004, U.S. regulators banned ephedra, and in 2006, California reached a $1 million settlement with Nutraquest, a diet-pill maker accused of using deceptive advertising to sell weight-loss products that contained ephedra.

When the FTC discovers deceptive ads, it usually requires advertisers to change or remove them from circulation. Although the FTC does not have the power to directly assess financial penalties, it can seek monetary civil penalties for consumer redress in court, and it occasionally requires an advertiser to run spots to correct the deceptive ads.

Product Placement

With consumers increasingly sophisticated about visual ad techniques and cynical about the ubiquity of advertising, product companies and ad agencies have become adept in recent years at strategically placing ads—in movies, TV shows, comic books, and most recently in video games—so they appear as part of a story's set environment (see "Tracking Technology: Online Games and Product Placement" on

" Clinically proven to increase fat-loss by an unprecedented 1,700 percent. **"**

—Deceptive ad claim by diet-pill maker Nutraquest (filed for bankruptcy in 2003)

page 422). This is called product placement. For example, a 2006 episode of the cable show *The Closer* promised a commercial-free hour, brought to us by Audi. However, embedded in the program was a Las Vegas scene that featured a silver Audi in a casino, which one of the main characters looked on admiringly. In 2005, Consumer Watch asked both the FTC and FCC to mandate that consumers be warned about product placement on television. Although the FTC rejected the petition, the FCC was considering a response in 2006. Commissioner Jonathan S. Adelstein said that he believed undisclosed product placement might constitute a form of illegal payola, particularly in sponsored shows that disguised themselves as news programs.

For many critics, product placement techniques have gotten out of hand in the quest to win consumers' hearts and minds. What started out as subtle appearances in realistic settings—like Reese's Pieces in the 1982 movie *E.T.*—has turned into Coca-Cola being almost an honorary "cast member" on Fox's *American Idol* set. The practice is now so pronounced that it became the subject of Hollywood parody in the 2006 summer film *Talladega Nights: The Ballad of Ricky Bobby*, starring Will Ferrell. But the irony is that the products that "star" in this satire about product sponsors and the culture of car racing got a great deal: ". . . none of the brands had to pay for its placements. With Ferrell and *Talladega* co-writer and director Adam McKay writing Wonder Bread, Perrier, and dozens of other brands into the script to poke fun at the over-the-top corporate sponsorship in NASCAR races, the filmmakers needed the brands' involvement just as much, if not more, than the brands wanted to be in the film."[30]

> " The level of integration on- and off-screen in *Talladega Nights* is unprecedented. I can't remember ever seeing this much product placement displayed, from the commercials to the trailers for the film to the publicity and press events. It's pretty incredible, and it's pretty unheard of . . . a new and great thing for the brands involved. "
>
> —Aaron Gordon, marketing executive, 2006

Advertising's Threat to Journalism

Much of the power advertising wields is subtle and difficult to monitor. One problem, particularly troubling for newspapers during economic recessions, occurs when reporters cover news issues that reflect poorly on a newspaper's major advertisers. Local real estate firms or car dealers, for instance, are no longer so dependent on newspapers as their main advertising channel. Companies can now take their ad business to direct mail, cable, and the Internet if they are unhappy with negative stories in the local newspaper. With many dailies facing financial difficulties in the 1990s and the early 2000s, some editors turned their investigative eyes away from controversial business stories in order to keep advertisers happy.

● Will Ferrell's 2006 movie *Talladega Nights: The Ballad of Ricky Bobby* satirized the over-the-top product placement advertising that supports Nascar.

In the early 1990s, a report by the nonprofit Center for the Study of Commercialism investigated fifty news stories that were allegedly "killed or downplayed by news media to appease advertisers."[31] In 1990, for example, car dealers in Hartford, Connecticut, withdrew advertising from the *Hartford Courant* over an article that urged consumers to be wary of shady dealers. After the *Courant*'s publisher apologized to the dealers, they ended their boycott, but many readers in the community were upset that the paper backed down. Two years later, one dealer in suburban Hartford reported that he had seen no more negative articles about dealers: "Consumer reporting is virtually nonexistent now."

By the early 2000s, despite deceptive ad practices by auto dealers nationwide, virtually no daily newspapers were initiating investigative stories on local and regional car dealerships; more often, papers merely reported on local government investigations. For example, the state of New York in 2001 reached out-of-court settlements with nearly fifty dealers accused of deceptive ads. (Some dealers were offering $2,500 to customers for trade-ins but then adding that cost to the price of a new car.) In the New York settlement, the dealers denied wrongdoing but agreed to pull the ads.[32]

Occasionally, newspapers stand up to their advertisers. Nordstrom, a large department store retailer, reduced its advertising in the *Seattle Times* in the early 1990s after the paper criticized the company's labor difficulties. In this case, the newspaper did not back down. Michael Fancher, then the executive editor of the *Times*, told the *Wall Street Journal:* "You can't just sell your soul in little bits and pieces and expect that readers will understand it. A lot of newspapers don't understand that."[33] Local television news outlets are also subject to advertiser pressure. A survey by the nonprofit Project for Excellence in Journalism in 2004 found that one-third of local journalists had been pressured by advertisers or corporate owners about what to write or broadcast.[34]

Advertising and the Internet

The earliest major form of Web advertising featured banner ads, the rectangular ads that load at the top of a Web page. But banner ads were losing favor by 2001, as click-through rates on the ads had fallen below 1 percent. To achieve higher click-through rates, the Interactive Advertising Bureau agreed on seven new larger "skyscraper" and "large rectangle" ad formats, which were embedded within the Web page text much like a newspaper layout. These larger ads were accompanied by a surge in pop-up, pop-under, flash multimedia ads, and **interstitials**, ads that pop up in new screen windows as the user attempts to access a new Web page—all provocative attempts to produce brand awareness and entice Web users to interact with the advertisement. More recently, though, paid search advertising has become the largest area for growth in Internet advertising. Even though their original mission was to provide impartial Web results, search sites such as Yahoo! and Google have quietly morphed into advertising companies, selling sponsored links associated with search terms and, in some cases, selling advertising links right within the search results themselves.[35]

Another form of Web advertising is through affiliate referrals on the Web. A Web site becomes an affiliate when it carries a hot button for an Internet business on its page; the affiliate then earns a commission—typically 7 to 15 percent—for any sales that it creates for the Web business. Amazon.com started its affiliate program in 1996 and now has more than 900,000 affiliate Web pages that carry its hot-button logos to refer customers to buy books, music, and other offerings. Other forms of Internet advertising include classified ads and unsolicited e-mail ads—known as **spam**—which accounted for more than 80 percent of e-mail in 2006.

The lure of the Internet to advertisers is its unique ability to record and track online users. Most ads are placed by Internet advertising agencies and are served to hundreds of client sites by the agencies' computers. The agencies then track ad impressions (how often the ads are seen) and click-throughs. By 2005, leading Web ad agencies included DoubleClick and 24/7 Real Media. Each of these businesses tracks millions of consumers by developing information profiles that help them to direct targeted advertisements to Web site visitors. Internet user information is gained through cookies and online surveys—for example, an ESPN.com contest required users to fill out a survey to be eligible to win sports tickets—or through sites such as nytimes.com, which requires users to provide demographic information for free access to that newspaper's site. Online and in-store retail sales data can be added to Internet user profiles as well, creating an unprecedented database of consumer information, but one that disturbs privacy advocates.

> ❝ Web surfers are becoming increasingly immune to the shriek of banner ads, the online equivalent of freeway billboards dotting the cyber landscape. ❞
>
> –Jonathan Gaw,
> *Los Angeles Times,* 1999

Even with all the technical innovations spurred by the Internet, the failure of so many dot-com companies and the stock market slide in the early 2000s dramatically affected online advertising. Yet, as the market for various Internet display advertising declined, the rise of paid search advertising created a new economic bubble—at least for search engine companies. All Internet advertising had rebounded and had grown into a $12.5 billion market by 2005, surpassing the outdoor (e.g., billboard) advertising business. The most troubling factor, though, is that most people aren't aware that the largest single category of Internet advertising—paid search—is actually advertising. According to a series of independent studies by *Consumer Reports WebWatch*, users frequently can't tell the difference between sponsored and nonsponsored search results, and the search sites often fail to provide clear disclosure that results are influenced by advertisers.[36]

Alternative Voices

One of the provisions of the government's multibillion-dollar settlement with the tobacco industry in 1998 established a nonprofit organization with the mission to counteract tobacco marketing and reduce youth tobacco use. That mission became a reality in 2000, when the American Legacy Foundation launched its antismoking/anti–tobacco-industry ad campaign.

Working with a coalition of ad agencies, a group of teenage consultants, and a $300 million budget, the foundation has created a series of stylish, gritty print and television ads that deconstruct the images that have long been associated with cigarette ads— macho horse country, carefree beach life, sexy bar scenes, and daring skydives. These ads show teens dragging, piling, or heaving body bags across the beach or onto a horse, and holding up signs that say "What if cigarette ads told the truth?" Other ads show individuals with lung cancer ("I worked where people smoked. I chose

> **"A lot of parents don't even know what Truth is."**
>
> —Joe Martyak,
> VP of American Legacy
> Foundation, 2006

● In 2005, The Truth, the national youth smoking prevention campaign, won a national Emmy award in the National Public Service Announcement (PSA) category. The Truth ads were created by the ad firms of Arnold Worldwide of Boston and Crispin Porter & Bogusky of Miami. Here a Truth ad reimagines a common image found in Marlboro cigarette ads.

Online Games and Product Placement

By Kasia Gruszkowska

You are the world's best undercover agent on a secret mission behind enemy lines. You've got your state-of-the-art weapon, body armor, night-vision goggles—and minty-fresh breath, thanks to Airwaves chewing gum. Wait a second—chewing gum?

Welcome to the world of high-profile videogame advertising. Videogame makers began putting real products in their games about a year ago, mostly as fixed advertisements—products featured on billboards or as props in the game—and advertisers have embraced the new medium. In Ubisoft's *Splinter Cell: Pandora Tomorrow,* agent Sam Fisher has to retrieve a message from a certain Sony Ericsson cell phone in order to move forward in the game. The firm's soon-to-be-released *CSI: Three Dimensions of Murder* has cops solving a crime by making use of Visa's fraud-protection services. Music also lends itself to videogame ads. Ubisoft has placed one advertisement for a band in *Splinter Cell: Chaos Theory,* and plans to do more.

The rise of online games means that game makers can change product-placement ads to cater to different consumers at different times—more like ads in that other video medium, television. For example, videogame advertising firm Massive, based in New York, coordinated a campaign for Warner Brothers in which online gamers playing Ubisoft's *Splinter Cell* saw ads for *Batman Begins* that were timed to when the movie was being released in local markets. Last summer, Funcom's game *Anarchy Online* featured audio ads triggered by the player's avatar. Walking past a billboard ad for a movie, for instance, triggers an audio promotion for the film. Similar ads will soon appear in Sony Online Entertainment games *Matrix* and *PlanetSide.*

Driving the trend is a change in the demographics of videogame players. The average gamer is not so much a teenager as a young investment banker with above-average education and income. Whereas men 18 to 34 watched 12 percent less TV last year than the year before, they spent 20 percent more time with the videogame console. "Games today are more mature and are catering to an older audience," says Deborah Coster, spokesperson for the Entertainment & Leisure Software Publishers Association. Industry executives are excited at the prospect of reaching these consumers. "You go where the eyeballs are," says analyst Michael Goodman of the research firm Yankee Group.

Massive has led the way in videogame advertisement since its founding in 2002. Mitch Davis, the company's founder and CEO, got the idea for tying ads into games while playing *Grand Theft Auto: Vice City.* He noticed that the game depicted fake advertising for a clothing firm called Goop, a play on Gap. "It struck me immediately that there was a way to change that advertising, in a way that would make it look better by adding realism and providing a new source of revenue for the industry," he says. Since then, Massive has signed contracts with high-profile game makers including Sony Online Entertainment, Ubisoft, and THQ.

The key to the success of videogame ads is the ability to fold the product realistically into the game. Advertisers can place products and billboards only where the player might encounter them in real life. For instance, a movie billboard in the jungle just wouldn't do.

So far, gamers seem to accept the ads. And they tend to remember them. Independent tests by Nielsen Entertainment show that videogame ads are remembered two and a half times better than television ads. That's good news for advertisers, at least for now. As gamers get older, they may also grow more skeptical.

● Is this the new background for video games?

Source: Kasia Gruszkowska, "Police! Freeze! Do You Accept Visa?" *Newsweek International,* February 27, 2006.

not to. But I got lung cancer anyway.") or illustrate how many people are indirectly touched by tobacco deaths ("Yeah, my grandfather died April last year.").

The TV and print ads all prominently reference the foundation's Web site, www.thetruth.com, which offers statistics, discussion forums, and outlets for teen creativity. For example, the site provides facts about addiction (more than 80 percent of all adult smokers started smoking before they turned eighteen) and tobacco money (tobacco companies make $1.8 billion from underage sales), and urges site visitors to organize the facts in their own customized folders. By 2006, with its jarring messages and cross-media platform, "The Truth" antitobacco campaign was recognized by 80 percent of teens and was ranked in the Top 10 "most memorable teen brands."[37]

Advertising, Politics, and Democracy

Advertising as a profession came of age in the twentieth century, facilitating the shift of U.S. society from production-oriented small-town values to consumer-oriented urban lifestyles. With manufacturers developing the products and advertisers producing the consumers, advertising became the central economic support system for our mass media industries. Through its seemingly endless supply of pervasive and persuasive strategies, advertising today saturates the cultural landscape. Its ubiquity raises serious questions about our privacy and the ease with which companies can gather data on our consumer habits. But an even more serious issue is the influence of advertising on our lives as democratic citizens. With fewer and fewer large media conglomerates controlling advertising and commercial speech, what is the effect of this trend on free speech and political debate? In the future, how easy will it be to get heard in a marketplace where only a small number of large companies control access to that space?

As advertising has become more pervasive and consumers more discriminating, ad practitioners have searched for ways to weave their work more seamlessly into the social and cultural fabric. Products now blend in as props or even as "characters" in TV shows and movies. In addition, almost every national consumer product now has its own Web site to market itself to a global audience 365 days a year. With today's digital technology, ad images also appear in places where they don't really exist—such as superimposed advertisements on the half wall behind the batter during a nationally televised baseball broadcast. Viewers at home see the ads but the ads can't be seen by fans at the game.

Among the more intriguing efforts to become enmeshed in the culture are the ads that exploit, distort, or transform the political and cultural meanings of popular music. In the 1990s and through the early 2000s, for instance, a number of formerly radical or progressive rock songs made their way into TV ads, muddying the boundary between art and commerce. The Beatles' "Revolution" (1968) promoted Nike shoes in the 1980s; more recently, "Come Together" (1969) morphed into the commercial theme for Nextel, and "Getting Better" (1967) accompanied Philips Electronics TV ads. Buffalo Springfield's "For What It's Worth" (1967) sold Miller beer—with the commercial stopping just short of the band's Vietnam War protest lyric, "There's a man with a gun over there." David Bowie's "Heroes" (1977) and the Rolling Stones' "Start Me Up" (1981) peddled Microsoft software, and Led Zeppelin's "Rock and Roll" (1971) sold Cadillac SUVs.

A more straightforward form of cultural blending is **political advertising**, the use of ad techniques to promote a candidate's image and persuade the public to adopt a particular viewpoint. Since the 1950s, political consultants have been imitating

> **"** The era of consumer resistance and control has begun.**"**
> —Yankelovich Partners, marketing services consultants, 2004

market-research and advertising techniques to sell their candidates. In the early days of television, politicians running for major offices either bought or were offered half-hour blocks of time to discuss their views and the issues of the day. As advertising time became more valuable, however, local stations and the networks became reluctant to give away time in large chunks. Gradually, TV managers began selling thirty-second spots to political campaigns just as they sold time to product advertisers.

In the late 1980s, a research team at the University of Pennsylvania's Annenberg School of Communication began critiquing political advertisements that reduce a candidate's ideas to a thirty-second advertising pitch. The research revealed that in using powerful visual images, these ads often attack other candidates and distract viewers through misleading verbal messages. Since the early 1990s, the major networks have been using the school's techniques in a news segment called Ad Watch. After critiquing a political ad, a commentator labeled it "true," "correct but. . . ," "misleading," or "false." As a result of Ad Watch, media consultants began paying more attention to the veracity of their ads. Unlike the ads that ran multiple times, Ad Watch pieces usually aired only once, and were viewed only by people who regularly watch the evening news.[38]

During the 1992 and 1996 presidential campaigns, third-party candidate Ross Perot restored the use of the half-hour time block when he ran political infomercials on cable and the networks. However, only very wealthy candidates can afford such promotional strategies because television does not usually provide free airtime to politicians. Questions about political ads continue to be asked: Can serious information on political issues be conveyed in thirty-second spots that many candidates can barely afford? Do repeated attack ads, which assault another candidate's character, so undermine citizens' confidence in the electoral process that they stop voting?[39] And how does a society ensure that alternative political voices, which are not so well financed or commercially viable, still receive a hearing in a democratic society?

Although broadcasters use the public's airwaves, they have long opposed providing free time for political campaigns and issues since political advertising is big business for television stations. TV broadcasters earned $400 million in 1996, took in more than $1.5 billion from political ads during the presidential election in 2004, and earned an estimated $2 billion in 2006.[40]

Although commercialism—through packaging both products and politicians—has generated cultural feedback that is often critical of advertising's pervasiveness, the growth of the industry has not diminished. Ads continue to fascinate. Many consumers buy magazines or watch the Super Bowl just for the advertisements. Adolescents decorate their rooms with their favorite ads and identify with the images certain products convey. For the year 2005, $143.3 billion was spent on U.S. advertising (nearly one-third of the money spent on ads worldwide) enough money to finance the budgets of several small countries. A number of factors have made possible advertising's largely unchecked growth. Many Americans tolerate advertising as a necessary "evil" for maintaining the economy, but many dismiss advertising as not believable and even trivial. As a result, unwilling to downplay its centrality to global culture, many citizens do not think advertising is significant enough to monitor or reform. Such attitudes have ensured advertising's pervasiveness and suggest the need to escalate our critical vigilance.

As individuals and as a society, we have developed an uneasy relationship with advertising. Favorite ads and commercial jingles remain part of our cultural world for a lifetime. But we detest irritating and repetitive commercials, using the remote control to mute the offenders on television. We realize that without ads many mass media would need to reinvent themselves. At the same time, we should remain critical of what advertising has come to represent: the overemphasis on commercial acquisitions and cultural images, and the disparity between those who can afford to live comfortably in a commercialized society and those who cannot.

www.

For review questions and activities for Chapter 11, go to the interactive *Media and Culture* Online Study Guide at *bedfordstmartins.com/ mediaculture*

REVIEW QUESTIONS

Early Developments in American Advertising

1. Whom did the first ad agents serve?

2. How did packaging and trademarks influence advertising?

3. Explain why patent medicines and department stores figured so prominently in advertising in the late 1800s.

4. What role did advertising play in transforming America into a consumer society?

The Shape of U.S. Advertising Today

5. What influences did visual culture exert on advertising?

6. What are the differences between boutique and mega-agencies?

7. What are the major divisions at most ad agencies? What is the function of each department?

8. What causes the occasional tension between the research and creative departments at some agencies?

Persuasive Techniques in Contemporary Advertising

9. How do the common persuasive techniques used in advertising work?

10. How does the association principle work, and why is it an effective way to analyze advertising?

11. What is the disassociation corollary?

Commercial Speech and Regulating Advertising

12. What is commercial speech?

13. What are four serious contemporary issues regarding health and advertising? Why is each issue controversial?

14. What is product placement? Cite examples.

15. What aspect of Internet advertising concerns privacy advocates?

Advertising, Politics, and Democracy

16. What are some of the major issues involving political advertising?

17. What role does advertising play in a democratic society?

QUESTIONING THE MEDIA

1. What is your earliest recollection of watching a television commercial? Do you have a favorite ad? A most-despised ad? What is it about these ads that you particularly like or dislike?

2. Why are so many people critical of advertising?

3. If you were (or are) a parent, what strategies would you use to explain an objectionable ad to your child or teenager? Use an example.

4. Should advertising aimed at children be regulated? Support your response.

5. Should tobacco (or alcohol) advertising be prohibited? Why or why not? How would you deal with First Amendment issues regarding controversial ads?

6. Would you be in favor of regular advertising on public television and radio as a means of financial support for these media? Explain your answer.

7. Is advertising at odds with the ideals of democracy? Why or why not?

SEARCHING THE INTERNET

http://www.adcouncil.org

The site of the nonprofit Ad Council, which uses the pro bono work of top ad agencies to create public service announcements on topics such as education and preventive health care.

http://www.adbusters.org

Satire with a sharp anticonsumerist critique, including spoofs of many advertisements, is the style of the Vancouver-based Adbusters Media Foundation, publisher of *Adbusters* magazine.

http://www.adage.com

Advertising Age is the leading advertising trade journal, with a large data portfolio of agency and brand rankings.

http://www.adweek.com

The online version of *Adweek,* a top advertising, marketing, and media publication.

http://www.clioawards.com

The official site for the advertising industry's major awards competition.

http://www.sric-bi.com/VALS

The site for the online VALS questionnaire, which categorizes adult consumers on the basis of their psychological characteristics and several key demographic factors.

KEY TERMS

product placement, 389
space brokers, 392
subliminal advertising, 395
slogan, 396
mega-agencies, 397
boutique agencies, 398
market research, 399
demographics, 399
psychographics, 399
focus groups, 399

Values and Lifestyles (VALS), 399
storyboard, 401
media buyers, 402
saturation advertising, 402
account executives, 403
account reviews, 403
famous-person testimonial, 404
plain-folks pitch, 404
snob-appeal approach, 404
bandwagon effect, 404

hidden-fear appeal, 404
irritation advertising, 404
association principle, 405
myth analysis, 406
commercial speech, 409
infomercials, 409
interstitials, 420
spam, 420
political advertising, 423

In Brief

As a class, consider the impact of advertising on your college campus. Are any buildings or sports facilities named after advertisers? Are any on-campus dining facilities run by fast-food franchises? Who has the soda franchise on your campus, and how much do they pay? What are the dominant companies that advertise on your campus, and where do they place their ads? Should college campuses be free of advertisements? Why or why not? Are there any places in society that are free of ads and corporate sponsorship?

In Depth

From a business perspective, magazine ads function to promote advertisers' goods or services over competing brands and to place these goods or services before consumers so that they can make informed buying decisions. We know, however, that ads mean more than what advertisers intend, because readers form their own opinions. We know, too, that ads function as popular culture. They operate on a symbolic level to affirm cultural values.

In a three- or four-page analysis, compare and critique three magazine ads. The ads should all feature the same type of product but should be taken from contrasting magazines (for example, three alcohol ads from women's and men's magazines, or three clothing ads from various kinds of publications).

Description. Take notes on your three choices, laying out what is going on in the ads. Briefly describe each ad. Is a narrative apparent here (setting, characters, conflict, etc.)? What different persuasive strategies seem to be at work?

Analysis. Figure out common patterns or differences that emerge among the three ads, and then develop an argument that you want to prove. For example, you may notice that one ad demonstrates more social responsibility than the others or provides better consumer information. In your critique, use the as-

sociation principle to deal with the ads' cultural meanings. Your analysis should go beyond the issue of whether the ads successfully market their products.

Interpretation. Now think about these questions in regard to the ads you have chosen: What's going on? What different sets of values are being sold (e.g., ideas about patriotism, family, sex, beauty, technology, tradition)? Are the ads selling a vision (or stereotype) of what it means to be male or female? of what it means to be young, old, or middle-aged? of what it means to be a member of a particular racial or ethnic group?

Evaluation. Make a judgment about which ad works best and why. Which ad is the best at treating both the product and consumer fairly and responsibly? Are any of the ads deceptive or irresponsible?

Again, your paper should have a central argument or thesis, drawing on evidence from your ads. To this end, organize your paper around an idea that is worth proving. For example, pointing out that your ads "sell their products in different ways" is not an argument. But if you state that an ad sells "the American dream as equal opportunity for all," or that it is racist or sexist, these arguments are worth proving.

Engagement. A number of projects and organizations bring a critical eye to advertising messages through education and activism. For example, the Gender Ads Project is a growing collection of more than twenty-three hundred advertisements (mostly from magazines), which are categorized into various topical areas in advertising (e.g., The Gaze, Social Class, Dolls, Males as Hero). Visit the site (www.genderads.com/gender.htm) and contribute to the project's image database, or offer your own commentary on issues related to gender and advertising. Also visit Adbusters, an organization that offers smart insights into our consumer culture, and join the Culturejammers network, "a global network of artists, activists, writers, pranksters, students, educators, and entrepreneurs who want to advance the new social activist movement of the information age" (www.adbusters.org).

public
relations
and framing the message

CHAPTER 12

Early Developments in Public Relations

The Practice of Public Relations

Tensions between Public Relations and the Press

Public Relations, Social Responsibility, and Democracy

● The delinquent in jeans: Marlon Brando in *The Wild One* (1953).

In the mid-1950s, the blue jeans industry was in deep trouble. After hitting a postwar peak in 1953, jeans sales began to slide. The durable one-hundred-year-old denim product had become associated with rock-and-roll and teenage troublemakers. Popular movies, especially *The Wild One* and *Blackboard Jungle,* featured emotionally disturbed, blue jeans–wearing "young toughs" terrorizing adult authority figures. A Broadway play about juvenile delinquency was even titled *Blue Denim.* The worst was yet to come, however. In 1957, the public school system in Buffalo, New

York, banned the wearing of blue jeans for all high school students. Formerly associated with farmers, factory workers, and an adult work ethic, jeans had become a reverse fashion statement for teenagers—something many adults could not abide.

In response to the crisis, the denim industry waged a public relations (PR) campaign to eradicate the delinquency label and rejuvenate denim's image. In 1956, the nation's top blue jeans manufacturers formed the national Denim Council "to put schoolchildren back in blue jeans

↓

through a concerted national public relations, advertising, and promotional effort."[1] First the council targeted teens, but its promotional efforts were unsuccessful. The manufacturers soon realized that the problem was not with the teens but with the parents, administrators, teachers, and school boards. It was the adults who felt threatened by a fashion trend that seemed to promote disrespect through casualness. In response, the council hired a public relations firm to turn the image of blue jeans around. Over the next five years, the firm did just that.

The public relations team determined that mothers were refusing to outfit their children in jeans because of the product's association with delinquency. To change this perception among women, the team encouraged fashion designers to update denim's image by producing new women's sportswear styles made from the fabric. Media outlets and fashion editors were soon inundated with news releases about the "new look" of durable denim.

The PR team next enlisted sportswear designers to provide

● The good citizen in jeans: former president Jimmy Carter, working with Habitat for Humanity.

new designs for both men's and women's work and utility clothes, long the backbone of denim sales. Targeting business reporters as well as fashion editors, the team transformed the redesign effort into a story that appealed to writers in both areas. They also planned retail store promotions nationwide, including "jean queen" beauty contests, and advanced positive denim stories in men's publications.

The team's major PR coup, however, involved an association with the newly formed national Peace Corps. The brainchild of the

Kennedy administration, the Peace Corps encouraged young people to serve their country by working with people from developing nations. Envisioning the Peace Corps as the flip side of delinquency, the Denim Council saw its opening. In 1961, it agreed to outfit the first group of two hundred corps volunteers in denim. As a result of all these PR efforts, by 1963 manufacturers were flooded with orders, and sales of jeans and other denim goods were way up. The delinquency tag disappeared, and jeans gradually became associated with a more casual, though not antisocial, dress ethic.

the blue jeans story illustrates a major difference between advertising and public relations: Advertising is controlled publicity that a company or an individual buys; public relations attempts to secure favorable media publicity (which is more difficult to control) to promote a company or client. In advertising, clients buy space or time for their products or services, and consumers know who paid for the messages. But with public relations the process is more subtle, requiring news media to accept the premise or legitimacy of a PR campaign and to use it as news. The transformation of denim in the public's eye was achieved primarily without the purchase of advertising. The PR team restyled denim's image mainly by cultivating friendly relations with reporters who subsequently wrote stories associating the fabric with a casual, dedicated, youthful America.

Publicity refers to one type of PR communication: messages that spread information about a person, corporation, issue, or policy in various media. Public relations today, however, involves many communication strategies besides publicity. In fact, much of what PR specialists do involves dealing with negative or unplanned publicity. For example, with obesity rates skyrocketing in the last few years, fast-food and processed-food companies suddenly found themselves under attack. Kraft Foods, Inc., which produces a fair number of fatty processed foods, reacted by launching a food education campaign. The company sent slick magazine-like spreads about healthy eating to households across the United States; created *Food & Family*, a free monthly magazine offering seasonal recipes for busy families (using Kraft products); established Kraftfoods.com, another recipe outlet; and scored a fifteen-minute radio slot on Radio Disney and a cable program on the Food Network to promote healthy living, healthy recipes, and Kraft foods.

Because it involves multiple forms of communication, **public relations** is difficult to define precisely. It covers a wide array of actions, such as shaping the image of a politician or celebrity, repairing the image of a major corporation, establishing two-way communication between consumers and companies, and molding wartime propaganda. Broadly defined, *public relations* refers to the entire range of efforts by an individual, an agency, or any organization attempting to reach or persuade audiences.[2]

The social and cultural impact of public relations, like that of advertising, has been immense. In its infancy, PR helped convince many American businesses of the value of nurturing the public, who had been redefined as purchasers rather than as producers of their own goods. PR also set the tone for the corporate image-building that characterized the economic environment of the twentieth century and transformed the profession of journalism by complicating the way "facts" could be interpreted. Perhaps PR's most significant effect, however, has been on the political process in which individuals and organizations—on both the Right and the Left—hire *spin doctors* to shape their media images.

Without public relations, the news profession would be hard-pressed to keep up with every upcoming event or complex issue. Although reporters and editors do not like to admit it, PR departments and agencies are a major source of story ideas and information. In this chapter, we will examine the impact of public relations and the historical conditions that affected its development as a modern profession—how it helped transform America into a more image-conscious society. We will begin by looking at nineteenth-century press agents and the role that railroads and utility companies played in developing corporate PR. We will then consider the rise of modern PR, particularly the influences of former reporters Ivy Lee and Edward Bernays. In addition, we will explore the major practices and specialties of public relations, the reasons for the long-standing antagonism between journalists and members of the PR profession, and the social responsibilities of PR in a democracy.

> **"** An image . . . is not simply a trademark, a design, a slogan, or an easily remembered picture. It is a studiously crafted personality profile of an individual, institution, corporation, product, or service.**"**
>
> –Daniel Boorstin, *The Image*, 1961

Early Developments in Public Relations

At the beginning of the twentieth century, the United States slowly shifted to a consumer-oriented, industrial society that fostered the rapid spread of advertising and publicity for new products and services. During this transformation from farm to factory, PR emerged as a profession, partly because businesses needed to fend off increased scrutiny from muckraking journalists and emerging labor unions.[3]

The first PR practitioners were simply theatrical **press agents**: those who sought to advance a client's image through media exposure, primarily via stunts staged for newspapers. The potential of these early PR techniques soon became obvious to business executives and to politicians. For instance, press agents were used by people like Daniel Boone, who engineered various land-grab and real estate ventures, and Davy Crockett, who in addition to heroic exploits was also involved in the massacre of Native Americans. Such individuals often wanted to repair and reshape their reputation as cherished frontier legends or as respectable candidates for public office.

P. T. Barnum, Buffalo Bill, and the Railroads

The most notorious theatrical agent of the 1800s was Phineas Taylor (P. T.) Barnum, who used gross exaggeration, fraudulent stories, and staged events to secure newspaper coverage for his clients, his American Museum, and, later, his circus. Barnum's best-known acts included the "midget" General Tom Thumb, Swedish soprano Jenny Lind, Jumbo the Elephant, and Joice Heth, who Barnum claimed was the 161-year-old nurse of George Washington (although she was actually 80 when she died). These performers became some of the earliest nationally known celebrities because of Barnum's skill in using the media for promotion. Decrying outright fraud and cheating, Barnum understood that his audiences liked to be tricked. In newspapers and on handbills, he later often revealed the strategies behind his more elaborate hoaxes.

From 1883 to 1916, former army scout William F. Cody, who once killed buffalo for the railroads, promoted himself in his "Buffalo Bill's Wild West and Congress of Rough Riders" traveling show. Cody's troupe—which featured bedouins, cossacks, and gauchos as well as "cowboys and Indians"—re-created dramatic gunfights, the Civil War, and battles of the Old West. The show employed sharpshooter Annie Oak-

> ❝ Public relations developed in the early part of the twentieth century as a profession which responded to, and helped shape, the public, newly defined as irrational, not reasoning; spectatorial, not participant; consuming, not productive. ❞
>
> –Michael Schudson, *Discovering the News*, 1978

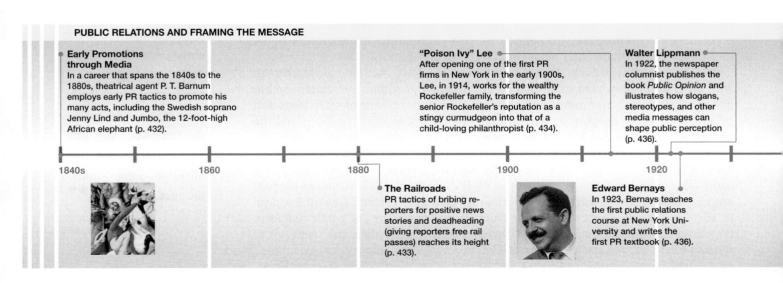

PUBLIC RELATIONS AND FRAMING THE MESSAGE

Early Promotions through Media
In a career that spans the 1840s to the 1880s, theatrical agent P. T. Barnum employs early PR tactics to promote his many acts, including the Swedish soprano Jenny Lind and Jumbo, the 12-foot-high African elephant (p. 432).

"Poison Ivy" Lee
After opening one of the first PR firms in New York in the early 1900s, Lee, in 1914, works for the wealthy Rockefeller family, transforming the senior Rockefeller's reputation as a stingy curmudgeon into that of a child-loving philanthropist (p. 434).

Walter Lippmann
In 1922, the newspaper columnist publishes the book *Public Opinion* and illustrates how slogans, stereotypes, and other media messages can shape public perception (p. 436).

1840s   1860   1880   1900   1920

The Railroads
PR tactics of bribing reporters for positive news stories and deadheading (giving reporters free rail passes) reaches its height (p. 433).

Edward Bernays
In 1923, Bernays teaches the first public relations course at New York University and writes the first PR textbook (p. 436).

ley and Lakota medicine man Sitting Bull, whose own legends were partially shaped by Cody's nine publicity agents. These agents were led by John Burke, who promoted the show for its thirty-four-year run. Burke was one of the first PR agents to use a variety of media channels: promotional newspaper stories, magazine articles and ads, dime novels, theater marquees, poster art, and early films. Burke's efforts successfully elevated Cody's show, which was seen by more than fifty million people in a thousand cities in twelve countries.[4] Burke and Buffalo Bill shaped many of the lasting myths about rugged American individualism and frontier expansion. Along with Barnum, they were among the first to use publicity to elevate entertainment-centered culture to an international level.

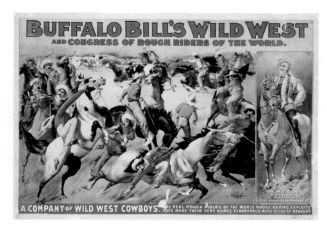

● Buffalo Bill's Wild West and Congress of Rough Riders of the World show, depicted in this 1899 poster, was internationally popular as a touring show for more than thirty years. William Frederick Cody (1846–1917) became popularly known as "Buffalo Bill" through dime-store novel stories adapted from his life by E. Z. C. Judson (under the pen name Ned Buntline). Prior to his fame as an entertainer, he worked as a Pony Express rider at age 14, and later as a buffalo hunter for the Kansas Pacific Railroad.

During the 1800s, America's largest industrial companies, particularly the railroads, also employed press agents to win favor in the court of public opinion. Initially, government involvement in railroad development was minimal; local businesses raised funds to finance the spread of rail service. Around 1850, however, the railroads began pushing for federal subsidies, complaining that local fund-raising efforts took too long. In its drive for government support, for example, Illinois Central promoted the following public strategy: "The railroad line would be expensive to construct; it would open up new land for economic development; without subsidy, the line might not be built; with subsidy the public interest would be served."[5] Illinois Central was one of the first companies to use government lobbyists to argue that railroad service between the North and the South would ease tensions, unite the two regions, and prevent a war.

The railroads successfully campaigned for government support by developing some of the earliest publicity tactics. Their first strategy was simply to buy favorable news stories through direct bribes. By the late 1880s, this practice was so common that a Chicago news reporter published his tongue-in-cheek rates: "For setting forth of virtues (actual or alleged) of presidents, general managers, or directors, $2 per line. . . . For complimentary notices of the wives and children of railroad officials, we demand $1.50 per line. . . . Epic poems, containing descriptions of scenery, dining cars, etc., will be published at special rates."[6] In addition to planting favorable articles in the press, the railroads engaged in *deadheading*: the practice of giving reporters free rail passes with the tacit understanding that they would write glowing

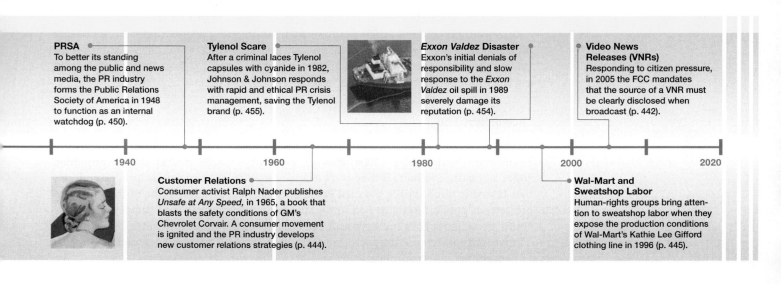

PRSA
To better its standing among the public and news media, the PR industry forms the Public Relations Society of America in 1948 to function as an internal watchdog (p. 450).

Tylenol Scare
After a criminal laces Tylenol capsules with cyanide in 1982, Johnson & Johnson responds with rapid and ethical PR crisis management, saving the Tylenol brand (p. 455).

***Exxon Valdez* Disaster**
Exxon's initial denials of responsibility and slow response to the *Exxon Valdez* oil spill in 1989 severely damage its reputation (p. 454).

Video News Releases (VNRs)
Responding to citizen pressure, in 2005 the FCC mandates that the source of a VNR must be clearly disclosed when broadcast (p. 442).

1940   1960   1980   2000   2020

Customer Relations
Consumer activist Ralph Nader publishes *Unsafe at Any Speed*, in 1965, a book that blasts the safety conditions of GM's Chevrolet Corvair. A consumer movement is ignited and the PR industry develops new customer relations strategies (p. 444).

Wal-Mart and Sweatshop Labor
Human-rights groups bring attention to sweatshop labor when they expose the production conditions of Wal-Mart's Kathie Lee Gifford clothing line in 1996 (p. 445).

> **"** Since crowds do not reason, they can only be organized and stimulated through symbols and phrases. **"**
>
> —Ivy Lee, 1917

reports about rail travel. Eventually, wealthy railroads received federal subsidies and increased their profits, while the public shouldered much of the financial burden for rail expansion.

In terms of power and influence, companies like Illinois Central and the Pennsylvania Railroad in the late 1800s were comparable to American automakers in the 1950s. Having obtained construction subsidies, the larger rail companies turned their attention to bigger game—lobbying the government to control rates and reduce competition, especially from smaller, aggressive regional lines. Railroad lobbyists argued that federal support would lead to improved service and guaranteed quality, because the government would be keeping a close watch. These lobbying efforts, accompanied by favorable publicity, led to passage of the Interstate Commerce Act in 1881, authorizing railroads "to revamp their freight classification, raise rates, and eliminate fare reduction."[7] Historians have argued that, ironically, the PR campaign's success actually led to the decline of railroads: Artificially maintained higher rates and burdensome government regulations forced smaller firms out of business and eventually drove many customers to other modes of transportation.

The Modern Public Relations Agent

Along with the railroads, utility companies such as Chicago Edison and AT&T also used PR strategies in the late 1800s to derail competition and eventually attain monopoly status. In fact, although both local and regional competitors existed at the time, AT&T's PR and lobbying efforts were so effective that they eliminated all telephone competition—with the government's blessing—until the 1980s.

The tactics of the 1880s and 1890s, however, would haunt public relations as it struggled to become a respected profession. In addition to buying the votes of key lawmakers, the utilities used a number of shady practices. These included hiring third-party editorial services, which would send favorable articles about utilities to newspapers; assigning company managers to become leaders in community groups; producing ghostwritten articles (often using the names of prominent leaders and members of women's social groups, who were flattered to see their names in print); and influencing textbook authors to write histories favorable to the utilities.[8]

As the promotional agendas of many companies escalated in the late 1800s, a number of reporters and muckraking journalists began investigating these practices. By the early 1900s, with an informed citizenry paying more attention, it became more difficult for large firms to fool the press and mislead the public. With the rise of the middle class, increasing literacy among the working classes, and the spread of information through print media, democratic ideals began to threaten the established order of business and politics—and the elite groups who managed them. Two pioneers of public relations—"Poison Ivy" Lee and Edward Bernays—emerged in this atmosphere to popularize an approach to public opinion that emphasized shaping the interpretation of facts and "engineering consent."

"Poison Ivy" Lee

Most nineteenth-century corporations and manufacturers cared little about public sentiment. By the early 1900s, though, executives realized that their companies could sell more products if they were associated with positive public images and values. Into this public space stepped Ivy Ledbetter Lee, considered one of the founders of modern public relations. Lee understood the undercurrents of social change. He counseled clients that honesty and directness were better PR devices than the deceptive corporate practices of the 1800s, which had fostered suspicion and an anti–big-business sentiment.

A minister's son and once an economics student at Princeton University, Lee, a former reporter, opened one of the first New York PR firms with a colleague in the early 1900s. Lee quit the firm in 1906 to work for the Pennsylvania Railroad, which, following a rail accident, wanted him to help downplay unfavorable publicity. Lee's advice, however, was that Penn Railroad admit its mistake, vow to do better, and let newspapers in on the story. These suggestions ran counter to what the utilities and railroads had been doing, yet Lee argued that an open relationship between the press and business would lead to a more favorable public image. In the end, Penn adopted Lee's strategies.

In 1914, Lee went to work for John D. Rockefeller, who by the 1880s controlled 90 percent of the nation's oil industry (Rockefeller once said, "It is my duty to make money and still more money").[9] Rockefeller suffered from periodic image problems, particularly after Ida Tarbell's powerful muckraking series in *McClure's Magazine* about Rockefeller's Standard Oil trust. Despite his philanthropic work, Rockefeller was often depicted in the press as a tyrant, as were other corporate bosses. The Rockefeller and Standard Oil reputations reached a low point in April 1914, when tactics to stop union organizing erupted in tragedy at a fuel and iron company in Ludlow, Colorado. During a violent strike, fifty-three workers and their family members, including thirteen women and children, died.

Lee was hired to contain the damaging publicity fallout. He immediately distributed a series of "fact" sheets to the press, telling the corporate side of the story and discrediting the United Mine Workers, which had been trying to organize the Ludlow workers. As he had done for Penn Railroad, Lee brought in the press and staged photo opportunities. John D. Rockefeller Jr., who by then ran his father's company, donned overalls and a miner's helmet and posed with the families of workers and union leaders. While Lee helped the company improve conditions for workers, the publicity campaign also kept the union out of the Ludlow coal mines. This was probably the first use of a PR campaign in a labor-management dispute. Over the years, Lee completely transformed the wealthy family's image, urging the discreet Rockefellers to publicize their charitable work. To improve his image, the senior Rockefeller took to handing out dimes to children wherever he went—a strategic ritual that historians attribute to Lee.

Called "Poison Ivy" by newspaper critics and corporate foes, Lee had a complex understanding of facts. He realized, better than most journalists of his day, that facts were open to various interpretations. For Lee, facts were elusive and malleable, begging to be forged and shaped. Interpreting facts so as to shine the best light on a client was not viewed as a particularly honorable practice, however. In the Ludlow case, for instance, Lee noted that the women and children who died while retreating from the charging company-backed militia had overturned a stove, which caught fire and caused their deaths. His PR fact sheet implied that they had, in part, been victims of their own carelessness.

In the 1930s, Ivy Lee was investigated by Congress for counseling German industries during the Nazi regime and for fraternizing with the Soviet Union under Joseph Stalin. Some critics thought that Lee's interest in a communist nation represented a curious contradiction for an avowed capitalist. In Lee's earlier work for railroads and utilities, however, he had advocated an anticompetition, pro-consolidation theme that he believed was in the best interests of his clients. Lee had argued for corporate-controlled monopolies, which benefited from protective government regulation. Thus Lee did share some common ground with foreign governments that ran state-controlled, anticompetitive business monopolies.

> ❝ It was the astounding success of propaganda during the war which opened the eyes of the intelligent few in all departments of life to the possibilities of regimenting the public mind. ❞
>
> —Edward Bernays, *Propaganda*, 1928

During World War I, PR pioneer Edward Bernays (1891–1995) worked for the federal Committee on Public Information (CPI). One of the main functions of the CPI was to create the poster art and print ads that would persuade reluctant or isolationist Americans to support the war effort against Germany.

Edward Bernays

The nephew of Sigmund Freud, former reporter Edward Bernays inherited the public relations mantle from Ivy Lee and dressed it up with modern social science. Bernays, who died in 1995 at age 103, was the first person to apply the findings of psychology and sociology to the business of public relations. He also referred to himself as a "public relations counselor" rather than as just a publicity agent. Over the years, Bernays's client list included General Electric, the American Tobacco Company, General Motors, *Good Housekeeping* and *Time* magazines, Procter & Gamble, RCA, the government of India, and the city of Vienna. In addition, he served as an adviser to President Coolidge in the 1920s, helping the president revamp his stiff, formal image.

Bernays made key contributions to public relations education.[10] He taught the first class called *public relations* — at New York University in 1923 — and wrote the field's first textbook, *Crystallizing Public Opinion*. For many years, his definition of PR was a standard: "Public relations is the attempt, by information, persuasion, and adjustment, to engineer public support for an activity, cause, movement, or institution." Bernays worked for the Committee on Public Information (CPI) during World War I, developing propaganda that supported America's entry into that conflict. Later, CPI helped create the image of President Woodrow Wilson as a peacemaker, among the first full-scale governmental attempts to mobilize public opinion.

Hired by the American Tobacco Company after World War I, Bernays was asked to develop a campaign that would make smoking more publicly acceptable for newly liberated women who had recently won the right to vote. Among other strategies, Bernays staged an event: placing women smokers in New York's 1929 Easter parade. He labeled cigarettes "torches of freedom" and encouraged women to smoke as a symbol of their newly acquired suffrage and independence from men. He also asked the women he placed in the parade to contact newspaper and newsreel companies in advance — to announce their symbolic protest. The campaign received plenty of free publicity from newspapers and magazines. Within five weeks of the parade, men-only smoking rooms in New York theaters began opening up to women.

Through much of his writing, Bernays suggested that emerging forms of social democracy threatened the established hierarchical order. He thought it was important for experts and leaders to keep business and society pointed in the right directions: "The duty of the higher strata of society — the cultivated, the learned, the expert, the intellectual — is therefore clear. They must inject moral and spiritual motives into public opinion."[11] Bernays saw a typical public relations campaign giving shape to public opinion — what he termed the "engineering of consent." Bernays believed that for any PR campaign to work, securing the consent of the people was the crucial ingredient.

Both Ivy Lee and Edward Bernays thought that public opinion was pliant and not always rational: In the hands of the right experts, leaders, and PR counselors, public opinion was ready for shaping in forms that people could rally behind.[12] Walter Lippmann, the newspaper columnist who wrote *Public Opinion* in 1922, also believed in the importance of an expert class to direct the more irrational twists and turns of public opinion. But he saw the development of public relations as "a clear sign that the facts of modern life [did] not spontaneously take a shape in which they can be known."[13] Lippmann lamented that too often PR professionals with hidden agendas, rather than detached reporters, were giving only their own meaning to the facts.

● Public relations pioneer Edward Bernays and his business partner and wife, Doris Fleischman, worked on behalf of a client, the American Tobacco Company, to make smoking socially acceptable for women. For one of American Tobacco's brands, Lucky Strike, they were also asked to change public attitudes toward the color green. (Women weren't buying the brand because surveys indicated that the forest green package clashed with their wardrobes.) Bernays and Fleischman organized events such as green fashion shows and sold the idea of a new trend in green to the press. By 1934, green had become the fashion color of the season, making Lucky Strikes the perfect accessory for the female smoker. Interestingly, Bernays forbade his own wife to smoke, flushing her cigarettes down the toilet and calling smoking a nasty habit.

Throughout Bernays's most active years, his business partner and later his wife, Doris Fleischman, worked on many joint projects as a researcher and coauthor. Beginning in the 1920s, she was one of the first women to work in advertising and public relations. She edited a pamphlet called *Contact,* which explained the emerging profession of public relations to America's most powerful leaders. Because it was a new quasi-profession not claimed entirely by men, PR was one of the few professions—apart from teaching and nursing—that was accessible to women who chose to work outside the home. Today, women outnumber men by more than three to one in the profession.

Pseudo-Events and Manufacturing News

Armed with its new understanding of public psychology, modern public relations changed not only the relationship between corporations and the public but also that among corporations, politics, and journalism. In his influential book *The Image,* historian Daniel Boorstin coined the term **pseudo-event** to refer to one of the key contributions of PR and advertising in the twentieth century. Basically, a pseudo-event is any circumstance created for the purpose of gaining coverage in the media. In other words, if no news media show up, there is no event.[14]

Typical pseudo-events are interviews, press conferences, TV and radio talk shows, the Super Bowl pregame show, or any other staged activity aimed at drawing public attention and media coverage. Such events depend on the participation of clients and performers and on the media's recording of the performances. With regard to national politics, Theodore Roosevelt's administration set up the first White House pressroom and held the first presidential press conferences in the early 1900s. By the early 2000s, presidential pseudo-events had evolved to a Bush administration event-staging team that included former producers at ABC and FoxNews Channel and a former NBC cameraman. The White House Communications Office has a multimillion dollar budget for staging media events.

As powerful companies, savvy politicians, and activist groups became aware of the media's susceptibility to pseudo-events, these activities proliferated. For example, to get free publicity, companies began staging press conferences to announce new product lines. During the 1960s, antiwar and civil rights protesters began their events only when the news media were assembled. One anecdote from that era aptly illustrates the principle of a pseudo-event: A reporter asked a student leader about the starting time for a particular protest; the student responded, "When can you get here?"

Politicians running for national office have become particularly adept at scheduling press conferences and interviews around 5:00 or 6:00 P.M. They realize that local TV news is live during these times, so they stage pseudo-events to take advantage of TV's appetite for live remote feeds and breaking news.

The Practice of Public Relations

Today, there are more than 2,900 PR firms worldwide, including 2,200 in the United States; thousands of companies and organizations also have in-house departments devoted to public relations functions. Especially since the 1980s, the formal study of public relations has grown significantly at colleges and universities. As certified PR programs have expanded (often featuring journalism as a minor), the profession has relied less and less on the ranks of reporters for its workforce. At the same time, new courses in professional ethics and issues management have expanded the responsibility of future practitioners.

The growth of formal PR education has been fairly dramatic. In the 1970s, the majority of students in communications and journalism programs indicated in surveys that they intended to pursue careers in news or magazine writing. By the late 1980s, however, similar surveys indicated that the majority of students wanted to enter public relations or advertising, both of which had higher entry-level salaries than journalism positions. By 2006, the Public Relations Student Society of America (PRSSA) had more than 8,500 members and 270 chapters in colleges and universities.

Approaches to Organized Public Relations

In 1988, the Public Relations Society of America (PRSA) offered this useful definition of PR: "Public relations helps an organization and its publics adapt mutually to each other." To carry out this mutual communication process, the PR industry follows two main approaches. First, many agencies function as independent companies whose sole job is to provide clients with PR services. (During the 1980s and 1990s, though, many large ad agencies acquired independent PR firms as subsidiaries.) Second, most companies, which may or may not hire the services of PR firms, maintain their own in-house staffs to handle routine PR tasks, such as writing press releases, managing various media requests, staging special events, and dealing with the public.

Public Relations Agencies

About twenty-two hundred U.S. companies identify themselves as public relations counseling firms. Many large ones are owned by, or affiliated with, multinational communications holding companies like WPP, Omnicom, and Interpublic. (See Figure 12.1.) Two of the largest PR agencies, Burson-Marsteller and Hill & Knowlton, generate nearly $1 billion in PR revenue annually for their parent corporation, the WPP Group. Founded in 1953, Burson-Marsteller has 103 offices in 58 countries, and lists

Figure 12.1

The Top 6 Holding Firms, with Public Relations Subsidiaries, 2006 (by Worldwide Revenue in U.S.$)

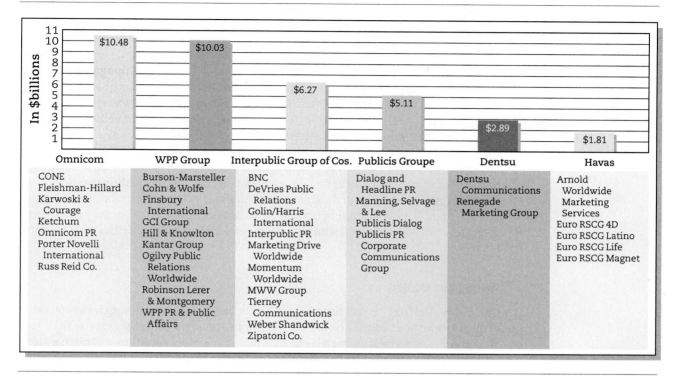

Source: "Agency Report," *Advertising Age*, May 1, 2006, http://adage.com/article?article_id=108906.

Coca-Cola, McDonald's, Old Navy, Wal-Mart, and the United Arab Emirates among its clients. Hill & Knowlton, founded in 1927, has seventy-one offices in forty countries, and clients that include American Express, Procter & Gamble, Starbucks, Pfizer Pharmaceuticals, and the United Kingdom.

Most independent PR firms are smaller and operated locally or regionally. New York–based Edelman, the largest independent firm, is an exception, with global operations and clients like Barnes & Noble, Boeing, Ericsson, Microsoft, Norwegian Cruise Line, and UPS.

In-House Services

In contrast to external agencies, the most common type of public relations is done in-house by companies and organizations. Although America's largest companies typically retain external PR firms, almost every company involved in a manufacturing or service industry has an in-house department. Such departments are also a vital part of many professional organizations, such as the American Medical Association, the AFL-CIO, and the National Association of Broadcasters, as well as large nonprofit organizations, such as the American Cancer Society, the Arthritis Foundation, and most universities and colleges.

Performing Public Relations

Public relations, like advertising, pays careful attention to the various audiences and clients that it interacts with or serves. These groups include not only consumers and the general public but company employees, shareholders, media organizations, government agencies, and community and industry leaders. Among potential clients,

> **" PR expands the public discourse, helps provide a wide assortment of news, and is essential in explaining the pluralism of our total communication system. "**
>
> –John C. Merrill, *Media Debates*, 1991

which constitute another public, are politicians, small businesses, industries, and nonprofit organizations.

Public relations involves a multitude of practices and techniques. The PRSA identifies a number of general activities associated with PR: publicity, communication, public affairs, issues management, government relations, financial PR, community relations, industry relations, minority relations, advertising, press agentry, promotion, media relations, and propaganda. This last activity, **propaganda**, is communication strategically placed, either as advertising or as publicity, to gain public support for a special issue, program, or policy, such as a nation's war effort.

The practice of public relations encompasses a wide range of activities. PR personnel produce employee newsletters, manage client trade shows and conferences, conduct historical tours, appear on news programs, organize damage control after negative publicity, and analyze complex issues and trends that may affect a client's future. Basic among these activities, however, are writing and editing, media relations, special events, research, and community and government relations. PR practice is generally divided into two roles: PR technicians, who handle daily short-term activities, and PR managers, who counsel clients and manage activities over the long term.

Writing and Editing

One of the chief day-to-day functions in public relations is composing news releases, or **press releases**: announcements, written in the style of news reports, that give new information about an individual, a company, or an organization and pitch a story idea to the news media. In issuing press releases, often called *handouts* by the news media, PR agents hope that their client information will be picked up and transformed into news. Through press releases, PR firms manage the flow of information; they often control which media get what material in which order. (A PR agent may reward a cooperative reporter through the strategic release of information.)

News editors and broadcasters sort through hundreds of releases daily to determine which ones contain the most original ideas or the most currency for their readers and viewers. The majority of large media institutions rewrite and double-check the releases, but small media companies and small-town newspapers often use them verbatim because of limited editorial resources or tight deadline constraints. Usually, the more closely a press release resembles actual news copy, the more likely it is to be used. (See Figure 12.2.)

Since the 1970s and the introduction of portable video equipment, PR agencies and departments have been using **video news releases (VNRs)**—thirty- to ninety-second visual PR stories packaged to mimic the style of a broadcast news report. Many large PR firms now operate their own TV studios, which enable them to create VNRs for their clients. Broadcast news stations in small TV markets regularly use video material from VNRs. Although large stations with more resources may get story ideas from VNRs, their news directors do not like to use video material obtained directly from PR sources; they prefer to assemble their own reports in order to maintain their independence. On occasion, news stations have been criticized for using video footage from a VNR without acknowledging the source. (See "Case Study—Video News Releases: Manufacturing the News" on page 442.)

In addition to issuing press releases, nonprofit groups also produce **public service announcements (PSAs)**: fifteen- to sixty-second reports or announcements for radio and television that promote government programs, educational projects, volunteer agencies, or social reform. As part of their requirement to serve the public interest, broadcasters historically have been encouraged to carry free PSAs. Since the deregulation of broadcasting began in the 1980s, however, there has been less pressure and no minimum obligation for TV and radio stations to air PSAs. When PSAs do

Figure 12.2

Differences between a Press Release and a News Story

News reporters can be heavily dependent on public relations for story ideas. At right below is a press release written by the News & Public Information Office at Miami University about students who started a finance business, and the magazine and newspaper articles inspired by the release (*at left and at bottom*).

ARE CREDIT UNIONS
RIGHT FOR ME?
By Jacob Dirr, University of Cincinnati

Whether it's for paying holiday bills or a new biology textbook, most college students are eventually bound to search out a loan. If so, borrowing from a credit union is an option that can offer advantages for first-time borrowers but frequently lacks consideration in comparison to traditional bank loans, credit experts say.

"Joe Student is always misspending with his debit card," says Dave DiCosola, a Generation Y Credit Union consultant. "Most students just need some money to get by and have never had a loan before."

DiCosola is also the president of First Miami Student Credit Union, at Miami (Ohio) University. One of two student-run credit unions in the country, First Miami offers students an education in financial literacy. Often though, students fail to consider credit unions when they are seeking loans, he says. His colleague has noticed the same thing.

However, Fritz Elmendorf, a spokesperson for the Consumer Bank Association, which represents banks nationwide, warns that while credit unions are enticing to students because they offer lower fees, it's not always the case.

"Students are particularly interested in ATM access," he says. "Credit unions typically only have one office. It's a question of where are the ATMs and how much do you pay to use them."

Online banking also attracts students, and even though credit unions offer the service, banks have more options, such as e-mail account alerts, he says. Still, credit unions offer their own advantages, such as lower rates on credit cards and a chance for young people to learn about the financial process.

"At credit unions we realize it is almost an education process," says DiCosola. "Sometimes we give members a break on fees; they will pile up and you have to help the kid out."

He likens credit scores and loans to a life-long game. "If you don't know the rules how do you plan on winning? This is a game you play if you want to or not, and you have to be educated early."

The first step to learning the game is establishing credit, done most easily by getting a credit card with a small spending limit.

"Buy a t-shirt, use your credit card and pay it off right away," says Brackman. "It is so much easier to get a loan when you start off with higher credit."

MIAMI UNIVERSITY **NEWS**

NEWS AND PUBLIC INFORMATION OFFICE   Oxford, Ohio 45056-3403   (513) 529-7592   www.new-info.muohio.edu

1 November 2005
OX (110-main)k

Contact: Holly Wissing
wissinhd@muohio.edu
office: (513) 529-7592
home: (513) 756-9728

STUDENT EXECS: GIVING CREDIT WHERE CREDIT IS DUE

OXFORD, Ohio – Overseeing $1 million in assets. Approving loans. Supervising more than 50 student interns. It's all in a day's work for two Miami University students who manage one of the last remaining student-run credit unions in the nation.

Doug Brackman, 20, is CEO and Dave DiCosola, 21, is president of the First Miami University Student/Alumni Federal Credit Union, an organization that provides 1,500 student members a full range of financial services ranging from checking and savings accounts to ATM cards and loans.

It's a task that can take 20 hours a week, but neither Brackman nor DiCosola get any academic credit or earn a penny. In fact, both moonlight at part-time jobs to earn pocket money. But their volunteer efforts are not entirely altruistic.

Brackman, a junior accounting major, and DiCosola, a senior marketing major, say they are "99.9 percent sure" they will land the specific job they want when they graduate. Experiences such as approving $15,000 car loans or successfully marketing ATM cards are priceless when it comes to selling yourself to potential employers.

In fact, since Miami's student credit union was founded in 1987, alumni from the credit union's executive committee have gone on to success in prestigious firms such as

d Bank, Cintas, JPMorganChase and Ernst & Young.

> The three top credit mistakes by college students, according to the Miami credit union execs:
>
> • Not keeping track of debit card use.
>
> • Taking advantage of credit card offers (often to get a 10 percent discount when purchasing an item) and not paying attention to the potential damage to one's credit rating from having multiple credit cards.
>
> • Not realizing how important one's credit score is after graduation. That score is going to be checked when you apply for many jobs, when you attempt to rent an apartment and when you apply for a car loan.

(MORE)

D8 | DAYTON DAILY NEWS   BUSINESS   SUNDAY, SEPTEMBER 4, 2005

College credit: Miami students run their union

FINANCE: Student-run credit union boasts $1 million in assets

By John Nolan
jnolan@DaytonDailyNews.com

OXFORD — Doug Brackman wears a shirt and tie in the classroom, not a common occurrence for today's college students.

He really raises eyebrows when he tells others on campus that he oversees the student-run credit union at Miami University and its $1 million in assets. Such is life for a budding administrator at one of the nation's few remaining credit unions that is run by students, for students.

Brackman, 20, a junior from Minster and accounting major at Miami, is chief executive officer of First Miami University Student/Alumni Federal Credit Union. He teams with Dave DiCosola, 21, the credit union's president and a senior from Hinsdale, Ill., to work with a manager and board of directors to run First Miami and serve its 1,500 student members.

They try to coach fiscal responsibility to students, who take out loans for everything from textbooks to

Getting loans

Reasons Miami University students cite for obtaining credit union loans:

➤ Textbooks and other school expenses
➤ Paying off personal debt
➤ Extra-curricular activities, including spring break trips
➤ Paying for court costs and fees

spring break trips and often obtain their first credit cards through the credit union. A loan for a spring break trip typically is for between $500 and $1,000, said DiCosola, a marketing major.

"It's very popular. There's a lot of students who really want to go on spring break with their friends ... and mom and dad aren't going to pay for it," DiCosola, who meets with student groups in residence halls to offer financial responsibility pointers, said of such loans. "We kind of preach that, just because you have that money, that's not a reason to spend the whole loan."

DAVE DICOSOLA (left) is president of the First Miami Credit Union and Doug Brackman (right) is CEO. The credit union is located in the Shriver Center on the campus of Miami University in Oxford.

LISA POWELL/DAYTON DAILY NEWS

First Miami has been around since 1989, created by student government leaders who received university support to get the credit union started.

It is among a handful of student-run credit unions that have survived, outlasting more than a dozen others which have either failed or been absorbed by professional credit unions within the past 20 years. Turnover among students, who typically serve as volunteers, makes the competitive pressure from banks which come onto campuses offering an array of financial services that

some student organizations cannot match has helped shrink their ranks.

Offering loans is a key to generating revenue and boosting the size of the customer base, said Willard Hopkins, a retired high school principal from Hamilton who has served on credit union boards. He joined First Miami as its manager five years ago to coach the student administrators.

"It's hard to survive when you're small," Hopkins said.

The Credit Union National Association, a trade organization,

lists other student-run credit unions at Georgetown University, the University of Pennsylvania, Kent State University, Rutgers University, the University of Missouri and Skidmore College in Saratoga Springs, N.Y.

Some have grown in clout. The Georgetown credit union boasts $10 million in assets and 7,000 members, and Pennsylvania's has $8.5 million in assets and nearly 2,500 members. But the Georgetown credit union faces stiff marketing competition from Chevy Chase Bank, while the Pennsylvania entity competes with banks serving Philadelphia including PNC, Citizens and Commerce.

Leaders of the student credit unions try to counter the competition by telling students they offer many of the same services — checking and savings accounts, loans, credit cards and debit cards — plus the convenience of on-campus offices and automated teller machines operated by the credit union. They also urge graduating students to using the credit unions' services as alumni.

"We have our unique advantages," said Casey Ching, 20, the president and CEO of the University of Pennsylvania campus credit union, who is also a finance and accounting

major from Vancouver, Canada.

The student administrators, who generally start as tellers and work their way up through supervisory positions, say the experience of running the credit union is helpful for landing jobs after graduation.

The hands-on financial management, work with boards and public visibility also provides memorable opportunities for some student administrators. DiCosola and Brackman have formed a consulting team to advise professional credit unions on how to market to young adults. The two have been invited to play golf with Ohio credit union industry leaders and to address them at a conference.

Ankit Bishnoi, chief executive of the Georgetown University Alumni and Student Federal Credit Union, said he met last year with executives of MBNA Corp. and they asked him what services they should strive to provide to Georgetown's students. He was 19 at the time, and was enthralled by the corporate attention.

"It was just really humbling," said Bishnoi, now a senior from Port Washington, N.Y., majoring in finance and accounting. "It's a great learning experience."

---

run, they are frequently scheduled between midnight and 6:00 A.M., a less commercially valuable time slot with relatively few viewers or listeners.

Public relations professionals often create brochures and catalogues as well as company newsletters and annual reports for shareholders in addition to writing or editing speeches. Today, the Internet is used for internal communications (such as a human resources newsletter) and external communications, including press release distribution and archives, press kit downloads, and campaign-related Web sites. Innovators such as Richard Edelman, president and CEO of Edelman, have also begun using blogs to increase dialogue and transparency between the industry and the general public. Started in 2004, Edelman's "6 A.M." blog (http://www.edelman.com/speak_up/blog/), candidly discusses PR issues and invites "feedback, blunt and quick."

CASE STUDY

Video News Releases: Manufacturing the News

You may have seen these seemingly innocuous stories on your local TV news over the summer: tips for staying in motels/hotels with pets; the importance of getting rental-car insurance; or how-to instructions for taking great digital photos of your vacation. These may not sound like traditional news stories, but they were broadcast because (a) a company called Medialink promoted them with text, photos, and digital video downloads from their Web site, and (b) three companies—Motel 6, Allstate Insurance, and Fuji Photo Film—paid Medialink to promote these stories (which subtly mention their products) as news.

Medialink, a $37-million business headquartered in New York City, specializes in video news releases (VNRs), a form of public relations that they pioneered in 1986. As Medialink boasted in its 2003 Annual Report, "Whether the situation calls for . . . an ongoing campaign to introduce a new consumer product or defeat proposed legislation, Medialink is an integral member of the client's strategy team."

Oftentimes, these VNRs aren't labeled as company-sponsored material, so local TV stations mistakenly treat them as real news. Other times, local affiliates are just plain understaffed or sloppy, and either take the VNRs as is or repackage them. Since the late 1980s, television stations across the country have been bombarded with VNRs from Medialink and other sources.

Medialink distributes the VNRs and even tracks the number of "plays" their clients' VNRs get on television stations around the world, providing a return on their clients' investment.

The obvious question might be, Why don't Motel 6, Allstate, Fuji, and other companies spend their money on advertising instead? The answer is that the news has more credibility.

The success of VNRs to disguise marketing as news hasn't been lost on some government officials, either. As reports in the *New York Times* and elsewhere in March 2005 revealed, the federal government has become a major originator of VNRs. During the first four years of George W. Bush's administration, $254 million in taxpayers' dollars was spent on public relations contracts. While the administration didn't invent government propaganda, it has taken it to a new level, spending almost double the amount as in the previous four years. A significant part of this spending was for VNRs—sometimes with PR officials posing as reporters—emanating from at least twenty different federal agencies, promoting the Bush agenda on issues such as the Medicare prescription drug law,

● The Army and Air Force Hometown News Service produces and distributes its "news products" to media outlets across the country. The story pictured (*above*) was made to promote a humanitarian mission of the Army.

post-invasion Iraq, military prison guard training, and agriculture programs.

This production of "good news" from the White House has one little problem. It's illegal. As Congress's General Accounting Office (GAO) noted, the federal government can't use covert propaganda—that is, VNRs that don't identify themselves as the work of government agencies. In fact, the GAO issued three opinions on the illegality of such VNRs and notified the White House to stop using them. The Bush administration told its federal agencies to ignore the GAO, Congress's investigative arm.

With the pressure of more than forty thousand citizen petitions to stop the government VNRs, the Federal Communications Commission (FCC) responded on April 13, 2005, with a public notice that stated, "Whenever broadcast stations and cable operators air VNRs, licensees and operators generally must clearly disclose to members of their audiences the nature, source and sponsorship of the material that they are viewing." As FCC Commissioner Jonathan Adelstein noted at the time, "People have a legal right to know the real source when they see something on TV that is disguised as 'news.'"

Yet, in a study from June 2005 to March 2006, the Center for Media and Democracy found that at least seventy-seven television stations across the country had used VNRs but failed to provide disclosure to viewers and, in more than one-third of the cases, aired the VNR in its entirety.[1]

Whether produced by the government or a company, VNRs are a pressing problem for local markets. Why? Local news directors often get their video from other larger news services, such as CNN Newsource, NBC News Channel, or ABC. These TV news services supply the video for national and international news stories that air on local TV. The problem is that these services are also sometimes paid to distribute VNRs in their news feeds as well. "If you're going to take that video, you're trusting that they went out and generated that video," Becky Lutgen-Gardner, news director at KCRG-TV, the ABC affiliate in Cedar Rapids, Iowa, says. But, "unless they flag it, I wouldn't know."

Media Relations

Through publicity, PR managers specializing in media relations promote a client or organization by securing favorable coverage in the news media. Media specialization often requires an in-house PR person to speak on behalf of an organization or to direct reporters to experts who can provide sources of information.

Media-relations specialists also perform *damage control* or *crisis management* when negative publicity occurs. Occasionally, in times of crisis—such as a scandal at a university or a safety recall by a car manufacturer—a PR spokesperson might be designated as the only source of information available to news media. Although journalists often resent being cut off from higher administrative levels and leaders, the institution or company wants to ensure that rumors and inaccurate stories do not circulate in the media. In these situations, a game often develops in which reporters attempt to circumvent the company spokesperson and induce a knowledgeable insider to talk *off the record*, providing background details without being named directly as a source.

PR agents who specialize in media relations also recommend advertising to their clients when it seems appropriate. Unlike publicity, which is sometimes outside a PR agency's control, paid advertising may help to focus a complex issue or a client's image. Publicity, however, carries the aura of legitimate news and thus has more credibility than advertising. In addition, media specialists cultivate associations with editors, reporters, freelance writers, and broadcast news directors to ensure that press releases or VNRs are favorably received. (See "Examining Ethics: Improving the Credibility Gap" on page 445.)

> **❝** I get in a lot of trouble if I'm quoted, especially if the quotes are accurate.**❞**
>
> –A congressional staff person, explaining to the *Wall Street Journal* why he can speak only "off the record," 1999

Special Events

Another public relations specialty involves coordinating special events. Since the late 1960s, for instance, the city of Milwaukee has run Summerfest, a ten-day music and food festival that attracts about a million people each year. As the festival's popularity grew, various companies sought to become sponsors of the event. Local manufacturers and the beer industry, for example, signed up to support different musical venues. The Miller Brewing Company sponsored a festival stage devoted to jazz. In exchange for sponsorship, the stage carried the Miller name, which also accompanied many items connected with Summerfest. In this way, Miller received favorable publicity by showing a commitment to the city that serves as the company's corporate headquarters.[15]

More typical of special-events publicity is the corporate sponsor that aligns its company image with a cause or an organization that has positive stature among the general public. For example, Liberty Mutual Insurance and the Scotts lawn products company are both national corporate contributors to *American Experience,* the long-running history series on PBS. At the local level, companies often sponsor a community parade or a charitable fund-raising activity. When a new professional sports team arrives in a community, a host of local companies may compete to associate themselves with the new franchise. In this kind of situation, a team's PR specialist attempts to identify those companies that will provide the most favorable publicity for the client.

Research

Just as advertising is driven today by demographic and psychographic research, PR uses similar strategies to project a client's image to the appropriate audience. Because historically it has been difficult to determine why particular campaigns succeed or fail, research has become the key ingredient in PR forecasting. Like advertising studies, PR research targets specific audiences. It makes use of mail and telephone surveys and of focus group interviews to get a fix on an audience's perceptions of an issue or a client's reputation.

Research can help focus a campaign's efforts. For example, the Liz Claiborne Foundation has been combating domestic violence with its Love Is Not Abuse campaign for more than a decade, but without much media visibility. In 2005, Liz Claiborne turned their focus to a subset of domestic violence—teen dating abuse—and hired Ruder Finn, a leading independent PR firm, for campaign assistance. The research phase began with a national survey of 683 teens between the ages of thirteen and eighteen. The results were sobering: one in three teenagers reported knowing someone who had been physically hurt by a partner; 13 percent of teenage girls reported being physically hurt in a relationship; and 80 percent of teenagers regarded verbal abuse as a serious issue for their age group. Ruder Finn helped its client develop a Love Is Not Abuse curriculum for high school students, and released the survey results and new curriculum in October 2005, in partnership with that month's *Marie Claire* magazine. Through newspaper, television, and radio talk show coverage about the new anti-abuse curriculum, the message reached an estimated fifty million people, and a number of schools adopted the curriculum.[16]

Community and Consumer Relations

Two other PR activities involve building relationships between companies and their communities. Companies have learned that sustaining close ties with their neighbors not only enhances their image but also promotes the idea that the companies are good citizens. Such ties expose a business to potential customers through activities such as plant tours, open houses, participation in town parades, and special events such as a company's anniversary.

Besides encouraging client employees to get involved in community activities, many PR firms like their clients to make charitable donations that build local bonds. Some companies offer their work sites to local groups for meetings and help in fundraising efforts. More progressive companies get involved in unemployment and job-retraining programs, and others donate equipment and workers to urban revitalization projects such as Habitat for Humanity.

In terms of customer relations, PR has become much more sophisticated since 1965, when Ralph Nader's *Unsafe at Any Speed* revealed safety problems concerning the Chevrolet Corvair. Nader's book gave General Motors a corporate migraine that resulted in the discontinuance of the Corvair line. More important, however, Nader's book lit the fuse that ignited a vibrant consumerism movement. During the 1960s, consumers became more sophisticated and, consequently, unwilling to readily accept the claims of those in power—including corporate leaders. Another cause of this movement was the trend toward large multinational corporate mergers and the rise of impersonal chain stores, both of which signaled a decreasing accountability to consumers.

For a while, the consumerism movement drew media attention. Many newspapers and TV stations hired consumer reporters, who tracked down the sources of customer complaints and often embarrassed companies by putting them in the media spotlight. Firms that were PR savvy responded by paying more attention to customers, establishing product and service guarantees, and ensuring that all calls and mail from customers were answered promptly. Some companies even produced consumer education literature about specific products and developed close ties with local consumer groups.

Today, the impact of the consumer movement is especially evident in the resources devoted to carefully training employees in good customer relations. Many product and service companies have also developed customer satisfaction questionnaires and "consumer creeds." For example, many restaurants and department stores go beyond asking consumers for advice, outlining what treatment customers

Improving the Credibility Gap

In the 1990s, a growing tide of Americans focused on the problems of outsourcing: using the production, manufacturing, and labor resources of foreign companies to produce American brand-name products, sometimes under deplorable working conditions. Outsourcing was pushed into the public eye in 1996 after major media attention focused on morning talk-show host Kathie Lee Gifford when investigations by the National Labor Committee revealed that part of her clothing line, made and distributed by Wal-Mart, came from sweatshops in New York and Honduras. The sweatshops paid less than minimum wages, and some employed child laborers. Human-rights activists claimed that in overseas sweatshops in particular, children were being exploited in violation of international child-labor laws.

Although some companies like Levi Strauss have distinguished themselves by pioneering public relations programs to guard against sweatshop practices, many leading clothing labels and retailers continue to ignore pressure from consumer and labor groups, and still tolerate sweatshop conditions in which workers take home minimal pay, sometimes less than a dollar an hour for working ten- to twelve-hour shifts six days a week.

In 2004, Gap Inc. — one of the world's largest clothing retailers with more than three thousand Gap, Banana Republic, and Old Navy stores — made a huge statement by publicizing its efforts to watch over labor conditions at its overseas factories — an enormous policy shift from the company's past defensiveness against allegations of worker exploitation. The Gap issued its first Social Responsibility Report in 2004 — the first time any company has ever detailed, and then made transparent, the production and labor information of the factories with which it contracts.

In explaining the genesis of the Social Responsibility Report, Paul Pressler, president and CEO of Gap, noted, "When I decided to join Gap Inc. in the fall of 2002, one of the first things my teenage daughter asked was 'Doesn't Gap use sweatshops?' I was able to tell her how the company was working to fight sweatshop practices and improve garment factory conditions around the world. Her question didn't surprise me, though. Our company hasn't done enough to tell people about our efforts."[1]

The report is Gap's effort toward improved transparency and better communication with its employees, shareholders, and those concerned about garment industry operations. Gap Inc. contracts with about three thousand factories in fifty different countries around the world. According to the report, which involved eighty-five hundred factory visits by the Gap's full-time monitors (as well as other visits by other independent monitors), a full 90 percent of the factories failed to meet minimum employment standards after an initial evaluation. Factories in China fared especially poorly in the report, where incidences of psychological coercion or verbal abuse against factory workers were frequently documented. Also documented were the use of underage workers, abuses of overtime, incidents of indentured labor, unsafe machinery, and forced pregnancy tests.

Beyond issuing the report, Gap has acted on the information by terminating contracts — forty-two in China, forty-two in Southeast Asia, thirty-one in India, and nine in Europe — and has rejected bids of hundreds more. "No garment factory is perfect," the report stated, "but this process helps ensure that we screen out the worst factories and look for those that have the ability to meet our standards." Gap's report isn't just window dressing, but instead a substantial change in how the apparel industry responds to sweatshop abuses. "It is historic," said Nikki Bas of Sweatshop Watch. "It's really a door-opening move toward more disclosure about labor practices." Clearly, however, this report — and Gap's subsequent reports — would never have been written had it not been for consumer complaints about overseas labor conditions and the company's decision to protect the credibility of its brands through proactive public relations efforts.[2]

● The nonprofit Rainforest Action Network uses public relations campaigns to "align the policies of multinational corporations with widespread public support for environmental protection." The group has worked to protect millions of acres of forests in Chile, Brazil, Indonesia, and Canada (*shown above*), and has convinced companies like Home Depot, Citigroup, Boise Cascade, and Goldman Sachs to change their practices.

should expect and what they should do when those expectations are not met. PR professionals routinely advise clients that satisfied customers mean not only repeat business but also new business, based on a strong word-of-mouth reputation about a company's behavior and image.

Government Relations and Lobbying

Public relations also entails maintaining connections with government agencies that have some say in how companies operate in a particular community, state, or nation. The PR divisions of major firms are especially interested in making sure that government regulation neither becomes burdensome nor reduces their control over their businesses. Specialists in this area monitor new and existing legislation, create opportunities to ensure favorable publicity, and write press releases and direct-mail letters to educate the public on the pros and cons of new regulations.

In many firms, government relations has developed into **lobbying**: the process of attempting to influence the voting of lawmakers to support an organization's or an industry's best interests. In seeking favorable legislation, some PR agents lobby government officials on a daily basis. In Washington, D.C., alone, there are more than 34,000 registered lobbyists—at least sixty-three lobbyists for each member of Congress. Lobbying in the U.S. capital has grown rapidly in the past decade, up from 11,000 lobbyists in 1995.[17]

One measure of lobbyists' work is legislative earmarks—specific spending directives slipped into bills to accommodate the interests of lobbyists. Earmarks in legislation jumped from just over 1,000 in 1995 to more than 13,000 in 2005. As the total value of earmarks ballooned into billions, corruption ensued. In fact, the multifaceted scandal linked to lobbyist Jack Abramoff (dubbed "The Man Who Bought Washington" on a *Time* magazine cover in 2006) led to the conviction of Abramoff and several of his associates, the resignation of leading House members, and voter disapproval of Congressional leaders in the 2006 elections.

Another form of public relations lobbying is **astroturf lobbying**, phony grass-roots public affairs campaigns engineered by public relations firms. U.S. senator Lloyd Bentsen of Texas coined the term (named after AstroTurf, the artificial grass athletic field surface) in the mid-1980s when he noticed that a letter-writing campaign to his office was coordinated by industry groups. Public relations firms deploy massive phone banks and computerized mailing lists to drum up support and create the impression that millions of citizens back their client's side of an issue. Astroturf lobbying also includes front groups with friendly sounding names that seem to represent grassroots citizen interests.

One such group, the Center for Consumer Freedom, was created by Washington, D.C.–based Berman & Co. (a PR firm that specializes in astroturf lobbying) and funded by restaurant, food, alcohol, and tobacco industries. According to Sourcewatch .org, which tracks astroturf lobbying, "Anyone who criticizes tobacco, alcohol, fatty foods or soda pop is likely to come under attack from CCF."

Public relations firms work on both sides of an issue, too. In 2005, the California Center for Public Health Advocacy, a nonpartisan, nonprofit organization, hired Brown-Miller Communications, a small California PR firm, to rally support for landmark legislation that would ban junk food and soda sales in the state's public schools. One of the main challenges was to get state legislators to see obesity not as a personal choice issue but as a public policy issue that they could impact. Brown-Miller helped tailor obesity studies for legislators and their districts, and then cultivated the editorial support of newspapers to compel legislators to sponsor the bills. By the end of the year, the legislature approved the bills with broad support, and California became the first state to remove sodas and junk food from its public schools.

Today, most major corporations, trade associations, labor unions, consumer groups, professional organizations, religious groups, and even foreign governments employ lobbyists. For example, the Saudi Arabian government began paying the PR firm Qorvis Communications about $200,000 a month to help repair its image with the American public after the September 11, 2001, terrorism attacks on the United States.[18] The Bush administration also engaged in extensive and sophisticated PR practices with its establishment of the White House Office of Global Communications (OGC) in 2002. The fully staffed bureau was created to repackage the image of U.S. Middle East policies and actions at home and abroad; to streamline the messages emanating from the Pentagon, the State Department, and military command in the Persian Gulf; and to engineer public consent for the U.S. invasion and occupation of Iraq. For example, the OGC spent $200 million in 2002 for a "PR blitz against Saddam Hussein" geared for both U.S. and foreign audiences.[19] The government also awarded public relations companies multimillion-dollar contracts to conduct PR campaigns in Iraq. One government contractor, the Lincoln Group of Washington, D.C., was investigated by the Pentagon in 2006 for misrepresenting its capabilities and connections, and secretly paying Iraqi newspapers to publish stories written by the U.S. military.[20]

> **"** Managing the outrage is more important than managing the hazard. **"**
>
> –Thomas Buckmaster, Hill & Knowlton, 1997

> **"** We're proud of the work we do for Saudi Arabia. It's a very challenging assignment. **"**
>
> –Mike Petruzzello, Qorvis Communications

Tensions between Public Relations and the Press

In 1932, Stanley Walker, an editor at the *New York Herald Tribune,* identified public relations agents and publicity advisers as "mass-mind molders, fronts, mouthpieces, chiselers, moochers, and special assistants to the president."[21] Walker added that newspapers and public relations agencies would always remain enemies, even if PR professionals adopted a code of ethics (which they did in the 1950s) to "take them out of the red-light district of human relations."[22] Walker's tone captures the spirit of one of the most mutually dependent—and antagonistic—relationships across mass media.

Much of this antagonism, directed at public relations from the journalism profession, is historical. Reporters have long considered themselves part of an older public service profession, whereas many regard PR as a pseudo-profession created to distort the facts that reporters work so hard to gather. Over time, reporters and editors developed a nationwide derogatory term for a PR agent—**flack**—which continues in usage to this day. The term derives from the military word *flak,* meaning the antiaircraft artillery shells fired to deflect aerial attack, and from the related flak jacket, the protective military attire worn to ward off enemy fire. For journalists, the word *flack* has come to mean PR people who insert themselves between their employers/clients and members of the press.

In the 1960s, an Associated Press manual for editors defined a flack as "a person who makes all or part of his income by obtaining space in newspapers without cost to himself or his clients." The AP depiction continued: "A flack is a flack. His job is to say kind things about his client. He will not lie very often, but much of the time he tells less than the whole story. You do not owe the PR man anything. The owner of the newspaper, not the flack, pays your salary. Your immediate job is to serve the readers, not the man who would raid your columns." This description, however, belies journalism's dependence on public relations. Many editors, for instance, admit that more than half of their story ideas each day originate with PR people.

Elements of Professional Friction

The relationship between journalism and PR is important and complex. Although journalism lays claim to independent traditions, the news media have become ever more reliant on public relations because of the increasing amount of information now available. Newspaper staff cutbacks, combined with television's need for local news events, have expanded the news media's need for PR story ideas.

Further depleting journalism, PR firms routinely raid the ranks of reporting for new talent. Because most press releases are written in a style that imitates news reports, the PR profession has always sought good writers who are well connected to sources and savvy about the news business. For instance, the fashion industry likes to hire former style or fashion news writers for its PR staff, and university information offices seek reporters who once covered higher education. It is interesting to note that although reporters frequently move into PR, public relations practitioners seldom move into journalism; the news profession rarely accepts prodigal sons or daughters back into the fold once they have left reporting for public relations. According to many reporters and editors, any profession that shapes images is considered manipulative or self-serving—and its practitioners may not be redeemable. Nevertheless, the professions remain co-dependent: PR needs journalists for publicity, and journalism needs PR for story ideas and access. Several historical explanations shed light on this type of discord and on the ways in which different media professions interact.

Undermining Facts and Blocking Access

Modern public relations redefined and complicated the notion of facts. PR professionals demonstrated that the same set of facts can be spun in a variety of ways, depending on what information is emphasized and what is downplayed. As Ivy Lee noted in 1925: "The effort to state an absolute fact is simply an attempt to achieve what is humanly impossible; all I can do is to give you *my interpretation* of the facts."[23] With practitioners like Lee showing the emerging PR profession how facts and news could be manipulated, the journalist's role as a custodian of accurate information became much more difficult. In fact, a 2000 survey of PR professionals gave some credence to public relations' worst image: "25 percent admit to lying on the job, 39 percent say they had exaggerated the truth, and 44 percent were uncertain of the ethics of the task they were required to perform."[24]

Journalists have also objected to PR flacks who block press access to key leaders. At one time, reporters could talk to such leaders directly and obtain quotable information for their news stories. Now, however, PR people insert themselves between the press and the powerful, thus disrupting the old ritual in which reporters would vie for interviews with top government and business leaders. If PR agents today want to manipulate or use reporters, they may give information to journalists who are likely to cast a story in a favorable light in return for getting the information first. On rarer occasions, a reporter's access to key sources might be cut off altogether if that journalist has written unfavorably about a PR agency's client.

Promoting Publicity and Business as News

Another explanation for the professional friction between the press and PR involves simple economics. The trade journal *Editor & Publisher* once called public relations agents "space grabbers"; what editors and publishers feared actually became a reality: PR agents helped companies "promote as news what otherwise would have been purchased in advertising."[25]

As Ivy Lee wrote to John D. Rockefeller after the oil magnate gave money to Johns Hopkins University: "In view of the fact that this was not really news, and that the newspapers gave so much attention to it, it would seem that this was wholly due to the manner in which the material was 'dressed up' for newspaper consumption. It seems to suggest very considerable possibilities along this line."[26] Many newspeople react strongly to this sort of manipulation. Critics worry that public relations is taking media space and time away from those who do not have the financial resources or the sophistication to become readily visible in the public eye. Beyond this lies another issue: If public relations can secure publicity for clients in the news, the added credibility of a journalistic context gives clients a status that the purchase of advertising cannot confer.

Today, however, something more subtle underlies journalism's contempt for public relations: Much of journalism actually functions in the same way. For instance, politicians, celebrities, and PR firms with abundant resources are clearly afforded more coverage by the news media than are their lesser-known counterparts. For example, workers and union leaders have long argued that the money that corporations allocate to PR leads to more favorable coverage for management positions in labor disputes. Standard news reports may feature subtle language choices, with

> **"**We need to amend our work product, to get away from message triangles, hyped-up press releases, and controlling access to our clients.**"**
>
> —Richard Edelman, Edelman CEO, 2006

"rational, cool-headed management making *offers*" and "hot-headed workers making *demands*." Walter Lippmann saw such differences in 1922 when he wrote: "If you study the way many a strike is reported in the press, you will find very often that [labor] issues are rarely in the headlines, barely in the leading paragraph, and sometimes not even mentioned anywhere."[27] Most newspapers now have business sections that focus on the work of various managers, but few have a labor, worker, or employee section. In fact, most large metro papers have eliminated the specialty beat of labor reporting.[28]

Business, economic, and stock "news" reports generated by corporate PR agents inundate newspapers and the evening news. A single business reporter at a large metro daily sometimes receives as many as a hundred press releases a day—far outnumbering the fraction of handouts generated by organized labor or grassroots organizations. This imbalance is particularly significant in that the great majority of workers are neither managers nor CEOs, and yet these workers receive little if any media coverage on a regular basis. Essentially, as a number of critics have pointed out, mainstream journalism best serves managers and the business status quo.

Managing the Press

Public relations, by making reporters' jobs easier, has often enabled reporters to become lazy. PR firms now supply what reporters used to work hard to gather for themselves. Instead of going out to beat the competition, many journalists have become content to wait for a PR handout or a good tip before following up on a story. Small community groups, social activists, and nonprofit organizations often cannot afford elaborate publicity. These groups argue that because of PR, large corporations and well-connected politicians enjoy easier access to reporters and receive much more frequent news coverage. Occasionally, also because of PR, powerful firms and individuals receive less critical scrutiny. Some members of the news media, grateful for the reduced workload that occurs when they are provided with handouts, may be hesitant to criticize a particular PR firm's clients.

Dealing with both a tainted past and journalism's hostility has often preoccupied the public relations profession, leading to the development of several image-enhancing strategies. Over the years, for example, as public relations has subdivided itself into specialized areas, it has used more positive descriptive phrases, such as "institutional relations," "corporate communications," and "news and information services." With the development of its own professional organization in 1948, PRSA (Public Relations Society of America), the PR industry has also enhanced its standing among the public and even the news media.[29] PRSA functions as an internal watchdog group that accredits individuals, maintains a code of ethics, and publishes newsletters and trade publications. Most PRSA local chapters and national conventions also routinely invite reporters and editors to speak to PR practitioners about

● President Bush shakes hands with the two Navy jet pilots who flew him to the USS *Abraham Lincoln* off the coast of California on May 1, 2003, where he announced that major military operations in Iraq were complete. White House spokesperson Ari Fleischer initially reported that the president's voyage to the aircraft carrier "will not be a helicopter arrival, because the ship is so far out at sea." Later it was revealed that use of the combat jet was more theatrical than necessary: The ship was only thirty miles off the coast of San Diego, easily within reach by helicopter.

The landing garnered massive news coverage. But the event (which inspired a Bush action figure) was later used by political opponents as a symbol of failure in Bush's foreign policy.

PRSA Member Statement of Professional Values

This statement presents the core values of PRSA members and, more broadly, of the public relations profession. These values provide the foundation for the Member Code of Ethics and set the industry standard for the professional practice of public relations. These values are the fundamental beliefs that guide our behaviors and decision-making process. We believe our professional values are vital to the integrity of the profession as a whole.

ADVOCACY

We serve the public interest by acting as responsible advocates for those we represent. We provide a voice in the marketplace of ideas, facts, and viewpoints to aid informed public debate.

HONESTY

We adhere to the highest standards of accuracy and truth in advancing the interests of those we represent and in communicating with the public.

EXPERTISE

We acquire and responsibly use specialized knowledge and experience. We advance the profession through continued professional development, research, and education. We build mutual understanding, credibility, and relationships among a wide array of institutions and audiences.

INDEPENDENCE

We provide objective counsel to those we represent. We are accountable for our actions.

LOYALTY

We are faithful to those we represent, while honoring our obligation to serve the public interest.

FAIRNESS

We deal fairly with clients, employers, competitors, peers, vendors, the media, and the general public. We respect all opinions and support the right of free expression.

Source: The full text of the PRSA Code of Ethics is available at http://www.prsa.org.

what the news media expect from their rival professionals. In addition, independent agencies, devoted to uncovering shady or unethical public relations activities, publish their findings in publications like *PR Tactics, PRWeek,* or *PR Watch.* Ethical issues have become a major focus of the PR profession, with self-examination of these issues routinely appearing in PR textbooks as well as in various professional newsletters (see Table 12.1).

Public relations' best press strategy, however, may be the limitations of the journalism profession itself. For most of the twentieth century, many reporters and editors clung to the ideal that journalism is, at its best, an objective institution that gathers information on behalf of the public. Reporters have only occasionally turned their pens, computers, and cameras on themselves to examine their own practices or their vulnerability to manipulation. Thus, by not challenging PR's more subtle strategies, many journalists have allowed PR professionals to interpret "facts" to their clients' advantage.

Limited by its reluctance or failure to identify and evade savvy public relations tactics, conventional journalism remains vulnerable. Consider this hypothetical situation: A wealthy and powerful development corporation decides to raze a homeless shelter to build condos. The firm uses public relations resources that overwhelm the protests of a few homeless activists. The major newspaper in town attempts to remain neutral on the issue. However, the strength of the corporation's PR unit has already tipped the balance of the issue in all of the town's media outlets. To recenter the scales, the newspaper in this case would have to take an advocacy position on behalf of the activists. But in conventional journalism, detachment prohibits this, and thus the corporate point of view typically triumphs—or, at least, gains most of the space and time in the news coverage. Although many alternative newspapers and advocacy reporters do a fine job of critiquing the limits of some questionable public relations activities, conventional journalism has few mechanisms for rebalancing the scales tipped by PR embellishment, whether advanced by government or business leaders.

Alternative Voices

Because public relations professionals work so closely with the press, their practices are not often the subject of media reports or investigations. Indeed, the multibillion-dollar industry remains virtually invisible to the public, most of whom have never heard of Burson-Marsteller, Hill & Knowlton, or Ketchum. John Stauber and Sheldon Rampton, investigative reporters who work for the Center for Media and Democracy in Washington, D.C., are concerned about the invisibility of PR practices and have sought to expose the hidden activities of large PR firms. As editors of *PR Watch,* a quarterly publication they launched in 1995, they publish investigative reports on the PR industry that never appear in mainstream mass media outlets. "*PR Watch* seeks to serve the public rather than PR," they explain. "With the assistance of whistleblowers and a few sympathetic insiders, we report about the secretive activities of an industry which works behind the scenes to control government policy and shape public opinion."[30] (See "Media Literacy and the Critical Process: The Invisible Hand of PR" on opposite page.)

Stauber and Rampton have also written books targeting public relations practices having to do with the Republican Party's lobbying establishment (*Banana Republicans*), U.S. propaganda on the Iraq War (*The Best War Ever*), industrial waste (*Toxic Sludge Is Good for You: Lies, Damn Lies, and the Public Relations Industry*), mad cow disease (*Mad Cow USA: Could the Nightmare Happen Here?*), and PR uses of scientific research (*Trust Us, We're Experts! How Industry Manipulates Science and Gambles with Your Future*). Their work helps bring an alternative angle to the well-monied battles over public opinion. "You know, we feel that in a democracy, it's very, very critical that everyone knows who the players are, and what they're up to," Stauber says.[31]

 ## Public Relations, Social Responsibility, and Democracy

From the days of PR's origins in the early 1900s, many people—especially journalists—have been skeptical of communications originating from public relations professionals. Yet early PR practitioners such as Ivy Lee and Edward Bernays were often very effective, and journalists have grown to rely on the public relations profession for information and ideas. Today, most public relations activity emerges from small

The Invisible Hand of PR

John Stauber, of the industry watchdog *PR Watch,* has described the PR industry as "a huge, invisible industry . . . that's really only available to wealthy individuals, large multinational corporations, politicians and government agencies."[1] How true is this? Is the PR industry so invisible?

Description. We decided to test the PR industry's so-called invisibility to see how often it is discussed in TV news. Using LexisNexis, we searched television, cable, and radio news transcripts over twelve months between 2003 and 2004 for any mention of three PR firms: Weber Shandwick Worldwide, Fleishman-Hillard, and Burson-Marsteller. All are among the largest five PR firms in the world. We found zero stories about Weber Shandwick, forty-one about Fleishman-Hillard, and zero about Burson-Marsteller.

Analysis. What are the patterns that emerged from our search? Foremost is the fact that *no stories* emerged about two of the three PR firms. In the case of Fleishman-Hillard, only twelve of the forty-one stories referencing it had anything to do with the actual business of the firm. (Those twelve stories were brief reports of a decision by the city of Los Angeles to drop its $3.6 million contract with Fleishman-Hillard after it was disclosed that the firm had made large donations to the mayor's election campaign.) Most of the remaining stories were mentions of a Fleishman-Hillard official who appeared as a budget expert on various business programs. Also notable is that most of the stories mentioning Fleishman-Hillard were not in general news programs but instead in business-oriented networks or programs (such as CNBC, PBS's *Nightly Business Report,* and Minnesota Public Radio's syndicated *Marketplace*).

Interpretation. Aside from the LA stories, which were more critical about the mayor than of Fleishman-Hillard, the firms and their practices remain largely invisible to the public. Indeed, the PR industry spends a good deal of effort placing positive stories about its clients in the news media. But clearly, reports *about* the PR industry itself—either positive or negative—do not exist in U.S. broadcast news coverage. Weber Shandwick, Fleishman-Hillard, and Burson-Marsteller alone managed to accumulate more than $10 billion in profits in 2003, but as enormous conglomerates, they are largely hidden from the sight of the American public.

Evaluation. PR firms—such as the heavyweights we examined—have enormous power in influencing the public images (and hence the practices) of both global and local corporations, entire nations, and important public policy initiatives in the United States and abroad. PR firms also have enormous influence over news content, generating tens of thousands of new stories a year. Yet the U.S. mass media are silent on this influence. Public relations firms certainly aren't going to be more public about their power, but should journalism be more public about its role as a publicity vehicle for PR?

Engagement. Visit the Center for Media and Democracy's PRWatch.org Web site and begin to learn about the underworld (and massive influence) of PR. Sign up for the organization's free weekly e-newsletter, the *Weekly Spin.* Read some of the organization's books, join forum discussions, or attend a PRWatch event. Visit the organization's wiki site, sourcewatch.org, and, if you can, do some research of your own on PR and contribute an entry.

in-house services, but the largest corporate clients and governments are usually served by the multinational PR subsidiaries of global communications firms.

Although the image of public relations professionals may not be as negative as that of advertisers, a cynical view of the profession nonetheless exists beyond the field of journalism. Given the history of corporate public relations, many concerned citizens believe that when a company or an individual makes a mistake or misleads the public, too often a PR counsel is hired to alter the image rather than to admit the misdeed and correct the problem. For example, in the aftermath of one of the largest

● Hurricane Katrina slammed into the Gulf Coast on August 29, 2005, creating the worst natural disaster in the nation's history and an unimaginable opportunity for crisis communications. Both Louisiana State University and Tulane University won awards from PRSA in 2006 for their crisis communication efforts after the storm. Tulane's New Orleans campus suffered major damage and used a Web-based strategy to communicate that it had survived the storm and would resume operations as quickly as possible. North of the coast in Baton Rouge, LSU immediately offered its facilities to support the relief effort as a media command center. Both the CBS affiliate in New Orleans and the *New Orleans Times-Picayune* newspaper temporarily relocated to the LSU campus.

environmental disasters of the twentieth century—the *Exxon Valdez* oil spill along the Alaska coast in 1989—the multinational corporation eventually changed the name of the tanker *Valdez* to *Mediterranean* in the 1990s. The name change was just a small tactic in a series of damage-control strategies that Exxon enacted to cope with the oil spill. Disaster management may reveal the worst—or best—attributes of the PR profession. How to enhance a company's image and, at the same time, encourage the company to be socially responsible remains a major challenge for public relations.

The *Exxon Valdez* case was a corporate as well as an environmental disaster, despite the company's outlay of $2 billion to clean up both its image and the spill. When eleven million gallons of crude oil spilled into Prince William Sound, contaminating fifteen hundred miles of Alaskan coastline and killing countless birds, otters,

seals, and fish, Exxon was slow to react to the crisis and even slower to accept responsibility. Although its PR advisers had encouraged a quick response, the corporation failed to send any of its chief officers immediately to the site to express concern. Many critics believed that Exxon was trying to duck responsibility by laying the burden of the crisis on the shoulders of the tanker's captain. A former president of NBC News, William Small, maintained that Exxon "lost the battle of public relations" and suffered "one of the worst tarnishings of its corporate image in American history."[32]

A decidedly different approach was taken in the 1982 tragedy involving Tylenol pain-relief capsules. Seven people died in the Chicago area after someone tampered with several bottles and laced them with poison. Like the oil spill, the case was a major news story. Discussions between the parent company, Johnson & Johnson, and its PR and advertising representatives focused on whether withdrawing all Tylenol capsules might send a signal that corporations could be intimidated by a single deranged person. Nevertheless, Johnson & Johnson's chairman, James E. Burke, and the company's PR agency, Burson-Marsteller, opted for full disclosure to the media and the immediate recall of the capsules nationally, costing the company an estimated $100 million. Before the incident, Tylenol had a market share of 37 percent, making it the leading pain-relief medicine. After the capsule withdrawal, Tylenol's share was cut nearly in half.

As part of its PR strategy to overcome the negative publicity and to restore Tylenol's market share, Burson-Marsteller tracked public opinion nightly through telephone surveys and organized satellite press conferences to debrief the news media. In addition, emergency phone lines were set up to take calls from consumers and health-care providers, who altogether sent two million messages to Johnson & Johnson. When the company reintroduced Tylenol three months after the tragedy began, it did so with tamper-resistant bottles that were soon copied by almost every major drug manufacturer. Burson-Marsteller, which received PRSA awards for its handling of the crisis, found that the public thought Johnson & Johnson had responded admirably to the crisis and did not hold Tylenol responsible for the deaths. In fewer than three years, Tylenol recaptured its former share of the market.

The Exxon and Tylenol incidents—and debates ranging from the value of government PR to the limits of corporate responsibility—demonstrate both dim and bright aspects of public relations, a profession that continues to provoke concern. The bulk of the criticism leveled at public relations argues that the crush of information produced by PR professionals overwhelms traditional journalism. In one example, former president Richard Nixon, who resigned from office in 1974 to avoid impeachment hearings regarding his role in the Watergate scandal, hired Hill & Knowlton to restore his post-presidency image. Through the firm's guidance, Nixon's writings, mostly on international politics, began appearing in Sunday op-ed pages. Nixon himself started showing up on *Nightline* and spoke frequently before groups such as the American Newspaper Publishers Association and the Economic Club of New York. In 1984, after a media blitz by Nixon's PR handlers, the *New York Times* announced: "After a decade, Nixon is gaining favor," and *USA Today* trumpeted: "Richard Nixon is back." Before his death in 1994, Nixon, who never publicly apologized for his role in Watergate, saw a large portion of his public image shift from that of an arrogant, disgraced politician to that of a revered elder statesman.[33] Many media critics have charged that the press did not balance the scales and treated Nixon too reverently after the successful PR campaign.

In terms of its immediate impact on democracy, the information crush delivered by public relations is at its height during national election campaigns. In fact, PR's most significant impact may be on the political process, especially when organizations hire spin doctors to favorably shape or reshape a candidate's media image. In the 2003 special recall election for governor in California, winning candidate Arnold Schwarzenegger used the media to his best advantage by avoiding tough interviews with political journalists and instead arranging interviews with friendly entertainment media. Thus, Schwarzenegger announced his candidacy on *The Tonight Show with Jay Leno* and gave extensive personal interviews with *Access Hollywood*'s Pat O'Brien, Oprah Winfrey, and Howard Stern, while his advisers shielded him from the difficult policy questions of political reporters.

Public relations has long been firmly ensconced in the White House as well. One of George W. Bush's closest advisers both when he was Texas governor and president has been Karen Hughes, his public relations counselor. Many events— from Bush's tee-ball games on the White House lawn to his long summer "working vacations" at his Texas ranch—were engineered by the White House communications staff to create an image that would differentiate Bush from his predecessor, Bill Clinton.

Though public relations often provides political information and story ideas, the PR profession bears only part of the responsibility for manipulating the news media; after all, it is the job of an agency to spin the news favorably for the individual or group it represents. PR professionals often police their own ranks for unethical or irresponsible practices, but the news media should also monitor the public relations industry, as they do other government and business activities. This media vigilance should be on behalf of citizens, who are entitled to robust, well-rounded debates on important social and political issues.

In a democracy, journalism and public relations need to retain their guarded posture toward each other. But journalism itself may need to institute changes that will make it less dependent on PR and more conscious of how its own practices play into the hands of spin strategies. Especially during elections, journalists need to become more vigilant in monitoring questionable PR tactics. A positive example of change on this front is that many major newspapers and news networks now offer regular critiques of the facts and falsehoods contained in political advertising.

Like advertising and other forms of commercial speech, publicity campaigns that result in free media exposure raise a number of questions regarding democracy and the expression of ideas. Large PR agencies and product companies, like well-financed politicians, have money to invest to figure out how to obtain favorable publicity. The question is not how to prevent that but how to ensure that other voices, less well financed and less commercial, receive an adequate hearing. To that end, journalists need to become less willing conduits in the distribution of publicity. PR agencies, for their part, need to show clients that participating in the democratic process as responsible citizens can serve them well and enhance their image.

> **"In politics, image [has] replaced action."**
>
> –Randall Rothenberg, *Where the Suckers Moon*, 1994

www.

For review questions and activities for Chapter 12, go to the interactive *Media and Culture* Online Study Guide at *bedfordstmartins.com/mediaculture*

REVIEW QUESTIONS

Early Developments in Public Relations

1. What did people like P. T. Barnum and Buffalo Bill Cody contribute to the development of modern public relations in the twentieth century?

2. How did railroads and utility companies give the early forms of corporate public relations a bad name?

3. What contributions did Ivy Lee make toward the development of modern PR?

4. How did Edward Bernays affect public relations?

5. What is a pseudo-event? How does it relate to the manufacturing of news?

The Practice of Public Relations

6. What are two approaches to organizing a PR firm?

7. What are press releases, and why are they important to reporters?

8. What is the difference between a VNR and a PSA?

9. What special events might a PR firm sponsor to build stronger ties to its community?

10. Why have research and lobbying become increasingly important to the practice of PR?

Tensions between Public Relations and the Press

11. Explain the historical background of the antagonism between journalism and public relations.

12. How did PR change old relationships between journalists and their sources?

13. In what ways is conventional news like public relations?

14. How does journalism as a profession contribute to its own manipulation at the hands of competent PR practitioners?

Public Relations, Social Responsibility, and Democracy

15. What are some socially responsible strategies that a PR specialist can use during a crisis to help a client manage unfavorable publicity?

16. In what ways does the profession of public relations serve democracy? In what ways can it impede democracy?

QUESTIONING THE MEDIA

1. What do you think of when you hear the term *public relations*? What images come to mind? Where did these impressions come from?

2. What might a college or university do to improve public relations with homeowners on the edge of a campus who have to deal with noisy student parties and a shortage of parking spaces?

3. What steps can reporters and editors take to monitor PR agents who manipulate the news media?

4. Can and should the often hostile relationship between the journalism and PR professions be mended? Why or why not?

5. Besides the *Exxon Valdez* and Tylenol cases cited in this chapter, investigate and research a PR crisis (such as the Bridgestone/Firestone–Ford Explorer tire problems, the mad cow disease beef scare in Europe, the recall of laptop batteries, or any number of campaigns described by PRWatch.org). How was the crisis handled?

SEARCHING THE INTERNET

http://www.prsa.org

The official site of the Public Relations Society of America, the leading U.S. professional PR organization. It provides information on membership, awards, conferences, PR publications, and links to other PR-related sites.

http://www.prssa.org

This site of the Public Relations Student Society of America gives information on local student chapters around the United States.

http://www.prmuseum.com

The Web site for the New York–based museum, which was established in 1997, includes interesting histories of Edward Bernays and other important figures in PR history.

http://www.odwyerpr.com

This site, linked to an influential and independent publisher of PR news and directories of PR firms, in-

cludes information about the field and statistics on numerous firms. Some parts of the site require a fee for access.

http://silveranvil.org

A resource center and archive for case studies of award-winning PR campaigns.

http://www.prwatch.org

This site is the online presence of the Center for Media and Democracy, a nonprofit public interest organization dedicated to investigative reporting on the PR industry.

http://www.sourcewatch.org

Created by the people at the Center for Media and Democracy, this Web site is "a directory of people, organizations, and issues, shaping the public agenda."

In Brief

Imagine that you work for a high-powered PR firm, and a controversial client (e.g., a tobacco company, a pharmaceutical company, the government of Saudi Arabia, etc.) hires your firm to reshape the client's image. To perform this job, what strategies would you employ and why? (Before you begin, your class may want to discuss clients you would refuse to work for.)

In Depth

What influence do press releases have? To find out, track three to five press releases, from the time they are released through any resulting news stories. First, check with a public relations organization that issues releases. For example, you can check with your university's public relations office or the athletic department's sports information office. Both offices may post their press releases on a Web site as well. On the day the press releases are issued, track the local print news stories that are generated. (Alternatively, you could track broadcast news stories.)

Description. Describe your list of stories. How many stories are there? Which newspaper(s) used the press release?

Analysis. What kinds of patterns emerge? Do most publications and broadcasts seem to be willing to print the information in the press release? Did the reporters do any additional investigation, or did they take the point of view of the release? Did certain types of releases fail to get any coverage? What kinds of stories received more prominence and coverage?

Interpretation. What changes, if any, were made between each public relations release and the corresponding news story? Why do you think these changes were made? Do newspapers ever print releases verbatim? Should they? Which version represented the best story—the press release or the news story? Why? (Keep in mind that each story has a different purpose and audience.)

Evaluation. How much should press releases drive a newspaper's coverage of an institution like a local college or university?

Engagement. Are there potentially significant stories on campus that don't get reported because they are not likely to be suggested to the press via a press release? Research some of these ideas, develop the information a little further, and then pitch the story idea to a local newspaper (via phone or e-mail).

KEY TERMS

publicity, 431
public relations, 431
press agents, 432
pseudo-event, 437
propaganda, 440
press releases, 440
video news releases (VNRs), 440

public service announcements
 (PSAs), 440
lobbying, 446
astroturf lobbying, 447
flack, 448

media economics

and the global marketplace

CHAPTER 13

Analyzing the
Media Economy

The Transition
to an Information
Economy

Social Issues in
Media Economics

The Media
Marketplace and
Democracy

Enron, the Houston-based energy trading firm that pumped up its stock price with phony accounting and later collapsed (only after its executives made off with millions of dollars), became the metaphor for a wave of corporate accounting scandals that emerged beginning in 2001.

Then in summer 2005, Bernard Ebbers, founder and CEO of global telecommunications giant WorldCom, was convicted in a record $11 billion fraud case that toppled his company. Late in 2005, former QWEST Communications CEO Joseph Nacchio

was indicted on forty-two federal charges. Earlier that year, QWEST had agreed to pay $250 million to settle fraud charges against the company.

As it turns out, several major media corporations that were reporting on the multibillion-dollar meltdowns of corporations like Enron, WorldCom, and QWEST got "Enronized" themselves. In cable television, Adelphia Communication's founder John Rigas and his son were convicted in June 2005 of looting their cable company and lying about its financial machinations.

↓

The Time Warner Center in New York City.

13

Investors soon lost confidence in the corporations' record profits, CEO salaries, and accounting schemes, shaking the very foundations of global stock markets.

Just a few years earlier, global media corporations giddily tried to outdo each other with rounds of media acquisitions. *Business Week* magazine called them the "moguls who shopped till they dropped."[1] And drop they did.

AOL Time Warner president Bob Pittman, Bertelsmann CEO Thomas Middlehoff, and Vivendi Universal CEO Jean-Marie Messier were all fired, with Messier undergoing the additional consequence of having his home raided by French police investigating his role in the possible falsification of Vivendi Universal accounts to inflate its stock price. Then, in 2003, Steve Case, the embattled chairman of the biggest media firm, AOL Time Warner, resigned in a storm of criticism and federal investigations of his company's finances.

Shortly afterward, Ted Turner—vice chairman of AOL Time Warner and a stern critic of the 2001 AOL–Time Warner merger—resigned as well. Turner's resignation came just after AOL Time Warner announced that its net losses for 2002 totaled nearly $100 billion—the largest corporate loss ever posted in the United States.

Richard Parsons, the new chairman and CEO at AOL Time Warner, vowed to do "no more silly deals" as he attempted to stabilize the giant firm. By the end of 2003, AOL Time Warner's new management elected to return to the original Time Warner name in an attempt to disassociate the corporation's name from mismanagement and its failing AOL brand. Meanwhile, Bertelsmann was left to sell many of its recent acquisitions at below-purchase prices. Vivendi, the French utility company that billed itself as Europe's rival to Time Warner when it bought Universal in 2000, entered 2003 with losses of $25.6 billion (the largest

corporate loss in French history).

The failure of these media conglomerates to capitalize on potential corporate synergies of their far-flung divisions doesn't mean an end to global media empire building, but instead just a reshuffling of the rankings as other media corporations buy up parts of the debt-ridden media conglomerates at discount prices to make themselves larger.

For example, in 2004 Vivendi sold controlling interest in its Universal entertainment assets (except Universal Music) to General Electric. With the acquisition, GE created NBC Universal, a media corporation that instantly vaulted onto the list of the Top 10 largest media firms. And in 2005, Viacom spun off CBS as a separate company (which it had taken over in 1999), but Viacom CEO Sumner Redstone in late 2006 still retained control of 72 percent of CBS Class A stock that had earned a total $24.5 million in 2005.

the rash of media mergers over the last two decades has made our world very distinct from that of earlier generations—at least in economic terms. In this chapter, we will explore the issues and tensions that have contributed to current economic conditions. We will look at the rise of the Information Age, distinguished by flexible, global, and specialized markets. We will discuss the breakdown of economic borders, focusing on media consolidation, corporate mergers, synergy, deregulation, and the emergence of an economic global village. We will also take up ethical and social issues in media economics, investigating the limits of antitrust laws, the concept of consumer control, and the threat of cultural imperialism. Finally, after examining the role of journalism in monitoring media economics, we will consider the impact of media consolidation on democracy and on the diversity of the marketplace.

Analyzing the Media Economy

Given the sprawling scope of the mass media, the study of their economic conditions poses a number of complicated questions. For example, does the government need to play a stronger role in determining who owns what mass media and what kinds of media products should be manufactured? Should the government step back and let competition and market forces dictate what happens to mass media industries? Should citizen groups play a larger part in demanding that media organizations help maintain the quality of social and cultural life? Does the rapid spread of American culture worldwide smother or encourage the growth of democracy and local cultures? Does the increasing concentration of economic power in the hands of several international corporations too severely restrict the number of players and voices in media markets? Answers to such questions span the economic spectrum. On the one hand, critics express concerns about the increasing power and reach of large media conglomerates. On the other hand, many free-market advocates maintain that as long as these structures ensure efficient operation and generous profits, they measure up as quality media organizations. In order to probe economic issues from different perspectives, we need to understand key economic concepts across two broad areas: media structure and media performance.[2]

The Structure of the Media Industry

In economic terms, three common structures characterize the media business: monopoly, oligopoly, and limited competition. First, a **monopoly** occurs when a single firm dominates production and distribution in a particular industry, either nationally or locally. At the national level, for example, until its breakup in the mid-1980s AT&T ran a rare government-approved and -regulated monopoly—the telephone business. Software giant Microsoft, accused of monopolistic practices for controlling

● Richard Parsons, Time Warner chairman and CEO, with Bugs Bunny, part of Time Warner's lucrative Looney Tunes franchise.

❝Unlike American automobiles, television sets, and machine tools, American cultural products—movies, TV programs, videos, records, cassettes, and CDs—are sweeping the globe.❞

–Richard J. Barnet and John Cavanagh, *Global Dreams*, 1994

more than 80 percent of computer operating systems worldwide, was ordered by a federal judge in 2000 to split into two separate companies. But, on appeal, Microsoft ultimately prevailed, and in 2002 it agreed to a court settlement that imposed restrictions on its business dealings with personal computer makers but left the company intact. On the local level, monopoly situations have been more plentiful, occurring in any city that has only one newspaper or one cable company. While the government has (since the 1970s) encouraged owner diversity by prohibiting a newspaper from operating a broadcast or cable company in the same city, many individual local media monopolies have been purchased by national and international firms. For instance, TCI and Time Warner—for years the nation's largest cable operators—own hundreds of small cable monopolies. And in 1999 AT&T swallowed TCI, a multibillion-dollar deal that married the world's largest phone company and the world's largest cable TV operation. Likewise, in the newspaper business, chain operators like Gannett own more than a hundred papers, most of which constitute a newspaper monopoly in their communities.

Second, an **oligopoly** describes an economic situation in which just a few firms dominate an industry. For example, the book publishing and feature-film businesses are both oligopolies. Each has five or six major players that control the production and distribution of the majority of that industry. Three multinational firms—News Corporation, Viacom, and Time Warner—have been major players in both the movie and the publishing oligopolies. Usually conducting business only in response to each other, such companies face little economic competition from small independent firms. Oligopolies often add new ideas and product lines by purchasing successful independents.

Third, **limited competition**, sometimes called *monopolistic competition,* characterizes a media market with many producers and sellers but only a few differentiable products within a particular category.[3] For instance, although the 1996 Telecommunications Act encouraged consolidation by lifting ownership restrictions on radio, hundreds of independently owned stations still operate in the United States. Most of these commercial stations, however, feature a limited number of formats—such as country, classic rock, and contemporary hits—from which listeners may choose. Because commercial broadcast radio is now a difficult market to enter, requiring an FCC license and major capital investment, most station managers play the few formats that attract sizable audiences. Under these circumstances, fans of blues, alternative country, or classical music may not be able to find the radio product that matches their interests. Given the high start-up costs of launching most

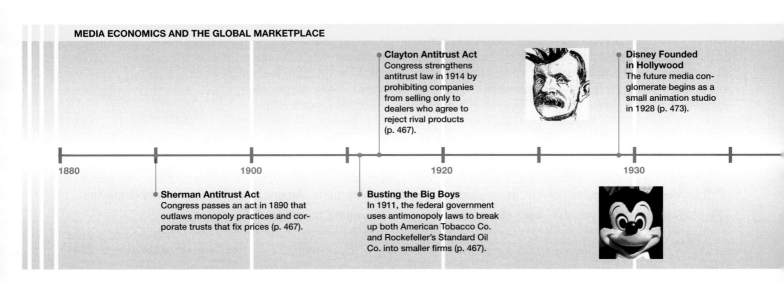

MEDIA ECONOMICS AND THE GLOBAL MARKETPLACE

Clayton Antitrust Act
Congress strengthens antitrust law in 1914 by prohibiting companies from selling only to dealers who agree to reject rival products (p. 467).

Disney Founded in Hollywood
The future media conglomerate begins as a small animation studio in 1928 (p. 473).

1880   1900   1920   1930

Sherman Antitrust Act
Congress passes an act in 1890 that outlaws monopoly practices and corporate trusts that fix prices (p. 467).

Busting the Big Boys
In 1911, the federal government uses antimonopoly laws to break up both American Tobacco Co. and Rockefeller's Standard Oil Co. into smaller firms (p. 467).

commercial media businesses, diverse players offering alternative products are becoming more rare in the twenty-first century.

The Performance of Media Organizations

A second important area in media economics involves analyzing the behavior and performance of media companies. Economists pay particular attention to the two ways the media collect revenues: through direct and indirect methods. **Direct payment** involves media products supported primarily by consumers, who pay directly for a book, a CD, a movie, an Internet service provider, or a cable TV subscription. **Indirect payment** involves media products supported primarily by advertisers, who pay for the quantity or quality of audience members that a particular medium delivers. Over-the-air radio and TV broadcasting, daily newspapers, and consumer magazines rely on indirect payments for the majority of their revenue. Through direct payments, consumers communicate their preferences immediately. Through indirect payments of advertiser-supported media, "the client is the advertiser, not the viewer or listener or reader."[4] Advertisers, in turn, seek media that persuade customers with discretionary income to acquire new products or switch brand loyalty. Many forms of mass media, of course, generate revenue both directly and indirectly, including newspapers, magazines, online services, and cable systems, which charge subscription fees in addition to selling commercial time to advertisers (see Table 13.1 on page 466).

In reviewing other behaviors of the media, economists look at many elements of the commercial process, including program or product costs, price setting, marketing strategies, and regulatory practices. For instance, marketers and media economists determine how high a local newspaper can raise its weekly price before enough disgruntled readers drop their subscriptions and offset the profits made from the price increase. Let's look at another example. In 1996, critics and government agencies began reviewing the artificially inflated price of CDs. They demonstrated that the **economies of scale** principle, which refers to the practice of increasing production levels so as to reduce the overall cost per unit, should have driven down the price of a CD in the same way that the price of blank videotapes and movie videos dropped in the 1980s. Yet it wasn't until October 2003 that any of the five major recording companies dropped their CD prices. At that time, Universal, trying to generate consumer demand in the face of illegal file sharing of music, cut the recommended retail price of music CDs by a third—to $12.98 each.

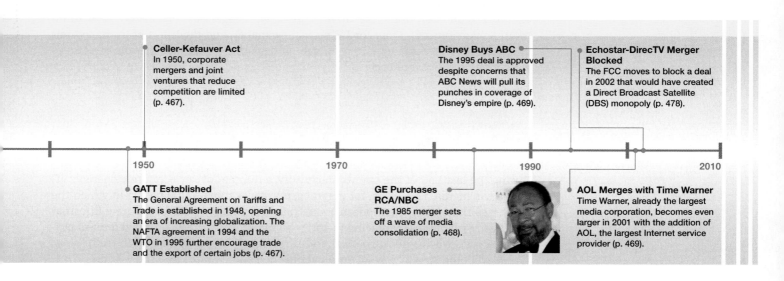

Celler-Kefauver Act
In 1950, corporate mergers and joint ventures that reduce competition are limited (p. 467).

Disney Buys ABC
The 1995 deal is approved despite concerns that ABC News will pull its punches in coverage of Disney's empire (p. 469).

Echostar-DirecTV Merger Blocked
The FCC moves to block a deal in 2002 that would have created a Direct Broadcast Satellite (DBS) monopoly (p. 478).

1950   1970   1990   2010

GATT Established
The General Agreement on Tariffs and Trade is established in 1948, opening an era of increasing globalization. The NAFTA agreement in 1994 and the WTO in 1995 further encourage trade and the export of certain jobs (p. 467).

GE Purchases RCA/NBC
The 1985 merger sets off a wave of media consolidation (p. 468).

AOL Merges with Time Warner
Time Warner, already the largest media corporation, becomes even larger in 2001 with the addition of AOL, the largest Internet service provider (p. 469).

Table 13.1 Consumer Spending per Person per Year on Selected Media, 2003–2007 (in $)

Year	Broadcast Radio/ Television	Cable & Satellite Television/ Radio	Home Video	Movies in Theaters	Recorded Music	Newspapers	Consumer Books	Consumer Magazines	Consumer Internet
2003	0.00	240.90	122.19	39.01	48.73	52.68	89.69	46.08	100.63
2004	0.00	256.51	125.31	38.79	49.39	51.62	89.67	46.88	113.48
2005	0.00	272.50	138.60	38.82	47.65	50.17	91.39	47.82	125.43
2006	0.00	287.60	151.09	39.11	45.77	48.97	91.27	47.59	138.83
2007	0.00	302.93	161.14	39.70	45.35	47.95	93.26	48.50	151.91

Hours per Person per Year Using Consumer Media, 2003–2007

Year	Broadcast & Satellite Radio	Broadcast Television	Cable & Satellite	Home Video	Movies in Theaters	Recorded Music	Daily Newspapers	Consumer Books	Consumer Magazines	Consumer Internet
2003	1,003	696	697	60	13	184	192	109	121	164
2004	986	678	719	67	12	185	188	108	124	176
2005	978	679	733	76	12	179	183	106	124	183
2006	975	684	737	84	12	175	179	106	122	190
2007	974	678	731	91	12	175	175	106	122	195

Source: Veronis Suhler Stevenson Communications Industry Forecast, 2004–05. Years 2005–07 are projections.

Over the years, economists, media critics, and consumer organizations have asked the mass media to meet certain performance criteria. Following are some of the key expectations of media organizations: introducing new technologies to the marketplace; making media products and services available to all economic classes; facilitating free expression and robust political discussion; acting as public watchdogs over wrongdoing; monitoring times of crisis; playing a positive role in education; and maintaining the quality of culture.[5] Although media industries live up to some of these expectations better than others, economic analyses permit consumers and citizens to examine the instances when the mass media fall short. For example, when corporate executives trim news budgets or use one reporter to do multiple versions of a story for TV, radio, newspaper, and the Internet to make their businesses leaner and increase profits, their decision jeopardizes the role of news as watchdog on the rest of society.

The Transition to an Information Economy

During the last half of the twentieth century, a number of key economic changes affected the media. The 1950s, for instance, marked a transitional period in which the machines that drove the modern Industrial Age changed gear in the new Information Age. With offices displacing factories as major work sites, centralized mass production gave way to decentralized and often low-paid service work. Indeed, today, Wal-Mart is the largest private employer in the United States and the world.

A major global change, which continues to unfold, accompanied this transformation. Bolstered by the passage of NAFTA (North American Free Trade Agreement), GATT (General Agreement on Tariffs and Trade), and the WTO (World Trade Organization), which succeeded GATT in 1995, global cooperation fostered the outsourcing of many U.S. jobs and the breakdown of economic borders. Transnational media corporations executed business deals across international terrain. Global companies took over high-profile brand-name industries, particularly the electronic equipment formerly associated with the United States. In 1995, for example, Matsushita, at the time the world's seventeenth-largest company according to *Fortune* magazine, produced VCRs under the General Electric, Magnavox, Sylvania, and J. C. Penney labels.

> **❝ Had anyone in 1975 predicted that the two oldest and most famous corporate producers and marketers of American recorded music [the RCA and CBS labels] would end up in the hands of German printers and publishers [Bertelsmann] and Japanese physicists and electronic engineers [Sony], the reaction in the industry would have been astonishment. ❞**
>
> –Barnet and Cavanagh, *Global Dreams*, 1994

The first half of the twentieth century emphasized mass production, the rise of manufacturing plants, and the intense rivalry of one country's products against another's. The contemporary era, however, emphasizes information distribution and retrieval as well as transnational economic cooperation. The major shift to an information-based economy began in the 1950s as various mass media industries began marketing music, movies, television programs, and computer software on a global level. During this time, the emphasis on mass production shifted to the cultivation of specialized niche markets. In the 1960s, serious national media consolidation began, escalating into the global media mergers of the 1980s and 1990s.

Deregulation Trumps Regulation

During the rise of industry in the nineteenth century, entrepreneurs such as John D. Rockefeller in oil, Cornelius Vanderbilt in shipping and railroads, and Andrew Carnegie in steel created giant companies that monopolized their respective industries. In 1890, Congress passed the Sherman Antitrust Act, outlawing the monopoly practices and corporate trusts that often fixed prices to force competitors out of business. In 1911, the government used the act to break up both the American Tobacco Company and Rockefeller's Standard Oil Company, which was divided into thirty smaller competing firms. In 1914, Congress passed the Clayton Antitrust Act, prohibiting manufacturers from selling only to dealers and contractors who agreed to reject the products of business rivals. The Celler-Kefauver Act of 1950 further strengthened antitrust rules by limiting any corporate mergers and joint ventures that reduced competition. Today, these laws are enforced by the Federal Trade Commission and the antitrust division of the Department of Justice.

In recent decades, government regulation has often been denounced as a barrier to the more flexible flow of capital. Although the Carter administration (1977–81) actually initiated deregulation, under President Reagan (1981–89) most controls on business were drastically weakened. Sometimes the deregulation and the decline in government oversight had severe consequences—such as the savings and loan

● During the late 1800s, John D. Rockefeller, Sr., was considered the richest man in the world, once controlling more than 90 percent of the U.S. oil refining business. But antitrust regulations were used in 1911 to bust Rockefeller's powerful Standard Oil into more than 30 separate companies. He later hired PR guru Ivy Lee to refashion his negative image as a greedy corporate mogul.

industry scandal, which cost consumers billions of dollars—but many businesses flourished in this new pro-commerce climate. Deregulation also led to easier mergers, corporate diversification, and increased tendencies in some sectors (airlines, energy, communications, and financial services) toward oligopolies.[6]

In the broadcast industry, the Telecommunications Act of 1996 lifted most restrictions on how many radio and TV stations one corporation could own. The act further welcomed the seven powerful regional telephone companies, known as the Baby Bells, into the cable TV business. In addition, cable operators not only regained the right to raise cable rates with less oversight but also were authorized to compete in the local telephone business (although high costs kept cable out of the phone business). Economists thought the new competition would bring down consumer prices for a time but would also encourage more mergers and eventually an oligopoly controlling *both* the telephone and the cable industries. This foreshadows a time when two or three megacorporations could control most of the wires entering a home and dictate both phone and cable TV pricing. Indeed, by 2006 the main battle featured phone companies (already permitted by the 1996 Telecommunications Act to buy cable companies)—like the newly remerged AT&T and BellSouth—lobbying for permission to home deliver video and television via phone lines along with the Internet and telephone services. Cable companies fought back, claiming that cable was the one competitor standing in the way of the reemergence of phone giants like AT&T.

Since the 1980s, a spirit of deregulation and special exemptions has guided communication legislation. For example, in 1995, despite complaints from NBC, Rupert Murdoch's Australian company News Corporation received a special dispensation from the FCC and Congress, allowing the firm to continue owning and operating the Fox network and a number of local TV stations. The Murdoch decision ran counter to the government decisions made right after World War I. At that time, the government feared outside owners and limited foreign investment in U.S. broadcast operations to 20 percent. In 2004, News Corporation moved its headquarters to the United States, where the company does about 80 percent of its business. (See "Media Literacy and the Critical Process: Local Newspaper Owners versus 'Absentee Landlords'" on page 475.)

Deregulation has also returned media economics to nineteenth-century principles, which suggest that markets can take care of themselves with little government interference. In this context, one of the ironies in broadcast history is that more than seventy years ago commercial radio broadcasters demanded government regulation to control technical interference and amateur competition. By the mid-1990s, however, the original impetus for regulation had reversed course. With new cable channels and Internet sites, broadcasting was no longer regarded as a scarce resource—once a major rationale for regulation as well as government funding of noncommercial and educational stations. Roughly thirteen thousand U.S. commercial and educational AM and FM stations and seventeen hundred commercial and educational VHF and UHF television stations now operate in U.S. cities.

Consolidation and Mergermania

In spite of the strong antitrust laws of the twentieth century, this legislation has been unevenly and curiously applied, especially in terms of the media. When International Telephone & Telegraph (ITT) tried to acquire ABC in the 1960s, loud protests and government investigations sank the deal. But when General Electric purchased RCA/NBC in the 1980s, the FTC, the FCC, and the Justice Department found few problems. Other actions have been even more significant. Even though the Justice Department broke up AT&T's century-old monopoly in the mid-1980s—creating

> 66 Big is bad if it stifles competition . . . but big is good if it produces quality programs. 99
> —Michael Eisner, CEO, Disney, 1995

> 66 It's a small world, after all. 99
> —Theme song, Disney theme parks

telephone competition—at the same time the government was also authorizing a number of mass media mergers that consolidated power in the hands of a few large companies.

Although the original Big Three TV networks—ABC, CBS, and NBC—constituted a prime-time oligopoly from the 1950s into the 1980s, competition from cable and VCRs changed the economic terrain. Eventually, the government allowed GE to buy back RCA for its NBC network in 1985. Then, in 1996, Microsoft joined with NBC to create a CNN alternative, MSNBC: a twenty-four-hour interactive news channel available on both cable and the Internet.

Among the world's biggest media deals, Disney acquired ABC in 1995 for $19 billion. To ensure its rank as the world's largest media conglomerate, Time Warner countered and bought Turner Broadcasting in 1995 for $7.5 billion. In 2001, Time Warner merged with AOL in the largest media deal in history, worth more than $160 billion. A year later, the federal government approved a $72 billion deal uniting AT&T's cable division with Comcast, creating a cable company twice the size of its nearest competitor (AT&T would later leave the merger).

Until the 1980s, antitrust rules had historically attempted to ensure diversity of ownership among competing businesses. Sometimes this happened, as in the breakup of AT&T, and sometimes it did not, as in the cases of local newspaper and cable monopolies. What has occurred consistently, though, is that media competition has been usurped by media consolidation. Today, the same anticompetitive spirit exists that once allowed a few utility and railroad companies to control their industries—in the days before antitrust laws.

Most media companies have skirted monopoly charges by purchasing diverse types of mass media rather than trying to control just one medium. For example, Disney, rather than trying to dominate one area, provides programming to a TV network, cable channels, and movie theaters. The company evades charges of monopoly by scattering products across many media ventures. In 1995, then Disney CEO Michael Eisner defended the ABC takeover on a number of ABC News shows. According to Eisner, as long as large companies remain dedicated to quality—and as long as Disney did not try to buy the phone lines and TV cables running into homes—such mergers benefit America. But Eisner's position raises questions: If companies cannot make money on quality products, what happens? If ABC News cannot make a substantial profit, should Disney's managers lay off their national or international news staff? How should the government and citizens respond?

Flexible Markets, "Downsizing," and the Wage Gap

In addition to the consolidation trend, today's information culture is also characterized by what business executives call flexibility. It emphasizes "the new, the fleeting . . . and the contingent in modern life, rather than the more solid values implanted" during Henry Ford's day, when relatively stable mass production drove mass consumption.[7] The new elastic economy features the expansion of the service sector (most notably in health care, banking, real estate, fast food, DVD rental, Internet ventures, and computer software) and the search for products to serve individual consumer preferences. This type of economy relies on cheap labor, sometimes exploiting poor workers in sweatshops, and on quick high-volume sales to offset the costs of making so many niche products for specialized markets.

Given that 80 to 90 percent of new consumer and media products typically fail (such as the failure of many dot-com companies), a flexible economy demands rapid product development and efficient market research. Companies need to score a few hits to offset investments in their failed products. For instance, during the peak summer movie season, studios premiere dozens of new feature films. A few are hits but many more miss, and studios hope to recoup their losses via DVD rentals. Similarly, TV networks introduce scores of new programs in the fall and then quickly replace those that fail to attract high numbers or the "right" kind of affluent viewers. At the same time, new music recordings are released daily on radio and in stores, while magazines vie for attention on supermarket shelves and through direct-mail solicitation. This flexible media system, of course, heavily favors large companies with greater access to capital over small businesses that cannot so easily absorb the losses incurred from failed products.

With the advantage to large companies in this flexible age, who is disadvantaged? The U.S. Department of Labor reported in 2005 that "30 million full-time American employees have gotten pink slips" since that department "belatedly started to count them in 1984." This phenomenon has been related to corporate "downsizing"—a euphemism for laying off workers—which is supposed to make companies "more productive, more competitive, more flexible."[8] This trend, spurred by government deregulation and a decline in worker protection, means that many employees today scramble for jobs, often working two or three part-time positions. In his 2006 book, *The Disposable American,* Louis Uchitelle reports that as of 2004 more than 45 percent of U.S. workers earned $13.45 an hour or less—or roughly $26,000 per year at the high end.[9] (Wal-Mart—the nation's largest private employer with 1.4 million workers—reported its average hourly pay in 2005 at $10.11—roughly $20,000 per year.) Uchitelle also noted that two side effects of downsizing include businesses that can no longer compete well because of fewer employees and a decline in innovation. He pointed out that the nation's most successful airline—Southwest—has refused to downsize. With so many workers "downsized," the main beneficiaries have been corporate CEOs—many who have overseen the downsizing. Princeton economist and *New York Times* columnist Paul Krugman reported in 2002 on the growing divide between corporate CEOs and the average worker: "Over the past 30 years most people have seen only modest salary increases: the average annual salary in America, expressed in 1998 dollars (that is, adjusted for inflation), rose from $32,522 in 1970 to $35,864 in 1999. That's about a 10 percent increase over 29 years—progress, but not much. Over the same period, however, according to *Fortune* magazine, the average real annual compensation of the top 100 CEOs went from $1.3 million—39 times the pay of an average worker—to $37.5 million, more than 1,000 times the pay of ordinary workers."[10]

Global Markets and Specialization

The era of downsizing coincided with the decline of workers who belong to labor unions. At their peak in 1955, labor unions represented 35 percent of U.S. workers. According to the U.S. Department of Labor, that figure fell to 20.1 percent in 1983 and 12.5 percent in 2005 (vs. 28.6 percent in Canada). (By 2006 Wal-Mart—a major player in sales of CDs, DVDs, and media electronics—had successfully fought all organized union attempts to represent its employees in its 3,850 U.S. stores; only one North American store—in Ontario, Canada—had managed to organize a union, although Wal-Mart ignored the union in its negotiations with that store's workers.)

With labor unions making strong gains on behalf of workers after World War II and throughout the early 1950s, manufacturers and other large industries began to look for ways to cut the rising cost of labor. With the shift to an information economy, many jobs, such as making CD players, TV sets, VCRs, and DVDs, were exported to avoid the high price of U.S. unionized labor. As large companies bought up small companies across national boundaries, commerce developed rapidly at the global level.

More recently, as global firms sought greater profits, they looked to even less economically developed countries that were short on jobs and lacked national health and safety regulations for workers. But in many cases global expansion by

● *Everybody Hates Chris*

Co-opting Consumers of Color

By Makani Themba-Nixon

They call it penetration—as in market penetration. The tentacles of the transnational mediopolies reach deeper into racial and ethnic communities than ever before. For some, this is a triumph in diversity. Big corporations reaching consumers of color is something they say we should celebrate. However, this market penetration has gone hand in hand with decreasing media ownership by people of color, resulting in loss of industry voice and jobs.

Flagship properties that were once trumpeted as success stories in black ownership—BET and *Essence* magazine—have become little more than shadows of their parent companies. The outlets' makeovers were designed to garner greater "synergy" and brand recognition for their corporate masters. As a result, BET looks more and more like VH1, complete with dog-eat-dog "reality" shows, cloying countdown lists, and decade retrospectives that work to remake history—even black history—into trivia. In fact, BET was the last place to tune in for Black History Month programming. Its main commemorative offering: a VH1 adaptation hosted by comedian Paul Mooney titled *BET's Top 25 Most @#%! Moments in Black History*. To many, it was fitting, as BET regularly programs what some regard as the most @#%! moments in black popular culture.

The remaking of *Essence* magazine has been more subtle. Celebrity profiles and gossipy features increase in page share, à la *People* magazine (both are Time Warner publications), while the names of *Essence* veterans have been disappearing from the masthead—mostly as a result of "restructuring" under editor and *Teen People* import Angela Burt-Murray.

The loss of *Essence*'s expert leadership is but one example of how diversity in staffing (especially at the top) is closely tied to diversity in ownership. According to a 2002 study by the Minority Media and Telecommunications Council, only 4.2 percent of radio outlets are minority-owned,

yet these outlets employ more than half of all the people of color in radio. Fewer minority-owned outlets has meant fewer minorities in media. And changes in regulation, like the elimination of tax incentives for outlet sales to minorities, are making things worse.

Television-staffing diversity has also been taking a real blow, especially since the merger of UPN with WB. According to a forthcoming study commissioned by the Writers Guild of America west, before the merger UPN had the single highest concentration of writers of color—63 percent of television writers of color in 2005–06 were employed by UPN. This was part of a conscious marketing strategy aimed at cornering the young black market to carve out a bankable niche. Some of the most controversial black programming on the air, including a short-lived, much-protested sitcom on slavery, was on CBS-owned UPN. But UPN [has merged] with WB to create a new network called CW. CW's fall scheduling plans show a safe mix of both networks' main stalwarts, which bodes deep cuts in UPN's black programming: Only a few appear to have survived, including *Girlfriends* and *Everybody Hates Chris*.

From Fox Sports en Español to the growing proliferation of affinity groups of color on MySpace (News Corporation's mega "e-community"), there are few spaces that Big Media hasn't invaded. And if that's not enough to keep you up at night, consider this: If public discourse in our communities becomes completely corporatized, what will become of our voices, our points of view, our interests? As history has shown, communities without access to media in their interest are vulnerable indeed.

Source: Makani Themba-Nixon, "The National Entertainment State," *The Nation,* July 3, 2006. Themba-Nixon is executive director of the Praxis Project, a media and policy advocacy center based in Washington, D.C.

U.S. companies ran counter to America's early-twentieth-century vision. Henry Ford, for example, followed his wife's suggestion to lower prices so workers could afford Ford cars. (In fact, with assembly-line production, Ford managed to drop the price of the average Model T from $850 in 1908 to $260 by 1925.) In many countries today, however, most workers cannot afford the stereo equipment and TV sets they are making primarily for U.S. and European markets.

The new globalism has coincided with the rise of specialization. The magazine, radio, and cable industries sought specialized markets both in the United States and overseas, in part to counter television's mass appeal at the national level. By the 1980s, however, even television—confronted with the growing popularity of home video and cable—began niche marketing, targeting eighteen- to thirty-four-year-old viewers, who controlled the bulk of consumer spending. Younger and older audiences were increasingly abandoned by the networks but were sought by other media outlets and advertisers. Magazines such as *Seventeen* and *Modern Maturity* (now *AARP The Magazine*) flourished. Cable channels such as Nickelodeon and the Cartoon Network served the under-eighteen market, while A&E and Lifetime addressed viewers over age fifty and women; in addition, cable channel BET targeted young African Americans, helping to define them as a consumer group for targeting by media outlets. (See "Case Study: Co-opting Consumers of Color" on page 471.)

Beyond specialization and national mergers, though, what really distinguishes current media economics is the extension of **synergy** to international levels. *Synergy* typically refers to the promotion and sale of different versions of a media product across the various subsidiaries of a media conglomerate (e.g., a Time Warner HBO cable special about "the making of" a Warner Brothers movie reviewed in *Time* magazine); however, it also refers to global companies like Sony buying up popular culture—movies studios and record labels—to play on its various electronic products. In Henry Ford's day, national companies competed against one another, and national pride was at stake. "Made in Japan," for instance, went from being a label of inferiority in the 1950s to a mark of superiority in the 1980s, especially in the automobile and electronics industries (for example, Toyota and Sony).

The global extension of America's vast popular media output occurred for a couple of key reasons. First, media technologies became cheaper and more portable, allowing proliferation both inside and outside national boundaries. Audiocassettes and CDs became compact enough to fit into a Sony Walkman, transportable to every room in the house and beyond. Thus, even when U.S. radio stations were not heard outside national borders, American music went everywhere. More recently, the swapping of audio and video files on the Internet (both legal and illegal instances) has expanded the global flow of popular culture. Furthermore, the transmission of visual images via satellite made North American and European TV available at the global level. Cable services such as CNN and MTV quickly took their national acts to the international stage, and by the twenty-first century, CNN and MTV were available in more than two hundred countries.

Second, as we have noted, American VCR, CD, DVD, and TV manufacturers lowered costs by moving production plants outside the country. In addition, global manufacturing permitted companies that lost money on products at home to profit in the international market. About 80 percent of American movies, for instance, do not earn back their costs in U.S. theaters and depend on foreign circulation as well as home video formats to recoup early losses.

In the global television market, certain programs were not particularly successful in the United States but became hits internationally. Consider the 1990s phenomenon *Baywatch*, which went into first-run syndication in 1991 after being canceled by NBC. The program's producers claimed that by the late 1990s *Baywatch*, a show about the adventures of underdressed lifeguards who make beaches safer for everyone, was the most-watched program in the world, with more than a billion viewers. The dialogue in the series, like that of action movies, was limited and fairly simple, making it easy and inexpensive to translate into other languages.

Disney: A Postmodern Media Conglomerate

To understand the contemporary story of media economics, we need only examine the transformation of Disney from a struggling cartoon producer to one of the world's largest media conglomerates. Walt Disney's first cartoon company, Laugh-O-Gram, went bankrupt in 1922, when Disney himself was twenty-one years old. But when Disney moved to Hollywood, he found his niche. After inventing Mickey Mouse (originally named Mortimer) in the first sound cartoons in the late 1920s, Disney developed the first feature-length cartoon, *Snow White and the Seven Dwarfs,* completed in 1937.

The first economic period for the Disney company—roughly from the late 1920s to the late 1940s—set the standard for popular cartoons and children's culture for much of the twentieth century. The *Silly Symphonies* series (1929–39), which featured classic cartoon shorts like "The Three Little Pigs," established the studio's production reputation for quality hand-drawn cartoons. The series ran before feature movies throughout the Great Depression, providing escape, humor, and morality tales. Although Disney remained a minor studio during this period, *Fantasia* and *Pinocchio*—the two top-grossing films of 1940—each made more than $40 million. Nonetheless, the studio barely broke even because cartoon projects took time—four years for *Snow White*—and commanded the company's entire attention.

● Building on the global reach and appeal of its ubiquitous cartoon characters—especially Mickey and Minnie Mouse—Disney opened theme parks in California and Florida as well as Japan, Paris, and Hong Kong. In 2005, 63 million people visited the U.S. parks.

The second Disney period, encompassing the 1950s and early 1960s, was marked by corporate diversification. With the demise of the cartoon film short in movie theaters, Disney expanded into other areas. In 1949, for example, the studio made its first nature documentary short, *Seal Island,* and in 1953 its first feature documentary, *The Living Desert.* In 1950, Disney also produced its first live-action feature, *Treasure Island.*

Disney was also among the first film studios to embrace television. In 1954, the company launched a long-running prime-time show, an even more popular venue than theaters for displaying its products. Then, in 1955, Disneyland opened in Southern California. Eventually, the theme parks would produce the bulk of the studio's revenues (Walt Disney World in Orlando, Florida, began operation in 1971).

In 1953, Disney started Buena Vista, its own distribution company. This was the first step in making the studio into a major player. The company also began exploiting the power of its early cartoon features. *Snow White,* for example, was successfully rereleased in theaters to new generations of children before going to videocassette.

In 1966, the death of Walt Disney triggered a period of decline for the studio. But in 1984 a new management team, led by Michael Eisner, initiated the third Disney period. Eisner inherited Disney's newly created Touchstone division, and its *Who Framed Roger Rabbit?* (1988) reinvented the live-action cartoon for adults as well as children. A string of hand-drawn animated hits followed, including *The Little Mermaid* (1989), *Beauty and the Beast* (1991), *The Lion King* (1994), *Mulan* (1998), *Fantasia 2000,* and *Lilo + Stitch* (2002). In a rocky partnership with Pixar Animation Studios, Disney also distributed a string of computer-animated blockbusters, including *Toy Story* (1995), *Monsters, Inc.* (2001), *Finding Nemo* (2003), *The Incredibles* (2004), and *Cars* (2006).

Although some critics regard synergy as a monopolistic practice, Disney epitomizes the synergistic possibilities of media consolidation. Disney can produce an animated feature for both theatrical release and DVD distribution. With its ABC network (purchased in 1995), it can spin off a cartoon version of the movie and place it on ABC's Saturday-morning schedule. A book version can be released through Disney's publishing arm, Hyperion, and "the-making-of" versions can appear on cable's Disney Channel or ABC Family, as well as in *Disney Adventures,* the company's popular children's magazine. Characters can become attractions at Disney's theme parks, which themselves have spawned Hollywood movies like the *Pirates of the Caribbean* movies (2003, 2006, 2007). Some Disney films have had upwards of seventeen thousand licensed products from clothing to toys to dog food bowls.

Throughout the 1990s, Disney continued to find new sources of revenue in both entertainment and distribution. Through its purchase of ABC, Disney also became the owner of the cable sports channels ESPN and ESPN2, and later expanded the brand with ESPNews and ESPN Classic channels, *ESPN The Magazine,* ESPN Radio, ESPN.com, and ESPN Zone, a sport-theme restaurant chain. Building on its sports interests, Disney bought—and later sold—both the NHL's Mighty Ducks and Major League Baseball's Angels, both located in Anaheim, near Disneyland. Across the country in New York, Disney renovated several theaters and launched theater versions of *Beauty and the Beast* and *The Lion King* as successful Broadway musicals.

Building on the international appeal of its cartoon features, in 1983 Disney extended its global reach by opening a successful theme park in Japan. In 1986, the company started marketing cartoons to Chinese television, attracting an estimated 300 million viewers per week. This stopped in 1990 because of the rampant counterfeiting in China of Disney-trademark products, but the studio resumed the deal in 1992. Disney also started a magazine in Chinese, opened several Disney stores and a theme park in Hong Kong, and signed a deal with Russian television, which began showing six hours of Disney programming each week. Disney received exclusive rights to sell ads during those programs.

In 1991, EuroDisney (now called Disneyland Paris) opened outside Paris. The French, though, did not eagerly embrace the theme park. It lost millions each month, well into the mid-1990s, before finally making money. Many Europeans continued to criticize the company for pushing out and vulgarizing classical culture. On the home front, a proposed historical park in Virginia, Disney's America, suffered defeat at the hands of citizens who raised concerns about Disney misinterpreting or romanticizing American history. Meanwhile, in 1995, shortly after the company purchased ABC, Disney suffered criticism for running a flattering company profile one evening on ABC's evening news program.

Despite criticism, little seemed to slow Disney's global expansion. Indeed, in 1997 Orbit—a Saudi-owned satellite relay station based in Rome—introduced Disney's twenty-four-hour premium cable channel to twenty-three countries in the

> **"In the States, going to Disneyland is a secular rite of passage, like visiting Mecca."**
>
> —Simon Hoggart, the *Guardian*, 1999

Local Newspaper Owners versus "Absentee Landlords"

Do newspaper media companies better serve communities when they are owned and operated by local area publishers? Investigate a national media company that owns or has recently bought local or smaller newspapers. This could be a newspaper chain like Gannett or McClatchy or News Corporation. Choose one paper and find out what it is doing to serve the town. (See if your hometown has a newspaper you can study.) If possible, find out what the local paper was like before the national media company came to town. Did the company make the paper better or worse, or did it stay the same? Use the five steps of the critical process for your investigation.

Description. Do a LexisNexis search and locate recent articles on your company. Find out in general what they own and where. Read the local paper for a three-day period and log a typical day's news coverage. Create categories of news and information based on what you read. How much local information is there? Also, log the ads: Are they local or national? What kinds of products and services are advertised?

Analysis. What patterns did you find in your company's coverage of the local community? What kinds of news are offered and what kinds of information are available about local events? Are things missing from the coverage? Are there patterns in the advertising?

Interpretation. Based on what you have discovered, what does it mean? Can you make an argument about whether or not the community is being well served by the national media company? If there is a local news company, is it serving the community well? Provide evidence.

Evaluation. Based on what you have found, is the company running the local paper doing a good or bad job? What is it doing well? What suggestions would you make to improve local coverage of news?

Engagement. Here you might do one or more of the following using face-to-face, phone, or e-mail interviews. Track down editors who manage the local paper. Ask them how well they think they are serving the local community. If they are working for a local publisher or owner, how do the owners influence the paper? If they work for national companies, what are those owners doing to support the local communities and employees?

If possible, interview people in the community who can offer critiques of the newspaper before and after the ownership may have changed. If the national company has been there a long time, interview a cross section of people and find out what they think about how the local paper is serving the community. Do you see any discrepancy or disconnect between what the community residents told you and what the local paper's managers told you about how the community is being served?

Middle East and North Africa. In the book *Global Dreams*, the authors set forth a formula for becoming a "great media conglomerate," a formula that Disney exemplifies: "Companies able to use visuals to sell sound, movies to sell books, or software to sell hardware would become the winners in the new global commercial order."[11] But even as Disney grew into the world's No. 2 media conglomerate in the early 2000s, the once proud cartoon pioneer experienced the multiple shocks of a recession, failed films and Internet ventures, expensive salaries for pro athletes, and declining theme park attendance. In addition, CEO Eisner's business moves had damaged Disney's relationships with a number of partners and subsidiaries, including Pixar (which had surpassed Disney in making highly profitable animated cartoons) and the film studio Miramax, which had produced a string of Oscar-winning movies, including *Shakespeare in Love, Chicago,* and *The Aviator.* In 2004 Eisner and Disney refused to distribute Michael Moore's controversial documentary *Fahrenheit 9/11* on the Iraq war, which Miramax financed (and eventually partnered with another distributor); the movie cost $7 million to make and went on to earn $119 million in U.S. theaters. By 2005, Disney had fallen to No. 5 among movie studios in U.S. box office sales—down from No. 1 in 2003. A divided and unhappy board of directors forced Eisner out in 2005 after twenty-one years as CEO.[12] In 2006, new CEO Robert Iger merged Disney with Pixar, making Pixar and Apple Computer founder and CEO Steve Jobs a Disney board member and its largest shareholder.

Social Issues in Media Economics

In recent years, we have witnessed billion-dollar takeovers and mergers between Time Inc. and Warner Communication, Viacom and Paramount, Disney and ABC, Viacom and CBS, Time Warner and Turner, AOL and Time Warner, AT&T and Bell South, UPN and the WB, and GE and Universal. This mergermania accompanied stripped-down regulation, which has virtually suspended most ownership limits on media industries. As a result, a number of consumer advocates and citizen groups have raised questions about deregulation and ownership consolidation.

One longtime critic of media mergers, Ben Bagdikian, author of *Media Monopoly*, has long argued that although there are abundant products in the market—"1,700 daily papers, more than 8,000 weeklies, 10,000 radio and television stations, 11,000 magazines, 2,500 book publishers"—only a limited number of companies are in charge of those products.[13] Bagdikian and others fear that this represents a dangerous anti-democratic tendency in which a handful of media moguls wield a disproportionate amount of economic control. (See "Case Study—From Fifty to a Few: The Most Dominant Media Corporations" on opposite page.)

The Limits of Antitrust Laws

The current consolidation of media owners has limited the number of independent voices and owners. Although meant to ensure multiple voices and owners, American antitrust laws have been easily subverted since the 1980s. As we have noted, most media companies diversify among different products, never fully dominating a particular media industry. Time Warner, for example, spreads its holdings among television programming, film, music, publishing, cable, and its Internet divisions. The media giant really only competes with a few other big companies.

Such diversification strategies, of course, promote oligopolies in which a few behemoth companies control media production and distribution. This kind of economic arrangement makes it difficult for many products—especially those offered outside an oligopoly—to compete in the marketplace. For instance, in broadcast TV, the few networks that control prime time—all of them now owned by film companies—offer programs that are selected from known production companies that the networks either contract with regularly or own outright. Thus even with a very good program or series idea, an independent production company, especially one that operates outside Los Angeles or New York, has a very difficult time entering the national TV market. The film giants even prefer buying from each other before dealing with independents.

Occasionally, independent voices raise issues that aid the Justice Department and the FTC in their antitrust cases. For example, when Echostar proposed to purchase DirecTV in 2001, a number of rural, consumer, and Latino organizations spoke out against the merger for a number of reasons. Latino organizations opposed the

From Fifty to a Few:
The Most Dominant Media Corporations

When Ben Bagdikian wrote the first edition of *The Media Monopoly,* published in 1983, he warned of the chilling control wielded by the fifty elite corporations that owned most of the U.S. mass media. By the publication of the book's seventh edition in 2004, the number of corporations controlling most of America's daily newspapers, magazines, radio, television, books, and movies had dropped from fifty to five: Time Warner, the Walt Disney Company, News Corporation, Viacom, and Bertelsmann. (Our own calculations would include Sony Corporation of America—the U.S. division of the Japanese conglomerate—in the elite group.) Some other companies are edging closer to the top few. General Electric (GE), for example, now has substantial media properties in its NBC Universal division, after recently combining its existing media holdings, such as NBC and various cable networks, with Universal's movie studios and television production and amusement park units. Most of the leading corporations have a high profile in the United States, particularly through ownership of television networks: Time Warner (WB), Disney (ABC), News Corporation (Fox), Viacom (CBS and UPN), and GE/NBC Universal (NBC).

The newspaper and magazine industries are somewhat less consolidated because of the great number of publications, but the trend toward greater consolidation is the same. In the newspaper industry, there are about 1,500 daily papers, but about two dozen large corporations like Gannett, the Tribune Company, and the New York Times Company dominate. Much of the magazine industry, with more than 12,000 commercial titles, is controlled by familiar corporations, particularly Time Warner, which owns titles such as *People, Sports Illustrated,* and *Time.*

The creep of consolidation over the past few decades requires us to think differently about how we experience the mass media on a daily basis. Potential conflicts of interest abound. For example, should we trust how NBC News covers GE or how ABC News covers Disney? Should we be concerned with the political tone of News Corporation's White House coverage (that is, on the Fox News Channel and in the *New York Post*) while the FCC is considering regulatory limits on media ownership? Should we be wary if *Time* magazine hypes a Warner Brothers film? More importantly, what actions can we take to ensure that the mass media function not just as successful businesses for stockholders but also as a necessary part of our democracy?

Most of the large media companies have been profiled in earlier chapters in the Media Ownership charts that illustrate these media companies' principal U.S. holdings. While the subsidiaries of these companies often change, the charts demonstrate the wide reach of large conglomerations. To get a better understanding of the largest media corporation, Time Warner, see its Media Ownership chart in the folded insert at the beginning of the book.

● Top 10 U.S. Media Companies, 2005			
Rank	Media Company	Net Media Revenue (in $billions)	% Increase
1	Time Warner	$37.0	6.6
2	Viacom	21.5	9.3
3	Comcast Corp.	20.1	10.9
4	Walt Disney Co.	17.4	6.8
5	NBC Universal (General Electric Co.)	12.5	14.3
6	News Corp.	11.4	8.7
7	DirecTV Group	9.8	26.9
8	Cox Enterprises	8.6	9.9
9	EchoStar Communications Corp.	6.7	23.4
10	Clear Channel Communications	6.5	5.7

Source: "Fact Pack 2006," *Advertising Age,* www.adage.com/datacenter, accessed August 2006.

> **"** [AOL Time Warner] turned into one of the biggest corporate disasters in U.S. history: America Online's business collapsed, synergies failed to materialize, the company missed its financial targets, and the stock price plunged. **"**
>
> – *Wall Street Journal*, 2003

merger because in many U.S. markets Direct Broadcast Satellite (DBS) service offers the only available Spanish-language television programming. The merger would have left the United States with just one major direct satellite broadcasting company, a virtual DBS monopoly for Echostar, which historically had fewer Spanish-language offerings than DirecTV. In 2002, the FCC declined to approve the merger, saying it would not serve the public interest, convenience, and necessity.

Because antitrust laws aim to curb national monopolies, most media monopolies today operate locally. For instance, although Gannett owns more than ninety daily newspapers, it controls less than 10 percent of daily U.S. newspaper circulation. Nonetheless, almost all Gannett papers are monopolies: They are the only papers in their various towns. Virtually every cable company has been granted monopoly status in its local community; these firms alone often decide which channels are made available and what rates are charged. Furthermore, antitrust laws have no teeth globally. Although international copyright laws offer some protection to musicians and writers, no international antitrust rules exist to prohibit transnational companies from buying up as many media companies as they can afford.

Consumer Choice versus Consumer Control

During the wave of mergers in the 1980s and 1990s, a number of consumer critics pointed to the lack of public debate surrounding the tightening oligopoly structure of international media. This lack of public involvement dates from the 1920s and 1930s. In that era, commercial radio executives, many of whom befriended FCC members, succeeded in portraying themselves as operating in the public interest while labeling their noncommercial counterparts in education, labor, or religion as mere voices of propaganda. In these early debates, the political ideas of democracy became closely allied with the economic structures of capitalism.

> **"** What they were really looking forward to was creating the biggest shopping mall in the world. **"**
>
> – Ben Bagdikian, author of *Media Monopoly*, on the AOL– Time Warner merger, 2000

Throughout the Cold War period in the 1950s and 1960s, it became increasingly difficult to even criticize capitalism, which had become a synonym for democracy in many circles. In this context, any criticism of capitalism became an attack on the free marketplace. This, in turn, appeared to be a criticism of free speech, because the business community often sees its right to operate in a free marketplace as an extension of its right to buy commercial speech. As longtime CBS chief William Paley told a group of educators in 1937: "He who attacks the fundamentals of the American system" of commercial broadcasting "attacks democracy itself."[14] Broadcast historian Robert McChesney, discussing the rise of commercial radio in the 1930s, has noted that leaders like Paley "equated capitalism with the free and equal marketplace, the free and equal marketplace with democracy, and democracy with 'Americanism.'"[15] The collapse of the former Soviet Union's communist economy in the 1990s is often portrayed as a triumph for democracy. As we know today, it was primarily a victory for capitalism and free-market economies.

As many economists point out, capitalism is arranged vertically, with powerful corporate leaders at the top and hourly wage workers at the bottom. But democracy, in principle, represents a more horizontal model in which each individual has an opportunity to have his or her voice heard and vote counted. In discussing free markets, economists also distinguish between *consumer control* over marketplace goods and freedom of *consumer choice*: "The former requires that consumers participate in deciding what is to be offered; the latter is satisfied if [consumers are] free to select among the options chosen for them by producers."[16] Most Americans and the citizens of other economically developed nations clearly have options among a range of media products. Yet consumers and even employees have limited power in deciding what kinds of media get created and circulated.

Cultural Imperialism

The influence of American popular culture has created considerable debate in international circles. On the one hand, the notion of freedom that is associated with innovation and rebellion in American culture has been embraced internationally. The global spread of media software and electronic hardware has made it harder for political leaders to secretly repress dissident groups because so much police and state activity (such as the 1989 student uprising and massacre in China) can now be documented on video and dispatched by satellite, Internet, and cell phones around the world. On the other hand, American media are shaping the cultures and identities of other nations. American styles in fashion and food, as well as media fare, dominate the global market—what many critics have identified as **cultural imperialism**. Today, numerous international observers contend that the idea of consumer control or input is even more remote in countries inundated by American fashion, food, movies, music, and television. Even mainstream U.S. newspapers report with skepticism on the 470,000 Brazilian Avon

Der coolste Job in
New York ist im
Vorzimmer
der Hölle.

Meryl
STREEP
Anne
HATHAWAY

DER
TEUFEL
TRÄGT
PRADA

Dieser Kinoherbst
wird höllisch trendy.

● Ever since Hollywood gained an edge in film production and distribution during World War I, U.S. movies have dominated the box office in Europe, in some years accounting for more than 80 percent of the revenues taken in by European theaters.

"beauty consultants," many of whom travel the backwaters of the Amazon jungle selling American cosmetics to women who can barely afford shoes.

Although many indigenous forms of media culture—such as Brazil's *telenovela* (a TV soap opera), Jamaica's reggae, and Ireland's Riverdance—are extremely popular, U.S. dominance in producing and distributing mass media puts a severe burden on countries attempting to produce their own cultural products. For example, American TV producers have generally recouped the costs of production in national syndication by the time their TV shows are exported. This enables American distributors to offer these programs to other countries at bargain rates, thereby undercutting local production companies trying to create original programs in their own language.

Defenders of American popular culture argue that because some of our culture challenges authority, national boundaries, and outmoded traditions, this creates an arena in which citizens can raise questions. Supporters also argue that a universal popular culture creates a global village and fosters communication across national boundaries. Critics, however, believe that although American popular culture often contains protests against social wrongs, such protests "can be turned into consumer products and lose their bite. Protest itself becomes something to sell."[17] The harshest critics have labeled American culture in the international arena a kind of cultural imperialism that both hampers the development of native cultures and negatively influences teenagers, who abandon their own rituals to adopt the tastes of their American counterparts. The exportation of U.S. entertainment media is sometimes viewed as "cultural dumping," because it discourages the development of original local products.

Perhaps the greatest concern regarding a global economic village is elevating expectations among people whose standards of living are not routinely portrayed in contemporary media. In 2005, about two-thirds of the world's population could not afford most of the products advertised on American, Japanese, and European television. Yet more and more of the world's populations were able to glimpse consumer abundance and middle-class values through satellite television and magazine distribution. Media managers as early as the 1950s feared political fallout—"the revolution of rising expectations"—in that ads and products would raise the hopes of poor people but not keep pace with their actual living conditions.[18] Furthermore, the conspicuousness of consumer culture makes it difficult for many of us to even imagine other ways of living that are not heavily dependent on the mass media and brand-name products.

The Media Marketplace and Democracy

In the midst of today's major global transformations of economies, cultures, and societies, the best way to monitor the impact of transnational economies is through vigorous news attention and lively public discussions. Clearly, however, this process is hampered. In the 1990s, for example, news organizations, concerned about the bottom line, severely cut back the number of reporters assigned to cover international developments. This occurred—especially after 9/11—just as global news became critical to an informed citizenry. We live in a society in which consumer concerns, stock market quotes, and profit aspirations, rather than broader social issues, increasingly dominate the media agenda. In response, critics have posed some key questions: As consumers, do we care who owns the media so long as most of us have a broad selection of products? Do we care who owns the media so long as multiple voices *appear* to exist in the market?

Merged and multinational media corporations will continue to control more aspects of production and distribution. Of pressing concern is the impact of mergers on news operations, particularly the influences of large corporations on their news subsidiaries. These companies have the capacity to use major news resources to promote their products and determine national coverage.

Because of the growing consolidation of mass media, it has become increasingly difficult to sustain a public debate on economic and ownership issues. From a monetary exchange perspective, the relationship of our mass media system to politics is highly functional. From a democratic perspective, the relationship of our mass media system to politics is highly dysfunctional. Politicians in Washington, D.C., regularly accept millions of dollars in contributions from large media conglomerates and their lobbying groups in order to finance their campaigns to stay in power. Those same media conglomerates use their money to influence deregulation that enables them to grow larger and be subjected to fewer civic rules.

Politicians then turn to the local television stations of many of the same media conglomerates and spend record amounts during each election period to get their political ads on the air. By 2000, politicians had become the third-best advertising client for network-affiliated local TV stations, just behind automobiles and retail

> 66 The top management of the networks, with a few notable exceptions, has been trained in advertising, research, or show business. But by the nature of the corporate structure, they also make the final and crucial decisions having to do with news and public affairs. Frequently they have neither the time nor the competence to do this. 99
>
> —Edward R. Murrow,
> broadcast news pioneer, 1958

stores. In 2004, with the unprecedented spending of the Bush/Kerry presidential campaign leading the way, local TV stations reaped an estimated $1.6 billion from political advertising. But, although broadcasters have been happy to take political ad money, they have been poor public citizens: In the weeks leading up to Election Day, more than 80 percent of local top-rated TV news broadcasts contained at least one political ad, but only 44 percent of the broadcasts contained any campaign coverage at all.[19] Yet, because the mass media system largely works to sustain those in power, there is not much incentive for those in power to change things.

One promising spot in the current economic atmosphere concerns the role of independent and alternative producers, artists, writers, and publishers. Despite the movement toward economic consolidation, the fringes of the media industry still offer a diversity of opinions and ideas. In fact, when independent views become even marginally popular, they are often pursued by large media companies that seek to make them subsidiaries or to capitalize on their innovations. Alternative voices in the mass media often tap into social concerns that are not normally discussed in corporate boardrooms. Moreover, business leaders "at the top" depend on independent ideas "from below" to generate new product lines. A number of transnational corporations encourage the development of local artists—talented individuals who might have the capacity to transcend the regional or national level and become the next global phenomenon.

One key paradox of the Information Age is that for economic discussions to be meaningful and democratic, they must be carried out in the popular media as well as in educational settings. Yet public debates about the structure and ownership of the media are often not in the best economic interests of media owners. Nonetheless, in some places, local groups and consumer movements are addressing media issues that affect individual and community life. Such movements—like the November–December 1999 Seattle protests against the World Trade Organization and subsequent protests at WTO and World Bank meetings around the globe—may be united by geographic ties, by common ethnic background, or by shared concerns about politics or technology. The Internet has made it possible for such groups to form globally, uniting around such issues as contesting censorship or monitoring the activities of multinational corporations.

Perhaps we are ready to question some of these hierarchical and undemocratic arrangements. Even in the face of so many media mergers, the public arena today seems open to such examinations, which might improve the global economy, worker conditions, and also serve the public good. By better understanding media economics, we can make a contribution to critiquing media organizations and evaluating their impact on democracy.

● Bill Moyers, one of the most recognized and respected journalists in the United States, founded *NOW,* an hour-long PBS weekly news series offering fresh perspectives and analysis on today's events, issues, and the ideas that are shaping our world.

NOW, created by Moyers's production company Public Affairs Television and hosted by David Brancaccio, has been one of the few broadcast news programs to discuss media economics on a regular basis. While most of the commercial news media have ignored the increasing consolidation and deregulation of ownership restrictions in the media, *NOW* has kept a constant watch on the story and has taken time to explain its ramifications.

www.

For review questions and activities for Chapter 13, go to the interactive *Media and Culture* Online Study Guide at *bedfordstmartins.com/ mediaculture*

REVIEW QUESTIONS

Analyzing the Media Economy

1. How are the three basic structures of mass media organizations—monopoly, oligopoly, and limited competition—different from one another?

2. What are the differences between direct and indirect payments for media products?

3. What are some of society's key expectations of its media organizations?

The Transition to an Information Economy

4. Why has the federal government emphasized deregulation at a time when so many media companies are growing so large?

5. How have media mergers changed the economics of mass media?

6. How do global and specialized markets factor into the new media economy? How are regular workers affected?

7. Using Disney as an example, what is the role of synergy in the current climate of media mergers?

Social Issues in Media Economics

8. What are the differences between freedom of consumer choice and consumer control?

9. What is cultural imperialism, and what does it have to do with the United States?

The Media Marketplace and Democracy

10. What do critics and activists fear most about the concentration of media ownership? How do media managers and executives respond to these fears?

11. What are some promising signs regarding the relationship between media economics and democracy?

QUESTIONING THE MEDIA

1. Are you exposed to popular culture from other countries? Why or why not? Give some examples.

2. Do you read international news? Why or why not?

3. What steps can reporters and editors take to cover media ownership issues in a better way?

4. How does the concentration of media ownership limit the number of voices in the marketplace? Do we need rules limiting media ownership?

5. Is there such a thing as a global village? What does this concept mean to you?

SEARCHING THE INTERNET

http://www.vss.com

Site for Veronis Suhler Stevenson, a leading research and investment firm devoted to publishing, broadcasting, cable, and new media industries.

http://www.hoovers.com

Site for Hoover's Inc., a Texas-based company devoted to tracking the nation's largest industries, including media; features links to related sites.

http://www.mediainfo.com

Site for *Editor & Publisher,* the trade publication for the newspaper industry; provides statistics and links to other companies.

http://www.cjr.org/tools/owners

The *Columbia Journalism Review*'s "Who Owns What" site, which lists the holdings of more than forty major media corporations.

http://www.fortune.com

This site provides overviews and summaries of revenues, assets, and other data on Fortune 500 companies.

http://www.aflcio.org/corporateamerica/paywatch

Part of the AFL-CIO labor-union site, PayWatch keeps track of the top U.S. CEOs' salaries.

http://www.usdoj.gov/atr/

The Antitrust Division of the U.S. Department of Justice, which includes current antitrust case information and antitrust laws.

Media Literacy
and the Critical Process

In Brief

Imagine that you are either a small independent record label or a book publisher. You have produced a high-quality product, but it has limited appeal. Without relying on signing distribution agreements with giant companies, how might you go about creating a market for your product and reaching the audience that might be interested in your product? Be specific.

In Depth

This project will help you get to know the small number of media corporations that control so much of U.S. and global culture, and help you understand what this influence may mean for democracy.

Description. Visit the "Who Owns What?" Web site (http://www.cjr.org/tools/owners/) and choose a media conglomerate to research (your instructor may also assign one to you). Then do more research by looking at news stories on Web sites like Lexis-Nexis, the corporation's own Web site, the corporation's annual reports, Web sites such as www.freepress.org, and the Federal Communication Commission's www.fcc.gov site (since big media corporations continually have business before the FCC).

1. Describe the company's history: When and how did it get so big?

2. Find out where the company is headquartered, where its many divisions are located, and where its products are distributed to get a general idea of the company's global expansiveness.

3. Note the company's latest revenue data and current standing among competitors.

4. Describe the company's chairperson and CEO, and, if relevant, the chairperson/CEO before the current ones. What are their credentials?

5. List all the company's many subsidiaries.

6. Describe the company's corporate values. What terms does the company's corporate Web site use to describe itself? How do descriptions directed to the general public differ from descriptions directed to shareholders? What can you learn from the company's latest annual report (usually located under "investor information" or "financial data" on the corporate Web site). What are some specific strategies for the company's future growth?

7. Go through a broad range of news reports about the company (independent media as well as mainstream). What can you learn about the company from these reports?

Analysis. Isolate a few patterns among your many findings. For example, what are some successes or failures of this company in leveraging its potential synergies? Or, focus on the company's news media holdings. How does this media giant use its news media divisions to its advantage?

Interpretation. What do these patterns mean? First discuss them from an investor's perspective. Then discuss them from a citizen's perspective. Are these interests the same or different?

Evaluation. Is this company good for democracy? Does it enable multiple points of view? Is this company good for the world? Why or why not? What might the mass media look like with more competition from more companies? Present your findings and conclusions in class, via either a spoken presentation or a poster.

Engagement. To express your perspective on media conglomeration, visit the FCC Web site and find out how you can officially comment on the regulatory process. The FreePress, a nonprofit organization focused on creating a more democratic media system, operates a Web site (www.freepress.net) that also provides resources to track and become involved in media policymaking.

KEY TERMS

monopoly, 463	direct payment, 465	synergy, 472
oligopoly, 464	indirect payment, 465	cultural imperialism, 479
limited competition, 464	economies of scale, 465	

the culture of journalism

values, ethics, and democracy

In 2006, the long-standing tension between government and the press continued as government leaders criticized the *New York Times* for publishing a story that "disclosed a secret Bush administration program to monitor" bank records of suspected terrorists—and millions of others.[1] While the *Los Angeles Times* and *Wall Street Journal* had also disclosed the tracking program, the White House came down hard only on the *Times* (which takes more liberal positions in its editorials), calling the report "disgraceful" and "very dangerous." At least one Republican member of Congress called the report an act of treason that should be prosecuted under the Espionage Act. Despite this demand and similar ones in the past, however, the U.S. government has "never once prosecuted the press for publishing government secrets."[2] At the time, some critics pointed out that President Bush himself had disclosed the program as early as 2001, and a book by reporter Ron Suskind, *The One Percent Doctrine*, had already reported that terrorists knew about the program and had stopped using electronic banking to move their money around.

In July 2006, NBC's *Meet the Press* featured a roundtable debate on tensions between the government and the press, and on the government's tendency to attack the news media when White House initiatives do poorly. (Actually, this attack followed two years of substantial criticism of the mainstream press from opponents of the Iraq war for not asking enough tough questions of the administration about the validity of the war; in fact, both the *Washington Post* and the *New York Times* issued apologies in 2004 for not being more skeptical of the White House's shifting rationale for the Iraq war.)[3]

Among other guests, the program featured conservative *Times* columnist William Safire, the *Post*'s Dana Priest, and William Bennett, a conservative spokesman for Republicans.

Priest had won a 2005 Pulitzer Prize for her coverage of "a covert program to capture terrorism suspects abroad and send them to secret prisons in Eastern Europe" (although at the Bush administration's request, the *Post* had not disclosed the location of these prisons).[4] Bennett had attacked Priest's reporting as "not worthy of an award" but instead "worthy of jail." And Safire had authored the famous 1968 speech by Republican Vice-President Spiro Agnew that attacked "pointy-headed liberals" in the major media as "nattering nabobs of negativism."

The *Meet the Press* program was a healthy debate about how the press has to weigh the public good against an administration's desire for secrecy when reporting about government operations. In the end, the debate revealed two surprising opposite camps. Opposing the publication of the *Times*'s banking story, William Bennett claimed that an elected president had the right to carry out a war as he saw fit. On the other side, supporting the story's publication, William Safire said the decision to publish was difficult but served the public's best interests. Safire argued that in the First Amendment our founders enabled the press to "act as a check and balance on government." And historically the Supreme Court has agreed with Safire, as Justice Hugo Black wrote in 1971, "The government's power to censor the press was abolished so that the press would remain forever free to censure the government. The press was protected so that it could bare the secrets of the government and inform the people."

news-related values receive special attention in this chapter because journalism is the only media enterprise that democracy absolutely requires—and it is the only media practice and business that is specifically mentioned and protected by the U.S. Constitution. However, with the gradual decline in traditional news audiences, the growing criticism of a corps of East Coast celebrity journalists, the rise of twenty-four-hour cable news, and Internet news blogs, mainstream journalists are searching for ways to reconnect with citizens. In this chapter, we examine the changing news landscape and definitions of journalism. We look at the implicit values underlying news practice and the ethical dilemmas confronting journalists. Next, we study the legacy of print-news conventions and rituals. We then turn to the impact of television and images on news. Finally, we take up recent controversial developments in journalism and democracy, specifically examining the public journalism movement and satirical forms of journalism.

> **"** A journalist is the lookout on the bridge of the ship of state. He peers through the fog and storm to give warnings of dangers ahead. . . . He is there to watch over the safety and the welfare of the people who trust him. **"**
> —Joseph Pulitzer, 1904

Modern Journalism in the Information Age

In modern America, serious journalism has sought to provide information that enables citizens to make intelligent decisions. Today, this guiding principle has been partially derailed. First, in a world entangled in media outlets and computer highways, we may be producing too much information. According to social critic Neil Postman, as a result of developments in media technology, society has developed an "information glut," transforming news and information into "a form of garbage."[5] Postman believed that scientists, technicians, managers, and journalists merely pile up mountains of new data, which add to the problems and anxieties of everyday life. As a result, too much unchecked data—especially on the Internet—and too little thoughtful discussion emanate from too many channels of communication.

A second, related problem suggests that the amount of information the media now provide has made little impact on improving public and political life. In fact, many people feel cut off from our major institutions, including journalism. As a result, many citizens are looking to take part in public conversations and civic debates—to renew a democracy in which many voices participate. In fact, one of the benefits of the controversial 2000 presidential election was the way its legal and political complications engaged the citizenry at a much deeper level than the predictable, staged campaigns themselves did. We will look at these issues—particularly information overload and public alienation—as we explore the culture of news.

> **"** When watchdogs, bird dogs, and bull dogs morph into lap dogs, lazy dogs, or yellow dogs, the nation is in trouble. **"**
> —Ted Stannard, former UPI reporter

What Is News?

In a 1963 staff memo, NBC news president Reuven Frank outlined the narrative strategies integral to all news: "Every news story should . . . display the attributes of fiction, of drama. It should have structure and conflict, problem and denouement, rising and falling action, a beginning, a middle, and an end."[6] Despite Frank's candid insights, most journalists today are not comfortable thinking of themselves as storytellers. Instead, they view themselves mainly as information-gatherers.

Over time, most journalists and journalism textbooks have come to define news by a set of conventional criteria for determining **newsworthiness**—information most worthy of transformation into news stories. Although other elements could be added to the list, news criteria generally include the attributes of timeliness, proximity, conflict, prominence, human interest, consequence, usefulness, novelty, and deviance.[7] Journalists are socialized professionally to select and develop news stories based on different combinations of these criteria.

Most issues and events that journalists select as news are *timely* or *new*. Reporters, for example, cover speeches, meetings, crimes, or court cases that have just happened. In order to rate as news, most of these events also have to occur close by, or in proximity to, readers and viewers. Although local papers usually offer some national and international news, readers and viewers expect to find the bulk of news devoted to their own towns and communities. In addition to being new and near, most news stories are narratives and thus contain a healthy dose of *conflict*—a key ingredient in narrative writing. In fact, in developing news narratives, reporters are encouraged to seek contentious quotes from those with opposing views. For example, stories on presidential elections almost always feature the most dramatic opposing Republican and Democratic positions. And stories in the aftermath of the terrorist attacks of September 11, 2001, often pit the values of the Eastern religions and other cultures against those of Western culture—for example, Islam versus Christianity or premodern traditional values versus contemporary consumerism.

For newsworthiness, *prominence* and *human interest* play a role as well. Reader and viewer surveys indicate that most people identify more closely with an individual than with an abstract issue. Therefore, the news media tend to report stories on powerful or influential people. Because these individuals often play a role in shaping the rules and values of a community, journalists have traditionally been responsible for keeping a watchful eye on them. But reporters also look for the human-interest story: extraordinary incidents that happen to "ordinary" people. In fact, good reporters can often relate a story about a complicated issue (such as unemployment, tax rates, health care, or homelessness) by illustrating its impact on one "average" person or family.

Two other criteria for newsworthiness, found less often in news stories, are *consequence* and *usefulness*. Stories about isolated or bizarre crimes, even though they might be new, near, or notorious, often have little impact on our daily lives. To balance these kinds of stories, many editors and reporters believe that some news must also be of consequence to a majority of readers or viewers. For example, stories about issues or events that affect a family's income or change a community's laws have consequence. Likewise, many people look for stories with a practical use: hints on buying a used car or choosing a college, strategies for training a pet or removing a stain.

Finally, news is often about the *novel* and the *deviant*. When events happen that are outside the routine of daily life, such as a seven-year-old girl trying to pilot a plane across the country or a pop music star driving with a baby in her lap, the news media are there. Reporters also cover events that appear to deviate from social norms, including murders, rapes, fatal car crashes, fires, political scandals, and gang activities. As tension in Iraq increased, by 2006, any suicide bombing in a Middle Eastern nation represented the kind of deviant behavior that qualifies as major news.

Although newsworthiness criteria are a useful way to define news, they do not reveal much about the cultural aspects of news. As culture, news is both a product and a process. It is both the morning paper or evening newscast and a set of subtle values and shifting rituals that have been adapted to historical and social circumstances, such as the partisan press ideals of the 1700s and the informational standards of the twentieth century. As culture, then, **news** in the twentieth century became the process of gathering information and making narrative reports—edited by individuals in for-profit news organizations—that offer selected frames of reference; within those frames, news helps the public make sense of prominent people, important events, and unusual happenings in everyday life.

Neutrality and Other Values in American Journalism

In 1841, Horace Greeley described the newly founded *New York Tribune* as "a journal removed alike from servile partisanship on the one hand and from gagged, mincing neutrality on the other."[8] Greeley feared that too much neutrality would make reporters look like wimps who stood for nothing. Yet the neutrality Greeley warned against is today a major value of conventional journalism. Such a value, ironically, is in the spirit of value-free science, with reporters assuming they are acting as detached and all-seeing observers of social experience. A news report, however, is seldom scientific; it remains essentially a literary or writing activity. As former reporter and journalism professor David Eason notes: "Reporters . . . have no special method for determining the truth of a situation nor a special language for reporting their findings. They make sense of events by telling stories about them."[9]

Even though journalists transform events into stories, they generally believe that they are—or should be—neutral observers who present facts without passing judgment on them. Conventions such as the inverted-pyramid news lead, the careful attribution of sources, the minimal use of adverbs and adjectives, and a detached third-person point of view all help reporters perform their work in a supposedly neutral way.

Like lawyers, therapists, and other professionals, many modern journalists believe that their credibility derives from personal detachment. Yet the roots of this view reside in less noble territory. Jon Katz, media critic and former CBS News producer, discusses the history of the neutral pose:

> The idea of respectable detachment wasn't conceived as a moral principle so much as a marketing device. Once newspapers began to mass market themselves in the mid-1880s, after steam- and rotary-powered presses made it possible to print lots of papers and make lots of money, publishers ceased being working, opinionated journalists. They mutated instead into businessmen eager to reach the broadest number of readers and antagonize the fewest. . . .
>
> Objectivity works well for publishers, protecting the status quo and keeping journalism's voice militantly moderate.[10]

To reach as many people as possible across a wide spectrum, publishers and editors realized as early as the 1840s that softening their partisanship might boost sales.

Neutral journalism remains a selective process. Reporters and editors turn some events into reports and discard many others. This process is governed by a deeper

set of subjective beliefs that are not neutral. Sociologist Herbert Gans, who studied the newsroom cultures of CBS, NBC, *Newsweek*, and *Time* in the 1970s, has generalized that several basic "enduring values" are shared by most American reporters and editors. The most prominent of these values are ethnocentrism, responsible capitalism, small-town pastoralism, and individualism.[11] By **ethnocentrism** Gans means that in most news reporting, especially foreign coverage, reporters judge other countries and cultures on the basis of how "they live up to or imitate American practices and values." Critics outside the United States, for instance, point out that CNN's international news channels portray world events and cultures primarily from an American point of view rather than through a neutral, global lens.

Gans also identified **responsible capitalism** as an underlying value, contending that journalists sometimes naively assume that businesspeople compete with one another not primarily to maximize profits but "to create increased prosperity for all." Gans points out that although most reporters and editors condemn monopolies, "there is little implicit or explicit criticism of the oligopolistic nature of much of today's economy."[12] In fact, by the 1990s, most journalists worked in monopoly newspaper towns or for oligopoly parent companies. Thus writing about the limitations of such economic structures constituted biting the hand that fed you.

Another value that Gans found was the romanticization of **small-town pastoralism**: favoring the small over the large and the rural over the urban. Reporters and editors, like most Americans, tend to prefer natural settings to their metropolitan counterparts. Many journalists equate small-town life with innocence and harbor deep suspicions of cities, their governments, and urban experiences. Consequently, stories about rustic communities with drug problems are usually framed as if the purity of country life had been contaminated by brutish city values.

Finally, **individualism**, according to Gans, remains the most prominent value underpinning daily journalism. Many idealistic reporters are attracted to this profession because it rewards the rugged tenacity needed to confront and expose corruption. Beyond this, individuals who overcome personal adversity are the subjects of many enterprising news stories. Often, however, journalism that focuses on personal triumphs fails to explain how large organizations and institutions work or fail. Many conventional reporters and editors are unwilling or unsure of how to tackle the problems raised by institutional decay. In addition, because they value their own individualism and are accustomed to working alone, many journalists dislike cooperating on team projects or participating in forums in which community members discuss their own interests and alternative definitions of news.[13]

Traditionally, reporters have aligned facts with an objective position and values with subjective feelings.[14] Within this context, news reports offer readers and viewers details, data, and description. It then becomes the citizen's responsibility to judge and take a stand about the social problems represented by the news. Given these assumptions, reporters are responsible only for adhering to the traditions of the trade—"getting the facts." As a result, many reporters view themselves as neutral "channels" of information rather than as selective storytellers and citizens actively

● As sociologist Herbert Gans notes, U.S. reporting tends to ethnocentrism and favors the main social classes who hold power. On April 10, 2006, in the National Day of Action for Immigrant Justice, millions of immigrants across the country—including these protestors near the Statue of Liberty—strategically argued that they, too, embraced the same ideals and values as other Americans. The peaceful protests became a major news story and changed the debate over immigration law reform.

involved in public life. (See "Media Literacy and the Critical Process: Telling Stories and Covering Terror" on page 492.)

Ethics and the News Media

The story at the beginning of this chapter speaks to a profound ethical dilemma that national journalists occasionally face, especially in the aftermath of 9/11: When is it right to protect government secrets and when should those secrets—obtained through reporting—be revealed to the public? How must editors weigh such decisions when national security bumps up against citizens' need for information? In 2006 Dean Baquet, editor of the *Los Angeles Times*, and Bill Keller, executive editor of the *New York Times*, wrestled with and wrote about this dilemma:

> Finally, we weigh the merits of publishing against the risks of publishing. There is no magic formula. . . . We make our best judgment.
>
> When we come down on the side of publishing, of course, everyone hears about it. Few people are aware when we decide to hold an article. But each of us, in the past few years, has had the experience of withholding or delaying articles when the administration convinces us that the risk of publication outweighed the benefits. . . .
>
> We understand that honorable people may disagree . . . to publish or not to publish. But making those decisions is a responsibility that falls to editors, a corollary to the great gift of our independence. It is not a responsibility we take lightly. And it is not one we can surrender to the government.[15]

What makes the predicament of these national editors so tricky is that in the government's war against terrorism, the administration claims that one value that terrorists truly hate is "our freedom"; and yet what is more symbolic of liberty than the freedom of an independent press—so independent that U.S. courts have protected the news media's right to criticize our political leaders and reveal government secrets for more than two hundred years?

Ethical Predicaments

What is the moral and social responsibility of journalists, not only for the stories they report but also for the actual events or issues they are shaping for millions of people? Wrestling with such media ethics involves determining the moral response to a situation through critical reasoning. Although national security issues raise problems for a few of our largest news organizations, the most frequent ethical dilemmas encountered in most newsrooms across the United States involve intentional deception, privacy invasions, and conflicts of interest.

Telling Stories and Covering Terror

Here are four opening sections—or leads—from news stories describing the bombing attacks on London in July 2005. Note both the similarities and the variety among these leads. Some are straightforward and some are very dramatic. Note the word choices used to represent this event symbolically.

New York Times (7/8/05)—"Bomb explosions tore through three subway trains and a red-painted double-decker bus in a coordinated terror attack during London's morning rush hour on Thursday, killing at least 37 people, wounding about 700 and leaving the city stunned and bloodied but oddly stoic."

Los Angeles Times (7/8/05)—"Bombs ripped through three Underground trains and a red double-decker bus in central London during the Thursday morning rush hour, killing at least 38 people and wounding more than 700 in the deadliest terrorist attack on British soil."

ABC's *World News Tonight* (7/7/05)—Charles Gibson: "Good evening. It has happened again. The world jolted by the horror of terrorism. It began as a typical morning commute in London. And then, the bombs started going off. Explosions at three separate subway stations tore through trains and ripped apart a double-decker bus like it was a tin can."

Fox News Network (7/7/05)—Brit Hume: "Next on 'Special Report,' deadly terrorist bombs kill dozens and injure hundreds more in London, shutting down the city's public transport system and throwing the G-8 summit in Scotland into disarray."

Although modern journalists claim objectivity as a goal, it is unlikely that a profession in the story-telling business can approximate any sort of scientific objectivity. The best journalists can do is be fair,

reporting and telling their stories in such a way that they best represent for their communities and nation the complicated experiences that they are symbolically converting into print or pictures.

After discussing these July 2005 leads in class, try this exercise using your own examples from local *crime* coverage in your area:

Description. Find print and broadcast news versions of the *same* crime story from two different days of the week. Make copies of each story. For the broadcast stories, make notes on the pictures chosen to tell the story.

Analysis. Find patterns in the coverage. How are the stories treated differently in print and on television? Are there similarities in the words chosen or images used? What kinds of crime are depicted? Who are the sources the reporters use to verify their information?

Interpretation. What do these patterns suggest? Can you make any interpretations or arguments based on the kinds of crime covered, sources used, areas of community covered, or words/images chosen? How prominently are the stories played in relationship to their importance to the entire community being served? How complex are these stories? Do they relate the events to the larger social problem of crime, or are the stories treated as isolated or individual problems?

Evaluation. Which stories are the strongest? Why? Which are the weakest? Why? Make a judgment on how well these crime stories serve your interests as a citizen and the interests of the larger community.

Engagement. In an e-mail or letter to the editor, report your findings to relevant editors and local TV news directors. How did they respond?

Deploying Deception

Ever since Nellie Bly faked insanity to get inside an asylum in the 1880s, investigative journalists have used deception to get stories. Today, journalists continue to use disguises and assume false identities to gather information on social transgressions. Beyond legal considerations, though, a key ethical question comes into play:

Does the end justify the means? For example, can a newspaper or TV newsmagazine use deceptive ploys to go undercover and expose a suspected fraudulent clinic that promises miracle cures at a high cost? By posing as clients desperate for a cure, are news professionals justified in using deception?

In terms of ethics, there are at least two major positions and multiple variations. First, *absolutist ethics* suggest that a moral society has laws and codes, including honesty, that everyone must live by. This means citizens, including members of the news media, should tell the truth at all times and in all cases. In other words, the ends (exposing a phony clinic) never justify the means (using deception to get the story). At the other end of the spectrum are *situational ethics,* which promote ethical decisions on a case-by-case basis. If a greater public good could be served by using deceit, many journalists would sanction deception as a practice. An editor who is an absolutist, however, would shun deceptive measures. Instead, he or she might cover this story by ordering a reporter to find victims who have been ripped off by the clinic, telling the story through their eyes.

Should a journalist withhold information about his or her professional identity to get a quote or a story from an interview subject? Many sources and witnesses are reluctant to talk with journalists, especially about a sensitive subject that might jeopardize a job or hurt another person's reputation. Journalists know they can sometimes obtain information by posing as someone other than a journalist, such as a curious student or an average citizen. Most newsrooms frown on such deception. In particular situations, though, such a practice might be condoned if reporters and their editors believed that the public needed the information. The ethics code adopted by the Society of Professional Journalists (SPJ) is fairly silent on issues of deception. The code "requires journalists to perform with intelligence, objectivity, accuracy, and fairness," but it also says that "truth is our ultimate goal."[16]

Invading Privacy

To achieve the truth, journalists routinely straddle a line between "the public's right to know" and a person's right to privacy. For example, journalists may be sent to hospitals to gather quotes from victims who have been injured. In many of these cases,

● In 2006, photographers caught Britney Spears driving illegally with her infant son on her lap. The public condemned her poor parenting skills, while Spears claimed that aggressive paparazzi had endangered her son. When photos of the incident appeared online, Spears threatened legal action, citing invasion of privacy. However, the infamous photos remain widely available, and the news media continue to follow Britney's every move, both public and private.

there is very little the public might gain from such a quote, but journalists worry that if they don't get the quote, a competitor might. In these instances, have the news media responsibly weighed the protection of individual privacy against the public's right to know? Although the latter is not constitutionally guaranteed, journalists invoke the public's right to know as justification for many types of stories.

Privacy issues also affect corporations and institutions. For example, in 1998 a *Cincinnati Enquirer* reporter got into trouble for illegally gaining access to the voice-mail system at Chiquita, a company best known for selling bananas. The reporter used voice-mail information to report on the company's business practices. Although a few journalists applauded the reporter's resourcefulness, many critics said such a technique represented a violation of the company's privacy rights. At the very least, in our digital age, when reporters can gain access to private e-mail messages as well as voice mail, such reporting practices raise serious questions about how far a reporter can or should go to get information.

In regard to both individual and institutional privacy, do the news media always ask the ethical questions: What public good is being served here? What significant public knowledge will be gained through the exploitation of a tragic private moment? Although journalism's code of ethics says, "The news media must guard against invading a person's right to privacy," this clashes with another part of the code, "The public's right to know of events of public importance and interest is the overriding mission of the mass media."[17] When these two ethical standards collide, journalists usually err on the side of the public's right to know.

Conflict of Interest

Journalism's code of ethics also warns reporters and editors not to place themselves in positions that produce a **conflict of interest** — that is, any situation in which journalists may stand to benefit personally from stories they produce. "Gifts, favors, free travel, special treatment or privileges," the code states, "can compromise the integrity of journalists and their employers. Nothing of value should be accepted."[18] For instance, at large mainstream news media that subscribe to the code, newspapers or broadcast stations pay for the game tickets of their sportswriters and for the meals of their restaurant critics. Small newspapers, however, with limited resources and poorly paid reporters, might accept such "freebies" from a local business or interview subject. This practice may be an economic necessity, but it does increase the likelihood of a conflict of interest that produces favorable or uncritical coverage.

On a broader level, ethical guidelines at many news outlets attempt to protect journalists from compromising positions. For instance, in most cities journalists do not actively participate in politics or support social causes. Some journalists will not reveal their political affiliations and occasionally will even refuse to vote. For these journalists, the rationale behind their decisions is straightforward: Journalists should not place themselves in a situation in which they might have to report on the misdeeds of an organization or political party to which they belong. If a journalist has a tie to any group, and that group is later discovered to be involved in shady practices or criminal activity, the reporter's ability to report on that group would be compromised — along with the credibility of the news outlet for which he or she works. Conversely, other journalists believe that not actively participating in politics or social causes means abandoning one's civic obligations. They believe that fairness, not total detachment from civic engagement, is their primary obligation.

Resolving Ethical Problems

When a journalist is criticized for ethical indiscretions or questionable reporting tactics, a typical response might be "I'm just doing my job" or "I was just getting the facts." In retrospect, such explanations are troubling because in responding this way, reporters are transferring personal responsibility for the story to a set of institutional rituals.

There are, of course, ethical alternatives to comments like "I'm just doing my job" that force journalists to think through complex issues. With the crush of deadlines and daily duties, most media professionals deal with ethical situations only on a case-by-case basis as dilemmas arise. However, examining major ethical models and theories provides a common strategy for addressing ethics on a general rather than a situational basis. Ethical and philosophical guidelines also offer universal measures for testing individual values and codes.

Although we cannot address all major moral codes here, a few key precepts can guide us. One principle entails the "categorical imperative," developed by German philosopher Immanuel Kant (1724–1804). A moral imperative or command maintains that a society must adhere to moral codes that are universal and unconditional, applicable in all situations at all times. For example, the Golden Rule—Do unto others as you would have them do unto you—operates as such an absolutist moral principle. The First Amendment, which prevents Congress from abridging free speech and other rights, also offers a model as a national unconditional law.

Another ethical principle, derived from British philosophers Jeremy Bentham (1748–1832) and John Stuart Mill (1806–1873), promotes "the greatest good for the greatest number," directing us "to distribute a good consequence to more people rather than to fewer, whenever we have a choice."[19] The most well-known ethical standard, the Judeo-Christian command to "love your neighbor as yourself," also provides the basis for constructing ethical guidelines.

Arriving at ethical decisions involves several stages. These include laying out the case; pinpointing the key issues; identifying involved parties, their intent, and their competing values; studying ethical models; presenting strategies and options; and formulating a decision. In terms of privacy issues, for instance, the goal would be to develop an ethical policy that the news media might implement in covering the private lives of people who have become prominent in the news. (See Figure 14.1 on page 496 for the SPJ Code of Ethics.)

Consider Richard Jewell, the Atlanta security guard who, for eighty-eight days, was the FBI's prime suspect in the park bombing at the 1996 Olympics. The FBI never charged Jewell with a crime, and he later successfully sued several news organizations for libel. Putting legal issues aside, the Jewell story involved a rivalry among various news media to report unusual or important developments before the competition could do so. The battle for newspaper circulation and broadcast ratings added a complex dimension. As has occurred in other instances, editors were reluctant to back away from the story once it had begun circulating in the major media.

At least two key ethical questions emerged from the Jewell story: (1) Should the news media have named Jewell as a suspect even though he was never charged with a crime? (2) Should the media have camped out daily in front of his mother's house in an attempt to interview him and his mother? The incidents surrounding the Richard Jewell case pit the

● For almost three months, security guard Richard Jewell was the FBI's main suspect in the July 1996 Olympic Park bombing that killed one person. When the FBI finally exonerated Jewell, he filed libel suits against the *Atlanta Journal-Constitution*, CNN, and NBC. In 2005, serial bomber Eric Rudolph pleaded guilty to the Olympics bombing and three other bomb attacks.

Figure 14.1
Society of Professional Journalists' Code of Ethics

Code Of Ethics

Preamble

Members of the Society of Professional Journalists believe that public enlightenment is the forerunner of justice and the foundation of democracy. The duty of the journalist is to further those ends by seeking truth and providing a fair and comprehensive account of events and issues. Conscientious journalists from all media and specialties strive to serve the public with thoroughness and honesty. Professional integrity is the cornerstone of a journalist's credibility.

Members of the Society share a dedication to ethical behavior and adopt this code to declare the Society's principles and standards of practice.

Seek Truth and Report It

Journalists should be honest, fair and courageous in gathering, reporting and interpreting information.

Journalists should:

- Test the accuracy of information from all sources and exercise care to avoid inadvertent error. Deliberate distortion is never permissible.
- Diligently seek out subjects of news stories to give them the opportunity to respond to allegations of wrongdoing.
- Identify sources whenever feasible. The public is entitled to as much information as possible on sources' reliability.
- Always question sources' motives before promising anonymity. Clarify conditions attached to any promise made in exchange for information. Keep promises.
- Make certain that headlines, news teases and promotional material, photos, video, audio, graphics, sound bites and quotations do not misrepresent. They should not oversimplify or highlight incidents out of context.
- Never distort the content of news photos or video. Image enhancement for technical clarity is always permissible. Label montages and photo illustrations.
- Avoid misleading re-enactments or staged news events. If re-enactment is necessary to tell a story, label it.
- Avoid undercover or other surreptitious methods of gathering information except when traditional open methods will not yield information vital to the public. Use of such methods should be explained as part of the story.
- Never plagiarize.
- Tell the story of the diversity and magnitude of the human experience boldly, even when it is unpopular to do so.
- Examine their own cultural values and avoid imposing those values on others.
- Avoid stereotyping by race, gender, age, religion, ethnicity, geography, sexual orientation, disability, physical appearance or social status.
- Support the open exchange of views, even views they find repugnant.
- Give voice to the voiceless; official and unofficial sources of information can be equally valid.
- Distinguish between advocacy and news reporting. Analysis and commentary should be labeled and not misrepresent fact or context.
- Distinguish news from advertising and shun hybrids that blur the lines between the two.
- Recognize a special obligation to ensure that the public's business is conducted in the open and that government records are open to inspection.

Minimize Harm

Ethical journalists treat sources, subjects and colleagues as human beings deserving of respect.

Journalists should:

- Show compassion for those who may be affected adversely by news coverage. Use special sensitivity when dealing with children and inexperienced sources or subjects.
- Be sensitive when seeking or using interviews or photographs of those affected by tragedy or grief.
- Recognize that gathering and reporting information may cause harm or discomfort. Pursuit of the news is not a license for arrogance.
- Recognize that private people have a greater right to control information about themselves than do public officials and others who seek power, influence or attention. Only an overriding public need can justify intrusion into anyone's privacy.
- Show good taste. Avoid pandering to lurid curiosity.
- Be cautious about identifying juvenile suspects or victims of sex crimes.
- Be judicious about naming criminal suspects before the formal filing of charges.
- Balance a criminal suspect's fair trial rights with the public's right to be informed.

Act Independently

Journalists should be free of obligation to any interest other than the public's right to know.

Journalists should:

- Avoid conflicts of interest, real or perceived.
- Remain free of associations and activities that may compromise integrity or damage credibility.
- Refuse gifts, favors, free travel and special treatment, and shun secondary employment, political involvement, public office and service in community organizations if they compromise journalistic integrity.
- Disclose unavoidable conflicts.
- Be vigilant and courageous about holding those with power accountable.
- Deny favored treatment to advertisers and special interests and resist their pressure to influence news coverage.
- Be wary of sources offering information for favors or money; avoid bidding for news.

Be Accountable

Journalists are accountable to their readers, listeners, viewers and each other.

Journalists should:

- Clarify and explain news coverage and invite dialogue with the public over journalistic conduct.
- Encourage the public to voice grievances against the news media.
- Admit mistakes and correct them promptly.
- Expose unethical practices of journalists and the news media.
- Abide by the same high standards to which they hold others.

Source: Society of Professional Journalists.

media's right to tell stories and earn profits against a citizen's right to be left alone.

Journalists' livelihoods partly depend on using stories that attract audiences and keep up with their competition. To defend their behavior toward the Jewells, for example, the news media might invoke their constitutional right to free expression or argue that their intent was to serve the public's right to know. Similar justifications were employed by the photographers who hounded Britain's Princess Diana in 1997, creating an atmosphere that contributed to events leading to her death. To criticize such media behavior, however, we might ask whether any significant public knowledge is gained by stalking a potential interview subject.

As journalists formally work through various ethical stages, they eventually formulate policies and ground them in an overarching moral principle, such as the commandment to "love your neighbor as yourself."[20] Would reporters, for instance, be willing to treat themselves, their families, or their friends the way they treated the Jewells? Ethical reporters could also invoke Aristotle's "golden mean": seeking moral virtue between extreme positions. In Richard Jewell's situation, this might have entailed developing guidelines that would attempt to balance the interests of the suspect and those of the news media. For example, during his eighty-eight-day ordeal, in reparation for using Jewell's name in early accounts, reporters might have called off their stakeout and allowed him to set interview times at a neutral site. At such a location, he might have talked with a small pool of journalists designated to relay information to other media outlets.

> " We should have the public interest and not the bottom line at heart, or else all we can do is wait for a time when sex doesn't sell. "
>
> —Susan Ungaro, editor, *Family Circle*, on media coverage of the Clinton-Lewinsky scandal, 1998

Reporting Rituals and the Legacy of Print Journalism

Unfamiliar with being questioned themselves, many reporters are uncomfortable discussing their personal values or their strategies for getting stories. Nevertheless, a stock of rituals, derived from basic American values, underlie the practice of reporting. These include focusing on the present, relying on experts, balancing story conflict, and acting as adversaries toward leaders and institutions.

Focusing on the Present

Historians mark the 1830s as the beginning of the transition between the partisan and modern press eras. Though American journalism began as a platform for partisan politics (debating issues such as constitutional amendments, slavery, and states' rights), in the 1800s publishers figured out how to sell news more profitably as a product. They used modern technology to substantially cut their costs; they also began to change news content to appeal to emerging middle- and working-class people, who could now afford a paper and had some leisure time to read one. Publishers realized that they needed more everyday content because many less affluent or educated readers were not particularly interested in the intricacies of partisan politics.

In the 1840s, when the telegraph first enabled news to crisscross America instantly, modern journalism was born. To complement the new technical advances, editors called for a dogged focus on the immediacy of the present. Modern print journalism de-emphasized political discussions and historical context, accenting instead the new and the now.

> **❝** [M]arathon mourning is now a hit show biz formula for generating ratings and newsstand sales. . . . The treacly theme music, the cheesy greeting-card art graphics, the New Age vocabulary of 'closure,' the ritualistically repeated slo-mo video clips.**❞**
>
> –Frank Rich, *New York Times* columnist, criticizing the excessive coverage of the 1999 plane crash that killed JFK Jr., Carolyn Bessette Kennedy, and Lauren Bessette

As members of an emerging modern profession, many journalists and newspapers ignored Joseph Pulitzer's call for news that maintained a continuity with the past. As a result, the profession began drawing criticism for failing to offer historical analyses. This is a pattern that continues today. In news stories about drugs, for example, individual characters—dealers, addicts, abusers, police, medical experts—pass through the frame of news, but only up to a point. Once these characters are no longer timely, they no longer meet the narrative requirements of daily news. For example, urban drug stories heavily dominated print and network news during the 1986 and 1988 election years. Such stories, however, virtually disappeared from the news by 1992, although the nation's serious drug and addiction problems had not diminished.[21] Drug stories simply became "yesterday's news."

Modern journalism tends to reject "old news" for whatever new event or idea disrupts today's routines. In the mid-1990s, when statistics revealed that drug use among middle-class high school students was rising, reporters again latched on to new versions of the drug story during the 1996 elections, but their reports made only limited references to the 1980s. And although drug problems and addiction rates did not diminish in subsequent years, these topics were virtually ignored by journalists during the 2000 and 2004 national elections. Indeed, given the space and time constraints of current news practices, reporters seldom link stories to the past or to the ebb and flow of history.

Getting a Good Story

Early in the 1980s, the Janet Cooke–Pulitzer Prize hoax demonstrated the difference between a reporter merely telling a good story and her social responsibility for the actual experience.[22] The main criticism against this former *Washington Post* reporter focused on her fabrication of an investigative report (for which she won a Pulitzer that was later revoked). She had created a cast of characters featuring a mother who contributed to the heroin addiction of her eight-year-old son. At the time the hoax was exposed, Chicago columnist Mike Royko criticized conventional journalism for allowing narrative conventions—getting a good story—to trump journalism's responsibility to the daily lives it documents: "There's something more important than a story here. This eight-year-old kid is being murdered. The editors should have said forget the story, find the kid. . . . People in any other profession would have gone right to the police."[23] Had editors at the *Post* demanded such help, Cooke's hoax would never have gone as far as it did.

According to Don Hewitt, the creator and longtime executive producer of *60 Minutes*, "There's a very simple formula if you're in Hollywood, Broadway, opera, publishing, broadcasting, newspapering. It's four very simple words—tell me a story."[24] For most journalists, the bottom line is getting a story—an edict that overrides most other concerns. Getting a timely story fills up a journalist's day and enables him or her to meet routine deadline demands. It is the standard against which reporters measure one another and their profession.

Getting a Story First

In a discussion on public television about the press coverage of a fatal airline crash in Milwaukee in the 1980s, a news photographer was asked to discuss his role in covering the tragedy. Rather than take up the poignant and heartbreaking aspects of witnessing the aftermath of such an event, the excited photographer launched into a dramatic recounting of how he had slipped behind police barricades to snap the first grim photos, which later appeared in the *Milwaukee Journal*. As part of their socialization into the profession, reporters often enjoy recounting how they evaded an authority figure to secure a story ahead of the competition.

The photographer's recollection points to the important role journalism plays in calling public attention to serious events and issues. Yet he also talked about the news-gathering process as a game that journalists play. Indeed, it's now routine for local television stations and newspapers to run self-promotions about how they beat competitors to a story. In addition, during political elections local television stations and networks project winners in particular races and often hype their projections when they are able to forecast results before the competition does. This led to the fiasco in November 2000 when the major networks and cable news services badly flubbed their predictions regarding the outcome of voting in Florida in the presidential election.

Journalistic *scoops* and exclusive stories attempt to portray reporters in a heroic light: They have won a race for facts, which they have gathered and presented ahead of their rivals. It is not always clear, though, how the public is better served by a journalist's claim to have gotten a story first. Certainly, enterprising journalists can get a story started by calling attention to an important problem or issue. But on occasion, as with the July 1999 plane crash that killed John F. Kennedy Jr., his wife, and his sister-in-law, scoop behavior has led to pack or **herd journalism**, which occurs when reporters stake out a house or follow a story in such large groups that the entire profession comes under attack for invading people's privacy and exploiting their personal tragedies. Although readers and viewers might value the tenacity of adventurous reporters, the earliest reports are not necessarily better or more significant than stories written days later with more context and perspective.

Relying on Experts

Another ritual of modern print journalism—relying on outside sources—has made reporters heavily dependent on experts. Reporters, though often experts themselves in certain areas by virtue of having covered them over time, are not typically allowed to display their expertise overtly. Instead, they must seek outside authorities to give credibility to seemingly neutral reports. What daily reporters know is generally subordinate to whom they know.

During the early 1900s, progressive politicians and leaders of opinion such as Woodrow Wilson and Walter Lippmann believed in the cultivation of strong ties among national reporters, government officials, scientists, business managers, and researchers. They wanted journalists supplied with expertise across a variety of areas. Today, a widening gap exists between citizens with expertise and those without it, creating a need for public mediators. Reporters have assumed this role, becoming surrogate citizens who represent both leaders' and readers' interests. With their access to experts, reporters are able to act as agents for citizens, transforming specialized knowledge into the everyday commonsense language of news stories.

In the quest for facts, reporters frequently use experts to create narrative conflict by pitting a series of quotes against one another. On occasion, reporters also use experts to support a particular position (which, because of neutrality requirements,

● The pressure on journalists to tell great stories and get them first has led to occasional problems. In May 2003, the *New York Times* revealed that one of its reporters, 27-year-old Jayson Blair (pictured on the left) made up facts, invented sources, stole quotes from other newspapers, and, in short, plagiarized dozens of articles. He even pretended to be reporting from Texas when he was actually at home in Brooklyn. In a 14,000-word report and self-examination, the *Times* called the episode "a low point" in the paper's storied history. Both the chief editor and managing editor of the *Times* resigned shortly after Blair's dismissal.

reporters are not allowed to state openly). In addition, the use of experts enables journalists to distance themselves from daily experience; they are able to attribute the responsibility for the events or issues reported in a story to those who are quoted.

In the ritual use of experts, journalists are required to make direct contact with a source—by phone or e-mail or in person. Journalists do not, however, heavily cite the work of other writers; that would violate the reporters' obligation not only to get a story first but to get it on their own. Telephone calls and face-to-face interviews are the stuff of daily journalism. More carefully researched interpretation is often assumed to be a different kind of writing, more the province of academics or magazine writers.

Of expert sources in general, *Newsweek*'s Jonathan Alter once called them the "usual suspects." Alter contended that "the impression conveyed is of a world that contains only a handful of knowledgeable people. . . . Their public exposure is a result not only of their own abilities, but of deadlines and a failure of imagination on the part of the press."[25] In addition, expert sources have historically been predominantly white and male. For example, based on a forty-month analysis of guests on ABC's *Nightline* between 1985 and 1988, Fairness and Accuracy in Reporting (FAIR) found that "89 percent of the U.S. guests were men, 92 percent were white, and 80 percent were professionals, government officials, or corporate representatives."[26] Beginning in 1995, coverage of the O.J. Simpson trials helped change this profile somewhat. Legal sources, especially on CNN and CNBC, featured a far more diverse array of expert participants. In 2003, though, the Iraq war marked the return on cable to predominantly white and male military experts and former officers. As journalists have increased their reliance on a limited pool of experts over the years, they have inadvertently alienated many readers, who feel they no longer have a stake in day-to-day social and political life—authoritative experts and knowledgeable journalists dominate the 24/7 news environment.

In the late 1990s, many journalists were being criticized for blurring the line between remaining neutral and being an expert. With shows like CNN's *Crossfire* (cancelled in 2005) pitting opinionated columnists and reporters against one another, the boom in twenty-four-hour cable news programs in the late 1990s led to a news vacuum that is now filled with talk shows and interviews with journalists willing to give their views on the hot stories of the day. During events with intense media coverage, such as the 2000 presidential election, 9/11, and the Iraq war, many print journalists appeared several times a day on various cable programs acting as experts on the story, sometimes providing factual information but mostly offering opinion and speculation. Some editors even encourage their reporters to go on these shows in the hope of selling more magazines and newspapers. Reporters and columnists from the *Washington Post*, for example, routinely appear in remote TV shots with the paper's logo prominently displayed in the background. Many critics contend that these practices erode the credibility of the profession by blending journalism with celebrity culture and commercialism.

Balancing Story Conflict

Embedded deep within journalism is a belief in the two-dimensionality of news. A reporter sent to cover property tax increases might be given this editorial advice: "Interview Republican and Democratic leaders from the district and have them fight it out in the story." Such "balance" is a narrative device that helps generate story conflict. For most journalists, balance means presenting all sides of an issue without appearing to favor any one position. Unfortunately, because time and space constraints do not always permit representing *all* sides, in practice this value has often been reduced to "telling both sides of a story." In recounting news stories as two-sided dramas, however, reporting often misrepresents the multifaceted complexity of social issues. (See "Case Study: Bias and the News" on page 506.) The abortion controversy, for example, is often treated as a story that pits two extreme positions (pro-life vs. pro-choice) against each other. Yet people whose views do not fall at either end of the spectrum are seldom represented; they are too far inside the outermost boundaries of a two-dimensional narrative conflict.

Although many journalists claim to be detached, they often stake out a moderate or middle-of-the-road position between the two sides represented in a story. In claiming neutrality and inviting readers to share their detached point of view, journalists circumvent their own values. The authority of their distant, third-person, all-knowing point of view (a narrative device that many novelists use as well) enhances the impression of neutrality by making the reporter appear value-free (or valueless).

The claim for balanced stories, like the claim for neutrality, disguises journalism's narrative functions. After all, when reporters choose quotes for a story, these are usually the most dramatic or conflict-oriented words that emerge from an interview, press conference, or public meeting. Choosing quotes often has more to do with enhancing drama than with being fair or establishing neutrality. The balance claim is also in the financial interest of modern news organizations that stake out the middle ground. William Greider, a former *Washington Post* editor, makes the connection between good business and balanced journalism: "If you're going to be a mass circulation journal, that means you're going to be talking simultaneously to lots of groups that have opposing views. So you've got to modulate your voice and pretend to be talking to all of them."[27]

Acting as Adversaries

Complementing the search for conflict, the value that journalists take the most pride in is their adversarial relationship with the prominent leaders and major institutions they cover. (See "The Global Village: How Independent Is Government-Controlled Public Broadcasting?" on page 502.) The prime narrative frame for portraying this relationship is sometimes called a *gotcha story,* which refers to the moment when the reporter nabs "the bad guy" or wrongdoer. This narrative strategy—part of the *tough-questioning style* of some reporters—is frequently used in political reporting. Many journalists assume that leaders are hiding something and that the reporter's main job is to ferret out the truth through tenacious fact-gathering and "gotcha" questions. An extension of the search for balance, this stance locates the reporter in the middle, between "them" and "us," between political leaders and the people they represent.

Critics of the tough-question style of reporting argue that it fosters a cynicism among journalists that actually harms the democratic process. Although journalists need to guard against becoming too cozy with their political sources, they sometimes go to opposite extremes. By constantly searching for what politicians may be hiding, some reporters may miss other issues.

News scholar Jay Rosen argues that "the essential problem is that the journalist's method of being critical is not disciplined by any political vision."[28] In other words, the bottom line for neutral or conventional journalists, who claim to have no political agenda, is maintaining an adversarial stance rather than improving the quality of political stories and discussions. When journalists employ the gotcha model to cover news, being tough often becomes an end in itself. Thus reporters believe they have done their job just by roughing up an interview subject or by answering the limited "What is going on here?" question. Yet the Pulitzer Prize, the highest award honoring journalism, often goes to the reporter who asks the ethically charged and open-ended questions, such as "Why is this going on?" and "What ought to be done about it?"

How Independent Is Government-Controlled Public Broadcasting?

By Anny Rey

On May 29, 2003, Andrew Gillighan, the defense correspondent for the BBC radio morning show *Today,* filed a report suggesting that the British government had asked British intelligence agencies to make the evidence they had of weapons of mass destruction in Iraq more convincing.

"The draft prepared by the Intelligence Agencies actually didn't say very much more than was public knowledge already," reported Gillighan. "And Downing Street [the residence of the British prime minister], our source says, a week before publication ordered it to be sexed up, to be made more exciting and ordered more facts to be discovered." Because the BBC is owned by the British government, one might have expected it to be more supportive of the government's policies, but far from being a mouthpiece for the government, the BBC has several times become embroiled in bitter fights with British authorities, most recently in its critical coverage of the Iraq war. Although a later and much criticized government inquiry came down hard on the BBC for poor editorial controls, the broadcaster's independence from the government remains certain and the assertions made by Gillighan's report were taken seriously.

The BBC is just one of many public broadcasters that sprang into existence in Western European democracies at

the dawn of broadcasting. In response to the chaos surrounding the ownership of radio stations and frequencies among private U.S. companies, European authorities decided to take control of the new medium themselves and created state monopolies.

The founding charters of many of these European public broadcasters specify that their mission is to entertain, educate, and inform without political interference or commercial pressure. They are thus held to a social pact: viewers and listeners pay annual license fees in return for which they can expect "their" public broadcasters to respect the plurality of their views.

Freed of having to generate profits or satisfy shareholders, most public broadcasters were able to set up important news operations and wide correspondent networks, which to this day continue to dwarf those of their private

competitors. They invested in documentaries as well as cultural and educational programs that most private investors would have shied away from.

By the 1980s, however, European public broadcasters started facing competition from the newly allowed private television stations. Noncommercial broadcasters now have to worry about ratings to justify their existence and are under increasing financial pressure. At the same time, growing competition and the globalization of news has made it harder for the government to influence coverage blatantly without incurring public outrage.

For example, terrorist attacks on commuter trains in Madrid, Spain, occurred on March 11, 2004, three days before national elections. In the following hours, the Aznar government led a massive disinformation campaign, attributing the attack to the Basque terrorist group ETA. The news directors of both the Spanish news agency EFE and the public broadcaster TVE were particularly active in sustaining the government's version. As increasing evidence linking the attack to Al-Qaeda surfaced in other media, angry Spaniards, already opposed to Aznar's Iraq policy, voted him out of office and called for the resignation of both the EFE and TVE news directors.

However, private media ownership is no guarantee of press freedom either. The Italian Prime Minister Silvio Berlusconi didn't hesitate to use his powerful media empire Mediaset, which includes Italy's three largest private television stations, to get elected and thereby take control of the only significant critical broadcaster remaining: the Italian state-funded RAI.

Although most European public broadcasters today are facing increasing challenges in meeting expectations in the face of diminishing resources and growing competition, they still invest far more in their news coverage than commercial broadcasters, and their flagship newscasts usually have the higher ratings.

Are public broadcasters a paradigm for independent journalism? Not always, but neither are commercial broadcasters. At least in a democratic society, public broadcasters still offer two guarantees over their private competitors: their bias is more easily detected, and the people attempting to misuse them are, after all, elected individuals facing regular elections and not media moguls with private agendas.

Anny Rey is a former CNN international assignment desk editor and CNN European producer. She has also headed the international coverage for three German TV networks. She holds a master's in journalism from the University of Michigan.

Journalism in the Age of Television

The rules and rituals governing American journalism began shifting in the 1950s. At the time, former radio reporter John Daly hosted the CBS game show *What's My Line?* When he began moonlighting as the evening TV news anchor on ABC, the fledgling network blurred the entertainment and information border, foreshadowing what by the 1990s had become a central criticism of journalism.

In those early days, the most influential and respected television news program was CBS's *See It Now*. Coproduced by Fred Friendly and Edward R. Murrow, *See It Now* practiced a kind of TV journalism lodged somewhere between the neutral and narrative traditions. Serving as the conscience of TV news in its early days, Murrow also worked as the program's anchor and main reporter, introducing the investigative model of journalism to television—a model that programs like *60 Minutes*, *20/20*, and *Dateline* would later imitate.

Generally regarded as "the first and definitive" news documentary on American television, *See It Now* sought "to report in depth—to tell and show the American audience what was happening in the world using film as a narrative tool."[29] In the early 1960s, *CBS Reports* carried on the traditions of *See It Now*, and as that decade unfolded, the literary model of reporting played a more significant role in the program. Friendly endorsed the importance of the narrative tradition to *CBS Reports*: "Though based on truth, the programs still have to have stories of their own, with the basic outline of beginning, middle and end."[30]

Differences between Print and Television News

Although TV news reporters share many values, beliefs, and conventions with their print counterparts, television has transformed journalism in a number of significant ways. First, broadcast news is often driven by its technology. If a camera crew and microwave-relay van (which bounces a broadcast signal back to the station) are dispatched to a remote location for a live broadcast, reporters are expected to justify the expense by developing a story, even if nothing significant is occurring. This happens, for instance, when a national political candidate does not arrive at the local airport in time for an interview on the evening news, leaving the news crew to report live on a flight delay. Print reporters, however, slide their notebooks or laptops back into their bags and report on a story when it actually occurs.

Second, although print editors must cut stories to fit a physical space around the slots allocated for ads, TV news directors have to time stories to fit news in between commercials. They are under pressure to condense the day's main events into a visual show. Despite the fact that a much higher percentage of space is devoted to print ads (more than 60 percent at most dailies), TV ads (which take up less than 25 percent of the time in a typical thirty-minute news program) generally seem more intrusive to viewers, perhaps because TV ads take up time rather than space.

Third, whereas modern print journalists are expected to be detached, TV news derives its credibility from live, on-the-spot reporting, believable imagery, and viewers' trust in the reporters and anchors who read the news. In fact, since the early 1970s, the annual Roper polls have indicated that the majority of viewers find television news a more credible resource than print news. Viewers tend to feel a personal regard for the local anchors who appear each evening on TV sets in their homes. Many print journalists have even come to resent operating in the relative anonymity of newspaper work while their TV counterparts become mini-celebrities.

By the mid-1970s, the public's fascination with the Watergate scandal, combined with the improved quality of TV journalism, helped local news departments realize profits. In an effort to retain high ratings, stations began hiring consultants, who advised news directors to invest in one of the national packaged formats, such as Action News or Eyewitness News (sometimes mocked as Eyewitless News). Traveling the country, viewers noticed similar theme music and opening visuals from market to market. Consultants also suggested that stations lead their newscasts with *crime blocks*: a group of TV stories that recount the worst criminal transgressions of the day. A cynical slogan soon developed in the industry: "If it bleeds, it leads."

A few stations around the country have responded to viewers and critics who complain about overemphasizing crime—especially given that FBI statistics show that crime and murder rates have been falling in most major urban areas since the 1990s. In 1996, the news director at KVUE-TV in Austin, Texas, concerned about crime coverage, launched a new set of criteria that had to be met for news reports to qualify as responsible crime stories. She asked that her reporters answer the following questions: Do citizens or officials need to take action? Is there an immediate threat to safety? Is there a threat to children? Does the crime have significant community impact? Does the story lend itself to a crime prevention effort? With KVUE's new standards, the station eliminated many routine crime stories. Instead, the station provided a context for understanding crime rather than a mindless running tally of what crimes were being committed each day.[31]

Sound Bitten

Beginning in the 1980s, the term **sound bite** became part of the public lexicon. The TV equivalent of a quote in print news, a sound bite is the part of a broadcast news report in which an expert, celebrity, victim, or person-on-the-street responds in an interview to some aspect of an event or issue. With the 1988 national elections, sound bites became the focus of intense criticism. Various studies revealed that during political campaigns the typical sound bite from candidates had shrunk from an average duration of forty to fifty seconds in the 1950s and 1960s to fewer than eight seconds by the late 1990s. With shorter comments from interview subjects, TV news sometimes seemed like dueling sound bites, with reporters creating dramatic tension by editing competing viewpoints together as if the individuals had actually been in the same location speaking to one another. Of course, print news also pits one quote against another in a story, even though the actual interview subjects may never have met. Once again, these reporting techniques are evidence of the profession's reliance on storytelling devices to replicate or create conflict.

Pretty-Face and Happy-Talk Culture

In the early 1970s, at a Milwaukee TV station, consultants advised the station's news director that the evening anchor looked too old. Showing a bit of gray, the anchor was replaced and went on to serve as the station's editorial director. He was thirty-two years old at the time. In the late 1970s, a woman reporter at the same station was fired because of a "weight problem," although that was not given as the official reason. Earlier that year, she had given birth to her first child. In 1983, Christine Craft, formerly a Kansas City television news anchor, initially won $500,000 in damages in a sex discrimination suit against station KMBC (she eventually lost the monetary award when the station appealed). She had been fired because consultants believed she was too old, too unattractive, and not deferential enough to men.

Such stories are rampant in the annals of TV news. They have helped create a stereotype of the half-witted but physically attractive news anchor, reinforced by popular culture images (from Ted Baxter on TV's *Mary Tyler Moore Show* to Ron Burgundy in the film *Anchorman*). Although the situation has improved slightly, a generation of national news consultants sets the agenda for what local reporters should cover—lots of local crime—as well as how they should look—young, attractive, pleasant, and with no regional accent. Essentially, news consultants—also known as *news doctors*—tried to replicate in modern local TV news the predominant male and female advertising images of the 1960s and 1970s.

● Formerly a star on NBC's long-running *Saturday Night Live*, Will Ferrell co-wrote and starred in *Anchorman: The Legend of Ron Burgundy*, released in summer 2004. Although a fictional comedy, the movie at times seems like a documentary in its portrayal of "pretty face-happy talk" culture and the low journalistic standards in place at some local TV news operations in the 1970s.

Another news strategy favored by news consultants has been *happy talk*: the ad-libbed or scripted banter that goes on among local news anchors, reporters, meteorologists, and sports reporters before and after news reports. During the 1970s, consultants often recommended such chatter to create a more relaxed feeling on the news set and to foster the illusion of conversational intimacy with viewers. Some news doctors also believed that happy talk would counter much of that era's "bad news," which included coverage of urban riots and the Vietnam War. A strategy still used today, happy talk often appears forced and may create awkward transitions, especially when anchors must report on events that are sad or tragic.

CASE STUDY

Bias and the News

ALL news is biased. News, after all, is primarily selective storytelling, not objective science. Editors choose certain events to cover and ignore others; reporters choose particular words or images to use and reject others. The news is also biased in favor of storytelling, drama, and conflict; in favor of telling "two sides of a story"; in favor of powerful and connected sources; and in favor of practices that serve journalists' space and time limits.

In terms of overt political bias, public perception says that mainstream news media operate mostly with a liberal bias. A June 2006 Harris Poll found 38 percent of adults surveyed detected a liberal bias in news coverage while 25 percent sensed a conservative bias (31 percent were "not sure" and 5 percent said there was "no bias").[1] This would seem supported by a 2004 Pew Research Center survey that found that 34 percent of national journalists self-identify as liberal, 7 percent as conservative, and 54 percent as moderate.[2] The Harris study also found that 20 percent of the public surveyed identified themselves as liberal, 29 percent as conservative, and 50 percent as moderate.

Given the primary dictionary definitions of liberal (adj., "favorable to progress or reform, as in political or religious affairs") and conservative (adj., "disposed to preserve existing conditions, institutions, etc., or to restore traditional ones, and to limit change"), it is not surprising that a high percentage of liberals and moderates gravitate to mainstream journalism. A profession that honors documenting change, checking power, and reporting wrongdoing would attract fewer conservatives, who are predisposed to "preserve existing conditions" and to "limit change." As sociologist Herbert Gans demonstrated in Deciding What's News, his 1970s landmark study of newsroom values, most reporters are socialized into a set of work rituals—especially getting the story first and telling it from "both sides" to achieve balance.[3] In fact, this commitment to "balance" mandates that if journalists interview someone on the Left, they must also interview someone on the Right. Ultimately, such a balancing act makes conventional news a middle-of-the-road proposition. In fact, most mainstream journalists (and 50 percent of Americans) identify themselves chiefly as political moderates.

Still, the "liberal bias" narrative persists. In 2001 Bernard Goldberg, a former producer at CBS News, published Bias. Using anecdotes from his days at CBS, he maintained that national news slanted to the left.[4] In 2003, Eric Alterman, a writer for The Nation, countered with What Liberal Media? Alterman admitted that mainstream news media do reflect more liberal views on social issues, but that they have become more conservative on politics and economics—displayed in their support for deregulated media and concentrated ownership.[5] Alterman says the liberal bias tale persists because conservatives keep repeating that story in the major media, what a former chair of the Republican Party calls "working the refs" until "you get the call." Conservative voices have been so successful at keeping the liberal bias charge going that a study in Communication Research reported "a fourfold increase over the past dozen years in the number of Americans telling pollsters that they discerned a liberal bias in the news. But a review of the media's actually ideological content, collected and coded over a 12-year period, offered no corroboration whatever for this view."[6]

Since journalists are primarily storytellers, and not scientists, searching for liberal or conservative bias should not be the main focus of our criticism. As The Daily Show's Jon Stewart told Bill Moyers in 2003 on PBS's NOW, much of the highest profile "noise" in the public sphere is made by 10 percent of the population—5 percent on the Left and 5 percent on the Right, while most of us remain somewhere in between. Under time and space constraints, most journalists serve the routine process of their profession, which calls on them to moderate their own political agendas. News reports, then, are always "biased," given human imperfection in storytelling and in communicating events/issues through the lens of language, images, and institutional values. Rather, fully critiquing news stories—whether they are fair, whether they represent an issue's complexity, whether they provide verification and documentation, whether they represent multiple views, and whether they serve democracy—should be our focus.

● Is There a Bias in Reporting of News?

	Total %	Political Party Affiliation			Political Philosophy		
		Republican %	Democrat %	Independent %	Conservative %	Moderate %	Liberal %
There is a liberal bias in the media	38	66	18	36	62	35	10
There is no bias in the media	5	1	8	7	3	5	9
There is a conservative bias in the media	25	13	37	26	13	24	47
Not at all sure	31	20	36	31	22	36	34

Note: Percentages add up to more than 100 percent due to multiple responses accepted.
Source: http://www.harrisinteractive.com/harris_poll; The Harris Poll® #52, June 30, 2006.

Visual Language and Critical Limits

The brevity of a televised report is often compared unfavorably with the length of print news. However, newspaper reviewers and other TV critics seldom discuss the visual language of TV news and the ways in which images may capture events more powerfully than words.

In contemporary America, the shift from a print-dominated culture to an electronic-digital culture requires thoughtful scrutiny. Instead, the complexity of this shift is often reduced to a two-dimensional debate about information versus entertainment. Yet over the past fifty years television news has dramatized America's key events and provided a clearinghouse for shared information. Civil Rights activists, for instance, acknowledge that the movement benefited enormously from televised pictures that documented the plight of southern blacks in the 1960s. Other enduring TV images, unfurled as a part of history to each new generation, are embedded in our collective memory: the Kennedy and King assassinations in the 1960s; the turmoil of Watergate in the 1970s; the first space shuttle disaster and the Chinese student uprisings in the 1980s; the Oklahoma City federal building bombing and the Clinton impeachment hearings in the 1990s; the terrorist attacks on the Pentagon and New York's World Trade Center in 2001; and the ongoing U.S. war in Iraq. During these critical events, TV news has been a cultural reference point marking the strengths and weaknesses of a nation.

In contrast, a disturbing TV news strategy developed in the mid-1980s. To cover crack cocaine stories, news operations used a visual shot in which news photographers, or *shooters* (using shaky, handheld cameras), leaped from the back of police vans and followed authorities as they raided crack houses. In such a shot, the news is actually representing only the authorities' point of view. Surprisingly, for a profession that prides itself on neutrality and its watchdog role, little criticism emerged about the appropriateness of this approach. But, TV news doesn't always tell a story from the authorities' viewpoint. When Hurricane Katrina hit the Gulf Coast in 2005, killing more than 1,800 people and displacing more than 500,000, the national TV news was there. In the first few days of the crisis, news anchors Brian Williams of NBC, Anderson Cooper of CNN, and Shepard Smith of Fox News, among others, traveled to the devastated areas and asked on camera how they had managed to make it there when disaster relief agencies like FEMA could not. They identified with the storm's victims and railed against the slow and inept government responses to the disaster.

Public Journalism, Fake News, and Democracy

In 1990, Poland was experiencing growing pains as it shifted from a state-controlled economic system to a more open market economy. The country's leading newspaper, *Gazeta Wyborcza*, the first noncommunist newspaper to appear in Eastern Europe since the 1940s, was also undergoing challenges. Based in Warsaw with a circulation of about 350,000 at the time, *Gazeta Wyborcza* had to report on and explain the new economy and the new crime wave that accompanied it. Especially troubling to the news staff and to Polish citizens were gangs that preyed on American and Western European tourists at railway stations. Apparently, an inner circle of thieves snatched purses, wallets, and luggage, sometimes assaulting tourists in the process. The stolen goods would then pass to an outer circle whose members transferred the goods to still another exterior ring of thieves. Even if the police caught the inner-circle members, the loot disappeared.

These developments triggered heated discussions in the newsroom. A small group of young reporters, some of whom had recently worked in the United States, argued that the best way to cover the story was to describe the new crime wave and relay the facts to readers in a neutral manner. Another group, many of whom were older and more experienced, felt that the paper should take an advocacy stance and condemn the criminals through interpretive columns on the front page. The older guard won this particular debate, and more interpretive pieces appeared.[32]

Resisting Conventional Journalism: Alternative Models for News

The Polish newsroom story illustrates the two competing models that have influenced American and European journalism since the early 1900s. The first—the *informational* or *modern model*—emphasizes describing events and issues from a seemingly neutral point of view. The second—a more *partisan* and *European model*—stresses analyzing occurrences and advocating remedies from an acknowledged point of view. In most American newspapers today, the informational model dominates the front page, whereas the partisan model remains confined to the editorial pages and an occasional front-page piece. Supplementing both models, photographs in newspapers and images on television tell parts of a story not easily captured in words. Alternative models of news—from the serious to the satirical—have emerged to challenge modern journalistic ideals.

The Public Journalism Movement

From the late 1980s through the 1990s, a number of papers experimented with ways to more actively involve readers in the news process. These experiments surfaced primarily at midsize daily papers, including the *Charlotte Observer*, the *Wichita Eagle*, the *Virginian-Pilot*, and the *Minneapolis Star Tribune*. Davis "Buzz" Merritt, editor and vice president of the *Wichita Eagle*, defined key aspects of **public journalism**:

- It moves beyond the limited mission of "telling the news" to a broader mission of helping public life go well, and acts out that imperative. . . .
- It moves from detachment to being a fair-minded participant in public life. . . .
- It moves beyond only describing what is "going wrong" to also imagining what "going right" would be like. . . .
- It moves from seeing people as consumers—as readers or nonreaders, as bystanders to be informed—to seeing them as a public, as potential actors in arriving at democratic solutions to public problems.[33]

Public journalism might best be imagined as a conversational model for journalistic practice. Modern journalism draws a distinct line between reporter detachment and community involvement; public journalism—driven by citizen forums, community conversations, and even talk shows—smudged this line.

The stimulus behind public journalism was the realization that many citizens felt and still feel alienated from participating in public life in a meaningful way. This alienation arises, in part, from watching passively as the political process plays out in the news media. The process stars the politicians who run for office, the spin doctors who manage the campaigns, and the reporters who dig into every nook and cranny. Meanwhile, readers and viewers serve as spectators, watching a play that does not seem to involve them.

The public journalism movement has drawn both criticism and praise. Though not a substitute for investigative reporting or the routine coverage of daily events, public journalism is a way to involve both the public and journalists more centrally in civic and political life. Editors and reporters interested in addressing citizen alienation—and reporter cynicism—began devising ways to engage people as conversational partners in determining the news. In an effort to draw the public into discussions about community priorities, these journalists began sponsoring reader

> 66 We need to see people not as readers, nonreaders, endangered readers, not as customers to be wooed or an audience to be entertained, but as a public, citizens capable of action. 99
>
> —Davis "Buzz" Merritt, *Wichita Eagle*, 1995

and citizen forums, where readers were supposed to have a voice in shaping aspects of the news that directly affected them.

Although isolated citizen projects and reader forums are sprinkled throughout the history of journalism, the public journalism movement began in earnest in 1987 and 1988, in Columbus, Georgia. The city was suffering from a depressed economy, an alienated citizenry, and unresponsive leadership. In response, a team of reporters from the *Columbus Ledger-Enquirer* surveyed and talked with community leaders and other citizens about the future of the city. Based on the findings, the paper published an eight-part series.

When the provocative series evoked little public response, the paper's leadership realized there was no mechanism or forum for continuing the public discussions about the issues raised in the series. Consequently, the paper created such a forum by organizing a town meeting. The editor of the paper, Jack Swift, organized a follow-up cookout at his own home at which concerned citizens created a new civic organization called United Beyond 2000, led by a steering committee with Swift as a leading member. Staffed by community volunteers, task forces formed around issues such as racial tension and teenage behavior. The committees spurred the city's managers and other political leaders into action. The Columbus project generated public discussion, involved more people in the news process, and eased race and class tensions by bringing various groups together in public conversations. In the newsroom, the *Ledger-Enquirer* reimagined the place of journalists in politics: "Instead of standing outside the political community and reporting on its pathologies, they took up residence within its borders."[34]

Another important public journalism project began in Wichita, Kansas, after the 1988 elections. Editor Davis Merritt was so discouraged by the *Wichita Eagle*'s typical and conventional political coverage that he led a campaign to use public journalism as a catalyst for reinventing political news. The *Eagle*'s first voter project during the 1990 campaign for governor used reader surveys and public forums to refocus the paper around a citizens' agenda. This involved dropping the tired horse-race metaphor—who's winning, who's losing—that usually frames political coverage. Merritt argued that "public life cannot regain its vitality on a diet of information alone." He believed that a new direction for journalism must "re-engage citizens in public life" through two steps: "(1) Add to the definition of our job the additional objective of helping public life go well, and then (2) Develop the journalistic tools and

> **"The idea is to frame stories from the citizen's view, rather than inserting man-in-the-street quotes into a frame dominated by professionals."**
> —NYU's Jay Rosen, 1995

● Sebastião Salgado, a Brazilian economist-turned-photographer, is renowned for his searing portraits of the world's dispossessed. Originally a news photographer, he turned to documenting refugee communities in Latin America, Southeast Asia, and Africa in books including *Migrations* (2000) and *The Children* (2000). While some critics contend that Salgado's work romanticizes the lives of the poor, others credit him with exposing to the affluent the desperate conditions in which billions of the world's poor live.

reflexes necessary to reach that objective."[35] The *Eagle's* project partially revitalized regional politics in Kansas in the early 1990s and into the new millennium. It influenced other papers as well, including the *Charlotte Observer*, which created a citizens' agenda to determine key issues for its election coverage throughout the 1990s.

Criticizing Public Journalism

By 2000, more than a hundred newspapers, many teamed with local television and public radio stations, practiced some form of public journalism. Yet many critics and journalists remained skeptical of the experiment, raising a number of concerns.[36] First, some editors and reporters argue that such journalism merely panders to what readers—and therefore corporate publishers—want and takes editorial control away from the newsrooms. They believe that very small focus group samples and poll research—tools of the marketing department—blur the boundary between the editorial and business functions of a paper. Journalists have traditionally viewed their work as a public service and seldom think of the news as a product or a commodity. Some journalists fear that as they become more active in the community they may be perceived as community boosters rather than as community watchdogs.

Second, some critics worry that public journalism might compromise the profession's credibility, which many believe derives from detachment. They argue that public journalism turns reporters into participants rather than observers. However, as Merritt points out, professionals who have credibility are regarded as "honest, intelligent, well-intentioned, trustworthy" and "share some basic values about life, some common ground about common good." Yet conventional journalists insist they "don't share values, with anyone; that [they] are value-neutral."[37] Merritt argues that modern journalism, as a result, actually has little credibility with the public. This view is buoyed by polls that reveal the public's basic distrust of most major news media. Research studies in 1988, for instance, indicated that 50 percent of surveyed respondents had "a great deal of confidence in newspapers"; by 1993 and into the early 2000s, similar polls showed that the confidence factor had dropped to less than 25 percent.[38]

Third, critics contend that public journalism undermines the both-sides-of-a-story convention by constantly seeking common ground and community consensus. Public journalists counter that they are trying to set aside more room for centrist positions. Such positions are often representative of many in the community but are missing in the mainstream news, which is more interested in the extremist views that make for a gripping story. Many journalists who seek to portray conflict by means of extreme viewpoints worry that in seeking a middle ground, public journalism runs the risk of dulling the rough edges of democratic speech.

Fourth, considered by many traditional reporters as merely a tool of marketers and business managers, public journalism had not addressed the changing economic structure of the news business. With more newspapers (and broadcast stations) in the hands of fewer owners, both public journalists and traditional reporters needed to raise tough questions about the disappearance of competing daily papers and the large profit margins generated by local monopoly newspapers. Facing little competition, will newspapers continue the 1990s trend of cutting reporting staffs or expensive investigative projects and reducing the space for news? Such a trend may increase profits and satisfy stockholders, but it also limits the voices and views in a community.

Fake News and Satiric Journalism

For many young people, the political system is broken, with two wealthy established parties—beholden to special interests and their lobbyists—controlling the nation's government. After all, 98 percent of congressional incumbents get reelected each year—not always because they've done a good job but often because they've used their time in office to make promises and do favors for the lobbyists and interests that helped get them elected in the first place. In fact, since 2000, registered lobbyists increased by 100 percent in Washington—from 17,000 to 34,750 in 2005.[39] Why shouldn't young citizens, then, be cynical about politics? It is this cynicism that has drawn more and more younger people to "fake news" shows like *The Daily Show with Jon Stewart* and *The Colbert Report* on cable's Comedy Central. Following in the tradition of *Saturday Night Live*'s "Weekend Update" sketches—which began in 1975—these half-hour cable satires tell their audiences something that seems truthful about politicians and the news media that cover them, and they do so with humor.

The Colbert Report satirizes cable "star" news hosts, particularly Fox's Bill O'Reilly and MSNBC's Chris Matthews, and the opinion-argument culture promoted by these programs. On the other hand, in critiquing the limits of news stories and politics, *The Daily Show*, "anchored" by Stewart, parodies the narrative conventions of the regular evening news programs: the clipped eight-second "sound bite" that limits meaning and the formulaic shot of the TV news "stand up," which depicts reporters "on location," apparently establishing credibility by revealing that they were really there. On *The Daily Show*, Stewart's cast of fake reporters (who seldom leave the studio) are digitally superimposed in front of exotic foreign locales or shot with the goofy graphic "Anytown, USA" appearing over their shoulder. In a 2004 exchange with "political correspondent" Rob Corrdry, Stewart asks him for his opinion about presidential campaign tactics. "My opinion? I don't have opinions," Corrdry answers, "I'm a reporter, Jon. My job is to spend half the time repeating what one side says, and half the time repeating the other. Little thing called objectivity; might want to look it up."

As news court jester, Stewart exposes the melodrama of TV news that nightly depicts the world in various stages of disorder while at the same time offering the stalwart presence of celebrity-anchors overseeing it all from their hi-tech command centers. Even before CBS's Walter Cronkite signed off the evening news with "And that's the way it is," network news anchors have offered a sense of order through the reassurance of their individual personalities. As a satirist, Stewart is not so sure, arguing that things are a mess and in need of repair. For example, while national news operations like MSNBC thought nothing of adopting the Pentagon slogan "Operation Iraqi Freedom" as its own graphic title, *The Daily Show* offered its satiric counter—"Mess O' Potamia." Even as a fake anchor, though, Stewart displays a much greater range of emotion— a range that may match our own—than we get from our detached "hard news" anchors: more amazement, irony, outrage, laughter, and skepticism.

Much of the unimaginative quality of traditional news stories that fake news shows critique has to do with news producers repeating familiar formulas rather than inventing new story forms. Although the world has changed, local TV news story formulas (except for splashy opening graphics and Doppler weather radar) have virtually gone unaltered since the 1970s, when *SNL*'s "Weekend Update" first started making fun of TV news. Newscasts still limit reporters' stories to two minutes or less and promote stylish male/female coanchors, a sports "guy," and a certified meteorologist as familiar personalities whom we invite into our homes each evening. The basic problem with mainstream news today—especially on local TV—is that a generation of young voters has been raised on the TV satire and political cynicism of "Weekend Update," Jay Leno, David Letterman, Conan O'Brien, *The Daily Show*, and now *The Colbert*

● A spin-off of *The Daily Show*, *The Colbert Report* (*below*) is a parody of political pundit news shows. The show coined the term "truthiness" in its first episode.

Online News Attracts Young Audience

By Peter Johnson

Meg Scholz, a senior at the University of Texas, goes online at least a few times every day to check her e-mail.

When she does, Scholz invariably scans several news websites and blogs to see what's going on in the world. She rarely picks up a newspaper or watches TV news, because for her, the Web serves virtually all her news needs.

"It's not that I have anything against reading a printed newspaper," says Scholz, 21. "But for my lifestyle, the Internet is more accessible."

Justin Ulahannan, 22, watches TV news occasionally and he reads the print edition of the *Wall Street Journal*, which he gets free as an intern at the U.S. Business Council in Washington.

But otherwise, he gets news online from CNN.com or BBC.com. "It's just a matter of convenience," Ulahannan says. "Why would I pay money (for a newspaper) when I can get the same thing online for free?"

A study released today by the Pew Internet & American Life project finds that for people like Scholz and Ulahannan, the Internet has become the primary news source on the average day.

"For many of these young broadband users, the Internet is their main course for news, and they don't always eat their vegetables or order dessert in the form of using other media," says study author John Horrigan.

Though this may not come as news to anyone under 35, the results have profound ramifications for mainstream media outlets, which need to integrate an online presence as quickly as possible or risk alienating the next generation of news consumers, Horrigan says.

"Mainstream media need to search for the right business model that integrates the online experience into what they do," Horrigan says. "We're seeing the beginnings of a significant segment of the population having their daily newsgathering habits formed by what they see on the Internet."

This compares with just five years ago, he says, when Pew researchers found that high-speed users "were using the Internet to fill in their news-gathering habits. Now, it governs where they go and what they do" to get news.

The report is based on a survey in December 2005 of 3,011 adult Americans, 1,931 of whom are Internet users and 1,014 of whom have high-speed connections at home.

Within a "high-powered" group of Internet users—those who use broadband four or more times a day—71% go online for news on an average day, while 59% get news from

Older Internet Users Branch Out for News

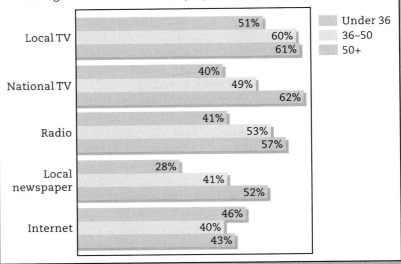

Younger online users are more likely to depend on the Internet as their main source of news; older users consume a wider variety of sources. Percentage of broadband users, by age, who regularly get news from:

Under 36 / 36–50 / 50+

- Local TV: 51%, 60%, 61%
- National TV: 40%, 49%, 62%
- Radio: 41%, 53%, 57%
- Local newspaper: 28%, 41%, 52%
- Internet: 46%, 40%, 43%

Source: Pew Internet & American Life Project, December 2005 survey of 1,014 home broadband Internet users, sampling error ±3 percentage points.

local TV, just over half from national TV and radio, and about 40% from local newspapers.

But especially for the under-36 age group, the local newspaper, local television, and national TV newscasts play lesser roles in their newsgathering, the study finds.

The study paints a bleak outlook for traditional ink-on-paper newspapers. But it also finds that younger readers—those under 36 who are often written off as not interested in news—are being drawn into the news habit earlier thanks to the appeal of the Internet.

"To maintain relevance in a community, a local print paper has to have a very robust online presence," Horrigan says. And if local newspapers quickly merge online technology into their print operations, they stand to draw younger, Internet-dependent readers "who find traditional media less relevant for them" but are drawn to local news Web sites.

"If my mother can set up her own broadband connection—and she did—then it has become a technology that is reasonably user-friendly to everybody," Horrigan says. "As more and more people go to the Internet just to pass the time, just for fun, it becomes a destination, just like turning on the TV traditionally has been."

Source: Peter Johnson, "Young People Turn to the Web for News," *USA Today*, March 23, 2006, D9.

Report. The slick and formulaic packaging of political ads or the canned and careful sound bites offered in news packages are simply not as persuasive.

Most importantly, journalism needs to break free from tired formulas—especially in TV news—and reimagine better ways to tell stories. In fictional TV, storytelling has evolved over time, becoming increasingly complex. As Steven Johnson argues, "One of the most complex social networks on popular television in the seventies [*Dallas*] looks practically infantile next to the social networks of today's hit dramas [e.g., *Desperate Housewives, CSI, Grey's Anatomy,* and *24,* among others]."[40] If fictional storytelling has developed and adapted, why has TV news remained virtually unchanged over the past forty years? Aren't there other or new ways to report the news? Even in print, the inverted pyramid lead has remained entrenched on the front pages of U.S. newspapers. It is no wonder then why young people are looking to *The Daily Show, The Colbert Report,* blogs, YouTube.com, and other alternatives for information. Maybe they want news that better matches the complicated storytelling that surrounds them in everything from TV dramas to interactive video games to their own conversations. As citizens we should demand news stories that better represent the complexity of our world. (See "Tracking Technology: Online News Attracts Young Audience" on opposite page.)

Democracy and Reimagining Reporting's Role

Journalism is central to democracy—that is, freedom requires that both citizens and the media have access to the information and stories that we all need to make important decisions. As this chapter illustrates, however, this is a complicated idea. For example, in the aftermath of 9/11, some government officials claimed that whenever the news media raised questions about fighting terrorism, invading Iraq, or secret programs, somehow reporters or columnists were being unpatriotic. But the basic principles of democracy require citizens and the media to ask questions. In fact, a counterargument could be made that patriotism demands that we question our leaders and our government. Isn't this, after all, what the American Revolution was originally all about?

Conventional journalists will fight ferociously for the overt principles that underpin reporting's basic tenets—questioning government, freedom of the press, the public's right to know, and two sides to every story. These are all worthy ideals, but they do have limitations. All these tenets, for example, generally do not acknowledge any moral or ethical duty for journalists to improve the quality of daily life. Rather, conventional journalism values its news-gathering capabilities and the well-constructed news narrative, leaving the improvement of civic life to political groups, nonprofit organizations, business philanthropists, and individual citizens.

Social Responsibility

Although reporters have traditionally thought of themselves first and foremost as observers and recorders, some journalists have occasionally acknowledged social responsibility. Among them was James Agee in the 1930s. In his book *Let Us Now Praise Famous Men,* which was accompanied by the Depression-era photography of Walker Evans, Agee regarded conventional journalism as dishonest, partly because the act of observing intruded on people and turned them into story characters, whom newspapers and magazines exploited for profit.

Agee also worried that readers would retreat into the comfort of his writing—his narrative—instead of confronting what for many families was the horror of the Great Depression. For Agee, the question of responsibility extended not only to journalism and himself but to the readers of his stories as well: "The reader is no less centrally involved than the authors and those of whom they tell."[41] Agee's self-conscious

> **"** Neither journalism nor public life will move forward until we actually rethink, redescribe, and reinterpret what journalism is; not the science of information of our culture but its poetry and conversation. **"**
>
> –James Carey,
> *Kettering Review,* 1992

● In *Let Us Now Praise Famous Men*, which begins with haunting photos taken by Walker Evans, author James Agee questioned the basic honesty of daily journalism in the late 1930s. He thought that professional journalists could too easily exploit interview subjects simply as news stories that serve a business enterprise without actively engaging in changing the conditions of social life.

analysis provides insights into journalism's hidden agendas and the responsibility of all citizens to make public life better.

Deliberative Democracy

According to advocates of public journalism, when reporters are chiefly concerned with maintaining their antagonistic relationship to politics and are less willing to improve political discourse, news and democracy suffer. *Washington Post* columnist David Broder thinks that national journalists like him—through rising salaries, prestige, and formal education—have distanced themselves "from the people that we are writing for and have become much, much closer to people we are writing about."[42] Broder believes that journalists need to become activists, not for a particular party but for the political process and in the interest of re-energizing public life. For the news media, this might involve spearheading voter registration drives or setting up pressrooms or news bureaus in public libraries or even in shopping malls, where people converge in large numbers.

By advocating a more active role for reporters and the news media, journalism at its best promises to reinvigorate both reporting and politics. Most of all, it offers people models for how to deliberate in forums, and then it covers those deliberations. This kind of community journalism aims to improve our standard *representative democracy*, in which most of us sit back and watch elected officials act on our behalf, by reinvigorating *deliberative democracy*, in which citizen groups, local government, and the news media together take a more active stand in shaping social, economic, and political agendas. In a more deliberative democracy, a large segment of the community discusses public life and social policy before advising or electing officials who represent the community's interests.

In 1989, the historian Christopher Lasch argued that "the job of the press is to encourage debate, not to supply the public with information."[43] Although he overstated his case—journalism does both and more—Lasch made a cogent point about how conventional journalism has lost its bearings. Adrift in data, mainstream journalism lost touch with its partisan roots. The early mission of journalism—to advocate opinions and encourage public debate—has been relegated to alternative magazines, the editorial pages, news blogs, and cable news channels starring elite East Coast reporters. Ironically, Lasch connected the gradual decline in voter participation, which began in the 1920s, to more responsible conduct on the part of professional journalists. With a modern "objective" press, he contended, the public increasingly began to defer to the "more professional" news media to watch over civic life on its behalf.

As the advocates of public journalism acknowledge, people have grown used to letting their representatives think and act for them. More community-oriented journalism and other civic projects offer citizens an opportunity to deliberate and to influence their leaders. This may include broadening the story frames they use to recount experiences; paying more attention to the historical and economic contexts of these stories; doing more investigative reports that analyze both news conventions and social issues; taking more responsibility for their news narratives; participating more fully in the public life of their communities; admitting to their cultural biases and occasional mistakes; and defending themselves better when they are attacked for performing their watchdog role.

Arguing that for too long journalism has defined its role only in negative terms, news scholar Jay Rosen notes: "To be adversarial, critical, to ask tough questions, to expose scandal and wrongdoing . . . these are necessary tasks, even noble tasks, but they are negative tasks." In addition, he suggests, journalism should assert itself as a positive force, not merely as a watchdog or as a neutral information conduit to readers but as "a support system for public life."[44]

www.

For review questions and activities for Chapter 14, go to the interactive *Media and Culture* Online Study Guide at *bedfordstmartins.com/ mediaculture*

REVIEW QUESTIONS

Modern Journalism in the Information Age

1. What are the drawbacks of the informational model of journalism?

2. What is news?

3. What are some of the key values that underlie modern journalism?

Ethics and the News Media

4. How do issues such as deception and privacy present ethical problems for journalists?

5. Why is getting a story first important to reporters?

6. What are the connections between so-called neutral journalism and economics?

Reporting Rituals and the Legacy of Print Journalism

7. Why have reporters become so dependent on experts?

8. Why do many conventional journalists (and citizens) believe firmly in the idea that there are two sides to every story?

Journalism in the Age of Television

9. How is credibility established in TV news as compared to print journalism?

10. With regard to TV news, what are sound bites and happy talk?

Public Journalism, Fake News, and Democracy

11. What is public journalism? How did it propose to make journalism better?

12. What are the major criticisms of the public journalism movement, and why do the mainstream national media have concerns about public journalism?

13. What role do satirical news programs like *The Daily Show* play in the world of journalism?

14. What is deliberative democracy, and what does it have to do with journalism?

QUESTIONING THE MEDIA

1. What are your main criticisms of the state of news today? In your opinion, what are the news media doing well?

2. If you were a reporter or an editor, would you quit voting in order to demonstrate your ability to be neutral? Why or why not?

3. Is there political bias in most front-page news stories? If so, cite an example.

4. How would you go about formulating an ethical policy with regard to using deceptive means to get a story?

5. For a reporter, what are the dangers of both detachment from and involvement in public life?

6. Do satirical news programs make us more cynical about politics and less inclined to vote? Why or why not?

7. What steps would you take to make journalism work better in a democracy?

SEARCHING THE INTERNET

http://www.journalism.org

The site for Project for Excellence in Journalism, initiated by concerns about standards. The site offers research studies and critical essays on topics related to journalism.

http://www.cjr.org

The Web site for the *Columbia Journalism Review*, one of the nation's premier critics of contemporary journalism. Run by the Columbia Graduate School of Journalism, the site not only contains current CJR magazine articles on national and international news coverage but also offers a valuable updated list of "who owns what" in the media.

http://ajr.org

The site for the *American Journalism Review*, another top national magazine that takes a critical look at contemporary journalism. Run by the Philip Merrill College of Jour-

nalism at the University of Maryland, the site features current articles from the magazine and links to useful resources.

http://www.aim.org

The Web site for the conservative media watchdog group Accuracy in Media (AIM). Among other issues, the site showcases articles from its national newsletter and tracks what AIM regards as anti-business bias in national news reporting.

http://www.fair.org

The Web site for the progressive and left-leaning media watchdog group Fairness and Accuracy in Reporting (FAIR). The site contains articles from its national magazine *EXTRA!* and a feature called "economic reporting review" that examines news coverage of money-related issues.

Media Literacy and the Critical Process

In Brief

Make a short list of questionable or illegal methods that a reporter might use to get a story (e.g., withholding her identity as a reporter). Discuss the circumstances under which these methods might be justified.

In Depth

The purpose of this project is to extend your critical approach to the news. With a partner, choose for reading and viewing one local daily paper, the *New York Times*, and one network, FoxNews, or CNN newscast—all from the same weekday.

Devise a series of charts and a descriptive scheme that will enable you to compare who gets quoted as expert sources in the stories for that particular day. For example, devise one chart that compares the occupations of the sources. Are they from academic, business, or government sectors? Or are they "ordinary" people? Throughout this project, limit your focus to local, national, or international news.

Description. Count the total number of sources used by each newspaper or network program. Look for quotes in news articles and for sound bites on television. Are all sources identified? How are they identified? Can you tell which area of the country these sources are from? What kinds of experts are quoted in the news? What jobs do they seem to hold? What gender are the news sources?

Analysis. After completing your charts, write one or two paragraphs discussing patterns that emerge. Who seems to get quoted most frequently? Among those quoted, what kinds of occupations generally appear? Do male or female sources dominate?

Interpretation. Write a one- or two-paragraph critical interpretation of your findings. How are the sources used? Why do you think certain sources appear in this day's news more frequently than others? Why do reporters seek out certain types of sources rather than others? Does the gender of sources mean anything?

Evaluation. Discuss the limitations of your study and whether you think print or television handles sources best. Did circumstances on the particular day you chose suggest why one type of expert appears more often than other types?

Engagement. Contact a print and TV reporter and/or editor responsible for your selected stories. Report your preliminary findings and document how they come to choose their sources.

(*Note:* This assignment works either as an in-class presentation or as a written project. Either way, it should include charts that help organize the material.)

KEY TERMS

newsworthiness, 487
news, 488
ethnocentrism, 490
responsible capitalism, 490
small-town pastoralism, 490

individualism, 490
conflict of interest, 494
herd journalism, 499
sound bite, 504
public journalism, 508

media effects

and cultural approaches to research

In 1966, NBC showed the Rod Serling made-for-television thriller *The Doomsday Flight,* the first movie to depict an airplane hijacking. In the story, a man plants a bomb and tries to extract ransom money from an airline. In the days following the telecast, the nation's major airlines reported a dramatic rise in anonymous bomb threats, some of them classified as teenage pranks. The network agreed not to run the film again.

In 1985, the popular heavy-metal band Judas Priest made headlines when two Nevada teenagers shot themselves after listening to the group's allegedly subliminal suicidal message on their 1978 *Stained Class* album. One teen died instantly; the other lived for three more years, in constant pain from severe facial injuries. The teenagers' parents lost a civil product liability suit against the British metal band and CBS Records.

In 1995, an eighteen-year-old woman and her boyfriend went on a killing spree in Louisiana after reportedly watching Oliver Stone's 1994 film *Natural Born Killers* more than twenty times.

15

The family of one of the victims filed a lawsuit against Stone and Time Warner, charging that the film—starring Juliette Lewis and Woody Harrelson as a demented, celebrity-craving young couple on a murderous rampage—irresponsibly incited real-life violence. Part of the family's case was based on a 1996 interview in which Stone said: "The most pacifist people in the world said they came out of this movie and wanted to kill somebody." Stone and Time Warner argued that the lawsuit should be dismissed on the grounds of free speech, and the case was finally thrown out in 2001. There was no evidence, according to the judge, that Stone had intended to incite violence.

In 1999, two heavily armed students wearing trench coats attacked Columbine High School in Littleton, Colorado. They planted as many as fifty bombs and murdered twelve fellow students and a teacher before killing themselves. In the wake of this tragedy many people blamed the mass media, speculating that the killers had immersed themselves in the dark lyrics of shock rocker Marilyn Manson and were desen-

● Woody Harrelson in *Natural Born Killers* (1994).

sitized to violence by "first-person shooter" video games such as *Doom.* Still others looked to the influence of films like *The Basketball Diaries,* in which a drug-using, trench-coated teenager (played by Leonardo DiCaprio) imagines shooting a teacher and his classmates.

In March 2005, a high school shooting that left ten dead in Red Lake, Minnesota, again brought attention to the mass media as a cause of violence. Reports cited that the sixteen-year-old shooter frequented a chat room on a neo-Nazi Web site and called himself "Angel of Death" in his postings. But the young man's life was complicated by other factors: a father who committed suicide, a

mother living in a nursing home due to a brain injury suffered in a car crash, an expulsion from school, and ready access to guns.

Each of these events has renewed long-standing cultural debates over the suggestive power of music, visual imagery, and screen violence. Since the emergence of popular music, movies, and television as influential mass media, the relationship between make-believe stories and real-life imitation has drawn a great deal of attention. Concerns have been raised not only by parents, teachers, and politicians but also by several generations of mass communication researchers as well.

**W**hen it comes to government- or university-sponsored mass media research, no social groups have been pondered and probed more than children and teens. The dominant strain of this research—known in shorthand as **media effects** because of its focus on attempting to understand, explain, and predict the effects of mass media on individuals and society—has focused on one particular area: the connection between aggressive behavior and violent media stories. In the late 1960s, government leaders—reacting to the social upheavals of that decade—first set aside $1 million to examine this connection. Since that time, thousands of studies have told us what most kindergarten teachers have come to believe instinctively: Violent scenes on television and in movies stimulate aggressive behavior in children—especially young boys. Over the years, children have imitated physical fight scenes from *Zorro, Mighty Mouse Playhouse, Batman, Teenage Mutant Ninja Turtles, Teen Titans,* and professional wrestling shows, leading generations of adults to suspect the effects of mass media.

In this chapter, we will examine the evolution of media research over time. After looking at some early research efforts, we will focus on two major directions in media research: effects research and cultural studies. We will investigate the strengths and limitations of these two approaches. Finally, we will consider how media research interacts with democratic ideals.

Early Developments in Media Research

In the early days of the United States, philosophical and historical writings tried to explain the nature of news and print media. For instance, Frenchman Alexis de Tocqueville, author of *Democracy in America,* noted differences between French and American newspapers in the early 1830s:

> In France the space allotted to commercial advertisements is very limited, and . . . the essential part of the journal is the discussion of the politics of the day. In America three quarters of the enormous sheet are filled with advertisements and the remainder is frequently occupied by political intelligence or trivial anecdotes; it is only from time to time that one finds a corner devoted to the passionate discussions like those which the journalists of France every day give to their readers.[1]

During the mid to late nineteenth century, the major models of media analysis were based on moral and political arguments, as suggested in de Tocqueville's writings.[2]

More scientific approaches to mass media research did not begin to develop until the late 1920s and 1930s. It was in 1920 that Walter Lippmann, in his book *Liberty and the News,* called on journalists to operate more like scientific researchers in gathering and analyzing factual material. Lippmann's next book, *Public Opinion,* published in 1922, applied principles of psychology to journalism. It is considered by many academics to be "the founding book in American media studies."[3]

In America, the emphasis on applied research led to an expanded analysis of the effects of the media, emphasizing data collection and numerical measurement. According to media historian Daniel Czitrom, by the 1930s "an aggressively empirical spirit, stressing new and increasingly sophisticated research techniques, characterized the study of modern communication in America."[4] Czitrom traces four early trends between 1930 and 1960 that contributed to the rise of modern media research: propaganda analysis, public opinion research, social psychology studies, and marketing research.

> **"** The pictures inside the heads of these human beings, the pictures of themselves, of others, of their needs, purposes, and relationships, are their public opinions. **"**
>
> —Walter Lippmann,
> *Public Opinion,* 1922

● One of the earliest forms of U.S. mass communication research—propaganda analysis—was prominent during the twentieth century's two world wars. Researchers studied the impact of war posters and other government information campaigns to determine how audiences could be persuaded through stirring media messages about patriotism and duty.

Propaganda Analysis

After World War I, some media researchers became interested in the ways in which propaganda had been used to advance the American war effort. They found that during the war, governments routinely relied on propaganda divisions as part of their "information" apparatus. Though propaganda was considered a positive force for mobilizing public opinion during the war, researchers after the war labeled propaganda as "partisan appeal based on half-truths and devious manipulation of communication channels."[5] Harold Lasswell's important 1927 study *Propaganda Technique in the World War* focused on media representations, defining propaganda as "the control of opinion by significant symbols, . . . by stories, rumors, reports, pictures and other forms of social communication."[6] *Propaganda analysis* became a major early focus of mass media research.

Public Opinion Research

Researchers soon extended the study of war propaganda to include general concerns about how the mass media filtered information and shaped public attitudes. In the face of growing media influence, Walter Lippmann distrusted the public's ability to function as knowledgeable citizens as well as journalism's ability to help the public separate truth from lies. In promoting the place of the expert in modern life, Lippmann celebrated the social scientist as part of a new expert class that could best make "unseen facts intelligible to those who have to make decisions."[7]

Today, Lippmann's expert class conducts citizen surveys in the form of *public opinion research,* which has become especially influential during political elections. On the upside, research on diverse populations has provided insights into citizen behavior and social differences, especially during election periods or following major national events. For example, in 2006 the level of enthusiasm for voting in the midterm election was higher among Democrats than Republicans. In a nationwide survey, 46 percent of Democratic voters versus 30 percent of Republican voters reported to be more enthusiastic about voting than usual, a reverse of the Republican voter excitement leading up to the 1994 election in which Republicans gained control of Congress.[8]

On the downside, the journalism profession has become increasingly dependent on political polls. Some critics ask whether this heavy reliance on measured public opinion has begun to adversely affect active political involvement. For example, there are numerous stories and studies about citizens who do not vote because they have already seen poll projections on television and decided that their votes would not make a difference in the outcome. Furthermore, because the public does not design a CBS News or Gallup poll, it is just passively responding to surveys that mainly measure opinions on topics of interest to business, government, academics, and the mainstream news media. Another problem is the pervasive use of unreliable **pseudo-polls**, typically call-in, online, or person-in-the-street polls that news media use to address a "question of the day." The National Council of Public Opinion Polls notes that "unscientific pseudo-polls are widespread and sometimes entertaining, if always quite meaningless," and discourages news media from conducting them.[9]

● Concerns about film violence are not new. This 1930 movie, *Little Caesar*, follows the career of gangster Rico Bandello (played by Edward G. Robinson, shown), who kills his way to the top of the crime establishment and gets the girl as well. The Motion Picture Production Code, which was established a few years after this movie's release, reined in sexual themes and profane language, set restrictions on film violence, and attempted to prevent audiences from sympathizing with bad guys like Rico.

Social Psychology Studies

Whereas opinion polls measure public attitudes, *social psychology studies* measure individual behavior and cognition. The most influential of these early investigations, the Payne Fund Studies, encompassed a series of thirteen research projects conducted by social psychologists between 1929 and 1932. Named after the private philanthropic organization that provided financial support for the research, the Payne Fund Studies emerged from a growing national concern about the effects of motion pictures, which had become a particularly popular pastime for young people in the 1920s. These beginning studies, which were later used by politicians to attack the movie industry, linked frequent movie attendance to juvenile delinquency, promiscuity, and other antisocial behaviors, arguing that movies took "emotional possession" of young filmgoers.[10]

In one of the Payne studies, for example, children were taken to a movie house and wired with electrodes to galvanometers, mechanisms that detect any heightened response via the subject's skin. The researchers interpreted any galvanic changes in the skin as evidence of emotional arousal. In retrospect, the findings hardly seem surprising: The youngest children in the group (nine-year-olds) had the strongest reaction to violent or tragic movie scenes, and the teenage subjects reacted most strongly to scenes with romantic and sexual content. The researchers concluded that films could be dangerous for young children and might foster sexual promiscuity among teenagers. The conclusions of this and other Payne Fund Studies contributed to the establishment of the film industry's production code, which tamed movie content from the 1930s through the 1950s. As forerunners of today's TV violence and aggression research, the Payne Fund Studies became the model for

> **66** Motion pictures are not understood by the present generation of adults. They are new; they make an enormous appeal to children; and they present ideas and situations which parents may not like. **99**
>
> – *Motion Pictures and the Social Attitudes of Children: A Payne Fund Study*, 1933

The TV industry continues to study its self-imposed rating categories, promising to fine-tune them to ensure that the government keeps its distance. These standards are one example of a policy that was shaped in part by media research. Since the 1960s, research has attempted to demonstrate links between violent TV images and increased levels of aggression among children and adolescents.

Figure 15.1
TV Parental Guidelines

The following categories apply to programs designed solely for children:

 All Children. *This program is designed to be appropriate for all children.*

 Directed to Older Children. *This program is designed for children age 7 and above.*

 Note: For those programs where fantasy violence may be more intense or more combative than other programs in this category, such programs will be designated **TV-Y7-FV**.

The following categories apply to programs designed for the entire audience:

 General Audience. *Most parents would find this program suitable for all ages.*

 Parents Strongly Cautioned. *This program contains some material that many parents would find unsuitable for children under 14 years of age.*

 Parental Guidance Suggested. *This program contains material that parents may find unsuitable for younger children.*

 Mature Audiences Only. *This program is specifically designed to be viewed by adults and therefore may be unsuitable for children under 17.*

 For programs rated **TV-PG**, **TV-14**, and **TV-MA**, labels are included to provide more information about contents, where appropriate:
D — suggestive dialogue
L — coarse language
S — sexual situations
V — violence

Source: TV Parental Guidelines Monitoring Board, http://www.tvguidelines.org, 7/10/06.

media research beginning in the late 1960s. (See Figure 15.1 for one example of a contemporary policy that has developed from media research. Also see "Examining Ethics: The Media Violence Myth" on opposite page, for part of the continuing debate over the theoretical link between media and violence.)

Marketing Research

A fourth influential area of media research, primarily private, developed through the efforts of advertisers and product companies. They began conducting surveys on consumer buying habits, known as *marketing research*. Specialized researchers, using improved audience sampling and statistical techniques, began selling their services to advertisers and media firms in the 1920s. The emergence of commercial radio led to the first ratings systems that measured how many people were listening on a given night. By the 1930s, radio networks, advertisers, large stations, and advertising agencies all subscribed to ratings services. However, compared with print media, whose circulation departments kept careful track of customers' names and addresses, radio listeners were more difficult to trace. This problem precipitated the development of increasingly sophisticated direct-mail diaries, television meters, phone surveys, the telemarketing industry, and eventually Internet tracking in trying to determine consumer preferences and measure media use worldwide.

> **❝ My idea of a good time is using jargon and citing authorities.❞**
>
> –Matt Groening,
> *School Is Hell,* 1987

EXAMINING ETHICS

The Media Violence Myth

By Richard Rhodes

A retired U.S. Army lieutenant colonel with an M.Ed. in counseling, formerly an ROTC professor at the University of Arkansas, [Dave] Grossman left the Army to dedicate himself to saving America from what he calls the "toxic waste" of "media violence" that is "being pumped into our nation and our children," the "electronic crack cocaine" of [TV] and video games that he claims are "truly addictive."

Grossman speaks to hundreds of organizations every year, from schools and colleges to Rotary Clubs, police departments, and veterans' groups. He's an effective speaker and polemicist. "We live in the most violent era in peacetime human history," he sets up his audiences. If someone reminds him that the murder rate was eight times as high in medieval Europe as it is in modern America, that murder rates have been declining steadily in the Western world for the past five hundred years, he claims it's an illusion. "Medical technology saves ever more lives every year," he says. "If we had 1930s medical technology today, the murder rate would be ten times what it is." He claims that people are trying to kill people ten times as often as they used to do back when there were no police and no common access to courts of law, but that modern emergency medicine is masking the increase.

It's easy to believe that violence is getting worse. . . . It's easy to believe that mock violence in media is influencing behavior: What other violence do suburban kids see? Without question, popular culture is a lot more raucous than it used to be. It's a wild pageant, and it scares the culture police. But however many national leaders and prestigious institutions endorse the theory, it's a fraud. There's no evidence that mock violence in media makes people violent, and there's some evidence that it makes people more peaceful.

To start with, take a look at Col. Dave's claim about improved medical technology saving potential homicides. Of 1.5 million violent crimes in the United States in 1998, 17,000 were murders. Of the remaining number, according to the FBI, only 20,331 resulted in major injuries (the rest produced minor physical injuries or none at all). So if all the assault victims with major injuries had also died—improbable even with 1930s medicine—the 1998 U.S. murder rate would only have been double what it was—that is, would have been about 13 per 100,000 population rather

than 6.3. But even 13 is well below the 23 per 100,000 murder rate of thirteenth-century England, the 45 per 100,000 of fifteenth-century Sweden, the 47 per 100,000 of fifteenth-century Amsterdam. We don't live in "the most violent era in peacetime human history"; we live in one of the least violent eras in peacetime human history.

Jib Fowles, a . . . media scholar at the University of Houston at Clear Lake, worked his way through the media effects literature carefully and thoroughly when he was researching a book on the subject, mischievously titled *The Case for Television Violence,* which was published last year. Although Grossman and others are fond of claiming that there have been more than 2,500 studies showing a connection between violent media and aggressive behavior (the number actually refers to the entire bibliography of a major government report on the subject), the independent literature reviews Fowles consulted identified only between one and two hundred studies, the majority of them laboratory studies. Very few studies have looked at media effects in the real world, and even fewer have followed the development of children exposed to violent media over a period of years.

The results of their laboratory experiments have been inconclusive. In some studies "aggression" increased following the "violent" television viewing; but in other studies the control kids who watched a neutral segment were more aggressive afterward. Sometimes kids acted up more after watching comedy. Boys usually acted up more than girls, but sometimes it was the other way around. "In the majority of cases," two investigators who reviewed a large number of laboratory studies found, "there was an increase in negative behaviors in the postviewing interval for both aggressive and non-aggressive television material." Contradictory results such as these prove, at best, no more than what everyone already knows: that watching movies or [TV] can stir kids up. They certainly don't prove that watching [TV] makes children violent. They don't prove anything about the real world, Fowles argues, because they're nothing like the real world.

Source: Excerpted from Richard Rhodes, *The Media Violence Myth,* http://www.abffe.com/myth1.htm, 2000. Rhodes is a Pulitzer Prize–winning writer and author of the book *Why They Kill* (New York: Knopf, 1999).

Research on Media Effects

As concern about public opinion, propaganda, and the impact of the media merged with the growth of journalism and mass communication departments in colleges and universities, media researchers looked more and more to behavioral science as a model. Between 1930 and 1960, "who says what to whom with what effect" became the key question "defining the scope and problems of American communications research."[11] Addressing these issues activated a major push in media effects research, with questions such as this: If children watch a lot of TV cartoons (stimulus or cause), will this repeated act influence their behavior toward their peers (response or effect)?

For most of the twentieth century, both media researchers and news reporters used different methods to answer similar sets of questions — who, what, when, and where — about our daily experiences. In practicing their professions, researchers and reporters have typically remained suspicious of concepts such as interpretation, subjectivity, and personal values, seeing them as problems to be avoided or even as dangerous contaminators of their work. An important difference exists between the two fields, however. Whereas daily news reporters *describe* what happens when teenagers watch violent movies, media researchers not only describe but also try to *explain* why it happens and attempt to predict whether it will happen again.

Media research generally comes from the private or public sector — each type with distinguishing features. *Private research,* sometimes called *proprietary research,* is generally conducted for a business, corporation, or even a political campaign. It is usually applied research in the sense that the information it uncovers typically addresses some real-life problem or need, such as determining consumer buying habits or market trends, trying to discover the hot-button issues for a political race, or measuring test audience responses to variations of a movie ending. *Public research,* on the other hand, usually takes place in academic and government settings. It involves information that is often more *theoretical* than applied; it tries to clarify, explain, or predict the effects of mass media rather than to address a consumer problem. Most public research is subject to examination and refutation by other academics. In contrast, private research is seldom shared, although the results of some private opinion polls or broadcast ratings may be released to the public with the owners' permission.

Key Phases in Research Approaches

A major goal of scientific research is to develop theories or laws that can consistently explain or predict human behavior. The varied impacts of the mass media and the diverse ways in which people make popular culture, however, tend to defy predictable rules. Historical, economic, and political factors influence media industries, making it difficult to develop

● Early media researchers were concerned about Adolf Hitler's use of national radio to control information and indoctrinate the German people throughout the 1930s. Germany's wartime international broadcasts, however, were considered failures. Trying to undermine morale using broadcasts aimed at Allied soldiers and British citizens, Germany hired British defector William Joyce ("Lord Haw Haw") and Ohioan Mildred Gillars ("Axis Sally"). Because so many media messages competed with Nazi propaganda in democratic countries, these radio traitors had little impact.

systematic theories that explain communication. What has developed instead are a number of small theories, or models, that help explain individual behavior rather than the impact of the media on large populations. But before these small theories began to emerge in the 1970s, mass media research followed several other models. Developing between the 1930s and the 1970s, these major approaches included the hypodermic-needle, minimal-effects, and uses and gratifications models.

Hypodermic-Needle Model

One of the earliest and least persuasive media theories attributed powerful effects to the mass media. A number of intellectuals and academics were particularly fearful of the popularity of film and radio, which became influential cultural forces in the 1920s and 1930s. Some of these observations were made by social psychologists and sociologists who arrived in this country after fleeing Hitler and Nazism in the 1930s. Having watched Hitler use radio, film, and print media as propaganda tools for Nazism, they worried that the popular media in America also had a strong hold over vulnerable audiences. This concept of powerful media affecting weak audiences has been labeled the **hypodermic-needle model**, sometimes also called the *magic bullet theory* or the *direct effects model*. It suggests that the media shoot their potent effects directly into unsuspecting victims.

One of the earliest challenges to the hypodermic-needle model of effects involved a study of Orson Welles's legendary October 30, 1938, broadcast of *War of the Worlds,* which presented a fictional news report of Martian invaders (see Chapter 4, page 133). Welles's radio program frightened millions of listeners who didn't realize that the show was an adaptation of the H. G. Wells science-fiction novel. In a 1940 book-length study, *The Invasion from Mars: A Study in the Psychology of Panic,* radio researcher Hadley Cantril argued that contrary to expectations according to the hypodermic-needle model, not all listeners thought the radio program was a real news report. Instead, Cantril noted—after conducting personal interviews and a nationwide survey of listeners, and analyzing newspaper reports and listener mail to CBS Radio and the FCC—that some people were more likely than others to believe in the report about a Martian invasion. Factors like the listening situation were found to be important, especially for people who tuned in late and missed the initial disclaimers for the program. Personal characteristics, too, were linked to the gullibility of certain audience members. For example, listeners with strong fundamentalist religious beliefs were more likely to think the invasion was an act of God and that the end of the world had indeed arrived.

Cantril's research helped to lay the groundwork for the minimal-effects model, which would become more popular in the following decades. Although the hypodermic-needle model has been disregarded or disproved by social scientists, many people still attribute such direct effects to the mass media, particularly in the case of children.

> 66 Theories abound, examples multiply, but convincing facts that specific media content is reliably associated with particular effects have proved quite elusive. 99
>
> —Guy Cumberbatch, *A Measure of Uncertainty,* 1989

Minimal-Effects Model

With the rise of empirical research techniques, social scientists began demonstrating that the media alone do not cause people to change their attitudes and behaviors. At this point, the limited or **minimal-effects model** emerged. Based on tightly controlled experiments and surveys, researchers generally argued that people engage in **selective exposure** and **selective retention** with regard to the media. That is, we selectively expose ourselves to media messages that are most familiar to us, and we retain messages that confirm values and attitudes we already hold. Minimal-effects researchers argued that in most cases the mass media reinforce existing behaviors and attitudes rather than change them.

The findings from the first comprehensive study of children and television, by Wilbur Schramm, Jack Lyle, and Edwin Parker in the late 1950s, best capture the minimal-effects tradition:

> For *some* children, under some conditions, some television is harmful. For *other* children under the same conditions, or for the same children under *other* conditions, it may be beneficial. For *most* children, under *most* conditions, *most* television is probably neither particularly harmful nor particularly beneficial.[12]

Joseph Klapper's important 1960 research review, *The Effects of Mass Communication,* found that the mass media influenced individuals who did not already hold strong views on an issue and that the media also had a greater impact on poor and uneducated heavy users. Solidifying the minimal-effects argument, Klapper concluded that strong media effects occur largely at an individual level and do not appear to have large-scale, measurable, and direct effects on society as a whole.[13]

Uses and Gratifications Model

Aside from difficulties in proving direct cause-effect relationships, the effects tradition usually assumed that audiences were passive and were acted upon by the media.

As early as the late 1950s, Schramm, Lyle, and Parker suggested that there were problems with this position:

> In a sense the term "effect" is misleading because it suggests that television "does something" to children. The connotation is that television is the actor, the children are acted upon. Children are thus made to seem relatively inert; television, relatively active. Children are sitting victims; television bites them. Nothing can be further from the fact. It is the children who are most active in this relationship. It is they who use television, rather than television that uses them.[14]

Indeed, as the authors observed, numerous studies have concluded that viewers—especially young children—are often *actively* engaged in the media, using various forms to guide their play.

A response to the minimal-effects theory, the **uses and gratifications model** was proposed in the 1940s to contest the notion of audience passivity. Under this model, researchers—usually using in-depth interviews to supplement survey questionnaires—studied the ways in which people used the media to satisfy various emotional or intellectual needs. The uses and gratifications

● In 1952, audience members at the Paramount Theater in Hollywood donned 3-D glasses for the opening night screening of *Bwana Devil,* the first full-length color 3-D film. The uses and gratifications model of research investigates the appeal of mass media, such as going out to the movies.

model represented a middle position between the hypodermic-needle and the minimal-effects models. Instead of asking, "What effects do the media have on us?" researchers asked, "Why do we use the media?"

Asking the *why* question enabled media researchers to develop inventories cataloguing how people employed the media. For example, individuals used the media to see authority figures elevated or toppled, to seek a sense of community and connectedness, to fulfill a need for drama and stories, and to confirm moral or spiritual values.[15] Though the uses and gratifications model addressed the *functions* of the mass media for individuals, it did not address the important questions related to the impact of the media on society. Once researchers had accumulated substantial lists of uses and functions, they often did not move in new directions. Consequently, the uses and gratifications model never became a dominant strain in media research.

Approaches to Media Effects

Most media research today, whether conducted in universities or in public policy institutes, has focused on the effects of the media on such issues as learning, attitudes, aggression, and voting habits. This research employs the **scientific method**, a blueprint long used by scientists and scholars to study phenomena in systematic stages. These steps include:

1. identifying the research problem
2. reviewing existing research and theories related to the problem
3. developing working hypotheses or predictions about what the study might find
4. determining an appropriate method or research design
5. collecting information or relevant data
6. analyzing results to see if the hypotheses have been verified
7. interpreting the implications of the study to determine whether they explain or predict patterns in human behavior

The scientific method relies on *objectivity* (eliminating bias and judgments on the part of researchers); *reliability* (getting the same answers or outcomes from a study or measure during repeated testing); and *validity* (demonstrating that a study actually measures what it claims to measure).

In scientific studies, researchers pose one or more **hypotheses**: tentative general statements that predict a relationship between a *dependent variable* that is influenced by an *independent variable*. For example, a researcher might hypothesize that heavy levels of TV viewing among adolescents (independent variable) cause poor performance (dependent variable) in traditional school settings. Or, another researcher might hypothesize that playing first-person shooter video games (independent variable) is associated with aggression (dependent variable) in children. Broadly speaking, the methods for studying media effects on audiences have taken two forms—experiments and survey research. To supplement these approaches, researchers also use content analysis as a technique for counting and documenting specific messages in mass media. We will look at all three.

Experiments

Like all studies that use the scientific method, **experiments** in media research isolate some aspect of content, suggest a hypothesis, and manipulate variables to discover a particular medium's impact on attitude, emotion, or behavior. To test whether a hypothesis is true, researchers expose an *experimental group*—the group under study—to a selected media program or text. To ensure valid results, researchers use a control group, which serves as a basis for comparison; this group is not exposed to the selected media content. Subjects are picked for each group through **random assignment**, which simply means that every subject has an equal chance of being placed in either group. Random assignment generally ensures that the variables researchers want to control are distributed to each group in the same way.

For instance, researchers might take a group of ten-year-old boys and randomly assign them to two groups. They expose the experimental group to a violent action movie that the control group does not see. Later, both groups are exposed to a staged fight between two other boys so that the researchers can observe how each group responds to an actual physical confrontation. Researchers then determine whether there is a statistically measurable difference between the two groups' responses to the fight. For example, perhaps the control subjects tried to break up the fight but the experimental subjects did not. Because the groups were randomly selected and the only measurable difference between them was the viewing of the movie, researchers may conclude that under these conditions the violent film caused a different behavior. (See the "Bobo doll" experiment photos on page 533.)

When experiments carefully account for variables through random assignment, they generally work well in substantiating direct cause-effect links. Such research takes place both in laboratory settings and in field settings, where people can be observed using the media in their everyday environments. In field experiments, however, it is more difficult for researchers to control variables. In lab settings, researchers have more control, but other problems may occur. For example, when subjects are removed from the environments in which they regularly use the media, they may act differently—often with fewer inhibitions—than they would in their everyday surroundings.

Experiments have other limitations as well. For instance, they are not generalizable to a larger population; they cannot tell us whether cause-effect results can be duplicated outside the laboratory. In addition, most academic experiments today are performed on college students, who are convenient subjects for research but are not representative of the general public. Although most experiments are fairly good at predicting short-term media effects under controlled conditions, they do not predict how subjects will behave months or years later in the real world.

Surveys

For long-term studies of the media, surveys usually work best. In its simplest terms, **survey research** is a method of collecting and measuring data taken from a group of respondents. Using random sampling techniques that give each potential subject an equal chance to be included in the survey, this research method draws on much larger populations than those used in experimental studies. Surveys are simply measuring instruments and do not control variables through randomly assigned groups. Survey investigators cannot account for all the variables that might affect media use; therefore, they cannot show cause-effect relationships. Survey research can, however, reveal *correlations*—or associations—between two variables. For example, a random questionnaire survey of ten-year-old boys might demonstrate that a correlation exists between aggressive behavior and watching violent TV programs, but it does not explain which causes which. Unlike experimental research, however, surveys are usually generalizable to the larger society.

Surveys are also useful measures for comparing voting behavior and levels of media use. To aid survey research, subjects are sometimes assigned to panel studies in which smaller groups of people are interviewed in depth on several occasions. In addition, surveys enable researchers to investigate various populations in long-term studies. For example, survey research might measure subjects when they are ten, twenty, and thirty years old to track changes in how frequently they watch television and what kinds of programs they prefer at different ages.

66 Writing survey questions and gathering data are easy; writing good questions and collecting useful data are not. **99**

—Michael Singletary,
*Mass Communication
Research*, 1994

It is important to note, though, that surveys are only as good as the wording of their questions and the answer choices they present. The validity of survey questions—measuring the effect that the study claims to measure—is a chronic problem for survey practitioners. For example, as NPR reported in 2006, "if you ask people whether they support or oppose the death penalty for murderers, about two-thirds of Americans say they support it. If you ask whether people prefer that murderers get the death penalty or life in prison without parole, then you get a 50-50 split."[16]

Using direct mail, personal interviews, telephone calls, e-mail, and Web sites, survey researchers can accumulate large amounts of information by surveying diverse cross sections of people. These data help to examine attitudes and demographic factors such as educational background, income levels, race, gender, age, lifestyle profiles, and political affiliations. Large government and academic survey databases are now widely available and contribute to the development of more long-range—or **longitudinal—studies**, which make it possible for social scientists to compare new studies with those conducted years earlier. In general, however, it is cheaper and easier to do short-term experimental and survey research, analyzing the effects of the media on particular individuals. Effects research focused on a large community or on societal responses to the media over time is much more difficult to conduct and sustain.

Content Analysis

Over the years, researchers recognized that traditional media effects studies generally ignored specific media messages. As a corrective, researchers developed a method known as **content analysis** to study the messages of print and visual media. Such analysis is a systematic method of coding and measuring media content.

Although content analyses were first used during World War II, more recent studies have focused on television, tracking the race, sex, and economic class of characters in daytime and prime-time programming. Probably the most influential content analyses have been conducted by George Gerbner and his colleagues at the University of Pennsylvania; since the late 1960s, they have coded and counted acts of violence on network television. Combined with survey methods, these annual "violence profiles" have shown that heavy watchers of television, including both children and retired Americans, tend to overestimate the amount of violence that exists in the actual world.[17]

The limits of content analysis have been well documented. This technique does not measure the effects of the media or explain why a particular media message gets produced in the first place. For example, a content analysis—sponsored by the Kaiser Family Foundation—of more than eleven hundred television shows found that 70 percent of television shows had sexual content.[18] But, the study doesn't tell us how viewers interpreted the content. (See "Media Literacy and the Critical Process: Counting Sexual Scenes on TV" on page 532.)

Problems of definition also occur. For instance, in the case of coding and counting acts of violence, how do researchers distinguish slapstick cartoon aggression from the violent murders or rapes in an evening police drama? Critics point out that such varied depictions may have diverse and subtle effects on viewers that are difficult to measure or quantify.

As content analysis grew as a primary tool in media research, it sometimes pushed to the sidelines other ways of thinking about television and media content. Broad questions concerning the media as a popular art form, as a democratic influence, or as a force for social control are difficult to address through strict measurement techniques. Critics of content analysis, in fact, have objected to the kind of social science that reduces culture to acts of counting. Such criticism has addressed

Media Literacy
and the Critical Process

Counting Sexual Scenes on TV

Every two years since 1999, the Kaiser Family Foundation, a nonprofit private foundation dedicated to "providing information and analysis on health care issues to policymakers, the media, the health care community, and the general public," releases a major study of sexual content on television. In 2005, the foundation released *Sex on TV 4*, and reported that the number of sexual scenes on television had nearly doubled since 1998.[1] But what does "sexual content" actually mean, and what do the study's results seem to suggest to policymakers? To address these questions, we will use the critical process to analyze the study.

Description. Central to any study using content analysis is developing a working definition of terms. For this study, "sex is defined as any depiction of sexual activity, sexually suggestive behavior, or talk about sexuality or sexual activity." What would you include or not include in a definition of sexual content?

Analysis. The study analyzed a sample of more than eleven hundred programs, covering a range of television genres, but excluding daily newscasts, children's shows, and sporting events. The main sample included shows from ABC, CBS, NBC, Fox, an independent WB affiliate, a PBS affiliate, Lifetime, TNT, USA Network, and HBO. The sample also included daytime soap operas, one of the genres with the highest percentage of sexual content. Do these genres represent the viewing environment of twelve to seventeen year-olds, the age group of greatest concern to the researchers?

Interpretation. Do jokes about a newlywed couple's sexual encounters (*Scrubs*), bedroom banter between a married couple (*According to Jim*), depictions of flirting (*Hope and Faith*), scenes with romantic kissing (*Joey*), dramatic discussions about sexually transmitted diseases (*Law & Order: Special Victims Unit*), and implied (*The OC*) or actual (*General Hospital*) depictions of sexual intercourse all have the same impact and meaning? This study treats them all as sex scenes. Do you think viewers would interpret these scenes the same way? How would audience studies—focusing on how people actually use and interpret this television content—help to clarify the interpretation of the content analysis?

Evaluation. The *Sex on TV 4* study notes that over the past decade "fewer teens are having sex, and more of those who are having intercourse are using protection—and the teen pregnancy rate is going down as a result." Does this admission seem to undermine the study's concerns that "the amount of sexual content on television continues to increase" and it "may be contributing to perceptions about peer norms regarding both sexual behavior (e.g., 'everybody is doing it') and safer sex practices"? How is it that sexual content, as measured by this study, is increasing on television, while teen sexual behavior is declining and becoming more safe?

Engagement. This series of studies has a big impact on the way policymakers understand media effects. There's bipartisan support in Congress to fund more studies that would analyze media effects on the health and development of children. How would you do this kind of study? Be ready to make an informed recommendation—critically read the series of studies for yourself at http://www.kff.org/entmedia/index.cfm.

the tendency by some researchers to favor measurement accuracy over intellectual discipline and inquiry.[19]

Explaining Media Effects

By the 1960s, the first departments of mass communication began graduating Ph.D.-level researchers schooled in experimental or survey techniques and content analysis. These researchers began documenting consistent patterns that can be found in mass communication. Four of the most influential contemporary frameworks that help explain media effects have been social learning theory, agenda-setting, the cultivation effect, and the spiral of silence.

Social Learning Theory

Some of the most well-known studies that suggest a link between the mass media and behavior are the "Bobo doll" experiments conducted on children by psychologist Albert Bandura and his colleagues at Stanford University in the 1960s. Bandura concluded that the experiments demonstrate a link between violent media programs, such as those that might be on television, and aggressive behavior.

Bandura theorized social learning as a four-step process: attention (the subject must attend to the media and witness aggressive behavior), retention (the subject must retain the memory for later retrieval), motor reproduction (the subject must be able to physically imitate the behavior), and motivation (there must be a social reward or reinforcement to encourage modeling of the behavior). Supporters of **social learning theory** often cite the anecdotal evidence of real-life imitations of media aggression (see the beginning of the chapter) as evidence of social learning theory at work. Yet critics note that many studies have found no link between media content and aggression. For example, millions of people have watched episodes of the Three Stooges with no subsequent aggressive behavior. In this view, critics say social learning theory simply makes television a scapegoat for larger social problems relating to violence. Others suggest that experiencing media depictions of aggression can actually help viewers to peacefully let off steam through a catharsis effect.

● These photos document the "Bobo doll" experiments conducted by Albert Bandura and his colleagues at Stanford University in the early 1960s. Seventy-two children from the Stanford University Nursery School were divided into experimental and control groups. The "aggressive condition" experimental group subjects watched an adult in the room sit on, kick, and hit the Bobo doll with hands and a wooden mallet while saying such things as "Sock him in the nose," "Throw him in the air," and "Pow." (In later versions of the experiment, children watched filmed versions of the adult with the Bobo doll.) Afterward, in a separate room filled with toys, the children in the "aggressive condition" group were more likely than the other children to imitate the adult model's behavior toward the Bobo doll.

Agenda-Setting

A key phenomenon posited by media effects researchers has been **agenda-setting**: the idea that when the mass media pay attention to particular events or issues, they determine—that is, set the agenda for—the major topics of discussion for individuals and society. Like the uses and gratifications approach, agenda-setting research has tried to strike a balance between the views of the mass media as all-powerful and as barely powerful. Essentially, agenda-setting researchers have argued that the mass media do not so much tell us what to think as *what to think about*. Traceable to Walter Lippmann's notion in the early 1920s that the media "create pictures in our heads," the first social science investigations of agenda-setting began in the 1970s.[20]

Over the years, agenda-setting research has demonstrated that the more stories the news media do on a particular subject, the more importance audiences attach to that subject. For instance, when the media seriously began to cover ecology issues after the first Earth Day in 1970, a much higher percentage of the population began listing the environment as a primary social concern in surveys. When *Jaws* became the top box-office movie in 1975, the news media started featuring more shark attack stories; even landlocked people in the Midwest began ranking sharks as a problem, despite the rarity of such incidents worldwide.

During the 1986 elections, local and national candidates often spoke about the problems of crime and illegal drugs. At the time, researchers documented a big leap in the media's attention to drugs, especially to crack cocaine; they found more than four hundred news stories dealing with cocaine over a forty-week period in America's major papers, newsmagazines, and newscasts.[21] Not surprisingly, the big jump in drug stories was accompanied by a parallel rise in concern over drugs as reflected in public opinion polls. In April 1986, only 2 percent of the respondents to a *New York Times*/CBS News poll identified drugs as the nation's most important problem. By early September 1986, however, a survey found that drugs topped the list, with 13 percent of 1,210 adults interviewed identifying drugs as the nation's most serious problem. This shift occurred even though government statisticians showed that despite rises in the use of crack cocaine, illicit drug use had generally dipped and leveled off since peaking in 1979–80.[22] Although many people's attitudes toward drugs were not affected by the increased coverage in news stories, the marked shift in public opinion is a good example of the agenda-setting effect of the news media.

More recently, a surge of reports on mad cow disease (BSE, bovine spongiform encephalopathy) on German TV news in late 2000 sparked a corresponding increase in public concern about the topic. As media coverage died down the following spring, so did public awareness of BSE in Germany.

The Cultivation Effect

Another mass media phenomenon—the **cultivation effect**—suggests that heavy viewing of television leads individuals to perceive reality in ways that are consistent with television portrayals. This area of effects research attempts to push researchers past the focus on individual behavior and toward larger ideas about the media's impact on society. The major research in this area grew from the TV violence profiles of George Gerbner and his colleagues, who attempted to make broad generalizations about the impact of televised violence on real life. The basic idea suggests that the more time an audience spends viewing television and absorbing its viewpoints, the more likely it is that the audience's own views of social reality will be "cultivated" by the images and portrayals they see on television.[23] For example, although fewer than 1 percent of Americans are victims of violent crime in any single year, people who watch a lot of television tend to overestimate this percentage. Such exaggerated perceptions, Gerbner and his colleagues argue, are part of a "mean world" syndrome in

which viewers with heavy, long-term exposure to television are more likely to believe that the external world is a mean and dangerous place.

According to the cultivation effect, media messages interact in complicated ways with personal, social, political, and cultural factors; they are one of a number of important factors in determining individual behavior and defining social values. Some critics have charged that cultivation research has provided limited evidence to support these findings. The cultivation framework, however, deserves close attention, especially with regard to findings about heavy television viewers who believe that the world is a meaner place than it actually is.

Spiral of Silence

Developed by German communication theorist Elisabeth Noelle-Neumann in the 1970s and 1980s, the **spiral of silence** is a theory that links the mass media, social psychology, and the formation of public opinion. It proposes that those who find that their views on controversial issues are in the minority will keep their views to themselves—i.e., become silent—for fear of social isolation. As those in the minority

● A consequence of the agenda-setting theory is that the stories that don't get attention from the mass media don't make it onto the public and political agendas. Each year Doctors Without Borders compiles a list of the most underreported humanitarian stories. In 2005, the list included the continuing war and disease ravaging the Democratic Republic of Congo (formerly Zaire) in Africa, where, since civil war broke out in 1998, millions have died or been forced into refugee camps like the one pictured above.

> **❝ Many studies currently published in mainstream communication journals seem filled with sophisticated treatments of trivial data, which, while showing effects . . . make slight contributions to what we really know about human mass-mediated communication. ❞**
>
> – Willard Rowland and Bruce Watkins,
> *Interpreting Television*, 1984

voice their views less often, it further diminishes the resonance of those views for themselves and others in the minority. The theory is based on social psychology studies, such as the conformity research of Solomon Asch. In a classic 1951 study on the effects of group pressure, Asch demonstrated that a test subject will more likely give clearly wrong answers to a test of determining line lengths if all of the others in the room (all secret confederates of the experimenter) unanimously state an incorrect answer. (The pressure to conform is much less if there is at least one true partner in dissent.)

For issues of public opinion, Noelle-Neumann argues, this effect of yielding to the majority is exacerbated by the mass media, particularly television, which can communicate a real or presumed majority public opinion widely and quickly. For example, one researcher notes that from the 1970s through the 1990s, the political Right in the United States was effective in using the media to frame liberals as an elite minority who protected special-interest groups such as atheists and criminals. At the same time, the Right was expounding the existence of a conservative Christian "moral majority" in the country. Instead of vigorously protesting that framing, liberals—apparently finding themselves already framed as a minority—retreated into silence.[24]

According to the theory, the mass media can help to create a false, overrated majority; that is, a true majority of people holding a certain position can grow silent when they sense an opposing majority view in the mass media. One criticism of the theory is that some people may not fall into a spiral of silence because they don't monitor the media, or they mistakenly perceive that more people hold their position than really do. Noelle-Neumann acknowledges that in many cases, "hard-core nonconformists" exist and remain vocal even in the face of social isolation and can ultimately prevail in changing public opinion.

Evaluating Research on Media Effects

The mainstream models of media research have made valuable contributions to our understanding of the mass media, submitting content and audiences to rigorous testing. This wealth of research exists partly because funding for studies regarding the effects of the media on young people remains popular among politicians and has drawn ready government support since the 1960s. Media critic Richard Rhodes argues that media effects research is inconsistent and often flawed but continues to resonate with politicians and parents because it generates an easy-to-blame social cause for real-world violence. "When violence among youths does erupt, as in the recent school shootings, parents look for a cause and blame the pale imitations of violence that their children watch on TV."[25]

Although the potential for government funding restricts the scope of some media research, other limits also exist, including the inability to address how the media affect communities and social institutions. Because most media research operates best in examining media and individual behavior, fewer research studies exist on media's impact on community and social life. Research has begun to address these limits and to turn more attention to the increasing impact of media technology on national life and international communication.

Cultural Approaches to Media Research

During the rise of modern media research, approaches with a stronger historical and interpretive edge developed as well, often in direct opposition to the scientific models. In the late 1930s, some social scientists began to warn about the limits of "gathering data and charting trends," particularly when research served advertisers and media organizations. Such private market research tended to be narrowly focused on individual behavior, ignoring questions like "Where are institutions taking us?" and "Where do we want them to take us?"[26]

It is important here to distinguish directions in American media studies from British-European traditions. In Europe, media studies have favored interpretive rather than scientific approaches; in other words, researchers there have approached media questions and problems as if they were literary or cultural critics rather than experimental or survey researchers. Such approaches built on the writings of political philosophers such as Karl Marx and Antonio Gramsci; these types of research investigated how the mass media have been used to maintain existing hierarchies in society. They examined, for example, the ways in which popular culture or sports distracted people from redressing social injustices. They also studied the subordinate status of some social groups in attempting to address some of the deficiencies of emerging social science research.

In the United States, early criticism of modern media research came from the Frankfurt School, a group of European researchers who emigrated from Germany to America after they fled Nazi persecution in the 1930s. Under the leadership of Max Horkheimer, T. W. Adorno, and Leo Lowenthal, this perspective pointed to at least three inadequacies of traditional scientific approaches, arguing that they (1) reduced large "cultural questions" to measurable and "verifiable categories"; (2) depended on "an atmosphere of rigidly enforced neutrality"; and (3) refused to place "the phenomena of modern life" in a "historical and moral context."[27] The researchers of the Frankfurt School did not reject outright the usefulness of measuring and counting data. They contended, however, that historical and cultural approaches would focus critical attention on the long-range processes of the mass media and their complex relations with audiences.

Cultural Studies

Since the time of the Frankfurt School, criticisms of the effects tradition and its methods have continued, with calls for more interpretive studies of the rituals of mass communication. Academics who have embraced a cultural approach try to understand how media and culture are tied to the actual patterns of communication in daily life. An important body of research—loosely labeled **cultural studies**—began challenging the mainstream media effects models in the 1960s. These studies have generally focused on how people make meaning, apprehend reality, and order experience through their use of cultural symbols in print and visual media. This research has attempted to make everyday culture the centerpiece of media studies, focusing on the subtle ways in which mass communication shapes and is shaped by history, politics, and economics. For example, in the 1970s Stuart Hall and his colleagues studied the British print media and the police as forms of urban surveillance. In *Policing the Crisis,* the authors revealed how political, economic, and cultural constraints aided the news media's success in mobilizing public opinion about crime.[28]

Cultural research focuses on the investigation of daily experience, especially on issues of race, gender, class, and sexuality, and on the unequal arrangements of power and status in contemporary society. Such research highlights the nature of cultural differences, emphasizing how some social groups have been marginalized and ignored throughout history. Consequently, cultural studies have attempted to recover lost or silenced voices, particularly among African American, Native American, Asian and Asian American, Arabic, Latino, gay and lesbian, and women's cultures. The major analytical approaches to cultural research are textual analysis, audience studies, and political economy.

> ❝ When people say to you, 'Of course that's so, isn't it?' that 'of course' is the most ideological moment, because that's the moment at which you're least aware that you are using a particular framework. ❞
>
> —Stuart Hall, 1983

CASE STUDY
Labor Gets Framed

● During the December 2005 Transit Worker Union (TWU) strike in New York City (TWU members operate the city's public transportation system, the largest in the country), the reasons behind the strike got less news coverage because the news focused on the millions of stranded commuters (*inset*) instead.

Labor union membership in the United States has dropped from a high of 34.7 percent of the workforce in 1954 to less than 12.5 percent (less than 8 percent in the private sector) by 2007. Given that most Americans do not belong to labor unions, that economic and social forces increasingly separate the "haves" from the "have-nots," and that popular media such as entertainment television and film rarely address labor issues, the news remains one of the few sites for any stories about labor and the working class.

Could the way in which news stories frame labor unions have an impact on how people in the United States understand them?

Analyzing the *frames* of news stories—that is, the ways in which journalists present them—is one form of textual analysis. Unfortunately, if one looks at the way in which the news media frame their reports about labor unions, one has to conclude that news coverage of labor is not at all good.

In a major study,[1] hundreds of network television news (ABC, CBS, and NBC) and national newspaper (*New York Times* and *USA Today*) reports involving labor over a ten-year period were analyzed to get a sense of how such stories are framed.

An interesting pattern emerged. Instead of discovering a straightforward bias against labor, the study found that news stories frame labor in a way that prioritizes the consumer perspective (as opposed to a citizen or worker perspective). That is, labor unions aren't portrayed as inherently bad, but any kind of collective action by workers, communities, and even consumers that upsets the American consumer economy and its business leaders and entrepreneurs is framed as a bad thing.

The classic example is the strike story. Even though less than 2 percent of all contract negotiations result in strikes, news stories seem to show union members regularly wielding picket signs. The real stars of strike stories, though, are the inconvenienced consumers—sour-faced

people who are livid about missed flights, late package delivery, or canceled ball games. And usually the reports don't explain why a strike is occurring; viewers and readers mainly learn that the hallowed American consumer is upset and if those darned workers would just be a little more agreeable, then none of this inconvenience would have happened.

The frame carries an interesting underlying assumption: If collective action is bad, then economic intervention by citizens should happen only at the individual level (e.g., tell your boss to "take this job and shove it" if you are dissatisfied, or "vote with your pocketbook" if you don't like something). Of course, individual action would preempt collective action on the part of organizations such as labor unions, which would be more democratic and potent.

Corporate news frames labor stories in ways that are in harmony with the media corporations' own economic priorities. (Corporations like General Electric, Disney, Gannett, and Wal-Mart all have long track records of either trying to weaken their unions or break them completely.) But they do so without giving the appearance of bias, which would undermine their credibility. So they frame these stories in the perspective of the consumer (indeed, in an advertising– and corporate sponsor–based media system, this is the familiar environment in which all media stories are framed).

With such framing, the news media's stories undercut a legal institution—labor unions—that might serve as a useful remedy to millions of American workers who want independent representation in their workplace for collective bargaining and dispute resolution, as well as a voice in the economy. In fact, national surveys have shown that the majority of American workers would like a stronger voice in their workplaces but have negative opinions about unions, so they aren't likely to consider joining them.[2]

And that's the disconnect that the framing study illustrates: People want independent workplace representation, but—according to the news—labor unions and similar forms of collective action are hardly a viable option.

Textual Analysis

In cultural research, the equivalent to measurement methods and content analysis has been labeled **textual analysis**: the close reading and interpretation of the meanings of culture, including the study of books, movies, and TV programs. Whereas content analysis approaches media messages with the tools of modern social science—replicability, objectivity, and data—textual analysis looks at rituals, narratives, and meanings. (See "Case Study: Labor Gets Framed" on opposite page.)

Although textual analysis has a long and rich history in film and literary studies, a significant shift occurred in 1974 with Horace Newcomb's *TV: The Most Popular Art,* considered the first serious academic book that analyzed television stories. Newcomb studied why certain TV programs became predominant, especially comedies, westerns, mysteries, soap operas, news, and sports. Newcomb took television programs seriously, examining patterns in the most popular programs at the time, such as the *Beverly Hillbillies, Bewitched,* and *Dragnet,* which traditional researchers had usually snubbed or ignored. Trained as a literary scholar, Newcomb argued that content analysis and other social science approaches often ignored artistic traditions and social context. For Newcomb, "the task for the student of the popular arts is to find a technique through which many different qualities of the work—aesthetic, social, psychological—may be explored" and to discover "why certain formulas . . . are popular in American television."[29]

Prior to Newcomb's work, textual analysis generally focused on "important" debates, films, poems, and books—either significant examples of democratic information or highly regarded works of art. But by the end of the 1970s a new generation of media studies scholars, who had grown up on television and rock and roll, became interested in less elite forms of culture. They extended the notion of what a "text" is to architecture, fashion, tabloid magazines, pop icons like Madonna, rock music, soap operas, movies, cockfights, shopping malls, TV drug news, hip-hop, and professional wrestling, trying to make sense of the most taken-for-granted aspects of everyday culture.

Often these seemingly minor elements of popular culture provide insight into broader meanings within our society. For example, a 1998 textual analysis examined the sexual etiquette endorsed for teenage women in popular magazines such as *YM, Teen, Seventeen, Glamour,* and *Mademoiselle.* The researchers looked at advice columns and features from a sample of magazines between 1974 and 1994. They concluded that the stories of sexual etiquette changed very little during those twenty years and that the magazines encouraged young women "to subordinate self for others and to be contained."[30]

Audience Studies

Cultural research that focuses on how people use and interpret cultural content is called *audience-* or *reader-response research.* For example, in *Reading the Romance: Women, Patriarchy and Popular Literature,* Janice Radway studied a group of midwestern women who were fans of the romance novel. Using her training in literary criticism but also employing interviews and questionnaires, Radway investigated the meaning of romance reading. She argued that this cultural activity functioned as personal time for some women, whose complex family and work lives provided very little time for themselves. The study also suggested that these particular romance-novel fans identified with the active, independent qualities of the romantic heroines they most admired. As a cultural study, Radway's work did not claim to be scientific, and her findings are not generalizable to a large group of women. Rather, Radway was interested in investigating and interpreting the relationship between reading popular fiction and ordinary life.[31]

James Carey
A Critical Reader

Eve Stryker Munson and Catherine A. Warren, editors

● James W. Carey, who spent many years teaching at the University of Illinois and Columbia University, was an influential figure in cultural and critical communication studies. Carey's most well-known contributions envisioned communication as a cultural ritual, rather than a mechanistic process of transmission. Carey died in 2006.

66 I take culture . . . and the analysis of it to be therefore not an experimental science in search of law but an interpretive one in search of meaning. 99

–Clifford Geertz, cultural anthropologist, 1973

As Radway's study demonstrated, cultural research uses a variety of interpretive methods and displays some common features. Most important, these studies define culture in broad terms, as being made up of both the *products* a society fashions and the *processes* that forge those products. As we discussed in Chapter 1, culture consists of the symbols of expression that individuals, groups, and societies use to make sense of daily life and articulate their values. Within this context, culture is viewed in part as a struggle over who controls symbols and meaning in society. For example, the battles over the meaning of jazz in the 1930s, of rock and roll in the 1950s, or of hip-hop in the 1980s were important cultural battles that addressed issues of race, class, region, and religion as well as generational differences.

Political Economy

The focus on the production of popular culture and the forces behind it are the topic of *political economy studies*. The greatest concern political economy studies have about the media is the increasing conglomeration of ownership, as noted in Chapter 13. This concentration of ownership means that the production of media content is being controlled by fewer and fewer organizations, investing those companies with more power. Moreover, the domination of public discourse by for-profit corporations may mean that the bottom line for all public communication and popular culture is money, not democratic expression.

Political economy studies work best when combined with the textual analysis and audience studies approaches, which provide a well-rounded context for understanding the cultural content, its production, and the audience's reception of it. For example, a major media corporation may, for commercial reasons, create a film and market it relentlessly through a number of venues (political economy), but the film's meaning or popularity makes sense only within the historical and narrative contexts of the culture (textual analysis), and it may be interpreted by various audiences in ways both anticipated and unexpected (audience studies).

Evaluating Cultural Approaches

In opposition to media effects research, cultural studies involve "reading" written texts and visual programs as a sequence of spoken or written symbols that contain interpretation. As James Carey has put it, a more cultural approach "does not seek to explain human behavior, but to understand it. . . . It does not attempt to predict human behavior, but to diagnose human meanings."[32] In other words, a cultural approach does not provide explanations for the laws that govern the mass media. Rather, it offers interpretations of the stories, messages, and meanings that circulate throughout our culture.

One of the main strengths of a cultural approach is the freedom it affords to broadly interpret the impact of the mass media. Because cultural work is not bound by the precise control of variables, researchers can more easily examine the ties between media messages and the broader social, economic, and political scene. For example, effects research on politics has generally concentrated on election polls and voting patterns, whereas cultural research has broadened the scope of politics to include class and income differences and the various uses of power by individuals and institutions in authority. Following Horace Newcomb, cultural investigators have also expanded the study of media content beyond "serious" works. They have studied many popular forms, including music, movies, and prime-time television.

Just as social science measurement has limits, so do cultural studies. Sometimes such studies have focused too heavily on the meanings of media programs or "texts," ignoring their effect on audiences. Some cultural studies, however, have tried to address this deficiency. For example, Elizabeth Bird's *For Enquiring Minds: A Cultural*

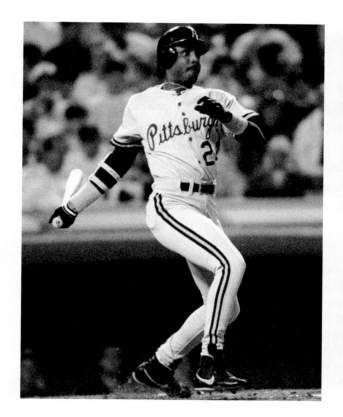

Study of Supermarket Tabloids set up a three-part analysis that included (1) interviews with the writers and editors of popular tabloids, (2) in-depth discussions with tabloid readers, and (3) an analysis of the form and content of tabloids. Bird's research demonstrated how individuals derive their own diverse meanings from this one ordinary form of popular culture, and how a researcher can combine textual analysis, audience studies, and political economy approaches.[33]

Both media effects and cultural researchers today have begun to look at the limitations of their work more closely, borrowing ideas from each other to better assess the complexity of the media's impact. For instance, in *Democracy without Citizens*, political scientist Robert Entman employed both perspectives to examine journalism and politics. He used cultural theories about economics and politics to reveal how journalists slant the news and oversimplify complex issues. He supplemented his cultural inquiry with surveys that measured the impact of slanted reports on public opinion. By combining the two approaches, Entman strengthened his argument, which called for substantial journalistic reform.[34]

● Cultural studies researchers are interested in the production, meaning, and audience response to a wide range of elements within communication culture, including the meaning and reception of sports figures like Barry Bonds, who is caught in a media controversy over performance-enhancing drugs. (*Above left,* Bonds in 1992; *above,* Bonds in 2006.)

Media Research, Ivory Towers, and Democracy ★❙❙❙❙

One charge frequently leveled at academic studies is that they fail to address the everyday problems of life; they often seem to have little practical application. With the growth of mass media departments in colleges and universities has come an increase in special terminology and jargon, which tend to intimidate nonacademics. Although media research has built a growing knowledge base and dramatically advanced what we know about individuals and societies, the academic world has paid a price. That is, the larger public has often been excluded from access to the research process. Researchers themselves have even found it difficult to speak to one another across disciplines because of the obscure language used to analyze and report findings.

The acceleration of jargon occurred with the splintering of academic life into narrow areas of specialization in the 1970s. We understand why chemistry, physics, math, and engineering require special symbols and languages. It is not as clear, however, why this practice extends to so many social science and humanities disciplines. Although cultural research has affected academic scholars in English, history, sociology, anthropology, and communication, they do not talk easily to one another about their work. Most social science research is intended only for other social scientists with similar training and experience. For example, understanding the elaborate statistical analyses used to document media effects requires special training. This kind of research advances knowledge, but it does not generally engage a larger public.

● As model contemporary intellectuals, Cornel West (*center*) and Henry Louis Gates Jr. (*right*) have dedicated much of their careers to communicating ideas to both the academic community and the larger public. Pictured here with Nobel Prize–winning Nigerian author Wole Soyinka (*left*), West and Gates write academic texts and mass market books, and also make appearances on radio and TV news and talk programs.

Even in cultural research, the language used is often incomprehensible to students and to other audiences who use the mass media. Cultural research tends to identify with marginalized groups, yet this scholarship can be self-defeating if its complexity is too removed from the daily experience of the groups it addresses and the students it is designed to educate.

A now famous hoax in 1996 pointed out just how inaccessible some academic jargon can be. Alan Sokal, a New York University physics professor, submitted an impenetrable article, "Transgressing the Boundaries: Toward a Transformative Hermeneutics of Quantum Gravity," to a special issue of the academic journal *Social Text* devoted to science and postmodernism. As he had expected, the article — a hoax designed to point out how dense academic jargon can sometimes mask sloppy thinking — was published. According to the journal's editor, about six reviewers had read the article but didn't suspect that it was phony. A public debate ensued after Sokal revealed his hoax. Sokal said he worries that jargon and intellectual fads cause academics to lose contact with the real world and "undermine the prospect for progressive social critique."[35]

In addition to the issue of specialized language, other problems have arisen involving media research and democracy. In the 1990s, lawmakers and the public had become increasingly concerned about the emphasis on research over teaching at most major universities. Throughout the 1990s and into the 2000s, as the government slashed support for student loans and university research, universities escalated their campaigns to raise money and become affiliated with corporations. The late historian Christopher Lasch, however, warned of the dangers "of corporate control of the universities" and the potential for "corruption" in higher education: "It is corporate control that has diverted social resources from the humanities into military and technological research, fostered an obsession with quantification that has destroyed the social sciences, replaced the English language with bureaucratic jargon, and created a top-heavy administrative apparatus whose educational vision begins and ends with the bottom line."[36]

Especially with the substantial tuition hikes at most universities across the United States in the early 2000s, it was also becoming more difficult for middle- and working-class students to attend college. This seemed to contradict the democratic progress that had been going on in higher education since the 1950s and 1960s, which brought government GI loans to war veterans and wider access to the universities spurred on by the women's and Civil Rights movements. These democratic movements also ushered in the study of popular culture and the mass media. The news media's coverage of the Watergate scandal alone sparked heightened interest in journalism as an undergraduate major throughout the country.

Ironically, while campuses were becoming more democratic, increasing specialization in the 1970s began isolating many researchers from life outside the university. Academics were once again locked away in their ivory towers. Early in the twentieth century, it was common for academics to operate as public intellectuals. But the proliferation of specialized fields widened the gap between the public and the university.

Facing a number of critical problems in higher education, more academics began stepping forward to broaden their ideas of research and to become active in political and cultural life by the 1980s and 1990s. For example, literary scholar Henry Louis Gates Jr. began writing essays for *Time* and the *New Yorker* magazines. Linguist Noam Chomsky, who tirelessly writes and speaks about excessive government and media power, was the subject of an award-winning documentary, *Manufacturing Consent: Noam Chomsky and the Media*. Steven D. Levitt, an economics professor at the University of Chicago, popularized his unconventional economics studies (answering questions like "If drug dealers make so much money, why do they still live with their mothers?") in his book *Freakonomics* (2005), with coauthor Stephen Dubner. And essayist and cultural critic Barbara Ehrenreich has written accessibly and potently about labor and economic issues in magazines such as *Time* and the *Nation*. The author of more than twelve books, she most recently completed *Bait and Switch: The (Futile) Pursuit of the American Dream*, an investigation of unemployed white-collar workers. Popular academic books ranging from conservative accounts (Allan Bloom's *The Closing of the American Mind*) to progressive accounts (Thomas Frank's *What's the Matter with Kansas?*) extended academic ideas beyond the boundaries of the university.

In recent presidential election campaign seasons, Kathleen Hall Jamieson, communication professor at the University of Pennsylvania, has made appearances on PBS and NPR to perform textual analyses of political advertising and presidential rhetoric. The TV coverage of the Gulf War in the early 1990s and the U.S.-led invasion of Iraq in 2003 has included many political scientists, military historians, and religion professors, who interpreted the events in the larger context of historic Middle Eastern struggles.

Like public journalists, public intellectuals based on campuses help to carry on the conversations of society and culture, actively circulating the most important new ideas of the day and serving as models for how to participate in public life.

> **"** In many ways the modern university has replaced its function as a creative/subversive institution with a fondness for structure and organization among its parts, and the rigid compartmentalization of knowledge within these structures. **"**
>
> –David Sholle and Stan Denski, *Media Education*, 1994

www.

For review questions and activities for Chapter 15, go to the interactive *Media and Culture* Online Study Guide at *bedfordstmartins.com/mediaculture*

REVIEW QUESTIONS

Early Developments in Media Research

1. What were the earliest types of media studies, and why weren't they more scientific?

2. What were the major influences that led to scientific media research?

Research on Media Effects

3. What are the differences between experiments and surveys as media research strategies?

4. What is content analysis, and why is it significant?

5. What are the differences between the hypodermic-needle model and the minimal-effects model in the history of media research?

6. What are the main ideas behind social learning theory, agenda-setting, the cultivation effect, and the spiral of silence?

7. What are some strengths and limitations of modern media research?

Cultural Approaches to Media Research

8. Why did cultural approaches to media studies develop in opposition to media effects research?

9. What are the features of cultural studies?

10. How is textual analysis different from content analysis?

11. What are some of the strengths and limitations of cultural research?

Media Research, Ivory Towers, and Democracy

12. How has specialization in academic research influenced universities?

13. How can public intellectuals and academics improve the relationship between campuses and the general public?

QUESTIONING THE MEDIA

1. What are your main concerns or criticisms about the state of media studies at your college or university?

2. One charge that has been leveled against a lot of media research—both the effects and the cultural models—is that it has very little impact on changing our media institutions. Do you agree or disagree, and why?

3. Can you think of an issue that a media industry and academic researchers could study together? Explain.

4. In looking at media courses in a college curriculum, what do you think is the relationship between theory and practice? Do hands-on, practical skills courses such as news reporting, advertising copywriting, or TV production belong in a liberal arts college or in a separate mass communication college? Explain your answer.

SEARCHING THE INTERNET

http://people-press.org/

The Pew Research Center for the People and the Press is an independent public opinion research group. The Center's surveys measure public attitudes about the media and also track how closely the public follows major news stories.

http://www.kff.org/entmedia/index.cfm

The Kaiser Family Foundation funds a number of media partnerships and studies, including national surveys on topics such as television and the Internet, with partners like National Public Radio, *The NewsHour with Jim Lehrer*, and the *Washington Post*.

http://www.aejmc.org/pubs/#jmcq

An online guide to recent issues of *Journalism and Mass Communication Quarterly*, one of the oldest journalism research journals. Includes full text of select articles and a searchable index dating back to 1984.

http://www.cjrdaily.org

A daily blog of media criticism from the *Columbia Journalism Review*.

In Brief

Consider the incidents outlined in the chapter's preview story, as well as any other recent media stories about violence, and discuss the following questions in class: Does media effects research support the charge that mass media should be responsible for the tragic instances of copycat behavior? How would you balance the First Amendment free-expression rights of the mass media with issues of social and moral responsibility?

In Depth

The purpose of this project is to extend your critical approach to media research. For the following assignment, comparatively analyze methodological approaches introduced in this chapter—a more social scientific method (such as experiments, surveys, or content analysis, or a creative combination thereof) or a cultural approach (such as textual analysis, audience study, or political economy study, or a creative combination thereof). Investigate the following argument (you can investigate other arguments as well): *College students are less informed about current news events than their parents are.*

Description. Describe how you could best investigate this argument using a social scientific method and then using a cultural approach. Explain fully how each study would be developed, step-by-step.

Analysis. Look at completed plans of study using each of the two methodological approaches, noting similarities and differences. Also, consider each methodology in terms of the potential breadth and depth of findings.

Interpretation. What kinds of questions are certain to be answered by each or both studies? How much does the way the research question or argument is stated determine the best methodological approach? What kind of approach seems to offer more definite, conclusive answers? Which approach offers more of a broader, big-picture point of view?

Evaluation. Based on the comparative analysis, if you had to do this study using only one methodological approach—social scientific or cultural—which would you use? Why? Would it ever be helpful, or even possible, to combine both approaches?

Engagement. Of course, actually completing one or both of the proposed studies would best answer the original question and direct you toward a plan of engagement. But for now, assume that college students should be even better informed and consider some feasible activities: How could campus news sources—including newspapers, radio stations, television or cable stations, Web sites, and bulletin boards—be better distributed to students? How can students be creatively engaged to care more about current events? How can students integrate more time into their day to learn about current events?

KEY TERMS

media effects, 521
pseudo-polls, 522
hypodermic-needle model, 527
minimal-effects model, 527
selective exposure, 527
selective retention, 527
uses and gratifications model, 528

scientific method, 529
hypotheses, 529
experiments, 529
random assignment, 529
survey research, 530
longitudinal studies, 531
content analysis, 531

social learning theory, 533
agenda-setting, 534
cultivation effect, 534
spiral of silence, 535
cultural studies, 537
textual analysis, 539

legal controls

and freedom of expression

We have our founding fathers to thank for this problem.

In 1787, they put the idea of copyright right into the U.S. Constitution. Article I, Section 8, says "Congress shall have power . . . to promote the progress of science and useful arts, by securing for limited times to authors and inventors the exclusive right to their respective writings and discoveries."

Then, passed just a few years later, the very first amendment to the Constitution says "Congress shall make no law . . . abridging the freedom of speech, or of the press. . . ."

We are left with contradictory goals that have only been exacerbated by the dawn of the digital age. On one hand, we have the tradition of copyright, which protects literary, dramatic, musical, artistic, and other intellectual works. On the other hand, we have the First Amendment, which guarantees free speech.

When Congress passed the first Copyright Act in 1790, it gave authors the right to control their published works for fourteen

16

years, with the opportunity for a renewal for another fourteen years. The copyright gives the author monopoly control over his or her work, determining any uses of the work and collecting the profits of its sale or licensing. After the end of the copyright period, the work enters the public domain, which gives the public free access to the work. The idea was that a period of copyright control would give authors financial incentive to create original works, and that the public domain gives others incentive to create derivative works.

Over the years, as artists lived longer, and—more importantly—corporate copyright owners became more common, copyright periods were extended by Congress. In 1976, Congress extended the copyright period to the life of the author plus 50 years, or 75 years for a corporate copyright owner. In 1998 (as copyrights on works such as Disney's Mickey Mouse were set to expire), Congress again extended copyright periods for twenty additional years. Corporate owners have millions of dollars to gain by keeping their properties out of the public domain. Disney, a

major lobbyist for the 1998 extension, would have lost its copyright to Mickey Mouse in 2004 but now will continue to earn millions on its movies, T-shirts, and Mickey Mouse watches through 2024. Warner/Chappell Music, which owns the copyright to the popular "Happy Birthday to You" song, will keep generating money on the song through 2030. And maybe even for longer—it is likely that around 2015 or 2020, there will be corporate pressure on Congress for another extension.

Is this what the Constitution meant by having "limited times" for authors and inventors to have the exclusive rights to their work? And what about free speech, when communicating with popular cultural symbols like Mickey Mouse and the Happy Birthday song always comes with a price tag attached? Kembrew McLeod, a communication studies professor at the University of Iowa, pointed out this problem in 1998 with a prank: he trademarked the phrase "freedom of expression®" as "an ironic comment that demonstrates how our culture has become commodified and privately owned."[1] (This was the same

year the U.S. Patent and Trademark Office awarded Fox News rights to "Fair and Balanced®.")

Since 2001, Creative Commons has offered an alternative approach to copyright—somewhere between a state where everything is permanently copyrighted, and where creators receive no compensation for their work. Founded in part by Lawrence Lessig, director of the Stanford Law School Center for Internet and Society, Creative Commons (http://creativecommons.org/) is designed to "reduce barriers to creativity" by helping artists "dedicate their creative works to the public domain—or retain their copyright while licensing them as free for certain uses, on certain conditions."

A Creative Commons license, which can be appended to any work, particularly work online, can permit users to copy, distribute, display, and perform a work, or make derivative works. Or it can require certain conditions, such as attribution of the original artist, noncommercial use, or a requirement that any derivative works be shared again with a Creative Commons license.

he cultural and social struggles over what constitutes "free" speech have defined the nature of American democracy. In 1989, when Supreme Court Justice William Brennan Jr. was asked to comment on his "favorite part of the Constitution," he replied, "The First Amendment, I expect. Its enforcement gives us this society. The other provisions of the Constitution really only embellish it." Of all the issues that involve the mass media and popular culture, none are more central, or explosive, than freedom of expression and the First Amendment. Our nation's fundamental development can often be traced to how much or how little we tolerated speech during particular historical periods.

The current era is a volatile time for free-speech issues. Our society has debated copyright issues, hate-speech codes on campuses, explicit lyrics in music, violent images in film, the swapping of media files on the Internet, and the right of the press to publish government secrets. In this chapter, we examine expression issues, focusing primarily on the implications of the First Amendment for a variety of mass media. We investigate the origins of *free* expression and the standard models that underlie press freedoms. We look at the definition of censorship and corresponding legal cases. Next, we study the types of expression that are not always protected as speech. Focusing on the impact of cameras in the courtroom, we will examine some of the clashes between the First and Sixth Amendments. With regard to film, we review the social and political pressures that gave rise to early censorship boards and the current film ratings system. We turn to issues in broadcasting and examine why it has been treated differently from print media. Among other topics, we inspect the idea of indecency in broadcasting and the demise of the Fairness Doctrine. Finally, we explore the newest frontier in speech—concerns about expression on the Internet.

> **"** Congress shall make no law respecting an establishment of religion, or prohibiting the free exercise thereof; or abridging the freedom of speech, or of the press; or the right of the people peaceably to assemble, and to petition the Government for a redress of grievances. **"**
>
> –First Amendment,
> U.S. Constitution, 1791

The Origins of Free Expression and a Free Press

When students from other cultures attend school in the United States, many are astounded by the number of books, news articles, editorials, cartoons, films, TV shows, and Web sites that make fun of U.S. presidents. When writer-director Hugh Wilson toured Spain after his comedy film *Police Academy* (1984) appeared there, he was astonished to discover that many Spanish citizens regarded him as a hero for "criticizing" the police. Many countries' governments throughout history have jailed, even killed, their citizens for such speech "violations." Between 2000 and mid-2006 alone, 580 journalists were killed in the line of duty, often because someone disagreed with what they wrote or reported.[2] In the United States, however, we have generally taken for granted our right to criticize and poke fun at elected officials, politicians, and the police. Many of us are unaware of the ideas that underpin the freedoms we have. Indeed, when reporters have surveyed unwitting Americans about the First Amendment to the U.S. Constitution, the majority of respondents, unfamiliar with the amendment's wording, have usually indicated that its freedoms are far too generous.

To understand the development of free expression in the United States, we must understand a key idea underlying the First Amendment. In Europe throughout the 1600s, in order to monitor—and punish, if necessary—the speech of editors and writers, governments controlled the circulation of ideas by requiring printers to obtain licenses. In 1644, English poet John Milton, author of *Paradise Lost*, published his essay *Areopagitica*, which opposed government licenses for printers and defended a free press. Milton argued that all sorts of ideas, even false ones, should circulate freely in a democratic society and that truth would eventually emerge. In 1695,

England stopped licensing newspapers, and most of Europe followed. In many democracies today, publishing a newspaper, magazine, or newsletter remains one of the few public or service enterprises that require no license.

Models for Expression and Speech

A recent international survey of the news media in 192 countries, conducted by the human rights organization Freedom House, reported that about 73 percent of the world's people lived in countries with a less than free press. This 2004 survey related that 71 nations had virtually no press freedom; those governments exercised tight control over the news media, and this included jailing, intimidating, and even executing journalists. Included in the rankings was Italy, which was briefly downgraded to the category Partly Free, as the nation's television environment became dominated by Prime Minister Silvio Berlusconi's media empire and his government's influence over Italy's public broadcaster, RAI.[3]

Since the mid-1950s, four conventional models for speech and journalism have been used to categorize the widely differing ideas underlying free expression.[4] These models include the authoritarian, communist, libertarian, and social responsibility concepts. They are distinguished by the levels of freedom permitted and by the attitudes of the ruling and political classes toward the freedoms granted to the average citizen. Today, given the diversity among nations, the experimentation of journalists, and the collapse of many communist press systems, these categories are no longer as relevant. Nevertheless, they offer a good point of departure for discussing the press and democracy.

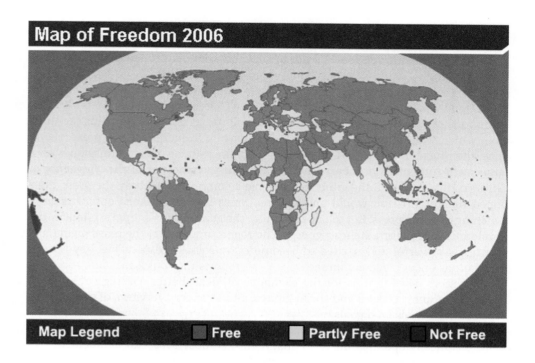

Map of Freedom 2006

Map Legend ■ Free ■ Partly Free □ Not Free

● The international human rights organization Freedom House comparatively assesses political rights and civil liberties in the world's 192 nations and 14 related and disputed territories. The most recent map counts 45 countries as Not Free, including Angola, Belarus, China, Cuba, Egypt, Iran, Iraq, North Korea, Russia, and Zimbabwe.

The **authoritarian model** developed about the time the printing press arrived in sixteenth-century England. Its advocates held that the general public, largely illiterate in those days, needed guidance from an elite, educated ruling class. Government criticism and public dissent were not tolerated, especially if such speech undermined "the common good"—an ideal that elites and rulers defined and controlled. Censorship was frequent, and the government issued printing licenses primarily to publishers who were sympathetic to government and ruling-class agendas.

Today, many authoritarian systems operate in developing countries throughout Asia, Latin America, and Africa, where journalism often joins with government and business to foster economic growth, minimize political dissent, and promote social stability. The leaders in these systems generally believe that too much outspoken speech and press freedom would undermine the delicate stability of their social and political infrastructures. In these societies, criticizing government programs may be viewed as an obstacle to keeping the peace, and both reporters and citizens may be punished if they question leaders and the status quo too fiercely.

Under most authoritarian models, the news is still controlled by private enterprise. But under the **communist** or **state model**, press control resides in government. Speaking for ordinary citizens and workers, state leaders believe they are enlightened and that the press should serve the common goals of the state. Although some state systems encourage media and government cooperation, political and military leaders still dictate the agendas for newspapers and the broadcast media. Some government criticism is tolerated, but ideas that challenge the basic premises of state authority are not. Although state media systems were in decline throughout the 1990s, they were still operating in China, Cuba, Iran, and North Korea, among other countries, in 2006.

The **libertarian model**, the flip side of state and authoritarian systems, encourages vigorous government criticism and supports the highest degree of freedom for individual speech and news operations. In a strict libertarian model, no restrictions are placed on the mass media or on individual speech. Libertarians tolerate the expression of everything, from publishing pornography to advocating anarchy. In North America and Europe, many political and alternative newspapers and magazines

> **❝Consider what would happen if—during this 200th anniversary of the Bill of Rights—the First Amendment were placed on the ballot in every town, city, and state. The choices: affirm, reject, or amend.**
>
> **I would bet there is no place in the United States where the First Amendment would survive intact.❞**
>
> **—Nat Hentoff, writer, 1991**

operate on such a model. Placing a great deal of trust in citizens' ability to distinguish truth from fabrication, libertarians maintain that the best way to fight outrageous lies and repulsive speech is not to suppress them but to speak out and write against them.

Along with the libertarian model, a **social responsibility model** characterizes the main ideals of mainstream journalism in the United States. The concepts and assumptions behind this model coalesced in the controversial 1947 Hutchins Commission, which was formed to examine the increasing influence of the press. Henry Luce, then head of the Time-Life magazine empire, funded the commission with a large grant to his friend Robert Maynard Hutchins, chancellor of the University of Chicago. Hutchins used the grant to assemble a committee to study the press. Luce hoped the commission would endorse free-press ideals and keep outsiders from watching over the press. But to Luce's dismay, the commission's report called for the development of press watchdog groups. The report argued that the mass media had grown too powerful and needed to become more socially responsible. Key recommendations encouraged comprehensive news reports that put issues and events in context, more news forums for the exchange of ideas, better coverage of society's range of economic classes and social groups, and stronger overviews of our nation's social values, ideals, and goals.

A socially responsible press is usually privately owned (although the government technically operates the broadcast media in most European democracies). In this model, the press functions as a **Fourth Estate**—that is, as an unofficial branch of government that monitors the legislative, judicial, and executive branches for abuses of power. In theory, private ownership keeps the news media independent of government. Thus they are better able to watch over the system on behalf of citizens. Under this model, which is heavily influenced by the libertarian view, the press supplies information to citizens so they can make wise decisions regarding political and social issues; the press also operates without excessive government meddling in matters of content.

Censorship as Prior Restraint

In the United States, the First Amendment has theoretically prohibited censorship. Over time, Supreme Court decisions have defined censorship as **prior restraint**. This means that courts and governments cannot block any publication or speech before it actually occurs, on the principle that a law has not been broken until an illegal act has been committed. In 1931, for example, the Supreme Court determined in *Near v. Minnesota* that a Minneapolis newspaper could not be stopped from publishing "scandalous and defamatory" material about police and law officials who were negligent in arresting and punishing local gangsters.[5] However, the Court left open the idea that the news media could be ordered to halt publication in exceptional cases. During a declared war, for instance, if a U.S. court judged that the publication of an article threatened national security, such expression could be restrained prior to its printing. In fact, during World War I the U.S. Navy seized all wireless radio transmitters. This was done to ensure control over critical information about weather conditions and troop movements that might inadvertently aid the enemy. In the 1970s, though, the Pentagon Papers decision and the *Progressive* magazine case tested important concepts underlying prior restraint.

The Pentagon Papers Case

In 1971, with the Vietnam War still in progress, Daniel Ellsberg, a former Defense Department employee, stole a copy of a forty-seven-volume document, "History of U.S. Decision-Making Process on Vietnam Policy." A thorough study of U.S. involvement in

Vietnam since World War II, the papers were classified by the government as top secret. Ellsberg and a friend leaked the study—nicknamed the Pentagon Papers—to the *New York Times* and the *Washington Post*. In June 1971, the *Times* began publishing articles based on the study. To block any further publication, the Nixon administration received a temporary restraining order to prepare its case, arguing that publishing the documents posed "a clear and present danger" to national security. The administration had five national security experts testify that publicizing the Pentagon Papers would impede the war effort.

A lower U.S. district court supported the newspaper's right to publish, but the government's appeal placed the case in the Supreme Court less than three weeks after the first articles were published. In a 6–3 vote, the Court sided with the newspapers. Justice Hugo Black, in his majority opinion, attacked the government's attempt to suppress publication: "Both the history and language of the First Amendment support the view that the press must be left free to publish news, whatever the source, without censorship, injunctions, or prior restraints."[6] (See "Media Literacy and the Critical Process: The First Amendment . . . and Publishing Government Secrets" on page 554.)

The *Progressive* Magazine Case

The issue of prior restraint surfaced again in 1979, when an injunction was issued to block publication of the *Progressive*, a national left-wing magazine; the editors had announced that they were running an article entitled "The H-Bomb Secret: How We Got It, Why We're Telling It." The dispute began when the editor of the magazine sent a draft to the Department of Energy to verify technical portions of the article. Believing that the article contained sensitive data that might damage U.S. efforts to halt the proliferation of nuclear weapons, the Energy Department asked the magazine not to publish it. When the magazine said it would proceed anyway, the government sued the *Progressive* and asked a federal district court to block publication.

Judge Robert Warren sought to balance the *Progressive*'s First Amendment rights against the government's claim that the article would spread dangerous information

● In 1971, Daniel Ellsberg surrendered to government prosecutors in Boston. Ellsberg was a former Pentagon researcher who turned against America's military policy in Vietnam and leaked information to the press. He was charged with unauthorized possession of top-secret federal documents. Later called the Pentagon Papers, the documents contained evidence on the military's bungled handling of the Vietnam War. In 1973, an exasperated federal judge dismissed the case when illegal government-sponsored wiretaps of Ellsberg's psychoanalyst came to light during the Watergate scandal.

The First Amendment . . . and Publishing Government Secrets

Enacted in 1791, the First Amendment supports not just press and speech freedoms but also religious freedom and the right of people to protest and to "petition the government for a redress of grievances." It also says that "Congress shall make no law" abridging or prohibiting these five freedoms. To investigate some critics' complaint that many citizens don't exactly know the protections offered in the First Amendment, conduct your own survey. Discuss with friends, family, or colleagues what they know or think about the First Amendment and about the news media's right under the law to report material about secret government activities during the continuing war on terrorism.

Description. Working alone or in small groups, find eight to ten people you know from two different age groups: (1) from your peers and friends or younger siblings; (2) from your parents' and/or grandparents' generations. (Do not choose students from your class.) Interview your subjects individually—either in person, by phone, or by e-mail—and ask them if Congress was considering the following law—then read the First Amendment (see page 549), but don't tell them what it is—would they approve? Then, also ask them to respond to this series of questions (and add some other questions that you think would be appropriate):

1. Do you agree or disagree with the freedoms? Explain.
2. Which do you support, and which do you think are excessive or provide too much freedom?
3. Do you think a law like this should protect the news media if they publish secret government documents? Why or why not? (Familiarize yourself with recent stories of the conflict between the government and the press over publishing articles about government secrets, as well as the Pentagon Papers case from the early 1970s.)
4. At the end of your interview, ask them if they recognize the law. Note how many identified it as

the First Amendment to the U.S. Constitution and how many did not. Note the percentage from each age group.
5. Optional: Find out each person's political leanings—Republican, Democrat, Independent, not sure, disaffected, apathetic, other, etc.

Analysis. What patterns emerge in the answers from the two groups? Are their answers similar or different? How? Note any differences in the answers based on their gender, levels of education, or occupations. Optional: Are their differences based on their political affiliations? Note these.

Interpretation. What do these patterns mean? Are your interview subjects supportive or unsupportive of the First Amendment? What are their reasons? Are your subjects supportive or unsupportive of the rights of the press to publish or broadcast government secrets? What are their reasons?

Evaluation. How do your interviewees judge the news media when their right to publish conflicts with government interests? What limits would they put on the news media in reporting government secrets? In general, what was your interview subjects' general knowledge of the First Amendment? What impressed you about your subjects' answers? Did you find anything alarming or troubling in their answers? Explain.

Engagement. Research free expression and locate any national studies that are similar to this assignment. Then, check the recent national surveys on attitudes toward the First Amendment at either www.freedomforum.org or www.firstamendmentcenter.org. Write a letter to a local TV station news director and a newspaper editor and find out what limits they would place on themselves when their rights to publish conflicted with the government's ability to protect secret operations. Share your study and research with your teacher and the class.

and undermine national security. In an unprecedented action, Warren sided with the government, deciding that "a mistake in ruling against the United States could pave the way for thermonuclear annihilation for us all. In that event, our right to life is extinguished and the right to publish becomes moot."[7] During appeals and further litigation, several other publications, including the *Milwaukee Sentinel* and *Scientific American*, published articles related to the H-bomb, getting much of their information from publications already in circulation. None of these articles, including the one published in the *Progressive*, contained the precise technical details needed to actually design a nuclear weapon; nor did they provide information on where to obtain the sensitive ingredients. Although the government dropped the case, Warren's injunction stands as the first time in American history that a prior-restraint order imposed in the name of national security actually stopped the initial publication of a controversial news report.

Unprotected Forms of Expression

In 1798, the Federalist Party, which controlled Congress, enacted the Sedition Act to silence opposition to an anticipated war against France. The act tried to curb criticism by the opposition Democratic-Republican Party. Led by President John Adams, the Federalists believed that defamatory articles might stir up discontent against the elected government and undermine its authority. Over the next three years, twenty-five individuals were arrested and ten were convicted under the act, which was also used to prosecute anti-Federalist newspapers. After failing to curb opposition, the Sedition Act expired in 1801 during Thomas Jefferson's presidency. Jefferson, a Democratic-Republican who had challenged the act's constitutionality, pardoned all defendants convicted under the Sedition Act.[8]

Despite the First Amendment's provision that "Congress shall make no law" restricting speech and press freedoms, the federal government has made other laws like the 1798 Sedition Act, especially during times of war. For instance, the Espionage Acts of 1917 and 1918, which were enforced during World Wars I and II, made it a federal crime to disrupt the nation's war effort. These acts also authorized severe punishment for seditious statements. In fact, in 2006 after the *New York Times*, the *Wall Street Journal*, and the *Los Angeles Times* all published articles on the Bush administration's secret program to track banking records of suspected terrorists, one congressman called for the *Times* "to be prosecuted for violating the 1917 Espionage Act" even though the effort had been revealed as early as 2001. And although the *Journal*'s news pages covered this story, their conservative editorial page condemned the *Times* (which features more liberal editorial positions) for "obstructing" the war on terror.[9]

Beyond the federal government, state laws and local ordinances have on occasion curbed expression, and over the years the court system has determined that some kinds of expression do not merit protection as speech under the Constitution. Today, for example, false or misleading advertising is not protected by law; nor are expressions that intentionally threaten public safety.

In the landmark *Schenck v. United States* appeal case during World War I, the Supreme Court upheld the conviction of a Socialist Party leader, Charles T. Schenck, for distributing leaflets urging American men to protest the draft, a violation of the recently passed Espionage Act. In upholding the act, Justice Oliver Wendell Holmes wrote two of the more famous interpretations and phrases in the First Amendment's legal history:

> But the character of every act depends upon the circumstances in which it is done. The most stringent protection of free speech would not protect a man in falsely shouting fire in a theater and causing a panic.

> The question in every case is whether the words used are used in such circumstances and are of such a nature as to create a clear and present danger that they will bring about the substantive evils that Congress has a right to prevent.

In supporting Schenck's sentence—a ten-year prison term—Holmes noted that the Socialist leaflets were entitled to First Amendment protection, but only during times

> **"** . . . were it left to me to decide whether we should have a government without newspapers or newspapers without a government, I should not hesitate a moment to prefer the latter.**"**
>
> –Thomas Jefferson, on the brutal press coverage of him by opposition party newspapers, 1787

of peace. In establishing the "clear and present danger" criterion for expression, the Supreme Court demonstrated the limits of the First Amendment. Beyond this judicial standard, several other kinds of expression are exceptions to the First Amendment's guarantee of free speech and press. These include copyright, libel, invasion of privacy, and obscenity.

Copyright

Appropriating a writer's or an artist's words or music without consent or payment is a form of expression that is not protected as speech. Hip-hop performers, in fact, have faced a number of court battles for copyright infringement; they have been accused of stealing other musicians' work by sampling their music, a technique fundamental to the genre. A **copyright** legally protects the rights of authors and producers to their published or unpublished writing, music and lyrics, TV programs and movies, or graphic art designs. As noted earlier, file-swapping on the Internet has raised an entirely new class of copyright concerns, not only in the music industry but also in every media sector. Copyright protection was extended with the Digital Millennium Copyright Act of 1998, which goes beyond traditional copyright protection to outlaw technology or actions that circumvent copyright protection systems. In other words, it may be illegal to merely create or distribute technology that enables someone to make illegal copies of digital content, such as a music CD or a DVD movie.

● In a 1994 landmark case, the Supreme Court ruled that the rap group 2 Live Crew's 1989 song "Pretty Woman" was a legitimate parody of the 1964 Roy Orbison song and was thus covered by the fair use exception to copyright.

Libel

The biggest single legal worry that haunts editors and publishers is the issue of libel, another form of expression that is not protected as speech under the First Amendment. Whereas **slander** constitutes spoken language that defames a person's character, **libel** refers to defamation of character in written or broadcast expression. Inherited from British common law, libel is generally defined as a false statement that holds a person up to public ridicule, contempt, or hatred or injures a person's business or occupation. Examples of potentially libelous statements include falsely accusing someone of professional dishonesty or incompetence (such as medical malpractice); falsely accusing a person of a crime (such as drug dealing); falsely charging a person with mental illness or unacceptable behavior (such as public drunkenness); or falsely accusing a person of associating with a disreputable organization or cause (such as the Mafia or a neo-Nazi military group). (See "Case Study: A False Wikipedia 'Biography'" on opposite page about online libel charges.)

To protect the news media's right to aggressively pursue wrongdoing and stories, courts since the mid-1960s have tried to make it more difficult for public officials to win libel suits. This has not, however, deterred some individuals and organizations from intimidating the news media by either threatening to file or actually filing libel suits. Such legal actions in civil law can prove costly, particularly to a small newspaper or magazine, even when the defendant wins the case. As a result, over the years many small news organizations have avoided tough, probing stories, and large organizations have hired lawyers to advise them on the libel implications of their more controversial investigative stories. In 2005, fourteen libel cases against the media went to trial, and of these, media defendants won seven. According to the Media Law Resource Center (www.medialaw.org), media firms have become more successful over the years at defending themselves against libel charges. In the 2000s, about fourteen libel cases go to trial each year, and media companies have won 53.8 percent of the cases; in the 1980s, about twenty-seven cases went to trial annually, and the media only won 36.3 percent of the time.

Since 1964, the *New York Times v. Sullivan* case has served as the standard for libel law. The case stems from a 1960 full-page advertisement placed in the *New York*

CASE STUDY

A False Wikipedia "Biography"

By John Seigenthaler

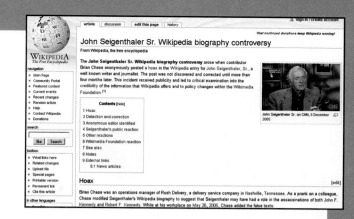

"John Seigenthaler Sr. was the assistant to Attorney General Robert Kennedy in the early 1960's. For a brief time, he was thought to have been directly involved in the Kennedy assassinations of both John, and his brother, Bobby. Nothing was ever proven."

—Wikipedia

This is a highly personal story about Internet character assassination. It could be your story. I have no idea whose sick mind conceived the false, malicious "biography" that appeared under my name for 132 days on Wikipedia, the popular, online, free encyclopedia whose authors are unknown and virtually untraceable. There was more: "John Seigenthaler moved to the Soviet Union in 1971, and returned to the United States in 1984," Wikipedia said. "He started one of the country's largest public relations firms shortly thereafter."

At age 78, I thought I was beyond surprise or hurt at anything negative said about me. I was wrong. One sentence in the biography was true. I was Robert Kennedy's administrative assistant in the early 1960s. I also was his pallbearer. It was mind-boggling when my son, John Seigenthaler, journalist with NBC News, phoned later to say he found the same scurrilous text on Reference.com and Answers.com. I had heard for weeks from teachers, journalists, and historians about "the wonderful world of Wikipedia," where millions of people worldwide visit daily for quick reference "facts," composed and posted by people with no special expertise or knowledge—and sometimes by people with malice.

At my request, executives of the three websites now have removed the false content about me. I phoned Jimmy Wales, Wikipedia's founder and asked, "Do you . . . have any way to know who wrote that?"

"No, we don't," he said. Representatives of the other two websites said their computers are programmed to copy data verbatim from Wikipedia, never checking whether it is false or factual. Naturally, I want to unmask my "biographer." And, I am interested in letting many people know that Wikipedia is a flawed and irresponsible research tool.

But searching cyberspace for the identity of people who post spurious information can be frustrating. I traced the registered IP (Internet Protocol) number of my "biographer" to a customer of BellSouth Internet. That company advertises a phone number to report "Abuse Issues." An electronic voice said all complaints must be e-mailed. My two e-mails were answered by identical form letters, advising me that the company would conduct an investigation but might not tell me the results. It was signed "Abuse Team."

After three weeks, hearing nothing further about the Abuse Team investigation, I phoned BellSouth's Atlanta corporate headquarters, which led to conversations between my lawyer and BellSouth's counsel. My only remote chance of getting the name, I learned, was to file a "John or Jane Doe" lawsuit against my "biographer." Major communications Internet companies are bound by federal privacy laws that protect the identity of their customers, even those who defame online. Only if a lawsuit resulted in a court subpoena would BellSouth give up the name.

Federal law also protects online corporations—BellSouth, AOL, MCI, Wikipedia, etc.—from libel lawsuits. Section 230 of the Communications Decency Act, passed in 1996, specifically states that "no provider or user of an interactive computer service shall be treated as the publisher or speaker." That legalese means that, unlike print and broadcast companies, online service providers cannot be sued for disseminating defamatory attacks on citizens posted by others.

Recent low-profile court decisions document that Congress effectively has barred defamation in cyberspace. Wikipedia's website acknowledges that it is not responsible for inaccurate information, but Wales, in a C-Span interview with Brian Lamb, insisted that his website is accountable and that his community of thousands of volunteer editors (he said he has only one paid employee) corrects mistakes within minutes.

My experience refutes that. My "biography" was posted May 26 [2005]. For four months, Wikipedia depicted me as a suspected assassin before Wales erased it from his website's history Oct. 5. The falsehoods remained on Answers.com and Reference.com for three more weeks.

And so we live in a universe of new media with phenomenal opportunities for worldwide communications and research—but populated by volunteer vandals with poison-pen intellects. Congress has enabled them and protects them.

Note: In 2006 Seigenthaler, with the help of some intrepid reporters, tracked down the man who posted the libelous content. Seigenthaler, however, chose not to sue him, deciding instead to speak out about the experience and to call on Wikipedia to require those who post entries to sign their names and take responsibility for their work. The controversy is now a part of his online Wikipedia bio and also has its own entry (*pictured*).

Source: John Seigenthaler, "A false Wikipedia 'biography,' " *USA Today,* November 30, 2005, p. 11A.

● This is the 1960 *New York Times* advertisement that triggered one of the most influential and important libel cases in U.S. history.

Times by the Committee to Defend Martin Luther King Jr. and the Struggle for Freedom in the South. Without naming names, the ad criticized the general law-enforcement tactics of southern cities, including Montgomery, Alabama, for the methods used to break up Civil Rights demonstrations. The ad condemned "southern violators of the Constitution" bent on destroying King and the movement. Taking exception, the city commissioner of Montgomery, L. B. Sullivan, sued the *Times* for libel, claiming the ad defamed him indirectly. Although Alabama civil courts awarded Sullivan $500,000, the newspaper's lawyers appealed to the Supreme Court, which unanimously reversed the ruling, holding that Alabama libel law violated the *Times*'s First Amendment rights.[10]

In the *Sullivan* decision, the Supreme Court asked future civil courts to distinguish whether plaintiffs are public officials or private individuals. (In later cases, *public figures* such as entertainment or sports celebrities were added to this mix.) Within this framework, private individuals have to prove three things to successfully argue a libel case:

1. that the public statement about them was false;
2. that damages or actual injury occurred, such as the loss of a job, harm to reputation, public humiliation, or mental anguish;
3. that the publisher or broadcaster was negligent.

But if a court determines that a plaintiff is a *public official* or figure, that person has to prove falsehood, damages, negligence, and **actual malice** on the part of the news medium. The latter test means that the reporter or editor knew the statement was false and printed or broadcast it anyway, or acted with a reckless disregard for the truth. Again, because actual malice is hard to prove, it remains difficult for public figures to win libel suits. The Court's rationale for the principle of actual malice not only protects the First Amendment rights of the media but, in theory, also allows news operations to aggressively pursue legitimate news stories without fear of continuous litigation. In practice, however, the mere threat of a libel suit still scares off many in the news media.

Under current libel law, civil courts determine, on a case-by-case basis, whether plaintiffs are public or private persons. In general, public officials must have substantial responsibilities in conducting government affairs; therefore presidents, senators, mayors, police detectives, and city managers count as examples of public officials. Citizens with more "ordinary" jobs, such as city sanitation employees, undercover police informants, nurses, or unknown actors, are normally classified as private individuals.

Judges often have a tough time deciding who is a public figure. Many vague categories exist, such as public high school teachers, police officers, and court-appointed attorneys. Individuals from these professions have ended up in either category depending on a particular court's ruling. The Supreme Court has distinguished two categories of public figures: (1) public celebrities or people who "occupy positions of such pervasive power and influence that they are deemed public figures for all purposes," and (2) individuals who have thrown themselves—usually voluntarily but sometimes involuntarily—into the middle of "a significant public controversy," such as a lawyer defending a prominent client, an advocate for an antismoking ordinance, a labor union activist, or a security guard like Richard Jewell.

Made famous by the news media, Jewell was initially suspected of setting off the pipe bomb that killed a woman at the 1996 Olympics in Atlanta, Georgia. After the FBI cleared Jewell, NBC News, ABC News, CNN, and the *New York Post* settled libel cases with him. His lawyers had charged that after media reports named him as the only suspect, he could not find work even though he was never charged with the crime. But the *Atlanta Journal-Constitution* did not settle out of court with Jewell, and a bitter libel lawsuit between them ensued. A Georgia court ruled that because Jewell had consented to media interviews, he was a public figure—thus he had to prove the Atlanta newspaper used actual malice, not just negligence. Even after Eric Rudolph pled guilty to the bombing in 2005, Jewell's libel case against the *Journal-Constitution* continued into 2006.

Defenses against Libel Charges

Since the 1730s, the best defense against libel in American courts has been the truth. In most cases, if libel defendants can demonstrate that they printed or broadcast statements that were essentially true, such evidence usually bars plaintiffs from recovering any damages—even if their reputations were harmed. To this end, the news media are particularly careful about using any direct quotes in which a source may have lied, employing legal staffs to check the veracity of controversial stories before publication. If a source, for instance, libels a private person in a news report, the paper may also be held accountable. Even if the reporter did not know the quote was false, he or she might be considered negligent for not checking the truthfulness of the statement more carefully.

Beyond the truth, there are other defenses against libel. Prosecutors, for example, receive *absolute privilege* in a court of law when they make potentially damaging statements about a defendant's reputation. When prosecutors accuse defendants of being murderers and they are later acquitted, lawyers are protected from libel on the legal theory that in public courtrooms the interests of an individual are overridden by the larger common good of the legal process. The reporters who print or broadcast statements made in court are also protected against libel. Entitled to conditional or **qualified privilege**, journalists are allowed to report judicial or legislative proceedings even though the public statements being reported may be libelous.

When police detectives, judges, or prosecutors make unsubstantiated claims about a defendant, or when legislators verbally attack each other during a session, reporters are allowed to report those incidents—even when potentially libelous statements are relayed secondhand by the reporter. As a condition for qualified privilege, the reporting of these public events must be fair and accurate. If a reporter, for instance, has prior knowledge that a public statement is untrue and still reports it as the truth, a judge may suspend qualified privilege and hold the reporter accountable for libel.

Another defense against libel concerns the area of *opinion and fair comment*. For example, after O.J. Simpson was acquitted of murder in October 1995 in his criminal case, many legal commentators and talk-show hosts continued to suggest that in their *opinion* he was guilty of killing his former wife, Nicole Brown, and her friend Ron Goldman. Generally, however, libel applies only to misstatements of factual information rather than opinion, although the line between fact and opinion is often hazy. Some libel cases turn on a plaintiff's ability to persuade a judge or jury that a defendant's statement was a factual error and not merely opinion or fair comment. For this reason, lawyers advise journalists to first set forth the facts on which a viewpoint is based and then to state their opinion based on those facts. In other words, journalists should make it clear that a statement is a criticism and not an allegation

> " You cannot hold us to the same [libel] standards as a newscast or you kill talk radio. If we had to qualify everything we said, talk radio would cease to exist. "
>
> —Lionel, WABC talk radio morning host, 1999

On Larry King's cable talk show in 1997, Moral Majority leader Rev. Jerry Falwell (*right*) discusses pornography and forgiveness with *Hustler* magazine publisher Larry Flynt (*center*)—their first face-to-face meeting since their 1984 libel trial.

of fact. Libel laws protect satire, comedy, and opinions expressed in reviews of books, plays, movies, or restaurants. Such laws may not, however, protect malicious statements in which plaintiffs can prove that defendants used their free-speech rights to mount a damaging personal attack.

One of the most famous tests of opinion and fair comment occurred in a case pitting conservative minister and political activist Jerry Falwell against Larry Flynt, publisher of *Hustler* magazine. The case became the subject of a major Hollywood movie, *The People vs. Larry Flynt* (1996). The actual *Falwell v. Flynt* case developed after a November 1983 issue of *Hustler* made an outrageous reference to Falwell. In a spoof of a Campari aperitif ad, the magazine asked readers to recall the "first time" they drank Campari. The parody stated that Falwell needed to be drunk before he could preach; it also described his "first time" as an incestuous encounter with his own mother. In fine print at the bottom of the page, a disclaimer read: "Ad parody — not to be taken seriously."

Often a target of Flynt's irreverence and questionable taste, Falwell sued for libel, asking for $45 million in damages. In the verdict, the jury rejected the libel suit but found that Flynt had intentionally caused Falwell emotional distress, awarding him $200,000. It was an unprecedented verdict in American legal history. Flynt's lawyers appealed, and in 1988 the Supreme Court unanimously overturned the verdict. Although the Court did not condone the *Hustler* spoof, the justices did say that the magazine was entitled to constitutional protection. The case drew enormous media attention and raised concerns about the erosion of the media's right to free speech. In affirming *Hustler*'s speech rights, the Court suggested that even though parodies and insults of public figures might indeed cause emotional pain, denying the right to publish them would undermine a key democratic principle and violate the spirit of the First Amendment.[11]

The Right to Privacy

Whereas libel laws safeguard a person's character and reputation, the right to privacy protects an individual's peace of mind and personal feelings. Any public figure who has ever been subjected to intense scrutiny by the media has experienced an invasion of privacy. But, in general, the news media have been granted wide protections under the First Amendment to subject public figures to the spotlight. Local municipalities and states, however, have passed laws that protect most individuals from unwarranted surveillance. Some courts have ruled that photographers must keep a certain distance away from celebrities, although powerful zoom lens technology usually overcomes this obstacle. But for some U.S. citizens, privacy rules here are too lax. In 2006, actors Brad Pitt and Angelina Jolie went to Namibia in Africa "to avoid photographers in the weeks leading up to the birth of their first child together." The government there placed strict security around their hotel and hospital, "set up large green barriers to protect their privacy from photographers, and refused to grant visas to any foreign journalists unless they had written permission from Jolie and Pitt to cover the birth."[12] Police in Namibia also arrested photographers and took their film. After the baby was born, Jolie and Pitt sold the baby's photo rights nationally and internationally to *People* and *Hello* magazines in multimillion-dollar deals, reportedly donating the money to charity.

● Must we know everything about the private lives of Brad Pitt and Angelina Jolie? The two movie stars decamped to Namibia to have a child in 2006 to take advantage of the African nation's stricter privacy laws.

Public figures have received some legal relief, but every year brings a few stories of a Hollywood actor or sports figure punching a tabloid photographer or TV cameraman who got too close. Similarly, actress Jennifer Aniston brought a privacy lawsuit against *Celebrity Skin* magazine in 2000 for printing photos of her sunbathing topless in her backyard. The suit claimed a photographer climbed a neighbor's fence to snap the photos. Such cases, as well as Princess Diana's death in 1997—partly attributed to harassment by paparazzi—have spawned a flurry of legislation attempting to protect celebrities and public figures from invasions of privacy. Such anti-paparazzi laws include prohibition of trespassing or using electronic devices that can capture images of a celebrity or crime victim engaged in personal activity on private property or outside public forums. In some states, the American Civil Liberties Union (ACLU) has challenged these laws as an infringement of the First Amendment rights of the news media. In 1999, the Supreme Court ruled that photographers and video news crews could not accompany police inside private property on authorized crime raids, such as a drug search, unless they received prior approval to enter the home or place of business from the occupants. Moreover, even in death there is a right to privacy. In 2004, the Supreme Court ruled—as an exception to the Freedom of Information Act—that families of prominent figures who have died have the right to object to the release of autopsy photos, so that the images may not be exploited.

In the simplest terms, **invasion of privacy** addresses a person's right to be left alone, without his or her name, image, or daily activities becoming public property. Invasions of privacy occur in different situations, the most common of which are listed here:

1. intrusion, in which unauthorized tape recorders, wiretaps, microphones, or other surveillance equipment are used to secretly record a person's private affairs.
2. the publication of private matters, such as the unauthorized disclosure of private statements about an individual's health, sexual activities, or economic status.
3. the unauthorized appropriation of a person's name or image for advertising or other commercial benefit.

As we have noted, the courts have generally given the news media a lot of leeway under the First Amendment. For instance, the names and pictures of both private individuals and public figures can usually be used without their consent in most news stories. If private citizens become part of public controversies and subsequent news stories, the courts have usually allowed the news media to record their quotes and use their images without the individuals' permission. The courts have even ruled that accurate reports of criminal and court records, including the identification of rape victims, do not normally constitute privacy invasions. Nevertheless, most newspapers and broadcast outlets use their own internal guidelines and ethical codes to protect the privacy of victims and defendants, especially in cases involving rape and child abuse.

Another privacy issue—especially significant in the age of the Internet—gets little sympathy from the general public: Are citizens' privacy rights protected when they go online to view the most controversial forms of pornography? The Child On-Line Protection Act makes it illegal to post "material that is harmful to minors," but an early version of the law was declared unconstitutional. Then in 2004 the Supreme Court prevented a revised version of the law from being enforced and "ordered a lower court to consider whether filtering software designed to block inappropriate content was a better way to achieve the law's aims."[13] By 2006, the Justice Department, which defended the law, was pitted against the American Civil Liberties Union because the Justice Department subpoenaed information from search-engine companies, including Google and AOL. Google challenged its subpoena but "a judge ordered the company to provide some information . . . but not information on individual searches, saying that had potential to violate the privacy of users."[14] Finally, the Justice Department did not ask for information that could be linked to the names of individual users. Yet, by fall 2006 hearings on the case continued in Congress.

Obscenity

Most privacy and libel issues are part of civil or private law: individuals filing personal lawsuits against another individual or a media organization. Anti-pornography legislation and obscenity issues, though, are guided by federal law and can be prosecuted as criminal offenses: a prosecutor making a case against a purveyor of obscene material on behalf of "the people."

For most of this nation's history, it has generally been argued that obscenity does not constitute a legitimate form of expression. The problem, however, is that little agreement has existed on how to define an obscene work. In the 1860s, a court could judge an entire book obscene if it contained a single passage believed capable of corrupting a person. In fact, throughout the 1800s certain government authorities outside the courts—especially U.S. post office and customs officials—held the power to censor or destroy written material they deemed obscene.

This began to change in the 1930s during the trial involving the celebrated novel *Ulysses* by Irish writer James Joyce. Portions of *Ulysses* had been serialized in the early 1920s in an American magazine, which was later seized and burned by postal officials. The publishers of the magazine, *Little Review*, were fined $50 and nearly sent to prison. Because of the four-letter words contained in the novel and the book-burning incident, British and American publishing houses backed away from the book, which was eventually published in Paris in 1922. In 1928, the U.S. Customs Office officially banned *Ulysses* as an obscene work. Ultimately, Random House agreed to publish the work in America only if it was declared "legal." Finally, in 1933, a U.S. judge ruled that *Ulysses* was an important literary work and removed it from unprotected status.

Battles over obscenity continued. In a landmark case, *Roth v. United States*, the Supreme Court in 1957 offered this test of obscenity: whether to an "average person," applying "contemporary standards," the major thrust or theme of the material,

> **❝ I shall not today attempt to define [obscenity]. . . . And perhaps I never could succeed in intelligibly doing so. But I know it when I see it.❞**
> —Supreme Court Justice Potter Stewart, 1964

"taken as a whole," appealed to "prurient interest" (in other words, was intended to "incite lust"). By the 1960s, based on *Roth*, expression no longer constituted obscenity if only a small part of the work lacked "redeeming social value." Refining *Roth*, the current legal definition of **obscenity** derives from the 1973 *Miller v. California* case, which involved sanctions for using the mail to promote or send pornographic materials. After a series of appeals, the Supreme Court argued that an obscene work had to meet three criteria:

1. The average person, applying contemporary community standards, would find that the material as a whole appeals to prurient interest.
2. The material depicts or describes sexual conduct in a patently offensive way.
3. The material, as a whole, lacks serious literary, artistic, political, or scientific value.

The *Miller* refinement of the *Roth* precedent contained two important ideas. First, it acknowledged that different communities and regions of the country have different values and standards; what is considered obscene in Fargo, North Dakota, for example, may not be judged obscene in Miami. The ruling sent various municipalities and states scrambling to develop lists of obscene acts and language that violated their communities' standards. (Some of these lists, when tested, were declared unconstitutional and had to undergo numerous revisions.) Second, the *Miller* decision also required that a work be judged *as a whole*. This removed a loophole in which some publishers would insert a political essay or literary poem to demonstrate in court that their publications contained redeeming features.

Since this decision, courts have granted great latitude to printed and visual pornography. By the 1980s and 1990s, major cases prosecuting obscenity had become rare—aimed mostly at child pornography—as the legal system advanced the concept that a free and democratic society must tolerate even repulsive kinds of speech.

First Amendment versus Sixth Amendment

Over the years, First Amendment protections of speech and the press have often clashed with the Sixth Amendment, which guarantees an accused individual in "all criminal prosecutions . . . the right to a speedy and public trial, by an impartial jury." In 1954, for example, the Sam Sheppard case, loosely the inspiration for the TV series *The Fugitive* and the subsequent 1994 film of the same name, involved enormous publicity. Featuring lurid details about the murder of Sheppard's wife, the Cleveland press editorialized in favor of Sheppard's quick arrest; some papers even pronounced him guilty. A prominent and wealthy osteopath, Sheppard was convicted of the murder. Twelve years later, though, Sheppard's new lawyer, F. Lee Bailey, argued before the Supreme Court that his client had not received a fair trial because of prejudicial publicity. The Court overturned the conviction and freed Sheppard.

Gag Orders and Shield Laws

One of the major criticisms of recent criminal cases concerns the ways in which defense lawyers use the news media to comment publicly on court matters outside the presence of a sequestered jury. After the Sheppard reversal in the 1960s, the Supreme Court suggested safeguards that judges could employ to ensure a fair trial in a heavily publicized case. These included sequestering juries (Sheppard's jury was not sequestered), moving cases to other jurisdictions, limiting the number of reporters, seating reporters in a particular place in courtrooms, and placing restrictions, or **gag orders**, on lawyers and witnesses. Historically, gag orders have been issued to prohibit the press from releasing preliminary information that might prejudice jury selection. In most instances, however, especially since a Supreme Court

> ❝ [Jailed *New York Times* reporter Judith Miller] does not believe, nor do we, that reporters are above the law, but instead holds that the work of journalists must be independent and free from government control if they are to effectively serve as government watchdogs. ❞
>
> —Reporters Committee for Freedom of the Press, 2005

● *New York Times* reporter Judith Miller spent eighty-five days in jail for refusing to testify about her confidential sources in connection with the leaked identity of CIA operative Valerie Plame. Bush administration officials had revealed Plame's CIA connection after the *Times* published an op-ed piece by her husband, U.S. ambassador Joseph Wilson, in which he challenged the accuracy of the prewar intelligence on Iraq's nuclear weapons program. Miller, who resigned from the *Times* in 2006, was released after she agreed to testify before a grand jury. She said that the source of her leak — Lewis "Scooter" Libby, Vice President Dick Cheney's chief of staff — released her from a pledge of confidentiality to protect his identity. Libby was indicted in 2005 for lying to the grand jury, with his trial set for 2007.

review in 1976, gag rules have been struck down as a prior-restraint violation of the First Amendment.

In opposition to gag rules, **shield laws** have favored the First Amendment rights of reporters, protecting them from having to reveal their sources for controversial information used in news stories. The news media have argued that protecting the confidentiality of key sources maintains a reporter's credibility, protects a source from possible retaliation, and serves the public interest by providing information citizens might not otherwise receive. In the 1960s, when the First Amendment rights of reporters clashed with Sixth Amendment fair-trial concerns, judges usually favored the Sixth Amendment arguments. In 1972, a New Jersey journalist became the first reporter jailed for contempt of court for refusing to identify sources in a probe of the Newark housing authority. After this case, a number of legal measures emerged to protect the news media. Thirty-one states and the District of Columbia now have some type of shield law. (See "Examining Ethics: Does It Matter That the Press Is under Siege?" on opposite page.)

Cameras in the Courtroom

When Sam Sheppard was originally convicted in the 1950s, television news was in its infancy and did not play a major role in the coverage of that trial. But by the mid-1990s, TV cameras in the courtroom had become central to public discussions of our legal system. More and more judges and lawyers had come to believe that the presence of cameras made the judicial system more accountable and helped the public learn how U.S. law operated.

This view, however, took a long time to evolve. The debates over intrusive electronic broadcast equipment and photographers actually date to the sensationalized coverage of the Bruno Hauptmann trial in the mid-1930s. Hauptmann was convicted and executed for the kidnap-murder of the nineteen-month-old son of Anne and Charles Lindbergh (the aviation hero who made the first solo flight across the Atlantic Ocean in 1927). During the trial, Hauptmann and his attorney had complained that the circus atmosphere fueled by the presence of radio and flash cameras prejudiced the jury and turned the public against him.

After the trial, the American Bar Association amended a professional ethics code, Canon 35, stating that electronic equipment in the courtroom detracted "from the essential dignity of the proceedings." Calling for a ban on photographers and radio equipment, the association believed that if such elements were not banned, lawyers would begin playing to audiences and negatively alter the judicial process. For years after the Hauptmann trial, almost every state banned photographic, radio, and TV equipment from courtrooms.

As broadcast equipment became more portable and less obtrusive, however, and as television became the major news source for most Americans, courts gradually reevaluated their bans on broadcast equipment. In fact, in the early 1980s the Supreme Court ruled that the presence of TV equipment did not make it impossible for a fair trial to occur, leaving it up to each state to implement its own system. In 2001, North Dakota became the last of the fifty states to end a complete ban on cameras in courtrooms. Most states still have certain restrictions on television coverage of courtrooms, though, often leaving it up to the discretion of the presiding judge. In 1991, U.S. federal courts began allowing limited coverage of trials. The Supreme Court still bans TV from its proceedings, but in 2000 the court broke its anti-radio rule by permitting delayed broadcasts of the hearings on the Florida vote recount case that determined the winner of the 2000 presidential election.

The judicial system got its very own national cable service when the Courtroom Television Network — Court TV — debuted in 1991. In 2006, the channel was available in eighty-three million homes, carrying both live and taped coverage of trials from

EXAMINING ETHICS

Does It Matter That the Press Is under Siege?

By Paul K. McMasters

Many of us view the increasingly intense struggle between the press and the government with a strange mix of fascination and detachment. We are tempted to believe this distant clash of titans has little impact on our daily lives and that we can't do anything about it anyway. Well, it does, and we can. In fact, it is one of those rare situations where merely paying attention is doing something about it. Yet for the most part we stand aloof.

For example, how much attention did we pay [in mid-2006] when five of our largest news organizations contributed to the government's settlement of a lawsuit filed by nuclear scientist Wen Ho Lee? In his suit, Lee claimed that the federal departments of Energy and Justice and the FBI had violated the Privacy Act and falsely branded him as a spy by leaking information from his files to the press.

Lee's lawyers subpoenaed five journalists to reveal who their government sources were. The journalists refused and eventually were ordered by the courts to divulge their sources or pay fines of $500 a day and possibly face jail. After more than four years of litigation, the government agreed to pay $895,000 to settle the lawsuit. The five news organizations agreed to pay a total of $750,000.

The journalists' employers paid up even though they were not parties to the lawsuit. Their reporting was not challenged. They were not accused of libel or of publishing classified information. They appealed all the way to the Supreme Court, to no avail.

The journalists and their lawyers said that every professional fiber in their beings was against making such a deal, but they had reached the end of the road. So they agreed to the least unappealing of a very ugly set of options. The settlement did allow them to protect their sources, to escape the threat of jail, and to halt the financial hemorrhaging from the legal battles—as well as to return full-time to what they do best: gathering and reporting the news. What does this unsettling and unprecedented action have to do with the rest of us?

First and foremost, it marks yet another loss of ground in journalists' efforts to report thoroughly and fairly on an increasingly secretive federal government. When news organizations break major stories about questionable government actions, members of Congress call for laws targeting the press more often than for investigation of the questionable actions. The Department of Justice warns darkly that it has the power to prosecute journalists for receiving or publishing classified information. A judge sends a reporter to federal prison for 85 days for refusing to reveal a source.

When the press is under a siege of this magnitude, the flow of vital information reaching the public is constricted and public policy is distorted. The major news organizations particularly are intimidated, distracted, or drained of resources to pursue the news aggressively and fight the legal battles that the public depends on.

It is little wonder that the USA has slipped to 44th place in the press-freedom rankings among other nations. What can be done?

We should resist the idea that the press deserves all this simply because at times it can be irritating, superficial, sensational, and invasive.

We should understand the necessity for the press on occasion to rely on sources that may not have the best of motives, as the police, the FBI, and the CIA do.

We should hope that to protect those sources Congress will pass a federal shield law and that the president will sign it. The Free Flow of Information Act, with bipartisan sponsorship, is moving toward a Senate vote.

Finally, we can remind government officials and the courts that there is interest by the public—by paying more attention.

Source: First Amendment Center, www.firstamendmentcenter.org/commentary.aspx?id-17024, June 18, 2006.

● Photographers surround aviator Charles A. Lindbergh (without hat) as he leaves the courthouse in Flemington, N.J., during the trial of Bruno Hauptmann on charges of kidnapping and murdering the Lindbergh baby boy in 1935.

❝The day you see a camera come into our courtroom, it's going to roll over my dead body.❞

–Supreme Court Justice
David Souter, 1996

around the United States in the daytime, and court-related dramas and reality shows in the evenings. The O.J. Simpson criminal trial—the most publicized case in history—gave Court TV its greatest boost in 1994. The channel provided the one "pool" camera allowed at the trial, supplying all local news channels and the networks with the only footage from inside the courtroom. Before and during the criminal trial, a number of national discussions took place regarding the impact of the courtroom camera. Judge Lance Ito threatened to pull the plug on at least two occasions—once when the camera briefly panned across an alternate juror, and another time when he thought the camera had zoomed in too tightly on the defendant taking notes. (In Simpson's civil trial, the judge banned TV coverage.)

Critical analysis of the first Simpson trial continued long after the outcome. In retrospect, many legal analysts thought that the nine-month duration of the trial—the longest in California history—resulted from too many lawyers overacting for a national audience. Certainly, such intense focus on the case took attention away from other issues that the news media might have covered more fully had the trial not occurred. Still, televising the criminal trial contributed to the democratic process in at least two important ways. First, the Simpson criminal trial gave many people their first sustained glimpse into the strengths and weaknesses of the U.S. legal system. Second, the TV trial focused national attention on the problems of spousal abuse, racial tension, and the need for judicial reform, creating national debates on these issues that went on for months after the trial ended.

The Clinton impeachment hearings in the late 1990s and subsequent trial again brought legal matters to the small screen. Covered round-the-clock by CNN, Court TV, MSNBC, CNBC, and Fox News, as well as by two C-Span channels, the Clinton affair gave many members of Congress, formerly unknown outside their own regions, a national platform. Throughout the hearings there just didn't seem to be enough legislators—or law professors—to fill all the talk time on these cable channels. During the 1999 Senate trial, U.S. senators often started their day with TV appearances, conducted their business in the Senate, then spent their evenings once more making the cable rounds to discuss Clinton and the trial.

Curbing the Law's Chilling Effect

As libel law and the growing acceptance of courtroom cameras indicate, the legal process has generally, though not always, tried to ensure that print and other news media are able to cover public issues broadly without fear of reprisals. Since the 1960s especially, legislators have sculpted laws that would not have a chilling effect on the news media, that would not curb their ability to actively pursue and report stories that are in the public interest. In a democracy, we expect journalists to act as watchdogs on public issues of vital importance. Such an expectation necessitates broad speech and press freedom. Because of this First Amendment freedom, as a society we occasionally tolerate pornography, hate speech, and other forms of expression that we may not support personally. We can, however, exercise our own free-speech rights and speak out against—or even boycott—language and expression that we find offensive, demeaning, or hateful.

Film and the First Amendment

When the First Amendment was ratified in 1791, even the most enlightened leaders of our nation could not have predicted the coming of visual media such as film and television. Consequently, new communication technologies have not always received the same kinds of protection as those granted to speech, pamphlets, newspapers, magazines, and books. For example, movies, in existence since the late 1890s, earned speech protection under the law only after a 1952 Supreme Court decision. In addition, broadcast stations, unlike newspapers or magazines, are licensed by the federal government and are subject to legislation that does not affect print media.

Social and Political Pressure on the Movies

During the early part of the twentieth century, movies rose in popularity among European immigrants and others from modest socioeconomic groups. This, in turn, spurred the formation of censorship groups, which believed that the popular new medium would threaten children, incite violence, and undermine morality. The number of nickelodeon theaters—often housed in ramshackle buildings—surged in 1905 and drew the attention of public health inspectors and city social workers. During this time, according to media historian Douglas Gomery, criticism of movies converged on four areas: "the effects on children, the potential health problems, the negative influences on morals and manners, and the lack of a proper role for educational and religious institutions in the development of movies."[15]

Film Review Boards

Public pressure on movies came both from conservatives, who saw them as a potential threat to the authority of traditional institutions, and from progressives, who worried that children and adults were more attracted to movie houses than to social organizations and urban education centers. Afraid that movies created an illusory dreamworld, civic leaders publicly escalated their pressure, organizing local review boards that screened movies for their communities. In 1907, the Chicago City Council created an ordinance that gave the police authority to issue permits for a movie's exhibition. By 1920, more than ninety cities in the United States had some type of movie censorship board made up of vice squad officers, politicians, or citizen groups. By 1923, twenty-two states had established such boards.

Pressure began to translate into law as politicians, wanting to please their constituencies, began to legislate against films. Support mounted for a federal censorship bill. When Jack Johnson won the heavyweight championship in 1908, boxing films became the target of the first federal law aimed at the motion-picture industry. In 1912, the government outlawed the transportation of boxing movies across state lines. The laws against boxing films, however, had more to do with Johnson's race than with concern over violence in movies. The first black heavyweight champion, he was perceived as a threat to the white community.

The first Supreme Court decision regarding film's protection under the First Amendment was handed down in 1915 and went against the movie industry. In *Mutual v. Ohio*, the Mutual Film Company of Detroit sued the state of Ohio, whose review board had censored a number of the Michigan distributor's films. On appeal, the case arrived at the Supreme Court, which unanimously ruled that film was not a form of speech but "a business pure and simple" and, like a circus, merely a "spectacle" for entertainment with "a special capacity for evil." This ruling would stand as a precedent for thirty-seven years. Although the U.S. movement to create a national censorship board failed, legislation to monitor and control movies, especially those from America, did pass in many other countries.

Industry Self-Regulation

As the film industry expanded after World War I, the impact of public pressure and review boards began to affect movie studios and executives who wanted to ensure control over their economic well-being. In the early 1920s, a series of scandals rocked Hollywood: actress Mary Pickford's divorce and quick marriage to actor Douglas Fairbanks; director William Desmond Taylor's unsolved murder; and actor Wallace Reid's death from a drug overdose. The most sensational scandal involved aspiring actress Virginia Rappe, who died a few days after a wild party in a San Francisco hotel hosted by popular silent-film comedian Fatty Arbuckle. After Rappe's death, the comedian was indicted for rape and manslaughter. Although two hung juries could not reach a verdict, Arbuckle's career was ruined. Censorship boards across the country banned his films. Even though he was acquitted at his third trial in 1922, the movie industry tried to send a signal about the kind of values and lifestyles it would tolerate: Arbuckle was banned from acting in Hollywood. He later directed several films under the name Will B. Goode.

In response to the scandals, particularly the first Arbuckle trial, the movie industry formed the Motion Picture Producers and Distributors of America (MPPDA) and hired as its president Will Hays, former Republican National Committee chair. Hays was paid $100,000 annually to clean up "sin city." Known as the Hays Office, the MPPDA attempted to smooth out problems between the public and the industry. Hays blacklisted promising actors or movie extras with even minor police records. Later, he developed an MPPDA public relations division, which stopped a national movement for a federal law censoring movies.

The Motion Picture Production Code

During the 1930s, the movie business faced a new round of challenges. First, various conservative and religious groups—including the influential Catholic Legion of Decency—increased their scrutiny of the industry. Second, deteriorating economic conditions during the Great Depression forced the industry to tighten self-regulation to keep harmful public pressure at bay. In 1927, the Hays Office had developed a list of "Don'ts and Be Carefuls" to steer producers and directors away from questionable sexual, moral, and social themes. Nevertheless, pressure for a more formal and sweeping code mounted. In the early 1930s, the Hays Office established the Motion Picture Production Code, whose overseers officially stamped almost every Hollywood film with a moral seal of approval.

The code laid out its mission in its first general principle: "No picture shall be produced which will lower the moral standards of those who see it. Hence the sympathy of the audience shall never be thrown to the side of crime, wrong-doing, evil or sin." The self-regulatory code dictated how producers and directors should handle "methods of crime," "repellent subjects," and "sex hygiene." A section on profanity outlawed a long list of phrases and topics, including "toilet gags" and "traveling salesmen and farmer's daughter jokes." In the late 1930s, the producers of *Gone with the Wind* had to seek a special dispensation so that actor Clark Gable could say "damn." Under "scenes of passion," the code dictated that "excessive and lustful kissing, lustful embraces, suggestive postures and gestures are not to be shown," and it required that "passion should be treated in such a manner as not to stimulate the lower and baser emotions." The section on religion revealed the influences of a Jesuit priest and a Catholic publisher, who helped write the code: "No film or episode may throw ridicule on any religious faith," and "ministers of religion . . . should not be used as comic characters or as villains."

Adopted by 95 percent of the industry, the code influenced nearly every commercial movie made between the mid-1930s and the early 1950s. It also gave the industry a relative degree of freedom, enabling the major studios to remain independent of outside regulation. When television arrived, however, competition from the new family medium forced movie producers to explore more adult subjects.

In 1952, the Supreme Court heard the *Miracle* case—officially *Burstyn v. Wilson*—named for the movie distributor who sued the head of the New York Film Licensing Board for banning Roberto Rossellini's film *Il Miracolo* (*The Miracle*). A few New York City religious and political leaders considered the 1948 Italian film sacrilegious and pressured the film board for the ban. In the film, an unmarried peasant girl is impregnated by a scheming vagrant (played by Federico Fellini, who also wrote the story). She believes the tramp's story: He is St. Joseph and she has conceived the baby Jesus. The importers of the film argued that censoring it constituted illegal prior restraint; because such an action could not be imposed on a print version of the story, the same freedom should attach to the film. The Supreme Court eventually agreed, declaring movies "a significant medium for the communication of ideas." The decision granted films the same protections as those enjoyed by the print media and other forms of speech. Even more important, the decision rendered most activities of

● Silent film comedian Roscoe "Fatty" Arbuckle never served jail time for the death of Virginia Rappe, but his career was ruined. Paramount canceled its $3 million contract with him, and he was blacklisted in Hollywood.

Figure 16.1
The Voluntary Movie Rating System

film review boards unconstitutional, because they had generally been engaged in prior restraint. Although a few local boards survived into the 1990s to handle complaints about obscenity, most of them had disbanded by the early 1970s.

Rating Movie Content

The current voluntary movie rating system—the model for the advisory labels the music business and television now use—developed in the late 1960s after another round of pressure over movie content. *The Pawnbroker* in 1965, for instance, contained brief female nudity, and in 1966 *Who's Afraid of Virginia Woolf?* featured a level of profanity that had not been heard before in a major studio film. In 1966, the movie industry hired Jack Valenti to run the MPAA (Motion Picture Association of America, formerly the MPPDA), and in 1968 he established an industry board to rate movies. Eventually, G, PG, R, and X ratings emerged as guideposts for the suitability of films for various age groups. In 1984, prompted by the releases of *Gremlins* and *Indiana Jones and the Temple of Doom*, the MPAA added PG–13 and sandwiched it between PG and R to distinguish slightly higher levels of violence or adult themes in movies that might otherwise qualify as PG (see Figure 16.1).

The MPAA copyrighted all ratings designations as trademarks, except for the X rating, which was gradually appropriated as a promotional tool by the pornographic film industry. In fact, between 1972 and 1989 the MPAA stopped issuing the X rating. In 1990, however, based on protests from filmmakers over movies with adult sexual themes that they did not consider pornographic, the industry copyrighted the NC–17 rating—no children age seventeen or under—and awarded the first NC–17 to *Henry & June*. In 1995, *Showgirls* became the first movie to intentionally seek an NC–17 to demonstrate that the rating was commercially viable. However, many theater chains in the mid-1990s refused to carry NC–17 movies, fearing economic sanctions and boycotts by their customers, religious groups, and other concerned citizens. Many newspapers also refused to carry ads for NC–17 films. Panned by the critics, *Showgirls* flopped at the box office. Since then, the NC–17 rating has not proved commercially viable and distributors avoid releasing films with the rating, preferring to label such films "unrated." When films such as *Clerks* (1994), *Eyes Wide Shut* (1999), and *Team America: World Police* (2004) initially received an NC–17 rating, the directors agreed to alter or cut graphic sexual scenes to secure an R rating. When director Atom Egoyan failed in his appeal to have his 2005 film, *Where the Truth Lies*, reclassified from NC–17 (or "unrated") to R, the film tanked at the box office. He said the combination of famous actors and "a nude homoerotic scene" doomed the film, a murder mystery starring Kevin Bacon, Colin Firth, and Alison Lohman.[16] The director, however, did cut both R and unrated versions for DVD release in 2006.

Expression over the Airwaves

During the Cold War, a vigorous campaign led by Joseph McCarthy, an ultraconservative senator from Wisconsin, tried to rid both government and the media of so-called communist subversives who were allegedly challenging the American way of life. In

1950, a publication called *Red Channels: The Report of Communist Influence in Radio and Television* aimed "to show how the Communists have been able to carry out their plan of infiltration of the radio and television industry." *Red Channels*, inspired by McCarthy and produced by a group of former FBI agents, named 151 performers, writers, and musicians who were "sympathetic" to communist or "left-wing" causes. Among those named were Leonard Bernstein, Will Geer (who later played the grandfather on *The Waltons*), Dashiell Hammett, Lillian Hellman, Lena Horne, Burgess Meredith, Arthur Miller, Dorothy Parker, Pete Seeger (the labor folksinger who in 1994 received a Kennedy Center Honors Award from President Clinton), Irwin Shaw, and Orson Welles. For a time, all were banned from working in television and radio even though no one on the list was ever charged with a crime.[17]

Although the First Amendment protects an individual's right to hold controversial political views, network executives either sympathized with the anticommunist movement or feared losing ad revenue. At any rate, the networks did not stand up to the communist witch-hunters. In order to work, a blacklisted or "suspected" performer required the support of the program's sponsor. Though *I Love Lucy*'s Lucille Ball, who in sympathy with her father once registered to vote as a communist in the 1930s, retained Philip Morris's sponsorship of her popular program, other performers were not as fortunate. Philip Loeb, who played the father on *The Goldbergs*, an early 1950s TV sitcom that came over from radio, found his name listed in *Red Channels*. Gertrude Berg, who owned and starred in the series, supported him. Nevertheless, boycott pressure on the program's sponsor, Sanka coffee, a General Foods brand, forced the company to abandon the program, which was dropped from CBS in 1951. After several months it resurfaced on NBC, but Loeb had been replaced. Four years later, depressed and unable to find work, he committed suicide. Although no evidence was ever introduced to show how entertainment programs circulated communist propaganda, by the early 1950s the TV networks were asking actors and other workers to sign loyalty oaths denouncing communism—a low point for the First Amendment.

The communist witch-hunts demonstrated key differences between print and broadcast protection under the First Amendment—differences that are perhaps best illustrated in legal history. On the one hand, licenses for printers and publishers have been outlawed since the eighteenth century. On the other hand, in the late 1920s commercial broadcasters themselves asked the federal government to step in and regulate the airwaves. At that time, they wanted the government to clear up technical problems, channel noise, noncommercial competition, and amateur interference. Ever since, most broadcasters have been trying to free themselves from the government intrusion they once demanded.

FCC Rules, Broadcasting, and Indecency

Drawing on the scarcity argument (that limited broadcast signals constitute a scarce national resource), the Communications Act of 1934 mandated in Section 309 that broadcasters operate in "the public interest, convenience, and necessity." Since the 1980s, however, with cable and later DBS increasing channel capacity, station managers have lobbied for "ownership" of their airwave assignments. Although the 1996 Telecommunications Act did not grant such ownership, stations continue to challenge the "public interest" statute. They argue that because the government is not allowed to dictate content in newspapers, it should not be allowed to control licenses or mandate any broadcast programming.

● In 1950, the 215-page *Red Channels*, published by American Business Consultants (a group of former FBI agents), placed 151 prominent writers, directors, and performers from radio, movies, and television on a blacklist, many of them simply for sympathizing with left-wing democratic causes. Although no one on the list was ever charged with a crime, many of the talented individuals targeted by *Red Channels* did not work in their professions for years.

> **"** It is the right of the viewers and listeners, not the right of the broadcasters, which is paramount. **"**
>
> —Supreme Court decision in *Red Lion Broadcasting Co. v. FCC*, 395 U.S. 367
> June 9, 1969
>
> **"** A responsible press is an undoubtedly desirable goal, but press responsibility is not mandated by the Constitution and like many other virtues it cannot be legislated. **"**
>
> —Supreme Court decision in *Miami Herald Publishing Co. v. Tornillo*, 418 U.S. 241
> June 25, 1974

Print vs. Broadcast Rules

Two cases—*Red Lion Broadcasting Co. v. FCC* (1969) and the *Miami Herald Publishing Co. v. Tornillo* (1974)—demonstrate the historic legal differences between broadcast and print. In the *Red Lion* decision, the operators of the small-town station in Red Lion, Pennsylvania, refused to give airtime to Fred Cook, author of a book that criticized Barry Goldwater, the Republican Party's presidential candidate in 1964. Cook then was verbally attacked by a conservative radio preacher and Goldwater fan, the Reverend Billy James Hargis, and asked for response time from the two hundred stations that carried the Hargis attack. Most stations complied, granting Cook free reply time. But WGCB, the Red Lion station, offered only to sell Cook time. He appealed to the FCC, which ordered the station to give Cook free time. The station refused, claiming that its First Amendment rights granted it control over its program content. On appeal, the Supreme Court sided with the FCC, deciding that whenever a broadcaster's rights conflict with the public interest, it is the public interest that is paramount. In 1969, interpreting broadcasting as different from print, the Supreme Court upheld the constitutionality of the 1934 Communications Act by reaffirming that broadcasters' responsibilities to program in the public interest may outweigh their rights to program whatever they want.

In contrast, five years later, in *Miami Herald Publishing Co. v. Tornillo*, the Supreme Court sided with the newspaper in a case in which a political candidate, Pat Tornillo Jr., requested space to reply to an editorial opposing his candidacy. Previously, Florida had enacted a right-to-reply law, which permitted a candidate to respond, in print, to editorial criticisms from newspapers. Counter to the *Red Lion* decision, the Court in this case struck down the Florida state law as unconstitutional. The Court argued that mandating that a newspaper give a candidate space to reply violated the paper's First Amendment rights to control what it chose to publish. The two decisions demonstrate that for most of the twentieth century the unlicensed print media received protections under the First Amendment that have not always been available to licensed broadcast media.

Dirty Words, Indecent Speech, and Hefty Fines

Although considered tame in a culture that now includes shock jock Howard Stern's lurid sexual programming, *topless radio* in the 1960s featured deejays and callers discussing intimate sexual subjects in the middle of the afternoon. The government curbed the practice in 1973, when the chairman of the FCC denounced topless radio as "a new breed of air pollution . . . with the suggestive, coaxing, pear-shaped tones of the smut-hustling host."[18] After an FCC investigation, a couple of stations lost their licenses, some were fined, and topless radio was checked temporarily. It reemerged in the 1980s, only with modern doctors and therapists—instead of deejays—offering intimate counsel over the airwaves.

In theory, communication law prevents the government from censoring broadcast content. Accordingly, the government may not interfere with programs or engage in prior restraint, although it may punish broadcasters for **indecency** or profanity after the fact. Over the years, a handful of radio stations have had their licenses suspended or denied after an unfavorable FCC review of past programming records. Concerns over indecent broadcast programming probably date from 1937. That year, NBC was scolded by the FCC after running a sketch featuring comedian-actress Mae West on ventriloquist Edgar Bergen's network program. West had the following conversation with Bergen's famous wooden dummy, Charlie McCarthy:

WEST: That's all right. I like a man that takes his time. Why don't you come home with me? I'll let you play in my woodpile . . . you're all wood and a yard long. . . .

CHARLIE: Oh, Mae, don't, don't . . . don't be so rough. To me love is peace and quiet.

WEST: That ain't love—that's sleep.[19]

After the sketch, West did not appear on radio for years. Ever since, the FCC has periodically fined or reprimanded stations for indecent programming, especially during times when children might be listening.

The current precedent for regulating broadcast indecency stems from one complaint to the FCC in 1973. In the middle of the afternoon, Pacifica's WBAI in New York aired George Carlin's famous comedy album about the seven dirty words that could not be uttered by broadcasters. A father, riding in a car with his fifteen-year-old son, heard the program and complained to the FCC, which sent WBAI a simple letter of reprimand. Although no fine was involved, the station appealed on principle and won its case in court. The FCC persisted, however, appealing all the way to the Supreme Court. Although no court has legally defined indecency, the Supreme Court's unexpected ruling in 1978 sided with the FCC and upheld the agency's authority to require broadcasters to air adult programming at later times. The Court ruled that so-called indecent programming, though not in violation of federal obscenity laws, was a nuisance (like a pig in a parlor, the Court said) and could be restricted to late-evening hours to protect children. The commission banned indecent programs from most stations between 6:00 A.M. and 10:00 P.M. In 1990, the FCC tried to ban such programs entirely. Although a federal court ruled this move unconstitutional, it still upheld the time restrictions intended to protect children. This ruling lies at the heart of the indecency fines that the FCC has leveled over the past several years against programs and stations that carried indecent or profane programming during daytime and evening hours.

● Howard Stern's broadcast radio show holds the record for FCC indecency fines, a fact that he and his cohost Robin Quivers used for material on the show. When Quivers commented, "I hear that the new [Harry Potter] movie is very scary," Stern replied, "You think that's scary? My kids' father is Howard Stern."

While Howard Stern and his various bosses own the record for racking up FCC indecency fines in the years before he moved to unregulated satellite radio, a $3.6 million fine was leveled in 2006 against 111 TV stations that broadcast a 2004 episode of the popular CBS program *Without a Trace* that depicted teenage characters taking part in a sexual orgy. (The fine was later reduced to $3.35 million when eight stations in Indiana and Tennessee noted their broadcasts came after 10 P.M.) After the FCC also leveled indecency fines against the *Billboard Music Awards* shows broadcast on Fox and an *NYPD Blue* episode on ABC, the four major networks sued the FCC on grounds that their First Amendment rights had been violated. (A federal appeals court planned to hear the case in 2007.) In their fining flurry, a conservative FCC was partly responding to the organized campaigns aimed at Howard Stern's popularity and vulgarity and the Janet Jackson exposed-breast incident during the 2005 Superbowl half-time show. In June 2006, President Bush signed a law that substantially increased the FCC's maximum allowable fine to $325,000 per indecent incident.

Political Broadcasts and Equal Opportunity

In addition to indecency rules, another law that the print media do not encounter is **Section 315** of the 1934 Communications Act, which mandates that during elections broadcast stations must provide equal opportunities and response time for qualified political candidates. In other words, if broadcasters give or sell time to one candidate, they must give or sell the same opportunity to others. Local broadcasters and networks have fought this law for years, complaining that it has required them to include poorly funded third-party candidates in political discussions. Broadcasters claim that because no Section 315–type rule applies to newspapers or magazines, the law violates their First Amendment right to control content. In fact, because of this rule, many stations have avoided all political programming. Ironically in these cases, a rule meant to serve the public interest by increasing communication backfired as stations decided to skirt the law.

The TV networks managed to get the law amended in 1959 to exempt newscasts, press conferences, and other events—such as political debates—that qualify as news. For instance, if a senator running for office appears in a news story, candidates running against him or her cannot invoke Section 315 and demand free time. Because of this provision, many stations from the late 1960s through the 1980s pulled TV movies starring Ronald Reagan. Because his film appearances did not count as bona fide news stories, politicians opposing Reagan as a presidential candidate could demand free time in markets that ran old Reagan movies. For the same reason, in 2003 TV stations in California banned the broadcast of Arnold Schwarzenegger movies when he became a candidate for governor, and dozens of stations nationwide preempted an episode of *Saturday Night Live* that was hosted by Al Sharpton, a Democratic presidential candidate.

Supporters of the equal opportunity law argue that it has provided forums for lesser-known candidates representing views counter to those of the Democratic and Republican parties. They further note that one of the few ways for alternative candidates to circulate their messages widely is to buy political ads, thus limiting serious outside contenders to wealthy candidates, such as Ross Perot, Steve Forbes, or members of the Bush or Kennedy families.

> ❝ There is no doubt about the unique impact of radio and television. But this fact alone does not justify government regulation. In fact, quite the contrary. We should recall that the printed press was the only medium of mass communication in the early days of the republic—and yet this did not deter our predecessors from passing the First Amendment to prohibit abridgement of its freedoms. ❞
>
> –Chief Judge David Bazelon,
> U.S. Court of Appeals, 1972

The Demise of the Fairness Doctrine

Considered an important corollary to Section 315, the **Fairness Doctrine** was to controversial issues what Section 315 is to political speech. Initiated in 1949, this FCC rule required stations (1) to air and engage in controversial-issue programs that affected their communities, and (2) when offering such programming, to provide competing points of view. Antismoking activist John Banzhaf ingeniously invoked the Fairness Doctrine to force cigarette advertising off television in 1971. When the FCC mandated antismoking public service announcements to counter "controversial" smoking commercials, tobacco companies decided not to challenge an outright ban rather than tolerate a flood of antismoking spots authorized by the Fairness Doctrine.

With little public debate, the Fairness Doctrine ended in 1987 after a federal court ruled that it was merely a regulation rather than an extension of Section 315 law. Over the years, broadcasters had argued that the doctrine forced many of them to play down controversial issues; they claimed that mandating opposing views every time a program covered a controversial issue was a burden not required of the print media. Since 1987, periodic support for reviving the Fairness Doctrine surfaces.

Its supporters argue that broadcasting is fundamentally different from—and more pervasive than—the print media, requiring greater accountability to the public. Although many broadcasters disagree, supporters of fairness rules insist that as long as broadcasters are licensed as public trustees of the airwaves—unlike newspaper or magazine publishers—legal precedent permits the courts and the FCC to demand responsible content and behavior from radio and TV stations.

By the mid-1990s, broadcast and cable operators were increasingly demanding the same First Amendment rights as the print media. This pressure, combined with a suspect belief (until the stock market collapse in 2001–02) that a free market can solve most economic problems, allowed a relaxation of the rules governing broadcasting and cable. Still, public concerns about visual violence, children's programming, and indecency kept regulatory issues prominent during recent presidential campaigns. But questions about the negative impact of concentrated media ownership rarely surfaced. In fact, when they did surface, they were raised most frequently by third-party presidential candidates such as Pat Buchanan and Ralph Nader. However, citizen action groups, such as MoveOn.org and FreePress.net, have worked to bring media ownership issues into the political mainstream.

Should deregulation accelerate, however, the remaining public and noncommercial broadcast outlets are at risk. For example, Jesse Ventura, the former Reform Party governor of Minnesota, made eliminating government funding of public radio and television a priority for his state in 1999. Public broadcasting already faced severe revenue cutbacks in the mid-1990s, so more deregulation of the communications industry might cause a recurrence of the problems of the late 1920s and early 1930s. As we noted in Chapter 4, the Great Depression crippled noncommercial broadcasters because many of them were forced to sell or transfer their licenses to commercial interests. Although Congress in 1996 mandated that the broadcast networks carry three hours of educational programs a week, public radio and television still offer the bulk of programming that is not commercially viable. Yet even public radio is doing less for free speech. A 1996 law required National Public Radio (NPR) affiliate stations to provide free airtime to political candidates. In 2000, after some candidates took notice of the law and asked for airtime in the election, NPR effectively lobbied Congress to be released from the requirement, before future candidates could make demands on public radio time. In addition, NPR, with the help of commercial radio's National Association of Broadcasters, successfully lobbied to have the FCC's plan for a new class of nonprofit, low-power FM stations curtailed before the first licenses were issued in 2001.[20]

The Internet, Expression, and Democracy

Since the beginnings of the United States more than two hundred years ago, there have been periods of war and heightened national security in which some in the government and some who consider themselves patriots attempt to suppress dissenting views. The time following the September 11, 2001, terrorist attacks and the 2003 invasion of Iraq mark two of those periods. Yet another concern for advocates of democratic expression has been the barriers to communicating in a commercialized mass media system that has generally favored corporate interests and media industries. For example, it is far easier for large corporations and advertisers such as Disney or General Motors to buy commercial speech than it is for small grassroots organizations that have important messages but limited finances. As a result, messages that counter mainstream culture might appear only in alternative magazines or on cable-access channels, where entry is cheap but audience reach is limited.

Communication Policy and the Internet

Another arena that increases the voices—and noise—circulating in culture is the Internet. Its current global expansion is comparable to the early days of broadcasting, when economic and technological growth outstripped law and regulation. At that time, noncommercial experiments by amateurs and engineering students provided a testing ground that commercial interests later exploited for profit. Indeed, before the Radio Act of 1927, many noncommercial groups experimented extensively with the possibilities of the new broadcast medium.

In much the same way, "amateurs," students, and various interest groups have explored and extended the communication possibilities of the Internet. They have experimented so successfully that commercial vendors raced to buy up pieces of the Internet. As in radio in the 1920s, the Internet's noncommercial developers in the 1990s and 2000s have been selling off services to commercial entrepreneurs. This is especially true of university consortiums, which had been running most of the regional Internet services. As in radio, experimenting and risk-taking took place at the noncommercial level before commercial adventurers stepped in to explore and exploit the profit possibilities.

The last serious widespread public debate on mass media ownership occurred in the early 1930s and ended with the passage of the 1934 Communications Act and the defeat of the Wagner-Hatfield Amendment (which would have reserved 25 percent of the broadcast spectrum for noncommercial radio). Public conversations about the Internet have not typically been about ownership questions. Instead, the debates—often triggered by the news media—have focused on First Amendment issues such as civility and pornography in cyberspace. Reporters, in fact, tend to view Internet issues as entrepreneurial business stories ("What company is marketing the next software breakthrough?") with free-speech implications ("Who is using the highway for pornographic purposes?"). Not unlike the public's concern over television's sexual and violent images, the scrutiny of the Internet is mainly about harmful images and information online, not about who controls it and for what purposes.

As we watch the rapid expansion of the Internet, an important question confronts us: Will the Internet continue to develop democratically rather than hierarchically, evading government or corporate plans to contain it, change it, and closely monitor who has access? In the early days of broadcasting, commercial interests became dominant partly because the companies running radio (such as the Hearst Corporation, which also owned chains of newspapers and magazines) did not report on ownership questions as serious news stories. It was not in their economic interest to do so. Today, once again, it has not been in the news media's economic interest to organize or lead the ownership debate; the major print and broadcast owners, after all, are heavily invested in the Internet.

Critics and observers hope that a vigorous debate will develop on new communication technologies—a debate that will go beyond First Amendment issues. The promise of the Internet as a democratic forum—adding millions of new users worldwide each month—encourages the formation of all sorts of regional, national, and global interest groups. Whether such virtual communities could eventually help to frame and solve society-level problems remains at issue.

> **66** One of the most striking paradoxes of Internet culture is that children are the most computer literate among us, but their vulnerability to online predators prevents their being able to enjoy or explore freely what is likely to be the defining medium of their lives. **99**
>
> –Denise Caruso,
> *New York Times*, 1998

● An anchorwoman for al-Jazeera, the Arab satellite news service originating in the small Persian Gulf nation of Qatar. Al-Jazeera was formed in 1996 to fill the gap after the British Broadcasting Corporation (BBC) closed its Arabic news service in Saudi Arabia. Although some have charged al-Jazeera with an anti-U.S. bias, it is actually the most independent news service in the Arab world and regularly covers controversial issues and dissenting political views in the region. In 2003, the news service launched its English-language Web site at http://english.al-jazeera.net, and in 2006 it announced its plans to start an English-language TV station.

● Filipino police officers crush approximately two million illegal video CDs, DVDs, and cassettes during a ceremony highlighting the Philippine government's fight against piracy. The pirated disks and tapes, including music and pornographic movies, were seized in three days of raids by police of sidewalk stalls and shops in Quezon City.

A positive sign is that global movements abound that use the Internet to fight political forms of censorship. The Digital Freedom Network, for example, has circulated material that has been banned or restricted in certain countries, including excerpts from dissident Chinese writer Wei Jingsheng and Indonesian novelist Pramoedya Ananta Toer, and it also conducts global online chats with people such as Myanmar's pro-democracy leader and Nobel Peace Prize–winner Aung San Suu Kyi. The organization also sends e-mail notices to members and helps them easily send letters of protest to international officials. In this example, the digital highway works as a global freeway—a democratic communication "weapon," bypassing both government bans and political restrictions. Just as fax machines, satellites, and home videos helped to document and expedite the fall of totalitarian regimes in Eastern Europe in the late 1980s, Internet services help to spread the word and activate social change today.

Watchdog Citizens

For most of our nation's history, citizens have counted on journalism to monitor abuses in government and business. During the muckraking period in the early part of the twentieth century, writers like Ida Tarbell, Upton Sinclair, and Sinclair Lewis made strong contributions in reporting corporate expansion and social change. Unfortunately, however, stories on business issues today are usually reduced to consumer affairs reporting. In other words, when a labor strike or a factory recall is covered, the reporter mainly tries to answer the question "How do these events affect consumers?" Although this is an important news angle, other questions remain: "How does the strike affect the families and future of workers and managers?" and

"What is the role of unions and manufacturing industries as we begin the twenty-first century?" At this point, citizen discussions about media ownership or labor-management ethics are not part of the news frame that journalists typically use. When companies announce mergers, reporters do not routinely question the economic wisdom or social impact of such changes. Instead, they tend to write stories about how individual consumers will be affected.

At one level, journalists have been compromised by the ongoing frenzy of media mergers involving newspapers, TV stations, radio stations, and Internet corporations. As Bill Kovach, former curator of Harvard's Nieman Foundation for Journalism, pointed out, "This rush to merge mainly entertainment organizations that have news operations with companies deeply involved in doing business with the government raises ominous questions about the future of watchdog journalism."[21] In other words, how can journalists adequately cover and lead discussions on issues of media ownership when the very companies they work for are the prime buyers and sellers of major news-media outlets?

With the news media increasingly compromised by their complex relations to their corporations, it is becoming increasingly important that the civic role of watchdog be shared by citizens as well as journalists. After all, the First Amendment protects not only the news media's free-speech rights but also the rights of all of us to speak out. Mounting concerns over who can afford access to the media go to the heart of free expression.

As we struggle to determine the future of converging print, electronic, and digital media and to broaden the democratic spirit underlying media technology, we need to stay engaged in spirited public debates about media ownership and control, about the differences between commercial speech and free expression. As citizens, we need to pay attention to who is included and excluded from the opportunities not only to buy products but also to speak out and shape the cultural landscape. To accomplish this, we need to challenge our journalists and our leaders. More important, we need to challenge ourselves to become watchdogs—critical consumers and engaged citizens—who learn from the past, care about the present, and map mass media's future.

> **❝ One thing is clear: media reform will not be realized until politicians add it to their list of issues like the environment, education, the economy, and health care. ❞**
>
> —Robert McChesney, freepress.net, 2004

www.

For review questions and activities for Chapter 16, go to the interactive *Media and Culture* Online Study Guide at *bedfordstmartins.com/ mediaculture*

REVIEW QUESTIONS

The Origins of Free Expression and a Free Press

1. What is the basic philosophical concept that underlies America's notion of free expression?

2. Explain the various models of the news media that exist under different political systems.

3. How has censorship been defined historically?

4. What is the significance of the Pentagon Papers and the *Progressive* magazine cases?

5. Why is the case of *New York Times v. Sullivan* so significant in First Amendment history?

6. What does a public figure have to do to win a libel case? What are the main defenses that a newspaper can use to thwart a charge of libel?

7. What is the legal significance of the *Falwell v. Flynt* case?

8. What issues are at stake when First Amendment and Sixth Amendment concerns clash?

Film and the First Amendment

9. Why were films not constitutionally protected as a form of speech until 1952?

10. Why did film review boards develop, and why did they eventually disband?

11. How did both the Motion Picture Production Code and the current movie rating system come into being?

Expression over the Airwaves

12. The government and the courts view print and broadcasting as different forms of expression. What are the major differences?

13. What is the significance of Section 315 of the Communications Act of 1934?

14. Why didn't broadcasters like the Fairness Doctrine?

The Internet, Expression, and Democracy

15. What are the similarities and differences between the debates over broadcast ownership in the 1920s and Internet ownership today?

16. Why is the Internet a potentially more democratic form than broadcasting?

QUESTIONING THE MEDIA

1. Have you ever had an experience in which you thought personal or public expression went too far and should be curbed? Explain. How might you remedy this situation?

2. If you owned a community newspaper and had to formulate a policy for your editors about which letters from readers appear in a limited space on your editorial page, what kinds of letters would you eliminate and why? Would you be acting as a censor in this situation? Why or why not?

3. The writer A. J. Liebling once said that freedom of the press belonged only to those who owned one. Explain why you agree or disagree.

4. Who is Judith Miller? Should the United States have a federal shield law to protect reporters?

5. What do you think of the current movie rating system? Should it be changed? Why or why not?

6. Should the Fairness Doctrine be revived? Why or why not?

SEARCHING THE INTERNET

http://www.freedomforum.org

The Freedom Forum deals with all First Amendment issues, including religion, free press, free speech, assembly, and technology. It also includes original articles as well as stories from the Associated Press.

http://www.freeexpression.org

The Free Expression Network is a national coalition of organizations and individuals united in the belief that free expression is the indispensable precondition of liberty.

http://www.rcfp.org

The Reporters Committee for Freedom of the Press, started in 1970, serves as a clearinghouse for press freedom and freedom of speech issues, including up-to-date reports on libel, freedom of information, and shield law cases.

http://ericnuzum.com/banned

Eric Nuzum maintains this site, which documents banned and censored (or otherwise altered) music, beginning in the 1950s, and keeps track of current music censorship issues.

http://www.fcc.gov/eb/oip

This site posts the Federal Communications Commission's enforcement policies on obscenity, indecency, and profanity, and lists recent violations of the regulations.

http://www.cpj.org

The nonprofit Committee to Protect Journalists works to defend press freedom around the world.

In Brief

If you were the owner of a community newspaper, what would be your policy on accepting advertising for pornographic movie theaters and movies rated NC–17? Justify whatever policy you develop.

In Depth

In small groups, investigate the age restriction policies of local retail outlets that carry media content for mature audiences.

Description. First, call or visit local movie theaters, video/DVD stores, music retailers, magazine shops, and outlets that carry video games. What are their respective policies for (1) selling tickets or selling/renting videos to the proper age groups for rated movies, especially those rated R and NC–17; (2) selling recordings with parental advisory labels; (3) displaying and selling adult magazines; and (4) selling video games rated "mature" or "adults only"? (You can review video game ratings from the Entertainment Software Rating Board at http://www.esrb.org/.) Second, you can also interview customers of these media outlets. Have their buying/renting experiences been restricted according to age, or do retailers ignore age guidelines?

Analysis. Look for patterns. Are there consistent policies across media outlets; for example, do all movie theaters have the same admissions policies? Are age policies consistent across all four types of outlets; for example, are magazine shops more or less strict on enforcement than music stores or video game retailers?

Interpretation. What are the meanings of the patterns? You might wish to consider the main clientele of each media outlet. For example, are movie theaters highly dependent on young audiences, even for R-rated films?

Evaluation. Are age restrictions for media content a good idea? Should enforcement be left up to retailers, or should some other entity become involved? Is censorship a concern? What responsibilities do marketers of media content have on this issue? What responsibilities do parents have? What responsibilities do underage customers have?

Engagement. With the aid of your course instructor, develop your findings into a more comprehensive audit on media retailers in your area and then release your report to the local press. Before you take the information public, make sure each small investigative group has clear documentation of its activities and that findings are fully disclosed. Give retailers the opportunity to respond to your findings and include those in the report as well. Also, consider the political implications of your public report. For example, does it suggest stronger self-enforcement of age restrictions by media retailers? Does it suggest government action? Or, perhaps, does it suggest a problem with retailers who use media-labeling systems as the default censorship system (i.e., they don't sell or rent any content with adult ratings or parental advisory labels)?

KEY TERMS

authoritarian model, 551
communist or state model, 551
libertarian model, 551
social responsibility model, 552
Fourth Estate, 552
prior restraint, 552

copyright, 556
slander, 556
libel, 556
actual malice, 558
qualified privilege, 559
invasion of privacy, 561

obscenity, 563
gag orders, 563
shield laws, 564
indecency, 573
Section 315, 574
Fairness Doctrine, 575

media and
culture

an extended case study

THE NEWS MEDIA AND WAR

Step 1: Description

Step 2: Analysis

Step 3: Interpretation

Step 4: Evaluation

Step 5: Engagement

Among the most difficult work news media do is war reporting. Of the 580 journalists who died "in the line of duty worldwide" between 1992 and mid-2006, 31 percent of those deaths occurred covering wars.[1] Eighty of these war-related deaths—which included 59 Iraqis and 2 Americans—happened in Iraq between 2003 and mid-2006. After war, the next highest category of reporter-related fatalities involves covering politics (24 percent). What also makes this job difficult for U.S. journalists—in addition to the physical danger—is the question of *how* to tell the stories of war: stories about actual combat and stories about why wars start, how wars are waged, and what wars mean. Covering these issues—especially in the politically charged environment that exists during wartime—often leads to two contradictory criticisms of the news media. First, reporters may be called "unpatriotic" if their work questions administration policy and performance. Second, reporters face criticism if they are perceived to be "soft" on political leaders, operating as cheerleaders for war rather than as watchdogs over the government.

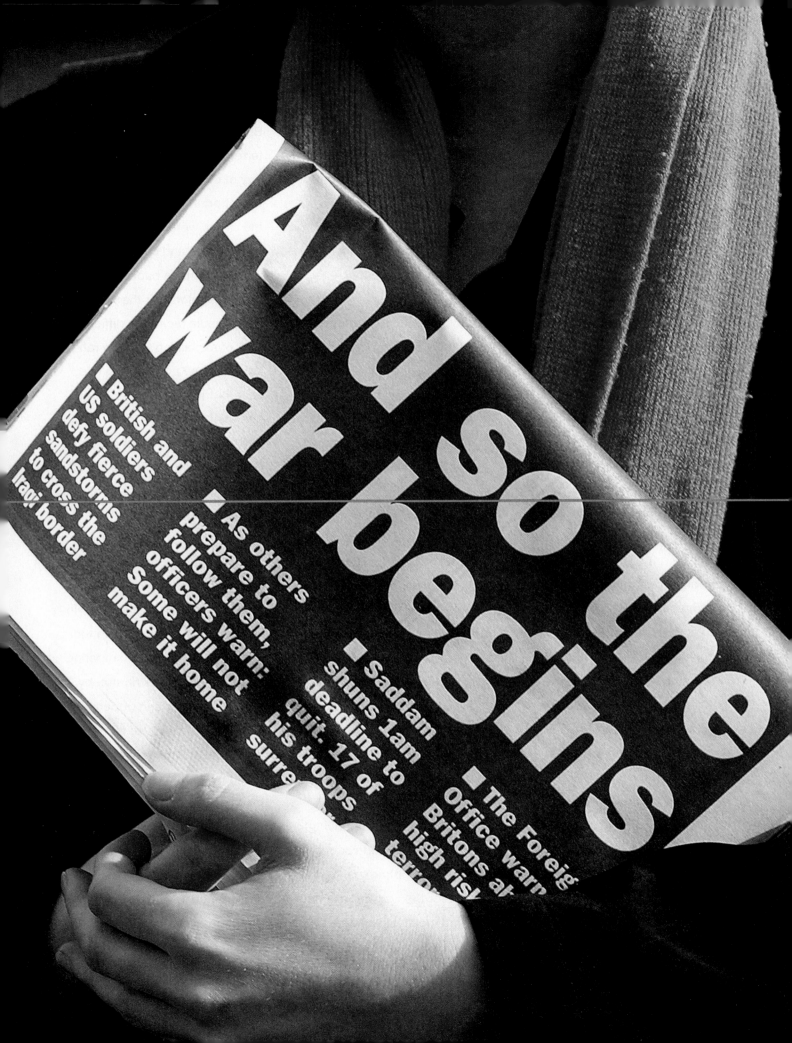

Additionally, there is intense pressure on journalists to report accurately on wars because politicians, activists, and citizens know the power the news media have to shape opinion and policy.

The war in Iraq, which started in 2003, provides an excellent example of the pressures placed on journalists when trying to cover major events that stretch over several years. At the outset, the Bush administration made a convincing case for war, providing apparent evidence that the Iraqi leader Saddam Hussein was building nuclear weapons and represented a threat to U.S. national security. The administration also argued that there was a connection between the Iraqi leadership and Al-Qaeda, the terrorist organization responsible for the attacks of 9/11. The case was so convincing at the time that surveys suggested a majority of Americans believed that most of the nineteen terrorists who died in the 9/11 plot were Iraqis, although none of them were.

Reporters often received praise for telling the stories of war during this early stage. But they also were faulted for appearing biased, as some TV anchors were criticized for wearing USA lapel pins on the air, and for not covering the conflict in a more straightforward and probing manner. Writing about this period, Craig Crawford, a *Congressional Quarterly* columnist, said that "the news media waited at least a year to ask critical questions about the war. They waited until public opinion polls showed declining support for the war, when the daily toll of American deaths was at an all-time high."[2]

Then, when both of the early justifications for war turned out not to be true, the White House offered a new set of arguments: Hussein was an evil dictator who needed to be taken down, and Iraq could then become an incubator for democracy and help stabilize the Middle East. As public support for the war declined and the news media began asking more questions, the administration offered a number of alternate stories for continuing the war and deployed various tactics in attempting to maintain support for the war. For example, in several political speeches leading up to the national 2006 midterm elections, President Bush and his supporters often referred to the "cut and run" strategy of those who opposed the war effort in Iraq, implying that the critics were "soft on terrorism" at best and cowardly at worst. Against a backdrop of shifting reasons for the war, the news media faced the difficult task of explaining the new rationales. At one point during this shift, both the *New York Times* and the *Washington Post* ran stories apologizing for not digging deeper into the evidence the administration used to justify going to war in the first place.

Shifting rhetoric offered by an administration is just one of the difficulties journalists face in covering a war. Not only do the news media confront competing stories and spin distributed by both supporters and opponents of a war, but they also face the challenge of what stories to tell and how best to tell them. The task for engaged citizens and critical consumers of the news media then is to sort through the news stories, the political rhetoric, and public opinion, and offer an informed critique of the job that news media actually do for us.

the case before us, then, is a limited critical investigation of mainstream U.S. news media's coverage of the Iraq war, as a way to explore how news media shape (and are shaped by) national conversations and stories about war. As a way of exploring this relationship between news media and contemporary culture, let's examine war coverage through the lens of the critical process by looking at professional studies of news content and then compare newspaper reports from 2003, when the war first started, and from late 2006. This case study will walk through some examples of the coverage and help you think through the critical process. To go deeper into this material on your own, look at two different weeks of war coverage, one from each of these time periods. For your stories, choose two newspapers from among the *New York Times*, the *Wall Street Journal*, *USA Today*, the *Los Angeles Times*, the *Washington Post*, or the *Chicago Tribune* (all of the stories from these papers are available in the LexisNexis database, or check your library). Also use one metro or regional daily paper from your area in order to compare how much information is available about the Iraq war at the local level.

As developed in Chapter 1, a media literate perspective involves mastering five overlapping critical stages that build on each other: (1) *description*: paying close attention, taking notes, and researching the subject under study; (2) *analysis*: discovering and focusing on significant patterns that emerge from the description stage; (3) *interpretation*: asking and answering the "What does that mean?" and "So what?" questions about one's findings; (4) *evaluation*: arriving at a judgment about whether something is good, bad, or mediocre, which involves subordinating one's personal taste to the critical assessment resulting from the first three stages; and (5) *engagement*: taking some action that connects critical interpretations and evaluations with responsibility as citizens to question our media institutions, adding our own voice to the process of shaping the cultural environment.

Step 1: Description

For the **description** phase, it is crucial first to look at models for organizing a case study and critically assessing a complex topic. So let's first look at the ongoing content studies at the Project in Excellence for Journalism (PEJ) Web site, www.journalism .org, particularly the State of the News Media studies from 2004, 2005, and 2006. In these studies, researchers break down news media coverage into a variety of story

● One crucial way we learn about a war is from the images that "embedded" photographers distribute in the media — allowing the public to come to know and understand war (*at left*, the Vietnam War; *at right*, the Iraq war).

Figure 1 Selected Story Topic Coverage in Print and Online Sources, 2006

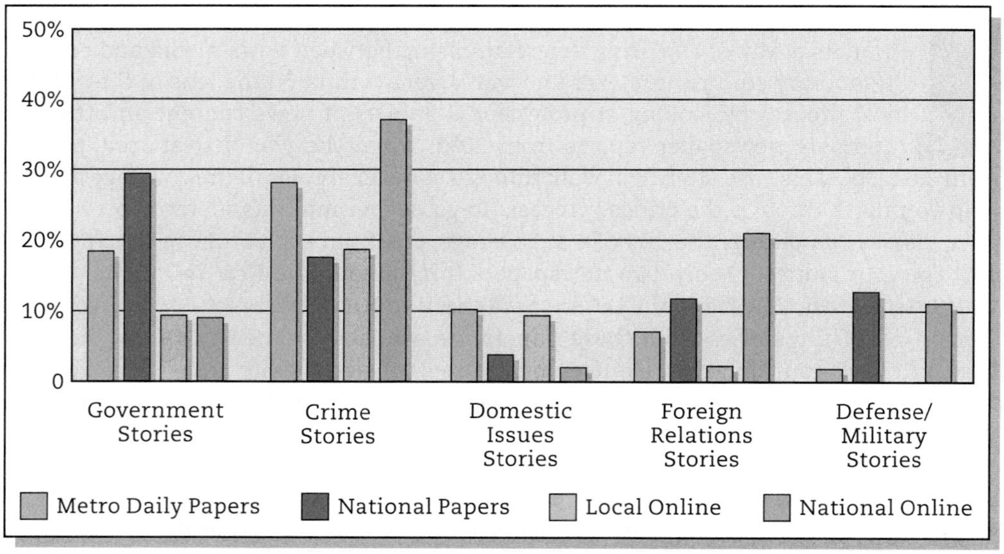

Source: www.stateofthemedia.com/2006/topline.pdf.

categories—elections, government, crime, business, domestic issues, science, accidents, and so forth—and then count what percentage of the news from particular days falls in these categories. For example, in the 2004 study, 29 percent of national newspaper stories were devoted to government stories, while metro or regional daily papers had 18 percent of their coverage in this category. Crime accounted for 17 percent of the news stories for the national papers, but 28 percent in the regional daily papers. (For a comparison to the 2006 study, see Figure 1.)

The State of the News Media studies also provide other statistics for newspapers on both national and local levels. For example, a 2004 count of the number of sources in a story found that metro papers presented 15 percent of their stories with no sources, 15 percent with one source, and 40 percent with four or more sources. The national papers included no stories with no sources, 2.9 percent with one source, but 78 percent with four or more sources. An alternate view on sources comes from a 2003 Pew study of war reporting that suggested 36 percent of respondents said "too much" commentary came from ex-generals and ex-military sources, while 48 percent thought that such commentary represented the "right amount" in the early news coverage of the war. This study also found that among 40 percent of respondents, antiwar sentiment appeared "too much," while 38 percent said antiwar sentiment appeared in the "right amount."[3] Although your own study is limited and therefore does not survey public opinion, you can document the number of ex-military personnel used as sources and contrast them with sources drawn from nonmilitary experts, from politicians, from frontline soldiers, and "ordinary" citizens in your story sample. What we want to assess here is *where* reporters are getting information so we can later see if multiple points of view are reported or if news reports are relying too heavily on too few sources or one particular kind of source and/or viewpoint.

With these various studies serving as background and as models, do a Lexis-Nexis search to identify the stories for your study, taking notes to compare a week's worth of coverage in 2003 and a week's worth of coverage in late 2006 or today. Drawing on the PEJ studies, create a classification system that separates war coverage from nonwar stories. Compare the percentage of the papers' overall news coverage

devoted to the Iraq war versus other news (for this task you can eliminate some sections of the paper such as local business news, sports, and entertainment sections). Next, come up with a classification system that distinguishes the different kinds of war stories—for example, battle reports, diplomacy stories, political reports, profile stories of individual soldiers or leaders, and so on. Count and classify the types of questions reporters ask as well as the photos used to accompany the stories. Take notes on the main "characters" and sources, on the conflicts and themes portrayed, and on settings and locales. Pay particular attention to military and political leaders and how much attention focuses on the daily experience of soldiers or the people in Iraq who are affected by the war. Are there stories here that you would call pro- or anti-American or pro- or anti-Iraqi? Note the language used to describe the United States and Iraq. Remember, the object of the description phase of the critical process is to collect as much information as possible from the stories you are investigating.

Step 2: Analysis

In the **analysis** phase, look for patterns and themes in sources, rhetoric, and images that emerged in 2003 and 2006 (or today) and that are used to construct the stories of war. Focus on the type of people that reporters talk to and quote, such as male and female sources, "experts" and "people on the street," or ex-military personnel. A number of studies on public perception of stories about the military and political leadership provide a complex and sometimes contradictory picture. In 2006, for example, the Pew Research Center for the People and the Press reported that "the percentage of people who believe that criticism of the military weakens American defenses has been rising . . . , and in 2005 reached its highest point (47%) since 1985."[4] On the other hand, although general public distrust of the mainstream news media persisted, the 2006 study also reported that "while there is doubt about the scrutiny of the military, there is enduring and even slightly growing support for the press as a watchdog over politicians. More Americans (60%) believe a critical press 'keeps leaders from doing things that shouldn't [be] done' than did in 2001 and 2003 (when the number was 54%)."[5]

For the analysis section, the patterns you discover should offer insights into how journalists frame the war—that is, how they "make sense" of war using language and images. What narrative strategies are employed in these news stories to help us understand something as complex and unwieldy as a protracted war? In studying the newspaper accounts, look for patterns in overall coverage and in specific word and photo choices. Note broad patterns in coverage, such as the number and style of pro- or anti-Iraqi stories and stories that seem pro-American or patriotic versus stories that seem to strive for a more neutral stance. Create categories to suggest how different kinds of stories are used to cover war: Do stories tend to frame the topic as "two-sided"

and construct print quotes that pit one set of characters against another, or do they give a view with more than two sides? How is antiwar sentiment portrayed? Do heroes and villains emerge from the stories?

For a contrasting point of view, also compare comic and satiric war coverage, drawing on *The Daily Show* or *The Colbert Report* on Comedy Central, NBC's *Saturday Night Live* sketches and its "Weekend Update" segment, or the print and online version of *The Onion*. For example, whereas cable's MSNBC has used the Pentagon slogan "Operation Iraqi Freedom" as its graphic label for its war coverage, *The Daily Show* uses the graphic "Mess O' Potamia." What do these differences in rhetoric and word choice suggest? How do these satiric or "fake" programs treat war and use sources? When they satirize the mainstream news media, what are they criticizing about war coverage?

Step 3: Interpretation

In the **interpretation** stage, try to determine the meanings of the patterns under analysis. The most difficult stage in criticism, interpretation demands an answer to "So what?" and "What does this all mean?" questions. Throughout the Iraq war, the news media and other survey firms also have been tracking public opinion on the war—and on journalistic coverage. For example, a CNN Poll conducted by Opinion Research Corporation revealed in early October 2006 that 32 percent of respondents approved of the Bush administration's handling of the war while 66 percent disapproved. And, as mentioned above, even though many of us may think that criticism of the military undermines the military and thus damages the war effort, we also seem to believe that the press should remain "neutral" and reject an obvious partisan or pro-American stance in reporting on war. If the military—or government—then makes mistakes, most of us think the press should report those errors. However, the media outlets themselves admitted that they didn't report them in the early stages of war. What does this mean and why wasn't mainstream media more critical at this time?

For the stories in your own sample, try to offer resolutions to issues such as what it means that particular kinds of sources are used and other kinds of sources are not. Are the stories mostly reflective of an administrative or "top down" viewpoint of war, or do they offer points of view from other perspectives, such as from frontline soldiers, military leaders critical of the war, or pro- and anti-administration citizens? If your study includes political stories about the war, how are various political officials and military leaders portrayed and used in these stories? How did your regional metro paper cover the war compared to the national papers? Depending on your findings, other approaches you might focus on include how casualties and victims are handled; are they shown in photos? How are pro- and antiwar attitudes handled in the stories? How are Iraqi people portrayed in these stories? Did the papers make clear distinctions among different sects of Iraqis, or among Iraqi civilians and Iraqi leaders?

Finally, a dominant value that often emerges in U.S. coverage of political stories and war news is rugged individualism—with leaders or soldiers portrayed as compe-

● Fake news, like the *Onion* and *The Daily Show* on cable, offer not only a critique of political leaders but a stinging satire of mainstream media.

tent individuals who can stand up against enemies and make a difference in our lives. If this value is portrayed in your stories, how does it play out? How do the voices of antiwar sources fit into this picture? Are these "characters" portrayed as rugged individuals or as some other character type? Of course, one of the limits of narrative, and this is true of news stories too, is that our lives don't usually play out like stories. In fact, most social progress—whether it's small cultural changes or big political decisions that affect war and our military system—is the result of group or collective action. (Think here of the dramatic shift in Congress as the result of voter decisions in the November 2006 elections.) Do the stories in your study pose questions that ask how the Iraq war might be solved as a shared national or international problem? Or do the stories suggest that the war is the responsibility of a few leaders who will act in the national or collective interest?

● Cindy Sheehan, whose son died in the Iraq war, became a symbol and a major leader for those who opposed the war. Since the Vietnam War, protestors have understood how to use mainstream media and visual images to champion their cause. How does the photo of Sheehan (*above*) demonstrate the famous slogan Vietnam War–era protestors used—"The whole world is watching"— to call attention to their antiwar position?

Step 4: Evaluation

Fourth, the **evaluation** stage of the critical process focuses on making informed judgments. Building on description, analysis, and interpretation, we are now better able to evaluate the fairness, accuracy, sense, and substance of mainstream news reports. Go back and look at the judgments made about the news media in some of the Pew studies reported here. For example, a study from June 2005 found that 80 percent of the respondents had a "favorable opinion" of daily or local newspapers, while only 61 percent had a favorable opinion of major national newspapers. (See Figure 2 on page 590.) After your study, do you now have a more or less favorable opinion of the national papers? Has your opinion of regional or local papers changed? If yes, in what ways?

In making other judgments about the papers in your study, do the stories seem complete? Are they fair? Can you think of things that are missing from the stories— or questions you might have asked had you been the reporter on these stories? Can you think of other ways to tell the story? Do these stories talk about the war in Iraq as part of the larger war on terrorism? Or do the stories treat these as separate wars or interrelated wars? Make a judgment about which papers did the best job covering the war over the period under study. Why are certain stories better than others? Did the stories' content change during the time frame studied? How?

Step 5: Engagement

Fifth, the **engagement** stage asks us to take some action that connects our critical interpretations and evaluations with our responsibility as citizens to question our news media, adding our own voice to the process. How would you go about producing an

Figure 2 Percent of Public with a Favorable Attitude toward Media Outlets 2001 vs. 2005

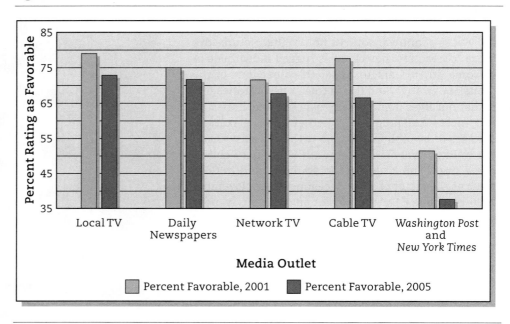

Source: www.stateofthemedia.com/2006/chartland.asp?id=494&ct=col&dir=&sort=&col1_box=1&col2_box=1.

alternative narrative strategy that would tell stories about war? Who would you talk to in your community about the war? What questions might you ask regular citizens? As an editor of a regional paper, how would you deal with the Iraq war and the war on terrorism? List some ideas you have that would tell these stories differently. Write a short letter or an e-mail to the editor and try to get it printed or read on the air. Your letter should either note a finding in your study or offer a suggestion on how to improve news coverage about war.

Then call, write, or e-mail the reporters and editors at the various news media in your study. Get comments from them. Let them know your key findings and ask them to respond. If they don't respond, note that too, but do what it takes to interview someone who is in charge of the news process at one of the papers in your sample. Throughout this process, recall that the point of media literacy and a critical approach is acknowledging that a healthy democracy requires the active participation of engaged citizens. In conclusion, discuss whether this study did anything to change your views of the mainstream news media and their coverage of war.

notes

CHAPTER 1

1. John Dunbar, Daniel Lathrop, and Robert Marlino, "Networks of Influence: The Political Power of the Communication Industry," October 28, 2004, www.publicintegrity.org/telecom/report.
2. Neil Postman, *Amusing Ourselves to Death: Public Discourse in the Age of Show Business* (New York: Penguin Books, 1985), 19.
3. James W. Carey, *Communication as Culture: Essays on Media and Society* (Boston: Unwin Hyman, 1989), 203.
4. Postman, *Amusing Ourselves to Death*, 65. See also Elizabeth Eisenstein, *The Printing Press as an Agent of Change*, 2 vols. (Cambridge: Cambridge University Press, 1979).
5. Roger Rosenblatt, "I Am Writing Blindly," *Time*, November 6, 2000, 142.
6. See Plato, *The Republic*, Book II, 377B.
7. For a historical discussion of culture, see Lawrence Levine, *Highbrow/Lowbrow: The Emergence of Cultural Hierarchy in America* (Cambridge, Mass.: Harvard University Press, 1988).
8. For an example of this critical position, see Allan Bloom, *The Closing of the American Mind: How Higher Education Has Failed Democracy and Impoverished the Souls of Today's Students* (New York: Simon & Schuster, 1987).
9. For overviews of this position, see Postman, *Amusing Ourselves to Death*; and Stuart Ewen, *Captains of Consciousness: Advertising and the Social Roots of the Consumer Culture* (New York: McGraw-Hill, 1976).
10. See Carey, *Communication as Culture*.
11. For more on this idea, see Cecelia Tichi, *Electronic Hearth: Creating an American Television Culture* (New York: Oxford University Press, 1991), 187–188.
12. See Jon Katz, "Rock, Rap and Movies Bring You the News," *Rolling Stone*, March 5, 1992, 33.

Case Study: The Sleeper Curve, p. 18

1. Steven Johnson, *Everything Bad Is Good for You: How Today's Popular Culture Is Actually Making Us Smarter* (New York: Riverhead Books, 2005). See book's subtitle.
2. Neil Postman, *Amusing Ourselves to Death: Public Discourse of Show Business* (New York: Penguin Books, 1985).
3. Ibid., 3–4.
4. Ibid., 129–131.
5. Steven Johnson, "Watching TV Makes You Smarter," *New York Times Magazine*, April 24, 2005, 55ff. Article adapted from Johnson's book *Everything Bad Is Good for You*. All subsequent quotations are from this article.

Examining Ethics: Covering the War, p. 24

1. Bill Carter, "Some Stations to Block 'Nightline' War Tribute," *New York Times*, April 30, 2004, p. A13.
2. For reference and guidance on media ethics, see Clifford Christians, Mark Fackler, and Kim Rotzoll, *Media Ethics: Cases and Moral Reasoning*, 4th ed. (White Plains, N.Y.: Longman, 1995); and Thomas H. Bivins, "A Worksheet for Ethics Instruction and Exercises in Reason," *Journalism Educator* (Summer 1993): 4–16.

The Global Village: Bedouins, Camels, Transistors, and Coke, p. 30

1. Václav Havel, "A Time for Transcendence," *Utne Reader*, January/February 1995, 53.
2. Dan Rather, "The Threat to Foreign News," *Newsweek*, July 17, 1989, 9.

An Extended Case Study: Video Games and Storytelling, p. 34

1. Stephen Poole, *Trigger Happy: Videogames and the Entertainment Revolution* (New York: Arcade Publishing, 2000), 208.
2. Ibid., 236.
3. See Sharon Waxman, "Study Finds Young Men Attending Fewer Films," *New York Times*, October 8, 2005, p. A17.
4. See John M. Broder, "Bill Is Signed to Restrict Video Games in California," *New York Times*, October 8, 2005, www.nytimes.com.
5. "Essential Facts about the Video and Computer Game Industry," Entertainment Software Association (ESA), www.theESA.com, 2005.

CHAPTER 2

1. Pat Kane, "Media: Saint of the Superhighway," *Independent* (London), April 28, 1997, p. 8.
2. Martin Walker, "Keyboard Whiz-Kid; William Gibson, the Novelist Who Created Cyberspace, Has Sony's Corporate Millions Riding on His Talent," *Guardian* (London), May 29, 1995, p. T8.
3. Bill Gates, "Shaping the Internet Age," speech to the Internet Policy Institute, December 2000, http://www.microsoft.com/billgates/shapingtheinternet.asp.
4. Philip P. Pan, "Reference Tool on Web Finds Fans, Censors," *Washington Post*, February 20, 2006, http://www.washingtonpost.com/wp-dyn/content/article/2006/02/19/AR2006021901335.html.
5. See the Open Net Initiative, http://www.opennetinitiative.net/. Also see Rebecca Mackinnon, RConversation, http://rconversation.blogs.com/rconversation/.

6. Daniel Burstein and David Kline, *Road Warriors: Dreams and Nightmares along the Information Highway* (New York: Dutton, 1995), 105.

7. U.S. data: "United States: Average Web Usage, Month of February 2006, Home Panel," Nielsen//NetRatings, http://www.nielsen-netratings.com/news.jsp?section=dat_to&country=us (accessed March 2006). Global data: Trends and Statistics. ClickZ Network, March 16, 2005, http://www.clickz.com/stats/web_worldwide/ (accessed March 2006).

8. Burstein and Kline, *Road Warriors*, 101–130.

9. Netcraft Internet Services, http://news.netcraft.com/archives/web_server_survey.html.

10. David Landis, "World Wide Web Helps Untangle Internet's Labyrinth," *USA Today*, August 3, 1994, p. 10D.

11. Robert Rossney, "Is It Worth Keeping All the Information on the Net?" *San Francisco Chronicle*, December 15, 1994, p. E4.

12. Pew Internet & American Life Project, "Reports: Online Activities and Pursuits," November 20, 2005, 207.21.232.103/PPF/r/167/report_display.asp.

13. Charles C. Mann, "The End of Moore's Law," *Technology Review*, May/June 2000, http://www.techreview.com/articles/may00/mann.htm.

14. Nicholas Negroponte, *Being Digital* (New York: Knopf, 1995), 23.

15. David Pogue, "Seeing Technology through Different Sets of Glasses," *New York Times* Circuits Newsletter, April 20, 2006, http://www.nytimes.com/packages/html/technology/circuits.html

16. Amy Harmon, "The Rebel Code," *New York Times Magazine*, February 21, 1999, 34–37.

17. Wikipedia contributors, "John Seigenthaler Sr. Wikipedia Biography Controversy," *Wikipedia, The Free Encyclopedia*, http://en.wikipedia.org/w/index.php?title=John_Seigenthaler_Sr._Wikipedia_biography_controversy&oldid=45268872 (accessed March 24, 2006).

18. Jim Giles, "Internet Encyclopaedias Go Head to Head," *Nature.com*, December 14, 2005, http://www.nature.com/news/2005/051212/full/438900a.html (accessed March 24, 2006).

19. Pew Internet & American Life Project, "The State of Blogging," January 2005, http://www.pewinternet.org/PPF/r/144/report_display.asp.

20. Janet Kornblum and Mary Beth Marklein, "What You Say Online Could Haunt You," *USA Today*, March 10, 2006, pp. 1A, 4A.

21. American Library Association, "Questions and Answers on Children's Internet Protection Legislation," http://www.ala.org/Content/NavigationMenu/Our_Association/Offices/ALA_Washington/Issues2/Civil_Liberties,_Intellectual_Freedom,_Privacy/CIPA1/Q_and_A/Q_and_A.htm#without%20also%20restricting%20access (accessed July 13, 2003).

22. Postini, "Postini Reports Increase in Spam, Decrease in IM Attacks during the Month of February," March 6, 2006, http://www.postini.com/news_events/pr/pr030606.php.

23. See Federal Trade Commission, *Privacy Online: Fair Information Practices in the Electronic Marketplace*, May 2000, http://www.ftc.gov/reports/privacy2000.pdf.

24. Also see Robert Scheer, "Nowhere to Hide," *Yahoo! Internet Life*, October 2000, 100–102.

25. Susannah Fox, Pew Internet & American Life Project, "Digital Divisions," October 5, 2005, http://www.pewinternet.org/PPF/r/165/report_display.asp. Also see Nielsen/Netratings, "Two-thirds of Active U.S. Web Populations Using Broadband," March 14, 2006, http://www.nielsen-netratings.com/pr/pr_060314.pdf.

26. Bill and Melinda Gates Foundation, "Toward Equality of Access: The Role of Public Libraries in Addressing the Digital Divide," February 25, 2004, http://www.gatesfoundation.org/Libraries/Announcements?Announce-040225.htm (accessed April 19, 2004).

27. See "Population Explosion!" ClickZ Stats, November 3, 2005, http://www.clickz.com/stats/sectors/geographics/article.php/5911_151151.

28. Douglas Gomery, "In Search of the Cybermarket," *Wilson Quarterly* (Summer 1994): 10.

Case Study: A Blog's Life, p. 67

1. David McClintick, "Towncrier for the New Age." *Brill's Content*, November 1998, 113–127.

2. Michael Barbaro, "Wal-Mart Enlists Bloggers in P.R. Campaign," *New York Times*, March 7, 2006, http://www.nytimes.com/2006/03/07/technology/07blog.html.

CHAPTER 3

1. Thomas Edison, quoted in Marshall McLuhan, *Understanding Media* (New York: McGraw-Hill, 1964), 276.

2. See Bruce Tucker, "'Tell Tchaikovsky the News': Postmodernism, Popular Culture and the Emergence of Rock 'n' Roll," *Black Music Research Journal* 9, no. 2 (Fall 1989): 280.

3. LeRoi Jones, *Blues People* (New York: Morrow Quill, 1963), 168.

4. Mick Jagger, quoted in Jann S. Wenner, "Jagger Remembers," *Rolling Stone*, December 14, 1995, 66.

5. See Mac Rebennack (Dr. John) with Jack Rummel, *Under a Hoodoo Moon* (New York: St. Martin's Press, 1994), 58.

6. Little Richard, quoted in Charles White, *The Life and Times of Little Richard: The Quasar of Rock* (New York: Harmony Books, 1984), 65–66.

7. Quoted in Dave Marsh and James Bernard, *The New Book of Rock Lists* (New York: Fireside, 1994), 15.

8. Tucker, "'Tell Tchaikovsky the News,'" 287.

9. Ed Ward, quoted in Ward, Geoffrey Stokes, and Ken Tucker, *Rock of Ages: The Rolling Stone History of Rock & Roll* (New York: Rolling Stone Press, 1986), 89.

10. Stuart Goldman, "That Old Devil Music," *National Review*, February 24, 1989, 29.

11. See Gerri Hershey, *Nowhere to Run: The Story of Soul Music* (New York: Penguin Books, 1984).

12. See Karen Schoemer, "Rockers, Models and the New Allure of Heroin," *Newsweek*, August 26, 1996, 50–54.

13. K. Tucker, in Ward, Stokes, and Tucker, *Rock of Ages*, 521.

14. Ibid., 560.

15. Stephen Thomas Erlewine, "Nirvana," in Michael Erlewine, ed., *All Music Guide: The Best CDs, Albums, & Tapes*, 2nd ed. (San Francisco: Miller Freeman Books, 1994), 233.

16. Bram Teitelman, quoted in Ricardo Baca, "Can Modern Rock Radio Be Saved?" *Denver Post*, May 29, 2005, p. F-1.

17. Ibid.

18. See Mikal Gilmore, "Puff Daddy," *Rolling Stone*, August 7, 1997, 50–56, 70–72.

19. *Billboard.com*, March 18, 2006.

20. Brian Garrity, "New Options Emerge for Music Vid Play," *Billboard.com*, November 20, 2004.

21. Steve McClure, "Utada, MTV Pin Hopes on Mobile Content Service Flux," *The Daily Yomiuri* (Tokyo), June 30, 2005, p. 14.
22. Emmanual Legrand and Michael Paoletta, "Music Makes the World Go 'Round," *Billboard.com,* April 30, 2005.
23. Saul Hansell, "Putting the Napster Genie Back in the Bottle," *New York Times,* November 20, 2005, sec. 3, p. 1.
24. IFPI, "Commercial Piracy Report 2003," http://www.ifpi.org/site-content/antipiracy/piracy2003.html (accessed May 13, 2004).
25. Oberst is quoted in Christian Bordal, "Independent Music Labels Showing Sales Gains While the Major Labels Continue to See Declines," *Day to Day* (National Public Radio), December 2, 2003 (4:00 PM ET).
26. Jeff Leeds, "The Net Is a Boon for Indie Labels," *New York Times,* December 27, 2005, p. E1.
27. Ibid.
28. Josh Belzman, "Bands and Fans Singing a New Tune on MySpace," *MSNBC.com,* February 13, 2006.
29. Ibid.
30. Tom Anderson, quoted in Belzman, "Bands and Fans."
31. Nat Hentoff, "Many Dreams Fueled Long Development of U.S. Music," *Milwaukee Journal*/United Press International, February 26, 1978, p. 2.

Tracking Technology: The Rise of MP3s and Digital Downloading, p. 81

1. "Instant Gratification," David Hajdu, *The New Republic,* March 6, 2006; "Tila Tequila for President," Jonah Weiner, *Salon,* April 11, 2006.

CHAPTER 4

1. Senator Byron Douglas, interview, "No Taste for Deregulation," *On the Media,* WNYC-Radio, April 2, 2004, http://www.wnyc.org/onthemedia/transcripts/transcripts_040204_regulation.html.
2. Tom Lewis, *Empire of the Air: The Men Who Made Radio* (New York: HarperCollins, 1991), 181.
3. Ibid., 32.
4. Ibid., 73.
5. For a full discussion of early broadcast history and the formation of RCA, see Eric Barnouw, *Tube of Plenty* (New York: Oxford University Press, 1982); Susan Douglas, *Inventing American Broadcasting, 1899–1922* (Baltimore: Johns Hopkins University Press, 1987); and Christopher Sterling and John Kitross, *Stay Tuned: A Concise History of American Broadcasting* (Belmont, Calif.: Wadsworth, 1990).
6. Lowell Thomas, quoted in Lawrence Lichty and Malachi Topping, *American Broadcasting: A Source Book on the History of Radio and Television* (New York: Hastings House, 1975), 229.
7. See Joe Mahoney, "Warner OKs 5M Payout for Payola," *Daily News* (New York), November 23, 2005, p. 6; and Jeff Leeds, "Spitzer Alleges Payola in Lawsuit," *New York Times,* March 9, 2006, p. C1.
8. Neil Strauss, "Pay-for-Play on the Air but This Rendition Is Legal," *New York Times,* March 31, 1998, pp. A1, A21.
9. Neil Strauss, "Birth and Rebirth on the Airwaves," *New York Times,* July 21, 1996, pp. 26–27.
10. See Ed Ward, Geoffrey Stokes, and Ken Tucker, *Rock of Ages: The Rolling Stone History of Rock & Roll* (New York: Rolling Stone Press, 1986), 484.
11. "Media Monopoly Made Simple: Corporate Ownership & the Problem with U.S. Media," http://www.freepress.net/media/tenthings.php (accessed May 25, 2004).
12. "Statement of FCC Chairman William E. Kennard on Low Power FM Radio Initiative," March 27, 2000, www.fcc.gov/Speeches/Kennard/Statements/2000/stwek024.html.
13. Paul Lehrman, "Attack of the Pod People," *Mix,* November 1, 2005, p. 28.
14. Tony Sanders, Duncan's American Radio, June 22, 2001, http://www.duncanradio.com/PR%20on%20Radio%20Ownership.htm.

CHAPTER 5

1. Dick Wolf, quoted in Tim Goodman, "Lucrative *Law & Order* Brand Deserves Limelight . . . ," *San Francisco Chronicle,* March 6, 2005, p. E1.
2. Paul Saffo, quoted in Timothy McNulty and Rob Owen, "Brave New Worlds: When TV Viewers Decide What's Prime Time," *Pittsburgh Post-Gazette,* November 13, 2005, P. A-1.
3. See Elizabeth Kolbert, "Americans Despair of Popular Culture," *New York Times,* August 20, 1995, sec. 2, pp. 1, 23.
4. J. Fred MacDonald, *One Nation under Television: The Rise and Decline of Network TV* (Chicago: Nelson-Hall Publishers, 1994), 132.
5. Ibid., 70.
6. Edgar Bergen, quoted in MacDonald, *One Nation under Television,* 78.
7. See Horace Newcomb, *TV: The Most Popular Art* (Garden City, N.Y.: Anchor Books, 1974), 31, 39.
8. Ibid., 35.
9. Paddy Chayefsky, quoted in Eric Barnouw, *Tube of Plenty: The Evolution of American Television,* rev. ed. (New York: Oxford University Press, 1982), 163.
10. Barnouw, *Tube of Plenty,* 163.
11. Ibid., 163.
12. MacDonald, *One Nation under Television,* 181.
13. See Richard Campbell, "Don Hewitt's Durable Hour," *Columbia Journalism Review* (September–October 1993): 25.
14. Stuart Elliott, "How to Value Ratings with DVR Delay," *New York Times,* February 13, 2006, p. C15.
15. "Who Is Paper Tiger Anyway?" December 15, 2002, www.papertiger.org.
16. Quoted in B. J. Bullert, "Public Television: Safe Programming and Faustian Bargains," *Chronicle of Higher Education,* September 19, 1998, B7.

Tracking Technology: Digital TV and the End of Analog, p. 164

1. See Joel Brinkley, "F.C.C. Clears New Standard for Digital TV," *New York Times,* December 25, 1996, pp. C1, C15.

Case Study: Anatomy of a TV "Failure," p. 183

1. See Andrew Pulve, "Now You See It: ABC Pulls the Plug on David Lynch's TV Series, *Mulholland Drive,*" *Guardian,* May 11, 2001, p. 10; and Andy Klein, "David Lynch: Still the Wizard of Weird," *Hamilton Spectator,* November 17, 2001, p. M16.
2. All Tim Reid and Hugh Wilson quotes from Jimmie L. Reeves and Richard Campbell, "Misplacing *Frank's Place:* Do You Know What It Means to Miss New Orleans?" *Television Quarterly* 24 (1989): 45–57.

CHAPTER 6

1. The Pew Research Center for the People and the Press, "Cable and Internet Loom Large in Fragmented Political News Universe," January 11, 2004, http://people-press .org/reports/display.php3?ReportID=200.
2. *United States v. Midwest Video Corp.*, 440 U.S. 689 (1979).
3. National Cable & Telecommunications Association, "Industry Statistics," March 2006, http://www.ncta.com/ ContentView.aspx?contentId=54.
4. Federal Communications Commission, Report on Cable Industry Prices, February 4, 2005, http://hraunfoss .fcc.gov/edocs_public/attachmatch/FCC-05-12A1.pdf.
5. National Cable & Telecommunications Association, 2006 Industry Overview, http://www.ncta.com/ contentview.aspx?contentId=S1, p. 14.
6. National Cable & Telecommunications Association, "Industry Statistics," March 2006, www.ncta.com.
7. "Tom Freston: The Pied Piper of Television," *Broadcasting & Cable*, September 19, 1994, 40.
8. Stephen Labaton, "AT&T's Acquisition of MediaOne Wins Approval by F.C.C.," *New York Times*, June 6, 2000, p. A1.
9. William J. Ray, "Private Enterprise, Privileged Enterprise, or Free Enterprise," January 28, 2003, www.glasgow-Ky .com/papers/#PrivateEnterprise.
10. Ibid.

CHAPTER 7

1. John Cawelti, *Adventure, Mystery, and Romance: Formula Stories as Art and Popular Culture* (Chicago: University of Chicago Press, 1976), 35.
2. See Charles Musser, *The Emergence of Cinema: The American Screen to 1907* (New York: Scribner's, 1991).
3. Douglas Gomery, *Shared Pleasures: A History of Movie Presentation in the United States* (Madison: University of Wisconsin Press, 1992), 18.
4. Douglas Gomery, *Movie History: A Survey* (Belmont, Calif.: Wadsworth, 1991), 53.
5. Ibid., 167.
6. See Cawelti, *Adventure, Mystery, and Romance*, 80–98.
7. See Barbara Koenig Quart, *Women Directors: The Emergence of a New Cinema* (New York: Praeger, 1988).
8. Ismail Merchant, "Kitschy as Ever, Hollywood Is Branching Out," *New York Times*, November 22, 1998, sec. 2, pp. 15, 30.
9. See Gomery, *Shared Pleasures*, 171–180.
10. See Eric Barnouw, *Tube of Plenty: The Evolution of American Television*, rev. ed. (New York: Oxford University Press, 1975, 1982), 108–109.
11. See Douglas Gomery, "Who Killed Hollywood?" *Wilson Quarterly* (Summer 1991): 106–112.
12. Sharon Waxman, "Swelling Demand for Disks Alters Hollywood's Arithmetic," *New York Times*, April 20, 2004.
13. Ken Belson, "A Star May Be Fading: As DVD Sales Slow, the Hunt Is on for a New Cash Cow," *New York Times*, June 13, 2006, p. C1, C10.
14. National Association of Theater Owners, "Total U.S. Admissions, 2005," http://www.natoonline.org/statistics admissions.htm.
15. "US Entertainment Industry: 2005 MPA Market Statistics," http://www.mpaa.org/researchstatistics.asp.
16. Jennifer Mann, "AMC Makes Surprise Bid for Rival Theater Chain," *Kansas City Star*, July 12, 2001, p. A1.
17. David Thorburn, "Television as an Aesthetic Medium," *Critical Studies in Mass Communication* (June 1987): 168.

Case Study: Breaking through Hollywood's Race Barrier, p. 245

1. Douglas Gomery, *Shared Pleasures: A History of Movie Presentation in the United States* (Madison: University of Wisconsin Press, 1992), 155–170.

CHAPTER 8

1. See Brooke Kroeger, *Nellie Bly: Daredevil, Reporter, Feminist* (New York: Times Books/Random House, 1994).
2. See Kay Mills, *A Place in the News: From the Women's Pages to the Front Page* (New York: Dodd, Mead, 1988).
3. Piers Brendon, *The Life and Death of the Press Barons* (New York: Atheneum, 1983), 136.
4. William Randolph Hearst, quoted in Brendon, *The Life and Death of the Press Barons*, 134.
5. Michael Schudson, *Discovering the News: A Social History of American Newspapers* (New York: Basic Books, 1978), 23.
6. See David T. Z. Mindich, "Edwin M. Stanton, the Inverted Pyramid, and Information Control," *Journalism Monographs*, no. 140 (August 1993).
7. John C. Merrill, "Objectivity: An Attitude," in Merrill and Ralph L. Lowenstein, eds., *Media, Messages and Men* (New York: David McKay, 1971), 240.
8. Roy Peter Clark, "A New Shape for the News," *Washington Journalism Review* (March 1984): 47.
9. Ibid., 143, 189.
10. See Edwin Emery, *The Press and America: An Interpretative History of the Mass Media*, 3rd ed. (Englewood Cliffs, N.J.: Prentice-Hall, 1972), 562.
11. Walter Lippmann, *Liberty and the News* (New York: Harcourt, Brace and Howe, 1920), 92.
12. American Society of Newspaper Editors, *Problems of Journalism* (Washington, D.C.: ASNE, 1933), 74.
13. Lippmann, *Liberty and the News*, 64.
14. Tom Wicker, *On Press* (New York: Viking, 1978), 3–5.
15. Jack Newfield, "The 'Truth' about Objectivity and the New Journalism," in Charles C. Flippen, ed., *Liberating the Media* (Washington, D.C.: Acropolis Books, 1973), 63–64.
16. Tom Wolfe, quoted in Leonard W. Robinson, "The New Journalism: A Panel Discussion," in Ronald Weber, ed., *The Reporter as Artist: A Look at the New Journalism Controversy* (New York: Hastings House, 1974), 67. See also Tom Wolfe and E. E. Johnson, eds., *The New Journalism* (New York: Harper & Row, 1973).
17. Jon Katz, "Online or Not, Newspapers Suck," *Wired*, September 1994, 5.
18. See Newspaper Association of America, www.naa.org, April 25, 2006. See also Project for Excellence in Journalism, "State of the News Media," www.journalism.org.
19. Ibid.
20. See Sreenath Sreenivasan, "As Mainstream Papers Struggle, the Ethnic Press Is Thriving," *New York Times*, July 22, 1996, p. C7.
21. Wil Cruz, "The New New Yorker: Ethnic Media Fill the Void," *Newsday*, June 26, 2002, p. A25.
22. See Phyl Garland, "The Black Press: Down but Not Out," *Columbia Journalism Review* (September–October 1982): 43–50.
23. American Society of Newspaper Editors, www.asne.org.
24. Dianiela Gevson, "Spanish-Language Dailies Expand a Bitter Battle," *New York Sun*, January 21, 2004, p. 2.
25. PR Newswire, "Joint Statement by UNITY, AAJA, NABJ, NAHJ, and NAJA on Annual American Society of Newspaper Editors Newsroom Census," April 21, 2004.

26. Ibid. See also Peter Johnson, "Hispanic Journalists Regroup in Post-Blair Era," *USA Today*, June 30, 2002, p. 3D.
27. American Society of Newspaper Editors, www.asne.org.
28. Ibid.
29. *PR Newswire*, "NAA Finds Newspaper Readership Steady in Top 50 Markets," May 3, 2004. See Newspaper Association of America at www.naa.org for updates.
30. Michael Emery and Edwin Emery, *The Press and America: An Interpretive History of the Mass Media*, 7th ed. (Englewood Cliffs, N.J.: Prentice-Hall, 1992), 536.
31. Newspaper Association of America, www.naa.org.
32. See Philip Meyer, "Learning to Love Lower Profits," *American Journalism Review* (December 1995): 40–44.
33. See William Glaberson, "Newspaper Owners Do the Shuffle," *New York Times*, February 19, 1996, pp. C1, C4.
34. See Katherine Q. Seelye, "Weighing Knight Ridder against Stubborn Worries" and Geraldine Fabrikant, "In a Big Bet on Newspapers, A Shy Investor Makes News," *New York Times*, December 8, 2005, p. C1; Katherine Q. Seelye and Andrew Ross Sorkin, "Newspaper Chain Agrees to a Sale for $4.5 Billion," *New York Times*, March 13, 2006, p. A1; Damon Darlin, "In Boomtown but Still Stuck on a Bubble: Why San Jose's Paper Is Being Left an Orphan," *New York Times*, March 23, 2006, p. C1; and Katherine Q. Seelye, "Philadelphia Investors Buy Two Newspapers," *New York Times*, May 24, 2006, p. A1.
35. Matt Wells, "*Big Issue* Faces Cash Crisis," *Guardian*, May 15, 2002, Home sec., p. 5; Sally Jackson, "Tide Turns for 'Good Read, Good Deed' Mag," *Australian*, July 18, 2002, p. M09.
36. Committee to Protect Journalists, "Journalists Killed in the Line of Duty during the Last Ten Years," www.cpj.org.
37. Marc Santora and Bill Carter, "War in Iraq Becomes the Deadliest Assignment for Journalists in Modern Times," *New York Times*, May 30, 2006, www.nytimes.com.

Case Study: Alternative Journalism: Dorothy Day and I. F. Stone, p. 299

1. Stone, quoted in Jack Lule, "I. F. Stone: Professional Excellence in Raising Hell," *QS News* (Summer 1989): 3.

CHAPTER 9

1. John Tebbel and Mary Ellen Zuckerman, *The Magazine in America, 1741–1900* (New York: Oxford University Press, 1991), 68.
2. See Theodore Peterson, *Magazines in the Twentieth Century* (Urbana: University of Illinois Press, 1964), 5.
3. See Richard Ohmann, *Selling Culture: Magazines, Markets, and Class at the Turn of the Century* (New York: Verso, 1996).
4. See Peterson, *Magazines*, 5.
5. Lincoln Steffens, quoted in Justin Kaplan, *Lincoln Steffens: A Biography* (New York: Simon & Schuster, 1974), 106.
6. See discussion in Peterson, *Magazines*, 228; and Tebbel and Zuckerman, *The Magazine in America*, 223.
7. Alexander Graham Bell, quoted in William H. Taft, *American Magazines for the 1980s* (New York: Hastings House, 1982), 60.
8. Harold Ross, quoted in John Tebbel, *The American Magazine: A Compact History* (New York: Hawthorn Books, 1969), 234.
9. Generoso Pope, quoted in Taft, *American Magazines for the 1980s*, 226–227.
10. See S. Elizabeth Bird, *For Enquiring Minds: A Cultural Study of Supermarket Tabloids* (Knoxville: University of Tennessee Press, 1992), 24.
11. See Taft, *American Magazines*, 229.

12. See Iver Peterson, "Media: Supermarket Tabloids Lose Circulation," *New York Times*, September 9, 1996, p. C5.
13. Ibid.
14. Katherine Q. Seelye, "As Magazine Readers Increasingly Turn to the Web, So Does Condé Nast," *New York Times*, April 3, 2006, p. C1.
15. Ibid.
16. See Deirdre Carmody, "Magazines Go Niche-Hunting with Custom-Made Sections," *New York Times*, June 26, 1995, p. C7.
17. See Robin Pogrebin, "The Number of Ad Pages Does Not Make the Magazine," *New York Times*, August 26, 1996, p. C1.
18. See Gloria Steinem, "Sex, Lies & Advertising," *Ms.*, July–August 1990, 18–28.
19. Robin Pogrebin, "Once a Renegade, Hachette Magazine Chief Gains Respect," *New York Times*, April 6, 1998, p. C1.

Media Literacy and the Critical Process: Uncovering American Beauty, p. 332

1. David Carr, "On Covers of Many Magazines, A Full Racial Palette Is Still Rare," *New York Times*, November 18, 2002.

Examining Ethics: *Ms.* Magazine's Latest Challenge, p. 341

1. Anita Chabria, "Ms. Understood; Can the Magazine That Helped Galvanize the Women's Movement Attract Readers Who See It as a Relic?" *Los Angeles Times Magazine*, August 31, 2003, part 9, p. 18.

CHAPTER 10

1. Harold Bloom, "The Wrong Stuff . . . ," *Los Angles Times*, September 24, 2003, p. A29.
2. Jack Zipes, quoted in Henry Kisor, "Way Too Many Books . . . ," *Chicago Sun-Times*, December 25, 2005, p. 9B.
3. See David Baddiel, "*The Da Vinci Code* Is as Dickensian as Miriam Margoyles in a Bonnet," *Times* (London), July 23, 2005, p. 3.
4. Anthony Lane, "Heaven Can Wait," *The New Yorker*, May 29, 2006, 76–78.
5. See Elizabeth Eisenstein, *The Printing Press as an Agent of Change* (Cambridge: Cambridge University Press, 1980).
6. See Quentin Reynolds, *The Fiction Factory: From Pulp Row to Quality Street* (New York: Street & Smith/Random House, 1955), 72–74.
7. For a comprehensive historical overview of the publishing industry and the rise of publishing houses, see John A. Tebbel, *A History of Book Publishing in the United States*, vol. 1, 1630–1865; vol. 2, 1865–1919; vol. 3, 1920–1940; vol. 4, 1940–1980 (New York: R. R. Bowker, 1972–1981).
8. National Association of College Stores, "FAQ on College Textbooks," http://nacs.org/common/research/faq_textbooks.pdf (accessed July 2, 2005).
9. Mary Jane Smetanka, "Students Sidestep High Cost of Books," *Minneapolis Star Tribune*, September 3, 2005, p. 1B.
10. For a historical overview of paperbacks, see Kenneth Davis, *Two-Bit Culture: The Paperbacking of America* (Boston: Houghton Mifflin, 1984).
11. See John P. Dessauer, *Book Publishing: What It Is, What It Does* (New York: R. R. Bowker, 1974), 48.
12. Patricia Nelson Limerick, "Dancing with Professors: The Trouble with Academic Prose," *New York Times Book Review*, October 31, 1993, p. 3.
13. David D. Kirkpatrick, "Report to the Authors Guild Midlist Books Study Committee," 2000, http://www.authorsguild.org/prmidlist.html.

14. See Doreen Carvajal, "Well-Known Book Clubs Agree to Form Partnership," *New York Times,* March 2, 2000, p. C2.
15. Jon Ortiz, "The Tale of the Little Guys . . . ," *Sacramento Bee,* September 1, 2005, p. D1.
16. Janet Forgrieve, "The Next Page . . . ," *Rocky Mountain News,* June 3, 2006, p. 1C.
17. Bibb Porter, "In Publishing, Bigger Is Better," *New York Times,* March 31, 1998, p. A27.
18. James Kaplan, "Inside the Club," *New York Times Magazine,* June 11, 1989, p. 62.
19. See Wilson Dizard Jr., *Old Media New Media: Mass Communication in the Information Age* (White Plains, N.Y.: Longman, 1994), 164.
20. Peter Wayner, "Technology Rewrites the Book," *New York Times,* July 20, 2006, p. C9.
21. National Endowment for the Arts, *Reading at Risk: A Survey of Literary Reading in America,* June 2004, http://www.nea.gov/pub/ReadingAtRisk.pdf.
22. See Bill Duryea, "Like Magic, They're Readers," *St. Petersburg Times,* July 15, 2005, p. 1A.
23. See Alvin Kernan, *The Death of Literature* (New Haven: Yale University Press, 1990).

CHAPTER 11

1. Marian Burros and Melanie Warner, "Bottlers Agree to a School Ban on Sweet Drinks," *New York Times,* May 4, 2006, p. A1.
2. Caroline Wilbert, Elizabeth Lee, and David Ho, "Beverage Industry Tightens Policy," *Atlanta Journal-Constitution,* May 4, 2006, p. 1A.
3. For a written and pictorial history of early advertising, see Charles Goodrum and Helen Dalrymple, *Advertising in America: The First 200 Years* (New York: Harry N. Abrams, 1990), 13–34.
4. Ibid.
5. Michael Schudson, *Advertising: The Uneasy Persuasion* (New York: Basic Books, 1984), 165. See also Arthur Marquette, *Brands, Trademarks, and Good Will* (New York: McGraw-Hill, 1967).
6. Goodrum and Dalrymple, *Advertising in America,* 31.
7. See Schudson, *Advertising,* 164.
8. Stuart Elliott, "Advertising's Big Four: It's Their World Now," *New York Times,* March 31, 2002, sec. 3 (Money and Business), p. 1.
9. Spotlight, "X-Ray Films Hits Target's Bull-Eye," *Shoot Magazine,* February 6, 2004.
10. Randall Rothenberg, *Where the Suckers Moon: An Advertising Story* (New York: Alfred A. Knopf, 1994), 20.
11. Stuart Elliott, "General Motors Accounts May Be Up for Grabs," *New York Times,* March 17, 2006, p. C3.
12. Leslie Savan, "Op Ad: Sneakers and Nothingness," *Village Voice,* April 2, 1991, p. 43.
13. "The 100 Top Brands," *Business Week,* August 2, 2004, 68–71, www.businessweek.com/pdfs/2004/0431_brands.pdf.
14. See Mary Kuntz and Joseph Weber, "The New Hucksterism," *Business Week,* July 1, 1999, 79.
15. Ibid.
16. Schudson, *Advertising,* 210.
17. Vance Packard, *The Hidden Persuaders* (New York: Basic Books, 1957, 1978), 229.
18. See Eileen Dempsey, "Auld Lang Syne," *Columbus Dispatch,* December 28, 2000, p. 1G; and John Reinan, "The End of the Good Old Days," *Minneapolis Star Tribune,* August 31, 2004, p. 1D.

19. See Schudson, *Advertising,* 36–43; and Andrew Robertson, *The Lessons of Failure* (London: MacDonald, 1974).
20. Kim Campbell and Kent Davis-Packard, "How Ads Get Kids to Say, I Want It!" *Christian Science Monitor,* September 18, 2000, p. 1.
21. David Lieberman, "Classics Are Back in Licensed Gear," *USA Today,* June 21, 2005, p. 4B.
22. See Jay Mathews, "Channel One: Classroom Coup or a 'Sham'?" *Washington Post,* December 26, 1994, p. A1+.
23. See Michael F. Jacobson and Laurie Ann Mazur, *Marketing Madness: A Survival Guide for a Consumer Society* (Boulder, Colo.: Westview Press, 1995), 29–31.
24. "Ads Beat News on School TVs," *Pittsburgh Post-Gazette,* March 6, 2006, p. A7.
25. Hilary Waldman, "Study Links Advertising, Youth Drinking," *Hartford Courant,* January 3, 2006, p. A1.
26. "Miller Brewing Sues Anheuser-Busch over Ads," *Adage Online Edition,* May 27, 2004, http://adage.com.
27. Douglas J. Wood, "Ad Issues to Watch For in '06," *Advertising Age,* December 19, 2005, p. 10.
28. For a discussion of deceptive ads, see Jacobson and Mazur, *Marketing Madness,* 143–148.
29. Associated Press, "Two Ephedra Sellers Fined for False Ads," *Washington Post,* July 2, 2003, p. A7.
30. Reuters News Service, "It's All Brand New," *Toronto Sun,* August 4, 2006, p. 15.
31. G. Pascal Zachary, "Many Journalists See a Growing Reluctance to Criticize Advertisers," *Wall Street Journal,* February 6, 1992, pp. A1, A6.
32. James McKinley Jr., "Car Dealers Settle with State," *New York Times,* August 10, 2001, sec. B, p. 4.
33. Ibid., p. A6.
34. The Project for Excellence in Journalism, "The State of News Media 2004," http://www.stateofthenewsmedia.org/index.asp (accessed June 18, 2004).
35. See Bettina Fabos, "The Commercialized Web: Challenges for Libraries and Democracy," *Library Trends* 53(4) (Spring 2005): 519–523.
36. *Consumer Reports* WebWatch, "Still in Search of Disclosure," June 9, 2005, http://www.consumerwebwatch.org/pdfs/search-engine-disclosure.pdf.
37. Beth Harskovits, "Corporate Profile: Legacy's Truth Finds Receptive Audience," *PR Week,* June 12, 2006, p. 9.
38. Kathleen Hall Jamieson, "Truth and Advertising," *New York Times,* January 27, 1996, p. 15.
39. See Stephen Ansolabehere and Shanto Iyengar, *Going Negative: How Attack Ads Shrink and Polarize the Electorate* (New York: Free Press, 1996).
40. Alliance for Better Campaigns, "Local Stations Are Big Winners in Campaign 2004," December 2004, http://www.bettercampaigns.org/standard/display.php?StoryID=322.

The Global Village: Smoking Up the Global Market, p. 414

1. Mark O'Neill, "Weeding Out the Profits," *South China Morning Post,* August 1, 2002, p. 1; and Rina Omar, "Light Up, Lights Out?" *New Strait Times* (Malaysia), May 31, 2002, p. 1.

CHAPTER 12

1. Matthew J. Culligan and Dolph Greene, *Getting Back to the Basics of Public Relations & Publicity* (New York: Crown Publishers, 1982), 90.
2. Ibid., 100.

3. See Stuart Ewen, *PR! A Social History of Spin* (New York: Basic Books, 1996).

4. Suzanne Heck, "Multimedia Sharpshooter Brought Buffalo Bill Fame," *Public Relations Journal* (October–November 1994): 12.

5. Marvin N. Olasky, "The Development of Corporate Public Relations, 1850–1930," *Journalism Monographs*, no. 102 (April 1987): 3.

6. Quoted in Alfred McClung Lee, *The Daily Newspaper in America* (New York: Macmillan, 1937), 436.

7. Olasky, "The Development of Corporate Public Relations," 14.

8. Ibid., 15.

9. See Ewen, *PR!* 47.

10. See Scott M. Cutlip, *The Unseen Power: Public Relations—A History* (Hillsdale, N.J.: Lawrence Erlbaum, 1994).

11. Edward Bernays, *Crystallizing Public Opinion* (New York: Horace Liveright, 1923), 217.

12. Michael Schudson, *Discovering the News: A Social History of American Newspapers* (New York: Basic Books, 1978), 136.

13. Walter Lippmann, *Public Opinion* (New York: Free Press, 1922, 1949), 218.

14. See Daniel Boorstin, *The Image: A Guide to Pseudo-Events in America* (New York: Atheneum, 1961), 11–12, 205–210.

15. The author of this book, Richard Campbell, worked briefly as the assistant PR director for Milwaukee's Summerfest in the early 1980s.

16. PRSA, 2006 Silver Anvil Awards, "Teaching Teens Love Is Not Abuse," http://www.prsa.org/_Awards/silver/index.asp.

17. Fareed Zakaria, ABC News, *This Week*, November 19, 2006.

18. Philip Shenon, "3 Partners Quit Firm Handling Saudis' P.R.," *New York Times*, December 6, 2002, http://www.nytimes.com/2002/12/06/international/middleeast/06SAUD.html?ex=1040199544&ei=1&en=c061b2d98376e7ba.

19. Tim Reid, "America Plans PR Blitz on Saddam," *Times* (London), September 17, 2002, http://www.timesonline.co.uk/article/o,,3-418110,00.html.

20. David S. Cloud, "Quick Rise for Purveyors of Propaganda in Iraq," *New York Times*, February 15, 2006, p. A1, A10.

21. Stanley Walker, "Playing the Deep Bassoons," *Harper's*, February 1932, 365.

22. Ibid., 370.

23. Ivy Lee, *Publicity* (New York: Industries Publishing, 1925), 21.

24. Luke Timmerman, "Are PR Firms Going Too Far? Survey Asks," *Seattle Times*, May 17, 2000, p. D2.

25. Schudson, *Discovering the News*, 136.

26. Ivy Lee, quoted in Ray Eldon Hiebert, *Courtier to the Crowd: The Story of Ivy Lee and the Development of Public Relations* (Ames: Iowa State University Press, 1966), 114.

27. See Lippmann, *Public Opinion*, 221.

28. See Jonathan Tasini, "Lost in the Margins: Labor and the Media," *Extra!* (Summer 1992): 2–11.

29. See J. David Pincus et al., "Newspaper Editors' Perceptions of Public Relations: How Business, News, and Sports Editors Differ," *Journal of Public Relations Research* 5(1) (1993): 27–45.

30. John Stauber and Sheldon Rampton, "Flack Attack," *PR Watch* 4(1) (1997), http://www.prwatch.org/prw_issues/1997-Q1/index.html.

31. John Stauber, "Corporate PR: A Threat to Journalism?" *Background Briefing: Radio National*, March 30, 1997, http://www.abc.net.au/rn/talks/bbing/stories/s10602.htm.

32. William Small, quoted in Walker, "Playing the Deep Bassoons," 174–175.

33. See Alicia Mundy, "Is the Press Any Match for Powerhouse PR?" in Ray Eldon Hiebert, ed., *Impact of Mass Media* (White Plains, N.Y.: Longman, 1995), 179–188.

Case Study: Video News Releases: Manufacturing the News, p. 442

1. Center for Media and Democracy, "Fake TV News: Widespread and Undisclosed," April 6, 2006, http://www.prwatch.org/fakenews/execsummary.

Examining Ethics: Improving the Credibility Gap, p. 445

1. Paul Pressler, "Executive Summary," Gap Inc. 2003 Social Responsibility Report, http://www.gapinc.com/social_resp/social_resp.htm.

2. Jenny Strasburg, "Gap Finds Problems at Thousands of Its Overseas Factories; Openness on Work Conditions Praised," *San Francisco Chronicle*, May 13, 2004, p. A1. Also see David Usborne, "Gap Draws Up a Map of Unfair Working Practices," *Sunday Tribune*, May 16, 2004, p. 13.

Media Literacy and the Critical Process: The Invisible Hand of PR, p. 453

1. John Stauber, "Corporate PR: A Threat to Journalism?" *Background Briefing: Radio INational*, March 30, 1997, http://www.abc.net.au/rn/talks/bbing/stories/s10602.htm.

CHAPTER 13

1. Ronald Grover, "Moguls Who Shopped Till They Dropped," *Business Week*, August 5, 2002.

2. For this section the authors are indebted to the ideas and scholarship of Douglas Gomery, a media economist and historian from the University of Maryland.

3. Douglas Gomery, "The Centrality of Media Economics," in Mark R. Levy and Michael Gurevitch, eds., *Defining Media Studies* (New York: Oxford University Press, 1994), 202.

4. Ibid., 200.

5. Ibid., 203–204.

6. David Harvey, *The Condition of Postmodernity: An Enquiry into the Origins of Cultural Change* (Oxford: Basil Blackwell, 1989), 171.

7. Ibid., 158.

8. Thomas Geoghegan, "How Pink Slips Hurt More Than Workers," *New York Times*, March 29, 2006, p. B8.

9. Louis Uchitelle, *The Disposable American: Layoffs and Their Consequences* (New York: Alfred A. Knopf, 2006).

10. Paul Krugman, "For Richer," *New York Times Magazine*, October 20, 2002, pp. 62ff.

11. Richard J. Barnet and John Cavanagh, *Global Dreams: Imperial Corporations and the New World Order* (New York: Simon & Schuster, 1994), 131.

12. James Stewart, *Disney War* (New York: Simon & Schuster, 2005).

13. Ben Bagdikian, *The Media Monopoly*, 6th ed. (Boston: Beacon Press, 2000), 222.

14. William Paley, quoted in Robert W. McChesney, *Telecommunications, Mass Media & Democracy: The Battle for Control of U.S. Broadcasting, 1928–1935* (New York: Oxford University Press, 1993), 251.

15. McChesney, *Telecommunications, Mass Media & Democracy*, 264.
16. Edward Herman, "Democratic Media," *Z Papers* (January–March 1992): 23.
17. Barnet and Cavanagh, *Global Dreams*, 38.
18. Richard J. Barnet and Ronald E. Muller, *Global Reach: The Power of Multinational Corporations* (New York: Simon & Schuster, 1974), 175.
19. The Lear Center Local News Archive, "Local TV News Coverage of the 2002 General Elections," http://www.localnewsarchive.org/pdf/LocalTV2002.pdf.

CHAPTER 14

1. Dean Baquet and Bill Keller, "When Do We Publish a Secret?" *New York Times*, July 1, 2006, p. A27; and see Frank Rich, "Can't Win the War? Bomb the Press!" *New York Times*, July 2, 2006, Sec. 4, p. 10.
2. Scott Sherman, "Chilling the Press," *Nation*, July 17/24, 2006, 4–5.
3. Helen Thomas, "Lap Dogs of the Press," *Nation*, March 27, 2006, 18–20.
4. See Katherine Q. Seelye, "Two Awards for Public Service after Katrina's Onslaught Lead the Pulitzers," *New York Times*, April 18, 2006, p. B7. See related story, p. C15.
5. Neil Postman, "Currents," *Utne Reader* (July–August 1995): 35.
6. Reuven Frank, "Memorandum from a Television Newsman," reprinted as Appendix 2 in A. William Bluem, *Documentary in American Television* (New York: Hastings House, 1965), 276.
7. For another list and alternative analysis of news criteria, see Brian S. Brooks et al., *The Missouri Group: News Reporting and Writing* (New York: St. Martin's Press, 1996), 2–4.
8. Horace Greeley, quoted in Christopher Lasch, "Journalism, Publicity and the Lost Art of Argument," *Gannett Center Journal* 4(2) (Spring 1990): 2.
9. David Eason, "Telling Stories and Making Sense," *Journal of Popular Culture* 15(2) (Fall 1981): 125.
10. Jon Katz, "AIDS and the Media: Shifting out of Neutral," *Rolling Stone*, May 27, 1993, 32.
11. Herbert Gans, *Deciding What's News* (New York: Pantheon, 1979), 42–48.
12. Ibid.
13. Ibid., 48–51.
14. See Michael Schudson, *Discovering the News: A Social History of American Newspapers* (New York: Basic Books, 1978), 3–11.
15. Baquet and Keller, "When Do We Publish a Secret?"
16. Code of Ethics, reprinted in Melvin Mencher, *News Reporting and Writing*, 3rd ed. (Dubuque, Iowa: William C. Brown, 1984), 443–444.
17. Ibid.
18. Ibid., 443.
19. For reference and guidance on media ethics, see Clifford Christians, Mark Fackler, and Kim Rotzoll, *Media Ethics: Cases & Moral Reasoning*, 4th ed. (White Plains, N.Y.: Longman, 1995); and Thomas H. Bivins, "A Worksheet for Ethics Instruction and Exercises in Reason," *Journalism Educator* (Summer 1993): 4–16.
20. Christians, Fackler, and Rotzoll, *Media Ethics*, 15.
21. See Jimmie Reeves and Richard Campbell, *Cracked Coverage: Television News, the Anti-Cocaine Crusade, and the Reagan Legacy* (Durham, N.C.: Duke University Press, 1994).

22. See David Eason, "On Journalistic Authority: The Janet Cooke Scandal," *Critical Studies in Mass Communications* 3(4) (December 1986): 429–447.
23. Mike Royko, quoted in "News Media: A Searching of Conscience," *Newsweek*, May 4, 1981, 53.
24. Don Hewitt, interview conducted at *60 Minutes*, CBS News, New York, February 21, 1989.
25. Jonathan Alter, "News Media: Round Up the Usual Suspects," *Newsweek*, March 25, 1985, 69.
26. William Hoynes and David Croteau, "All the Usual Suspects: MacNeil/Lehrer and Nightline," *Extra!* Special Issue 3(4) (Winter 1990): 2. This article reports on the original *Nightline* study and offers a follow-up study on both *Nightline* and *MacNeil/Lehrer*, which reveals roughly the same gender patterns. See Hoynes and Croteau, "Are You on the Nightline Guest List?" *Extra!* 2(4) (January–February 1989): 2–15.
27. William Greider, quoted in Mark Hertsgaard, *On Bended Knee: The Press and the Reagan Presidency* (New York: Farrar, Straus & Giroux, 1988), 78.
28. Jay Rosen, "Politics, Vision, and the Press: Toward a Public Agenda for Journalism," in Jay Rosen and Paul Taylor, *The New News v. the Old News: The Press and Politics in the 1990s* (New York: Twentieth Century Fund, 1992), 6.
29. Bluem, *Documentary in American Television*, 94.
30. Fred Friendly, quoted in Joseph Michalak, "CBS Reports Covers Assortment of Topics," *New York Times*, December 13, 1959, sec. 2, p. 21.
31. See Joe Holley, "Should the Coverage Fit the Crime?" *Columbia Journalism Review* (May–June 1996), www.cjr.org/year/96/coverage.asp.
32. Based on notes made by the author's wife, Dianna Campbell, after a visit to Warsaw and discussions with a number of journalists working for *Gazeta Wyborcza* in 1990.
33. Davis "Buzz" Merritt, *Public Journalism & Public Life: Why Telling the News Is Not Enough* (Hillsdale, N.J.: Lawrence Erlbaum, 1995), 113–114.
34. Rosen, "Politics, Vision, and the Press," 14.
35. Davis Merritt and Jay Rosen, "Imagining Public Journalism: An Editor and a Scholar Reflect on the Birth of an Idea," *Roy W. Howard Public Lecture* (Bloomington: Indiana University), no. 5, April 13, 1995, 11.
36. See Jonathan Cohn, "Should Journalists Do Community Service?" *American Prospect* (Summer 1995): 15.
37. Merritt and Rosen, "Imagining Public Journalism," 12.
38. Poll statistics cited in Merritt, *Public Journalism & Public Life*, xv–xvi; see Philip Meyer, "Raising Trust in Newspapers," *USA Today*, January 11, 1999, p. 15A; and Project for Excellence in Journalism, www.journalism.org, and the Pew Research Center, www.people-press.org/reports, for current research data.
39. Jeffrey Birnbaum, "The Road to Riches Is Called K Street . . . ," *Washington Post*, June 22, 2005, p. A1.
40. Stephen Johnson, *Everything Bad Is Good for You: How Today's Popular Culture Is Actually Making Us Smarter* (New York: Riverhead Books, 2005), 8.
41. James Agee and Walker Evans, *Let Us Now Praise Famous Men* (Boston: Houghton Mifflin, 1960), xiv.
42. David Broder, quoted in "Squaring with the Reader: A Seminar on Journalism," *Kettering Review* (Winter 1992): 48.
43. Christopher Lasch, "Journalism, Publicity and the Lost Art of Argument," *Gannett Center Journal* 4 (2) (Spring 1990): 1.
44. Jay Rosen, "Forming and Informing the Public," *Kettering Review* (Winter 1992): 69–70.

Case Study: Bias and the News, p. 506

1. Harris Poll #52, "News Reporting Perceived as Biased . . . ," June 30, 2006, www.harrisinteractive.com/harris_poll/index.asp?PID=679.
2. Pew Research Center for the People and the Press, "Bottom-Line Pressures Now Hurting Coverage, Say Journalists," May 23, 2004, www.people-press.org/reports/display.php3?PageID=829.
3. Herbert Gans, *Deciding What's News* (New York: Vintage, 1980).
4. See Bernard Goldberg, *Bias: A CBS Insider Exposes How the Media Distort the News* (New York: Perennial, 2003).
5. See Eric Alterman, *What Liberal Media? The Truth about Bias and the News* (New York: Basic Books, 2003).
6. M. D. Watts et al., "Elite Cues and Media Bias in Presidential Campaigns: Explaining Public Perceptions of a Liberal Press," *Communications Research* 26 (1999), 144–175.

CHAPTER 15

1. Alexis de Tocqueville, *Democracy in America* (New York: Modern Library, 1835, 1840, 1945, 1981), 96–97.
2. Steve Fore, "Lost in Translation: The Social Uses of Mass Communications Research," *Afterimage*, no. 20 (April 1993): 10.
3. James Carey, *Communication as Culture: Essays on Media and Society* (Boston: Unwin Hyman, 1989), 75.
4. Daniel Czitrom, *Media and the American Mind: From Morse to McLuhan* (Chapel Hill: University of North Carolina Press, 1982), 122–125.
5. Ibid., 123.
6. Harold Lasswell, *Propaganda Techniques in the World War* (New York: Alfred A. Knopf, 1927), 9.
7. Walter Lippmann, *Public Opinion* (New York: Macmillan, 1922), 18.
8. Pew Research Center for the People and the Press, "Democrats More Eager to Vote, but Unhappy with Party," June 27, 2006, http://people-press.org/reports/display.php3?ReportID=279.
9. Sheldon R. Gawiser and G. Evans Witt, "20 Questions a Journalist Should Ask about Poll Results," 2nd ed. http://www.ncpp.org/qajsa.htm (accessed July 11, 2004).
10. See W. W. Charters, *Motion Pictures and Youth: A Summary* (New York: Macmillan, 1934); and Garth Jowett, *Film: The Democratic Art* (Boston: Little, Brown, 1976), 220–229.
11. Czitrom, *Media and the American Mind*, 132. See also Harold Lasswell, "The Structure and Function of Communication in Society," in Lyman Bryson, ed., *The Communication of Ideas* (New York: Harper and Brothers, 1948), 37–51.
12. Wilbur Schramm, Jack Lyle, and Edwin Parker, *Television in the Lives of Our Children* (Stanford, Calif.: Stanford University Press, 1961), 1.
13. See Joseph Klapper, *The Effects of Mass Communication* (New York: Free Press, 1960).
14. Schramm, Lyle, and Parker, *Television*, 1.
15. For an early overview of uses and gratifications, see Jay Blumler and Elihu Katz, *The Uses of Mass Communication* (Beverly Hills, Calif.: Sage, 1974).
16. National Public Radio, "Death-Penalty Option Varies Depending on Question," *Weekend Edition*, July 2, 2006.
17. See George Gerbner et al., "The Demonstration of Power: Violence Profile No. 10," *Journal of Communication* 29, no. 3 (1979): 177–196.
18. Kaiser Family Foundation, *Sex on TV 4* (Menlo Park, Calif.: Henry C. Kaiser Family Foundation, 2005).
19. Robert P. Snow, *Creating Media Culture* (Beverly Hills, Calif.: Sage, 1983), 47.
20. See Maxwell McCombs and Donald Shaw, "The Agenda-Setting Function of Mass Media," *Public Opinion Quarterly* 36, no. 2 (1972): 176–187.
21. See Stephen D. Reese and Lucig H. Danielton, "A Closer Look at Intermedia Influences on Agenda Setting: The Cocaine Issue of 1986," in Pamela J. Shoemaker, ed., *Communication Campaigns about Drugs: Government, Media, and the Public* (Hillsdale, N.J.: Lawrence Erlbaum, 1989), 47–66; and Peter Kerr, "Anatomy of the Drug Issue: How, after Years, It Erupted," *New York Times*, November 17, 1986, p. A12.
22. See Craig Reinarman and Harry G. Levine, "Crack in Context: Politics and Media in the Making of the Drug Scare," *Contemporary Drug Problems* (Winter 1989): 546; see also Adam Clymer, "Public Found Ready to Sacrifice in Drug Fight," *New York Times*, September 2, 1986, pp. A1, D16.
23. See Nancy Signorielli and Michael Morgan, *Cultivation Analysis: New Directions in Media Effects Research* (Newbury Park, Calif.: Sage, 1990).
24. Em Griffin, "Spiral of Silence of Elisabeth Noelle-Neumann," from *A First Look at Communication Theory* (McGraw-Hill, 1997) http://www.afirstlook.com/archive/spiral.cfm?source=archther.
25. Richard Rhodes, "The Media-Violence Myth," *Rolling Stone* (November 23, 2000): pp. 55–58.
26. Robert Lynd, *Knowledge for What? The Place of Social Science in American Culture* (Princeton, N.J.: Princeton University Press, 1939), 120.
27. Czitrom, *Media and the American Mind*, 143; and Leo Lowenthal, "Historical Perspectives of Popular Culture," in Bernard Rosenberg and David White, eds., *Mass Culture: The Popular Arts in America* (Glencoe, Ill.: Free Press, 1957), 52.
28. See Stuart Hall et al., *Policing the Crisis: Mugging, the State, and Law and Order* (London: Macmillan, 1978).
29. Horace Newcomb, *TV: The Most Popular Art* (Garden City, N.Y.: Anchor Books, 1974), 19, 23.
30. Ana Garner, Helen M. Sterk, and Shawn Adams, "Narrative Analysis of Sexual Etiquette in Teenage Magazines," *Journal of Communication* 48, no. 4 (Autumn 1998): 59–78.
31. See Janice Radway, *Reading the Romance: Women, Patriarchy and Popular Literature* (Chapel Hill: University of North Carolina Press, 1984).
32. James Carey, "Mass Communication Research and Cultural Studies: An American View," in James Curran, Michael Gurevitch, and Janet Woollacott, eds., *Mass Communication and Society* (London: Edward Arnold, 1977), 418, 421.
33. See S. Elizabeth Bird, *For Enquiring Minds: A Cultural Study of Supermarket Tabloids* (Knoxville: University of Tennessee Press, 1992).
34. Robert M. Entman, *Democracy without Citizens* (New York: Oxford University Press, 1989).
35. Scott Janny, "Postmodern Gravity Deconstructed, Slyly," *New York Times*, May 18, 1996, p. 1. See also The Editors of Lingua Franca, eds., *The Sokal Hoax: The Sham That Shook the Academy* (Lincoln, Nebr.: Bison Press, 2000).

36. Christopher Lasch, "Politics and Culture," *Salmagundi* (Winter–Spring 1990): 33.

Media Literacy and the Critical Process: Counting Sexual Scenes on TV, p. 532

1. Kaiser Family Foundation, *Sex on TV 4* (Menlo Park, Calif.: Henry C. Kaiser Family Foundation, 2005).

Case Study: Labor Gets Framed, p. 538

1. Christopher Martin, *Framed! Labor and the Corporate Media* (Ithaca, N.Y.: Cornell University Press, 2003).
2. Richard B. Freeman and Joel Rogers, *What Workers Want* (Ithaca, N.Y.: Cornell University Press, 1999).

CHAPTER 16

1. Kembrew McLeod, "My Freedom of Expression Trademark," http://www.kembrew.com/pranks/mytrademark of.html.
2. See Committee to Protect Journalists, "Journalists Killed in the Line of Duty," http://www.cpj.org/killed/Ten_Year _Killed/stats.html, September 1, 2006.
3. Freedom House, "Press Freedom Survey 2004," http:// www.freedomhoudr.org/rresearch/pressurvey.htm (accessed July 12, 2004).
4. Fred Siebert, Theodore Peterson, and Wilbur Schramm, *Four Theories of the Press* (Urbana: University of Illinois Press, 1956).
5. See Douglas M. Fraleigh and Joseph S. Tuman, *Freedom of Speech in the Marketplace of Ideas* (New York: St. Martin's Press, 1997), 125.
6. Hugo Black, quoted in "New York Times Company v. U.S.: 1971," in Edward W. Knappman, ed., *Great American Trials: From Salem Witchcraft to Rodney King* (Detroit: Visible Ink Press, 1994), 609.
7. Robert Warren, quoted in "U.S. v. The Progressive: 1979," in Knappman, ed., *Great American Trials,* 684.
8. See Fraleigh and Tuman, *Freedom of Speech,* 71–73.
9. See Eric Alterman, "The Liberal Media: The *Times* Is Us," *Nation,* July 31/August 7, 2006, 10.
10. See Knappman, ed., *Great American Trials,* 517–519.
11. Ibid., 741–743.
12. "Doctor: Brangelina's Shiloh 'a Healthy Baby,'" *Newsday,* May 29, 2006, p. A13.
13. Saul Hansell, "More Subpoenas in Suit over Obscenity Law," *New York Times,* March 31, 2006, p. C7.
14. Ibid.
15. Douglas Gomery, *Movie History: A Survey* (Belmont, Calif.: Wadsworth, 1991), 57.
16. Susan Dunne, "Rated or Not, 'Truth' Works," *Hartford Courant,* March 2, 2006, Sect. CAL, p. 20.
17. See Eric Barnouw, *Tube of Plenty: The Evolution of American Television,* rev. ed. (New York: Oxford University Press, 1982), 118–130.
18. Dean Burch, quoted in Peter Fornatale and Joshua Mills, *Radio in the Television Age* (Woodstock, N.Y.: Overlook Press, 1980), 85.
19. See "Dummy and Dame Arouse the Nation," *Broadcasting-Telecasting,* October 15, 1956, p. 258; and Lawrence Lichty and Malachi Topping, *American Broadcasting: A Source Book on the History of Radio and Television* (New York: Hastings House, 1975), 530.
20. Stephen Labaton, "Congress Severely Curtails Plan for Low-Power Radio Stations," *New York Times,* December 19, 2000, http://www.nytimes.com/2000/12/19/business/ 19RADI.html.
21. Bill Kovach, "Big Deals, with Journalism Thrown In," *New York Times,* August 3, 1995, p. A17.

An Extended Case Study: The News Media and War, p. 582

1. See Committee to Protect Journalists, www.cpj.org.
2. Craig Crawford, *Attack the Messenger: How Politicians Turn You against the Media* (Lanham, Maryland: Rowman & Littlefield, 2006), 74.
3. See the Pew Research Center for the People and the Press, www.people-press.org/reports.
4. Pew Research Center for the People and the Press, conducted in association with the Project for Excellence in Journalism, "Public More Critical of the Press, but Goodwill Persists," June 26, 2005. See www.journalism.org/ stateofthenewsmedia.com/2006.
5. Ibid.

A&R agents short for artist & repertoire agents, these talent scouts of the music business discover, develop, and sometimes manage performers.

absolutist ethic the principle that in a moral society legal or ethical codes must be followed without exception; no one is above the law or above a society's fundamental moral principles.

access channels in cable television, a tier of nonbroadcast channels dedicated to local education, government, and the public.

account executives in advertising, client liaisons responsible for bringing in new business and managing the accounts of established clients.

account reviews in advertising, the process of evaluating or reinvigorating an ad campaign, which results in either renewing the contract with the original ad agency or hiring a new agency.

acquisitions editors in the book industry, editors who seek out and sign authors to contracts.

actual malice in libel law, a reckless disregard for the truth, such as when a reporter or an editor knows that a statement is false and prints or airs it anyway.

adult contemporary (AC) one of the oldest and most popular radio music formats, typically featuring a mix of news, talk, oldies, and soft rock.

advocacy journalism often associated with a journalistic trend in the 1960s but actually part of a tradition that dates to the early days of the partisan press, this approach to journalism features the reporter actively promoting a particular cause or viewpoint.

affiliate stations radio or TV stations that, though independently owned, sign a contract to be part of a network and receive money to carry the network's programs; in exchange, the network reserves time slots, which it sells to national advertisers.

agenda-setting a media-research argument that says when the mass media pay attention to particular events or issues, they determine—that is, set the agenda for—the major topics of discussion for individuals and society.

album-oriented rock (AOR) the radio music format that features album cuts from mainstream rock bands.

alternative rock nonmainstream rock music, which includes many types of experimental music and some forms of punk and grunge.

AM amplitude modulation; a type of radio and sound transmission that stresses the volume or height of radio waves.

analog recording a recording that is made by capturing the fluctuations of the original sound waves and storing those signals on records or cassettes as a continuous stream of magnetism—analogous to the actual sound.

analysis the second step in the critical process, it involves discovering significant patterns that emerge from the description stage.

anthology drama a popular form of early TV programming that brought live dramatic theater to television; influenced by stage plays, anthologies offered new teleplays, casts, directors, writers, and sets from week to week.

ARPAnet the original Internet, designed by the U.S. Defense Department's Advanced Research Projects Agency (ARPA).

association principle in advertising, a persuasive technique that associates a product with some cultural value or image that has a positive connotation but may have little connection to the actual product.

astroturf lobbying phony grassroots public affairs campaigns engineered by public relations firms; coined by U.S. Senator Lloyd Bentsen of Texas (named after AstroTurf, the artificial grass athletic field surface).

attack ad a type of political ad that uses repeated negative assaults on another candidate's character.

audiotape lightweight magnetized strands of ribbon that make possible sound editing and multiple-track mixing; instrumentals or vocals can be recorded at one location and later mixed onto a master recording in another studio.

authoritarian model a model for journalism and speech that tolerates little criticism of government or public dissent; it holds that the general public needs guidance from an elite and educated ruling class.

bandwagon effect an advertising strategy that incorporates exaggerated claims that everyone is using a particular product, so you should, too.

barter deal in TV syndication, an arrangement in which no money changes hands between the local station and the syndicator; instead, a syndicator offers a new program to a local TV station in exchange for a portion of the advertising revenue.

basic cable in cable programming, a tier of channels composed of local broadcast signals, nonbroadcast access channels (for local government, education, and general public use), a few regional PBS stations, and a variety of popular channels downlinked from communication satellites.

Big Five/Little Three from the late 1920s through the late 1940s, the major movie studios that were vertically integrated and that dominated the industry. The Big Five were Paramount, MGM, Warner Brothers, Twentieth Century Fox, and RKO. The Little Three were those studios that did not own theaters: Columbia, Universal, and United Artists.

bits a computer term coined from BInary digiTS, which refers to information that represents two values, such as yes/no, on/off, or 0/1.

"black box" technologies any of the newly emerging TV technologies—such as TiVo—that permits viewers to record and save TV programs by digital storage means rather than onto tape via older VCR formats.

block booking an early tactic of movie studios to control exhibition involving pressuring theater operators to accept marginal films with no stars in order to get access to films with the most popular stars.

blockbuster the type of big-budget special effects films that typically have summer or holiday release dates, heavy promotion, and lucrative merchandising tie-ins.

block printing a printing technique developed by early Chinese printers, who hand-carved characters and illustrations into a block of wood, applied ink to the block, and then printed copies on multiple sheets of paper.

blogger an individual who posts or publishes an ongoing personal or opinion journal or log online (from the term *Web-log*).

blues originally a kind of black folk music, this music emerged as a distinct category in the early 1900s; it was influenced by African American spirituals, ballads, and work songs in the rural South, and by urban guitar and vocal solos from the 1930s and 1940s.

books on tape audiotape books that generally feature actors or authors reading abridged versions of popular fiction and nonfiction trade books.

book superstore a large retail business that sells books, recordings, and new media; this contemporary trend in bookselling adapts the large retail store concept to the publishing industry.

bootlegging the illegal counterfeiting or pirating of CDs, cassettes, and videos that are produced and/or sold without official permission from the original songwriter, performer, or copyright holder.

boutique agencies in advertising, small regional ad agencies that offer personalized services.

broadcasting the transmission of radio waves or TV signals to a broad public audience.

browsers information-search services, such as Netscape's Navigator and Microsoft's Internet Explorer, that offer detailed organizational maps to the Internet.

button fatigue in TV audience measurement, the phenomenon of weary viewers failing to log on and report their viewing.

cable franchise in cable television, a local monopoly business awarded by a community to the most attractive cable bidder, usually for a fifteen-year period.

cable music the commercial-free, format-music services offered via cable or DBS.

cash deal in TV syndication, an arrangement in which the distributor of a program offers a series to the highest bidder in a TV market or to a station trying to fill a particular time slot.

cash-plus deal in TV syndication, an arrangement in which the distributor of a program offers a series to the highest bidder in a TV market but retains some time to sell national commercial spots.

CATV (community antenna television) an early cable system that originated where mountains or tall buildings blocked TV signals; because of early technical and regulatory limits, CATV contained only twelve channels.

CD-ROM a computer term coined from Compact-Disc Read-Only Memory; a CD technology that permits the storage of vast amounts of computer software and information (one CD-ROM can store as much information as seven hundred conventional floppy disks).

CD-Rs recordable compact discs that can be recorded only once.

CD-RWs rewriteable compact discs that can be recorded over many times.

celluloid a transparent and pliable film that can hold a coating of chemicals sensitive to light.

channel in mass communication, a medium that delivers messages from senders to receivers.

chapter shows in television production, any situation comedy or dramatic program whose narrative structure includes self-contained stories that feature a problem, a series of conflicts, and a resolution from week to week (for contrast, see **serial programs** and **episodic series**).

cinema verité French term for *truth film*, a documentary style that records fragments of everyday life unobtrusively; it often features a rough, grainy look and shaky, handheld camera work.

clearance rule established in the 1940s by the Justice Department and the FCC, this rule mandated that all local affiliates are ultimately responsible for the content of their channels and must clear, or approve, all network programming.

coaxial cable a system for transmitting TV signals via a solid core of copper-clad aluminum wire encircled by an outer axis of braided wires; these bundles of thin wire accommodate fifty or more separate channels running side by side with virtually no interference.

codex an early type of book in which paperlike sheets were cut and sewed together along the edge, then bound with thin pieces of wood and covered with leather.

commercial speech any print or broadcast expression for which a fee is charged to the organization or individual buying time or space in the mass media.

common carrier a communication or transportation business, such as a phone company or a taxi service, that is required by law to offer service on a first-come, first-served basis to whoever can pay the rate; such companies do not get involved in content.

communication the process of creating symbol systems that convey information and meaning (for example, language, Morse code, film, computer codes).

communist or state model a model for journalism and speech that places control in the hands of an enlightened government, which speaks for ordinary citizens and workers in order to serve the common goals of the state.

compact discs (CDs) playback-only storage discs for music that incorporate pure and very precise digital techniques, thus eliminating noise during recording and editing sessions.

complementary copy positive, upbeat articles—often about food, fashion, and cosmetics—that support the ads carried in various consumer magazines.

conflict of interest considered unethical, a compromising situation in which a journalist stands to benefit personally from the news report he or she produces.

conflict-oriented journalism found in metropolitan areas, newspapers that define news primarily as events, issues, or experiences that deviate from social norms; journalists see their role as observers who monitor their city's institutions and problems.

consensus narrative cultural products that become popular and command wide attention, providing shared cultural experiences.

consensus-oriented journalism found in small communities, newspapers that promote social and economic harmony by providing community calendars and meeting notices and carrying articles on local schools, social events, town government, property crimes, and zoning issues.

contemporary hits radio (CHR) originally called Top 40 radio, this radio format encompasses everything from hip-hop to children's songs; it remains the most popular format in radio for people ages eighteen to twenty-four.

content analysis in social science research, a method for studying and coding media texts and programs.

continuity editing an editing technique that makes space and time seem continuous and seamless; it is used in most traditional Hollywood films.

control group in social-science research, the group that serves as a basis for comparison to the experimental group; the control group has not been exposed to the particular phenomenon or media content being studied.

controlled circulation the process of earning magazine revenue from advertising or corporate sponsorship by targeting captive audiences, such as airline passengers or association members, who receive the publications free.

cookies information profiles about a user that are usually automatically accepted by the Web browser and stored on the user's own computer hard drive.

copy editors the people in magazine, newspaper, and book publishing who attend to specific problems in writing such as style, content, and length.

copyright the legal right of authors and producers to own and control the use of their published or unpublished writing, music, and lyrics; TV programs and movies; or graphic art designs.

Corporation for Public Broadcasting (CPB) a private, nonprofit corporation created by Congress in 1967 to funnel federal funds to nonprofit radio and public television.

counterfeiting the unauthorized copying of CDs, cassettes, and their packaging.

country claiming the largest number of radio stations in the United States, this radio format includes such subdivisions as old-time, progressive, country-rock, western swing, and country-gospel.

cover music songs recorded or performed by musicians who did not originally write or perform the music; in the 1950s, cover music was an attempt by white producers and artists to capitalize on popular songs by blacks.

crisis management in public relations, the strategic response to uncontrolled negative publicity about an individual, client, or company; also known as *damage control*.

critical process the process whereby a media-literate person or student studying mass communication forms and practices employs the techniques of description, analysis, interpretation, evaluation, and engagement.

cultivation effect in media research, the idea that heavy television viewing leads individuals to perceive reality in ways that are consistent with the portrayals they see on television.

cultural imperialism the phenomenon of American media, fashion, and food dominating the global market and shaping the cultures and identities of other nations.

cultural studies in media research, the approaches that try to understand how the media and culture are tied to the actual patterns of communication used in daily life; these studies focus on how people make meanings, apprehend reality, and order experience through the use of stories and symbols.

culture the symbols of expression that individuals, groups, and societies use to make sense of daily life and to articulate their values; a process that delivers the values of a society through products or other meaning-making forms.

cyberspace the region to which the networks of computer communication transport their users—a territory that does not recognize conventional geographic boundaries or social hierarchies.

day parts in radio programming, the division of each day into time blocks—usually 6 to 10 A.M., 10 A.M. to 3 P.M., 3 to 7 P.M., and 7 P.M. to 12 midnight—in order to reach various listening audiences.

DBS (direct broadcast satellites) See **direct broadcast satellites**.

deficit financing in television, the process whereby a TV production company leases its programs to a network for a license fee that is actually less than the cost of production; the company hopes to recoup this loss later in rerun syndication.

deliberative democracy a political culture in which citizen groups, local governments, and the news media join together to actively shape social and political agendas.

demographic editions national magazines whose advertising is tailored to subscribers and readers according to occupation, class, and zip-code address.

demographics in market research, the study of audiences or consumers by age, gender, occupation, ethnicity, education, and income.

description the first step in the critical process, it involves paying close attention, taking notes, and researching the cultural product to be studied.

design managers publishing industry personnel who work on the look of a book, making decisions about type style, paper, cover design, and layout.

desktop publishing a computer technology that enables an aspiring publisher/editor to inexpensively write, design, lay out, and even print a small newsletter or magazine.

developmental editors in book publishing, the editors who provide authors with feedback, make suggestions for improvements, and obtain advice from knowledgeable members of the academic community.

digital communication images, texts, and sounds that use pulses of electric current or flashes of laser lights and are converted (or encoded) into electronic signals represented as varied combinations of binary numbers, usually ones and zeros; these signals are then reassembled (decoded) as a precise reproduction of a TV picture, a magazine article, or a telephone voice.

digital divide the socioeconomic disparity between those who do and do not have access to digital technology and media, such as the Internet.

digital recording music recorded and played back by laser beam rather than by needle or magnetic tape.

digital video the production format that is replacing celluloid film and revolutionizing filmmaking because the cameras are more portable and production costs are much less expensive.

digital video recorder (DVR) A device that enables users to find and record specific television shows (and movies) and store them in a computer memory to be played back at a later time or record them onto a DVD.

dime novels sometimes identified as pulp fiction, these cheaply produced and low-priced novels were popular in the United States beginning in the 1860s.

direct broadcast satellites (DBS) satellite-based services that for a monthly fee downlink hundreds of satellite channels and services; they began distributing video programming directly to households in 1994.

directories review and cataloguing services that group Web sites under particular categories (e.g., Arts & Humanities, News & Media, Entertainment).

direct payment in media economics, the payment of money, primarily by consumers, for a book, a music CD, a movie, an online computer service, or a cable TV subscription.

disassociation corollary in advertising, a persuasive technique that tries to distance the consumer from a large product manufacturer or parent company.

distribution the network of individuals or companies in the mass-media business that delivers media products to various regional, national, and international markets.

documentary a movie or TV news genre that documents reality by recording actual characters and settings.

domain names extensions on Web addresses, such as ".edu," that indicate the origination of a Web site.

domestic comedy a TV hybrid of the sitcom in which characters and settings are usually more important than complicated situations; it generally features a domestic problem or work issue that characters have to solve.

dramedy in TV programming, a narrative that blurs serious and comic themes.

drive time in radio programming, the periods between 6 and 10 A.M. and 4 and 7 P.M., when people are commuting to and from work or school; these periods constitute the largest listening audiences of the day.

DVD digital video disc, a digital storage format that looks like a CD but has greater capacity, enabling it to handle feature-length films as well as graphics, video, multichannel audio, and interactivity.

e-books electronic books that can be downloaded to portable e-book reading devices.

e-commerce electronic commerce, or commercial activity, on the Web.

economies of scale the economic process of increasing production levels so as to reduce the overall cost per unit.

electromagnetic waves invisible electronic impulses similar to visible light; electricity, magnetism, light, broadcast signals, and heat are part of such waves, which radiate in space at the speed of light, about 186,000 miles per second.

electronica often referred to as "techno," an underground music genre that developed in the 1990s; it features keyboards, drum machine beats, and music samples often sequenced with computers.

electronic publisher a communication business, such as a broadcaster or a cable TV company, that is entitled to choose what channels or content to carry.

e-mail electronic mail messages sent by the Internet; developed by computer engineer Ray Tomlinson in 1971.

episodic series a narrative form well suited to television because main characters appear every week, sets and locales remain the same, and technical crews stay with the program; episodic series feature new adventures each week, but a handful of characters emerge with whom viewers can regularly identify (for contrast, see **chapter shows**).

e-publishing Internet-based publishing houses that design and distribute books for comparatively low prices for authors who want to self-publish a title.

ethnocentrism an underlying value held by many U.S. journalists and citizens, it involves judging other countries and cultures according to how they live up to or imitate American practices and ideals.

evaluation the fourth step in the critical process, it involves arriving at a judgment about whether a cultural product is good, bad, or mediocre; this requires subordinating one's personal taste to the critical assessment resulting from the first three stages (description, analysis, and interpretation).

evergreens in TV syndication, popular and lucrative enduring network reruns such as the *Andy Griffith Show* or *I Love Lucy*.

exhibition the individuals or companies in the mass media business who exhibit media products; the term usually refers to companies that control movie theaters.

experiment in regard to the mass media, research that isolates some aspect of content, suggests a hypothesis, and manipulates variables to discover a particular medium's impact on attitudes, emotions, or behavior.

experimental group in social science research, the group under study that has been exposed to a particular phenomenon or media content.

Fairness Doctrine repealed in 1987, this FCC rule required broadcast stations to both air and engage in controversial-issue programs that affected their communities and, when offering such programming, to provide competing points of view.

famous-person testimonial an advertising strategy that associates a product with the endorsement of a well-known person.

feature syndicates commercial outlets or brokers, such as United Features and King Features, that contract with newspapers to provide work from well-known political writers, editorial cartoonists, comic-strip artists, and self-help columnists.

Federal Communications Act of 1934 the far-reaching act that established the FCC and the federal regulatory structure for U.S. broadcasting.

Federal Communications Commission (FCC) an independent U.S. government agency charged with regulating interstate and international communications by radio, television, wire, satellite, and cable.

Federal Radio Commission (FRC) established in 1927 to oversee radio licenses and negotiate channel problems.

feedback responses from receivers to the senders of messages.

fiber-optic cable thin glass bundles of fiber capable of transmitting thousands of messages converted to shooting pulses of light along cable wires; these bundles of fiber can carry broadcast channels, telephone signals, and all sorts of digital codes.

film noir French for *black film,* this film genre is usually shot in black and white, uses low-lighting techniques, shows few daytime scenes, displays bleak urban settings, and explores the sinister side of human nature.

Financial Interest and Syndication Rules (fin-syn) FCC rules that prohibited the major networks from running their own syndication companies or from charging production companies additional fees after shows had completed their prime-time runs; most fin-syn rules were rescinded in the mid-1990s.

first-run syndication in television, the process whereby new programs are specifically produced for sale in syndication markets rather than for network television.

flack a derogatory term that journalists use to refer to a public relations agent.

FM frequency modulation; a type of radio and sound transmission that offers static-less reception and greater fidelity and clarity than AM radio by accentuating the pitch or distance between radio waves.

focus group a common research method in psychographic analysis in which a moderator leads a small-group discussion about a product or an issue, usually with six to twelve people.

folk music music performed by untrained musicians and passed down through oral traditions; it encompasses a wide range of music, from Appalachian fiddle tunes to the accordion-led zydeco of Louisiana.

folk-rock amplified folk music, often featuring politically overt lyrics; influenced by rock and roll.

format radio the concept of radio stations developing and playing specific styles (or formats) geared to listeners' age, race, or gender; in format radio, management, rather than deejays, controls programming choices.

Fourth Estate the notion that the press operates as an unofficial branch of government, monitoring the legislative, judicial, and executive branches for abuses of power.

franchise fees the money a cable company pays a city annually for the right to operate the local cable system;

these fees are limited by law to no more than 5 percent of the company's gross annual revenue.

fringe time in television, the time slot either immediately before the evening's prime-time schedule (called *early fringe*) or immediately following the local evening news or the network's late-night talk shows (called *late fringe*).

gag orders legal restrictions prohibiting the press from releasing preliminary information that might prejudice jury selection.

gangster rap a style of rap music that depicts the hardships of urban life and sometimes glorifies the violent style of street gangs.

gatekeepers editors, producers, and other media managers who function as message filters, making decisions about what types of messages actually get produced for particular audiences.

general-interest magazine a type of magazine that addresses a wide variety of topics and is aimed at a broad national audience.

genre a narrative category in which conventions regarding similar characters, scenes, structures, and themes recur in combination.

geo-synchronous orbit the orbit in space, 22,300 miles above the earth, where communication satellites traveling at about 6,800 miles per hour can maintain the same position (or "footprint") above the earth as the planet rotates on its axis.

gotcha stories news reports in which journalists nab evil-doers or interview subjects who were caught in an act of deception.

grunge rock music that takes the spirit of punk and infuses it with more attention to melody.

halo effect in TV audience measurement, the phenomenon of viewers reporting not what they actually watched but what they think they should have watched.

happy talk in TV journalism, the ad-libbed or scripted banter that goes on among local news anchors, reporters, meteorologists, and sportscasters before and after news reports.

headend a cable TV system's computerized nerve center, where TV signals from local broadcast stations and satellites are received, processed, and distributed to area homes.

herd journalism a situation in which reporters stake out a house or follow a story in such large groups that the entire profession comes under attack for invading people's privacy or exploiting their personal tragedies.

hidden-fear appeal an advertising strategy that plays on a sense of insecurity, trying to persuade consumers that only a specific product can offer relief.

high culture a symbolic expression that has come to mean "good taste"; often supported by wealthy patrons and corporate donors, it is associated with fine art (such as ballet, the symphony, painting, and classical literature), which is available primarily in theaters or museums.

high-definition television (HDTV) a new digital standard for U.S. television sets that has more than twice the resolution of the system that served as the standard from the 1940s through the 1990s.

hip-hop music that combines spoken street dialect with cuts (or samples) from older records and bears the influences of social politics, male boasting, and comic lyrics carried forward from blues, R&B, soul, and rock and roll.

Hollywood Ten the nine screenwriters and one film director subpoenaed by the House Un-American Activities Committee (HUAC) who were sent to prison in the late 1940s for refusing to discuss their memberships or to identify communist sympathizers.

HTML (HyperText Markup Language) the written code that creates Web pages and links; a language all computers can read.

human-interest stories news accounts that focus on the trials and tribulations of the human condition, often featuring ordinary individuals facing extraordinary challenges.

hypertext a data-linking feature of the World Wide Web, it enables a user to click on a highlighted word or phrase and skip directly to other files related to that subject in other computer systems.

hypodermic-needle model an early model in mass communication research that attempted to explain media effects by arguing that the media shoot their powerful effects directly into unsuspecting or weak audiences; sometimes called the *bullet theory* or *direct effects model*.

hypotheses in social science research, tentative general statements that predict a relationship between a dependent variable and an independent variable.

illuminated manuscripts books from the Middle Ages that featured decorative, colorful designs and illustrations on each page.

independent station a TV station, such as WGN in Chicago or WTBS in Atlanta, that finds its own original and syndicated programming and is not affiliated with any of the major networks.

indies independent music and film production houses that work outside industry oligopolies; they often produce less mainstream music and film.

indirect payment in media economics, the financial support of media products by advertisers, who pay for the quantity or quality of audience members that a particular medium attracts.

individualism an underlying value held by most U.S. journalists and citizens, it favors individual rights and responsibilities over group needs or institutional mandates.

infomercials thirty-minute late-night and daytime programs that usually feature fading TV and music celebrities, who advertise a product in a format that looks like a talk show.

information highway the circulation of both personal communication and mass media on personal computers and modems, high-speed telephone links, communication satellites, and television screens.

infotainment a type of television program that packages human-interest and celebrity stories in TV news style.

ink-jet imaging a computer technique that enables a magazine publisher or advertiser to print personalized messages to individual subscribers.

instant book in the book industry, a marketing strategy that involves publishing a topical book quickly after a major event occurs.

instant messaging services a Web feature that enables users to chat with buddies in real time via pop-up windows assigned to each conversation.

interactive cable television two-way cable channels that enable users to connect to their local services, such as banks and the fire department, and also offer two-way entertainment, such as play-along versions of game shows and the ability to guess the next play during a football game.

interactivity a communication process that allows immediate two-way communication (as via telephones or e-mail) between senders and receivers of media messages.

Internet the vast central network of high-speed telephone lines designed to link and carry computer information worldwide.

Internet2 (I2) the next generation of online technology, deployed on an experimental basis in 1999, that is expected to be one thousand times faster than today's Internet.

Internet radio online radio stations that either "stream" simulcast versions of on-air radio broadcasts over the Web, or are created exclusively for the Internet.

Internet service provider (ISP) a company that provides Internet access to homes and businesses for a fee.

interpretation the third step in the critical process, it asks and answers the "What does that mean?" and "So what?" questions about one's findings.

interpretive journalism a type of journalism that involves analyzing and explaining key issues or events and placing them in a broader historical or social context.

interstitials advertisements that pop up in a new screen window as a user attempts to access a new Web page.

invasion of privacy the violation of a person's right to be left alone, without his or her name, image, or daily activities becoming public property.

inverted-pyramid style a style of journalism in which news reports begin with the most dramatic or newsworthy information—answering *who, what, where,* and *when* (and less frequently *why* or *how*) questions at the top of the story—and then tail off with less significant details.

irritation advertising an advertising strategy that tries to create product-name recognition by being annoying or obnoxious.

jazz an improvisational and mostly instrumental musical form that absorbs and integrates a diverse body of musical styles, including African rhythms, blues, big band, and gospel.

joint operating agreement (JOA) in the newspaper industry, an economic arrangement, sanctioned by the government, that permits competing newspapers to operate separate editorial divisions while merging business and production operations.

kinescope before the days of videotape, a 1950s technique for preserving television broadcasts by using a film camera to record a live TV show off a studio monitor.

kinetograph an early movie camera developed by Thomas Edison's assistant in the 1890s.

kinetoscope an early film projection system that served as a kind of peep show in which viewers looked through a hole and saw images moving on a tiny plate.

leased channels in cable television, channels that allow citizens to buy time for producing programs or presenting their own viewpoints.

libel in media law, the defamation of character in written expression.

libertarian model a model for journalism and speech that encourages vigorous government criticism and supports the highest degree of freedom for individual speech and news operations.

limited competition in media economics, a market with many producers and sellers but only a few differentiable products within a particular category; sometimes called *monopolistic competition.*

linotype a technology introduced in the nineteenth century that enabled printers to set type mechanically using a typewriter-style keyboard.

literary journalism news reports that adapt fictional storytelling techniques to nonfictional material; sometimes called *new journalism.*

lobbying in government public relations, the process of attempting to influence the voting of lawmakers to support a client's or an organization's best interests.

longitudinal studies a term used for research studies that are conducted over long periods of time and often rely on large government and academic survey databases.

low culture a symbolic expression allegedly aligned with the questionable tastes of the "masses," who enjoy the commercial "junk" circulated by the mass media, such as soap operas, rock music, talk radio, comic books, and monster truck pulls.

low power FM (LPFM) a new class of noncommercial radio stations approved by the FCC in 2000 to give voice to local groups lacking access to the public airwaves; the 10-watt and 100-watt stations broadcast to a small, community-based area.

magazine a nondaily periodical that comprises a collection of articles, stories, and ads.

manuscript culture a period during the Middle Ages when priests and monks advanced the art of bookmaking.

market research in advertising and public relations agencies, the department that uses social science techniques to assess the behaviors and attitudes of consumers toward particular products before any ads are created.

mass communication the process of designing and delivering cultural messages and stories to diverse audiences through media channels as old as the book and as new as the Internet.

mass customization the process whereby product companies and content providers customize a Web page, print ad, or other media form for an individual consumer.

mass market paperbacks low-priced paperback books sold mostly on racks in drugstores, supermarkets, and airports, as well as in bookstores.

mass media the cultural industries—the channels of communication—that produce and distribute songs, novels, news, movies, online computer services, and other cultural products to a large number of people.

mass media channel newspapers, books, magazines, radio, television, or the Internet.

mechanical royalty the copyright fee, usually about one-half cent for each CD or audiotape sold, received by songwriters and publishers when they allow their music to be recorded.

media buyers in advertising, the individuals who choose and purchase the types of media that are best suited to carry a client's ads and reach the targeted audience.

media convergence the process whereby old and new media are available via the integration of personal computers and high-speed satellite-based phone or cable links.

media effects research the mainstream tradition in mass communication research, it attempts to understand, explain, and predict the impact—or effects—of the mass media on individuals and society.

media literacy an understanding of the mass communication process through the development of critical thinking tools—description, analysis, interpretation, evaluation, engagement—that enable a person to become more engaged as a citizen and more discerning as a consumer of mass media products.

mega-agencies in advertising, large firms or holding companies that are formed by merging several individual agencies and that maintain worldwide regional offices; they provide both advertising and public relations services and operate in-house radio and TV production studios.

megaplexes movie theater facilities with fourteen or more screens.

messages the texts, images, and sounds transmitted from senders to receivers.

microchips/microprocessors miniature circuits that process and store electronic signals, integrating thousands of electronic components into thin strands of silicon along which binary codes travel.

minimal-effects model a mass communication research model based on tightly controlled experiments and survey findings; it argues that the mass media have limited effects on audiences, reinforcing existing behaviors and attitudes rather than changing them.

miniseries a serial television program that runs over a two-day to two-week period, usually on consecutive nights.

modern period a historical era spanning the time from the rise of the Industrial Revolution in the eighteenth and nineteenth centuries to the present; its social values include celebrating the individual, believing in rational order, working efficiently, and rejecting tradition.

monopoly in media economics, an organizational structure that occurs when a single firm dominates production and distribution in a particular industry, either nationally or locally.

Morse code a system of sending electrical impulses from a transmitter through a cable to a reception point; developed by the American inventor Samuel Morse.

movie palaces ornate, lavish single-screen movie theaters that emerged in the 1910s in the United States.

MP3 short for MPEG-1 Layer 3, an advanced type of audio compression that reduces file size, enabling audio to be easily distributed over the Internet and to be digitally transmitted in real time.

muckraking a style of early-twentieth-century investigative journalism that referred to reporters who were willing to crawl around in society's muck to uncover a story.

multiple-system operators (MSOs) large corporations that own numerous cable television systems.

multiplexes contemporary movie theaters that exhibit many movies at the same time on multiple screens.

must-carry rules rules established by the FCC requiring all cable operators to assign channels to and carry all local TV broadcasts on their systems, thereby ensuring that local network affiliates, independent stations (those not carrying network programs), and public television channels would benefit from cable's clearer reception.

myth analysis a strategy for critiquing advertising that provides insights into how ads work on a cultural level; according to this strategy, ads are narratives with stories to tell and social conflicts to resolve.

narrative the structure underlying most media products, it includes two components: the story (what happens to whom) and the discourse (how the story is told).

narrative films movies that tell a story, with dramatic action and conflict emerging mainly from individual characters.

narrowcasting any specialized electronic programming or media channel aimed at a target audience.

National Public Radio (NPR) noncommercial radio established in 1967 by the U.S. Congress to provide an alternative to commercial radio.

network a broadcast process that links, through special phone lines or satellite transmissions, groups of radio or TV stations that share programming produced at a central location.

network era the period in television history, roughly from the mid-1950s to the late 1970s, that refers to the dominance of the Big Three networks—ABC, CBS, and NBC—over programming and prime-time viewing habits; the era began eroding with a decline in viewing and with the development of VCRs, cable, and new TV networks.

news the process of gathering information and making narrative reports—edited by individuals in a news organization—that create selected frames of reference and help the public make sense of prominent people, important events, and unusual happenings in everyday life.

newsgroups organized computer conferences consisting of bulletin boards and individual messages, or postings, that are circulated twenty-four hours a day via the Internet and cover a range of topics.

newshole the space left over in a newspaper for news content after all the ads are placed.

newspaper chains large companies that own several papers throughout the country.

newsreels weekly ten-minute magazine-style compilations of filmed news events from around the world organized in a sequence of short reports; prominent in movie theaters between the 1920s and the 1950s.

news/talk the fastest-growing radio format in the 1990s.

newsworthiness the often unstated criteria that journalists use to determine which events and issues should become news reports, including timeliness, proximity, conflict, prominence, human interest, consequence, usefulness, novelty, and deviance.

nickelodeons the first small makeshift movie theaters, which were often converted cigar stores, pawnshops, or restaurants redecorated to mimic vaudeville theaters.

O & Os TV stations "owned and operated" by networks.

objective journalism a modern style of journalism that distinguishes factual reports from opinion columns; reporters strive to remain neutral toward the issue or event they cover, searching out competing points of view among the sources for a story.

objectivity in social science research, the elimination of bias and judgments on the part of researchers.

obscenity expression that is not protected as speech if these three legal tests are all met: (1) the average person, applying contemporary community standards, would find that the material as a whole appeals to prurient interest; (2) the material depicts or describes sexual conduct in a patently offensive way; (3) the material, as a whole, lacks serious literary, artistic, political, or scientific value.

off-network syndication in television, the process whereby older programs that no longer run during prime time are made available for reruns to local stations, cable operators, online services, and foreign markets.

offset lithography a technology that enabled books to be printed from photographic plates rather than metal casts, reducing the cost of color and illustrations and eventually permitting computers to perform typesetting.

oligopoly in media economics, an organizational structure in which a few firms control most of an industry's production and distribution resources.

open-source software noncommercial software shared freely and developed collectively on the Internet.

opt-in/opt-out policies controversial Web site policies over personal data gathering: *opt in* means Web sites must gain explicit permission from online consumers before the site can collect their personal data; *opt out* means that Web sites can automatically collect personal data unless the consumer goes to the trouble of filling out a specific form to restrict the practice.

option time now considered illegal, a procedure whereby a radio network paid an affiliate station a set fee per hour for an option to control programming and advertising on that station.

Pacifica Foundation a radio broadcasting foundation established in Berkeley, California, by journalist and World War II pacifist Lewis Hill; he established KPFA, the first nonprofit community radio station in 1949.

paid circulation the process of earning magazine revenue from consumers who pay either for regular subscriptions or for individual copies at newsstands or supermarkets.

paperback books books made with cheap paper covers, introduced in the United States in the mid-1800s.

papyrus one of the first substances to hold written language and symbols; obtained from plant reeds found along the Nile River.

Paramount decision the 1948 Supreme Court decision that ended vertical integration in the film industry by forcing the studios to divest themselves of their theaters.

parchment treated animal skin that replaced papyrus as an early pre-paper substance on which to document written language.

partisan press an early dominant style of American journalism distinguished by opinion newspapers, which generally argued one political point of view or pushed the plan of the particular party that subsidized the paper.

pass-along readership the total number of people who come into contact with a single copy of a magazine.

pay-for-play up-front payments from record companies to radio stations to play a song a specific number of times.

payola the unethical (but not always illegal) practice of record promoters paying deejays or radio programmers to favor particular songs over others.

pay-per-view (PPV) a cable-television service that allows customers to select a particular movie for a fee, or to pay $25 to $40 for a special onetime event.

penny papers (also *penny press*) refers to newspapers that, because of technological innovations in printing, were able to drop their price to one cent beginning in the 1830s, thereby making papers affordable to working and emerging middle classes and enabling newspapers to become a genuine mass medium.

people meters in TV audience measurement, devices that are hooked up to a random sample of households to determine their viewing behavior.

performance royalty the copyright fee paid to songwriters and performers whenever their music is used on radio, television, or other media channels.

photojournalism the use of photos to document events and people's lives.

piracy the illegal uploading, downloading, or streaming of copyrighted material, such as music.

plain-folks pitch an advertising strategy that associates a product with simplicity and the common person.

podcasting enables listeners to download audio program files from the Internet for playback on computers or digital music players.

political advertising the use of ad techniques to promote a candidate's image and persuade the public to adopt a particular viewpoint.

pop music popular music that appeals either to a wide cross section of the public or to sizable subdivisions within the larger public based on age, region, or ethnic background; the word *pop* has also been used as a label to distinguish popular music from classical music.

portal an entry point to the Internet, such as a search engine.

postmodern period a contemporary historical era spanning the 1960s to the present; its social values include opposing hierarchy, diversifying and recycling culture, questioning scientific reasoning, and embracing paradox.

precision journalism a type of journalism that attempts to push news reporting in the direction of science, maintaining that by applying rigorous social science methods, such as using poll surveys and questionnaires, journalism can better offer a valid portrait of social reality.

premium channels in cable programming, a tier of channels that subscribers can order at an additional monthly fee over their basic cable service; these may include movie channels and interactive services.

press agent the earliest type of public relations practitioner, who sought to advance a client's image through media exposure.

press release in public relations, an announcement—written in the style of a news report—that gives new information about an individual, a company, or an organization and pitches a story idea to the news media.

prime time in television programming, the hours between 8 and 11 P.M. (or 7 and 10 P.M. in the Midwest), when networks have traditionally drawn their largest audiences and charged their highest advertising rates.

Prime-Time Access Rule (PTAR) an FCC rule that in 1970 took the 7:30 to 8 P.M. time slot (6:30 to 7 P.M. Central) away from the TV networks and gave it exclusively to local stations in the nation's fifty largest television markets.

printing press a fifteenth-century invention whose movable metallic type technology spawned modern mass communication by creating the first method for mass production; it reduced the size and cost of books, made them the first mass medium affordable to less affluent people, and provided the impetus for the Industrial Revolution, assembly-line production, modern capitalism, and the rise of consumer culture.

prior restraint the legal definition of censorship in the United States, which prohibits courts and governments from blocking any publication or speech before it actually occurs.

production the network of individuals or companies in the mass media business in charge of creating movies, TV programs, music recordings, magazines, books, and other media products.

product placement the advertising practice of strategically placing products in movies, TV shows, comic books, and video games so the products appear as part of a story's set environment.

professional books technical books that target various occupational groups and are not intended for the general consumer market.

program-length commercials thirty-minute cartoon programs developed for TV syndication primarily to promote a line of toys.

propaganda in advertising and public relations, a communication strategy that tries to manipulate public opinion to gain support for a special issue, program, or policy, such as a nation's war effort.

pseudo-event in public relations, any circumstance or event created solely for the purpose of obtaining coverage in the media.

pseudo-polls typically call-in, online, or person-in-the-street polls that news media use to address a "question of the day."

psychographics in market research, the study of audience or consumer attitudes, beliefs, interests, and motivations.

Public Broadcasting Act of 1967 the act by the U.S. Congress that established the Corporation for Public Broadcasting, which oversees the Public Broadcasting Service (PBS) and National Public Radio (NPR).

Public Broadcasting Service (PBS) the noncommercial television network established in 1967 as an alternative to commercial television.

public journalism a type of journalism, driven by citizen forums, that goes beyond telling the news to embrace a broader mission of improving the quality of public life; also called *civic journalism*.

public relations the total communication strategy conducted by a person, a government, or an organization attempting to reach and persuade its audiences to adopt a point of view.

publicity in public relations, the positive and negative messages that spread controlled and uncontrolled information about a person, corporation, issue, or policy in various media.

public service announcements (PSAs) reports or announcements, carried free by radio and TV stations, that promote government programs, educational projects, voluntary agencies, or social reform.

publishing houses companies that try to identify and produce the works of good writers.

puffery bordering on deception, advertisements that use hyperbole and exaggeration.

pulp fiction a term used to describe many late nineteenth-century popular paperbacks and dime novels, which were constructed of cheap machine-made pulp material.

punk rock rock music that challenges the orthodoxy and commercialism of the recording business; it is characterized by loud, unpolished qualities, a jackhammer beat, primal vocal screams, crude aggression, and defiant or comic lyrics.

qualified privilege a legal right allowing journalists to report judicial or legislative proceedings even though the public statements being reported may be libelous.

rack jobbers sales agents in the music business who contract with general retailers such as Wal-Mart to stock their racks or shelves with the latest CDs, audiocassettes, and music videos.

Radio Act of 1912 the first radio legislation passed by Congress, it addressed the problem of amateur radio operators increasingly cramming the airwaves.

Radio Act of 1927 the second radio legislation passed by Congress; in an attempt to restore order to the airwaves, it stated that licensees did not own their channels but could license them as long as they operated in order to serve the "public interest, convenience, or necessity."

Radio Corporation of America (RCA) a company developed during World War I that was designed, with government approval, to pool radio patents; the formation of RCA gave the United States almost total control over the emerging mass medium of broadcasting.

radio waves a portion of the electromagnetic wave spectrum that was harnessed so that signals could be sent from a transmission point and obtained at a reception point.

random assignment a social science research method for assigning research subjects; it ensures that every subject has an equal chance of being placed in either the experimental group or the control group.

rating in TV audience measurement, a statistical estimate expressed as a percentage of households tuned to a program in the local or national market being sampled.

receivers the target of messages crafted by a sender.

reference books dictionaries, encyclopedias, atlases, and other reference manuals related to particular professions or trades.

regional editions national magazines whose content is tailored to the interests of different geographic areas.

reliability in social science research, getting the same answers or outcomes from a study or measure during repeated testing.

religious books Bibles, hymnals, and other materials related to religious observances.

rerun syndication in television, the process whereby programs that stay in a network's lineup long enough to build up a certain number of episodes (usually four seasons' worth) are sold, or syndicated, to hundreds of TV markets in the United States and abroad.

responsible capitalism an underlying value held by many U.S. journalists and citizens, it assumes that businesspeople compete with one another not primarily to maximize profits but to increase prosperity for all.

retransmission consent consent periodically given by commercial broadcast stations permitting cable companies to retransmit their signal on cable, usually in exchange for monetary compensation from the cable companies.

rhythm and blues (R&B) music that merged urban blues with big-band sounds.

rockabilly music that mixed bluegrass and country influences with those of black folk music and early amplified blues.

rock and roll music that mixed the vocal and instrumental traditions of popular music; it merged the black influences of urban blues, gospel, and R&B with the white influences of country, folk, and pop vocals.

rotation in format radio programming, the practice of playing the most popular or best-selling songs many times throughout the day.

satellite radio pay radio services that deliver various radio formats nationally via satellite.

saturation advertising the strategy of inundating a variety of print and visual media with ads aimed at target audiences.

scientific method a widely used research method that studies phenomena in systematic stages; it includes identifying the research problem, reviewing existing research, developing working hypotheses, determining appropriate research design, collecting information, analyzing results to see if the hypotheses have been verified, and interpreting the implications of the study.

scoop an exclusive story obtained by a journalist, who publicly presents the story ahead of all rivals.

search engines computer programs that allow users to enter key words or queries to find related sites on the Internet.

Section 315 part of the 1934 Communications Act; it mandates that during elections, broadcast stations must provide equal opportunities and response time for qualified political candidates.

seditious libel in law, the act of defaming a public official's character in print.

selective exposure the phenomenon whereby audiences seek messages and meanings that correspond to their preexisting beliefs and values.

selective retention the phenomenon whereby audiences remember or retain messages and meanings that correspond to their preexisting beliefs and values.

senders the authors, producers, agencies, and organizations that transmit messages to receivers.

serial programs radio or TV programs, such as soap operas, that feature continuing story lines from day to day or week to week (for contrast, see **chapter shows**).

servers individual "host" computer centers run (or hosted) by universities, corporations, and government agencies, all of which are connected to the Internet by special high-speed phone lines.

share in TV audience measurement, a statistical estimate of the percentage of homes tuned to a certain program, compared with those simply using their sets at the time of a sample.

shield laws laws protecting the confidentiality of key interview subjects and reporters' rights not to reveal the sources of controversial information used in news stories.

shortwave radio a type of radio transmission, used mostly by amateur—or ham—radio operators and governments, that can bounce a radio signal off the ionosphere to locations halfway around the world.

situational ethics the principle that in a moral society ethical decisions are arrived at on an individual or case-by-case basis.

situation comedy (sitcom) a type of comedy series that features a recurring cast and set as well as several narrative scenes; each episode establishes a situation, complicates it, develops increasing confusion among its characters, and then resolves the complications.

sketch comedies short television comedy skits that are usually segments of TV variety shows; sometimes known as *vaudeo*, the marriage of vaudeville and video.

slander in law, spoken language that defames a person's character.

slogan in advertising, a catchy phrase that attempts to promote or sell a product by capturing its essence in words.

small-town pastoralism an underlying value held by many U.S. journalists and citizens, it favors the small over the large and the rural over the urban.

snob appeal an advertising strategy that attempts to convince consumers that using a product will enable them to maintain or elevate their social station.

social responsibility model a model for journalism and speech, influenced by the libertarian model, that encourages the free flow of information to citizens so they can make wise decisions regarding political and social issues.

soul music music that mixes gospel, blues, and urban and southern black styles with slower, more emotional, and melancholic lyrics.

sound bite in TV journalism, the equivalent of a quote in print; the part of a news report in which an expert, a celebrity, a victim, or a person on the street is interviewed about some aspect of an event or issue.

space brokers in the days before modern advertising, individuals who purchased space in newspapers and sold it to various merchants.

spam a computer term referring to unsolicited e-mail.

spin doctors political consultants who manage campaigns and attempt to favorably shape the news media's image of a candidate.

split-run editions editions of national magazines that tailor ads to different geographic areas.

spyware software with secretive codes that enable commercial firms to "spy" on users and gain access to their computers.

stereo the recording of two separate channels or tracks of sound.

stereotyping the process of assigning individuals to groups, whose members are falsely assumed to act as a single entity and to display certain characteristics, which are usually negative.

storyboard in advertising, a blueprint or roughly drawn comic-strip version of a proposed advertisement.

stripping in TV syndication, the showing of programs—either older network reruns or programs made for syndication—five days a week.

studio system an early film production system that constituted a sort of assembly-line process for moviemaking; major film studios controlled not only actors but also directors, editors, writers, and other employees, all of whom worked under exclusive contracts.

subliminal advertising a 1950s term that refers to hidden or disguised print and visual messages that allegedly register on the unconscious, creating false needs and seducing people into buying products.

subsidiary rights in the book industry, selling the rights to a book for use in other media forms, such as a mass market paperback, a CD-ROM, or the basis for a movie screenplay.

supermarket tabloids newspapers that feature bizarre human-interest stories, gruesome murder tales, violent accident accounts, unexplained phenomena stories, and malicious celebrity gossip.

superstations local independent TV stations, such as WTBS in Atlanta or WGN in Chicago, that have uplinked their signals onto a communication satellite to make themselves available nationwide.

survey research in social science research, a method of collecting and measuring data taken from a group of respondents.

sweeps in TV ratings, month-long measurement periods—conducted four times a year (six times in larger markets)—that determine both local and national ad rates.

syndicated exclusivity (syndex) repealed in 1980, FCC rules that gave local stations exclusive rights in their area to syndicate TV programs, such as off-network reruns, that they had purchased.

synergy in media economics, the promotion and sale of a product (and all its versions) throughout the various subsidiaries of a media conglomerate.

talkies movies with sound, beginning in 1927.

Telecommunications Act of 1996 the sweeping update of telecommunications law that led to a wave of media consolidation.

telegraph invented in the 1840s, it sent electrical impulses through a cable from a transmitter to a reception point, transmitting Morse code.

textbooks books made for the el-hi (elementary and high school) and college markets.

textual analysis in media research, a method for closely and critically examining and interpreting the meanings of culture, including architecture, fashion, books, movies, and TV programs.

time shifting the process whereby television viewers tape shows and watch them later, when it is convenient for them.

Top 40 format the first radio format, in which stations played the forty most popular hits in a given week as measured by record sales.

trade books the most visible book industry segment, featuring hardbound and paperback books aimed at general readers and sold at bookstores and other retail outlets.

transistor invented by Bell Laboratories in 1947, this tiny technology, which receives and amplifies radio signals, made portable radios possible.

transponders the relay points on a communication satellite that receive and transmit telephone and TV signals.

TV newsmagazines a TV news program format, pioneered by CBS's *60 Minutes* in the late 1960s, that features multiple segments in an hour-long episode, usually ranging from a celebrity or political feature story to a hard-hitting investigative report.

UHF ultrahigh frequency; in broadcasting, the band in the electromagnetic spectrum that the FCC allocated for TV channels 14 through 69.

underground press radical newspapers, run on shoestring budgets, that question mainstream political policies and conventional values; the term usually refers to a journalism movement of the 1960s.

university press the segment of the book industry that publishes scholarly books in specialized areas.

urban one of radio's more popular formats, primarily targeting African American listeners in urban areas with dance, R&B, and hip-hop music.

uses and gratifications model a mass communication research model, usually employing in-depth interviews and survey questionnaires, that argues that people use the media to satisfy various emotional desires or intellectual needs.

validity in social science research, demonstrating that a study actually measures what it claims to measure.

Values and Lifestyles (VALS) a market-research strategy that divides consumers into types and measures psychological factors, including how consumers think and feel about products and how they achieve (or do not achieve) the lifestyles to which they aspire.

vellum a handmade paper made from treated animal skin, used in the Gutenberg Bibles.

vertical integration in media economics, the phenomenon of controlling a mass media industry at its three essential levels: production, distribution, and exhibition; the term is most frequently used in reference to the film industry.

VHF very high frequency; in broadcasting, the band in the electromagnetic spectrum that the FCC allocated for TV channels 2 through 13.

videocassette recorders (VCRs) recorders that use a half-inch video format known as VHS (video home system), which enables viewers to record and play back programs from television or to watch movies rented from video stores.

video news release (VNR) in public relations, the visual counterpart to a press release; it pitches a story idea to the TV news media by mimicking the style of a broadcast news report.

video-on-demand (VOD) cable television technology that enables viewers to instantly order programming such as movies to be digitally delivered to their sets.

virtual communities groups of computer users who are separated geographically but connected nationally and globally by their shared interests or business and their access to an online service or the Internet.

vitascope a large-screen movie projection system developed by Thomas Edison.

Webzines magazines that publish on the Internet.

weighting in TV audience measurement, assigning more weight to a particular respondent in an attempt to correct the underrepresented group in the original sample.

wireless telegraphy the forerunner of radio, a form of voiceless point-to-point communication; it preceded the voice and sound transmissions of one-to-many mass communication that became known as broadcasting.

wireless telephony early experiments in wireless voice and music transmissions, which later developed into modern radio.

wire services commercial organizations, such as the Associated Press, that share news stories and information by relaying them around the country and the world, originally via telegraph and now via satellite transmission.

world music sometimes called *international* or *ethnic songs*, this category includes the many different styles of popular regional and folk music from cultures throughout the world; it usually excludes classical music and the most popular forms of American or European music.

World Wide Web (WWW) a free and open data-linking system for organizing and standardizing information on the Internet; the WWW enables computer-accessed information to associate with—or link to—other information no matter where it is on the Internet.

yellow journalism a newspaper style or era that peaked in the 1890s, it emphasized high-interest stories, sensational crime news, large headlines, and serious reports that exposed corruption, particularly in business and government.

zapping using a VCR to edit out commercials during the videotaping process.

zines self-published magazines produced on personal computer programs or on the Internet.

zipping using a VCR to fast-forward a videotaped program through the ads during the recorded viewing.

credits

Text Credits

6, David Halberstam. Quote from "Why America Napped." This article first appeared in Salon.com at http://www .Salon.com. October 1, 2001. Copyright (c) 2001. An online version remains in the Salon archives. Reprinted with permission. 2001. Reprinted with permission of Salon.com. All rights reserved. **14,** Table 1.1: "Hours per Person per Year Using Consumer Media." Veronis Suhlar Stevenson Communications Industry Forecast. Reprinted with permission. **47,** Figure 2.1: "Distributed Networks." Excerpted data from p. 59 in *Where Wizards Stay Up Late* by Katie Hafner and Matthew Lyon. (c) 1996 by Katie Hafner and Matthew Lyon. Reprinted with permission of Simon & Schuster Adult Publishing Group. **55,** Amy Harmon. Brief quote from *The New York Times,* 1998. Copyright (c) 1998 by The New York Times Company. Reprinted with permission. Table 2.1: "Top 10 Internet Parent Companies in the United States." From Nielsen/Netratings "Top 10 Web Sites by Parent Company," March 14, 2006. Copyright (c) 2006. www.nielsen-netratings.com. **63,** Tom Zeller Jr. "Keylogging." Excerpted from "Cyberthieves Silently Copy as You Type," in *The New York Times,* February 27, 2006, A1. Copyright (c) 2006 by The New York Times Company. Reprinted with permission. **79,** Figure 3.1: "Annual Record, Tape, CD, DVD, and Digital Sales." From Recording Industry Association of America, 2005. Reprinted with permission. **112,** Sharon LaFraniere. "In the Jungle, the Unjust Jungle, a Small Victory." Excerpted from "In the Jungle, the Unjust Jungle, a Small Victory," in *The New York Times,* March 22, 2006, p. A1. Copyright (c) 2006 by The New York Times Company. Reprinted with permission. **142,** Figure 4.4: "Most Popular Radio Formats in the United States." From Arbitron, www.arbitron.com (Fall 2005). Reprinted with permission. **143,** David Foster Wallace. "Host: The Origins of Talk Radio." Excerpted from "Host: The Origins of Talk Radio." Originally published in *Atlantic,* April 2005, 66–68. Reprinted with permission of the Frederick Hill-Bonnie Nadell Incorporated Literary Agency on behalf of the author. **146,** Table 4.1: "Number of Stations Owned by Top Broadcasting Companies, 2006." Copyright (c) 2006 by BIA Financial Network, Inc. The contents of this report are the property of BIA Financial Network and are protected by copyright and other intellectual property laws. No part of this material may be reproduced or transmitted by any means, electronic or mechanical, including photocopying or recording in information storage and retrieval systems, unless there is written permission from BOA Financial Network or a license agreement with them for such use. All rights reserved. BIA FINANCIAL NETWORK, BIAfn, INVESTING IN RADIO, INVESTING IN TELEVISION, INVESTING IN NEWSPAPER, RADIO YEARBOOK, TELEVISION YEARBOOK, and MEDIA ACCESS PRO are trademarks of BIA Financial Network, Inc. *Warning:* COPYRIGHT VIOLATIONS WILL BE PROSECUTED. BIAfn shares 10% of the net proceeds of settlements and jury awards with individuals who provide essential evidence of illegal copying or electronic distribution. To report violations, please contact 703-818-2425 or e-mail violations@bia.com. **151,** Katy Bachman. "Satellite Radio: Defying Gravity." Excerpted from "Satellite Radio: Defying Gravity" in *Billboard Radio Monitor,* February 3, 2006. **172,** Table 5.1: "Selected Situation and Domestic Comedies Rated in the Top 10 Shows." Adapted from data published in *The Complete Directory to Prime Time Network and Cable TV Shows,* 7th edition, edited by Tim Brooks and Earle Marsh. Copyright (c) 1999 by Tim Brooks and Earle Marsh. Reprinted with permission of Ballantine Books, a division of Random House, Inc.; *Times Almanac 1999,* published by Information Please, L.L.C. Copyright (c) 1998 Information Please, L.L.C., and A. C. Nielsen Media Research, 2005–06. Reprinted with permission. **181,** Figure 5.2: "Top 12 TV Station Groups by $ Revenue and % of U.S. Households Reached." Adapted from "Special Report: This Time They Like What They See" in *Broadcasting & Cable,* January 23, 2006, p. 34. Copyright (c) 2006 Broadcast Cable. Reprinted with permission. **191,** Table 5.2: "The Top 10 Highest-Rated TV Series, Individual Programs." Adapted from data in *The World Almanac and Book of Facts 1997,* published by World Almanac Books, 1996, p. 296; *TV Facts* by Cobbett Steinberg. Published by Facts on File, 1985. A. C. Nielsen Media Research. **207,** Figure 6.2: "U.S. Cable Systems, 1970–2010." Adapted from data posted on www.ncta.com. Reprinted with the permission of the National Cable & Telecommunications Association. **210,** Figure 6.3: "The Top Cable Networks, 2006." From www.ncta.com, May 2006. Reprinted with the permission of the National Cable & Telecommunications Association. **220,** Leslie Cauley. "Cable TV a la Carte." Originally titled "How We Pay for Cable May Be about to Change." From *USA TODAY,* March 2, 2006, p. 1A. Copyright (c) 2006 USA TODAY. Reprinted with permission. **235,** Table 7.1: "The Top 10 Box-Office Champions, 2006." Excerpted data from "All Time Top 100 Grossing Films," October 4, 2006. www.movieweb.com. (c) 2006 MovieWeb. Reprinted with permission of MovieWeb, Inc. All Rights Reserved. **262,** Figure 7.1: "DVD Profits and Sales." From "A Star May Be Fading: As DVD Sales Slow, the Hunt Is on for a New Cash Cow," from *New York Times,* June 13, 2006, C1. Copyright (c) 2006 The New York Times Company. Reprinted with permission. **263,** Figure 7.2: "Gross Revenues from Box-Office Sales, 1984–2005." From "U.S. Market Statistics: 2005." www.mpaa.org. (c) 2005 Motion Picture Association. Reprinted with permission. All rights reserved. **266,** Figure 7.3: "Top Movie Theater Chains in North America." Adapted data from the National Association of Theatre

allocation of frequency space, 136
anti-network regulations, 180–81
and cable television, 178, 209
and deregulation of broadcasting, 116
and digital television, 164
establishment of, 131
Fairness Doctrine, 143
and indecency, 572–74
mandates access channels, 206
must-carry rules, 205–6
and Pacifica Foundation, 148
and payola, 139
and pirate radio stations, 149–50
and print vs. broadcast rules, 572
regulation of tobacco ads, 412
Telecommunications Act of 1996, 144–45
television licensing, 162–65
television technical standards, 161
on video news releases, 442
and *War of the Worlds* broadcast, 134
Federal Food and Drug Act, 393
Federal Radio Commission (FRC), 131
Federal Trade Commission (FTC)
and advertising regulation, 396, 418
and antitrust legislation, 467
ends RCA monopoly, 129
and online privacy, 62, 64
and product placement, 419
and watchdog organizations, 416
feedback, communication, 11
feeder cables, 204
Felicity (television program), 182
Fellini, Federico, 253, 569
Felt, Mark, 489
Feminine Mystique, The (Friedan), 407
Fenske, Mark, 399
Fenton, Roger, 322
Ferber, Edna, 359
Ferrell, Will, 419, 505
Fessenden, Reginald, 123
FHM, 333, 334
Fibber McGee and Molly (radio program), 131
fiber optics, 45, 53, 203
Field, Sally, 252
Figgis, Mike, 270
file sharing, 61, 62, 79, 106, 110
film exchanges, 242
film festivals, 257
film noir, 249, 250, 261
film review boards, 568
film technology, development of, 9, 237–38
Filo, David, 48
Financial Interest and Syndication Rules (fin-syn), 180–81, 188
Finding Nemo (motion picture), 474
Finn, Ruder, 444
Finnegan's Wake (Joyce), 20
fin-syn (Financial Interest and Syndication Rules), 180–81, 188
Firefox (web browser), 50
fireside chats, 131, 132

First Amendment
and commercial speech, 409, 410
and movies, 567–68
print vs. broadcast rules, 572
and Sixth Amendment, 563–67
text of, 546, 549
as unconditional law, 495
and Zenger case, 278
first-run syndication, 189
FitTV (cable channel), 213
Fitzgerald, F. Scott, 359
Five Great Tragedies (Shakespeare), 364
flacks, 447, 449
Flaherty, Robert, 254
flat disk recordings, 76–77
Fleischer, Ari, 450
Fleischman, Doris, 437
Fleisher, Michael, 69
Fleishman-Hillard, 453
Flix (cable channel), 217
Flynt, Larry, 560
FM radio, 135–36
focus groups, 399
Fodor's Travel Publications, 374
Fog of War, The (documentary film), 256
folk music, 95–96
Food and Drug Administration (FDA), 393, 416
Food & Family, 431
Food Network (cable channel), 212, 219, 338
football bowl games, 386
Forbes, 337
Forbes, Steve, 575
Ford, Henry, 472
Forden, Diane, 340
foreign films, 253–54
ForeignFilms.com, 265
For Enquiring Minds: A Cultural Study of Supermarket Tabloids (Bird), 540–41
format radio, 137–38, 141–42
Fornatale, Peter, 147
Forrest Gump (motion picture), 265
Fortune, 323
Foster, Jodie, 252
Fourth Estate, 552
Four Tops, 94
Fowles, Jib, 525
Fox, William, 240
Fox Film Corporation, 240, 246
Fox Network, 170, 182, 325
FoxNews, 212, 214
Fraggle Rock (television program), 218
framing study, 538
franchising, cable, 206–7
Frank, Reuven, 487
Frank, Thomas, 543
Franken, Al, 145
Frankenstein (Shelley), 17, 379
Frankfurt School, 537
Franklin, Aretha, 93
Franklin, Benjamin, 278, 279, 293, 315, 316, 357
Franklin, James, 277–78
Franklin Delano Roosevelt: A Memorial, 364–65

Frank's Place (television program), 183
Frasier (television program), 173
fraud, online, 62
Frazier, Joe, 178
Freakonomics (Levitt and Dubner), 543
Freaks and Geeks (television program), 188
Freed, Alan, 85, 86, 87, 89, 91
freedom of expression
and broadcast media, 570–71
Fairness Doctrine, 575–76
FCC rules, 571–74
political broadcasts, 574–75
and democracy, 578–79
and the Internet, 576–78
models of expression, 550–52
and movie industry
Motion Picture Production Code, 569–70
movie ratings, 570
social and political pressures, 567–68
and music industry, 111–13
origins, 549–50
unprotected forms of expression, 555–56
copyright, 556
libel, 556–60
obscenity, 562–63
right to privacy, 560–62
Freedom of Information Act, 561
Freedom's Journal, 293–94
freelance writers, 340
FreePress.net, 576
frequencies, airwave, 162
Frey, James, 354
Friedan, Betty, 407
Friedkin, William, 251
Friendly, Fred, 503
Friends (television program), 166, 173, 185, 191
fringe time, 188
Frontline (television program), 6
FTC. *See* Federal Trade Commission
Fugitive, The (television program), 191
Full Monty, The (motion picture), 257
Fuse (cable channel), 215, 217
Fust, Johann, 357
FX channel, 211

Gable, Clark, 569
gag orders, 563–64
Gala, 345
Gallo advertising campaign, 406
Gallo Studios, 112
Game Informer, 331
game shows, television, 166–68
gangster films, 249
gangster rap, 101
Gannett Company, Inc., 301–3
Gans, Herbert, 490, 506
GAO (General Accounting Office), 442
Gap, Inc., 445
Garland, Judy, 166
Garrett, Lynn, 365
gatekeepers, communication, 11

Gates, Bill, 40
Gates, Henry Louis, Jr., 542, 543
GATT (General Agreement on Tariffs and Trade), 467
Gaw, Jonathan, 420
gay- and lesbian-oriented magazines, 335
Gaye, Marvin, 95, 414
Gazeta Wyborcza, 507–8
GE. *See* General Electric
Geer, Will, 571
Geertz, Clifford, 540
Geffen, David, 267
Gelbart, Larry, 172
General Accounting Office (GAO), 442
General Agreement on Tariffs and Trade (GATT), 467
general assignment reporters, 298
General Electric (GE)
advertising, 404
and Edward Bernays, 436
media holdings, 477
and NBC, 127, 184, 468
and RCA, 129
and wireless technology, 123, 124, 125
General Hospital (television program), 177
general-interest magazines
Life, 321, 324, 325, 327, 328
Reader's Digest, 320
Saturday Evening Post, 319–20
Time, 320–21
TV Guide, 324–25
General Magazine and Historical Chronicle, 315
General Motors
advertising by, 212, 404, 406
and car radios, 128
and Edward Bernays, 436
and Ralph Nader, 444
General Motors Family Party (radio program), 134
General Tom Thumb, 432
genres, Hollywood, 247–50
Gentleman's Agreement (motion picture), 261
Gentleman's Magazine, 314
geography magazines, 331–33
geosynchronous orbit, 203
Gerbner, George, 534
Gershwin, George, 82
Get on the Bus (motion picture), 245, 251
"Getting Better" (Beatles), 423
G.I. Joe (television program), 410
Gibson, Charles, 170
Gibson, Don, 90
Gibson, Mel, 258
Gibson, William, 40, 174
Gifford, Kathie Lee, 445
Gillars, Mildred, 526
Gillette razors, 418
Gillighan, Andrew, 502
Gillis, Willie, 320
Gilmore Girls (television program), 182
Ginsberg, Allen, 296
Girlfriends (television program), 182, 471
Glamour, 333, 338, 539

revocation of monopoly status, 129
sells NBC-Blue, 131
radio deejays, 85, 89, 90–91, 131, 138
radio group, 127
radio waves, 120–21
Radway, Janice, 540–41
Raging Bull (motion picture), 250, 251
Raiders of the Lost Ark (motion picture), 251
railroads, public relations methods of, 433–34
Rainforest Action Network, 446
Raise the Red Lantern (motion picture), 255
Raitt, Bonnie, 85
Ramones, The, 98
Rampton, Sheldon, 452
Rand Corporation, 46
Rand McNally, 359
random assignment, 529–30
Random House, 359, 369, 374, 562
Ranger Rick, 333
Rappe, Virginia, 568, 569
Rather, Dan, 30, 67, 169
ratings, television, 190–91
ratings system, movie. *See* Motion Picture Production Code
Raw, 363
Rawlins, Tom, 500
Ray, Johnnie, 86
Ray, Rachel, 338
Ray, Satyajit, 253
Raza, La, 295
RCA. *See* Radio Corporation of America
reader-response research, 539–40
readers, e-book, 377
Reader's Digest, 320, 324, 327, 328, 333, 334, 345
Reader's Digest Selecciones, 336
readership, newspaper, 300–301
Reading at Risk (National Endowment for the Arts), 381
Reading the Romance: Women, Patriarchy, and Popular Literature (Radway), 540–41
Reagan, Ronald, 143, 467, 575
reality shows, 156, 158, 182, 185, 192, 216
Real World, The (television program), 216
Reasoner, Harry, 169, 341
Rebel without a Cause (motion picture), 260, 261
receivers, communication, 11
Recording Industry Association of America, 110
records vs. radio, 80–82
Redbook, 327
Red Bulls (formerly MetroStars), 388
Red Channels: The Report of Communist Influence in Radio and Television, 571
Redding, Otis, 89
Redford, Robert, 174, 217
Red Lion Broadcasting Co. v. FCC, 572
Red Riding Hood (film short), 239

Red Skelton Show (television program), 171
Redstone, Sumner, 462
reference books, 365–67
Reformer, 336
regional cable services, 213
regional magazine editions, 328
Reid, Tim, 183
Reid, Wallace, 568
Reiner, Carl, 172
Reinventing Comics (McCloud), 363
religious publications
books, 365
magazines, 316
R.E.M., 99
Remington, Mark, 119
rentals, movie, 180
Replacement Killers, The (motion picture), 255
reporters, newspaper, 298
Reporters without Borders, 42
Report of the Warren Commission on the Assassination of President Kennedy, 365
representative democracy, 514
Republic, The (Plato), 12
Requiem for a Heavyweight (television drama), 174
reruns, 158, 185, 188–89
Respiro (motion picture), 254
responsible capitalism, 490
retransmission consent, 208
Reuters, 300
Revere, Paul, 315
Review, 314
"Revolution" (Beatles), 423
Rey, Anny, 502
Reynolds, Frank, 169
Rhodes, Richard, 525
rhythm and blues, 84–85, 89–90
Rice, Anne, 369
Rich, Frank, 159, 498
Rich, Mokoto, 380
Richard III (motion picture), 166
Richards, Keith, 106
Richardson, Samuel, 357
Rich Man, Poor Man (television miniseries), 177
Rigas, John, 460
Riis, Jacob, 322
Ring, 336
Ring, The (motion picture), 255
Ring Two, The (motion picture), 255
Ringu (motion picture), 255
rituals, journalistic
acting as adversaries, 501
balancing story conflict, 500–501
focusing on the present, 497–99
relying on experts, 499–500
RKO, 244
Road Rules (television program), 216
Roadrunner, 49
Robertson, Robbie, 82
Robinson, Jackie, 294
Robinson, Max, 169
Robinson, Smokey, 94
"Rock, The," 378
rockabilly, 87
rock and roll
alcohol and drug influences, 96–97

alternative rock, 98–100
becomes mainstream, 97–98
blues and R&B foundations, 83–85
British invasion, 92–93
country and western influences, 87–88
folk influences, 95–96
gender issues, 86–87
gospel influences, 89
and hip-hop, 100–101
northern and southern influences, 88
payola scandals, 90–91
and race issues, 85–86
and soul music, 93–94
taming of, 91–92
"Rock and Roll" (Led Zeppelin), 423
"Rock around the Clock," 89
Rockefeller, John D., 318, 435, 449, 467
Rockford Files (television program), 176
Rockwell, Norman, 320
Rocky (motion picture), 264
Roc (television program), 182
Roger and Me (documentary), 254, 256
Rogers, Fred, 193
Rogers, Mark C., 362–63
Rolling Stone, 289, 331
Rolling Stones, 85, 89, 92, 94, 96, 423
romance films, 248
Romanowski, William, 26
Rome, Jim, 139, 145
Romeo Must Die (motion picture), 255
Ronettes, 92
Roosevelt, Franklin Delano, 124, 131, 132, 364–65
Roosevelt, Theodore, 318, 319, 437
Roots (television miniseries), 177
Rorty, James, 392
Rose, Reginald, 174, 175
Roseanne (television program), 173, 185
Rosen, Jay, 307, 509, 515
Rosenbaum, Jonathan, 252
Rosenblatt, Roger, 12, 333
Rosing, Boris, 161
Ross, Diana, 94, 95
Ross, Harold, 335
Ross, Lillian, 335
Rossellini, Roberto, 569
rotation, 137
Rotenberg, Mark, 208
Rothafel, Samuel "Roxy," 244
Rothenberg, Randall, 457
Roth v. United States, 562–63
Rounder Records, 111
Rowdy Journal, 281
Rowland, William, 535
Rowling, J. K., 350, 378
royalties, 109, 112
Royko, Mike, 498
Rudolph, Eric, 495
Run-DMC, 100
Rushdie, Salman, 382
Rush Limbaugh Show, The (radio program), 143, 145, 152

Ruskin, Gary, 416
Russert, Tim, 377

Saatchi & Saatchi, 397
Sacramento Bee, 305
Safari (web browser), 50
Saffo, Paul, 158
Safire, William, 486
Salaam Bombay (motion picture), 257
Salgado, Sebastião, 509
Salinger, J. D., 381
Salon, 338, 339
Salten, Felix, 364
Salt-N-Pepa, 100
Sam Goody, 105
San Francisco Examiner, 283
San Jose Mercury News, 303
SANS Institute, 63
Santa Barbara (television program), 29
Sarnoff, David, 127–28
and FM radio, 135–36
and television sponsorship, 165
Satanic Verses, The (Rushdie), 382
satellite broadcasting, 150–51, 164, 178, 221–22
satellite technology, 202–4
Satrapi, Marjane, 363
saturation advertising, 402–3
Saturday Evening Post, 316, 319–20, 325, 327
Saturday Night Live (television program), 171, 200, 511, 575
Saudi Arabia, 447
SBC Communications, 49
scanning disk, 160
Schieffer, Bob, 169
Schiffrin, André, 367
Schindler's List (motion picture), 250
Schlessinger, Laura, 139, 145
Schmidt, Eric E., 43
Schofield, Jack, 270
scholarly journals, 329
Scholz, Meg, 512
schools
advertising in, 412–13
sale of beverages in, 388
shootings in, 520
Schramm, Wilbur, 528
Schudson, Michael, 290, 390, 432
Schwarzenegger, Arnold, 37, 456, 575
science, postmodern attitiude toward, 27
Science Fiction Book Club, 371
scientific method, 529
Sci-Fi Channel, 211
scoops, 498–99
Scorsese, Martin, 251
Scott, Ridley, 26
Scotts lawn products, 443
screenwriters, 266
scribes, 355–56
Scribner's (publishing house), 359
Scripps, Edward Wyllis, 302
Scrubs (television program), 173
Se7en (motion picture), 249, 250
Seabiscuit (Hillenbrand), 377
Seal Island (documentary short), 473
search engines, 48, 50–51, 57, 367